APPLIED SPORT PSYCHOLOGY

FIFTH EDITION

APPLIED SPORT PSYCHOLOGY

PERSONAL GROWTH TO PEAK PERFORMANCE

Jean M. Williams, Editor

University of Arizona

Boston   Burr Ridge, IL   Dubuque, IA   Madison, WI   New York   San Francisco   St. Louis
Bangkok   Bogotá   Caracas   Kuala Lumpur   Lisbon   London   Madrid   Mexico City
Milan   Montreal   New Delhi   Santiago   Seoul   Singapore   Sydney   Taipei   Toronto

Higher Education

APPLIED SPORT PSYCHOLOGY: PERSONAL GROWTH TO PEAK PERFORMANCE
Published by McGraw-Hill, a business unit of The McGraw-Hill Companies, Inc., 1221 Avenue of the Americas, New York, NY, 10020. Copyright © 2006, 2001, 1998, 1993, 1986 by The McGraw-Hill Companies, Inc.

This book is printed on acid-free paper.

2 3 4 5 6 7 8 9 0 FGR/FGR 0 9 8 7 6

ISBN-13: 978-0-07-284383-5
ISBN-10: 0-07-284383-7

Editor in Chief: *Emily Barrosse*
Publisher: *Bill Glass*
Executive Editor: *Nicholas Barrett*
Developmental Editor: *Lynda Huenefeld*
Executive Marketing Manager: *Pamela S. Cooper*
Managing Editor: *Jean Dal Porto*
Project Manager: *Emily Hatteberg*
Senior Media Producer: *Lance Gerhart*
Art Director: *Jeanne Schreiber*
Associate Designer: *Marianna Kinigakis*
Interior Designer: *Kiera Pohl*
Cover Credit: © *Getty Images/Alan Thornton*
Senior Media Project Manager: *Ron Nelms*
Associate Production Supervisor: *Jason I. Huls*
Composition: *9/11 Stone Serif, by International Typesetting and Composition*
Printing: *45 # New Era Matte, Quebecor World Fairfield Inc.*

Library of Congress Cataloging-in-Publication Data

Applied sport psychology : personal growth to peak performance/Jean M. Williams, editor.—5th ed.
    p. cm.
Includes bibliograhical references and indexes.
    ISBN 0-07-284383-7 (softcover : alk. paper)
    1. Sports—Psychological aspects. 2. Coaching (Athletics) I. Williams, Jean M. (Jean Marie)
GV706.4.A66 2006
796'.01—dc22   2005050509

www.mhhe.com

WE DEDICATE THIS FIFTH EDITION TO THE MEMORY OF DOROTHY V. HARRIS AND BRUCE C. OGILVIE. BOTH ARE ORIGINAL CONTRIBUTORS TO APPLIED SPORT PSYCHOLOGY: PERSONAL GROWTH TO PEAK PERFORMANCE AND WORLD-RENOWNED PIONEERS IN THE FIELD. DOT AND BRUCE HELPED PROVIDE THE VISION AND INSPIRATION FOR MUCH OF THE GROWTH WITHIN APPLIED SPORT PSYCHOLOGY. THEY ARE GREATLY APPRECIATED AND SORELY MISSED.

BRIEF CONTENTS

CONTENTS

21 Development and Implementation of Coach-Training Programs: Cognitive-Behavioral Principles and Techniques 458
Frank L. Smoll, Ronald E. Smith

PART FIVE—PSYCHOLOGICAL ISSUES: REFERRAL, DRUG ABUSE, BURNOUT, INJURY, TERMINATION FROM ATHLETICS, AND EXERCISE

22 When to Refer Athletes for Counseling or Psychotherapy 483
Mark B. Andersen, David Tod

23 Drug Abuse in Sport: Causes and Cures 505
Mark H. Anshel

24 Burnout in Sport: Understanding the Process—From Early Warning Signs to Individualized Intervention 541
Kate Goodger, David Lavallee, Trish Gorely, Chris Harwood

PREFACE

An increasing number of coaches and athletes have turned to applied sport psychology to gain a competitive edge—to learn, among other things, ways to manage competitive stress, control concentration, improve confidence, increase communication skills, and promote team harmony.

The first edition of *Applied Sport Psychology: Personal Growth to Peak Performance,* which was published 20 years ago, was one of the first books written specifically to introduce coaches and sport psychologists to psychological theories and techniques that could be used to enhance the performance and personal growth of sport participants from youth sport to elite levels. The book focused primarily on three dimensions: (1) techniques for developing and refining psychological skills to enhance performance and personal growth, (2) suggestions for establishing a learning and social environment that would enhance the effectiveness of coaches and maximize the skill and personal growth of athletes, and (3) special issues such as staleness and burnout, psychology of injury and injury rehabilitation, and retirement from athletics.

Later editions had the same focus but were expanded to cover more topics. New chapters were added on motivation, training youth sport coaches, improving communication, referring athletes for professional counseling, drug abuse in sport, and exercise psychology. The last chapter reflected the growing importance to applied sport psychology of understanding the psychological benefits and risks of exercise and the psychological and behavioral principles for enhancing exercise adoption and adherence.

The same important topics, focus, and organizational structure have been retained for this fifth edition, but the revision reflects the latest research, practice, and anecdotal examples in applied sport psychology.

Applied Sport Psychology is particularly well suited as a text for classes in applied sport psychol-

ogy and psychology of coaching. The book will also be a valuable reference for practicing coaches, sport psychologists, and psychologists who did not have the opportunity for such training in their own formal education. Here are some of the reasons the fifth edition continues to be exceptionally well suited for these classes and individuals.

Written Specifically for Sport Psychologists and Coaches

The growing body of knowledge and interest in applied sport psychology is perhaps best indicated by the approximately 300 books that have been published on mental skills for peak performance. Most of these books continue to be written primarily for the sport participant. Their coverage is not comprehensive enough for the sport psychologist or coach who must apply psychological constructs across a wide variety of situations and deal with many different sport participants. Books written for sport psychologists and coaches are typically general textbooks that attempt to cover the entire field of sport psychology. Thus their coverage of applied issues—and particularly psychological interventions for enhancing sport performance, personal growth, and exercise participation—is superficial compared to the in-depth coverage provided in this text. Other applied textbooks do not have the comprehensive coverage of this book, the expertise of the contributors, or as clear a presentation of the theories and research that provide the foundation for application.

Based on the Latest Research and Practice

The knowledge and experiential base in applied sport psychology has greatly expanded since the initial publication of this book. Each new edition has reflected the latest research and cutting-edge practice in applied sport psychology. Although the primary focus of the fifth edition continues to be on application, each chapter provides theoretical and research foundations when appropriate. When using the book as a textbook for a graduate course, the instructor may want to supplement the book with readings from the research studies cited by the contributors.

Comprehensive Coverage of Topics

No other text in applied sport psychology encompasses the comprehensive approach taken here. The first chapter discusses the past, present, and future of sport psychology. The remainder of the book is divided into five parts.

Part One covers learning, feedback, motivation, and effective leadership. Part Two covers social interactions such as effective groups, communication, and coach–parent relationships. For clarity and simplicity, some of these chapters have been written in the vernacular of the coach. The reader is cautioned, however, not to conclude that these chapters are only useful for coaches. Sport psychologists frequently find it necessary to work with coaches in areas such as improving communication skills, building team rapport, and fostering more effective leadership behaviors. Also, the same principles of learning, motivation, and social interaction that help to increase a coach's effectiveness apply to the sport psychologist teaching mental skills and interacting with athletes. Thus the knowledge and insight gained from reading the chapters in Part Two are as appropriate for current and prospective sport psychologists as they are for coaches.

Part Three of the book discusses mental training for enhancing performance. This section begins with a chapter on the psychological characteristics of peak performance; other chapters discuss identifying ideal performance states, setting and achieving goals, managing stress and energy levels, training in imagery, identifying optimal attentional styles, control-

ling concentration, and building confidence. Part Four deals with implementing training programs. The first chapter provides suggestions for the integration and implementation of a psychological skills training program. The second chapter provides guidance on how to conduct sport psychology training programs with coaches.

Part Five addresses the referral of sport competitors for professional counseling, drug abuse in sport, burnout, injury risk and rehabilitation, termination from sport competition, and psychology of exercise. No sport psychology book has dealt with all of these issues, even though they are crucial to sport performance, personal development, and the enhancement of exercise participation and benefits.

The appropriateness of these chapters for certain courses will depend on the students' backgrounds and interests. The book was planned to provide complete coverage of psychological theories, techniques, and issues relevant to the enhancement of personal growth and to sport and exercise participation and performance. Instructors may select those chapters that are appropriate for their courses. For example, Chapters 2 and 3 concern motor skills learning and principles of reinforcement and feedback; this material might be redundant if students already have a thorough background in motor learning. Chapter 10, on coach–parent relationships, may interest only those individuals who are working, or plan to work, in a setting where sport participants are still living with their parents; whereas Chapter 26, on termination from sport competition, may interest only individuals who work with athletes who are nearing retirement or dropping out of sport competition.

Written by Leading Experts in Sport Psychology

The contributors to this volume are leading scholars and practitioners in sport and exercise psychology. They work with sport participants from youth sport to Olympic and professional levels, and most have illustrious backgrounds as elite athletes or coaches.

Integrated Organization and Writing Style

The book has the major advantage of drawing on the diverse expertise and perspectives of 46 sport and exercise psychologists and 3 motor learning experts, but it avoids the common disadvantage of disparate coverage and diverse writing styles frequently found in edited textbooks. The content and sequencing of chapters have been carefully coordinated to ensure comprehensive coverage and progressive development of concepts while eliminating undesirable overlap and inconsistency in terminology. Writing focus, styles, and organization have been standardized as much as possible. Each chapter cites appropriate research and theory, makes application to the world of sport and/or exercise, and provides examples and intervention exercises whenever appropriate. Each chapter also begins with an introduction that highlights the content of the chapter and ends with a conclusion or summary of the major psychological constructs and skills and study questions for students.

Application Examples

The numerous examples given throughout the book greatly facilitate the translation of psychological theory and constructs into everyday practice. Many of these examples involve well-known professional and amateur sportspeople. The examples cut across more than 40 sports and provide important anecdotal evidence that can be used to motivate individuals to develop psychological and behavioral skills for their sport and exercise participation. These real-life examples are frequently supplemented with hypothetical examples created by the authors to clarify appropriate applications.

Applied Sport Psychology Provides Many Benefits

The rewards are many for those who choose to dedicate themselves to the pursuit of excellence and personal growth through use of the theories and techniques of applied sport and exercise psychology. Coaches and sport participants acknowledge the importance of mental factors in sport development and performance, yet the time individuals actually spend practicing mental skills belies this view. In publishing this book, we have made a serious effort to help abolish that inconsistency by supplying the knowledge necessary for providing a salutary psychological climate. The benefits that can be derived from this text will arise not just in sport performance but in overall performance outside of sport and, perhaps most important, in general personal growth and increased physical and mental health.

Acknowledgments

I wish to thank all the contributors who participated in this project and thus shared their vast expertise with the readers. The high acceptance given to earlier editions of this book and the fact that we are going into our fifth edition 20 years later is due primarily to their efforts, and I am greatly indebted to them. Whatever contribution this book continues to make to applied sport and exercise psychology will be in large measure a consequence of their efforts.

Thanks are also due to Robert Baker, Ashland University; Shane G. Frehlich, California State University, Northridge; Robert W. Grossman, Kalamazoo College; and Christine M. Kelly, University of Great Falls, Williams, England, for their insightful reviews of this edition. In addition, preparation of Chapters 3, 10, and 21 was supported in part by Grant 22-97 to Ronald E. Smith and Frank L. Smoll from the William T. Grant Foundation.

I am also indebted to the fine editorial staff at McGraw-Hill, most particularly Lynda Huenefeld, for her support and skill. I also wish to thank Emily Hatteberg for her efficiency and thoroughness in overseeing the production process for this edition.

Jean M. Williams

CONTRIBUTORS

Jean M. Williams is a professor in the Department of Psychology at the University of Arizona. She teaches courses in stress and coping and psychology of excellence. Dr. Williams has done consulting with intercollegiate athletes, teams, and coaches and with top amateur and professional athletes. She has more than 10 years of coaching experience in men's and women's fencing, including coaching nationally ranked teams. Dr. Williams has edited two books in sport psychology and published more than 100 research and professional articles. She is a past president of the Association for the Advancement of Applied Sport Psychology (AAASP) and past chair of the American Alliance of Health, Physical Education, Recreation and Dance (AAHPERD) Sport Psychology Academy.

Mark B. Andersen is a registered psychologist and associate professor at Victoria University in Melbourne, Australia. He teaches in the School of Human Movement and coordinates the master of applied psychology degree (sport and exercise psychology emphasis) in the Department of Psychology. He received his doctorate from the University of Arizona in 1988 and immigrated to Australia in 1994. He teaches subjects in research design, psychology of rehabilitation, and the professional practice of psychology. His areas of research interest include the psychology of injury and rehabilitation; the role of exercise in mental health, well-being, and quality of life; the training and supervision of graduate students; and the practice of sport psychology service delivery. He is the former editor of the Professional Practice section of the international journal *The Sport Psychologist*. He has published more than 80 refereed journal articles and book chapters and has made over 90 national and international conference presentations. Dr. Andersen has worked for many years counseling athletes ranging from 12-year-old juniors to American and Australian Olympians.

Mark H. Anshel is a professor in the Department of Health, Physical Education, and Recreation at Middle Tennessee State University in Murfreesboro. His academic degrees and specializations include B.S., physical education (Illinois State University), M.A., psychology of motor performance (McGill University in Montreal), and Ph.D., motor learning/sport psychology (Florida State University). He has authored three books, *Sport Psychology: From Theory to Practice* (4th ed.), *Applied Exercise Psychology: A Guide to Consulting Exercise Participants*, and *Concepts in Fitness: A Balanced Approach to Good Health*. He has also published numerous chapters in books and articles in scientific journals. His research has focused on coping with stressful events in sport and drugs in sport. Current research interests include perfectionism in sport and intervention effectiveness in promoting exercise adherence. He is on the editorial board for the *Journal of Sport Behavior* and is a reviewer of submitted articles for 11 scientific journals. Dr. Anshel is a certified sport psychology consultant with the AAASP, and has counseled many athletes and coaches, from youth sports through professional levels. He is a former competitive baseball player at the high school and college levels.

Shawn M. Arent is an assistant professor in the Department of Exercise Science and Sport Studies at Rutgers University. He completed his doctorate in exercise science at Arizona State University. Dr. Arent is currently the director of the honors program in exercise science and is also the director of research for the Youth Sport Research Council. His research focuses on the physiological and psychological mechanisms underlying biological and behavioral responses to sport and exercise. He has received a national research-writing award for his work on the arousal–performance relationship. Dr. Arent is a member of the national staff for the U.S. Soccer Federation and has served as a performance consultant for various college and professional coaches and athletes. He is also a certified strength and conditioning specialist through the National Strength and Conditioning Association (NSCA).

Janet Buckworth is an associate professor of exercise science at The Ohio State University. She is part of the Physical Activity and Exercise Behavior Research Group and her research areas are exercise adherence and the psychobiology of exercise and mental health. Dr. Buckworth has masters' degrees in clinical social work and community health education. She directed a campus wellness program before earning her Ph.D. in exercise psychology at the University of Georgia. She advises graduate students studying psychological and physiological correlates and consequences of acute and chronic physical activity. Dr. Buckworth was principal investigator on a 3-year grant funded by the National Institute of Health (NIH) to study exercise adherence in college students and is the co-author with Dr. Dishman of *Exercise Psychology*, published in 2002. Dr. Buckworth is a fellow of the American College of Sports Medicine.

Linda K. Bunker is director of the motor learning laboratory and professor of kinesiology at the University of Virginia where she is the Parrish Professor of Education. She is a certified sport psychology consultant (AAASP) and has worked extensively with professional golfers and tennis players. Dr. Bunker is a well-known scholar in the areas of applied motor learning and sport psychology and was selected as the 2000–2001 Alliance Scholar for the AAHPERD. She has written more than 100 articles and authored 15 books, including *Motivating Kids Through Play, Parenting Your Superstar, Golf: Steps to Success,* and *Mind Mastery for Winning Golf.* Her involvement in sport has been both active and scholastic. She is on the Advisory Board of the Womens Sports Foundation, *SHAPE* magazine, and the Melpomene Institute and was a nationally ranked tennis player and four-sport athlete at the University of Illinois.

Shauna M. Burke is a Ph.D. student in the Department of Health Sciences at the University of Western Ontario, where her primary research interests relate to group dynamics in sport and exercise. Shauna has presented her research at several national and international scientific and professional conferences, and she is currently a Canadian Regional Student Representative for the AAASP.

Albert V. Carron received an Ed.D. from the University of California, Berkeley in 1967 and M.A. (1965) and B.P.E. (1963) degrees from the University of Alberta, Edmonton. He has taught at the University of Western Ontario for 28 years. Dr. Carron has been an author or co-author of 14 books and monographs, 30 chapters in edited texts, and 125 refereed publications. Professionally, he is a fellow in the American Academy of Kinesiology and Physical Education (AAKPE), the AAASP, and the Canadian Society for Psychomotor Learning and Sport Psychology (SCAPPS). He is a past president of the Canadian Association for Sport Sciences and a former member of the board of directors of the Sports Medicine Council of Canada. In 1998, Carron was a co-recipient of the International Council of Sport Science and Physical Education's Sport Science Award of the International Olympic Committee President.

Packianathan (Chella) Chelladurai is currently a professor of sport management in the School of Physical Activity and Educational Services at The Ohio State University. He is a frequent reviewer for the *Journal of Sport and Exercise Psychology* and the *Journal of Applied Sport Psychology.* He is a former editor of the *Journal of Sport Management.* He was honored by the North American Society for Sport Management as the first recipient of its prestigious Earle F. Zeigler Award. He received his doctorate from the University of Waterloo. He conducts research in the areas of organization theory and organizational behavior, including leadership in sports. Dr. Chelladurai is the author of *Sport Management: Macro Perspectives, Management of Human Resources in Sport and Recreation,* and *Managing Organizations for Sport and Physical Activity* and coauthor of monographs titled *Leadership* and *Group Cohesion and Sport.* He was a national basketball player, referee, and coach in India.

Cheryl Coker received her doctorate from the University of Virginia and is currently an associate professor with the Department of Physical Education, Recreation and Dance at New Mexico State University. She has coached at the Division I level in both track and field and strength and conditioning and continues to consult with several teams. This coaching experience together with her experiences as an international competitor in track and field have contributed to her research. In addition to numerous publications and presentations on coaching and motor behavior, Dr. Coker is the author of the textbook *Motor Learning and Control for Practitioners.*

Sean P. Cumming is a postdoctoral research associate in the Department of Psychology at the University of Washington. He is currently investigating the impact of coach and parent education programs upon children's experiences in youth sports. His research interests also include the behavioral and psychological correlates of growth and maturation in the context of youth sports. Hailing from the Orkney Isles in Scotland, Dr. Cumming gained an honors degree in psychology from the University of Edinburgh, Scotland, an M.Sc. in Exercise and Sport Psychology from the University of Exeter, England, and a Ph.D. in Kinesiology from Michigan State University. While studying at Michigan State University, Dr. Cumming worked as a consultant and researcher at the Institute for the Study of Youth Sports.

Paul W. Dennis is the development coach for the Toronto Maple Leafs of the National Hockey League, a position that requires technical and applied sport psychology expertise. His primary responsibility with the Maple Leafs is to assist team members and potential prospects with their psychological skills development. His main research interest is in the area of group dynamics. He received his doctorate from the University of Western Ontario under the supervision of Dr. Albert V. Carron.

Rod K. Dishman is a professor of exercise science and an adjunct professor of psychology at the University of Georgia. He advises graduate students studying behavioral neuroscience and interventions to increase physical activity. Dr. Dishman received his Ph.D. at the University of Wisconsin, Madison and has focused his research on neurobiological aspects of the mental health outcomes associated with physical activity and on the behavioral determinants of physical activity. He is a fellow of the American College of Sports Medicine, the American Psychological Association (APA), and the AAKPE. He has served as a consultant on exercise for the National Institutes of Health, the Sports Medicine Council for the United States Olympic Committee, and the Olympic Prize subcommittee of the Medical Commission of the International Olympic Committee. He also was one of 22 founding members of the International Olympic Committee (IOC) Academy of Sport Sciences.

Joan L. Duda is a professor of sports psychology in the School of Sport and Exercise Sciences at The University of Birmingham, UK. She is past president of the AAASP; has been a member of the executive boards of the North American Society for the Psychology of Sport and Physical Activity (NASPSPA), the Sport Psychology Academy, Division 47 of the APA, and the International Society for Sport Psychology; and is currently on the Scientific Committee of the European Congress of Sport Science. She was editor of the *Journal of Applied Sport Psychology* and is on the editorial board of several other leading journals in the field. A fellow of the AAASP and the AAKPE, Dr. Duda has edited one book (*Advances in Sport and Exercise Psychology Measurement* in 1998) and authored over 170 publications focused on motivation in the physical domain and the psychological aspects of sport and exercise performance and participation. She is certified as a mental skills consultant by the AAASP, is accredited as a sport psychology consultant by the British Association for Sport and Exercise Sciences, and is listed on the U.S. Olympic Registry. At The University of Birmingham, she works with sport scholars, other elite athletes, and also offers consultation with respect to performance excellence and motivational issues among professional ballet dancers. Her hobbies include music, playing club tennis, and traveling.

Mark A. Eys received his Ph.D. and master's from The University of Western Ontario under the supervision of Dr. Albert V. Carron. He is currently an assistant professor at Laurentian University in sport psychology, and his research interests include group dynamics in sport and exercise with a specific focus on individual roles within a group environment. Dr. Eys is an active member of professional associations such as the AAASP, the NASPSPA, and the Canadian Society for Psychomotor Learning and Sport Psychology. He is a former intercollegiate basketball player and has coached soccer at the club and university levels.

Mark G. Fischman is a professor in the Department of Health and Human Performance at Auburn University. He received his doctorate in motor learning from the Pennsylvania State University. Dr. Fischman is associated with the Motor Behavior Center at Auburn, where he conducts research on theories of response programming, factors that constrain grip selection in humans, and divided attention. Dr. Fischman served as president of the NASPSPA, and is a fellow of the American Academy of Kinesiology and Physical Education and the Research Consortium of AAHPERD. Dr. Fischman is a former collegiate swimmer and has coached collegiate and age-group swimming.

Kate Goodger is currently a Ph.D. student and teaching assistant in sport and exercise psychology at Loughborough University in the U.K. She is an accredited sport psychologist by the British Association of Sport and Exercise Sciences and a practicing consultant with the English Institute of Sport, English Football Association, RYA Great Britain Junior Program, and Nottingham Ice Center. As a performer herself, she represented the South of England in netball and regional squads in hockey and badminton.

Trish Gorely is a faculty member in the School of Sport and Exercise Sciences at Loughborough University. She received a master's degree and doctorate in sport and exercise psychology from The University of Western Australia. She has research interests in commitment, and physical activity and health. Dr. Gorely plays golf and racquet sports in her leisure time.

Daniel Gould is the director of the Institute for the Study of Youth Sports and a professor in the Department of Kinesiology at Michigan State University. A specialist in applied sport psychology, he focuses his research on competitive stress and coping, athlete motivation, and the effectiveness of psychological skills training interventions for coaches and athletes. He is also heavily involved in coaching education and children's sports. Dr. Gould has been a consultant to elite international athletes in a wide variety of sports ranging from figure skating and dressage to wrestling and baseball. Formerly a wrestler and football and baseball player, he remains an avid fitness enthusiast. Dr. Gould was the founding co-editor of *The Sport Psychologist*. He served as president of the AAASP, chaired the U.S.A. Wrestling Science and Medicine Committee, served on the U.S. Olympic Coaching Development Committee, the U.S. Olympic Sport Science and Technology Committee, and presently serves as vice chair of the United States Tennis Association Sport Science Committee.

Christy Greenleaf is an assistant professor in the Department of Kinesiology, Health Promotion, and Recreation at the University of North Texas. She is also a member of the university's Center for Sport Psychology and Performance Excellence. Dr. Greenleaf's research focuses on body image, eating attitudes and behaviors, and gender issues within exercise and sport contexts. She has consulted with figure skaters and synchronized skaters, as well as figure skating coaches and parents. Dr. Greenleaf is an active figure skater and a competitive member of an adult synchronized skating team.

Dorothy V. Harris, now deceased, was a professor and coordinator of the graduate program in sport psychology at Pennsylvania State University. She was a world-renowned educational sport psychologist, past president of the NASPSPA, a member of the Managing Council of the International Society of Sport Psychology (ISSP), ISSP-treasurer, and editor of the ISSP Newsletter.

Dr. Harris was a prolific author who wrote two books, edited five, and contributed to numerous others. She was also an accomplished speaker. She spent a sabbatical at the Olympic Training Center in 1980 and continued to work with numerous Olympic and national teams and athletes.

Chris Harwood is a faculty member in the School of Sport and Exercise Sciences at Loughborough University. He received both his master's and doctoral degrees from Loughborough University, and was awarded the AAASP doctoral dissertation award in 1998 for his applied research in achievement motivation. An active practitioner accredited by the British Association of Sport and Exercise Sciences and a registered psychologist of the British Olympic Association, his applied work centers on coach, parent, and athlete education in high performance environments. Dr. Harwood plays tennis for a regional men's team and is a keen golfer and runner.

Thelma Sternberg Horn received her doctoral degree from Michigan State University and is currently an associate professor in the Department of Physical Education, Health, and Sport Studies at Miami University in Ohio. Her research interests center around children's perceptions of their physical competence and the influence of teacher, coach, and parent behavior on children's psychosocial growth. She is also working on an interdisciplinary project designed to examine the relationship between exercise and stress reactivity in adolescents and young children. Dr. Horn is a former editor of the *Journal of Sport and Exercise Psychology* and is currently editing the third edition of *Advances in Sport Psychology*. Prior to her graduate work in sport psychology, Dr. Horn taught physical education and English at the high school level in Michigan and Colorado. She has had extensive coaching experience at both interscholastic and intercollegiate levels and continues to work as a consultant and clinician with coaches and teachers in youth sport and interscholastic programs.

Vikki Krane is the director of the Women's Studies program and a professor with the School of Human Movement, Sport, and Leisure Studies at Bowling Green State University. She teaches courses in sport psychology and gender and sport. Her research is grounded in a feminist perspective, specifically focusing on body image issues and heterosexism in sport. She is the former editor of *The Sport Psychologist* and is on the editorial board of the *Journal of Applied Sport Psychology*. Dr. Krane also is a fellow of the AAASP and a certified consultant with the organization. As a psychological skills consultant, Dr. Krane has worked with a variety of athletes, including high school, rising elite adolescents, and college athletes.

Francisco (Paco) Labrador received a bachelor's degree in psychology and exercise science from Hiram College in Ohio and a master's degree in sport studies from Miami University. After spending several years as an assistant volleyball coach with the women's intercollegiate volleyball team at Miami University, Mr. Labrador recently accepted a position as head volleyball coach of the women's intercollegiate team at Wittenberg University in Ohio. Mr. Labrador's research interests include the study of coaching leadership styles and behaviors and their relationship to athletes' level of motivation and sport commitment. Mr. Labrador played 4 years of intercollegiate volleyball at Hiram College and also served as the assistant coach for the Hiram College women's intercollegiate volleyball team.

Daniel M. Landers is a regents' professor of kinesiology at Arizona State University. He was the founding editor of the *Journal of Sport and Exercise Psychology*. Dr. Landers also served as president of the Research Consortium of AAHPERD, the Division of Exercise and Sport Psychology of the APA, and the NASPSPA. In 1995, he received the NASPSPA Distinguished Scholar Award, and in 2003, the APA-Div. 47 Award for Distinguished Scientific and Research Contributions to Exercise and Sport Psychology. Dr. Landers has been a member of an ad hoc National Academy of Science Committee, a member of the Sport Psychology and Sport Science and Technology Committees of the U.S. Olympic Committee, and a member of the Prize Selection Committee of the International Olympic Committee. His research has focused on the arousal–performance relationship, including attention/concentration and stress-reducing coping strategies. He has served as a sport psychologist for collegiate teams, professional teams, and national Olympic teams in the United States, Canada, and Korea.

David Lavallee is a faculty member in the School of Sport and Exercise Sciences at Loughborough University. He received a master's degree in counseling psychology from Harvard University and doctorate in sport and exercise psychology from The University of Western Australia. He is an associated fellow and chartered psychologist of The British Psychological Society and has applied and research interests in counseling in sport and exercise settings. Dr. Lavallee serves as associate editor of *The Psychologist*. He is also a former All-American soccer player.

Curt L. Lox is a professor of kinesiology and health education and an associate dean in the School of Education at Southern Illinois University, Edwardsville. His research interests center broadly around the psychological and emotional aspects of exercise in special populations. Dr. Lox has coached at the youth and high school levels and continues to serve as a sport psychology consultant to players and coaches at the interscholastic, intercollegiate, and professional levels in the greater St. Louis area. He is a member of the editorial board for the *Journal of Sport and Exercise Psychology* and serves as a reviewer for a number of additional journals, including *The Sport Psychologist, Journal of Applied Social Psychology, Journal of Applied Sport Psychology, Journal of Aging and Physical Activity, Journal of Social Behavior and Personality, Research Quarterly for Exercise and Sport*, and the *European Journal of Sport Science*. Dr. Lox is also co-author of an exercise psychology text titled *The Psychology of Exercise: Integrating Theory and Practice*, which is currently at press in its second edition.

Betty L. Mann received her doctorate from Springfield College, where she is a professor of Physical Education. She is the assistant vice president of graduate education and research and serves as the coordinator for graduate studies in physical education. Her areas of expertise are sport psychology, sport law, and administration. Dr. Mann has made numerous presentations on leadership and has written articles about that topic. She has coached women's basketball at the college and high school levels and taught middle school physical education.

Mimi C. Murray is a professor of physical education at Springfield College. Dr. Murray has been a very successful gymnastics coach: Her teams at Springfield College won three Division I National Championships, she was selected to coach the U.S. team for the World University Games, and was named "Coach of the Year." She authored *Gymnastics for Women: The Spectator, Gymnast, Coach and Teacher*. She has been a television sports commentator. As a sport psychology consultant, Dr. Murray has published many articles and lectured throughout the world and has worked with Olympic and professional athletes, including the U.S. equestrian team and the 1996 U.S. field hockey team. She is listed on the U.S. Olympic Committee's Sport Psychology Registry, is past president of the National Association for Girls and Women in Sport (NAGWS), AAHPERD, and is currently president of International Council For Health, Physical Education, Recreation, Sport, & Dance (ICHPER-SD).

Robert M. Nideffer has been a professor on the faculties of the University of Rochester, the California School of Professional Psychology, and California State University at San Diego. He has been involved in sport psychology since 1969 and is the chief executive officer and founder of Enhanced Performance Systems. Dr. Nideffer has published extensively in the sport psychology and stress management areas, with 10 books and more than 100 articles to his credit. He has worked with Olympic-level and professional athletes in a wide variety of sports and has been a member of policy-setting committees in the United States, Canada, and Australia.

Bruce C. Ogilvie, now deceased, was professor emeritus in the Department of Psychology at California State University, San Jose. Dr. Ogilvie was a world-renowned pioneer in applied sport psychology, having researched, consulted, and published in the area of performance and the high-performance person since 1955. He contributed to more than 150 publications on issues including children in sport, identification of psychological factors that contribute to performance success, and the development of performance-enhancing strategies. Dr. Ogilvie served as team psychological consultant for numerous U.S. Olympic teams as well as professional football, basketball, baseball, hockey, and soccer teams. He was also a private-practice consultant for elite athletes from various sports.

Joseph B. Oxendine is currently chancellor emeritus of The University at North Carolina at Pembroke where he served as chancellor from 1989 until 1999. After competing in 3 sports at the college level, he played professional baseball for 3 years in the Pittsburgh Pirate minor league system. Dr. Oxendine served for 30 years at Temple University as professor, department chairman, and founding dean of the College of Health, Physical Education, Recreation and Dance. He has conducted research on practice conditions, information feedback, and the role of arousal on motor performance. He has written three books, including *Psychology of Motor Learning* and *American Indian Sports Heritage.*

Erik Peper is an international authority on biofeedback and self-regulation. He is professor and director of the Institute for Holistic Healing Studies/Department of Health Education at San Francisco State University, president of the Biofeedback Foundation of Europe, and past president of the Association for Applied Psychophysiology and Biofeedback. He received the 2004 California Governor's Safety Award for his work on the Healthy Computing Program and was the behavioral scientist (sport psychologist) for the United States Rhythmic Gymnastic team. He is an author of numerous scientific articles and books. His most recent co-authored books are *Healthy Computing with Muscle Biofeedback, Make Health Happen: Training Yourself to Create Wellness* and *De Computermens.* He is also the co-producer

of the weekly *Healthy Computing E-mail Tips*. His re-search interests focus on psychophysiology of healing, voluntary self-regulation, holistic health, healthy computing, respiratory psychophysiology, and optimizing health with biofeedback.

Kenneth Ravizza is a professor in the Department of Kinesiology and Health Promotion at California State University at Fullerton. His research examines the nature of peak performance in a variety of domains. He has developed and implemented performance-enhancement programs for business groups, health care and school staffs, cancer patients, police officers, and physicians. He has worked with his university's baseball, softball, and gymnastics teams for the past 15 years. He worked with the U.S. baseball and water polo teams in the 1996 Olympics, and the U.S. softball team for the 2000 Olympics. He was a sport psychology consultant for the Anaheim Angels for 16 years. He spent 3 years (1986–1988) working with the University of Nebraska football team, and he worked with the New York Jets between 1993 and 1995. For the past 8 years he has done extensive work with Olympic-level figure skaters. He also has consulted with numerous athletic departments in the area of coaching effectiveness (UCLA, Texas, L.S.U., Harvard). Ken enjoys working in his garden to recharge himself.

Carrie B. Scherzer is an assistant professor in the psychology department at the State University of New York College at Potsdam. She completed her doctoral studies at the University of Arizona in clinical psychology, with an emphasis in sport psychology. Dr. Scherzer received her B.A. in psychology from Concordia University and her M.S. in athletic counseling at Springfield College. Her research interests include rehabilitation from injury, incorporating sport psychology in the athletic training room, eating disorders, and professional training and development. She has served as a regional student representative for the AAASP and is a member of the graduate training committee. She has done performance enhancement, injury rehabilitation, and academic counseling with intercollegiate athletes.

Andrea B. Schmid is professor emeritis of kinesiology at San Francisco State University. A two-time Olympian, she received gold, silver, and bronze medals in gymnastics. She coached the 1975 U.S. world championship team and judged 13 world championships and 3 Olympic Games in rhythmic gymnastics. She has published books and articles and given lectures on sport psychology at national and international conferences. Her research focuses on optimal performance. She is a member of the Federation of International Gymnastics and is the international consultant to the U.S. Gymnastics Federation. Dr. Schmid has served as sport psychology consultant to several college athletes and the U.S. Olympic rhythmic gymnasts and synchronized swimmers.

Ronald E. Smith is a professor of psychology and the director of clinical psychology training at the University of Washington. He received his bachelor's degree from Marquette University and his Ph.D. in clinical psychology from Southern Illinois University. He completed his advanced clinical training at the Neuropsychiatric Institute and Hospital, University of California, Los Angeles. Dr. Smith has held faculty positions at Purdue University and the University of Washington, as well as visiting appointments at Marquette University, the University of Hawaii, the University of New Mexico, and UCLA. His major research interests are in personality, stress and coping, and sport psychology research and intervention. For 12 years, he directed a psychological skills training program for the Houston Astros professional baseball organization. He has also served as a training consultant to the Oakland Athletics and Major League Soccer and as Team Counselor for the Seattle Mariners. Dr. Smith is a fellow of the Division of Exercise and Sport Psychology of the APA and a past president of the AAASP. He is the recipient of a Distinguished Alumnus Award from the UCLA Neuropsychiatric Institute for his contributions to the field of mental health. At the University of Washington, he has served as head of the social psychology and personality area and as co-director of the sport psychology graduate training program and Husky Sport Psychology Services in the Department of Intercollegiate Athletics. Dr. Smith has published more than 160 scientific articles and book chapters in his areas of interest. He also has authored or co-authored 23 books on introductory psychology, stress and stress management, sport psychology, and human performance enhancement. Sport-related books include *Psychological Skills in Professional Baseball, Children and Youth in Sport: A Biopsychosocial Perspective, Way to Go, Coach! A Scientifically-Proven Approach to Coaching Effectiveness, Coaches Who Never Lose: A 30-minute Primer for Coaching Effectiveness*, and *Sports and Your Child: A 50-Minute Guide for Parents*.

Frank L. Smoll is a professor in the Department of Psychology at the University of Washington. He is co-director (with Ronald Smith) of the sport psychology graduate program. Dr. Smoll's research focuses on coaching behaviors in youth sports and on the psychological effects of competition on children and adolescents. He has authored more than 100 scientific articles and book chapters, and he has co-authored or edited 15 books and manuals on children's athletics. Dr. Smoll is a fellow of the APA, the AAKPE, and the AAASP. He is a certified sport consultant and was the recipient of AAASP's Distinguished Professional Practice Award. In the area of applied sport psychology, Dr. Smoll has extensive experience in conducting psychologically oriented coaching clinics and workshops for parents of young athletes.

Bill Straub is a retired professor of sport psychology and sport biomechanics. Most recently he has taught sport psychology classes part-time at Binghamton and Syracuse Universities. In addition, he does sport psychology consulting work with high school, and college and university teams. Unusual for a sport psychologist, Straub is an avid videographer. His Sport Science International company specializes in sport video production. He makes recruiting tapes for high school athletes, and college and university teams. Bill received his Ph.D. from the University of Wisconsin, Madison and has earned master's degrees in education (State University of New York, Albany) and psychology (New School for Social Research). He is the author of many publications that have focused on such topics as team cohesion, mental training, and other important aspects of sport psychology.

Jim Taylor has been a consultant to Olympic sports federations and has worked with junior-elite, collegiate, world-class, and professional athletes for 19 years. He is currently in private practice, specializing in sports performance, parent education, corporate training, and injury rehabilitation. Dr. Taylor received his bachelor's degree from Middlebury College in Vermont and earned his M.A. and Ph.D. in psychology from the University of Colorado. He is a former associate professor in the School of Psychology at Nova University in Ft. Lauderdale. Dr. Taylor is the author of 8 books, has published over 400 popular and scholarly articles, and has given more than 500 workshops throughout North America and Europe. He competed internationally as an alpine ski racer, holds a second degree black belt in karate, and is a marathon runner and Ironman triathlete.

David Tod is a doctoral student at Victoria University in Melbourne, Australia. His dissertation is focused on professional practice and the training of sport psychology practitioners. His research interests also include cognitive factors in strength performance. Prior to beginning his Ph.D., David was employed at the Wiakato Institute of Technology in Hamilton, New Zealand, where he taught sport psychology and provided applied services to student-athletes. He was a consultant with the New Zealand Academy of Sport (Northern Institute) and has worked with athletes from a wide variety of sports. His master's degree is from the University of Otago, and he has twice received the New Zealand Sport Science award for best sport science article in the *New Zealand Coach Journal*. David's "performance" extends beyond sport and academic endeavors. He also performs on stage as an actor in local productions in Melbourne.

Darren Treasure holds an adjunct associate professor position in the Department of Psychology at Arizona State University. He currently serves as CEO of Competitive Advantage International Performance Systems, which offers a comprehensive and integrated approach in the assessment, development, and delivery of performance in sport and business. Darren received his doctoral degree from the University of Illinois at Urbana-Champaign in 1993. He has published over 50 scientific articles and book chapters and made over 100 presentations worldwide on motivation and the psychology of peak performance including keynote presentations at conferences in France, Norway, and the UK. As a sport psychology consultant, his past and present clients include Major League Baseball, the National Football League, the Ladies Professional Golf Association, the Women's United Soccer Association, Olympic champions, NCAA national champions, all-American athletes at a number of different universities, and elite adolescent performers in a wide range of sports. Darren is an editorial board member of the *Journal of Sport and Exercise Psychology* and *The Sport Psychologist*. He is also a member of the United States Soccer Federation National Coaching Staff and Sport Medicine Advisory Committee.

Brian A. Turner is an assistant professor of sport management in the School of Physical Activity and Educational Services at The Ohio State University. Prior to his current position, he was director of sport management at DeSales University and a visiting assistant professor at the University of Oklahoma. His primary research interests lie in the general area of organizational behavior, specifically focusing on athletic teams. Dr. Turner completed his Ph.D. under the supervision of Dr. Packianathan Chelladurai at The Ohio State University in 2001. Before starting his doctoral work, he was a high school basketball coach in Texas.

Robin S. Vealey is a professor in the Department of Physical Education, Health, and Sport Studies at Miami University. Dr. Vealey's research interests include self-confidence in sport, competitive activation and burnout, coaching effectiveness, and mental skills training. She has authored two books: *Coaching for the Inner Edge* and *Competitive Anxiety in Sport*. She has served as a sport psychology consultant for the U.S. Nordic Ski Team, U.S. Field Hockey, elite golfers, and athletes and teams at Miami University and in the Cincinnati area. Dr. Vealey is a fellow, certified consultant, and past president of the AAASP and former editor of *The Sport Psychologist*. A former collegiate basketball player and coach, she now enjoys the mental challenge of golf.

Robert S. Weinberg is a professor in the Department of Physical Education, Health, and Sport Studies at Miami University. He has published more than 140 journal articles as well as 6 books and 22 book chapters. He serves on the editorial boards of several sport psychology journals, including the *Journal of Sport and Exercise Psychology* and the *International Journal of Sport Psychology*. In addition, he was editor-in-chief of the *Journal of Applied Sport Psychology*. He has served as president of AAASP and NASPSPA and chair of the AAHPERD Sport Psychology Academy. He is a certified consultant of AAASP and a member of the U.S. Olympic Committee's Sport Psychology Registry. He has worked extensively with young athletes developing psychological skills in a variety of individual and team sports. He has been a varsity athlete in tennis, football, and basketball and has coached these three sports.

Vietta E. "Sue" Wilson is a professor at York University, where she teaches sport psychology, coaching, and self-regulation courses. She is a certified Biofeedback Certification Institute of America senior fellow in biofeedback and a fellow in electroencephalogram (EEG) biofeedback (neurofeedback). Her current work is the practical application of biofeedback-assisted relaxation for enhancing performance while her research centers on the use of EEG to assess and enhance performance. She has worked with a variety of sports, from archery to yachting, and a variety of people, from novice athletes to Olympic and world champions. Sue delivers performance enhancement services to corporations, schools, counseling, and medical clinics. She was an athlete and coach in three sports, taught for the Canadian Coaching

Certification Program, and she remains physically active.

David Yukelson is the coordinator of sport psychology services for the Penn State University Athletic Department. Through the Morgan Academic Support Center for Student-Athletes, he provides counseling and support to coaches and athletes in the areas of motivation and goal setting, leadership and communication skills, group cohesion and team building, mental training techniques for managing peak performance under pressure, coping skill strategies for handling multiple demands and stress effectively, personal and performance excellence in sport and life, and issues pertaining to the interpersonal growth and developmental needs of student-athletes. He is a past president, fellow, and certified consultant in the AAASP; has published numerous articles in professional refereed journals; and has served on the Editorial Boards for the *Journal of Applied Sport Psychology* and the *Journal of Sport and Exercise Psychology*. In addition, he is a consultant and member of the USA Track and Field Sport Psychology Registry, an associate with Lane Management Group in England, an advisory board member for Mushin Inc., and an internationally renowned lecturer on applied sport psychology interventions.

Nate Zinsser is director of the Performance Enhancement Program for the Center for Enhanced Performance at the United States Military Academy. He supervises a team of sport psychology trainers and conducts team and individual training for 600 cadet-athletes each year. Dr. Zinsser also provides sport psychology services to the U.S. Army's world-class athlete program; professional athletes; and "white collar" athletes in law, sales, and management. Dr. Zinsser is the author of *Dear Dr Psych*, the first sport psychology guidebook for youth sport participants, and he contributed a sport psychology advice column to *Sports Illustrated for Kids* for 5 years. His formal training in sport psychology from the University of Virginia is complemented by his experience as a state wrestling champion, world-class mountaineer, and third degree black belt in karate.

CHAPTER

1

Sport Psychology: Past, Present, Future

Jean M. Williams, *University of Arizona*
William F. Straub, *Sport Science International*

Within the past 30–35 years, the academic community and the public have recognized a new field of sport science. It is called **sport psychology,** and it is concerned with both the psychological factors that influence participation and performance in sport and exercise and the psychological effects derived from them. Sport psychologists study motivation, personality, violence, leadership, group dynamics, exercise and psychological well-being, thoughts and feelings of athletes, and many other dimensions of participation in sport and physical activity. Among other functions, modern-day sport psychologists teach sport psychology classes, conduct research, and work with athletes, coaches, and exercise participants to help improve performance and enhance the quality of the sport and exercise experience.

Coaches showed interest in the psychological aspects of athletic competition even before there was a science called sport psychology. For example, in the 1920s Knute Rockne, the football coach of the fighting Irish of Notre Dame, popularized the pep talk by making it an important part of his coaching. We should note, however, that Rockne did not attempt to psych up his team for every contest. He only used the pep talk for special occasions. Coaching interest in contemporary sport

psychology also involves more than a mere concern for psyching up athletes for competition.

Applied sport psychology focuses on only one facet of sport psychology, that of identifying and understanding psychological theories and interventions that can be applied to sport and exercise to enhance the performance and personal growth of athletes and physical activity participants. Applied sport psychology has grown tremendously in recent years, as evidenced by the number of coaches and athletes now looking to sport psychology for a competitive edge. These individuals have turned to various psychological training programs to learn, among other things, ways to manage competitive stress, control concentration, improve confidence, and increase communication skills and team harmony.

One goal of psychological interventions is to learn to consistently create the ideal mental climate that unleashes those physical skills that allow athletes to perform at their best. An additional goal, for exercise psychologists, is to use interventions to enhance physical and mental health by increasing exercise participation. In addition to these two broad goals, there are many specific intervention goals. What follows are a few situations that identify the diverse circumstances under which individuals might turn to the field of sport psychology for help.

When to use sport psychology

Val is only a third-year coach but already has the reputation of coaching players with excellent physical fundamentals and conditioning. Her team's poor play comes more from mental lapses and from not handling pressure. Val's goal this season is to increase her players' mental toughness.

Tim is a student athletic trainer. After taking a sport psychology workshop, he recognizes that he could be more effective in helping his injured athletes heal and be ready mentally to return to play if he incorporated psychological skills into their injury rehabilitation program.

Matt is a sport psychology consultant who was just hired by a professional team that rarely plays up to its potential because of internal dissention and too much concern with personal stats. His task is to help resolve the conflicts and enhance cohesiveness and team play.

Andrew is a fitness trainer at a health resort. Most of the guests either have led sedentary lives or have started exercise programs but quit within a few months. Andrew's job is to help the guests set fitness goals and plan strategies that will achieve those goals.

Brian arrives as a new wrestling coach at a major university. He discovers that some of his wrestlers are on steroids and others have eating disorders. What should he do?

Jennifer is a recreational golfer who has played for over 20 years. She loves golf but has become quite frustrated with her putting. Her normally excellent putting game has gone into a 2-year slump. She knows it's mental but can't seem to correct it.

Kimberly is a first-year physical education teacher who is having difficulty motivating many of her students to actively participate in class. How can she improve her teaching?

The authors of subsequent chapters will present psychological principles and interventions that can be used to enhance performance, personal growth, and health. These principles and interventions provide the foundation for effectively dealing with the preceding situations as well as many others that athletes, coaches, sport psychology consultants, athletic trainers, fitness trainers, and physical educators might encounter.

But, first, in this chapter we will provide a brief overview of the past, present, and future of sport psychology. Primary emphasis will be given to sport psychology practices in North America and the countries of Eastern Europe. The coverage is not all-inclusive but selective to the focus of the book.

History of Sport Psychology in North America

According to Mahoney (1989), sport psychology's conceptual roots lie in antiquity. For example, in early Greek and Asian cultures the interdependence of mind and body was not only acknowledged but emphasized as central to both performance and personal development. However, the scientific foundation of sport psychology emerged primarily during the last 35 years. Although modern sport psychology's roots and development lie largely within the domains of physical education and exercise science, psychologists also conducted some of the early influential sport psychology investigations.

Coleman Griffith, a psychologist who is considered by many to be the father of sport psychology in North America, was the first person to research sport psychology over an extended period of time. Griffith was hired by the University of Illinois in 1925 to help coaches improve the performance of their players. He wrote two books, *Psychology of Coaching* (1926) and *Psychology of Athletics* (1928), that are considered to be classics. He also established the first sport psychology laboratory in North America and taught the first course in sport psychology. By modern definition, Griffith was as much interested in motor learning as he was in sport psychology. Besides studying reaction time and flexibility, Griffith corresponded with Notre Dame coach Rockne about psychological and motivational aspects of coaching and athletics. Later Griffith served as a team psychologist and researcher for the Chicago Cubs baseball team. His personality study of the Cubs is of particular interest and importance because it was the forerunner of one of the first research emphases in sport psychology.

Following Griffith's work and up until the 1960s very little writing occurred in sport psychology, except for occasional research studies on personality and stress and a book, *Psychology of Coaching,* published in 1951 by John Lawther, a psychologist who also headed the Pennsylvania State University basketball team. Coaches were particularly interested in Lawther's treatment of such topics as motivation, team cohesion, personality, feelings and emotions, and handling athletes.

The 1960s: Birth of Applied Sport Psychology and Supporting Organizations

During the 1960s, two San Jose State University psychologists, Bruce Ogilvie and Tom Tutko (1966), created considerable interest in sport psychology with their research and their book *Problem Athletes and How to Handle Them.* According to Ogilvie, this book "moved the coaching world off dead center." After extensively researching the personality of athletes, Ogilvie and Tutko developed the controversial Athletic Motivation Inventory, a paper-and-pencil test that purported to measure the motives of athletes. Despite some criticism of their work, Ogilvie and Tutko were the leading applied sport psychologists of the 1960s. They did considerable consulting with college and professional teams and did much to foster public interest in sport psychology. Because of Ogilvie's

numerous contributions, many in the field have called him the father of applied sport psychology in North America.

The 1960s also witnessed the first attempts to bring together groups of individuals interested in sport psychology. Sport psychology began to organize on an international level with the formation in Rome in 1965 of the International Society of Sport Psychology (ISSP). Dr. Ferruccio Antonelli, an Italian psychiatrist, was elected the first president and provided leadership during the early years. The ISSP publishes the *International Journal of Sport Psychology* and hosts worldwide meetings. These gatherings provide a forum for sharing research and fostering the exchange of ideas by sport psychologists from different countries. At the First International Congress in Sport Psychology, more than 400 attendees representing 27 countries came to Rome.

The second meeting of the ISSP was hosted in 1968 at Washington, DC, by the newly formed North American Society for the Psychology of Sport and Physical Activity (NASPSPA). The first annual meeting of NASPSPA was held in 1967 prior to the American Alliance for Health, Physical Education, Recreation and Dance (AAHPERD) conference in Las Vegas, Nevada. Dr. Arthur Slatter-Hammel of Indiana University was the first president. NASPSPA hosts annual meetings that focus on research in the subareas of motor learning and control, motor development, and sport psychology.

The late 1960s also saw the formation of the Canadian Society for Psychomotor Learning and Sport Psychology (CSPLSP), also referred to as SCAPPS, to reflect the French translation of the name. Founded by Robert Wilberg at the University of Alberta in 1969, SCAPPS was initially under the auspices of the Canadian Association for Health, Physical Education and Recreation, but it became independent in 1977. The members and leaders of NASPSPA and CSPLSP were extremely influential in building the research base in sport psychology and gaining acceptance of the field. During this same time period, the equivalent can be said within Europe for sport psychologists who, in 1969, created the European Federation of Sport Psychology (FEPSAC—acronym reflects the

French translation of the name) and elected Ema Geron (then from Bulgaria, now Israel) as its first president.

Learn more about sport and exercise psychology by accessing the following Web sites:

Organizations in North America

American Alliance for Health, Physical Education, Recreation and Dance
http://www.aahperd.org

American College of Sports Medicine
http://www.acsm.org

Association for the Advancement of Applied Sport Psychology
http://www.aaasponline.org

Canadian Society for Psychomotor Learning and Sport Psychology
http://www.scapps.org

Division 47 of the American Psychological Association
http://www.psyc.unt.edu/apadiv47

Organizations Around the World

Asian South Pacific Association of Sport Psychology
http://www.humankinetics.com/associations/aspasp/index.cfm

Board of Sport Psychologists of the Australian Psychological Society
http://www.psychsociety.com.au/units/colleges/sport/

European Federation of Sport Psychology
http://www.fepsac.org

International Society of Sport Psychology
http://www.issponline.org

The 1970s: Field Grows and Moves Toward Interactionism and Cognitive Focus

The 1970s saw further organizational growth with sport psychology being added to the conference programs of the American College of Sports Medicine (ACSM) and AAHPERD. The Sport Psychology Academy (SPA), formed within AAHPERD in 1975, was the first group for which a major goal

was to bridge the gap between the researcher and practitioner by providing an opportunity for sport psychologists to share their research and expertise with coaches and physical education teachers.

The decade of the 1970s was the period in which sport psychology in North America began to flourish and to receive recognition as a separate discipline within the sport sciences. Systematic research by ever-increasing numbers of sport psychologists played a major role in this coming of age. In fact, the primary goal of sport psychologists in the 1970s was advancing sport psychology's knowledge base through experimental research. We should note, however, that no clear focus or agreement existed as to an appropriate knowledge base for the field. Consequently, research topics were very diverse and were directed toward many target populations. Topics typically came from mainstream psychology and from motor learning.

The earlier interest in personality research declined in the 1970s because of heated debates about the validity of personality traits and the paper-and-pencil tests used to assess the personality traits of athletes. Many sport psychologists continued to believe that internal mechanisms (i.e., traits) govern behavior, but these psychologists also became aware of the effect of environmental variables. The **interactionism paradigm,** which considers person and environmental variables and their potential interaction, surfaced and began to gain credibility. Today interactionism is the most viable approach to the understanding of sport and exercise behavior.

In the late 1970s and early 1980s sport psychology began to reflect a more cognitive focus by devoting increasing attention to athletes' thoughts and images. How athletes think influences how they perform. Negative thinking, the "I can't" attitude, seems to be associated with performance failure. The 1983 New York City Marathon provides an excellent example of how inner dialogue can influence the performance of runners. Geoff Smith, an Englishman, led for most of the race. Within approximately 300 meters of the finish line, Rod Dixon, a New Zealander, passed Smith and won the race. The difference between first and second place was 9 seconds, or about 50 yards. William P. Morgan (1984), a well-known sport psychology authority, indicated that

Dixon's success may have been aided by his cognitive strategy. According to newspaper reports, Dixon stated, "With a mile to go I was thinking, 'A miler's kick does the trick,' and 'I've got to go, I've got to go.'" By contrast, with 600 yards to go, Smith is reported to have said, "My legs have gone." Later Smith noted, "I was just running from memory. I thought I was going to stumble and collapse." In fact, Smith did collapse at the finish line. Today many sport psychologists who work in the area of applied sport psychology have developed techniques to train athletes to think positively by focusing on what they want to happen as opposed to what they do *not* want to happen. Perhaps the results of the 1983 New York Marathon would have differed had Smith employed these techniques.

The growth of cognitive sport psychology has also led to renewed interest in visualization. Athletes who naturally visualize themselves performing well or who are trained to image successful performances appear to both learn and perform better. Consequently, imagery and cognitive interventions have become an integral part of most mental training programs. See Chapters 17 and 18 for a detailed description of how these procedures work and how they can be trained.

The interest in cognitive sport psychology paralleled an increase in field research in sport psychology, which advanced knowledge in the area. Research has been conducted on topics such as identifying coaching behaviors most effective in promoting learning and personal growth; discovering ways to enhance team harmony and coach-athlete communications; learning how to set and use goals; determining psychological characteristics of successful performers; and developing psychological and behavioral interventions for enhancing performance, personal growth, and exercise participation.

The 1980s: Increased Research, Acceptance, and Breadth

An important development of the 1980s was better documentation of the effectiveness of psychological interventions at enhancing performance (see the chapters that follow and a meta-analysis by Greenspan and Feltz, 1989, for examples of research documentation from this era). In addition to this performance enhancement research, the 1980s saw increased attention given to exercise and health psychology issues such as the psychological effects of exercise and overtraining, factors influencing participation in and adherence to exercise programs, exercise addiction, psychology of injury and injury rehabilitation, and the relationship of exercise to stress reactivity. Although much still needs to be learned and tested in regard to these topics in applied sport psychology, important advances have been made. The advances that are integral to enhancing sport performance, personal growth, and exercise participation will be discussed specifically in the following chapters.

Journals. Perhaps the best reflection of the quality and volume of work in any academic area is the number of research journals devoted strictly to the discipline. By the start of the 1970s, there were two such journals for the field of sport psychology, and the 1980s saw the addition of two more. The first sport psychology journal was the *International Journal of Sport Psychology,* published initially in 1970, and in 1979 the second was established, the *Journal of Sport Psychology.* Its name was changed in 1988 to *Journal of Sport and Exercise Psychology* to reflect an expanding research base dealing with exercise and health psychology issues. The tremendous growth in applied sport psychology is exemplified by the establishment of *The Sport Psychologist* in 1987 and the *Journal of Applied Sport Psychology* in 1989. Both of these journals are devoted exclusively to applied sport psychology. *The Sport Psychologist* publishes research and professional practice articles that deal primarily with performance enhancement questions, and the *Journal of Applied Sport Psychology* encompasses the areas of social, health, performance enhancement, and clinical/counseling psychology.

USOC recognition. Considerable growth and recognition of applied sport psychology also occurred because of publicity stemming from sport psychologists working with athletes, particularly Olympic athletes. In 1978 the United States Olympic Committee (USOC) recruited expert advisers in four branches of sport science: biomechanics, exercise physiology, nutrition, and sport psychology. This development was the first indication of the USOC's interest in using sport psychologists to help elite athletes enhance their performance. Later, in 1983, the USOC established an official Sport Psychology Committee and a registry of qualified sport psychologists. Following intensive review of an individual's credentials and experiences, he or she could be recognized as either a research, educational, or clinical sport psychologist. As a result of the USOC's development of its sport psychology program, sport psychologists played an increasingly prominent and visible role in the 1984 and 1988 Olympics (see Suinn, 1985, and issue #4, 1989, *The Sport Psychologist*). Television and written coverage of various sport psychology topics and interventions with Olympic athletes also created considerable interest among professionals and laypersons. Involvement by sport psychologists in the Olympic movement and on the professional level (see issue #4, 1990, *The Sport Psychologist*) and intercollegiate level continues to grow.

Formation of AAASP and APA Division 47. The interest and knowledge base in sport psychology also is reflected by the number and quality of its national and international organizations. In addition to the ISSP, NASPSPA, CSPLSP, SPA, and ACSM, the Association for the Advancement of Applied Sport Psychology (AAASP) was formed in 1985. John Silva, a University of North Carolina sport psychologist, played the primary role in forming AAASP and served as its first president. The purpose of AAASP is to provide a forum to address applied aspects of sport psychology such as the promotion of applied research in the areas of social, health, and performance enhancement psychology; the promotion of the appropriate application of these research findings; and the examination of professional issues such as ethical standards, qualifications for becoming a sport psychologist, and certification of sport psychologists. Another objective is to promote the field of sport psychology within general psychology and to encourage membership from interested individuals trained in general psychology and other relevant disciplines as well as sport psychologists

trained through physical education and exercise and sport science departments. AAASP appears to have met the latter objective, as approximately half of its 1,000+ members are individuals with degrees in psychology or equivalent departments.

Additional support for the growing recognition of sport psychology within mainstream psychology comes from the American Psychological Association (APA). In 1987 the APA officially recognized a sport psychology division, Division 47. Bill Morgan, a University of Wisconsin sport psychologist, served as the first president. Division 47 provides APA members with an opportunity to share research and discuss relevant sport psychology issues.

The 1990s–Present: Progress in Research, Application, and Professional Issues

The last 15 years have been characterized by exciting growth in knowledge and practice of sport psychology and considerable progress regarding professional issues in sport psychology.

Research. Particularly impressive, and relevant to this book, is the research into the effectiveness of interventions to enhance the performance of athletes and to increase the physical activity levels of all types of individuals. For a quantitative review of these intervention studies, see the meta-analysis of Meyers, Whelan, and Murphy (1996) for the sport performance studies and Dishman and Buckworth (1996) for the exercise adoption and adherence studies. See Chapters 11 to 21 and 27 in this book for a discussion of intervention advances since the publication of these meta-analyses. Although more research is needed, particularly regarding the efficacy of interventions and what influences their effectiveness, the findings from the last 15 years should quiet critics who have questioned whether sufficient knowledge exists to justify ethical delivery of sport psychology services.

Also noteworthy is the growth in qualitative research. Before the 1990s, research consisted almost exclusively of quantitative paradigms. A recent review of publications from 1990 to 1999 in three sport psychology journals indicated 84 articles (approximately 1 out of 7) used a qualitative data collection technique such as interviews, observation, and open-ended questions (Culver, Gilbert, & Trudel, 2003). Qualitative studies have the potential to add greatly to knowledge in applied sport psychology because rather than statistically analyzing numbers or ratings, they involve researchers looking for trends and patterns in what people say and how they act.

Sport psychology books. Another reflection of the increase in knowledge in sport psychology and its application comes from the tremendous growth in the number of books dealing with applied sport psychology. In a 1991 critique of psychological skills training books in applied sport psychology, Sachs identified 48 books. The list had grown to 187 books by 1998 (Sachs & Kornspan, 1998) and to 282 by 2004 (Burke, Sachs, & Gomer, 2004)!

Training of sport psychology consultants. What is the necessary minimum curriculum to produce the scholarly base, competencies, and practitioner skills for the would-be sport psychology consultant? Answering that question, and then monitoring the impact that the resulting standardized curriculum would have on graduate programs, the training of graduate students, and the use of sport psychology consultants, has been a major professional focus of the last 15 years. One answer to the question occurred in 1991 when AAASP established a curricular model for individuals to become certified by AAASP to provide services such as performance enhancement interventions for athletes. AAASP's standards encompass 14 criteria, including a doctoral degree from an accredited institution of higher education and knowledge that bridges the disciplines of psychology (e.g., basic skills in counseling, psychopathology, and its assessment) and kinesiology (e.g., physiological bases of sport or biomechanics; historical, philosophical, social, or motor behavior bases of sport). Also required is knowledge in sport psychology (equivalent of three courses), training in professional ethics and standards, and a supervised practicum with a qualified individual (i.e., one who has an appropriate background in applied sport psychology). Two changes have occurred since 1991. The supervision requirement was made more stringent in 1994 by increasing

the required hours to 400, and in 2002 AAASP approved standards and a process for certifying individuals with a Master's degree. See AAASP's Web site (http://www.aaasponline.org) for the specific criteria and process for becoming a certified consultant.

Tracking surveys of the 1989 to 1994 (Andersen, Williams, Aldridge, & Taylor, 1997) and 1994 to 1999 (Williams & Scherzer, 2003), graduates of sport psychology programs found that most of the 14 criteria for obtaining certified consultant status had been met by high percentages of Master's and doctoral graduates who had consulting as a career goal. One disturbing finding, however, was that the 1994 to 1999 doctoral graduates were less prepared to meet the criteria than those from 1989 to 1994. Whether good or bad, it appears that this curricular model has influenced the program of study of most graduate students in the United States who have an interest in consulting. Another indication of the acceptance of AAASP's certification standards is that, starting in 1996, the USOC requires consultants who wish to work with Olympic programs to be AAASP-certified. Unfortunately, it is highly unlikely that other consumers are equally aware of the importance of picking qualified consultants.

Another training issue during the 1990s was who would house sport psychology graduate programs. The preceding tracking surveys found that 20% and 12%, respectively, of the doctoral graduates from the first and second 5-year blocks received their degrees from psychology/counseling departments. Although taking coursework that bridges the disciplines of psychology and kinesiology is common, it appears that sport science and physical education departments remain the primary home department for sport psychology programs.

Ethical standards. Another professional issue on which the 1990s provided much progress is that of setting standards for ethical behavior. Although the growth in applied sport psychology led to a tremendous boon for individuals interested in consulting, negative by-products resulted, such as unqualified individuals providing the services and unethical practitioners promising more than they can deliver. These concerns, and others, led AAASP in 1994 and 1996 to approve ethical standards and guidelines for sport psychologists (see Burke, Sachs, & Gomer, 2004, for a copy). Individuals certified by AAASP have to agree to observe these ethical standards.

Consulting job market. Tremendous growth has occurred over the last 15 years in the opportunities that exist for applied sport psychologists to do consulting. For example, of the 1994 to 1999 sport psychology graduates in the Williams and Scherer (2003) tracking study, 52% of the doctoral graduates and 41% of the Master's graduates indicated that they did some paid sport psychology consulting. In most of the cases, the work was part rather than full time. Only 13 (12%) of the doctoral graduates and 7 (5%) of the Master's graduates held a full-time position doing performance enhancement consulting. Some of this consulting occurred in domains outside of sport such as music, business, and health (e.g., injury rehabilitation in medical centers). When asked about the ease or difficulty in finding paid consulting work, almost equal numbers of the doctoral graduates responded very easy or moderately easy, moderately difficult, very difficult, or did not seek such work. Although progress has occurred from the findings with 1989 to 1994 graduates, it is still unrealistic to expect to find full-time work doing sport psychology consulting. For example, of 51 (53% of the sample) NCAA Division I universities that provide sport psychology services, only 7 (14%) of the athletic departments employed a full-time sport psychology consultant (Voight & Callaghan, 2001).

Academic job market. The last 15 years have shown a tremendous growth in academic positions as an increasing number of colleges and universities recognized the contribution that sport psychologists can make to their research mission and to the education of future coaches, physical education teachers, athletic trainers, fitness specialists, and psychologists. For example, the graduate tracking studies found that 54 of the 92 doctoral respondents from 1989 to 1994 obtained positions in kinesiology departments (Andersen et al., 1997) compared to a figure of 66 of 107 for the 1994 to 1999 graduates (Williams & Scherzer,

2003). In contrast, an even earlier study of just kinesiology doctoral graduates from 1984 to 1989 found that only 23 of the 34 respondents obtained positions in colleges/universities (Waite & Pettit (1993). From 1989 to 1999, academic appointments in psychology departments dropped from 12 to 5 over the two 5-year time spans, but this drop was probably more a reflection of fewer graduates from psychology departments (12 vs. 20). When the 1994 to 1999 graduates were asked if they held a replacement or new academic position, 19 indicated new positions (16 in kinesiology and 3 in psychology departments). All the new positions, except for two in kinesiology, were described as having a primary emphasis in sport psychology. As promising as this growth appears, enthusiasm should be tempered by the fact that we do not know how many sport psychology positions were lost over this time span.

Growth in exercise psychology. Another important development of the last 15 years is that exercise psychology has become a highly viable area of specialization, particularly within the academic community. Although the content within this domain is meritorious in its own right (e.g., identifying why people exercise and how to increase and maintain exercise behavior), much of the growth has been driven by widespread grant support. For example, funding opportunities have occurred because of recent attention to the exercise goals in Healthy People 2000 and the position statements from the ACSM and Centers for Disease Control on the importance of exercise in reducing risk of disease and all-cause mortality. See Chapter 27 for a presentation of the latest knowledge and interventions in exercise psychology.

History of Sport Psychology in Eastern Europe

Sport psychology in the former iron curtain countries of Eastern Europe is of particular importance to people interested in peak performance. These nations have a long history of giving a great deal of attention to the applied aspects of sport psychology—more specifically, to enhancing elite athletes' performance through applied research and direct intervention. As a consequence of this emphasis, sport psychologists in Eastern Europe played an active role at all levels in the selection, training, and competitive preparation of athletes.

Before the breakup of the Soviet Union and the fall of communist control, sport psychology in Eastern Europe was a highly esteemed field of academic and professional concern as evidenced by state support and the acceptance of sport psychologists in national psychological associations. In some nations, sport psychologists were even awarded the title of academician, a title that elevated the recipient to the level of a national hero. All of this occurred because the countries perceived sport excellence as an important propaganda tool in advancing the communist political system, and sport psychologists were viewed as central figures in facilitating the athlete's quest for excellence.

Vanek and Cratty (1970) reported that the first interest in sport psychology in Eastern Europe can be traced to a physician, Dr. P. F. Lesgaft, who described in 1901 the possible psychological benefits of physical activity. The first research articles were published by Puni and Rudik in the early 1920s. The Institutes for Physical Culture in Moscow and Leningrad also were established in the early 1920s, and the beginning of sport psychology can be traced to them.

Garfield (Garfield & Bennett, 1984), who visited with a group of Soviet sport psychologists and physiologists while lecturing in Milan in 1979, reported that "the extensive investment in athletic research in the communist countries began early in the 1950s as part of the Soviet space program" (p. 13). Russian scientists successfully explored the possibility of using ancient yogic techniques to teach cosmonauts to control psychophysiological processes while in space. These techniques were called **self-regulation training** or **psychic self-regulation** and were used to voluntarily control such bodily functions as heart rate, temperature, and muscle tension, as well as emotional reactions to stressful situations such as zero gravity. Nearly 20 years passed before these methods were systematically applied

to the Soviet and East German sport programs. According to Kurt Tittel, then director of the Leipzig Institute of Sports (a 14-acre sport laboratory that during the 1970s employed 900 people, over half of whom were scientists), new training methods similar to psychic self-regulation were responsible for the impressive victories by East German and Soviet athletes during the 1976 Olympics (Garfield & Bennett, 1984).

Salmela (1984) reported that sport psychology research in Eastern European countries was more limited in scope than in North America because of greater governmental control. Rather narrowly focused 5-year research plans were determined by the state with the advice of its sport psychologists. All sport psychology researchers within the country were required to coordinate and streamline their research efforts to accomplish the stated research objective. Salmela (1981) also indicated that this research focus tended to be of a field variety and applied primarily toward top-level achievement in sport. This focus is not surprising considering each state's heavy emphasis on sport excellence and the easy access by sport psychologists to elite athletes. Most of the Eastern European sport institutes where the athletes were trained had teams of sport psychologists. For example, Salmela (1984), on a visit to a major sport institute in Bucharest, Romania, reported meeting with a team of eight sport psychologists. A sport psychology faculty of that size is considered normal for that type of sport institute. In contrast, in North America it is uncommon for an institution to have more than one or two people specifically trained in sport psychology.

Although most North American sport psychologists would find government-dictated research endeavors abhorrent, a large-scale, unified approach to a particular research topic does have advantages. Salmela (1984) cited one positive example that was a consequence of knowledge gained from a constrained focus of attention. All Eastern European countries successfully inaugurated as many as 30 hours of theory and practice of training in self-control for all elite athletes. Equivalent types of programs have been implemented on only a limited basis in North America.

The exact training techniques employed by the Eastern European sport psychologists remain vague; however, a book by a Russian sport psychologist indicates that autogenic training, visualization, and autoconditioning (self-hypnosis) were key components (Raiport, 1988). Because of its government-funded research and widespread integration of sophisticated mental training programs with rigorous physical training, many authorities believed Eastern Europe was ahead of North America and the rest of the world in the development and application of applied sport psychology. Whatever gap that initially existed has closed as North Americans complemented their growing research base with experience in implementing performance-enhancement interventions with athletes. With the late 1980s and the 1990s bringing the termination of communist control in Eastern Europe and the breakup of the Soviet Union, the status of sport and sport psychology has changed in these previously called Iron Curtain countries. With the considerable decline in state support, many sport psychology consultants that worked with elite athletes have either lost their positions or moved to other countries. Another consequence of these changes is a broadening of interests (e.g., noncompetition) among the remaining sport psychologists (Kantor & Ryzonkin, 1993).

Future Directions in North American Applied Sport Psychology

What should be the future directions in sport psychology research? Will the effectiveness of performance-enhancement techniques be rigorously tested with elite athletes? Will we continue to bridge the gap between research and practice? What will be the impact on graduate curriculums of AAASP's certification standards? Will the training of future sport psychologists more rigorously merge the disciplines of psychology and sport science? Will future sport psychology practitioners be certified? Will the acceptance of sport psychology by mainstream psychology continue to grow? How much consulting growth will occur in psychology of excellence domains outside of sport?

Will exercise psychologists dominate the academic market because of their potential for greater external research funding? Will professional organizations do a better job marketing the field of sport psychology and the services of qualified sport psychology consultants?

As these questions indicate, many challenges remain for the field of sport psychology. Its future nature and scope hinge on the answers to these questions and others. We offer a few observations and predictions regarding some of the questions. One certainty in this new millennium is that both knowledge and interest in sport psychology will continue to grow and even larger numbers of individuals will seek the services of a sport psychology consultant or express interest in becoming a sport psychologist. The appropriate training of these future sport psychologists will depend on their career goals. For those who aspire to do consulting work, we believe AAASP's certified consultant requirements will remain the dominant curricular model for their training and that efforts will continue to increase flexibility in meeting the requirements. Because of a tremendous growth in the knowledge base within sport and exercise psychology, we predict even greater specialization in the training of future students. The growth in specialization will particularly continue within health and exercise psychology, driven largely by ever-increasing opportunities in external research funding and the resulting potential for academic positions.

The tracking studies of graduate students indicate that more career opportunities are needed for sport psychologists. We predict the academic job market will remain strong, but it must be supplemented by greater growth in consulting and nontraditional career options. The most consulting opportunities in the future, including full-time ones, will probably come from applied sport psychologists who recognize the potential for using their training in sport psychology not just in sport settings but also to enhance performance in domains such as the performing arts, music, business, and the military. For example, Gould (2002) noted that the 2001 American Psychological Association Convention contained many sessions on corporate "coaching," that is, helping businesspersons achieve performance excellence. With only minimal additional training and preparation, who is better qualified than sport psychology consultants to do such coaching? (See the December 2002 issue of the *Journal of Applied Sport Psychology,* which was devoted to moving beyond the psychology of athletic excellence, for articles regarding these types of consulting.) Other less traditional realms for future career growth are areas such as youth life-skills development through sport, injury prevention and rehabilitation (e.g., hospitals, sports medicine, and physical therapy centers), and exercise and wellness promotion (e.g., insurance companies, employee wellness programs, medical centers, and treatment centers for substance abuse). Good examples of programs in youth life-skills development are The First Tee (Petlichkoff, 2004; http://www.thefirsttee.org) and Play It Smart (Petitpas, Van Raalte, Cornelius, & Presbrey, 2004; http://playitsmart.footballfoundation.com).

In the future, we anticipate even greater acceptance of sport psychology within mainstream psychology. One new impetus for greater acceptance comes from what sport psychology has to offer the call for psychologists to put more emphasis on studying positive psychology, which seeks to understand positive emotion and build one's strengths and virtues (Seligman & Csikszentmihalyi, 2000). The field of sport psychology has been doing this since its inception! Although greater acceptance will result in things such as more overlap in research questions and professional practice and more sport psychology and psychology of excellence course offerings in psychology departments, we do not anticipate that they will lead to appreciable increases in sport psychology appointments within psychology departments.

In conclusion, as great as the growth of sport psychology has been, the future looks even brighter. We are confident that the field of sport psychology has much to offer you, the reader of this book. We are hopeful that you will use the content in this book to enhance your own performance and personal growth.

Summary

Sport psychology, the youngest of the sport sciences, is concerned with the psychological factors that influence participation and performance in sport and exercise and with the psychological effects derived from participation. Today many athletes and coaches look to sport psychology for a competitive edge by seeking psychological training programs to learn, among other things, ways to manage competitive stress, control concentration, improve confidence, and increase communication skills and team harmony.

The roots of sport psychology in North America go back to Coleman Griffith, a psychologist who was hired in 1925 by the University of Illinois to help improve the performance of its athletes. Griffith taught the first course in sport psychology, established the first sport psychology laboratory in North America, and wrote the first psychology of coaching book (1926). Following Griffith's contributions in the 1920s and 1930s, very little happened in sport psychology until the 1960s. The 1960s witnessed the first attempts to bring together groups of individuals interested in sport psychology, which resulted in the formation of several sport psychology associations. During the 1970s, sport psychology in North America began to flourish. Systematic research by increasing numbers of sport psychologists played a major role in this coming of age. Research topics were very diverse and were channeled toward many populations.

During the 1980s a shift occurred from primarily laboratory to field research. It became popular to apply psychological theories and interventions to sport to enhance the performance and personal growth of athletes. Increased attention also was given to exercise and health psychology issues. The growth in applied sport psychology resulted in the formation of an additional sport psychology organization and two new journals. The last 15 years saw a tremendous growth in knowledge and increased career opportunities in academia and consulting, including performance enhancement work with nonsport populations such as performing artists and businesspeople. Exercise psychology became an even stronger specialization area. Great strides were made in addressing critical professional issues such as trying to identify minimal standards for training and certifying sport psychologists and establishing a code of ethics. During this same time, sport psychology became more acceptable to mainstream psychology, and an increasing number of psychologists became active in sport psychology.

In contrast, sport psychology in the countries of Eastern Europe has a long history of devoting a great deal of attention to enhancing the performance of elite athletes through applied research and direct intervention. Sport psychologists in these countries were viewed as central figures in facilitating an athlete's quest for excellence. Thus, they were held in great esteem because sport excellence was considered an important propaganda tool in advancing the communist political system of Eastern Europe. With the breakup of communist party control in Eastern Europe and the reduction in governmental support of sport psychology researchers and practitioners, the future for sport psychology in Eastern Europe does not look as bright as its past.

Many questions and challenges remain for the field of sport psychology, but one certainty is that both knowledge and interest in sport psychology will continue to grow. Key future challenges will be trying to grow the job market at a rate that parallels the increasing number of individuals interested in becoming a sport psychologist and then ensuring that these future sport psychologists are appropriately trained for the job market. We predict the academic job market will remain strong, and particularly so for individuals specializing in exercise psychology, but it must be supplemented by greater growth in consulting and nontraditional career options. The increased emphasis on positive psychology within mainstream psychology will have the effect of increasing sport psychology's visibility and acceptance within mainstream psychology. As great as the growth of sport psychology has been, the future looks even brighter.

Study Questions

1. Define what is meant by applied sport psychology and when it might be used.

2. How are sport psychologists trained and what do they do?

3. Briefly describe the development of sport psychology in North America.

4. Contrast the development of sport psychology in Eastern Europe to that in North America.

5. If you designed and ran a really good study that might be publishable or given as a talk, what journals and organizations would you want to check out?

6. What are some of the concerns and questions that sport psychologists must address in the future?

7. What relationship does sport psychology have to the call for psychologists to put more emphasis on positive psychology?

8. Describe some of the nontraditional job opportunities that sport psychologists might pursue.

References

Andersen, M. B., Williams, J. M., Aldridge, T., & Taylor, T. (1997). Tracking the training and careers of graduates of advanced degree programs in sport psychology, 1989 to 1994. *The Sport Psychologist, 11,* 326–344.

Burke, K. L., Sachs, M. L., & Gomer, S. (Eds.). (2004). *Directory of graduate programs in applied sport psychology* (7th ed.). Morgantown, WV: Fitness Information Technology.

Culver, D. M., Gilbert, W. D., & Trudel, P. (2003). A decade of qualitative research in sport psychology journals: 1990–1999. *The Sport Psychologist, 17,* 1–15.

Dishman, R. K., & Buckworth, J. (1996). Increasing physical activity. A quantitative synthesis. *Medicine and Science in Sports and Exercise, 28,* 706–719.

Garfield, C. A., & Bennett, H. Z. (1984). *Peak performance.* Los Angeles: Tarcher.

Gould, D. (2002). Sport psychology in the new millennium: The psychology of athletic excellence and beyond. *Journal of Applied Sport Psychology, 14,* 137–139.

Greenspan, M. J., & Feltz, D. L. (1989). Psychological interventions with athletes in competitive situations: A review. *The Sport Psychologist, 3,* 219–236.

Griffith, C. R. (1926). *Psychology of coaching.* New York: Scribner.

Griffith, C. R. (1928). *Psychology of athletics.* New York: Scribner.

Kantor, E., & Ryzonkin, J. (1993). Sport psychology in the former USSR. In R. N. Singer, M. Murphey, & L. K. Tennant (Eds.), *Handbook of research on sport psychology* (pp. 46–49). New York: Macmillan.

Lawther, J. D. (1951). *Psychology of coaching.* Englewood Cliffs, NJ: Prentice Hall.

Mahoney, M. J. (1989). Sport psychology. In I. Cohen (Ed.), *The G. Stanley Hall lecture series* (Vol. 9, pp. 97–134). Washington, DC: American Psychological Association.

Meyers, A. W., Whelan, J. P., & Murphy, S. M. (1996). Cognitive behavioral strategies in athletic performance enhancement. In M. Hersen, R. M. Eisler, & P. M. Miller (Eds.), *Progress in behavior modification, v. 30* (pp. 137–164). Pacific Grove, CA: Brooks/Cole.

Morgan, W. P. (1984). Mind over matter. In W. F. Straub & J. M. Williams (Eds.), *Cognitive sport psychology* (pp. 311–316). Lansing, NY: Sport Science International.

Ogilvie, B., & Tutko, T. (1966). *Problem athletes and how to handle them.* London: Pelham.

Petitpas, A. J., Van Raalte, J. L., Cornelius, A., & Presbrey, J. (2004). A life skills development program for high school student-athletes. *The Journal of Primary Prevention, 24,* 325–334.

Petlichkoff, L. M. (2004). Self-regulation skills in children and adolescents. In M. R. Weiss (Ed.), *Developmental sport and exercise psychology: A lifespan perspective* (pp. 273–292). Morgantown, WV: Fitness Information Technology, Inc.

Raiport, G. (1988). *Red gold: Peak performance techniques of the Russian and East German Olympic victors*. New York: Tarcher.

Sachs, M. L. (1991). Reading list in applied sport psychology: Psychological skills training. *The Sport Psychologist, 5,* 88–91.

Sachs, M. L., Burke, K. L., & Gomer, S. (Eds.). (1998). *Directory of graduate programs in applied sport psychology* (5th ed.). Morgantown, WV: Fitness Information Technology.

Sachs, M. L., & Kornspan, A. S. (1998). Reading list in applied sport psychology: Psychological skills training. In M. L. Sachs, K. L. Burke, & S. Gomer (Eds.), *Directory of graduate programs in applied sport psychology* (5th ed., pp. 264–274). Morgantown, WV: Fitness Information Technology.

Salmela, J. H. (1981). *The world sport psychology sourcebook*. Ithaca, NY: Mouvement Publications.

Salmela, J. H. (1984). Comparative sport psychology. In J. M. Silva III & R. A. Weinberg (Eds.), *Psychological foundations of sport* (pp. 23–24). Champaign, IL: Human Kinetics.

Seligman, M., & Csikszentmihalyi, M. (2000). Positive psychology: An introduction. *American Psychologist, 55,* 5–14.

Suinn, R. M. (1985). The 1984 Olympics and sport psychology. *Journal of Sport Psychology, 7,* 321–329.

U.S. Olympic Committee. (1983). U.S. Olympic Committee establishes guidelines for sport psychology services. *Journal of Sport Psychology, 5,* 4–7.

Vanek, M., & Cratty, B. J. (1970). *Psychology and the superior athlete*. New York: Macmillan.

Voight, M., & Callaghan, J. (2001). The use of sport psychology services at NCAA Division I universities from 1998–1999. *The Sport Psychologist, 15,* 91–102.

Waite, B. T., & Pettit, M. E. (1993). Work experiences of graduates from doctoral programs in sport psychology. *Journal of Applied Sport Psychology, 5,* 234–250.

Williams, J. M., & Scherzer, C. B. (2003). Tracking the training and careers of graduates of advanced degree programs in sport psychology, 1994 to 1999. *Journal of Applied Sport Psychology, 15,* 335–353.

Learning, Motivation, and Effective Leadership

Motor Skill Learning for Effective Coaching and Performance

Cheryl A. Coker, *New Mexico State University*
Mark G. Fischman, *Auburn University*
Joseph B. Oxendine, *University of North Carolina at Pembroke*

It's not necessarily the amount of time you spend at practice that counts; it's what you put into the practice.

—Eric Lindros

Effective coaching depends on many factors. Coaches must have excellent knowledge of their sport and be innovative strategists, skilled motivators, and effective personal counselors. However, at the core of successful coaching is an understanding of the motor learning process. First and foremost, effective coaches must be good teachers. Most sports comprise a diverse array of complex motor skills. Athletes enter the sporting arena with different abilities and prior experiences. The coach must understand both how the novice performer acquires brand-new skills and how the experienced athlete maintains, and possibly improves, peak performance on well-learned skills. This understanding will enable the coach to structure effective practices and to provide clear, effective feedback to the athlete about performance errors. For the sport psychologist, this understanding serves as the basis for a more comprehensive assessment of athlete behavior and of potential intervention strategies that will enhance performance.

This chapter's goal is to present coaches and sport psychologists with information concerning the essentials of motor skill learning. We begin by providing a formal definition of the term **motor learning**, and then we describe a three-phase model of the learning process. Next, we proceed to two topics that are among the most critical determinants of skill learning and performance: practice considerations and information feedback. Clearly, a wealth of other topics also are important for motor skill learning. However, the topics chosen were selected because of their immediate relevance to the practical world of coaching. The principles and recommendations in this chapter are based on knowledge derived from motor learning research but with the understanding that in some areas the current state of research may be less than adequate for making generalizations to applied sport settings.

Motor Learning Defined

Motor skill learning should be understood as a set of internal processes, associated with practice or experience, leading to relatively permanent changes in the capability for skilled movement behavior. **Capability** means that once a skill has been learned, the potential, or likelihood, for exhibiting skilled performance is quite high, although we realize that even highly skilled athletes do occasionally make errors. Because motor learning is internal, taking place within the athlete's central nervous system, we cannot observe learning directly. We can, however, monitor an athlete's *performance*, which is observable behavior, and draw an inference about learning. For example, a beginning swimmer's first attempts at the butterfly stroke will likely proceed in an awkward, step-by-step manner. As the swimmer practices, form, timing, and coordination improve. By monitoring these changes in performance, we infer that the swimmer is learning. It is also important that the changes in performance are relatively permanent; that is, the athlete should be able to demonstrate the skill repeatedly, even after a period of no practice.

Phases of Motor Skill Learning

As athletes progress from the novice stage to an advanced level, they go through different phases or steps. These phases commonly are characterized by the goal of the athlete in each (Gentile, 2000), as well as their behavioral tendencies (Fitts & Posner, 1967). Such information is useful, as it provides the coach a basis from which to make informed decisions that will optimize the learning of his or her athletes. Consequently, the section that follows describes three phases through which athletes traverse based on Fitts and Posner's model (1967), and the role of the coach in each. It would, however, be misleading to think of these phases as distinct because, as learning progresses, one phase blends gradually into another so that no clear transition between them is evident (Christina & Corcos, 1988; Fitts & Posner, 1967). Thus, the phases of learning should be thought of as a continuum, with some overlap occurring between them (see Figure 2-1).

The Cognitive Phase

In the cognitive or beginning phase of skill learning, athletes focus on gaining an understanding of how the skill is to be performed. The coach or instructor assists the athlete in this process by describing the skill's key elements. In addition, he or she will typically provide demonstrations, films, charts, or other visual cues to help the learners "picture" the new skill. During this period, the athletes use cognition, or mental processes, to gain

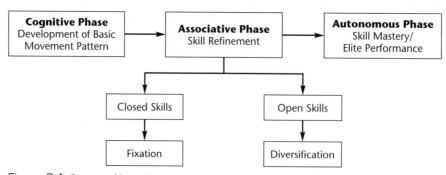

Figure 2-1 **Stages of learning**

an understanding of how the task is to be performed. The cognitive phase is characterized by much verbal activity by the athletes; they "talk" themselves through the movements.

Based on the explanation and demonstrations provided by the coach, athletes begin to develop a **motor program** for that skill. A motor program is an abstract, internal representation of the skill, similar to a computer program that contains a set of instructions to guide the movement. These instructions are written in the language of the individual's nervous and muscular systems and allow athletes to begin practicing the skill. At first the motor program may be very crude, containing just enough details to allow the athletes to make a "ballpark" response. There also are likely to be errors in the program, just as there would be in the initial attempts to write a complex computer program. However, with practice and feedback, both from the athlete's sensory systems and from the coach, the motor program is revised and refined so that it gradually becomes more effective at controlling performance.

Much conscious attention is directed toward the details of the movement in this phase and athletes are unable to focus on aspects of the environment as a result. In other words, they will be unable to attend to external events such as the positions of teammates or movements of defensive players. The movements produced in this phase will lack synchronization and appear choppy and deliberate. This phase is also characterized by inconsistency, and the production of numerous errors that are typically gross in nature. Athletes will be highly dependent on the coach at this point as they lack the capability to determine the specific cause of an error and its subsequent correction (Coker, 2004). Finally, the dominant sensory system in the cognitive phase of learning is *vision*; we visually monitor our limbs when first practicing a new skill. For example, observe a young child learning to dribble a basketball: the child intently watches both the hand and the ball, knowing that, without such visual guidance, the dribble will be lost. Vision of the limbs also is important in the beginning phase of learning skills that do not involve manipulating another object, such as learning a new gymnastics routine.

Role of the coach. The role of the coach during the cognitive phase is to facilitate the athlete's development of a basic movement pattern by clearly communicating the critical aspects of the skill through verbal instructions and demonstrations. There is much truth in the saying "a picture is worth a thousand words," and a demonstration will help learners create a reference image of the skill so that practice can begin. However, a correctly performed demonstration does not necessarily ensure that the athletes' attention was focused on the most important part of the demonstration. Verbal cues should be used to direct athletes' attention in conjunction with the demonstration (McCullagh, Steihl & Weiss, 1990; Weiss & Klint, 1987; Zetou, Tzetzis, Vernadakis, & Kioumourtzoglou, 2002). The coach must tell the athletes *specifically* what to look for, whether it be the pattern of racket movement in a looped tennis backswing, the position of the recovery elbow in the freestyle, or the entire pattern of coordination in a baseball swing. Magill (2004) further recommends that those cues be short and concise rather than providing "continuous verbal commentary while demonstrating the skill" (p. 259) to avoid overloading the athlete with information.

How important is it that a demonstration be performed correctly? Is it possible for an athlete to learn by viewing incorrect performances? Research comparing expert demonstrators, or "models," versus novice models who exhibit errors in their performance has explored these questions in simple timing tasks (McCullagh & Caird, 1990), complex video games (Pollock & Lee, 1992), and sport skills such as tennis (Hebert & Landin, 1994) and weight-lifting (McCullagh & Meyer, 1997). Results suggest that observing a learning model can be as effective as observing a skilled model, provided that the observer has access to the feedback given to the model. Psychological benefits may also be derived from watching a learning model in terms of improved self-esteem and self-efficacy.

Once athletes have been exposed to several demonstrations, they must be afforded the opportunity to practice the skill. Accordingly, the role of the coach also entails the design of practice experiences for initial motor program development.

This practice should allow for numerous repetitions (blocked practice) in which the athletes can allocate their undivided attention to the details of the movement itself to encourage the discovery of effective performance strategies. Furthermore, the provision of feedback is important in this phase to reinforce, motivate, and guide athletes in modifying their performance. Specific details regarding practice design and feedback will be addressed in a later section.

Duration of the cognitive phase. The cognitive phase of learning is a relatively short period in the overall learning process. It may last only a few minutes, as in teaching a simple skill to older athletes, or it may involve a longer period if the skill is complex and the athletes are very young. The cognitive phase is complete when the athletes can reasonably execute the skill the way it was demonstrated (Christina & Corcos, 1988).

The Associative Phase

The focus of the associative or intermediate phase of skill learning is refinement. Through practice, the learner moves from having a general idea of how to execute the movement to being able to perform the skill both accurately and consistently. The coach's role during this phase shifts to one that mainly involves planning and implementing effective practice conditions as well as providing feedback for skill enhancement.

During the associative phase of learning, the motor program is further developed and athletes gradually eliminate extraneous movements and make fewer, less gross errors. They improve their speed, accuracy, coordination, and consistency. As athletes progress through this phase, their movement will become more automated and they will have to attend less and less to the physical execution of the skill. Some attention can now be devoted to other aspects of the environment, such as planning strategy. Visual control of movement, which was dominant during the cognitive phase of learning, is gradually replaced by **proprioceptive control,** or "feel." Returning to the example of learning to dribble a basketball, the child can now effectively dribble without looking at the

ball or his or her hand and could probably dribble it with the eyes closed. Were proprioceptive cues not available during the early phases of learning? They were available, but the athletes were simply not yet sensitive to them. It takes many practice trials before athletes come to associate the feel of their movements with the outcomes that these movements produce. Schmidt (1975) referred to the generation of "expected sensory consequences," meaning that we expect our movements to feel a certain way, and we can use such sensory feedback to evaluate the correctness of our movements. In other words, using this information, the athlete not only learns to identify the cause of performance errors but, over time, will also develop the capability to generate strategies for their correction.

Another aspect of vision that changes with increases in skill is visual search patterns, or what the athlete actually monitors in the environment. Research shows that there are marked differences in visual search strategies between beginners and experts. For example, when waiting to receive a serve, beginning tennis players direct more time looking at the server's head region than do experts (Singer, Cauraugh, Chen, Steinberg, & Frehlich, 1996). In badminton and squash, Abernethy (1991) found that experts were better than novices at using earlier occurring cues from the opponent's arm to predict the speed and direction of the forthcoming shot. Williams, Davids, Burwitz, and Williams (1994) investigated anticipation and visual search strategies in soccer and found that inexperienced players tend to focus more frequently on the ball and the players passing the ball, whereas experienced players focus on the positions and movements of other players. Also in soccer, as a kicker approached the ball, the focus of experienced goalkeepers progressed from the kicker's head to the nonkicking foot, then the kicking foot and finally to the ball, whereas novices focused more on the trunk, arms, and hips (Savelsbergh, Williams, van der Kamp, & Ward, 2002). Furthermore, the experienced goalkeepers directed their attention toward the ball more than twice the time of novices. Finally, comparisons between elite and near elite athletes recently have been conducted. Differences in gaze behaviors of

Team Canada ice hockey players who displayed exceptional defensive abilities and those known for making tactical errors during games were revealed (Vickers & Martell, 2004). The knowledge gained through these studies provides invaluable information to coaches that have important implications for designing training programs to improve anticipation, selective attention, and decision-making skills. This will be explored further in the next section.

The role of the coach. During the associative phase, the coach must design effective practices to optimize skill refinement. Understanding the nature of the skill is the first step to accomplishing this objective. A skill can be categorized as falling on a continuum between being closed and open according to the predictability of the environment in which that skill is performed. Closed skills are those performed in a relatively stable, predictable environment such as bowling, target archery, free throw shooting, and tennis serving. Successful performance of such skills requires that the athlete be able to consistently and accurately replicate the movement pattern (*fixation*). Practice should therefore reflect this objective of mastering the movement pattern. Some closed skills, however, involve intertrial variability. An example of a closed skill with intertrial variability is putting. Each time a putt is attempted in a round of golf, it is from a different position in relation to the hole. For these types of skills, consistency in technique is important, but the performer also must be able to utilize that technique in a variety of situations. Accordingly, the athlete should practice on different greens, a variety of slopes, and from different locations and distances from the hole. Open skills are those in which the environment is changing and unpredictable. Examples of open skills include returning a punt in football, executing a breakaway in field hockey or soccer, and driving through heavy rush-hour traffic. Because the performer must constantly conform his or her actions to those of the environment, the objective of practice is to *diversify* the movement pattern or teach the athlete to be able to quickly adapt to the demands of the performance situation. Practice should therefore be gamelike so that the athlete becomes better at anticipating changes in the environment, which results in more time to prepare an action.

As indicated earlier, athletes in the associative phase are increasingly able to direct their attention toward aspects of the performance environment. Given the nature of open skills, learning where to direct one's attention to locate appropriate cues is critical to successful performance. Research has shown that anticipatory skills can be acquired and enhanced through specific training in visual search strategies (Abernethy, Wood, & Parks, 1999). By directing athletes to focus on the areas in which the critical cues for performance occur and providing a variety of practice experiences in which athletes must identify and respond to those cues, coaches can assist athletes in developing effective visual search strategies (Magill, 1998).

Finally, the provision of effective feedback continues to be an important role of the coach throughout this phase. That feedback not only should guide the athletes in correcting movement errors but should help them develop their error detection and correction capabilities by teaching them to relate the feelings associated with a movement to the resulting performance outcome.

Duration of the associative phase. The associative phase of skill learning is a much longer period than the cognitive phase, ranging from perhaps a few hours for learning simple skills to several years for mastering complex ones. In fact, not all learners will transition to the final stage of learning as it represents the highest level of skill proficiency.

The Autonomous Phase

The autonomous or advanced phase of learning emerges when the learner can perform the skill at a maximal level of proficiency. As the term implies, performance is quite automatic; the learner seems to require very little conscious thought or attention to the details of movement. In fact, asking highly skilled performers to consciously focus on their movements will seriously disrupt performance, especially in high-speed activities such as performing a routine on the uneven bars in gymnastics or executing a dodge and kick for a goal in soccer.

Automatic Behavior

To experience what happens when elite athletes consciously focus on their movements, perform the following:

Everyone has a natural walking pace. Determine your natural pace by walking across the room several times. Describe your thought process during this activity as well as what happened to your gait. (From Coker, 2004; p. 107)

In the autonomous phase, the athletes' understanding of the skill is excellent. Their motor program for generating the correct movements is highly developed and well established in memory. Free from having to concentrate on executing the skill, they can concentrate on other things besides technique. For example, the NBA's Jason Kidd can dribble the basketball down court at full speed on a fast break and does this without looking at the ball and while planning the best strategy for getting the ball to the basket. During such a play, he considers the position and movements of his opponents as well as his teammates. He considers delivering a bounce pass to the right or to the left or perhaps faking in one direction and, if the defensive player takes the fake, driving for the basket himself, or pulling up short and shooting a 15-foot jump shot. He also has the option of slowing down and taking the ball outside to set up a new play. Kidd does all this while dribbling the ball at full speed, giving no thought to the mechanics of dribbling, and there is rarely an error in the dribble itself. He is "programmed" to perform the fundamental skills of basketball, which include dribbling. A similar analysis would apply to Mia Hamm bringing a soccer ball down the field, or to Michelle Kwan, the figure skater, performing a complex routine. They perform their skills while devoting little thought to the actual movements involved.

Each of these tasks—basketball dribbling, soccer, and figure skating—is a complex motor skill that requires some native ability as well as a great deal of practice before one reaches the autonomous phase. Yet each of these experts began as a novice, comparable to a child beginning to walk, or an adult attempting to use chopsticks for the first time. Progressing from the cognitive through the associative and arriving at the autonomous phase of learning requires an amount of practice and a period of time that depends on the abilities of the individual, the complexity of the task itself, the learner's prior movement experiences, and the efficiency of the learning environment. Certainly high-speed dribbling and complex figure skating maneuvers require more time and practice to master than does a vertical jump or a simple forward roll. In fact, some speculate that it requires a minimum of 10 years and over a million repetitions to produce high-level performance in major sports such as football, basketball, baseball, and gymnastics (Ericsson, Krampe, & Tesch-Römer, 1993).

Role of the coach. Instruction during the autonomous phase of learning basically serves two purposes: first, to help the athletes maintain their level of skill, and, second, to motivate the athletes to continue to want to improve. Once a consistently high level of skill is achieved, it must be maintained not only during a single season but also from season to season. Recall that our definition of motor learning referred to changes in the capability for skilled behavior that are relatively permanent. Also, it would be a mistake to assume that learning has ended in the autonomous phase and that performance cannot be improved. Although the level of competence an athlete may achieve in a skill has certain limits, and performance may be approaching some arbitrary standard of perfection, the progression to this point usually occurs so gradually that it is rarely possible to claim that athletes have reached their highest level of achievement (Christina & Corcos, 1988; Ericsson, 1996). However, because of the difficulty in improving performance as one approaches the highest levels of skill, even though practice continues, athletes may lose motivation to strive for improvement. Thus, the role of the coach as a motivator becomes very important during this phase of learning. The use of goal setting and reinforcement can help skilled athletes maintain motivation. These topics will be discussed in detail in later chapters.

Error correction and the learning process. An understanding of the motor learning process and the phases of skill learning is important for teaching new skills to novice athletes. However, an understanding of the phases of learning is also important when a coach desires to *change* a

highly skilled athlete's well-learned technique (see Table 2-1). Making a minor change in technique, such as widening a baseball player's batting stance, is simple and can usually be accomplished easily. Having a tennis player change from an Eastern forehand grip to the continental grip also should be accomplished with little difficulty. This is because changes such as these require very little relearning. However, when you ask athletes to make a major change in technique, such as

Table 2-1 **Performer Characteristics and Role of the Coach for Each Stage of Learning**

Stage of Learning	Performer Characteristics	Role of the Coach
Cognitive	High degree of cognitive activity	Motivate to want to learn the skill
	Use of self-talk	Provide verbal instructions and demonstrations to help learners gain a basic understanding of the skill
	Development of initial motor program	
	Much conscious attention to details of movement	Design experience for initial development of motor program
	Inability to attend to external events	
	Lack synchronization and appear choppy and deliberate	Assist learner by providing feedback regarding errors and prescribing corrections
	Inconsistent	Encourage
	Production of numerous errors	
	Errors are large	
	Lack capability to determine specific cause of errors and subsequent corrections	
	Vision is the dominant sensory system	
Associative	Fewer errors	Plan and implement appropriate practice opportunities (Fixations vs. Diversification)
	Improvements in speed, accuracy, coordination, and consistency	Teach visual search strategies
	Attend less to physical execution of skill	Continue to provide feedback to reinforce, motivate, and correct performance
	Can devote attention to environment	
	Proprioceptive control replaces visual	Help athletes to develop error detection and correction capabilities
	Refining motor program	
	Developing capability to identify errors and generate strategies for their correction	
Autonomous	Highly proficient	Still planning appropriate practice opportunities
	Performance is automatic	Provision of feedback when needed
	Focus completely directed to environment and decision making	Motivation

going from a two-hand backhand in tennis to a one-hand backhand, you are essentially asking them to return to the cognitive phase of learning and progress through the associative to the autonomous phases again. When you consider that it may have taken years of practice to perfect the motor program for the original technique, you realize that learning the new technique will require a great deal of time. Thus, major changes in technique should probably be undertaken during the off-season. Furthermore, when athletes are in the process of relearning a skill, performance initially will suffer. This can be very discouraging, and the athletes may hold the coach responsible. The coach should be prepared to accept this responsibility and take some of the pressure off the athletes by providing much encouragement. Ultimately, when relearning is accomplished, the athlete's performance should be better than it was with the old technique.

Practice Considerations

Most writers agree that the single most important factor in the control of learning is **practice,** the repeated performance of a skill so as to become proficient. In general, the greater the number of practice trials, the better the learning. Current knowledge suggests that the necessary conditions for reaching international-level performance in many different domains is at least 10 years of effortful practice under optimal training conditions (Ericsson, 1996, 2003; Ericsson et al., 1993). Such conditions require a well-defined task of appropriate difficulty for the athlete, information feedback, and sufficient opportunities for repetition and correction of errors. Ericsson and his colleagues use the term *deliberate practice* to characterize training activities that contain all of these elements.

Deliberate practice by itself, however, is not enough to enable athletes to learn a skill correctly. For practice to be effective, the athletes must be motivated to learn. The old adage "practice makes perfect" is not necessarily true; athletes must practice with the *intent* to improve. This means that skill learning involves more than simply going through the motions physically. Without the goal to constantly improve the level of performance, practice can lead to a mediocre level of proficiency or, worse, a deterioration of skill (Christina & Corcos, 1988; Ericsson et al., 1993).

Given athletes who are motivated to learn, the coach is faced with the task of organizing and scheduling practice so that maximal learning occurs. The next sections of this chapter present several topics important in organizing effective practice sessions. One topic that we will not cover here is mental practice, the cognitive rehearsal of a skill without overt movement. This important topic is covered later in this book (see Chapter 16).

Teaching Several Skills: Blocked Versus Random Practice

In most sports, athletes are challenged to learn a variety of different skills. Swimmers, for example, must learn four strokes, along with starts and turns. Gymnasts must learn many routines on several pieces of equipment. Tennis players must learn forehand and backhand ground strokes, several different serves, net play, and appropriate strategies. Golfers are charged with learning to hit many different clubs over a variety of distances and often through various obstacles. Novice athletes have to learn the many skills of their sport before the first competition. Experienced athletes have to practice these many skills in order to maintain peak performance.

Considering the large number of skills most sports comprise and the often-restricted practice time available, coaches are forced to teach more than one skill in a week; often, several skills must be taught in a single practice session. How can a coach sequence the practice of several tasks during the practice period to maximize learning?

Suppose that an age group swim team practices four times a week for an hour per session. The coach would like to devote 2 weeks to teaching the four competitive strokes: butterfly, backstroke, breaststroke, and freestyle. A commonsense approach to scheduling would be to practice the butterfly for two sessions, then the backstroke for two sessions, and so on until all four strokes are completed.

This schedule of practice is called **blocked practice,** where all the trials of a given task are completed before moving on to the next task. Note that the order in which the strokes are practiced could be arbitrary, as long as practice on one stroke is completed before beginning practice on the next stroke. Intuitively, blocked practice seems to make sense because it allows the swimmers to concentrate on one stroke at a time without worrying about interference from the other strokes.

An alternative approach to scheduling would be to practice all four strokes within each practice period but to do so in a random order so that the swimmers never practice the same stroke on two consecutive trials. This is called a **random practice** schedule. It is important to note that, at the end of the 2-week period, both practice schedules would have provided the same amount of practice on each of the four strokes.

Which of these practice schedules might produce more efficient learning in our swimmers? At first glance, the obvious answer would be blocked practice as it would appear that random practice would present a more difficult environment for the athlete because of the constant switching between tasks. Indeed, if we plotted the swimmers' performance of the four strokes over the 2-week learning period, we would probably find better performance under blocked practice. However, a sizable body of research seems to contradict this intuitive view about practice. The results of many laboratory-based experiments indicate that blocked practice produces better acquisition performance than random practice, but poorer long-term learning, as measured by delayed retention and **transfer,** the application of the practiced skill in a new situation (Lee & Magill, 1983; Li & Wright, 2000; Shea & Morgan, 1979; Shea & Zimny, 1983, 1988; Tsutsui, Lee & Hodges, 1998). Studies using more real-world sport skills, such as learning different badminton serves (Goode & Magill, 1986; Wrisberg & Liu, 1991), forehand and backhand ground strokes in tennis (Hebert, Landin & Solmon, 1996), and different snowboarding skills (Smith, 2002) lend additional support to this notion. This phenomenon is known as the **contextual interference** effect, based on the early work of Battig (1966). (For a comprehensive

review of contextual interference, see Magill and Hall [1990] and Brady [1998].)

Essentially, contextual interference proposes that making the practice environment more difficult for the learner, as with random practice, leads to better learning, even though performance during acquisition is depressed. This is certainly a counterintuitive idea, and we are challenged to understand how a practice structure that degrades acquisition performance can produce more learning. Attempts to explain why random practice is more effective than blocked practice for learning suggest two possible mechanisms. First, when several tasks are present in the athletes' working memory at the same time, they have to use more elaborate processing strategies to keep the tasks distinct. The more effortful processing produces better memory representations for the tasks (Shea & Zimny, 1983, 1988). Second, when athletes practice a task on Trial 1 but do not repeat that task until several trials later, there may be some forgetting of the "solution" to the task. Consequently, the athletes are forced to go through more solution generations with random practice, which ultimately leads to better retrieval (Lee & Magill, 1983).

Although the research on contextual interference discussed thus far implies that a random practice schedule would optimize learning, one additional factor should be considered. Evidence exists indicating that during the initial stage of skill acquisition, when the learner is getting the idea of the movement, blocked practice conditions may be more beneficial than random practice (Del Rey, Whitehurst, & Wood, 1983; Hebert, Landin, & Solmon, 1996; Landin & Hebert, 1997). However, once the basic movement pattern is acquired, the amount of contextual interference must be increased. Aside from doing so through random practice, Landin and Hebert (1997) propose the use of a third approach to scheduling, **repeated blocked practice,** which may combine the advantages of both blocked and random practice. Using the swimming example, rather than practicing the butterfly for two sessions followed by the backstroke for two sessions and so on until all four strokes are completed (blocked practice) or practicing all four strokes within each practice period where the same stroke is never practiced

Practice Strategy	Time	Session 1	Session 2	Session 3	Session 4	Session 5	Session 6	Session 7	Session 8
Blocked Practice	40 min	FLY	FLY	BK	BK	BR	BR	FR	FR
Repeated Blocked Practice	5 min 5 min 5 min 5 min × 2	FLY BK BR FR	FLY BK BR FR	FLY BK BR FR	FLY BK BR FR	FLY BK BR FR	FLY BK BR FR	FLY BK BR FR	FLY BK BR FR
Random Practice	40 min	FLY BK BR FR BR FR BK FLY BR FR FLY BK FLY BR FR BK BR FR FLY BK Etc.	FLY BR FR BK BR FR BR FLY BK BR FLY FR BR FR BK FLY BK FR FLY BK Etc.	BK BR FR BK FR FLY BR FR BK BR FR FLY BR FLY BK FLY BK FLY BR FR Etc.	FR BR FLY BK BR FLY FR BR FR BK FLY BR FR BK BR FLY BR FR FLY BK Etc.	BK BR FR BR FR FLY BR FR BK BR FR FLY BR FR FLY BK FLY BK FR FLY Etc.	FLY BK FR BK BR FR BR FLY BK BR FLY FR BR FR BK FLY BR FR FLY BK Etc.	FR BR FLY BK BR FLY FR BK BK BK FLY BR FR BK BR FLY BR FR FLY BK Etc.	FLY BK BR FR BR FR BK FLY BR FR FLY BK FLY BR FR BK BR FR FLY BK Etc.

Figure 2-2 **Three practice variations for practicing swimming strokes (FLY = butterfly; BK = backstroke; BR = breaststroke; FR = freestyle)**

consecutively (random practice), repeated blocked practice would be organized such that several successive trials of each stroke are performed with the rotation repeated throughout the practice period. Figure 2-2 shows sample practice variations for all three strategies.

More field-based research in a variety of sports is needed before we can be truly confident about the learning benefits of repeated blocked and random practice. Nevertheless, the available research should encourage coaches to at least think about some of their deeply rooted traditional practice methods. Sometimes we can be led astray by following the intuitively obvious.

Teaching Several Variations of a Skill: Variable Practice

In the preceding discussion, the coach's goal was to teach several *different* tasks. There also are times, however, when only a single task is to be learned during a practice session, such as shooting a jump shot, kicking a field goal, or fielding a ground ball. How should the coach structure practice for these situations to maximize learning?

Consider the task of developing one of the skills needed by a shortstop in softball, specifically, fielding a ground ball and throwing to first base.

This task essentially involves perceiving a stimulus (the ground ball), moving the body in front of the ball, getting down to field it, and making an accurate throw. Coach A believes the best way to learn this task would be to practice under **constant** conditions. She will give her shortstop 100 ground balls to field, but each one will be thrown by a pitching machine, have constant velocity, come to the same spot on the field, and have exactly the same bounce and roll characteristics. Coach A feels that this type of practice will allow her shortstop to master the fundamentals of fielding and to "groove" her response.

Coach B adopts a **variable** practice approach. She also will give her shortstop 100 balls to field, but each one will be hit by a batter, possess different bounce and roll characteristics, and go to different spots on the field forcing the player to move to multiple locations and adapt to the ever changing demands presented. Coach B reasons that in the real game no two ground balls are exactly alike, so variability of practice would be more likely to produce the specific skills needed by a shortstop. This type of drill more realistically simulates actual game conditions. It is also possible that in an actual game a shortstop will have to field a ball that is slightly different from any of the 100 variations experienced during practice.

The variable practice approach adopted by Coach B has been shown to result in better learning than the constant conditions offered by Coach A's practice (e.g., Ota & Vickers, 1999; Shoenfelt, Snyder, Maue, McDowell, & Woolard, 2002). Coach B's shortstop would be more likely to experience success when faced with a "novel" fielding situation than Coach A's shortstop because of all the practice received at similar versions of the task. What is actually being learned through variable practice is more than simply the specific actions practiced. The shortstop develops a general capability to produce "fielding" responses, a capability that enhances generalizability, allowing athletes to transfer their learning to actions not specifically experienced in practice. According to schema theory (Schmidt, 1975; Schmidt & Wrisberg, 2004), variable practice allows the learner to discover relationships among environment conditions (her location on the field, speed and bounce characteristics of the ball, distance from first base); what she "told" her muscles to produce (how fast to move, where to put her glove, how hard to throw); and the outcomes that these movements produced (missed/caught the ball, threw too far or too short). Through variable practice, the athlete's understanding of these relationships becomes stronger, and she develops a set of "schemas," or rules, that relate the initial environment conditions, such as distance of the throw, to the force and trajectory requirements that must be selected to produce a correct throw. When the shortstop is called on to execute a "new" fielding response, one that she has never experienced before, her variable practice experiences allow her to better estimate the response specifications needed by her motor program to produce the new response. The athlete who has experienced only one version of the task, through constant practice, may be able to execute that version very well but will be limited in developing a repertoire of responses that may be needed in the criterion activity.

Before we leave the topic of variable practice, a word of caution may be in order. As discussed with blocked and random practice, the skill level of the athlete should be considered prior to deciding whether to employ constant or variable practice. When athletes have no prior experience in an activity, such as may be common with very young children or even adult novices, then it may be advantageous to begin with constant practice at one version of the task, shooting a jump shot from one spot on the court, for example, before introducing variable practice. Initial constant practice will allow the pure beginner to master the "basics" of the skill and pass through the cognitive phase of learning. Once this is accomplished, however, variable practice should be introduced to develop the schemas needed in the actual sport.

Whole Versus Part Practice

Many of the sport skills an athlete must learn are quite complex, such as a floor exercise routine in gymnastics, a reverse lay-up in basketball, or a forward double somersault with two twists in diving. Even a relatively simple skill, such as a

2-foot putt in golf, may seem very complex to the beginner. One of the most important decisions for a coach is whether to present all aspects of such skills to the athlete at once for practice or to divide the skill into smaller, meaningful units that can be practiced separately and then combined into the whole skill.

Whole and part methods of practice should be thought of as the extreme ends of a continuum. The **whole** method requires that the athletes practice the activity or skill in its entirety, as a single unit. At the other end of the continuum, the **part** method requires that the athletes practice each component of the activity or skill separately and then combine the parts into the whole skill. Between these two extremes we have a variation known as the **progressive-part** method, in which the first two parts of a skill are practiced separately and then combined and practiced as a unit. The third part is practiced next and then combined with the first two, and so on until the skill is performed in its entirety.

There are distinct advantages to both the whole and part methods of practice, and there are circumstances under which one or the other is preferable. The part method of practice is of greatest value when a skill is very complex and involves separate, independently performed parts. For example, a gymnastics floor exercise routine is suited to the part method of practice because each individual trick can be practiced independently. Also, using this method, the gymnast can devote more practice time to particularly difficult tricks in the routine without practicing the easier ones, thus making practice more efficient. However, as Gestalt psychologists emphasized years ago, "the whole is greater than the sum of its parts." The successful gymnastics or figure skating routine is more than a series of well-executed individual movements. The transitions between individual elements must be executed smoothly so that the entire performance "flows" as a coherent unit. Most serial activities of reasonably long duration are characterized by an inherent timing or rhythmic structure among certain components. The coach must be careful to identify the components within the routine that "go together" and have the athletes practice them as a unit so as not to disrupt the essential timing.

The undue adherence to the part method can also result in the development of a series of well-learned components that are disconnected and are performed in a disjointed and segmented fashion when combined into a whole. Learning a skill through the part method therefore requires both learning the individual parts and *connecting* them into a cohesive unit. By demonstrating the whole skill before breaking it down for part practice, and explaining how the parts are associated, coaches can facilitate the athletes' understanding of how the parts fit into the whole.

The whole may be greater than the sum of its parts, but it also may be different from its parts. For example, teaching the swimming strokes would seem to be suited to the part method of practice because the arm and leg actions can be practiced independently. However, in the front and back crawl strokes, the kick, when practiced in drills with a kickboard, is performed in a vertical plane. In the whole stroke, though, the kick occurs in a diagonal plane because of the body roll (Counsilman, 1968). Therefore, how much transfer of learning can we expect between the kick performed in isolation and the kick as performed in the whole stroke?

The transfer of learning principle underlies the use of part methods of practice. In some cases the part of a task practiced in isolation is nearly identical to that part in the whole task; thus, transfer from the part to the whole should be almost perfect. In other situations the isolated part may be quite different from the whole task, leading to very little transfer. The amount of transfer from parts of a skill to the whole skill, and thus the effectiveness of part practice, depends on the nature of the skill.

Another advantage of teaching complex activities by the part method is that it usually provides the learners with a sense of having accomplished something. The more success athletes experience, the more motivated and confident they are likely to become. Building confidence is a critical factor in successful athletic performance.

The decision to practice a motor skill as a whole or by parts should be based on the nature of the skill *and* the nature of the learner. Christina and Corcos (1988) provide several excellent suggestions for how to do this. In general, the whole method is favored if (a) the skill is not too complicated and can be understood in a meaningful way; (b) the skill is not too dangerous and can be practiced with a reasonable degree of success (many gymnastics and diving routines, certain wrestling maneuvers, and pole vaulting, for example, because of the potential for injury, lend themselves to part practice); (c) you are working with capable athletes, highly motivated, who have an extensive background in various sports; and (d) the athletes' attention span is long enough to deal with the whole. Skills with components that are highly interdependent also are best served by whole practice.

There also are times when parts of an activity should be practiced separately. For example, when one particular skill or phase of the overall activity is causing difficulty, such as a tennis player having problems tossing the ball accurately and consistently, concentration and practice on this particular component are appropriate for a time. This allows additional practice where it is most needed. However, too much part practice on an isolated component can cause it to become disconnected from the surrounding components. The coach should seek to integrate the troublesome part back into the whole skill as quickly as possible.

Feedback: Its Functions and Use in Skill Learning and Performance

If practice is number one in importance for successful motor skill learning, then running a close second is **feedback,** the information athletes receive about their performance. Chen (2001) suggests that feedback is the most critical form of guidance that a coach can provide an athlete. After all, if people do not know how they are doing, there is no reason for them to change their behavior. Furthermore, if they arbitrarily make a change, there is no assurance that it will be in the right direction. (For a review of recent research on feedback and motor learning, see Swinnen [1996] and Magill [2001].)

Kinds of Feedback

Information available to athletes about their movements can be of two types: intrinsic feedback and augmented feedback. **Intrinsic feedback** is information athletes receive as a natural consequence of moving; it is provided by the athletes' own sensory systems. For example, when basketball players shoot the ball, they can *feel* the proprioceptive sensations coming from their muscles, joints, and tendons. They can *hear* the sound of the ball hitting the rim, or perhaps swishing through the net. Finally, they can *see* whether the ball went into the basket or not. All these sensations provide the athletes with information about the outcome of their shot in terms of achieving the environmental goal. In many sports, information about the success in achieving some goal is readily apparent to performers intrinsically. For example, it is easy to see where the arrow lands in the archery target, whether one clears the bar in the high jump, how many pins are knocked down in bowling, or whether the tennis ball lands in the service area. In these activities it is not necessary for anyone to provide information as to the results of the performances. This information is clearly evident to the athlete.

Augmented feedback is information athletes receive that is not a natural consequence of executing a response. It must be provided by some external source such as a coach, teammate, stopwatch, judge's score, videotape replay, and so on. Augmented feedback is supplied beyond intrinsic feedback and supplements the information naturally available. It can provide information about the outcome of the performance or about the movement pattern that the athletes have just made.

In many sports the performers have no clear idea of how well they are doing. In track, the runner does not know his or her time in a 400-meter trial run until informed by another person or a clock. Neither does the long jumper know the distance of the jump until a measure is taken and reported by an official. Gymnasts, divers, and figure skaters have minimal information about the quality of their performance until they receive the judges' score or are informed by the coach or other observers.

The augmented feedback a coach gives athletes should not be redundant with the intrinsic feedback the athletes have already obtained. It is absurd for a football coach to tell a receiver, "You dropped the ball." The athlete knows this.

Feedback should provide specific information directed at correcting errors or reinforcing correct performance. For example, a bowler sees that the ball is repeatedly veering off into the left gutter but has no idea of what is causing it. A coach may be able to point out that during the follow-through the arm is pulling across the left shoulder, therefore pulling the ball off to the left. Consequently, focusing the athlete's attention on executing a follow-through that is straight past the visual line may correct the problem.

Function of Feedback

Feedback serves at least three important functions in skill learning and performance: (a) motivation, (b) reinforcement or punishment, and (c) error correction information (see Figure 2-3).

Feedback as motivation. How hard would you try or how long would you persist at learning a task in which you had no idea how well you were performing? Feedback can play a powerful role in energizing and directing athletes' behavior in a particular task. A casual comment from a coach, such as "You're doing great, Jason, only two more repeats to go!" can help Jason get through a grueling practice and perhaps put out even a little more effort. Notice that this comment is of a general nature in that it did not convey specific information about Jason's performance. Nevertheless, the extra effort such feedback can cause athletes to bring to the task can only benefit them in terms of increased performance.

Feedback also can influence motivation in terms of goal setting and goal evaluation. Most athletes, with the help of their coaches, set performance goals for themselves, both immediate and long range. Feedback (intrinsic or augmented) informs the athletes about their progress toward those goals. If the feedback indicates that the athletes are improving, then this kind of information can be very satisfying to them, causing them to try to improve present performance until the goal is achieved. If the feedback indicates very little or no improvement is occurring, then this can either lower the athletes' incentive to keep trying to learn the skill, or it may reveal that the original goals were unrealistic and need to be adjusted. More about motivation and goal setting will be covered in later chapters of this book.

Feedback as reinforcement or punishment. **Reinforcement** is any event that *increases* the likelihood that a specific action will occur again under similar circumstances. **Punishment** is just the opposite; it is any event that *decreases* the likelihood that a specific action will occur again. The reinforcing and punishing properties of feedback operate according to Thorndike's (1927) empirical **law of effect,** which essentially says that actions followed by rewarding consequences tend to be repeated, whereas actions followed by unpleasant, or punishing, consequences tend *not* to be repeated.

An example of intrinsic feedback that may serve as positive reinforcement is the satisfaction of seeing your tennis serve go untouched for an "ace" because you served it exactly where you wanted to and sensing (via proprioception) that your body moved just as you intended it to move when executing the serve. To experience these rewarding sensations again you will try to perform the serve in the same way in the future under similar conditions.

Examples of augmented feedback that may serve as reinforcement are compliments or praise from the coach, such as "Good job," "Nice shot,"

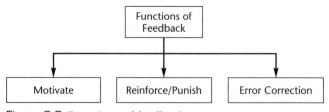

Figure 2-3 **Functions of feedback**

"Your form was excellent that time," and "Way to hustle," and nonverbal types of communication, such as a thumbs up, a smile, or a high five. Athletes receiving these kinds of rewarding augmented feedback right after performing a skill will try to perform the skill in the same way in the future under similar circumstances.

Based on the proceeding discussion, it should be easy to see how intrinsic and augmented feedback also can operate as punishment. When Hilary lands on her back following a dive, her pain receptors provide powerful feedback that an error occurred. She may or may not know precisely what was wrong, but she knows she must change something on her next attempt to avoid this unpleasant experience. Intrinsic feedback does not necessarily have to be associated with physical pain to be offensive. When Mike attempts a field goal, seeing the ball veer off wide to the left and feeling the sensations associated with that kick also should be unpleasant and cause Mike to modify his next attempt. Essentially, athletes will try to avoid punishing feedback by learning not to perform the response being punished.

In the preceding examples, augmented feedback from coaches, such as verbally expressing disapproval of the incorrect performance or nonverbally expressing disapproval (shake of the head, scowl), also could serve as punishment to stop Hilary and Mike from repeating their errors. It is important to note, however, that if a coach elects to use augmented feedback as punishment, the undesirable behavior, the performance error, should be the focus, not the athlete. The coach should praise sincere effort and any part of the skill that was performed correctly, thereby reinforcing these desirable aspects of the performance. A more detailed discussion of the implications of using positive reinforcement versus punishment is presented in the next chapter.

Feedback as error correction information. There is little doubt that the most important component of feedback for motor skill learning is the information it provides about patterns of movement, specifically, errors in the movement pattern. This feedback about errors, prescribing ways for modifying performance, is the reason the coach's role as a teacher is so important for skill learning. Only a skilled teacher can know the correct technique, the proper movement pattern, to provide information feedback.

In some sports, because of the nature of the scoring system, the criterion for successful performance *is the* movement pattern itself. Examples include diving, figure skating, gymnastics, and synchronized swimming. Because it is impossible to receive a high score in these sports without producing technically correct patterns of movement, the coach's augmented feedback must be directed at helping the athletes achieve the correct mechanics. In other sports, however, successful performance outcomes are possible even in the absence of textbook-perfect movement patterns. For example, it does not matter how a basketball player shoots the free throw as long as the ball goes into the basket, how a runner swings her arms as long as she crosses the finish line first, or how a golfer grips the club as long as the result is a 250-yard drive straight down the fairway. Nevertheless, the probability of producing successful performance outcomes is greater when athletes use proper mechanics than when they use improper mechanics. Therefore, coaches should teach and reinforce the use of correct fundamental movement patterns in *all* sports.

How does information feedback operate in skill learning? What does information about errors cause the learner to do? First and foremost, giving information helps to guide the learners toward the movement goal (Salmoni, Schmidt, & Walter, 1984; Schmidt & Wrisberg, 2004). This guidance is very important during the early stages of learning, when performance errors are quite large and tend to occur often. Continued use of augmented feedback from the coach helps keep errors to a minimum and allows them to be corrected quickly, thus bringing performance close to the goal and helping to maintain it there. Although this would seem to be good for learning, recent studies have shown that the guidance properties of feedback may cause learners to become too dependent on the feedback, using it as a "crutch," so that performance can be maintained only when the feedback is present (Butki & Hoffman, 2003; Lee, White, & Carnahan, 1990; Salmoni et al., 1984; Schmidt,

Young, Swinnen, & Shapiro, 1989). When the feedback is withdrawn, as it must be during actual competition, the athletes may have trouble performing. The constant provision of augmented feedback also may distract athletes from processing their own sensory feedback. If the athletes know that the coach will give feedback on every practice attempt, they simply have to wait for it, without attending to the rich sources of intrinsic feedback that can be important for learning. A strategy that may help athletes focus more on intrinsic feedback is to have them subjectively estimate, or "guess," their error following a particular performance, before providing augmented feedback.

The practical implications here seem clear. A high frequency of augmented feedback is important during the early stage of learning to bring performance close to the goal. As proficiency increases, augmented feedback should gradually become less and less frequent so that the athlete learns to become less dependent on it for successful performance (Winstein & Schmidt, 1990). When a high degree of proficiency is attained, the athletes need only an occasional dose of information feedback to be certain that performance is correct. This method, whereby augmented feedback is gradually reduced as performance improves, is called *faded feedback* (Nicholson & Schmidt, 1991; Winstein & Schmidt, 1990).

Another method for reducing the frequency of augmented feedback is *bandwidth feedback* (Butler & Fischman, 1996; Butler, Reeve, & Fischman, 1996; Cauraugh, Chen, & Radlo, 1993; Lai & Shea, 1999; Lee & Carnahan, 1990; Lee & Maraj, 1994; Sherwood, 1988), in which the coach identifies an acceptable error tolerance, or "bandwidth," and provides feedback only when the athlete's performance falls outside this acceptable range. Early in learning, the athlete's performances are more likely to fall outside the bandwidth, and so the coach would provide feedback more frequently. As performance improves and more responses start to fall inside the bandwidth, the frequency of feedback is reduced. This method appears to have a great deal of merit because it is based on the athlete's actual performance, rather than some arbitrary, fixed schedule. Earlier studies of bandwidth feedback relied mainly on laboratory-type tasks, but recent

work by Smith, Taylor, and Withers (1997) shows that the method can be successfully applied to learning a golf chip shot.

Learner-regulated feedback, in which augmented feedback is only provided to the athlete when he or she requests it, is an alternative strategy that has recently been shown to be effective (Chen, 2001; Chen, Kaufman, & Chung, 2001; Chiviacowsky & Wulf, 2002; Janelle, Barba, Frehlich, Tennant, & Cauraugh, 1997; Janelle, Kim, & Singer, 1995). Because athletes control when augmented feedback is given, feedback frequency is individualized. Moreover, the athlete is thought to benefit by becoming actively engaged in the learning process.

Diagnosing and Correcting Errors

Providing timely and effective feedback to athletes is not a simple matter. First, prescribing modifications for skill improvement is dependent on the coach's capability to accurately identify performance errors. Second, even when the movement faults are obvious to the coach and the appropriate corrective responses are clear, transmitting this information to learners so that they can comprehend and use it is not always easy. Frequently, the athletes are unable to translate the verbiage into meaningful movement behavior. At other times they simply may not believe or "buy into" what they are being told. Consequently, the following sections offer strategies for both analyzing a skill and providing the athlete with augmented feedback.

Analyzing the Skill

Before giving augmented feedback designed to correct errors in performance, the coach should first do a careful, thorough analysis of the athlete's technique. Christina and Corcos (1988) advocate a three-step process for analyzing skill technique. The first step is to compare the athlete's technique with correct technique. The key here is to focus on the basic movement pattern rather than on small idiosyncrasies in individual style. The coach asks, "Is this athlete's technique fundamentally sound?" It may take several observations of the skill to evaluate the seriousness of observed errors, and the coach should avoid the mistake of offering feedback too quickly. Errors in technique should be corrected if they will substantially improve performance or increase safety.

The second step in analyzing technique is to select which error to correct. With beginners especially there are probably several performance errors occurring simultaneously. If the coach tried to give feedback about every error observed, the athlete would likely be overloaded with too much information, resulting in very little correction on the next trial. Consequently, only one error should be addressed at a time.

Given multiple errors, where does one begin? The coach should try to identify the error that is most fundamental or critical and give feedback only about it. Very often, one error is the cause of other errors, and if this critical error can be corrected, others may be eliminated. When the fundamental aspect is mastered, then attention can be devoted to the next most important error. When multiple errors seem unrelated, a good strategy is to select the one that is easiest to learn and leads to the greatest improvement. The benefits here may be twofold. First, the athlete's respect for the coach's knowledge may be enhanced, and, second, improved performance will contribute to the athlete's motivation to continue learning the skill. Finally, a third strategy is to identify the critical error that occurs earliest in the sequence. For example, in diving, if the approach on the board is incorrect, the takeoff, the dive itself, and the entry will likely be adversely affected. By correcting the faulty approach, the errors that emerged later in the sequence as a consequence are likely to be eliminated. For more information on these and other strategies, see Knudson and Morrison (2002).

The final step in analyzing technique is to determine the cause of the error and what the athlete must do to correct it. Causes of errors can range from the relatively simple, such as forgetting to concentrate on some aspect of the skill, to the very difficult, such as a subtle change in mechanics. If the coach determines that forgetting is the cause of an error, then the correction is a simple reminder. "Square up your racket to the net" may be all a young tennis player needs to correct a short volley. Determining the cause of a nonpropulsive breaststroke kick may be more difficult, however, because the problem may lie in poor body position, incorrect timing, position of the ankle, and so on. Further analysis, perhaps through filming, may be necessary.

If the coach cannot isolate the cause of an error or is uncertain about how to correct it, he or she should not experiment with random suggestions. If the hasty suggestions do not lead to improved performance, athletes may come to doubt their coach's ability, as well as experience a great deal of frustration. Coaches should think through the situation carefully and watch the performance many times before prescribing modifications.

Providing Augmented Feedback

Once the coach has completed the analysis, a positive approach to correcting the identified performance error(s) is advocated (Christina & Corcos, 1988; Martens, 2004). To confirm the athlete's progress, effort and any parts of the technique that were correct should be reinforced. Coaches should be specific when conveying what aspects of the performance were correct and only reinforce real progress or they could lose credibility (Rink, 2002). To facilitate skill acquisition, the coach should give simple, precise, error correction information. Adhere to the "KISS" principle—"Keep It Short and Simple." Feedback must provide sufficient information to benefit the athletes, but it must not provide too much or it may become confusing. Also, the coach should be sure to verify the athletes' understanding of the feedback by asking them to repeat it and explain how they will attempt to make the correction. Finally, the coach should motivate the athlete to incorporate the prescribed modifications. Notice that this approach simply takes advantage of the three functions of feedback, with error correction information being sandwiched between reinforcement and motivation. The following is an example: "Good, Susan. You are rotating your head to the side much better now. Remember to blow all of your air out underwater though *before* you turn to breathe. You'll be able to get more air and swim a greater distance before running out of breath."

A teacher or coach who can provide accurate and understandable feedback is important to athletes at all levels of the performance scale, from novice to elite. Clearly, the beginner in any sport needs early and consistent instruction as well as regular feedback. What is not as often understood is that performers at average and even advanced levels also need effective feedback. Major league pitchers at the peak of their careers sometimes run into slumps that are not attributable to any physical or emotional problem they can detect. At this point, the pitching coach must set aside a period to work with such pitchers and attempt to determine what they are doing differently and how the problem can be corrected. At this high level of performance, problems are usually very subtle; errors in technique are so slight that only a highly skilled coach, who is thoroughly familiar with the particular player, can detect them and prescribe appropriate modifications for their correction.

Summary

This chapter has focused on one of the *most important* roles of a coach, that of a teacher of motor skills. The motor learning process is incredibly complex, and we have attempted to provide a basic understanding of that process. We began by defining the term *motor learning* and then describing a three-phase model of motor skill learning, consisting of the cognitive (beginning), associative (intermediate), and autonomous (advanced) phases. Understanding the phases of learning is important both for teaching novice athletes a brand-new skill and for changing well-learned techniques of highly skilled athletes.

Practice and feedback are two of the most important determinants of motor learning and performance, and we have provided some guidelines for structuring effective practice sessions and for providing effective feedback to learners. In some instances, current research findings run counter to some of our long-held beliefs about practice and feedback.

Study Questions

1. Define the term *motor learning* and explain why learning must remain an inference based on performance.

2. Briefly describe Fitts and Posner's three phases of motor skill learning.

3. What are the important points to remember when demonstrating a new skill for learners?

4. How is proprioception, or "feel," important in motor performance?

5. What are the effects of asking highly skilled performers to consciously attend to their movements?

6. Explain why the coach's role as motivator is so important during the autonomous phase of learning.

7. Describe how a coach should proceed to change a highly skilled athlete's well-learned technique.

8. How could one use blocked practice to teach several skills? Random practice? Which would be more effective and why?

9. Give an example of how a coach could use variable practice to teach several variations of a skill.

10. What are schemas, and how does variable practice contribute to their development?

11. What general guidelines should a coach consider in deciding to use the whole method versus the part method of practice?

12. What are the two major types of feedback? Give three examples of each type.

References

Abernethy, B. (1991). Visual search strategies and decision-making in sport. *International Journal of Sport Psychology, 22,* 189–210.

Abernethy, B., Wood, J. M., & Parks, S. (1999). Can anticipatory skills of experts be learned by novices? *Research Quarterly for Exercise and Sport, 70*(3), 313–318.

Battig, W. F. (1966). Facilitation and interference. In E. A. Bilodeau (Ed.), *Acquisition of skill* (pp. 215–244). New York: Academic Press.

Brady, F. (1998). A theoretical and empirical review of the contextual interference effect and the learning of motor skills. *Quest, 50,* 266–293.

Butki, B. D., & Hoffman, S. J. (2003). Effects of reducing frequency of intrinsic knowledge of results on the learning of a motor skill. *Perceptual and Motor Skills, 97*(2), 569–580.

Butler, M. S., & Fischman, M. G. (1996). Effects of bandwidth feedback on delayed retention of a movement timing task. *Perceptual and Motor Skills, 82,* 527–530.

Butler, M. S., Reeve, T. G., & Fischman, M. G. (1996). Effects of the instructional set in the bandwidth feedback paradigm on motor skill acquisition. *Research Quarterly for Exercise and Sport, 67,* 355–359.

Cauraugh, J. H., Chen, D., & Radlo, S. J. (1993). Effects of traditional and reversed bandwidth knowledge of results on motor learning. *Research Quarterly for Exercise and Sport, 64,* 413–417.

Chen, D. D. (2001). Trends in augmented research and tips for the practitioner. *JOPERD, 72*(1), 32–36.

Chen, D. D., Kaufman, D., & Chung, M. W. (2001). Emergent patterns of feedback strategies in performing a closed motor skill. *Perceptual and Motor Skills, 93,* 197–204.

Chiviacowsky, S., & Wulf, G. (2002). Self-controlled feedback: Does it enhance learning because performers get feedback when they need it? *Research Quarterly for Exercise and Sport, 73*(4), 408–415.

Christina, R. W., & Corcos, D. M. (1988). *Coaches guide to teaching sport skills.* Champaign, IL: Human Kinetics.

Coker, C. A. (2004). *Motor learning and control for practitioners.* St. Louis, MO: McGraw-Hill.

Counsilman, J. E. (1968). *The science of swimming.* Englewood Cliffs, NJ: Prentice-Hall.

Del Rey, P., Whitehurst, M., & Wood, J. M. (1983). Effects of experience and contextual interference on learning and transfer by boys and girls. *Perceptual and Motor Skills, 56,* 581–582.

Ericsson, K. A. (2003). Development of elite performance and deliberate practice: An update from the perspective of the expert performance approach. In J. L. Starkes & K. A. Ericsson (Eds.), *Expert performance in sports: Advances in research on sport expertise* (pp. 49–83). Champaign, IL: Human Kinetics.

Ericsson, K. A. (1996). The acquisition of expert performance: An introduction to some of the issues. In K. A. Ericsson (Ed.), *The road to excellence: The acquisition of expert performance in the arts and sciences, sports, and games* (pp. 1–50). Mahwah, NJ: Erlbaum.

Ericsson, K. A., Krampe, R. T., & Tesch-Römer, C. (1993). The role of deliberate practice in the acquisition of expert performance. *Psychological Review, 100,* 363–406.

Fitts, P. M., & Posner, M. I. (1967). *Human performance.* Pacific Grove, CA: Brooks/Cole.

Gentile, A. M. (2000). Skill acquisition: Action, movement, and the neuromotor processes. In J. H. Carr, R. B. Shepard, J. Gordon, A. M. Gentile, & J. M. Hind (Eds.), *Movement science: Foundations for physical therapy in rehabilitation* (pp. 111–187). Rockville, MD: Aspen.

Goode, S., & Magill, R. A. (1986). Contextual interference effects in learning three badminton serves. *Research Quarterly for Exercise and Sport, 57,* 308–314.

Hebert, E. P., & Landin, D. (1994). Effects of a learning model and augmented feedback on tennis skill acquisition. *Research Quarterly for Exercise and Sport, 65*(3), 250–257.

Hebert, E. P., Landin, D., & Solmon, M. A. (1996). Practice schedule effects on the performance and learning of low- and high-skilled students: An applied study. *Research Quarterly for Exercise and Sport, 67,* 52–58.

Janelle, C. M., Barba, D. A., Frehlich, S. G., Tennant, L. K., & Cauraugh, J. H. (1997). Maximizing performance feedback effectiveness through videotape replay and a self-controlled learning environment. *Research Quarterly for Exercise and Sport, 68*(4), 269–279.

Janelle, C. M., Kim, J., & Singer, R. N. (1995). Subject-controlled feedback and learning a closed skill. *Perceptual and Motor Skills, 81,* 627–634.

Knudson D. V., & Morrison, C. S. (2002). *Qualitative Analysis of Human Movement.* Champaign, IL: Human Kinetics.

Lai, Q., & Shea, C. H. (1999). Bandwidth knowledge of results enhances generalized motor program learning. *Research Quarterly for Exercise and Sport, 70,* 79–83.

Landin, D., & Hebert, E. P. (1997). A comparison of three practice schedules along the contextual interference continuum. *Research Quarterly for Exercise and Sport, 68,* 357–361.

Lee, T. D., & Carnahan, H. (1990). Bandwidth knowledge of results and motor learning: More than just a relative frequency effect. *Quarterly Journal of Experimental Psychology, 42A,* 777–789.

Lee, T. D., & Magill, R. A. (1983). The locus of contextual interference in motor-skill acquisition. *Journal of Experimental Psychology: Learning, Memory, and Cognition, 9,* 730–746.

Lee, T. D., & Maraj, B. K. V. (1994). Effects of bandwidth goals and bandwidth knowledge of results on motor learning. *Research Quarterly for Exercise and Sport, 65,* 244–249.

Lee, T. D., White, M. A., & Carnahan, H. (1990). On the role of knowledge of results in motor learning: Exploring the guidance hypothesis. *Journal of Motor Behavior, 22,* 191–208.

Li, Y., & Wright, D. L. (2000). An assessment of the attention demands of random and blocked practice. *Quarterly Journal of Experimental Psychology, 53A,* 591–606.

Magill, R. A. (2004). Motor learning and control: Concepts and applications. *Motor learning: Concepts and applications.* St. Louis, MO: McGraw-Hill.

Magill, R. A. (2001). Augmented feedback in motor skill acquisition. In R. N. Singer, H. A. Hausenblaus, & C. M. Janelle (Eds.), *Handbook of research on sport psychology* (pp. 86–114). New York: John Wiley & Sons.

Magill, R. A. (1998). Knowledge is more than we talk about: Implicit learning in motor skill acquisition. *Research Quarterly for Exercise and Sport, 69*(2), 104–110.

Magill, R. A., & Hall, K. G. (1990). A review of the contextual interference effect in motor skill acquisition. *Human Movement Science, 9,* 241–289.

Martens, R. (2004). *Successful coaching.* Champaign, IL: Human Kinetics.

McCullagh, P., & Caird, J. K. (1990). Correct and learning models and the use of model knowledge of results in the acquisition and retention of a motor skill. *Journal of Human Movement Studies, 18,* 107–116.

McCullagh, P., & Meyer, K. N. (1997). Learning versus correct models: Influence of model type on the learning of a free-weight squat lift. *Research Quarterly for Exercise and Sport, 68,* 56–61.

McCullagh, P., Steihl, J., & Weiss, M. R. (1990). Developmental modeling effects on the quantitative and qualitative aspects of motor performance acquisition. *Research Quarterly for Exercise and Sport, 61,* 344–350.

Nicholson, D. E., & Schmidt, R. A. (1991). Scheduling information feedback to enhance training effectiveness. In *Proceedings of the Human Factors Society 35th Annual Meeting* (pp. 1400–1402). San Francisco.

Ota, D., & Vickers, J. M. (1999). The effects of variable practice on the retention and transfer of two volleyball skills in Club-Level Athletes. *International Journal of Volleyball Research, 1*(1), 18–24.

Pollock, B. J., & Lee, T. D. (1992). Effects of the model's skill level on observational motor learning. *Research Quarterly for Exercise and Sport, 63,* 25–29.

Rink, J. E. (2002) *Teaching physical education for learning.* St. Louis, MO: McGraw-Hill.

Salmoni, A. W., Schmidt, R. A., & Walter, C. B. (1984). Knowledge of results and motor learning: A review and critical reappraisal. *Psychological Bulletin, 95,* 355–386.

Savelsbergh, G. J. P., Williams, A. M., van der Kamp, J., & Ward, P. (2002). Visual search, anticipation and expertise in soccer goal keepers, *Journal of Sport Sciences, 200,* 279–287.

Schmidt, R. A. (1975). A schema theory of discrete motor skill learning. *Psychological Review, 82,* 225–260.

Schmidt, R. A., & Wrisberg, C. A. (2004). *Motor learning and performance: A problem based learning approach.* Champaign, IL: Human Kinetics.

Schmidt, R. A., Young, D. E., Swinnen, S., & Shapiro, D. C. (1989). Summary knowledge of results for skill acquisition: Support for the guidance hypothesis. *Journal of Experimental Psychology: Learning, Memory, and Cognition, 15,* 352–359.

Shea, J. B., & Morgan, R. L. (1979). Contextual interference effects on the acquisition, retention, and transfer of a motor skill. *Journal of Experimental Psychology: Human Learning and Memory, 5,* 179–187.

Shea, J. B., & Zimny, S. T. (1983). Context effects in memory and learning movement information. In R. A. Magill (Ed.), *Memory and control of action* (pp. 345–366). Amsterdam: North-Holland.

Shea, J. B., & Zimny, S. T. (1988). Knowledge incorporation in motor representation. In O. G. Meijer & K. Roth (Eds.), *Complex movement behaviour: "The" motor-action controversy* (pp. 289–314). Amsterdam: Elsevier Science Publishers B.V.

Sherwood, D. E. (1988). Effect of bandwidth knowledge of results on movement consistency. *Perceptual and Motor Skills, 66,* 535–542.

Shoenfelt, E. L., Snyder, L. A., Maue, A. E., McDowell, C. P., & Woolard, C. D. (2002). Comparison of constant and variable practice conditions on free throw shooting. *Perceptual and Motor Skills, 94,* 1113–1123.

Singer, R. N., Cauraugh, J. H., Chen, D., Steinberg, G. M., & Frehlich, S. G. (1996). Visual search, anticipation, and reactive comparisons between highly skilled and beginning tennis players. *Journal of Applied Sport Psychology, 8,* 9–26.

Smith, P. J. K. (2002). Applying contextual interference to snowboarding skills. *Perceptual and Motor Skills, 95,* 999–1005.

Smith, P. J. K., Taylor, S. J., & Withers, K. (1997). Applying bandwidth feedback scheduling to a golf shot. *Research Quarterly for Exercise and Sport, 68,* 215–221.

Swinnen, S. P. (1996). Information feedback for motor skill learning: A review. In H. N. Zelaznik (Ed.), *Advances in motor learning and control* (pp. 37–66). Champaign, IL: Human Kinetics.

Thorndike, E. L. (1927). The law of effect. *American Journal of Psychology, 39,* 212–222.

Tsutsui, S., Lee, T. D., & Hodges, N. J. (1998). Contextual interference in learning new patterns of bimanual coordination. *Journal of Motor Behavior, 30,* 151–157.

Vickers, J. N., & Martell, S. G. (2004). *How elite ice hockey players read tactical plays as they defend against opponents.* Paper presented at the meeting of the American Alliance for Health, Physical Education, Recreation and Dance, New Orleans, LA.

Weiss, M. R., & Klint, K. A. (1987). "Show and tell" in the gymnasium: An investigation of developmental differences in modeling and verbal rehearsal of motor skills. *Research Quarterly for Exercise and Sport, 58,* 234–241.

Williams, A. M., Davids, K., Burwitz, L., & Williams, J. G. (1994). Visual search strategies in experienced and inexperienced soccer players. *Research Quarterly for Exercise and Sport, 65,* 127–135.

Winstein, C. J., & Schmidt, R. A. (1990). Reduced frequency of knowledge of results enhances motor skill learning. *Journal of Experimental Psychology: Learning, Memory, and Cognition, 16,* 677–691.

Wrisberg, C. A., & Liu, Z. (1991). The effect of contextual variety on the practice, retention, and transfer of an applied motor skill. *Research Quarterly for Exercise and Sport, 62,* 406–412.

Zetou, E., Tzetzis, G., Vernadakis, N., & Kioumourtzoglou, E. (2002). Modeling in learning two volleyball skills. *Perceptual and Motor Skills, 94,* 1131–1142.

3

Positive Reinforcement, Performance Feedback, and Performance Enhancement

Ronald E. Smith, *University of Washington*

I try never to plant a negative seed. I try to make every comment a positive comment. There's a lot of evidence to support positive management.

　　　　　　　　　　　　　　　　　—*Jimmy Johnson, Former College and Professional Football Coach*

To really win, you have to get every player to go beyond his capabilities. He must feel great about himself. . . . He must feel that his coaches or supervisors have total confidence in his ability, and he must feel that his weaknesses are small and his strengths are much bigger. You do that by positive reinforcement, making sure that no one thinks negatively at any time.

　　　　　　　　　　　　　　　　　—*Rick Pitino, Basketball Coach, University of Louisville*

If a pitcher throws one good pitch during the whole morning, you have something to work on. Let him know it. That will give him all the incentive he needs. He too sees that he can do a certain thing. He may not know exactly how he did it. He has to find that out from his own study.

　　　　　　　　　　　　　　　　　—*The Late Branch Rickey, Legendary Baseball Executive*

Much of human interaction consists of attempts to influence the behavior of other people. Influence attempts occur constantly in virtually every life setting. Sometimes the attempts are directed at influencing attitudes, motives, values, or emotions. At other times social interactions or task performance are the targets of influence attempts.

Sport is a setting where all of these targets of influence—thoughts, emotions, motivational factors, and behaviors—are relevant. Influence attempts occur constantly as athletes interact with teammates, opponents, officials, and their coaches. In the discussion to follow I will focus on influence attempts directed by coaches to their athletes and provide a conceptual framework to which other topics in this book, such as goal setting (Chapter 13) and intervention programs directed toward coaches and parents (Chapters 10 and 21), may be related. My focus will be primarily on enhancing sport performance, although, as you shall see, this goal is intimately related to the psychosocial climate created by interactions among coaches and athletes.

Coaches try to influence their players in many important ways. One of their most important goals is to create a good learning situation where athletes can acquire the technical skills needed to succeed as individuals and as a team. Another priority for most coaches is to create a social environment where the participants can experience positive interactions with one another. This is certainly a key factor in building team cohesion, in making athletes more receptive to technical instruction, and in fostering a supportive environment where athletes can develop teamwork, dedication, "mental toughness," and other valued traits. Indeed, virtually everything coaches do can be viewed as attempts to increase certain desired behaviors and to decrease undesirable behaviors.

The "psychology of coaching" essentially may be regarded as a set of strategies designed to increase a coach's ability to influence the behavior of others more effectively. It is often said that stripped of its jargon and complexities psychology is basically the application of common sense. I believe the principles discussed in this chapter—positive (as opposed to aversive) control, reinforcement, and performance feedback—make good sense. But more important, they have been shown in many scientific studies to be among the most effective ways to increase motivation, morale, enjoyment of the athletic situation, and performance (Smith, Smoll, & Christensen, 1996).

The ABCs of Behavior Control

To understand what motivates people and controls their behavior, we must take into account the relations between people and their environment. In psychology one influential approach to this task is the study of **operant conditioning,** which considers in part the manner in which our behaviors are influenced by their consequences (Martin & Pear, 2002).

The operant analysis of behavior involves the study of relations between three kinds of events: **antecedents** (A), or environmental stimuli; behaviors (B) in which the person engages; and consequences (C) that follow the behaviors and either strengthen or weaken them. The relations that exist among these "if, then" elements are called **contingencies.** The ABCs of contingencies can be expressed in the following way:

IF antecedent stimuli (A) are present

AND behavior (B) is emitted,

THEN consequence (C) will occur.

Two aspects of these relations are of interest. The first is the relation between antecedents and behaviors (A and B); the second is the contingency between behavior and its consequences (B and C).

Antecedents: Stimulus Control of Behavior

Through experience we learn which behaviors have which consequences under which conditions. Antecedents that signal the likely consequences of particular behaviors in given situations are known as **discriminative stimuli.** These signals help guide our behavior so that it is "appropriate" and most likely will lead to positive consequences. Much skill learning in sports involves learning to "read" the environment and respond appropriately. Thus, a basketball player learns how to set up the offense when the opponent switches from one defense to another. The same player also may learn that it is not a good idea to crack jokes in the presence of the coach after a tough loss. When antecedents are influential in governing a behavior, that behavior is said to be under **stimulus control.** With experience in sports many behaviors come under stimulus control, and we react automatically and mindlessly to changing stimulus conditions. The same thing occurs in the realm of social behaviors.

Response Consequences

The key feature in operant conditioning is what happens after a response is made. Psychologists have done a great deal of research on how

	Present	Remove
Positive Stimuli	Positive reinforcement *(strengthens behavior)*	Extinction *(weakens behavior)* Response cost punishment *(weakens behavior)*
Aversive Stimuli	Punishment *(suppresses/weakens behavior)*	Negative reinforcement *(strengthens behavior)*

Figure 3-1 **Five basic response consequences created by the presentation or removal of positive or negative stimuli and their effects on behavior**

different types of consequences affect behavior. In general consequences always involve either the presentation, the nonoccurrence, or the removal of a positive or an aversive stimulus. For example, in the coach–athlete interaction a positive stimulus may be a word of praise or a smile, and an aversive stimulus may be a critical comment made by the coach.

Figure 3-1 shows five basic response consequences that result from the presentation or removal of positive or aversive stimuli in response to a given behavior. Presentation of a positive stimulus is called **positive reinforcement,** and it increases the likelihood that the behavior will occur in the future under the same conditions. Removal of a positive stimulus that has in the past followed the behavior results in **extinction,** reducing the likelihood of the behavior. Extinction of operant behaviors occurs when reinforcement stops. When previously reinforced behaviors no longer "pay off," we are likely to abandon them and replace them with more successful ones. It follows, therefore, that an effective way to change someone's negative behaviors is to make sure he or she gets no reinforcement for the undesirable behaviors while at the same time reinforcing alternative behaviors that are more desirable. This principle is also useful for approaching disciplinary issues, which will be discussed in a later section.

Other consequences involve either presentation or removal of aversive stimuli. **Punishment** entails presentation of aversive stimuli, with the effect of suppressing the behavior. Thus, a coach

who harshly criticizes an athlete for being late for practice will probably find a marked reduction in tardiness in the future. Another form of punishment, known as response cost, also involves removal of a positive stimulus, but not the one that is reinforcing the behavior. It is discussed in the next section. **Negative reinforcement** involves removal or avoidance of aversive stimuli, the effect being a strengthening of the behavior that results in successful escape or avoidance. For example, an athlete may drop out of a sport program to escape an abusive coach, or a gymnast who has been injured may avoid performing a particular routine because of anxiety concerning possible reinjury. In the latter case the avoidance response may become stronger over time because each time it occurs it is negatively reinforced by anxiety reduction. The term *negative reinforcement* is sometimes used synonymously with punishment, but the two are clearly different. Punishment reduces the likelihood of a behavior, whereas negative reinforcement, like positive reinforcement, strengthens the behavior.

Positive and Aversive Approaches to Influencing Behavior

As suggested by our cursory examination of response consequences and their influence on behavior, there are two basic approaches to influencing the behavior of others. Psychologists refer to these as **positive control** and **aversive control** (Sarafino, 2004). Both forms of control are based on the fact that behavior is strongly influenced by the consequences it produces. Responses that lead to positive or desired consequences (from the perspective of the responder) are strengthened and their likelihood of occurring in the future is increased. In more technical terms, **positive reinforcers** are consequences that increase the probability of behaviors that produce them. Conversely, behaviors that result in undesirable or unpleasant consequences (as perceived by the responder) are less likely to recur. **Punishment** is thus defined as a consequence that weakens or suppresses a behavior that produces it. Positive reinforcement and punishment are the respective cornerstones of positive and aversive control of behavior. Positive and aversive control, in turn, underlie the *positive approach* and the *negative approach* to coaching (see Chapters 4 and 5 of this volume, and Smith & Smoll, 2001).

The positive approach is designed to strengthen desired behaviors by motivating players to perform them and by reinforcing the behaviors when they occur. The second approach, the negative approach, involves attempts to eliminate unwanted behaviors through punishment and criticism. The motivating factor in this approach is fear. Observational studies of coaches indicate that most coaches use a combination of positive and aversive control (Smith, Zane, Smoll, & Coppel, 1983).

In our society, aversive control through punishment is perhaps the most widespread means of controlling behavior. Our system of laws is backed up by threats of punishment. Similarly, fear of failure is one means of promoting school achievement, social development, and other desired behaviors. The reason punishment is the glue that holds so much of our society's fabric together is that, for the most part, it seems to work. It is the fastest way to bring behavior under control (Zirpoli, 2004). In sports it finds one mode of expression in the negative approach to coaching.

Frequently in sport we hear the statement, "The team that makes the fewest mistakes will win"—and, indeed, this is usually the case. Many coaches, therefore, develop coaching tactics oriented toward eliminating mistakes. The most natural approach is to use aversive control. To get rid of mistakes, we simply punish and criticize athletes who make them. The assumption is that if we make players fearful enough of making mistakes they are more likely to perform well. We do not have to look far to find examples of highly successful coaches who are "screamers" and whose teams seem to perform like well-oiled machines. Other less experienced coaches may conclude that this is the most effective way to train athletes. They too adopt this aspect of the successful coaches' behavior, perhaps to the exclusion of other teaching techniques that probably are the true keys to the success of the "screamers."

Negative Side Effects of Punishment

There is clear evidence that punishment and criticism can decrease unwanted behaviors. Unfortunately, the evidence is equally compelling that punishment has certain undesirable side effects that can actually interfere with what a coach is trying to accomplish (Maag, 2003).

First and foremost is the fact that punishment works by arousing fear. If used excessively, punishment promotes the development of fear of failure, and this is undoubtedly the least desirable form of athletic motivation. If it becomes the predominant motive for athletic performance, it not only decreases enjoyment of the activity but also increases the likelihood of failure. The high fear of failure athlete is motivated not by a positive desire to achieve and enjoy "the thrill of victory" but by a dread of "the agony of defeat." Athletic competition is transformed from a challenge into a threat. Because high anxiety disrupts motor performance and interferes with thinking, the high fear of failure athlete is prone to "choke" under pressure because he or she is concentrating more on the feared consequences of mistakes or failure than on what needs to be done in a positive sense. Research has shown that athletes having high fear of failure not only perform more poorly in competition but also are at greater risk for injury, enjoy the sport experience less, and are more likely to drop out (Smith, Smoll, &

Passer, 2002). The research literature also shows that the quickest and most effective way to develop fear of failure is by punishing people when they fail (Petri & Govern, 2004). Thus, coaches who create fear of failure through the use of punishment may, ironically, increase the likelihood that their athletes may indeed make the very mistakes they are trying to prevent. Moreover, high levels of fear may have a generally depressing effect on behavior and make athletes afraid to take risks of any kind.

Punishment has other potential side effects that most coaches wish to avoid. A predominance of aversive control makes for an unpleasant teaching situation. It arouses resentment and hostility, which may be masked by the power differential that exists between coach and athlete. It may produce a kind of cohesion among players based on their mutual hatred for the coach, but most coaches would prefer other bases for team cohesion. It is even possible that players may consciously or subconsciously act in ways that sabotage what the coach is trying to accomplish. Moreover, coaches occupy a role that is admired by athletes, and they should not overlook their importance as models for young people who are developing socially. The abusive "screamer" is certainly not exhibiting the kind of behavior that will contribute to the personal growth of athletes who emulate the coach.

Does this mean coaches should avoid all criticism and punishment of their athletes? Not at all. Sometimes these behaviors are necessary for instructional or disciplinary purposes, but they should be used sparingly and with a full appreciation for their potential negative side effects. The negative approach should never be the primary approach to athletes. This is particularly the case where child athletes are concerned, but it also applies at higher competitive levels, including professional sports (Smith & Johnson, 1990).

Although abusive coaches may enjoy success and may even be admired by some of their players, they run the risk of losing other players who could contribute to the team's success and who could profit personally from an athletic experience. Those who succeed through the use of aversive control usually do so because (a) they are also able to communicate caring for their players as people, so that the abuse is not "taken personally"; (b) they have very talented athletes; (c) they recruit thick-skinned athletes who are less affected by aversive feedback; or (d) they are such skilled teachers and strategists that these abilities overshadow their negative approach. In other words, such coaches win in spite of, not because of, the negative approach they espouse.

Response Cost: Punishment through Removal of Noncontingent Reinforcers

Up to now, we have been discussing aversive punishment, in which an unpleasant stimulus, such as yelling or criticism, is made contingent on a behavior in order to suppress it. There is another type of punishment that involves contingently taking away something valued by the athlete.

> The legendary baseball umpire Bill Klem once called a batter out on a close third strike. The enraged batter flung his bat high into the air and whirled around to argue the call. Klem whipped off his mask, fixed the batter with a steely gaze, and said, "If that bat comes down, it'll cost you 100 bucks." (Smith, 1993, p. 280)

Fines, loss of desirable activities (such as batting practice), and "benchings" are all examples of a second form of punishment that involves the removal of *noncontingent* reinforcers. That is, the reinforcers that are taken away are not those that maintain the behavior. (If they were, we would be dealing with extinction.) For example, a monetary consequence (having $100) was not the "reason" the batter threw the bat into the air in the example above, and being late for practice is not done in order to get increased playing time. Yet a fine or a loss in playing time can be powerful forms of punishment. Appropriately, this form of punishment is called **response cost** (as in, "That'll cost you").

Punishment through deprivation has two distinct advantages over aversive punishment. First, even though response cost may arouse temporary frustration or anger, it does not create the kind of fear that aversive punishment does (Sarafino, 2004). It is therefore less likely to cause avoidance of the punisher or the punishing situation, and it may actually increase the attractiveness of the withdrawn reinforcer (which can then be used to reinforce desired alternative behaviors). Second, the punisher is not modeling physical aggression, so that there is less opportunity for learning of aggression through imitation. For these reasons, the response cost procedure is a preferred alternative to aversive punishment. In using such punishment, it is useful to verbalize the contingency in a matter of fact fashion, without expressing anger, for example, "I don't like to do this, but because you were late for practice, it automatically means you get less playing time during our next game."

The Positive Alternative

Fortunately, there is an alternative to the negative approach. As a means of influencing behavior, it can accomplish everything aversive control does and much more—without the harmful side effects. The positive approach is aimed at strengthening desired behaviors through the use of encouragement, positive reinforcement, and sound technical instruction carried out within a supportive atmosphere. From this point of view the best way to eliminate mistakes is not to try to stamp them out with punishment but to strengthen the correct or desired behaviors. The motivational force at work here is a positive desire to achieve rather than a negative fear of failure. Mistakes are seen not as totally negative occurrences but as, in the words of John Wooden, "stepping stones to achievement" that provide the information needed to improve performance. The positive approach, through its emphasis on improving rather than on "not screwing up," fosters a more positive learning environment and tends to promote more positive relationships among coaches and athletes. Research has clearly shown that athletes like positive coaches better, enjoy their athletic experience more and report higher team cohesion when playing for them, and perform at a higher level when positive control techniques are used (Martin & Hyrcaiko, 1983). Even negative control procedures work more effectively if they occur within a context of positive interactions. Thus, Jimmy Johnson,

a highly successful college and professional football coach, once noted, "We rely ninety percent on positive reinforcement, so when we do use punishment, it really makes an impact" (*Orlando Sentinel,* July 24, 1996, p. C2).

The cornerstone of the positive approach is the skillful use of positive reinforcement to increase motivation and to strengthen desired behaviors. Another highly effective technique is the use of performance feedback. Let's discuss these specific techniques.

Positive Reinforcement: Getting Good Things to Happen

As noted earlier, positive reinforcement is any consequence that increases the likelihood of a behavior that it follows. For our present purposes, positive reinforcement can be viewed as related to the more familiar concept of "reward," as long as we keep in mind that a consequence that may be "rewarding" from the perspective of one person may not function as a reinforcer for another person who is not motivated to receive that consequence. Thus, a compliment from a coach who is despised by her athletes may have no positive impact on their behavior. (Likewise, rat food is a highly effective reinforcer for the white rat, but notoriously ineffective for children.) Reinforcement can take many possible forms: verbal compliments, smiles or other nonverbal behaviors that convey approval, increased privileges, awards, and so on.

The effective use of reinforcement to strengthen behavior requires that a coach (a) find a reinforcer that works for a particular athlete, (b) make the occurrence of reinforcement dependent on performance of the desired behavior, and (c) make sure the athlete understands why the reinforcement is being given. The relations between behaviors and their consequences are termed **reinforcement contingencies.**

Choosing Effective Reinforcers

Choosing a reinforcer is not usually difficult, but in some instances the coach's ingenuity and sensitivity to the needs of individual athletes may be tested. Potential reinforcers include social behaviors such as verbal praise, smiles, nonverbal signs such as applause, or physical contact such as a pat on the back. They also include the opportunity to engage in certain activities (such as extra batting practice) or to play with a particular piece of equipment.

Social reinforcers are most frequently employed in athletics, but even here the coach must decide what is most likely to be effective with each athlete. One athlete might find praise given in the presence of others highly reinforcing, whereas another might find it embarrassing. The best way for a coach to find an effective reinforcer is to get to know each athlete's likes and dislikes. In some instances a coach may elect to praise an entire unit or group of athletes; at other times reinforcement may be directed at one athlete. If at all possible, it is a good idea to use a variety of reinforcers and vary what one says and does so that the coach does not begin to sound like a broken record. In the final analysis the acid test of one's choice of reinforcer is whether it affects behavior in the desired manner.

The effectiveness of verbal reinforcement can be increased by combining it with a specific description of the desirable behavior the athlete just performed. For example, a coach might say, "Way to go, Bob. Your head stayed right down on the ball on that swing." In this way the power of the reinforcement is combined with an instructional reminder of what the athlete should do. This also cues the athlete to what the coach wants him to concentrate on.

Selecting and Reinforcing Target Behaviors

Systematic use of reinforcement forces coaches to be specific in their own minds about exactly which behaviors they want to reinforce in a given athlete at a particular time. Obviously, they will not want to reinforce everything an athlete does correctly, lest the power of the reinforcer be diluted. The most effective use of "reward power" is to strengthen skills an athlete is just beginning to master. In many instances complex skills can be broken down into their component subskills, and coaches can concentrate on one of these

subskills at a time until it is mastered. For example, a football coach might choose to concentrate entirely on the pattern run by a pass receiver, with no concern about whether or not the pass is completed. This is where a coach's knowledge of the sport and of the mastery levels of individual athletes is crucial. Athletes can enjoy lots of support and reinforcement long before they have completely mastered the entire skill if coaches are attentive to their instructional needs and progress. Such reinforcement will help to keep motivation and interest at its maximum.

Shaping

We have all marveled at the complex behaviors performed by animals in circuses, at amusement parks, and in the movies. These behavioral feats are brought about by the use of a positive reinforcement procedure known as **shaping.** At the beginning of training the animal was incapable of anything even approximating the desired behavior. The trainer chose some behavior the animal was already performing and began reinforcing that behavior. Then, over time, the requirements for reinforcement were gradually altered so that the animal had to perform acts that more and more closely resembled the final desired behavior until that behavior had been "shaped" by the systematic application of reinforcement.

The products of operant conditioning go far beyond rats pressing bars and pigeons pecking discs in Skinner boxes, and even beyond the feats performed by trained animals. Humans also learn many complex behaviors through shaping. Shaping is involved in learning a language and in developing educational skills. If we want to train children to be mathematicians, we do not expect them to solve complex calculus problems spontaneously. We start by teaching them basic arithmetic operations, and we successively build on what they have already learned. On a broader level, our acquisition of the behaviors, values, and attitudes of our society involves a great deal of shaping on the part of parents, teachers, and peers.

Shaping can also be used to enhance athletic skills. Start with what the athlete is currently capable of doing, and then gradually require a more skillful level of performance before reinforcement is given. It is important that the shift in demands be realistic and that the steps be small enough so that the athlete can master them and be reinforced. For example, a youth softball coach may at first praise novice infielders whenever they stop a ball (with any part of their anatomy). As proficiency increases, however, she may require that the players field the ball in the correct position, and later that they field the ball cleanly in the correct position and make an accurate throw. Used correctly, shaping is one of the most powerful of all the positive control techniques.

An Example of a Successful Positive Reinforcement Program

A comprehensive review of research on the effectiveness of behavioral techniques for enhancing sport performance revealed a consistently high success rate for the systematic use of positive reinforcement techniques (Smith et al., 1996). Let us consider an example from youth sports.

The systematic use of positive reinforcement to improve the performance of a youth football team's offensive backfield was described by Judi Komaki and Fred Barnett (1977). Three different offensive plays were selected by the coach. Each of the plays was broken down into five stages judged to be crucial to the execution of the play and was presented to the players accordingly. For example, one of the plays included the following stages: (1) quarterback-center exchange; (2) quarterback spin and pitch; (3) right halfback and fullback lead blocking; (4) left halfback route; and (5) quarterback block. Breaking down the play in this manner allowed the coach to respond to the elements that were run correctly and to give specific feedback to the players about their execution of each of the five stages.

During the first phase of the experiment, data were carefully collected on how often the stages of each play were executed correctly. Then the coach began to systematically apply reinforcement procedures to Play A. Each time the play was run in practice, the coach checked off which of the elements had been successfully executed and

praised the players for the stages that were run successfully. Reinforcement was not applied when Plays B and C were run. After a period of time the reinforcement procedure was shifted to Play B only, and later to Play C only. Applying the technique to only one play at a time permitted a determination of the specific effects of reinforcement on the performance of each of them.

A comparison of the percentage of stages executed correctly before and after introduction of the reinforcement procedure indicated that performance increased for all three plays, but only after reinforcement was introduced. The level of performance for Play A improved from 61.7% to 81.5% when reinforcement was applied, but execution of B and C did not improve until reinforcement was also applied to them. When this occurred, execution of play B improved from 54.4% to 82%, and execution of Play C improved from 65.5% to 79.8%. Clearly, the systematic use of reinforcement led to a substantial improvement in performance. Other studies have shown similar performance improvement in gymnastics, swimming, baseball, golf, and tennis (see Martin & Hyrcaiko, 1983).

Schedules and Timing of Reinforcement

One of the most frequently asked questions is how often and how consistently reinforcement should be given. Fortunately, a great deal of research has been done concerning the effects of so-called **schedules of reinforcement** on behavior change. Reinforcement schedules refer to the pattern and frequency with which reinforcement is administered. Although there are many different kinds of schedules, the most important distinction is between continuous and partial schedules. On a continuous schedule, *every* correct response is reinforced. On partial schedules, some correct responses are reinforced and some are not.

A coach has two related challenges. First, athletes must be instructed in specific skills until they master them. Then the coach must figure out ways to maintain the skills so players will continue to perform them at a high level of proficiency. A knowledge of the effects of reinforcement schedules can assist in meeting both challenges.

During the initial stages of training, reinforcement is best given on a continuous schedule. Frequent reinforcement not only helps strengthen the desired response but also provides the athlete with frequent feedback about how well he or she is doing. Once the behavior is learned, however, reinforcement should be shifted to a partial schedule. Research has shown that behaviors reinforced on partial schedules persist much longer in the absence of reinforcement than do those that have been reinforced only on a continuous schedule (Skinner, 1969). For example, people will put a great many coins into slot machines, which operate on partial schedules. In contrast, they are unlikely to persist long in putting coins into soft drink machines that do not deliver because these machines normally operate on a continuous schedule. Thus, the key principle in using schedules is to start with continuous reinforcement until the behavior is mastered, then to shift gradually to partial reinforcement to maintain a high level of motivation and performance (Martin & Pear, 2002).

The timing of reinforcement is another important consideration. Other things being equal, the sooner after a response that reinforcement occurs, the stronger are its effects on behavior. Thus, whenever possible, try to reinforce a desired behavior as soon as it occurs. If this is not possible, however, try to find an opportunity to praise the athlete later on.

Reinforcing Effort and Other Desirable Behaviors

To this point, I have discussed the use of reinforcement to strengthen skills. It is important to realize, however, that reinforcement can be used to strengthen other desirable behaviors as well. For example, the positive approach can be used to reduce the likelihood of disciplinary problems by reinforcing compliance with team rules. There is no reason a coach should not recognize and reinforce exemplary conduct on the part of particular athletes or the team as a whole. One of the most effective ways of avoiding disciplinary problems is by strengthening the opposite (desired) behaviors through reinforcement (Smith & Smoll, 2001).

Similarly, instances of teamwork and of athletes' support and encouragement of one another should be acknowledged and reinforced from time to time. Doing so not only strengthens these desirable behaviors but also creates an atmosphere in which the coach is actually serving as a positive model by supporting them. Research has shown that the best predictor of liking for the coach and desire to play for him or her in the future is not the won-lost record of the team but how consistently the coach applies the positive approach and avoids the use of punishment (Smith & Smoll, 1991).

I have saved one of the most important points of all until last. *What* coaches choose to reinforce is of critical importance. It's easy to praise an athlete who has just made a great play. It is less natural to reinforce an athlete who tried but failed. A good principle is to reinforce effort as much as results. After all, the only thing athletes have complete control over is the amount of effort they make; they have only limited control over the outcome of their efforts. Coaches have a right to demand total effort, and this is perhaps the most important thing of all for them to reinforce. If athletes have had good technical instruction, are free from self-defeating fear of failure, and are giving maximum effort (all of which should be promoted by the use of the positive approach), then performance and winning will take care of themselves within the limits of the athletes' ability. John Wooden, the legendary "Wizard of Westwood," placed great emphasis on this concept:

> You cannot find a player who ever played for me at UCLA that can tell you he ever heard me mention "winning" a basketball game. He might say I inferred a little here and there, but I never mentioned winning. Yet the last thing that I told my players, just prior to tipoff, before we would go on the floor was, "When the game is over, I want your head up—and I know of only one way for your head to be up—and that's for you to know that you did your best. . . . This means to do the best YOU can do. That's the best; no one can do more. . . . You made that effort. (personal communication, 1975)

The beneficial effects of focusing on effort—and the potentially damaging effects of focusing on ability—were demonstrated in a study by Claudia Mueller and Carol Dweck (1998). In a series of experiments, fifth-grade children worked on a number of academically oriented tasks. Some were reinforced for their successes by being told that they were very intelligent, had excellent ability, or were "very good" at the activity. Others were commended for their effort when they performed successfully. The two groups of children were then tested on a series of additional tasks. Children who had been praised for intelligence cared more about performance goals (succeeding) as opposed to learning goals (getting better or gaining skills) than did children praised for effort. After failure, those praised for intelligence displayed less task persistence, less task enjoyment, poorer task performance, and more low-ability attributions. As described by the authors,

> After they faced failure, these children used low-ability, rather than low-effort, attributions to account for their poor performance more than did children praised for hard work, who preferred to ascribe their failures to low effort. Thus, the children who were explicitly told that they were smart after success were the ones who most indicted their ability on the basis of poor performance. This indictment of ability also led children praised for intelligence to display more negative responses in terms of lower levels of task persistence, task enjoyment, and performance than their counterparts who received commendations for effort. (p. 48)

Reinforcement and Intrinsic Motivation

An important distinction is often made between **intrinsic motivation** and **extrinsic motivation.** When people are motivated to perform an activity for its own sake, they are said to be **intrinsically motivated.** When they perform the activity only to obtain some external reward, they are **extrinsically motivated.**

Concerns are often raised about the potential negative impact of positive reinforcement on intrinsic motivation. If external rewards are suddenly introduced for performance of a behavior that is intrinsically rewarding, a person may come to attribute his or her performance to the extrinsic reward and cease performing the behavior if the external reward is withdrawn. Thus, in one study children who loved drawing with pens were offered external reinforcement (a "good player" award) for drawing with the pens. Later, when the good player award was withdrawn, the children showed a sharp decrease in their tendency to draw with the pens (Lepper & Greene, 1978).

Most of us would like athletes to be intrinsically motivated to participate in athletics. Is it possible that the positive approach, with its emphasis on reinforcement from the coach, could undermine their "love of the game" for its own sake?

It now appears that if extrinsic reinforcement is given to acknowledge a specific level of performance, it is unlikely to undermine intrinsic motivation (Deci, Koestner, & Ryan, 1999). Rather, it provides important information to an athlete that she has met a standard of excellence and thereby provides a basis for positive self-reinforcement by the athlete. Positive internal self-evaluations can strengthen behavior and also maintain and even increase intrinsic motivation (Cervone, 1992). Thus, it is a good idea for coaches to instill self-pride in their athletes with statements like "Great job! You ought to feel proud of yourself for that effort." There is considerable evidence that standards for self-reinforcement are often adopted from other people, and a coach can be an influential source of standards of excellence that can be internalized by the athletes, particularly if the coach has developed a strong positive relationship with them.

Positive Reinforcement and Motivational Climate

Positive reinforcement can be made contingent on virtually any behavior. For example, we could choose to reinforce effort, persistence, and improvement, or we could give reinforcement only when an athlete is outperforming others, both teammates and opponents. The positive approach described earlier has emphasized reinforcement for effort, improvement, and meeting internal standards of performance. This approach is designed to foster a *task-oriented motivational climate*, in which athletes will feel successful and competent when they have learned something new, witnessed skill improvement, mastered the task at hand, or given their best effort. Importantly, even if athletes perceive themselves as possessing lower ability than others, they can still feel competent and successful if focused on mastery achievement goals (Nicholls, 1989).

By contrast, when young athletes are in a state of *ego involvement*, their definitions of personal success and demonstrated competence are *other-referenced*. The goal here is to show that one is superior to relevant others (approach ego orientation), or to avoid appearing inferior to others (avoidance ego orientation). When coaches make reinforcement contingent on outperforming others or winning, punish unsuccessful performance, and fail to attend to effort and developing personal goals for improvement, they can easily create an *ego-oriented motivational climate*.

Research on the effects of task- versus ego-motivational climates in both educational and sport settings reveal that the motivational climate created by teachers and coaches has strong effects on achievement goals, standards of success, and behavior. Research in the educational domain indicates that children are more likely to invest in learning, develop intrinsic motivation, and adopt adaptive achievement strategies in task-involving environments, in which the emphasis in on learning, personal improvement, and developing new skills rather than on interpersonal evaluation and social comparison with others. By contrast, maladaptive achievement strategies, fear of failure, and motivational problems tend to occur in ego-involving motivational climates, in which mistakes are punished, children with greater ability receive more encouragement and rewards, and social comparison is emphasized (Ames, 1992). As described in the next chapter (Duda & Treasure, Chapter 4, this volume), similar findings have been reported in the sport environment, and we can safely conclude that a task-oriented motivational climate is greatly preferable to an ego-oriented one (McArdle & Duda, 2002). As John Wooden and other progressive coaches have recognized, focusing on effort, preparation, and dedication to personal improvement pays dividends not only in performance but also in the development of healthy attitudes and values concerning sport participation. Especially noteworthy is the fact that athletes report greater enjoyment of their sport experience when coaches create a task-oriented motivational climate. Knowing what to reinforce is a key to creating such a climate.

Performance Feedback

Positive reinforcement serves not only as a reward for desirable behavior but also as a form of performance feedback. In other words, providing "knowledge of results" communicates the message that performance has met or exceeded the coach's standards. When it is possible to measure desired and undesired behaviors objectively, the coach can utilize the highly effective tool of performance feedback to increase motivation and performance.

In recent years there has been a surge of interest in objective feedback as a technology for improving job performance in business, industry, and other settings (Huberman & O'Brien, 1999; Latham & Seijts, 1999; Tauer & Harackiewicz, 1999). The evidence indicates that performance feedback is a highly effective tool. One review of 18 studies carried out in a variety of job settings found increases in objective performance indicators averaging 53% after systematic performance feedback procedures were instituted (Kopelman, 1982–83). Specific work behaviors improved an average of 78%, and overall productivity an average of 16%. These increases were recorded over intervals ranging from 8 weeks to 4 years.

Performance feedback is a prominent feature of what many successful coaches do. For example, psychologists Ronald Gallimore and Roland Tharp (2004) charted all of John Wooden's behaviors during 15 practice sessions. They found that 75% of Wooden's comments to his players contained instructional feedback.

Most of his comments were specific statements of what to do and how the players were or were not doing it. Indeed, Wooden was five times more likely to inform than to merely praise or reprimand.

How Feedback Motivates

Objective feedback is so consistently effective in motivating increased performance for a variety of reasons. For one thing, feedback can correct misconceptions. Athletes, like other people, often have distorted perceptions of their own behavior. Objective evidence in the form of statistics or numbers can help correct such misconceptions and may motivate corrective action. For example, it can be a sobering experience for a basketball player who fancies himself a great ball handler to learn that he has more turnovers than assists. Performance feedback can have powerful informational effects that can help enhance behavior (Latham & Seijts, 1999).

Feedback also creates internal consequences by stimulating athletes to experience positive (or negative) feelings about themselves, depending on how well they performed in relation to their standards of performance. An athlete who is dissatisfied with his or her level of performance may not only be motivated to improve but will experience feelings of self-satisfaction that function as positive reinforcement when subsequent feedback indicates improvement. Such self-administered reinforcement can be even more important than external reinforcement from the coach in bringing about improved performance (Cervone, 1992). Promoting self-motivation in athletes also reduces the need for coaches to reinforce or punish. When feedback is public, as in posting statistics, the actual or anticipated reactions of others to one's performance level can serve as an additional motivator of increased effort and performance. Improvement is also likely to result in reinforcement from teammates.

A final motivational function of objective feedback is in relation to formal goal-setting programs. Because goal setting is discussed in detail in Chapter 13, I will simply point out that successful goal-setting programs provide clear feedback that informs workers as to their performance in relation to the goal (Locke & Latham, 1990). Without such feedback, goal setting does not improve performance, and without clear and specific goals that are either assigned by others or set internally, performance feedback has little effect on performance. For example, in a study by Albert Bandura and Daniel Cervone (1983) participants engaged in a strenuous aerobic task on an arm-powered exercise bicycle. Four experimental conditions were created by the presence/absence of challenging assigned goals and the presence/absence of performance feedback. Over the three performance periods, those who had both assigned goals and feedback improved their level of performance 59%. The performance improvements in the other three experimental conditions ranged from 20% to 25%. The presence of both challenging goals and performance feedback provided a powerful motivational boost to task performance. Such motivation is maximized if the person also has a high level of self-efficacy (the belief that he or she can succeed) and if the goal is highly prized (Cervone, 1992). In the study just described, the largest performance increases on the aerobic task occurred for participants who (a) had both goals and feedback, (b) were performing below the goal, (c) were dissatisfied with this state of affairs, and (d) had high self-efficacy for improvement.

Performance feedback can also result in increases in self-efficacy. In one study, participants performed an athletic task, in this case, the hurdles. Performance feedback contributed to subsequent self-efficacy, choice of more difficult hurdles, and performance (Escarti & Guzman, 1999).

Instructional Benefits of Feedback

Feedback has not only motivational but also instructional effects (see Chapter 2, this volume). It helps direct behavior. Objective performance feedback provides information about (a) the specific behaviors that should be performed, (b) the levels of proficiency that should be achieved in each of the skills, and (c) the athlete's current level of proficiency in these activities. This instructional function of feedback can be especially valuable when execution of a given skill is broken down into its stages or components, as was done in the football study described earlier. When the skill is a highly complex one, such as hitting a baseball, objective feedback on how frequently a hitter executes each of the essentials (keeping the bat in the correct position, shifting one's weight correctly, striding with the hips closed, keeping one's head down during the swing, and so on) can be very valuable in pinpointing areas of strength and weakness so that attention can be directed toward correcting mistakes. The information provided by subsequent objective feedback allows both coach and athlete to monitor progress in a more useful fashion than by depending on a more global measure of proficiency, such as batting average.

The foregoing discussion suggests a number of principles for giving effective feedback to athletes. Feedback should be contingent on what the athlete has just done, and it should be framed so that it can help the athlete continue to improve. The athlete is provided with feedback both on correct aspects of performance and on errors that were made. However, the athlete should then be told very specifically how to correct the error and encouraged to attempt the change. Expressions of confidence that with effort and time correct performance will result are likely to help maintain or even increase the athlete's own self-efficacy (Bandura, 1997).

Sometimes coaches need to give feedback that focuses on unfavorable aspects of performance. Such feedback is not always welcomed by the athlete. Indeed, much research in business organizations has shown that such feedback often results in negative emotional reactions and can actually create resistance to changing the problematic behavior. A recent study of factors that help counteract these negative reactions to unfavorable feedback showed that employees were more motivated to improve their job performance when the source of the corrective feedback was viewed as credible, the feedback was specific and of high quality, and the feedback was delivered in a considerate, supportive manner (Steelman & Rutkowski, 2004). Thus, to the extent that coaches can communicate to athletes that the corrective feedback is intended to help

them achieve their own performance goals, it is more likely they are to be receptive to it and utilize it in the intended manner.

Implementing a Performance Measurement and Feedback System

As in the application of positive reinforcement, a successful feedback program requires that coaches identify specific and measurable behaviors or consequences—something that can be counted. The performance measures can be fairly global (e.g., number of rebounds per minute) or more specific and dealing with subskills (e.g., percentage of rebound plays in which the opponent is boxed out). Because successful execution does not always result in a successful outcome, it is sometimes preferable to use a measure of successful execution. For example, some baseball coaches keep statistics on the percentage of times the batter hits either a line drive or a hard ground ball in preference to batting average. In other words, select the specific behaviors you want to track, and then develop a system for measuring them. At this stage it is important to communicate with players so that they are in agreement with the coach that the behaviors are important ones. A coach should try to elicit suggestions from the athletes so that they feel a sense of involvement in the program.

In many instances, coaches can choose between measuring a desired behavior or its undesirable counterpart. In line with the positive approach to coaching, I strongly recommend choosing the correct behavior for feedback rather than the mistake (or, at the very least, presenting both). This puts a coach in the position of reinforcing improvement rather than punishing or criticizing mistakes. It also focuses players' attention on what they should do rather than on what they should *not* do.

The measurement and feedback system coaches choose is limited only by their own ingenuity and awareness of the specific behaviors they want to promote. Some coaches have developed "total performance indexes" that include a variety of behaviors. For example, basketball coach Lute Olson devised an index in which negative behaviors such as turnovers, missed free throws, and defensive mistakes were subtracted from positive behaviors such as points scored, rebounds, and assists. Many college football coaches have highly detailed performance feedback systems that chart the percentage of plays during games and scrimmages in which each player successfully carries out his specific assignment. The measures are derived from game films and posted after every game and scrimmage. Such statistics also can provide an objective basis for selecting starters and allocating playing time.

Finally, it is important to note that performance feedback measures can be derived not only for individual players but also for subgroups or even for the team as a whole. Such measures can help to promote team cohesion by emphasizing the importance of teamwork and by providing a specific measure of group performance. As we saw in the Bandura and Cervone (1983) study, a negative discrepancy between the goal and the individuals' performance stimulated the greatest amount of performance improvement. In another study, participants received information on how both they and their group were doing in relation to specific individual and group goals. Performance improvement was stimulated by negative performance-goal discrepancies on the part of either the individual or the group. When the group was lagging behind, individuals tried harder to do their part to improve group performance. When individuals were not achieving their individual goals, they felt compelled to work harder to "pull their share of the load" (Matsui, Kakuyama, & Onglatco, 1987). This suggests the effectiveness of establishing both individual and group performance-unit goals.

Positive reinforcement and performance feedback techniques can be applied to sports in many ways. Given the success they have enjoyed in a wide variety of performance settings, these strategies have the potential to increase coaching effectiveness at all competitive levels, from children's programs to the demanding and exacting realm of elite and professional sports. Table 3-1 presents some practical guidelines based on the positive approach emphasized in this chapter.

Table 3-1 Getting Positive Things to Happen: Some Practical Guidelines

Administering positive reinforcement

1. Be liberal with reinforcement, particularly in the early stages of learning.

2. Have realistic expectations and consistently reinforce compliance with your standards.

3. Try to reinforce desired behaviors as soon as they occur.

4. Reinforce effort and perseverance, not just results.

5. Pair reinforcement with a statement of what the athlete did correctly (e.g., "Way to go, you blocked out really well").

6. Verbally reinforce compliance with team rules to help prevent disruptive behavior.

7. Help athletes set positive, individualized, behavioral performance goals. Use written or statistical performance feedback to track improvement and stimulate self-reinforcement processes in athletes.

Reacting to mistakes

1. Regard mistakes as learning opportunities.

2. Ask the athlete what should have been done instead to reinforce the performance principle.

3. If the athlete knows how to correct the mistake, give encouragement. If not, demonstrate.

4. The "positive sandwich" is an excellent way to combine instruction with encouragement and reinforcement. First, find something the athlete did right and reinforce it (e.g., "You did a good job of getting to that fly ball"). Then tell the athlete how to correct the mistake, emphasizing the good things that will happen as a result (e.g., "Now, if you catch the ball with both hands, you'll hang onto it and make that play"). Finally, end with an encouraging statement (e.g., "Keep working on this and you're going to be a good fielder").

5. Restrict criticism to behaviors that are in the athlete's control, such as lack of effort.

6. Avoid aversive punishment as much as possible. It builds fear of failure, the athlete's worse enemy. Response cost is a more desirable alternative if punishment is used.

Source: Adapted with permission from Smith, R. E., & Smoll, F. L. (2002). *Way to go, Coach! A scientifically proven approach to coaching effectiveness* (2nd ed.) Portola Valley, CA: Warde Publishers.

Summary

In this chapter I have focused on some of the advantages of a positive approach to coaching that uses reinforcement (a) to strengthen desired behaviors and (b) to promote the development of a positive motivation for success rather than fear of failure. Objective performance feedback on specific aspects of performance is a highly successful motivational and instructional technique. Both systematic reinforcement and objective feedback require that the coach identify specific behaviors that are important to individual and team success. This is in itself a highly desirable practice, because it focuses both coach and player attention on exactly what needs to be mastered and executed. It also promotes goal setting based on specific behaviors rather than on more general goals that are difficult to measure. Systematic use of positive reinforcement and objective feedback has yielded impressive results in many performance settings, including sports, and their utilization is appropriate at all competitive levels of athletics.

Study Questions

1. In what ways can coaching be viewed as attempts to influence behavior?
2. What are the ABCs of behavior control within an operant conditioning analysis of behavior?
3. Define the four basic consequences created by the presentation or removal of positive or aversive stimuli, and explain their effects on behavior.
4. Differentiate between negative reinforcement and punishment.
5. Define positive reinforcement and contrast it with punishment in terms of its effects on behavior and the motivational factors that underlie its effectiveness.
6. What are the direct effects and undesirable side effects of punishment? Distinguish between aversive punishment and response cost. How can we explain the fact that highly punitive coaches are sometimes very successful in eliciting high levels of athlete performance?
7. What are reinforcement contingencies, and how are they applied in shaping?
8. Summarize the schedules of reinforcement described in the text, as well as their effects on performance.
9. What is the importance of reinforcing effort rather than focusing entirely on outcome? What empirical evidence is provided by the Mueller and Dweck study?
10. How can the positive approach be used to reduce disciplinary problems?
11. Differentiate between intrinsic and extrinsic motivation. Under what conditions can intrinsic motivation be undermined by positive reinforcement, and what can be done to reduce this danger?
12. How would you use positive reinforcement to create (a) a task-oriented motivational climate and (b) an ego-oriented motivational climate?

13. What are the effects of performance feedback on task performance, and what are the mechanisms whereby feedback is assumed to motivate behavior? What is the instructional value of feedback?

14. What are some of the key principles in implementing a performance feedback program? How are these related to the positive approach to coaching?

References

Ames, C. (1992). Achievement goals and adaptive motivational patterns: The role of the environment. In G. C. Roberts (Ed.), *Motivation in sport and exercise* (pp. 161–176). Champaign, IL: Human Kinetics.

Bandura, A. (1997). *Self-efficacy: The exercise of control.* New York: Freeman.

Bandura, A., & Cervone, D. (1983). Self-evaluative and self-efficacy mechanisms governing the motivational effects of goal systems. *Journal of Personality and Social Psychology, 45,* 1017–1028.

Cervone, D. (1992). The role of self-referent cognitions in goal setting, motivation, and performance. In M. Rabinowitz (Ed.), *Applied cognition* (pp. 79–96). New York: Ablex.

Deci, E. L., Koestner, R., & Ryan, R. M. (1999). A meta-analytic review of experiments examining the effects of extrinsic rewards on intrinsic motivation. *Psychological Bulletin, 125,* 627–668.

Escarti, A., & Guzman, J. F. (1999). Effects of feedback on self-efficacy, performance, and choice on an athletic task. *Journal of Applied Sport Psychology, 11,* 83–96.

Gallimore, R., & Tharp, R. (2004). What a coach can teach a teacher, 1975–2004: Reflections and reanalysis of John Wooden's teaching practices. *The Sport Psychologist, 18,* 119–137.

Huberman, W. L., & O'Brien, R. M. (1999). Improving therapist and patient performance in chronic psychiatric group homes through goal-setting, feedback, and positive reinforcement. *Journal of Organizational Behavior Management, 19,* 13–36.

Komaki, J., & Barnett, F. T. (1977). A behavioral approach to coaching football: Improving the play execution of an offensive backfield on a youth football team. *Journal of Applied Behavior Analysis, 10,* 657–664.

Kopelman, R. E. (1982–83). Improving productivity through objective feedback: A review of the evidence. *National Productivity Review, 24,* 43–55.

Latham, G. P., & Seijts, G. H. (1999). The effects of proximal and distal goals on performance on a moderately complex task. *Journal of Organizational Behavior, 20,* 421–429.

Lepper, M. R., & Greene, D. (1978). *The hidden costs of reward: New perspectives on the psychology of motivation.* Hillsdale, NJ: Erlbaum.

Locke, E. A., & Latham, G. P. (1990). *A theory of goal setting and task performance.* Englewood Cliffs, NJ: Prentice Hall.

Maag, J. W. (2003). *Behavior management: From theoretical implications to practical applications.* Pacific Grove, CA: Wadsworth.

Martin, G. L., & Hyrcaiko, D. (1983). *Behavior modification and coaching: Principles, procedures, and research.* Springfield, IL: Charles C. Thomas.

Martin, G., & Pear, J. (2002). *Behavior modification: What it is and how to do it* (7th ed.). Englewood Cliffs, NJ: Prentice Hall.

Matsui, T., Kakuyama, T., & Onglatco, M. L. U. (1987). Effects of goals and feedback on performance in groups. *Journal of Applied Psychology, 72,* 407–415.

McArdle, S., & Duda, J. K. (2002). Implications of the motivational climate in youth sports. In F. L. Smoll & R. E. Smith (Eds.), *Children and youth in sport: A biosocial perspective* (2nd ed.). Dubuque, IA: Kendall/Hunt.

Mueller, C. M., & Dweck, C. S. (1998). Praise for intelligence can undermine children's motivation and performance. *Journal of Personality and Social Psychology, 75,* 33–52.

Nicholls, J. G. (1989). *The competitive ethos and democratic education.* Cambidge, MA: Harvard University Press.

Petri, H. L., & Govern, J. (2004). *Motivation: Theory, research, and applications* (5th ed.). Belmont, CA: Wadsworth/Thomson Learning.

Sarafino, E. P. (2004). *Behavior modification: Principles of behavior change.* Long Grove, IL: Waveland Press.

Skinner, B. F. (1969). *Contingencies of reinforcement: A theoretical analysis.* New York: Appleton-Century-Crofts.

Smith, R. E. (1993). *Psychology.* Minneapolis, MN: West.

Smith, R. E., & Johnson, J. (1990). An organizational empowerment approach to consultation in professional baseball. *The Sport Psychologist, 4,* 347–357.

Smith, R. E., & Smoll, F. L. (1991). Behavioral research and intervention in youth sports. *Behavior Therapy, 22,* 329–344.

Smith, R. E., & Smoll, F. L. (2001). *Way to go, Coach: A scientifically-proven approach to coaching effectiveness.* (2nd ed.). Portola Valley, CA: Warde Publishers.

Smith, R. E., & Smoll, F. L. (1997). Athletic performance anxiety. In H. Leitenberg (Ed.), *Handbook of social and evaluation anxiety* (pp. 417–454). New York: Plenum.

Smith, R. E., Smoll, F. L., & Christensen, D. S. (1996). Behavioral assessment and interventions in youth sports. *Behavior Modification, 20,* 3–44.

Smith, R. E., Smoll, F. L., & Passer, M. W. (2002). Sport performance anxiety in young athletes. In F. L. Smoll & R. E. Smith (Eds.), *Children and youth in sport: A biosocial perspective* (2nd ed.). Dubuque, IA: Kendall/Hunt.

Smith, R. E., Zane, N. S., Smoll, F. L., & Coppel, D. B. (1983). Behavioral assessment in youth sports: Coaching behaviors and children's attitudes. *Medicine and Science in Sports and Exercise, 15,* 208–214.

Steelman, L. A., & Rutkowshi, K. A. (2004). Moderators of employee reactions to negative feedback. *Journal of Managerial Psychology, 19,* 6–18.

Tauer, J. M., & Harackiewicz, J. M. (1999). Winning isn't everything: Competition, achievement orientation, and intrinsic motivation. *Journal of Experimental Social Psychology, 35,* 209–238.

Zirpoli, T. J. (2004). *Behavior management: Applications for teachers.* Upper Saddle River, NJ: Prentice Hall.

4

Motivational Processes and the Facilitation of Performance, Persistence, and Well-Being in Sport

Joan L. Duda, *The University of Birmingham*
Darren C. Treasure, *Arizona State University*

I've always believed that if you put in the work, the results will come. I don't do things halfheartedly. Because I know if I do, then I can expect half-hearted results. That's why I approached practices the same way I approached games. You can't turn it on and off like a faucet. I couldn't dog it during practice and then, when I need that extra push late in the game, expect it to be there.

—Michael Jordan, National Basketball Association MVP 1988, 1991, 1993, 1996, and 1998

The principle is competing against yourself. It's about self-improvement, about being better than you were the day before.

—Steve Young, MVP Super Bowl XXIX

Michael Jordan and Steve Young speak to the very essence of why understanding motivation is of such interest to coaches, parents, sport psychologists, and athletes alike. Motivation is the foundation of sport performance and achievement. Without it, even the most talented athlete is unlikely to reach his or her full potential. Motivation is also pertinent to how the athlete experiences and responds to sport. That is, whether or not sport contributes positively or negatively to athletes' welfare is linked to motivation-related factors. In spite of its significance in the athletic milieu, however, motivation is one of the most misunderstood psychological constructs in all of sports.

What is motivation, and how does an athlete optimize it? Some think that whether an athlete is high or low in motivation is somehow inherent in the athlete's personality—a relatively unchangeable characteristic of the person. Others believe coaches "motivate" athletes, perhaps in their pregame pep talks or in the techniques they use in practice to foster their athletes' focus and intensity. There is, perhaps, some truth in each of these perspectives, although sport motivation is more complex and multifaceted than either.

Contemporary research shows motivation to be dependent both on some malleable, psychological tendencies of the athletes themselves and on aspects of the social environment in which they develop, train, and compete. In particular, variations in motivation are held to be a function of the diverse ways in which athletes *interpret* their sport-related experiences.

How do we decide if an athlete is motivated? Is good or poor performance the best or only indicator? In general, researchers suggest that motivation is inferred from variability in **behavioral patterns.** For example, John, a club tennis player, seeks out opponents who really challenge his game. Whether practicing or competing, John tries his hardest to get to every shot and to hit it well, even when down 40–love in a game or behind 5–1 in a set. John maximizes the tennis talent that he has. When an athlete such as John tries hard, seeks out challenge, persists in the face of adversity, and performs up to his ability level on a reasonably consistent basis, we typically conclude that this person is highly motivated. In contrast, if John were to hold back in training or a match and not give his best effort, prefer to play opponents or work on drills that are too easy or way beyond his capabilities, regularly experience performance impairment or fail to live up to his potential, and contemplate dropping out or actually quit tennis, we infer that motivational problems abound.

A number of factors need to be considered before we can determine whether a sport participant is motivated or not. It is important to take into account how much motivation the individual has (i.e., the *quantity* of motivation) as well as the quality of that motivation (Duda, 2001, in press). Typically, the quantity of motivation is reflected in how "into" her/his sport the athlete is at the present time and how well she/he is currently performing. The quality of motivation is inferred by the athlete's sustained and positive engagement in the sport. This includes both the athlete's accomplishments and the degree of enjoyment and psychological and physical benefits associated with sport involvement. Understanding motivation requires that we focus on divergence in motivational processes rather than only discrepancies in motivational outcomes.

The quantity and quality of motivation are intricately linked with how athletes think before, during, and after their sport experiences.

What thoughts appear critical to variations in motivation? Researchers (e.g., DeCharms, 1968; White, 1959) have shown that individuals feel and act more motivated when they think they have the competence to meet the demands of the task at hand and believe they have some control, or autonomy, in regard to their participation. Competence and control are basic human needs that all of us (athletes included) strive for (Deci & Ryan, 1985). The assumption that perceptions of ability and autonomy are critical to motivational patterns is fundamental to a number of popular contemporary theories of motivation. Four of those theoretical frameworks, which have provided a foundation for research and practice on sport motivation, will be reviewed here. These are (1) self-efficacy or social cognitive theory, (2) attribution theory, (3) cognitive evaluation and self-determination theories, and (4) achievement goal theory. Goal-setting theory (Locke & Latham, 1990), which examines the principles of effective goal setting and their effect on motivation, is addressed in Chapter 13.

Believing That One Can: The Construct of Self-Efficacy

> *I don't even think about the prospect of not winning—it never occurs to me. I really am that confident.*
>
> —*Daley Thompson, 1984 and 1988 Olympic decathlon champion*

> *Negative thoughts lead to a negative performance; the connection is as straightforward as that.*
>
> —*Sally Gunnell, Olympic gold medalist, world record holder, and world champion 400 meter hurdler*

Although not exactly synonymous with the concept of self-efficacy, the words of Daley Thompson, one of the world's greatest ever athletes, is a clear testament to the "power of positive thinking." The words of Sally Gunnell also provide insight into the effect of negative thinking—namely, that if you don't think you can do it you won't. Positive thinking is thought to be a very important antecedent of motivation, especially in challenging, achievement-oriented contexts such as competitive sport. Athletes think positively when they believe they can do something effectively, that is, when they think in a self-efficacious manner. (See Chapter 17 for a more complete discussion of positive versus negative thinking.) **Self-efficacy** is defined as a person's judgment about her or his capability to successfully perform a particular task (Bandura, 1986). Such judgments relate to the *level* of performance expected, the *strength* or certainty of those attainment beliefs, and the *generality* of those beliefs to other related tasks or domains. Bandura (1995, 1997) refined the definition of self-efficacy to encompass those beliefs regarding individuals' capabilities to produce performances that will lead to anticipated outcomes, and the term **self-regulatory efficacy** now encompasses a social cognitive approach that articulates the role cognition plays in performance above and beyond simple behavioral or skill beliefs.

Bandura (1986) has argued that (1) our efficacy beliefs mediate subsequent thought patterns, affective responses, and action and that (2) self-efficacy is positively related to positive motivational patterns. In general, sport research has shown that self-efficacy is a positive predictor of motor skill acquisition, execution, and competitive sport performance (see Bandura, 1997, for a review; Treasure, Monson, & Lox, 1996). Self-efficacy is one among a variety of mechanisms that is associated with higher performance. Athletes with high self-efficacy are more likely to try harder, choose challenging tasks, experience positive emotions, and be less anxious. The influence of self-efficacy on performance and motivation also seems to be intertwined with the goal-setting process (see Chapter 13). That is, although self-efficacy may directly relate to variations in performance, its impact may be because of its effect on athletes' personal goal setting and the development and employment of self-regulation skills (Kane, Marks, Zaccaro, & Blair, 1996; Schunk, 1995).

It is interesting to note, however, that previous performance tends to be a better predictor of subsequent pretask self-efficacy than efficacy judgments are of ensuing performance (Feltz, 1992). The athlete's incentives (whether intrinsic or extrinsic) to try to turn that self-efficacy into reality have an impact on the predictive utility of those initial task-specific confidence judgments. Further, if high performance is defined with respect to successful competitive outcomes, the athlete has relatively less control over achieving those outcomes than if the performance standard is self-referenced. That is, high self-efficacy does not always translate into a win. It does increase the probability, however, that the athlete will do well in terms of the facets of performance within her or his personal control. Coaches, sport psychologists, and athletes themselves would be wise to optimize efficacy judgments prior to the athletes' engaging in training or competitive-related activities. In other words, it is important for athletes to think (and act!) confidently if they want to perform optimally.

Implications for Practice

How do we increase self-efficacy? Thankfully, existing theoretical frameworks (e.g., Bandura, 1997) and sport research provide some insight into the antecedents of task-specific confidence in the athletic domain. Six key determinants of self-efficacy are emphasized (Figure 4-1):

1. The most influential determinant of self-efficacy is *past performance*. Especially when the task is difficult, we tend to feel more confident about performing a particular task when we have demonstrated mastery of that activity before—success breeds success. Therefore, when learning a new aspect of technique or strategy or gaining experience in sport competitions, it is important for athletes to accumulate progressively more demanding accomplishments to build their sense of competence. Breaking down the task into manageable "chunks" or decreasing the difficulty of early-in-the-season opponents are two ways of increasing the probability of initial positive performance and, thus, fostering athletes' self-efficacy.

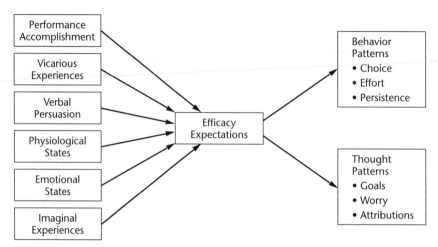

Figure 4-1 **The relationship between sources of self-efficacy, efficacy expectations, and behavior and thought patterns**
Source: Adapted from Feltz, 1988.

2. Another antecedent of athletes' efficacy judgments is *vicarious experience* (Bandura, 1986). For example, watching someone else successfully perform the activity, especially if this person is deemed to be similar to the athlete in question, can facilitate self-efficacy. This is a more salient source of efficacy information among younger athletes and those who have had limited experience with the task at hand. By watching or modeling others, athletes can learn how to do things. Also, if done in an informative rather than a comparative manner, coaches can use vicarious experiences to help athletes believe "if he or she can do it, so can I!" **Participation modeling,** where the athlete engages in the task while observing someone else do it (and, thus, works his or her way through the activity), can be particularly efficacy building (Feltz, 1992).

3. *Verbal persuasion* from coaches, sport psychologists, and significant others is another antecedent of self-efficacy. This can be in the form of feedback ("Here's how to do this") or motivational ("Come on, you can do it!") statements. If the person conveying the efficacy-enhancing information is considered credible and knowledgeable, the verbal persuasion is likely to be more influential. Athletes also often employ verbal persuasion

(or positive self-talk, see Chapter 17) to help themselves feel efficacious about what they are about to do. As there is a tendency to act according to how we think, positive self- and task-related statements made by athletes can increase their self-efficacy, too.

4. It is important to remember that our heads are attached to our bodies (and vice versa). With respect to formulating efficacy judgments, athletes also may look to their *physiological state* in deciding whether they can successfully meet specific task demands. More specifically, athletes appraise their physiological condition—state of autonomic arousal, fear, pain, fatigue, and so on—and make judgments as to their readiness to "rise to the occasion." By mastering techniques such as progressive muscle relaxation and deep breathing, which help them modify physiological conditions such as the heightened muscle tension, heart rate, and respiration rate associated with stress (Chapter 15), athletes can facilitate their preperformance self-efficacy. Similarly, for those athletes who have difficulty "getting up" for competition, energizing strategies may be effective in increasing arousal levels that will, for example, enhance perceptions of precompetition self-efficacy.

5. Similar to a consideration of their physiological state, athletes also appraise their *emotional state,* or mood, prior to performing when they decide on their level of confidence (Maddux, 1995). Consequently, emotional control techniques should be helpful in enhancing task-specific confidence among athletes who find themselves being debilitated by anger, frustration, and other negative mood states. Our thoughts can precipitate different emotional responses, and cognitive interventions such as "negative thought stopping" (see Chapter 17) can also result in higher efficacy judgments among sport competitors, not only decreasing negative mood states but also, and perhaps more significantly, increasing positive mood states (Treasure et al., 1996).

6. Finally, *imaginal experiences* are assumed to have an impact on task-specific self-confidence (Maddux, 1995). If athletes go through the demands of a sport activity in their minds before performing, those demands might not seem so daunting or unfamiliar, and the athletes' perceptions of their ability to meet those demands should be increased. Seeing (and feeling) yourself doing something successfully before actually doing it can also enhance your perceptions of ability (see Chapter 16 on imagery in sport).

Keep in mind that these critical antecedents to self-efficacy can be interdependent. For example, an athlete can use imagery to help reduce over-activation (e.g., imaging a peaceful setting to diminish one's muscular tension or high heart rate) or to attenuate the cognitive anxiety associated with an upcoming competition. In this way imaginal strategies are employed to influence the physiological and emotional states that subsequently feed an athlete's preperformance efficacy judgments.

Explaining Our Sport Successes and Failures: The Importance of Attributions

As players, when we are having a bad day, we tend to think in melodramatic terms, that we've lost it, that everything's gone wrong, but usually all you have to do is correct one small element of your game and everything else will fall into place.

—Mia Hamm, Member of the U.S. women's soccer World Cup 1999 winning team

Hard work is the basic building block of every kind of achievement: Without it, everything else is pointless.

—Rick Pitino, former NBA coach and current head coach of the University of Louisville men's basketball team

Without downplaying the importance of self-efficacy, any astute observer of motivational differences among people also quickly notes that merely being successful does not automatically translate into someone feeling confident and being motivated. Similarly, experiencing "failures" does not necessarily lead to diminished confidence and low motivation. According to attribution theory (Weiner, 1986), variations in motivated behavior are dependent on more than a consideration of whether an athlete is successful or unsuccessful in terms of performance outcomes. Specifically, it is assumed that the athlete's explanations for those outcomes are also pertinent to subsequent achievement striving (Biddle, 1993). Especially if the outcome was unexpected or experienced as a failure, we seek to answer the question, "Why did this occur?"

The determinants of sport performance are diverse and numerous. Consequently, a competitor can give a myriad of responses when explaining her or his positive or negative outcomes. For example, one's sport success can be attributed to "getting the lucky breaks," "the poor showing of the other team," the fact that "I trained harder than my opponent," or that "I had a good game." When an athlete fails, she or he can think that this was because of "those blind refs!," "the other team (or one's opponent) being better," "not giving my best effort," or the view that "I am just not good enough."

The attributional framework suggests that it is not the particular cause that we give to explain successes or failures that is most important (Weiner, 1986). Rather, it is characteristics that underlie those causes that have motivational significance (Figure 4-2). Specifically, causal attributions for

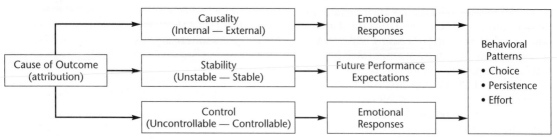

Figure 4-2 **Attribution process in sport**
Source: Adapted from Weiner, 1986.

poor and good performance in sport can be considered (in the mind of the athlete) to be more or less stable, internal or external, and controllable or uncontrollable.

When an athlete explains a success or failure to being physically strong or being "good" at the sport, the cause of the outcome is relatively stable. This element (whether it is something about the athlete or the sport environment) was present today, and it will likely be present the next time the individual is in the same or a similar situation. In contrast, a cause of success or failure that is less stable, for example, luck, the officials, or "everything went right," is viewed as being more dynamic (it was here today but might be gone tomorrow!). The stability of athletes' attributions has ramifications for their performance expectations. Simply put, if the athlete succeeds and feels that it is due to something stable, he or she is likely to have positive expectations for success the next time around. A parallel logic holds in the case of failures attributed to stable causes; negative performance expectations are likely to ensue. In contrast, a successful outcome that is explained by an unstable cause does not promote positive performance expectations. Similarly, failures explained by unstable determinants will not necessarily diminish the athlete's expectations for doing well next time.

Why are athletes' expectations regarding their forthcoming performance important? Our previous discussion of preperformance efficacy judgments has shed light on the relevance of performance expectations for achievement patterns. Moreover, the literature on competitive stress in

sport indicates that performance expectations are inversely related to precompetition state anxiety responses of athletes (Scanlan & Lewthwaite, 1984; Scanlan & Passer, 1978). That is, the lower the performance expectation, the more likely the athlete will be anxious before competing.

The attributions athletes evoke to explain success and failure also can be classified along an internal to external continuum. This has important ramifications for athletes' emotional responses following positive and negative sport events (Biddle & Hill, 1992). When success is realized and linked to internal reasons, the athlete is likely to feel pride and personal satisfaction. Although relatively positive emotions might be experienced (such as happiness, relief, or pleasant surprise), sport-related successes viewed as being caused by external elements do not result in affective responses that enhance self-esteem. If an athlete experiences subjective failure and attributes this failure to internal reasons, negative emotions (such as shame, guilt, and disappointment) are likely to be experienced. When sport failure is seen as being a consequence of external reasons, quite different affective reactions, such as frustration and anger, are more likely to emerge. The experience of self-esteem enhancing as well as potentially self-esteem damaging emotional reactions is also contingent on whether the causes of success and failure, respectively, are deemed to be based on things the athlete can influence. Similar to the predictions regarding the perceived stability and internality/externality of the attributions provided, athletes' views regarding their control over determinants of performance outcomes are expected to correspond to their emotional responses and future performance expectations.

How do sport competitors who vary in motivation tend to think about the reasons they succeeded or failed? Consistent with Anderson's personal changeability hypothesis (Anderson, 1983), motivated athletes in sport tend to attribute their sport successes to controllable, internal, and stable causes. As a result, positive outcomes are maximized for athletes who are "go-getters." Such experiences enhance performance expectations and leave the athlete feeling good about what she or he has just accomplished. Those who are motivated do not "pass the buck" (by blaming others) or feel the situation is insurmountable when difficult times arise in their sport training or competitions. Specifically, they are more likely to attribute failure to internal, controllable, and unstable factors. Failure is not usually regarded as something beyond their control (in terms of overcoming) or here to stay. Moreover, although they don't feel good about what just happened, motivated athletes tend to take responsibility for such negative outcomes; they attribute the causes of failure internally to such things as poor preparation, tactical or mental errors, or technical deficiencies. These are causes within their control that can be improved upon.

What about the attributions of athletes who are prone to motivational difficulties? Attribution theory and related sport research suggests that these competitors, who are often referred to as being **learned helpless** (Dweck, 1999), do not maximize their successful experiences because they are less likely to think this achievement occurred due to internal, controllable, or stable reasons. Learned helpless athletes typically attribute failure to internal, uncontrollable, and stable causes: "I'm not good enough, and I can't change this fact!"

In the sport environment, few learned helpless athletes compete at the higher levels. Most have dropped out by this point in their career because sport, unlike other educational pursuits, is usually voluntary. It is possible, though, that some athletes with motivationally maladaptive attribution patterns have managed to climb the ladder of athletic competition. Perhaps because of their very high sport ability, these athletes may not yet have encountered "failure." When they do, it is possible that they will become learned helpless.

Implications for Practice

Although more research needs to be conducted on this topic, sport work has successfully incorporated attributional principles to initiate positive behavioral, emotional, and cognitive change in athletes (Orbach, Singer, & Murphey, 1997; Orbach, Singer, & Price, 1999). In general, this line of investigation places athletes in a "failure" situation and then determines their responses to such negative outcomes. The individuals targeted in these studies are the ones who tend to attribute such failures as internal, stable, and uncontrollable (i.e., they are characterized as learned helpless). In attribution retraining, research experimenters typically provide some athletes in this group with controllable and unstable explanations for their poor fortunes. Other athletes are provided with uncontrollable and stable reasons. There is usually a control group in which there is no manipulation of their attributions for failure. The findings regarding attribution retraining interventions in sport suggest that athletes' dimensional ratings of the determinants of failure can be modified. For example, those in the controllable and unstable condition tend to rate the perceived cause of their failure as more controllable and unstable following the intervention. Furthermore, there tends to be a parallel increase in performance (and performance expectations) as well as positive emotions among those athletes who now view the causes of failure as more under their volitional control and unstable over time.

The "take-home" messages stemming from the sport attribution literature are quite clear. Coaches, sport psychologists, and significant others need to be more cognizant of the reasons they give for athletes' successes and, especially, their failures. It is important to make attributions for athletes' performances that are likely to enhance rather than undermine motivation. In essence, athletes should be made to feel accountable for their performance outcomes (whether positive or negative) and encouraged to believe there is hope when failures are encountered.

Work on causal attributions also calls attention to those in sport settings who may be "at risk." Motivational challenges may lie ahead for sport competitors who do not take credit (at least in their own hearts and mind) for their achievements and who fail to perceive that the precursor to each success is something (preferably a personal attribute or action) that they can control and count on tomorrow. In particular, we should intervene to enhance the perceived competence and control in those athletes who, when they experience failure, think "I'm not good at this. I never will be . . . and there is nothing I can do about it!"

Doing It for the Joy: The Determinants of Intrinsic Motivation

I don't like the glamour. I just like the game.

—Ben Hogan, professional golfer, winner of 63 PGA tournaments including 9 major championships; Player of the Year 1948, 1950, 1951, and 1953

When athletes are **intrinsically motivated,** they participate in sport for its own sake. That is, the motivation for sport engagement primarily revolves around the inherent pleasure of doing the activity. Someone or something else does not instigate athletes' sport participation in this case. Rather, they play sport out of personal choice. The motivation literature suggests that in various achievement activities, including sport, intrinsic motivation is associated with positive affect and maximal engagement (Vallerand & Losier, 1999).

It is assumed that our motivation has two sources; that is, we have intrinsic and extrinsic reasons for participating in an activity. When athletes feel that they are the cause of their involvement (as well as their performance outcomes) in a sport activity, they are more intrinsically motivated. When individuals view the determinants of their sport engagement to be external (i.e., dependent on rewards, which are

usually social or material), they are more **extrinsically motivated.** In this instance, athletes engage in sport as a means to an end, namely, to obtain something they want or to avoid realizing something they don't desire.

There are different types of intrinsic and extrinsic motivation. According to Deci and Ryan (1985, 1992), these types of intrinsic and extrinsic motivation vary along a self-determination continuum (Figure 4-3). We will start by describing the least self-determined types of motivation and move toward a portrayal of more autonomous motivational regulations.[1] First are those athletes characterized by **amotivation.** These athletes have no sense of personal control with respect to their sport engagement, and there are no extrinsic (or intrinsic) reasons for doing the activity. Amotivated athletes are no longer sure of why they are playing their sport and are considered to be similar to the learned helpless athletes described in the previous section.

Next on the continuum come three forms of extrinsic motivation, with the least autonomous being **external regulation.** Here behavior is performed to satisfy an external demand or stems from the external rewards an athlete expects to secure. For example, an athlete might say "I'm going to practice today but only because my scholarship depends on it." With the second form of extrinsic motivation, **introjected regulation,** athletes participate because, inside, they feel they *have* to play sport. Such motivation is still extrinsic in nature; it only replaces the external source of control with an internal one such as self-imposed guilt. For example, "I'm going to practice today because I can't deal with the guilt I will feel if I miss." With the third type of extrinsic motivation, **identified regulation,** behavior is undertaken out of free choice but as a means to an end, with the athlete often not considering the behavior itself pleasurable. For example, an athlete who wants to improve his fitness level chooses not to miss any sessions during off-season conditioning and preseason training, even though the activity is very demanding and unpleasant. At the opposite end of the

[1]Vallerand (2001).

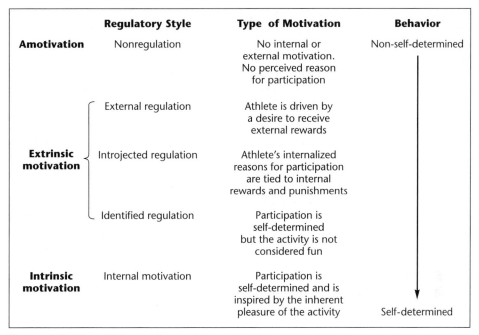

Regulatory Style	Type of Motivation	Behavior

Amotivation — Nonregulation — No internal or external motivation. No perceived reason for participation — Non-self-determined

Extrinsic motivation — External regulation — Athlete is driven by a desire to receive external rewards

Introjected regulation — Athlete's internalized reasons for participation are tied to internal rewards and punishments

Identified regulation — Participation is self-determined but the activity is not considered fun

Intrinsic motivation — Internal motivation — Participation is self-determined and is inspired by the inherent pleasure of the activity — Self-determined

Figure 4-3 **The self-determination continuum**
Source: Deci & Ryan, 1985, 1992.

self-determination continuum is the classic state of **intrinsic motivation,** in which an athlete participates in an activity for its inherent satisfactions. It is highly autonomous and represents the quintessential state of self-determination (Ryan & Deci, 2000).

It is proposed by Deci and Ryan (1992; Ryan & Deci, 2000) that all of us, athletes and nonathletes alike, need to feel competent (i.e., feel sufficiently efficacious), autonomous (i.e., perceive we are acting according to our own volition and have options), and connected with others (i.e., view relationships with important individuals as being supportive and respectful) within our various life domains. When the sport environment meets those three needs, we expect to witness greater intrinsic motivation, investment, and well-being in the athletic setting (Reinboth, Duda, & Ntoumanis, 2004).

Not surprisingly, athletes who are amotivated are expected to exhibit maladaptive motivational patterns. Most likely, we would have lost amotivated athletes along the way as they would have quit. With respect to the three types of extrinsic motivation discussed earlier (i.e., identified, introjected, and external regulations), the literature suggests that athletes who manifest such less self-determined reasons for sport engagement tend to report lower enjoyment of sport, and appear to be at risk for maladaptive responses such as over training and burnout (Lemyre, Roberts, Treasure, Stray-Gundersen, & Matt, 2004). Such athletes are particularly prone to not trying as hard as possible or dropping out if the extrinsic reinforcements and constraints that maintain their involvement begin to wane or completely disappear. This is because their sport participation is not especially, if at all, self-determined.

At all competitive levels, there are those athletes who play sport for intrinsic reasons. The sources of that intrinsic interest may vary. It may be the continuous learning that sport affords, the possibility of personal accomplishment and mastery, or the opportunity to experience pleasant sensations whether they be sensory or aesthetic (Vallerand, 2001). All in all, intrinsically motivated athletes find sport pleasurable in and of itself and are maximally motivated both quantitatively and qualitatively. Indeed, we would argue that it is most unlikely that athletes, even multimillionaires, would be able to sustain high levels of motivation and commitment throughout their careers if they did not have high levels of intrinsic motivation for engaging in their sport, particularly during periods of adversity, duress, and poor performance.

From youth sport onward, competitive athletics is dominated by extrinsic reinforcements. One can win medals and trophies. Fame and fortune may be the consequences of sport involvement for some. Talented college athletes in the United States may be rewarded with scholarships. Athletes at the professional level are paid for their sport achievements. An interesting question, therefore, is: What is the effect of extrinsic rewards on intrinsic motivation? The answer to this question is, "It depends." Athletes who are intrinsically motivated and receive extrinsic rewards are not necessarily more motivated. Indeed, research has indicated that extrinsic rewards can diminish intrinsic interest (Lepper & Greene, 1978; Vallerand, Deci, & Ryan, 1987). Rewards, however, also can foster intrinsic motivation. What seems to be critical in sport is to consider how extrinsic reinforcements are interpreted by individual athletes. That is, what do these rewards mean to the athlete?

There is a *controlling* aspect to extrinsic rewards. The use of extrinsic reinforcements by coaches and parents can provide athletes with a sense of "who is pulling the strings" in terms of their sport involvement. Rewards are detrimental to intrinsic motivation when they take away from athletes' sense of self-determination. Consider how a coach might refer to an intercollegiate athlete's scholarship and the resulting impact on that athlete's intrinsic interest in the sport. Perhaps, during the recruitment process, the coach repeatedly used the scholarship to coax the athlete to come play for his or her team. In this case the athlete's decision to play for this coach might be

more likely to be perceived as contingent on this external reward rather than being self-determined. When that athlete performs poorly, if the coach says, "How can you play like that? We're paying you to perform!" the athlete might think of his or her participation as more like work and less like an inherently enjoyable activity, which may lead to motivational difficulties.

Extrinsic reinforcements also can have different meanings. Sometimes rewards inform us about our level of competence and worth. When receiving the reward is contingent on personal performance and an athlete obtains the reward, this should increase his or her perceived ability while not undermining self-determination. As a result, intrinsic motivation should be fostered. The social environment that surrounds athletes (which is created by coaches, parents, sport psychologists, peers, the media, and fans) has a huge impact on the meaning of extrinsic rewards. Whether extrinsic reinforcements are likely to be viewed as controlling or informational regarding one's ability is a function of characteristics of these environments. In sport situations that allow athletes little autonomy, the rewards are more likely to be interpreted in a controlling manner.

Implications for Practice

The literature on intrinsic motivation in sport provides another rationale for cultivating perceived competence and control among sport participants. In essence, perceived adequate ability and internal control are the fuel that fire athletes' intrinsic motivation. Caution in the use (and especially the *overuse*) of extrinsic reinforcements in athletic settings is required. Extrinsic rewards must be salient to the athletes to have any influence, positive or negative, and should be used sparingly so that athletes are less likely to construct a behavior–reward contingency (i.e., "If I do this, I will get that"). This can promote an external locus of control in the athlete's sport involvement. The goals cooperatively set between coach, sport psychologist, and athlete (see Chapter 13) should be performance- rather than primarily outcome-based (Burton, 1989). They also should be realistic, that is, optimally challenging with the exertion of effort. Achieving these goals will enhance perceptions of competence and are more within the athlete's personal control than goals tied to competitive outcomes.

So that they are less likely to take on a controlling flavor, the reinforcements we use to reward athletes should ideally be based on reaching these personally referenced goals. We should strive to make the external rewards available in the sport domain more informative about what an athlete has achieved and can accomplish. Sport practitioners also might consider doing all that is possible to emphasize the intrinsic challenge, personal satisfaction, and sources of enjoyment fundamental to engaging in sport. This can help take the athlete's mind off the extrinsic reinforcements that often run rampant in the athletic arena.

Finally, there are other ways in which coaches and other significant people in athletes' lives can foster their self-determination (Reinboth et al., 2004). Considering the athletes' perspective and allowing them to make choices in training and competition events should cultivate autonomy. Committed and compatible coach-athlete relationships (Jowett & Chaundy, 2004) and the fostering of positive social exchanges between and cooperation among team members should lead to an enhanced sense of relatedness. As described above, when athletes feel more autonomous and connected in sport, there is a greater possibility that they will be more intrinsically motivated to play.

Achievement Goals: The Importance of How We Judge Our Competence

I never played to get into the Hall of Fame. I only tried to be the best that I could be.

—*Walter Payton, member of the National Football League Hall of Fame*

Another area of research that may assist athletes, coaches, and sport psychologists in understanding and enhancing motivation in sport is based on contemporary achievement goal frameworks. These frameworks assume that differences in goal perspectives, or the ways in which individuals judge their competence and perceive success, are the critical antecedents to variations in the direction and intensity of behavior. These models of motivation, similar to the three theoretical approaches just described, assume that perceptions of competence (how able we think we are) do relate to motivational patterns. However, achievement goal frameworks also state that how we decide whether we have been able or not is essential to the prediction of the quantity and quality of our motivation (Duda, 2001).

Fundamental to achievement goal models is that there are, at least, two central achievement goal perspectives (task and ego) that govern the way athletes think about achievement and guide subsequent decision making and action (Nicholls, 1984, 1989). According to Nicholls (1989), task and ego goal states entail distinct ways of processing an activity and can fluctuate throughout the course of an event. When task involved, an athlete's main purposes are to gain skill or knowledge, to exhibit effort, to perform at one's best, and to experience personal improvement. This athlete is focused on what he or she is doing and is thinking primarily about how to accomplish the task. If such purposes are achieved, the individual feels competent and successful. When ego is involved, athletes are preoccupied with the adequacy of their ability and the demonstration of superior competence compared to others. Perceptions of competence and subjective achievement, in this case, entail social comparisons with others. High ability is demonstrated for the ego-involved athlete when his or her performance is perceived to exceed that of others or to be equivalent with less effort exerted. The athlete's focus is on whether he or she is good enough (if confidence is low) and how to prove (rather than improve) his or her high level of competence (if confidence is high).

When task involvement is manifested, it is assumed that the athlete will think, act, and feel in a motivated manner regardless of his or her level of perceived ability. Ego involvement, too, can correspond with positive achievement patterns (e.g., high performance, or persistence) as long as the athlete is quite certain that her or his ability is high. When an athlete is ego-involved, however, and thinks the possibility of demonstrating superior competence is "slim to none," the achievement-related cognitions, emotions, and behaviors displayed are far less than optimal. That is, the quantity and, in particular, the quality of motivation is diminished.

Achievement goal theory states that an individual's goal perspective state—task or ego involvement—is the result of both individual differences and situational criteria. With respect to the former, an athlete's proneness for task and ego involvement is thought to be captured by his or her dispositional task and ego goal orientations. We will first discuss the nature and implications of these goal orientations in the athletic domain.

Significance of Goal Orientations

Achievement goal orientations are not bipolar opposites (Nicholls, 1989). Rather, they are independent dimensions. As a result, an athlete can be high ego/low task, high task/low ego, high task/high ego, or low task/low ego. From both a theoretical and applied perspective it is important to consider athletes' degree of proneness for both task and ego goals to get a more complete view of their motivational processes.

Findings from studies involving male and female athletes from a variety of competitive levels and age groups show that an adaptive achievement profile is one of high task and high ego orientation (e.g., Fox, Goudas, Biddle, Duda, & Armstong, 1994; Roberts, Treasure, & Kavussanu, 1996). But why might this be the case? Some researchers have suggested that a high task orientation might, to some degree, insulate highly ego-oriented individuals from the negative consequences of low perceived ability when they are performing poorly and, thus, be motivationally advantageous "over the long haul" (Duda, 1992; Nicholls, 1989; Roberts et al., 1996). Athletes who are high in both task and ego orientation have multiple sources of subjective success and perceived competence. They have the flexibility of focusing on either task or ego goals at different times in their training or competi-

tions to enhance their motivation (Duda, 1996, 2001). It should be noted that there are some questions regarding whether a high-task/high-ego orientation profile is most adaptive when the focus is on indices of the *quality* of motivation (Duda, 2001). For example, research examining the subjective well-being and moral functioning of athletes suggests that high-task/high-ego participants can be similar to their low-task/high-ego counterparts in views about and responses to sport (Reinboth & Duda, 2004a).

In general, a significant body of research has revealed that task and ego goal orientations are associated with qualitatively different behavioral, cognitive, and affective patterns in sport that are likely to have an impact not only on short-term performance but also on the quantity and quality of long-term participation. Researchers have found a task orientation to be related to positive motivational outcomes—for example, the belief that effort is a cause of success, the use of problem-solving and adaptive learning strategies, enjoyment, satisfaction, and intrinsic interest (Duda & White, 1992; Lochbaum & Roberts, 1993; Roberts & Ommundsen, 1996). Previous work has also revealed a task orientation to be associated with the belief that one's level of physical ability is changeable and unstable (Sarrazin et al., 1996). This is very important in the context of sport, because elite level performers usually reach their potential only after years of training. If an athlete believed this commitment to training was not going to lead to increases in ability (i.e., the view that sport ability is "fixed"), it is unlikely that the athlete would be optimally motivated to train over time.

In contrast, an ego orientation has been found to be associated with boredom, the belief that deception is a cause of success, and reported anxiety (Duda & White, 1992; Hall & Kerr, 1997; Lochbaum & Roberts, 1993; Roberts & Ommundsen, 1996). Ego orientation also has been found to be related to the belief that ability is an important determinant of success and the idea that sport competence is stable and a "gift" (Sarrazin et al., 1996). Such a belief system may lead an athlete who is questioning his or her ability not to be as motivated or committed to long-term training.

These individuals believe that ultimately "You've either got it or you haven't," and the possession of "it" is deemed a prerequisite to sport achievement.

Achievement goal models state that individuals in a state of ego involvement who have high perceptions of perceived ability are likely to respond in a fashion similar to competitors who are task involved, regardless of whether their perceived competence is high or low. This has lead a number of leading sport psychology researchers to contend that a high ego orientation may not be detrimental to performance. Indeed, Hardy and colleagues have argued that it is hard to see how an individual could succeed, particularly at the elite level, without having a strong ego orientation (Hardy, 1997; Hardy, Jones, & Gould, 1996). The assumption here is that elite athletes are motivated by winning and outperforming others. Although acknowledging that the combination of ego orientation with low perceptions of ability may have a detrimental effect on performance, Hardy and colleagues assume that elite athletes are and should be strongly ego-oriented and that this will be predictive of positive short-term performance as well as long-term motivation.

Although we would agree that all elite level athletes perceive success in an ego-involving fashion at certain times, we would caution those who want to promote ego orientation. Indeed, high levels of ego orientation may not be motivating at the elite level of sport over time as even these athletes sometimes doubt their ability (e.g., due to injury, during a performance slump). At such times a predominant ego orientation coupled especially with moderate or low task orientation puts individuals at jeopardy for feeling incompetent because their focus is primarily on their performance compared to others (Ames, 1992; Dweck, 1986; Nicholls, 1989). Because of the social comparative nature of sport and the high demands placed on athletes, both in training and competition, athletes (particularly those who are elite) are involved in an activity that is designed to challenge their perceived ability on a day-to-day basis.

Pertinent to any debate of the advantages or disadvantages of an ego orientation in sport are contemporary extensions of achievement goal models (Middleton & Midgley, 1997; Skaalvik, 1997). That is, recently some researchers have called for a reconsideration of dichotomous task/ego approaches to achievement goals and have instead advocated consideration of approach and avoidance aspects of an ego goal focus. An athlete would be considered ego-approach oriented when he/she is preoccupied with demonstrating superior ability compared to others. In contrast, an athlete emphasizing an ego-avoidance goal would be most concerned about not revealing his or her inferiority. For this athlete, the most important thing is to avoid showing that he or she does not possess adequate levels of ability. Central to this elaboration of the two-goal model of achievement goals (Dweck, 1999; Nicholls, 1989) is that an ego approach goal orientation would positively relate to achievement striving, whereas an ego avoidance goal emphasis would be coupled with negative motivational outcomes.

Our understanding of the nature, antecedents, and consequences of ego avoidance goals, especially in contrast to an ego-approach goal perspective, is still in its infancy (Duda, in press). Not surprisingly, highly ego avoidance athletes have been found to report lower perceived competence when compared to highly ego avoidance athletes. Other work has suggested that an ego avoidance focus would prove most problematic in the sport domain. More specifically, an ego avoidance perspective on achievement has been linked to greater fear of failure, stronger beliefs that sport ability is fixed or unchangeable, heightened anxiety, and lower intrinsic motivation (Cury, DaFonseca, Rufo, Peres, & Sarrazin, 2003; Cury, Elliot, Sarrazin, Da Fonseca, & Rufo, 2002; Halvari & Kjormo, 1999).

Regardless of skill level, or whether their ego goal focus is approach- or avoidance-oriented, those who are particularly concerned about how they are doing compared to others (ego-involved athletes) will become prime candidates for questioning their competence (Hall, 1990). This might be a regular occurrence for those of us who are less talented but could strike *any* athlete at *any* time. It is important at this point to remember that we are discussing *perceived* ability here, not *actual* ability.

Although actual ability may not change during a game of tennis or a round of golf, for example, athletes' perceptions of ability can and do change, often in a relatively short period of time, and are seldom stable over a long period of time.

How can ego involvement set the stage for performance impairment? Nicholls (1989) has suggested that the negative relationship between ego involvement and performance is instigated by the expectation an individual holds about looking incompetent. This expectation of looking low in ability can result in a decrease in performance in a number of ways. First, in an attempt to protect one's perception of competence, it may cause an athlete to select sport tasks that are too easy or too difficult. Although choosing to engage in less challenging tasks prevents the unhappy prospect of making errors and appearing to be less able, it simultaneously hinders an individual from developing a variety of sport skills to the maximum. Likewise, selecting tasks that are much too hard provides the athlete with a ready-made justification for the unsuccessful outcome as he or she is able to state, "I failed, but so did everyone else." This strategy, however, will be costly for the athlete in terms of maintaining or enhancing his or her development over time.

Second, the expectation of looking incompetent can result in a lack of trying when failure is looming and when it looks like one will look incompetent compared to others. For example, athletes who back off at the end of a race because the outcome is already determined and coast to the finish line or athletes who begin to engage in inappropriate achievement strategies or unsportspersonlike behavior when it looks like they will not be the best on that day are unlikely to ever reach their full potential.

Finally, if the expectation of demonstrating low ability becomes chronic, it may lead to regular and high levels of anxiety and, eventually, a devaluing of, and loss of interest in, the activity. If this chain of events occurs, it is likely that these athletes may find themselves in a state of amotivation and be characterized as learned helpless (Deci & Ryan, 1985; Vallerand, 2001). At the very least, if such athletes stay in sport, they should

become strongly ego avoidance goal-oriented (Duda, in press).

Significance of the Sport Context

A key variable in determining the motivation of athletes is situational and relates to the salience of task- and ego-involving cues in the achievement context. The focus here is on how the *perceived* structure of the environment, often referred to as the **motivational climate** (Ames, 1992), can make it more or less likely that a particular goal state is manifested in training or competition. This perception of the motivational climate affects the achievement patterns of individuals through their view of what goals are reinforced in that setting (Treasure, 1997). In essence, perceptions of the goal perspectives emphasized in these social environments are assumed to be predictive of variability in motivational processes.

Sport research has shown that a perceived task-involving setting is characterized by the athletes' view that the coach does reinforce high effort, cooperation among team members, learning and improvement, and the perception that everyone on the team (regardless of ability level) contributes to the team's achievements (Newton & Duda, 1999; Ommundsen, Roberts, & Kavussanu, 1998; Seifriz, Duda, & Chi, 1992; Treasure, Standage, & Lochbaum, 1999; Walling et al., 1993). A perceived ego-involving team climate, in contrast, is marked by athletes' perceiving that the coach punishes their mistakes, fosters rivalry among team members, and gives much of his or her attention to the most talented athletes on the team.

A recent meta-analysis demonstrated that, overall, a task-involving climate is associated with more adaptive motivational and affective patterns than perceptions of a performance climate in the contexts of physical education and sport (Ntoumanis & Biddle, 1999). For example, recent research has shown perceptions of a task involving climate to be negatively related to claimed self-handicapping behavior in elite level sport (Kuczka & Treasure, in press). Self-handicapping (Prapavessis, Grove, & Eklund, 2004; Prapavessis, Grove, Maddison, & Zillmann, 2003) is evident when athletes, who might be concerned about not performing well, "set the stage" so that there is an excuse or "scapegoat" evident that could explain their poor subsequent performance. In so doing, failure could be attributed to the "handicap" rather than any inadequacy in personal ability. Such a strategy also allows athletes to "save face" in front of others. Other work has found perceptions of an ego-involving climate to positively predict indices of physical ill-being among athletes (e.g., reported physical exhaustion and symptoms; Reinboth & Duda, 2004b). Moreover, the degree to which the sport environment is deemed ego-involving appears to have implications for athletes' level of self-esteem and the degree to which their self-worth is tied to athletic performance (Reinboth & Duda, 2004b). When athletes train and compete in a highly ego-involving motivational climate and have some doubts about their sport competence, they also are more likely to question their worth as a person overall.

One of the key elements of achievement goal theory is that dispositional goal orientations and perceptions of the climate are considered two independent dimensions of motivation that interact to affect behavior (Nicholls, 1989). Specifically, the theory calls for examination of a Person × Situation interaction effect. For example, let us consider a basketball player with a predominantly ego-oriented goal orientation (high ego/low task) who finds herself in a situation where the task- and ego-involving cues are vague or weak. In this case it is likely that the athlete's goal orientation will be most predictive of her goal state. In a situation in which the cues are in favor of an ego-involving climate, it is likely that these perceptions will complement the athlete's goal orientation in predicting a strong state of ego involvement. For a state of task involvement to emerge for this basketball player, the perceptions of a task-involving climate would have to be extremely strong. The stronger the goal orientation, the less probable it is to be overridden by situational cues and the stronger the situational cues must be. Alternatively, the weaker the disposition, the more easily it may be altered by situational cues (see Swain & Harwood, 1996; Treasure & Roberts, 1998).

Consideration of situational criteria would not be complete, particularly in the context of youth sport, without taking into account the influence peers (Vazou, Ntoumanis, & Duda, in press) and parents (Roberts, Treasure, & Hall, 1994; White, 1996) have in the development of children's and adolescents' achievement motivation. The majority of the work on the motivational climates created by other significant others in the sport setting *besides the coach* has concentrated on parental influence. Research has shown that the perceived situational goal structure initiated by parents has an impact on children's responses in sport (Roberts et al., 1994; White & Duda, 1993) Not only is there a relationship between the way parents define success for their children and the child's goal orientation, but there is also a relationship between a child's goal orientation and what the child perceives is of importance to the parents. Specifically, White and Duda (1993) found that children high in task orientation perceived that their parents valued their learning and enjoyment in sport and frowned on low levels of effort. In contrast, youth sport participants who had high levels of ego orientation perceived their parents to hold a definition of success that reflected the value of being superior, even if that meant that one does well with low effort (Roberts et al., 1994). This latter finding confirms what all children know—namely, that the worst 20 minutes in youth sport can be the drive home, at least for those children whose parents are ego involved.

Implications for Practice

The research conducted to date that has established the links between task and ego goals (whether dispositional or situational in nature) and various motivational patterns has contributed to our understanding of the motivation process in sport. But how do we enhance motivation based on the achievement goal model? High ego/low task athletes are the most susceptible to motivational difficulties. The evidence suggests that a sport psychology consultant should try to enhance the dispositional task goal orientation for these athletes, perhaps by introducing goal-setting or self-regulation techniques (Schunk, 1995; see Chapter 13). We should consider implementing strategies that encourage athletes to focus on gains in skill or knowledge, effort levels, and self-referenced criteria for success. It may be very difficult in the ego-involving milieu of sport to reduce an athlete's ego orientation, and it is likely that many athletes and coaches will be unwilling to reduce what they believe is a vital ingredient in developing motivation in sport—namely, focusing on winning and being superior. A high ego orientation is not necessarily detrimental to achievement striving, but it is especially problematic when coupled with low task orientation, low perceived competence, or grounded in a fear of looking incompetent. All in all, techniques designed to increase task orientation are likely to be more readily accepted by practitioners in the sport world and probably will be a more effective strategy for an applied sport psychologist to pursue.

Focusing on the individual to enhance the quality of motivation by affecting his or her dispositional goal orientations may seem a viable option, but practically speaking this strategy may be most suitable for an elite athlete who has access to a sport psychologist on a regular basis. Concentrating on individual change in dispositional tendencies may not be the most efficient and feasible alternative for a team or, especially, in the youth sport setting where the goal should be the development of *all* players rather than the performance of a select few. Findings from some recent studies in the more controlled environment of physical education suggest that devoting time and energy to developing strategies and instructional practices that facilitate the creation of a task-involving motivational climate may be an effective way to foster task involvement and enhance motivation in the sport setting (Lloyd & Fox, 1992; Solmon, 1996; Treasure & Roberts, 1995; Parish & Treasure, 2003; Sarrazin, Roberts, Cury, Biddle, & Famose, 2002; Standage, Duda & Ntoumanis, 2003).

Fostering a state of task involvement may be a particular challenge in the context of sport because ego involvement is inherent in the activity (Duda, 1992). However, in a relatively short period of time, a coach may be able to structure a context in such a way as to influence athletes' recognition of a task-involving motivational climate. In so doing, the coach can have an impact on the quality of athletes' sport participation.

Strategies employed at the individual or team level by the coach or sport psychologist can be easily undermined, however, by the policies and procedures of sport leagues and by the behavior and expectations of parents. For example, a coach's attempts to reward athletes privately for effort and improvement will be subverted by a leaguewide end of season award ceremony at which the winners—the most able athletes—are publicly acknowledged. Similarly, the coach who decides to give equal playing time to all athletes will struggle in a league in which all other coaches only allow their best athletes to play. It is clear that it will be difficult to develop and sustain changes at individual athlete or team levels without dealing with the wider sport environment.

In addition to youth sport coaches, interventions designed to enhance motivation should target the attitudes and behaviors of "Moms and Dads" (Roberts et al.,1994; White, 1996;). By making certain types of goals and performance feedback salient, a parent can influence young athletes' views about themselves, perceptions of the sport activity per se, and the criteria they use to evaluate success and failure. For example, when a young sport participant returns from a weekly tennis game and a parent asks, "Did you win?" the athlete receives a rather clear message as to what the parent considers most important. This message may counter or compromise the efforts of a coach or sport psychologist to enhance task involvement. We would suggest, therefore, that any intervention designed to promote task involvement in sport recognize the role parents and other significant adults and peers (Vazou et al., in press) may play in determining a young athlete's sport experience.

By emphasizing certain cues, rewards, and performance expectations a coach, parent, peer/teammate, or sport psychologist can encourage a particular goal state and in so doing affect the way an athlete perceives the sport. For the remaining discussion, the focus will be on intervention strategies relevant to adult in contrast

Table 4-1 Description of TARGET Structures and Strategies That Enhance Task Involvement

TARGET Structure	Strategies
Task. What athletes are asked to learn and what tasks they are given to complete (e.g., training activities, structure of practice conditions).	Provide the athlete with a variety of moderately demanding tasks that emphasize individual challenge and active involvement. Assist athletes in goal setting. Create a developmentally appropriate training environment by individualizing the demands of the tasks set.
Authority. The kind and frequency of participation in the decision-making process (e.g., athlete involvement in decisions concerning training, the setting and enforcing of rules).	Encourage participation by your athletes in the decision-making process. Develop opportunities for leadership roles. Get athletes to take responsibility for their own sport development by teaching self-management and self-monitoring skills.
Recognition. Procedures and practices used to motivate and recognize athletes for their progress and achievement (e.g., reasons for recognition, distribution of rewards, and opportunities for rewards).	Use private meetings between coach and athlete to focus on individual progress. Recognize individual progress, effort, and improvement. Ensure equal opportunities for rewards to all.
Grouping. How athletes are brought together or kept apart in training and competition (e.g., the way in-groups are created during practice).	Use flexible and mixed ability grouping arrangements. Provide multiple grouping arrangements (i.e., individual, small group, and large group activities). Emphasize cooperative solutions to training problems set.
Evaluation. Standards set for athletes' learning and performance and the procedures for monitoring and judging attainment of these standards.	Develop evaluation criteria based on effort, improvement, persistence, and progress toward individual goals. Involve athletes in self-evaluation. Make evaluation meaningful. Be consistent.
Timing. Appropriateness of the time demands placed on learning and performance (e.g., pace of learning and development, management of time and training schedule).	Training programs should recognize that athletes, even at the elite level, do not train, learn, or develop at the same rate. Provide sufficient time before moving on to the next stage in skill development. Spend equal time with all athletes. Assist athletes in establishing training and competition schedules.

to potential peer or teammate influences. To enhance motivation, coaches, parents, and sport psychologists should critically evaluate what they do and how they do it in terms of task and ego goals. For example, how do you define sport success for your players or children? Is it in terms of development and effort, or winning and losing? As a coach, do you design practice sessions that optimally challenge your players, or do you repeat well-learned skills that may delay or stifle development even though they increase the probability of winning? How do you evaluate performance? What behaviors do you consider desirable? Do you congratulate players and your children when they win and outperform others or when they try hard and improve? How do you react when the team, your athlete, or your child loses? If you feel that you coach, parent, or consult in a task-involving manner, then you are probably fostering athletes' motivation and promoting adaptive beliefs and positive achievement strategies. If your style of coaching, parenting, or consulting is ego-involving, you may be setting up your athletes or children, even those who are currently the most successful, for motivational difficulties in the future.

To assist the coach, parent, or sport psychologist in modifying the motivation-related atmosphere being created for athletes, Table 4-1 lists some suggestions on how to develop a task-involving motivational climate (Ames, 1992; Duda, 1996; Treasure, 2001; Treasure & Roberts, 1995). These suggestions have been organized around the task, authority, recognition, grouping, evaluation, and timing (TARGET) situational structures Epstein (1988, 1989) has argued make up the "basic building blocks" of achievement contexts such as sport.

Summary

Based on both anecdotal and scientific evidence, we know that elevated motivation is essential to maximal involvement in sport. Research and the wisdom gleaned from practice also suggest that motivational factors are fundamental to maximizing that participation. Sport allows for achievement, satisfaction, enjoyment, and interest, and athletes have an opportunity to develop in body, mind, and spirit. Motivation is a key ingredient in athletes' success, and we need to recognize that the quantity and quality of athletes' motivation is inferred from a constellation of behaviors, emotions, and cognitive variables—not from competitive sport performance alone. Indeed, indices of athletes' mental and physical welfare should be taken into account when we evaluate whether a particular motivational approach is desirable or not (Duda, 2001).

Athletes are more likely to exhibit optimal motivation when they feel they have the necessary capabilities to match the psychological and physical challenges of the sport in question, have a sense of autonomy, and feel connected to others in regard to their sport involvement. Motivation deficits appear when an athlete doesn't think he or she "has what it takes," perceives him or herself to be like "a pawn on a chessboard," and feels disenfranchised from relevant others in the sport setting. In other words, understanding variations in sport motivation means paying attention to athletes' thoughts regarding issues of competence, personal control, and connectedness to others in the sport domain.

With respect to perceptions of competence, number of elements contribute to athletes' perceived self-efficacy. For example, by providing effective models, "setting the stage" for success when athletes are learning a new skill or starting the competitive season, and verbal persuasion, coaches and sport psychologists can augment the confidence level of their athletes. Through learning and mastering psychological skills (e.g., arousal regulation, imagery), athletes make it more likely that their self-efficacy is elevated and resistant to vacillation.

Athletes' confidence in their ability to perform tends to stay strong and buoyant when they attribute their good performances to internal, controllable, and stable reasons and define poor performances with respect to internal, controllable, and unstable causes. The attributions coaches, sport psychologists, and significant others provide for the successes and setbacks of athletes in training and during competition can influence athletes' post-performance reasoning about these outcomes and, consequently, influence future behavior. When sport participants feel competent and "captains of their destiny," their motivation to participate is more likely to be intrinsic. When athletes "play" sport for the love of the game and other self-determined reasons, they do not need external rewards to encourage or legitimize their involvement. As a consequence, coaches, sport psychologists, and other significant social agents in athletes' lives need to be careful when considering the use of extrinsic reinforcements as a means to increase motivation. These reinforcements can become the primary incentive for participation and soon the activity will feel more like work than play. External reward contingencies can sustain intrinsic motivation if they inform athletes about their gains in competence and are not employed in overabundance. Otherwise, they may cause more harm than good.

Finally, notwithstanding the importance of athletes' sense of autonomy and relatedness to others, perceptions of competence are a significant predictor of adaptive, more self-determined motivational patterns among athletes. However, research on achievement goals has indicated that how athletes judge their competence level is also critical to motivation. There are several advantages to a focus on task involvement in the athletic setting, including that the source of subjective success is more within the athlete's control and is less likely to result in feelings of incompetence. Defining sport competence in terms of self-referenced effort or task mastery criteria repeatedly stokes the motivation fire.

An emphasis on ego involvement can advance on athlete's desire to excel too but it can also have its motivational costs. First, a strong ego focus, whether approach or avoidance oriented, means that others are individuals to be outdone and surpassed or from whom an athlete should hide his/her inadequacies. Opponents and teammates become primarily reference points for feeling more or less competent, rather than cohorts with whom we learn from, collaborate with to improve individually and collectively, or cooperate with to compete. Thus, an emphasis on ego goals can jeopardize an athlete's sense of connectedness in the sport environment.

Second, when aiming to reach ego-centered goals, the criteria for success (showing superiority or avoiding the demonstration of inferiority) are less within the athlete's control. This means that the maintenance of an autonomous perspective on sport achievement is endangered when the athlete's inclination is toward ego approach or ego avoidance goals. The criteria underlying success, in both cases, are external to the athlete and her or his performance.

Finally, no matter the degree of athletic prowess or the competitive level of the athlete, targeting ego goals can prove detrimental if that individual's confidence starts to waiver and he or she possesses a weak task orientation. In this instance, the athlete desperately wants to be the best, fears he or she will not be, and has no other meaningful way of redefining his or her goals and sense of competence to feel good about the performance. Because the world of sport is competitive, challenging, and conducive to competence questioning, coaches, parents, and sport psychologists should encourage task involvement in an attempt to optimize sport motivation.

Study Questions

1. What are the behavioral characteristics that reflect whether an athlete's motivation is high or low?

2. What is the difference between the quantity and quality of motivation among athletes?

3. What is self-efficacy, and why is it supposed to affect motivation?

4. Provide examples for each of the six antecedents of self-efficacy in a sport setting.

5. Describe the three dimensions of Weiner's (1986) attribution theory. When do athletes typically engage in an attempt to understand why a certain outcome occurred?

6. Describe the typical attributional patterns in terms of successful and unsuccessful outcomes for a motivated athlete and one who suffers from motivational difficulties.

7. What do we mean when we say that an athlete is intrinsically motivated?

8. Describe the process by which external rewards can influence the intrinsic motivation of athletes.

9. How do task- and ego-involved athletes differ in the way they judge their competence and perceive success in sport?

10. What are the distinctions between and consequences of being more ego-approach or ego-avoidance goal-oriented?

11. Provide examples of how being primarily oriented to ego goals can set the stage for performance impairment and motivational difficulties.

References

Ames, C. (1992). Achievement goals, motivational climate, and motivational processes. In G. C. Roberts (Ed.), *Motivation in sport and exercise* (pp. 161–176). Champaign, IL: Human Kinetics.

Anderson, C. A. (1983). Motivational and performance deficits in interpersonal settings: The effect of attributional style. *Journal of Personality and Social Psychology, 45*, 1136–1147.

Bandura, A. (1986). *Social foundations of thought and action: A social cognitive theory.* Englewood Cliffs, NJ: Prentice Hall.

Bandura, A. (1995). On rectifying conceptual ecumenism. In J. E. Maddux (Ed.), *Self-efficacy, adaptation, and adjustment: Theory, research, and application* (pp. 347–375). New York: Plenum Press.

Bandura, A. (1997). *Self-efficacy. The exercise of control.* New York: W. H. Freeman.

Biddle, S. J. H. (1993). Attribution research and sport psychology. In R. Singer, M. Murphy, & L. K. Tennant (Eds.), *Handbook of research in sport psychology* (pp. 437–464). New York: Macmillan.

Biddle, S. J. H., & Hill, A. B. (1992). Attributions for objective outcome and subjective appraisal of performance: Their relationships with emotional reactions in sport. *British Journal of Social Psychology, 31*, 215–226.

Burton, D. (1989). Winning isn't everything: Examining the impact of performance goals on collegiate swimmers' cognitions and performance. *The Sport Psychologist, 3,* 105–132.

Cury, F., Da Fonseca, D., Rufo, M., Peres, C., & Sarrazin, P. (2003). The trichotomous model and investment in learning to prepare a sport test: A mediational analysis. *British Journal of Educational Psychology, 73,* 529–543.

Cury, F., Elliot, A., Sarrazin, P., Da Fonseca, D., & Rufo, M. (2002). The trichotomous achievement goal model and intrinsic motivation: A sequential mediational analysis. *Journal of Experimental Social Psychology, 38,* 473–481.

DeCharms, R. (1968). *Personal causation: The internal affective determinants of behavior.* New York: Academic Press.

Deci, E. L., & Ryan, R. M. (1985). *Intrinsic motivation and self-determination in human behavior.* New York: Plenum.

Deci, E. L., & Ryan, R. M. (1992). The initiation and regulation of intrinsically motivated learning and achievement. In A. K. Boggiano & T. S. Pittman (Eds.), *Achievement and motivation: A social-developmental perspective* (pp. 77–114). Cambridge: Cambridge University Press.

Deci, E. L., & Ryan, R. M. (2002). (Eds.). *Handbook of self-determination research.* Rochester, NY: University of Rochester Press.

Duda, J. L. (1992). Motivation in sport settings: A goal perspective approach. In G. C. Roberts (Ed.), *Motivation in sport and exercise* (pp. 57–92). Champaign, IL: Human Kinetics.

Duda, J. L. (1996). Maximizing motivation in sport and physical education among children and adolescents: The case for greater task involvement. *Quest, 48,* 290–302.

Duda, J. L. (2001). Goal perspective research in sport: Pushing the boundaries and clarifying some misunderstandings. In G. C. Roberts (Ed.), *Advances in motivation in sport and exercise* (pp. 129–182). Champaign, IL: Human Kinetics.

Duda, J. L. (in press). Motivation in sport: The relevance of competence and achievement goals. In A. J. Elliot & C. S. Dweck (Eds.), *Handbook of competence and motivation.* New York: Guildford Publications.

Duda, J. L., & White, S. A. (1992). The relationship of goal perspectives to beliefs about success among elite skiers. *The Sport Psychologist, 6,* 334–343.

Dweck, C. S. (1986). Motivational processes affecting learning. *American Psychologist, 41,* 1040–1048.

Dweck, C. S. (1999). *Self-theories and goals: Their role in motivation, personality, and development.* Philadelphia, PA: Taylor & Francis.

Dweck, C. S., & Leggett, E. L. (1988). A social-cognitive approach to motivation and personality. *Psychological Review, 95,* 265–273.

Elliott, E., & Dweck, C. S. (1988). Goals: An approach to motivation and achievement. *Journal of Personality and Social Psychology, 54,* 5–12.

Epstein, J. (1988). Effective schools or effective students? Dealing with diversity. In R. Haskins & B. MacRae (Eds.), *Policies for America's public schools* (pp. 89–126). Norwood, NJ: Ablex.

Epstein, J. (1989). Family structures and student motivation: A developmental perspective. In C. Ames & R. Ames (Eds.), *Research on motivation in education: Vol. 3* (pp. 259–295). New York: Academic Press.

Feltz, D. L. (1988). Self-confidence and sports performance. In K. B. Pandolf (Ed.), *Exercise and sport sciences reviews: Volume 16* (pp. 423–457). New York: MacMillan.

Feltz, D. L. (1992). Understanding motivation in sport settings: A self-efficacy perspective. In G. C. Roberts (Ed.), *Motivation in sport and exercise.* Champaign, IL: Human Kinetics.

Fox, K. R., Goudas, M., Biddle, S. J. H., Duda, J. L., & Armstrong, N. (1994). Children's task and ego goal profiles in sport. *British Journal of Educational Psychology, 64,* 253–261.

Hall, H. K. (1990). *A social-cognitive approach to goal setting: The mediating effects of achievement goals and perceived ability.* Unpublished doctoral dissertation. University of Illinois at Urbana-Champaign.

Hall, H. K., & Kerr, A. W. (1997). Motivational antecedents of pre-competitive anxiety in youth sport. *The Sport Psychologist, 11,* 24–42.

Halvari, H., & Kjormo, O. (1999). A structural model of achievement motives, performance approach and avoidance goals and performance among Norwegian Olympic athletes. *Perceptual and Motor Skills, 89,* 997–1022.

Hardy, L. (1997). Three myths about applied consultancy work. *Journal of Applied Sport Psychology, 9,* 277–294.

Hardy, L., Jones, G., & Gould, D. (1996). *Understanding psychological preparation for sport. Theory and practice of elite performers.* Chichester, England: Wiley.

Jowett, S., & Chaundy, V. (2004). An investigation into the impact of coach leadership and coach-athlete relationship on group cohesion. *Group Dynamics: Theory, Research and Practice, 8,* 302–311.

Kane, T., Marks, M., Zaccaro, S., & Blair, V. (1996). Self-efficacy, personal goals, and wrestlers' self-regulation. *Journal of Sport and Exercise Psychology, 18,* 36–48.

Kuczka, K. K., & Treasure, D. C. (in press). Self-handicapping in competitive sport: Influence of the motivational climate, self-efficacy and perceived importance. *Psychology of Sport and Exercise.*

Lemyre, P.-N., Roberts, G. C., Treasure, D. C., Stray-Gundersen, J., & Matt, K. (2004). Psychological and physiological determinants of overtraining and burnout in elite athletes. *Journal of Sport and Exercise Psychology, Supplement,* 144–145.

Lepper, M. R., & Greene, D. (1978). Overjustification research and beyond: Toward a means-end analysis of intrinsic and extrinsic motivation. In M. R. Lepper & D. Greene (Eds.), *The hidden costs of reward* (pp. 109–148). Hillsdale, NJ: Erbaum.

Lloyd, J., & Fox, K. (1992). Achievement goals and motivation to exercise in adolescent girls: A preliminary intervention study. *British Journal of Physical Education Research Supplement, 11,* 12–16.

Lochbaum, M., & Roberts, G. C. (1993). Goal orientations and perceptions of the sport experience. *Journal of Sport and Exercise Psychology, 15,* 322–341.

Locke, E. A., & Latham, G. P. (1985). The application of goal setting to sports. *Journal of Sport Psychology, 7,* 205–222.

Locke, E. A., & Latham, G. P. (1990). *A theory of goal setting and task performance.* Englewood Cliffs, NJ: Prentice Hall.

Maddux, J. E. (1995). Self-efficacy theory: An introduction. In J. E. Maddux (Ed.), *Self-efficacy, adaptation, and adjustment* (pp. 3–33). New York: Plenum.

Middleton, C., & Midgley, C. (1997). Avoiding the demonstration of lack of ability: An unexplored aspect of goal theory. *Journal of Educational Psychology, 89,* 710–718.

Newton, M., & Duda, J. L. (1999). The interaction of motivational climate, dispositional goal orientation and perceived ability in predicting indices of motivation. *International Journal of Sport Psychology, 30,* 63–82.

Newton, M. L., Duda, J. L., & Yin, Z. (2000). Examination of the psychometric properties of the perceived motivational climate in sport questionnaire-2 in a sample of female athletes. *Journal of Sports Sciences, 18,* 275–290.

Nicholls, J. (1984). Conceptions of ability and achievement motivation. In R. Ames & C. Ames (Eds.), *Research on motivation in education: Student motivation Vol. 1* (pp. 39–73). New York: Academic Press.

Nicholls, J. (1989). *The competitive ethos and democratic education.* Cambridge, MA: Harvard University Press.

Ntoumanis, N., & Biddle, S. J. H. (1999). A review of motivational climate in physical activity. *Journal of Sports Sciences, 17,* 643–665.

Ommundsen, Y., Roberts, G. C., & Kavussanu, M. (1998). Perceived motivational climate and cognitive and affective correlates among Norwegian athletes. *Journal of Sports Sciences, 16,* 153–164.

Orbach, I., Singer, R., & Murphey, M. (1997). Changing attributions with an attribution training technique related to basketball dribbling. *The Sport Psychologist, 11,* 294–304.

Orbach, I., Singer, R., & Price, S. (1999). An attribution training program and achievement in sport. *The Sport Psychologist, 13,* 69–82.

Parish, L. E., & Treasure, D. C. (2003). Physical activity and situational motivation in physical education: Influence of the motivational climate and perceived ability. *Research Quarterly for Exercise and Sport, 74*(2), 173–182.

Prapavessis, H., Grove, J. R., & Eklund, R. C. (2004). Self-presentational issues in competition and sport. *Journal of Applied Sport Psychology, 16,* 19–40.

Prapavessis, H., Grove, J. R., Maddison, R., & Zillmann, N. (2003). Self-handicapping tendencies, coping, and anxiety responses among athletes. *Psychology of Sport and Exercise, 4,* 357–375.

Reinboth, M., & Duda, J. L. (2004a). The relationship between perceptions of the motivational climate and achievement goal orientations to indices of positive deviance in sport. *2004 Proceedings of the Association for the Advancement of Applied Sport Psychology* (p. 28). Middleton, WI: AAASP.

Reinboth, M., & Duda, J. L. (2004b). Relationship of the perceived motivational climate and perceptions of ability to psychological and physical well-being in team sports. *The Sport Psychologist, 18,* 237–251.

Reinboth, M., Duda, J. L., & Ntoumanis, N. (2004). Dimensions of coaching behavior, need satisfaction, and the psychological and physical welfare of young athletes. *Motivation and Emotion, 28,* 297–313.

Roberts, G. C., & Ommundsen, Y. (1996). Effect of goal orientation on achievement beliefs, cognition and strategies in team sport. *Scandinavian Journal of Medicine and Science in Sports, 6,* 46–56.

Roberts, G. C., & Treasure, D. C. (1992). Children in sport. *Sport Science Review, 2,* 46–64.

Roberts, G. C., Treasure, D. C., & Hall, H. K. (1994). Parental goal orientations and beliefs about the competitive sport experience of their child. *Journal of Applied Social Psychology, 24,* 631–645.

Roberts, G. C., Treasure, D. C., & Kavussanu, M. (1996). Orthogonality of achievement goals and its relationship to beliefs about success and satisfaction in sport. *The Sport Psychologist, 10,* 398–408.

Roberts, G. C., Treasure, D. C., & Kavussanu, M. (1997). Motivation in physical activity contexts: An achievement goal perspective. In M. L. Maehr & P. R. Pintrich (Eds.), *Advances in motivation and achievement. Vol. 10* (pp. 413–447). Greenwich, CT: JAI Press.

Ryan, R. M., & Deci, E. L. (2000). Self-determination theory and the facilitation of intrinsic motivation, social development, and well being. *American Psychologist, 55,* 68–78.

Sarrazin, P., Biddle, S. J. H., Famose, J.-P., Cury, F., Fox, K. R., & Durand, M. (1996). Goal orientations and conceptions of sport ability in children: A social cognitive approach. *British Journal of Social Psychology, 35,* 399–414.

Sarrazin, P., Roberts, G. C., Cury, F., Biddle, S. J. H., & Famose, J.-P. (2002). Exerted effort and performance in climbing among boys: The influence of achievement goals, perceived ability and task difficulty. *Research Quarterly for Exercise and Sport, 73,* 425–436.

Scanlan, T. K., & Lewthwaite, E. (1984). Social psychological aspects of competition for male youth sport participants: I. Predictors of competitive stress. *Journal of Sport Psychology, 6,* 208–226.

Scanlan, T. K., & Passer, M. W. (1978). Factors relating to competitive stress among male youth sport participants. *Medicine and Science in Sports, 10,* 103–108.

Schunk, D. H. (1995). Self-efficacy, motivation, and performance. *Journal of Applied Sport Psychology, 7,* 112–137.

Seifriz, J., Duda, J. L., & Chi, L. (1992). The relationship of perceived motivational climate to intrinsic motivation and beliefs about success in basketball. *Journal of Sport and Exercise Psychology, 14,* 375–391.

Skaalvik, E. (1997). Self-enhancing and self-defeating ego orientations: Relations with task and avoidance orientation, achievement, self-perceptions, and anxiety. *Journal of Educational Psychology, 89,* 71–81.

Solmon, M. A. (1996). Impact of motivational climate on students: Behaviors and perceptions of a physical education setting. *Journal of Educational Psychology, 88,* 731–738.

Standage, M., Duda, J. L., & Ntoumanis, N. (2003). A model of contextual motivation in physical education: Using constructs from self-determination and achievement goal theories to predict physical activity intentions. *Journal of Educational Psychology, 95,* 97–110.

Swain, A. B. J., & Harwood, C. G. (1996). Antecedents of state goals in age group swimmers: An interactionist perspective. *Journal of Sport Sciences, 14,* 111–124.

Treasure, D. C. (1997). Perceptions of the motivational climate and elementary school children's cognitive and affective response. *Journal of Sport and Exercise Psychology, 19,* 278–290.

Treasure, D. C. (2001). Enhancing young people's motivation in physical activity. In G. C. Roberts (Ed.), *Advances in motivation in sport and exercise* (pp. 79–100). Champaign, IL: Human Kinetics.

Treasure, D. C., Monson, J., & Lox, C. (1996). Relationship between self-efficacy, wrestling performance, and affect prior to competition. *The Sport Psychologist, 10,* 73–83.

Treasure, D. C., & Roberts, G. C. (1995). Applications of achievement goal theory to physical education: Implications for enhancing motivation. *Quest, 47,* 475–489.

Treasure, D. C., & Roberts, G. C. (1998). Relationship between adolescent females' achievement goal orientations, perceptions of the motivational climate, beliefs about success and sources of satisfaction in basketball. *International Journal of Sport Psychology, 29,* 211–230.

Treasure, D. C., Standage, M., & Lochbaum, M. (1999, September). *Perceptions of the motivational climate and situational motivation in elite youth sport.* Paper presented at the annual meeting of the Association for the Advancement of Applied Sport Psychology, Banff, Canada.

Vallerand, R. (2001). A hierarchical model of intrinsic and extrinsic motivation in sport and exercise. In G. C. Roberts (Ed.), *Advances in motivation in sport and exercise* (pp. 263–320). Champaign, IL: Human Kinetics.

Vallerand, R., Deci, E. L., & Ryan, R. M. (1987). Intrinsic motivation in sport. In K. Pandolf (Ed.), *Exercise and sport science reviews: Volume 15* (pp. 389–425). New York: MacMillan.

Vallerand, R., & Losier, G. (1999). An integrative analysis of intrinsic and extrinsic motivation in sport. *Journal of Applied Sport Psychology, 11,* 142–169.

Vazou, S., Ntoumanis, N., & Duda, J. L. (in press). Peer motivational climate in sport: A qualitative inquiry. *Psychology of Sport and Exercise.*

Walling, M. D., Duda, J. L., & Chi, L. (1993). The perceived motivational climate in sport questionnaire: Construct and predictive validity. *Journal of Sport and Exercise Psychology, 15,* 172–183.

Weiner, B. (1986). *An attributional theory of motivation and emotion.* New York: Springer-Verlag.

White, R. W. (1959). Motivation reconsidered: The concept of competence. *Psychological Review, 66,* 297–333.

White, S. A. (1996). Goal orientation and perceptions of the motivational climate initiated by parents. *Pediatric Exercise Science, 8,* 122–129.

White, S. A., & Duda, J. L. (1993). Dimensions of goals and beliefs among young adolescent athletes with physical disabilities. *Adapted Physical Activity Quarterly, 10,* 125–136.

CHAPTER

5

The Self-Fulfilling Prophecy Theory: When Coaches' Expectations Become Reality

Thelma Sternberg Horn, *Miami University*
Curt L. Lox, *Southern Illinois University*
Francisco Labrador, *Wittenberg University*

I couldn't believe it! This kid came to the first day of Little League draft tryouts with bright purple and spiked hair! Me and all of the other coaches . . . none of us wanted him on our team. But, in the last round of draft picks, I got stuck with him. The funny thing is that by the end of the season, he turned out to be our team's Most Valuable Player! Once you got past the purple hair, the kid was a real solid baseball player.

—Coach of a Little League Baseball Team

In 1968 Rosenthal and Jacobson published the results of an experiment they had conducted with teachers and students in 18 elementary school classrooms. This research study, which was appropriately titled "Pygmalion in the Classroom," had been designed to determine whether the academic progress of students could actually be affected by their teachers' expectations or beliefs concerning their intellectual abilities. To investigate this issue, Rosenthal and Jacobson informed the sample of teachers that certain children in each of their classes had been identified, via scores on a standardized test of academic ability, as latent achievers or "late bloomers" who could be expected to show big gains in academic achievement over the coming school year.

In actuality, the identified children had been selected at random from the total group, and there was no reason to expect that they would show any greater academic progress than their classmates. At the end of the school year, however, many of the targeted children, especially those in the lower elementary grades, had made greater gains intellectually than had children who were not so identified. Rosenthal and Jacobson concluded that the false information given to the teachers had led them to hold higher expectations for the targeted children and then to act in ways that would stimulate better performance from those students. Thus, the authors were suggesting that the teachers' expectations served as self-fulfilling prophecies by initiating a series of events that ultimately caused the expectations to be fulfilled.

The publication of this study elicited considerable interest among other researchers, some of whom responded with criticism of the Pygmalion study for a variety of methodological and statistical flaws (Elashoff & Snow, 1971; Thorndike, 1968). The ensuing controversy concerning the legitimacy of the self-fulfilling prophecy phenomenon stimulated an impressive amount of research during the next several decades. Although most of these investigations were oriented toward the study of expectancy effects in the academic classroom, some of them were conducted in physical education classrooms or in competitive sport contexts (e.g., Bibik, 1999; Cousineau & Luke, 1990; Horn, 1984; Markland & Martinek, 1988; Martinek, 1988; Martinek & Karper, 1984, 1986; Papaioannou, 1995; Rejeski, Darracott, & Hutslar, 1979; Sinclair & Vealey, 1989; Solomon, 2001; Solomon & Kosmitzki, 1996; Solomon, DiMarco, Ohlson, & Reece, 1998; Solomon, Golden, Ciapponi, & Martin, 1998; Solomon, Striegel et al., 1996; Solomon, Wiegardt et al., 1996; Trouilloud, Sarrazin, Martinek, & Guillet, 2002). Several excellent reviews of this literature have been compiled (e.g., Brophy, 1983; Cooper & Tom, 1984; Harris & Rosenthal, 1985; Jussim, 1991; Jussim & Eccles, 1995; Jussim, Smith, Madon, & Palumbo, 1998; Martinek, 1989). Based on a thorough examination of the expectancy research, the authors of these reviews have generally concluded that teachers' expectations certainly do have the potential to affect the academic progress of individual students. However, these writers also caution that the overall effects of teacher expectations on student learning and performance appear to be relatively small, with effect sizes ranging from .1 to .3. Despite this relatively small effect size, there does appear to be considerable variability between teachers (and, by extension, coaches) in the degree to which their expectations can and do affect their own behavior as well as the learning and performance of their student-athletes. Several recent studies (e.g., Jussim, Eccles, & Madon, 1996; Snyder, 1992) have found, for example, that under some conditions (i.e., in some instructional situations) the impact of teachers' expectations on student learning and performance is much more powerful than what the average effect size would suggest. Thus, although many teachers and coaches are not Pygmalion-prone (i.e., they do not allow their expectations to affect the performance or the achievement of their students and athletes), there certainly does appear to be a subset of teachers and coaches who do exhibit expectancy biases in educational and sport settings.

Such variation among teachers and coaches implies that those who are aware of and understand the self-fulfilling prophecy phenomenon can avoid becoming Pygmalion-type coaches or teachers. Therefore, it is the purpose of this chapter to present coaches with information concerning the expectation–performance process. In the following pages, we will examine how coaches' expectations or judgments of their athletes can influence the athletes' performance and behavior. Specifically, we will identify (a) the processes by which coaches form expectations concerning individual athletes, (b) the ways in which such expectations influence the coaches' behavior, (c) the processes by which expectancy-biased coaches' behavior can affect the athletes' performance and psychological growth, (d) how the athletes' performance and behavior can ultimately conform to the coaches' original expectations, and, finally, (e) how expectancy effects can be particularly negative for selected athletes. The chapter will conclude with a discussion of ways coaches can individualize their interactions with athletes to avoid behaving in expectancy-biased ways and thus facilitate the performance of all athletes.

The Expectation–Performance Process

According to the self-fulfilling prophecy theory, the expectations coaches form about the ability of individual athletes can serve as prophecies that dictate or determine the level of achievement each athlete will ultimately reach. Several researchers who have studied the self-fulfilling prophecy phenomenon in educational contexts

(Brophy, 1983; Cooper & Tom, 1984; Harris & Rosenthal, 1985; Jussim, 1986) have proposed a sequence of steps to explain how the expectation–performance connection is accomplished. These models or sequences of events can be adapted to describe how the self-fulfilling prophecy phenomenon can also occur in sport settings.

Step 1: The coach develops an expectation for each athlete that predicts the level of performance and type of behavior that athlete will exhibit over the course of the year.

Step 2: The coach's expectations influence his or her treatment of individual athletes. That is, the coach's behavior toward each athlete differs according to the coach's belief concerning the athlete's competence.

Step 3: The way in which the coach treats each athlete affects the athlete's performance and rate of learning. In addition, differential communication tells each athlete how competent the coach thinks he or she is. This information affects the athlete's self-concept, achievement motivation, and level of aspiration.

Step 4: The athlete's behavior and performance conform to the coach's expectations. This behavioral conformity reinforces the coach's original expectation, and the process continues.

We will now examine each of these steps in detail.

Step 1: Coaches Form Expectations

At the beginning of an athletic season most coaches form expectations for each athlete on their teams. These expectations are really initial judgments or assessments regarding the physical competence or sport potential of each athlete and are based on certain pieces of information available to the coach. In particular, the research indicates that teachers and coaches most often use three types, or categories, of information.

The first category contains what we can label as **person cues** and includes such informational items as the individual's socioeconomic status, racial or ethnic group, family background, gender, physical attractiveness, body size, physique, and style of dress. The exclusive use of any or all of these person cues to form judgments about an athlete's physical competence would certainly lead to inaccurate and very stereotypic expectations (see last section of this chapter). Fortunately, according to the research on expectancy effects, not all coaches form their expectations solely on demographic or physical appearance cues; they also use behaviorally based information. Thus, many coaches use additional **performance information** such as the athlete's scores on certain physical skills tests, the athlete's past performance achievements (e.g., previous season statistics or related sport accomplishments), as well as other teachers' or coaches' comments concerning the athlete's performance and behavior. Coaches also base initial impressions of athletes on observation of their behavior in practice or tryout situations (e.g., observation of the player's motivation, work ethic, enthusiasm, pleasantness, response to criticism, interaction with teammates).

A third and more recently identified category of information sources that coaches can and do use to evaluate their athletes' performance potential includes **psychological characteristics**. Specifically, Solomon's recent (2001) study with intercollegiate male and female athletic teams demonstrated that the evaluations that coaches formed regarding the trait sport confidence levels of individual athletes on their teams were an important factor affecting the link between coaches' preseason expectations of their athletes' performance potential and the athletes' subsequent level of performance over the season. Other psychological characteristics of athletes that may serve as cues coaches might use to form their expectations or judgments of each athlete's performance potential might be athletes' level of anxiety as well as their motivational orientation, their degree of "coachability," or any other aspect of their personalities.

Although the initial expectations formed by most coaches are based on information from a variety of sources, individual coaches probably differ in regard to the weight they assign to each source. That is, some coaches may particularly value the comments of other coaches in evaluating an athlete during recruitment or at the beginning of the season, whereas other coaches may place greater emphasis on the player's physical attributes (e.g., speed, size, strength, body build). Therefore, two coaches could form very different sets of expectations for the same athlete on the basis of what sources of information each valued most.

It obviously follows, then, that a coach's initial judgment of an athlete may be either accurate or inaccurate depending on the sources of information used. Accurate assessments of a player's competence generally pose no problem as they usually do not adversely affect the player's subsequent performance. However, inaccurate expectations (i.e., expectations that are either too high or too low) that are *also* inflexible can be very disruptive for athletes and can interfere with their optimal athletic progress. Consider, for example, the coach who misjudges a particular athlete at the beginning of the season and falsely believes that individual to be less competent than he or she really is. If the coach's expectation or judgment is flexible (i.e., changes when the athlete demonstrates better performance than expected), then the initial false expectation does not cause a problem. In contrast, a coach who is very inflexible and resistant to modifying her or his initial beliefs may well "see" only what she or he expects to see from that player. That is, all evidence of skill errors by the athlete will reinforce the coach's belief that the athlete is incompetent, and all skill success will either be ignored or simply considered by the coach to be "lucky" events and not indicative of the athlete's sport skill. Solomon and her colleagues (e.g., Solomon & Kosmitzki, 1996; Solomon, Golden et al., 1998) have recently referred to this characteristic of coaches as "perceptual flexibility" or, by extension, "perceptual inflexibility." Coaches who develop expectations of players at the beginning of the season and who do not allow those expectations to remain flexible or fluid tend to perceive individual athletes' performance and behavior from a very rigid perspective. That is, these coaches will perceive in their athletes' performance and behavior exactly what they expected to see. This type of situation is illustrated in Example 1. In this example the coach's initial expectations or judgments concerning the relative basketball ability of both Greg and Robert are formed on the basis of information provided by a colleague. These initial expectations, which may *not* be accurate, cause the coach to *perceive* the two players' performance differently. Such differential perceptions, in turn, affect the way the coach reacts or responds to that player. This type of situation leads to the second step in the sequence of events composing the self-fulfilling prophecy phenomenon.

Step 2: Coaches' Expectations Affect Their Behavior

Example 1

The new coach of a junior high basketball team is informed by the principal that the team has two point guards returning from last year. The first player, Greg, is described as a talented athlete, and the other player, Robert, is portrayed as having been a member of last year's squad "only because he was the coach's son." At practice the first day, Robert dribbles fast up the court but then loses control of the ball. The coach, who has developed the expectation that Robert is not a talented athlete, sees this error as proof of Robert's lack of innate basketball ability. Thus, the coach responds by telling Robert to slow down. Moments later, Greg also mishandles the ball during the same dribbling drill. The coach, who believes Greg to be an excellent dribbler, assumes that the error occurred because the basketball is either worn and slippery or overinflated (and thus difficult to dribble). Based on this perception, the coach orders that the ball not be used again and that Greg should get another ball and try again.

The expectations that coaches typically form for each athlete at the beginning of an athletic season do not necessarily or automatically act as self-fulfilling prophecies. Expectations do, however, have the potential for doing so if they affect the coaches' treatment of their athletes.

Much of the research on the self-fulfilling prophecy phenomenon in competitive sport situations has focused on this issue by asking the crucial question, "Do coaches treat athletes they believe have high ability (i.e., high-expectancy individuals) differently from athletes they believe have low ability (i.e., low-expectancy individuals)?" Generally this question has been studied by observing and recording the type, frequency, and quality of instructional behavior coaches exhibit toward individual athletes. Again, the overall conclusion from this research (see studies by Horn, 1984; Krane, Eklund, & McDermott, 1991; Rejeski et al., 1979; Sinclair & Vealey, 1989; Solomon & Kosmitzki, 1996; Solomon, DiMarco et al., 1998; Solomon, Golden et al., 1998; Solomon, Striegel et al., 1996) indicates that *some* coaches do indeed show differential instructional behaviors to these two groups of athletes. Applying the results of this research to any specific athletic setting, we could expect the Pygmalion-type coach to show differential behavior to high- and low-expectancy athletes in regard to (a) the frequency and quality of interactions the coach has with the individual athletes, (b) the quantity and quality of instruction given to each athlete, and (c) the frequency and type of performance feedback given to each athlete.

In the first behavioral category, **frequency and quality of coach–athlete interactions,** a Pygmalion-prone coach typically shows less tendency to initiate interpersonal contact (either of a social or a skill-related nature) with athletes he or she believes to be less skilled. As a result, the coach spends significantly more time with athletes who are highly skilled (see Example 2). In addition, the quality of coach–athlete interactions may also differ, with high-expectancy players being shown more warmth and positive affect (e.g., smiling, head nodding, and personal contact) than their low-expectancy teammates.

Example 2

Jen and Kari, who are teammates on their school's varsity basketball team, stay after practice to play a game of one-on-one. Their coach comes over to watch. When Jen (a high-expectancy athlete) executes a successful fake and drive, the coach responds with approval but also stops the game to provide Jen with further instruction (i.e., what she should do in a similar situation if the weak side defender had moved across the key). Later when Kari (a low-expectancy player) executes the same successful fake and drive, the coach responds with approval only ("Good move, Kari") but then goes on to show Jen how she should have prevented or defended against such an offensive move.

Perhaps of greater consequence is the differential treatment that high- and low-expectancy players may receive in regard to the **quantity and quality of instruction.** If a coach firmly believes certain players on her or his team do not have the requisite athletic competencies to be successful (i.e., the low-expectancy players), that coach may, first of all, reduce the amount of material or skills those players are expected to learn, thus establishing a lower standard of performance for them. Second, the coach may allow the low-expectancy players less time in practice drills. As a result, these athletes may spend relatively more practice time in non-skill-related activities such as shagging balls, waiting in line, and keeping score. Finally, the coach may be less persistent in helping low-expectancy athletes learn a difficult skill. The Pygmalion-prone coach tends to give up on a low-expectancy player who fails after two or three attempts to learn a new skill but will persist in working with a high-expectancy player who is having the same difficulty (see Example 3).

In addition to differences in the quality of instruction, researchers have also found differences in the **type and frequency of feedback** that coaches give to high- and low-expectancy players.

Example 3

During a practice scrimmage, Jen (the high-expectancy player in Example 2) is having problems running a particularly difficult offensive pattern. The coach stops the team drill and spends 3 or 4 minutes helping Jen learn the pattern. When Kari (the low-expectancy athlete) later evidences the same difficulty, the coach removes her from the scrimmage team by saying to another player, "Sally, come here and take Kari's place. Let's see if you can run this play."

Example 4

During the course of a varsity volleyball match, a hitter approaches the net for a spike. Seeing her opponents put up a single block, she reaches out to "tip" the ball around the block. No point is scored, but the ball is kept in play. The athlete, who is a high-expectancy player, is told by her coach, "OK, Keisha, at least you kept the ball in play. But next time you go up against a single block, hit *the ball. Your spike is good enough to get it through that block." If, however, a low-expectancy player executes the same play, the Pygmalion-type coach might respond with approval only: "Great work, Whitney, you kept the ball away from the block. That was smart."*

One of the primary ways coaches respond differently to individual athletes is in their use of praise and criticism. Some researchers investigating expectancy issues in the classroom or in the sport setting (Brophy & Good, 1970; Cooper & Baron, 1977; Martinek & Johnson, 1979; Martinek & Karper, 1982; Rejeski et al., 1979; Solomon, DiMarco et al., 1998; Solomon, Striegel et al., 1996) have found that teachers and coaches give high-expectancy students and athletes more reinforcement and praise after a successful performance than they do low-expectancy individuals. In contrast, other researchers have found that low-expectancy students and athletes are the ones who receive proportionately more reinforcement (Horn, 1984; Kleinfeld, 1975; Martinek, 1988; Weinstein, 1976). However, some of these latter researchers have additionally noted that the higher frequency of reinforcement or praise given by coaches and teachers to these low-expectancy individuals may actually be qualitatively suspect because the reinforcement is often given inappropriately (i.e., given for a mediocre performance or for success at a very easy task) (see Example 4). Therefore, it appears that Pygmalion-prone coaches may (a) provide low-expectancy athletes with less frequent reinforcement and (b) give them less appropriate and less beneficial feedback after successful performances.

Observation of teachers' and coaches' feedback also has revealed differences in the amount of corrective or technical instruction given.

In the sport setting such differential treatment may be especially evident in the feedback coaches provide their athletes following a performance. As illustrated in Example 5, high-expectancy performers receive informational and corrective feedback that tells them how to improve their performance. In contrast, low-expectancy performers receive a positive communication from the coach but no accompanying technical information to tell them what they can do to improve their performance. These differences in feedback responses may well be due to the different expectations the coach holds for the various athletes. For example, because the coach fully expects Dan's performance to improve, he is more apt to provide Dan with technical information to help him achieve skill success. However, the low expectations the coach holds for Pete lead the coach to believe that corrective instruction may be fruitless and certainly not useful for Pete.

Finally, coaches may also differ in the type of attribution they use to explain the cause of the high- and low-expectancy athletes' successful or unsuccessful performances. Although this aspect of performance feedback has received very little research attention, we certainly might speculate that a coach's beliefs concerning the competence

Example 5

Dan and Pete have both joined an age-group swimming team. Although both swimmers begin the season at the same level of performance, their coach has very high expectations for Dan's improvement and ultimate success because of his "natural" physical attributes. The coach does not have the same high expectations for Pete. At the first meet of the season, both swimmers take fifth place in their respective events. The coach responds to Dan's performance by telling him that he can considerably reduce his time if he improves his technique on the turns. The coach concludes with the comment, "We'll work on those turns all next week so you'll be ready for the next meet." In contrast, the coach responds to Pete's fifth place performance by saying, "Good job, Pete. Hang in there."

Example 6

During a baseball game, Steve (a low-expectancy athlete) hits a pitched ball sharply toward the left side of the infield. The shortstop makes a nice backhanded move for the ball and fields it. Although he then slightly mishandles it, he does throw it hard to first for a close play, with the runner (Steve) being called safe. The coach comments, "What a break, Steve! We were lucky he [the shortstop] bobbled it, or you would have been out." However, in a similar situation with Scott (a high-expectancy player) as the batter/runner, the coach responds to the same performance by exclaiming, "Way to hit the hole, Scott, and great speed! You beat the throw again!"

Example 7

Later in the game described in Example 6, Scott (the high-expectancy player) attempts to steal second without the coach's giving a steal sign. Scott is easily thrown out. As he reaches the dugout, the coach tells him, "Good try, Scott. That would have been a good pitch to steal on, but you didn't have a big enough lead to go. Next time, you should . . ." When Steve (the low-expectancy player) attempts the same performance, the coach angrily responds, "What are you doing out there? I didn't tell you to go . . . you're too slow to steal second, especially on that catcher."

or incompetence of selected players on his or her team would induce that coach to verbalize different attributions for the athletes' performance outcome. For instance, the coach in Example 6 holds different perceptions or expectations concerning the physical competence of Scott (a high-expectancy player) and Steve (a low-expectancy player). These expectations lead the coach to attribute these players' performance to different causes. When Steve reaches first base safely, the coach immediately, and in this case verbally, attributes that success to the opposing team's error (i.e., a lucky break for Steve). In comparison, the coach verbally attributes the same performance by Scott to Scott's ability (i.e., his batting prowess and speed). Similarly, the coach's response to these athletes' performance errors may also be affected by the coach's judgment of each player's ability. In Example 7 the coach attributes Scott's lack of success in stealing a base to poor positioning and thus suggests that the performance can be corrected. The coach attributes a similar failure by Steve to Steve's lack of ability (i.e., his lack of speed).

These examples illustrate how the expectations coaches form for individual athletes on their teams can affect coaches' perceptions of actual events. Such different perceptions, in turn, can lead to differences in coaches' responses to athletes' performances.

Although the research clearly suggests that some teachers and coaches treat high- and low-expectancy athletes and students differently, we need to exercise caution in regard to those findings. Specifically, we must not jump to the conclusion that it is essential for coaches to treat all athletes on their teams in exactly the same way. Because athletes differ in their skills as well as in their personalities, coaches are well advised to individualize their instructional behavior to accommodate the uniquenesses of each athlete. Therefore, it is important at this point to emphasize that observable differences in a coach's behavior toward individual athletes on his or her team do not automatically imply that the coach is acting in a biased manner and that the athletes' progress will be impeded. If the differences in the coach's behavior are designed to and actually do facilitate the performance and achievement of *each* athlete, then such differential coaching behavior is appropriate. However, if the differential treatment an athlete or a group of athletes *consistently* receives from their coach in practices and games limits the athletes' ability or opportunity to learn, then such differential coaching behavior is dysfunctional, and the coach's expectations may be serving as self-fulfilling prophecies.

Step 3: Coaches' Behavior Affects Athletes' Performance and Behavior

The third step in the sequence of events in the self-fulfilling prophecy phenomenon occurs when a coach's expectancy-biased treatment of an individual athlete affects that athlete's performance and psychological growth. It is easy to understand how the biased behavior described in the preceding section is likely to maximize the athletic progress of high-expectancy athletes while limiting the achievements of their low-expectancy teammates. Players who are *consistently* given less effective and less intensive instruction or who are allowed less active time in practice drills will not show the same degree of skill improvement as their teammates who are given optimal learning opportunities. In Examples 2 and 3, Jen and Kari are obviously not being given the same quality of instruction. If this instructional behavior is typical of the treatment these athletes receive from their coach over the season, we might well anticipate that after a certain period of time Jen's basketball skills will be considerably better than Kari's. Their coach will

attribute these skill differences to what she believes to be the innate differences in Jen's and Kari's basic athletic talent. Given the observed variation in the coach's instructional behavior toward these two athletes, it is equally likely that the coach's original expectation or judgment concerning each athlete's sport potential actually *determined,* rather than just *predicted,* the level of achievement that Jen and Kari reached. The coach's expectations, then, served as self-fulfilling prophecies by setting in motion a series of events (i.e., consistent differences in the quality of instruction) that ultimately caused the original expectations to be fulfilled.

In addition to the negative effects that a coach's biased instructional behavior has on an athlete's rate of learning and level of achievement, such behavior can also affect the athlete's psychological growth. Recent research in sport psychology has demonstrated that the type of instructional behaviors a coach exhibits in games and in practices is correlated with, and can actually cause, changes in athletes' self-concept, perceived competence, intrinsic motivation, and level of competitive trait anxiety over a season (e.g., Allen & Howe, 1998; Amorose & Horn, 2000, 2001; Black & Weiss, 1992; Baker, Cote, & Hawes, 2000; Horn, 1985; Kenow & Williams, 1992, 1999; Smith, Smoll, & Barnett, 1995; Smith, Smoll, & Curtis, 1979; Williams, Jerome, Kenow, Rogers, Sartain, & Darland, 2003). This association between coaches' behavior and changes in athletes' self-perceptions, intrinsic motivation, and anxiety is quite consistent with several developmental, cognitive, and social psychological theories (e.g., Bandura, 1997; Eccles, Jacobs, & Harold, 1990; Harter, 1981; Ryan & Deci, 2000, 2002; Schunk, 1984; Vallerand, 2001; Vallerand & Losier, 1999; Weiner, 1992) that suggest that the evaluation or feedback adults provide is an important source of information that children and adolescents use to determine how competent or incompetent they are.

In the athletic setting, then, the type of feedback coaches give to individual athletes may affect the athletes' self-perceptions (e.g., their self-confidence, self-efficacy, and anxiety) by communicating to the athletes how competent or skilled the coach thinks they are. Occasionally, of course, the coach communicates this evaluative information directly to the athletes. More commonly, however, coaches communicate their judgments or beliefs concerning the athletes' abilities in more subtle or indirect ways. Specifically, the coach's reinforcement patterns (i.e., the level of performance or type of behavior the coach rewards) provide athletes with information that tells them how skilled the coach thinks they are. In Example 4, Keisha and Whitney have demonstrated the same level of performance, but each receives a different response from the coach. This differential feedback may be communicating to these athletes what standard of performance each is expected to achieve. Whitney, who is clearly reinforced for that level of performance, may be receiving information telling her that she is at the maximum level she is capable of achieving. Keisha, however, is led to believe her performance, although acceptable, can and should be improved because she has the requisite skills to perform at a higher level.

Similarly, the amount and frequency of corrective instruction a coach provides after a skill error may also tell each athlete how competent or skillful the coach thinks he or she is. In Example 5, for instance, the coach responds to Dan's fifth-place performance with corrective feedback, thus overtly telling him that his performance can be improved with effort and covertly supplying him with the perception that he is capable of a higher level of skill. In contrast, although the coach gives Pete a positive and encouraging response for a similar level of performance, the coach does not provide Pete with the additional information to tell him that he can improve his performance and that he is capable of achieving at a higher level. Thus, the coach has indirectly communicated his expectations or judgments concerning each athlete's level of ability.

In a study investigating coaches' feedback in the interscholastic athletic context (Horn, 1984), it was found that junior high softball coaches gave their low-expectancy female athletes proportionately more reinforcement or praise in response to skill successes during games than they gave their high-expectancy athletes. In response to skill errors, however, these coaches provided their high-expectancy athletes with more criticism and corrective instruction but tended more frequently to ignore (give no response to) the mistakes of their low-expectancy athletes.

These findings are consistent with research reported in the educational psychology literature (Graham, 1990; Meyer, 1982, 1992) that has demonstrated that differential feedback responses do indeed provide performers with information concerning their abilities. Individuals who received more reinforcement than other performers for the same level of performance were perceived by themselves and others to have lower ability. In situations where performers exhibited the same performance errors, the individuals who received criticism were perceived by themselves and others to be more competent than those who received a neutral response following failure. It appears, then, that the evaluative feedback given by coaches to individual athletes is indeed providing the athletes with information concerning their competence. Certainly the differential feedback that low- and high-expectancy athletes receive from Pygmalion-prone coaches may affect the athletes' perceptions or beliefs concerning their own skill competence.

Similarly, there would be reason to believe that the differential feedback received by high- and low-expectancy athletes would also affect these athletes' levels of anxiety in sport contexts. In a study conducted by Smith et al. (1995), a sample of Little League Baseball coaches participated in a preseason coaching workshop. In this workshop, coaches were taught to increase the frequency with which they responded to their players' performances in games and practices with reinforcement (for effort as well as for good performance) and with mistake-contingent encouragement, corrective instruction, and technical instruction. A corresponding sample of coaches who did not participate in the workshop served as the control group. Pre- and postseason measures of athletes' levels of competitive trait anxiety were obtained. Analyses of the data showed that players who played for the trained coaches showed significant reductions in trait anxiety over the course of the season, whereas the players of the control group coaches showed no change in anxiety. As these results suggest, athletes who receive higher frequencies of technically instructive and corrective feedback, delivered by coaches in a positive and encouraging way, may have fewer problems with performance anxiety in sport contexts. Thus, the differential type of feedback that high- and low-expectancy athletes receive from their coaches not only may affect the athletes' perceptions of their sport ability but also may have an effect on the degree of anxiety they will experience in performance situations.

Finally, as noted in the previous section, coaches also may affect their athletes' self-perceptions by the attributions they make for their athletes' performance. Such attributions provide each athlete with information concerning his or her competence. When a coach attributes an athlete's successful performance to the athlete's innate ability (e.g., Example 6) the athlete develops a high expectancy for future success and a positive attitude toward the sport activity. In contrast, when a coach attributes successful performance to luck, the attribution does not encourage an athlete to believe that he or she can attain the same performance in the future and provides the athlete with no information concerning personal competence. Similarly, a coach who attributes an athlete's skill error to lack of effort, lack of practice, or some other athlete-controlled factor will do more to facilitate future motivation, decrease feelings of helplessness, and encourage a positive attitude than attributing the athlete's failure to lack of ability. In Example 7, Scott's performance failure is attributed by his coach to incorrect skill execution (a controllable and correctable error), whereas Steve's failure is attributed to his lack of speed (a less controllable and less correctable cause). The differential messages carried via these coaching communications may affect each athlete's future performance and motivation.

Step 4: The Athlete's Performance Conforms to the Coach's Expectations

The final step in the chain of events in the self-fulfilling prophecy phenomenon occurs when the athlete's performance and behavior conform to the coach's original expectation. This behavioral conformity is, in itself, a very important component in the chain of events because it reinforces for the coach that his or her initial judgment of the athlete was accurate. This confirms for the Pygmalion-prone coach that he or she is a very astute judge of sport potential and can recognize true athletic talent at the beginning of the season. Unfortunately, such "success" may reinforce or intensify the coach's Pygmalion tendencies.

As a final point in regard to the self-fulfilling prophecy process, it is important to recognize that *not* all athletes allow their coach's behavior or expectations to affect their performance or psychological responses. Just as all coaches are not Pygmalion prone, so, too, all athletes are not susceptible to the self-fulfilling prophecy. Earlier research in the coaching effectiveness area (as summarized in Smoll & Smith, 1989) has suggested that the self-perceptions of some athletes are more easily affected by their coach's evaluative feedback than are the self-perceptions of their teammates. It is likely that individuals who tend to be very dependent on their coach's feedback to provide them with information concerning their competence would be most easily "molded" by their coach's expectations. In contrast, those athletes who are resistant to the Pygmalion process may not use the coach's feedback as a sole source of information to tell them how competent they are. If these "resistant" athletes do receive biased feedback from a coach, they may respond by discounting that information and using other informational sources (e.g., feedback from peers, parents, or other adults) to form their perceptions of how competent or skilled they are. Recent research in the educational psychology literature (e.g., Madon, Jussim, & Eccles, 1997) has suggested that high-achieving students in academic classrooms are almost completely invulnerable to negative teacher perceptions/expectations, whereas their lower-achieving classmates are very susceptible to their teachers' expectations (i.e., their academic achievement over the school year was significantly predicted by their teachers' initial expectations of their academic potential). Assuming that such interindividual variability in susceptibility to adult expectations also occurs in the athletic setting, it would be reasonable to believe that there are some athletes (perhaps the higher achieving ones) who will be resistant to their coaches' expectations. Thus, even if a coach shows biased treatment of an individual athlete, the self-fulfilling prophecy process will short-circuit if the athlete is resistant to the coach's bias. It is important to note, then, that all four steps in the sequence are essential if the self-fulfilling prophecy phenomenon is to occur in the athletic setting.

Sport Applications

The research and theory detailed in the previous pages describe the processes by which coaches' expectations and behavior can affect the performance and psychological growth of individual athletes on their team. Some of this information is based on research work that has been conducted in the academic classroom and that is then applied to the sport domain. Although there are certainly many similarities between these two instructional contexts, there also are some factors that make each domain unique. In this section, four expectancy-related issues that are particularly relevant to the sport context are discussed. The first three of these issues are important because they describe how selected groups of athletes may be at an especially high risk for negative expectancy effects. The last issue concerns the leadership styles and personal characteristics that may place individual coaches at highest risk for exhibiting expectancy-biased behavior.

Expectancy Effects in Youth Sport Programs

Although Pygmalion-prone coaches can almost certainly be found at any level within the sport system (e.g., from youth sports through the professional level), the negative effects of a coach's expectancy-biased behavior may be particularly devastating at the younger age levels. There are three reasons this may be the case. First, because children's initial experience with any particular

sport is typically through a youth sport program, their interest in and enjoyment of that particular activity is being formed. Ineffective or expectancy-biased feedback from the coach during these early years may cause children to develop extremely negative feelings about that activity and subsequently to discontinue participation before they have had an opportunity to learn the skills.

Second, a series of research studies recently conducted with children ranging in age from 8 to 18 years (see summary of this research by Horn, 2004) shows that the self-perceptions of younger children (those under the age of 10) are based, to a large extent, on the feedback of significant adults. That is, these children are very much apt to evaluate how "good" or "bad" they are at a sport or physical activity based on what their parents, coaches, or teachers say to them. For example, a child in this age range is apt to say, "I know that I am a good runner because my mom says I am" or "I don't think that I'm a very good soccer player because my coach is always yelling at me." Thus, for children under 10, the feedback of a coach can have significant effects on the child's self-esteem and self-confidence in that sport.

Third, based on research information obtained from the motor development literature (e.g., Thomas, Gallagher, & Thomas, 2001), children in the early and mid-childhood years (4 to 10 years) should be acquiring a variety of fundamental motor and sport-specific skills. Specifically, children should be learning to throw, catch, kick, jump, and run using mature and efficient movement patterns. In addition, this is a good time for children to learn some fundamental sport-specific skills (e.g., dribbling, passing, trapping). If children do not acquire these fundamental motor and sport skills during the formative years, it will be difficult for them to participate with any degree of skill in the more competitive sport programs such as those offered to children after the age of 10 years. Because Pygmalion-prone coaches tend to act in ways that impede the skill progress of their low-expectancy players, these children will be prevented from learning the necessary fundamental motor and sport skills. This, in turn, serves as a limiting factor in regard to their subsequent participation in the more advanced sport programs. Thus, again, the negative effects of a coach's expectancy-biased behavior may be particularly devastating in the early and mid-childhood years.

Maturational Rates and the Sport Expectancy Process

A second expectancy issue, which is related to the first, is that children vary considerably in the rate at which they grow and mature. Children who mature early will reach full physical maturation 2 to 3 years earlier than children who mature at a more average rate. Furthermore, children who mature late will not reach full physical maturation until 2 or 3 years later than their average maturing peers and 4 to 5 years later than the early maturing child. As a result, within any given chronological age group, there will likely be considerable variation in children's physical status. Such differences in maturational rates may be a factor that not only affects children's and adolescents' performance and behavior in sport situations but also causes coaches to hold differential expectancies for individual athletes.

On a seventh-grade basketball team, for example, all boys may be between 12 and 13 years old chronologically, but they may differ in terms of their biological and physical status. The early maturing 12-year-old boy may be at a stage of physical development comparable to that of the average 14- or 15-year-old boy. In contrast, a late maturing 12-year-old may be at a stage of development comparable to that of a 9- or 10-year-old boy. Given such obvious differences in rate of maturation, the early maturer's physical and motor abilities are likely to be superior to those of the late maturer. It is important to know, however, that the late maturing boy's disadvantage is only temporary—he will eventually catch up to and may even surpass his early maturing peers in physical size and athletic performance. Unfortunately, however, because the late maturing boy in many youth sport programs is falsely diagnosed by unwitting coaches to be a low-expectancy athlete (i.e., a child who is not now and never will be physically competent), that

child may not receive optimal instruction, adequate playing time, or effective performance feedback and may even, in fact, be cut from the program. Thus, even though the late maturing boy could develop into a proficient athlete, he may be inhibited from doing so because of expectancy-biased coaching behaviors. Therefore, we should consider late maturing boys to be at an especially high risk for negative expectancy effects.

A more complicated pattern of expectancy bias may occur for girls in sport. Although early maturing girls may have the same advantages as early maturing boys during the childhood years (before the age of 12), the reverse may be true after this age. That is, early maturing girls could begin experiencing the effects of a negative expectancy bias on the part of their coaches around or after the time that these girls reach puberty. This could occur because some of the physical changes that girls experience as they reach puberty (e.g., breast development, menarche, increase in hip width, increase in body fat) are typically not perceived in our society as conducive to sport proficiency. Thus, some coaches may perceive or believe that these physical changes, which occur at an earlier age for the early maturing girls, will be detrimental to their sport proficiency and performance. In addition, gender-biased coaches may believe girls who are becoming more "womanly" in appearance may no longer be interested in sport, because participation in sport is still perceived by gender-biased individuals as antithetical to femininity. Thus, early maturing girls (i.e., girls who reach puberty earlier than their female peers) may suddenly be seen by gender-biased coaches as less physically competent and less interested in sport participation.

This argument is consistent with the biosocial hypothesis developed by Malina (1983, 1994, 2002) to explain the correlational relationship that links girls' participation in intensive sport training with a delay in age of menarche. As Malina suggests, a linear body build (narrow hips, flat chest, relatively low body fat), which is more typical of a late rather than an early maturing girl, may be used by coaches to select athletes into particular sport programs such as gymnastics, dance, track, volleyball, swimming, and diving. Thus, early maturing girls who no longer exhibit a linear build may either be cut from sport programs once they reach puberty or be socialized out of sport (i.e., be encouraged to turn to more feminine activities).

Girls' maturational status during the childhood and adolescent years could serve as a factor that causes their coaches to develop inaccurate and inflexible expectations concerning their sport ability. Similar to boys, early maturing girls may be favored during the childhood years, but these same girls may be at a disadvantage once they reach the age of 11 or 12.

Another issue relating to maturation and expectancy effects in the sport setting concerns the concept of "developmental vulnerability." Specifically, recent research in the educational setting (e.g., Rudolph, Lambert, Clark, & Kurlakowsky, 2001; Valeski & Stipek, 2001) has indicated that children and adolescents may be more susceptible to socioenvironmental factors at particular times in their educational careers. These particularly vulnerable times appear to be at important transition points (e.g., from kindergarten to first grade and from elementary to middle or junior high school). The increased vulnerability of children and adolescents to experience academic or psychological problems at these timepoints is likely because of the uncertainty, unfamiliarity, or novelty that are characteristic of a new achievement situation as well as the increased demands that are placed on them in the new (higher level) achievement context (see arguments on this point by Eccles & Midgley, 1989; Eccles, Wigfield, & Schiefele, 1998). Applying this concept to expectancy effects in the sport setting, we might hypothesize that individual children may be more susceptible to their coaches' expectancy-biased behavior when such children make transitions from the recreational to the more "select" or competitive level (i.e., from sport programs in which everyone makes the team to programs where tryouts are held and only select players make the team). Similarly, transitions from middle school or junior high programs to high school sport programs, and, eventually, from junior varsity to varsity programs, may result in

greater susceptibility of children/adolescents to their coaches' expectancy-biased behavior. This notion regarding critical developmental timepoints in the psychological vulnerability of children and adolescents supports the overall concept that not all children and adolescents at all timepoints in their athletic career will be susceptible to the effects of the self-fulfilling prophecy.

Sport Stereotypes and the Expectancy Process

A third expectancy issue concerns selected stereotypes that are related to the performance and behavior of individuals in sport situations. The two most pervasive stereotypes in the sport setting are those concerning ethnicity and gender. In regard to ethnicity, it is commonly believed that African American individuals are "naturally" gifted in particular sports and physical activities (e.g., basketball, sprinting events). Although this may initially appear to be a positive stereotype, there are certain negative ramifications for those African American children who are not "as good as they are supposed to be." An African American child who, for example, does not score *higher* than his Euro-American (white) peers on a series of sport skills tests may be perceived by his or her coach to be either lazy or "untalented." That is, even though he may have performed as well as his Euro-American peers, he is perceived by the Pygmalion-prone coach to be less than adequate. Such perceptions may be reflected in the fact that African American athletes in some programs must either make the starting lineup or be cut from the team (i.e., they will not make the team unless they are significantly more talented than the other athletes). Thus, African American children may be held to a higher standard of performance in these sports because of the stereotypes concerning their physical prowess.

Another aspect of ethnically biased stereotypes is that involving perceptions concerning athletes' mental capabilities. Specifically, although African American athletes are perceived to be very competent in regard to physical capabilities (e.g., speed, reaction time, strength), it is the Euro-American athletes who are perceived to be better in regard to mental capabilities (i.e., they are believed to be better decision makers and leaders). Pygmalion-prone coaches who subscribe to such ethnic stereotypes will act in ways that reflect these biased beliefs. Thus, African American athletes may not be considered for sport leadership or decision-making positions (e.g., football quarterback, basketball point guard, volleyball setter, baseball catcher). Even if they are given the opportunity to practice or play at such positions, their "mistakes" will be perceived as evidence of their innate inability to perform well in these roles rather than as an indicator that they may need more instruction or practice to acquire the necessary skills.

The situations described in the above paragraphs only illustrate *some* of the ethnicity-related stereotypes that abound in the sport context. There are certainly many more (see, for example, Brooks & Althouse, 2000). The examples given in the previous paragraphs were provided to show that expectations based on ethnicity are not accurate and certainly can inhibit the progress of individual athletes or groups of athletes. Support for this idea is evident in the educational psychology literature where researchers (e.g., Jussim et al., 1996) have found that teacher expectations or teacher stereotypes have greater effects on the academic achievement of African American students and students from lower socioeconomic backgrounds than they do on children who are not from these two backgrounds. Other support for the effect of negative racial and gender stereotypes on academic performance comes from the work of Steele (1997) and his colleagues (e.g., Steele & Aronson, 1995).

In regard to gender stereotypes, it is commonly believed that females are less physically capable than males. Although these beliefs are based to some extent on research showing that postpubertal males and females do differ on selected physical characteristics (e.g., height, body composition, limb length) (Malina, 1994, 2002; Ransdell, 2002), they also are based on inaccurate stereotypes concerning the performance and behavior of females. In particular, the available research indicates that there are very few physiological or biological differences

between boys and girls prior to puberty (particularly before 10 years of age) (Malina, 1994, 2002). Despite these research findings, many teachers, coaches, and parents continue to believe that girls from early childhood on are not "naturally talented" in the physical activity area. Because of such stereotyped beliefs, girls in coeducational youth sport programs may be more apt to be treated as low-expectancy athletes. That is, they may be given less instruction by their coaches in practice and less playing time in games. When they do play in games, they may be relegated to positions where they are inactive for large amounts of time. (For interesting detail regarding gendered behavior in children's sport contexts, see recent observational studies by Landers & Fine, 1996, and Messner, 2000.) Even on all-girl teams, a coach's stereotyped belief that girls are not and cannot be physically competent may cause her or him to establish lower standards of performance for them and to give greater amounts of inappropriate praise (i.e., to accept and praise mediocre performance accomplishments). Again, such expectancy-biased behavior is particularly negative during the childhood years because girls may then be less apt to develop the necessary fundamental motor and sport skills. As was indicated earlier in this section, failure to acquire these skills during the childhood years serves as an inhibitor of sport performance in the postpubertal years. Thus, as several researchers and writers have recently suggested, the rather large differences in the physical performance capabilities of postpubertal males and females may be due as much to inadequate instruction, participation, and training during the childhood years as to actual physiological or biological differences between males and females (Smoll & Schutz, 1990; Thomas & French, 1985). Furthermore, although there certainly are postpubertal sex differences in strength, speed, power, and endurance, this does not necessarily mean that all girls are less strong or less fast than all boys. Thus, coaches who develop expectations concerning the physical competencies of children and adolescents based solely or primarily on gender ignore the reality that there is as much (or more) variation within each sex as there is between sexes. Thus, coaches' expectations should be based to a greater extent on characteristics specific to each individual child rather than on the ethnic group or biological sex to which that child belongs.

The information provided in this section clearly indicates that selected children may be more apt to be perceived as low-expectancy athletes by their coaches than are other children. The specific concern here is that because such expectancies are based either on inaccurate stereotypes (e.g., ethnicity and gender) or on coaches' lack of knowledge concerning the physical growth and maturation process, these expectancies do have the potential to seriously inhibit children's sport development. Thus, we need to consider such children as at greater risk for negative expectancy effects than their peers.

Coaches' Personal Characteristics, Their Leadership Styles, and the Sport Expectancy Process

As noted earlier in this chapter, the research conducted to date suggests that not all coaches are expectancy biased. That is, not all coaches will allow their initial judgments of each athlete's sport ability to affect the quantity and quality of their interactions with those athletes. Given this variability among coaches in their tendency to be Pygmalion prone, it would seem to be of interest to determine what types of coaches are most apt to fall into this category. That is, what characteristics distinguish those coaches who act in expectancy-biased ways from coaches who do not do so?

Many characteristics of coaches could be investigated as possible correlates or predictors of expectancy-biased behavior. Based on the research concerning gender stereotypes in sport settings (see, for example, a recent chapter by Gill, 2002, as well as books by Messner, 1992, and Lenskyj, 1987), it might be hypothesized that coaches of male athletes who hold strong gender-stereotyped and homophobic beliefs would act very positively toward the players on their team who "fit" the masculine stereotype (i.e., those who have broad shoulders, high muscle mass,

and who act in aggressive ways) while acting less positively toward the players who do not "fit" this masculine stereotype (i.e., players who have a more linear body shape, lower amounts of muscle mass, and who do not exhibit aggressive behaviors). Similarly, gender-biased and homophobic coaches of female athletes might act more positively to the athletes on their team who conform to the "feminine" ideal (i.e., female athletes who have longer hair, have boyfriends, wear makeup off the court) than to those athletes who do not conform to this image.

Other personal characteristics of coaches that may be linked to their tendencies to exhibit expectancy-biased behavior would be the degree to which individual coaches possess critical thinking skills or are very self-reflective (see Abraham & Collins, 1998, for a discussion of these coaching characteristics). Also, Smoll and Smith (1989) have suggested that coaches who are high self-monitors (i.e., those individuals who are continually aware of their own behavior and its effects on others) may be more responsive to cues in the sport context and thus more flexible in their interactions with individual athletes. Such coaches should be less apt to exhibit expectancy-biased behavior in their interactions with individual athletes on their team.

From the cognitive psychology (e.g., Skinner, 1996) theoretical literature as well as from the teacher education research literature (e.g., Cooper, 1979; Guskey, 1981), it appears that we might want to examine individual coaches' perceptions or locus of control with regard to their job responsibilities. That is, coaches may differ in how much they perceive that they personally can control the performance outcomes their teams can achieve. Coaches who possess an external locus of control would believe that the degree to which their teams will be successful over a season (i.e., have a high win-loss record) will be a function of external factors (e.g., "Do I have good athletes this year?" "Will we have any significant injuries?"). In contrast, coaches with an internal perception or locus of control might believe that a successful season would be, at least in large part, under their own personal control (i.e., "if I design my practices well," "if I work hard to teach my athletes the basic skills," "if I choose and implement the right offensive and defensive strategies," "if I maximize my athletes' level of conditioning"). Based on these different perceptions or beliefs on the part of the coaches, their behaviors toward and with their athletes might differ. Because coaches with an internal perception of control have a stronger belief that they can personally affect the degree to which their athletes can learn skills, such coaches might be more apt to persist in their efforts to teach all athletes the basic skills and to spend extra time with those who need more help or more repetitions. In contrast, coaches who generally believe successful outcomes are not under their own control but, rather, are more dependent on the athletes themselves may be more apt to "give up" on individual athletes who cannot perform the skills the right way the first time and focus all of their practice time and attention on the higher skilled athletes. Thus, we might well find that coaches who have such an external perception or locus of control with regard to seasonal outcomes also would tend to be Pygmalion-prone coaches (i.e., act in expectancy-biased ways).

A more recent concept that certainly may be related to coaches' perceptions of control concerns their implicit theories regarding individuals' traits or abilities. This concept was introduced by Carol Dweck and her colleagues (e.g., Chiu, Hong, & Dweck, 1997; Dweck, Chiu, & Hong, 1995; Erdley & Dweck, 1993; Levy, Stroessner, & Dweck, 1998) to describe two types of individuals. Entity theorists are those individuals who believe that people's traits and abilities are fixed. In contrast, incremental theorists are those individuals who believe that traits and abilities are malleable (i.e., that abilities can be changed or improved over time or with effort). In a series of experiments, Dweck and her colleagues (e.g., Chiu et al., 1997; Erdley & Dweck, 1993; Levy et al., 1998) have shown that these two types of theorists differ in their perceptions and beliefs about others. Specifically, entity theorists, as compared to incremental theorists, (a) made more extreme judgments about others' traits and abilities based on a small sample of their behavior; (b) believed more strongly that individuals will show a high degree of consistency in their behavior over time; (c) showed a lesser tendency to adjust

their initial trait judgments of another person even when exposed to information that was contrary to their initial trait judgment of that individual; and (d) more strongly agreed with societal stereotypes regarding particular ethnic and occupational groups. In contrast, incremental theorists viewed people's behavior as varying across time and contexts. Thus, for incremental theorists, the initial information they received about a person's characteristics or traits served as only tentative or provisional descriptors of their future performance and behavior. Assuming that coaches also can be identified or categorized as either entity or incremental theorists, it would follow that such a global perspective or worldview regarding the fixedness or malleability of athletes' traits or abilities would predict the degree to which coaches would exhibit expectancy-biased behavior. Coaches who adhere to an entity perspective (i.e., that an athlete's traits and abilities are fixed) should be more apt to be Pygmalion-prone whereas coaches who adhere to an incremental perspective (i.e., that an athlete's traits and abilities are malleable) should be less at risk for developing and exhibiting Pygmalion-prone behaviors.

From a somewhat different perspective, we could also look at the research on coaches' leadership styles to identify possible predictors of Pygmalion-prone behaviors. Based on research conducted to date on the topic of leadership styles in coaches (see Chapter 7 and reviews by Chelladurai, 1993, and Horn, 2002), it is clear that coaches do differ in the type of leadership styles they employ in sport contexts. Furthermore, the research shows that the types of leadership styles individual coaches exhibit are related to, and may even be predictive of, differences in athletes' performance, level of satisfaction, intrinsic motivation, and perceptions of competence. That is, certain leadership styles appear to be more effective than others in facilitating high levels of performance and positive self-perceptions in athletes.

An examination of some of these leadership styles may reveal possible links to the expectancy-bias process. For example, a highly autocratic coaching style might be associated with a tendency to act in expectancy-biased ways.

As explained by Chelladurai and Saleh (1980), coaches who exhibit an autocratic leadership style tend to stress their own personal authority in working with athletes. These coaches are the source of all rules, and they make all decisions. They also demand strict compliance from their athletes in following these rules. Of necessity, autocratic coaches also tend to separate themselves from their athletes. That is, they remain emotionally distant or aloof from players on their team. In contrast, coaches who exhibit a democratic leadership style encourage and solicit the participation of their athletes in making decisions pertaining to group goals, practice methods, game tactics, and strategies. Such coaches also tend to interact more frequently with individual athletes to solicit their opinions and feedback regarding team rules, practices, and games. Given such contrasting styles, it would seem reasonable to hypothesize that coaches who adopt a more autocratic leadership style would be more apt to act in expectancy-biased ways than would coaches who adopt a more democratic style.

From a somewhat different but related perspective, we can contrast coaches who create a more **mastery-oriented** team climate with coaches who create a more **performance-oriented** team climate. Based on the work of several researchers and writers (e.g., Ames, 1992; Duda, 1996; Ntoumanis & Biddle, 1999; Ommundsen & Roberts, 1999; Treasure & Roberts, 1995; Weiss & Ebbeck, 1996), we can describe coaches who create a performance-oriented climate as those who place heavy emphasis in practices and games on performance outcomes (e.g., winning/losing). Such coaches also create a team environment that encourages between-player rivalries (e.g., coaches try to motivate athletes to outperform each other) and focuses attention on a limited number of players (e.g., only the "stars" get attention from the coach). In addition, in this type of team climate, player mistakes are perceived as extremely negative and deserving of punishment. In contrast, coaches who create a mastery-oriented team climate place greatest emphasis in practices on the development of individual players' skills (e.g., reinforcement and rewards given to all individuals who work hard and who show improvement in skills). Such coaches also view player mistakes as part of the learning process and distribute their time and attention to all players on the team and not just the "stars." Again, based on behavioral differences between these two contrasting leadership styles, we could hypothesize that performance-oriented coaches would be more apt to exhibit expectancy-biased behaviors than would mastery-oriented coaches. Of course, the validity of this hypothesis awaits further research.

As the comments in this section indicate, certain coaching characteristics, attitudes, beliefs, and leadership styles may be more conducive than others to the occurrence of expectancy effects in the sport setting. A summary of these personal factors is provided in Table 5-1. Coaches who adopt, assume, or exemplify the characteristics, beliefs, attitudes, and behaviors descriptive of the "Pygmalion-prone coach" may certainly be at risk for undermining the performance and behavior of individual athletes on their team.

Behavioral Recommendations for Coaches

The information on how coaches' expectations and behavior can affect the performance and psychological growth of individual athletes on their team can and should be used to promote positive coach–athlete interactions. Therefore, the following recommendations are offered to coaches and prospective coaches for their use in evaluating and perhaps modifying their own behavior in the athletic setting.

1. *Coaches should determine what sources of information they use to form preseason or early season expectations for each athlete.* Performance-based information sources are generally more reliable and accurate predictors or indicators of an individual's physical competence than are person cues such as the athlete's gender, ethnic background, socioeconomic status, or physical appearance.

2. *Coaches should realize that their initial assessments of an athlete's competence may be inaccurate*

Table 5-1 **Characteristics, Attitudes, Beliefs, and Behaviors of Pygmalion-Prone and Non-Pygmalion-Prone Coaches**

	Pygmalion-Prone Coach	Non-Pygmalion-Prone Coach
Beliefs about Athletic Ability	"Good athletes are just born that way."	"Athletic ability is something that can be developed through practice and good training."
Beliefs about Coaching Success	"I can be a successful coach if I recruit/get good athletes." "If my team does not have a successful season, it's because I did not have good athletes, or because my athletes did not do what they could/should have done to be successful. I don't have to change any of my strategies or behaviors next season. I just need to get better athletes or more cooperative athletes."	"I can be a successful coach if I work hard to design and conduct good practices and institute the right game strategies and tactics." "If my team does not have a successful season, I will consider the possibility that I could/should have done something differently. I will likely change some of my strategies, behaviors, and tactics next season in an effort to improve my coaching effectiveness."
Stereotypic Beliefs	The Pygmalion-prone coach holds stereotypic beliefs regarding gender, race/ethnicity, country of origin, and socioeconomic status. These stereotypic beliefs affect or determine the coach's attitude toward, and behaviors with, individual athletes.	The non-Pygmalion-prone coach does not subscribe to stereotypic beliefs regarding gender, race/ethnicity, country of origin, or socioeconomic status. The coach's behaviors toward and with athletes are individualized.
Preseason Expectations	This coach tends to form preseason expectations for individual athletes based on "person" cues (e.g., race/ethnicity, gender, body size, and appearance).	This coach forms preseason expectations for individual athletes based primarily on performance-related information sources (i.e., how athletes perform in drills, scrimmages, and other performance contexts).
Perceptual Flexibility	This coach's preseason expectations are rigid and fixed. Thus, coach sees in each athlete's performance and behavior in practices and games exactly what he/she expected to see.	This coach's preseason expectations are fluid and flexible. Thus, expectations for individual athletes may change as the athlete's performance and behavior in practices and games provide new information for the coach to use in evaluating that athlete.
Leadership Style	This coach exhibits an autocratic or controlling leadership style. Source of power lies within the coach. Athletes are not consulted about any team decisions, rules, strategies, or practices. Coach is central source of authority, and he/she conveys the attitude that "it's my way or the highway."	This coach exhibits a democratic or autonomous leadership style. Although coach is clearly the team leader, he/she regularly consults with athletes regarding team decisions, team rules, strategies, practices, etc. Coach encourages athletes to take personal responsibility for their own behaviors, motivation levels, training, etc.

(continued)

Table 5-1 **Characteristics, Attitudes, Beliefs, and Behaviors of Pygmalion-Prone and Non-Pygmalion-Prone Coaches (*Continued*)**

	Pygmalion-Prone Coach	Non-Pygmalion-Prone Coach
Team Climate	This coach creates a climate in practices and games that is performance-oriented or ego-involving. In this climate, player mistakes are punished, better players receive more attention, encouragement, and rewards, and intrateam rivalry is encouraged.	This coach creates a team climate in practices and games that is mastery-oriented or task-involving. In this climate, each team member is perceived to be a valuable contributor, emphasis is placed on individual effort and skill improvement, and mistakes are viewed as opportunities to learn and improve.

and thus need to be revised continually as the season progresses. As the research literature in the motor learning area suggests, individuals do not always learn or progress at the same rate. Some individuals may show rapid progress early in the season but then slow down or even plateau toward the middle and end of the season. Other athletes may start slowly but then evidence a rapid increase in performance during the latter part of the season. Given such interindividual variation in learning and performance rates, it is obvious that expectations based on initial assessments of an athlete's capabilities may soon become inaccurate. Thus, coaches at all levels of play should maintain a certain degree of flexibility with regard to their expectations or judgments concerning individual athletes' abilities.

3. During practices, *coaches need to keep a running count of the amount of time each athlete spends in non-skill-related activities* (e.g., shagging balls, waiting in line, sitting out of a scrimmage or drill). Certainly it is advisable for coaches to ask a friend or another coach to observe their practices and record the amount of time a starter (usually a high-expectancy athlete) and a nonstarter (usually a low-expectancy athlete) spend in practice drills.

4. *Coaches should design instructional activities or drills that provide all athletes with an opportunity to improve their skills.* In planning practice activities, the Pygmalion-type coach typically uses

skill drills that are most appropriate for the highly skilled players. When the less skilled athletes cannot keep up, the coach then gives up on these athletes because he or she believes their failure is inevitable because of low skill abilities. The more effective coach, upon finding that his or her less skilled players cannot master the skill, will implement instructional activities designed to help them ultimately achieve success (e.g., break the skill down into component parts, employ performance aids, or ask the athlete to stay a few minutes extra after practice for more intensive work).

5. As a general rule, *coaches should respond to skill errors with corrective instruction* that tells each athlete what she or he can do to improve the skill performance. Also, praise and criticism should be given contingent to or consistent with the level of performance that was exhibited.

6. *Coaches should emphasize skill improvement as a means of evaluating and reinforcing individual athletes* rather than using absolute performance scores or levels of skill achievement. To the degree that a coach conveys the attitude that *all* athletes can *improve* their skill performance, no matter what their present level, then positive expectations can be communicated to each athlete.

7. *Coaches should interact frequently with all athletes on their team to solicit information concerning athletes' perceptions, opinions, and* *attitudes regarding team rules and practice organization.* Such individual coach–athlete interactions should allow each athlete to feel like a valued member of the team no matter what his or her level of skill is.

8. *Coaches should try to create a mastery-oriented climate in team practices.* Such a climate is most conducive to the development of skill in all players and to the maintenance of a team-oriented attitude.

Summary

Coaches' preseason judgments of individual athletes can serve as self-fulfilling prophecies by initiating a series of events that cause the coaches' initial expectations to become reality. This self-fulfilling prophecy phenomenon can be most detrimental when a coach forms an initial expectation that is inaccurate and underestimates an athlete's true ability. The coach's biased judgment of the athlete's sport potential, in turn, causes the coach to provide that player with less frequent and less effective instruction. Not only does such biased coaching behavior ultimately interfere with the athlete's opportunity to learn, but it also has a negative effect on his or her motivation and self-confidence. When the athlete subsequently exhibits an inability to perform well and a lack of motivation in practice situations, the coach's original but false judgment of incompetence is fulfilled.

Fortunately, the research that has been conducted in academic classrooms as well as in physical activity settings shows that all coaches are not Pygmalion prone. That is, some coaches do not allow their preseason judgments of individual athletes to affect the quality of their interaction with those players. It seems likely that coaches who are made aware of the effects that their expectations may have on athletes and who are trained to monitor their own instructional behavior may become more effective in working with individual athletes. The results of this research demonstrate that it is important that researchers and coaches more closely examine coaching behavior as one of the major factors that affect the performance and psychological growth of young athletes.

Study Questions

1. Identify and briefly describe the four steps in the expectation–performance process.

2. What sources of information might coaches use to form initial expectations for individual athletes on their team?

3. A coach's initial expectations for an individual athlete can vary along two dimensions (accuracy and flexibility). Briefly describe the consequences of the four possible combinations.

4. Should coaches form expectations at the beginning of the season for individual athletes? Why or why not?

5. What are the three primary ways coaches' expectations influence their behavior toward individual athletes?

6. Do all coaches show expectancy-biased behavior? Explain what is meant by the term *Pygmalion-prone* coach.

7. Why might the negative effects of a coach's expectancy-biased behavior be particularly devastating for children in youth sport programs?

8. Explain what the term *late maturing child* means, and then explain why late maturing boys may be at an especially high risk for negative expectancy effects.

9. Explain why early maturing girls may be at greater risk for negative expectancy effects once they reach puberty.

10. Describe the stereotypes in the sport setting associated with ethnicity. Explain how such stereotypes may affect selected groups of athletes.

11. Explain what the term *high self-monitor* means. How might this personal characteristic be related to a coach's behavior in practice situations?

12. Describe how internal and external locus of control coaches might differ in their assessment of their team and its chances for success at the beginning of a new season. How would such preseason perceptions affect their practice behaviors?

13. Define the terms *entity theorist* and *incremental theorist*. Explain why coaches who adhere to an entity theorist perspective of athletic ability might be more apt to be Pygmalion-prone in their interactions with individual athletes.

14. Compare and contrast the behaviors of an autocratic and a democratic coach.

15. Explain how a mastery-oriented team climate differs from a performance-oriented one.

16. What actions might a coach take to avoid or eliminate Pygmalion-prone behaviors?

References

Abraham, A., & Collins, D. (1998). Examining and extending research in coach development. *Quest, 50,* 59–79.

Allen, J. B., & Howe, B. (1998). Player ability, coach feedback, and female adolescent athletes' perceived competence and satisfaction. *Journal of Sport and Exercise Psychology, 20,* 280–299.

Ames, C. (1992). Achievement goals, motivational climate, and motivational processes. In G. C. Roberts (Ed.), *Motivation in sport and exercise* (pp. 161–176). Champaign, IL: Human Kinetics.

Amorose, A. J., & Horn, T. S. (2000). Intrinsic motivation: Relationships with collegiate athletes' gender, scholarship status, and perceptions of their coaches' behavior. *Journal of Sport and Exercise Psychology, 22,* 63–84.

Amorose, A., & Horn, T. S. (2001). Pre- to post-season changes in the intrinsic motivation of first year collegiate athletes: Relationships with coaching behavior and scholarship status. *Journal of Applied Sport Psychology, 13,* 355–373.

Baker, J., Cote, J., & Hawes, R. (2000). The relationship between coaching behaviors and sport anxiety in athletes. *Journal of Science and Medicine in Sport, 3*(2), 110–119.

Bandura, A. (1997). *Self-efficacy: The exercise of control.* New York: Freeman.

Bibik, J. M. (1999). Factors influencing college students' self-perceptions of competence in beginning physical education classes. *Journal of Teaching in Physical Education, 18,* 255–276.

Black, S. J., & Weiss, M. R. (1992). The relationship among perceived coaching behaviors, perceptions of ability, and motivation in competitive age-group swimmers. *Journal of Sport and Exercise Psychology, 14,* 309–325.

Brooks, D., & Althouse, R. (Eds.). (2000). *Racism in college athletics: The African-American athlete's experience* (2nd ed.). Morgantown, WV: Fitness Information Technology.

Brophy, J. (1983). Research on the self-fulfilling prophecy and teacher expectations. *Journal of Educational Psychology, 75,* 631–661.

Brophy, J., & Good, T. (1970). Teachers' communication of differential expectations for children's classroom performance: Some behavioral data. *Journal of Educational Psychology, 61,* 365–374.

Chelladurai, P. (1993). Leadership. In R. N. Singer, M. Murphey, & L. K. Tennant (Eds.), *Handbook of research on sport psychology* (pp. 647–671). New York: Macmillan.

Chelladurai, P., & Riemer, H. A. (1998). Measurement of leadership in sport. In J. L. Duda (Ed.), *Advances in sport and exercise psychology* (pp. 227–253). Morgantown, WV: Fitness Information Technology.

Chelladurai, P., & Saleh, S. (1980). Dimensions of leader behavior in sports: Development of a leadership scale. *Journal of Sport Psychology, 2,* 34–45.

Chiu, C., Hong, Y., & Dweck, C. S. (1997). Lay dispositionism and implicit theories of personality. *Journal of Personality and Social Psychology, 73,* 19–30.

Cooper, H. M. (1979). Pygmalion grows up: A model for teacher expectancy communication and performance influence. *Review of Educational Research, 49,* 389–410.

Cooper, H., & Baron, R. (1977). Academic expectations and attributed responsibility as predictors of professional teachers' reinforcement behavior. *Journal of Educational Psychology, 69,* 409–418.

Cooper, H. M., & Tom, D. Y. H. (1984). Teacher expectation research: A review with implications for classroom instruction. *The Elementary School Journal, 85,* 77–89.

Cousineau, W. J., & Luke, M. D. (1990). Relationships between teacher expectations and academic learning time in sixth grade physical education basketball classes. *Journal of Teaching in Physical Education, 9,* 262–271.

Duda, J. (1996). Maximizing motivation in sport and physical education among children and adolescents: The case for greater task involvement. *Quest, 48,* 290–302.

Dweck, C. S., Chiu, C., & Hong, Y. (1995). Implicit theories and their role in judgments and reactions: A world from two perspectives. *Psychological Inquiry, 6,* 267–285.

Eccles, J. S., Jacobs, J., & Harold, R. D. (1990). Gender-role stereotypes, expectancy effects, and parents' role in the socialization of gender differences in self-perceptions and skill acquisition. *Journal of Social Issues, 46,* 183–201.

Eccles, J. S., & Midgley, C. (1989). Stage-environment fit: Developmentally appropriate classrooms for young adolescents. In R. E. Ames & C. Ames (Eds.), *Research on motivation in education* (Vol. 3, pp. 139–181). New York: Academic Press.

Eccles, J. S., Wigfield, A., & Schiefele, U. (1998). Motivation to succeed. In N. Eisenberg (Ed.), W. Damon (Series Ed.), *Handbook of child psychology: Vol. 4. Personality and social development.* New York: John Wiley & Sons.

Elashoff, J., & Snow, R. (1971). *Pygmalion reconsidered.* Worthington, OH: Jones.

Erdley, C. A., & Dweck, C. S. (1993). Children's implicit personality theories as predictors of their social judgments. *Child Development, 64,* 863–878.

Gill, D. L. (2002). Gender and sport behavior. In T. S. Horn (Ed.), *Advances in sport psychology* (2nd ed.), (pp. 355–376). Champaign, IL: Human Kinetics.

Graham, S. (1990). Communicating low ability in the classroom: Bad things that good teachers sometimes do. In S. Graham & V. S. Folkes (Eds.), *Attribution theory: Applications to achievement, mental health, and interpersonal conflict* (pp. 17–36). Hillsdale, NJ: Erlbaum.

Guskey, T. (1981). Measurement of the responsibility teachers assume for academic successes and failures in the classroom. *Journal of Teacher Education, 32,* 44–51.

Harris, M., & Rosenthal, R. (1985). Mediation of interpersonal expectancy effects: 31 meta-analyses. *Psychological Bulletin, 97,* 363–386.

Harter, S. (1981). The development of competence motivation in the master of cognitive and physical skills: Is there still a place for joy? In G. C. Roberts & D. M. Landers (Eds.), *Psychology of motor behavior and sport—1980* (pp. 3–29). Champaign, IL: Human Kinetics.

Horn, T. S. (1984). Expectancy effects in the interscholastic athletic setting: Methodological considerations. *Journal of Sport Psychology, 6,* 60–76.

Horn, T. S. (1985). Coaches' feedback and changes in children's perceptions of their physical competence. *Journal of Educational Psychology, 77,* 174–186.

Horn, T. S. (2002). Coaching effectiveness in the sport domain. In T. S. Horn (Ed.), *Advances in sport psychology* (2nd ed., pp. 309–354). Champaign, IL: Human Kinetics.

Horn, T. S. (2004). Developmental perspectives on self-perceptions in children and adolescents. In M. R. Weiss (Ed.), *Developmental sport and exercise psychology: A lifespan perspective* (pp. 101–141). Morgantown, WV: Fitness Information Technology.

Jussim, L. (1986). Self-fulfilling prophecies: A theoretical and integrative review. *Psychological Review, 93,* 429–445.

Jussim, L. (1991). Social perception and social reality: A reflection-construction model. *Psychological Review, 98,* 54–73.

Jussim, L., & Eccles, J. S. (1995). Naturally occurring interpersonal expectancies. *Review of Personality and Social Psychology, 15,* 74–108.

Jussim, L., Eccles, J., & Madon, S. (1996). Social perception, social stereotypes, and teacher expectations: Accuracy and the quest for the powerful self-fulfilling prophecy. In M. P. Zanna (Ed.), *Advances in experimental social psychology* (Vol. 28, pp. 281–388). San Diego, CA: Academic Press.

Jussim, L., Smith, A., Madon, S., & Palumbo, P. (1998). Teacher expectations. *Advances in Research on Teaching, 7,* 1–48.

Kenow, L. J., & Williams, J. M. (1992). Relationship between anxiety, self-confidence, and evaluation of coaching behaviors. *The Sport Psychologist, 6,* 344–357.

Kenow, L., & Williams, J. (1999). Coach–athlete compatibility and athlete's perception of coaching behaviors. *Journal of Sport Behavior, 22,* 251–260.

Kleinfeld, J. (1975). Effective teachers of Eskimo and Indian students. *School Review, 83*, 301–344.

Krane, V., Eklund, R., & McDermott, M. (1991). Collaborative action research and behavioral coaching intervention: A case study. In W. K. Warren, A. LeUnes, & J. S. Picou (Eds.), *The applied research in coaching and athletics annual* (pp. 119–147). Boston: American.

Landers, M. A., & Fine, G. A. (1996). Learning life's lessons in tee ball: The reinforcement of gender and status in kindergarten sport. *Sociology of Sport Journal, 13*, 87–93.

Lenskyj, H. (1987). *Out of bounds: Women, sport, and sexuality.* Toronto: Women's Press.

Levy, S. R., Stroessner, S. J., & Dweck, C. S. (1998). Stereotype formation and endorsement: The role of implicit theories. *Journal of Personality and Social Psychology, 74*, 1421–1436.

Madon, S., Jussim, L., & Eccles, J. (1997). In search of the powerful self-fulfilling prophecy. *Journal of Personality and Social Psychology, 72*, 791–809.

Malina, R. M. (1983). Menarche in athletes: A synthesis and hypothesis. *Annals of Human Biology, 10*, 1–24.

Malina, R. M. (1994). Physical growth and biological maturation of young athletes. In J. O. Holloszy (Ed.), *Exercise and sport science reviews* (Vol. 22, pp. 388–433). Baltimore, MD: Williams & Wilkins.

Malina, R. M. (2002). The young athlete: Biological growth and maturation in a biocultural context. In F. L. Smoll & R. E. Smith (Eds.), *Children and youth in sport: A biopsychosocial perspective* (2nd ed., pp. 261–292). Dubuque, IA: Kendall/Hunt.

Markland, R. D., & Martinek, T. J. (1988). Descriptive analysis of coach augmented feedback given to high school varsity female volleyball players. *Journal of Teaching in Physical Education, 7*, 289–301.

Martinek, T. (1988). Confirmation of a teacher expectancy model: Student perceptions and causal attributions of teaching behaviors. *Research Quarterly for Exercise and Sport, 59*, 118–126.

Martinek, T. (1989). Children's perceptions of teaching behaviors: An attributional model for explaining teacher expectancy effects. *Journal of Teaching in Physical Education, 8*, 318–328.

Martinek, T., & Johnson, S. (1979). Teacher expectations: Effects on dyadic interactions and self-concept in elementary age children. *Research Quarterly, 50,* 60–70.

Martinek, T., & Karper, W. B. (1982). Canonical relationships among motor ability, expression of effort, teacher expectations, and dyadic interactions in elementary age children. *Journal of Teaching in Physical Education, 1,* 26–39.

Martinek, T., & Karper, W. B. (1984). Multivariate relationships of specific impression cues with teacher expectations and dyadic interactions in elementary physical education classes. *Research Quarterly for Exercise and Sport, 55,* 32–40.

Martinek, T., & Karper, W. B. (1986). Motor ability and instructional contexts: Effects on teacher expectations and dyadic interactions in elementary physical education classes. *Journal of Classroom Interaction, 21,* 16–25.

Messner, M. A. (1992). *Power at play: Sports and the problem of masculinity.* Boston: Beacon Press.

Messner, M. A. (2000). Barbie girls versus sea monsters: Children constructing gender. *Gender and Society, 14*, 765–784.

Meyer, W. (1982). Indirect communications about perceived ability estimates. *Journal of Educational Psychology, 74*, 888–897.

Meyer, W. (1992). Paradoxical effects of praise and criticism on perceived ability. In W. Stroebe & M. Hewstone (Eds.), *European Review of Social Psychology*. (pp. 259–283). New York: John Wiley & Sons.

Ntoumanis, N., & Biddle, S. J. H. (1999). A review of motivational climate in physical activity. *Journal of Sports Science, 17*, 643–665.

Ommundsen, Y., & Roberts, G. C. (1999). Effects of motivational climate profiles on motivational indices in team sport. *Scandinavian Journal of Medicine and Science in Sports, 9*, 389–397.

Papaioannou, A. (1995). Differential perceptual and motivational patterns when different goals are adopted. *Journal of Sport and Exercise Psychology, 17*, 18–34.

Ransdell, L. B. (2002). The maturing young female athlete: Biophysical considerations. In F. L. Smoll & R. E. Smith (Eds.), *Children and youth in sport: A biopsychosocial perspective* (2nd ed., pp. 311–338). Dubuque, IA: Kendall/Hunt.

Rejeski, W., Darracott, C., & Hutslar, S. (1979). Pygmalion in youth sports: A field study. *Journal of Sport Psychology, 1*, 311–319.

Rosenthal, R., & Jacobson, L. (1968). *Pygmalion in the classroom: Teacher expectations and pupils' intellectual development.* New York: Holt, Rinehart & Winston.

Rudolph, K. D., Lambert, S. F., Clark, A. G., & Kurlakowsky, K. D. (2001). Negotiating the transition to middle school: The role of self-regulatory processes. *Child Development, 72*, 929–946.

Ryan, R. M., & Deci, E. L. (2000). Self-determination theory and the facilitation of intrinsic motivation, social development, and well-being. *American Psychologist, 55*, 68–78.

Ryan, R. M., & Deci, E. L. (2002). An overview of self-determination theory: An organismic-dialectical perspective. In E. L. Deci & R. M. Ryan (Eds.), *Handbook of self-determination research* (pp. 3–33). Rochester, NY: University of Rochester Press.

Schunk, D. (1984). Self-efficacy perspective on achievement behavior. *Educational Psychologist, 19*, 48–58.

Sinclair, D. A., & Vealey, R. S. (1989). Effects of coaches' expectations and feedback on the self-perceptions of athletes. *Journal of Sport Behavior, 12*, 77–91.

Skinner, E. A. (1996). A guide to constructs of control. *Journal of Personality and Social Psychology, 71*, 549–570.

Smith, R. E., Smoll, F. L., & Barnett, N. P. (1995). Reduction of children's sport anxiety through social support and stress-reduction training for coaches. *Journal of Applied Developmental Psychology, 16*, 125–142.

Smith, R. E., Smoll, F. L., & Curtis, B. (1979). Coach effectiveness training: A cognitive-behavioral approach to enhancing relationship skills in youth sport coaches. *Journal of Sport Psychology, 1*, 59–75.

Smoll, F. L., & Schutz, R. W. (1990). Quantifying gender differences in physical performance: A developmental perspective. *Developmental Psychology, 26,* 360–369.

Smoll, F. L., & Smith, R. E. (1989). Leadership behaviors in sport: A theoretical model and research paradigm. *Journal of Applied Social Psychology, 19,* 1522–1551.

Snyder, M. (1992). Motivational foundations of behavioral confirmation. In M. P. Zanna (Ed.), *Advances in experimental social psychology* (Vol. 25, pp. 67–114). San Diego, CA: Academic Press.

Solomon, G. B. (2001). Performance and personality impression cues as predictors of athletic performance: An extension of expectancy theory. *International Journal of Sport Psychology, 32,* 88–100.

Solomon, G. B., DiMarco, A. M., Ohlson, C. J., & Reece, S. D. (1998). Expectations and coaching experience: Is more better? *Journal of Sport Behavior, 21,* 444–455.

Solomon, G. B., Golden, A. J., Ciapponi, T. M., & Martin, A. D. (1998). Coach expectations and differential feedback: Perceptual flexibility revised. *Journal of Sport Behavior, 21,* 298–310.

Solomon, G. B., & Kosmitzki, C. (1996). Perceptual flexibility and differential feedback among intercollegiate basketball coaches. *Journal of Sport Behavior, 19,* 163–176.

Solomon, G. B., Striegel, D. A., Eliot, J. F., Heon, S. N., Maas, J. L., & Wayda, V. K. (1996). The self-fulfilling prophecy in college basketball: Implications for effective coaching. *Journal of Applied Sport Psychology, 8,* 44–59.

Solomon, G. B., Wiegardt, P. A., Yusuf, F. R., Kosmitzki, C., Williams, J., Stevens, C. E., & Wayda, V. K. (1996). Expectancies and ethnicity: The self-fulfilling prophecy in college basketball. *Journal of Sport and Exercise Psychology, 18,* 83–88.

Steele, C. M. (1997). A threat in the air. How stereotypes shape intellectual identity and performance. *American Psychologist, 52,* 613–629.

Steele, C. M., & Aronson, J. (1995). Stereotype threat and the intellectual test performance of African-Americans. *Journal of Personality and Social Psychology, 69,* 797–784.

Thomas, J. R., & French, K. E. (1985). Gender differences across age in motor performance: A meta-analysis. *Psychological Bulletin, 98,* 260–282.

Thomas, K. T., Gallagher, J. D., & Thomas, J. R. (2001). Motor development and skill acquisition during childhood and adolescence. In R. N. Singer, H. A. Hausenblas, & C. M. Janelle, *Handbook of sport psychology* (2nd ed.). New York: John Wiley & Sons.

Thorndike, R. (1968). Review of Pygmalion in the classroom. *American Educational Research Journal, 5,* 708–711.

Treasure, D. C., & Roberts, G. C. (1995). Applications of achievement goal theory to physical education: Implications for enhancing motivation. *Quest, 47,* 475–489.

Trouilloud, D. O., Sarrazin, P. G., Martinek, T. J., & Guillet, E. (2002). The influence of teacher expectations on student achievement in physical education classes: Pygmalion revisited. *European Journal of Sport Psychology, 32,* 591–607.

Valeski, T. N., & Stipek, D. J. (2001). Young children's feelings about school. *Child Development, 72,* 1198–1213.

Vallerand, R. J. (2001). A hierarchical model of intrinsic and extrinsic motivation in sport and exercise. In G. C. Roberts (Ed.), *Advances in motivation in sport and exercise* (pp. 263–320). Champaign, IL: Human Kinetics.

Vallerand, R. J., & Losier, G. F. (1999). An integrative analysis of intrinsic and extrinsic motivation in sport. *Journal of Applied Sport Psychology, 11,* 142–169.

Weiner, B. (1992). *Human motivation: Metaphors, theories, and research.* Newbury Park, CA: Sage.

Weinstein, R. (1976). Reading group membership in first grade: Teacher behaviors and pupil experience over time. *Journal of Educational Psychology, 68,* 103–116.

Weiss, M. R., & Ebbeck, V. (1996). Self-esteem and perceptions of competence in youth sport: Theory, research, and enhancement strategies. In O. Bar-Or (Ed.), *The encyclopaedia of sports medicine: Vol. VI. The child and adolescent athlete* (pp. 364–382). Oxford: Blackwell Science Ltd.

Williams, J. M., Jerome, G. J., Kenow, L. J., Rogers, T., Sartain, T. A., & Darland, G. (2003). Factor structure of the Coaching Behavior Questionnaire and its relationship to athlete variables. *The Sport Psychologist, 17,* 16–34.

Leadership Effectiveness

Mimi C. Murray, *Springfield College*
Betty L. Mann, *Springfield College*

. . . one does not lead by hitting people over the head—that's assault, not leadership.
—President Dwight D. Eisenhower

Having great leadership is a big key to success. Our team will go as far as our leaders are willing to take us.
—Mike Candrea, University of Arizona softball coach

In every great group, "there is one person who acts as maestro, organizing the genius of the others. He or she is a pragmatist dreamer, a person with an original but attainable vision. Ironically, the leader is able to realize his or her dream only if the others are free to do exceptional work . . . like [a] great conductor, [the leader] may not be able to play Mozart's First Violin Concerto, but he or she has a profound understanding of the work and can create the environment to realize it" (Bennis & Biederman, 1997, pp. 199–200). "Leadership is vision," says Peter Drucker. Or, as expressed in Proverbs 29:18, "Where there is no vision, the people perish" (Senge et al., 1999).

Leaders are those who significantly influence the thoughts, behaviors, and feelings of others (Gardner, 1995). Harry Truman suggested, "A leader is a person who has the ability to get other people to do what they don't want to do and like it." The process by which one influences and inspires others is leadership.

Social scientists and behavioral psychologists have studied leadership for many decades. With more than 350 definitions of leadership and thousands of empirical investigations of leaders (Bennis & Nanus, 1985), there still appears to be no universally accepted definition of leadership, nor is there clear understanding of what distinguishes successful leaders from less successful leaders or what distinguishes leaders from followers. Burns (1978), author of *Leadership,* a Pulitzer prize–winning book, observes that leadership is one of the least understood phenomena on earth. Yet the search for qualities that lead to effective leadership is a quest that continues to occupy the attention of numerous investigators. Unfortunately, despite the varied interpretations and still incomplete analysis of leadership, there is a paucity of research and conceptual literature about leadership in sport situations.

When people are asked, "Who is a leader?" successful coaches such as Lombardi, Bryant,

Stagg, Torre, Shanahan, Holtz, Landry, Stengel, Durocher, Lasorda, Auerbach, Hixon, Vanderveer, Stringer, Wooden, Head-Summitt, Thompson, and Robinson are frequently included in their lists. Because coaches are leaders, coaching effectiveness can be maximized through understanding the concepts of leadership. Sport psychology consultants also serve in a leadership capacity, although from a different perspective than that of coaches. Thus, although this chapter is often written in the lexicon of the coach and may initially appear to be aimed exclusively at coaches, this is not the case. Knowledge of the basic principles of leadership presented in this chapter will help individuals in sport psychology deal more effectively with athletes; it will also help them to more fully understand effective coach–athlete communications, help coaches to become more effective leaders, as well as help coaches develop player leadership within a team. This chapter describes several approaches to leadership and relates these theoretical frameworks to dimensions of leadership behavior in sports.

What Is Leadership?

Leadership is the art and science of influencing others through credibility, capability, and commitment. Some authorities (Barrow, 1977; Stogdill, 1974) define leadership as the behavioral process of influencing the activities of an organized group toward specific goals and achievement of those goals. Others simply define leadership as the process whereby an individual influences others to do what he or she wants them to do. But leadership is often far more complex than the latter definition implies. Attempts to understand leadership should be concerned with *why* people comply as well as with how one person influences another.

Schein (1970) suggested that people comply because of a psychological contract. This hypothesis implies that individuals will do many things because they believe they should, and they expect reciprocation for what they do in the form of remuneration, perks, and privileges. Coaches and sport consultants need to be aware of the

rewards or reinforcements their athletes expect. The athlete who complies with the wishes or demands of the leader might expect to win, to be positively reinforced, to get to play, or to receive a higher status. In essence, the cost–benefit ratio needs to balance. Consequently, both the leader and the athlete strike a bargain, or a psychological contract, with each other and with the team. Whether or not an athlete complies may be somewhat dependent on how she or he views authority. Individuals have learned to respond to authority through their experiences with parents, teachers, coaches, and other authority figures. Indirectly, individuals also learn how to respond to authority through the modeling portrayed in books, magazines, TV, and the movies. *Legitimate power* is often granted to coaches and sport psychology consultants when athletes feel it is right for these people to tell them what to do. In a later section of this chapter, we will discuss ways leaders can increase their potential influence or power.

Leadership Theories and Implication

Researchers interested in leadership have attempted to identify personal qualities and behaviors that are most likely to result in leader effectiveness and to determine what influence, if any, specific situational factors have on these variables. It was hoped that such knowledge could be used in both the selection and training of individuals who are likely to become effective leaders. Much of the work defined by contemporary theorists who have investigated selected situational variables was founded on an integration of earlier theoretical assumptions regarding personality traits and behavioral dimensions thought to be relevant to leadership effectiveness. Over the past several decades, researchers have investigated trait, behavioral, situational, transformational, leader member exchange, and cognitive approaches to leadership theory. We will discuss each of these. We have only briefly described Smoll and Smith's (1989) model of leadership behavior in sport, which encompasses constructs from many of these theories. A detailed explanation of the model is presented and discussed in Chapter 21.

Trait Approach

Assessing personality characteristics and traits to determine whether effective leaders have similar qualities is the same approach as one that was initially directed at trying to understand why certain people are successful athletes. The findings of trait or factor theory studies as applied to athletes and coaches have left us without conclusive results or information. No readily identifiable personality traits are related to leadership status or leadership effectiveness in *all* situations. A more viable explanation for effective leadership is that leadership qualities are situationally specific. Furthermore, characteristics related to leadership do not operate separately but in combination.

If we could begin to address significant qualities or traits as **dispositional,** we might gain more valuable insights. Dispositional means that behavior associated with a given trait can vary from situation to situation, but individuals keep the same relative position regardless of the situation; that is, the most assertive individual will respond with the highest level of assertiveness. Research on traits associated with successful business executives indicates that these individuals are dominant, self-confident, assertive, high in levels of aspiration, and generally successful throughout life (Dunette, 1965). In 1971 Ghiselli found the following traits or dispositions related to leadership success as determined by upward mobility and rated job success: self-perceived intelligence, initiative, supervisory ability, and self-assurance. For more information on traits associated with successful leaders, refer to Stogdill (1974) for an excellent review.

The work of Hendry (1972, 1974) established the stereotypical coach/physical educator as someone who needs to be in control and is inflexible, domineering, and emotionally inhibited. Sage (1975) did not concur with these findings, which seemingly indicate that coaches are highly authoritarian, dogmatic, and manipulative. Sage's reservations were based on the small number of samples and the sampling techniques employed. Even if this stereotype is incorrect, these dispositions may be necessary for successful leadership under many situations found in sport, such as stressful game situations. For example, during a 30-second time-out the coach should be informing the athletes of the strategies to use when the game resumes. This is obviously not the time for participatory or democratic decision making. Furthermore, authoritarianism in coaches may be only part of their sport personalities and is not necessarily present or apparent in other situations in their lives.

The authoritarian personality profile merits further explanation and understanding because it is a typical description of sport leadership—whether a false one or not. Authoritarians generally avoid unstructured situations because such situations are perceived as threatening. The inability to cope with ambiguous situations may result from the authoritarian's continuing use of old responses for new stimulus conditions, even when these responses provide less than satisfactory results. Such inability could help explain the "this is the way I was coached; it was good enough for me, and it is good enough for them" syndrome often found in coaching. Unfortunately, the practices of many coaches are frequently at odds with the most current sport knowledge in motor learning, sport psychology, exercise physiology, and biomechanics. Is it because many coaches cannot cope with change? This attitude may also explain why so many coaches can be threatened by insignificant social change such as longer hairstyles for men a few years ago and, more currently, male athletes wearing an earring. Those male authoritarians who are most threatened by social changes probably define their masculinity in and through sport. Thus, anything perceived as deviating from their masculine image, based on their older, unchanged social values, might be difficult for them to understand.

Higher need for social approval, impulsiveness in decision making, and greater frequency in making errors have been noted as authoritarian traits (Podd, 1972). Some examples of typical authoritarian behaviors are to harass referees, humiliate players, and throw clipboards and chairs during a game. Can these aggressive behaviors be ethically justified, and do they provide an appropriate leadership role model?

According to Triandis (1971), authoritarians typically avoid introspection, approve of severe punishment, and tend to hold strong prejudices. Could this help explain why sport in some situations is still sexist and racist and is sometimes filled with physical and psychological abuses of athletes by both male and female coaches? A study of authoritarianism and associated attitudes sheds some light on the behavior of some male coaches and athletic directors toward females in sport. Males who were more concerned with winning at the expense of fair play/sportsmanship and who also were the highest in authoritarianism had negative attitudes about women, admired the traditional male roles, and were opposed to equality (Maier & Laurakis, 1981). An example of this type of behavior comes from remarks of Bobby Knight, Indiana basketball coach: "I don't like people very well because most of them lack intestinal fortitude or they lack integrity. Women in particular bother me. I don't like women at all. I can't bear all the small talk and social amenities that women put you through." When asked what he said during an animated chat with a player, Knight responded, "I told him to take a picture of his testicles so he'd have something to remember them by if he ever took another shot like the last one. For you ladies, that's t-e-s-t-i-c-l-e-s." Former President Dwight D. Eisenhower suggested, "One does not lead by hitting people over the head—that's assault, not leadership" (Safire & Safir, 2000, p. 29). We know John Wooden didn't use verbal or physical abuse to intimidate his players. This great coach was a teacher not only of the game but of life's important lessons.

Interestingly, Hendry (1972) found the personality profiles of successful athletes and coaches to be alike. Further, the profiles of coaches evidenced high levels of enthusiasm, need to achieve, and energy (Andrud, 1970; Gagen, 1971). In summary, the factor/trait approach to examining leadership has attempted to determine whether there is a universal personality for leadership success. This approach is also called the great person (man) theory of leadership. Irrefutably, character, morality/ethics, and conceptual skills

matter (Senge et al., 1999). There are some commonalities found in the literature that describe leaders as being bright, confident, extroverted, and even tall, but the overall results of research on leadership personality characteristics and traits have been quite equivocal. This approach isolates and focuses on hero-leaders. Ironically, "our contemporary views of leadership are entwined with our notions of heroism, so much so that the distinction between "leader" and "hero" (or celebrity, for that matter) often becomes blurred. In our society leadership is too often seen as an inherently individual phenomenon (Bennis & Biederman, 1997, p. 1). Nor does this approach explain differences in leadership style. Therefore, researchers directed their efforts toward examining characteristic behaviors of effective leaders rather than assessing distinguishing personality traits.

Behavioral Theories

More recent research on leadership theory has focused on actual leadership behaviors, or how a leader leads rather than what a leader is. This approach examines the behavior of leaders and their group effectiveness, or the productivity and satisfaction of group members.

Researchers on behavioral theories have investigated the influence different leaders allow others in decision making. From such research a classification system was developed by which leaders were described as autocratic, or dictatorial; participative, or democratic; or laissez-faire, or free rein. Little attention will be given here to leadership types because they are covered in Chapter 7.

The concern with leadership behaviors first emerged in business management areas, as did the factor/trait approach to studying leadership. The majority of early studies (1940s and 1950s) were conducted by researchers at The Ohio State University (Halpin, 1957; Halpin & Winer, 1957). From these studies, two leader behavior characteristics related to group effectiveness emerged. The first was consideration, and the second was initiating structure. **Consideration** reflects job relationships in which there is mutual trust, respect for the ideas of others, and attention to others' feelings.

Leaders who scored high in consideration had good rapport and communication with others. **Initiating structure** refers to how leaders define and structure their roles for goal attainment. Leaders who scored high in initiating structure were active in directing group activities, communicating, scheduling, and experimenting with new ideas. According to the Ohio State Studies, successful leaders score high on both consideration and initiating structure.

After World War II, some interesting studies on organizational effectiveness were conducted at the University of Michigan. The Michigan studies described a leader as being either production centered (high in initiating structure) or employee centered (high in consideration structure) (Stogdill, 1974), but not both. These classifications are self-evident. Later studies have revealed that leaders *can* be both employee centered and production centered, and the most effective leaders tend to score high on both behaviors.

When these various behavioral theories were applied to sport, it was found that the behaviors of coaches most desired by athletes were training for competitiveness, providing social support, and being rewarding (Chelladurai & Saleh, 1978). In another study, Hoffman (2003) gleaned that the important perceived behaviors that athletes most often reported were work ethic, knowledge, and preparation. In a study of leadership and competitive rowers, Neil and Kirby (1985) found that less skilled and younger rowers preferred coaches who demonstrated person-oriented behaviors. Weiss and Friedrichs (1986) found that coaches of losing basketball teams were high on social support. Therefore, we cannot assume that social support only leads to success. When coaches are more encouraging and give instruction, whether winning or losing, their athletes had higher levels of competence (self-efficacy) in their own abilities, thought of themselves as successful, and gave more effort (Black & Weiss, 1992). Interestingly, Feltz, Chase, Moritz, and Sullivan (1999) found that more confident coaches used praise and encouragement more than less confident coaches. Furthermore Sullivan and Kent (2003) suggested that motivation and teaching technique are

important components of coaching efficacy. Coaching efficacy was defined as the "extent to which coaches believe they have the capacity to affect learning and performance of their athletes" (Feltz et al., 1999, p. 765). Massimo (1973) asked a large number of gymnasts what behaviors they desired most in a coach and found desired behaviors were ordered in importance from "use minimal verbiage," "have a sense of humor," "use individual psychology," and "have technical competency" to "appreciate the sociology of the team." We will use Massimo's statements and expand on them. Although the desirable leadership behaviors were initially identified for coaches and are expanded in coaching terminology, most of the behaviors are probably equally viable for sport psychology consultants and their interactions with athletes.

1. *Use minimal verbiage.* Too many people overcoach/overteach. An example of how to correct this is to select only one correction for a group or an athlete to work on in each skill or effort. Once these corrections are selected, *briefly* verbalize the key analysis points for each correction and perhaps physically demonstrate the correct movements. Then put the athletes in an appropriate drill to practice the correct response.

2. *Have a sense of humor.* Although this behavior is desirable, one must be careful not to overuse humor. Sarcasm is not a desirable form of humor. Humor involves laughing at oneself and with others, not at another.

3. *Use individual psychology.* This implies dealing with each team member as an individual. Some athletes need considerable coaching and attention, and others can almost coach themselves. Fairness matters greatly to athletes, but there is no way a coach can appear to be completely fair. Some athletes will get more of the coach's attention on a given day than will others. Perhaps if the team understands why the coach is giving more time to a certain athlete, other members will be more understanding. This involves good communication skills. All athletes have different needs, and coaches should attempt to determine those needs and, within their own philosophy, provide for them.

4. *Have technical competency.* Anyone who is willing to learn and cares enough to take the time to understand correct movement mechanics, strategies, and fundamental principles of exercise physiology, motor learning, and psychology can effectively coach most sports. A person can acquire knowledge of a particular sport and factors influencing the learning process. This knowledge should not be equated with personal skill in performing. One can be a very effective coach and not be able personally to perform well, just as one can be an outstanding athlete and not have the technical competencies and personal skills to be an effective coach.

5. *Appreciate the sociology of the team.* The coach must deal not only with the individuals on the team but also with how those individuals interact. The coach should not blow minor animosities between team members out of perspective; but if animosities go too far, then the coach should end them, diplomatically and emphatically.

Although there has been support for behavioral theories, there are sufficient inconsistencies in the literature to suggest that leadership is far more complex than to be relegated to explanations based on traits or behaviors alone. It appears that both situational and individual factors, and the interactions of these factors, determine who will emerge as a successful leader. "Nobody is more powerful than a passionate leader, particularly in terms of his or her impact on others" (Senge et al., 1999, p. 108).

Situational Theories

Some situational factors that are important to leadership success are the characteristics of subordinates, the organizational situation, and the demands of the specific situation. Of particular interest to those of us in sport are the interactions of coaches and sport consultants (leaders) with athletes (subordinates) in a specific situation. Fiedler (1967) in his contingency model argues that leadership behavior, or leader–member relations, the task structure, and the leader's position relative to authority and power interact to affect group performance and satisfaction. Fiedler believes a leader's style results from the leader's own needs and personality. He also suggests that leadership style is a stable personality characteristic that is well established. According to Fiedler, the two categories of leadership behavior are people centered or task centered. If leadership style is not flexible and the organization is not productive, he proposed that the organizational structure should be changed or the leader replaced. If one accepts this theory, then leadership style is generalizable regardless of the situation. Accordingly, leadership can be improved in a given situation in two ways. The first is to change the leader's personality—not an easy task even if the leader wishes to change. The second is to change the situation, including the organizational structure, so that it is more compatible with the leader's personality. Personalities and situations should be matched and congruent for maximum leadership effectiveness. The studies in sport using Fiedler's contingency approach have proved interesting. Danielson (1976) found that the most effective coaching in ice hockey was person-oriented rather than task-oriented. In a study involving volleyball, Bird (1977) found that winning women's volleyball coaches in the more skilled Division I programs were person-oriented. The results were the opposite in less skillful Division II programs.

The application of Fiedler's model to sport might imply that a coach who is successful in one situation may not be so in another—for example, Perkins for Bryant. Ray Perkins had been a fairly successful professional football coach with the New York Giants; upon Bear Bryant's retirement at Alabama, Perkins took the helm and had a few fairly unsuccessful seasons. Conversely, there are examples of successful coaches in sport who have traveled from one team to another with success following each move. Pat Riley left a great Lakers team to lead the Knicks, with much improvement and success, then to coaching the Miami Heat. Is the difference because the situations for Riley are similar, moving from one professional basketball team to another, whereas Perkins moved from a professional to a collegiate team? What about Calipari, and Pitino who went from head coach of successful collegiate teams to head coach of professional teams. The leader should invent a leadership style that is compatible with the group (Bennis & Biederman, 1997, p. 199). Can Fiedler's model help explain this?

Fiedler's (1967) contingency theory posits that leaders' personality and leadership style are relatively inflexible. Thus, leadership can be most effective when situations are favorable and compatible. In other situation-specific theories the focus is on the situationally specific *behaviors* of leaders and how these behaviors affect followers. These other situation-specific theories to be briefly mentioned here are the life-cycle and path-goal theories.

Hersey and Blanchard (1969, 1977, 1982) proposed that effective leaders can and should adjust their leadership style to respond to the **life-cycle** needs of their followers and to the environment. Hersey and Blanchard (1982) suggested that an appropriate leadership style for a specific situation is determined by the maturity of the followers. Thus, the emphasis is on the subordinate and not the leader. Maturity is defined as "the ability and willingness of people to take responsibility for directing their own behavior" (Hersey & Blanchard, 1982, p. 151). The behavior of the leader in relation to the followers is then based on three variables: (1) the amount of guidance and direction a leader gives, or initiating behavior; (2) the amount of socioemotional support a leader gives, or consideration behavior; and (3) the maturity level of the followers as they perform a task. Case (1984) illustrates the importance of adapting leadership style to the needs of the followers within a particular situation by asking us to consider differences in leadership style that would be appropriate when coaching 9-year-old soccer players as compared to Division I collegiate soccer players. The experience, maturity, and skill level of the players may influence the leadership styles that would be most effective within the specific environment.

In the **path-goal theory** the leader is viewed as a facilitator who helps others achieve their goals (House, 1971). As the term implies, the leader provides a path by which the followers can reach their goals. The specific characteristics of each situation should determine the leader behaviors that should most successfully aid the follower. A swim coach who determines that her athlete wants to decrease her time in her event so she can qualify for a regional championship would provide the appropriate and specific conditioning and training program so that her swimmer could qualify for regionals. The coach would be operationalizing the path-goal theory of leadership by focusing on her athlete's goal. Furthermore, by utilizing this theory one could predict that each athlete might prefer specific behaviors from his or her coach. Neither of these situation-specific theories, life-cycle or path-goal, has been applied to any great extent in sport. The results of the few studies that have done so are contradictory and inconclusive (Carron, 1984; Chelladurai & Carron, 1978; Chelladurai & Saleh, 1978; Von Strache, 1979).

In 1973 Vroom and Yetton developed the normative model of decision making for sport settings. Other researchers have examined the interactions of various decision-making models (Chelladurai, Haggerty, & Baxter, 1989; Chelladurai & Quek, 1995). The potential for the application of these approaches to a better understanding of sport leadership is vast.

There appear to be no direct and simple answers to questions such as "Is group effectiveness caused by how a leader behaves, or does the leader behave in a certain way because of the group's performance?" It would be extremely difficult and unwise to assume any cause–effect relationships on the basis of the limited and somewhat contradictory research evidence available. Flexibility, which can be very disturbing for many authoritarians, would appear to be an ideal approach to coaching because of the situational nature of the varying sport milieu. Chelladurai reaches a similar conclusion in Chapter 7 when he discusses leadership style and decision making.

Transformational Leadership

Since the 1980s, transformational leadership paradigms have become the focus of the study of leadership. In *The Next American Frontier* (1983) author Robert Reich's major emphasis is that traditional management in the United States is the greatest threat to American prosperity. Reich views

Table 6-1 **What Do Workers Want from Their Jobs?**

	Supervisors	Workers
Good working conditions	4	9
Feeling "in" on things	10	2
Tactful discipline	7	10
Full appreciation for work done	8	1
Management loyalty to workers	6	8
Good wages	1	5
Promotion and growth with company	3	7
Sympathetic understanding of personal problems	9	3
Job security	2	4
Interesting work	5	6

Factors were rated from 1 to 10, with 1 being the highest priority.

traditional management as being bureaucratic, top-heavy, and authoritarian and very much in contrast to the new, flexible, adaptive, organic management systems in which the worker is viewed as a vital resource.

John Naisbitt (1984) believes, if people are to be affected by decisions, they should be part of the decision-making process. Workers, increasingly, are struggling for this recognition. Table 6-1 presents the results of a study conducted in 1948 that asked workers and supervisors to rank in order of importance what workers want from their jobs. Interestingly, this study has been replicated several times over the past 50 years, and the results have been similar. Workers continue to seek appreciation for work done, want to be "in" on things, and seek promotion and growth, whereas supervisors perceive that workers are more interested in and motivated by wages and job security.

More recent interpretations of effective leadership reflect the needs of workers. We learn from Bennis and Nanus (1985), for example, that three major contexts shape a more responsive work environment: commitment, complexity, and credibility. These concepts refer to the nature of the work ethic, the dynamic changes of knowledge age society, and the need to be fair and trustworthy. Through their research, Bennis and

Nanus discovered four strategies or themes that seemed to be common among competent leaders. They titled the first strategy "attention through vision." In a speech at Smith College in 1995 Jane Blalock, former Ladies Professional Golf Association superstar and currently a successful businesswoman, stated "you must dream in order to make things happen . . . keep striving but keep focused and your thoughts and dreams will become reality." A second strategy, according to Bennis and Nanus, is "meaning through communication." The competent leader has a vision, an intense focus on outcome and results, a realistic strategy to carry out the vision, and the ability to communicate the vision and rally the support of others.

The term *vision* is used more and more frequently in the business literature. The authors of *Lessons in Leadership* (Lund & Finch, 1987) write that successful leaders must possess a vision. There are four factors inherent in vision, including what was, what is, what can be, and what should or shouldn't be. Applying the first factor to sport, "what was" deals with understanding the history and traditions of the sport team, previous coaches, academic discipline, and institution. The future should be based on the social foundation of the past. The harvest for the future begins with the seeds of the past. "What is" has to do with the present and includes knowledge of the organization/institution, the players, other coaches, consultants, administrators, policies, regulations, and goals. Having a vision or sense of the potential is the "what can be"; it is the leader's dream for the future. Gardner (1995) emphasizes the importance of this factor in his development of the cognitive framework for leadership. What vision does the president, coach, or consultant have for the organization, team, or athletes? The "what should or shouldn't be" is an exposition on values: what is right or wrong, what is ethical, and what is not. For too long many leaders in sport have neglected this part of the vision and focused only on "win at any cost." We know this costs much too much in terms of the positive growth and development of athletes. Once appropriate values regarding the vision are determined, they should be reflected in the establishment of the priorities by which the vision/dream becomes reality.

A third theme that emerged from Bennis and Nanus's research is "trust through positioning." This reflects the undeniable importance of trust and accountability. "Trust is the glue that maintains organizational integrity" (Bennis & Nanus, 1985, p. 44). The final strategy is the "deployment of self through positive self-regard." The competent leader realizes his or her sense of worth and creates in others a sense of confidence and high but reasonable expectations. In other words, leaders have a vision for the future that they can communicate; they are trustworthy; and they exhibit respect for others and self. Furthermore, these powerful people accomplish much with tact and diplomacy. With their power, competence, and confidence, they empower others. Leaders need to be secure enough to believe in and surround themselves with talented people "with rare gifts and [work] together as equals" (Bennis & Biederman, 1997, p. 199).

DePree (1987) commented that the "signs of outstanding leadership appear primarily among the followers. Are the followers reaching their potential? Are they learning? Do they achieve required results?" (p. 10). As previously described, researchers have attempted to identify situation variables that best explain and predict

an effective, productive leader–follower relationship. House (1971) suggests that the personal characteristics of subordinates and task or job demands help determine the most appropriate leadership style. For example, a player with an internal locus of control who believes she is in control of her successes and her failures may perform better with the direction of a leader characterized as relationship-oriented. The individual with an external locus of control may be more compatible with a task-oriented coach. Hersey and Blanchard (1982) would suggest that coaches need to change their leader style (initiation or consideration) according to the maturity level of the followers to enhance satisfactory performance and satisfaction of the followers.

Another variable that has been studied by theorists for years (House, 1976; Weber, 1968) but is recently receiving increased attention is charisma. A study of transformational leadership, or charismatic leadership, may offer more insight into the question "What leader characteristics best facilitate the efforts and satisfaction of the worker?" Komives (1991) reminds us that research on charismatic leadership paralleled the fate of trait theories in the 1920s and 1930s. With renewed interest in the last 20 years, however, there is some agreement among researchers that transformational, or charismatic, leaders are those who inspire others to work to achieve a shared vision.

Seltzer and Bass (1990) looked beyond the two behavioral dimensions of leadership, initiation, and consideration, and found support for considering transformational leadership characteristics as important to a better understanding of leadership. They defined transformational leadership as superior leadership performance that is "seen when leaders broaden and elevate the interests of their followers, when they generate awareness and acceptance among their followers of the purposes and mission of the group, and when they move their followers to transcend their own self-interests for the good of the group" (pp. 693–694). According to Bennis and Biederman (1997), "the standard models, especially the command-and-control style, simply won't work. [Leaders] have to act decisively, but never arbitrarily. They have to make decisions without limiting the perceived autonomy of the other participants. Devising and maintaining an atmosphere in which others can put a dent in the universe is the leader's creative act" (p. 199). To illustrate the essence of a transformational leader, the following quotation is presented from a letter written to Laurence L. Doggett, President of Springfield College, 1896–1936, from a professor who was in his 25th year of "service with the college." To President Doggett, the professor wrote: "It is a great thing . . . to play in a team whose captain has the power to keep the players in the spirit of the game and arouse latent capacity and energy. To be able to unlock the hidden sources of power is the supreme gift of leadership. Our captain has it and our appreciation of it grows with the years" (Hall, 1964, p. 76).

The influence of the leader on his or her associates or followers is critical to understanding the distinction between transformational theory and previous theories that have been described by some as transactional theories (Bass & Avolio, 1995; Burns, 1978). Transactional theories, according to Bass and Avolio (1995), may be more closely associated with management than leadership. Doherty and Danylchuk (1996) further explained that transactional leadership involves a leader–worker "exchange relationship in which rewards are provided, or punishment is withheld, in return for performance" (p. 295). Transformational leaders, by contrast, influence others by their ability to inspire, to empower, and to intellectually stimulate others to achieve beyond expectations toward the fulfillment of higher order needs (Bass & Avolio, 1995).

Based on research conducted by House (1976), charismatic or transformational leaders have high expectations of their associates, possess high levels of referent power, and are viewed as being credible, trustworthy, confident, and competent. Kotter (1990) suggested that a "big challenge to leaders is to get people to believe the message," keeping in mind that a good track record, integrity, and consistency between words and actions are important contributors to the credibility factor. In contrast to the transformational leader, consider the impatient, reactive CEO who has a viable message and vision but is unable to communicate that vision and is unable to foster supportive, meaningful relationships with those who surround him or her. Perhaps those who are encumbered by feelings of self-importance, arrogance of power, or stress and bottom-line issues tend to isolate others and themselves (Grant, 1996).

Weese (1995), Weese and Bourner (1995), and Prujin and Boucher (1995) have examined transformational and transactional leadership in the sport setting. Doherty and Danylchuk (1996), utilizing the transformational/transactional model (Bass, 1985) of leadership, examined interuniversity athletic administrators. The results of the study present a profile of predominantly transformational as opposed to transactional or nonleadership behavior. Leader-centered behavior was used more often than subordinate-centered behavior by the participants. Satisfaction of coaches with their respective administrators was positively associated with transformational leadership and contingent reward behavior. Negative relationships were found for management-by-exception, passive, and nonleader behavior.

According to Komives (1991), both men and women are capable of scoring high as transformational leaders. Rosener (1990) found that women managers tended to view their leadership style as transformational, particularly those with managerial responsibilities in medium-size, nontraditional organizations. Rosener also found that women were more likely to be described as charismatic leaders. These findings further support the notion that the traditional male-oriented command and control style of managing may not be advantageous or the most suitable in all situations. Rosener supports the value of an interactive leader style utilizing referent power rather than formal authority within an environment in which participation is encouraged and power is shared, but she also recognizes the value in diversity of styles.

Leader–Member Exchange Theory

In 1975, Graen and Cashman proposed the leader–member exchange theory, which was originally referred to as the vertical dyad linkage.

This approach to leadership is from the role theory perspective. Role development between leader and subordinates is a result of the role exchanges within an organization. Because of time restraints and various pressures, within this approach leaders develop close relationships with only a very limited number of key subordinates. These subordinates are termed the "in group." Leader relationships and exchanges with the other members of the group, who are considered the "out group," are far more limited.

Members of the in group are likely to enjoy open communication with the leader, greater influence in decision making, support for their respective actions, consideration, and demonstrated confidence in them. The reciprocity from the member to the leader can be noted in the greater availability and commitment to success of the group. Dienesch and Linden (1986) proposed that in-group members might become advisors or assistants to the leader. Members of the out group have less influence and are required to comply with the leader's directions and role expectations. If out-group members comply, they receive the standard benefits (what everyone else receives). Once role expectations are established, they are unlikely to change and will remain stable. Compatibility, competence, and dependability are determinants for membership in the in group (Graen & Cashman, 1975).

The leader–member exchange model (LMX) differs from other leadership theories in its emphasis on the development processes between the leader and the subordinates, which influence member satisfaction (Graen, Novak, & Sommerkamp, 1982; Scandura, Graen, & Novak, 1986). LMX is assessed by the Leader–Member Exchange Scale (Graen & Cashman, 1975). Although the LMX has great potential for application in the sport milieu, it has been utilized infrequently. Case (1998) examined starters as members of the in group and nonstarters as the out group in a summer basketball camp. The researcher concluded that LMX has potential for adding to our insight regarding leadership in sport. Traditionally, we have assumed that leadership for members on teams is consistent and standard. The results of the study contradicted

that assumption. In-group members, or starters, had higher performance levels, scoring significantly higher on the LMX Scale (Graen & Cashman, 1975) than the out-group nonstarters. Consequently, coaches should be aware of the differences in exchanges between in and out groups and adjust the exchanges for the out group so that their performances may also be enhanced. Case (1998) further suggested that a multidimensional approach to leadership in sport be embraced through the application not only of the trait, behavioral, situational, and transformational approaches but through the role development approach (LMX) as well.

Cognitive Framework

Howard Gardner (1995), in his book *Leading Minds: An Anatomy of Leadership,* provides a highly original framework of leadership that includes an examination of the minds of leaders and their followers. This innovative approach contains traditional ideas of how to judge great leaders, such as in the great person theory; however, the mind of the leader, not the personality, is considered. This cognitive approach to the thinking of great leaders and how their ideas developed is the antithesis of the behavioral approach, which focuses only on leaders' actions. Gardner emphasizes that the nature and processes of leadership can be understood by examining the minds of leaders and their followers.

As an approach to discerning effective leadership, the needs and demands of the audience or followers as well as the nature of the times are essential factors. For example, Lou Holtz, Notre Dame Head Football Coach from 1986 to 1996 with a 100–30–2 record, observed that "the difference between athletes now and 25 years ago is that today everybody wants to talk about his [her] rights and privileges, whereas 25 years ago people talked about their obligations and responsibilities." As leaders, we need to be cognizant of the characteristics of those growing up in the millennium age. Leadership can best be understood, then, with a cognitive, cultural, and contextual appreciation. According to Gardner, the previously described models of leadership have been unable to adequately explain the leadership phenomena, and he suggests that the missing link is a knowledge of the mental structures activated in the effective leader, which is called cognition.

In applying the cognitive framework, Gardner (1995) introduces six constants of leadership: the story, the audience, the organization, the embodiment, direct and indirect leadership, and the issue of expertise. Each constant explains leadership as a cognitive enterprise, which is a dynamic process between and within the minds of the leader and the followers.

The story. Great leaders achieve power through the stories they relate. In these stories the leader is able to put words and symbols to the longings and needs of others. This central story or message should become the leader's central mission and should address the sense of the individual as well as the group. Martin Luther King's story was built on religion and history and was well circulated, yet he was able to synthesize and present this message in a new and fresh way, a way by which many were able to hear, learn, and grow. His message was inclusionary. Other leaders have capitalized on exclusionary stories, for example, Hitler, by attempting to exclude all but white Aryans from his Nazi Germany, or the tribalism now rampant in the countries that once were Yugoslavia.

Gardner divides leaders into three types according to the stories they relate. The "ordinary leader" is one who relates a traditional story of his or her group as effectively as possible. An ordinary leader from politics is Gerald Ford; from sport, Vince Lombardi might be considered an ordinary leader in this sense, for his football strategy was based on a team steeped in sound fundamentals.

Gardner's "innovative leader" takes a latent story of his or her group and brings new attention as well as a new twist to it. Innovative leaders in politics would include Margaret Thatcher or Charles deGaulle; from sport, Bear Bryant from Alabama might be considered an innovative leader, for he was noted for his commitment to sound, thorough planning and preparation harking back to earlier days of football.

The rarest of leaders is the "visionary leader," one who creates a new story. The founders or those credited with founding the world's great religious traditions are visionary leaders—for example, Moses, Confucius, Jesus, Buddha, and Mohammed. To suggest that there are visionary sport leaders is not to suggest that sport is as significant as the religious movements named above, although Harry Edwards refers to sport as the "universal religion."

Two of the earlier "Muscular Christians" of Springfield College, Amos Alonzo Stagg and James Naismith, were visionary leaders in sport. Stagg, considered the Father of American Football, with his football inventions, including the T formation, unbalanced line, lateral, forward pass, placekick, numbers on jerseys, hip pads, flankers, and wingbacks, as well as his winning record, was a visionary leader in sport. So, too, was Naismith, for he invented the game of basketball. Both Naismith and Stagg are sport leaders from whom we could learn much. They were visionary leaders whose stories changed the sports world.

The audience. The relationship between the leader and the audience or the followers is an elusive, mysterious, complex, and very interactive one. The interaction occurs between the desires of the audience and the leader's story. It seems the leader's best chances for success rest in a steadfast concentration on the same core message, flexibility in presentation of the story, and the audience's openness to comprehending the message. What is it about Naismith's game of basketball that has been able to resonate with a truly international audience?

The organization. Although leaders can share their stories with eager and receptive audiences so that bonding occurs between the leader and audience, to endure, there is a need for an organizational or institutional basis. Certainly, the early visionary religious leaders embodied their stories, and their stories resonated with the resulting bonding with their followers. Would these stories or religions have endured without a strong religious institutionalization?

Would basketball still be played had it not been initially embraced by the YMCA leaders who graduated from Springfield College and spread the "word" of basketball throughout the world? A strong and viable institution or organization is essential for effective leadership. Could this also explain the popularity and success of intercollegiate sport, housed within U.S. colleges and universities and in large degree controlled by national organizations such as the National Collegiate Athletic Association (NCAA), National Association of Intercollegiate Athletics (NAIA), or National Junior College Athletic Association?

The embodiment.   The leader should in some way embody the story. If the leader's story and life are inconsistent or the leader appears hypocritical, the story becomes unconvincing. Consider the conduct of the leaders of Enron and Tyco. They were the antithesis of their stories.

Examples of sport leaders who are the embodiment of their stories are Amos Alonzo Stagg and John Thompson. Stagg, for instance, ran to and from practice every day until he was 95 years of age and participated in all of his teams' conditioning programs until his late 70s.

John Thompson of Georgetown University was a successful coach and a very powerful man. He knows what he wants and goes after it. He has done everything he asks of his players. He has triumphed over overwhelming obstacles and reached his potential through hard work, perseverance, and belief in himself. Evidently his mother inspired him with the following:

> You can do anything you think you can.
> It's all in the way you view it.
> It's all in the start you make, young man.
> You must feel that you are going to do it.
> (Shapiro, 1991, p. 99)

Thompson and his parents were told he couldn't make it in grade school, and in fifth grade he was asked to leave the Catholic school. A determined public school teacher realized Thompson had a vision problem that made it hard for him to read. With glasses, he caught up quickly and eventually earned a degree in economics from Providence College. He was raised in poverty by parents who demonstrated the ultimate of the committed work ethic. He, through his own work ethic, has

become a millionaire. Thompson taught his players to know their limits and to find inner strength through hard work as he guided them to winning seasons and winning lives. He was so dedicated to the importance of academics that 98% of his players graduate from college—the highest graduation rate in the NCAA. His dedication inspired his players. He is the embodiment of his story.

Direct and indirect leadership.   Leaders seem to exert their influence in either a "direct" or "indirect" way (Gardner, 1995). Winston Churchill is an example of a leader whose influence was direct, whereas Einstein (*Time* magazine's "Person of the Century"), through the ideas he developed and how his thoughts were presented in the form of a theory, is an example of an indirect leader. In sport, John Wooden of basketball fame is an example of a leader who has been influential in both the direct and indirect ways. His thoughts and influence on his players, other coaches, and administrators were direct; and his "pyramid of success," a formalized collection of life's principles, building blocks for both personal and professional achievement, will endure as an indirect approach to effective coaching and will continue to influence others indirectly in the future.

The issue of expertise.   Individuals who aspire to be effective leaders will be perceived as credible if their work is of a high quality. For those involved in direct leadership, as most coaches are, it is more difficult to retain technical expertise from direct knowledge due to the excessive demands of the position. Indirect leaders, in contrast, such as sport psychology consultants, can proceed on the basis of direct knowledge and, through their academic and professional activities, contribute to the body of direct knowledge.

There are coaches at certain levels of competition who can and do remain technically competent, but today those at the elite level will find it exceedingly difficult to remain technically competent in all of the areas or domains that can affect athlete performance. Hence, astute leaders will form a support team of knowledgeable people. Pam Hixon, head coach of the University of Massachusetts field hockey team and head coach of the 1996 U.S. Olympic team, formed what she termed a "team around the team" of experts in the areas of conditioning and strength training, sports medicine, athletic training, nutrition, and, of course, sport psychology. What a sage and productive approach. Some conservative coaches might find this approach threatening or perceive it as a coaching weakness. This is an approach of strength. Furthermore, in such situations, there is no doubt who the head coach is and where "the buck stops."

Leadership effectiveness may depend on a workable match between the leader's style and situational variables, and we may better understand the nature of leadership by examining the minds of leaders and followers. But Goleman (1998) is convinced that the common denominator among effective leaders is a high degree of emotional intelligence. The importance of cognitive ability and technical skills is well recognized; however, the ability to work effectively with others may be more closely linked to strong leadership performance. The five components of emotional intelligence are defined as follows (Goleman, 1998, p. 95):

Self-awareness is "the ability to recognize and understand your moods, emotions, and drives and their effect on others." A person who is highly self-aware has self-confidence and is willing to candidly and realistically assess his or her capabilities.

Self-regulation is "the ability to control or redirect disruptive impulses and moods . . . and the propensity to think before acting." Trustworthiness, integrity, and openness to change are hallmarks of a person who exhibits self-regulation.

Motivation is a passion to work for reasons that go beyond money or status and "a propensity to pursue goals with energy and persistence." The motivation component of emotional intelligence is associated with a strong drive to achieve, optimism, and organizational commitment.

Empathy is "the ability to understand the emotional makeup of other people . . . and skill in treating people according to

their emotional reactions." A person who exhibits empathy is likely to possess cross-cultural sensitivity and is able to build and retain talent.

Social skill is "proficiency in managing relationships and building networks . . . finding common ground and building rapport." Individuals with good social skills are persuasive and effective in leading change. Appropriate social skills are key ingredients of effective managerial and leader effectiveness.

Weinberg and McDermott (2002), in a study comparing sport and business leaders, found similarities in preferences for an interactional style emphasizing a democratic approach, if possible. The leaders suggested matching the leadership style to the situation.

By definition leaders work with and influence others. A successful leader realizes the importance of getting along with others, communicating his or her passion and vision to others, and doing so in a trusting, respectful, fair, and caring manner. Sport leaders have a responsibility to promote such behaviors by teaching, enforcing, advocating, and modeling ethical principles (Arizona Sport Summit Accord, 1999).

Women in Sport

The dearth of women in sport leadership positions is of grave concern to many who are committed to increasing sport opportunities for girls and women. The number of women officiating, coaching, and administrating sport programs for girls and women has significantly decreased since Title IX was enacted. This is a critical time, and in looking at the role of women in leadership, it may be time to reevaluate the qualities of leadership.

Researchers such as Acosta and Carpenter (2002), Hart, Hasbrook, and Mathes (1986), and Sisley and Capel (1986) have provided valuable information about the dramatic decrease in the number of women coaching females: a change from approximately 90% 25 years ago to 44% today. Acosta and Carpenter (2002) reported that of the 8,132 head coaching jobs of women's NCAA teams, 90.3% of the new coaching jobs in women's athletics since 2000 have been filled by males. We view this decline as more than unfortunate. Some investigators have attempted to explain the decrease in women coaching females (Eitzen & Pratt, 1989; George, 1989; Holmen & Parkhouse, 1981; Parkhouse & Williams, 1986). One explanation often presented is the "lack of qualified female coaches." The use of the term "qualified" is, of course, prejudicial. It is often assumed in sport that males, regardless of training or experience, are more qualified than females. Anderson and Gill (1983) found that hiring standards for male coaches of female teams were lower than for women or men coaching same-sex teams. Ironically, Eitzen and Pratt (1989) found that most female coaches have physical education backgrounds (which, we believe, is the ideal background from which to coach), whereas males coaching females were primarily from other areas in education. Acosta and Carpenter (2002) are convinced that discrimination in hiring practices continues and female coaches are recruited and paid differently than male coaches.

Other researchers have explored gender coaching preferences of athletes. These studies have tended to find a pro-male bias (George, 1989; Parkhouse & Williams, 1986; Weinberg, Reveles, & Jackson, 1984). We believe this bias is due to sport being perceived as a male domain and to female gender socialization, as well as to the patriarchal nature of sport. These factors tend to devalue women; hence, female athletes may also devalue women.

One possible framework for understanding this decline and pro-male bias in hiring coaches in sport can be found within Knoppers's (1987, 1989) application of Kanter's work on corporate organization in sport. Kanter believes the workplace shapes the worker, whereas much of the literature states the opposite.

Kanter is an internationally recognized expert on corporate entrepreneurship and organizational change. In her 1977 book *Men and Women of the Corporation,* she delineates the ways in which rigid job hierarchies can constrain employees. In particular she demonstrates that subtle and overt discrimination affects performance. She shows that the problems and failures of women in management often stem from powerlessness, and she calls on companies to abandon rigid pyramidal structures and to empower employees, especially women.

Knoppers's application of Kanter's theory to sport relies on the same structural determinants that Kanter identifies as present in the workplace: opportunity, power, and proportion of women. These factors are believed to determine work roles and may account for the decline in the number of female coaches. A few examples may help to illustrate this point.

First, to have opportunities is to have visible career ladders with the potential to experience more satisfaction than obstacles. What opportunities do neophyte women coaches perceive? Do they see opportunities for advancement to head coach or for administrative positions? The previously mentioned research on percentages of female coaches indicates that these opportunities are rapidly and dramatically declining. Second, to have power is to have access to resources and information. Are these available to women coaches? Although Susan Schafer, from the Department of Education in Colorado, has shown women in sport ways this access can be obtained, equal access to sport information in general remains an unrealized goal.

Third is the issue of proportion: The gender ratio for women in sport leadership positions is low. Through extrapolation, the percentage of full-time women coaches (at all ranks) would be about 25%. Coaching is male dominated, and the skewness is increasing. This is in sharp contrast to other professions such as law and medicine where the number of women is steadily increasing.

Knoppers (1987, 1989) also says that institutional factors figure in the low number of women coaches. An example of such an institutional factor is homophobia, which, according to Lenskji (1986), precludes some women from getting jobs in coaching. This irrational fear is based on the false assumption that there are more lesbians in sport than in other professions. Perhaps more damaging is the false assumption that lesbians, as coaches, are more likely to seduce their female athletes. Although no physical/sexual involvement is or can be condoned between an athlete and a coach, it is worthwhile to note from the literature in psychology that the percentages of males compared to females who become sexually involved with their subordinates are considerably greater (Diesenhouse, 1989; Pope, Keith-Speigel, & Tabachnick, 1986).

Occupation stereotypes that grow out of gender typing are major barriers to women seeking leadership positions in sport. The generally lower self-concepts that females hold, as compared to males, often result in self-limiting behaviors that are expressed in phrases such as "I can't" or "I wonder if I am qualified." Another part of gender typing is stereotyping by which women view their tasks as of lesser value than male tasks. This belief is often confounded in organizational systems such as sport, which is traditionally defined as a male domain; therefore, women are assigned roles, if at all, in middle management levels in sport. These assigned roles result in organizational discrimination.

This phenomenon of organizational discrimination is paralleled in corporate America, where there exists a "glass ceiling" or invisible barrier that blocks women and minorities from top management jobs, despite legislative support for equal jobs. Although there is rapid growth in the number of women and minorities entering the workforce, there is not a corresponding or proportional increase in these groups within senior vice president levels and above. Is there an explanation other than sociocultural conditions and discrimination? The glass ceiling initiative was created by the Department of Labor under the direction of former Secretary of Labor Elizabeth Dole to determine the nature and extent of job advancement and barriers and scrutinize hiring and promotional practices of U.S. businesses.

In sport, organizational discrimination is evidenced in fewer women coaching, officiating, and administering athletic programs. Only 17.9% of women's collegiate athletic programs are directed by females (Acosta & Carpenter, 2002). Discrimination is also shown by fewer

women in high positions within sport governance such as the national governing bodies, the USOC, the state high school federations, and the NCAA. Self-limiting behaviors and organizational discrimination are among the components of occupational gender typing.

It would be beneficial for today's women to bring to the workplace, and in particular the sport workplace, their own unique and valuable qualities. Carole Oglesby has argued for the feminization of sport so that sport can be transformed into a more humane environment for all without decreasing (in fact, increasing) the skill levels and the physical prowess of our athletes.

Women in leadership need to use their female strengths rather than totally adopting what is alien to them: the male role. Women have the ability to create, to care, and to encourage growth in the context of concern for others. Women in sport need to approach leadership with courage, tolerance, and humor while addressing personal and organizational gender typing. This can be accomplished by communication with women and men about the negative aspects of gender stereotypes for both.

In sport it would be refreshing to see decisions questioned and well thought out from an ethical vantage point. The business world is addressing an outdated "macho" management style's detrimental effects and suggesting it be replaced with the teamwork concept, which involves trust, cooperation, point-of-view communication, and an emphasis on strengths, not weaknesses. Is this not the humanization of business? Could sport not benefit from this approach as well? Both Joe Torre of the New York Yankees and Mike Shanahan of the Denver Broncos have had extremely successful coaching careers. They focus on their strengths rather than their weaknesses. Both possess very different coaching/management styles. Torre is known for his ability to deal with all kinds of personalities from the massive egos of some professional ball players to that of owner George Steinbrenner, communicate effectively, and make difficult decisions (Torre & Dreher, 1999), whereas Mike Shanahan has the ability to focus on many, many small details, thus taking care of things that might otherwise distract the players (Shanahan & Shafter, 2000).

We predict that the most effective leadership well into the 21st century will involve a "softer approach" in that the way we treat others makes a critical difference. Excellent coaches, administrators, and teachers have acted as such.

Richard Hagberg advises chief executives on the points of leadership. At his firm there is a compilation within a database on the characteristics of 511 CEOs. The research indicates that those who fail were still utilizing an outdated macho management style, and they tend to be impatient, impulsive, manipulative, dominating, self-important, and critical of others (Grant, 1996).

According to Hagberg, the three pillars of leadership are having a vision, managing implementation, and building relationships with subordinates. Companies and colleges have mission statements or applied strategic plans. It is important to stop revisiting the plan and implement what is there. Effective leaders do have plans as to how they will achieve their goals. As Yogi Berra said, "If you don't know where you are going you might end up someplace else."

This new management model is a product of the empowerment movement begun in the 1960s and a by-product of the women's movement. Readers will recognize many of the buzzwords for this new management model in the following principles:

- Delegate and nurture. The General Patton/ autocratic approach to leadership is out.

- Empower subordinates through democracy and consensus, remembering that consensus leads to synergy.

- Relate to all people in the institution/ organization. Hagberg's third pillar of leadership is to build a relationship with subordinates. Good leaders are demanding, but have a connection to their people/ athletes that builds a sense of loyalty.

- Encourage ownership. Having a stake in the job, company, team, or school is a valuable

incentive. Ownership is demonstrated when the leader goes the "extra mile."

- Pursue learning for all members, top down and bottom up, by going to conventions and conducting programs and seminars, for example.

- Build teamwork. CEOs in business tend to have a high need for autonomy and control, just as many coaches do. Often, the more they need to be in control, the weaker their communication skills become. They tend to forget the words of management guru W. Edwards Deming: "Listen, Learn, Help, Lead." Basically, let everyone talk and then decide.

- Have fun. The concept of fun was not in vogue in the 1980s and early 1990s. Today, those who laugh together profit together. Humor or laughter helps us think more clearly and boosts health and creativity.

How Leaders Can Increase Their Influence or Power

Power is the basis of followers complying with a leader's wishes. When a leader/coach is successful at influencing another person, he or she has demonstrated power. It has been said about Willie Shoemaker, considered one of racings finest jockeys, that he possessed the lightest touch on the reins; horses never knew he was there until they needed him. Power comes partly from being in a position of authority. Thousands of years ago, the Greek philosopher Seneca said, "He who has great power should use it lightly." The coach by virtue of her or his position has control and is perceived as more valid than other members of the team. Consequently, the coach can exert a great deal of influence of either a positive or negative nature on the behaviors of team members. To a lesser extent, the same can be said of a sport psychologist assigned to work with a team.

What specific measures can leaders take to ensure greater influence or power other than that granted by virtue of position? Paying attention to appearance, demonstrating self-confidence and expertise, appropriately allocating rewards and sanctions, and being an example to admire and emulate are all ways coaches and sport psychologists can increase their potential influence.

Appearance: First Impression

Visualize Tom Landry, the perennially successful coach of the Dallas Cowboys; or Eddie Robinson, one of the all-time top winning football coaches (with Stagg, Bryant, Paterno, and Bowden) of Grambling University; or Pat Riley of the Lakers, Knicks, and Miami Heat. What were your first impressions of these great coaches? They are always well groomed, dressed in a tie and jacket at games; appear to be fit; seemingly in complete control of themselves and their teams regardless of the circumstances or intensity of the situations. At the other extreme, what are your impressions of a coach who never changes from a practice warm-up jacket and shirt, is overweight and out of shape or smokes on the sidelines, shouts obscenities at athletes and officials, and appears to be gearing up for a volcanic explosion in tense and close situations?

Pat Head-Summitt, women's basketball coach at the University of Tennessee, National Championship coach, and prior U.S. Olympic coach; Tara Vanderveer, Stanford University coach and 1996 U.S. Olympic basketball coach; Pam Hixon, former University of Massachusetts and 1996 U.S. Olympic field hockey coach; and Vivian Stringer of the University of Iowa and now Rutgers are other examples to be admired. Athletes' immediate impressions of them are that they are extremely well-groomed, dynamic, enthusiastic, intense, fit, and in total control. Because of these first impressions and the influence that emanates from them, they must be formidable recruiting forces.

We may want to resist as "superficial" the notion that appearance is or should be important in effective leadership, and yet it is. Often our first impressions of people are inadequate and distorted, yet these approximations are critical starting points for predicting influence and the quality of social interaction to follow. Certainly, there are and have been successful coaches whose

appearance and behavior have been less than exemplary, but they are the exceptions.

The "Rosenthal effect," or a self-fulfilling prophecy, can be initiated by the coach who looks and acts like a winner. That is, the coach who behaves like a winner is more likely to be a winner.

Expert and Referent Power

Expert power is task and knowledge specific and is more likely to occur when an individual such as a coach or sport psychology consultant demonstrates skill or competence at certain tasks or has expert power granted because of his or her education or experience. Identification with a leader occurs when the leader possesses personal characteristics and qualities valued by the group or team, such as appearance, demonstrated knowledge, and the ability to express the values and concerns of his or her followers. Laios, Theodorakis, and Gargalianos (2003) examined leadership effectiveness and the five sources of power and found that coaches rated expert power as the most important dimension of power.

Charisma

Some leaders receive loyalty and commitment because they possess the illusive quality called **charisma.** This kind of influence is unique to the leader and group and thus cannot be transferred to another person. Political history is punctuated by charismatic leaders: John F. Kennedy, Martin Luther King Jr., Adolf Hitler, Ghandi, Eleanor Roosevelt, Gloria Steinem, and Oprah Winfrey are a few examples.

Who would be on your list of charismatic coaches? If these coaches retired or resigned, would those who follow in their positions exhibit the same charisma? Obviously not. Unfortunately, in many instances the charismatic leader is the most difficult of all to replace. The most inappropriate and ineffective behavior for the new coach is to attempt to emulate or behave like the previous charismatic coach. Coaches need to develop and establish their own styles. How very different from one another were outstanding coaches from the past such as Lombardi, Bryant, Hayes, Auerbach, and Wooden—all uniquely distinct individuals. No one else could exactly duplicate their leadership style and charisma. We are all individuals, and our personalities differ greatly; therefore, we should not attempt to imitate someone else's behavior. Seltzer and Bass (1990) noted that charisma "operates at the leader-individual level rather than at the leader-group level" (p. 702). Charisma cannot be copied; it is individually created and perceived.

Allocation of Rewards and Sanctions

If a leader can influence others, it is frequently because others depend on her or him. As previously discussed, this influence can arise from psychological identification because the leader has the power to allocate rewards or sanctions. The rewards can be objective or subjective. For example, some professional and college coaches have the authority to provide objective rewards such as salaries, tuition, room and board, books, and the like as well as subjective rewards such as approval or disapproval. The majority of coaches regularly give subjective, largely intangible rewards.

Some athletes are able to motivate themselves completely (internal motivation), whereas others need help from their peers, family, coach, and additional significant others (external motivation). The leader's role is much easier when he or she is involved with an athlete who is internally motivated. The leader's influence will be lessened if he or she does not appropriately motivate the athlete who needs external motivation. For example, when Jerry Kramer was asked how his coach, Vince Lombardi, motivated individual players, Kramer responded by saying that Lombardi knew who needed pats on the back, who needed to be kicked, and who needed various shades between the extremes. Lombardi had the ability to differentiate among the athletes and knew how to motivate each athlete effectively and at the proper time (Kaplan, 1983). (See Chapters 2 and 3 for specific suggestions regarding effective motivation.)

Expectations for Coaches

Interestingly, often coach and athlete perceptions of the coach's behaviors are very different (Kenow & Williams, 1992; Smith, Smoll, & Curtis, 1978). Kenow and Williams (1992) found that coaches believed that their behaviors were more positive than they actually were.

A model of coaching behaviors that influence athlete's perceptions of the coach has been suggested by Smoll and Smith (1989). This model is comprised of actual coaching behaviors, athlete's perceptions of the coaching behaviors, athlete's evaluation of the coaching behaviors, and situational factors, including coach and athlete differences and coach perception of the athlete's attitudes. Certainly, the nature of the sport, level of competition, practice or game situation, prior success or failure, and cohesiveness are other influential factors to be considered regarding specific coach behaviors.

Williams et al. (2003) found, for example, that "athletes with higher anxiety and lower self-confidence and compatibility with the coaches were more likely to negatively evaluate coaching behaviors" (p. 16). For more information on coaching behavior, Hoffman (2003) and Williams et al. (2003) evaluated the psychometric properties of coaching behavior scales.

Coaches should be aware of the sources of stress for athletes. In a study of organizational stress in elite athletes, Fletcher and Hanton (2003) found categories of stress including environmental, personal leadership, and team issues. Environmental issues were player selection, finances, training environment, accommodations, travel, and competitive environment. The personal issues included nutrition, injury, goals, and expectations. Coaching and coaching styles comprised the issues of leadership, whereas team issues were team atmosphere, support network, roles, and communication.

In addition, coaches should be aware of athlete gender differences in preferred leadership behavior. Riemer and Toon (2001) used Riemer and Chelladurai's (1998) *Athlete Satisfaction Scale* and found that females preferred positive feedback behavior from the coach whereas males preferred more autocratic behavior than females. The researchers further suggested coaches of individual sport athletes should avoid autocratic type behaviors if athlete satisfaction is to be maximized.

Social support behavior for male coaches compared to female coaches was more preferred by female athletes.

In a study by Martin, Jackson, Richardson, and Weiller (1999) children were asked what they thought was the most important duty of a coach. The adolescents age 10–18 rated skill instruction and positive feedback as most important. They also rated democratic behavior higher than autocratic behavior. Furthermore, females more than males preferred democratic coaching styles. Social support also was an important factor. The parents had similar ratings to their respective children.

Leadership in terms of influencing others to maintain programs of physical activity was studied by Fox, Rejeski, and Gauvin (2000). They found that participants were more likely to enjoy and to continue to participate in physical activity when the leader demonstrated personal interest in them and when the participants were able to positively interact with each other, thus, demonstrating the efficacy of social support.

A coach must not expect any more from an athlete than what the coach is willing to give or be. Athletes will emulate the coach's behavior. This means that the coach should be committed to exemplifying as well as enforcing the rules for the players. For example, if there is a punctuality rule, then the coach should abide by it, too.

Control of emotions is another expectation most coaches have for their athletes. This is a worthy expectation, for people cannot function maximally in terms of physical performance or interpersonal relations if they lose emotional control. Decision making, information processing, speed and coordination, objectivity, reasonableness, and the acuity of the senses are just a few of the factors that are adversely affected by loss of emotional control. Coaches who lose emotional control are not performing at their optimal level, and they are also presenting a negative role model. If coaches can misbehave on the sidelines, why can't athletes misbehave on the sidelines or lose their tempers while performing? Research also shows that athletes, and particularly athletes with higher anxiety and less confidence, rate coaching behaviors more negatively when they perceive their coach to lack emotional control

(Kenow & Williams, 1992, 1999). The athletes also felt that such behavior made them nervous and contributed to their not playing well.

Planning and commitment are also behaviors coaches expect from their athletes. In an interview with Rapaport (1993), Bill Walsh, renowned football coach at both the collegiate and professional levels, stressed the importance of precise, "minute-by-minute," well-planned, and tightly structured practices. "It's all in the way you prepare" (p. 115); ". . . you need to have a plan for every scenario" (p. 113). Bill Walsh sets a standard of competence and excellence for his players and believes that "those coaches who are most successful are the ones that have demonstrated the greatest commitment to their players" (p. 112). The preparation begins with setting goals and identifying the skills and strategies needed to compete successfully.

Dick Vermeil coached the 2000 Super bowl Champion St. Louis Rams after a 15-year layoff from previous successful coaching. The layoff was voluntary and self-described as burnout. The burnout was due to perfectionism and compulsive planning—beware. Vermeil retired again after the Superbowl win.

Goal setting is appropriate and important for athletes, but it is critical for coaches and sport psychology consultants. The emphasis should be on short-range goals. Setting goals is only the beginning. Goals can be used to plan athletic practices and psychological interventions down to the smallest detail. Such practices are extremely positive ways for a coach or sport leader to facilitate teaching and learning. For example, during games, Bear Bryant carried reminders on a piece of paper. Among the things that he had written down were "Don't forget—use timeouts intelligently—double timeouts—run clock down last play—ORDERLY BENCH." (For detailed information on how to set effective goals and what strategies help to achieve these goals, see Chapter 13.)

In summary, having an appropriate appearance, exhibiting conduct that exemplifies the behavior expected from athletes, balancing the cost–benefit reinforcement ratio for complying with the leader's wishes, and complete planning and commitment are specific behaviors all leaders can use to improve their credibility and influence. Improvement in any of these areas can potentially increase one's effectiveness as a leader.

Developing Leadership Within the Team

In identifying leaders within a team, a coach should be attuned to functional leadership that arises spontaneously in a climate of trust. Such a climate is present when coaches accept the uniqueness of each team member—including what might appear as deviant behavior, provided this behavior does not have a negative impact on the effectiveness of the team or the satisfaction of its members. Leadership within a team should go to the most competent. Natural leaders will usually surface if there is a climate of acceptance and if athletes are encouraged to provide input and leadership. A coach can help certain athletes demonstrate or develop their leadership abilities by giving those individuals responsibilities, small at first, and then positively reinforcing their successful attempts at leadership. Wright and Cote (2003), in a qualitative study of six leader–athletes, indicated that leadership development in sport focused on high skill, strong work ethic, sport knowledge, and good people skills. Leader–member exchange theory supports these suggestions.

Human relations within a team can be improved if everyone is aware of expectations, if the rules and regulations are clearly stated, if team procedures are well written and available, and if responsibilities that do not overlap are clearly defined. Here are some suggestions for building effective team leaders:

1. Identify potential leaders and provide opportunities for leadership within the team.

2. Use these athlete leaders, as well as leaders such as athletic trainers, managers, and assistant coaches, wisely by delegating authority and responsibility to them.

3. Deal with all athletes and assistant leaders as individuals.

4. Keep communication open and direct rather than having team leaders serve as a "buffer" between the coach and other athletes.

Developing Morale Within the Team

Morale is an elusive quality, like charisma. Morale is a feeling created within each team member that is generated by a sense of caring that is communicated within the team. Positive morale includes an awareness that each individual on the team is important and the knowledge that hard work and sacrifices are recognized and appreciated. These two behaviors generate an ambiance that causes an increase in loyalty and productiveness.

Morale may determine motivation, which directs energy in either acceptable or unacceptable ways on the team. When morale is positive, it is worth more than anything money can buy. The reverse is true too. Morale can be enhanced if the leaders' behavior tells the truth. Coaches should not try to fool athletes. They should "walk the talk, walk the walk." Positive morale cannot be purchased; therefore, material incentives are not the answer. Leaders at every level are responsible for morale, from the equipment manager, to trainer, to assistant coaches, to the head coach.

Further, morale is based on trust. If the players don't believe the coach or director of athletics is working in their best interests, morale declines. Morale is resistant to change so that once trust is established the players are more tolerant of setbacks. Negative morale is also resistant to change. Without trust, it is very hard for players to move beyond defensive postures, and defensiveness impedes creativity, innovation, decision making, and productivity.

Morale is highly contagious. Morale is often communicated by the coach's or institution's attitude toward the team members as people. Both positive and negative information spreads like wildfire, horizontally. Player-to-player communication consistently reinforces positive or negative perceptions of the team, its management, and management's motives. Influencing player-to-player communication must be a primary goal of any team effort if one wishes to build positive morale.

Positive morale can create a strong emotional bond to and within the team. When morale is low, player departure or disgruntlement increases. To increase positive morale, basic player security is required. Either too much security (intolerance or laziness is tolerated) or too little ("will I be next?") affects morale. Positive morale necessitates that competency is valued. Often low morale occurs when playing or starting time is based on player longevity or "who you know" or school/team politics rather than skill level. When players see this, even the most dedicated become negative or cynical.

How can a coach or athletics director assess team morale? By looking and listening informally to:

- *Humor.* Is it filled with anger, hostility, deep cynicism, or is there no humor at all? Look for upbeat humor while laughing at the funny side of life.

- *The grapevine.* When morale is positive, the talk on the informal communication network is about the "comings and goings and doings" of people players know. When morale is low, the talk is strong and defensive, "What's the coach or A.D. going to do now?"

- *Griping and complaints.* This exists no matter how high morale is, but it typically is not serious.

- *Coach/administrator responsiveness.* Communication is usually pretty good from the top down, but what about bottom up? Are players listened to?

Coaches can boost morale when they make the environment an emotionally secure one in which a sense of caring and appreciation are communicated. Players feel a sense of belonging to something good. A positive sense of self-esteem is validated, and appreciation is expressed in positive, personally validating ways for the athletes. Further, they also feel free to change and grow. Healthy relationships within a team can be built by savvy coaches. Enhanced morale results in fewer player problems, a more upbeat attitude, and better performance—a win-win situation for all.

Ethical Leadership

Most individuals would agree that leaders in sport have a moral responsibility and obligation to facilitate the utmost of ethical situations. Unfortunately, the American values demonstrated, reinforced, and learned in sport are not all positive or praiseworthy. The most pervasive and potentially immoral value in sport and in society is that of "win at any cost." Such a costly attitude can be noted in the rampant use in sport of performance-enhancing drugs, violence, cheating, and practices that keep athletes eligible but fail to educate them. The unethical behaviors that emanate from this doctrine are destructive for the athlete, coach, spectator, the credibility of education, and, ultimately, society.

Granted, it is awful to lose. Anyone who competes has felt the sting. Vince Lombardi, in response to his quote—"Winning isn't everything, it's the only thing," said, "I wish to hell I'd never said the damn thing. I meant having a goal. . . . I sure as hell didn't mean for people to crush human values and morality" (Michener, 1976, p. 432). Dramatic ethical and moral changes could be made in sport, and thus in society, through ethical leadership. Ethical leadership should insist that all in sport follow the letter and spirit of the rules and cease and desist from valuing the cheater, the "get away with whatever you can" ethic. Character should be the basis for our personal and social ethics. Virtue—doing the right thing—should be our goal in sport. James Naismith, the inventor of basketball mentioned earlier, had one goal in life, to "do good." How simple, and yet how profound.

It has been suggested by John Wooden that "if you know in your heart that you've made the effort to do the best of which you are capable, that's not failure, that's success. And I want each individual to feel that. It doesn't matter if it's in business or in the classroom or on the athletic field." Ethical leadership also should concern itself with racism and sexism. Just as racism and sexism are ever prevalent in our society, so too are they glaringly evident in sport. It should be a goal of leaders in sport to provide equitable opportunities for all athletes regardless of race, gender, or sexual preference. The "isms" are significant social problems that need addressing and amelioration, in society and in sport.

If we provide virtuous leaders (e.g., coaches, sport psychologists, administrators, parents) who demand, expect, reward, and practice virtue, we will be contributing through sport to a better world. As Sophocles claimed, "I would prefer to fail with honor than to win by cheating." "On May 25, 1999, nearly 50 sports leaders issued the Arizona Sports Summit Accord to emphasize the ethical and character-building aspects of athletic competition—with the hope that the framework of principles and values set forth will be adopted and practiced widely" (Arizona Sport Summit Accord, 1999).

Summary

Successful coaches create environments in which trust, respect, and consideration grow and flourish. When these aspects are present in daily interactions with others, a high quality of life is returned to organizations, teams, students, players, and colleagues, resulting in greater productivity and service. This makes work much more manageable and enjoyable. An effort should be made to keep our teams, schools, organizations, disciplines, and professions safe from pollutants such as fear, selfishness, bigotry, abuse, deceit, and prejudice.

We would like to suggest 10 qualities for effective leadership that offer only positive benefits for those who employ them. They are symbolic derivatives of the original "magic words," please and thank you. They are effective and help others work better. They are fundamental to human relationships.

1. *Trust* is given as a gift, although once given it must be nurtured, because it is so fragile it can be broken by one lie. When we trust others, they trust us. As a leader, "dig into the problem, not the person."

2. *Fairness* is like beauty, for it is often "in the eye of the beholder." Whether or not fairness is achieved or perceived, it must be our goal. Athletes will accept a coach's actions even if they disagree with them, as long as they believe the coach acted out of the principle of fairness.

3. *Generosity* is forgiving past grievances or mistakes. It is giving the benefit of the doubt. It involves providing opportunities for others to shine. It is demonstrated by speaking more often of "we" than "I."

4. *Respect* is showing and treating others with esteem, consideration, and regard.

5. *Consideration* is demonstrating concern for others as individuals. In current society the stress and pressure to succeed are high. There are ways of dealing with stress that avoid acting disrespectfully toward others.

6. *Gratefulness* is appreciating and being thankful for everything. Although many athletes demonstrate a sense of entitlement, we are not entitled to anything in this world. Entitlements are gifts from others; therefore, take no one or no pleasure for granted. Grateful leaders see opportunities where the entitled see problems and despair.

7. *Dignity* is carrying oneself with pride and self-respect. It shines through at all times, especially during trying times. Leaders with dignity look the part. If we don't recognize our own dignity and that of others, our respect is lost. Dignity is something we have and do not want damaged, whereas respect is something we give to others. Coaches who forget their own dignity find that others lose regard for them. Coaches who snivel, whine, make excuses for poor performance (such as blaming others), or seek special privileges compromise their respect. Coaches/leaders need to find ways to help others preserve their dignity as well. The "isms" are ways we prevent giving respect, which takes dignity away from those who may be different.

8. *Integrity* is to be integrated psychologically, spiritually, intellectually, ethically, and socially. Leaders with integrity don't speak out of both sides of their mouths. Having integrity has potential benefits as well as pain for the leader. The positive side of having integrity is that the leader has predictable values that can be relied on. The painful part of having integrity is that holding to a core principle can cost one personally. Integrity does not mean rigidity; it means holding dear to various parts of your life, to yourself.

9. *Caring candor* is giving feedback that shows you are concerned about the person, especially if the feedback is critical. When using caring candor, the coach does not hang a person and then give him or her a fair trial. Caring candor is descriptive rather than punitive, so it is not *brutal* honesty. Coaches who lose their tempers do not motivate others. Athletes want no part of coaches who invade their space and scream and carry on in what amounts to tantrums. Tantrums are selfish and self-centered. Today there are few successful bullies.

10. *Responsiveness* is being dependable. It is reacting easily or readily to suggestion or appeal, or closing the communication gap. Coaches who are unresponsive might be procrastinators, or they might say "yes," but lack follow-through. Responsive leaders are on time, make calls and decisions, write reports, do the paperwork, confront when necessary, pay compliments, and do more than what is required or expected. When a coach makes a commitment, it is to be honored.

In the 21st century, leadership will be through persuasion and goodwill; it will replace leadership through power and intimidation. These qualities are not intended to manipulate others. They are basic humanistic contentions about dignity and worth of others.

Because of the significant role coaches play in the skill and personal development of their athletes, their influence, power, and effect cannot be negated. Being a good leader involves an appreciation of leadership theory and knowledge of how a coach can maximize influence and followership through positive role modeling, planning, preparation, and being true to oneself. Coaches must accept their athletes' individuality as well as their own.

In leadership theory as well as coaching experience, it is evident that there are specific implications of what coaches, athletics directors, and sport psychology consultants who are responsible professionals and successful leaders should do:

- Master and apply current knowledge of sport physiology, psychology, and biomechanics.

- Develop interpersonal skills including the communication skills of speaking, writing, observing, understanding defensive mechanisms, motivating, and listening. Of all the communication skills, coaches are generally the weakest at listening. Interpersonal interactions are critical to sport success, and communication is the key (Mancini & Agnew, 1978). See Chapter 9 for a discussion of effective communication skills.

- Eliminate all sexist, ageist, heterosexist, racist, ableist, and dehumanizing language.
- Eliminate any attitude that involves the humiliation of losers and the glorification of winners.
- Encourage the athletes as well as him- or herself to view the opponent as a challenge and not an enemy.
- Understand the effects of social reinforcement on individual performance.
- Control his or her own arousal level and be an example for the athletes of the emotionality needed for successful performance.
- Help athletes set their *own* goals. Emphasize the process (participation and playing as well as possible) and not the outcome (winning). This is an important concept because goals should be something that an individual can accomplish or control. Athletes can control their own performance but not the opponents'.
- Live in the present. Do not constantly remind athletes of past winners or of the potential for team success 2 years hence.
- Provide opportunities for success through well-planned practices, good game conditions, sensible scheduling, and a pleasant atmosphere. The administrative aspects of a coach's job cannot be overlooked. Planning, preparation, and budgeting are important functions that affect leadership performance. A coach must be a teacher, a leader, and an administrator.
- Be rational and humanistic.

As coaches and sport psychology consultants, we should commit to leadership in sport that is dedicated to the ethics and morality of positive growth for all athletes. "Great coaching is artful, compassionate, and incisive" (Senge et al., 1999).

Study Questions

1. Why is leadership of particular interest to sport psychology consultants?
2. Describe your perception of the relationship between power and leadership.
3. Describe the authoritarian personality profile.
4. Distinguish between the trait and behavioral leadership theories.
5. Is there a difference in expectations between what coaches and athletes prefer for leadership in the sport environment?
6. Describe in detail one situational theory. How do situational theories differ from trait and behavioral theories?
7. Identify the status of women in leadership positions in sport. In your discussion, describe causes and barriers to the existing status as well as prospects for the future.
8. Explain the 10 suggested qualities for successful leadership.
9. Explain the significance of a role model in relation to leader–member exchange theory.
10. List four suggestions for building effective team leaders.

11. Identify factors, traits, and behaviors that you believe are important for the effective leader.

12. Describe the behaviors of a transformational or charismatic leader.

13. Discuss ways in which the five theories of leadership are related or integrated.

14. Identify the dangers associated with a "win at all cost" approach to coaching.

15. Identify ways to foster and model ethical behavior.

16. Discuss Gardner's cognitive framework for leadership and how it might be assessed.

References

Acosta, R. V., & Carpenter, L. J. (2002). *Women in intercollegiate sport: A longitudinal study—twenty-five year update.* Unpublished manuscript, Smith College and Brooklyn College of the City University of New York.

Anderson, D. F., & Gill, K. S. (1983). Occupational socialization patterns of men's and women's inter-scholastic basketball coaches. *Journal of Sport Behavior, 6,* 105–116.

Andrud, W. E. (1970). *The personality of high school, college, and professional football coaches as measured by the Guilford-Zimmerman temperament survey.* Unpublished master's thesis, University of North Dakota, Grand Forks.

Arizona Sport Summit Accord (1999). Pursuing victory with honor [Online]. Available: http://www.charactercounts.org

Barrow, J. C. (1977). The variables of leadership: A review and conceptual framework. *Academy of Management Review, 2,* 233–251.

Bass, B. M. (1985). *Leadership and performance beyond expectations.* New York: The Free Press.

Bass, B., & Avolio, B. (1995). *MLQ: Multifactor Leadership Questionnaire.* Palo Alto, CA: Mind Garden.

Bennis, W., & Biederman, P. W. (1997). *Organizing genius: The secrets of creative collaboration.* Reading, MA: Addison-Wesley.

Bennis, W., & Nanus, B. (1985). *Leaders.* New York: Harper & Row.

Bird, A. (1977). Team structure and success as related to cohesiveness and leadership. *Journal of Social Psychology, 103,* 217–233.

Black, S. J., & Weiss, M. R. (1992). The relationship among perceived coaching behaviors, perceptions of ability, and motivation in competitive age-group swimmers. *Journal of Sport and Exercise Psychology, 14,* 309–325.

Burns, J. M. (1978). *Leadership.* New York: Harper & Row.

Carron, A. V. (1984). *Motivation: Implications for coaching and teaching.* London, ON: Sports Dynamics.

Case, R. (1984). Leadership behavior in sport: A field test of situational leadership theory. *International Journal of Sport Psychology, 18,* 256–268.

Case, R. (1998). Leader member exchange theory and sport. *Journal of Sport Behavior, 21,* 387–395.

Chelladurai, P., & Carron, A. V. (1978). *Leadership*. Canadian Association for Health, Physical Education and Recreation, Sociology of Sport Monograph Series. Ottawa, Ontario.

Chelladurai, P., Haggerty, T. R., & Baxter, P. R. (1989). Decision style choices of university basketball coaches and players. *Journal of Sport and Exercise Psychology, 11*, 201–215.

Chelladurai, P., & Quek, C. B. (1995). Decision style choices of high school basketball coaches: The effects of situational and coach characteristics. *Journal of Sport Behavior, 18*, 91–108.

Chelladurai, P., & Saleh, S. (1978). Preferred leadership in sport. *Canadian Journal of Applied Sport Sciences, 3*, 85–97.

Danielson, R. (1976). *Contingency model of leadership effectiveness: For empirical investigation of its application in sport. Motor learning, sport psychology, pedagogy, and didactics of physical activity.* Monograph 5. Quebec City, Canada.

DePree, M. (1987). *Leadership is an art.* New York: Doubleday.

Dienesch, R. M., & Linden, R. C. (1986). Leader–member exchange model of leadership: A critique and further development. *Academy of Management Journal, 11*, 618–634.

Diesenhouse, S. (1989, August 20). Therapists start to address damage done by therapists. *New York Times*, p. 5.

Doherty, A. J., & Danylchuk, K. E. (1996). Transformational and transactional leadership in interuniversity athletics management. *Journal of Sport Management, 10* (3), 292–309.

Dunette, M. (1965). *Personnel selection and placement.* Belmont, CA: Wadsworth.

Eitzen, D. S., & Pratt, S. (1989). Gender differences in coaching philosophy: The core of female basketball teams. *Research Quarterly for Exercise and Sport, 60*, 152–158.

Feltz, D. L., Chase, M. A., Moritz, S. E., & Sullivan, P. J. (1999). A conceptual model of coaching efficacy: Preliminary investigation and instrument development. *Journal of Educational Psychology, 91*, 765–776.

Fiedler, F. (1967). *A theory of leadership effectiveness.* New York: McGraw-Hill.

Fletcher, D., & Hanton, S. (2003). Sources of organizational stress in elite sports performers. *The Sport Psychologist, 17*, 175–195.

Fox, L. D., Rejeski, W. J., & Gauvin, L. (2000). Effects of leadership style and group dynamics on enjoyment of physical activity. *American Journal of Health Promotion, 14*(5), 277–283.

Gagen, J. J. (1971). *Risk-taking within football situations of selected football coaches.* Unpublished master's thesis, Kent State University, Kent, Ohio.

Gardner, H. (1995). *Leading minds: An anatomy of leadership.* New York: Basic Books.

George, J. J. (1989). Finding solutions to the problem of fewer female coaches. *The Physical Educator, 46* (1), 2–8.

Ghiselli, E. (1971). *Explorations in managerial talent.* Santa Monica, CA: Goodyear.

Goleman, D. (1998). What makes a leader? *Harvard Business Review, 76*, 93–102.

Graen, G., & Cashman, J. F. (1975). A role-making model of leadership in formal organizations: A developmental approach. In J. G. Hunt & L. L. Larson (Eds.), *Leadership frontiers* (pp. 143–165). Kent, OH: Kent State University Press.

Graen, G., Novak, M., & Sommerkamp, P. (1982). The effects of leader-member exchange and job design on productivity and satisfaction: Testing a dual attachment model. *Organizational Behavior and Human Performance, 30,* 109–131.

Grant, L. (1996, June 24). Rambos in pinstripes: Why so many CEOs are lousy leaders. *Fortune,* 147.

Hall, L. K. (1964). *Doggett of Springfield.* Lebanon, PA: Sowers.

Halpin, A. W. (1957). *Manual for the leader behavior description questionnaire.* Columbus, OH: Bureau of Business Research.

Halpin, A. W., & Winer, B. J. (1957). A factorial study of leader behavior descriptions. In R. M. Stodgill & A. E. Coons (Eds.), *Leader behavior: Its description and measurement* (pp. 399–451). Columbus, OH: Bureau of Business Research.

Hart, B. A., Hasbrook, C. A., & Mathes, S. A. (1986). An examination of the reduction in the number of female interscholastic coaches. *Research Quarterly for Exercise and Sport, 57*(1), 68–77.

Hendry, L. B. (1972). The coaching stereotype. In H. T. A. Whiting (Ed.), *Readings in sport psychology.* London: Kingston.

Hendry, L. (1974). Human factors in sport systems. *Human Factors, 16,* 528–544.

Hersey, P., & Blanchard, K. H. (1969). Life style theory of leadership. *Training and Development Journal, 23,* 26–34.

Hersey, P., & Blanchard, K. H. (1977). *Management of organizational behavior.* Englewood Cliffs, NJ: Prentice Hall.

Hershey, P. G., & Blanchard, K. (1982). Leadership style: Attitudes and behavior. *Training and Development Journal, 36* (5), 50–52.

Hoffman, J. D. (2003). *Development and validation of the perceived coaching behavior inventory.* Unpublished doctoral dissertation, Springfield College, Springfield, MA.

Holmen, M. G., & Parkhouse, B. L. (1981). Trends in the selection of coaches for female athletes: A demographic inquiry. *Research Quarterly for Exercise and Sport, 52*(1), 9–18.

House, R. J. (1971). A path–goal theory of leader effectiveness. *Administrative Science Quarterly, 16,* 321–338.

House, R. J. (1976). A 1976 theory of charismatic leadership. In J. G. Hunt & L. L. Larson (Eds.), *Leadership: The winning edge.* Carbondale: Southern Illinois University Press.

Kanter, R. M. (1977). *Men and women of the corporation.* New York: Basic Books.

Kaplan, E. (1983, January 30). The legend of Vince Lombardi. *Family Weekly.*

Kenow, L. J., & Williams, J. M. (1992). Relationship between anxiety, self-confidence, and evaluation of coaching behaviors. *The Sport Psychologist, 6,* 344–357.

Kenow, L., & Williams, J. (1999). Coach–athlete compatibility and athlete's perception of coaching behaviors. *Journal of Sport Behavior, 22,* 251–259.

Knoppers, A. (1987). Gender and the coaching profession. *Quest, 39,* 9–22.

Knoppers, A. (1989). Coaching: An equal opportunity occupation? *Journal of Physical Education, Recreation, and Dance,* March, pp. 38–43.

Komives, S. R. (1991, March). Gender differences in the relationship of hall directors' transformational and transactional leadership and achieving styles. *Journal of College Student Development, 32,* 155–165.

Kotter, J. P. (1990, May–June). What leaders really do. *Harvard Business Review,* 103–111.

Laios, A., Theodorakis, N., & Gargalianos, D. (2003, Winter). Leadership and power: Two important factors for effective coaching. *International Sports Journal,* 150–154.

Lenskji, H. (1986). *Out of bounds: Women, sport, and sexuality.* Toronto: Women's Press.

Lund, D. R., & Finch, L. W. (1987). *Lessons in leadership: Mostly learned the hard way.* Staples, NY: Adventure.

Maier, R., & Laurakis, D. (1981). Some personality correlates of attitudes about sports. *International Journal of Sport Psychology, 12,* 19–22.

Mancini, V., & Agnew, M. (1978). An analysis of teaching and coaching behaviors. In W. Straub, (Ed.), *Sport psychology: An analysis of athlete behavior.* Ithaca, NY: Mouvement Publications.

Martin, S. B., Jackson, A. W., Richardson, P. A., & Weiller, K. H. (1999). Coaching and preferences of adolescent youths and their parents. *Journal of Applied Sport Psychology, 11,* 247–262.

Massimo, J. (1973). *A psychologist's approach to sport.* Presentation to New England Gymnastic Clinic, Newton, Mass.

Michener, J. A. (1976). *Sports in America.* Greenwich, CT: Fawcett.

Millard, L. (1996). Differences in coaching behaviors of male and female high school soccer coaches. *Journal of Sport Behavior, 19,* 19–31.

Naisbitt, J. (1984). *Megatrends.* New York: Warner Books.

Neil, G. I., & Kirby, S. L. (1985). Coaching styles and preferred leadership among rowers and paddlers. *Journal of Sport Behavior, 8,* 3–17.

Parkhouse, B. L., & Williams, J. M. (1986). Differential effects of sex and status on evaluation of coaching ability. *Research Quarterly for Exercise and Sport, 57* (1), 53–59.

Podd, M. (1972). Ego identity status and morality: The relationship between two developmental contracts. *Developmental Psychology, 6,* 497–507.

Pope, K. S., Keith-Speigel, P., & Tabachnick, B. G. (1986). Sexual attraction to clients. *American Psychologist, 41* (2), 147–158.

Prujin, G. H. J., & Boucher, R. L. (1995). The relationship of transactional and transformational leadership to the organizational effectiveness of Dutch National Sport Organizations. *European Journal for Sport Management, 2,* 72–87.

Rapaport, R. (1993, January–February). To build a winning team: An interview with head coach Bill Walsh. *Harvard Business Review, 71*(1), 111–120.

Reich, R. (1983). *The next American frontier.* New York: Times Books.

Riemer, H. A., & Chelladurai, P. (1998). Development of the Athlete Satisfaction Questionnaire (ASQ). *Journal of Sport and Exercise Psychology, 20,* 127–156.

Riemer, H. A., & Toon, K. (2001). Leadership and satisfaction in tennis: Examination of congruence, gender, and ability. *Research Quarterly for Exercise and Sport, 72*(3), 243–256.

Rosener, J. B. (1990, November–December). Ways women lead. *Harvard Business Review,* 119–125.

Safire, W., & Safir, L. (2000). *Leadership.* New York: Galahad.

Sage, G. (1975). An occupational analysis of the college coach. In D. Ball & L. Loy (Eds.), *Sport and social order.* Reading, MA: Addison-Wesley.

Scandura, T. A., Graen, G. B., & Novak, M. A. (1986). When managers decide not to decide autocratically: An investigation of leader–member exchange and decision influence. *Journal of Applied Psychology, 71,* 579–584.

Schein, E. (1970). *Organizational psychology.* Englewood Cliffs, NJ: Prentice Hall.

Seltzer, J., & Bass, B. M. (1990). Transformational leadership: Beyond initiation and consideration. *Journal of Management, 16,* 693–703.

Senge, P., Kleiner, A., Roberts, C., Ross, R., Roth G., & Smith, B. (1999). *The dance of change.* New York: Currency Doubleday.

Shanahan, M., (with) Shefter, A. (2000). *Think like a champion: Building success one victory at a time.* New York: Harper Collins.

Shapiro, L. (1991). *Big man on campus.* New York: Holt.

Sisley, B. L., & Capel, S. A. (1986). High school coaching: Filled with gender differences. *Journal of Physical Education, Recreation, and Dance, 57*(3), 39–43.

Smith, R. E., Smoll, F. L., & Curtis, B. (1978). Coaching behaviors in Little League Baseball. In F. L. Smoll & R. E. Smith (Eds.), *Psychological perspectives in youth sports* (pp. 173–201). Washington, DC: Hemisphere.

Smith, R. E., Smoll, F. L., & Curtis, B. (1979). Coach effectiveness training: A cognitive-behavioral approach to enhancing relationship skills in youth sport coaches. *Journal of Sport Psychology, 1,* 59–75.

Smoll, F. L., & Smith R. E. (1989). Leadership behaviors in sport: A theoretical model and research paradigm. *Journal of Applied Social Psychology, 19,* 1522–1551.

Stagg, A. A., & Stoudt, W. W. (1927). *Touchdown!* New York: Longmans and Green.

Stogdill, R. (1974). *Handbook of leadership: A survey of theory and research.* New York: Free Press.

Sullivan, P. J., & Kent, A. (2003). Coaching efficacy as a predictor of leadership style in intercollegiate athletes. *Journal of Applied Sport Psychology, 15,* 1–11.

Torre, J., (with) Dreher, H. (1999). *Joe Torre's ground rules for winners: 12 keys to managing team players, tough bosses, set backs and success.* New York: Hyperion Press.

Triandis, H. C. (1971). *Attitude and attitude change.* New York: Wiley.

Von Strache, C. (1979). Players' perceptions of leadership qualities for coaches. *Research Quarterly, 50,* 679–686.

Vroom, V. H., & Yetton, P. W. (1973). *Leadership and decision making.* Pittsburgh: University of Pittsburgh Press.

Weber, M. (1968). *Economy and society: An outline of interpretive sociology.* New York: Bedminster Press.

Weese, W. J. (1995). A synthesis of leadership theory and a prelude to the five "C" model. *European Journal of Sport Management, 2,* 59–71.

Weese, W. J., & Bourner, F. (1995). Effective leadership and organizational effectiveness in the Canadian Hockey League. *European Journal of Sport Management, 2,* 88–100.

Weinberg, R., & McDermott, M. (2002). A comparative analysis of sport and business organizations: Factors perceived critical for organizational success. *Journal of Applied Sport Psychology, 14,* 282–298.

Weinberg, R., Reveles, M., & Jackson, A. (1984). Attitudes of male and female athletes toward male and female coaches. *Journal of Sport Psychology, 6,* 448–453.

Weiss, M. R., & Friedrichs, W. D. (1986). The influence of leader behaviors, coach attributes, and institutional variables on performance and satisfaction of collegiate basketball teams. *Journal of Sport Psychology, 8,* 332–346.

Williams, J. M., Jerome, G. J., Kenow, L. J., Rogers, T., Sartain, T. A., & Darland, G. (2003). Factor structure of the coaching behavior questionnaire and its relationship to athlete variables. *The Sport Psychologist, 17,* 16–34.

Wooden, J., & Jamison, S. (1997). *Wooden: A lifetime of observations on and off the court.* New York: McGraw-Hill Trade.

Wright, A., & Cote, J. (2003). A retrospective analysis of leadership development through sport. *The Sport Psychologist, 17,* 268–291.

7

Styles of Decision Making in Coaching

P. Chelladurai, *The Ohio State University*
Brian A. Turner, *The Ohio State University*

Sure, I listen to the players when they talk to me and make suggestions, just as Coach Smith (former head basketball coach at University of North Carolina) did. But when it's time to make a decision for the good of the team, like Coach Smith, I'm a Benevolent dictator. Great leaders know what it means to make tough decisions, even if they sometimes aren't popular with the people they're leading.

—Roy Williams, head basketball coach at the University of North Carolina

All the activities carried out by a coach involve **decision making,** which is defined as the process of selecting an alternative from among many choices to achieve a desired end. For example, the coach has to decide what performance goals to pursue, what activities or programs will lead to the attainment of those goals, who of the available athletes should be selected, what should be the assignments for the selected athletes, and what are ways of motivating the athletes. In addition to these fundamental concerns, the coach needs to make decisions about practice and tournament schedules, travel arrangements and uniform selection, and other routine matters. Every decision the coach makes has a strong impact on the team and its performance. Thus, as has been said of management, coaching is in essence the art and science of decision making.

The coach must be primarily concerned with making good decisions that will effectively and efficiently move the group toward its goals. To that extent, the coach must also be concerned with how much participation in decision making he or she should allow the members of the team. This is an important concern because member participation may ensure that good decisions will be made and may also enhance the motivation of the athletes. Because the coach has sole authority over the degree and manner of members' participation, he or she must have a clear grasp of the advantages and disadvantages of such participation and the conditions under which the participation will be most fruitful. This chapter focuses on the specific issue of participation in decision making and discusses theory and research on the topic.

Decision-Making Processes

We must begin, however, with an overview of the decision-making process from two perspectives: as a cognitive process and as a social process.

Decision Making as a Cognitive Process

The emphasis in decision making as a cognitive process is on the **rationality** of the decision. That is, the concern is with evaluating the available alternatives and selecting the best one to achieve a desired end. Decision makers can arrive at rational decisions only after defining the problem clearly, identifying relevant constraints, generating possible and plausible alternatives, evaluating and ranking the alternatives according to some selected criterion, and then selecting the best alternative in terms of some prespecified criterion. For example, in the establishment of a team's competitive schedule the coach must consider all possible opportunities, then evaluate and prioritize those opportunities with regard to such constraints as time and financial cost to attend, level of competition, and ability of the team. Based on that evaluation, the competitive opportunities that are most likely to help the team achieve its goals will be selected. In this view, generating alternatives and evaluating them become crucial to decision making. Thus, the focus here is on the objective and optimal use of available information.

Decision Making as a Social Process

In the context of coaching the **social process** refers to the degree to which members of the team are allowed to participate in decision making and the varying degrees of influence the members have on the decisions. Thus, the social process of decision making may vary from strictly autocratic decision making by the coach to varying degrees of participation by members (e.g., consultation with one or a few members, consultation with all members, group decision making, and delegation). These variations have been called the **decision styles** of the coach (Chelladurai & Haggerty, 1978). As Vroom (2000) noted, the focus in the social process is not on what should be decided but on how it should be decided and who should be involved.

Confounding Factors

Before continuing, we must isolate decision style from other factors that may confound our understanding of the decision-making process. Three confounding factors in the coaching context are the leader's personality, the leader's mannerisms, and the substance of a decision.

Decision Making and Personality

The issue of decision styles in coaching has been clouded by the exclusive focus on the personality of the coach. For instance, a number of authors have suggested that coaches, influenced by their personality, tend to be either autocratic or democratic in all instances without reference to the nature of the problems facing them. That is, a coach with an autocratic or authoritarian personality will make all decisions single-handedly, whereas a coach with a more democratic and flexible personality will share or even delegate responsibility for decision making with others. However, instead of labeling coaches as autocratic or democratic, recent theorists suggest that we should be analyzing the problem situation and designating it as calling for an autocratic or democratic decision-making style. That is, effective decision making will be determined more by the nature of the problem and an appropriate decision-making style than by the personality of the coach.

Decision Making and Leader's Mannerisms

One also must guard against confusing the coach's mannerisms and affectations with his or her decision style. For instance, consider a football coach who presents his playbook for the season to the quarterback with the apparently menacing command: "This is your bible. You better master it." In contrast, another coach may present his playbook with a smile and the comment: "Here is the playbook I drew up during the summer. You may get a kick out of reading it." The obvious difference in their mannerisms should not be allowed to mask the fact that both coaches autocratically decided on the plays.

Style and Substance of Decisions

An important issue regarding decision making is that the "style" of decision making has been confounded with the "substance" of the decision. For instance, in Fiedler's (1967) contingency model of leadership effectiveness, a leader is deemed to be either task oriented, focusing primarily on task accomplishment, or relations oriented, focusing on the people who carry out the task. In addition, Fiedler's model suggests that a task-oriented leader, let us say a coach who is concerned with the successful completion of a practice, will be more autocratic and a relations-oriented leader, let us say a coach who is concerned with the athletes'

development as a result of the practice, will be more democratic.

However, there have been some attempts to separate the decision style of the leader from other leadership behaviors. To illustrate, five dimensions of leader behavior in coaching are identified and described in Table 7-1. Of these, training and instruction and positive feedback relate more directly to the task and its performance, whereas social support relates to the personal needs of the athletes. The remaining two dimensions refer to the social process of decision making.

There is support for the distinction among these leader behaviors. For example, it has been found that experienced male athletes prefer more autocratic behavior and at the same time more social support than less experienced athletes (Chelladurai & Carron, 1982). The point is that in earlier leadership theories an autocratic style of decision making and socially supportive behavior

Table 7-1 **Leader Behavior Dimensions in Sport**

Dimension	Description
Training and instruction	Behavior of the coach aimed at improving the athlete's performance by emphasizing and facilitating hard and strenuous training; by instructing them in the skills, techniques, and tactics of the sport; by clarifying the relationship among the members; and by structuring and coordinating the activities of the members.
Democratic behavior	Behavior of the coach that allows greater participation by the athletes in decisions pertaining to group goals, practice methods, and game tactics and strategies.
Autocratic behavior	Behavior of the coach that involves independence in decision making and stresses personal authority.
Social support	Behavior of the coach characterized by a concern for the welfare of individual athletes, positive group atmosphere, and warm interpersonal relations with members.
Positive feedback	Behavior of the coach that reinforces an athlete by recognizing and rewarding good performance.

Source: Chelladurai and Saleh, 1980.

were deemed to be negatively related, but recent theories and research indicate that these dimensions of leader behavior are independent of each other. In other words, athletes' desire for authoritarianism in their team coach does not preclude or negate their desire for social support from that same coach.

Participative Decision Making

There are advantages and disadvantages of team members' participation in decision making.

Advantages

Participation by athletes in decision making beneficially affects the team and its performance in three specific ways. First, such participation enhances the rationality of the decision insofar as there is more information available in a group to generate and evaluate alternate pathways to a goal. Thus, the quality of the decision is enhanced. Second, once a participative decision is made, the members feel that it is their own decision, and such feelings of ownership result in proper and efficient execution of the decision. Member participation increases the acceptance of as well as commitment to the decision. All of these advantages contribute to the success of the decisions made. This view is supported by Nutt's (2002) finding that although over half of the decisions made by organizations failed, 80% of the decisions where significant members participated in the decisions succeeded. Finally, participation in decision making is said to contribute to the personal growth of the members by enhancing their feelings of self-worth and self-confidence and by facilitating development of their problem-solving skills. This humanistic point of view has led several theorists to emphasize increased participation by members. In the athletic context, Sage (1973) advised that coaches should become more aware of the needs of their athletes and should allow greater participation in deciding on team membership, practice methods, team strategy, and so forth. Consider, for example, the case of the sprint relay team in which a decision needs to be made regarding the order of the runners to ensure optimal success. Relay team members may be asked for their suggestions based on their perception of the ability of each member. This participation will enhance their sense of responsibility for the decision and consequently for its execution.

Disadvantages

Three notable disadvantages are associated with participative decision making. First, participative decisions are time consuming. Anyone who has ever served on a committee has experienced tangential discussions and arguments over trivial issues. This may be the case when a coach asks for players' input into the team's practice schedule and individual rather than group interests become the focus.

A second disadvantage is that groups are relatively less effective in solving complex problems that require the decision maker(s) to keep a number of factors in perspective and to think through a series of steps and procedures that link all the relevant factors. Under such circumstances, the group is less likely to make an optimal decision than the best member in the group.

Kelley and Thibaut (1969) provide a good example of the contrast between a simple and complex problem: the solution of a crossword puzzle versus the construction of a crossword puzzle. The solution of a crossword puzzle is a relatively simple problem in which the group will be more proficient than individual members. This is because the group can generate a greater number of alternatives, each of which can easily be judged as correct or incorrect according to the criteria provided. Furthermore, one need not be concerned with all the words in the puzzle at the same time. The construction of a crossword puzzle is more complex, because the whole set of words and associated criteria must be kept in perspective and linked in a coherent and logical manner. According to Kelley and Thibaut (1969), the best individual in the group is likely to be more efficient than the group as a whole in this type of task.

A sport-specific example of the same concept would be to involve the defensive football squad in identifying why they are having trouble defending against a specific offensive pattern and then to have them follow up by planning what kind of practice is needed to correct the weakness. This relatively simple problem could easily be resolved by means of participative decision making. The decision would probably result in much more effective action by the players in resolving the problem than if the coach had merely told them what to do. Although there is merit in involving athletes in simple problems like this, it would probably be inefficient and ineffective to expect the defensive squad to deal with the more complex problem of drawing up the entire defensive game plan for an upcoming competition.

The third disadvantage of participative decision making is that its efficacy is heavily dependent on the degree of integration within the group. If the group is marked by internal conflict and rivalry, participation in decision making may result in one of two negative outcomes. First, the internal conflict may be further accentuated; one subgroup may feel that it has won the argument, but the other may not accept the decision. This conflict is not conducive to effective implementation of the decision. The other possibility is that the subgroups may "smooth over" the issue and arrive at a compromise solution that is not optimal. Consider, for example, the situation in which members are asked for their input into the determination of team goals or priority competitions. One subgroup of veteran players on a basketball team may want to focus on avenging a loss to a rival, whereas another subgroup may want to focus on winning a major tournament. The decision will result in either one group feeling slighted and less committed, or both subgroups compromising their focus.

In addition to the disadvantages described here, which may be inherent in participation per se, a number of attributes of a problem situation may preclude or restrict member participation in decision making. Thus, it is necessary to analyze the mix of relevant characteristics of the situation before selecting the appropriate decision style. The following sections describe a framework purported to facilitate such analyses and the research results thereof.

A Normative Model of Decision Styles in Coaching

In 1978 Chelladurai and Haggerty proposed a normative model of decision styles in coaching, based largely on the works of Vroom and his associates (Vroom & Jago, 1974; Vroom & Yetton, 1973) and on heuristics. Briefly, their model identifies the following seven problem attributes deemed relevant to the athletic context:

1. *Time pressure.* Many of the decisions in the sport context, as in the case of military units in action, have to be made under great time pressure. The lack of time may preclude participative decisions.

2. *Decision quality required.* Some problems require optimal solutions (e.g., the selection of a quarterback in football), but in other cases the coach may be satisfied with any one of several minimally acceptable alternatives (e.g., the selection of a captain). Several members can carry out the functions of a captain. In fact, some teams elect a different captain for each game. But the quarterback's function is more instrumental to the team's success, and the best person(s) with the necessary abilities should be selected. Therefore, the coach should be more concerned about the quality of the decision in selecting a quarterback than in selecting a captain. Vroom (2000) felt that decision quality was the most important attribute.

3. *Information location.* Information is the basis of high-quality decisions in any context. Such information in athletics relates to the strategies and tactics of the sport; its rules and their interpretations; and to the athletes, their capabilities, attitudes, needs, and preferences. The decision style adopted by the coach will be affected by the level of information possessed by the coach in relation to the information possessed by the athletes. For example, the coach may have a relatively greater amount of knowledge than the athletes regarding the interpretation of a rule, but the athletes may have greater

information about their personal needs. The coach should ensure that an optimal amount of information is made available so that a high-quality decision can be made. At the same time, the coach should guard against the "pooling of ignorance," which results when members without the necessary expertise and knowledge participate in decisions.

4. *Problem complexity.* On the basis of Kelley and Thibaut's (1969) work discussed earlier, Chelladurai and Haggerty suggested that when a problem is complex the coach or one player with the necessary information is more likely to make the optimal decision than a group. The selection of plays for a football team is an example of a complex problem in which the relative abilities of team members and opponents, the sequence of events, and the various options and their consequences all must be held in perspective.

5. *Group acceptance.* It was noted previously that the acceptance of a decision by the group, which is essential for effective implementation of the decision, is facilitated by member participation. However, acceptance of some decisions may not be critical. For instance, the decision to use a full-court press would be successful only if the players accept the press as appropriate and as within their capabilities. In contrast, acceptance of a decision to practice foul shots every day is not critical, as it is quite specific and its execution can easily be monitored.

6. *Coach's power.* To the extent that group acceptance of a decision is important, that acceptance may be affected by the coach's power over the group.[1] The coach's power base may consist of one or more of the following: (a) control over rewards; (b) control over punishments; (c) the authority residing

in the position of a coach; (d) the interpersonal liking and admiration the athletes have for the coach; and (e) the expertise, superior knowledge, and past performance of the coach. It should be pointed out that group acceptance emanating from the coach's referent and expert power is of real essence. The other three bases of power (reward, coercion, and legitimacy) only elicit compliance, not acceptance.

7. *Group integration.* Group integration encompasses the quality of interpersonal relations on the team and the relative homogeneity of members in ability and tenure. If the team is not integrated, the participative process will not yield optimal decisions and may weaken the already fragile team consensus and team spirit.

The next component of the normative model is the specification of the following three decision styles:

- *Autocratic style.* In the autocratic style the coach makes the final decision. Although consultation with one or more players is included within the autocratic style in this model, other authors (Vroom & Yetton, 1973) prefer to treat this consultation process as a separate style of decision making.

- *Participative style.* In participative decision making, the group, which includes the coach as just another member, makes the decision.

- *Delegative style.* In the delegative style the coach delegates the decision making to one or more members. The coach's involvement is restricted to announcing the decision and implementing it.

Having specified the attributes of a problem situation and the three decision styles, Chelladurai and Haggerty presented the model in the form of a flowchart as shown in Figure 7-1. The attributes are listed as questions at the top of the chart. The decision maker is required to follow the branches of the flowchart as indicated by the yes or no responses to the questions. At the terminal nodes the appropriate decision styles are indicated.

[1]Our description of the coach's power follows French and Raven's (1959) original conception of five bases of social power: reward power, coercive power, referent power, expert power, and legitimate power.

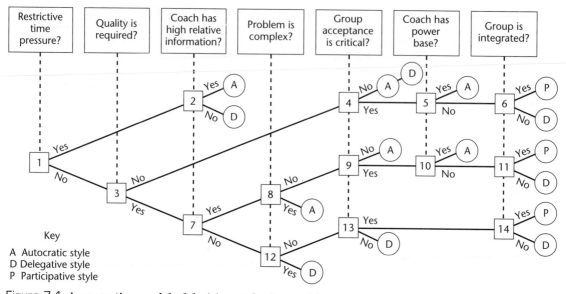

Figure 7-1 **A normative model of decision styles in coaching**
    Source: Reprinted from "A Normative Model of Decision-Making Styles in Coaching," by P. Chelladurai and
    T. R. Haggerty, 1978, *Athletic Administration, 13*(1), p. 8. Used with permission.

Although Chelladurai and Haggerty (1978) acknowledged that their model was fashioned after the framework provided by Vroom and Yetton (1973), there are considerable differences between the two approaches. Therefore, the results of empirical research carried out with the Vroom and Yetton model cannot be used to substantiate the Chelladurai and Haggerty model. Thus, the latter remains a heuristic model without any empirical base. Furthermore, the two studies conducted in this regard are not entirely supportive of the model. The next section further elucidates these research efforts.

Research on Decision Styles in Coaching

Research Strategy

The method used in the following research studies of Chelladurai and his associates was to present a set of cases representing all possible configurations of the presence or absence (yes-no or high-low) of selected problem attributes. For example,

Chelladurai, Haggerty, and Baxter (1989) and Chelladurai and Quek (1995) used five problem attributes (quality requirement, coach's information, problem complexity, acceptance requirement, and team integration). The complete crossing of high-low dichotomy of five problem attributes resulted in 32 cases ($2 \times 2 \times 2 \times 2 \times 2$). Following each case, a set of decision styles were presented for the respondents to indicate the one style they would choose or prefer in that particular case.

Early Studies at University Level

A study by Gordon (1983) was the only attempt to test the Chelladurai and Haggerty model in its entirety. Gordon's study was concerned with soccer coaches' self-reports on what decision styles they would use in any given situation and on what other coaches would use in the same situation, as well as with soccer players' preferences for a specific decision style in a given situation and their perceptions of what decision style their coaches would use in the same situation.

Chelladurai and Arnott's study (1985) was concerned only with the preferences of university-level basketball players of both sexes. Furthermore, their study included only four of the seven problem attributes (quality requirement, coach's information, problem complexity, and group integration). They argued that these four attributes were more critical in the determination of players' preferences.

In both studies the categories of decision styles were autocratic, consultative, participative, and delegative. It must be noted that these authors, in contrast to Chelladurai and Haggerty (1978), separated the consultative style from the autocratic style. The consultative style was defined as the coach's making the final decision after consulting with one or more members of the team.

Table 7-2 presents the percentage distribution of each decision-style choice totaled over all various configurations of problem attributes. The notable finding of both studies was that the delegative style was totally rejected by the respondents. Obviously, this finding is contrary

to the normative model (see Figure 7-1), wherein the delegative style was prescribed in 7 of the 15 situations. The normative model prescribed the delegative style only under the simultaneous occurrence of the conditions that (1) the coach does not have the necessary information, which prohibits him or her from making the decision, and (2) the group is not integrated, which precludes the participative style. However, we must consider the relative influence of the coach and team members in the decision styles. For instance, Chelladurai and Arnott (1985) argued that the four decision styles could be placed on a continuum on the basis of the degree of the coach's influence in the decisions. That is, the coach's influence ranges from 100% in the autocratic style to 0% in the delegative style, as shown in Figure 7-2. It is unlikely that the coach would want to relinquish decision control completely and therefore would be unlikely to simply delegate in any situation. From the players' perspective both the autocratic style and the delegative style exclude them from participation (see Figure 7-2).

Table 7-2 **Percentage Distribution of Decision-Style Choices**

	Decision Styles			
	A	C	G	D
University Soccer (Gordon, 1983)				
Coaches' own choices	46.3	33.3	18.5	1.9
Coaches' perceptions of other coaches	45.5	41.2	12.5	0.8
Players' preferences	31.2	41.9	12.5	0.8
Players' perceptions of coaches' choices	43.0	39.6	15.4	2.0
University Basketball (Chelladurai & Arnott, 1985)				
Players' preferences				
Females	33.0	18.1	46.9	2.0
Males	38.9	25.8	34.1	1.2

A = Autocratic; C = Consultative; G = Group; D = Delegative

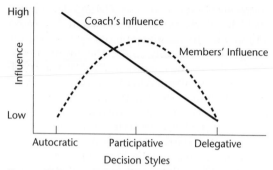

Figure 7-2 **Coach's and members' relative influence in three decision styles**

Apparently, members would forego their influence in favor of the coach rather than in favor of another teammate(s). . . . One possible explanation for this result could be that sharing of the decision-making power with one or more (but limited) members from the

group is antithetical to the egalitarian notion inherent in a team. That is, such delegation to a few athletes may be construed as preferential treatment by the rest of the team. (Chelladurai & Arnott, 1985, pp. 21–22)

High School Studies Based on Vroom and Yetton Decision Styles

Based on the earlier findings that delegation is not a viable option in team sports, Chelladurai, Haggerty, and Baxter (1989) and Chelladurai and Quek (1995) used the five decision styles prescribed by Vroom and Yetton for group problems. These five decision styles are described in Table 7-3.

Furthermore, only five of the problem attributes specified by Chelladurai and Haggerty—quality requirement, coach's information, problem complexity, acceptance requirements, and team integration—were included in these two studies. Time pressure was excluded because its presence automatically led to the autocratic or delegative

Table 7-3 **Decision Styles in Coaching**

Autocratic I (*AI*)	The coach solves the problem himself/herself, using the information available to him/her at the time.
Autocratic II (*AII*)	The coach obtains the necessary information from relevant players, then decides himself/herself. The coach may or may not tell the players what the problem is in getting the information. The role played by the players is clearly one of providing information to the coach, rather than generating or evaluating solutions.
Consultative I (*CI*)	The coach consults with the players *individually* and then makes the decision himself/herself. The coach's decision may or may not reflect the players' influence.
Consultative II (*CII*)	The coach consults with his/her players *as a group* and then makes the decision himself/herself. The coach's decision may or may not reflect the players' influence.
Group (*G*)	The coach shares the problem with his/her players. Then the coach and the players jointly make the decision without any influence on the coach's part.

Source: Modified from Vroom and Yetton, 1973[a]

[a]Recently Vroom (2000, 2003) has changed the names for the decision styles into (a) *Decide* for AI and AII, *Consult Individually* for CI, *Consult Group* for CII, and *Facilitate* for G. A new decision style named *Delegate,* in which the decision is delegated to the whole group, has been added to the list.

style based only on coach's information without reference to the other attributes. Coach's power was excluded because it was expected to be similar across comparable institutions (i.e., universities within one province).

The subjects in the Chelladurai, Haggerty, and Baxter (1989) study were 22 coaches (males = 15; females = 7), and 99 players (males = 53; females = 46) from university basketball teams in Ontario, Canada. The coaches indicated their choice of a decision style in specific situations, and the athletes expressed their preferences of a particular decision style in the same situations. Chelladurai and Quek's (1995) study was concerned with the decision-style choices of 51 coaches of high school boys' basketball teams in and around Toronto, Canada.

The results of the two studies are presented in Table 7-4. Referring to the Chelladurai, Haggerty, and Baxter (1989) study, the distribution of decision-style choices was significantly associated with group membership (coaches, male players, and female players). Also, within each group the actual distribution was significantly different from the expected equal distribution across the five decision styles. The *AI* style (coach making decision alone) was chosen more often than any other style by each group. The *CII* style (consultation with all players on a group basis) was the

second most popular choice in all three groups. It must also be noted that the participative style (*G*) was chosen less than 20% of the time in all three groups. When the *AI*, *AII*, and *CI* styles are combined (because they involve minimal influence from the members), the total percentage amounts to 64.8% for coaches, 59.4% for male players, and 57.3% for female players.

The frequency distribution of the total choices in Chelladurai and Quek's (1995) study is presented in Table 7-4 along with those of Chelladurai, Haggerty, and Baxter (1989). Autocratic style without getting more information (*AI*) was the most preferred choice (32.5%) and consultation with a few individuals (*CI*) was the least preferred choice (9.7%) of the total decision-style choices.

As noted earlier, the results shown in Tables 7-2 and 7-4 are drawn from the total frequencies of decision-style choices summed over all cases included in a study (16 or 32 cases). These results show that all of the decision styles (four or five as the case may be) were acceptable to varying degrees. It must also be noted that in all the studies reported in Tables 7-2 and 7-4, the subjects chose or preferred different decision styles according to situational characteristics (i.e., in each of the 16 or 32 situations). Insofar as both the players and the coaches were influenced more or less to the same degree by the variations in the

Table 7-4 **Percentage Distribution of Decision-Style Choices**

	Decision Styles[a]				
	AI	AII	CI	CII	G
University Basketball (Chelladurai, Haggerty, & Baxter, 1989)					
Coaches' choices	34.8	20.2	9.8	20.2	15.1
Male players' preferences	28.5	16.8	13.9	21.3	19.5
Female players' preferences	30.1	14.0	13.2	25.8	16.3
High School Basketball (Chelladurai & Quek, 1995)					
Coaches' choices	32.5	15.4	9.7	21.3	21.1

[a]See Table 7-3 for a description of the decision styles.

problem situation, it is appropriate to dub the *situation* as democratic or autocratic rather than labeling the coaches as democratic or autocratic.

Future Research

It must be noted that the preceding studies were concerned with team sports (soccer and basketball). The efficacy of specific decision styles needs to be verified in the context of differing types of sports (e.g., small versus large teams, open versus closed sports, individual versus team sports). For instance, the delegative style that was rejected by the soccer players (Gordon, 1983) and basketball players (Chelladurai & Arnott, 1985) could indeed be a viable decision style in individual sports that present a dyadic setting instead of a group setting as in the case of a team. That is, an individual sport team consists of numerous but distinct units consisting of the coach and each individual athlete, whereas there is only one unit in the case of a team sport (the coach and all athletes). Thus, the individual sport coach is not burdened as much with the task of coordinating the activities of the athletes as is a team sport coach. Furthermore, the individual sport coach need not be unduly concerned about consistency of his or her behavior toward all athletes. Therefore, delegating the decision-making authority to some athletes and not to others may be acceptable in individual sports.

It was alluded to earlier that the delegative style is antithetical to the egalitarian orientations of team sports. But the notion of egalitarianism may not be relevant in sports characterized by a hierarchical substructure that places one or more players in a superior position (e.g., the quarterback in North American football). Even in sports without a formal hierarchy, there may exist an informal and socially acceptable "pecking order." Such stratified patterns of interactions may permit the delegation of decision making to those informal leaders.

There have been reports that females prefer more participation than males do (e.g., Chelladurai & Saleh, 1978). In contrast, Sherman, Fuller, and Speed (2000) found no gender differences in preferences for participation. Similar contradictory results also were found in the two studies of decision styles, which verified gender differences. Chelladurai and Arnott (1985) found that the females preferred more participation, but Chelladurai, Haggerty, and Baxter (1989) did not find any gender difference. These latter authors argued that "the gender differences reported earlier were a function of less explicit description of the decision situations and the inclusion of fewer decision styles" (p. 213). Additional research is needed before any definitive statements can be made on this issue.

It has been reported that athletes from different countries and cultures have varying preferences for their participation in decision making (e.g., Chelladurai, 1993; Hastie, 1993). But these results reflected a general orientation toward participation in decision making without references to the problem attributes. It is necessary to extend this line of research to verify if athletes from different countries or cultures vary in their preferences for participation in a given problem situation and if they react differently to the problem attributes.

The availability of relevant information is fundamental to effective decision making. Hence, it is not surprising that the normative model and the subsequent studies included coaches' information and athletes' information as two of the problem attributes. A unique feature of athletics is the prolonged and intense interactions between coaches and athletes. During these interactions, coaches gain a knowledge of the skills and abilities of the athletes through directing, monitoring, and evaluating their activities. In addition, coaches also glean some insights into the psychological makeup and motivational patterns of their athletes. These pieces of information, coupled with coaches' knowledge of the sport and the opponents in the league, should make coaches more knowledgeable than any single player. Directive leaders who have the information make the best use of the information and make better decisions than do nondirective leaders (Larson, Foster-Fishman, & Franz, 1998). These assumptions could underlie the preference of athletes for more autocratic decisions from their coaches. Future research investigating decision styles of coaches may also verify whether coaches have the relevant information, and whether athletes believe their coaches have the necessary information.

Endorsement of the autocratic style by most of the athletes in these studies could be based on the assumption that the coaches' decisions will be fair to everyone. This sense of fairness of decisions is known as **organizational justice.** There are two aspects to organizational justice: procedural justice and distributive justice. **Procedural justice** refers to whether the procedures employed in coming to a decision are fair and would address these questions (Folger, 1987):

- Is the coach consistent across situations and players?
- Is he or she unbiased in making decisions?
- Is the decision based on accurate information?
- Does the process include the concerns of all?
- Is the decision ethical and moral?
- Is the coach willing to correct a bad decision?

Distributive justice refers to the fairness in the distribution of resources and rewards to organizational members (Cohen, 1987). In our context, distributive justice answers these questions:

- Does the coach reward players based on their contributions?
- Does coach's use of players reflect their relative talents and abilities?
- Does the coach punish players based on the severity of rule violations?
- Does the coach provide social support to players based on their need?

Given these notions of justice, the autocratic style of decision making may be considered fair and humanistic if these questions are addressed. One future avenue of research is to verify the extent to which justice, as perceived by athletes, is related to the coach's style of decision making.

An overriding consideration in the choice of a decision style by a coach may be his or her inability to successfully engage in participatory procedures. As Vroom and Jago (1988) point out, the skills required to make autocratic decisions are different from those required to make participative decisions. To make an effective autocratic decision the coach must be able to identify alternatives, evaluate them, and then choose the best alternative. In more participative decision processes the coach needs the skills of a facilitator and a discussion leader. More specifically, the coach needs the skills to (a) state the problem in clear terms, (b) conduct the discussion making sure that it does not go off in tangents, and (c) assist the group in reaching a good decision without polarizing into cliques. Some coaches may choose more autocratic decisions because they feel that they do not possess the unique skills necessary to make participative decisions. It is important, therefore, that future research relate the decision-style choices of coaches to their abilities in participative procedures. It is also important that training in participative procedures become part of coach development programs.

The studies reported here were based on Vroom and Yetton's (1973) model, but future research in the area should include the additional characteristics of the problem attributes as suggested by Vroom and Jago (1988). More specifically, Vroom and Jago added four more problem attributes to the original eight attributes. These are (a) time constraint, which may limit member participation; (b) geographical dispersion of subordinates, which may increase the cost of participation; (c) motivation–time, which refers to the leader's motivation to minimize the time taken for a decision; and (d) motivation–development, which reflects the leader's motivation to develop subordinates through participation. Of these, geographical location is not relevant to the athletic context because a coach and his or her team are assembled in one location almost all the time. Time constraint was already included in Chelladurai and Haggerty's (1978) normative model but was not used in subsequent research because according to that model the presence of time constraint led directly to an autocratic or delegative decision depending on whether the coach had the information or not (see Figure 7-1). Given Vroom and Jago's (1988) emphasis on time constraint, future research in sport may follow suit.

The remaining two new attributes—motivation–time and motivation–development—are meaningful in the context of sports. From one perspective, a coach's concerns with minimizing decision time and maximizing player development may be seen as reflective of Fiedler's (1967) dichotomy of task orientation and people orientation. From another perspective, either of these concerns may be seen to be part of the situation. This would be particularly true of athletics in educational institutions. High school and collegiate coaches are faced with these two different and, at times, conflicting demands. It is likely that the relative emphasis placed on these two requirements may vary from one situation to another. Thus, it is necessary to assess the effects of these two attributes in the choice of a decision style in athletics.

Recently, Dirks (2000) found that trust in the coach had a significant effect on the performance of NCAA basketball teams. He defined trust as "an expectation of belief that the team can rely on the leader's action or words and that the leader has good intentions toward the team" (p. 1004). Dirks argued that as the decisions made by the leader are of great importance to the team, they must be embraced by members for the team to perform well. And acceptance of those decisions is a function of players' trust in the coach. Following this line of reasoning, future research may verify the relationships between members' trust in the coach and their preferences for varying decision styles in different problem situations.

Group integration may influence the choice of a decision style. An alternative perspective is presented by a recent finding that perceived democratic behavior of the coach as being strongly associated with cohesion of the team (Shields, Gardner, Bredemeier, & Bostro, 1997). It follows that if a coach adopts a more participative decision style, he or she is likely to foster group integration. It also follows that group integration and participative decision styles could have reciprocal influence on each other. Thus supposition needs to be verified in future research.

Summary

Theories relating to the social process of decision making and the related research indicate that it is more useful to assume that situations call for autocratic or participative decision making rather than merely to categorize coaches as autocratic or democratic. This is not to deny the influence of the coach's personality but to point out that the coach's personality is only part of the total situation, which includes the team members' personalities and preferences and the type of problem involved.

There is a common tendency to view the autocratic style as something evil, indulged in only by despots and dictators as a device for furthering their own interests. Contrastingly, the participative style is viewed as a humanistic approach aimed at the welfare of the members. Coaches and athletes need to understand that these contrasting decision styles are not value laden and that the autocratic style can be associated with humanism and benevolence.

Finally, research in the area of decision styles, although rather limited, clearly shows that the autocratic style is quite acceptable to the athletes in certain circumstances. It appears that coaches need to select a decision style appropriate to the particular situation rather than being guided by a belief that participative decisions are always superior or always preferred.

Study Questions

1. List and explain briefly three factors that may "cloud" the issue of participation in decision making.

2. Categorize each leader behavior dimension in Table 7-1 as task, social, or decision-making oriented.

3. Distinguish between the cognitive and social processes of decision making. Give examples from sport.

4. Describe the advantages and disadvantages of participative decision making in team sports.

5. List the seven problem attributes that Chelladurai and Haggerty (1978) deemed relevant to decision styles in the athletic context.

6. The results of a study showed that both coaches and players rejected the delegative style. How is this result explained in terms of coaches' and players' perceived influence across each of the three styles (autocratic, participative, and delegative)?

7. Give examples of situations in which the coach should make a decision (a) without consultation (*AI*), (b) after consulting with the whole group (*CII*), and (c) jointly with group members (*G*). Explain why.

8. Give examples of how decision-style choices might differ in individual as opposed to team sport.

9. What factors within the coach make him or her more autocratic or more participative in decision making?

References

Chelladurai, P. (1993). Leadership. In R. N. Singer, M. Murphy, & K. Tennant (Eds.), *The handbook on research in sport psychology.* (pp. 647–671). New York: Macmillan.

Chelladurai, P., & Arnott, M. (1985). Decision styles in coaching: Preferences of basketball players. *Research Quarterly for Exercise and Sport, 56*(1), 15–24.

Chelladurai, P., & Carron, A. V. (1982, May). *Task characteristics and individual differences, and their relationship to preferred leadership in sports.* Paper presented at the annual meeting of the North American Society for the Psychology of Sport and Physical Activity, College Park, MD.

Chelladurai, P., & Haggerty, T. R. (1978). A normative model of decision styles in coaching. *Athletic Administration, 13,* 6–9.

Chelladurai, P., Haggerty, T. R., & Baxter, P. R. (1989). Decision styles choices of university basketball coaches and players. *Journal of Sports and Exercise Psychology, 11,* 201–215.

Chelladurai, P., & Quek, C. B. (1995). Decision style choices of high school coaches: The effects of situational and coach characteristics. *Journal of Sport Behavior, 18*(2) 91–108.

Chelladurai, P., & Saleh, S. D. (1978). Preferred leadership in sports. *Canadian Journal of Applied Sport Sciences, 3,* 85–92.

Chelladurai, P., & Saleh, S. D. (1980). Dimensions of leader behavior in sports. Development of a leadership scale. *Journal of Sport Psychology, 2*(1), 34–45.

Cohen, R. L. (1987). Distributive justice: Theory and research. *Social Justice Research, 1,* 19–40.

Dirks, K. T. (2000). Trust in leadership and team performance: Evidence for NCAA basketball. *Journal of Applied Psychology, 85,* 1004–1012.

Fiedler, F. E. (1967). *A theory of leadership effectiveness.* New York: McGraw-Hill.

Folger, R. (1987). Distributive and procedural justice in the workplace. *Social Justice Research, 3,* 141–183.

French, J. R. P., & Raven, B. (1959). The bases of social power. In D. Cartwright (Ed.), *Studies in social power* (pp. 150–167). Ann Arbor, MI: University of Michigan, Institute for Social Research.

Gordon, S. (1983, July). *Decision-making styles in university soccer coaching.* Paper presented at the FISU conference, World University Games, Edmonton, Canada.

Hastie, P. A. (1993). Coaching preferences of high school girl volleyball players. *Perceptual and Motor Skills, 77,* 1309–1310.

Kelley, H. H., & Thibaut, J. W. (1969). Group problem solving. In G. Lindzey & E. Arconson (Eds.), *The handbook of social psychology* (2nd ed., Vol. 4, pp. 1–101). Reading, MA: Addison-Wesley.

Larson, J. R., Foster-Fishman, P. G., & Franz, T. M. (1998). Leadership style and the discussion of shared and unshared information in decision-making groups. *Personality and Social Psychology Bulletin, 24,* 482–496.

Nutt, P. C. (2002). *Why decisions fail: Avoiding the blunders and traps that lead to debacles.* Williston, VT: Berrett-Koehler.

Sage, G. H. (1973). The coach as management: Organizational leadership in American sport. *Quest, 19,* 35–40.

Sherman, C. A. Fuller, R., & Speed, H. D. (2000). Gender comparisons of preferred coaching behaviors in Australian sports, *Journal of Sport Behavior, 23*(4), 389–406.

Shields, D. L. L., Gardner, D. E., Bredemeier, B. J. L., & Bostro, A. (1997). The relationship between leadership behaviors and group cohesion in team sports. *The Journal of Psychology, 131*(2), 196–210.

Vroom, V. H. (2000). Leadership and the decision-making process. *Organizational Dynamics, 28*(4), 82–94.

Vroom, V. H. (2003). Educating managers for decision making and leadership. *Management Decision, 41*(10), 968–978.

Vroom, V. H., & Jago, A. G. (1974). On the validity of the Vroom-Yetton model. *Journal of Applied Psychology, 63,* 151–162.

Vroom, V. H., & Jago, A. G. (1988). *The new leadership: Managing participation in organizations.* Englewood Cliffs, NJ: Prentice-Hall.

Vroom, V. H., & Yetton, R. N. (1973). *Leadership and decision making.* Pittsburgh: University of Pittsburgh Press.

Williams, R. (2004). [Foreword]. In D. Smith & G. D. Bell, *The Carolina Way: Leadership lessons from a life in coaching* (pp. ix–xiv). New York: The Penguin Press.

Social Interactions

The Sport Team as an Effective Group

Mark A. Eys, *The University of Western Ontario*
Shauna M. Burke, *The University of Western Ontario*
Albert V. Carron, *The University of Western Ontario*
Paul W. Dennis, *Toronto Maple Leafs Hockey Club*

I'm humiliated, not for the loss—I can always deal with wins and losses—but I'm disappointed because I had a job to do as a coach, to get us to understand how we're supposed to play as a team and act as a team, and I don't think we did that.

—United States Men's Olympic Basketball Coach Larry Brown after losing to Puerto Rico in the preliminary rounds of the Athens 2004 Summer Games

Membership and involvement in groups is a fundamental characteristic of our society. We band together in a large number and variety of groups for social reasons or to carry out more effectively some job or task. Thus, each of us interacts daily with numerous other people in group settings—in the family, at work, in social situations, on sport teams. The result is a reciprocal exchange of influence; we exert an influence on other people in groups, and, in turn, those groups and their members have an influence on us. The following two examples illustrate just how powerful this influence can be.

In January 1980, Tony Conigliaro, a former Boston Red Sox baseball player, was driving with his brother when he suffered a massive heart attack—he experienced "sudden death." At least

6 minutes passed before CPR was administered and his heart was stimulated into activity. However, he remained in a coma for 4 days, and the prognosis for any significant recovery was bleak. A lack of oxygen to the brain for as few as 4 minutes can produce permanent brain damage. Also, people who are comatose for the length of time experienced by Conigliaro are almost never able to walk, talk, or look after themselves totally again.

Conigliaro's family refused to believe the prognosis. They were at his side constantly, talking, encouraging, providing love and affection. Slowly Conigliaro fought back, began to talk, and showed improvements that astounded his doctors. In fact, as Maximillian Kaulback, one of his doctors, stated, "This case is beyond science. . . . I wouldn't be surprised if someday it was proven that the input of the family in cases like this is significant" (as quoted in McCallum, 1982, p. 72). The incident is powerful and moving; it also illustrates the importance of the family's positive influence—its love, concern, and physical and emotional support. The second illustration, however, shows another side of group influence.

In August of 2003, members of a high school football team in Pennsylvania attended a preseason camp. During the week of practices and team bonding, three members of the team were subjected to the common practice of hazing, a process of humiliating new members of the group. However, in this instance, the actions of the more senior members not only humiliated the freshmen but caused two members to seek medical treatment for their injuries. As a result, a number of spiraling events occurred that included the suspension of the team, first-degree felony charges for the perpetrators, and a media frenzy around the small community. Wahl and Wertheim (2003) described the situation:

> As the hazing inquiry intensified and the severity of the acts became more apparent, investigators from the criminal justice system . . . confronted an impenetrable wall of silence. The victims had spoken, albeit reluctantly, but no other players were willing to provide firsthand accounts. Nuwer says this is typical behavior: "Until you get to be about 25 years old, loyalty to the group is more important than moral qualms. We're more likely to agree as a group that we should turn on this victim than we are to confront one another."

These anecdotes show the dramatic influence groups can have on their members. In the Conigliaro case the influence was a positive one, whereas in the hazing case the influence was negative and destructive. The fundamental question is how groups can come to exert such influence. From a coaching perspective, insight into this issue could produce possible prescriptions for the development of a positive, productive sport group—an effective, cohesive team. In this chapter, both the nature of groups and group cohesion are discussed, and some suggestions for the development of effective groups in sport settings are offered.

The Nature of Groups

Definition

As Carron and Hausenblas (1998) note, "every group is like all other groups, like some other groups, and like no other group" (p. 11). What this means, of course, is that every group not only contains characteristics that are common to every other group but they also possess characteristics that are unique to themselves. The uniqueness or diversity among groups has led group dynamics theoreticians to advance a variety of definitions in an attempt to portray what a group is. Carron and Hausenblas categorized these definitions into five general categories. In the first category, the *common fate* of members serves to highlight the nature of a group. Another category of definition focuses on the fact that groups are a source of *mutual benefit* for members. Also, groups are characterized by a *social structure;* that is, members of groups behave in a manner that demonstrates the presence of roles, norms, status differences, and positional differences. A fourth category highlights the fact that groups are characterized by a variety of *group processes* such as communication, cooperation, task and social interactions, and so on. The fifth general category of definition is based on the fact that members of groups engage in *self-categorization;* that is, they consider themselves to be part of a "we" that differentiates them from "they."

Carron and Hausenblas drew on these various definitions of a group to define a sport team:

> a collection of two or more individuals who possess a common identity, have common goals and objectives, share a common fate, exhibit structured patterns of interaction and modes of communication, hold common perceptions about group structure, are personally and instrumentally interdependent, reciprocate interpersonal attraction, and consider themselves to be a group. (pp. 13–14)

A university basketball team can be used to illustrate each of these definitional components. Such teams are typically composed of 12 athletes (i.e., two or more individuals), all of whom consider themselves to be members of a group representing the university in intercollegiate competitions (i.e., common identity). Every team has explicit or implicit short- and long-term goals such as, for instance, winning upcoming games or eventually winning the conference (i.e., common goals and objectives). Success or failure in the achievement of these goals is experienced by the team as a whole (i.e., common fate). To increase the chances for team success, the coaching staff implements and emphasizes team offensive plays and defensive formations (i.e., structured pattern of interaction). In the heat of game competition, the athletes (or coaching staff) communicate various offensive or defensive options using either nonverbal communications or coded verbal communications (i.e., structured modes of communication). Over time, team positions become fixed, individual roles such as leadership become established, and common expectations for behavior develop (i.e., group structure). In order for the team to function effectively, team social gatherings and team competitions must be attended by a minimum quorum of athletes (i.e., personal and task interdependence). Because of the constant contact athletes have in a team context, friendships typically develop (i.e., interpersonal attraction). Finally, athletes on any team consider themselves to be members of that group (i.e., self-categorization).

Groups Versus Collections of Individuals

Individuals who study groups often make an important distinction between a group and a collection of individuals. Alvin Zander (1982), the former director of the Research Center for Group Dynamics at the University of Michigan, highlighted this issue when he pointed out that

> a group is a collection or set of individuals who interact with and depend on each other. A number of persons jointly engaged in an activity—traveling on a sightseeing tour, picking apples in an orchard, working in a personnel department, attending a seminar—are not necessarily a group, but it may become one. (pp. 1–2)

Zander went on to say that 10 characteristics that differentiate a group from a collection of individuals are that people in groups (1) talk freely, (2) are interested in the welfare of the collective as a whole, (3) feel that their associates are helpful, (4) try to assist those associates, (5) refer to the collection of individuals as "we" and to other collections as "they," (6) faithfully participate in group activities, (7) are not primarily interested in individual accomplishments, (8) are concerned with the activities of other members, (9) do not see others as rivals, and (10) are not often absent.

Sport teams including teams in the so-called individual sports of wrestling, swimming, and golf possess all of these characteristics—they are groups in every sense of the word. And any group can become more effective. On a sport team, coaches or leaders must facilitate the development of the sense of "we" and reduce the importance of "I." Associated with the development of a stronger sense of "we" is an increase in group cohesiveness. The terms *cohesion* and *group* are tautological—if a group exists, cohesion is present.

Group Cohesion

Definition

Groups are dynamic, not static. They exhibit life and vitality, interaction, and activity. Their vitality may be reflected in many ways—some positive, others negative. For example, at times the group and its members may be in harmony; at other times, conflict and tension may predominate. Sometimes communication may be excellent between leaders and members, but at other times, it may be nonexistent. Also, commitment to the group's goals and purposes may vary over time. All these variations represent different behavioral manifestations of an underlying, fundamental group property that is referred to as "cohesiveness."

In an early, classic definition advanced by Festinger, Schachter, and Back (1950), **cohesiveness** was viewed as the sum of the forces that cause members to remain in the group. Subsequently, a second, classic definition was proposed by Gross and Martin (1951), who considered it to be the resistance of the group to disruptive forces. More recently, Carron, Brawley, and Widmeyer (1998) proposed that cohesion is "a dynamic process which is reflected in the tendency for a group to stick together and remain united in the pursuit of its instrumental objectives and/or for the satisfaction of member affective needs" (p. 213).

Several points should be made about this last definition because it explicitly highlights the nature of cohesiveness as it is manifested in most groups. First, cohesion is multidimensional. Groups stick together and remain united as a result of many factors. The contributing factors causing one group to stick together may not be evident in another apparently identical group. Nevertheless, both groups manage to stick together. For example, a basketball team may be highly united around its task objectives and, at the same time, may experience open conflict from a social perspective. Another similar basketball team may have an absence of task unity but may be united socially.

Second, the use of the word *dynamic* is an acknowledgment that cohesion is not as transitory as a state, but neither is it as stable as a trait. The factors contributing to cohesion can change over time with experiences.

The third point surrounds the instrumental nature of cohesion. Regardless of whether groups are formed for task or social reasons, all groups have a purpose. Thus, members of a social group meeting to develop or maintain better friendships are cohering for instrumental reasons. As a result, the instrumentality that characterizes cohesion stems from the motivational base of the group (Sherif & Sherif, 1969).

The fourth issue is that cohesion has an affective dimension. Social relationships among group members may be present in a group initially, or they might evolve over time. But even in highly task-oriented groups—work crews, sport teams, military units—social cohesion generally develops as a result of members' instrumental and social interactions and communications.

Finally, the goals and objectives of all groups are complex and varied. Consequently, cohesiveness has many dimensions or aspects—it is perceived in multiple ways by different groups and their members. It has been proposed (Brawley,

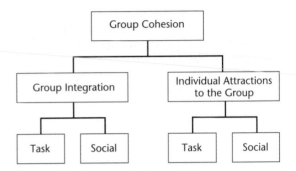

Figure 8-1 A conceptual model for group cohesiveness
Source: Brawley, Carron, and Widmeyer, 1987; Carron, Widmeyer, and Brawley, 1985; Widmeyer, Brawley, and Carron, 1985.

Carron, & Widmeyer, 1987; Carron, Widmeyer, & Brawley, 1985; Widmeyer, Brawley, & Carron, 1985) that these multidimensional perceptions of the group are organized and integrated by individual members into two general categories (Figure 8-1). The first category, **group integration**, represents each individual's perceptions of the group as a total unit, set, or collection. The second, **individual attractions to the group**, represents each individual's personal attractions to the group. Both of these categories of perceptions about the degree of unity within the group are also assumed to be manifested in two principal ways: in relation to the group's *task* and in terms of the *social* aspects of the group. This conception of cohesiveness is depicted in Figure 8-1. As the figure shows, cohesion within sport groups is considered to have four facets: individual attractions to the group–task, individual attractions to the group–social, group integration–task, and group integration–social.

The Correlates of Cohesiveness

Because cohesiveness is multidimensional, it is associated with a wide variety of correlates or factors. Carron and Hausenblas (1998) have provided a framework to discuss the main correlates of cohesion in sport teams. As Figure 8-2 shows, one general category is referred to as *environmental factors,* which are situational. Cohesiveness in sport

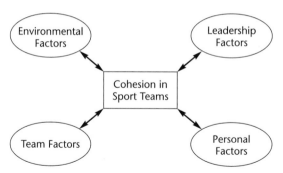

Figure 8-2 **A general framework for examining the correlates of cohesion in sport teams**
Source: Reprinted by permission from Carron and Hausenblas, 1998.

teams is related to aspects of the social setting, the physical environment, and various structural characteristics of the group. Characteristics of individual team members are also associated with the nature and amount of cohesiveness that is present; the category *personal factors* represents these correlates. *Leadership factors,* the third general category, is an acknowledgment that decision styles, leader behaviors, and leader–member relations are also related to team cohesion. The fourth category, *team factors,* represents the group-based aspects that are associated with a stronger bond, a sense of "we," and a commitment to the collective. In the following sections, some of the main correlates within each general category are identified.

Developing a Team Concept: Correlates of Cohesion

Environmental Factors

Individuals who are in close **proximity,** who are physically close to each other, have a greater tendency to bond together. Physical proximity by itself is not always sufficient for producing cohesiveness, but being in close contact and having the opportunity for interaction and communication does hasten group development. Some situations in sport that ensure physical proximity among group members include

having a specific team locker room, residence, or training table. In youth sport situations, scheduling games that require the team to travel together in a bus or car is also beneficial. The important point is that group members should be placed in situations where interaction is inevitable.

A second situational factor associated with the development of cohesiveness is **distinctiveness.** As a set of individuals becomes more separate, more distinctive from others, feelings of oneness and unity increase. Traditionally, distinctiveness is achieved through team uniforms and mottos, by having special initiation rites, by providing special privileges, or by demanding special sacrifices.

Many of the factors that make athletes distinct from the general population are taken for granted. These include year-round intensive training programs and reduced time for social activities or part-time employment. The coach should highlight such factors to develop a stronger feeling of commonality. Finally, emphasizing the sense of tradition and the history of the organization or team can contribute to the feeling of distinctiveness.

The team's **size** is also associated with the development of cohesiveness. Research by Widmeyer, Brawley, and Carron (1990) has shown that there is an inverted-*U* relationship between social cohesion and team size in intramural basketball teams. That is, moderate-sized groups showed the greatest cohesiveness, and larger and smaller groups exhibited the least. In research by Widmeyer and Williams (1991) using only the travel rosters of women's NCAA golf teams, however, social cohesion did not vary with team size.

Research with intramural basketball teams (Widmeyer et al., 1990) has also shown that task cohesiveness decreases with increasing group size. Widmeyer and colleagues felt that this decrease could be attributed to the fact that it is more difficult to obtain consensus and task commitment in larger groups. In their research with women's NCAA golf teams, Widmeyer and Williams (1991) found that increasing team size was associated with increasing task cohesion. However, they only tested the 4–5 competitors on the travel rosters who were actually involved in the competition.

The maximum team size among the teams examined was 12. Consequently, it is possible that the responses from the 7–8 golfers who were not on the travel rosters might have substantially altered the profile of the team's cohesiveness.

Personal Factors

There are a number of personal factors that have been shown to be associated with cohesion. Arguably the most important personal factor associated with the development of both task and social cohesion in sport teams is individual **satisfaction.** Satisfaction is derived from many sources (Widmeyer & Williams, 1991). The quality of the competition is one element; having opportunities for social interactions with teammates is another. In order to feel satisfied, athletes also need to feel that they are improving in skill. Satisfaction also results from the recognition of others—parents, coaches, teammates, fellow students, the public. And, of course, the athlete's relationship with his or her coach is yet another potential source of satisfaction or dissatisfaction. When these elements are satisfying, cohesiveness is enhanced.

Another personal factor that has been shown to be related to cohesion is **competitive state anxiety.** Prapavessis and Carron (1996) found that athletes who perceived their teams to be higher in task cohesion seemed to experience less cognitive anxiety. They suggested that this might be the case because members of more cohesive teams could experience less pressure to (a) carry out the responsibilities of the group and (b) satisfy other members' expectations of themselves. In addition, Eys, Hardy, Carron, and Beauchamp (2003) extended the above work and found that those athletes who perceived greater task cohesion were more likely to view their symptoms of both cognitive (e.g., worry) and somatic (e.g., sweaty palms) anxiety as facilitative (i.e., beneficial) and necessary for their competition.

The degree to which athletes engage in **social loafing** is another personal factor related to cohesion. Social loafing reflects "the reduction in individual effort when people work in groups versus when they work alone" (Carron & Hausenblas,

1998, p. 253). There are a number of potential reasons why individuals feel they can reduce their effort in a group. These include the fact that once more people take part in a task it is easier to get lost in the crowd and, thus, not expend as much effort. However, McKnight, Williams, and Widmeyer (1991) found that individuals who were members of swimming relay teams that were high in task cohesion were less likely to be a "social loafer."

A fourth factor often cited as a correlate of cohesion is the **similarity** of group members. This incorporates similarity in attitudes, aspirations, commitments, and ability. As Zander (1982) noted:

> Birds of a feather flock together, and create a more distinct entity when they do. People too form a better unit if they are alike, and an effective leader develops oneness within a set by encouraging likeness among members. To do this, she recruits persons who will interact well because of similar purpose, background, training, experience, or temperament. . . . Persons whose beliefs do not fit together well have a hard time forming a strong group. (p. 3)

However, in their study with golf teams, Widmeyer and Williams (1991) noted that similarity in terms of playing background (i.e., whether the golfer came from a country club or public courses) and number of years of experience on the team did not correlate with cohesiveness. Therefore, similarity in all aspects may not be critical in sport teams, and differences in personality, ethnicity, racial background, economic background, ability, and numerous other factors are inevitable. The coach's challenge is to work to develop a similarity in attitude about other factors, such as the group's performance goals, expectations for individual behavior, and codes of conduct for practices, games, and situations away from the sport environment.

Finally, other personal factors that are related to increased cohesion include a tendency to assume greater responsibility for negative events/ outcomes (Brawley, Carron, & Widmeyer, 1987), greater commitment to the team/organization (Widmeyer & Williams, 1991), and an increase in sacrifice behaviors (Carron & Hausenblas, 1998).

These all demonstrate the positive nature of group cohesion.

Leadership Factors

The interrelationships among the coach, the athlete, cohesiveness, and performance are complex. In a mutiny, for example, cohesion is high, the leader–subordinate relationship is poor (and the leader is excluded from the group), and performance from an organizational perspective is poor. One example of the complex interrelationship between coach, athlete, cohesiveness, and performance comes from a study by Widmeyer and Williams (1991). They had golf coaches rate the importance that they attached to task cohesion, the importance that they attached to social cohesion, and the number of techniques that they used to foster cohesiveness. These measures were not related to their athletes' perceptions of the amount of team cohesiveness. In short, in the Widmeyer and Williams study, coaches were not crucial to the development of group cohesion.

Another example of the complex relationship arises when a leader is on the fringe of the group from the perspective of cohesiveness—this can produce problems. The perceptions a group has about itself, about other groups, and about nongroup members often become distorted with increased group cohesiveness. The group tends to be very favorable in its perception of its own members and to overvalue its own contributions, importance, and performance. Also, the group tends to undervalue the contributions, importance, and performance of other groups or nongroup members. This turning inward can lead to some difficulties for a new, formally appointed leader such as a coach. The new leader may not be readily accepted, and any proposed changes to existing practices may be met with resistance (Jewell & Reitz, 1981).

This situation is often encountered in sport when a new coach replaces a highly popular, highly successful predecessor. The group makes constant comparisons between the two leaders' personalities, methods, and so on. And because a cohesive group tends to overvalue its own membership and undervalue outsiders, the new coach will encounter initial difficulties in being accepted.

When people have ownership over a decision, they tend to support that decision more strongly. Consequently, the coach's *decision style* can have an influence on the level of cohesiveness within the team. Team members engage in behaviors more persistently, with greater intensity, and for a longer duration when they have had an opportunity to participate in decision making. In short, as Westre and Weiss (1991) found when they examined the relationship between coaching behaviors and the perceptions of team cohesion by high school football players, coaches who are viewed as engaging in more democratic behaviors will be more likely to have teams with higher cohesion.

The *compatibility* between coaches and athletes (and the athlete and team as a whole) is also related to the level of cohesiveness. Carron and Chelladurai (1981) tested athletes and coaches from high school basketball and wrestling teams in their orientations/motivations toward the group activities. Three orientations were examined: task (individuals are motivated toward the group's goals), self (individuals are motivated toward personal rewards and outcomes), and affiliation (individuals are motivated to develop and maintain harmonious relationships within the group). The most important predictors of the athlete's perceptions of cohesiveness were compatibility between the athlete and his coach and between the athlete and his teammates in task motivation.

Team Factors

When a set of individuals is brought together with the intention of performing as a group, cohesion can be influenced by a number of structural characteristics that emerge as the group develops (e.g., roles and norms), processes that take place between group members (e.g., group goals, communication), and group performance outcomes that occur throughout the duration of its existence. The emergence of these factors is inevitable and essential if the set of individuals is to become a more cohesive group.

Roles. A role is a set of behaviors that are expected from the occupants of specific positions within the group. Thus, when we think of the "role of a coach," a number of expectations for behavior come to mind: instruct athletes; set up the team's offensive and defensive alignments; communicate with parents, media, and the general public; organize practices; and so on.

Within every group there are two general categories of roles, formal and informal (Mabry & Barnes, 1980). As the term suggests, **formal roles** are explicitly set out by the group or organization. Coach, team captain, and manager are examples of explicit leadership roles within a team. Spiker and setter in volleyball; forward, guard, and center in basketball; and scrum half and prop in rugby are examples of explicit performance roles. The sport team as an organization requires specific individuals to carry out each of these roles. Thus, individuals are trained or recruited for these roles, and specific expectations are held for their behavior. **Informal roles** evolve as a result of the interactions that take place among group members. Some examples of the informal roles that often emerge on a sport team are leader (which may or may not be the team captain), enforcer, police officer, social director, and team clown.

There are a variety of elements associated with athletes' roles that determine how effective they can be performed. One element is the degree to which athletes understand, or do not understand, what constitutes their role. The term **role ambiguity** is often used to describe this element of role involvement and is defined as the lack of clear consistent information regarding one's role (Kahn, Wolfe, Quinn, Snoek, & Rosenthal, 1964). Beauchamp, Bray, Eys, and Carron (2002) noted that it is important for athletes to understand four aspects with regard to their role: (a) the scope of their responsibilities or generally what their role entails; (b) the behaviors that are necessary to successfully fulfill their role responsibilities; (c) how their role performance will be evaluated; and (d) what the consequences are should they not successfully fulfill their role responsibilities. In general, previous research has shown that athletes who understand their roles better are more

satisfied (Eys, Carron, Bray, & Beauchamp, 2003), experience less anxiety (Beauchamp et al., 2003), and are likely to view their teams as more cohesive (Eys & Carron, 2001).

A National Hockey League coach once observed that the worst thing that could happen to a team was to have its "enforcer" score a few goals in successive games. The enforcer would then begin to see himself as and prefer the role of goal scorer, to the detriment of the team as a whole. The roles that individuals are expected to perform should be clearly spelled out.

A second element of role involvement that has been shown to be related to group cohesiveness (e.g., Bray, 1998) is the degree to which athletes accept their role responsibilities. It is beneficial to set out any contingencies associated with role performance. "We plan to use you as a defensive specialist only. If you cannot or do not want to play this role, you will probably get very little playing time this year." Role acceptance is also enhanced when the coach minimizes the status differences among roles. Thus, the success of the total team and the importance of all roles for team success should be continually emphasized. When all group members perceive that their responsibilities are important and make a contribution to the common good, they more willingly accept and carry them out.

There are a number of interventions, although not empirically tested, that could potentially improve role clarity and role acceptance. One very simple intervention that serves to open communication channels and clarify roles is to arrange for individual meetings between the athlete and his or her coach. Another method is to utilize an effective goal setting program. Goal setting serves four important functions: (a) directs the individual's attention and actions toward appropriate behaviors; (b) mobilizes and increases effort toward the task; (c) increases persistence in the task; and (d) motivates the individual to develop strategies and action plans to accomplish the task (Locke, Shaw, Saari, & Latham, 1981). All of these contribute to role clarity and acceptance.

Finally, other elements of role involvement that are extremely important to the group environment and are likely contributors to the cohesiveness of sport teams include **role efficacy** (i.e., athletes' beliefs about their capabilities to carry out role responsibilities; Bray, Brawley, & Carron, 2002), **role conflict** (i.e., athletes' perceiving others to be sending incongruent expectations; Kahn et al., 1964), **role overload** (i.e., athletes' having too many role expectations and/or unable to prioritize them appropriately), and **role satisfaction** (i.e., how happy athletes are with their given role on the team). The applied practitioner or coach should be conscious of these role elements when working with sport teams.

Norms. The presence of **norms** is also associated with increased cohesiveness (Gammage, Carron, & Estabrooks, 2001). A norm is a standard for behavior that is expected of members of the group. It may be task irrelevant or task relevant; in either case, a norm reflects the group's consensus about behaviors that are considered acceptable. The treatment of team managers (Gammage, Carron & Estabrooks, 2001) or trainers by the athletes is one example of a task-irrelevant norm. On one team the manager might be regarded and treated as little more than an unpaid servant; on another team he or she might be considered a member of the coaching team. In both cases new team members quickly become aware of the standard of behavior considered acceptable in their interactions with the manager and begin to act accordingly.

In a sport setting, Munroe and her colleagues (1999) asked athletes to identify the types of norms that exist within their teams. What they found was that important norms existed in four different contexts. First, the two most important norms in the context of *competition* were that teammates put forth maximum effort toward the task and that they supported the other members of the team. These two norms also were the most relevant in the second context, *practice*. The third context for the existence of norms was the *off-season*. In this context the most relevant norms for members of sport teams were to continue training/development as well as maintaining contact with other group members. Finally, norms also were identified for social situations in which group members

had expectations to attend social events (e.g., parties) and have respect for each other.

The relationship between the presence of group norms and the degree of group cohesiveness is circular. The development of norms contributes to the development of cohesiveness. With increased group cohesiveness there is also greater conformity to group standards for behavior and performance. A recently formed group has minimal influence over its members. But as the group develops and becomes more cohesive, adherence to norms for behavior increases. Failure to conform can lead to different sanctions or types of punishment. For example, the group can control the amount of interaction it permits members, their degree of involvement in decision making, and their accessibility to task and social rewards. Controlling the opportunity to interact and to influence the group is probably the most powerful sanction the group possesses. As a group increases in cohesiveness, its members place increasing value on social approval and the opportunities to interact with other group members. Therefore, they show an increasing tendency to adhere to the group norms and to give in to the group influence—even if that influence is negative. Some examples of negative influence are the performance of deviant behavior (such as was the case in the high school football team hazing incident) or the maintenance of an inappropriately low work quota (low standards for productivity).

One of the best-known, most heavily researched issues relating to task-relevant norms is the **norm for productivity**. One example of this occurs in industrial settings when a level or rate of performance is established by the group as acceptable. Then productivity above (rate busting) or below (malingering) that standard is not tolerated by the group. Cohesion and the norm for productivity jointly influence group productivity and achievement. Traditionally it was assumed that there is a direct, positive relationship between cohesion and productivity: As the former increased, the latter was improved. Research in management science, psychology, and sport, however, has shown that the picture is not quite that simple. For example, when Stogdill (1972) reviewed 34 studies that had been carried

Table 8-1 **Interactive Effects of Group Cohesiveness and Group Norm for Productivity on Individual and Group Performance**

		Group Cohesion	
		High	Low
Group Norm for Productivity	High	Best performance (1)	Intermediate performance (2)
	Low	Worst performance (4)	Intermediate performance (3)

out with a variety of different groups, he found that cohesiveness was positively related to performance in 12, negatively related in 11, and unrelated to performance in 11. According to Stogdill, the key factor that influences the relationship between cohesion and performance is the group's norm for productivity (Table 8-1). If group cohesiveness is high and the norm for productivity is high, performance will be positively affected (number 1). Conversely, if cohesion is high and the norm for productivity is low (number 4), performance will be low or negatively affected. When cohesiveness is low, groups with a high norm (number 2) will outperform groups with a low norm (number 3).

A group places a great deal of pressure on members to conform to its norms. In the movie *Chariots of Fire,* for example, the British sprinter Harry Abrahams was chided by his Cambridge dons for hiring a professional trainer—for becoming too serious. Similarly, when Pete Rose broke into major league baseball, he was nicknamed "Charlie Hustle" for the intensity he brought to all aspects of his behavior on the field—sprinting to first base after a walk, for example. The implication was that he was too intense.

Another important aspect of group norms is their *stability.* It has been demonstrated experimentally that an arbitrary norm can persist for four or five generations after the original members have been removed from the group (Jacobs & Campbell, 1961). Thus, if a sport team develops negative norms, such as abusive behavior toward officials or other team members, a laissez-faire attitude toward

training, a reliance on individual versus team goals, those norms could persist over a number of seasons unless steps are taken to eliminate them.

Establishing positive group norms is extremely important in sport teams, particularly if an inappropriate norm is in place. One technique that has been used successfully is to enlist the formal and informal leaders of the group as active agents. If group leaders (in addition to the coach) accept and adhere to specific standards, other group members soon follow.

In some instances the group leaders may be resistant to change. This poses a problem because on sport teams the formal and informal leaders are usually the most highly skilled. If this is the case, the coach must decide how important the new standard is to the long-term success of the organization. In the event that the new standard is considered to be very important, the coach may have to release the resistant team members.

Group processes. Another important team factor that influences the development of a team concept and task cohesion is the interactive processes that occur among the members. One process is the establishment of *group goals and rewards.* In most group activities, including track and field, swimming, baseball, and even basketball, hockey, and soccer, there is an opportunity for the gifted individual competitor to obtain special recognition and rewards. This is inevitable. However, to ensure that a concept of unity develops, the coach must emphasize the group's goals and objectives as well as the rewards that will accrue to the group if these are achieved. Individual goals and rewards should be downplayed.

Communication is another group process associated with increased group cohesiveness, but the relationship is circular. As the level of communication relating to task and social issues increases, cohesiveness is enhanced. And as the group becomes more cohesive, there is also increased communication. Group members are more open with one another, they volunteer more, they talk more, and they listen better. In short, the exchange of task information and social pleasantries increases with cohesiveness. For suggestions on enhancing intrateam communication, see the section on team building.

Performance outcome. As has been the case with so many other factors, the relationship between cohesion and performance outcome is a circular one. More specifically, cohesiveness contributes to performance success and with performance success there is increased cohesiveness. In fact, Carron, Colman, Wheeler, and Stevens (2002) conducted a meta-analysis to examine a number of issues related to the cohesion-performance relationship. Their results demonstrated that *both* task and social cohesion were positively related to performance and that the relationship was cyclical as mentioned earlier. That is, the strength of the cohesion to performance relationship was as strong as performance to cohesion. In addition, it was shown that these relationships existed equally for interactive (e.g., volleyball) and coacting (e.g., track and field) sports, were present across the spectrum of skill and competitive levels, but seemed to be stronger in female teams. Overall, performance success is an important team factor for developing cohesion. Consequently, if it is at all possible, a coach should try to avoid an excessively difficult schedule early in a season.

Team Building

> *If everybody can find a way to put their personal agendas aside for the benefit of the team, ultimately they will gain for themselves in the long run. But I think what often happens is people think they have to take care of themselves first and the team second. Then the infrastructure*

> *breaks down and nobody's accountable. You have to sacrifice yourself for the good of the team, no matter what role you play on the team—whether you're playing 30 minutes or two minutes a game.*
>
> —Mark Messier (as quoted in Miller, 2001, p. 152)

As this quote by Mark Messier illustrates, the importance of cohesion in sport teams is recognized by even those who are best known for their individual prowess. Because it is critical for group development, group maintenance, and the group's collective pursuit of its goals and objectives, cohesion has been identified as the most important small group variable (see Golembiewski, Hilles, & Kagno, 1974). Consequently, at the core of any team building program is the expectation that the intervention will produce a more cohesive group.

Coaches, either alone or with the help of a sport psychologist, invariably seek ways to build an effective team. It's not enough for the coach to proclaim to his or her charges, "Let's act like a team." Consequently, coaches or sport psychology specialists often engage in what is known as **team building.** As Carron and Hausenblas (1998) noted, team building can be defined as "team enhancement or team improvement for both task and social purposes" (p. 332). Thus, it would seem prudent for coaches and sport psychologists to implement certain strategies to foster team building so that athletes may have meaningful experiences that ultimately may lead to a greater sense of unity and cohesiveness.

However, sport is not the only physical activity domain in which team building has been shown to be effective. Research by Carron and Spink (1993) and Spink and Carron (1993) has shown that a team-building intervention program can have a substantial impact on perceptions of cohesiveness as well as on individual adherence behavior. In short, the group has a substantial stabilizing influence on its membership. Given that 50% of adults who initiate an exercise program drop out within the first 6 months (Dishman, 1994), this seems an important area for intervention. Thus, this chapter will conclude with suggestions for implementing a team-building protocol in both sport and exercise settings.

Owing to its distinct nature, the implementation of team-building interventions in sport and exercise settings is *indirect*. The coach/leader is generally the primary arbitrator of group goals, individual roles, and leadership style. As a consequence of this, all of the team-building interventions in these settings become more indirect as they must be filtered through the coach/leader in each instance.

One approach to team-building interventions adopted by Carron, Spink, and Prapavessis (Carron & Spink, 1993; Prapavessis, Carron, & Spink, 1996; Spink & Carron, 1993) involved the use of a four-stage process comprising an *introductory stage*, a *conceptual stage*, a *practical stage*, and an *intervention stage*. The purpose of the introductory stage was to provide the coach/leader with a brief overview of the general benefits of group cohesion. For example, in team building with sport teams, the relationship between perceptions of cohesiveness and enhanced team dynamics was discussed (Prapavessis, Carron, & Spink, 1996). In team building with exercise groups, the introductory stage consisted of a discussion of the relationship between perceptions of cohesiveness and increased adherence to the exercise program (Carron & Spink, 1993).

The conceptual stage was used to accomplish three purposes: (a) to facilitate communication with the coaches/leaders about complex concepts (e.g., groups, cohesiveness); (b) to highlight the interrelatedness of various components of the team building protocol; and (c) to identify the focus for possible interventions (Carron & Spink, 1993).

The purpose of the practical stage was to have coaches/leaders, in an interactive brainstorming session, generate as many specific strategies as possible to use for team building in their group. This was thought to be desirable for three reasons. First, coaches/leaders differ in personality and preferences; therefore, a strategy that might be effectively implemented by one coach/leader might not be by another. Second, groups differ, and coaches/leaders are the individuals most familiar with their groups. An intervention strategy that might be effective in one group might be ineffective in another. Finally,

de Charms's (1976) origin-pawn research has shown that motivation is enhanced when individuals are given greater control over personal behavior. Thus, coaches and exercise leaders are likely to be motivated to employ various team-building strategies because (a) they are given the opportunity to participate in the brainstorming session, and (b) they have control over which strategies they use with their team or class.

Research by Carron and Spink (1993) and Spink and Carron (1993) in the exercise domain provides a good illustration of the type of activities characteristic of the practical stage. Carron and Spink encouraged fitness instructors to develop specific strategies to use in their classes. Table 8-2 contains examples of some of the specific team-building strategies identified by fitness leaders in the practical stage, as well as suggested strategies for coaches of sport teams.

In the intervention stage, the team-building protocols were introduced and maintained by the coaches or exercise leaders in order to increase the level of task cohesiveness of the groups. One team-building intervention that was implemented in a sport setting used elite male soccer teams (Prapavessis et al., 1996). The coaches involved in the team-building intervention attended a workshop 2 weeks before the beginning of the season, at which the specific strategies for implementing a team-building program were established. Throughout the preseason and then during 6 weeks of the season, the coaches emphasized the team-building strategies. Perceptions of cohesiveness were assessed in the preseason and after 8 weeks. No differences in cohesiveness were found, however, between the team-building, attention-placebo, and control conditions.

One possible explanation advanced to account for these results was that many sport coaches inevitably engage in team-building strategies on their own. That is, they establish goals and objectives, work to ensure conformity to group norms, facilitate role clarity and role acceptance, and so on. Also, in sport teams, cohesion is an inevitable by-product of group processes (e.g., communication), an evolving group structure (e.g., development of roles), and group outcomes (e.g., winning/losing). Thus, a team-building

Table 8-2 **Examples of Specific Team-Building Strategies for Coaches and Fitness Class Instructors**

Factor		Examples of Intervention Strategies
Distinctiveness	Sport[a]	Provide the team with unique identifiers (e.g., shirts, logos, mottos, etc.). Emphasize any unique traditions and/or history associated with the team.
	Exercise[b]	Have a group name. Make up a group T-shirt. Hand out neon headbands or shoelaces. Make up posters/slogans for the class.
Individual positions	Sport[a]	Create a team structure in which there is a clear differentiation in team positions/roles.
	Exercise[b]	Use three areas of the pool depending on fitness level. Have signs to label parts of the group. Use specific positions for low-, medium-, and high-impact exercisers. Let them pick their own spot and encourage them to remain in it throughout the year.
Group norms	Sport[c]	Show individual team members how the group's standards can contribute to more effective team performance and a greater sense of team unity. Point out to all team members how their individual contributions can contribute to the team's success. Reward those team members who adhere to the group's standards and sanction those who do not.
	Exercise[b]	Have members introduce each other to increase social aspects. Encourage members to become fitness friends. Establish a goal to lose weight together. Promote a smart work ethic as a group characteristic.
Individual sacrifices	Sport[a]	Encourage important team members to make sacrifices for the team (e.g., ask a veteran athlete to sit out in order to give a novice athlete more playing time).
	Exercise[b]	Use music in aqua fitness (some do not want music). Ask two or three people for a goal for the day. Ask regulars to help new people—fitness friends. Ask people who aren't concerned with weight loss to make a sacrifice for the group on some days (more aerobics) and people who are concerned with weight loss to make a sacrifice on other days (more mat work).
Interaction and communication	Sport[d]	Provide opportunities for athlete input; create an environment that fosters mutual trust and respect so that athletes will feel comfortable communicating. [e]Have all players identify (on paper) why they want their fellow players on the team, then create a summary sheet for each player.
	Exercise[b]	Use partner work and have them introduce themselves. Introduce the person on the right and left. Work in groups of five and take turns showing a move. Use more partner activities.

[a]Bull, Albinson, and Shambrook, 1996
[b]Adapted from Carron and Spink, 1991; Spink and Carron, 1991
[c]Zander, 1982
[d]Yukelson, 1984
[e]Munroe, Terry, and Carron, 2002

program in a sport team would most likely combine in an interactive way with ongoing concomitants of cohesion. The lack of research in sport on the impact of team building on cohesiveness makes it difficult to arrive at any definitive conclusions. Perhaps practitioners and researchers engaged in team building in sport might wish to consider the athletes' opinions on collective areas of concern (i.e., targets for team-building strategies). For example, a needs assessment could reveal that team members understand and accept their roles and are well aware of the team's goals and objectives but perceive group cooperation to be minimal. Also, the inclusion of selected high-status members of the team (captains, co-captains, highly skilled athletes) in implementing the team-building program could then be designed around this feedback. In this regard, Yukelson (1984) presented nine effective ways to enhance coach-athlete communication systems and team harmony in sport teams:

- Open communication channels by providing opportunities for athlete input. Communication is a group process, and mutual trust and respect are essential in order to keep the channels open.

- Develop pride and a sense of collective identity within the group by setting out realistic team, individual, and subunit goals. Feelings of pride and satisfaction develop when individuals and groups attain challenging but realistic goals.

- Strive for common expectations on what types of behavior are appropriate. "An organizational philosophy should specify not only the desired objectives the group is striving to achieve but also the strategy, operating procedures, or means to reach these goals as well" (pp. 236–237).

- Value unique personal contributions by emphasizing the importance of each of the roles that are necessary for group performance.

- Recognize excellence by rewarding exceptional individual performance. If realistic objectives are set out and each individual clearly understands his or her role, the outstanding execution of that role should be recognized to enhance feelings of pride and commitment in the group and its members.

- Strive for consensus and commitment by involving the total team in goal-setting activities.

- Use periodic team meetings to resolve conflicts. Many explosive situations can be resolved by encouraging open communication within the team.

- Stay in touch with the formal and informal leaders in the team. The team members with high prestige and status are not only a barometer for assessing the group's attitudes and feelings; they also are effective agents for implementing necessary changes.

- Focus on success before discussing any failures. A positive group climate is developed if the positive aspects of group and individual performance are highlighted before errors and omissions are discussed.

Summary

Groups are dynamic, not static; they exhibit life and vitality, interaction, and activity. Athletic teams are simply a special type of group. One important implication of this is that they are therefore subject to change, to growth, to modification, and to improvement. The coach is probably in the best position to influence change in a positive direction. To do this efficiently and effectively, it is beneficial to draw on the wealth of research information that has been developed over a number of years in management science, social psychology, sociology, and physical education. Given the influence that groups have on their members, a knowledge of group structure, group dynamics, and group cohesiveness is essential for coaches. This understanding will provide an excellent base from which to weld athletes into a more effective team.

Study Questions

1. Using Carron's definition of a group, briefly describe the six features that characterize groups.

2. List at least six of Zander's characteristics that distinguish a group from a collection of individuals.

3. Define cohesiveness. What are the four specific facets of cohesion?

4. List the four factors that contribute to cohesiveness and give one specific example of each.

5. Discuss the relationship of team size to group cohesiveness.

6. Describe the environmental, personal, and leadership factors that contribute to the development of cohesiveness.

7. Four team factors related to cohesion are roles, norms, group processes, and performance outcome. Distinguish between each of these factors and describe how the factors might be manipulated or modified to enhance team cohesion.

8. Give at least one example (using a sport of your choice or an exercise class) of a strategy that could be used by a coach, fitness leader, or sport psychologist to enhance group cohesiveness using each of the following factors: (a) distinctiveness, (b) individual positions, (c) group norms, (d) individual sacrifices, and (e) interaction and communication.

References

Beauchamp, M. R., Bray, S. R., Eys, M. A., & Carron, A. V. (2002). Role ambiguity, role efficacy, and role performance: Multidimensional and mediational relationships within interdependent sport teams. *Group Dynamics: Theory, Research, and Practice, 6*(3), 229–242.

Beauchamp, M. R., Bray, S. R., Eys, M. A., & Carron, A. V. (2003). The effect of role ambiguity on competitive state anxiety. *Journal of Sport and Exercise Psychology, 25*(1), 77–92.

Brawley, L. R., Carron, A. V., & Widmeyer, W. N. (1987). Assessing the cohesion of teams: Validity of the Group Environment Questionnaire. *Journal of Sport Psychology, 9,* 275–294.

Bray, S. R. (1998). *Role efficacy within interdependent teams: Measurement development and tests of theory.* Unpublished doctoral thesis. University of Waterloo, Waterloo, Canada.

Bray, S. R., Brawley, L. R., & Carron, A. V. (2002). Efficacy for interdependent role functions: Evidence from the sport domain. *Small Group Research, 33,* 644–666.

Bull, S. J., Albinson, J. G., & Shambrook, C. J. (1996). *The mental game plan: Getting psyched for sport.* Eastborne, UK: Sports Dynamics.

Carron, A. V., Brawley, L. R., & Widmeyer, W. N. (1998). The measurement of cohesiveness in sport groups. In J. L. Duda (Ed.), *Advancements in sport and exercise psychology measurement* (pp. 213–226). Morgantown, WV: Fitness Information Technology.

Carron, A. V., & Chelladurai, P. (1981). The dynamics of group cohesion in sport. *Journal of Sport Psychology, 3,* 123–139.

Carron, A. V., Colman, M. M., Wheeler, J., & Stevens, D. (2002). Cohesion and performance in sport: A meta-analysis. *Journal of Sport and Exercise Psychology, 24,* 168–188.

Carron, A. V., & Hausenblas, H. A. (1998). *Group dynamics in sport* (2nd ed.). Morgantown, WV: Fitness Information Technology.

Carron, A. V., & Spink, K. S. (1991). *Team building in an exercise setting: Cohesion effects.* Paper presented at the Canadian Psychomotor Learning and Sport Psychology Conference, London, ON.

Carron, A. V., & Spink, K. S. (1993). Team building in an exercise setting. *The Sport Psychologist, 7,* 8–18.

Carron, A. V., Widmeyer, L. R., & Brawley, L. R. (1985). The development of an instrument to assess cohesion in sport teams: The Group Environment Questionnaire. *Journal of Sport Psychology, 7,* 244–266.

de Charms, R. (1976). *Enhancing motivation: Change in the classroom.* New York: Halstead.

Dishman, R. K. (1994). *Exercise adherence: Its impact on public health.* Champaign, IL: Human Kinetics.

Eys, M. A., & Carron, A. V. (2001). Role ambiguity, task cohesion, and task self-efficacy. *Small Group Research, 32,* 356–372.

Eys, M. A., Carron, A. V., Bray, S. R., & Beauchamp, M. R. (2003). Role ambiguity and athlete satisfaction. *Journal of Sports Sciences, 21,* 391–401.

Eys, M. A., Hardy, J., Carron, A. V., & Beauchamp, M. R. (2003). The relationship between task cohesion and competitive state anxiety. *Journal of Sport and Exercise Psychology, 25,* 66–76.

Festinger, L., Schachter, S., & Back, K. (1950). *Social pressures in informal groups: A study of human factors in housing.* Stanford, CA: Stanford University Press.

Gammage, K. L., Carron, A. V., & Estabrooks, P. A. (2001). Team cohesion and individual productivity: The influence of the norm for productivity and the identifiability of individual effort. *Small Group Research, 32,* 3–18.

Golembiewski, R. T., Hilles, R., & Kagno, M. S. (1974). A longitudinal study of flexi-time effects: Some consequences of an O.D. structural intervention. *Journal of Applied Behavioral Science, 10,* 485–500.

Gross, N., & Martin, W. (1951). On group cohesiveness. *American Journal of Sociology, 57,* 533–546.

Jacobs, R. C., & Campbell, D. T. (1961). The perpetuation of an arbitrary tradition through several generations of a laboratory microculture. *Journal of Abnormal and Social Psychology, 62,* 649–658.

Jewell, L. N., & Reitz, H. J. (1981). *Group effectiveness in organizations.* Glenview, IL: Scott, Foresman.

Kahn, R. L., Wolfe, D. M., Quinn, R. P., Snoek, J. D., & Rosenthal, R. A. (1964). *Occupational stress: Studies in role conflict and ambiguity.* New York: Wiley.

Locke, E. A., Shaw, K. N., Saari, L. M., & Latham, G. P. (1981). Goal setting and task performance: 1969–1980. *Psychological Bulletin, 90,* 125–152.

Mabry, E. A., & Barnes, R. E. (1980). *The dynamics of small group communication.* Englewood Cliffs, NJ: Prentice Hall.

McCallum, J. (1982). Faith, hope, and Tony C. *Sports Illustrated, 57,* 58–72.

McKnight, P., Williams, J. M., & Widmeyer, W. N. (1991, October). *The effects of cohesion and identifiability on reducing the likelihood of social loafing.* Presented at the Association for the Advancement of Applied Sport Psychology Annual Conference, Savannah, GA.

Miller, S. L. (2001). *The complete player: The psychology of winning hockey.* Toronto, ON: Soddart.

Munroe, K., Estabrooks, P., Dennis, P., & Carron, A. V. (1999). A phenomenological analysis of group norms in sport teams. *The Sport Psychologist, 13,* 171–182.

Munroe, K., Terry, P., & Carron, A. (2002). Cohesion and teamwork. In B. Hale & D. Collins (Eds.), *Rugby tough* (pp. 137–153). Champaigne, IL: Human Kinetics.

Prapavessis, H., & Carron, A. V. (1996). The effect of group cohesion on competitive state anxiety. *Journal of Sport and Exercise Psychology, 18,* 64–74.

Prapavessis, H., Carron, A. V., & Spink, K. S. (1996). Team building in sport. *International Journal of Sport Psychology, 27,* 269–285.

Sherif, M., & Sherif, C. (1969). *Social psychology* (rev. ed.). New York: Harper Row.

Spink, K. S., & Carron, A. V. (1991, October). *Team building in an exercise setting: Adherence effects.* Paper presented at the Canadian Psychomotor Learning and Sport Psychology Conference, London, ON.

Spink, K. S., & Carron, A. V. (1993). The effects of team building on the adherence patterns of female exercise participants. *Journal of Sport and Exercise Psychology, 15,* 39–49.

Stogdill, R. M. (1972). Group productivity, drive and cohesiveness. *Organizational Behavior and Human Performance, 8,* 26–43.

Wahl, G., & Wertheim, L. J. (2003). A rite gone terribly wrong. *Sports Illustrated, 99*(24), 68.

Westre, K. R., & Weiss, M. R. (1991). The relationship between perceived coaching behaviors and group cohesion in high school football teams. *The Sport Psychologist, 5,* 41–54.

Widmeyer, W. N., Brawley, L. R., & Carron, A. V. (1985). *The measurement of cohesion in sport teams: The Group Environment Questionnaire.* London, ON: Sports Dynamics.

Widmeyer, W. N., Brawley, L. R., & Carron, A. V. (1990). The effects of group size in sport. *Journal of Exercise and Sport Psychology, 12,* 177–190.

Widmeyer, W. N., & Williams, J. M. (1991). Predicting cohesion in a coaching sport. *Small Group Research, 22,* 548–570.

Yukelson, D. P. (1984). Group motivation in sport teams. In J. M. Silva & R. S. Weinberg (Eds.), *Psychological foundations of sport.* Champaign, IL: Human Kinetics.

Zander, A. (1982). *Making groups effective.* San Francisco: Jossey-Bass.

CHAPTER

9

Communicating Effectively

David P. Yukelson, *The Pennsylvania State University*

I wish my coach was a little clearer with me. I wish I knew where I stood with her. I wish she believed in me more. Right now, I feel like I'm working really hard but nothing ever seems to be good enough. Anytime I go into my coach's office to talk, things get turned around and I'm always on the defensive. I wish the communication between us was better and more open.

—*Penn State University Student–Athlete*

In my work with intercollegiate student-athletes, I am often asked to address the topic of communication, particularly as it pertains to group cohesion, team dynamics, and interpersonal relationships. Effective communication is critical to the success of any team or organization and its members. It affects attitudes, motivation, expectations, emotional dispositions, and behaviors. The ability to express one's thoughts, feelings, and needs effectively, and reciprocally to be able to understand the thoughts, feelings, ideas, and needs of others, is central to good communication.

One day following a workshop on communication and team building, a football player came up to me and remarked that, to him, communication is what teamwork and group chemistry are all about. From a group perspective, it is tied to oneness of thought, synchronization of roles, and everyone being on the same page. He elaborated by saying, "If I can walk up to the line of scrimmage and know that the offensive tackle next to me is thinking the same thing I am, has internalized what needs to be done on this particular play,

transmits to me a nonverbal signal indicating it's time to take care of business, then I know with great confidence, we are going to execute the upcoming play with precise timing, intensity, and cohesiveness."

His remarks reminded me that there is much more to communication than meets the ear. From a global perspective, communication goes beyond talking and listening; rather, it's about connecting with people in a meaningful way. In the context of team it involves internalization of team goals and standards, respecting the values and norms that govern the team, and being a loyal and valued teammate, someone people can rely on, trust, and respect.

Although coaches, athletes, and sport psychologists talk about the importance of effective communication, very little has been written about the subject, particularly as it pertains to sport (Anshel, 1997; Connelly & Rotella, 1991; Harris & Harris, 1984; Henschen & Miner, 1989; Martens, 1987, 2004; Orlick, 1986; Rosenfeld & Wilder, 1990; Yukelson, 1997). Hence, the purpose of this chapter is to explore what effective communication is as it relates to sport, identify barriers to effective communication, and develop strategies for improving communication processes within athletic environments.

Communication Defined

Effective communication has been identified as a very important part of team success (Connelly & Rotella, 1991; Harris & Harris, 1984; Janssen & Dale, 2002; Krzyzewski, 2000; Martens, 2004; Orlick, 1986; Salmela, 1996). Unfortunately, consensus among researchers as to what the word *communication* means is equivocal. For instance, Dance and Larson (1976) surveyed a wide variety of diverse journals and publications in the literature and found 126 different definitions. According to the *American Heritage Dictionary* (1983), communication refers to an act of transmitting or exchanging information, knowledge, thoughts, and/or feelings by means of written or verbal messages. However, as we will come to learn in the chapter, the message transmitted is not always the message received.

Moving beyond a simplistic dictionary definition to a deeper and richer context, the philosopher and social theorist John Dewey notes the word communication shares the same etiology or root as the word "community," and is the result of people feeling engaged in shared projects and meaningful social interactions (Stuhr, 1997). At the core of this issue of community is the notion of engaged communication processes and connecting with people in a meaningful way. When an individual feels engaged in conversation, it connotes a feeling the other person genuinely cares. The quote at the beginning of the chapter points to the importance of engagement and the athlete's desire to connect with her coach on a meaningful level.

Along these lines, it has been my experience that many interpersonal problems in teams (and society in general) result from individuals' lack of understanding of each others needs and feelings. As Orlick astutely notes, "It is difficult to be responsive to another's needs or feelings when

you do not know what they are. Similarly, it is difficult to respect another person's perspective if you do not understand what it is or where it came from" (Orlick, 2000, p. 184). Consequently, an important goal of interpersonal communication is to simply express oneself so the other person is in a better position to understand. As such, I believe effective communication is linked to mutual sharing and mutual understanding (Orlick, 1986). It represents an engaged process by which people come to understand others and, in turn, endeavor to be understood by them (Anderson, 1959).

Communication involves sending, receiving (encoding), and interpreting (decoding) messages through a variety of sensory modalities (Harris & Harris, 1984; Schramm, 1954). These messages can be verbal (as in written or spoken communication) or nonverbal (facial expressions, body language, body positioning, and symbolic gestures and signals) and can be distinguished in terms of content and emotion. The way a message is expressed will influence how the message is received and interpreted. Likewise, communication does not exist in a vacuum; rather, content and context interact to produce meaning in every communication episode (Clampitt, 2005).

Communication can be expressed in many different ways; it can be interpersonal (one-on-one or in a group context), intrapersonal (within one's organism, such as self-talk), written (books, diagrams, playbooks, other printed material), or visual (modeling, observational learning, pictures, video analysis). Although our dominant communication channels are vision and hearing, we also communicate through the senses of touch, taste, smell, and feel.

Many factors affect the way messages are expressed, transmitted, received, and interpreted. Stress, selective attention, perceptual filtering, and psychological expectancies can all influence the way messages are received (Henschen & Miner, 1989; Norman, 1976; Tubbs & Moss, 1987). In the process of interpreting verbal and nonverbal messages, information may be lost or distorted (Henschen & Miner, 1989). Sometimes we think we hear a person say one thing when, in fact, he or she said something different. We then act on the basis of what we think the person said. Many communication problems are rooted in this kind of misunderstanding.

In addition, interpersonal communication is a dynamic process influenced by both person and situation variables. An individual's personality, upbringing, values, beliefs, and style of communication interact with a variety of situation-specific circumstances to influence the way messages are transmitted and received. Some people are didactic and believe effective communication is telling people what they should think (with authority and conviction by the way). Others are more attuned to listeners' needs and feelings and, as such, view communication as a two-way process involving a dynamic interplay between an active sender and active receiver. Likewise, other contextual factors come into play such as your relationship with the other person (e.g., history you share, perceived level of trust, power and control issues), the environment you find yourself in (e.g., office, practice field, before or after competition, public or private setting), the cultural context from which communication is to take place (e.g., learned rules and behaviors that are supposed to be followed), and interpretation rules for abstracting the meaning out of a message. Although there are individual differences in the way people respond, understanding the dynamics that surround these contexts can attenuate misunderstanding and influence individuals' interpersonal effectiveness (Beebe, Beebe, & Redmond, 1996; Clampitt, 2005).

Emotional stress can also cause perceptual distortions and breakdowns in communication (McCloskey, Larson, & Knapp, 1971). Tom Perrin, a sport psychologist and former assistant basketball coach at the University of Virginia, provides an illustration of how good intentions can be misinterpreted due to stress, selective filtering, or emotional mood states. During a practice, an athlete misses an offensive rebound, yet the coach compliments him for demonstrating good positioning, footwork, and intensity. Stressed over a variety of things going on in his life (e.g., he has two midterms coming up, he has seen limited playing time the past two weeks, he broke up with his girlfriend the night before), the athlete

processes the compliment as an insult. For reasons not apparent to the coach, tension builds and tempers fly. Angry over the turn of events, the coach verbally denounces the athlete's reaction as stupid, mumbles to himself, "I can't control how he took it," and benches the athlete. Consequently, a wall is formed, communication blocked, and the intent of the message is never received.

Likewise, during the course of a long competitive season, coaches in particular are susceptible to heightened job stress, emotional mood swings, and possible burnout (Dale & Weinberg, 1990; Smith, 1986; Vernacchia, McGuire, & Cook, 1992), which in turn can have an adverse effect on how messages are transmitted and received. I recall a situation midway through the course of a season; a coach was not happy with the way her team was playing. The pressure to win, coupled with increased travel demands and injuries to key personnel, resulted in the coach (and the entire team) being extremely stressed out. Frustrated and impatient toward the end of practice, the coach yelled and chastised a young, inexperienced freshman for making a mistake. The coach's comments were so demeaning and degrading, her tone of voice so penetrating and hurtful, her nonverbal body language so piercing that the athlete shut down and tuned out anything positive that was said thereafter. The whole situation was unfortunate because the athlete, talented yet low in self-confidence, began to fear failure, was scared to make a mistake, and never quite recovered for the rest of the season.

These examples show how communication is an attitude that goes beyond the content and emotion of what is said and done. How a coach says things is just as important as what the coach has to say, especially in stressful situations (Henschen & Miner, 1989). Consequently, coaches and athletes must make certain the message conveyed is the message received. Tone of voice, facial expressions, body posture/spatial distance, and eye contact are some of the nonverbal cues and body language to be aware of. Coaches who have good communication skills find different ways, verbally and nonverbally, to get their intended message across. A good rule of thumb is to become aware of how you come across to others, and make sure you say what you mean and mean what you say.

Communication in Sport

With regard to sport, so much of what goes on in athletics revolves around communication. Communication affects motivation, team dynamics, internalization of team goals and objectives, and expectations coaches and athletes have for one another. It can affect teaching of sport skills, strategy and skill acquisition, concentration and confidence, as well as individual attitudes, feelings, and behaviors.

Research regarding communication in athletic settings has primarily emphasized the importance of leadership and communication styles as they relate to a number of variables, including motivation, team cohesion, principles of feedback and reinforcement, and conflict resolution skills (Anshel, 1997; Carron & Hausenblas, 1998; Connelly & Rotella, 1991; Martens, 1987; Orlick, 1986; Smith, Smoll, & Curtis, 1979). For instance, leadership style has been shown to have a direct influence on the quality of participants' athletic experiences (see Chapters 6 and 7; Martens, 1987; Wooten, 1992). Although styles of communication vary from coach to coach, it is important to communicate in a manner consistent with one's own personality and coaching philosophy (Vernacchia, McGuire, & Cook, 1996; Wooten, 1992). In terms of communication styles, Martens (1987) notes that clear, honest, and direct communication with no hidden agenda is what coaches should strive for in developing successful coach–athlete relationships. Furthermore, empathy, consistency, and responsiveness to individual differences have also been shown to be critical elements for effective communication in sport settings (Martens, 2004; Smith et al., 1979; Yukelson, 1997).

As noted earlier, communication is a dynamic process that involves mutual sharing and mutual understanding (Martens, 1987; Orlick, 1986). Mutual sharing implies reciprocal participation (e.g., two parties sharing thoughts, feelings, ideas, or information about a particular subject). Likewise, to truly understand or comprehend another

individual's perspective, people need to be adept at the art of listening. In essence mutual sharing leads to mutual understanding (through sharing, the other person is in a better position to truly understand). In the team context, if a group is to function effectively, its members must be able to communicate openly and honestly with one another about the efficiency of group functioning and the quality of interpersonal relationships (Yukelson, 1997). Effective communication is apparent when team members listen to one another and attempt to build on each other's strengths and contributions (Sullivan, 1993).

For coaches, the foundation for effective communication skills is having credibility in the eyes of athletes and developing trust and mutual respect (Yukelson, 1984). Credibility is reflected in the athletes' attitudes about the trustworthiness of what you say and do (Martens, Christina, Harvey, & Sharkey, 1981). Trust is linked to the concepts of honesty, integrity, sincerity, and truthfulness. Lack of honesty and betrayal of trust can lead to many interpersonal problems within a team, including feelings of tension, anger, hostility, resentment, and jealousy (Tubbs & Moss, 1987). It is very difficult to regain someone's trust once it is broken.

Athletes seem to be motivated most by coaches for whom they have a lot of respect (Halliwell, 1989; Lynch, 2001). Respect is not often communicated directly in words; rather, it is demonstrated through actions, a sense of genuineness, sincerity, and social influence (Egan, 1994). Athletes will lose respect for their coaches if they feel betrayed, manipulated, or perceive that they are not being listened to. To illustrate the latter point, I remember a situation where a coach "heard through the grapevine" that a particular athlete violated a long-standing team rule. The coach, who liked to be in control of everything, failed to garner all the facts. She solicited information from other teammates as to what had happened, but never talked directly to the person in question. As a consequence, the athletes felt betrayed, angry, respect for the coach was shattered, and interpersonal relations among the athletes became strained. A good rule of thumb is to solicit all the facts before passing judgment, and treat people exactly the way you want to be treated yourself! Being able to put yourself in the shoes of others and "see" things from their perspective (i.e., empathy) builds credibility, trust, and mutual respect.

Coaches who are good communicators have credibility in the eyes of their athletes. They establish open lines of communication; they are honest, fair, sincere, and consistent. They accept individuals for who they are and genuinely care about them as people outside of athletics. This values-based orientation is consistent with recent qualititative research from Janssen and Dale (2002), who found credible coaches to possess the following commonalities: they were character-based, competent, committed, caring, consistent, confidence builders, and good communicators.

Coaches who are good communicators explain, clarify, and individualize instruction to meet the athlete's needs and personality. They observe performance analytically and are able to help athletes improve performance by providing clear and constructive behavioral feedback in a nonthreatening manner (Smith, 1986; Martin & Hrycaiko, 1983). The following discussion between a coach and a fencer between competitive bouts highlights the point: "Kathy, you are too anxious on the strip. You are telegraphing messages to your opponent as to what your intentions are. Relax, see things develop, trust your decisions and actions, and when you see the window of opportunity open up, go for it! In addition, fence with confidence, keep your focus, and remember to take it one touch at a time." The importance of giving constructive feedback in relation to goals an individual or team is striving to accomplish cannot be overstated.

Athletes react in various ways to how coaches communicate with them. They know the characteristics they like and dislike in coaches. In general, research in the area of youth sports indicate young athletes like coaches who are knowledgeable and instructive, supportive and encouraging, enthusiastic and motivated, reliable, fair, and consistent (Martens, 2004; Martens et al., 1981; Smith, Smith, & Smoll, 1983). In contrast, young athletes dislike coaches who are judgmental, manipulative, capricious, indifferent, inconsistent,

or constantly negative. Personally, I believe the same principles hold true for older athletes as well. It has been my observation over the years that at the intercollegiate level, athletes seem to respond best to coaches who are open, honest, sincere, approachable, consistent, fair, and understanding. They do not mind being yelled at as long as deep down inside they know the coach cares. One of our coaches at Penn State notes "creating players who respect you as a coach is a difficult task. You want the players to feel comfortable around you, but at the same time, realize you are the authority figure." He goes on to say, "Gaining trust is the first step toward building respect. A coach can gain trust with their athletes by being honest and approachable. I try to get my athletes to respect me by attempting to be fair in my decisions and truthful when giving assessment and advice. By listening to my athletes and taking into account suggestions they might have, I feel I establish some form of credibility with my athletes, and hopefully, they will think of me as a more understanding coach."

Again, from a philosophical perspective, this example points to the importance of engaging athletes in the communication processes, creating an atmosphere that reflects a "community" of caring. Athletes want to feel a sense of connection with their coach on a genuine and meaningful level. They expect to be treated with dignity and respect, and should give the same thing back in return. Similarly, athletes (and people in general) want to know their role is valued and contributions appreciated. When the communication process is working properly, mutual understanding should lead to mutual trust and respect.

Communication and Groups

One of the most gratifying experiences a coach or athlete can have is to be a member of a team that gets along well and works together efficiently in a cohesive, harmonious, task-oriented manner (Orlick, 2000; Yukelson, 1984). At Penn State University, much of my work with athletic teams deals with group cohesion, team building, and team performance.

When individuals work together in groups, communication, coordination, and interaction are essential (Carron & Hausenblas, 1998). In fact, communication lies at the heart of group process. If a group is to function effectively, members must be able to communicate easily and efficiently with one another (Shaw, 1981). Because communication directly affects group solidarity, collective efficacy, and team performance (Zaccaro, Blair, Peterson, & Zazanis, 1995), I spend a great deal of time talking with teams about group process, team dynamics, and methods for improving harmonious team relations. Team building comes from a shared vision of what the group is striving to achieve and is tied to commitment, individual and mutual accountability, collaboration, communication, and teamwork. A shared vision that has meaning and purpose creates synergistic empowerment. Likewise, in successful teams, coaches and athletes talk openly and honestly about interpersonal and task related issues that affect them directly, and everyone works together to develop a positive group atmosphere/team culture conducive for team success (Cannon-Bowers & Salas, 2001; Janssen, 1999; Katzenbach & Smith, 1993; Yukelson, 1997).

Unfortunately, not every group functions cohesively. Many interpersonal problems on teams stem from poor communication. Interpersonal conflict is often the result of misunderstanding or miscommunication of feelings. Henschen and Miner (1989) have identified five types of misunderstandings that often surface within groups: (1) a difference of opinion resolvable by common sense, (2) a clash of personalities in the group, (3) a conflict of task or social roles among group members, (4) a struggle for power between one or more individuals, and (5) a breakdown of communication between the leader and the group or among members of the group itself. Misunderstandings are also the result of inaccessibility to relevant information (not being privy to certain sources of information); inattentiveness (failing to listen, not paying attention, being distracted); lack of assertiveness (failure to speak up) or misperceiving someone's motives, intentions, or behavior (inference mind reading). Similarly, people are often afraid to express how they truly feel for fear of being ridiculed or rejected for saying what is truly on their minds (Orlick, 1986).

Several teams I have worked with have had their fair share of interpersonal communication problems and conflict. Problems have ranged from interpersonal jealousies within the team to power struggles, control issues, perceived injustices, and coach–athlete as well as athlete–athlete inequities. Learning how to express oneself in a constructive manner and communicate effectively is an important initial step in preventing and solving problems.

It has been stated that the more open you can be with each other, the better are your chances of getting along and achieving both individual and team goals (Orlick, 1986). Thus, it is important for coaches and athletes to learn how to express their thoughts and feelings about various issues that affect them directly. Team building requires a group climate of openness in which airing problems and matters of concern is not just appropriate but encouraged. Orlick expounds by saying, "Harmony grows when you really listen to others and they listen to you, when you are considerate of their feelings and they are considerate of yours, when you accept their differences and they accept yours, and when you help them and they help you" (Orlick, 2000, p. 143).

Team Communication Dynamics

As already mentioned, many communication problems on teams are the result of misunderstanding or miscommunication between the coach and the team or among athletes themselves. Harris and Harris (1984) offer an interesting framework to examine communication processes in athletic teams. The framework consists of coach–team, coach–athlete, athlete–coach, and athlete–athlete interactions.

Coach–team communications. From a coach–team perspective group synergy and team chemistry are of vital importance. According to DePree (1989), group synergy comes from leaders (in this case coaches) sharing a vision of what could be if everyone puts his or her skills and resources together to achieve team goals and objectives.

Individual and mutual accountability, passion and belief, and a genuine commitment to a common team goal are needed. Athletes unite behind common goals, so it is important to get athletes to think in terms of the philosophy, operating procedures, and values that govern the team (Yukelson, 1984). Similarly, homogenous attitudes and expectations (e.g., unity of purpose) as well as shared ideals and covenants to live by are required (Riley, 1993; Walsh, 1998). In terms of shared ideals, it is important to obtain *consensus and commitment* from the team regarding team goals, operating procedures, rules of engagement, and normative behaviors including appropriate methods for achieving them (Carron & Hausenblas, 1998; Martens, 1987). To this end, the coach should solicit input from team members regarding their perceptions of what needs to be done for everyone to come together and be an effective team (Janssen, 1999; Katzenbach & Smith, 1993; Kouzes & Posner 1995; Yukelson, 1997). Everyone on the team must be on the same page, working together with a collective desire to be successful.

To achieve these ends, a coach may find these communication principles useful: impart, inspire, monitor, clarify, and reinforce.

- *Impart* relevant information regarding team rules, expectations, operating procedures, and goals the group is striving to achieve. Clarify the team's mission, outline strategies and action plans to reach team goals and objectives, and involve staff and athletes in decisions that affect them directly.

- *Inspire* athletes to reach for their best. Communicate with a sense of inspired enthusiasm. Be honest, direct, and sincere. Instill a sense of pride, passion, belief, and team spirit. Strive to make everyone on the team feel valued and significant.

- *Monitor the progress team is making.* Set up a goal-setting program (e.g., goal boards are often very helpful), monitor, evaluate, and adjust goals as needed. Give athletes feedback on how they are doing in relation to individual and team goals, challenge everyone involved to become better.

- *Clarify* how things are going. Talk openly about the commitment that is required to achieve team goals and what needs to be done to keep things on task. Challenge everyone to take responsibility for their own actions and to work with continued effort, purpose, and focus.

- *Reinforce* behavior that you want repeated. Catch people doing things right; provide lots of support, encouragement, and positive reinforcement; discipline athletes according to your coaching philosophy and team mission statement; correct errors in a positive way.

Coach–athlete communications. As for coach–athlete lines of communication, coaches should build a psychological and social environment conducive to goal achievement and team success. They should take the time to get to know their athletes as unique goal-oriented individuals and find out what their strengths, interests, and needs are. Martens' (1987) ideas regarding transformational leadership and reciprocal influence are applicable in the context of athletes and coaches working together to meet each other's needs and goals. Coaches should be open, honest, and upfront with athletes about various decisions that affect them directly. This will ease many misunderstandings that can often lead to hurt feelings, dissension, or turmoil within the team.

Similarly, another area coaches should address with athletes is communication at the competition site (Orlick, 2000). Recognizing individual differences in the way athletes prepare and respond in competition, it is suggested that coaches assess ahead of time what their athletes' needs and preferences are. Prior to competition, some athletes like to be left alone; others appreciate a word of encouragement or a task-oriented cue that reminds them to concentrate and bring their best focus forward. The same holds true for postcompetition feedback. Some athletes are very emotional after competition and don't want to be disturbed; others want feedback immediately. Thus, a coach–athlete communication plan for competition helps to alleviate stress and possible misunderstandings that may arise.

As for athlete–coach interactions, athletes need feedback as to where they stand and how they are progressing in relation to individual and team goals. Research indicates that *evaluative feedback* is an important part of the goal-setting process (see Chapter 13 and Locke & Latham, 1990) and is directly tied to communication. Unfortunately, some coaches are not very good at giving feedback in a positive and supportive manner (Orlick, 2000). This can lead to motivation problems and performance inconsistencies. In contrast, many athletes have difficulty internalizing feedback for what it is and, as a consequence, take feedback personally as opposed to constructively.

In addition to providing tangible feedback about performance accomplishments, many athletes will seek out their coach to talk about things outside of sport that may be affecting their lives and self-esteem. In intercollegiate settings, this might include concerns about various transition and adjustment issues, motivation, and confidence; things pertaining to academic matriculation; ways to navigate interpersonal relationships; and strategies for handling pressure. Thus, a coach is often asked to take on many mentoring roles (e.g., counselor, confidant, teacher, friend, role model, and sometimes substitute parent). For these reasons, it is important that lines of communication be open between athlete and coach, and that a trusting relationship be established.

As for breakdowns in coach–athlete communications, many athletes do not feel confident approaching a coach if they do not trust or respect him or her. Although it is common for coaches to have a so-called open-door policy, many athletes find it difficult to walk through the door if they feel the coach is not going to listen to their concerns with genuine interest, or if they perceive a hidden agenda. Connelly and Rotella (1991) note that some athletes go so far as to "fake honesty"— tell coaches what they think they want to hear so the athletes don't have to deal with the situation at hand.

Likewise, situations often arise during the course of a season that can cause communication problems between the coach and athlete (e.g., frustration associated with losing, poor performance, lack of playing time, stress and fatigue,

personality clashes, and injury, to name just a few). In situations like these, athletes often perceive the coach as being insensitive, unappreciative, unapproachable, or uninterested. As a result, it is not unusual for an athlete to feel apprehensive about approaching the coach. Rather than clam up, athletes need to learn how to express themselves in an assertive manner. A practical technique I have found to be useful is to have athletes write down on a cue card three main points they would like to express to the coach. We then role-play and simulate potential scenarios. Athletes visualize themselves communicating their message in a confident and successful manner. This type of preparation helps to build confidence and desensitize athletes to situations they perceive to be stressful.

Coaches should create an environment that encourages athletes to initiate communication freely. Athletes must feel that communication lines are truly open and things could be voiced without fear of reprisal. Communication is a two-way street; hence, both the coach and the athlete have a responsibility to make it work!

In terms of coach–athlete communications, Anshel (1997), Janssen and Dale (2002), Lynch (2001), Orlick (2000), Martens (1987, 2004), and Thompson (1993) offer several practical cognitive-behavioral interventions to facilitate improved relations. Some key considerations include being honest, sincere, direct, positive, and empathetic. Below is a summary of tips for improving coach–athlete communications. If these suggestions don't work, it might be appropriate for a sport psychologist to intervene.

- To communicate successfully, you must understand that each person with whom you communicate has had different experiences than you.

- Use a style of communication that is comfortable for you. Whether you are laid back, animated, relaxed, vocal, or somewhere in between, communicate in a manner that is consistent with your personality and coaching philosophy.

- Recognize individual differences in the way people respond to you. Do not assume that you (the communicator) and the other person(s) (the receiver) will interpret the information in the same manner.

- Characteristics of effective communication include being honest, sincere, genuine, fair, and consistent. Sarcasm, ridicule, and degrading or demeaning comments are poor communication techniques and should be discouraged.

- Never underestimate the power of positive social influence techniques. Focus on the positive; catch people doing things correct. Be generous with praise, encouragement, and positive reinforcement. The skillful use of positive reinforcement can increase motivation and strengthen a person's self-esteem (see Chapters 2 and 3).

- Be a good role model; influence by example!

- Work to improve nonverbal communication skills. Remember the axiom: "Your actions speak louder than words."

- Recognize the importance of emotional self-control. Stress and losing can have an impact on emotions. When coaches lose control of their emotions, frustration may override the content element of communication and what gets heard.

- Work on developing empathy skills. Put yourself in the shoes of your athletes. Show genuine concern for them as people. Listen attentively to their feelings and concerns and work jointly with them to find appropriate solutions.

- Reduce uncertainty: Be supportive. As a coach, you play a vital role in helping athletes feel worthy and important. Strive to create a supportive atmosphere in which athletes feel their efforts and contributions to the team are appreciated and valued.

- Convey rationales as to why athletes should or should not do certain behaviors.

- If you have an open-door policy, show athletes (and your assistants) that you are sincere about using it!

- Evaluate and monitor group process. Set aside time with the team to discuss openly how things are going (e.g., what is working, what is not, what you need more or less of from coaches, teammates, trainers, sport psychologist, support staff). This is an excellent way to open communication channels and show athletes you care about their feelings and opinions.

Athlete–athlete communications. As for athlete–athlete communication, it is important that teammates establish and maintain harmonious working relationships with each other. Ideally, they should show genuine support and care for each other both on and off the athletic field. In fact, some of the most cohesive teams I have ever been associated with had a special relationship off the field (i.e., a "bonding together feeling") that propelled them to be successful as a team during competitions. This was particularly evident during pressure situations within a competitive contest when they needed to trust each other most.

Along these lines, athletes can be a great source of support for one another; they often spend a lot of time together and share common experiences that are unique to their own peer subculture. In order for teams to get to know one another better and develop a sense of team camaraderie, I often employ team-building activities that promote personal disclosure through mutual sharing. For instance, I might have a team go around a circle discussing individual and team assets and strengths, or a life event that significantly influenced them as a person or team (Yukelson, 1997). These team disclosures promote diversity, team cohesion, and lend depth to understanding teammates. Recent qualitative research by Dunn & Holt (2004) as well as anecdotal accounts from coaches (Yukelson, Sullivan, Morett, & Dorenkott, 2003) noting the benefits of using personal disclosure/mutual sharing team-building activities before major competitions has been documented in the literature (Cannon-Bowers & Salas, 2001; Dunn & Holt, 2004, Yukelson et al., 2003).

It takes a great deal of dedication, commitment, time, and discipline to excel in sport.

In many cases, athletes can become encapsulated in their own athletic world; they don't have time for themselves and can take it out on each other. Unfortunately, if interpersonal relationships and team dynamics break down, the experience can be quite stressful.

Athletic teams are very much like families. Some degree of tension, frustration, and conflict is inevitable. Several teams I have worked with have had their fair share of interpersonal communication problems and conflict. Problems have ranged from roommate problems (e.g., incompatibility, intolerance, general needs not being met), to interpersonal jealousies within the team, to boyfriend–girlfriend problems, to coach–athlete inequities, and to freshmen adjustment issues. Typically, the underlying issues revolve around misunderstanding, insensitivity, sense of betrayal, distrust, and athletes feeling, in general, like they are not being heard.

Likewise, in a multicultural athletic environment some degree of conflict or misunderstanding is unavoidable. When teammates come from different racial, ethnic, religious, or socioeconomic backgrounds, dissimilarities due to deeply rooted cultural systems often lead to intercultural misunderstandings (Tubbs & Moss, 1987). Because values, beliefs, relational roles, and attitudes in one culture are often different from those held in another, athletes need to learn to be tolerant, accepting, respecting, and understanding (Parham, 1996).

Learning how to communicate effectively is an important first step in developing satisfying interpersonal team relationships. Recognizing that it is difficult to be responsive to someone else's thoughts, feelings, ideas, and needs when you don't know what they are, I have found Orlick's (1986) writings on communication and mind reading, and suggestions for improving interpersonal relations and team harmony, to be quite helpful. Although it is easier said than done, I am in total agreement with Orlick when he states, "The most important thing you can do to increase team harmony is to make a commitment to do so" (Orlick, 1986, p. 98).

Here are some suggestions derived from Orlick (1986, 2000) and from my personal experiences to help you improve interpersonal communication processes within a team:

- Make sure everyone is pulling in the same direction (team comes first). Recognize that the more open you can be with each other, the better are your chances of getting along and achieving your goals.

- Discuss strategies for improving team harmony, including ways to support and help each other both on and off the athletic field. In addition, do whatever is necessary to make teammates feel valued, appreciated, and accepted.

- Listen to others; they will listen to you! Put yourself in the shoes of others; try to understand the other person's perspective.

- Learn how to give and receive feedback or criticism constructively. Listen to the *intent* of what is being said; avoid taking things personally.

- Learn how to tolerate each other better. Accept team members for who they are, including their flaws, personality quirks, idiosyncrasies, and funny little habits that make them unique.

- Avoid backstabbing and gossiping about teammates. Interpersonal cliques and petty jealousies will destroy team morale quickly.

- Keep confrontations private. Deal with the person directly (e.g., "Here is what your behavior is like," "This is how your behavior makes others feel," "Here is how your behavior influences others and is perceived by others").

- Recognize that not all conflicts can be resolved, but most can be managed more effectively if both parties communicate.

Assertiveness Training: The Need for Expression

At times athletes need to stand up for their rights and be able to express themselves in a forthright yet respectful manner. **Assertiveness** refers to the honest and straightforward expression of a person's thoughts, feelings, and beliefs in a socially appropriate way that does not violate or infringe on the rights of others (Connelly & Rotella, 1991; Lazarus, 1973).

People have difficulty being assertive for a variety of reasons. They include social consequences (e.g., being hesitant to speak up for fear of hurting someone's feelings); lack of awareness (i.e., failure to learn how to be assertive); lack of confidence (i.e., it takes courage to be assertive); and vulnerability (i.e., risk of making oneself known has potential negative consequences) (Connelly & Rotella, 1991; Egan, 1994). For instance, some freshmen may be afraid to speak up in team meetings for fear of looking bad in the eyes of upperclassmen. Respect of teammates is something that is earned, and it takes time to develop. Likewise, some freshmen might feel intimidated by their coach and be hesitant to ask for help. In addition, cultural and socialization factors within a team may affect one's decision to be assertive. For example, it may be awkward for a newcomer of Asian or Latin American descent to feel comfortable speaking up in North American surroundings.

Assertiveness is a learned social behavior that takes practice to be perfected. Effective interpersonal skills such as assertiveness cannot be taught in one session; rather, a more comprehensive approach that incorporates assertiveness with other cognitive-behavioral mental training skills such as goal setting, coping rehearsal techniques, positive self-talk, and self-monitoring strategies is recommended (Connelly, 1988). It is suggested that athletes learn how to express their thoughts, needs, feelings, and preferences in a positive, direct, and considerate manner. The following *DESC* formula proposed by Greenberg (1990) is a good example of how people can express themselves more assertively:

1. *Describe* the situation as you see it, paint a verbal picture of the other person's behavior or the situation to which you are reacting: "What I see happening is this . . ."; "When my play is criticized, I feel. . . ."

2. *Express* your feelings regarding the other person's behavior or the situation you have just described: "When you do this, it makes me feel like . . ."; "I get angry and frustrated when you talk behind my back."

3. *Specify* what changes you would like to see take place: "I would prefer you give me feedback in a more constructive, less degrading manner"; "I would appreciate it if you did not talk behind my back."

4. *Consequences* to expect: "If you don't get off my case, I will ask coach to meet with us to straighten this situation out."

It should be noted there is a difference between being assertive and overly aggressive. It is okay to assert oneself in a respectful and considerate manner when trying to express one's views, but it is not okay for someone to be dogmatic and lose their composure when trying to make a point. Assertiveness is a learned social skill that takes time, patience, and practice to be perfected.

The Sport Psychologist as a Skilled Helper

Throughout the chapter I have talked about the importance of coaches and athletes developing good listening and communication skills. Likewise, sport psychologists must develop good interpersonal communication skills to work effectively with coaches, athletes, and teams. For sport psychologists to do a good job, they must be able to develop rapport, listen attentively, speak the appropriate sport language, and earn the trust of both the coach and athlete.

In my own day-to-day interactions I find myself working with a variety of people within the intercollegiate athletics hierarchy: student-athletes, coaches, parents, athletic administrators, academic counselors and support personnel, sports medicine doctors and athletics trainers, strength trainers, and alumni. These people have a wealth of information and experience to draw upon. They all have their own personality and comfort level from which they work and communicate. There are certain protocols to follow, appropriate chains of command to work through, written and unwritten rules and policies that can't be violated. But it is impossible to implement a thorough and effective applied sport psychology program if one is unable to gain the trust and support of key personnel at all levels of the athletics organization.

Similarly, it takes time and patience to integrate mental training techniques into already existing structures. Thus, sport psychologists working in applied settings should take time to develop rapport and establish a good working relationship with the people with whom they interact (Ravizza, 1988). Personally, I feel applied sport psychologists must first earn the trust and respect of the coaching staff before they can expect to work effectively on an individual or collective basis with their athletes. This can be accomplished by establishing open lines of communication with the coaching staff, by listening, being patient, gathering facts, and observing as much as possible about the dynamics surrounding the team. Gaining entry and building the trust of the coaching staff takes time. It is important that the sport psychologist be able to fit in and relate well with both athletes and staff. In order to achieve these ends, they must be confident, creative, flexible, adaptable, and focused (Orlick & Partington, 1987; Partington & Orlick, 1987; Ravizza, 1988).

With regard to individual consultations, the sport psychologist must be a skilled interviewer, adept at listening, good at probing, able to draw out an individual's strengths and weaknesses, and creative with regard to individualizing a mental skills training program based on the person's needs and concerns. Again, good communication skills are essential.

Drawing from counseling theory, general communication skills that sport psychologists need in order to be effective include genuineness (responding with honesty, sincerity, and integrity); openness (accepting others as they are, even if you don't agree with them); warmth (helping people feel at ease when expressing intimate thoughts and feelings); empathetic (accepting and understanding the other person's point of view); adept at interviewing (good listening and probing skills); creative and skillful (helping athletes generate alternative ways of looking at problems); and trustworthy (being able to maintain confidences) (Corey, 1977; Danish, D'Augelli, & Ginsberg, 1984; Egan, 1994; Ivey, 1983). Although a variety of verbal and nonverbal communication skills are essential in developing a healthy helping relationship, perhaps none is more important than being able to listen.

Active Listening and Empathy

Whether you are a sport psychologist, coach, athlete, administrator, or friend, listening is an essential interpersonal skill to develop. People listen for appreciation, comprehension, and self-understanding (Rosenfeld & Wilder, 1990). Whereas most of us have been trained to listen to facts, true listening means tuning into what the other person is feeling (Pietsch, 1974).

Rosenfeld and Wilder (1990) have identified three levels of listening, each representing a different degree of listening effectiveness. **Active listening** is the preferred mode of listening in which the listener is concerned about the content, intent, and feelings of the message being transmitted. The second level of listening is called **superficial** or **inattentive listening.** In this situation, listeners tune out quickly once they think they have enough information to decipher what the speaker's intent is. Although listeners at this level may grasp the basic meaning of the message, they often fail to comprehend the emotional feeling or underlying concepts of what is being communicated. Level three listening could be characterized as **arrogant listening.** Here, listeners seem to be more interested in what they have to say as opposed to what the other person is saying. These individuals wait for pauses in the conversation so they can jump in and hear themselves speak.

By far the most useful tool for improving listening is active listening (Martens, 1987). When people talk about themselves, they do so in terms of experiences (things that happen to them), behaviors (what they do or fail to do), and affect (the feelings and emotions that accompany these experiences and behaviors) (Egan, 1994). Effective listening means demonstrating that we care enough to hear the other person's viewpoint (Pietsch, 1974). Elements of good listening skills include attending physically and psychologically to the person you are working with (e.g., adopt a posture that indicates active involvement), listening to become more aware of what it is the person is really trying to say (both verbally and nonverbally), paraphrasing or clarifying to ensure your understanding is correct, and some form of summarizing statement to pull everything together in a respectful empathetic way (Corey, 1977; Egan, 1994). Along these lines, good counselors use a variety of nonverbal microskills to facilitate the attending process. The SOLER technique outlined in Egan (1994) has proven to be very useful: *Square* and face the client (adopt a posture that indicates involvement); espouse an *Open* posture to communicate openness and availability to the client; *Lean* toward your client (this connotes you are interested in what the client has to say); maintain good *Eye* contact (this deepens your level of engagement); *Relax* body position (being natural puts people at ease).

Reflective listening is one of the most powerful methods of demonstrating to the person you are working with that you are actively listening and striving to understand. It has been said that reflective listening is to verbal communication as video feedback is to physical skill instruction (Henschen & Miner, 1989). The skills of questioning, encouraging, paraphrasing, reflecting, and summarizing make up the basic listening sequence. The following reflective listening techniques (Egan, 1994; Ivey, 1983) may facilitate better communication between athlete and sport psychologist:

- *Questioning.* Use open-ended questions and statements that encourage the athlete to continue speaking. ("How are you feeling about the injury?" "Tell me more about what happened") As a general rule, avoid initial "why" questions. This may put the person you are talking with on the defensive. Wait until he or she has reached an appropriate comfort level.

- *Clarifying.* Make clear to the other person what has been heard. Clarifying does not mean "I agree with your opinion," but rather, it lets the speaker know someone cares enough to listen. Some good lead-ins include "What I hear you saying is . . ."; "I am not sure I quite understand, but it sounds as though you are angry with the coach because she benched you. Is that it?"

- *Encouraging.* Use a variety of verbal and nonverbal statements or mannerisms to prompt athletes to keep talking. These include head nods, gestures, a phrase such as "uh-huh," or the simple repetition of key words the athlete has uttered.

- *Paraphrasing.* Check whether the responder understands the message. This encourages the sharer to go on and explore his or her feelings and ideas further. Similar to reflective listening, paraphrasing involves using one's own words, in concise comments, to feed back to the athlete the essence of what has just been said.

- *Reflecting.* Let the person know you hear the content and feelings of what is being said. ("You're sad because . . ."; "You feel confident of your ability to play at this level but worry about getting in.")

- *Understanding.* Use empathy to keep the person you are dealing with focused on important issues. ("It must be hard for you to sit and watch teammates practice while you are recovering from arthroscopic knee surgery.")

- *Summarizing.* Pull together all the main ideas and feelings of what has been said. ("It sounds as if you have mixed feelings about the situation. On one hand, you have more time for yourself, but are also apprehensive about getting your starting job back.") Summaries may be used to begin or end a conversation, for transition to a new topic, or to provide clarity when dealing with lengthy or complex issues or statements.

The skills of attending, listening, and influencing are not always sufficient in and of themselves to provide quality relationships with people. Of primary interest is the concept of **empathy.** Empathy is a special kind of understanding. In essence, it means putting yourself in the shoes of the other person, trying to understand what the other person is experiencing from his or her own perspective.

Empathy is not the same thing as sympathy. Rather, it is an acquired skill that reflects an attitude of caring, concern, and genuine interest (Egan, 1994). The previously mentioned attending and reflective listening skills are deeply rooted in empathy (Ivey, 1983). Empathetic listeners reflect what they hear by restating the ideas heard in their own words and by asking good probing questions (Rosenfeld & Wilder, 1990). The following example gives two responses, one low and one high in empathy:

Athlete: I really get mad when my coach criticizes me without letting me explain anything. I get angry not because he criticizes me, but because he does it in such a degrading way.

Sport psychologist (low empathy): "You don't like being criticized."

Sport psychologist (high empathy): "You get really mad when he criticizes you and his insulting manner makes you feel personally attacked."

Sport psychologists should also be sensitive to things that could inhibit effective communication processes when working with people, such as information overload (saying too much at one time), telling someone what she or he should do (e.g., "If I were you, I would . . ."), ordering or directing ("You should speak your mind to the coach"), warning or threatening ("You will regret it if you . . ."), or preaching and moralizing ("That's not right").

In summary, developing effective communication skills takes time, patience, and practice. In addition, it is important to remember that not all problems can be resolved and not all people want help. Listen to what the athlete is asking for, and respond accordingly. Perhaps the following guidelines will help you be a more effective listener:

- *Focus* on the person who is talking. Be attentive, genuine, and supportive.
- Listen for both *content* and *feelings*.
- Show that you *understand* what is being said.
- *Summarize* the main points.
- Promote alternative perspectives. Set *goals* based on action-oriented understanding. Work on role-playing scenarios and coping rehearsal strategies to help the individual feel prepared to take immediate action.

Summary

Communication is a multifaceted phenomenon that involves the transmission or exchange of thoughts, ideas, feelings, or information through verbal and nonverbal channels. Effective communication involves mutual sharing and mutual understanding. Its foundation is based on trust and mutual respect. Open lines of communication can help alleviate many problems that arise within sport environments.

Characteristics of effective and ineffective communication styles have been presented. Although there are many ways to motivate athletes, it has been suggested that coaches adopt a communication style that is consistent with their personality and coaching philosophy.

An important aspect of communication that has been highlighted is the need to be honest, sincere, and consistent. Because messages transmitted are not always received and interpreted the same way, coaches, athletes, and sport psychologists must strive to be consistent in their verbal and nonverbal communications. Many times when incongruent messages are transmitted, the receiver can become confused as to the true meaning of the message, thus leaving the door open for miscommunication and misunderstanding.

Although much of this chapter has focused on coach–athlete communications, many principles discussed carry over to the applied sport psychologist working in an athletics environment. The communication skills we teach coaches and athletes are the same skills we use as effective consultants. Gaining entry, building rapport, developing trust, and individualizing a mental skills training program based on the needs and desires of coaches and athletes all require good listening and communication skills. Drawing from counseling theory, the chapter has presented a variety of general communication skills sport psychologists need to be effective, with a strong emphasis on developing empathy, being genuine and expressive, and practicing active listening skills.

Study Questions

1. Why is communication an important tool for a coach and sport psychologist to possess?

2. There is no true definition of communication in the literature. How would you define communication in sport?

3. What factors interfere with effective communication processes in sport?

4. Give some behavioral examples of verbal and nonverbal communication in sport.

5. What role does communication play in teaching mental skills to coaches and athletes?

6. As a sport psychologist, what are some things you would do to improve coach–athlete communications?

7. As a coach or sport psychologist, what would you do to intervene if interpersonal conflict arose among team members that resulted in disruption of group cohesion and team harmony?

8. The volleyball team at Nike University has a tendency to clam up when the going gets tough (i.e., communication breaks down; the team loses its intensity, enthusiasm, and focus in critical situations and fails to make appropriate adjustments to things that are going on during competition). How would you intervene as either a sport psychologist or coach to deal with this situation?

9. Why are active listening and empathy such important skills for a sport psychologist to develop in working with coaches and athletes?

10. What are some things you could do to become a better listener?

References

American heritage dictionary. (1983). New York: Dell.

Anderson, M. P. (1959). What is communication? *The Journal of Communication, 9,* 5.

Anshel, M. (1997). *Sport psychology: From theory to practice* (3rd ed.). Scottsdale, AZ: Gorsuch Scarisbrick.

Beebe, S. A., Beebe, S. J., & Redmond, M. V. (1996). *Interpersonal communication: Relating to others.* Boston: Allyn and Bacon.

Cannon-Bowers, J. A., & Salas, E. (2001). Reflections on shared cognition. *Journal of Organizational Behavior, 22,* 105–202.

Carron, A. V., & Hausenblas, H. A. (1998). *Group dynamics in sport* (2nd ed.). Morgantown, WV: Fitness Information Technology.

Clampitt, P. G. (2005). *Communicating for managerial effectiveness* (3rd ed.). Thousand Oaks, CA: Sage Publications.

Connelly, D. (1988). Increasing intensity of play in nonassertive athletes. *The Sport Psychologist, 2,* 255–265.

Connelly, D., & Rotella, R. J. (1991). The social psychology of assertive communication: Issues in teaching assertiveness skills to athletes. *The Sport Psychologist, 5,* 73–87.

Corey, G. (1977). *Theory and practice of counseling and psychotherapy.* Pacific Grove, CA: Brooks/Cole.

Dale, J., & Weinberg, R. (1990). Burnout in sport: A review and critique. *Journal of Applied Sport Psychology, 2,* 67–83.

Dance, F. E., & Larson, C. E. (1976). *The functions of human communication: A theoretical approach.* New York: Holt, Rinehart, and Winston.

Danish, S., D'Augelli, A. R., & Ginsberg, M. (1984). Life development intervention: Promotion of mental health through the development of competence. In S. Brown & R. Lent (Eds.), *Handbook of counseling psychology* (pp. 520–544). New York: John Wiley.

DePree, M. (1989). *Leadership is an art.* New York: Doubleday.

Dunn, J. G. H., & Holt, N. L. (2004). A qualitative investigation of a personal-disclosure mutual-sharing team building activity. *The Sport Psychologist, 18,* 363–380.

Egan, G. (1994). *The skilled helper: A problem management approach to helping* (5th ed.). Pacific Grove, CA: Brooks/Cole.

Greenberg, J. S. (1990). *Coping with stress: A practical guide.* Dubuque, IA: William C Brown.

Halliwell, W. (1989). What sport psychologists can learn from coaches and athletes about the psychology of sport. *AAASP Newsletter,* p. 7.

Harris, D. V., & Harris, B. L. (1984). *Sports psychology: Mental skills for physical people.* Champaign, IL: Leisure Press.

Henschen, K., & Miner, J. (1989). *Team principles for coaches.* Ogden, UT: Educational Sport Services.

Ivey, A. E. (1983). *Intentional interviewing and counseling.* Pacific Grove, CA: Brooks/Cole.

Janssen, J. (1999). *Championship team building.* Tucson, AZ: Winning the Mental Game.

Janssen, J., & Dale, G. (2002). *The seven secrets of successful coaches: How to unlock and unleash your team's full potential.* Cary, NC: Winning the Mental Game.

Katzenbach, J. R., & Smith, D. K. (1993). *The wisdom of teams.* Boston: Harvard Business School Press.

Kouzes, J. J., & Posner, B. Z. (1995). *The leadership challenge: How to keep getting extraordinary things done in organizations* (2nd ed.). San Francisco: Jossey-Bass.

Krzyzewski, M. (2000). *Leading with the heart.* New York: Warner Books.

Lazarus, A. A. (1973). On assertive behavior: A brief note. *Behavior Therapy, 4,* 697–699.

Locke, E. A., & Latham, G. P. (1990). *A theory of goal setting and task performance.* Englewood Cliffs, NJ: Prentice Hall.

Lynch, J. (2001). *Creative coaching.* Champaign, IL: Human Kinetics Publishers.

Martens, R. (1987). *Coaches guide to sport psychology.* Champaign, IL: Human Kinetics.

Martens, R. (2004). *Successful coaching* (3rd ed.). Champaign, IL: Human Kinetics.

Martens, R., Christina, R. W., Harvey, J. S., & Sharkey, B. J. (1981). *Coaching young athletes.* Champaign, IL: Human Kinetics.

Martin, G., & Hrycaiko, D. (1983). Effective behavioral coaching: What's it all about? *Journal of Sport Psychology, 5,* 8–20.

McCloskey, J. C., Larson, C. E., & Knapp, M. L. (1971). *An introduction to interpersonal communication.* Englewood Cliffs, NJ: Prentice Hall.

Norman, D. A. (1976). *Memory and attention: An introduction to human information processing.* New York: John Wiley and Sons.

Orlick, T. (1986). *Psyching for sport.* Champaign, IL: Human Kinetics.

Orlick, T. (2000). *In pursuit of excellence* (3rd ed.). Champaign, IL: Human Kinetics.

Orlick, T., & Partington, J. (1987). The sport psychology consultant: Analysis of critical components as viewed by Canadian Olympic athletes. *The Sport Psychologist, 1,* 4–17.

Parham, W. D. (1996). Diversity within intercollegiate athletics: Current profile and welcomed opportunities. In E. F. Etzel, A. P. Ferrante, & J. W. Pinkney (Eds.), *Counseling college student-athletes* (pp. 27–54). Morgantown, WV: Fitness Information Technology.

Partington, J., & Orlick, T. (1987). The sport psychology consultant: Olympic coaches views. *The Sport Psychologist, 1,* 95–102.

Pietsch, W. V. (1974). *Human being: How to have a creative relationship instead of a power struggle.* New York: New American Library.

Ravizza, K. (1988). Gaining entry with athletic personnel for season long consulting. *The Sport Psychologist, 2,* 243–254.

Riley, P. (1993). *The winner within.* New York: Putnam.

Rosenfeld, L., & Wilder, L. (1990). Communication fundamentals: Active listening. *Sport Psychology Training Bulletin, 1*(5), 1–8.

Salmela, J. H. (1996). *Great job coach.* Ottawa, ON: Potentium.

Schramm, W. (1954). How communication works. In W. Schramm (Ed.). *The process and effects of mass communication.* Urbana: University of Illinois Press.

Shaw, M. E. (1981). *Group dynamics: The psychology of small group behavior* (3rd ed.). New York: McGraw-Hill.

Smith, N. J., Smith, R. E., & Smoll, F. L. (1983). *Kidsports: A survival guide for parents.* Reading, MA: Addison-Wesley.

Smith, R. E. (1986). Toward a cognitive-affective model of athletic burnout. *The Journal of Sport Psychology, 8,* 36–50.

Smith, R. E., Smoll, F., & Curtis, B. (1979). Coach effectiveness training: A cognitive-behavioral approach to enhancing relationship skills in youth sport coaches. *Journal of Sport Psychology, 1,* 59–75.

Stuhr, J. (1997). *Genealogical pragmatism: Philosophy, experience, and community.* Albany: State University of New York.

Sullivan, P. A. (1993). Communication skills training for interactive sports. *The Sport Psychologist, 7,* 79–91.

Thompson, J. (1993). *Positive coaching: Building character and self-esteem through sports.* Dubuque, IA: William C. Brown.

Tubbs, S. L., & Moss, S. (1987). *Human communication* (5th ed.). New York: Random House.

Vernacchia, R. A., McGuire, R. T., & Cook, D. L. (1992). *Coaching mental excellence: It does matter whether you win or lose.* Dubuque, IA: William C. Brown and Benchmark.

Walsh, B. (1998). *Finding the winning edge.* Champaign, IL: Sports Publishing Inc.

Wenburg, J. R., & Wilmot, W. W. (1982). *The personal communication process.* Malabar, FL: Krieger Publishing.

Wooten, M. (1992). *Coaching basketball effectively.* Champaign, IL: Human Kinetics.

Yukelson, D. (1984). Group motivation in sport teams. In J. Silva & R. Weinberg (Eds.), *Psychological foundations in sport* (pp. 229–240). Champaign, IL: Human Kinetics.

Yukelson, D. (1997). Principles of effective team building interventions in sport: A direct service approach at Penn State University. *Journal of Applied Sport Psychology, 9,* 73–96.

Yukelson, D., Sullivan, B. A., Morett, C., & Dorenkott, B. (2003). *Coaches' perspectives on applying sport psychology into their coaching.* Invited symposium presented at the annual meeting of the Association for the Advancement of Applied Sport Psychology, Philadelphia, PA.

Zaccaro, S. J., Blair, V., Peterson, C., & Zazanis, M. (1995). Collective efficacy. In J. Maddox (Ed.), *Self-efficacy, adaptation, and adjustment* (pp. 305–328). New York: Plenum Press.

Enhancing Coach–Parent Relationships in Youth Sports: Increasing Harmony and Minimizing Hassle*

Frank L. Smoll, *University of Washington*
Sean P. Cumming, *University of Washington*

Parents should be observers and supporters of their athletically inclined children, but never pushers.

—Wayne Gretzky, National Hockey League Hall of Famer

Athletic competition for children and youth is firmly entrenched in the fabric of North American society. Historical research by Berryman (2002) and by Wiggins (2002) has shown that the first programs in the United States were instituted in public schools in the early 1900s when it was recognized that physical activity was an important part of education. The programs emerged as after-school recreation activities, but they soon acquired a highly competitive "win-at-all-costs" orientation. This change resulted in condemnation and subsequent withdrawal of support by educators. Over time, sponsorship and control of some sports shifted to a host of local and national agencies. The diversified mix of autonomous organizations offered a wide array of sport programs that grew in scope and popularity.

*Preparation of this chapter was supported in part by Grant 2297 to Ronald E. Smith and Frank L. Smoll from the William T. Grant Foundation.

The rate of growth of youth sports has been phenomenal. For example, Little League Baseball originated in 1939 in Williamsport, Pennsylvania, as a three-team league for 8- to 12-year-old boys. The program was so popular that it spread rapidly. During its 50-year anniversary season, there were some 16,000 chartered leagues in 25 countries and territorial possessions around the world, providing opportunities for more than 2.5 million boys and girls 6 to 18 years of age (Smith & Smoll, 2002a). Programs in other sports have also shown rapid growth. As a result, some 47 million youngsters between the ages of 6 and 18 participate in youth sports, approximately 6 to 7 million of which do so under the auspices of the school systems (Ewing & Seefeldt, 2002).

Moving from the sandlot to the more formalized programs that now exist has required the involvement of increasing numbers of adults. Approximately 7.5 million men and women

volunteer their time as coaches, league administrators, and officials. As programs have become
more highly organized, parental involvement has
also increased, and research has shown that parents influence children's socialization into sport
as well as the psychological consequences that
accrue (see Brustad, 2003; Brustad, Babkes, &
Smith, 2001; Brustad & Partridge, 2002; Coté,
1999; Coté & Hay, 2002; Greendorfer, Lewko, &
Rosengren, 2002).

Through their cooperative efforts, many parents are productive contributors to youngsters'
sport experiences. Unfortunately, however, the
negative impact of a rather small minority is all
too obvious. Indeed, because of the increased frequency of cases of parents engaging in abusive
and violent behavior, some organizations have
implemented preventative measures. For example,
the American Youth Soccer Organization has team
officials educate parents of participants below 8
years of age on issues such as sportsmanship and
behavioral conduct. Another concern is that parents of young athletes are exercising too much
control over their children. Increasing tuition
costs, the competition for collegiate scholarships,
and the lure of professional sports has motivated
many parents to commit their children to specialized training regimens at an early age (American
Academy of Pediatrics, 2000). Parents are investing a greater amount of time and finance into the
athletic development of their children. Moreover,
parents' decisions to send or transfer children to
and from academic institutions are increasingly
based on the athletic and not the academic reputation of the schools (Frenette, 1999). Although
such actions are supposedly taken in the child's
"best interests," there is growing concern that the
overinvolvement of parents may undermine the
basic goals of youth sports and rob youngsters of
benefits they could derive from participation.

The so-called athletic triangle, consisting of
coach, athlete, and parent, is a natural aspect of
youth sports, and a coach's role in relating to parents is very important to the success of a program
(Coté & Salmela, 1996; Hellstedt, 1995). Coaches
are in a position to channel parents' genuine concerns and good intentions in a way that heightens
the value of athletes' sport experiences. The purpose of this chapter is to assist coaches in working
effectively with parents, thereby increasing the
harmony and minimizing the hassle for all concerned. The objective is to foster better understanding of (a) the difference between youth and
professional models of sport, (b) the goals of youth
sports, including a healthy philosophy of winning, (c) parental responsibilities and challenges,
(d) how to achieve effective two-way communication with parents, and (e) how to organize and
conduct sport meetings with parents.

Developmental Versus Professional Models of Sport

An important issue is the difference between youth
and professional models of sport. Youth sports provide an educational medium for the development
of desirable physical and psychosocial characteristics. The sport environment is viewed as a micro-
cosm of society in which children and youth can
learn to cope with realities they will face in later
life. Thus, athletics provide a developmental setting within which an *educational process* can occur.

In contrast, professional sports are an explicitly commercial enterprise. Their goals, simply
stated, are to entertain and, ultimately, to make
money. Financial success is of primary importance and depends heavily on a *product orientation*, namely, winning. Is this wrong? Certainly
not! The professional sports world is a part of the
entertainment industry, and as such, it is enor-
mously valued in our society.

What, then, is the problem? Most of the negative consequences of youth sports occur when
adults erroneously impose a professional model on
what should be a recreational and educational
experience for youngsters. When excessive emphasis is placed on winning, it is easy to lose sight of
the needs and interests of the young athlete.

Objectives of Youth Sports

Participation in youth sports can yield many benefits. Some of them are physical, such as acquiring
sport skills and increasing health and fitness.

Others are psychological, such as developing leadership skills, self-discipline, respect for authority, competitiveness, cooperativeness, sportsmanship, and self-confidence. These are many of the positive attributes that fall under the heading of "character." Youth sports are also an important social activity in which children can make new friends and acquaintances and become part of an ever-expanding social network. Furthermore, the involvement of parents in the athletic enterprise can serve to bring families closer together and strengthen family unity. Finally, of course, youth sports are (or should be) just plain *fun!*

The basic right of the young athlete to have fun participating should not be neglected. One of the quickest ways to reduce fun is for adults to begin treating children as if they were varsity or professional athletes. Coaches and parents alike need to keep in mind that young athletes are not miniature adults. They are children, and they have the right to play as children. Youth sports are first and foremost a play activity, and youngsters deserve to enjoy sports in their own way. In essence, it is important that programs remain child centered and do not become adult dominated.

What about *winning*? The common notion in sports equates success with victory. However, with a "winning is everything" philosophy, young athletes may lose opportunities to develop their skills, to enjoy participation, and to grow socially and emotionally. As emphasized in Chapter 21, well-informed coaches realize that success is not equivalent to winning games, and failure is not the same as losing. Rather, the most important kind of success comes from striving to win and giving maximum *effort.* The only thing athletes can control is the amount of effort they give. They have incomplete control over the outcome that is achieved. Athletes at all levels of competition should be taught that they are never "losers" if they give maximum effort in striving for excellence. This philosophy of success is relevant to parents as well as coaches. In fact, it may be more important for parents to understand its meaning. They can apply it to many areas of their child's life in addition to athletics.

What are some criteria for determining when winning is out of perspective? Martens (1978) suggested that winning is out of perspective (a) when a display of comradeship with an opponent is considered a sign of weakness, or when laughter is judged to be a lack of competitiveness; (b) when a coach instructs athletes in strategies designed to take unfair advantage of an opponent; (c) when youngsters are given drugs, coaxed to cheat, and intimidated to excel; or (d) when winning the game becomes more important than winning friends, respect, self-confidence, skill, health, and self-worth. The philosophy of the American Sport Education Program—*Athletes First, Winning Second*—reflects a proper perspective on winning (Martens, 2004). In other words, the most important product is not a won-lost record; it is the value of the experience provided for the athletes.

What about the objectives that young athletes seek to achieve? A survey of more than 100,000 youth sport participants in the state of Michigan indicated that young athletes participated for the following reasons (listed in the order of their importance): (a) to have fun, (b) to improve skills and learn new skills, (c) for thrills and excitement, (d) to be with friends or make new friends, and (e) to succeed or win (Universities Study Committee, 1978). In a report based on data derived from a national survey of approximately 8,000 boys and girls, these same items were included in lists of the 10 most frequently selected reasons youngsters play non-school and interscholastic sports (Seefeldt et al., 1992). Coaches may wish to consider these reasons when establishing goals for the season. Furthermore, coaches should be aware that none of these outcomes is achieved automatically through participation in sports. Coaches, parents, and sport administrators should be part of a team trying to accomplish common goals. By working together to reduce chances of misunderstanding and problems, the objectives can be attained. In this regard, parents should be encouraged to view their involvement in youth sports as an integral part of their child-rearing responsibilities.

Parents' Responsibilities and Challenges

When a child enters a sport program, parents automatically take on some obligations. Some parents do not realize this at first and are surprised to find what is expected of them. Others never realize their responsibilities and miss opportunities to help their children grow through sports, or they may actually do things that interfere with their children's development.

To begin with, parents must realize that children have a right to participate in sports. This includes the right to choose *not* to participate (Martens & Seefeldt, 1979). Although parents might choose to encourage participation, children should not be pressured, intimidated, or bribed into playing. In fulfilling their responsibility, parents should counsel their children, giving consideration to the sport selected and the level of competition at which the children want to play. And, of course, parents should respect their children's decisions.

Sometimes the best decision is not to participate. Participation in sports, although desirable, is not necessarily for everyone. For those children who wish to direct their energies in other ways, the best program may be no program. Many parents become unnecessarily alarmed if their child does not show an interest in sports—particularly if the parents themselves had positive sport experiences. They think that a child who would rather do other things must somehow be abnormal. But forcing a child into sports against his or her will can be a big mistake. Sometimes the wisest decision is to encourage the child to move into other activities that may be more suited to his or her interests and abilities, at least until an interest in sports develops.

Parents can enjoy their children's participation more if they acquire an understanding and appreciation of the sport. This includes knowledge of basic rules, skills, and strategies. Coaches can serve as valuable resources by answering parents' questions and by referring parents to a community or school library or a bookstore for educational materials (books and videos). In addition, coaches should devote part of an early season practice to a lecture/demonstration of the fundamentals of the sport. Parents having little background in the sport should be encouraged to attend this session.

The Reversed-Dependency Trap

Parents often assume an extremely active role in youth sports, and in some instances, their influence becomes an important source of children's stress (see Brustad, Babkes, & Smith, 2001; Brustad & Partridge, 2002; Passer, 1984; Scanlan, 1986). One factor in parent-induced stress is what has been labeled the *reversed-dependency trap* (Smith & Smoll, 2002b). All parents identify with their children to some extent and thus want them to do well. Unfortunately, in some cases, the degree of identification becomes excessive, and the child becomes an extension of the parents. When this happens, parents begin to define their own self-worth in terms of their son's or daughter's successes or failures. The father who is a "frustrated jock" may seek to experience through his child the success he never knew as an athlete. The parent who was a star may be resentful and rejecting if the child does not attain a similar level of achievement. Some parents thus become "winners" or "losers" through their children, and the pressure placed on the children to excel can be extreme. A child *must* succeed or the parent's self-image is threatened. Much more is at stake than a mere game, and the child of such a parent carries a heavy burden. When parental love and approval depend on adequacy of performance, sports are bound to be stressful (see Smoll & Smith, 1990, 2005).

Coaches may be able to counteract this tendency by explaining the identification process to parents. They can tell parents that placing excessive pressure on children can decrease the potential of sports for enjoyment and personal growth. A key to reducing parent-produced stress is to impress on parents that youth sport programs are for young athletes and that children and youth are *not* adults. Parents must acknowledge the right of each child to develop athletic potential in an atmosphere that emphasizes participation, personal growth, and *fun*.

Commitments and Affirmations

Other important challenges must be met by youth sport parents as well. To contribute to the success of a sport program, parents must be willing and able to commit themselves in many different ways. The following questions serve as thought-provoking reminders of the scope of parents' responsibilities, questions to which parents must honestly answer "Yes" (Smoll & Smith, 2005):

1. *Can parents share their son or daughter?* This requires putting the child in the coach's charge and trusting him or her to guide the sport experience. It involves accepting the coach's authority and the fact that the coach may gain some of the admiration and affection the child once directed solely at the parent. This commitment does not mean that parents cannot have input, but the coach is the boss! If parents are going to undermine the coach's leadership, it is best for all concerned not to have their child join the program.

2. *Can parents accept their child's disappointments?* Every child athlete experiences "the thrill of victory and the agony of defeat" as part of the competition process. In addition to enjoying triumphs, parents are called on to support their children when they are disappointed and hurt. This may mean not being embarrassed, ashamed, or angry when their son or daughter cries after losing a contest. When an apparent disappointment occurs, parents should be able to help their children learn from the experience. By doing this without denying the validity of their feelings, parents can help their children see the positive side of the situation and thus change their children's disappointment into self-acceptance.

3. *Can parents show their child self-control?* Parents should be reminded that they are important role models for their children's behavior. It is not surprising that parents who lose control of themselves often have children who are prone to emotional outbursts and poor self-discipline. Coaches can hardly be expected to teach sportsmanship and self-control to youngsters whose parents obviously lack these qualities.

4. *Can parents give their child some time?* Parents need to decide how much time can be devoted to their children's sport activities. Conflicts arise when they are very busy yet are also interested and want to encourage their children. To avoid this, the best advice coaches can give parents is to deal honestly with the time-commitment issue and not promise more time than they can actually deliver. Coaches should recommend that parents ask their children about their sport experiences and make every effort to watch some of their contests.

5. *Can parents let their child make his or her own decisions?* Accepting responsibility for one's own behavior and decisions is an essential part of growing up. Coaches should encourage parents to offer suggestions and guidance about sports, but ultimately, within reasonable limits, they should let the child go his or her own way. All parents have ambitions for their child, but they must accept the fact that they cannot dominate their child's life. Sports can offer an introduction to the major parental challenge of letting go.

Conduct at Sport Events

The most noticeable parent problem is misbehavior at games. As part of their responsibilities, parents should watch their children compete in sports. But their behavior must meet acceptable standards. In addition to acknowledging some obviously inappropriate actions (using profanity, drinking alcohol, throwing objects, and so forth), these rules for parental behavior (*do's* and *don'ts*) have been recommended (Smoll & Smith, 2004):

1. *Do* remain in the spectator area during the event.

2. *Don't* interfere with the coach. You must be willing to give up the responsibility for your child to the coach for the duration of the practice or game.

3. *Do* express interest, encouragement, and support to your child. Be sure to cheer good effort as well as good performance. Communicate repeatedly that giving total effort is all you expect.

4. *Don't* shout instructions or criticisms to the children.

5. *Do* lend a hand when a coach or official asks for help.

6. *Don't* make abusive comments to athletes, parents, officials, or coaches of either team.

What about parents who violate the rules of conduct? Good sportsmanship among spectators is a goal worth working for. Parents have the obligation not only to control their own behavior but also to remind others, if necessary. When parents misbehave, it is the duty of other parents and league administrators to step in and correct the situation. The rule of thumb for all spectators is that nothing in their actions should interfere with any child's enjoyment of the sport.

Two-Way Communication

Parents have both the right and the responsibility to inquire about *all* activities that their children are involved in, including sports. For this reason, coaches should be willing to answer questions and remain open to parents' input. Remember that *communication is a two-way street.* If coaches keep the lines of communication open, they will be more likely to have constructive relations with parents.

Fostering two-way communication does not mean that parents are free to be disrespectful toward coaches in word or action. Rather, it is an open invitation for parents to express their genuine concerns with the assurance that they will be heard by the coach. There is, however, a proper time and place for parent–coach interaction. That time is not during practice or a contest, and it is never in the presence of the youngsters. Coaches should tell parents what times and places are best suited for discussions.

The most common cause of coach–parent conflicts is a difference of opinions about the young athlete's abilities. In this regard, the use of a performance measurement system (described in Chapter 3) not only provides valuable feedback to athletes but can be an objective source of performance evaluation for parents. Nevertheless,

sometimes parents will disagree with what coaches are doing. The main thing is for coaches not to get defensive. They should listen to what the parents have to say. They might find some parents' suggestions helpful. However, even if they do not agree, coaches can at least *listen* and evaluate the message. They should realize that they have the final say and that no coach can please everyone. No one can ask any more than what coaches ask of their athletes—doing the very best job they can and always looking for ways to improve.

In some instances, it is desirable to have an athletic director or league official serve as a mediator for a coach–parent consultation. The presence of a third person reduces the likelihood of conflict or hostility and can potentially contribute to the resolution process. It is also desirable to bring documentation that supports one's position or actions. This could include an established parent code of conduct, league or team rules and regulations, or educational materials. The objective is to reach a clear and shared solution that is stated in behavioral terms—that is, specific actions that a coach, parent, or athlete should or should not engage in.

In establishing good relations with parents, coaches should be aware that most parents are really enthusiastic and have a true concern for their children. Sometimes, however, parents simply do not realize the trouble they are causing. Instead of being angry with them, coaches should recognize that they have a problem—one that the coaches can help solve. The task is to point out to these people, tactfully and diplomatically, the negative influences of their actions and get them to become more constructive and helpful. Some common types of "problem parents" are identified in the following section. In addition to describing their traits, recommendations are included for dealing with them.

Disinterested Parents

Distinguishing characteristics. The most noticeable characteristic of disinterested parents is their absence from team activities to a degree that is upsetting to their child.

What coaches should do. Coaches should find out why the parents do not participate and contribute, and let them know that their involvement is welcome. Coaches should avoid the mistake of misjudging parents who are actually interested but have good reasons (work, sickness, etc.) for missing activities. Explaining the value of sports and how they can draw children and parents closer together may provide parents with a new interest in the activities of their children. In this situation, the athletes need help, too. Coaches should encourage the athletes and show that they are really interested in them as people.

Overcritical Parents

Distinguishing characteristics. Overcritical parents often scold and berate their child. Such parents are never quite satisfied with their child's performance. They give the impression that it is more "their" game than it is the athlete's.

What coaches should do. As discussed earlier, some parents unconsciously relate the success or failure of their child with their own success or failure. As a result, they are often hard on their children. Coaches should attempt to make overcritical parents aware of this problem as tactfully as possible. They can explain how constant criticism can cause stress and emotional turmoil for their youngster—irritation that actually hinders performance. They can tell the parents why they prefer to use praise and encouragement to motivate and instruct young people, and how parents can do the same.

What coaches can say. "Mr. Jones, I know you're only trying to help Billy, but when you criticize him, he gets so nervous that he plays worse, and that certainly takes any fun out of it for him." *Or* "Mr. Jones, I've found that Billy responds much better to encouragement and praise than he does to criticism. If you were to encourage your son instead of criticizing him so much, sports would be a lot more enjoyable for both of you. After all, it's the kids' game. They play for fun, and too much criticism spoils it for them."

Parents Who Scream from Behind the Bench

Distinguishing characteristics. Some parents seem to have "leather lungs" and large vocal chords. They often sit directly behind the bench, which makes them a distinct danger to the well-being of coaches' eardrums. They frequently rant and rave and virtually drown out everyone else speaking in the area, including the coach. Everyone is the target for their verbal abuse—team members, opponents, coaches, officials.

What coaches should do. Coaches must not get into an argument with a screaming parent. It will not do any good and will probably make things worse. During a break in the contest (half time, between periods), coaches can calmly, tactfully, and privately point out to the person that such yelling is a poor example for the young athletes. Coaches can ask other people to help out by working with this person during games. Also, coaches can give the disruptive parent a job that will help the team (scouting opponents, keeping stats, looking after equipment, etc.). This may provide a greater sense of responsibility and help the screamer to keep quiet. If the screaming persists, coaches should seek assistance from league administrators.

What coaches can say. "I know it's easy to get excited, but these kids are out here to have a good time. Try not to take the game so seriously, okay?" *Or* "Listen, why don't we get together after the game and you can give me some of your ideas on coaching. I'd rather have them afterward because during the game, they're very confusing."

Sideline Coaches

Distinguishing characteristics. Parents who assume the role of sideline coaches are often found leaning over the bench making suggestions to athletes. They may contradict the coach's instructions and disrupt the team.

What coaches should do. Again, coaches should not confront such a parent right away. Coaches should advise their athletes that during practices and games they are the coach and they want the athletes' full attention. Listening to instructions from others may become confusing. Coaches should tell the parent privately how confusing it is for the athletes when two or more people are telling them what to do. Coaches might ask the parent to be either a full-time assistant coach or a full-time spectator.

What coaches can say. "Ms. Slavin, I appreciate your concern and enthusiasm for the team. But when you are coaching Becky from the sidelines, it becomes confusing and distracting to her. I know you've got some good ideas, and I want to hear them. But please, after the game."

Overprotective Parents

Distinguishing characteristics. Most often, over-protective parents are the mothers of the athletes. Such parents are characterized by their worried looks and comments whenever their son or daughter is playing. Overprotective parents frequently threaten to remove their child because of the dangers involved in the sport.

What coaches should do. Coaches must try to eliminate the fear of injury by reassuring the parent that the event is fairly safe. They can explain the rules and equipment that protect the athlete. Point out how good coaching, program administration, and officiating add to the safety of the sport.

What coaches can say. "Ms. Smith, we try to make the game as safe as possible for the athletes. You've got to remember that I wouldn't be coaching kids if I didn't care about them or if I thought the sport was dangerous for them." *Or* "Ms. Smith, I care about each one of these kids, and I would never let any of them do anything that I thought would endanger them."

The Coach–Parent Meeting

Coaches unselfishly devote a tremendous amount of time and effort to providing a worthwhile experience for youngsters. All too often they are asked to do "just one more thing." However, successful coaches are aware of the importance of securing the aid and support of well-informed parents. Rather than facing the task of dealing with problem parents, a preseason meeting is the *key* to reducing the chance of unpleasant experiences. In other words, having a coach–parent meeting is well worth the additional time and effort!

This part of the chapter is a *guide* for planning and conducting effective coach–parent meetings. Because each coach is unique, coaches should evaluate the information and suggestions and make modifications to suit their personal situation.

Purposes of the Meeting

The objectives of a coach–parent meeting are (a) to improve parents' understanding of youth sports, and (b) to gain their cooperation and support. Their input can then increase the value of sport participation for their children's physical, psychological, and social development.

Planning and Preparation

It is not unusual for coaches to be hesitant about conducting a coach–parent meeting because they feel insecure about leading a group of adults. People are often unwilling to do things for which they have had little training or previous experience. Coaches who have held meetings with parents indicate that it is not an overtaxing experience, and the benefits make the meeting a good investment.

It will take approximately 1-1/4 hours to cover the necessary topics. The meeting does not have to be elaborate to be successful. However, the importance of being well prepared and organized cannot be overemphasized. To improve organizational quality, develop and follow a written program outline.

The coach should schedule the meeting as early in the season as possible, and be sure that the facility selected is easily accessible and has a meeting room of adequate size, with appropriate seating, lighting, and other amenities. Should athletes attend the meeting? Some coaches have no objections and believe it helps improve communication among all those involved. Other coaches find it more productive to conduct the meeting without the athletes present. The coach's personal preference will determine the policy adopted. However, if the athletes are excluded, the coach should make special arrangements for parents who might not be able to attend without their children. For example, an additional room might be sought in which the children could be shown an educational sport film under the supervision of an assistant coach.

Parents should be sent a personal letter of invitation, including brief statements about the objective of the meeting, its importance, and information about the date, time, location, directions, and attendance by youngsters. A team roster with addresses and telephone numbers should accompany the letter. Follow-up telephone calls are recommended to remind parents about the meeting. This could be accomplished by enlisting the aid of parents to set up a chain-calling system.

Content and Conduct of the Meeting

As stated earlier, effective communication is based on two-way sharing. Therefore, in conducting the meeting, the coach should draw parents into the discussion instead of lecturing to them. The coach can do this (a) by encouraging parents to ask questions and (b) by directing questions to them from time to time. Also, in creating an open atmosphere for exchange, it is very important to show respect for the parents. They should feel that they are a contributing part of the meeting, rather than a mere audience.

Opening (5 minutes). The coach begins the meeting by introducing himself or herself and the assistant coach(es). In welcoming the parents it is important to let them know that their interest and concern are appreciated. In praising their attendance the coach can point out that they are taking an important step toward assuring a quality sport experience for their children. Next, the coach establishes credibility by giving

pertinent background information. The coach tells parents about his or her experience in the sport, experience as a coach, and special training that he or she has had (e.g., workshops, clinics). Finally, the coach points out the purposes of the meeting and tells parents how he or she will provide information about fundamentals of the sport (invite them to attend a practice session).

A note of caution is in order. Coaches conducting a coach–parent meeting for the first time, or who have little experience in leading adults, should not begin the meeting by announcing this as a personal shortcoming or by asking for the parents' tolerance. Such statements may reduce parents' trust and support. Self-degrading remarks may also cause parents to question the coach's ability to conduct the meeting. To gain respect, coaches must show confidence in leading the session.

Objectives of youth sports (10 minutes). A discussion of the objectives of children's athletics, including a healthy philosophy of winning, should follow the opening remarks. The coach should focus on those goals and values that are a major part of his or her coaching. Also, the coach should find out which objectives the parents would like to have emphasized. As pointed out earlier, if coaches and parents work together to reduce misunderstandings, the objectives can be achieved.

Details of the sport program (10 minutes). The coach presents details about the operation of the sport program. In addition to other items that he or she might think of, consideration should be given to the following: (a) equipment needed and where it can be purchased, (b) sites and schedules for practices and contests, (c) length of practices and contests, (d) team travel plans, (e) major team rules and guidelines, (f) special rule modifications to be used at this level of competition, (g) medical examinations, (h) insurance, (i) fundraising projects, (j) communication system for cancellations and so on, and (k) midseason and postseason events.

The coach should also provide information about what is expected of the athletes and parents relative to the program details. Some coaches find it useful to organize a parent committee, giving this committee the task of coordinating parent involvement in many activities of the season.

Coaching roles and relationships (10 minutes). Parents will benefit from knowing about the coach's leadership style. In addition to describing the *positive approach* that he or she will be using (see Chapter 21), the coach should encourage parents to reinforce this approach in interactions with their children.

Parents' responsibilities and challenges (20 minutes). Informing parents about the responsibilities the coach expects them to fulfill is the most important part of the meeting. The coach should discuss the following topics, which were covered earlier in this chapter:

1. Counseling children about sports selection and the level of competition at which they want to play—conferring with and *listening* to them.

2. Dangers of the reversed-dependency trap—the negative impact of this process.

3. Parent commitments and affirmations—the five important questions (see page 196) to which parents must be able to honestly answer "Yes."

4. Rules of conduct at sports events—the coach is responsible for the team, and the parents are responsible for their own behavior.

Coach–parent relations (5 minutes). The coach should tell parents of his or her willingness to discuss any problems that might arise—that all-important two-way communication! He or she should let parents know what times and places are best suited for discussions.

Closing (20–30 minutes). The coach–parent meeting should be concluded with a question-and-answer session. For this to be worthwhile, a coach must be ready to cover a wide range of parents' concerns. Preparation is best accomplished by reading a manual such as *Sports and Your Child* (Smoll & Smith, 2005), which provides brief answers to the most frequently asked questions about youth sports, including participation issues and youngsters' physical and psychological development.

An effective technique for starting a question-and-answer period is for the coach to take the lead in raising questions. He or she can stimulate parent involvement by asking the first few questions, and then guide the discussion. If the coach does not know the answer to a question, he or she should not be ashamed to admit it. The parents will appreciate the honesty. Rather than giving a weak or incorrect response, the coach can offer to seek the answer along with the parent, or perhaps someone in the group will be able to provide the answer. The coach should not give the impression that he or she must address every question. Finally, at the end of the meeting, the coach should thank the parents again for attending.

The coach–parent meeting is a vitally important tool for developing parent involvement and support. A successful meeting will help solidify the athletic triangle (the coach–athlete–parent triad) and lead to positive youth sport experiences.

Follow-Up Meetings

If possible, it is highly desirable to schedule a midseason meeting with parents. This will provide an opportunity to present refresher points, discuss the athletes' progress, and cooperatively seek solutions to existing problems.

A postseason celebration is an excellent way to end the season. This could take the form of a family dinner planned by the parents. In addition to having good fellowship and fun, coaches could take some time to obtain parents' evaluations of the program and their coaching. In such conversations, the coach asks parents to point out things that went well and gets their suggestions for making improvements.

Summary

This chapter has dealt with a frequently neglected aspect of youth sports, namely, interactions between coaches and parents. Consideration was given to promoting effective coach–parent relationships to improve the quality of the athletes' sport experiences. In so doing, the following major points were emphasized:

1. Coaches and parents play important roles in determining the outcomes of participation in youth sports.

2. In a developmental model sports provide an arena for learning, where success is measured in terms of personal growth and development.

3. Participation in youth sports can improve physical skills and fitness, build character, promote social competence, bring families closer together, and provide enjoyable recreational experiences for young people.

4. Fun is the essence of play, and it constitutes the core of successful youth sport experiences.

5. Young athletes should be taught that they are never "losers" if they give maximum effort in striving for excellence.

6. Youngsters participate in sports to have fun, to improve skills, for thrills and excitement, and to make friends. The goal of winning is relatively unimportant to them as compared with these other objectives.

7. Parents should not pressure, intimidate, or bribe their children into playing a sport.

8. Parents should learn basic sport rules, skills, and strategies.

9. Coaches should serve as valuable resources and answer parents' questions as best as possible.

10. A key to reducing parent-produced stress is to impress on them that youth sports are for the young athletes.

11. Parents must be able to endorse their child's participation in youth sports and support the coach's program.

12. Parents must conform to acceptable standards of behavior at contests.

13. In working with parents, it is essential to develop and maintain open, healthy communication with them.

14. Effective communication is a two-way street requiring both speaking and listening skills.

15. Holding a preseason coach–parent meeting is the key to avoiding unpleasant experiences.

16. The main objectives of a coach–parent meeting are to improve parents' understanding of youth sports and to gain their cooperation and support.

Study Questions

1. What are the components of the "athletic triangle," and what impact does this triad have on youth sports?

2. Describe the major differences between developmental and professional models of sport. Why is it important that coaches and parents understand these distinctions?

3. What responsibilities do parents have with respect to counseling their children about sports selection and guiding their entry into specific programs?

4. Explain the reversed-dependency trap that might underlie parent-induced stress in youth sports.

5. Discuss the implications of these sport-related responsibilities of parents: (a) sharing their child, (b) accepting their child's disappointments, (c) demonstrating self-control, (d) giving their child some time, and (e) allowing their child to make decisions.

6. What are the major rules of conduct (do's and don'ts) for parent behavior at youth sport contests?

7. What are some keys to establishing and maintaining open channels of communication with parents of young athletes?

8. Describe the distinguishing characteristics of the following types of problem parents and indicate how they might be dealt with: (a) disinterested parents, (b) overcritical parents, (c) parents who scream from behind the bench, (d) sideline coaches, and (e) overprotective parents.

9. What are the main purposes of a preseason coach–parent meeting?

10. What are the most important considerations in planning a coach–parent meeting?

11. Briefly describe the content of each of these components of a coach–parent meeting: (a) opening, (b) objectives of youth sports, (c) details of the sport program, (d) coaching roles and relationships, (e) parents' responsibilities and challenges, (f) coach–parent relations, and (g) closing.

12. What kinds of follow-up meetings can be held with parents, and of what value are they?

References

American Academy of Pediatrics: Committee on Sports Medicine and Fitness. (2000). Intensive training and sports specialization in young athletes. *Pediatrics, 106* 154–157.

Berryman, J. W. (2002). The rise of boys' sports in the United States, 1900 to 1970. In F. L. Smoll & R. E. Smith (Eds.), *Children and youth in sport: A biopsychosocial perspective* (2nd ed., pp. 5–17). Dubuque, IA: Kendall/Hunt.

Brustad, R. J. (2003). Parental roles and involvement in youth sports: Psychosocial outcomes for children. In R. M. Malina & M. A. Clark (Eds.), *Youth sports: Perspectives for a new century* (pp. 127–138). Monterey, CA: Coaches Choice.

Brustad, R. J., Babkes, M. L., & Smith, A. L. (2001). Youth in sport: Psychosocial considerations. In R. N. Singer, H. A. Hausenblas, & C. M. Janelle (Eds.), *Handbook of sport psychology* (2nd ed., pp. 604–635). New York: John Wiley & Sons.

Brustad, R. J., & Partridge, J. A. (2002). Parental and peer influence on children's psychosocial development through sport. In F. L. Smoll & R. E. Smith (Eds.), *Children and youth in sport: A biopsychosocial perspective* (2nd ed., pp. 187–210). Dubuque, IA: Kendall/Hunt.

Coté, J. (1999). The influence of the family in the development of talent in sport. *The Sport Psychologist, 13,* 395–417.

Coté, J., & Hay, J. (2002). Family influences on youth sport performance and participation. In J. M. Silva III & D. E. Stevens (Eds.), *Psychological foundations of sport* (pp. 503–519). Boston: Allyn and Bacon.

Coté, J., & Salmela, J. H. (1996). The organizational tasks of high-performance gymnastic coaches. *The Sport Psychologist, 10,* 247–260.

Ewing, M. E., & Seefeldt, V. (2002). Patterns of participation in American agency-sponsored youth sports. In F. L. Smoll & R. E. Smith (Eds.), *Children and youth in sport: A biopsychosocial perspective* (2nd ed., pp. 39–56). Dubuque, IA: Kendall/Hunt.

Frenette, G. (1999, August). The parent trap. *American Football Monthly, 5,* 65–67.

Greendorfer, S. L., Lewko, J. H., & Rosengren, K. S. (2002). Family and gender-based influences in sport socialization of children and adolescents. In F. L. Smoll & R. E. Smith (Eds.), *Children and youth in sport: A biopsychosocial perspective* (2nd ed., pp. 153–186). Dubuque, IA: Kendall/Hunt.

Hellstedt, J. C. (1995). Invisible players: A family systems model. In S. M. Murphy (Ed.), *Sport psychology interventions* (pp. 117–146). Champaign, IL: Human Kinetics.

Martens, R. (1978). *Joy and sadness in children's sports.* Champaign, IL: Human Kinetics.

Martens, R. (2004). *Successful coaching* (3rd ed.). Champaign, IL: Human Kinetics.

Martens, R., & Seefeldt, V. (1979). *Guidelines for children's sports.* Washington, DC: American Alliance for Health, Physical Education, Recreation, and Dance.

Passer, M. W. (1984). Competitive trait anxiety in children and adolescents: Mediating cognitions, developmental antecedents and consequences. In J. M. Silva & R. S. Weinberg (Eds.), *Psychological foundations of sport and exercise* (pp. 130–144). Champaign, IL: Human Kinetics.

Scanlan, T. K. (1986). Competitive stress in children. In M. R. Weiss & D. Gould (Eds.), *Sport for children and youths* (pp. 113–118). Champaign, IL: Human Kinetics.

Seefeldt, V., Ewing, M. E., & Walk, S. (1992). *Overview of youth sport programs in the United States.* Washington, DC: Carnegie Council on Adolescent Development.

Smith, R. E., & Smoll, F. L. (2002a). *Way to go, coach! A scientifically-proven approach to coaching effectiveness.* Portola Valley, CA: Warde.

Smith, R. E., & Smoll, F. L. (2002b). Youth sports as a behavior setting for psychosocial interventions. In J. L. Van Raalte & B. W. Brewer (Eds.), *Exploring sport and exercise psychology* (2nd ed., pp. 341–371). Washington, DC: American Psychological Association.

Smoll, F. L., & Smith, R. E. (1990). Psychology of the young athlete: Stress-related maladies and remedial approaches. *Pediatric Clinics of North America, 37,* 1021–1046.

Smoll, F. L., & Smith, R. E. (2004). *Behavior at sport events* [Brochure]. Palo Alto, CA: Warde.

Smoll, F. L., & Smith, R. E. (2005): *Sports and your child: Developing champions in sports and in life* (2nd ed.). Palo Alto, CA: Warde.

Universities Study Committee. (1978). *Joint legislative study on youth sports programs: Phase II. Agency sponsored sports.* East Lansing: Michigan Institute for the Study of Youth Sports.

Wiggins, D. K. (2002). A history of highly competitive sport for American children. In F. L. Smoll & R. E. Smith (Eds.), *Children and youth in sport: A biopsychosocial perspective* (2nd ed., pp. 19–37). Dubuque, IA: Kendall/Hunt.

Mental Training for Performance Enhancement

Psychological Characteristics of Peak Performance

Vikki Krane, *Bowling Green State University*
Jean M. Williams, *University of Arizona*

Trying to articulate the zone is not easy because it's such an indescribable feeling. That moment doesn't happen often, and when it does happen, you feel like you're playing out of your head! You aren't feeling any tension or any pressure and physically your strokes are just flowing, every ball you hit is going in. Emotionally you're really calm. There's no strain involved. It's a euphoric feeling. The feeling that whatever you touch turns to gold. Whatever you do, whatever decision you make on the court, whatever stroke or shot you try, you know it's going to work.

—Chris Evert, Tennis Champion

Peak performances are those magic moments when an athlete puts it all together—both physically and mentally. The performance is exceptional, seemingly transcending ordinary levels of play. Privette defined **peak performance** as "behavior which exceeds one's average performance" (1982, p. 242) or "an episode of superior functioning" (1983, p. 1361). Competitively, these performances often result in a personal best. They are the ultimate high, the thrilling moment that athletes and coaches work for in their pursuit of excellence. Unfortunately, they also are relatively rare and, according to many athletes, nonvoluntary. But are they truly nonvoluntary? Can athletes be trained so that peak performances occur more frequently? If not to produce a peak performance, can athletes be

trained so they consistently play closer to their optimal level?

To answer these questions, it is first necessary to know if there are any common characteristics that identify peak performances. For example, is there an ideal body/mind state associated with peak performance? If so, is this ideal state similar from one athlete to another or one sport to another? More important, if common qualities are identified, can they be learned and developed?

First it is safe to assume that peak performance is a consequence of both physical and mental factors. Mind and body cannot be separated. A precondition to peak performance is a certain level of physical conditioning and mastery of the physical skills involved in performance. For many decades, athletic and sport science communities have been devoted to improving physical training programs.

Obviously, the higher the level of physical skill and conditioning, the more potential control the athlete has over his or her performance. Within this minimal physical skill framework, one must realize that peak performance is relative-contingent on each athlete's present level of ability.

Peak performances are most likely to occur when athletes' skills level match the demand or challenge of the situation (Csikszentmihalyi, 1990; Jackson, 2000). Absolute skill level is not important; rather, it is important that the athlete has the skills to match the expected level of play. Thus, concern for enhancing peak performance is as relevant to coaches and sport psychologists who work with less skilled and youth sport athletes as it is to coaches and sport psychologists who work with professional or elite amateur athletes.

Overview of Peak Performance

This chapter is not concerned per se with physical skill characteristics and physical training programs that enhance the likelihood of peak performance. Instead, the focus is on the mental side of peak performance and how the mind interacts with the body in ultimately producing performance. Most athletes and coaches will acknowledge that at least 40% to 90% of success in sports is due to mental factors. The higher the skill level, the more important the mental aspects become. In fact, on the elite competitive level, it is not uncommon to hear that the winner invariably comes down to who is the strongest athlete—mentally—on a given day! Rushall (1989) has stated that "psychology is the key to athletic excellence" (p. 165). In *Golf My Way,* Jack Nicklaus states that mental preparation is the single most critical element in peak performance. This is not a particularly surprising statement considering that Nicklaus believes golf is 90% mental.

When the physical, technical, and mental readiness of Olympic athletes was assessed, only mental readiness significantly predicted Olympic success (Orlick & Partington, 1988). A study of professional baseball players (Smith & Christensen, 1995) showed psychological skills, but not physical skills, significantly predicted pitching performance. When examining batting performance, psychological and physical skills contributed equally to performance success. Additionally, psychological skills significantly predicted whether players would still be involved in professional baseball 2 and 3 years later.

If the mental side of performance is so important to success, then perhaps an ideal internal psychological climate exists during peak performance. Over the last 20 years, there has been a tremendous surge of research on psychological aspects of peak performance. The remainder of this chapter will reflect what has been learned from this research and from the insights of people who have worked with athletes in psychological training. Before identifying some of these research findings and insights, we must offer a caution. Do not think that the field of sport psychology has found all the answers. It certainly has not, and the evidence to support some of its answers is still quite tenuous. In addition to not having all of the answers, sport psychologists have probably not even identified all of the questions yet! There is, however, a growing foundation for understanding the mental side of performance and possibilities for improving performance through psychological skills training. This chapter, and the following chapters in this section, reflect the latest state of knowledge and the current thinking and practices of those involved in mental training for peak performance.

The Peak Performance Psychological Profile

Before we can think in terms of psychological skills training, it is necessary to know if there is an optimal psychological state for peak performance. If such a state can be identified for programs or for a given individual, then there is a foundation for developing a mental skills training program. There are many excellent sources for identifying the psychological characteristics underlying successful athletic performance. In initial research in this area, researchers asked athletes to recall their thoughts, feelings, and perceptions during a peak or best ever sport performance. Later researchers distinguished between peak performance and flow and focused on identifying individualized emotional patterns for successful performance. Another source of data comes from studies that compared the psychological characteristics of successful and less successful athletes—for example, athletes who were Olympic qualifiers compared to nonqualifiers, or collegiate athletes who were nationally ranked compared to less successful collegiate athletes. Recent twists on this type of study are to query highly successful athletes (e.g., Olympic champions, world-ranked international competitors) about mental states associated with exceptional performance or to compare the psychological aspects of successful athletes' personal best and worst performances. Much current research focuses on identifying the mental preparation strategies and psychological skills used by successful elite athletes. Further insights come from asking top coaches and scouts what it takes to make it in sport.

Psychological Characteristics During Peak Experiences in Sport

Ken Ravizza (1977), the author of Chapter 12, was one of the first sport psychologists to publish a study on the subjective experiences of athletes during their "greatest moment" in sport. He interviewed 20 male and female athletes from a variety of competitive levels who related experiences in 12 different sports. Over 80% of the athletes reported having the following perceptions:

- Loss of fear—no fear of failure

- No thinking of performance

- Total immersion in the activity

- Narrow focus of attention

- Effortless performance—not forcing it

- Feeling of being in complete control

- Time/space disorientation (usually slowed down)

- Universe perceived to be integrated and unified

- Unique, temporary, involuntary experience

In trying to determine where mental toughness comes from and to answer other questions about the mental aspects of sports training, Jim Loehr interviewed hundreds of athletes. He asked them to describe how they felt when they were playing at their best. What were their psychological experiences prior to and during a peak athletic experience? The athletes gave surprisingly similar accounts. According to Loehr (1984), "It was," they said, "like playing possessed, yet in complete control. Time itself seemed to slow down, so they never felt rushed. They played with profound intensity, total concentration and an enthusiasm that bordered on joy" (p. 67). Loehr further clarified the relationship between optimal sport performance and confidence and arousal by compiling the following composite of athletes' interview statements:

> I felt like I could do almost anything, as if I were in complete control. I really felt confident and positive. [Regarding arousal,] I felt physically very relaxed, but really energized and pumped up. I experienced virtually no anxiety or fear, and the whole experience was enjoyable. I experienced a very real sense of calmness and quiet inside, and everything just seemed to flow automatically. . . . Even though I was really hustling, it was all very effortless. (as cited in Garfield & Bennett, 1984, pp. 37, 95)

Loehr concluded that the probability of good performance could be substantially increased if the following combination of feelings could be triggered and maintained: high energy (challenge, inspiration, determination, intensity); fun and enjoyment; no pressure (low anxiety); optimism and positiveness; mental calmness; confidence; being very focused; and being in control.

Loehr's research has been corroborated by Charles Garfield (Garfield & Bennett, 1984). In interviews with hundreds of elite athletes, Garfield identified eight mental and physical conditions that athletes described as being characteristic of the feelings they have at those moments when they are doing something extraordinarily well: mentally relaxed, physically relaxed, confident/optimistic, focused on the present, highly energized, extraordinary awareness, in control, and in the cacoon (feeling of being completely detached from the external environment and any potential distractions).

A study of competitive golfers (Cohn, 1991) further substantiated these findings. Collegiate golfers and touring and teaching professionals were queried concerning their peak performance experiences. Psychological characteristics associated with peak performance acknowledged by these golfers included:

- A narrow focus of attention, typically on one specific thought or action

- Feeling that performance was automatic and effortless—being immersed in the present

- Feelings of control over emotion, thoughts, and arousal

- Feeling highly self-confident

- An absence of fear

- Feeling physically and mentally relaxed

Each of these qualities of peak performance was reported by at least 80% of the golfers interviewed. Many of the golfers associated this state with fun or enjoyment. These golfers also indicated that peak performance was considered a temporary phenomenon that typically lasted no longer than the length of a tournament (four rounds of golf).

Privette and Bundrick (1997) compared the mental states associated with peak, average, and failing performances of nonelite athletes. Using a questionnaire assessing characteristics of peak performance, they found peak performances were considered more fulfilling compared to average and failing performances and more playful compared to failing experiences. Privette and Bundrick further identified what they called the "peak performance dyad" (p. 331), which encompassed full focus on the activity and "self in process." They described it this way: "focusing fully on the relevant task of the game, whether narrowly on the placement of the ball or broadly over the entire field, while simultaneously being acutely aware of self as the doer, underlay peak performance"

(p. 331). They concluded that peak performances are personally meaningful, rewarding, and fulfilling.

Flow and Peak Performance

Often associated with peak performance is the psychological construct **flow.** Csikszentmihalyi (1985) has considered flow the basis of intrinsically motivated experiences or self-rewarding activity. It is "the state in which people are so involved in an activity that nothing else seems to matter" (Csikszentmihalyi, 1990, p. 4). Flow is not analogous to peak performance. One may be in flow and not necessarily be having a peak performance; however, when an athlete experiences peak performance, he or she appears to be in a flow state.

Jackson (1996) distinguished between flow and peak performance, suggesting that flow may be a precursor to or the psychological process underlying peak performance, and it has been found to be positively related to performance (Jackson, Thomas, Marsh, & Smethurst, 2001). Nine dimensions of flow have been described (Csikszentmihalyi, 1990; Jackson, 2000; Jackson & Csikszentmihalyi, 1999). When athletes are in flow, they experience the following:

1. The challenge of the situation matches the skills of the athlete, and these challenges and skills are at a personal high level.

2. Awareness and action merge, so that movement is perceived as effortless and the athlete "ceases to be aware of herself as separate from her action" (Jackson, 2000, p. 142).

3. Goals are clear; "there is clarity about what one is to do" (Jackson, 2000, p. 142).

4. Unambiguous feedback indicates that what is being done is correct.

5. Total and complete concentration on the task at hand occurs.

6. There is a paradox of control, or the sense of being in complete control without actively attempting to be in control. This also has been described as a clear sense of being in control of performance so that it feels effortless and without fear of failure.

7. Loss of self-consciousness whereby one is aware of performing but is not concerned with self-evaluation.

8. A transformation of time in which time may seem to speed up or slow down.

9. An autotelic experience in which the activity is enjoyable and participation becomes its own reward.

Interviews with elite, international level athletes revealed psychological states that coincided with these characteristics of flow (Jackson 1992, 1996). They described feeling in complete control, total confidence, complete absorption in the activity, and a sense that they "could do no wrong" (Jackson, 1992). The most salient aspects of flow experiences for these athletes were the autotelic nature of the experience, merging of action and awareness, task-focused concentration, and the paradox of control (Jackson, 1996). These characteristics are very similar to those reported to accompany peak performances.

Subsequent research has examined the factors perceived by athletes to facilitate or disrupt flow. Elite figure skaters identified five factors that enhanced the likelihood of getting into flow: (a) a positive mental attitude (including confidence, positive thinking, and motivation to do well); (b) positive affect (e.g., being relaxed, controlling anxiety, enjoying what one is doing); (c) maintaining an appropriate focus; (d) physical readiness; and (e) partner unity (Jackson, 1992). Factors identified by the skaters perceived to interfere with flow included (a) having physical problems or making mistakes; (b) an inability to maintain their focus; (c) a negative mental attitude; and (d) a lack of audience response. Interviews with college athletes revealed similar findings (Russell, 2000). In another study with elite athletes in a variety of sports (Jackson, 1995), the athletes identified factors that facilitated the likelihood of achieving flow. Mental preparation that enhanced flow states included the following:

• Maintaining confidence and a positive attitude

• Following precompetitive plans and preparation

• Optimal physical preparation prior to competition

• Attaining optimal arousal

• Achieving appropriate motivation to perform

• Being in tune with movements and performance—feeling good

• Being focused on the task

• Having optimal environmental and situational conditions

• Having positive team interactions

• Having experience with flow states

Studies employing flow questionnaires have found that athletes who experience flow, compared to those who do not, have higher preevent self-confidence (Catley & Duda, 1997; Stein, Kimiecik, Daniels, & Jackson, 1995). Also, high perceived ability, a task goal orientation, and low anxiety are positively associated with flow (Jackson & Roberts, 1992; Jackson, Kimiecik, Ford, & Marsh, 1998).

Additionally, intrinsic motivation (Kowal & Fortier, 2000) and athletic self-concept (Jackson, Thomas, Marsh, & Smethurst, 2000) have been found to be positively related to flow experiences. Jackson et al. (1998) concluded that high perceptions of one's athletic abilities appear to be crucial to the experience of flow. As they stated, "athletes who believe in their capabilities are probably more likely to experience a balance between challenge and skills, even when the challenge of a specific sport competition is relatively high" (p. 373).

When considering the characteristics of flow and the factors that facilitate or disrupt it, it seems that psychological skills may enhance the likelihood of experiencing flow. This notion was explored by Jackson et al. (2000) in a study of competitors in surf life saving, orienteering, and road cycling. They found "the avoidance of negative thinking, combined with good emotional control, relaxation, appropriate activation levels, and, to a lesser extent, setting goals, use of imagery, and positive self-talk facilitated flow" (p. 148). In a rare intervention study aimed to enhance flow, Pates, Cummings, and Maynard

(2002) tested the effect of a hypnosis intervention. Using an ideographic (i.e., individualized), multiple baseline design, five athletes provided many baseline scores on a questionnaire assessing flow experiences during a basketball shooting task (i.e., three-point shots). Then, during the intervention, they were taught how to use hypnosis, and, finally, they completed several postintervention flow assessments. The hypnosis intervention consisted of relaxation, imagery, hypnotic induction and regression, and use of a trigger. The results showed that the intensity of flow experienced during the shooting task increased after learning to use hypnosis, as did their performance.

These findings suggest that athletes can learn prerequisite skills that may enhance the likeliness of experiencing flow. Athletes who learn to be confident, focus their attention on the task at hand, control their anxiety, and have appropriate and challenging goals may experience flow and peak performance more often.

The Individualized Zone of Optimal Functioning

Another approach to examining psychological states of successful athletes focuses on performance-related emotions (Hanin, 2000a). The **Individualized Zone of Optimal Functioning** (IZOF) model (Hanin, 2000b) attempts to identify emotional patterns associated with individual athletes' successful performances. This approach is **ideographic,** or individually focused. Hanin (1997) acknowledges that each athlete has her or his own unique emotional state in which successful performances are most likely. Thus, individual athletes' emotional states associated with their better and worse performances are compared, with the goal of identifying an IZOF for the individual. Optimal performance states include both positive and negative emotions (Hanin, 2000b). Four groups of emotional states are recognized: positive performance-enhancing, positive performance-impairing, negative performance-enhancing, and negative performance-impairing. For example, elite Finnish athletes described feeling energetic

as a positive, performance-enhancing emotion, whereas easygoing was considered a positive emotion that was performance-impairing (Hanin, 2000c). Tense and dissatisfied were described as negative performance-enhancing emotions, whereas feeling tired was considered negative and performance-impairing.

To identify individuals' IZOFs, athletes complete an assessment identifying emotions related to their successful and unsuccessful performances. Different athletes may include different emotions in their profiles. This assessment results in identifying a range of optimal and dysfunctional emotions, and an IZOF iceberg profile emerges. As seen in Figure 11-1, both positive and negative emotions considered performance-enhancing comprise the optimal zone, and performance-impairing emotions comprise the dysfunctional zones. Athletes whose emotional states are within their IZOF are more successful than athletes with emotional profiles out of their IZOFs (Hanin, 2000c). For example, successful junior soccer players had emotional profiles that were close to their optimal zones and outside of their dysfunctional zones (Syrja, Hanin, & Pesonen, 1995, as cited in Hanin, 2000c). The soccer players who had poor performances had emotional profiles outside of their optimal zones prior to competition, and they never entered their IZOFs once the match began. Similarly, successful international competitors in squash and badminton had emotions that were close to their optimal zones and outside of their dysfunctional zones (Syrja, Hanin, & Tarvonen, 1995, as cited in Hanin, 2000c).

Elite competitors in blackbelt karate had emotional responses that differed prior to successful and less successful performances (Robazza, Bortoli, & Hanin, 2004). When these athletes compared their emotion scores at actual competitions to their worst-ever emotion score, better performances were associated with larger differences (or greater distance from worst-ever emotions). Robazza and Bortoli (2003) compared the emotional profiles of elite (competed in major national or international championships) and nonelite athletes from a variety of sports. Their findings showed that the more

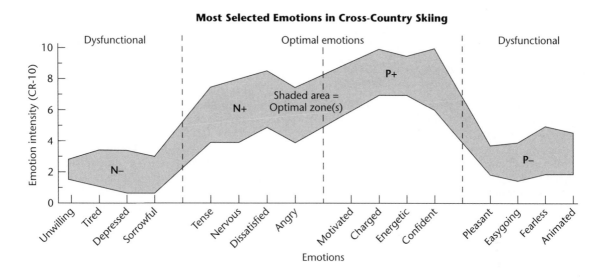

Most Selected Emotions in Cross-Country Skiing

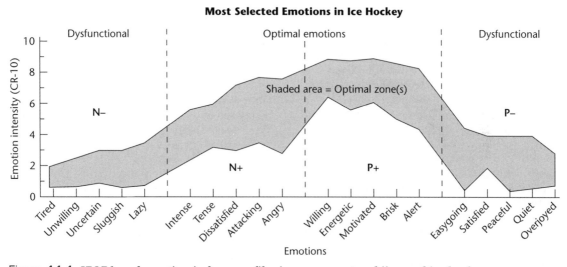

Most Selected Emotions in Ice Hockey

Figure 11-1 **IZOF-based-emotion iceberg profiles in cross-country skiing and ice hockey**
Source: Reprinted from Hanin, Y. L. (2000c). Successful and poor performance and emotions. In Y. L. Hanin (Ed.),
Emotions in sport (p. 185). Champaign, IL: Human Kinetics.

elite athletes had a higher intensity of facilitating-positive emotions than the less elite athletes.

This research supports that performance-enhancing and performance-impairing IZOFs can be identified for individual athletes. Interestingly, these patterns of optimal and dysfunctional emotions differed not only across athletes but also across contexts. For example, elite Finnish cross-country skiers identified different IZOFs for races, intensive training, and technical training (Hanin & Syrja, 1997). Teaching athletes to maintain their emotional state within their performance-enhancing zones may increase the likelihood of peak performance or assist athletes to perform more consistently.

Psychological Attributes and Skills of Successful and Less Successful Athletes

Another source of peak performance information comes from researchers who have examined the psychological attributes and skills of athletes. Although it is interesting to understand the psychological characteristics associated with skilled athletes, and good performances, it may be considered even more important to know how athletes achieve these psychological states. Hence, much of the current research examining the psychological characteristics related to peak performance also assessed the psychological skills that successful athletes use. A common focus of these studies was to compare more and less successful athletes with the goal of learning why some individuals outperform others.

In the mid-1970s, Mahoney and Avener designed an objective questionnaire to assess various psychological factors such as confidence, concentration, anxiety, self-talk, imagery, and dreams. This basic tool, or variations of it, has been used by researchers to study athletes in the sports of gymnastics, wrestling, tennis, racquetball, and diving. When Mahoney and Avener (1977) compared 1976 U.S. Olympic qualifiers and nonqualifiers in men's gymnastics, they found that the finalists coped more easily with competitive mistakes, were better able to control and utilize anxiety, had higher self-confidence and more positive self-talk, had more gymnastics-related dreams, and had more frequent imagery of an internal versus external nature. **External imagery** occurs when a person views himself or herself from the perspective of an external observer, such as seeing oneself on television or videotape. **Internal imagery** requires an approximation much more like the actual perspective when the skill is performed physically—that is, imagining being inside the body and experiencing the same sensations as one might expect in actual physical execution.

Studies employing a design similar to Mahoney and Avener's have found consistent results across varied samples. National team qualifiers have often been compared to nonqualifiers (Highlen & Bennett, 1979, 1983) and more and less successful collegiate athletes have been compared (Gould, Weiss, & Weinberg, 1981; Meyers, Cooke, Cullen, & Liles, 1979). Typically the more successful athletes had high self-confidence and few self-doubts. The more successful athletes also used imagery more often and controlled their anxiety better than the less successful athletes. Additionally, placers, compared to nonplacers, in a Big Ten wrestling tournament reported more frequent use of attentional focusing to prepare for the meet and were more positively affected by seeing themselves as the underdog (Gould et al., 1981).

A comparison of golfers with handicaps less than 11 or more than 20 revealed that the more skilled golfers had better mental preparation, concentration, automaticity, and commitment (Thomas & Over, 1994). In a subsequent study, Thomas, Schlinker, and Over (1996) found skilled (average of 170 or more), compared to less skilled (average of 135 or less), ten-pin bowlers had greater mental toughness, competitiveness, confidence in their equipment and technique, interest in improving, and consistency. The skilled bowlers also used more planning and evaluation, and fewer luck attributions.

Most of the studies in this area discussed so far have used questionnaires developed specifically for that study. In an attempt to improve our ability to compare findings across studies, researchers have developed a variety of scales that measure psychological skills used by athletes. Mahoney, Gabriel, and Perkins (1987) developed the Psychological Skills Inventory for Sport (PSIS) that measured anxiety management, concentration, self-confidence, motivation, mental preparation, and team emphasis. Using this scale, they examined differences in use and effectiveness of psychological skills in elite, preelite, and collegiate athletes in a variety of sports. Elite athletes reported that they experienced fewer anxiety problems, had better concentration before and during competition, were more self-confident, used internal and kinesthetic imagery in their mental preparation, were more focused on individual rather than team performance, and were more highly motivated to do well than less elite athletes. Other studies using the PSIS found similar results. For example, highly skilled collegiate rodeo athletes reported better anxiety management, concentration, confidence, and motivation compared to their less skilled counterparts (Meyers, LeUnes, & Bourgeois, 1996). A comparison of elite and subelite equestrian athletes revealed the elite athletes had better anxiety management and concentration (Meyers, Bourgeois, LeUnes, & Murray, 1998).

The Test of Performance Strategies (TOPS; Thomas, Murphy, & Hardy, 1999) was developed to assess the frequency with which athletes used goal setting, relaxation, activation, imagery, self-talk, attentional control, negative thinking, emotional control, and automaticity. Athletes rate how frequently they use the various skills in competitive and practice situations. Initial findings using this scale have shown that male international competitors scored higher on goal-setting, imagery, and activation compared to less elite athletes (Thomas et al., 1999). Female international athletes had higher self-talk, emotional control, goal-setting, imagery, activation, negative thinking, and relaxation compared to their less elite peers. College softball and baseball players who reported high use of mental skills assessed by the TOPS also revealed higher perceptions of success compared to the players who reported moderate or low use of mental skills in both practice and competition (Frey, Laguna, & Ravizza, 2003).

The Ottawa Mental Skill Assessment Tool (Durand-Bush, Salmela, & Green-Demers, 2001) measures athletes' use of goal setting, stress reactions, fear control, relaxation, activation, focusing, refocusing, imagery, mental practice, mental planning, as well as confidence and commitment. When this scale was administered to Canadian elite (national or international competitors) and competitive (college or provincial sport club) athletes, the elite athletes had higher scores on confidence, commitment, stress reactions, focusing, and refocusing compared to the competitive athletes. Across a wide array of studies, it seems that regardless of how it is measured, elite and successful athletes consistently report

using the following psychological skills, which likely contribute to their high-level performances:

- imagery
- attentional focusing
- maintaining concentration
- controlling anxiety and activation
- positive self-talk
- goal-setting

Also, athletes who consider anxiety as facilitative or helpful to performance have been found to be more successful than athletes who interpret their anxiety negatively or as debilitative to performance (Jones, Swain, & Hardy, 1993). Similarly, elite athletes have been found to interpret their anxiety as facilitative whereas less elite athletes interpret anxiety as debilitative (Jones & Swain, 1995). Subsequent research has shown that athletes who employed a facilitative interpretation of their anxiety also associated more positive emotional states with their athletic performance compared to the athletes who had a debilitative interpretation of anxiety (Mellalieu, Hanton, & Jones, 2003). In this study, elite athletes also reported higher self-confidence and lower cognitive and somatic anxiety and they interpreted their anxiety as less debilitating and unpleasant compared to the nonelite athletes.

Hanton and Jones (1999a) interviewed elite swimmers who acknowledged that they did not always interpret their anxiety in a facilitative manner. Rather, as they gained experience, they learned that these anxiety symptoms actually assisted them in performances. Building on this, Hanton and Jones (1999b) taught nonelite swimmers strategies to reinterpret their anxiety. At the end of the intervention the swimmers had redefined their anxiety as facilitative to performance, supporting the idea that a positive interpretation of anxiety is learned. These athletes also improved their performance.

So far, most of the studies discussed that compared more and less successful athletes have used questionnaires. Although these studies provide a strong foundation for understanding psychological characteristics of peak performance, another type of research also is used in this area: qualitative research. Generally, qualitative researchers examining peak performance have interviewed athletes to obtain a more detailed description of the athletes' perceptions and experiences than can be expressed through questionnaires. In some studies, both questionnaire and interview data are collected and analyzed. The explosion of qualitative research with Olympic and other elite athletes has greatly expanded our understanding of psychological attributes associated with peak performances.

Orlick and Partington (1988) conducted an extensive investigation of Olympic athletes in their study of "mental links to excellence" with Canadian Olympic athletes. Seventy-five athletes were interviewed, and another 160 athletes completed questionnaires assessing factors related to optimal mental readiness and psychological elements of success. "Total commitment to pursuing excellence" (p. 129) was common to all of these elite athletes. Another distinctive characteristic was high-quality training that included daily goal setting, competition simulation, and imagery training. These athletes obviously cultivated their mental skills, as they had well-developed plans for competition, competition focusing, and coping with distractions. These plans typically included mental imagery, positive thoughts, and attentional focus strategies. Through postcompetition evaluations, which also were common among these athletes, their mental approach was continually refined.

As previously mentioned studies revealed, imagery was an important skill for peak performance in these Olympic athletes. Interviews with the best athletes (Olympic and world medalists) indicated that they had well-developed imagery skills, used an internal perspective, and used imagery on a daily basis. The questionnaire data revealed that 99% of the athletes reported using imagery as a mental preparation strategy. "On average, preplanned, systematic imagery was used at least once a day, 4 days per week, for about 12 minutes each time" (Orlick & Partington, 1988, p. 125).

Research with the Canadian Olympians also revealed three things that interfered with peak performance: changing preparation/performance patterns that worked, late selection onto the Olympic team, and an inability to refocus attention after distractions (Orlick & Partington, 1988). Olympic athletes with an ineffective focus of attention were preoccupied with self-doubts, concerns about competitors, concern with current standings or score, thoughts of the possible outcome, or were thinking too far ahead. This is in contrast to an effective focus of attention that zeroed in on the present task and was associated with an appropriate arousal level, positive self-statements, "clear and ever-present awareness of executing the task or plan without distraction" (p. 126), and feelings of confidence, determination, power, and control.

Gould and his colleagues conducted a comprehensive assessment of the 1988 U.S. Olympic wrestling team (Gould, Eklund, & Jackson, 1992a, 1992b). They examined the wrestlers' use of psychological skills, compared athletes' descriptions of their all-time best and worst performances, and compared the responses of medalists and nonmedalists. Similar to the findings with the Canadian Olympians (Orlick & Partington, 1988), the wrestlers reported using a variety of psychological skills. When comparing the wrestlers' best and worst performances, positive expectancies, total concentration, high confidence, a task-relevant focus, heightened arousal and intensity, and heightened effort and commitment were related to athletes' all-time best performances. In contrast, feeling listless, over- or underarousal, lack of concentration, irrelevant or negative thoughts, worries about losing, nonadherence to normal preparation routines, and negative physical feelings (e.g., tired, inadequate warm-up) were associated with all-time worst performances.

Gould et al. (1992a, 1992b) also compared the responses of medalists and nonmedalists. The more successful Olympic wrestlers were able to cope effectively with distractions and unforeseen events and adhered to their mental preparation plans and precompetition routines more than the nonmedalists. The most salient difference between the medalists and nonmedalists was the extent that their coping strategies were practiced and internalized. The successful athletes had highly developed techniques for coping with distractions, which acted as "automatized buffers" that reduced the impact of negative unforeseen events or allowed the wrestlers to interpret these occurrences positively. Specific coping strategies of the successful wrestlers included using positive thinking; a narrow, specific focus of attention; and changing their environment (e.g., avoiding potential irritants, moving away from others). The less successful wrestlers abandoned competitive plans when under pressure, lost competitive focus, and did not rigorously adhere to the mental preparation plans.

Similar findings have emerged in studies with athletes in subsequent Olympic Games (Greenleaf, Gould, & Dieffenbach, 2001). Psychological preparation, using mental skills, and having a positive attitude were noted as especially important by athletes in the 1996 Games. In particular, Olympic athletes who met or exceeded their expectations perceived the Olympics as a "time to shine." An interesting study compared the mental preparation of teams who met or exceeded their goals in the 1996 Atlanta Olympics to teams that failed to meet expectations at the Games (Gould, Guinan, Greenleaf, Medbury, & Peterson, 1999). Both coaches and athletes on these teams were interviewed. Members of the more successful teams described having total commitment, a strong performance focus, mental preparation to cope with the stress of Olympic competition, and an ability to "reframe negative events in a more positive light." Less successful team members reported a lack of focus and commitment, and an inability to cope well with distractions. In a separate study, Olympic athletes who expected to win a medal but did not described that departing from their normal routines seemed to be a primary obstacle to success (Greenleaf et al., 2001).

Gould, Dieffenbach, and Moffett (2002) administered a battery of measures and interviewed Olympic champions who were "'consistent' outstanding performers" (p. 177). The psychological profiles of these athletes were similar to previous descriptions of successful elite athletes. Their profiles included the following:

- They had high confidence, concentration, and emotional control.
- They had low worry.
- They used goal setting.

- They controlled their activation and relaxation levels.
- They peaked under pressure.

Adding to previous findings, these Olympic champions revealed that they had high optimism, high levels of dispositional hope (i.e., a sense of control in setting and achieving goals), high productive perfectionism (i.e., personal standards), and low unproductive perfectionism (i.e., concerns about mistakes, parental criticism and expectations, doubts). These champion athletes also possessed "sport intelligence," which Gould and colleagues identified as analyzing skills and performances, being innovative regarding technique, making good decisions, being a quick learner, being "a student of the sport," and "understanding the nature of elite sport" (p. 199).

Eklund (1994, 1996) replicated the Olympic findings with collegiate wrestlers. Interestingly, unlike other studies, Eklund (1994) noted that the collegiate wrestlers experienced some doubts before peak performances. However, the athletes' doubts turned into confidence during the match, suggesting that some temporary self-doubts do not necessarily rule out the possibility of a peak performance.

Additionally, Eklund (1994, 1996) compared collegiate wrestlers' mental states at high, moderate, and low levels of performance, revealing somewhat of a continuum of mental states leading to peak performance. Overall, as performance improved, wrestlers experienced an increase in positive affect and a concomitant decrease in negative affect. One of the clearest patterns was that task-relevant thoughts increased and irrelevant thoughts decreased as performances improved. The quality of task-relevant thoughts also improved, with a noticeable lack of focus in poor performances and an intense competitive focus in best performances. Additionally, activation levels changed as performance improved. Low levels of performance were associated with feeling listless and lethargic, moderate performance was associated with "normal nervousness" (Eklund, 1996, p. 126), and high levels of performance were associated with high positive activation and intensity. Changes in confidence were also evident. Low-level performance was accompanied by a lack of confidence and self-doubts, moderate-level performance was accompanied by low confidence and self-doubts, and high-level performance was accompanied by high and persistent confidence.

McCaffrey and Orlick (1989) interviewed top touring professional golfers, all of whom had won professional tournaments. The interviews revealed the following "elements of excellence":

- total commitment
- quality rather than quantity of practice
- clearly defined goals
- imagery practice on a daily basis
- focusing totally on one shot at a time
- recognizing, expecting, and preparing to cope with pressure situations
- practice and tournament plans
- tournament focus plan
- distraction control strategies
- posttournament evaluation
- a clear understanding of what helps them play well versus play poorly

Across all these studies, there appear to be some commonalities in the psychological characteristics of more successful athletes. These attributes almost identically parallel the attributes of "mental toughness" identified by the elite athletes studied by Jones, Hanton, and Connaughton (2002). For successful athletes, the most consistent finding is that they are highly confident. Without exception, the research shows that elite and more successful athletes believed in themselves more than less successful athletes. These athletes also used a wide array of psychological skills. In particular, they used imagery and had well developed plans for competition and for refocusing if distracted. They tended to be "psyched up" rather than "psyched out" by demanding competitive situations, such as the Olympics or World Championships. Additionally, the successful athletes were less likely to be distracted and had a higher ability to rebound from mistakes. One may conjecture that this could be a consequence of high self-confidence, optimal control of anxiety, and superior concentration skills. The psychological

characteristics associated with elite athletes include the following:

- highly self-confident
- total commitment
- strong performance focus
- coped well with stress
- coped well with distractions
- optimistic, positive attitude
- high personal standards
- well developed competitive plans
- controlled emotions and remained appropriately activated
- viewed anxiety as beneficial
- set performance goals

Team, Coach, and Organizational Influences on Peak Performance

To this point, we have emphasized factors within athletes that help or hinder peak performance. Another consideration is the effect that other people may have on high level athletic performance, such as teammates, coaches, and administrators. For example, Olympic athletes believed that team cohesion was an important contributor to their success (Gould, Greenleaf, Chung, & Guinan, 2002; Greenleaf et al., 2001). In particular, having a positive team leader and strong team chemistry were considered helpful while lacking trust and confidence in one's teammates interfered with optimal performance. Athletes on Olympic teams that achieved their team goals described having high cohesion and strong athlete leadership as well as positive social support from friends and family (Gould, Guinan, Greenleaf, Medbery, & Peterson, 1999). Conversely, members of less successful teams noted poor team cohesion and a lack of trust among team members. See Chapter 8 for a fuller discussion of cohesion and its role in performance.

Coaches also can be quite influential on athletes. Ideally, coaches help athletes learn the psychological, physical, and tactical skills needed to be successful. However, coaches may unintentionally interfere with success. U.S. Olympic athletes identified that coaches with strong commitment and those who implemented a clear performance plan assisted successful performances (Gould, Greenleaf, Chung, & Guinan, 2002; Gould, Greenleaf, Guinan, & Chung, 2002). Conversely, they considered the following coach attributes to hinder team success:

- inability to deal with crises
- unrealistic expectations
- overcoaching and excessive interactions with team members
- inability to make decisive and fair decisions
- inability to "keep it simple"

Coaches and athletes who were on teams that did not meet their Olympic expectations also believed that negative attitudes toward the coach and poor coach-athlete communications were at least partially to blame (Gould Greenleaf, Guinan, & Chung, 2002).

Another issue affecting athletes' ability to perform optimally is organizational stress, or concerns that arise because of the management of teams. Interviews with British Olympic and elite (i.e., international competitors) athletes revealed that they experienced concerns related to finances, travel, accommodations, team selection, coaching styles, and team atmosphere (Fletcher & Hanton, 2003; Woodman & Hardy, 2001). Some athletes overtly expressed that when faced with interpersonal or financial difficulties, they had less than ideal performances (Woodman & Hardy, 2001). Interviews with U.S. Olympic athletes corroborated these findings. U.S. athletes who competed at the Atlanta and Nagano games indicated that a wide range of variables influenced their performances, including transportation difficulties, housing problems, getting event tickets for family, media distractions, and team selection issues (Gould, Greenleaf, Guinan, & Chung, 2002; Greenleaf et al., 2001). All of these factors are aspects of organizational stress. In all, it seems that team and environmental factors affect the likelihood of peak performance.

Organizational stress can arise from any of the following:

- team selection
- transportation
- housing
- family accommodations and event tickets
- media control
- finances
- communication among and with administrators
- coaching style
- communication among and with coaching staff

Psychological Characteristics of Elite Athlete Talent Development

After devoting so much space to describing the psychological factors that influence peak performances, one may wonder about the psychological processes involved in *becoming* an elite athlete. Contemporary researchers have begun investigating the psychological aspects of expert talent development in sport. In general, talent development occurs in clearly defined stages, such as initiation, development, and perfection (Bloom, 1985) or sampling, specializing, investment, and maintenance (Cote, 1999; Durand-Bush & Salmela, 2002). Common premises across these models are that talent is nurtured, requires years of intense commitment, and involves continuous learning. Nurturing talent involves a strong support system. In their study of 10 Olympic champions, Gould, Dieffenbach, and Moffett (2002) uncovered the central role that parents and family members played in this support network. Families of rising elite athletes voiced their belief in the athlete's ability to succeed, encouraged a "can do attitude," and created an "optimistic achievement oriented climate" (p. 200). Similarly, Cote's (1999) interviews with young Canadian national level athletes showed the critical role families played in development of athletic talent. Gould et al. also revealed that coaches influenced athletes' psychological development by emphasizing "hard work and discipline or having fun, having characteristics that facilitated athlete trust, providing encouragement and support, directly teaching or fostering mental skills, and by understanding these athletes" (2002, p. 200).

Through interviews with 10 athletes who won at least two gold medals in separate Olympic Games or World Championships, Durand-Bush and Salmela (2002) identified the psychological factors influential in the investment and maintenance stages of talent development. These athletes expressed that confidence, competitiveness, and motivation were essential during both investment and maintenance. They employed cognitive skills such as imagery, self-talk, and relaxation while in pursuit of elite performance, during the investment stage. Developing a keen focus and "an acute sense of awareness of their environment" (p. 160) also was important at this time. Through experience, these athletes became more confident and enhanced their ability to cope with pressure. They also began using post-competition evaluation in the investment phase of development. During maintenance, becoming independent, being mentally tough, having a strong work ethic, and striving to learn and improve were essential. Although self-talk and imagery were important at both stages, becoming innovative, creative, and connecting with the process of performing emerged as indispensable during maintenance. As Durand-Bush and Salmela (2001) concluded, "expert athletes are extremely confident and dedicated individuals who are willing to do anything to become the best" (p. 283). In becoming an elite performer, highly motivated athletes develop confidence, commitment, and the mental skills necessary for peak performances.

Conclusion: What It Takes to "Make It"

There seems to be a pretty strong consensus that to become a successful elite athlete takes commitment, dedication, mental toughness, and the ability to pursue a dream in a rational manner. When top coaches and scouts in the National Hockey League were asked what determines who does and does not make it at the professional level, they used words such as desire, determination, attitude, heart, and self-motivation (Orlick & Reed, cited in Orlick, 1980). Olympic coaches felt that athletes needed confidence, social support, and cohesive teams (Gould, Guinan, et al., 1999; Gould, Guinan, Greenleaf, & Chung, 2002) and needed to be able to maintain their composure, be prepared to cope with distractions, and have a sound competitive plan (Gould, Guinan, et al., 2002). All of these attributes may be developed or enhanced by using psychological skills. Gould, Guinan, et al. (2002) concluded that, according to Olympic coaches, "the role of psychological variables was perceived as especially salient and reinforces the need for psychological skills training" (p. 248).

Junior tennis coaches also believed in the need for mental skills training (Gould, Medberry, et al., 1999). They considered the following skills as particularly essential to the success of their athletes: enjoyment/fun, focus/concentration, self-confidence, and emotional control. These findings are consistent with studies of intercollegiate and national team coaches who also acknowledged the importance of athletes' psychological skills (Gould, Hodge, Peterson, & Giannini, 1989).

That mental preparation was important for success in elite level sport was a consistent theme across studies of Olympic athletes (e.g., Gould et al., 1999; Greenleaf et al., 2001; Orlick & Partington, 1988). The Canadian Olympians in Orlick and Partington's (1988) study believed that through psychological skills training they improved their performance level and learned to perform more consistently at their best. Many of the Olympic athletes interviewed by Orlick and Partington stated that they could have obtained their best performances much sooner had they strengthened their mental skills earlier in their athletic careers. As U.S. Olympic athletes that met or exceeded their goals expressed, mental preparation was essential (Gould et al., 1999), whereas athletes on less successful teams felt that they did not spend enough time on mental preparation.

At this point, a word of caution is needed regarding the interpretation of the research summarized in this chapter. All of the studies presented were either descriptive or correlational. What this means is that they generated descriptions of successful athletic experiences or identified relationships between psychological skills and peak performances. Based on this type of research, we cannot make any cause-and-effect relationships—we cannot say certain mental states cause peak performances; we can only note that they are related. When considering the question, "Are the psychological differences between successful and less successful athletes critical to performance differences?" we cannot be absolutely sure. There seems to be a lot of evidence suggesting that there are psychological characteristics associated with peak performances. Still, we do not know if athletes first learned the psychological skills necessary to achieve an ideal mental state or if by being consistently successful they developed these characteristics (e.g., being successful leads to being confident of having continued success) (Heyman, 1982). It also is plausible that athletes with certain psychological strengths are drawn to elite level sport. We may never know what causes an ideal mental state. However, given the weight of the evidence presented, it seems safe to assume that athletes use psychological skills in pursuit of their athletic goals and they have consistent psychological profiles when they compete at elite levels.

Summary

This chapter began with the questions "Is there an ideal body/mind state associated with peak self-control?" and "If so, is this ideal state similar from one athlete to another or one sport to another?" Across a wide range of sources, a certain psychological profile appears to be linked with successful athletic performance. Although there are numerous individual variations, in most cases this general profile is depicted by the following characteristics:

- high self-confidence and expectations of success
- self-regulation of arousal (energized yet relaxed)
- feeling in control
- total concentration
- keen focus on the present task
- viewing difficult situations as exciting and challenging
- productively perfectionist (i.e., have high standards, yet flexibility to learn from mistakes)
- positive attitude and thoughts about performance
- strong determination and commitment

Mental states associated with poor performances include self-doubts, acting contrary to normal performance routines, focusing on distractions, concerns about the outcome or score, over- or underarousal, and lack of concentration.

According to Loehr (1984) and others, this ideal performance state does not just happen. Top level athletes have identified their own ideal performance state and have learned, intentionally or subconsciously, to create and maintain this state voluntarily so that their talents and physical skills thrive. Achieving one's own ideal internal psychological climate is not a simple task. As Orlick and Partington (1988) stated, "Mental readying is derived from a number of learned mental skills that must be continually practiced and refined for an athlete to perform to potential and on a consistent basis" (p. 129). Accordingly, elite athletes employ meticulous planning for competitive performances. Generally, this involved:

- setting goals
- using imagery
- developing competition and refocusing plans
- practicing coping skills so they become automatic
- competitive simulation

Successful athletes also have highly developed coping skills that they use to deal with the demands of practice and competition. They are quite diverse and typically encompass:

- thought control strategies
- arousal management techniques
- interpreting anxiety as facilitative to performance
- attention control and refocusing skills

The high-level talent of successful athletes has been nurtured through years of intense commitment and continuous learning. These athletes also have strong support networks that include their families, friends, teammates, and coaches. Having high team cohesion, good communication and relationships with coaches, and minimal organizational stress also are associated with elite performances.

Conversely, team, coach, and administrative factors have been found to interfere with peak performances. Lacking team cohesion, trust, or confidence in one's teammates or coach hampers good performances. When coaches make poor decisions, have unrealistic expectations, or have poor coping or communication skills, they can interfere with athletes' optimal functioning. Problems with travel and accommodations, concerns about team selection, financial problems, and other administrative issues also may negatively affect athletes.

The commonalities in mental states and psychological skill use have led researchers and practitioners to conclude that the right psychological climate helps mobilize mental and physical reactions that are essential to performing at one's best. Conversely, things that create a negative mental climate will impede the likelihood that an athlete can perform optimally. Through teaching athletes to control unproductive mental states and enhance the productive ones, athletes will be more likely to create ideal performance states. Psychological skills are learned through knowledge and practice, just as physical skills and competitive strategies are learned. Some gifted athletes may perfect these mental states on their own, but most need to be taught specific training techniques.

The remaining chapters in this section of the book specifically address the psychological states associated with peak performance and, when appropriate, provide techniques for learning to create and maintain desirable mental and physiological states. Chapter 12 is unique in that its purpose is to help coaches and sport psychologists learn how to assist each athlete in identifying his or her own internal psychological climate for peak performance and to identify those factors that tend to enhance or detract from this ideal climate. Such an awareness is the first step in mental skills training. In the chapters that follow, it becomes obvious that peak performance need not be a unique, temporary, involuntary experience. It is a product of the body and mind, and it can be trained. Just as improving physical skills, strategies, and conditioning increases the likelihood of peak performance, learning to control psychological readiness and the ideal mental climate for peak performance also enhances performance.

Study Questions

1. Define peak performance.

2. Think back to your own best sporting performance. What were the psychological states that you experienced? How does your experience compare to the descriptions about the psychological characteristics of peak performance in the research?

3. Summarize the psychological states typically associated with peak performances.

4. Define flow and describe its dimensions.

5. What are factors that will enhance and hinder flow experiences?

6. What is the individualized zone of optimal functioning (IZOF) and how does it relate to peak performance?

7. What are the primary psychological characteristics that distinguish between more and less successful athletic performances?

8. Summarize the major psychological characteristics of elite athletes.

9. What are the primary psychological skills that elite athletes use? What is the association between these skills and peak performance?

10. Describe how athletes' relationships with their teammates may influence optimal performance.

11. What are things that coaches may do that will interfere with peak performance?

12. What is organizational stress and how might it influence athletes' performances?

13. If you were a coach or administrator, how would you minimize the problems faced by Olympic athletes who did not achieve their goals?

References

Bloom, B. S. (Ed.). (1985). *Developing talent in young people.* New York: Ballantine.

Catley, D., & Duda, J. L. (1997). Psychological antecedents of the frequency and intensity of flow in golfers. *International Journal of Sport Psychology, 28,* 309–322.

Cohn, P. J. (1991). An exploratory study on peak performance in golf. *The Sport Psychologist, 5,* 1–14.

Cote, J. (1999). The influence of the family in the development of talent. *The Sport Psychologist, 13,* 395–417.

Csikszentmihalyi, M. (1975). *Beyond boredom and anxiety.* San Francisco: Jossey-Bass.

Csikszentmihalyi, M. (1985). *Emergent motivation and the evolution of the self.* In D. Kleiber & M. Maehr (Eds.), *Advances in motivation and achievement* (Vol. 4, pp. 93–119). Greenwich, CT: JAI.

Csikszentmihalyi, M. (1990). *Flow: The psychology of optimal experience.* New York: Harper & Row.

Csikszentmihalyi, M., Rathunde, K., & Whalen, S. (1993). *Talented teenagers: The roots of success and failure.* New York: Cambridge University Press.

Durand-Bush, N., & Salmela, J. H. (2001). The development of talent in sport. In R. N. Singer, H. A. Hausenblas, & C. M. Janelle (Eds.), *Handbook of sport psychology* (pp. 269–289). New York: John Wiley & Sons.

Durand-Bush, N., & Salmela, J. H. (2002). The development and maintenance of expert athletic performance: Perceptions of World and Olympic champions. *Journal of Applied Sport Psychology, 14,* 154–171.

Durand-Bush, N., Salmela, J. H., & Green-Demers, I. (2001). The Ottawa Mental Skills Assessment Tool (OMSAT-3). *The Sport Psychologist, 15,* 1–19.

Eklund, R. C. (1994). A season long investigation of competitive cognition in collegiate wrestlers. *Research Quarterly for Exercise and Sport, 65,* 169–183.

Eklund, R. C. (1996). Preparing to compete: A season-long investigation with collegiate wrestlers. *The Sport Psychologist, 10,* 111–131.

Fletcher, D., & Hanton, S. (2003). Sources of organizational stress in elite sports performers. *The Sport Psychologist, 17,* 175–195.

Frey, M., Laguna, P., & Ravizza, K. (2003). Collegiate athletes' mental skill use and perceptions of success: An exploration of the practice and competition settings. *Journal of Applied Sport Psychology, 15,* 115–128.

Garfield, C. A., & Bennett, H. Z. (1984). *Peak performance: Mental training techniques of the world's greatest athletes.* Los Angeles: Tarcher.

Gould, D., Dieffenbach, K., & Moffett, A. (2002). Psychological characteristics and their development in Olympic champions. *Journal of Applied Sport Psychology, 14,* 172–204.

Gould, D., Eklund, R. C., & Jackson, S. A. (1992a). 1988 U.S. Olympic wrestling excellence: I. Mental preparation, precompetitive cognition, and affect. *The Sport Psychologist, 6,* 358–382.

Gould, D., Eklund, R. C., & Jackson, S. A. (1992b). 1988 U.S. Olympic wrestling excellence: II. Thoughts and affect occurring during competition. *The Sport Psychologist, 6,* 383–402.

Gould, D., Greenleaf, C., Chung, Y., & Guinan, D. (2002). A survey of U.S. Atlanta and Nagano Olympians: Variables perceived to influence performance. *Research Quarterly for Exercise and Sport, 73,* 175–186.

Gould, D., Greenleaf, C., Guinan, D., & Chung, Y. (2002). A survey of U.S. Olympic coaches: Variables perceived to have influenced athlete performance and coach effectiveness. *The Sport Psychologist, 16,* 229–250.

Gould, D., Guinan, D., Greenleaf, C., Medbery, R., & Peterson, K. (1999). Factors affecting Olympic performance: Perceptions of athletes and coaches from more and less successful teams. *The Sport Psychologist, 13,* 371–394.

Gould, D., Hodge, K., Peterson, K., & Giannini, J. (1989). An exploratory examination of strategies used by elite coaches to enhance self-efficacy in athletes. *Journal of Sport and Exercise Psychology, 11,* 128–140.

Gould, D., Medbery, R., Damarjian, N., & Lauer, L. (1999). A survey of mental skills training knowledge, opinions, and practices of junior tennis coaches. *Journal of Applied Sport Psychology, 11,* 28–50.

Gould, D., Weiss, M., & Weinberg, R. (1981). Psychological characteristics of successful and nonsuccessful Big Ten wrestlers. *Journal of Sport Psychology, 3,* 69–81.

Greenleaf, C., Gould, D., & Dieffenbach, K. (2001). Factors influencing Olympic performance: Interviews with Atlanta and Nagano U.S. Olympians. *Journal of Applied Sport Psychology, 13,* 154–184.

Hanin, Y. L. (1997). Emotions and athletic performance: Individualized zones of optimal functioning model. *European Yearbook of Sport Psychology, 1,* 29–72.

Hanin, Y. L. (2000a). *Emotions in sport.* Champaign, IL: Human Kinetics.

Hanin, Y. L. (2000b). Individual zones of optimal functioning (IZOF) model: Emotion-performance relationships in sport. In Y. L. Hanin (Ed.), *Emotions in sport* (pp. 65–89). Champaign, IL: Human Kinetics.

Hanin, Y. L. (2000c). Successful and poor performance and emotions. In Y. L. Hanin (Ed.), *Emotions in sport* (pp. 157–187). Champaign, IL: Human Kinetics.

Hanin, Y. L., & Syrja, P. (1997). Optimal emotions in elite cross-country skiers. In E. Muller, H. Schwameder, E. Kornexl, & C. Raschner (Eds.), *Science and skiing* (pp. 408–419). London: SPON.

Hanton, S., & Jones, G. (1999a). The acquisition and development of cognitive skills and strategies: I. Training the butterflies to fly in formation. *The Sport Psychologist, 13,* 1–21.

Hanton, S., & Jones, G. (1999b). The acquisition and development of cognitive skills and strategies: II. Training the butterflies to fly in formation. *The Sport Psychologist, 13,* 22–41.

Heyman, S. R. (1982). Comparisons of successful and unsuccessful competitors: A reconsideration of methodological questions and data. *Journal of Sport Psychology, 4,* 295–300.

Highlen, P. S., & Bennett, B. B. (1979). Psychological characteristics of successful and nonsuccessful elite wrestlers: An exploratory study. *Journal of Sport Psychology, 1,* 123–137.

Highlen, P. S., & Bennett, B. B. (1983). Elite divers and wrestlers: A comparison between open- and closed-skill athletes. *Journal of Sport Psychology, 5,* 390–409.

Jackson, S. A. (1992). Athletes in flow: A qualitative investigation of flow states in elite figure skaters. *Journal of Applied Sport Psychology, 4,* 161–180.

Jackson, S. A. (1995). Factors influencing the occurrence of flow states in elite athletes. *Journal of Applied Sport Psychology, 7,* 138–166.

Jackson, S. A. (1996). Toward a conceptual understanding of the flow experience in elite athletes. *Research Quarterly for Exercise and Sport, 67,* 76–90.

Jackson, S. A. (2000). Joy, fun, and flow state in sport. In Y. L. Hanin (Ed.), *Emotions in sport* (pp. 135-156). Champaign, IL: Human Kinetics.

Jackson, S. A., & Csikszentmihalyi, M. (1999). *Flow in sport.* Champaign, IL: Human Kinetics.

Jackson, S. A., & Roberts, G. C. (1992). Positive performance states of athletes: Toward a conceptual understanding of peak performance. *The Sport Psychologist, 6,* 156–171.

Jackson, S. A., Kimiecik, J. C., Ford, S. K., & Marsh, H. W. (1998). Psychological correlates of flow in sport. *Journal of Sport & Exercise Psychology, 20,* 358–378.

Jackson, S., Thomas, P. R., Marsh, H. W., & Smethurst, C. J. (2001). Relationships between flow, self-concept, psychological skills, and performance. *Journal of Applied Sport Psychology, 13,* 129–153.

Jones, G., & Swain, A. (1995). Predispositions to experience debilitative and facilitative anxiety in elite and non-elite performers. *The Sport Psychologist, 9,* 201–211.

Jones, G., Hanton, S., & Connaughton, D. (2002). What is this thing called mental toughness? An investigation of elite sport performers. *Journal of Applied Sport Psychology, 14,* 205–218.

Jones, J. G., Swain, A., & Hardy, L. (1993). Intensity and direction dimensions of competitive state anxiety and relationships with performance. *Journal of Sports Sciences, 11,* 525–532.

Kowal, J., & Fortier, M. S. (2000). Testing relationships from the hierarchical model of intrinsic and extrinsic motivation using flow as a motivational consequence. *Research Quarterly for Exercise and Sport, 71,* 171–181.

Loehr, J. E. (1984, March). How to overcome stress and play at your peak all the time. *Tennis,* 66–76.

Mahoney, M. J. (1989). Psychological predictors of elite and non-elite performance in Olympic weightlifting. *International Journal of Sport Psychology, 20,* 1–12.

Mahoney, M. J., & Avener, M. (1977). Psychology of the elite athlete: An exploratory study. *Cognitive Therapy and Research 1,* 135–142.

Mahoney, M. J., Gabriel, T. J., & Perkins, T. S. (1987). Psychological skills and exceptional athletic performance. *The Sport Psychologist, 1,* 181–199.

McCaffrey, N., & Orlick, T. (1989). Mental factors related to excellence among top professional golfers. *International Journal of Sport Psychology, 20,* 256–278.

Mellalieu, S. D., Hanton, S., & Jones, G. (2003). Emotional labeling and competitive anxiety in preparation and competition. *The Sport Psychologist, 17,* 157–174.

Meyers, A. W., Cooke, C. J., Cullen, J., & Liles, L. (1979). Psychological aspects of athletic competitors: A replication across sports. *Cognitive Therapy and Research, 3,* 361–366.

Meyers, M. C., Bourgeois, A. E., LeUnes, A., & Murray, N. G. (1998). Mood and psychological skills of elite and sub-elite equestrian athletes. *Journal of Sport Behavior, 22,* 399–409.

Meyers, M. C., LeUnes, A., & Bourgeois, A. E. (1996). Psychological skills assessments and athletic performance in collegiate rodeo athletes. *Journal of Sport Behavior, 19,* 132–146.

Miller, P. S., & Kerr, G. A. (2002). Conceptualizing excellence: Past, present, and future. *Journal of Applied Sport Psychology, 14,* 140–153.

Nicklaus, J. (1974). *Golf My Way.* New York: Simon and Schuster.

Orlick, T. (1980). *In pursuit of excellence.* Champaign, IL: Human Kinetics.

Orlick, T., & Partington, J. (1988). Mental links to excellence. *The Sport Psychologist, 2,* 105–130.

Pates, J., Cummings, A., & Maynard, I. (2002). The effects of hypnosis on flow states and three-point shooting performance in basketball players. *The Sport Psychologist, 16,* 34–47.

Privette, G. (1982). Peak performance in sports: A factorial topology. *International Journal of Sport Psychology, 13*, 242–249.

Privette, G. (1983). Peak experience, peak performance, and flow: A comparative analysis of positive human experiences. *Journal of Personality and Social Psychology, 45*, 1361–1368.

Privette, G., & Bundrick, C. M. (1997). Psychological processes of peak, average, and failing performance in sport. *International Journal of Sport Psychology, 28*, 323–334.

Ravizza, K. (1977). Peak experiences in sport. *Journal of Humanistic Psychology, 17*, 35–40.

Robazza, C., & Bortoli, L. (2003). Intensity, idiosyncratic content and functional impact of performance-related emotions in athletes. *Journal of Sport Sciences, 21*, 171–189.

Robazza, C., Bortoli, L., & Hanin, Y. (2004). Precompetition emotions, bodily symptoms, and task-specific qualities as predictors of performance in high level karate athletes. *Journal of Applied Sport Psychology, 15*, 151–165.

Rushall, B. S. (1989). Sport psychology: The key to sporting excellence. *International Journal of Sport Psychology, 20*, 165–190.

Russell, W. D. (2000). An examination of flow state occurrence in college athletes. *Journal of Sport Behavior, 24*, 83–107.

Smith, R. E., & Christensen, D. S. (1995). Psychological skills as predictors of performance and survival in professional baseball. *Journal of Sport and Exercise Psychology, 17*, 399–415.

Stein, G. L., Kimiecik, J. C., Daniels, J. L., & Jackson, S. A. (1995). Psychological antecedents of flow in recreational sport. *Personality and Social Psychology Bulletin, 21*, 125–135.

Thomas, P. R., & Over, R. (1994). Psychological and psychomotor skills associated with performance in golf. *The Sport Psychologist, 8*, 73–86.

Thomas, P. R., Murphy, S. M., & Hardy, L. (1999). Test of Performance Strategies: Development and preliminary validation of a comprehensive measure of athletes' psychological skills. *Journal of Sports Sciences, 17*, 697–711.

Thomas, P. R., Schlinker, P. J., & Over, R. (1996). Psychological and psychomotor skills associated with prowess at ten-pin bowling. *Journal of Sports Sciences, 14*, 255–268.

Woodman, T., & Hardy, L. (2001). A case study of organizational stress in elite sport. *Journal of Applied Sport Psychology, 13*, 207–238.

CHAPTER

12

Increasing Awareness for Sport Performance

Kenneth Ravizza, *California State University at Fullerton*

The end of the soccer game results in a critical penalty kick. Both teams have played hard and well and now it gets down to one player shooting the shot that determines the outcome. All too often, the coach's instruction is "Just relax" or "Concentrate," and frequently this results in even more perceived pressure by the athlete, because now the coach knows she is not relaxed or focused.

The underlying basis of psychological interventions for performance enhancement involves teaching athletes the importance of the recognition, or awareness, of the need to do something to gain control. Athletes will not be aware of the need to gain control unless they first identify their own ideal performance state (see Chapter 11) and can contrast that state with the present one. Thus, **awareness** is the first step to gaining control of any pressure situation. The athlete must "Check in" and determine if his or her arousal level, emotional state, thought processes, and focus are where they need to be and, if not, adjust them to give the best opportunity for success. For example, the athlete must be aware of too low or too high arousal level and adjust it as needed to reach the optimal arousal level for performance. Then the athlete must attend to the appropriate focal points that will fine-tune or lock in his or her concentration. For example, a

softball player will only get two or three great pitches to hit in a game. The player must be fully focused on each pitch so that when the appropriate pitch comes she is ready to make solid contact. The lack of awareness demonstrated by many athletes is often a by-product of the sport socialization process, whereby the athlete is encouraged to follow orders and not to question the coach's authority. More and more, coaches are beginning to take a less dogmatic approach because they realize that dependence often results from a strictly authoritarian coaching style.

Furthermore, lack of awareness in athletes is almost always the result of excessive concern with achieving the end result. For example, the baseball player in the pressure situation focuses on the end result of getting a hit. Awareness and control are part of the process of skill execution—specifically, execution in the present moment. The anxiety lies in the end result. Thus, the field-goal kicker in football must focus on the key components of kicking such as wind, ground conditions, the opponents' alignment, getting proper distance, and his target. At this point the athlete is totally focused on the task at hand and is ready to react spontaneously to the situation with controlled intensity. This type of appropriate **focus of attention** is essential to maximize performance.

The athlete's challenge is to focus on basic skills even when the athlete's pulse rate may increase significantly. The situation can be perceived as speeded-up or out-of-the-usual perspective because of the perceived threat of the situation. This chapter does not suggest a multitude of performance changes; instead, it suggests that athletes be encouraged to become aware of their own ideal performance state and *routine behaviors* they are already using to achieve this state. Many of the techniques we talk about in sport psychology are performed instinctively by the athlete. Awareness of these instinctive routines provides athletes with something to focus on to regain control. Sport psychology consultants have contributed to enhancing performance by providing a structure or consistent framework for the various mental skills athletes have often developed and practiced haphazardly.

This structure clarifies for athletes the fact that there is a relationship between the various things that they do to maximize performance. When they can begin to understand that the imagery skills that are used for pregame preparation can also be used for concentration and relaxation training (as well as for academic studies), they have a better sense of control. **Control** is the key issue because an athlete's anxiety level tends to decrease with a feeling of control.

The purpose of this chapter is to discuss the importance of awareness in reaching peak performance in sport. Awareness will be presented as the first essential step in goal setting and self-regulation as it relates to skill development and the management of performance stress and other psychological factors. The final section will discuss specific methods athletes can use to develop heightened awareness.

The Importance of Awareness in Athletics

Peak performance is about compensating and adjusting. An athlete is not in the flow state most of the performance. I have found athletes to be in the "zone" 10–20% of the time. So, why is the athlete so concerned with feeling just right and

surprised when they aren't? Lou Pinella, a veteran professional baseball manager, claimed, "A player must learn to feel comfortable being uncomfortable." "So what, deal with it!" is what I tell athletes. But this is only after they have practiced dealing with adversity in practice and recognizing that they have "something to go to" (mental skills) to get them refocused. But, in order to compensate and adjust, one must first be aware that they are not where they need to be. As the athlete works on this ability to deal with adversity in practice, it only increases his and her confidence in knowing they don't have to feel great to perform well. For example, in one of the most high-performance fields, astronaut training, they do not just have positive thoughts and use positive imagery. They practice dealing with adversity in the simulator so that, when adversity occurs, they are prepared to deal with it with confidence and focus.

Every sport requires athletes to execute basic skills. Athletes must stand alone and accept responsibility for their performance. During the off-season, individual responsibility is an even more crucial aspect since it is then that athletes must put in hours of isolated, rigorous training, and self-coaching to develop and refine essential skills. Athletes must perform the skills, reflect on the feedback gained from the performance, make corrections and refinements, and then make the skills feel natural through a multitude of repetitions and refinements.

Athletes must recognize their strengths and weaknesses so that they can maximize their strengths and correct their weaknesses. Goal setting can be used to facilitate performance enhancement. At first, athletes want to be told what their goals should be, but it is essential that they make the major contribution to establishing individual goals. This requires athletes to reflect on and evaluate past performance. The coach gains a great deal of insight about the athletes' awareness on the basis of this evaluation of perceived strengths and weaknesses. The goals should be **performance goals,** such as "I will be more consistent at the foul line by shooting 50 shots a day with the goal of hitting over 60% by the end of two weeks and 65% after one month." This is different from an **outcome goal,** such as "I want to improve my foul shooting." The goals should be as specific as possible and of various durations: short-term, intermediate, and long-range. (See Chapter 13 for additional guidelines for goal setting and strategies for achieving goals.)

A good way for a player to develop more of an awareness in this area is to have the player write a scouting report on his or her self. What is the opponent saying about them? Also, have them write about what they would like the opponent to say about them. Julie Wilhout, Loyola Marymount's women's basketball coach, uses this technique to help the players obtain a better grasp of their awareness of where they need to direct their attention. Another practical way to remind players to have a mission for practice is to have them establish a routine. For example, when you put on your shoes, set two goals for today's practice or game, and when you take your shoes off, evaluate how you did. The athlete took 2 hours out of her life; what did she learn to get better? The reality is that each day we take a step toward our goal, or remain the same, or take a step back. Always remember, failure can be a step forward if you learn from it. Failure is positive feedback if you are aware of it and use the information to get better.

Goal setting requires awareness because the athlete first sets the goals, then strives to reach them, then proceeds to evaluate the performance feedback, and, finally, adjusts the goals appropriately (Harris & Harris, 1984; McClements & Botterill, 1979).

Awareness as It Relates to Skill Development

Athletes must learn the difference between merely performing skills and experiencing skills. For example, try this exercise. Raise your right arm over your head five times—one . . . two . . . three . . . four . . . five—and halt. Now deeply inhale as you slowly raise your right arm over your head. Breathe slowly and steadily as you feel the movement, experience the muscles involved, feel the gentle stretch through the different muscles,

feel that extension all through the arm, and now slowly let the arm down.

The difference between just going through the motions and really experiencing the skills hinges on the awareness involved. Feldenkrais (1972), a movement specialist, offers the following analogy:

> A man without awareness is like a carriage whose passengers are the desires, with the muscles for horses, while the carriage itself is the skeleton. Awareness is the sleeping coachman. As long as the coachman remains asleep the carriage will be dragged aimlessly here and there. Each passenger seeks a different destination and the horses pull different ways. But when the coachman is wide awake and holds the reins the horses will pull and bring every passenger to his proper destination. (p. 54)

Like the coachman, athletes must gain control of muscles, emotions, and thoughts and integrate them into a smooth performance. When athletes are aware and focused on the sport experience, they exert more control over the situation. They recognize sooner when their balance is off, when too much tension is present in certain muscle groups, or when thoughts have become self-defeating. Aware athletes are more attuned to subtle fluctuations in the flow of the contest and can adjust that much sooner. Aware athletes can conserve vital energy by exerting no more than the needed intensity.

Learning the Basics

Awareness requires that athletes totally focus their attention on the task. This ability must be developed in practice. Coaches want their athletes to be intense and totally involved in practice because this aids in creating quality practice time. Many coaches also realize the importance of mental training for performance, but the challenge is to find time for it. For this reason, it is important to incorporate awareness training with the physical skills that are already being performed in practice. For example, coaches and sport psychology consultants should encourage athletes to develop concentration as they stretch before practice by feeling the stretch and breathing into it. This type of stretching develops concentration in that the athletes are tuned in to their body as they stretch.

With the 1984 U.S. Olympic women's field hockey team we established a set warm-up procedure for practice to aid the athletes in mentally and physically preparing for practice. The players began by stretching, then hit the ball back and forth to work out any kinks, and finally executed **focused hitting.** Focused hitting involves hitting the ball to exact locations—for example, to the receiver's right, middle, and left. This sequence is followed for 5 minutes. These are basic field hockey skills, but there is a difference when they are done with awareness. If the player's attention is on other aspects of the day, such as a party coming up or an argument with a friend, consistency in the focused hitting drill will be impossible.

This type of drill has two major advantages for the coach. First, visible objective performance demonstrates whether or not the athlete is concentrating. More important, awareness training is incorporated into the practice of basic skills. As a result, additional practice time is not required for mental training. This sophisticated approach to basic skills allows coaches to make the most of practice time by integrating mental or awareness skills training with basic fundamentals.

During one practice the Cal State Fullerton baseball team engaged in a focused bat and catch drill for 90 minutes because they had not been hitting exact locations consistently. This emphasis on basics was crucial because the players realized the coach was serious about executing the basics. The difference between performing the basics and focusing on the basics lies in the players' awareness. Athletes must learn to concentrate when the pressure is on, and the focal points for concentration become the task-relevant cues. Augie Garrido, Cal State Fullerton's baseball coach, gives the following example:

> We are really working on having the players clear their minds. Yesterday one player was given a bunt signal and he proceeded to pop out. His next time at the plate he was in a bunting situation and tried to bunt but missed. So I called him over and said, "You've tried two times and failed, and you are about to fail again because you still have the other

two times on your mind. Give yourself the best chance to be successful by seeing the ball and bunting the ball. You can do that. Stay right with the ingredients of bunting. You've done it a hundred times, but you have to get the other times off your mind." The player proceeded to lay down a perfect bunt. (1982)

When athletes practice physical skills and mental skills together, their confidence increases because they are ready and experienced in the subtle skill of concentration.

The days of doing sport psychology on Wednesdays from 12 to 1 must be replaced by doing it during practice as an intricate component of quality practice. This necessitates that coach integrates it into his or her skill development. It is my belief that mental skills can be developed like physical skills, but they must be practiced, and awareness is the way of obtaining that quality of performance.

The All-or-None Syndrome

Awareness develops in the process of participating in sport, and this is where athletes experience self-control. Gymnasts learning new moves cannot expect to master them immediately. A series of progressions must be worked through. Often, in the midst of this process, gymnasts feel they have *either* hit the move *or* missed. If they hit it, they are delighted, but if they miss, frustration begins to set in. The challenge is to maintain motivation throughout the hours of practice.

At Cal State Fullerton, we have established gradations of execution for the gymnasts to evaluate their skill development. For example, even if a move is "missed," certain aspects of the movement were probably successful, and it is important that they be identified. Similarly, in baseball a pitcher is told that he needs to raise his arm on a fastball release. The number 5 is given for the ideal release distance, and a 1 is given for a side-arm release. After each pitch the player is asked to assign a numerical value from 1 to 5 to the arm location. It is essential that the athlete reflect on the position of his arm because this requires awareness. The coach can then give an evaluation from 1 to 5. This aids the athlete in beginning to adjust his awareness to what the proper position feels like (based on a principle from Gallwey, 1974). If a video recorder is available, the performance feedback is even more specific.

When athletes gain more awareness, they can make more accurate adjustments in their performance. This ability to refine the subtle intricacies of performance is a critical skill as athletes reach for maximum performance. In addition to improving self-control, the athletes experience a feeling of growing success. Even though the outcome is not perfect, players develop a more positive attitude about the skill and will keep their motivation level where it needs to be.

Playing the Edge of Peak Performance

To reach their full sport potential, athletes must learn to play the **performance edge.** For example, they must learn to control that delicate balance between power and grace. Every sport has components that must be balanced appropriately to maximize performance. This type of control necessitates that athletes be aware. They must monitor their performance to recognize when it is at its peak. In athletic training and conditioning, there are many times when athletes push too hard or do not push hard enough. At such times the athletes need to relate to their movement experience with the precision of a surgeon so that they can make needed adjustments. For example, runners constantly monitor their body for subtle messages so that they can make adjustments to reach that edge of peak performance.

One awareness technique I use with runners is the blindfold run. A blindfolded runner and a partner run a specified distance together, with the partner providing physical support and removing any dangers. The blindfold alters the runner's perspective, as the runner is now totally focused on the present moment. Usual thoughts and distractions are suspended by the new perspective. After about 5 minutes into the run, the athlete experiences running in a more aware fashion.

Coaches and sport psychology consultants are encouraged to discuss with their athletes this idea of playing the edge so that each athlete can begin to understand and identify where that edge is for him or her. Figure 12-1 and the chapter appendix suggest ways of keeping records of the mental aspects of performance.

Awareness in Managing Performance Stress

To move consistently toward peak performance, each athlete must know and be aware of his or her own experience of optimal performance. Athletes must learn to control the excitement of the sport situation so that their energy can be channeled into the performance, or to reorganize when the arousal level is too low and activate it as needed. To gain this control athletes must learn how competitive stress affects individual performance. (See Chapter 14 for more information on this topic.) The first step is to be aware of one's **arousal level** and then to adjust it as needed. The athlete must recognize which situations or stressors tend to negatively affect his or her performance. Knowledge of stressful areas allows for the development of a strategy to prepare and cope effectively with them. For example, playing in front of a crowd or in the presence of scouts is stressful; thus, the athlete can mentally prepare to deal with the situation to avoid surprise. The athlete has time to get support from teammates and the coaching staff and also to develop his or her own strategy.

Once the athlete understands the stressors, the next step is to be aware of the way that stress is experienced, because the manifestations of stress vary greatly among individuals. For example, "As the pressure mounts, my shoulders and neck tighten, my thoughts jump around, and I tend to get jittery." Changes in breathing are another bodily cue that often signals too much stress. Athletes should be trained to become sensitive to how their breathing responds to stress. For example, do they start to breathe more rapidly and shallowly? Do they hold their breath? Do they have difficulty breathing? These manifestations of stress may be perceived as problems, but they can be used as signals to provide feedback to the athlete as to whether the arousal level is appropriate. The athlete gains this personal knowledge by reflecting on previous performances and essentially using sport experiences like a biofeedback machine.

PERFORMANCE FEEDBACK SHEET

Name _____

Opponent _____

1. What were your stressors for today's game?

2. How did you experience the stress (thoughts, actions, body)?

3. How was your level of arousal for today's game? What were your feelings at these various points?

   a. Bus ride to game: _____
   b. Warm-up on field, court, etc.: _____
   c. Just before the game: _____
   d. During the game: _____

   0 ————— 5 ————— 10
   Too Low   Perfect   Too High

4. What techniques did you use to manage the stress and how effective were you in controlling it?

5. How was your self-talk? (Describe.)

6. What did you learn from today's game that will help you in your next game?

7. What mental training techniques were most effective for you?

8. Briefly describe one play or segment of the game that you enjoyed.

9. How would you rate your play? _____

10. Briefly describe how you felt about today's game.

    0 ————— 5 ————— 10
    Terrible   OK   Great

11. Anything you want to say?

Figure 12-1 **Sample performance feedback sheet**

To help athletes understand the concept of self-monitoring as a way to increase awareness, the coach or sport psychologist can use the analogy of a traffic signal light (Ravizza & Hanson, 1994). Sport performance is similar to driving a car. Most of the time that we are driving, we are not thinking about the mechanics or technical aspects of driving. When we come to a signal light, we must be aware of the light, or check in; if it is green, we continue. Similarly, when athletes are playing well, there is no need to think about it, but they must check in for that split second. When we are driving and the light is yellow, we have to observe the intersection in more detail to determine whether it is safe to continue as well as check our rearview mirror for a police officer. When the light is red, we must stop.

Using this analogy, the athlete must be aware of his or her signal lights and recognize the impact they have on his or her arousal level, self-talk, breathing patterns, and ability to focus. Thus, if the athlete can be aware of when he or she is shifting from a green light to a yellow light, and it is recognized early, it can be turned around more easily. When the signal light is not recognized until it is red, it is much more difficult to get it turned around. So the first use of the signal lights is to serve as an indicator of the way the athlete experiences the situation.

The second use of the signal lights is to help the athlete in preparing for consistent performance by monitoring the potential stressors that he or she may confront. For example, the field conditions may be a yellow light, the officials may be a red light, the opponent may be a red light. By acknowledging these signals, the athlete can develop contingency plans to cope effectively with them. This is part of solid mental preparation, as the athlete will be confident in handling them.

The most useful part of the signal light analogy is that it provides a vocabulary to address the awareness aspects of performance. Also, there are many times for athletes when the lights are green; then there is minimal awareness, and they are just playing the game when they are not in that ideal state. The traffic light analogy is useful as a symbol for how the athlete is experiencing the situation as well as the potential stressors that must be confronted in the competition.

And it is this signal light analogy that provides a method to give the athlete a symbol and vocabulary to discuss his or her awareness level. With young athletes, this is an effective tool to have them learn to "check in" and make the needed adjustments. For example, a young tennis player is working on his serve; when the results don't happen, he works harder and faster and often his performance gets worse and his frustration rises. At this point, one has to remember the goal is to work on "quality" serves, not the quantity, or what I call "aerobic serving."

The athlete's consistent focus on his or her thoughts and feelings and use of appropriate interventions allows the athlete to maintain an optimal performance state. Interventions may include relaxation and activation techniques, concentration methods, thought control, and basic breathing techniques. (See Chapters 15–19 for specific techniques.) There are also times when the athlete must recognize that it is time just to flow with the experience and let it happen (Ravizza, 1984; Ravizza & Osborne, 1991). Once again, the sport journal described in the chapter appendix helps the athlete develop this awareness because it provides a mechanism for recording, evaluating sport performance, and processing the information learned from the act of participation.

Techniques for Developing Awareness

There are many techniques to increase awareness. One valuable technique is keeping a sport journal. The sport journal provides a structured method to reflect on sport performances and to capitalize on the wealth of experiential knowledge gained from the performance. The journal guidelines in the appendix ask questions about stressors, manifestations of stress, and feelings associated with performance, concentration, and skill execution. After teams play a game, they can discuss what the members have learned so that, with the coach, they can establish new goals or modify earlier ones.

Following selected performances, coaches can give players feedback sheets similar to the one shown in Figure 12-1 so that they can process the subjective information gained from each contest. This procedure helps the players systematically learn from the experience and bring closure to their performance so that they can begin to focus on the next performance. This is particularly helpful in tournament play when the athletes have to perform many times during a short period, because it is critical to bring **closure,** or let go of one performance before beginning another.

With the athletes' permission, coaches and sport psychologists can read these journals and feedback sheets, using the information as a foundation for better understanding the athlete and what behavior or intervention might best facilitate performance and personal growth. Writing feelings in a journal or on a feedback sheet is often perceived by athletes as less threatening than verbal discussions. Such writing often forges an understanding that promotes discussion. (In some cases coaches have also worked with English teachers to capitalize on the athletes' interest in writing about the experiential aspects of sport performance to develop English writing skills.)

Some coaches and sport psychologists have helped athletes glean information regarding ideal psychological states for peak performance by having them fill out psychological questionnaires just before beginning performance. Ideally, this should be done prior to a number of competitions, enabling a comparison between performance and scores on the questionnaires. The intention is to find what psychological state(s) typically occurred when athletes performed at their best. The Competitive State Anxiety Inventory-2 (CSAI-2) (Martens, Vealey, & Burton, 1990) is one example of an appropriate questionnaire for this purpose. The CSAI-2 assesses the athlete's current cognitive anxiety, somatic anxiety, and self-confidence. We know from the research discussed in Chapter 11 that each of these psychological states may be relevant to performance. See some of the questionnaires discussed in other chapters for additional examples of potentially appropriate instruments. It should be noted that not all sport psychology consultants find these questionnaires useful. It is

critical that the consultant discuss the results with the athletes to determine whether the information obtained is accurate for that athlete.

Monitoring relevant physiological systems is another tool for gaining awareness regarding ideal performance states. Purportedly, Eastern European sport psychologists frequently use this procedure when working with elite athletes. Heart rate, blood pressure, brain waves, muscle tension, galvanic skin response, and catecholamine levels are all examples of types of physiological monitoring that might be appropriate for identifying an athlete's psychological state and its relationship to performance. Research and interventions in this area are still in their infancy in North America. Work by Landers and his students provides one example of what the future might hold when sophisticated technology is more common (Landers et al., 1991; Salazar et al., 1990). Even without sophisticated technology, heart rate can be monitored right before a number of critical competitions and then compared with subsequent performance to determine an optimal pulse rate. According to Dr. Alexeev of the Moscow Research Institute of Physical Culture, this is one of the best ways to discover an athlete's optimal level of anxiety (Raiport, 1988).

Athletes who are good imagers can use imagery to gain awareness of their ideal performance state. This technique is particularly effective if the athletes are in the off-season or in a situation where actual competition is not possible. Imagery is used to relive previous excellent performance, with particular attention given to identifying what feelings, arousal level, thoughts, muscle tension, attentional focus, and so forth might have occurred. There also may be merit in imaging previous bad performances in order to contrast their psychological state with what appears to be a more optimal state.

Imagery can be an effective tool as well for creating awareness when filling out performance feedback sheets after an actual performance. Athletes who are unsure of exactly what happened can replay their performance to determine what they were thinking, feeling, and attending to at any given moment.

Group discussion is another method that coaches and sport psychology consultants can use to increase athlete awareness. Coaches should provide their athletes with an opportunity to discuss a performance by encouraging but not requiring them to do so. Sport psychology consultants should do the same thing after practice of certain mental training techniques. Sometimes coaches and sport psychology consultants can foster this form of communication through one-on-one discussions. Coach/sport psychology practitioners should share their perspective or expertise but also encourage the athletes to talk about the experience. They should ask questions about arousal and confidence levels, stressors, and manifestations. Every team is capable of this type of interaction, but such dialogue is frequently difficult to facilitate at first. As the athletes become much more aware of the needs of their teammates, team cohesion will be more likely to result. In turn, athletes gain new insights into their own

sport performances. For example, one athlete responds to stress by withdrawing. An understanding of this by teammates relieves stress because other people now know that this is one method used to mentally prepare for performance. There is nothing wrong with an athlete who is quiet.

A good time to begin group discussions is after a positive experience because the feelings are nonthreatening. For example, after a great practice, the coach can ask the athletes to discuss what made the practice so good. How was it different from a nonproductive practice session?

In regard to specific methods of increasing awareness, it is important that practitioners do what they are comfortable with. However, it is strongly suggested that coaches and sport psychology consultants slowly integrate the various methods discussed in this chapter.

Summary

Developing awareness is a critical element of peak performance because it provides athletes with the experiential knowledge to gain control of the performance. Awareness is the first step in raising self-control in sport participation. Initially, athletes need to become aware of their ideal performance state. Next, athletes need to recognize when they are no longer at that ideal state. As athletes develop awareness skills, they will recognize earlier when they are not focused or aroused appropriately. This early recognition aids athletes in gaining control before it is lost. The sooner a deviation is recognized, the easier it is to get back on course. Athletes with a range of interventions can use them to get their mental-emotional and physical states to more nearly approximate what they have found leads to peak performance. Journal keeping, performance feedback sheets, assessing precompetitive performance states through psychological questionnaires and physiological monitoring, using imagery to relive past performances, and group discussions are all effective techniques for developing awareness. Depending on the athlete's preferences and the circumstances, certain techniques may be more effective than others at any given moment.

Study Questions

1. Why is it important that athletes be aware of their ideal performance state?

2. What is the difference between merely performing skills and experiencing skills?

3. Why is it important to incorporate awareness training with the physical skills that are already being performed in practice?

4. Give an example of focused practice.

5. Describe how the all-or-none syndrome can be overcome.

6. What is meant by playing on the edge? What techniques can help an athlete become aware of this skill?

7. How can a sport journal and performance feedback sheets be used to increase awareness? Describe what might be included in a journal and feedback sheets.

8. How can psychological questionnaires and physiological monitoring be used to increase awareness of ideal performance states?

9. When might imagery and group discussion be used to increase awareness?

References

Feldenkrais, M. (1972). *Awareness through movement.* New York: Harper & Row.

Gallwey, T. (1974). *The inner game of tennis.* New York: Random House.

Garrido, A. (1982, December 7). Interview with author. Fullerton, CA.

Harris, D., & Harris, B. (1984). *The athlete's guide to sport psychology: Mental skills for physical people.* New York: Leisure Press.

Landers, D., Petruzello, S., Salazar, W., Cruz, D., Kubitz, K., Gannon, T., & Han, M. (1991). The influence of electrocortical biofeedback on performance in pre-elite archers. *Medicine and Science in Sports and Exercise, 23,* 123–129.

Martens, R., Vealey, R. S., & Burton, D. (1990). *Competitive anxiety in sport.* Champaign, IL: Human Kinetics.

McClements, J., & Botterill, C. (1979). Goal setting in shaping of future performance of athletes. In P. Klavora & J. Daniel (Eds.), *Coach, athlete and the sport psychologist.* Champaign, IL: Human Kinetics.

Raiport, G. (1988). *Red gold: Peak performance techniques of the Russian and East German Olympic victors.* Los Angeles: Tarcher.

Ravizza, K. (1984). Qualities of the peak experience in sport. In J. Silva & R. Weinberg (Eds.), *Psychological foundations for sport.* Champaign, IL: Human Kinetics.

Ravizza, K., & Hanson, T. (1994). *Heads-up baseball: Playing the game one pitch at a time.* Indianapolis: Masters Press.

Ravizza, K., & Osborne, T. (1991). Nebraska's 3R's: One play-at-a-time preperformance routine for collegiate football. *The Sport Psychologist, 5,* 256–265.

Salazar, W., Landers, D., Petruzello, S., Han, M., Cruz, D., & Kubitz, K. (1990). Hemispheric asymmetry, cardiac response, and performance in elite archers. *Research Quarterly in Exercise and Sport, 61,* 351–359.

Guidelines for Keeping a Sport Journal

The sport journal is a tool to help you further develop your mental skills for sport performance. The first step in gaining self-control is to develop an awareness of your sport performance so that you can recognize when you are pulled out of the most appropriate mental state for you. The journal provides you with an opportunity to record the different intervention strategies that you experiment with to regain control. The long-range goal is to develop various techniques that you can implement in stressful situations to perform to your utmost ability.

If you choose to, the journal also can be a place to record your feelings and the personal knowledge that you are gaining about yourself, the game, your teammates, and any other factors. This is one of the few times in your life that you will ever direct so much energy toward one specific goal. There is a lot to learn from your pursuit of excellence. This journal will give you something to reflect on after your high-level participation is completed.

The journal also can serve as a place where you can express your feelings in writing and drawings. It is beneficial to get these feelings out in some way so that they don't build up and contribute to unproductive tension. The use of colored pens is often helpful to express yourself. You do not have to make an entry every day, but date the entries you do make. The journal is an informal record of your thoughts and experiences as you train for high-level performance.

If you choose to have someone read your journal, please feel free to delete any parts that you think are too personal to share. The intention of someone who is reviewing your writing should be to guide you and make *suggestions* that may facilitate your self-exploration in reaching your goals.

I would suggest that you try this technique, but it is not for everyone. If you choose not to, that is your choice. If you try the technique, assess the following areas with the accompanying questions/descriptors:

1. *Peak Performance.* What does it feel like when you play or practice at your best? Describe some of your most enjoyable experiences playing your sport. What have you learned from these moments when you are fully functioning?

2. *Stressors.* Outside the sport: write down your thoughts about various events outside your sport that are distracting to you—for example, parents, boy/girlfriends, peers, job hassles, financial issues, community (hometown expectations). On the field: do the same for distractions on the field, such as importance of contest, location, and spectators.

3. *Coaching Staff.* What do you need from your coaches? What can you give them in order to reach your goals? What can you do to make your relationship with your coaches more productive?

4. *Teammates.* What do you want from your teammates? What can you give them? How do you relate and work with your teammates? Write about your relationship with other teammates. Any unfinished business?

5. *Confidence.* At this time how confident are you in regard to achieving your goals? What can you do differently to feel more confident? What can you ask of yourself, coach, or teammates?

6. *Manifestations of Your Stress.* How do you experience high levels of anxiety in performance? Assess your thoughts and physiological and behavioral reactions. What did you do to intervene and keep in balance?

7. *Awareness and Concentration.* What changes do you observe in your performance when you are aware? What concentration methods are you experimenting with? What are your focal points for various skills?

8. *Relaxation Training.* How are your relaxation skills developing? Are there any parts of your body that are more difficult than others to relax? What method is best for you? How are you able to relate this to your play? How quickly can you relax?

9. *Thought Control.* How is your self-talk affecting your performance? Write out some of your negative self-talk and make it positive.

10. *Centering/Concentration Skills.* What are you doing to concentrate appropriately before the contest and during the contest? What has been successful? Unsuccessful? Describe your preperformance routine.

11. *Imagery.* How are your imagery skills developing? Do you see a TV screen–type image or is it more of a feeling image? At what point do you notice lapses in concentration? How clear are your images? Can you control the speed and tempo of the image?

12. *Controlling Your Arousal Level.* What are you doing to control your arousal level? What are you doing to increase arousal and intensity? What are you experimenting with to reduce arousal levels? What is working for you and what is not working?

13. *Pressure Situations.* How are you handling pressure situations? What are you doing differently? What are you doing to learn to cope more effectively?

14. *Quality Practice Time.* What do you do to mentally prepare for practice? How do you keep your personal difficulties from affecting your play? What are you doing to take charge? What works for you and what hasn't worked?

15. *Anything You Want to Address.*

13

Goal Setting for Peak Performance

Daniel Gould,[1] *Michigan State University*

Without goals you are like a ship without a rudder—heading in no particular direction.
　　　　　　　—Roy Williams, head basketball coach at the University of North Carolina

In recent years, a number of psychological strategies have been identified as ways of assisting athletes in achieving personal growth and peak performance. Goal setting is one such technique. In fact, goal setting has not only been shown to influence the performance of athletes of varied age and ability levels but also been linked to positive changes in important psychological states such as anxiety, confidence, and motivation. It is clearly a technique that coaches and sport psychologists should regularly employ.

Unfortunately, goal setting is not always effectively employed by coaches and sport psychologists. It is falsely assumed, for example, that because athletes set goals on their own these goals will automatically facilitate performance. This is seldom the case, however, as many athletes set inappropriate goals or do not set goals in a systematic fashion. Similarly, coaches and sport psychologists often forget to initiate the follow-up and evaluation procedures that are necessary

if goal setting is to be effective. To use goal setting effectively, coaches and sport psychologists must understand the goal-setting process and the many factors that can affect it.

This chapter has a fourfold purpose. First, psychological and sport psychological research and theory on goal setting will be briefly examined. Second, a number of fundamental goal-setting guidelines will be discussed. Third, a system for effectively initiating goal-setting procedures with athletes will be presented. And, fourth, common problems that arise when setting goals will be identified and solutions will be offered. The principles and recommendations derived in this chapter are based both on research and on what sport psychologists have learned while utilizing goal-setting interventions with athletes in a variety of settings.

Goal-Setting Research and Theory

Before examining the research on goal setting and theoretical explanations for the relationships between goal setting and performance, we must

[1]The author would like to thank Linda Bump, Linda Petlichkoff, and Jeff Simons for their helpful comments on early versions of this chapter.

first define goals and distinguish between various types of goals.

Defining Goals

Locke and his colleagues (1981) have generated the most widely accepted definition for the term *goal*. For these investigators, a **goal** is defined as "attaining a specific standard of proficiency on a task, usually within a specified time limit" (Locke, Shaw, Saari, & Latham, 1981, p. 145). From a practical perspective, then, goals focus on achieving some standard, whether it be increasing one's batting average by 10 percentage points, lowering one's time in the 800 meters, or losing 5 pounds. This definition also implies that such performance standards will be achieved within some specified unit of time, such as by the end of the season, within 2 weeks, or by the end of practice.

Even though the definition by Locke and his associates provides a good general description of a goal, sport psychologists have at times found it useful to make specific distinctions between types of goals. McClements (1982), for instance, has differentiated between **subjective goals** (e.g., having fun, getting fit, or trying one's best), **general objective goals** (e.g., winning a championship or making a team), and **specific objective goals** (e.g., increasing the number of assists in basketball or decreasing a pitcher's earned run average in softball).

Similarly, Martens (1987) and Burton (1983, 1984, 1989) have made distinctions between **outcome goals,** which represent standards of performance that focus on the results of a contest between opponents or teams (e.g., beating someone), and **performance goals,** which focus on improvements relative to one's own past performance, (e.g., improving one's time in the mile). Finally, Hardy, Jones, and Gould (1996) extended the outcome-performance goal distinction to include **process goals,** which specify the procedures in which the performer will engage during performance (e.g., a skier focusing on keeping his hands in front of him during a downhill run, a tennis player on keeping her feet moving when fatigued). These distinctions are important because evidence suggests that certain types of

goals are more useful in changing behavior than other types of goals.

Goal-Effectiveness Research

Extensive psychological research has been conducted on the topic of goal setting (see Locke et al., 1981; Locke & Latham, 1990; Mento, Steel, & Karren, 1987; Tubbs, 1991, for extensive reviews). Typically, this research has involved a comparison of the performance of individuals who set goals or certain types of goals (e.g., specific-explicit goals) with the performance of individuals who are simply told to do their best or are given no goals. Studies sometimes manipulate other factors, such as individual characteristics (e.g., race, educational level, personality) or situational variables (e.g., the presence or absence of feedback).

Psychological research on goal setting is impressive in that it has been conducted in a variety of laboratory and field settings and has used a wide variety of tasks, ranging from truck loading to brainstorming sessions; it has employed diverse samples, including elementary schoolchildren, uneducated laborers, managers, and scientists. In addition, a clear pattern of results has emerged with ready implications for sport psychology specialists and coaches alike.

The most important result generated from this line of research is that goal setting clearly and consistently facilitates performance. In their excellent and comprehensive review of well over a hundred studies on goal setting, for example, Locke and colleagues (1981) concluded that "the beneficial effect of goal setting on task performance is one of the most robust and replicable findings in the psychological literature. Ninety percent of the studies showed positive or partially positive effects. Furthermore, these effects are found just as reliable in the field setting as in the laboratory" (p. 145). Thus, a review of the psychological research clearly shows that goal setting is a powerful technique for enhancing performance.

Given the abundance of research on goal setting and the consistent pattern of results found in the psychological literature in general, it is surprising that until the 1980s the topic was rarely discussed in the sport psychology literature. In fact, prior to 1985, only a few studies had been conducted on the topic (Botterill, 1977; Burton, 1983, 1984).

Nevertheless, the results of these initial investigations showed much promise. Botterill (1977), for instance, had youth ice hockey players perform an exercise endurance task under various combinations of goal difficulty, goal explicitness specificity, and goal type (group, individual, or experimenter-set) conditions. Consistent with the psychological literature, the results revealed that goal setting facilitated performance. Similarly, difficult goals were more effective in enhancing performance than easy goals, and explicit goals were more effective than general "do your best" goals. Finally, it was concluded that explicit, difficult, and group-set goals were most effective in enhancing endurance task performance.

In an important field investigation, Burton (1983, 1989) examined the effects of a goal-setting training program on the performance and cognitions (e.g., levels of self-confidence, motivation, and state anxiety) of male and female intercollegiate swimmers. In a 5-month goal-setting program, performance as opposed to outcome goals were employed, and an attempt was made to explain why goal setting influences performance by relating goals to other psychological constructs such as confidence and state anxiety. The results revealed that swimmers who participated in the goal-setting training program learned to focus highest priority on performance goals and that those swimmers high in goal-setting ability demonstrated better performance and more positive cognitions. Furthermore, a related study conducted with National Sports Festival swimmers supported these findings, demonstrating that goals were positively related to performance and positive psychological attributes (Burton, 1984).

Although goal setting was not widely studied by sport psychology researchers prior to 1985, increased attention has been placed on this topic over the last two decades. Much of this interest in goal-setting research was spurred by a 1985 *Journal of Sport Psychology* review article written by noted goal-setting researchers Locke and Latham, in which it was suggested that goal-setting research principles found in the general

psychological literature were applicable to the sport context. This has led to a series of sport psychology studies testing Locke and Latham's proposition in the sport environment. (See Burton, Naylor, & Holliday, 2002, for an excellent review of these studies.)

More recent sport psychology goal-setting research investigations have examined such issues as whether specific goals are more effective than general "do your best" goals, the effectiveness of long-term versus short-term goals, and the relationship between goal difficulty and task performance. Results of these studies have shown that goal setting works well in sport, but not as well as in other settings such as business (Burton et al., 2002). Robert Weinberg, one of the leading sport psychology researchers in the area, has indicated that research efforts are characterized by a number of methodological problems such as spontaneous setting of goals by control group participants, competition between comparison group participants, and the failure to control levels of participant motivation and commitment (Weinberg, 1994). Burton et al. (2002) also noted that athletes often operate closer to their performance potential, task complexity, and the failure to use appropriate goal implementation strategies. Hence, these problems have limited the implications that can be derived from this research and made it somewhat difficult to determine when and where goal setting works in sport. Goal setting, then, is more complex to apply in sport than it might appear on the surface.

Despite the fact that the recent sport psychology goal-setting research has not been as fruitful as was hoped, it has shown that goal setting can and does influence performance in sport settings. In fact, in a meta-analytic statistical review of 36 independent sport and exercise goal-setting studies conducted by Kyllo and Landers (1995), it was concluded that goal setting was a successful technique for improving performance.

Field studies (Anderson, Crowell, Doman, & Howard, 1988; Brosbst & Ward, 2000; Filby, Maynard, & Graydon, 1999; Lambert, Moore, & Dixon, 1999; Swain & Jones, 1995; Wanlin, Hrycaiko, Martin, & Mahon, 1997; Ward & Carnes, 2002; Weinberg, Stitcher, & Richardson, 1994) have shown that goal setting facilitates athlete performance. In particular, Anderson et al. (1988) examined goal setting along with publicly posted performance and praise on "checking" in a collegiate ice hockey team. The results of this within-subject design showed that this behavioral intervention increased checking behavior over a baseline and that the goal-setting component was associated with improved performance. It was concluded not only that goal setting was associated with improved performance but that performance feedback moderates these effects.

In another study, Swain and Jones (1995) examined goal setting in four university basketball players over a series of matches. Using a single-subject baseline design, results revealed goal setting had positive consequences on three out of four identified behaviors. Hence, goal setting was found to be effective in changing desired behaviors.

Finally, in a very well-designed single-subject multiple baseline study using four female speed skaters, Wanlin et al. (1997) had participants take part in a goal-setting package. This package involved developing an overall mission (general subjective goal), a long-term goal, subgoals and practice goals, self-talk, and goal visualization. It was taught to each skater, and performance was compared prior to and after the goal-setting package was used. Results revealed that the goal-setting package was effective in influencing the skaters to work harder and show fewer off-task behaviors. Race times also decreased. Hence, goal setting was effective in facilitating desirable behaviors and performance in the skaters and decreasing undesirable behaviors.

Taken together, these field studies support the earlier findings of Burton (1983, 1989). They also reinforce a main contention of this chapter; that is, goal setting will only be effective when a systematic approach is adopted and a knowledgeable professional customizes the goal-setting process to his or her particular setting and athletes.

In summary, although not unequivocal, the results of the psychological and sport psychology research literature provide strong support for using goal-setting procedures to facilitate athletic performance. Moreover, these findings are further strengthened by the fact that they have been demonstrated in studies using varied tasks and largely different populations in both laboratory and field settings. A survey of leading sport psychology consultants working with U.S. Olympic athletes has also shown that goal setting is the most often used psychological intervention in both individual athlete–coach and group consultations (Gould, Tammen, Murphy, & May, 1989). Data from Orlick and Partington's (1988) extensive study of Olympic athletes supports the survey results from the sport psychologists. The athletes reported daily goal setting as a part of their training program.

Examining Athletes' and Coaches' Uses of Goal Setting

A recent development in sport psychology goal-setting research is the study of the goal-setting practices actually employed by athletes and coaches. Weinberg and his colleagues (Burton, Weinberg, Yukelson, & Weigand, 1998; Weinberg, Burton, Yukelson, & Weigand, 2000; Weinberg, Butt, Knight, & Perritt, 2001) have spearheaded this line of research. For example, Burton et al. (1998) studied 321 male and 249 female collegiate athletes representing 18 sports who were surveyed regarding their goal-setting practices. Findings revealed that most of the athletes set goals but rated them as only moderately effective, preferred moderate to very difficult goals, and more often reported problems with setting goals that were too hard versus easy.

Most interesting was the researchers' comparison between more and less effective goal setters, which found that more effective goal setters used all types of goals and implemented productive goal-setting strategies more frequently than did their less effective counterparts. Based on these results, it was concluded that coaches and athletes underutilize goal setting and need further goal-setting education. In particular, more emphasis must be placed on teaching athletes about process-oriented performance goals, the relationship between long- and short-term goals, skill and fitness goals, and implementing goals in practice and competition.

The most recent studies in this line of research showed that Olympic athletes all set some type of goals (Weinberg et al., 2000). Interviews with collegiate coaches from a variety of sports also showed that they used individual, team, practice, and competition goals (Weinberg et al., 2001), although there was some divergence in how systematic the coaches were in their use of goal setting.

Theoretical Explanations for the Relationship Between Goal Setting and Performance

The old adage that there is nothing more practical than a good theory is an appropriate way to view the goal-setting process. It is important to know that goal setting influences performance, but it is equally important for coaches and sport psychologists to understand how and why goal setting is effective, especially when problems occur in goal setting and these individuals must assess the situation and make adjustments.

Three explanations have been proposed to describe how goals influence performance. Locke and his associates (1981) suggested a mechanistic theory to explain the goal-performance relationship in general. In contrast, Burton (1983) and Garland (1985) have proposed more cognitively oriented theories to explain how goal setting influences performance.

In their mechanistic theory, Locke and colleagues (1981) contend that goals influence performance in four ways. First, goals direct the performer's attention and action to important aspects of the task. For example, by setting goals a basketball player will focus attention and subsequent action on improving specific skills such as blocking out under the boards or decreasing turnovers as opposed to becoming a better ball player in general. Second, goals help the performer mobilize effort. For example, by setting a series of practice goals, a swimmer will exhibit greater practice effort in attempting to achieve these objectives. Third, goals not only increase immediate effort but help prolong effort or increase persistence. As a case in point, the boredom of a long season is offset and persistence is increased when a wrestler sets a number of short-term goals

throughout the year. Finally, research has shown that performers often develop and employ new learning strategies through the process of setting goals. Golfers, for instance, may learn new methods of putting in an effort to achieve putting goals that they have set in conjunction with their coach or sport psychologist.

In contrast to the Locke and associates' theory (1981), Burton's cognitive theory (1983) focuses solely on how goal setting influences performance in athletic environments. Athletes' goals are linked to their levels of anxiety, motivation, and confidence. That is, when athletes focus solely on outcome or winning goals, unrealistic future expectations often result; such expectations can lead to lower levels of confidence, increased cognitive anxiety, decreased effort, and poor performance. Unlike outcome goals, performance goals are both in the athlete's control and flexible. Moreover, when properly employed, performance goals assist the athlete in forming realistic expectations. This, in turn, results in optimal levels of confidence, cognitive anxiety, and motivation, and, ultimately, in enhanced performance.

More recently, Burton and Naylor (2002) further developed his theoretical view of goal setting. The most interesting aspect of this update was the contention that an athlete's goal orientation interacts with perceived ability to produce one of three goal styles: a performance orientation where the athlete defines success based on learning and self-improvement and has high perceived ability; a success orientation where the athlete defines success on social comparison and winning and has high perceived ability; and a failure orientation where the athlete defines success on social comparison and winning but has low perceived ability. They predict that goal setting should best increase performance for the performance oriented athlete, moderately increase performance for the success oriented athlete, and slightly decrease performance for the failure oriented athlete. Goal setting, then, interacts with a variety of personal and situational factors and these motivational factors must be taken into consideration in any goal setting program. The implication is that the goal setting will work differently depending on one's goal setting style.

Like Burton (1983), Garland (1985) contends that goals influence one's performance through one's cognitive or thought processes. In particular, he contends that when an individual sets a task goal, that goal affects performance by influencing the individual's performance expectancy and performance valence.

Performance expectancy is an athlete's self-efficacy of confidence relative to reaching a range of performance levels. One aspect of performance expectancy is the athlete's confidence in achieving a specific goal. Moreover, it is predicted that the more confidence the athlete has about achieving a specific task goal, the better he or she will perform. **Performance valence** refers to the range of satisfactions an athlete anticipates he or she will derive from achieving various performance levels. Hence, an athlete anticipates certain satisfactions by setting a specific task goal and achieving a specific level of performance. When task goals are achieved, the person becomes more satisfied (performance valence increases), and the person becomes less motivated to improve performance.

Unfortunately, little research (particularly sport psychology research) has been conducted to directly test Garland's cognitive mediation theory. The theory does, however, provide researchers with some ideas for explaining how goals may influence performance.

When setting goals, then, coaches and sport psychologists should make every effort to become aware of the mechanisms causing performance changes to occur. Simply stated, theorists indicate that performance changes occur because of the influence of goals on such psychological attributes as anxiety, confidence, satisfaction, and motivation; the directing of attention to important aspects of the skill being performed; the mobilization of effort; increases in persistence; and the fostering of the development of new learning strategies.

Life Skills Goal-Setting Programs

Much of the research, theory, and practical goal-setting literature in sport psychology has focused on using goals to enhance athletic performance, but goals can also be used to enhance personal development. For example, sport psychologist Steve Danish and his colleagues have used goal setting as a cornerstone of programs designed to enhance life skills, particularly in at-risk populations (Danish, Nellen, & Owens, 1996; Danish, Petitpas, & Hale, 1995). In particular, these scholars have initiated intervention programs that are designed to promote health-enhancing behaviors (e.g., learn how to learn, stay healthy) and decrease health-compromising behaviors (e.g., drug and alcohol use) in participants, particularly at-risk youth. Because of the importance of sport in the lives of many youth, these programs focus on identifying and then transferring valuable skills learned in the sport environment to other more general life situations. One fundamental skill that is stressed is goal setting (Danish et al., 1992; Danish et al., 1995). Organizers focus on effectively setting and achieving sport goals by helping athletes clarify their training and competition objectives. Efforts are then made to "teach for transfer" by helping participants apply their new goal-setting skills to other life contexts. An example of the steps followed in such a program is given in Danish et al. (1996):

> (a) the identification of positive life goals, (b) the importance of focusing on the process (not the outcome) of goal attainment, (c) the use of a general problem solving model, (d) the identification of health-comprising behaviors that can impede goal attainment, (e) the identification of health-promoting behaviors that can facilitate goal attainment, (f) the importance of seeking and creating social support, and (g) ways to transfer these skills from one life situation to another. (p. 215)

Finally, these steps are implemented in a series of 10 one-hour workshops.

Additional research on the efficacy of programs to develop goal-setting-based life skills is needed, but initial reports are encouraging. Moreover, these programs clearly demonstrate the importance of looking beyond goal setting as simply an athletic performance enhancement technique to looking at it as a general skill that can positively influence all aspects of one's life. The programs also emphasize the need to teach for transfer and not assume that just because a person can effectively set goals in sport he or she will automatically use goal setting in other life contexts.

Goal-Setting Guidelines

The research clearly shows that goal setting facilitates performance. It is misleading to think, however, that all types of goals are equally effective in enhancing athletic performance. Research reviews conducted by Burton et al. (2002) and Locke and Latham (1990), Weinberg (1994), and Kyllo and Landers (1995) indicate that this is not the case. Their work has produced specific guidelines concerning the most effective types of goals to use. Similarly, sport psychologists (Bell, 1983; Botterill, 1983; Carron, 1984; Gould, 1983; Harris & Harris, 1984; McClements & Botterill, 1979; O'Block & Evans, 1984; Orlick, 1990) who have had extensive experience in employing goal-setting techniques with athletes have been able to derive a number of useful guidelines for those interested in utilizing such techniques, the most important of which are summarized here.

Set Specific Goals in Measurable and Behavioral Terms

Explicit, specific, and numerical goals are more effective in facilitating behavior change than general "do your best" goals or no goals at all. Therefore, it is of the utmost importance that in the athletic environment goals be expressed in terms of specific measurable behaviors. Goals such as doing one's best, becoming better, and increasing one's strength are least effective. More effective goals include being able to high jump 6 feet 5 inches by the end of the season or increasing one's maximum lift on the bench press to 240 pounds. If athletes are to show performance improvements, specific measurable goals must be set!

Set Moderately Difficult But Realistic Goals

Locke and his associates (1981) have found a direct relationship between goal difficulty and task performance. That is, the more difficult the goal, the better the performance. It must be remembered, however, that this relationship is true only when the difficulty of the goal does not exceed the performer's ability. Unrealistic goals that exceed the ability of an athlete only lead to failure and frustration. In fact, in their meta-analysis, Kyllo and Landers (1995) found that moderately difficult (as opposed to extremely difficult) goals lead to the best performance. Thus, it is recommended that goals be set so that they are difficult enough to challenge athletes but realistic enough to be achieved (McClements, 1982).

Set Short-Range as Well as Long-Range Goals

When asked to describe their goals, most athletes identify long-range objectives such as winning a particular championship, breaking a record, or making a particular team. However, a number of sport psychologists (Bell, 1983; Carron, 1984; Gould, 1983; Harris & Harris, 1984; O'Block & Evans, 1984) have emphasized the need to set more immediate short-range goals. The superiority of combining short- and long-term goals as compared to focusing only on long-term goals was also demonstrated in the Kyllo and Landers (1995) meta-analysis. Short-range goals are important because they allow athletes to see immediate improvements in performance and in so doing enhance motivation. Additionally, without short-range goals, athletes often lose sight of their long-range goals and the progression of skills needed to obtain them.

An effective way to understand the relationship between short- and long-range goals is to visualize a staircase (see Figure 13-1). The top stair represents an athlete's long-range goal or objective and the lowest stair his or her present ability. The remaining steps represent a progression of short-term goals of increasing difficulty that lead from the bottom to the top of the stairs. In essence, the performer climbs the staircase of athletic achievement by taking a step at a time, accomplishing a series of interrelated short-range goals.

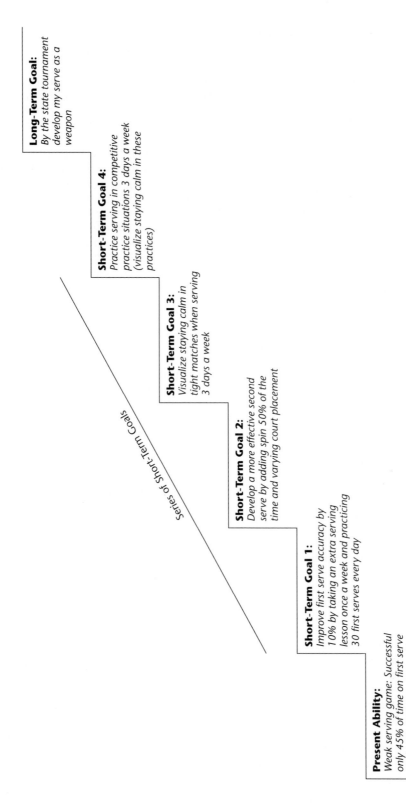

Long-Term Goal:
By the state tournament develop my serve as a weapon

Short-Term Goal 4:
Practice serving in competitive practice situations 3 days a week (visualize staying calm in these practices)

Short-Term Goal 3:
Visualize staying calm in tight matches when serving 3 days a week

Short-Term Goal 2:
Develop a more effective second serve by adding spin 50% of the time and varying court placement

Short-Term Goal 1:
Improve first serve accuracy by 10% by taking an extra serving lesson once a week and practicing 30 first serves every day

Series of Short-Term Goals

Present Ability:
Weak serving game: Successful only 45% of time on first serve and no variation on second serve

Figure 13-1 **Goal Staircase example series of short-term goals leading to long-term goals for improved tennis serve**

247

Set Process and Performance Goals as well as Outcome Goals

North American society places tremendous emphasis on the outcome of athletic events. Because of this, most athletes are socialized to set only outcome goals (e.g., winning, beating a particular opponent). However, outcome goals have been shown to be less effective than performance goals (Burton, 1984, 1989; Burton et al., 2002).

It has been theorized that focusing on outcome goals has several inherent weaknesses (Burton, 1984, 1989; Martens, 1987). First, athletes have, at best, only partial control over outcome goals. For example, a cross-country competitor can set a personal best but fail to achieve the outcome goal of winning because he or she came in second. Despite his or her superior effort, this runner could not control the behavior of the other competitors.

A second important weakness of outcome goals is that when they are employed by athletes the athletes usually become less flexible in their goal-adjustment practices. For example, an athlete who sets an outcome goal of winning every game but loses the initial contest will often reject goal setting altogether. However, an athlete who sets an individual performance goal such as decreasing his or her 100-meter breaststroke time by $\frac{3}{10}$ of a second and fails to achieve this goal is more likely to reset the goal to $\frac{1}{10}$ of a second.

Finally, process goals (e.g., watch the ball longer by focusing on the pitcher's release, get back on defense) orient the athlete to focus on task-relevant strategies and procedures that need to be executed to have a good performance. Focusing on outcome goals can distract athletes, as they tend to worry about the event outcome and do not attend to task-relevant strategies (Hardy et al., 1996).

Although focusing on outcome goals, especially at the time of competition, has weaknesses, this does not mean outcome goals have no benefits. They can facilitate short-term motivation by helping athletes set long-term priorities and may be especially useful away from competition when athletes may lack the motivation to practice. Athletes with high levels of confidence may also be less affected by the negative side effects of outcome goals (Hardy et al., 1996). It is clear, however, that at or near competitions it is best to emphasize process and performance goals and that focusing exclusively on outcome goals is ineffective.

A study by Filby, Maynard, and Graydon (1999) provides additional empirical support for the idea of setting performance and process as well as outcome goals. Specifically, these investigators had physical education students perform a soccer wall volley test under one of five goal conditions: outcome goals only; outcome plus process goals; process goals only; outcome, performance, and process goals; and a control no goal condition. Results revealed that the groups using multiple goal strategies performed best, indicating that it is important to balance outcome, process, and performance goals. It was also concluded that the "benefits of adopting an outcome goal are realized only when the outcome goal is combined with the prioritization of a 'process orientation' immediately before, and during performance" (Filby et al., 1999, p. 242). Moreover, looking across all goals Burton et al. (2002) reported that 9 out of 10 studies supported the notion of using a combination of process, performance, and outcome goals.

In summary, by emphasizing personal performance and process goals in an environment where outcome goals predominate, coaches create greater opportunities for meeting the success needs of all athletes. Those highly gifted competitors who easily exceed the performances of their opponents learn to compete against themselves and, in turn, reach new performance heights. Similarly, the less skilled athletes on the team are no longer doomed to failure; they learn to judge success and failure in terms of their own performance, not solely on the basis of peer comparisons. Finally, focusing on process goals directs the athlete's attention away from outcome and puts it on task-relevant cues.

Set Goals for Practice and Competition

When implementing a goal-setting program, people frequently make the mistake of only setting goals that relate to competition. This does not imply that setting competitive performance goals is inappropriate; rather, it suggests that *practice* goals should not be forgotten (Bell, 1983). In fact, Orlick and Partington (1988) found that one characteristic of highly successful Olympians was their practice of setting clear daily practice goals.

Common practice goals may include starting practice on time, making five sincere positive statements to teammates during practice, running to and from all drills, and achieving various performance standards. These are typically not the most frequently cited goals of athletes, but they take on special significance when one considers the amount of time athletes spend in practice as opposed to competition. Moreover, most athletes report that it is easier to get "up" and motivated for a game or match, whereas additional motivation is often needed for daily practices.

Set Positive Goals as Opposed to Negative Goals

Goals can be stated in either positive (e.g., increase the percentage of good first serves in tennis) or negative terms (e.g., decrease the percentage of bad first serves in tennis). Although it is sometimes necessary for athletes to set goals in negative terms, it has been suggested that, whenever possible, goals should be stated positively (Bell, 1983). That is, identify behaviors to be exhibited as opposed to behaviors that should not be exhibited. Instead of having goal tenders in ice hockey strive to decrease the number of unblocked shots, have them set goals of increasing the number of saves they can make. This positive goal-setting procedure helps athletes focus on success instead of failure.

Identify Target Dates for Attaining Goals

Not only should goals describe the behavior of focus in specific measurable terms, but they should identify target dates for goal accomplishment. Target dates help motivate athletes by reminding them of the urgency of accomplishing their objectives in realistic lengths of time.

Identify Goal-Achievement Strategies

All too often goals are properly set but never accomplished because athletes fail to identify goal-achievement strategies. That is, the athlete fails to understand the difference between setting goals and developing and initiating effective goal-achievement strategies. An important ingredient for any effective goal-setting program, then, is identification of ways of achieving goals. For example, a basketball player who has set a goal of increasing her field goal percentage by 5 percentage points may want to identify a goal-achievement strategy of shooting 25 extra foul shots after every practice. Similarly, a wrestler needing to lose 10 pounds prior to the start of the season should identify an achievement strategy of cutting out a midafternoon snack and running an additional 2 miles a day.

Record Goals Once They Have Been Identified

It is easy for athletes to focus attention on their goals soon after those goals have been set. Over the course of a long season, however, goals are sometimes forgotten. Therefore, it is useful for athletes to record their goals in written form and place them where they will be seen (e.g., in their lockers). In fact, in the previously mentioned Wanlin et al. (1997) speed skating study, it was concluded that using a log book was a particularly important component of the successful goal-setting package used. Additionally, Harris and Harris (1984) recommend that athletes keep notebooks recording goals, goal-achievement strategies, and goal progress on a daily or weekly basis. Finally, Botterill (1983) suggests that the coach develop a contract stating all goals and goal-achievement strategies for each athlete. Each athlete then signs his or her contract, and the coach keeps the contracts on file. Later the coach can use the contracts to remind the athletes of their goals.

Provide for Goal Evaluation

Based on their review of the research, Locke and his associates (1981) concluded that evaluative feedback is absolutely necessary if goals are to enhance performance. Therefore, athletes must receive feedback about how present performance is related to both short- and long-range goals. In many cases feedback in the form of performance statistics such as batting average, assists, goals scored, or steals made is readily available. Other goals, however, require that coaches make special efforts to provide evaluative feedback. For instance, a coach helping an athlete control his or her temper on the field may have a manager record the number of times the player loses his or her temper in practice. Similarly, a softball coach helping outfielders attain their goal of efficiently backing up one another may have an observer record the number of times players move into correct positions after the ball is hit. In Chapter 17, the authors suggest that the sport psychologist trying to help an athlete become more aware of his or her negative thoughts might have the athlete put a box of paper clips in a pocket; then during practice the athlete transfers one paper clip at a time to another pocket for each negative thought.

Provide Support for Goals

A goal-setting program will not succeed unless it is supported by those individuals who are paramount in the athlete's life. This typically includes the coach, the athlete's family, and teammates. Therefore, efforts must be made to educate these individuals as to the types of goals the athlete sets and the importance of their support in encouraging progress toward the goals. For instance, if an athlete sets performance goals as opposed to outcome goals but significant others in the athlete's life only stress the outcome of the game or match, it is unlikely that performance goals will change behavior. Simply stated, significant others must understand the goal-setting process and support it!

Set Group Goals

Although the bulk of sport psychologists' attention has focused on individual athlete goals, Widmeyer and Ducharme (1997) emphasized the need to set group goals. A particularly important point these authors make is that understanding group goals involves more than knowing individual athlete's goals. The group task must be clearly specified along with the process for achieving group goals. When setting group goals, long-term team objectives should be identified, clear sequences of short- and long-term goals specified, team goal progress assessed, progress toward group goals rewarded, and team confidence fostered in group goals. All team members should have input into the team goal-setting process.

Dawson, Bray, and Widmeyer (2002) also have recently shown that when setting group goals, the process involves more than setting collective goals. In contrast, they found evidence for four types of goals on any team: (1) an individual member's goals for self (e.g., be the leading scorer on the team); (2) an individual's goal for the team (e.g., qualify for post season play by finishing in the top half of the league); (3) the group's goals (e.g., win the league title); and (4) the group's goal for the individual member (e.g., lead the team in assists). They also showed that individual goals and expectations might differ from those generated by the collective. For example, one athlete might see his role as the point scorer on the team while the team sees him as an assist leader. Therefore, it is of the utmost importance that coaches and team leaders discuss and integrate individual goals with team goals. Role clarification and definition are critical if effective team performance is to result.

A Goal-Setting System for Coaches

Goal-setting research and guidelines provide coaches with the information necessary for implementing goal-setting techniques with athletes. To be successful in implementing goal-setting procedures, however, coaches must develop and employ a goal-setting system. Botterill (1983) has outlined the essentials of such a system in detail. Of the many elements Botterill discusses, three seem paramount and can be incorporated into a three-phase goal-setting system: (1) the planning phase, (2) the meeting phase, and (3) the follow-up/evaluation phase.

The Planning Phase

Coaches will be ineffective if they attempt to set goals without first spending considerable time planning them. Before discussing goals with athletes, for instance, coaches must identify individual and team needs. These needs may focus on any number of areas such as player fitness, individual skills, team skills, playing time, sportsmanship, and enjoyment.

Following this needs analysis, coaches must identify potential team and individual goals. Most coaches can identify a large number of potential goals for their athletes, so it is important for them to consider how likely it is that their athletes will agree to and accomplish the goals. In doing so, coaches should consider the athletes' long-range goals, individual potential, commitment, and opportunity for practice. Finally, coaches must begin to consider possible strategies that they can use to help athletes achieve their goals. For example, a segment of each practice could be devoted to the accomplishment of identified goals, or extra practices could be held.

In essence, goal setting involves commitment and effort on the part of coaches as well as athletes. Therefore, coaches must be ready to initiate the goal-setting process with well-planned assessments of their athletes' abilities and established priorities.

The Meeting Phase

Once coaches have considered individual athlete and team needs, they should schedule goal-setting meetings. The first of these meetings should include the entire team. At the first meeting, coaches should convey basic goal-setting information (e.g., the value of setting goals, areas in which to set goals, types of goals to set, the importance of performance and process goals) and ask the athletes to think about their general objectives for participation, as well as specific team and individual goals. Coaches must then give the athletes time to reflect on their reasons for participation and to formulate potential goals.

A few days after the initial meeting, a second meeting should be held for the purpose of discussing some of the athletes' goals. It is especially important to examine goals in respect to their importance, specificity, and realistic nature. It is also desirable to examine possible strategies for achieving these goals.

In most cases it will be impossible to set specific goals for each athlete during these initial group meetings. Therefore, coaches must also hold a number of meetings with individual athletes and small subgroup meetings (e.g., forwards, centers, and guards in basketball). In these meetings individual goals should be recorded, specific strategies for achieving these goals identified, and goal evaluation procedures determined. Before and after practice are often the most effective times for holding such meetings.

The Follow-Up/Evaluation Phase

As previously stated, goal setting will not be effective unless evaluative feedback is provided to athletes. Moreover, recent research shows that public postings and oral feedback are critical for goal success. Unfortunately, because of the hectic nature of the season, this is often forgotten. It is therefore a good idea to schedule goal evaluation meetings throughout the season. At these meetings, subgroups of athletes should discuss their goals and progress made toward achieving them and reevaluate unrealistic goals or goals that cannot be achieved because of injury or sickness.

Finally, to facilitate goal follow-up and evaluation, coaches should develop systematic ways of providing feedback. Figure 13-2 contains such a system for the sport of basketball. Prior to the season, the coach prints goal-achievement cards that are completed by the athlete during the preseason or seasonal meetings. These cards contain places for the athletes to rate their present skills, identify specific goals, describe goal achievement strategies, and develop goal evaluation schedules. In addition, performance evaluation cards are printed (see Figure 13-2) and

Goal Achievement Card—Basketball

Name B. Jones					Date 9-27-04		
Position Forward					Years Experience 2		

Skill–Activity	Strong	Average	Needs improvement	Specific goal	Strategy	Target date
Shooting				To correctly execute 8 out of 10 jump shots from the 8' to 10' range	Shoot 4 sets of 10 jump shots before practice every day	
lay-ups	✓					Oct. 27
jump shots			✓			
free throws		✓				
Ball handling		✓				
Rebounding	✓					

Performance Evaluation Card—Basketball

Name B. Jones		Date 12-4-04
Position Forward		Game 3

Skill–Activity	Available statistics/Coach performance rating (0–100%)	Comments
Overall offensive play	80%	
Overall defensive play	94%	
Shooting	70%	Jump shot release ball at peak of jump
lay-ups	2 for 2	
jump shots	2 for 6	
free throws	3 for 4	
Ball handling	90%	
turnovers	1	
Rebounding	90%	

Figure 13-2 **Sample goal-achievement and performance evaluation cards for the sport of basketball**

used to evaluate performance on a percentage scale (0% = poor; 100% = excellent). The evaluation cards are completed after various competitions and, when combined with other available statistics, serve as feedback for weekly goal follow-up meetings. Although written in the vernacular of the coach, this goal-setting system can also be used by sport psychologists as they work with athletes on goal setting. The suggestions are equally appropriate for goals in the physical and mental skills domains, but they may need to be somewhat modified for sport psychologists working with an individual rather than the entire team.

Common Problems in Setting Goals

Goal setting is not a difficult psychological skill to use. However, it would be a misconception to think that problems do not arise when setting goals. Some of the more frequently encountered problems include attempting to set too many goals too soon, failing to recognize individual differences in athletes, setting goals that are too general, failing to modify unrealistic goals, failing to set performance and process goals as opposed to outcome goals, understanding the time and commitment needed to implement a goal-setting program, setting only technique-related goals, and failing to create a supportive goal-setting atmosphere. Each of these problems is addressed in the next sections.

Setting Too Many Goals Too Soon

A natural mistake that occurs when one first implements a goal-setting system is to set too many goals too soon. For example, it is not uncommon for coaches and athletes to set 5 or 10 specific goals. This usually has negative results. The athletes have so many individual goals that they cannot properly monitor performance, or if they do monitor performance, they find the record keeping to be overwhelming and lose interest. A more effective approach is to prioritize goals and focus on accomplishing the one or two most important ones. When these goals

are achieved, the athletes then focus on the next most important prioritized goals. As the athletes become more experienced in goal setting, they also learn to handle greater numbers of goals more efficiently. In essence, coaches and sport psychologists must first teach their athletes how to set and accomplish goals so that later on the athletes can set goals independently.

Failing to Recognize Individual Differences

Not all athletes will be excited about setting goals, and some may even have negative attitudes about doing so. Coaches and sport psychologists must expect this and not overreact. *Forcing* athletes to set goals is ineffective, for individual commitment is needed. Rather, expose all of the athletes to goal setting, and then work with those who show interest. Over time, their success will convince other less committed athletes to begin setting goals.

The importance of recognizing individual differences when setting goals with athletes was recently demonstrated in an investigation by Lambert, Moore, and Dixon (1999). In a study of female gymnasts it was found that the most effective type of goal setting depended on the participant's locus of control. Specifically, gymnasts characterized by an internal locus of control (those who felt they could control what happened to them) spent more time on task when they set their own goals. In contrast, external locus of control gymnasts (those who felt they had little control over what happened to them) responded better to coach-set goals. Hence, goal-setting effectiveness was dependent on the gymnast's personality.

An especially important individual difference factor to consider when setting goals with athletes is the individual's goal perspective (Duda, 1992). High ego-oriented athletes base their success/failure competence evaluations on how they perform relative to other individuals and tend to focus on outcome goals. In contrast, high task-oriented athletes base their competence evaluations on how they perform relative to their own previous performances and tend to focus on performance goals. Thus, athletes differing in their goal perspectives may adopt different goals. Unfortunately, only one study (Tenenbaum, Spence, & Christensen, 1999) has examined this issue and definitive results were not evident. Special efforts then need to be made to get ego-oriented individuals to focus on performance and process goals as opposed to outcome goals. Ego-oriented athletes with low confidence will often set unrealistically high or low goals as well.

Setting Goals That Are Too General

Throughout this chapter, the emphasis has been on the need for setting specific, measurable goals. Unfortunately, this does not always occur. Inexperienced goal setters will often set goals that are too general. Improving one's first serve in tennis, executing a better Yamashita vault in gymnastics, and lessening the frequency of negative thoughts are too vague. These goals are more effectively stated as increasing the number of good first serves from 50% to 55% in tennis, improving the Yamashita vault by sticking the landing 8 out of 10 times, and reducing negative thoughts to five or less during each practice session. When stating goals, always ask, "How can we make this goal measurable and specific?"

Failing to Modify Unrealistic Goals

In his extensive 5-month study of goal setting, Burton (1989) found that competitive collegiate swimmers had problems readjusting goals once they were set. Although the swimmers had little difficulty raising their goals once they were achieved, a number of athletes failed to lower goals that became unrealistic because of illness or injury. Coaches must recognize this problem and continually emphasize the appropriateness of lowering goals when necessary.

Failing to Set Process and Performance Goals

The work of Martens (1987), Burton (1984, 1989), and Filby et al. (1999) has demonstrated the value of setting performance and process goals as opposed to outcome goals. For too many athletes, however, winning or outcome goals are the only worthy goals. This is psychologically destructive and illogical but occurs because of the tremendous emphasis Americans place on winning. Coaches must be aware of this problem and continually emphasize the attainment of performance and process goals. For instance, coaches must continually remind athletes that great performances will typically lead to the best possible outcomes. Finally, coaches must realize that changing their athletes' perception of the importance of outcome versus performance/process goals may take a long-term effort.

Understanding the Time Commitment Needed to Implement a Goal-Setting Program

It is not uncommon for a coach to become interested in goal setting and to begin to implement a goal-setting program with his or her athletes during the preseason or early season. However, as the season progresses, less and less time is spent on goal setting. By the end of the season the goal-setting program is all but forgotten.

Like other psychological skills, goal setting takes time to implement. It must be recognized that a good deal of commitment on the part of the coach is needed. When planning your goal-setting program, think about the busiest time of your team's season and how much time is available to commit to goal setting. It is much better to devote 20 minutes a week to goal setting throughout the season and follow through on that plan than to say you will devote 20 minutes a day to goal setting and not follow through on it. Similarly, time spent in preseason planning and organization (e.g., mass-producing goal-achievement cards and goal-evaluation forms) makes the goal-setting process much more efficient and realistic to implement.

Finally, consider program efficiency when organizing your program. One collegiate basketball coach, for example, simply had her athletes write down a practice goal on index cards for the next day's practice. The coaching staff would then evaluate and provide feedback relative to these practice goals during each postpractice cool-down period. This was a time-efficient yet effective program that was easy to implement for the entire season.

Setting Only Technique-Related Goals

When setting goals with athletes, it is very easy to focus all of one's attention on technique-related goals (e.g., shooting statistics, faster running times). However, as previously mentioned, there are a number of other areas in which the performer may want to use goal setting. For example, a high school volleyball coach who was having trouble with his team's cohesion found it useful to have several key players set goals of giving sincere positive feedback to teammates at least five times per practice, and the team manager recorded the number of positive remarks made during practice. Similarly, an injured runner set specific goals relative to the number of times per week she would practice imagery. Finally, a football coach whose team seemed unenthusiastic and burned out at the end of a long season had considerable success asking the players to identify what elements of football were most fun for them (e.g., lineman throwing and catching the football) and then setting team goals to incorporate specified amounts of fun activities in every practice.

As I discussed earlier, a coach may also adopt a life skills approach by helping an athlete who has learned to set goals in the sport domain (e.g., improve free throw shooting percentage by shooting 20 extra shots a day) to transfer this goal-setting ability to other life contexts (e.g., improve his or her math grades by setting a goal of studying 30 additional minutes a day).

Failing to Create a Supportive Goal-Setting Atmosphere

To reiterate, coaches and sport psychologists cannot set goals for their athletes or force them to participate in the goal-setting process. The athletes must be self-motivated and committed to the program. For this reason, the goal-setting leader needs to create a supportive goal-setting atmosphere, and in creating such an atmosphere, communication style is critical. Coaches and sport psychologists must act as facilitators of goal-setting discussions, not as dictators (Botterill, 1983). They must share limitations with athletes and identify unrealistic goals, while simultaneously avoiding pessimistic remarks and putdowns. In essence, the leader must adopt a positive communication style that includes good listening skills, a sincere orientation, and a positive approach.

Summary

This chapter has provided strong empirical and experiential support for the utility of using goal setting in helping athletes attain personal growth and peak performance. Goals are effective because they influence psychological states such as self-confidence, direct attention to important aspects of the task, mobilize effort, increase persistence, and foster the development of new learning strategies. A number of recognized guidelines should be followed when setting goals with athletes. These include setting behaviorally measurable goals, difficult yet realistic goals, short-range as well as long-range goals, performance/process goals as well as outcome goals, practice and competition goals, and positive as opposed to negative goals. Equally important guidelines are identifying target dates for attaining goals, identifying goal-achievement strategies, recording goals once they have been identified, providing goal evaluation procedures, providing for goal support, and setting group goals. Lastly, common problems that arise when setting goals must be recognized. These include setting too many goals too soon, failing to recognize individual differences, setting goals that are too general, failing to modify unrealistic goals, failing to set process and performance goals, not understanding the time and commitment needed to implement a goal-setting program, setting only technique-related goals, and failing to create a supportive goal-setting atmosphere. These problems can be easily avoided or controlled if they are recognized at the onset of the goal-setting process.

Like other psychological skills, goal setting is not a magic formula that guarantees success. Goal setting is a tool, a very effective tool, that when combined with hard work and discipline can help coaches, athletes, and sport psychologists reap the fruits of personal athletic growth and peak performance. It is highly recommended, then, that coaches and sport psychologists at all levels of competition engage in goal setting with their athletes.

Study Questions

1. Define what a goal is and differentiate between the following types of goals: (a) subjective, (b) general objective, (c) specific objective, (d) outcome, (e) performance, and (f) process goals.

2. Briefly describe Locke and colleagues' (1981) mechanistic, Burton's (1983) cognitive, and Garland's (1985) cognitive mediation explanations for the relationship between goal setting and performance.

3. Describe what is meant by saying life skill goal-setting programs teach for goal-setting transfer.

4. Think of your own sport and physical activity involvement and identify two goals you have set in the past. Evaluate your two goals relative to the 12 goal-setting guidelines presented in this chapter.

5. Describe the three phases of a goal-setting system for coaches and sport psychologists.

6. Indicate why failing to set performance/process goals is a common problem when setting goals with athletes.

7. Is it easier to adjust goals upward or downward? Explain.

8. Give an example of goal setting that is not technique related.

9. Four types of group goals have been set: individual group members' goals for themselves; the group's goals for individual members; the group's goals for the group; and individual members' goals for the group. Imagine that you are a member of a basketball team and provide an example of each type of goal. For your team to be effective, how best should these goals be related?

10. How can a coach create a supportive goal-setting atmosphere?

References

Anderson, D. C., Crowell, D. R., Doman, M., & Howard, G. S. (1988). Performance posting, goal setting, and activity-contingent praise as applied to a university hockey team, *Journal of Applied Psychology, 73,* 87–95.

Bell, K. F. (1983). *Championship thinking: The athlete's guide to winning performance in all sports.* Englewood Cliffs, NJ: Prentice Hall.

Botterill, C. (1977, September). *Goal setting and performance on an endurance task*. Paper presented at the Canadian Psychomotor Learning and Sport Psychology Conference, Banff, Alberta.

Botterill, C. (1983). Goal setting for athletes with examples from hockey. In G. L. Martin & D. Hrycaiko (Eds.), *Behavior modification and coaching: Principles, procedures, and research* (pp. 67–85). Springfield, IL: Thomas.

Brosbst, B., & Ward, P. H. (2002). Effects of public posting, goal setting, and oral feedback on the skills of female soccer players. *Journal of Applied Behavior Analysis, 35,* 247–257.

Burton, D. (1983). *Evaluation of goal setting training on selected cognitions and performance of collegiate swimmers*. Unpublished doctoral dissertation, University of Illinois, Urbana.

Burton, D. (1984, February). Goal setting: A secret to success. *Swimming World,* 25–29.

Burton, D. (1989). Winning isn't everything: Examining the impact of performance goals on collegiate swimmers' cognitions and performance. *The Sport Psychologist, 3,* 105–132.

Burton, D., & Naylor, S. (2002). The Jekyll/Hyde nature of goals: Revisiting and updating goal-setting in sport. In T. S. Horn (Ed.), *Advances in sport psychology* (2nd ed., pp. 459–499). Champaign, IL: Human Kinetics.

Burton, D., Naylor, S., & Holliday, B. (2002). Goal setting in sport. In R. N. Singer, H. A. Hausenblas, & C. M. Janelle (Eds.), *Handbook of sport psychology* (2nd ed., pp. 497–528). New York: John Wiley & Sons.

Burton, D., Weinberg, R., Yukelson, D., & Weigand, D. (1998). The goal effectiveness paradox in sport: Examining the goal practices of collegiate athletes. *The Sport Psychologist, 12,* 404–418.

Carron, A. V. (1984). *Motivation: Implications for coaching and teaching*. London, ON: Sports Dynamics.

Danish, S. J., Mash, J. M., Howard, C. W., Curl, S. J., Meyer, A. L., Owens, S. S., & Kendall, K. (1992). *Going for the goal leader manual*. Richmond: Virginia Commonwealth University: Department of Psychology.

Danish, S. J., Nellen, V. C., & Owens, S. S. (1996). Teaching life skills through sport: Community-based programs for adolescents. In J. K. Van Raalte & B. W. Brewer (Eds.), *Exploring sport and exercise psychology* (pp. 205–225). Washington, DC: American Psychological Association.

Danish, S. J., Petitpas, A., & Hale, B. (1995). Psychological interventions: A life development model. In S. Murphy (Ed.), *Clinical sport psychology* (pp. 19–38). Champaign, IL: Human Kinetics.

Dawson, K. A., Bray, S. R., & Widmeyer, W. N. (2002). Goal setting by intercollegiate sport teams and athletes. *Avante, 8*(2), 14–23.

Duda, J. L. (1992). Motivation in sport settings: A goal perspective approach. In G. C. Roberts (Ed.), *Motivation in sport and exercise* (pp. 57–92). Champaign, IL: Human Kinetics.

Filby, W. C. D., Maynard, I. W., Graydon, J. K. (1999). The effect of multiple-goal strategies on performance outcomes in training and competing. *Journal of Applied Sport Psychology, 11,* 230–246.

Garland, H. (1985). A cognitive mediation theory of task goals and human performance. *Motivation and Emotion, 9,* 345–367.

Gould, D. (1983). Developing psychological skills in young athletes. In N. L. Wood (Ed.), *Coaching science update.* Ottawa, ON: Coaching Association of Canada.

Gould, D., Tammen, V., Murphy, S., & May, J. (1989). An examination of U.S. Olympic sport psychology consultants and the services they provide. *The Sport Psychologist, 3,* 300–312.

Hardy, L., Jones, G., & Gould, D. (1996). *Understanding psychological preparation for sport: Theory and practice of elite performers.* Chichester, UK: Wiley.

Harris, D. V., & Harris, B. L. (1984). *The athlete's guide to sports psychology: Mental skills for physical people.* New York: Leisure Press.

Kyllo, L. B., & Landers, D. M. (1995). Goal setting in sport and exercise: A research synthesis to resolve the controversy. *Journal of Sport and Exercise Psychology, 17,* 117–137.

Lambert, S. M., Moore, D. W., & Dixon, R. S. (1999). Gymnasts in training: The differential effects of self- and coach-set goals as a function of locus of control. *Journal of Applied Sport Psychology, 11,* 72–82.

Locke, E. A., & Latham, G. P. (1985). The application of goal setting to sports. *Journal of Sport Psychology, 7,* 205–222.

Locke, E. A., & Latham, G. P. (1990). *A theory of goal setting and task performance.* Englewood Cliffs, NJ: Prentice Hall.

Locke, E. A., Shaw, K. N., Saari, L. M., & Latham, G. P. (1981). Goal setting and task performance. *Psychological Bulletin, 90,* 125–152.

Martens, R. (1987). *Coaches guide to sport psychology.* Champaign, IL: Human Kinetics.

McClements, J. (1982). Goal setting and planning for mental preparations. In L. Wankel & R. B. Wilberg (Eds.), Psychology of sport and motor behavior: Research and practice. *Proceedings of the Annual Conference of the Canadian Society for Psychomotor Learning and Sport Psychology* (pp. 165–172). Edmonton: University of Alberta.

McClements, J. D., & Botterill, C. B. (1979). Goal setting in shaping of future performance of athletes. In P. Klavora & J. Daniel (Eds.), *Coach, athlete and the sport psychologist* (pp. 199–210). Champaign, IL: Human Kinetics.

Mento, A. J., Steel, R. P., & Karren, R. J. (1987). A meta-analytic study of the effects of goal setting on task performance: 1966–1984. *Organizational Behavior and Human Decision Processes, 39,* 52–83.

O'Block, F. R., & Evans, F. H. (1984). Goal setting as a motivational technique. In J. M. Silva & R. S. Weinberg (Eds.), *Psychological foundations of sport* (pp. 188–196). Champaign, IL: Human Kinetics.

Orlick, T. (1990). *In pursuit of excellence* (2nd ed.). Champaign, IL: Human Kinetics.

Orlick, T., & Partington, J. (1988). Mental links to excellence. *The Sport Psychologist, 2,* 105–130.

Swain, A. B. J., & Jones, G. (1995). Goal attainment scaling: Effects of goal setting interventions on selected subcomponents on basketball performance. *Research Quarterly for Exercise & Sport, 66,* 51–63.

Tenenbaum, G., Spence, R., & Christensen, S. (1999). The effect of goal difficulty and goal orientation on running performance in young female athletes. *Australian Journal of Psychology, 51*(1), 6–11.

Tubbs, M. E. (1991). Goal setting: A meta-analytic examination of the empirical evidence. *Journal of Applied Psychology, 71*, 474–483.

Wanlin, C. M., Hrycaiko, D. W., Martin, G. L., & Mahon, M. (1997). The effects of a goal-setting package on the performance of speed skaters. *Journal of Applied Sport Psychology, 9*, 212–228.

Ward, P., & Carnes, M. (2002). Effects of posting self-set goals on collegiate football players' skill execution during practice and games. *Journal of Applied Behavior Analysis, 35*, 1–12.

Weinberg, R. S. (1994). Goal setting and performance in sport and exercise settings: A synthesis and critique. *Medicine & Science in Sport & Exercise, 26*, 469–477.

Weinberg, R. S., Burton, D., Yukelson, D., & Weigand, D. (1993). Goal setting in competitive sport: An exploratory investigation of practices of collegiate athletes. *The Sport Psychologist, 7*, 275–289.

Weinberg, R., Burton, D., Yukelson, D., & Weigand, D. (2000). Perceived goal setting practices of Olympic athletes: An exploratory investigation. *The Sport Psychologist, 14*, 279–295.

Weinberg, R., Butt, J., Knight, B., & Perritt, N. (2001). Collegiate coaches' perceptions of their goal-setting practices: A qualitative investigation. *Journal of Applied Sport Psychology, 13*, 374–398.

Weinberg, R. S., Stitcher, T., & Richardson, P. (1994). Effects of seasonal goal setting on lacrosse performance. *The Sport Psychologist, 8*, 166–175.

Widmeyer, W. N., & Ducharme, K. (1997). Team building through team goal setting. *Journal of Applied Sport Psychology, 9*, 61–72.

14

Arousal–Performance Relationships

Daniel M. Landers, *Arizona State University*
Shawn M. Arent, *Arizona State University*

Most athletes at some time or another have experienced an unexpected breakdown in their performance. Consider, for a moment, the following illustrative examples. A U.S. Olympic weight lifter in international competition surprisingly deviates from his customary preparatory routine before a clean and jerk and totally forgets to chalk his hands. As might be expected, the lift is missed. A gymnast preparing for a high flyaway dismount from the still rings suddenly focuses on self-doubts concerning his ability to perform the stunt without the presence of a spotter. These doubts, coupled with an increased fatigue level brought about by a long routine, cause him to freeze and release the rings prematurely. Finally, a sprinter who appears lackadaisical and lethargic during precompetition warm-up records one of her worst 100m times.

These are just a few examples of what athletes and coaches usually refer to as lack of concentration, "choking" under pressure, or failure to get the athlete "up" for competition. Sport competition can generate much anxiety and worry, which in turn can affect physiological and thought processes so dramatically that performance often deteriorates. In your own athletic or coaching experience, you have probably perceived a racing heartbeat, a dry mouth, butterflies in your stomach, cold and clammy hands, trembling muscles, or an inability to clearly focus thoughts. In these situations you may have told yourself that you were "too tight" or tense or that you "couldn't think straight." Common expressions like these often prompt practical questions concerning whether the athlete should be fired up as much as possible or relaxed as much as possible before an important competition. Or perhaps there is some in-between state that should be sought.

These concerns are generally related to the topic of motivation and, more specifically, to the concept of arousal. Understanding arousal and its effects on athletic performance, finding ways to estimate the arousal demands of a particular sport, and assessing arousal levels of individual athletes form the focus of this chapter. In the first section we will describe arousal and its effects and then outline a model for understanding its influence on athletic performance. In the second section we will describe the major hypotheses and research evidence for the arousal–performance relationship. Finally, in the third section we will describe a method whereby the coach or sport psychologist can estimate the optimal arousal level for a specific sport skill and for specific athletes.

The Nature of Arousal

Before considering how arousal is related to performance, it is necessary to clarify the nature of the arousal construct. This will be done by first defining arousal, followed by a discussion of its origin and how it is generated. Finally, various techniques for measuring arousal will be presented.

Defining Arousal and Related Constructs

In the psychological literature behavior is viewed as varying on only two dimensions—intensity and direction. The term *arousal* is used synonymously with the term *activation*, and these terms both refer to the intensity level of behavior (Duffy, 1957). Both of these terms also refer to a nondirective generalized bodily activation or arousal dimension. According to Malmo (1959), **arousal** consists of neural excitation on a continuum ranging from a comatose state to a state of extreme excitement as might be manifested in a panic attack. Conceptually, Duffy (1962) argues that any given point on this continuum is determined by "the extent of release of potential energy, stored in the tissues of the organism, as shown in activity or response" (p. 17). For our purposes, arousal will be viewed as an energizing function that is responsible for harnessing the body's resources for intense and vigorous activity (Sage, 1984).

Using Martens's (1974) analogy, the energy produced by increases in arousal can be likened to the engine of an automobile which, when the car is in neutral or park, can be varied along a revolutions per minute (rpm) continuum without affecting the direction (forward or reverse) of the car. The nondirectional term *arousal* has no more positive or negative connotations than the rpm continuum described here. However, like the human, when the car is in motion and the speed is too fast for the road conditions, inappropriate levels of energy in the automobile (rpm) can disrupt efficient driving performance. The ideal rpm intensity should match the requirements for the desired task outcome (e.g., quick acceleration) to produce the greatest performance efficiency. Sometimes, however, this is not the case. The engine may be racing with the car in a forward gear but with the emergency brake on. This unnatural state is akin to what we will refer to later as a **performance disregulation,** in which extraneous influences (e.g., the brake or anxiety brought about by negative, self-defeating thought processes) interfere with the natural coordinative action of the skill being performed. The human engine refers to both the activation of the brain and the innervation of different physiological systems. Without the proper arousal athletes may simply be left "spinning their wheels."

Unlike the car engine, our human engine cannot be turned off—at least not while we are alive! Even as you sleep, there is electrical activity in your brain as well as small amounts in the muscles. Thus, arousal is a natural, ongoing state. However, when arousal levels become extremely high, you may experience unpleasant emotional reactions associated with the autonomic nervous system. This maladaptive condition is often referred to as *stress* or *state anxiety* or *distress* (Selye, 1950). Although anxiety, stress, and arousal are related concepts, they are not conceptually the same (Figure 14-1). There has been considerable confusion in the research literature resulting from these terms being used interchangeably. Recall that arousal is nondirective generalized bodily arousal-activation, and anxiety is an unpleasant emotional state.

According to Spielberger (1975), the condition of anxiety is an emotional state or reaction

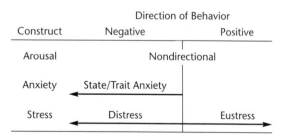

Figure 14-1 **Direction of behavior for arousal, anxiety, and stress**

characterized by (a) varying intensity; (b) variation over time; (c) the presence of recognizable unpleasant feelings of intensity, preoccupation, disturbance, and apprehension; and (d) a simultaneous pronounced activation of the vegetative (autonomic) nervous system. Like anxiety, stress also identifies the direction the behavior takes. Selye (1950) maintains that stress can be either positive (called *eustress*) or negative (called *distress*) in direction. In the psychological literature distress and anxiety both describe the kind of negative emotional state Spielberger (1975) is referring to in his definition. Thus, anxiety and distress can occur when arousal levels are high, but they do not have to occur at higher levels of arousal if athletes maintain control over all aspects of their performance. Thus, these terms are not conceptually and operationally the same as arousal.

Eustress is associated with one's ability to use stress in a constructive way that is beneficial to performance. Each of the theories presented here has something to say about the amount of arousal that may be conducive to producing eustress. Levels of anxiety and distress are influenced by perceptions of certainty/uncertainty and whether one can control the situation at hand. When there is total assurance of being successful, the competition is often taken for granted and the resulting underaroused state is maladaptive for effective performance. Basically, we know that some degree of uncertainty is necessary to increase arousal and motivation, but too much uncertainty can be anxiety producing. Thus, the anxiety response associated with higher states of arousal is typically related to an athlete's perceived inability to deal with the specific situation (e.g., task difficulty or demands). As we will see in a later section of this chapter, anxiety reactions to competition can result in ineffective performance, faulty decision making, and inappropriate perception. Helping athletes harness arousal so that it will not become an uncontrollable anxiety response is one of the major tasks performed by sport psychologists. It is important to bear in mind that

sport psychologists do not seek to make people unemotional zombies but instead attempt to teach skills that will enable athletes to better control arousal and, thereby, more effectively cope with anxiety.

Origin of Arousal States

The structures for controlling arousal are located in the brain and primarily involve the cortex, reticular formation, the hypothalamus, and the limbic system. These centers interact with the adrenal medulla and the somatic and autonomic systems to determine overall arousal. We can demonstrate the integration of these different systems in an athletic situation by means of the following example.

A field hockey goalie sits in the dressing room minutes before an important match. She *begins to worry* about an upcoming game, *which happens to be the* biggest game of the season. These thoughts lead to anxiety about her performance. Her worrying may not be realistic, but to her body that does not matter. Technically speaking, as her worrying ensued messages were being sent by a quick route to the amygdala, and another message by a longer route to the thalamus and then on to the cerebral cortex (Gorman, 2002). The amygdala, an almond-shaped cluster of cells in the midbrain, reacts quickly by activating physiological responses that are associated with fear, worry, and threat. Even before the source of the fear can be verified by higher brain centers (i.e., cerebral cortex), the amygdala activates the sympathetic nervous system causing the adrenal medulla to pump the catecholamines epinephrine and norepinephrine (also called adrenaline and noradrenaline) into the bloodstream (Gorman, 2002; Krahenbuhl, 1975). The rapid increase in these catecholamines and cortisol prepares her body and mind for an emergency "fight or flight" situation. Autonomic nervous system measures such as heart rate, blood pressure, and breathing begin to increase, and muscles in general begin to tighten. The blood supply begins to be shunted away from the digestive system

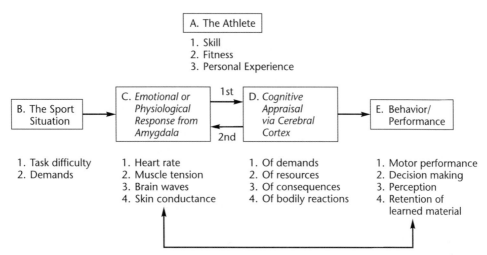

Figure 14-2 **A model illustrating factors that affect the arousal–performance relationship**

and redirected to the larger muscles of the arms and legs through vasodilation. While all of these physiological reactions are already underway, the cerebral cortex begins to receive information on the worry or fear that this athlete is experiencing. The cerebral cortex analyzes this information to determine whether or not a threat exists. If through analysis, the situation the athlete is in is not perceived to be a threat, the prefrontal cortex sends out an "all-clear signal" to the amygdala and the physiological responses described above are terminated. By contrast, if the cerebral cortex perceives the situation the athlete currently faces as a threat, then a fear label is attached to it and this is sent to the amygdala. In this case, the amygdala continues to send out a "fear alarm" and the already initiated physiological responses continue or may even increase. Having conscious awareness, she may interpret these changes as further support for her lack of ability and readiness, leading to a debilitating cycle of worry and physiological disruption of homeostasis (i.e., disregulation). The hockey goalie is now in an overly aroused or anxious state. Needless to say, we would not expect her to perform well in this condition.

How Arousal Is Generated

From the foregoing example, we can see that the athlete's fleeting self-doubt was the starting point of a chain reaction that ultimately led to an overaroused state. This chain reaction along with the host of other factors involved in the arousal–performance relationship is outlined in Figure 14-2.

Our hockey goalie had a self-doubt that led to physiological and subsequent cognitive appraisal that led her to conclude that her capabilities did not meet the demands of the upcoming game. This combination of an important meaningful event and doubts about her ability was responsible for generating anxiety and worry. Whether this process starts with an internal thought or an external stimulus, the amygdala triggers a physiological reaction in advance of full-fledged cognitive appraisal (Gorman, 2002). Once cognitive appraisal is initiated and the threat or doubt is confirmed, physiological reactions described in Figure 14-2 (see entries 1–4 under D) are heightened. When these physiological reactions are heightened, she begins to interpret the feelings as well (see entry 4 under D). Not knowing how to cope with the physiological reactions can create even more worry and appre-hension (see entries 1–4 under D). Notice also that, once performance begins, aspects of the athlete's behavior (see entries 1–4 under E) are fed back for cognitive appraisal (see entries 1–4 under D) that may further intensify anxiety. As we will see later, this process can be influenced by individual difference variables such as skill level, personality, physical and psychological fit-ness, and competitive experience.

Measurement of Arousal

Because arousal affects so many bodily func-tions, it appears to be an easy construct to mea-sure. Unfortunately, this is not the case. We will discuss three types of arousal measurement and two types of anxiety measurement and high-light the advantages and disadvantages of each (Table 14-1).

Physiological measures. In sport psychology research much frustration has resulted from the lack of consistent agreement among different physiological variables and questionnaire mea-sures. However, this poor correspondence has occurred because many investigators believed similar results would be found with a physio-logical arousal-activation measure and an anxi-ety questionnaire measure. It would not be expected that nondirective physiological mea-sures of generalized bodily activation or arousal state would necessarily be consistent with ques-tionnaire measures of negative emotional states like anxiety.

A more important concern is the low corre-lation found among physiological measures explained by Lacey, Bateman, and Van Lehn's (1953) principle of "autonomic response stereo-typy." For example, in the same stressful situa-tion, athlete A might display an elevated heart rate, and athlete B might show an increase in blood pressure. This principle suggests that averaging one physiological variable (e.g., heart rate) across the group may conceal individual arousal reactions.

To overcome this problem, Duffy (1962) has recommended the use of multiple physiological

measures as an index of the arousal response. From these multiple measures, if athlete A is found to be a heart rate responder when exposed to stres-sors like competition, this measure would be sin-gled out for comparison of athlete A in conditions varying in levels of perceived stress. By using each person's most responsive autonomic measure, greater differentiation can be achieved and thus more meaningful information can be gleaned.

The current view concerning physiological measures is that they are far more complex than first thought. However, with increased under-standing of physiological processes and the con-tinuing trend of cheaper, more sophisticated equipment, physiological measures have consid-erable potential as reliable indicators of the arousal response.

Biochemical measures. The adrenal gland is responsible for the release of epinephrine and norepinephrine into the bloodstream in times of stress. Also, a variety of corticosteroids enter the blood during high arousal. Increases in amines or cortisol have been examined primarily by analyz-ing either the blood or urine. Blood analysis usu-ally involves drawing blood from the athlete by syringe or catheter. The analysis is complex and requires sophisticated equipment. Another disad-vantage is that drawing blood can be traumatic or stressful to some athletes, thus confounding the results of the study. Urine analysis is less invasive but suffers from the same cost and time disadvan-tages as blood analysis. Furthermore, there is a dif-ference in the usefulness of the analyses due to the speed at which the hormones of interest show up in the blood or urine. At this point it is also unclear how accurately serum measures reflect the brain's overall hormonal levels.

Questionnaires. Many questionnaires have been used to measure arousal, but unfortunately most of these are anxiety measures and not arousal mea-sures. Only two questionnaires are specifically designed to assess nondirective generalized bodily activation, or arousal. These are the Activation-Deactivation Adjective Checklist (AD-ACL, Thayer, 1986) and the Somatic Perception Questionnaire (SPQ, Landy & Stern, 1971). The AD-ACL has been

Table 14-1 **Some Common Physiological, Biochemical, and Questionnaire Measures of Arousal and Anxiety**

Measure and Description

I. Arousal Measures

   A. Physiological

   1. Central

      Electroencephalography (EEG). Changes occur in brain wave patterns from an alpha or relaxed state (8–14 Hz) to beta or a more aroused state (14–30 Hz).

   2. Automatic

      Electrical properties of the skin. This measure assesses either the amount of skin conductance or resistance to an electric current. Elevations in arousal cause increased perspiration, which increases the flow of the current.

      Heart rate. Increases in heart rate, the pattern of beats, and heart rate variability can all be indices of arousal.

      Blood pressure. Increases in blood pressure are also associated with increased arousal levels and can be measured by cannulation or by the stethoscope and pressure-cuff method.

      Muscle activity. Muscle tension can be measured by electromyography (EMG), which measures the firing rate of motor units by means of surface electrodes attached to the muscle.

   B. Biochemical

   1. Epinephrine. Epinephrine is released from the adrenal medulla during times of stress. This can be measured in the urine and blood.

   2. Norepinephrine. Also elevated during stressful activities, this catecholamine can be measured by the same techniques used to analyze epinephrine.

   3. Cortisol. This steroid hormone is released from the adrenal cortex when the organism is confronted with either physical/emotional stressors or declining blood glucose levels.

   C. Questionnaires

   1. Somatic Perception Questionnaire (Landy & Stern, 1971)

   2. Activation Deactivation Adjective Checklist (Thayer, 1967)

II. Anxiety Measures

   A. Unidimensional Questionnaires

   1. State-Trait Anxiety Inventory (Spielberger, Gorsuch, & Lushene, 1970)

   2. Sport Competition Anxiety Test (Martens, 1977)

   B. Multidimensional Questionnaires

   1. Cognitive-Somatic Anxiety Questionnaire (Schwartz, Davidson, & Goleman, 1978)

   2. Competitive State Anxiety Inventory-2 (CSAI-2); Martens, Burton, Vealey, Smith, & Bump, 1983; Martens, Burton, Vealey, Bump, & Smith, 1990)

   3. Sport Anxiety Scale (SAS; Smith, Smoll, & Schutz, 1990)

---

used in the exercise and sport literature. Unlike the SPQ, it contains two bipolar activation dimensions. Within the broader dimension of energetic arousal, which is generalized, nondirective bodily activation, the AD-ACL has two subscales of Energy (General Activation) and Tiredness (Deactivation-Sleep). The other dimension, which is a directional measure of one's mood state, consists of the subscales of Tension (High Activation) and Calmness (General Deactivation). There is some evidence that the AD-ACL yields a better assessment of global arousal-activation than do individual physiological measures (Thayer, 1967, 1970). These questionnaire measures have broader use in a variety of sport settings. They are quick and easy to administer and are less cumbersome and intrusive than most physiological measures. However, the physiological measures are less dependent on athletes' linguistic and cultural background and are also less susceptible to behavioral artifacts (e.g., halo effects, demand characteristics, social desirability).

Anxiety Measures

The majority of sport studies published on the topic of arousal contain information derived from anxiety questionnaires. As has been pointed out earlier, it is a mistake to use the terms "arousal" and "anxiety" interchangeably. Recall that arousal is considered a nondirectional energizing function, whereas anxiety is negative in direction in that it is an emotional state or reaction characterized by unpleasant feelings of intensity, preoccupation, disturbance, and apprehension. Although the constructs of arousal and anxiety may at times be highly related, arousal is conceptually and operationally not the same as anxiety, and therefore, theories based on the construct of arousal should not be replaced by anxiety-based theories (Anderson, 1990; Neiss, 1988).

Even though anxiety measures are not appropriate for examining the arousal-performance relationship, the fact that they are so prevalent in this literature warrants some discussion of these measures. Most of these *anxiety* questionnaires focus on cognitive and physiological manifestations associated with an anxiety response. Some measure cognitive and physiological responses by differentiating between them (CSAI-2, SAS), whereas others (STAI) contain cognitively and physiologically related items, but no differentiation is made between them (see Table 14-1).

Many questionnaires are designed to assess both trait and state forms of anxiety. **Trait anxiety** is a *general* predisposition to respond across many situations with high levels of anxiety. To assess trait anxiety, individuals are asked to rate how they generally feel. **State anxiety** is much more specific, referring to an individual's anxiety at a particular moment. People who are high in trait anxiety are expected to respond with higher levels of state anxiety, or situationally specific anxiety. The State-Trait Anxiety Inventory (Spielberger, Gorsuch, & Lushene, 1970) is a popular example of a well-researched questionnaire that assesses both dimensions of anxiety.

A more recent development in the construction of anxiety questionnaires is the trend toward multidimensional instruments. Three questionnaires, one non–sport specific (Schwartz, Davidson, & Goleman, 1978) and the others sport specific (Martens et al., 1983, 1990; Smith, Smoll, & Schutz, 1990), have subdivided anxiety into the components of somatic and cognitive aspects. The CSAI-2 (Martens et al., 1983, 1990) has somatic and cognitive state anxiety subscales plus a self-confidence scale. The SAS (Smith et al., 1990) has a somatic trait anxiety scale and two cognitive trait anxiety scales—one for worry and one for concentration disruption. Somatic or bodily anxiety is assessed by questions such as "How tense are the muscles in your body?" Cognitive anxiety would be indicated by affirmative responses to questions such as "Do you worry a lot?" By subdividing anxiety into its component parts, more will be understood about its nature and more effective therapies can thus be designed.

The Relationship Between Arousal and Motor Performance

In the motor behavior literature two hypotheses have been advanced to explain the relationship between arousal and performance. We will first consider the drive theory hypothesis and then the inverted-*U* hypothesis.

Drive Theory

Although this is not a view held by all psychologists, for our purposes we will equate the term *drive* with *arousal*. In other words, drive and arousal convey what we referred to earlier as the intensity dimension of behavior.

Drive theory, as modified by Spence and Spence (1966), predicts that performance (P) is a multiplicative function of habit (H) and drive (D): $P = H \times D$. The construct of habit in this formulation refers to the hierarchical order or dominance of correct or incorrect responses. According to this hypothesis, increases in arousal should enhance the probability of making the dominant responses. When performance errors are frequently made, as in the early stages of skill acquisition, the dominant responses are likely to be incorrect responses. Conversely, when performance errors are infrequent, the dominant response is said to be a correct response. Increases in arousal during initial skill acquisition impair performance, but as the skill becomes well learned, increases in arousal facilitate performance. This latter situation would be likened to a eustress state.

For example, a novice basketball player shooting free throws only sinks 3 shots out of 10; therefore, the incorrect response (a miss) is dominant. The drive theory hypothesis would predict that given greater pressure the novice player is likely to miss more than 7 shots out of 10. By contrast, the all-star basketball player may average 8 successful shots for every 10 attempted. In this case, because the dominant response is a correct response, an increase in arousal should enhance the player's chance of sinking more than 8 shots out of 10.

It is questionable whether a linear relationship between arousal and performance can be found for accuracy tasks such as free throw shooting. However, Oxendine (1984) argues that linear relationships, as depicted in Figure 14-3, do exist for gross motor activities involving strength and speed. These types of activities are typically overlearned, with strongly formed habit patterns. It seems likely, therefore, that a very high level of arousal is desirable for optimal performance in these types of gross motor skills. Support for this view comes from anecdotal evidence regarding superhuman feats performed in emergency situations in which unexpected physical strength and speed were required (e.g., a mother lifting a station wagon off her trapped child).

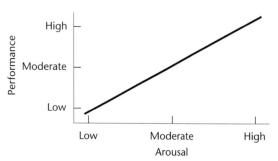

Figure 14-3 **The linear relationship between arousal and performance as suggested by drive theory**

At first glance these examples seem to provide ample evidence to support a drive theory explanation for sport skills involving strength and speed. Contrary to Oxendine's analysis, however, we would like to argue on conceptual grounds that the "fight or flight" arousal responses produced in these emergency situations are not appropriate comparisons to the sport situation. The sport setting is highly structured, often involving complex decision making and perceptual strategies in addition to the performance of a motor skill. The surge of adrenaline resulting from an emergency situation may enhance strength and speed in an uncontrolled manner, which may actually be detrimental to actual sport performances. For example, there are many instances of overaroused sprinters recording false starts in intense competition. Similarly, many superenergized weight lifters have forgotten to chalk up or have lifted the barbell in a biomechanically inefficient way in major competitions. Thus, on experiential grounds it appears that even among weight lifters and sprinters there are limits to the amount of arousal the athlete can tolerate without suffering performance decrements.

The drive theory has not fared much better when the experimental evidence from the motor behavior literature has been examined. For example, Freeman (1940) has shown that, with high levels of arousal, reaction times are slower than when arousal levels are in the moderate range. Furthermore, in other arousal-producing situations (e.g., audience effects) where the drive theory has

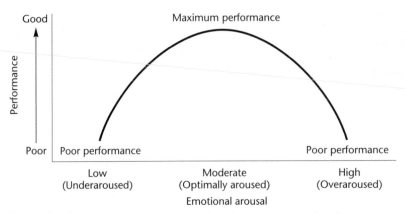

Figure 14-4 **The inverted-*U* relationship between arousal and performance**

received extensive support, it is now known that these effects were so small as to be of trivial practical significance (Bond & Titus, 1983; Landers, Snyder-Bauer, & Feltz, 1978). Thus, it appears that other hypotheses, such as the inverted-*U*, need to be considered to explain the highly complex network of skills characteristic of sport performance.

Inverted-*U* Hypothesis

The inverted-*U* relationship between arousal and performance is shown in Figure 14-4. The **inverted-*U* hypothesis** predicts that as arousal increases from drowsiness to alertness there is a progressive increase in performance efficiency. However, once arousal continues to increase beyond alertness to a state of high excitement, there is a progressive decrease in task performance. Thus, the inverted-*U* hypothesis suggests that behavior is aroused and directed toward some kind of balanced or optimal state. In Selye's (1950) terms this balanced state could also be termed eustress.

The idealized curve shown in Figure 14-4 is not usually seen with actual data that is based on relatively small sample sizes and only a few levels of manipulated arousal. As presented in statistics classes, most things in nature will resemble symmetrical bell-shaped curves, provided there are

hundreds of cases and numerous (i.e., >30) levels of the independent variable. With nearly all of the tests of the inverted-*U* hypothesis having fewer than 20 subjects and only 3–5 levels of arousal, it is unrealistic to expect perfectly symmetrical bell-shaped curves (i.e., idealized inverted-*U*); instead, the curve usually resembles an unsymmetrical inverted *V*. The key point is that the relationship between arousal and performance is curvilinear with best performance occurring at an intermediate point within the range of arousal being examined.

The curvilinear relationship between arousal and performance is observed across studies with considerable regularity. This can be seen in Figure 14-5, where the curve for the difficult task looks more like an inverted *V*. This curve may have more closely resembled an inverted-*U* if 1-second increments in seconds of delay had been used. Other motor behavior laboratory studies (Martens & Landers, 1970; Wood & Hokanson, 1965) have shown support for the curvilinear relationship predicted by the inverted-*U* hypothesis. Other experiments do not show inverted-*U* curves (Murphy, 1966; Pinneo, 1961). In these studies investigators have manipulated incentive or threat to produce changes in arousal. Therefore, most of the research on this topic is limited, because in most studies arousal has been examined as a

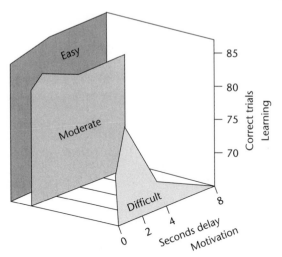

Figure 14-5 **A three-dimensional model illustrating the Yerkes-Dodson Law. Rats were held underwater and deprived of air for varying numbers of seconds, after which they were allowed to escape by selecting the correct door. The optimal level of motivation for learning depended on task difficulty**
Source: Broadhurst, 1957.

dependent rather than independent variable. Anderson (1990) and Neiss (1988) both argued that, if one wished to examine the effects of arousal on performance, data can't be derived from anxiety or incentive manipulations. Furthermore, these arousal manipulations should be relative to arousal levels of each participant. In other words, arousal should be standardized as a percentage of a person's maximum arousal to control for baseline differences because of factors such as fitness, experience, and genetics.

Fortunately the few studies (Babin, 1966; Levitt & Gutin, 1971; Arent & Landers, 2003) that have manipulated arousal by increasing levels of physical activity have found support for the inverted-*U* hypothesis. For example, in the Arent and Landers study, participants were randomly assigned to one of eight arousal groups and they were all told they were competing for a

cash prize. The eight arousal groups were 20, 30, 40, 50, 60, 70, 80, or 90% of relative heart rate reserve (HRR). The use of HRR, which is highly correlated to maximal oxygen uptake, allowed for standardization of arousal relative to each participant. While participants rode a bicycle ergometer at their assigned percentage of HRR they responded to 12 stimulus presentations, and measures of reaction time, movement time, and overall response time were assessed. The results showed a statistically significant curvilinear relationship between arousal and reaction- and response-time performance (see Figure 14-6), accounting for 13.2% and 14.8% of the variance in performance, respectively. For movement time, the results showed a significant linear relationship between arousal and performance, accounting for 9.7% of the performance variance. Arent and Landers attributed the differences in measures of movement time to task characteristics and complexity issues that will be examined next.

Task characteristics. From an arousal perspective, the characteristics of a skill or activity are essential determinants of performance. In the early 1900s it was known that the optimal level of arousal varied among different tasks. Using laboratory animals, Yerkes and Dodson (1908) found that, on more complex tasks, the decrement in performance under increasing arousal conditions occurred earlier than it did for less complex tasks. The interaction of task complexity with arousal level is clearly illustrated in Broadhurst's (1957) experiment (see Figure 14-5). In this study arousal was created by holding rats underwater for zero, 2, 4, or 8 seconds prior to allowing them to swim underwater to complete a two-choice maze. In one condition the choice was made easier by making the correct escape door more obvious (brightly painted lines), whereas in the more difficult condition the doors were nearly the same. As shown in Figure 14-5, decrements in time to negotiate the maze occurred much earlier (after 2 seconds of submergence) in the more complex decision-making situation. Thus, higher levels of arousal can be tolerated on simpler tasks before performance is curtailed.

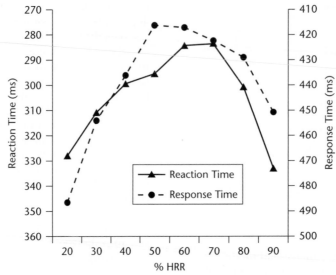

Figure 14-6 **Reaction and response time as a function of percent of maximum heart rates reserve**
Source: Arent & Landers, 2003

What does all of this mean for the performance of sport skills? Basically, the complexity characteristics of the motor skill need to be analyzed to determine how much arousal is optimal. A number of factors that must be considered appear in Table 14-2. Take, for example, the precision and steadiness characteristics required for successful execution of a skill (Figure 14-7). For very precise fine motor skills that involve steadi- ness or control of unwanted muscle activity (e.g., putting a golf ball), very little arousal can be tolerated without accompanying performance decrements. However, for tasks such as weight lifting that involve gross motor skills, a much higher level of arousal can be achieved before performance is impaired.

In addition to considering factors associated with the motor act itself, it is important to

Table 14-2 **The Complexity of Motor Performance**

Decision	Perception	Motor Act
Number of decisions necessary	Number of stimuli needed	Number of muscles
Number of alternatives per decision	Number of stimuli present	Amount of coordinative actions
Speed of decisions	Duration of stimuli	Precision and steadiness required
Sequence of decisions	Intensity of stimuli Conflicting stimuli	Fine motor skills required

Source: Based on Billing, 1980.

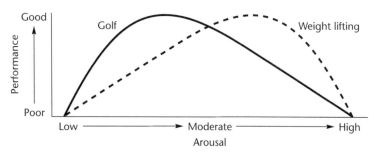

Figure 14-7 **Sport-specific optimal levels of arousal**

consider the decisional and perceptual characteristics of the task. The underwater swimming of the rats in Broadhurst's (1957) experiment was an example of varying the complexity of alternative *decisions*. Generally speaking, tasks with higher decisional demands require lower arousal levels for optimal performance compared to tasks with lower decisional demands.

The relationship of *perception* to the inverted-*U* hypothesis has been studied primarily in situations where individuals are attending to potentially conflicting stimuli. A number of studies (see Landers, 1978, 1980, for reviews) have shown that when dual tasks are performed individuals will generally allocate more attention to one of them to maintain or better their performance. This strategy is typically chosen because it is believed humans have very limited spare attentional capacity for focusing attention on task-irrelevant cues when they are performing complex motor skills.

There are many examples of attention being shifted away from secondary tasks to enhance the concentration necessary to perform the primary task. The experimental situation called the *dual-task paradigm* involves creating differing levels of arousal while subjects are performing a primary task and, at the same time, periodically reacting to a tone or a visual stimulus (Landers, Wang, & Courtet, 1985; Weltman & Egstrom, 1966).

From similar studies in which the dual-task paradigm has been used, Bacon (1974) offers the generalization that arousal effects depend on the degree of attention the stimuli attract, with "sensitivity loss systematically occurring to those

cues which initially attract less attention" (p. 86). Other investigators (e.g., Easterbrook, 1959) suggest that arousal acts to narrow the range of cue utilization, which results in the inverted-*U* function previously described. The underaroused performer, for example, has a broad perceptual range and, therefore, either through lack of effort or poor selectivity accepts irrelevant cues uncritically. Performance in this case is understandably poor. When arousal increases to a moderate or optimal level, perceptual selectivity increases correspondingly and performance improves, presumably because the performer tries harder or is more likely to eliminate task-irrelevant cues. Arousal increases beyond this optimal point result in further perceptual narrowing, and performance deteriorates in accord with the inverted-*U* hypothesis. For instance, a highly anxious football quarterback may focus attention too narrowly and therefore not be able to perceive task-relevant cues such as a cheating safety or his third receiver open downfield. The ideas of both Bacon (1974) and Easterbrook (1959) suggest that the effects of arousal impair performance through a loss of perceptual sensitivity by interfering with athletes' capacity to process information.

Individual differences. The optimal level of arousal for a particular task is also dependent on factors that are unique to the individual. Coaches who routinely give pep talks to all athletes on their team before competitions may not be aware that these arousing talks may not be beneficial for all athletes. Because of inherent personality differences and strength of dominant habits associated with the sport skill, some athletes can perform effectively at much higher levels of arousal than other athletes. People differ in the amount of prior experience with a task as well as the amount of practice they have had. As we discussed earlier, the strength of the correct habit response varies from one person to the next. The person who has greater skill—that is, has a stronger habit hierarchy—may be better able to offset the detrimental effects of increased arousal more effectively than the individual who is less skillful and possesses a weaker habit strength.

Of course, habit patterns may not always be appropriate. Landers (1985) has indicated that subtle changes in habit patterns may lead to **disregulation,** which is defined as a physiological measure of arousal that either negatively correlates with performance or creates some degree of discomfiture for the performer. For example, in our work with a world champion archer, we found that he had developed a habit of tightly squinting his nonsighting eye following the release of the arrow. At the end of several hours of shooting, this resulted in a tension headache. With the archer having to concentrate so much on the act of shooting, it was difficult for him to focus on the source of his problem. To correct this, it was necessary for us to bring the disregulation to his conscious awareness by providing an electromyographic signal of the electrical activity around his nonsighting eye. After several shots with this type of biofeedback, the squinting, which lasted for

several seconds, was reduced to a blink and the headaches disappeared.

Perhaps the greatest individual difference factor is personality. The most relevant personality variables affecting optimal arousal levels are anxiety and extroversion/introversion. For instance, in the aforementioned study by Arent and Landers (2003), somatic anxiety as measured by Sport Anxiety Scale (SAS) (Smith, Smoll & Schutz, 1990), significantly contributed to the amount of reaction- and response-time variance over and above the amount of variance explained by physiological arousal alone. Neither cognitive (as measured by either the Cognitive-Somatic Anxiety Questionnaire 2 [CSAI-2] or the SAS) nor somatic anxiety (as measured by the CSAI-2) accounted for a significant amount of performance variance. Arent and Landers suggested that the failure of the CSAI-2 somatic measure to predict performance is probably related to the better psychometric characteristics of the SAS. These findings suggest that if an athlete is high strung and intolerant of stressful situations (i.e., high perceived somatic anxiety or introverted), even a small amount of arousal can put him or her over the top an the inverted-U curve (Figure 14-8). By contrast, if the athlete is calm, cool, and collected (i.e., low perceived somatic anxiety or extroverted), he or she will be able to tolerate much higher levels of arousal without suffering a performance impairment.

Another factor emphasized by Mahoney (1979) is the ability of the individual to cope with relatively high levels of arousal. This coping

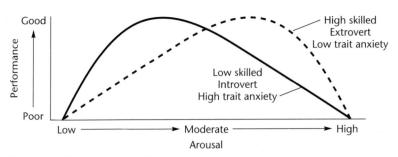

Figure 14-8 **Athlete-specific optimal levels of arousal**

model emphasizes the individual's reaction to and ability to deal with arousal, since this may be "a significant determinant of its course and its effects on performance" (p. 436). For instance, if two athletes have a high absolute heart rate of 120 bpm, one athlete may be able to cope with this level of sympathetic disturbance and the other may not. With this view, there is less concern with physiological departures from normal levels and more emphasis on teaching athletes psychological skills (e.g., relaxation, imagery, self-talk). This view recognizes that a certain amount of energy (arousal) is needed for sporting activities, and a greater amount of arousal is not necessarily bad as long as the athlete can cope with it.

This point was recognized several years ago in research on rifle and pistol shooters (Landers et al., 1980). At that time some sport psychologists (Coleman, 1977; Nideffer, 1978) believed that better shooters actually decreased their heart rates below preshooting, resting levels while performing. However, research results (Landers et al., 1980; Tretilova & Rodmiki, 1979) showed that elite shooters invariably increased their heart rate above resting levels when they fired. In fact, if they did not increase heart rate at least 5 bpm above preshooting levels, they displayed poor performance (Tretilova & Rodmiki, 1979). Some elite gold medalist shooters had heart rates in excess of 50 bpm above preshooting levels and performed quite well. According to Mahoney (1979), when considering the inverted-U notion, the important factor is determining what level of arousal (usually a range) an individual athlete can cope with and still perform optimally.

Given individual differences in personality, habit patterns associated with the skills, and ability to cope with arousal and stress, it is clear that the relationship between arousal and performance is best assessed on an individual basis. Somewhere between the very diverse extremes of comatose state and panic attack, each athlete will have a "zone of optimal functioning" (Hanin, 1978). This is referred to as the individualized zone of optimal functioning (IZOF; Hanin, 2000). For some this arousal zone will be much higher than is evident for other athletes (Landers, 1981). The trick is to know where this zone is for each

athlete and then to help the athlete reproduce this arousal state more consistently from one competition to the next.

Unfortunately, in the sport psychology literature the IZOF model has only been operationalized with measures of anxiety. The questionnaires employed do not measure arousal per se, and, thus, the results of these studies should not be used to make direct inferences to the inverted-U hypothesis (Anderson, 1990; Neiss, 1988). In addition, the study by Arent and Landers (2003) shows that physiological measures of arousal explain double the amount of performance variance than measures of somatic anxiety. If performance enhancement is the desired goal, then investigators need to use either physiological measures or questionnaires that can directly measure arousal. However, the techniques presented for determining the IZOF are instructive and can be used in future research employing physiological measures or the AD-ACL. One technique, presented by Hanin (1978), had divers and gymnasts recollect and evaluate, with the aid of a retrospective anxiety scale, "how they felt before or at the time of a definite competition in the past" (Hanin 1978, p. 240). Furthermore, they were asked to recollect that state "in which they found themselves to act most effectively and achieve the highest result" (p. 242). This retrospectively determined "health anxiety" was then used to help determine an IZOF for each individual athlete. This was done by having an athlete recollect and rate his or her precompetitive anxiety prior to four favorable past competitions. If these ratings yielded values varying by only four points, the IZOF for this athlete would range, for example, between the extremes of these values, with the athlete's optimal level being the midpoint between these extremes.

Hanin (1978) believes these ratings of typical past behavior "allow one, with some credibility, to predict his emotional and behavioral manifestations and actions in situations of competitive stress" (p. 240). These retrospective ratings could then be used to estimate the level of anxiety in forthcoming competitions. If the athlete is outside his or her individually determined IZOF, the anxiety level needs to be raised or lowered by

(a) altering the subjective significance of the upcoming activity; (b) increasing the athlete's confidence in his or her ability to cope with the upcoming competition; (c) limiting the number of people giving input to the athlete; and (d) creating a less stressful social environment (Hanin, 1978).

A similar approach has been used by Sonstroem and Bernardo (1982) without reliance on retrospective ratings of precompetition state anxiety. Using the State-Trait Anxiety Scale (Spielberger et al., 1970), they had athletes give ratings before each game. Over time, a pattern of ratings began to appear for each athlete, and these were then used to predict *optimal* anxiety levels from which individual IZOFs could be computed. Using a variety of different sports, Hanin (1978) and Sonstroem and Bernardo (1982) have shown that if athletes are outside their IZOFs, the outcome is typically poorer performance.

Suggested Modifications and Alternatives to the Inverted-*U* Hypothesis

The inverted-*U* hypothesis does not provide a theoretical explanation for the arousal–performance relationship; it merely posits that this relationship is curvilinear without explaining what internal state or process produces it. There are explanations for this hypothesis, but only a few have been tested in a sport context. Three of these theories/models have been presented within the confines of the inverted-*U* hypothesis—Easterbrook's cue utilization theory as a description of the interaction of task characteristics and perception, Mahoney's coping model as an explanation of individual differences in coping ability, and Hanin's IZOF model as a technique for operationally defining individual anxiety differences at the level of the individual athlete. Other theories go beyond simply clarifying certain aspects of the arousal–performance relationship predicted by the inverted-*U* hypothesis. These more recent theories have been motivated by discontent with the ability of the inverted-*U* hypothesis as a way of predicting exactly where in the expansive range between panic attack and comatose states performance is at an optimal level. In this case, investigators have provided conceptual distinctions that,

like the IZOF model, mistakenly equate anxiety with arousal and view anxiety as multidimensional. Thus, these models/theories differ dramatically from the concepts in the inverted-*U* hypothesis and were proposed as alternatives in an attempt to better explain the relationship between arousal and performance. The two alternative explanations presented here are the multidimensional anxiety theory and the catastrophe cusp model.

Multidimensional anxiety theory related to performance. This theory, developed by Burton (1988) and Martens et al. (1990), posits that anxiety has two different components: a cognitive component associated with fear about the consequences of failure and a somatic component reflecting perceptions of the physiological response to psychological stress. Although this theory assumes a sort of Cartesian dualism between mind and body, the authors maintain that mind and body are intertwined, but not completely. Martens et al. (1990) predicted that cognitive anxiety remains high and essentially stable prior to competition, whereas somatic anxiety peaks later (i.e., immediately prior to arrival at the site of the competition). This hypothesis has been tested in a "time to competition" paradigm and has generally been confirmed (Barnes, Sime, Dienstbier, & Plake, 1986; Burton, 1988; Gould, Petlichkoff, Simons, & Vevera, 1987; Gould, Petlichkoff, & Weinberg, 1984; Jones & Cale, 1989; Martens et al., 1990; Parfitt, 1988; Parfitt & Hardy, 1987; Speigler, Morris, & Liebert, 1968). However, this hypothesis does not deal directly with how these anxiety components influence arousal levels or the inverted-*U* relationship between arousal and performance.

To link this theory to performance, another prediction from multidimensional theory (Martens et al., 1990, pp. 123–124) is that somatic anxiety dissipates once performance begins, whereas cognitive anxiety can vary throughout performance because the subjective probability of success can change throughout performance. Thus, Martens et al. (1990) predicted an inverted-*U* relationship between somatic anxiety and performance and a linear negative relationship between cognitive anxiety and performance. Despite the initial popularity that multidimensional theory has had in predicting performance, there are many problems with these performance predictions.

1. This theory has little relevance to the inverted-*U* relationship between arousal and performance since arousal measures have been rarely employed.

2. Multidimensional theorists have used the CSAI-2 questionnaire to measure cognitive and somatic anxiety. In an experimental study in which arousal was manipulated, Arent and Landers (2003) showed that CSAI-2 anxiety measures do not reliably predict performance. Other nonexperimental studies that have not manipulated arousal (Burton, 1988; Gould et al., 1984) have actually shown contradictory results that are not supportive of the theory. Likewise meta-analytic findings (Craft, Magyar, Becker, & Feltz, 2003) of 29 CSAI-2 studies (175 effect sizes and 2,905 participants) showed that the relationship between somatic/cognitive anxiety and performance was –.03 and .01, respectively, and these correlations were not significant from zero. Furthermore, cognitive anxiety consistently showed a positive rather than a negative performance relationship.

3. Among CSAI-2 nonexperimental studies that have tested for an inverted-*U* relationship between anxiety and performance (Burton, 1988; Gould et al., 1987; Randle & Weinberg, 1997; Woodman, Albinson, & Hardy, 1997), the only consistent relationship has been a curvilinear relationship between somatic anxiety and performance. However, an experimental arousal study (Arent & Landers, 2003) failed to find a significant CSAI-2 somatic anxiety-performance relationship, but did find a significant relationship with SAS somatic anxiety.

In summary, there is now mounting evidence that cognitive and somatic anxiety are not linearly related to sport performance. There is, however, consistent evidence that there is a curvilinear relationship between somatic anxiety and performance. In terms of the cognitive anxiety/performance relationship, research findings have not supported the hypothesized negative linear relationship derived from multidimensional anxiety theory.

Catastrophe cusp model. One problem with the multidimensional anxiety theory "is that it attempts to explain the three-dimensional relationship between cognitive anxiety, somatic anxiety and performance in terms of a series of two-dimensional relationships" (Hardy & Parfitt, 1991).

The three-dimensional model proposed by Hardy and Parfitt is derived from Zeeman's (1976) catastrophe cusp model, which was originally designed to describe ocean wave action. Hardy and Fazey (1987) suggest that the inverted-*U* relationship between physiological arousal and performance varies along another dimension defined as a *splitting factor,* which they arbitrarily identified as cognitive anxiety. They argued that this splitting factor determines whether the effects of physiological arousal (on performance) are smooth and small, large and catastrophic, or somewhere in between these extremes. According to Hardy and Fazey (1987), physiological arousal is not necessarily detrimental to performance, particularly if the skill is simple or well learned. However, when cognitive anxiety is high and dominant, "the curve is discontinuous and represents a catastrophic fall off in performance once the optimal peak is passed" (p. 29). When discontinuity, or sudden large jumps, occur along the normal factor (i.e., physiological arousal continuum) this is referred to as *hysteresis*. A visual example of what this may look like is the difficult conditions in Figure 14-5, where there is a sharp decline in performance with relatively low levels of arousal. It is suggested that this may occur because cognitive anxiety distracts the athlete or creates doubt (consciously or unconsciously) about what is beneficial and what is detrimental physiological arousal.

A better way of addressing the catastrophe cusp theory is to experimentally examine the inverted-*U* relationship between arousal and performance and then determine if cognitive and somatic anxiety alter the shape of the curve or predict performance. Arent and Landers (2003) have done this and did not find support for the catastrophe cusp theory. When physiological arousal levels were from 70% to 90% of maximum heart rate reserve, the catastrophic fall off in performance predicted by Hardy and Fazey was not at all evident (Figure 14-6). Analysis of the effects of anxiety on performance indicated that only SAS somatic anxiety predicted a curvilinear relationship with performance. The failure of the CSAI-2 cognitive measure to show any relationship to performance also supports the idea that Hardy and Fazey may have used an ineffectual splitting factor in their catastrophe cusp model. It may be that, for tasks of this type in which the cognitive load is relatively low, cognitive anxiety does not predict performance well.

The studies that have thus far been conducted have not supported the catastrophe cusp model. For many of these studies, there have been problems in the methodology employed (i.e., extremely small sample sizes and questionable statistical analyses). Furthermore, because of its complexity, Gill (1994) believes the model is of dubious value because it is difficult to test. The three-dimensional cusp catastrophe is only the second level of complexity, and Fazey and Hardy (1988) have suggested five additional higher dimensional catastrophes (i.e., swallowtail, butterfly, hyperbolic, elliptic, and parabolic). Hardy (1996) has responded to Gill's criticism with the argument that "complexity is an insufficient reason for rejecting any theory or model . . ." (p. 140). Actually, in the philosophy of science, there are adequate grounds for rejecting needlessly complex models and theories. The principle of parsimony maintains that given a simple and a complex description for the same phenomenon, each with empirical support, the simple description should prevail. Therefore, rather than viewing the simplicity of the inverted-*U* as a weakness (Gould & Krane, 1992), it is seen as a scientific advantage.

Estimating the Relationship Between an Athlete's Optimal Arousal and Performance

As indicated previously, the optimal arousal level will depend on task characteristics as well as individual difference factors. To help athletes learn to regulate arousal during the competition, it is important that the coach or sport psychologist compare the arousal demands of the sport task to the athlete's typical competitive arousal state. We recommend the following guidelines. Select a specific task such as playing the quarterback position in football. Avoid global activities such as gymnastics, football, or basketball, and be as task specific as you can! Once you zero in on the task, answer the questions in Table 14-3. For example, high scores (3s and 4s) in the sport of archery on motor act characteristics (C.1–4) would produce high total task scores. In short sprints, however, the decision/perceptual processes would in general receive low values (1s and 2s), and the gross motor nature of sprinting would keep the overall task score at a relatively low level. When using this table, bear in mind that it is only a rough guideline for estimating the complexity of your sport.

Total your scores and see where your chosen skill falls on the range in Table 14-4. If the skill has a low score, this indicates that the average athlete can be psyched up to a greater extent and still perform optimally. If an athlete performing this task is low trait anxious and typically responds to competition in a constantly laid-back way, you may need to supplement normal psych-up procedures by teaching the athlete some of the energizing techniques presented in Chapter 15. However, if the athlete scores over 32 in the specific skill you have selected, he or she will not usually be able to tolerate as much arousal. In this case it is important for the coach to extensively train the athlete in the basic skills so as to develop correct habits that are less susceptible to the debilitating effects of arousal. For those more complex skills coaches should particularly avoid implementing last-minute changes in technique; a weak habit strength for the skill will make the athlete more susceptible to the disruptive effects of arousal.

In addition to reinforcing the strength of correct habits, it is also important (in complex skills) to pay greater heed to the relaxation, imagery, and cognitive coping strategies presented in Chapters 15, 16, and 17. Athletes who display consistent, high-level performance during practice or unimportant competition but then fail to perform effectively in major competitions will have

Table 14-3 **Estimating Complexity of Motor Performance**

A. Decision of Characteristics of Skill

1. Number of decisions necessary	0 None	1 Few	2 Some	3 Several	4 Many
2. Number of alternatives per decision	0 None	1 Few	2 Some	3 Several	4 Many
3. Speed of decisions	0 Not relevant	1 Very slow	2 Slow	3 Fast	4 Very fast
4. Sequence of decisions	0 Not relevant, only one decision	1 Sequence of 2	2 Sequence of 3	3 Sequence of 4	4 Sequence of 5 or more

B. Perception Characteristics of Skill

1. Number of stimuli needed	0 None	1 Few	2 Some	3 Several	4 Many
2. Number of stimuli present	0 Very few	1 Few	2 Some	3 Several	4 Many
3. Duration of stimuli	0 More than 20 sec	1 More than 10 sec	2 More than 5 sec	3 More than 2 sec	4 Less than 2 sec
4. Intensity of stimuli	0 Very intense	1 Intense	2 Moderately intense	3 Low intensity	4 Very low intensity
5. Clarity of correct stimulus among conflicting stimuli	0 Very obvious	1 Obvious	2 Moderately obvious	3 Subtle difference	4 Very subtle difference

C. Motor Act Characteristics of Skill

1. Number of muscle actions to execute skill	0 1–2	1 3–4	2 5–6	3 7–8	4 9 or more
2. Amount of coordination of actions	0 Minimal	1 A little	2 Some	3 Several coordinative actions	4 A great deal
3. Precision and steadiness required	0 None	1 Minimal	2 Some	3 Considerable	4 A great deal
4. Fine motor skill required	0 None, only gross motor skill	1 Minimal	2 Some	3 Considerable	4 A great deal

an even greater need to practice these coping techniques regularly.

To determine an optimal level of arousal for a given skill, athletes should be examined individually. This is most easily done by administering one of the arousal questionnaires (preferably the AD-ACL) listed in Table 14-1. By using either retrospective arousal ratings (Hanin, 1978) or ratings before each competition and noting performance levels associated with the arousal scores, a coach

Table 14-4 **Optimum Arousal Level and Complexity Scores for a Variety of Typical Sport Skills**

Level of Arousal	Complexity Score Range	Sport Skills
5 (extremely excited)	0–10	Football blocking, running 200 meters to 400 meters
4 (psyched up)	11–16	Short sprints, long jump
3 (medium arousal)	17–21	Basketball, boxing, judo
2 (some arousal)	22–31	Baseball, pitching, fencing, tennis
1 (slight arousal)	32+	Archery, golf, field goal kicking

Source: Based on Oxendine, 1984, and Billing, 1980.

or sport psychologist should eventually be able to determine the athlete's IZOF. Having this as a basis, the athlete's arousal in a given competition can be compared to the arousal score associated with a personal best performance. If these arousal scores are discrepant, the coach or sport psychologist should use energizing techniques (Chapter 15) or relaxation, imagery, or other psychological skills (Chapters 15, 16, 17) to bring the athlete's arousal levels in closer alignment with the predefined IZOF.

Armed with the information in this chapter and the techniques described in Chapter 13, the athletes with whom coaches work will be better equipped to select, develop, and use the arousal self-regulation skills presented in Chapter 15. Often, coaches and sport psychologists want to identify athletes with inappropriate arousal levels for the tasks they are performing. Figure 14-2 suggests some areas that will serve as a guide in the identification process. The situation (B) of greatest interest, of course, is competition. The cognitive (C), physiological (D), and behavioral (E) response of athletes in the competitive situation can be compared to responses in noncompetitive situations (i.e., practice conditions). Marked discrepancies in these responses, accompanied by a poor competitive performance, may provide clues that the athlete is overaroused or underaroused.

At the level of cognitive appraisal (C), the coach or sport psychologist should look for signs of distraction before competition. This is usually indicated by an athlete who is not paying attention to the coach's pregame instructions. The athlete may express more concern than is normal by making statements that indicate a certain degree of self-doubt about his or her ability to meet the competitive demands. This identification process is often simplified at a cognitive appraisal level when the athlete recognizes the excessive worry and comes to the coach or sport psychologist for help.

Even without this self-disclosure, many times it is possible to detect physiological or emotional responses (D) that relate to cognitive appraisal (C) as described in Figure 14-2. Where there is a consistent shift to poor performance from practice to competition, the coach or sport psychologist should look for obvious signs of emotional reactivity (e.g., flushed face, sweaty palms, dilated pupils). Another way of getting more direct verification of the arousal mismatch is to administer various measures of arousal (e.g., AD-ACL) throughout the competitive season. Some physiological measures are also quite easy for a coach or sport psychologist to use. For instance, Landers (1981) and Tretilova and Rodmiki (1979) tracked heart rates of top U.S. and Soviet rifle shooters and found an optimal heart rate increase above resting values where best performance scores were fired.

Finally, at a behavioral level (Figure 14-2.E) much can be gained from careful observation of the athlete's motor activity, actions, and speech characteristics. Hyperactivity before a performance can be gleaned from erratic behaviors such as pacing, fidgeting, and yawning. An unusually high or low energy level before or during competition may also indicate an inappropriate level of arousal. Rapid speech that sounds abnormal for a particular athlete may provide a reason for the coach or sport psychologist to inquire further into an athlete's arousal state.

The above-mentioned cognitive, physiological, and behavioral manifestations of arousal should not be the last step of the identification process. These factors are only indicators or clues that can serve as a basis for discussions with the athlete. Don't mistake fidgeting because the athlete needs to go to the bathroom as a sign of overarousal. Check out these possible signs of arousal to see what meaning the athlete gives to them. This interpretation is essential in the final determination of overarousal. As we will see in the next three chapters, interpretation is also important for designing interventions to help bring arousal levels under control.

Summary

In this chapter we have attempted to provide a basic understanding of arousal–performance relationships. The drive theory and inverted-U hypothesis were presented, the former theory emphasizing the development of correct habits to insulate the athlete against the effects of arousal and the latter hypothesis stressing the determination and maintenance of an optimal arousal level for the task to be performed. To determine optimal arousal levels, several task characteristics as well as individual differences in state anxiety and skill must be considered.

In addition, two recent theories/models, which have been advocated as possible replacements for the inverted-U, were addressed and found to have conceptual and methodological flaws in many of the studies examining them. Although some scientific problems with tests of the inverted-U have been reported, a recent study (Arent & Landers, 2003) that has been designed to overcome these problems has still found support for the inverted-U hypothesis. Thus, the weight of the scientific evidence continues to favor the inverted-U hypothesis as the best description for how arousal affects performance.

We have provided guidelines to help coaches and sport psychologists estimate the arousal demands in reference to the complexity of the task to be performed. Finally, we have made suggestions to help identify athletes who are over- or underaroused. We anticipate that, by increasing their understanding of arousal–performance relationships, coaches and sport psychologists will be able to better assess the task demands and more accurately determine appropriate arousal levels for their athletes.

Study Questions

1. Diagram (see figure on p. 280) the predictions of drive theory and the inverted-U theory under conditions of a well-learned skill and under conditions of a novice performer learning a new skill. After diagramming, explain in words exactly where the two theories predict different performance outcomes.

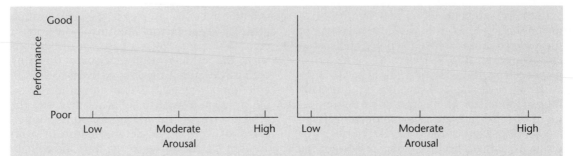

2. In 1965 Zajonc proposed a drive theory explanation for the effects of a passive audience on an individual's performance. Zajonc hypothesized that an audience produced an increase in an individual's arousal level. Assuming that Zajonc was correct and arousal is increased by an audience, how would such an increase affect the performance of a novice performer and an elite performer? According to drive theory, would you desire an audience for the novice or elite performer?

3. Describe Easterbrook's theory of cue utilization and how it provides an explanation for the inverted-*U* relationship between arousal and performance.

4. You are aware of two athletes at your school who display markedly different patterns of emotional excitement when practicing and competing. The 200-meter sprinter becomes much more emotional than the golfer. They both seem to perform well in their respective psychological states. Describe why these vastly different states may make sense in terms of the inverted-*U* hypothesis.

5. Describe what is meant by the term *arousal*. How does arousal relate to the term *anxiety?* Under what conditions might the arousal state of an individual trigger an anxiety response?

6. Describe the ways in which arousal has been measured. What do you consider to be the strengths and weaknesses of these measures?

7. What two factors are known to modify the shape of the inverted-*U* relationship?

8. How would you go about determining the complexity of motor skills such as free throw shooting in basketball versus maneuvering against three players to shoot a layup? According to the task complexity score, which task is more prone to the disruptive effects of arousal?

9. Which of the following athletes would you be most concerned about in terms of holding up under the effects of stress in an upcoming competition? Explain your choice.

   • Athlete A is an outgoing individual who is relatively unskilled.

   • Athlete B is an introverted person but is one of your most skilled players.

   • Athlete C tends to be highly anxious and has recently made some changes in her tennis serving technique.

- Athlete D is low in anxiety and is also relatively unskilled.

- Athlete E is extroverted and is only moderately skilled.

10. According to the inverted-*U* hypothesis, a moderate or "optimal" level of arousal is needed for effective performance. Throughout the season, how would you go about helping an athlete achieve an optimal arousal state prior to each competition?

References

Anderson, K. J. (1990). Arousal and the inverted-*U* hypothesis: A critique of Neiss's "Reconceptualizing arousal." *Psychological Bulletin, 107,* 96–100.

Arent, S. M., & Landers, D. M. (2003). Arousal, anxiety, and performance. A reexamination of the inverted-*U* hypothesis. *Research Quarterly for Exercise & Sport, 74,* 436–444.

Babin, W. (1966). *The effect of various work loads on simple reaction latency as related to selected physical parameters.* Unpublished doctoral dissertation, University of Southern Mississippi, Hattiesburg.

Bacon, S. J. (1974). Arousal and the range of cue utilization. *Journal of Experimental Psychology, 103,* 81–87.

Barnes, M. W., Sime, W., Dienstbier, R., & Plake, B. (1986). A test of construct validity of the CSAI-2 questionnaire in male elite college swimmers. *Journal of Sport Psychology, 17,* 364–374.

Billing, J. (1980). An overview of task complexity. *Motor Skills: Theory Into Practice, 4,* 18–23.

Bond, C. F., & Titus, L. J. (1983). Social facilitation: A meta-analysis of 241 studies. *Psychological Bulletin, 94,* 265–292.

Broadhurst, P. L. (1957). Emotionality and the Yerkes-Dodson Law. *Journal of Experimental Psychology, 54,* 345–352.

Burton, D. (1988). Do anxious swimmers swim slower?: Reexamining the elusive anxiety–performance relationship. *Journal of Sport and Exercise Psychology, 10,* 45–61.

Coleman, J. (1977, December). Normal stress reactions in shooting. *The Rifleman,* 19–20.

Cox, R. H. (1990). *Sport psychology: Concepts and applications.* Dubuque, IA: Brown.

Craft, L. L., Magyar, T. M., Becker, B. J., & Feltz, D. L. (2003). The relationship between the Competitive State Anxiety Inventory-2 and athletic performance: A meta-analysis. *Journal of Sport & Exercise Psychology, 25,* 44–65

Duffy, E. (1957). The psychological significance of the concept of "arousal" and "activation." *Psychological Review, 64,* 265–275.

Duffy, E. (1962). *Activation and behavior.* New York: Wiley.

Easterbrook, J. A. (1959). The effect of emotion on cue utilization and the organization of behavior. *Psychological Review, 66,* 183–201.

Fazey, J. & Hardy, L. (1988). The Inverted-*U* Hypothesis: Catastrophe for sport psychology. *British Association of Sports Sciences Monograph No. 1.* Leeds, UK: The National Coaching Foundation.

Freeman, G. L. (1940). The relationship between performance level and bodily activity level. *Journal of Experimental Psychology, 26,* 602–608.

Gill, D. L. (1994). A sport and exercise psychology perspective on stress. *Quest, 44,* 20–27.

Gorman, C. (2002, June 10). The science of anxiety. *Time Magazine,* 47–54.

Gould, D., & Krane, V. (1992). The arousal–performance relationship: Current status and future directions. In T. Horn (Ed.), *Advances in sport psychology* (pp. 119–141). Champaign, IL: Human Kinetics.

Gould, D., Petlichkoff, L., Simons, J., & Vevera, M. (1987). Relationship between competitive state anxiety inventory-2 subscale scores and pistol shooting performance. *Journal of Sport Psychology, 9,* 33–42.

Gould, D., Petlichkoff, L., & Weinberg, R. (1984). Antecedents of, temporal changes in, and relationships between CSAI-2 subcomponents. *Journal of Sport Psychology, 6,* 289–304.

Hanin, Y. L. (1978). A study of anxiety in sports. In W. F. Straub (Ed.), *Sport psychology: An analysis of athlete behavior* (pp. 236–256). Ithaca, NY: Mouvement Publications.

Hanin, Y. L. (2000). Successful and poor performance and emotions. In Y. L. Hanin (Ed.), *Emotions in sport* (pp. 157–187). Champaign, IL: Human Kinetics.

Hardy, L. (1996). Testing the predictions of the cusp catastrophe model of anxiety and performance. *The Sport Psychologist, 10,* 140–156.

Hardy, J. P. L., & Fazey, J. A. (1987). *The inverted-U hypothesis—a catastrophe for sports psychology and a statement of a new hypothesis.* Paper presented at a meeting of the North American Society for the Psychology of Sport and Physical Activity, Vancouver, Canada.

Jones, J. G., & Cale, A. (1989). Relationships between multidimensional competitive state anxiety and cognitive and motor subcomponents of performance. *Journal of Sport Sciences, 7,* 129–140.

Krahenbuhl, G. S. (1975). Adrenaline, arousal and sport. *Journal of Sports Medicine, 3,* 117–121.

Lacey, J. I., Bateman, D. E., & Van Lehn, R. (1953). Heart rate feedback-assisted reduction in cardiovascular reactivity to a videogame challenge. *The Psychological Record, 39,* 365–371.

Landers, D. M. (1978). Motivation and performance: The role of arousal and attentional factors. In W. Straub (Ed.), *Sport psychology: An analysis of athletic behavior.* Ithaca, NY: Mouvement Publications.

Landers, D. M. (1980). The arousal–performance relationship revisited. *Research Quarterly, 51,* 77–90.

Landers, D. M. (1981). Reflections of sport psychology and the Olympic athlete. In J. Segrave & D. Chu (Eds.), *Olympism* (pp. 189–200). Champaign, IL.: Human Kinetics.

Landers, D. M. (1985). Psychophysiological assessment and biofeedback: Applications for athletes in closed skill sports. In J. H. Sandweis & S. Wolf (Eds.), *Biofeedback and sport science* (pp. 63–105). New York: Plenum.

Landers, D. M., Christina, R. W., Hatfield, B. D., Daniels, F. S., Wilkinson, M., & Doyle, L. A. (1980, April). Research on the shooting sports: A preliminary report. *The American Rifleman, 128* (4), 36–37, 76–77.

Landers, D. M., Snyder-Bauer, R., & Feltz, D. L. (1978). Social facilitation during the initial stage of motor learning: A reexamination of Martens's audience study. *Journal of Motor Behavior, 10*, 325–337.

Landers, D. M., Wang, M. Q., & Courtet, P. (1985). Peripheral narrowing among experienced and inexperienced rifle shooters under low- and high-stress conditions. *Research Quarterly, 56*, 57–70.

Landy, F. J., & Stern, R. M. (1971). Factor analysis of a somatic perception questionnaire. *Journal of Psychosomatic Research, 15*, 179–181.

Levitt, S., & Gutin, B. (1971). Multiple choice reaction time and movement time during physical exertion. *Research Quarterly, 42*, 405–410, 423–443.

Mahoney, M. J. (1979). Cognitive skills and athletic performance. In P. C. Kendall & S. D. Hollon (Eds.), *Cognitive-behavioral interventions: Theory, research, and procedures*. New York: Academic Press.

Malmo, R. B. (1959). Activation: A neuropsychological dimension. *Psychological Review, 66*, 367–386.

Martens, R. (1974). Arousal and motor performance. In J. H. Wilmore (Ed.), *Exercise and sport science reviews* (pp. 155–188). New York: Academic Press.

Martens, R. (1977). *Sport competitive anxiety test*. Champaign, IL: Human Kinetics.

Martens, R., Burton, D., Vealey, R. S., Bump, L. A., & Smith, D. E. (1990). Development and validation of the competitive state anxiety inventory-2. In R. Martens, R. S. Vealey, & D. Burton, *Competitive anxiety in sport* (pp. 123–124, 160). Champaign, IL: Human Kinetics.

Martens, R., Burton, D., Vealey, R., Smith, D., & Bump, L. (1983). *The development of the competitive state anxiety inventory-2 (CSAI-2)*. Unpublished manuscript.

Martens, R., & Landers, D. M. (1970). Motor performance under stress: A test of the inverted-*U* hypothesis. *Journal of Personality and Social Psychology, 16*, 29–37.

Murphy, L. E. (1966). Muscular effort, activation level and reaction time. *Proceedings of the 74th Annual Convention of the American Psychological Association* (p. 1). Washington, DC: APA.

Neiss, R. (1988). Reconceptualizing arousal: Psychobiological states in motor performance. *Psychological Bulletin, 103*, 345–366.

Nideffer, R. M. (1978). *Predicting human behavior: A theory and test of attentional and interpersonal style*. San Diego: Enhanced Performance Associates.

Oxendine, J. B. (1984). *Psychology of motor learning*. Englewood Cliffs, NJ: Prentice Hall.

Parfitt, C. G. (1988). *Interactions between models of stress and models of motor control*. Unpublished doctoral dissertation, University College of North Wales.

Parfitt, C. G., & Hardy, L. (1987). Further evidence for the differential effects of competitive anxiety upon a number of cognitive and motor subcomponents. *Journal of Sport Sciences, 5*, 62–63.

Pinneo, L. R. (1961). The effects of induced muscle tension during tracking on level of activation and on performance. *Journal of Experimental Psychology, 62*, 523–531.

Randle, S., & Weinberg, R. (1997). Multidimensional anxiety and performance: An exploratory examination of the zone of optimal functioning hypothesis. *The Sport Psychologist, 11,* 169–174.

Sage, G. (1984). *Motor learning and control.* Dubuque, IA: Brown.

Schwartz, G. E., Davidson, R. J., & Goleman, D. (1978). Patterning of cognitive and somatic processes in the self-regulation of anxiety: Effects of meditation versus exercise. *Psychosomatic Medicine, 40,* 321–328.

Selye, H. (1950). *Stress.* Montreal: Acta.

Smith, R. E., Smoll, F. L., & Schutz, R. W. (1990). Measurement and correlates of sport-specific cognitive and somatic trait anxiety: The sport anxiety scale. *Anxiety Research, 2,* 263–280.

Sonstroem, R. J., & Bernardo, P. (1982). Intraindividual pregame state anxiety and basketball performance: A reexamination of the inverted-*U* curve. *Journal of Sport Psychology, 4,* 235–245.

Speigler, M. D., Morris, L. W., & Liebert, R. M. (1968). Cognitive and emotional components of test anxiety: Temporal factors. *Psychological Reports, 22,* 451–456.

Spence, J. T., & Spence, K. W. (1966). The motivational components of manifest anxiety: Drive and drive stimuli. In C. D. Spielberger (Ed.), *Anxiety and behavior* (pp. 291–326). New York: Academic Press.

Spielberger, C. D. (1975). Anxiety: State-trait process. In C. D. Spielberger & I. G. Sarason (Eds.), *Stress and anxiety* (Vol. 1, pp. 115–143). New York: Hemisphere.

Spielberger, C. D., Gorsuch, R. L., & Lushene, R. E. (1970). *Manual for the State-Trait Anxiety Inventory (STAI).* Palo Alto, CA: Consulting Psychologists Press.

Thayer, R. E. (1967). Measurement of activation through self-report. *Psychological Reports, 20,* 663–679.

Thayer, R. E. (1970). Activation states as assessed by verbal report and four psychophysiological variables. *Psychophysiology, 7,* 86–94.

Thayer, R. E. (1986). Activation-deactivation adjective checklist: Current overview and structural analysis. *Psychological Reports, 58,* 607–614.

Tretilova, T. A., & Rodmiki, E. M. (1979). Investigation of emotional state of rifle shooters. *Theory and Practice of Physical Culture, 5,* 28.

Weltman, A. T., & Egstrom, G. H. (1966). Perceptual narrowing in novice divers. *Human Factors, 8,* 499–505.

Wood, C. G., & Hokanson, J. E. (1965). Effects of induced muscle tension on performance and the inverted-*U. Journal of Personality and Social Psychology, 1,* 506–510.

Woodman, T., Albinson, J. G., & Hardy, L. (1997). An investigation of the zones of optimal functioning hypothesis within a multidimensional framework. *Journal of Sport and Exercise Psychology, 19,* 131–141.

Yerkes, R. M., & Dodson, J. D. (1908). The relation of strength of stimulus to rapidity of habit formation. *Journal of Comparative Neurology of Psychology, 18,* 459–482.

Zeeman, E. C. (1976). Catastrophe theory. *Scientific American, 234,* 65–83.

Relaxation and Energizing Techniques for Regulation of Arousal

Jean M. Williams, *University of Arizona*
Dorothy V. Harris, *Deceased, Formerly of Pennsylvania
State University*

He didn't stay relaxed like I told him. If he did, he'd have run in the 9.7s.

—*Trevor Graham, coach of Justin Gatlin, after Gatlin won the gold medal
with a time of 9.85 seconds in the 100 meters at the 2004 Olympics.*

Somehow the misconception persists that if one practices and trains hard enough physically for a competition, everything else will magically come together. In fact, during a given competition, or between two competitions that closely follow each other, there is usually no marked change in an athlete's skill level, physiological capacity, or biomechanical efficiency. The fluctuation in performance is generally caused by the fluctuation in the athlete's mental control. The athlete simply does not lose and gain stamina, skill, strategy, or conditioning during the ebb and flow of a competition. What the athlete does lose is control of cognitive factors such as the ability to concentrate, to process relevant cues, and to focus on positive self-talk. In the final analysis the athlete is inappropriately aroused, which we will refer to as activated, or some appropriate derivative, throughout the rest of the chapter.

Consistent high-level performance begins with the discovery of those factors and conditions that accompany superior performance. (See Chapter 12 for suggestions on how to discover the mental and bodily states typically associated with an athlete's superior performance.) Beyond that, acceptance of the fact that each of us has control over our own behavior and activation allows athletes to learn and develop skills and strategies necessary to consciously regulate their responses and maintain an optimal level of performance. Although it is unrealistic, wouldn't it be great if all athletes responded to competition the way Michelle Akers, a member of the 1999 U.S. World Cup soccer team, did during a game leading to the team winning the World Cup. After the semifinal game with Brazil, a reporter asked Michelle if she was nervous about being chosen to take the penalty kick with a trip to the World Cup final still hanging in the balance. Akers smiled and replied, "Nervous? I was like,

'Yeah baby, give me that.' Those are the moments you live for" (*USA Today,* July 6, 1999).

Elmer Green and Alyce Green (1977) have studied the effects of the mental control of the **autonomic functions,** including the muscular and hormonal changes that occur in sport performance. In their experiments measuring the influence of the mental control of bodily functions, they studied yogis from India. The Greens found that yogis were voluntarily able to alter their brain waves, heart rate, breathing, blood pressure, body temperature, and other bodily processes that are generally regulated by the autonomic nervous system. The researchers also discovered that the ability to voluntarily control these processes could be taught to others with ease in a relatively short period of time. The Greens concluded that each of us possesses a highly complex, sophisticated, and effectively integrated network between the mind and body. They further concluded that every change in the mental-emotional state is consciously or unconsciously accompanied by an appropriate change in the bodily state. This conclusion provides strong support for the idea that we think with our entire body. Accepting this, we can learn to exercise much greater mastery and control over all of our functions and responses. Our bodies tend to do what they are told to do; the trick is to learn how to communicate with our bodies. This is the principle of learning how to self-regulate arousal and relaxation. The same principle applies to activating and psyching ourselves up to reach an optimal level of performance. Once an athlete has learned to identify which mental-emotional and bodily states and feelings accompany superior performance, he or she can learn to program these responses voluntarily to set the stage for another superior performance.

Readiness, being psyched, energized, mentally tough, activated, aroused, or whatever you may want to call it, is an integration of the mind–body feelings and thoughts that provide the athlete with a feeling of confidence, of mastery and control. The athlete can learn to reach this state voluntarily by practicing the skills and strategies included in this book; learning to regulate activation level, the subject of this chapter, is one

important part of the process. Once an athlete has identified his or her optimal level of arousal for maximizing performance, the athlete can use appropriate relaxation or energizing techniques and strategies to reduce or increase that activation as needed. (See Chapter 14 for ways of determining optimal level of activation for consistent, high-level performance and a discussion of the factors that influence optimal activation level.)

Obviously, all athletes need a certain amount of arousal or motivation to accomplish a task; however, some need more than others to perform at the same level. Too much activation is detrimental; that is more often the problem than needing a "win one for the Gipper" speech to psych up a team. Some athletes will respond positively to a highly charged motivational speech, whereas others will become overactivated. Traditionally, most coaches and athletes have tended to emphasize the psyching up aspect of preparation for performance; most sport psychologists have focused on lowering activation.

As noted in the preceding chapters, a combination of physiological, psychological, and behavioral responses occurs when an athlete is worried and afraid of not performing as desired. Each athlete has to learn his or her particular pattern of overactivation resulting from worry and anxiety about performance. Learning to relax is essential to regulating these responses to avoid any detrimental effects on performance. When a muscle tenses up, as it usually does with worry and anxiety, it contracts or is shortened. This contraction involves nerves as well. Approximately half of the nerves alert the muscles to respond to the messages from the brain, and the other half carry the messages back to the brain.

The voluntary muscles in humans (and animals) are arranged in pairs. When a muscle tightens because of perceived stress, its opposite sets up a counter tension to hold the segment of the body in place. The resulting double pull can build up formidable heights of tension over much of the body yet remain unidentified by most people. This double pull explains why a person can be scared stiff, become rigid with anger, be unable to move because of fright, and so forth. It also explains why an athlete shoots air balls, blows a short putt, passes with too much force, or overhits a tennis ball. The principle of the **double pull,** sometimes referred to as *bracing,* has great significance for the athlete. When muscular tension occurs with anxiety and worry, it interferes with performance because it prevents appropriately coordinating movement. Proper form in any movement involves using just the right amount of tension at any given time in the relevant muscles; too much tension interferes with the execution of the skill. We can learn the right amount of contraction, that is, expend only those energies necessary to accomplish our purposes without waste. This is called **differential relaxation.**

Excessive muscular tension can be triggered by mental input generated by worry and anxiety about not performing well. When the nerve pathways are occupied by impulses alerting the system of stress, to fight or flee, the impulses necessary for skillful, coordinated movement are inhibited to some degree. The more muscular tension in the body, the more difficult it is to execute good form or the proper coordination in any type of movement task.

Exercise for illustrating how excessive tension disrupts speed and coordination:

Rest your dominant forearm and hand palm down on a desk or tabletop. Tense all the muscles in the hand and fingers and then try to alternately tap the index and middle fingers back and forth as quickly as possible. Relax all the muscles in the forearm and hand and repeat the exercise.

With the preceding exercise athletes discover how too much tension makes their movements slow and clumsy.

We often have observed coaches and teachers shout "relax" to an athlete or learner whose performance was suffering because of too much muscular tension, for example, a beginning swimmer going into the deep end for the first time or a skilled athlete becoming frustrated because performance is not up to expectations. Although the instruction to relax was certainly appropriate, more often than not the performers were clueless as to how to relax, particularly so when in their uptight state. To learn to avoid too much tension, athletes need to be taught to recognize unwanted tension and to relax or release the tension. The tension sensation comes from the contraction of skeletal muscle fibers. Relaxation comes from no more than releasing the tension from the contracted muscle. Total relaxation means letting go and doing absolutely nothing with the muscles so that no messages are traveling either to or from the brain.

As a coach or sport psychologist, you may be wondering why any athlete would want to be completely relaxed. Athletes need some activation and muscular tension to perform; some need maximal tension to accomplish their sport. However, in learning to train the muscles to relax totally, athletes develop a much greater sensitivity to their bodily feelings and responses. Once athletes become aware of bodily responses and learn to associate them with certain types of behavior and performance, they can learn to regulate different levels of tension to deal with the environment actively and effectively.

Once trained in relaxation, athletes can use this skill to lower general muscular tension under any condition. Relaxation can assist in removing localized tension such as that occurring with headaches or lower back pain or that surrounding injuries. Relaxation can facilitate recovery when athletes have only a short time between events or when they are fatigued. Relaxation also promotes the onset of sleep and reduces insomnia problems that plague many athletes prior to competition. Probably the most important contribution that relaxation can make to athletes is to teach them the regulation of muscular tension so that nerve pathways to the muscle are never overcharged.

Reviews of research findings clearly indicate the effectiveness of relaxation techniques in enhancing sport performance (Greenspan & Feltz, 1989; Meyers, Whelan, & Murphy, 1996). For example, the Meyers et al. meta-analysis identified

25 relaxation interventions that combined for an effect size of .73 ($SD = 1.64$, $p < .01$). Little is known, however, about the relative effectiveness of different relaxation techniques. Nor do we know much about individual differences among athletes in their success at relaxing, their preferences for different relaxation techniques, and their willingness to practice the techniques. More frequent practice of stress reduction methods should result in more rapid learning and powerful effects, and, obviously, individual characteristics and the motivational effects of the various techniques will influence rate of practice.

Research with nonathlete populations does offer possible insights for teaching relaxation skills to athletes. After reviewing studies with a nonathlete population, Lehrer and Woolfolk (1993) concluded that individuals with an internal locus of control and positive expectancy for success master relaxation techniques more easily and adhere better to outside practice regimens. They also indicated that their own work suggested that individuals enjoyed meditating more than practicing progressive relaxation (PR), and that they enjoyed PR more than autogenic training (AT). They cautioned, however, that these were group differences and that some individuals preferred to meditate, others to relax their muscles, others to talk about their thoughts and feelings, and so forth. These nonathlete findings suggest that for maximum effectiveness in teaching relaxation skills the sport psychologist or coach should expose athletes to several relaxation techniques and convince them of the benefits that will result from practicing the techniques. They should also convince the athletes that, with practice, they can learn to recognize and, at will, get rid of unwanted tension.

In choosing the potentially most effective technique to practice, the coach, sport psychologist, and athlete may want to consider matching the stress management intervention with whether the symptoms of the anxiety complaint manifest themselves primarily cognitively, somatically, or both equally. Some evidence exists in the field of behavioral medicine that greater reduction in muscular problems follows muscular interventions and that disorders that primarily involve cognitive processes tend to respond particularly well to cognitive therapies (Lehrer, Carr, Sarganaraj, & Woolfolk, 1993). Little equivalent research exists in sport psychology, except for recent research by Maynard and his colleagues. Their findings with athletes also suggest that stress management interventions may be more effective when relaxation strategies are matched to the precise mode of the anxiety response (e.g., Maynard, Hemmings, & Warwick-Evans, 1995; Maynard, Warwick-Evans, & Smith, 1995).

This chapter primarily discusses physical stress management interventions, but more often than not anxiety problems manifest themselves both cognitively and somatically, suggesting that the most effective intervention will integrate physical and cognitive techniques. See Chapter 17 for a discussion of cognitive interventions that athletes can use to build confidence and manage stress resulting from self-doubt and worry and an inability to concentrate. Even without an integrated approach, some crossover benefit often occurs. That is, reducing cognitive anxiety helps the body release physical tension and eliminating unwanted physical tension helps lessen cognitive anxiety.

Although some overlap exists, the techniques of relaxation in this chapter can be divided into two categories. The first category includes techniques that focus on the bodily aspects, the **muscle-to-mind techniques.** Breathing exercises and Jacobson's (1930) scientific neuromuscular relaxation or progressive relaxation (PR) fall into this category. The objective of PR is to train the muscles to become sensitive to any level of tension and to be able to release that tension. The second category of techniques work from **mind-to-muscle.** Benson's relaxation response (1975), meditation, autogenic training, and imagery all approach relaxation from the mind-to-muscle perspective. Either approach is effective; the point is to disrupt the stimulus–response pattern of half of the nerves leading to the brain or away from the brain. Learning to reduce the sensation in either half of the circuit will interrupt the stimulation necessary to produce unwanted muscular tension.

Relaxation skills must be practiced on a regular basis just like any sport skill. When teaching relaxation to athletes, it is more effective to begin the training after a workout because it is easier to let go after having had some exercise. It is more difficult to hold muscular tension when physically fatigued. In addition, exercise is nature's best tranquilizer and tends to lower general anxiety and tension.

As previously mentioned, some athletes take longer to develop relaxation skills than others, but most should show improvement after a week or two weeks of regular practice. Emphasize the fact that it takes time to develop the skills, and encourage athletes to continue to practice for several weeks even though they may not always detect improvement.

The degree of relaxation attainable varies to some extent. Within that variation, athletes should learn how to relax and withdraw completely from the environment as well as to relax momentarily. The ability to relax completely serves a different function from relaxing momentarily. After a hard training session, before falling asleep at night, when fatigue sets in, or when an athlete is worried, sick, or under emotional stress, deep, complete relaxation is desirable. Learning to relax completely provides a reference point for the athlete to learn what a **zero-activation level** feels like. It also provides an opportunity to increase awareness of both mental and physical responses and how integrated they are. In the process the athlete learns to recognize patterns of feelings, thoughts, and behaviors and how they affect performance. As a result, the athlete can develop procedures for changing behaviors that interfere with performance. The athlete can learn through deep relaxation how to become detached from the environment and be in full control without interference. The ability to relax completely produces a positive, pleasurable, and beneficial experience that provides the central nervous system with a rest. That, in turn, allows regeneration of physical, mental, and emotional states with the athlete in control.

Finally, the ability to relax completely provides the foundation for learning the skill of **momentary relaxation.** Momentary relaxation skills are extremely important for athletes because they can be used to reduce overactivation at any point during practices and competition. When the nerves are carrying worry messages instead of the stimuli for smooth, coordinated, integrated efforts, the performance suffers. With momentary relaxation, excessive muscular tension and, hopefully, worry and anxiety stimuli are removed, resulting in an enhanced kinesthetic awareness. The momentary respite also allows the athlete to return to a point of controlled balance. Every aspect of performance is enhanced: concentration, attentional focus, awareness, confidence, precision, speed, and so on.

Momentary relaxation can be used just before and during warm-up. In fact, during stretching in preparation for competition is a good time to utilize the strategies of momentary relaxation and to focus on the upcoming game. The more uptight the athlete is prior to performance, the longer the session of momentary relaxation should be. After the competition, this type of relaxation can be used to return to the controlled, balanced state. During the competition, depending on the specific sport and position within the sport, brief periods or lapses in play allow for momentary relaxation as needed. The athlete must learn to become aware of tension and activation levels and adjust them as necessary.

The learning of skills and strategies for a sport is enhanced when one is in a relaxed state, particularly if periods of learning are alternated with periods of relaxation. This is true for academic learning as well as athletic learning. Relaxation preparation also facilitates concentration and imagery practice because it reduces and eliminates other thoughts and stimulation that interfere with the single-minded focus necessary for such practice.

Muscle-to-Mind Relaxation Skills and Strategies

Most athletes respond positively to muscle-to-mind techniques, perhaps because of their more physical lifestyle. When learning these relaxation techniques, athletes should be in a comfortable position and in a quiet, warm environment. Once athletes are trained, they should be able to relax in any environment under any condition. Learning, however, should occur under ideal conditions.

Breathing Exercises[1]

Breathing properly is relaxing, and it facilitates performance by increasing the amount of oxygen in the blood. This carries more energy to the muscles and facilitates the removal of waste products. Unfortunately, many individuals have never learned deep, diaphragmatic breathing, and those who have often find their breathing patterns disrupted under stress. Athletes who get stressed out during a high-pressure performance situation find their breathing is usually affected in one of two ways—they either hold their breath or breathe rapidly and shallowly from the upper chest. Both of these adjustments create even more tension and impairment of performance.

Exercise for feeling shallow, chest breathing:

Raise your shoulders way up and notice what happens to your breathing. This posture forces your breathing to move into just the upper chest and to become rapid and shallow.

The preceding exercise increases athletes' awareness of what it feels like when their breathing has become ineffective. It also replicates, usually unbeknownst to the performer, what often occurs when uptight.

Fortunately, with practice, breathing is one of the easiest physiological systems to control. Learning to take a deep, slow, complete breath will usually trigger a relaxation response. This relaxing, complete breath is the basis for a variety of breathing exercises. Suggestions for specific exercises for breathing control to increase relaxation follow. Depending on the exercise and how it is practiced, these techniques can be used for both deep and momentary relaxation. Some coaches and sport psychologists even choreograph breaths into the performance of certain skills such as gymnastic and figure skating routines.

[1]Several of these exercises are adaptations from Mason (1980).

Complete breath. Proper breathing comes from the *diaphragm,* the thin muscle that separates the lung and abdominal cavities. During inhalation, the diaphragm should move down slightly, thus pushing the abdomen out and creating a vacuum in the lungs. This fills the lungs up from the bottom. For practicing a deep, complete breath, have the athletes imagine that their lungs are divided into three levels or parts. Have the athletes concentrate on filling the lower section of the lungs with air, first by pushing the diaphragm down and forcing the abdomen out. Have them continue by filling the middle portion of the lungs by expanding the chest cavity and raising the rib cage. Finally, have the athletes fill the upper portion of the lungs by raising the chest and shoulders slightly. All three stages progress continuously and smoothly. The athletes should hold the breath for several seconds, then exhale by pulling the abdomen in (which pulls the diaphragm up) and lowering the shoulders and chest to empty the lungs. Finally, instruct the athletes to pull the abdomen in further to force out the last bit of air from the lungs. They should let go of all muscular action at the end of the exhalation so the abdomen and chest are completely relaxed.

Stress to the athletes that during the exhalation they should feel as if the air drains out of the bottom of the lungs, first emptying the upper part, then the middle, and finally the lower part. Repeat this exercise many times with instructions. Once athletes are comfortable with the sequential complete breath, emphasize that on the inhalation they should take a long, slow, deep inhalation through the nose, inhaling as much air as possible. Emphasize that the exhalation should be slow and complete and that the athletes should focus on feeling all tension leaving the body as the air is exhaled.

Exercise for confirming diaphragmatic breathing:

Put one hand on your abdomen and the other on your upper chest. If you are taking a deep, complete breath from the diaphragm, the hand on your abdomen will move out with the inhalation and in with the exhalation, while the hand on the chest remains relatively still.

After learning the procedure, the athletes should take at least 30 to 40 deep breaths each day. Associating deep breathing with events that naturally occur during the day will facilitate practice. Suggest to the athletes that each time the phone rings, they should take a deep breath, exhaling fully and completely before answering. Some stress therapists suggest affixing to a person's wristwatch dial a tiny colored paper disc so that each time the person looks at the watch, he or she is reminded to relax by taking a deep breath. Another good time for athletes to practice this breathing exercise is during the time they are waiting for class to begin or when they need momentary relaxation, such as before a free throw shot, tennis serve, or golf putt.

Sighing with exhalation. Sighing aids in reducing tension. Instruct the athletes as follows: "Inhale slowly and then hold your breath for 10 seconds, feeling the tension building in the throat and chest. Exhale through the mouth with a slight sigh as you let go of the tension in the rib cage. Do nothing about inhaling—let that happen naturally. Hold your breath and repeat the sigh with the exhalation as you force the air out of the lungs."

The quietest or calmest time of the breath is at the end of the exhalation and just before the inhalation. Stress that athletes feel the stillness at the moment directly after fully exhaling and sighing. If athletes can feel this quietness, they are learning how to relax. Practice again, but without holding the breath. As athletes exhale fully and completely, they should feel all the tension leaving the body. Be aware of this quiet time during the breath. Whenever athletes feel themselves getting too tense, they should try to re-create this moment of peace and calm by momentarily practicing this exercise.

Rhythmic breathing. Have the athletes inhale to a count of 4, hold for a count of 4, exhale to a count of 4, and pause for a count of 4 before repeating the sequence. You can alter the rhythm of their breathing by changing the count.

1:2 ratio. Have the athletes take a deep, full breath and then exhale fully and completely. Have them breathe again, only this time to a count of 4 on the inhalation and a count of 8 on the exhalation. If the athletes run out of breath before reaching 8, suggest that next time they take a deeper breath and exhale more slowly. Emphasize awareness of a full inhalation and exhalation. With more practice and deepened relaxation on the part of the athletes, you may need to change the count to 5:10 or 6:12. This exercise is a very powerful relaxer if done properly.

5-to-1 count. Instruct the athletes as follows: "Say to yourself and visualize the number 5 as you take a deep, full, slow breath. Exhale fully and completely. Mentally count and visualize the number 4 with your next inhalation. During the exhalation, say to yourself, 'I am more relaxed now than I was at number 5.' Do not rush the thought. Inhale while mentally counting and visualizing the number 3. With the exhalation, say to yourself, 'I am more relaxed now than I was at number 4.' Allow yourself to feel the deepening relaxation. Continue until you reach number 1. As you approach number 1, you should feel totally calm and relaxed."

The complete exercise takes 1 to 2 minutes. If done properly, it should lead to more relaxation than practicing a single complete breath. Use this exercise before or during practices and competition, depending on how much time is available and how much relaxation is needed.

Concentration breathing. Have the athletes concentrate on focusing their attention on their breathing rhythm. Tell them that if their mind wanders to some other thought between inhaling and exhaling to redirect their attention back to their next breath, letting the intruding thought disappear. Instruct them to think of becoming more relaxed with each exhalation as they continue to focus on the rhythm of their breathing. This is a good exercise for athletes to practice when they are having problems with distracting thoughts.

Progressive Relaxation Exercises[2]

Working under the assumption that an anxious mind cannot exist within a relaxed body, Jacobson (1930) developed the concept of **progressive relaxation (PR),** another muscle-to-mind approach to relaxation. PR consists of a series of exercises that involve contracting a specific muscle group, holding the contraction for 5–7 seconds, then relaxing. The exercises progress from one muscle group to another. The contraction phase teaches an awareness and sensitivity to what muscular tension feels like. The letting go, or relaxation phase, teaches an awareness of what absence of tension feels like and that it can voluntarily be induced by passively releasing the tension in a muscle. Thus, in the learning process, one simply identifies a local state of tension, relaxes it away, and then contrasts the tension sensations with the ensuing relaxation that comes from the elimination of tension. By practicing this internal sensory observation, the athlete can become quite proficient at recognizing unwanted tension sensations wherever they may occur and can then easily release the tension. The ultimate goal of PR is for athletes to develop *automaticity,* whereby they automatically, unconsciously, and effortlessly identify and relax tensions that interfere with the smooth execution of movement skills. At a minimum, the athletes should be able to do PR on a conscious level.

The initial training program devised by Jacobson required much more time in training each muscle group than many of the modifications that have been developed over the years. Jacobson (1964) would have used the following sequence and time frame: left arm, 7 days; right arm, 7 days; left leg, 10 days; right leg, 10 days; trunk, 10 days; neck, 6 days; eye region, 12 days; visualization, 9 days; speech region and speech

imagery, 19 days. Each practice session would take an hour, and as an example, the 7-day left arm sequence would consist of Day 1, bend the hand back; Day 2, bend the hand forward; Day 3, relax only; Day 4, bend the arm at the elbow; Day 5, press the wrist down on books; Day 6, relax only; and Day 7, progressive tension and relaxation of the whole arm.

The modified exercises evolved because the original PR technique proved lengthy and painstaking. For many of the modified Jacobsonian procedures, including the one in this chapter, initial practices require only 25–30 minutes and entail relaxing all the muscle groups. Once skill is acquired, shorter practice sessions and variations can occur.

The coach or others knowledgeable about relaxation should personally lead the exercises. Tape recordings of instructions are available, but coaches and sport psychologists can make the instructions more relevant to a particular sport and situation. There is some evidence that live presentations are more effective than tape-recorded ones (Paul & Trimble, 1970). Encourage athletes to practice outside of the teaching session on their own to improve their skills. Be sure to mention that practice should not occur within an hour after eating a meal. Providing athletes with tapes or written handouts of relaxation exercises may facilitate the likelihood of practicing, but discourage reliance on tapes. With increased experience, these will not be needed.

Begin the relaxation session in a normal, conversational tone. Over the course of the session, however, your voice should progressively and subtly become smoother, quieter, and more monotonous while giving the relaxation phase instructions. In contrast, during the tension phase, your voice should increase slightly in volume and speed. These changes in voice will help athletes distinguish between the phases and the contrast between the sensations of tension and relaxation.

Pace the instructions by doing the exercises with the athletes. Pause about 20 to 30 seconds after each contraction so relaxation can continue for brief periods. Tense larger muscle groups longer than the smaller ones. Repetition is the

---

[2]Several of these exercises are adaptations from Bernstein and Carlson (1993).

key to learning, so continue to practice the same muscle groups until the athletes can relax quickly without producing additional tension. Before you begin, explain to the athletes why excessive physical tension occurs, how it interferes with effective movement (e.g., finger tap technique previously described), and how they can, with practice, learn to recognize and eliminate unwanted tension. Also explain that muscle twitches and spasms are to be expected as muscle fibers begin to let go. If there is a great deal of tension, an entire muscle group may let go, producing involuntary movement. On occasion, this happens just before one falls asleep if there is a tremendous buildup of muscular tension. The flexor pair lets go before the extensors and they take up the slack, resulting in a sudden jerk throughout the body.

Restlessness is a signal to let go and relax further. If you are working with a single athlete or a small group, you may want the participants to signal when they are fully relaxed by raising a finger. As they become proficient in relaxing, there is a tendency not to follow instructions. Emphasize the importance of following instructions passively. This is particularly essential during the relaxation phase. Just let the relaxation happen— don't force it. Relaxation requires no effort. Any effort to relax causes tension. "The process of relaxing is one in which the individual gives up the tension—just lets it go and allows the muscle fibers to elongate" (McGuigan, 1993, p. 39).

Practice PR either sitting or lying down. The latter is usually more conducive to relaxation, but athletes should sit up if they tend to fall asleep. The lying down position is on the back with the head, neck, and trunk in a straight line. The legs should be straight and 6–12 inches apart with the heels inward and the toes pointing outward. Rest the arms comfortably at the sides with the hands a little way from the thighs, palms up, and fingers comfortably bent. Put a small pillow (rolled up sweats are a good substitute) under either the knees or neck (not both) for additional comfort. If using a sitting position the athletes should sit upright, hips against the backrest, with the arms and legs uncrossed and the feet flat on the floor. The hands rest comfortably on the thighs (palms down). If no

chairs are available, athletes can lean against the gymnasium wall.

Athletes wearing hard contact lenses can either remove them or keep their eyes open while practicing PR. They should also remove or loosen any constrictive clothing such as belts or shoes. The body should be completely supported by the chair, floor, mat, or whatever is being used. Regardless of which PR exercise is being practiced, the preceding protocol is a good one to follow.

Active PR. Read the following script but keep your voice from sounding canned: "Sit or lie down in a comfortable position and try to put yourself in a relaxed state. Close your eyes and take a long, slow, deep breath through your nose, inhaling as much air as you can. Then exhale slowly and completely, feeling the tension leaving your body as you exhale. Take another deep breath and let the day's tensions and problems drain out of you with the exhalation. [Pause.] Relax as much as possible and listen to what I say. Remember not to strain to relax. Just let it happen. During the session, try not to move any more than necessary to stay comfortable. Particularly, try not to move muscles that have already been relaxed.

"As we progress through each of 12 muscle groups, you will first tense the muscle group for approximately 5 to 7 seconds and then relax for 20–30 seconds. Do not start the tensing until I say 'NOW.' Continue to tense until I say 'OKAY.' or 'RELAX,' at which time immediately let go of all the tension.

"Begin with tensing the muscles in the dominant hand and lower arm by making a tight fist and bending your hand back at the wrist NOW. Feel the tension in the hand and up into the lower arm. . . . Okay, relax by simply letting go of the tension. Notice the difference between tension and relaxation [pause 20 to 30 seconds]. . . . Make another fist NOW [pause 5 to 7 seconds]. Okay, relax. Just let the relaxation happen by stopping the contraction; don't put out any effort [pause 25 to 30 seconds].

"Next tense the muscles of the dominant upper arm by pushing your elbow down against the floor or back of the chair. Tense NOW. Feel the tension in the biceps without involving the muscles in the lower arm and hand. . . . Okay, release the tension all at once, not gradually. Just let it happen. Let it all go. . . . Tense NOW. . . . Okay, release it. Contrast the difference between tension and letting go into relaxation. Relaxation is no more than the absence of tension.

"With your nondominant hand, make a tight fist and bend your wrist back NOW. Feel the tension in your hand and lower arm, but keep the upper arm relaxed. . . . Okay, relax by simply draining all of the tension out. . . . NOW tense again. . . . Okay, relax and feel the difference between the tension and relaxation. . . . NOW push the elbow down or back to tighten the nondominant upper arm. . . . Okay, relax. . . . NOW tense the upper arm again. Note the discomfort. . . . RELAX. Let all the tension dissolve away. . . . Enjoy the feelings of relaxation. . . . Notice the sensations you have in the muscles of both arms and hands. . . . Perhaps there is a sort of flow of relaxation—perhaps a feeling of warmth and even heaviness in these muscles. Notice and enjoy this feeling of relaxation.

"Turn your attention to the muscles in your face. Tense the muscles in your forehead by raising your eyebrows NOW. Feel the tension in your forehead and scalp. [Pause for only 3- to 5-second contractions with these smaller muscle groups.] Okay, relax and smooth it out. . . . Enjoy the spreading sensation of relaxation. . . . NOW frown again. . . . RELAX. Allow your forehead to become smooth again. . . . Your forehead should feel smooth as glass. . . .

"Next squint your eyes very tightly and at the same time pucker your lips and clinch your teeth, but not so tightly that it hurts. Tense NOW. Feel the tension. . . . Okay, relax. . . . Let the tension dissolve away. . . . NOW tense again. . . . Okay, let all the tension go. . . . Your lips may part slightly as your cheeks and jaw relax.

"Next tense the muscles of the neck and shoulders by raising your shoulders upward as high as you can while pulling your neck down into your shoulders. Tense NOW. . . . feel the discomfort. . . . RELAX. Drop your shoulders back down and feel the relaxation spreading through your neck, throat, and shoulders. . . . Let go more and more. . . . Tense NOW by raising your shoulders and sinking your neck. . . . Okay, relax. Let go more and more. Enjoy the deepening sensation of relaxation. . . . Remember relaxation is simply the absence of tension."

"Next tighten your abdomen as though you expect a punch while simultaneously squeezing the buttocks together. Tense NOW. You should feel a good deal of tightness and tension in the stomach and buttocks. . . . RELAX, release the tension, let it all drain out. Just let it happen. . . . NOW tense again. . . . Okay, relax. Feel the spreading sensation of relaxation. Let go more and more. . . .

"Turn your attention to your right leg. Tighten the muscles in your right thigh by simultaneously contracting all the muscles of your thigh. Tense NOW. Try to localize the tension only to your thigh. . . . Note the sensation. Okay, relax. Contrast the tension and relaxation sensations. Remember relaxation is merely the absence of tension; it takes no effort except merely releasing the tension. . . . NOW tighten the right thigh again. . . . Okay, release the tension—just passively let it drain out. Enjoy the feeling of relaxation. . . .

"Next flex your ankle as though you are trying to touch your toes to your shin. Tense NOW. You should be feeling tension all through your calf, ankle, and foot. Contrast this tension with when you tensed the thigh. Okay, relax. Simply release the tension; let go of any remaining tension. . . . NOW tense again. . . . Okay, slowly release all the tension. . . .

"Next straighten your legs and point your toes downward. Tense NOW. Note the discomfort. . . . Okay, relax. Feel the spreading sensation of relaxation as you relax deeper and deeper. . . . NOW straighten your legs. . . . RELAX. Release all the tension. Let go more and more. . . ."

"Relax all the muscles of your body—let them all go limp. You should be breathing slowly and deeply. Let all last traces of tension drain out of your body. Scan your body for any places that might still feel tension. Wherever you feel tension, do an additional tense and relax. You may notice a sensation of warmth and heaviness throughout your body, as though you are sinking deeper and deeper into the chair or floor. Or you may feel as though you are as light as air, as though you are floating on a cloud. Whatever feelings you have, go with them. . . . Enjoy the sensation of relaxation. . . . Relax deeper and deeper. . . .

"Before opening your eyes, take several deep breaths and feel the energy and alertness flowing back into your body. Stretch your arms and legs if you wish. Open your eyes when you are ready."

After taking your athletes through their first few PR practices, take several minutes to discuss their reactions. Get them to identify what it felt like and how successful they thought they were at relaxing. For those who had difficulty relaxing, stress again the importance of the absence of efforting, of being passive and just letting it happen. Also remind them of the need to practice regularly. Just like any physical skill, PR takes practice. See if any of the athletes became aware of places in their body where they tend to hold tension. The goal is to spot this tension and release it before it causes any pain, such as headaches and backaches, or performance problems. When taking an athlete or team through a PR exercise, signs to look for that indicate difficulty relaxing are a wrinkled forehead, frowning, darting eyes, exaggerated or rapid breathing, and habits of fidgeting (McGuigan, 1993). When too many of these occur, or they occur frequently, stop the PR exercise and discuss what is causing difficulty. When resuming practice, it may be necessary to take more time to try and learn how to relax the given muscle group.

Have the athletes practice this lengthy active PR exercise daily for several weeks or until they gain some proficiency. If less time is available, and when they become more proficient, do only one repetition of each muscle group. In successive practices, put progressively more emphasis on keeping the rest of the body totally relaxed while tensing only the muscle group in question. Once athletes have achieved some skill, have them practice the differential PR procedure described in the next section.

Differential PR. The differential PR exercise is performed with the same sequence of muscle groups as the preceding exercise. The difference is in the amount of tension generated. Rather than doing an all-out contraction twice for each muscle group, do an initial all-out contraction followed by relaxation; then generate half as much tension and relax, and finally just enough tension to identify and let it go. Thus, differential active PR consists of studying and releasing tension of ever-decreasing intensity. Throughout the exercise, stress that tension should only occur in the muscle group being contracted and only at the predetermined level of intensity.

This exercise is an important way to help athletes become aware of differential relaxation. As noted earlier, relaxing all muscle groups as completely as one can almost never occurs in sport; neither does only total muscle contraction. Differential relaxation is far more common. **Differential relaxation** involves learning to relax all of the muscles except those that are needed for the task at hand. The muscles that are used should only be tensed to the level needed. Learning appropriate differential relaxation leads not only to better performance but also to less fatigue. With proper training in the active PR exercise, followed by practice of this exercise, athletes can better accomplish differential relaxation during practice and competition, as well as throughout the day, because they become more sensitive to the slightest unwanted tension in different muscle groups and more confident in their ability to control the level of tension.

Abbreviated active PR. Once the athletes have learned the PR technique, you can have them use a shorter procedure to achieve deep muscle relaxation by combining some of the muscle groups. Tense each group for 5 to 10 seconds and then relax for 30 to 40 seconds. Read the following directions:

"Make a tight fist with both hands, tighten the biceps and forearms, hold, and relax for 20 to 30 seconds.

"Tense all of the facial and neck muscles. . . . Relax. . . .

"Raise the shoulders while making the stomach hard and tightening the buttocks. HOLD. . . . Relax and let go. . . . [Give the instructions quickly so the tension buildup is continuous.]

"Tighten the muscles of both legs and feet by straightening your knees and pulling your toes toward your shins. HOLD. . . . Relax and let go of all the tension. . . ."

It you think the preceding procedure might require too big of a jump for the athletes, modify it by doing each arm separately and each leg separately. Once the athletes can successfully do the abbreviated exercise, which, according to Bernstein and Carlson (1993), normally takes several weeks of practice, an even shorter version is to have the athletes put as much tension as possible into the entire body. Hold this total body tension 5 to 10 seconds, and then completely release the tension, letting go into a totally relaxed state. Repeat this procedure several times, trying to deepen the relaxation state with each successive practice. Just as with the longer PR exercise, individuals will benefit from practicing the abbreviated PR exercises with the differential contraction protocol rather than just an all-out contraction.

Passive PR. Once the athletes have learned the skill of active, deep muscle relaxation, they can relax the muscles without first tensing them. Many people find this passive form of relaxation more effective and pleasant than the active form. With passive PR, the participant merely lets go from whatever level of muscular tension is in the muscle group. There is a slow progression from one part of the body to another as the participant relaxes each body part more deeply by letting go of any remaining tension. The same sequence of complete or abbreviated body parts can be used for passive PR as for active PR. (Some people prefer to progress from the feet up or from the head down.)

After a general lead-in to the exercise, progress through the specific body parts with directions such as the following: "Turn your attention to your dominant hand. Just tune in to how this hand feels. Become aware of any tension that might be in it and let go of the tension—even more and more. Let go of all the muscles in your dominant hand. Allow it gradually to become looser and heavier. Think about letting go further. Now go to your nondominant hand. Think of your nondominant hand getting looser, heavier, just letting go of the muscles in your nondominant hand. Let go further, more deeply, and now feel the relaxation coming into your left and right forearms. Feel your forearms getting looser and heavier. Enjoy the relaxation that is now coming into your forearms. . . ."

Quick body scan. The quick body scan is an abbreviated passive PR technique that is a helpful momentary muscle relaxation exercise best used during performance, such as just before serving, shooting a free throw, batting, or even while running, particularly middle or long distances. Quickly scan the body from head to toe (or toe to head). Stop only at muscle groups where the tension level is too high. Release the tension and continue the scan down (or up) the body.

Neck and shoulder check. It is very common for athletes to carry excessive tension in the neck and shoulders when they are worried or anxious. Once they have learned to spot tension and relax, instruct your athletes to scan their neck and shoulders periodically for any undue signs of tension. If they feel tension in the neck, they should release it passively or roll the neck around the shoulders. Releasing excessive tension in these two areas tends to spread relaxation to the rest of the body; it may also have a calming effect on the mind.

Mind-to-Muscle Relaxation Techniques

The majority of additional relaxation techniques and strategies focus on **efferent nerve control,** or the stimulation from the brain to the muscles. Among these techniques are meditation, visualization, and autogenic training. The techniques should be practiced initially in a comfortable position in a quiet environment. Any of the positions suggested for progressive relaxation practice can be used.

Meditation

The regular practice of meditation helps one teach a state of deep relaxation, and it facilitates concentration by disciplining the mind. Four basic components are common to most types of meditation: a quiet environment, a comfortable position, a mental device, and a passive attitude. A mental device, such as a mantra or fixed gazing at an object, helps to shift the mind from logical, externally oriented thought by providing a focus of attention on something that is nonarousing and nonstimulating. A **mantra** is a nonstimulating, meaningless rhythmic sound of one or two syllables that a person regularly repeats while meditating.

It is critical that athletes not worry about how well they are performing the technique because this disrupts effective meditation. Stress their adopting a "let it happen" attitude. The passive attitude is perhaps the most important element in learning to meditate. Distracting thoughts or mind wandering may occur, but this is to be expected and does not mean that the technique is being performed incorrectly. When these thoughts occur, simply redirect attention to the mental device, focusing on this cue and letting all other thoughts move on through consciousness with a passive attitude, making no attempt to attend to them.

The **relaxation response** developed by Herbert Benson (1975), a physician at Harvard Medical School, is an excellent meditative technique to teach athletes. This technique is a generalized version of a variety of Eastern and Western religious, cultic, and lay meditation practices. It has the advantage, however, of being a noncultic technique, with all reference to mysticism and unusual postures eliminated. In fact, the technique does not even need to be called meditation. For a mental device, Benson recommended the word *one*. However, *one* is a very stimulating word for achievement-oriented athletes. A better word might be *calm* or a word or sound of their choosing. The following are directions for meditation based on a variation of Benson's relaxation response:

1. Sit in a comfortable position in a quiet place.

2. Close your eyes.

3. Deeply relax all your muscles, beginning at your feet and progressing up to the top of your head (head to feet if you prefer). Keep them relaxed.

4. Breathe through your nose. Concentrate on your breathing. As you breathe out, say the word *calm* or some other word or nonsense sound silently to yourself. For example, breathe IN . . . OUT . . . "calm"; IN . . . OUT . . . "calm"; and so forth. Breathe easily and naturally.

5. You may open your eyes to check the time, but do not use an alarm. When you finish, sit quietly for several minutes, at first with your eyes closed and later with your eyes open. Do not stand up for a few minutes.

Do the preceding for 5 minutes initially and, with practice, build to 15–20 minutes. Do not worry about whether you are successful in achieving a deep level of relaxation. Try to remain passive by just letting the relaxation happen. Practice the technique once or twice daily, but not within one hour after any meal, since the digestive processes seem to interfere with the elicitation of the relaxation response.

Visualization

If athletes have been trained in imagery and can visualize easily, visualizing being in a place conducive to relaxation is another successful technique for eliciting relaxation. For example, an athlete might visualize lying on a beach feeling the warm sand and sun on the body while listening to the continuous rhythm of breaking waves and smelling the salt air. Other images might be sitting in the midst of a beautiful mountain scene or lying in a grassy valley by a gentle, gurgling stream. Whatever image provides the athlete with a sense of calm and relaxation is the one he or she should use.

Autogenic training.[3] Developed in Germany in the early 1930s by Johannes Schultz, **autogenic training** has been used extensively with European athletes. The training consists of a series of exercises designed to produce two physical sensations, warmth and heaviness. Basically, it is a technique of autohypnosis or self-hypnosis. Attention is

---

[3]Some of these exercises have been modified from Linden (1993).

focused on the sensations one is trying to produce. As in meditation, it is important to let the feeling happen in a very passive manner. There are six stages in the training. Have the athletes learn each stage before progressing to the next stage. Some people suggest that trainees spend 2 weeks at each stage; however, the progression can be modified to suit athletes' learning rates as well as the training program and length of season of the sport. It usually takes several months of regular practice of 10 to 40 minutes, total one to six times per day, to become proficient enough to experience heaviness and warmth in the limbs and to produce the sensation of a relaxed, calm heartbeat and respiratory rate accompanied by warmth in the abdomen and coolness in the forehead. Once athletes have reached that level of training and can attain a relaxed state, they can use imagery to increase the depth of relaxation.

The first autogenic stage involves focusing attention in a passive manner on the dominant arm while silently saying: (1) "My right (left) arm is very heavy" (this phrase is repeated six times); (2) "I am very quiet" (or, "I am at peace") (this is said only once and then alternates with the first step until completing three to six cycles of these two steps). Then cancel out the effect by having the athletes bend the arm, take a deep breath, and open their eyes. The canceling out should always occur with each part of the heaviness stage in order to ultimately maximize the effect. Practice just the preceding two or three sessions a day (takes only 1 or 2 minutes each time) until the heaviness starts to spread to the opposite arm. When this occurs, replace "my right arm" with "my arms." Once the heaviness starts to generalize to the legs, replace "my arms" with "my arms and legs are heavy." Ultimately, the entire body starts to feel heavy. If the mind wanders, emphasize passively redirecting attention back to the task at hand. Some athletes may be able to produce a sense of heaviness immediately; others may take 1 or 2 weeks of three or more times of practice daily to accomplish the sensation.

Once the heaviness experience has been well trained and can be induced rapidly and reliably, move on to the second stage, which is warmth and may take longer to achieve. Instructions for the warmth stage follow the same general content and format as the first stage except "heavy" is replaced with "warmth." Before practicing the warmth phrases, however, begin by repeating the suggestions for the preceding stage:

1. "My arms and legs are very heavy" (repeat a total of six times).

2. "I am very quiet" (or "at peace"; say only once).

3. "My right (left) arm is very warm" (and so forth, as done in stage one).

Do not move on to the third stage until the athletes have mastered the heaviness and warmth sensations.

If athletes are having difficulty feeling the appropriate sensation, sometimes learning can be facilitated by having them physically experience the sensation. For example, if trying to achieve heaviness in the right arm, put a pillow over the arm and, if need be, a book or two on top of the pillow. For the warmth sensation, have the athletes immerse their hands in hot water or put a heating pad or hot water bottle over the hands while they initially do the exercise.

Regulation of the heartbeat is the third stage. It consists of the autosuggestion "My heartbeat is regular and calm" or "My heart is beating quietly and strongly." Because awareness of heart activity varies considerably among people, you may need to sensitize the trainees to their own heart activity by having them put their hand over their heart when initially doing the exercise. Again, follow the same careful and progressive procedure as that described previously, only this time begin with the phrase, "My arms and legs are heavy. My arms and legs are warm." Follow the same type of protocol for the fourth, fifth, and sixth stages, which consist of the following:

Stage 4: Breathing rate
"My breathing rate is slow, calm, and relaxed: It breathes me."

Stage 5: Warmth in the solar plexus
"My solar plexus is warm" (hand placed on upper abdominal area); or say, "Sun rays are streaming quiet and warm."

Stage 6: Coolness of the forehead
"My forehead is cool."

During Stage 4, the trainee becomes aware of the breathing rate but does not try consciously to change it. Stage 5 deals with self-regulation of the visceral organs. The trainee focuses on the area of the solar plexus because it is the most important nerve center for the inner organs. You may prefer the second phrase because it helps to depict the image that this nerve center is that of a sun from which warm rays extend into the other body areas (Linden, 1993). The well-known relaxing effect of a cool cloth on the forehead forms the basis for Stage 6. Just as warmth is associated with vasodilation, the experience of coolness on the forehead leads to a localized vasoconstriction. Normally it takes about one week of practice each to learn stages 4 to 6.

Once the athlete has learned all the stages, the entire sequence can be practiced as follows:

"My arms and legs are heavy" six times; "quiet" once.

"My arms and legs are very warm" six times; "quiet" once.

"My heartbeat is regular and calm" six times; "quiet" once.

"It breathes me" six times; "quiet" once.

"Sun rays are streaming quiet and warm" six times; "quiet" once.

"My forehead is cool" six times; "quiet" once.

Linden (1993) advises that daily training of the total exercise for another 4 to 6 months will lead to more profound and stronger sensations and the targeting of generalization of training to different environments. With proficiency, it may take fewer than six repetitions for each of these exercises to achieve the desired effect.

Autogenic Training With Visualization

After athletes have mastered the six stages of autogenic training and can induce the desired state in a few minutes and sustain it for 30 minutes to an hour, they are ready to move to the next phase of training, which combines autogenic exercises with visualization. The progression goes from first doing the autogenic exercise to then visualizing the desired feeling or objective. For example, an athlete might build confidence by imaging some *flow,* winning, or peak experience when everything went just right. An athlete might program success by imaging her- or himself performing exactly the proper execution of a skill or strategy for an upcoming competition. The visualization applications are without limit, but the athlete may first need to gain skill at imagery if he or she lacks it (see Chapter 16).

As indicated earlier, autogenic training takes a relatively long time to master. As a result, it is less popular in the United States because athletes seldom train under the same coach or sport psychologist for such long periods of time. In addition, the competitive seasons are frequently too short to introduce and learn autogenic training. However, prior to the fall of communism, it was used extensively in many Eastern European countries where athletes were housed in sport training centers for several years working with a relatively stable staff of coaches and sports medicine personnel. Despite the time required to become proficient in autogenic training, many athletes find it a satisfactory means of training for relaxation and imagery. This approach will be particularly appealing to those athletes who respond to autosuggestion.

When Relaxation Training Fails

Sometimes efforts to teach athletes relaxation skills will fail or the athletes may be able to relax when practicing the relaxation skill, but cannot do it when it counts most—during frustrating practices and stressful competitions. There are a number of potential sources for difficulty in learning and achieving relaxation. For example, if the individual teaching the relaxation intervention has not developed sufficient rapport with the athlete, the athlete may not be comfortable enough to consider relaxing, let alone deeply relaxing. An athlete referred by a coach may feel coerced and thus not be a willing participant. Whether from coercion or another source for lack of motivation, a failure to practice relaxation techniques sufficiently and to self-monitor frequently for the need to implement a quick relaxation intervention are common reasons for ineffective relaxation training. Other situations may activate personal issues for the athlete. Someone who feels a great need for personal control or who has a great fear of losing control may respond with increasing levels of anxiety when asked to relax. In each of the preceding situations, more effective relaxation training would occur if strategies to overcome the difficulties were first introduced.

For athletes who know how to relax but have difficulty doing it in performance situations, more success might occur with greater practice reducing muscular tension in situations that more closely simulate the actual performance environment. An example might be a basketball player who gets really anxious when he has to shoot free throws during critical game times. Having this athlete practice his free throws using imagery that puts him on the foul line with the game on the line could create a more gamelike situation to practice staying relaxed when shooting free throws. The coach may even want to tape crowd noise and play it loudly over the PA system or invite people to watch to create more social evaluation. Teammates waiting their turn to practice could verbally harass the shooter. In this practice situation, the player should precede his shot by relaxing with a deep-breathing technique (e.g., diaphragmatic breathing) or a quick body scan followed by a brief imagery (see Chapter 16), wherein he sees himself successfully performing the skill while remaining loose and positively focused.

Research suggests that when some high-anxious individuals are in stressful circumstances and try to relax their effort can backfire by producing the ironic effect of intensifying the anxiety and tension (Wegner, Broome, & Blumberg, 1997). In other words, just as athletes most want to relax the desire to be calm and collected may be the culprit in creating even more unwanted cognitive anxiety and somatic effects. Wegner (1994, 1997) explains these paradoxical effects with a theory he calls ironic processes of mental control. Doing the opposite of what one intends has been found for not only relaxation but also cognitions (see Chapter 17). Although the implications this theory has for sport psychology research and interventions have been discussed (e.g., see Janelle, 1999), there is no intervention research to suggest how best to deal with athletes suffering from the phenomena, but Wegner et al.'s research findings and suggestions provide some guidance. Their experimental manipulations indicated a less pronounced effect with more detailed relaxation instructions rather than the general comment, "relax." They also suggest downplaying the importance of mental control, not providing highly motivational instructions, and that even capitulating to our anxieties may be more effective than intentional relaxation.

Apter's (1989) reversal theory also offers possible insights into how to best intervene with athletes who experience ironic effects. Apter proposed that athletes in a "telic" (i.e., goal-minded, serious) motivational state are likely to perceive their high arousal as anxiety, whereas athletes in a "paratelic" (i.e., seeking fun, performing for its own sake) state are likely to perceive their high arousal as excitement, not threat. If correct, rather than focusing on trying to reduce the symptoms (e.g., physical tension) of anxiety through relaxation techniques, a better procedure might be helping these athletes put the fun back into sport. Such an approach initially entails identifying the sources of stress and disputing the underlying irrational beliefs or distortions in thinking that probably led to them. The cognitive restructuring intervention (rational emotive cognitive) described in Chapter 17 is one excellent method for accomplishing the preceding (see also Kerr, 2001). Once done, the athlete should find it easier to focus on the excitement of competition, having fun, and playing for its own sake. The preceding approach is certainly worth a try but, until more is known, coaches and sport psychologists may well have to use trial and error in trying to help the athletes who need it most to relax.

Skills and Strategies for Learning How to Increase Activation and Energy

Once athletes have been taught how to slow down the heart rate and respiration rate and to increase blood flow and temperature in the extremities, they can also learn to develop skills to speed up the heart rate and respiration rate and get the physiological systems ready for action. These skills are essential for generating energy on short notice or when brief bursts of energy are needed.

Just as there are a variety of effective techniques for decreasing activation, there are many techniques for energizing or increasing activation. Such skills and strategies should be used to build appropriate activation when athletes are not psyched up enough for practice or for competition. They can also be used to reduce fatigue during practice and competition. The coach should encourage athletes to practice and develop these skills and strategies. Not only should athletes identify primary energizing techniques that tend to work for them, but they should also have backup techniques in the event that the effectiveness of the primary techniques diminishes over time. Meyers, Whelan, and Murphy's meta-analysis of sport psychology intervention studies found support for the effectiveness of psych-up procedures in enhancing performance ($n = 5$, $d = 1.23$, $SD = .73$).

First, the athletes need to identify when energizing is generally needed in their particular sport or in specific positions or situations within the sport. The coach and sport psychologist should try to become sensitive to each athlete's optimal level of activation; some athletes are much more likely than others to need energizing. The athletes also need to learn how to recognize signs and symptoms of low energy and activation and where they are located in the body. As an example, a track athlete may need to learn how to energize dead legs during a race. Or a weight lifter may want to put all available energy into the legs and arms to attain a particular lift.

We turn now to 10 specific skills and strategies athletes can use to increase their activation and energy.

Breathing

Breathing control and focus work as effectively in producing energy as in reducing tension. Instruct your athletes to focus on a regular, relaxed breathing rhythm. Now have them consciously increase that rhythm and imagine with each inhalation that they are generating more energy and activation. With each exhalation the athletes should imagine that they are getting rid of any waste products or fatigue that might prevent them from being at their best. Ask them to feel in full control, supplying sufficient oxygen and energy for any task that they have to perform. Have the athletes increase their breathing rate as they increase their level of energy generation. Along with the accelerated breathing rate, athletes may want to say "Energy in" with each inhalation and "Fatigue out" with each exhalation.

Using Energizing Imagery

Using imagery skills, have the athletes imagine that they are machines capable of generating energy at will. As an example, have them imagine that they are a train that is just beginning to move, building up steam, momentum, and power with each deep breath. There are literally hundreds of images that can be conjured up as cues for generating energy: animal images, machine images, forces of nature, and so on. Instruct the athletes to develop a supply of imagery cues that work for them in various situations encountered in their particular sport. Instruct them to establish a plan for using these cues ahead of time and to practice and prepare to use them on a regular basis. Some sports have lapses in action that are much more conducive to using cues for activation and energizing than others. Help your athletes to become aware of and to plan for the times when they can use these strategies with self-talk, concentration, and imagery. They are particularly effective when fatigue is beginning to set in, when a series of points have been lost, or when a sudden burst of energy is needed to finish a play.

Formulating Energizing Verbal Cues

In the midst of a performance, depending on the sport or position, there are many occasions when the athletes do not have enough time to prepare imagery techniques to generate energy. In preparation for such times, think of word cues and images with which they can quickly associate energy buildup. Words such as *explode, charge, psych up, go,* and the like, as well as any image representing energy, can be used. Then have the athletes select the cues that are appropriate to their sport and to the tasks that they perform during competition.

Athletes need to get to know themselves well enough to learn what types of thoughts, images, and cue words serve to activate and energize them during practice and competitive performance.

Combining Energizing Cues, Images, and Breathing

Raiport (1988), a former Russian sport psychologist, described in a recent book several exercises that Eastern European sport psychologists teach athletes to help them self-induce activation. Each of these exercises combines a verbal phrase with imagery and a certain breathing pattern. The breathing pattern is one of exhaling on the first part of the phrase and inhaling on the italicized part. For example, take the phrase "I've had *a good rest.*" The most meaningful part of the phrase (italics) is combined with the inhalation, which is physiologically connected with tensing up the muscles and thus facilitates energizing. When time permits, take a two-breath pause between each repetition of the phrase. The following exercises come from Raiport's 1988 book:

> "I am breathing *deeper, inhaling energy*" (repeat twice). During the pauses between the phrases, visualize yourself inhaling a tiny cloud of white energy that spreads throughout your entire body. [Some athletes may prefer an energizing color such as red or yellow.]
>
> "My body is *becoming lighter*" (repeat four times). Imagine that the white cloud of energy you inhale is a very light gas, like helium. Feel your body becoming light and energized.
>
> "Strength is *flowing into my body*" (repeat three times). Visualize a stream of vibrating energy pouring into your body with each breath. It fills you with freshness and vigor. Feel yourself overflowing with this purifying energy; it now radiates from every pore of your body. [Some athletes may benefit from giving the stream of vibrating energy an energizing color.]
>
> "I am *vigorous and alert*" (repeat three times). Imagine strength, power, and a keen awareness of life expanding throughout your body.
>
> "My muscles are *quivering with energy*" (repeat four times). Feel your muscles twitching in impatient anticipation for action.

You feel energized yet relaxed. Strongly clench your fists and jaws several times.

Transferring Energy

Help your athletes learn to convert energy from other sources into a positive and useful force for athletic performance. Activation and arousal that result from aggression, anger, frustration, or some other emotion that tends to interfere with performance need to be converted into energy to accomplish performance goals.

Storing Excess Energy for Later Use

Many athletes have found that the strategy of storing excess energy that is frequently generated just prior to competition accomplishes two purposes: It provides them a means of transferring that energy somewhere else, and it provides a well of energy from which to draw on at some later point. If an athlete has a problem with overarousal, suggest that the athlete store away that energy and use it later when he or she feels fatigued or discouraged.

Using the Environment

Some athletes have learned how to draw energy from the spectators to use for their own performance. This type of strategy provides the home team with an advantage. Athletes need to learn how to take all types of energy available in the sport environment and put it to their own use through imagery, word cues, self-talk, and the like. They can even draw energy from their opponents, particularly when it appears that the opponents have the momentum going for them.

Listening to Music

Music is often a good relaxer and energy provider, depending on the music selected. With the availability of cassette players and headphones, athletes can readily select and listen to the music that works best for them. However, the coach should ensure that the practice or competitive environment is not saturated with loud music that may detract from the optimal level of activation for many athletes.

Improving Pacing

Athletes become underactivated in some sports because of fatigue. This tiredness is often caused by inappropriate pacing and unnecessary sources of energy drain. The alert coach can spot athletes who have difficulty rationing out their energy over time. Appropriate physical practice plus teaching the athlete to become more sensitive to physical signs and symptoms can improve pacing. Pacing is also improved when unnecessary sources of energy drain are eliminated; these sources include too much muscle tension for a particular skill or situation, anger, frustration and undue response to officiating calls, and anxiety or worry over one's own performance or that of teammates.

Using Distraction

Another way to deal with underactivation caused by fatigue is to focus one's attention away from the state of fatigue being experienced. Most athletes do just the opposite; the more fatigued they become, the more they tune into it. This just increases the sense of fatigue as well as its detrimental effects on performance. Instead, suggest to the athletes that they apply their concentration skills and focusing ability on what is happening and about to happen within the performance setting. Remind the athletes to think about what they are doing rather than about how they are feeling.

Exercise for applying what you know about interventions:

Use the following case studies to design an optimal intervention for the particular scenario described in the case study.

1. *David, a football quarterback, goes to a sport psychologist because the demands of professional football have him so stressed that he is having difficulty sleeping. During games, he is so tense that his throws are often erratic and he can't find his secondary receivers. He reports that it seems like "he's looking at the field through a roll of toilet paper." What relaxation interventions might a coach or sport psychology consultant implement to help David? Indicate how to sequence them and describe how they might be practiced.*

2. *Jeff, a sport psychologist, finds that his relaxation training with Jenny, a promising intercollegiate pitcher, results in ironic processing when she pitches in important games. What is happening to Jenny and how might the sport psychologist help her deal with this consequence?*

3. *Sue, a high school coach, finds that her team usually competes up to its potential. She is frustrated, however, with their play during practice. She feels that the team's development is not what it could be because the players often lack intensity and focus during practice. What might the coach do to try and correct this problem?*

Summary

It is the coach's and sport psychologist's responsibility to teach the athlete strategies and techniques for achieving an optimal level of activation for practice and competition. Acquiring the ability to self-regulate arousal enhances not only one's learning and performance of athletic skills but also one's functioning in many nonathletic situations.

It is important for coaches to know that poor performance during competition is more frequently a consequence of overactivation than underactivation. All too often coaches assume the opposite and partially contribute to the continuation of the problem by berating athletes to try harder when intervening with some calming strategy would be much more appropriate. This chapter has described techniques for achieving total relaxation and momentary or partial relaxation. Such techniques rid the muscles of disruptive tension that interferes with performance and help quiet the rest of the body and the mind. They also promote confidence in the athlete's ability to lessen or eliminate the effects of undesirable thoughts and feelings.

Energizing skills and strategies that can be used to increase activation and lessen the effects of fatigue were also described in this chapter

No single control strategy is effective or desirable for all athletes. Consequently, coaches and sport psychologists will need to teach their athletes a variety of techniques. Athletes should be encouraged to identify and practice the primary techniques that tend to work best for them as well as some backup techniques in the event that the primary ones lose their effectiveness.

Study Questions

1. Discuss how relaxation skills are useful to an athlete.
2. Compare conceptually the two major types of relaxation techniques (muscle to mind and mind to muscle).
3. Give four examples of breathing relaxation techniques.
4. Briefly describe the technique of progressive relaxation (active, passive, differential).
5. Give an example of a meditation relaxation technique.
6. How can visualization be used to achieve relaxation?
7. What is autogenic training? Give an example of an autogenic relaxation technique.
8. Briefly describe and give an example of at least six different types of techniques for increasing activation.
9. A sport psychologist is having great difficulty getting Ashley, an elite diver, to learn the skill of deep muscle relaxation. What factors might be contributing to her difficulty at relaxing?

References

Apter, M. J. (1989). *Reversal theory: Motivation, emotion, and personality.* London: Routledge.

Benson, H. (1975). *The relaxation response.* New York: Avon Books.

Bernstein, D. A., & Carlson, C. R. (1993). Progressive relaxation: Abbreviated methods. In P. M. Lehrer & R. L. Woolfolk (Eds.), *Principles and practice of stress management* (2nd ed., pp. 53–87). New York: The Guilford Press.

Green, E., & Green, A. (1977). *Beyond biofeedback.* New York: Dell.

Greenspan, M. J., & Feltz, D. L. (1989). Psychological interventions with athletes in competitive situations: A review. *The Sport Psychologist, 3,* 219–236.

Jacobson, E. (1930). *Progressive relaxation.* Chicago: University of Chicago Press.

Jacobson, E. (1964). *Self-operations control: A manual of tension control.* Chicago: National Foundation for Progressive Relaxation.

Janelle, C. (1999). Ironic mental processes in sport: Implications for sport psychologists. *The Sport Psychologist, 13,* 201–220.

Kerr, J. H. (2001). *Counseling athletes: Applying reversal theory.* London: Routledge.

Lehrer, P. M., Carr, R., Sarganaraj, D., & Woolfolk, R. L. (1993). Differential effects of stress management therapies in behavioral medicine. In P. M. Lehrer & R. L. Woolfolk (Eds.), *Principles and practice of stress management* (2nd ed., pp. 571–605). New York: The Guilford Press.

Lehrer, P. M., & Woolfolk, R. L. (1993). Specific effects of stress management techniques. In P. M. Lehrer & R. L. Woolfolk (Eds.), *Principles and practice of stress management* (2nd ed., pp. 481–520). New York: The Guilford Press.

Linden, W. (1993). The autogenic training method of J. H. Schultz. In P. M. Lehrer & R. L. Woolfolk (Eds.), *Principles and practice of stress management* (2nd ed., pp. 205–229). New York: The Guilford Press.

Mason, L. J. (1980). *Guide to stress reduction.* Culver City, CA: Peace Press.

Maynard, I. W., Hemmings, B., & Warwick-Evans, L. (1995). The effects of a somatic intervention strategy on competitive state anxiety and performance in semiprofessional soccer players. *The Sport Psychologist, 9,* 51–64.

Maynard, I. W., Warwick-Evans, L., & Smith, M. J. (1995). The effects of a cognitive intervention strategy on competitive state anxiety and performance in semiprofessional soccer players. *Journal of Sport and Exercise Psychology, 17,* 428–446.

McGuigan, F. J. (1993). Progressive relaxation: Origins, principles, and clinical applications. In P. M. Lehrer & R. L. Woolfolk (Eds.), *Principles and practice of stress management* (2nd ed., pp. 17–52). New York: The Guilford Press.

Meyers, A. W., Whelan, J. P., & Murphy, S. M. (1996). Cognitive behavioral strategies in athletic performance enhancement. In M. Hersen, R. M. Eisler, & P. M. Miller (Eds.), *Progress in behavioral modification,* (Vol. 30, pp. 137–164). Pacific Grove, CA: Brooks/Cole.

Paul, G. L., & Trimble, R. W. (1970). Recorded vs. "live" relaxation training and hypnotic suggestion: Comparative effectiveness for reducing physiological arousal and inhibiting stress response. *Behavior Therapy, 1,* 285–302.

Raiport, G. (1988). *Red gold peak performance techniques of the Russian and East German Olympic victors.* Los Angeles: Tarcher.

Wegner, D. M. (1994). Ironic processes of mental control. *Psychological Review, 101,* 34–52.

Wegner, D. M. (1996). Why the mind wanders. In J. D. Cohen & J. W. Schooler (Eds.), *Scientific approaches to consciousness* (pp. 295–315), Hillsdale, NJ: Lawrence Erlbaum Associates.

Wegner, D. M., Broome, A., & Blumberg, S. J. (1997). Ironic effects of trying to relax under stress. *Behavioral Research and Therapy, 35,* 11–21.

Seeing Is Believing: Understanding and Using Imagery in Sport

Robin S. Vealey, *Miami University*
Christy A. Greenleaf, *University of North Texas*

We taped a lot of famous pictures on the locker-room door: Bobby Orr, Potvin, Beliveau, all holding the Stanley Cup. We'd stand back and look at them and envision ourselves doing it. I really believe if you visualize yourself doing something, you can make that image come true. . . . I must have rehearsed it ten thousand times. And when it came true it was like an electric jolt went up my spine.

—Wayne Gretzky (as quoted in Orlick, 1998, p. 67)

"I'll believe that when I *see* it!" Have you ever said this? Of course, we've all made this statement numerous times because it's true—seeing *is* believing. It is especially true in relation to our own accomplishments. If you've seen yourself sink par putts under pressure, then you believe you're a clutch golfer. If you've seen yourself serve well, hit strong ground strokes, and react at the net with crisp volleys in competition, then you believe you're a successful tennis player. Seeing yourself perform well in these circumstances creates positive beliefs about your ability to succeed in sport—seeing is believing.

But do we *literally* have to see ourselves perform a skill in a certain situation (actually experience it) before we believe we can do it? Absolutely not! Albert Einstein describes how he was able to conceptualize his theory of relativity by visualizing how the world would look to him as he traveled inside a beam of light. Einstein didn't actually travel at light speed, but he saw the world as if he did, which allowed him to believe in a wondrous theoretical development in science. Annika Sorenstam, top female golfer in the world for several years and winner of an incredible 13 of 24 LPGA tournaments in 2002, explains how she "believes by seeing." "When I'm on the golf course, I see a big green, a huge hole, just the positive things. I don't see out-of-bounds on the left or a water hazard over there. I put the ball on the ground. I see the fairway. I hit it. I just grab a club and trust it."

Tiger Woods's father recalls asking his son, then a second-grader playing in his first international tournament, what he was thinking about on the first tee as he stood with all the other nervous young golfers and prepared to hit his first shot. Tiger's answer was simple: "Where I wanted the ball to go, Daddy." Although Tiger Woods was experiencing his first major competition and could have chosen to worry about embarrassing himself or disappointing his parents, he chose instead to demonstrate exceptional mental skill and simply see himself hitting the ball perfectly. And, by the way, he did rip a perfect drive in that situation, and then went on to become a three-time U.S. Amateur Champion and the number one professional golfer in the world as a member of the PGA circuit.

Albert Einstein, Annika Sorenstam, and Tiger Woods took advantage of their most powerful weapon—their minds. They harnessed the power of imagery to provide the vision they needed to reach the upper limits of human potential. Imagery is simply a mental technique that programs the mind and body to respond optimally. By using imagery as a mental training tool, athletes have the capacity to see and believe, which gives them the confidence and focus to perform successfully. All athletes possess the ability to use imagery effectively. In fact, many athletes use imagery, but most do not use it systematically and many are unable to control their images. Evidence supports the effectiveness of imagery in improving sport performance, but only through controlled, systematic practice.

The purpose of this chapter is to introduce imagery as a basic mental training tool that can be used in simple and systematic ways to help athletes perform better. The chapter is divided into five main sections. First, imagery is defined and explained as a mental training tool available to all athletes. Second, research literature is presented to demonstrate that imagery does work to enhance athletes' performance. Third, several explanations are provided to explain how imagery works to enhance athletes' performance. In the fourth and fifth sections, practical uses of imagery in sport are presented as well as tips to make imagery training more effective with athletes.

What Is Imagery?

Imagery may be defined as using all the senses to re-create or create an experience in the mind. Research indicates that when individuals engage in vivid imagery, their brains interpret these images as identical to the actual stimulus situation (Marks, 1983). This is what makes imagery so powerful! An Alpine skier can imagine herself skiing a downhill run, and her brain will interpret her images as if she actually was skiing the course. The power of imagery allows athletes to practice sport skills, strategies, and mental skills without physically being in the training or competitive environment (e.g., pool, ski slope, gymnasium).

Imagery as Re-creating or Creating

Through imagery we are able to re-create as well as to create experiences in our mind. We re-create experiences all the time. Have you ever watched someone perform a certain skill and then gone out and done it yourself? Or have you ever improved a fundamental aspect of a sport skill after spending hours teaching it to your athletes or to youngsters at a sports camp? We are able to imitate the actions of others because our mind takes a picture of the skill that we use as a blueprint for our performance. In essence, this is imagery. Imagery is based on memory, and we experience it internally by reconstructing external events in our minds.

Athletes spend a lot of time re-creating their performances in their minds. We all can remember the nights after competition when we went over and over our performances in our heads. Athletes often get stuck in this type of imagery by focusing on their mistakes and failures, and they replay these miscues without any type of planned strategy for dealing with these negative images. The key for athletes is to learn to use imagery in a productive and controlled manner to learn from performance mistakes and to program their minds and bodies to respond optimally. A good example of productive re-creating using imagery comes from Bob Rotella's book *Golf Is Not a Game of Perfect* (1995). Rotella, a renowned mental training consultant for professional golfers, was questioned by Fred Couples about whether the mental strategy he (Couples) was using prior to each shot was effective. Couples explained that before hitting a six-iron, he simply visualized in his mind the best six-iron shot he had ever hit. Rotella applauded this strategy used by Couples, which, although it sounds simple, actually is the best strategy you could use! Imagery doesn't have to be complicated or lengthy but should be simple and easily used in competitive conditions, such as the strategy used by Couples. He re-created his best-ever performances in his mind in an attempt to program his body to execute a perfect golf shot.

We can also use imagery to create new experiences in our minds. Although imagery is essentially a product of memory, our brain is able to put the pieces of the internal picture together in different ways. As programmers of their own imagery programs, athletes can build images from whatever pieces of memory they choose. Nancy Kerrigan developed an imagery script to prepare for her figure skating performance in the 1994 Olympic Games. In her mind, Kerrigan created and rehearsed her ideal performance from the dressing room, through her entire routine, to the exhilarating moments after leaving the ice in which she felt intense joy and pride in her accomplishment.

Football quarterbacks may use imagery in this way to create offensive game plans based on the defensive tactics of upcoming opponents. By viewing films of the opponent's defense, a quarterback can create an offensive game plan and visualize the successful execution of this strategy without having previously played against that particular opponent. Coach Tara Van Derveer of the 1996 U.S. Olympic Women's basketball team conducted a mock medal ceremony at the Olympic basketball arena in Atlanta months before the Olympic Games so that each player experienced the gold medal being placed around her neck. Van Derveer wanted her athletes to create in their minds the emotional exhilaration of winning the gold medal to enhance their motivational drive and commitment. Of course, several months later, they all got to experience the thrill of winning the gold medal for real! At the elite levels of international competition, athletes view photographs or video tapes of upcoming competition sites for world championships or the Olympic games. Athletes study these photographs of the various pools, fields, arenas, dressing rooms, and warm-up areas so they can create effective images of themselves performing in those particular contexts. Creating these types of images serves to familiarize athletes with the environment far in advance of actual competition. Athletes should use imagery to prepare mentally for hostile crowds on the road or difficult travel conditions, by creating effective responses such as, "What will it be like?" and "How will you respond?" Research shows that elite athletes create mental focus plans for competition and regularly mentally practice these plans for the way they will respond productively to various competitive stressors (Greenleaf, Gould, & Dieffenbach, 2001).

Interestingly, research supports that athletes choose to use imagery to either create or re-create based on the demands of their sport (White & Hardy, 1998). For example, slalom canoeists used imagery more to review (re-create) their previous performance because they complete one practice and two competitive runs of the course at each competition. Conversely, gymnasts reported using imagery to create the perfect routine in their minds prior to actually performing it, because they perform each routine only once during a competition. Thus, athletes should re-create and create effective images based on the specific needs of their sport.

Imagery as a Polysensory Experience

The second key to understanding imagery is realizing that imagery can and should involve all the senses, or that it is a **polysensory** experience. Although imagery is often termed visualization or seeing with the mind's eye, sight is not the only significant sense. All of our senses are important in experiencing events. Images can and should include as many senses as possible, including visual, auditory, olfactory, gustatory, tactile, and kinesthetic senses. Auditory refers to sound, such as hearing the crack of the bat in baseball or the sweet sound of a perfect golf drive. Olfactory refers to smell, such as a swimmer smelling chlorine in the pool. Tactile is the sensation of touch, such as feeling the grip of a golf club or the textured leather of a basketball. Gustatory refers to the sense of taste, such as tasting salty sweat in your mouth. **Kinesthetic** sense is the feel or sensation of the body as it moves in different positions. The kinesthetic sense would be important for a gymnast using imagery to practice a balance beam routine or a diver using imagery to feel the rotations before reaching for the water. Professional golfer Bob Tway states that a consistent golf swing requires turning all of your mechanical thoughts into a feeling, which is simply a kinesthetic image of the perfect golf swing.

So although seeing is believing, seeing yourself via imagery means that you should incorporate as many senses as possible to increase the vividness of the image. The more vivid the image, the more effective it is. Let's use the example of a wide receiver in football to stress the importance of using different senses. The receiver uses his visual sense to read the defense and focus on the ball before catching it. He uses his auditory sense to listen to the snap count barked by the quarterback. He uses his tactile and kinesthetic senses to run his pattern, jump in the air, catch a hard thrown ball, and touch both feet inbounds. He might also smell freshly mown grass and the sweat of his opponent's jersey when he is tackled. He may even taste the saltiness of his own sweat. All senses should be utilized when practicing imagery to create vivid images of sport experiences.

In addition to the senses just discussed, the emotions associated with various sport experiences are also an important part of imagery. In using imagery to help control anxiety, anger, or pain, athletes must be able to re-create these emotions in their minds. For example, athletes could re-create their thoughts and feelings experienced during competition to understand how and why anxiety hurt their performance. In using imagery to re-create past outstanding performances, athletes should feel the emotions associated with those experiences such as elation, satisfaction, pride, and self-esteem.

Imagery as a Mental Training Tool

Imagery is simply a polysensory experience in one's mind. Dreaming and daydreaming qualify as forms of imagery, as most of us can attest based on vivid dreams we have experienced. However, the focus in this chapter is on understanding and using imagery as a mental training tool with athletes. Dreaming is a form of imagery, but it is not a mental training tool.

Athletes must use imagery in a continuous and systematic manner for it to qualify as mental training. Dreaming or random imagery is not systematic, and there is no evidence that these forms of imagery enhance athletes' performance. This doesn't mean that athletes have to spend numerous hours a day engaged in imagery for it to help their performance. However, there must be some sort of systematic, continuing use of imagery in an organized manner, even if it is in small doses, for it to have the desired effect on one's performance. This is similar to physical training, in which random, occasional physical practice won't do much to increase an athlete's skills. However, systematic, repetitive physical (and mental) practice clearly pays off in performance improvement in any sport.

Athletes must learn to control their imagery to use it effectively as a mental training tool. **Controllability** is the ability of athletes to imagine exactly what they intend to imagine, and also the ability to manipulate aspects of the images that they wish to change. Dreams are for the most part uncontrollable—we simply experience them during sleep. Imagery, by contrast, must be controllable so that athletes can manipulate images in productive ways to program themselves for optimal performance. As we all remember as athletes, often our images become uncontrollable such as when we "choke" under pressure or experience dreaded performance slumps. Thus, coaches and sport psychology consultants must help athletes gain control of their images so that imagery can be used effectively in mental training. In addition to controllability, the other key to using imagery effectively in mental training is vividness. **Vividness** refers to how clearly athletes can see an image and how detailed the image appears to them. Vividness involves such features as whether the image is in color, how many senses are being used, and the emotion or physical sensations experienced when engaging in imagery.

Overall, imagery as a mental training tool involves the systematic practice and use of imagery to engage in vivid and controllable polysensory images to enhance performance. When athletes first begin using imagery, it is typical to lack vividness and especially controllability of images. However, systematic practice has been shown to be very effective in increasing imagery ability (Evans, Jones, & Mullen, 2004; Rodgers, Hall, & Buckolz, 1991). Also, imagery has been shown to be more effective in helping athletes perform (Isaac, 1992). It is important to encourage athletes if they are not skilled in their initial attempts at imagery. Let them know that imagery is a skill that takes time to train, but it is a learnable skill that they can improve with practice. This is true with even world-class athletes, as seen in the following quote:

> It took me a long time to control my images and perfect my imagery, maybe a year, doing it every day. At first I couldn't see myself, I always saw everyone else, or I would see my dives wrong all the time. I would get an image of hurting myself, or tripping on the board, or I would "see" something done really bad. As I continued to work at it, I got to the point where I could see myself doing a perfect dive and the crowd yelling at the Olympics. But it took me a long time. . . . I started to see myself on the board doing my perfect dive. But some days I couldn't see it, or it was a bad dive in my head. I worked at it so much it got to the point that I could do all my dives easily. Sometimes I would even be in the middle of a conversation with someone and I would think of one of my dives and "see" it. Olympic gold medalist, springboard diving. (Orlick & Partington, 1988, p. 114)

Internal and External Imagery Perspectives

When you spontaneously engage in imagery, do you see yourself as if you're watching a videotape or do you see yourself from behind your own eyes? This question differentiates between an external imagery perspective and an internal imagery perspective. Athletes who use an **external imagery perspective** see the image from outside their bodies as if they are viewing themselves from behind a video camera. When athletes use

an **internal imagery perspective,** they see the image from behind their own eyes as if they were inside their bodies. Consider the different imagery perspectives used by athletes in the following examples:

> My imagery is more just feel. I don't think it is visual at all. When I'm watching it on video I look visually at it and then I get this internal feeling. When I'm actually doing it I get the same feeling inside. It is a very internal feeling that is hard to explain. You have to experience it, and once you do, then you know what you are going after. I can even get a feeling for an entire program. . . . I get this internal feeling . . . and usually I'm fresh and usually it will be a perfect program. I just don't step out there in training and just say, here we go, another program. Canadian Olympic figure skater. (Orlick & Partington, 1988, p. 113)
>
> In mental imagery. . . . I would think about the last time I actually did it, "Why did I miss that one move? Okay, I know what happened, I pulled my body in too close to the apparatus and it . . . went off. Okay, now how do I avoid that?" Then I try to see myself doing it correctly in imagery. Sometimes you look at it from a camera view, but most of the time I look at it as what I see from within, because that's the way it's going to be in competition. It is natural [that way] because I do the routines so many times that it's drilled in my head, what I see and how I do it. . . . I think of it as the way I've done it so many times, and that's from within my body. Olympic rhythmic gymnast. (Orlick & Partington, 1988, p. 114)

Research has shown that elite athletes are more likely to practice imagery from an internal perspective as compared to nonelite athletes, who are more likely to practice imagery from an external perspective (Orlick & Partington, 1988; Rotella, Gansneder, Ojala, & Billing, 1980; Salmon et al., 1994). Also, internal imagery has been shown to produce more neuromuscular activity than external imagery (Hale, 1982; Harris & Robinson, 1986). Research also has shown that both imagery perspectives can enhance performance (e.g., Hardy & Callow, 1999). Thus, athletes should experiment to find the imagery

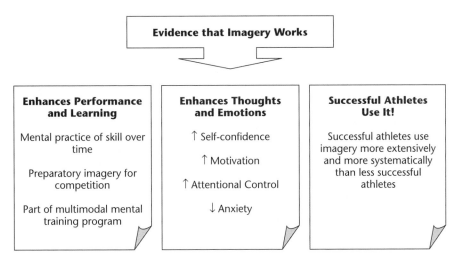

Figure 16-1 **Summary of research support for the effectiveness of imagery**

perspective that is most helpful to them for specific situations.

Many athletes frequently shift back and forth between perspectives when using imagery, and they should be encouraged to practice both perspectives to be competent and comfortable with each. A suggested way to develop athletes' imagery ability is to have them actually perform the skill (e.g., serve a volleyball, noting all the sensations) and then immediately close their eyes and try to replay the serve using an internal perspective (as if from inside their body). Repeat until the athlete can discern little difference between actual and imaged performance. Do this physical-mental practice routine again, only this time with an external imagery perspective (as if seen on videotape). Once athletes are more skilled in imagery, they may prefer to keep their eyes open and may discover a preference for using one perspective more than another.

Does Imagery Work to Enhance Athletes' Performance?

Now that you have a basic understanding about imagery, your next question should be: "That's great, but does it work?" The answer is a resounding

"yes!" As shown in Figure 16-1, research evidence supporting the effectiveness of imagery as a mental training tool is divided into three areas. First, imagery has been shown to enhance sport performance and learning. Second, imagery has been shown to enhance thoughts and emotions in athletes that are critical to athletes' performance. And, third, research shows that successful athletes use imagery more extensively and systematically than less successful athletes.

Enhancing Sport Performance and Learning

Of primary interest to coaches and athletes is the effectiveness of imagery in enhancing athletes' performance. It is intriguing to think that an internal sensory experience has the power to help athletes learn more easily and to perform better. The research in this area is divided into three sections: mental practice of skill over time, preparatory imagery for competition, and imagery as part of multimodal mental training programs (see Figure 16-1).

Mental practice research. Using imagery to perform a specific sport skill repetitively in the mind is called **mental practice.** Typically, mental practice occurs across a period of time in an intermittent learning style similar to a distributed physical practice schedule. The first study of mental practice effects on motor skills took place in 1934 (Vandall, Davis, & Clugston, 1934). Since that time, a plethora of research has been conducted in this area, and comprehensive reviews have concluded that mental practice enhances performance and is better than no practice at all (Feltz & Landers, 1983; Martin, Moritz, & Hall, 1999). Improvement in the following sport skills has been documented through mental practice: basketball shooting, volleyball serving, tennis serving, golf, football placekicking, figure skating, swimming starts, dart throwing, alpine skiing, karate skills, diving, trampoline skills, competitive running, dance, rock climbing, and field hockey performance.

Research has begun to examine how different ways of delivering imagery interventions influence the impact of mental practice on performance. In an imagery training program designed to improve golf putting, putting performance was enhanced more by mental practice using audiotapes and videotapes of successful performance than by mental practice using written scripts that were read by the golfers (Smith & Holmes, 2004). It may be that the auditory and visual cues in the audio- and videotapes used in conjunction with mental practice stimulated more neural pathways involved in the execution of the golf putt, thus enhancing performance to a greater degree.

Keep in mind that this research is not saying that mental practice is better than physical practice. It certainly is not, as nothing takes the place of deliberate, repetitive physical practice in refining sport skills! For example, total physical practice was shown to be more effective in enhancing performance than the combination of mental and physical practice (Hird et al., 1991). However, mental practice is better than no practice, and is useful in complementing the rigorous physical practice schedules of athletes. Athletes can only engage in physical practice for finite periods of time, because of fatigue and attentional overload. Mental practice allows athletes to refine their mental blueprints of sport skills without having to physically engage in the activity. Thus, athletes should augment their physical training through mental practice to build strong and clear mental blueprints to program their minds and bodies for automatic and flawless skill execution. The following quote by a Canadian Olympic gold medalist in the bobsled emphasizes this point:

> In bobsledding, you can only do two or three runs per day. I would have liked to do 20 of them but I couldn't. The physical demands were too high. . . . So I did a lot of imagery instead and it was a real learning process. . . . Each track filled up a videotape in my head. (Durand-Bush & Salmela, 2002)

Preparatory imagery. Research has also shown that using imagery immediately before performance can help athletes perform better. Often, imagery is used just prior to performing to "psych up," calm down, or focus on relevant aspects of the task. Consider how Larry Bird, three-time NBA champion and MVP, used imagery during the playing of the national anthem just prior to games:

> People have noticed that during the national anthem at home games I am always looking up to the Boston Garden ceiling. . . . The thing I look at up there are our championship flags. I focus on the three championships my teams have won and I always look at them in order. I start at 1981, move to 1984 and shift over to 1986. I try to capture how I felt when we won each one and play the championship through my mind. It doesn't take very long to zip through that. (Bird, 1989)

Imagery as a preparatory strategy used prior to performance has improved performance on strength tasks (Shelton & Mahoney, 1978; Tynes & McFatter, 1987), muscular endurance tasks (Gould, Weinberg, & Jackson, 1980; Lee, 1990), and golf putting (Murphy & Woolfolk, 1987; Woolfolk, Parrish, & Murphy, 1985). Imagery also has been shown to be an effective part of athletes' pre-performance routines, which involve a planned sequence of thoughts and behaviors that lead to automatic performance execution (Lidor & Singer, 2003).

Situation Study

Multimodal Mental Training Intervention for a Tennis Player

Christy was a 14-year-old tennis player ranked in the top 25 of her age group nationally. Working with a mental trainer, she needed to improve on two key aspects of her performance. First, she had a poor net game, and was fearful of coming to the net for volleys. Second, she tended to "choke" on her second serve, worrying about double-faulting, even though she had the technical talent to execute a successful second serve. Thus, her mental training goals were to overcome her fear of the net game and to develop a focused and confident mental routine to allow her to execute a successful "kick" second serve.

Christy began working on her net game by physically practicing net volleys on shots that began very easy and progressed to harder. She verbalized the cue word "seams" out loud that made her focus her attention on the seams of the ball coming toward her and also occupied her mind to prevent negative thinking or worry. Before and after training, she mentally practiced net volleys in various situations, using her cue word to create the correct visual picture. Using imagery, she mentally practiced various net tactics for different competitive situations. A performance goal was set for her to hit at least one winner per game from the net. In training, she did not win the game or end the drill until she accomplished this goal. Her net performance improved over the course of the 25-week intervention so that she won, on average, 4 points per match from the net.

To deal with her double-fault problem, Christy developed a preservice routine using relaxation, thought-stopping, self-talk, and imagery. The routine started with bouncing the ball four times and catching it. Then she took a relaxation breath, during which she imagined air passing through her body and dissipating any tension in it. She used the cue word "smooth" to program a relaxed, smoothly executed serve. She then used the kinesthetic image of her racquet making contact with the ball for a perfect kick serve and a visual image of the ball "kicking" successfully within her opponent's service box. She had extensively practiced thought-stopping, and used the word "stop" to put any irrelevant and worrisome thoughts out of her mind. This routine was developed and practiced in parts, and was completed and refined over three months of practice. Christy was able to gain fluidity and smoothness in her second serve, and significantly decrease her double-fault percentage as the result of the mental training (modified from Mamassis & Doganis, 2004).

Multimodal mental training interventions. The effects of imagery on performance and learning also have been examined within multimodal mental training interventions that are implemented with athletes over a period of time. For example, a mental training program consisting of imagery, relaxation, and self-talk training was implemented with basketball players during the season to improve their defensive skills (Kendall, Hrycaiko, Martin, & Kendall, 1990). The program was clearly effective in enhancing the players' defensive skills in competition. Similar programs have been shown to be successful in enhancing performance in basketball (Hall & Erffmeyer, 1983; Savoy, 1993; Wrisberg & Anshel, 1989), swimming (Hanton & Jones, 1999), gymnastics (Lee & Hewitt, 1987), figure skating (Ming & Martin, 1996; Mumford & Hall, 1985), tennis (Daw & Burton, 1994; Efran, Lesser, & Spiller, 1994; Mamassis & Doganis, 2004; Noel, 1980), golf putting (Beauchamp, Halliwell, Fournier, & Koestner, 1996), and triathlon (Thelwell & Greenlees, 2001).

Enhancing Competition-Related Thoughts and Emotions

In addition to helping athletes perform better, imagery also has been shown to enhance the competition-related thoughts and emotions of athletes. This is important because a basic objective of sport psychology is to help athletes think better—to enable them to manage their thoughts and emotions effectively to create a productive competitive focus.

Research has supported the effectiveness of imagery in enhancing self-confidence (Callow, Hardy, & Hall 2001; Evans et al., 2004; Garza & Feltz, 1998; Hale & Whitehouse, 1998; Mamassis & Doganis, 2004; McKenzie & Howe, 1997; Short, Bruggeman, Engel, Marback, Wang, Willadsen, & Short, 2002), motivation (Beauchamp et al., 1996; Martin & Hall, 1995), and attentional control (Calmels, Berthoumieux, & d'Arripe-Longueville, 2004), in athletes. Imagery combined with other mental training methods (relaxation, stress inoculation training) has been shown to help athletes decrease or control precompetitive anxiety (Cogan & Petrie, 1995; Kerr & Leith, 1993; Lee & Hewitt, 1987; Ryska, 1998; Savoy, 1997). Research has also shown that specific types of imagery are effective in changing athletes' perceptions of anxiety from harmful and negative to facilitative and challenging (Evans et al., 2004; Hale & Whitehouse, 1998; Mamassis & Doganis, 2004; Page, Sime, & Nordell, 1999).

A highly successful Olympic pistol shooter states:

> As for success imagery, I would imagine to myself, "How would a champion act? How would a champion feel? How would she perform on the line?" This helped me find out about myself, what worked and didn't work for me. . . . That helped me believe that I would be the Olympic champion. (Orlick & Partington, 1988, p. 113)

Professional golfer Bob Ford, admired by peers for his ability to clear his mind for competition, describes his unique imagery practice of imagining himself on an elevator as he walks to the first tee at a tournament. When he gets to the first tee, the doors open and he envisions being on a "whole new floor." Ford explains this image allows him to leave all problems and extraneous thoughts behind on another "floor," and enables him to focus in on the "competition floor." Thus, imagery has been shown to help athletes create a productive and motivational competitive focus for the way they want to think and feel in responding to the challenge of competition.

Incidence of Imagery Use

A lot of really successful athletes use imagery! More successful, elite athletes use imagery more extensively, more systematically, and have better imagery skill than less successful and accomplished athletes (Calmels, d'Arripe-Longueville, Fournier, & Soulard, 2003; Cumming & Hall, 2002; Hall, Rodgers, & Barr, 1990; Salmon, Hall, & Haslam, 1994).

Of 235 Canadian Olympic athletes who participated in the 1984 Olympic Games, 99% reported using imagery (Orlick & Partington, 1988). These athletes estimated that during training they engaged in preplanned systematic imagery at least once a day, 4 days per week, for about 12 minutes each time. At the Olympic site, some reported engaging in imagery for 2 to 3 hours in preparation for their events. Coaches attending a mental skills training workshop indicated that they used imagery more than any other mental training technique and felt that imagery was the most useful mental technique that they used with their athletes (Hall & Rodgers, 1989). Eighty-six percent of the U.S. Olympic sport psychology consultants in 1988 used imagery in their mental training programs with athletes (Gould, Tammen, Murphy, & May, 1989). An analysis of the mental preparation strategies of U.S. wrestlers during the 1988 Olympics found that the wrestlers' best performances involved adherence to mental routines, including positive imagery before the matches (Gould, Eklund, & Jackson, 1992). More recently, mental training (including imagery) to develop systematic competitive routines and plans was found to be a critical factor in the successful performance of athletes at the 1996 Olympic Games (Gould, Guinan, Greenleaf, Medbery, & Peterson, 1999).

Research also has examined *how* and *why* athletes use imagery. Elite gymnasts and canoeists report using imagery extensively to rehearse skills and difficult moves, to optimize concentration and quality of training, and to enhance self-confidence and motivation (White & Hardy, 1998). Also, individuals who used imagery to practice golf skills were shown to set higher goals, spend more time practicing, and demonstrate more realistic self-expectations as compared to individuals who did not use imagery (Martin & Hall, 1995).

Experiential Evidence That Imagery Works

Perhaps it would be helpful to learn firsthand from athletes themselves about how imagery works for them. Several athletes who have at one time been the best in the world at their sport advocate the use of imagery. Jack Nicklaus, perhaps the greatest golfer of all time, says that playing the ball to a certain place in a certain way is 50% mental picture. Nicklaus sees and believes before he hits any shot.

> I never hit a shot, not even in practice, without having a very sharp, in-focus picture of it in my head. It's like a color movie. First, I "see" the ball where I want it to finish, nice and white and sitting up high on bright green grass. Then the scene quickly changes and I "see" the ball going there; its path, trajectory and shape, even its behavior on landing. Then there is sort of a fade-out, and the next scene shows me making the kind of swing that will turn the images into reality. (Nicklaus, 1974, p. 79)

Certainly, Jack Nicklaus has won more major championships than anyone else because of his enormous physical talent. Yet experts feel that his concentration skills carried him to a level above all other golfers. It may be that Nicklaus's systematic practice of imagery facilitates the concentration that has been the key to his success.

Greg Louganis reached the pinnacle of his magnificent diving career by winning gold medals in both the springboard and platform events at the 1984 and 1988 Olympic Games. He speaks of how he used imagery to practice each dive and of his particular technique of setting his dives to music as he practiced them in his head. Chris Evert, the great tennis champion, admitted that she practiced imagery before important matches by painstakingly visualizing opponents' specific styles of play and then visualizing her successful responses to these opponents. Pat Summitt, the highly successful women's basketball coach at the University of Tennessee, described in an interview how her team uses imagery for relaxation before big games, mental practice of specific performance situations, and pregame preparation (Wrisberg, 1990). Phil Mickelson, one of the top five golfers in the world, states, "When I see a shot, I see in my mind's eye a 'window' I want the ball to pass through at the apex of its flight."

Colleen Hacker, sport psychology consultant for the U.S. women's soccer team which won the 1996 and 2004 Olympic Games and the 1999 World Cup, created individualized audio and video imagery tapes for the players prior to these competitions as well as every other major world event. The tapes are full of confidence-building trigger words, phrases, and images, all set to each player's favorite songs. The tapes became a powerful source of team chemistry when the players ended up watching the tapes as a group. Kristine Lilly, who made a key header save in the World Cup final against China, stated: "The tapes give me that little extra confidence, remind me about who I am and what I can give. I'm inspired watching my teammates' tapes. And I'm reminded of what they do well, so I'll never second-guess them" (Lieber, 1999, p. 2c).

The following excerpt from an interview with a Canadian Olympic diver attests to this athlete's extreme commitment to and belief in imagery (Orlick & Partington, 1988):

> I did my dives in my head all the time. At night, before going to sleep, I always did my dives. Ten dives. I started with a front dive, the first one that I had to do at the Olympics, and I did everything as if I was actually there. I saw myself on the board with the same bathing suit. Everything was the same. . . . If the dive was wrong, I went back and started

over again. It takes a good hour to do perfect imagery of all my dives, but for me it was better than a workout. Sometimes I would take the weekend off and do imagery five times a day.

Similarly, observe the commitment to imagery by Alex Baumann, Olympic double gold medalist in swimming:

> The best way I have learned to prepare mentally for competition is to visualize the race in my mind. . . . In my imagery I concentrate on attaining the splits I have set out to do. About 15 minutes before the race I visualize the race in my mind. I think about my own race and nothing else. I try to get those splits in my mind, and after that I am ready to go. My visualization has been refined more and more over the years. That is what really got me the world record and Olympic medals. (Orlick, 1998, p. 70)

Summary of Evidence Supporting Effectiveness of Imagery in Enhancing Performance

Overall, there is a great deal of research and experiential evidence supporting the effectiveness of imagery in enhancing the performance and psychological responses of athletes. In short, imagery works! Two additional questions should be addressed in relation to the effectiveness of imagery in enhancing athlete performance.

The first question addresses whether imagery is more beneficial for beginning athletes or more highly skilled performers. Research has indicated that although both novice and expert performers can gain skill by using imagery (Hall, Schmidt, Durand, & Buckolz, 1994), experienced athletes have shown greater gains in performance via imagery practice (Feltz & Landers, 1983). This is probably because of clearer and more accurate images that elite athletes have of specific sport skills, as compared to novices who are just beginning to form mental representations of skills in their minds. However, it is appropriate to encourage athletes at all skill levels to use imagery. Novice performers may use imagery to get a basic mental blueprint of the movement and to stay motivated for skill improvement, whereas highly skilled athletes may use imagery to more deeply ingrain the perfect mental blueprint as well as to develop strategy and build confidence.

The second question addresses whether imagery is more effective in enhancing performance when athletes are higher in imagery ability. The answer is, of course it is! The fact that imagery is more effective when athletes are higher in imagery ability (Goss, Hall, Buckolz, & Fishburne, 1986; Hall, 1985; Isaac, 1992) emphasizes that athletes must work to improve the vividness and controllability of their images so that their performance may subsequently be improved. It is important that athletes realize that imagery is a skill that takes time to train, especially if they are not skilled in their initial attempts at imagery. Even Olympic athletes did not initially have good control over their imagery, but they perfected their imagery skills through persistent daily practice (Orlick & Partington, 1988). Systematic imagery training has been shown to be very effective in increasing both visual and kinesthetic imagery ability (Evans et al., 2004; Rodgers et al., 1991). So athletes should practice and hone their imagery skills to enhance the positive effect of imagery training on their performance.

How Does Imagery Enhance Athletes' Performance?

Several theoretical explanations for how imagery facilitates performance have been advanced in the literature. In this section, four popular explanations of imagery are presented and discussed in relation to sport performance. The explanations presented include psychoneuromuscular theory, symbolic learning theory, bioinformational theory, and the attentional-arousal set explanation.

Psychoneuromuscular Theory: Muscle Memory

As athletes engage in various sport movements, their brains are constantly transmitting impulses to the muscles for the execution of the movements.

The **psychoneuromuscular theory** suggests that similar impulses occur in the brain and muscles when athletes imagine the movements without actually performing them. Thus, the psychoneuromuscular theory asserts that vivid imagined events produce innervation in our muscles similar to that produced by the actual physical execution of the event. This innervation is theorized to provide kinesthetic feedback that can be used by athletes to improve their skills (Richardson, 1967). It is helpful to use the term *muscle memory* when explaining this theory to athletes. Emphasize to them that through imagery they are strengthening their muscle memories by having the muscles fire in the correct sequence without actually physically executing the movement.

Scientific evidence supports the notion that vivid imagined events produce innervation in our muscles similar to the actual physical execution of the event. Jacobson (1931) first supported this phenomenon. He demonstrated that the imagined movement of bending the arm created contractions in the flexor muscles of the arm. Jacobson's findings have been supported in the sport psychology literature (Bird, 1984; Hale, 1982; Harris & Robinson, 1986; Jowdy & Harris, 1990). Richard Suinn (1980) tested this phenomenon by having a downhill skier re-create a race using imagery. Suinn monitored the electrical activity in the skier's leg muscles as he imagined the downhill run. Suinn found that the printed output of muscle firings mirrored the terrain of the ski run. Muscle firings peaked at certain points during imagery that corresponded to times in which greater muscle contraction would be expected due to turns and rough sections on the course.

Thus, whether athletes actually perform movements or vividly imagine performing them, similar neural pathways to the muscles are used, although the muscle activity is far less during imagery as compared to actual movement. However, although research clearly supports that vivid imagery can produce low-level innervation of muscles, research has not demonstrated that this slight muscle innervation produced by imagery actually facilitates performance (Slade, Landers, & Martin, 2002; Smith, Collins, & Holmes, 2003).

Symbolic Learning Theory: Mental Blueprint

The second explanation of how imagery may facilitate sport performance suggests that imagery may function as a coding system to help athletes acquire or understand movement patterns. All movements that we make must first be encoded in our central nervous system—we must have a blueprint or plan for this movement. The **symbolic learning theory** suggests that imagery facilitates performance by helping individuals to blueprint or code their movements into symbolic components, thus making the movement more familiar and perhaps more automatic. For example, a gymnast can use imagery to cue herself on the temporal and spatial elements involved in performing a balance beam routine. It is helpful to use the term *mental blueprint* when talking to athletes about this theory and emphasize that by using imagery they are strengthening their mental blueprint (or the mental code they use to perform the skill) to make the skill more automatic.

Symbolic learning theory was first proposed by Sackett (1934), who stated that imagery enables performers to rehearse the sequence of movements as symbolic components of a task. This theoretical position has been supported by studies that have demonstrated greater performance improvement through imagery on movement tasks that required cognitive coding as opposed to pure motor tasks (Feltz & Landers, 1983; Feltz, Landers, & Becker, 1988; Hird, Landers, Thomas, & Horan, 1991; Ryan & Simons, 1981, 1983; Wrisberg & Ragsdale, 1979). This theory has also been supported by research showing improved free throw shooting (Hall & Erffmeyer, 1983) and motor performance (Housner, 1984) when imagery is used to mentally encode modeled movement behaviors.

Bioinformational Theory: Response Set

Bioinformational theory assumes that a mental image is an organized set of propositions, or characteristics, stored in the brain's long-term memory (Lang, 1977, 1979). When individuals engage in imagery, they activate **stimulus**

characteristics that describe the content of the image for them and **response characteristics** that describe what their responses are to the stimuli in that situation. For example, imagining shooting a basketball free throw in the final seconds of a close game would involve the stimulus characteristics of the feel of the ball in the hand, the sight of the basket, and the sound of the crowd. The response characteristics for this image might include muscular tension in the shooting arm, increased perspiration, feelings of anxiety, and the joyous sight of the ball swishing through the net. According to bioinformational theory, for imagery to facilitate sport performance, response characteristics must be activated so they can be modified, improved, and strengthened. By repeatedly accessing response characteristics for a particular stimulus situation and modifying these responses to represent perfect control and execution of a skill, imagery is predicted to enhance performance.

Research has shown that response-oriented imagery results in greater physiological reactivity than stimulus-oriented imagery (Bakker, Boschker, & Chung, 1996) and also that images of situations with which athletes have personal experience create greater physiological reactivity than less familiar images (Hecker & Kaczor, 1988). Moreover, athlete performance has been improved to a greater degree through imagery that included both stimulus and response characteristics, as opposed to imagery that just included stimulus characteristics (Smith & Collins, 2004; Smith, Holmes, Whitemore, Collins, & Devenport, 2001). Interestingly, response-oriented imagery has been shown to create more "priming" responses in the brain as measured by electroencephalographic (EEG) activity when compared to stimulus-oriented imagery (Smith & Collins, 2004). In addition, bioinformational theory is supported by findings that experienced athletes benefit more from imagery than do novices (Feltz & Landers, 1983), which indicates that experienced athletes have a network of successful response characteristics stored in memory that they can activate during imagery.

An important implication from this is that coaches, athletes, and sport psychologists involved in imagery training should include many response characteristics when using imagery. Specifically, images should contain not only the conditions of the situation (swimming in a pool, water is rough, championship meet) but also the athlete's behavioral (swimming strongly, right on pace), psychological (feeling confident, focusing on the race), and physiological (feeling energized) responses to the situation. By including these positive responses, the image will be more vivid and should result in psychophysiological changes in the body and thus improved performance. (Note the positive responses to an upcoming competition described in the sample imagery script provided in Appendix A.) Also, it is important to encourage use of kinesthetic imagery to emphasize feeling the physical sensations of performing a specific skill, which will further strengthen effective response characteristics.

It may be helpful to use the term *response set* when talking about this theory to athletes. Practically, imagery can be explained as a way of enhancing performance by programming personalized and appropriate responses to specific situations, or creating the perfect response set. Emphasize that behavioral, psychological, and physiological responses should all be included in imagery. Another practical concern of bioinformational theory is that the meaning of particular images is very individualized so that response sets should be unique and personally meaningful to each athlete (Ahsen, 1984).

Attentional-Arousal Set Explanation: Mental Set

The attentional-arousal set explanation of how imagery works is not a theory but an intuitive description of the role of imagery in helping athletes to optimize arousal and attention. Athletes commonly use imagery to psych up or calm down to meet the energy demands of a particular sport, as well as to visualize aspects of the upcoming competition to sharpen the focus they need to be successful. For example, a wrestler may use imagery before a match to psych himself up to a high energy level and to focus his attention on the specific strategies and moves he needs to use against a particular opponent.

Research has shown that imagery is effective in optimizing arousal and attention in athletes (Calmels et al., 2004; Hale & Whitehouse, 1998; Page et al., 1999). A national level gymnast explains that imagery "helped her to think more clearly and 'not get all worked up,'" and an elite canoeist described imagery as helping her "feel 'switched on' and able to keep 'away from everybody'" (White & Hardy, 1998). The term *mental set* can be used to describe this explanation about imagery to athletes, and it can be emphasized that imagery can help them perform better by creating the right mental set (optimal energy and concentration) for competition.

Summary of Explanations for How Imagery Enhances Athletes' Performance

Each of the four theories/explanations for how imagery works to enhance athletes' performance helps our understanding of how imagery works in sport. The psychoneuromuscular theory explains to us that imagery is psychophysiological, or that simply imagining a skill creates innervation in the muscles similar to the actual physical execution of the skill. However, the psychoneuromuscular theory is wrong in suggesting that performance is improved by this low-grade innervation in the muscles via imagery. This has not been supported by any research that has tested psychoneuromuscular theory.

Symbolic learning theory correctly predicts that imagery enhances performance based on its effects on information processing in the brain, and that through systematic imagery training, athletes can develop and enhance well-grooved mental blueprints of their skills to enhance their performance. Bioinformational theory provides the important theoretical premise that for imagery to be effective, athletes must systematically mentally practice appropriate and productive mental and physical responses to the competitive demands of their sports. Research has supported both symbolic learning theory and

bioinformational theory as correct explanations for how imagery enhances athletes' performance. The attentional-arousal set explanation, although not a formal theory, emphasizes that imagery gets athletes mentally "set" for competition, by directing their attention on what they need to do and creating an optimal energy level for performance.

Can Imagery Hurt Athletes' Performance?

Often, coaches and athletes ask if imagery can ever hurt their performance. It's a good question. The answer to the question is yes, imagery *can* hurt athletes' performance *if* they focus on the *wrong* images at the *wrong* times.

When individuals used negative imagery, or imagined performing unsuccessful putts, their golf putting accuracy declined (Short et al., 2002; Woolfolk, Parrish, & Murphy, 1985; Woolfolk, Murphy, Gottesfeld, & Aitken, 1985). This research indicates that imagery can hurt athletes' performance if they systematically imagine bad performance. This doesn't mean that athletes should not use imagery, as the point of imagery training is to enable athletes to control their previously uncontrollable images. Athletes are going to experience images whether they engage in mental training or not, so it seems productive to enable them to become more skillful in their use of imagery to avoid the debilitating effects of negative imagery. The point is for athletes to create a mental blueprint for perfect responses, NOT create a mental blueprint for disastrous responses! Consider how Ken Dryden, then a 23-year-old rookie goalie for the Montreal Canadiens, created the wrong mental blueprint the night before he was to face the Boston Bruins in Game 7 of the quarterfinals at hostile Boston Garden:

> [I turned on the television in my hotel, and] the only thing I could find was *The Bruins Week in Review*. All they kept showing was the Bruins' scoring goal after goal. "Esposito scores! Orr scores! Esposito scores again!" I was already nervous, and I turned downright depressed. I went to bed and dreamed about those goals. (McCallum, 2004, p. 56)

Additional research has shown that constant attempts to suppress negative thoughts and images from conscious awareness can increase the probability that these negative thoughts and images will influence performance (Beilock, Afremow, Rabe, & Carr, 2001). In this study, individuals in a golf putting task were told, "Be careful to try not to image hitting the ball short of the target. Don't image undershooting the target!" When individuals were given "negative" image instructions (told what not to image), they performed poorly, even when they attempted to suppress these negative images. From a practical perspective, this indicates that athletes should not program themselves to not do something, or constantly focus on negative images and attempt to suppress them. Likewise, coaches should refrain from "negative coaching," or giving verbal feedback such as "Don't pop up!" or "Watch out for the out-of-bounds on the left." These well-meaning, yet negative, coaching comments often create mental blueprints in athletes' heads of the exact performance the coach is suggesting that they not do.

So there is a grain of truth in the popular notion that "thinking too much" can hurt an athlete's performance. The key is to think productively and to simplify one's thinking to the point of automatic performance. This may be difficult during a performance slump, when one's controllability of images slips a bit and negative images pop up during competition. However, the goal of systematic imagery training is to develop more and more skill in controlling one's thoughts and images. To resist mental training because it causes athletes to "think too much" is like an ostrich putting its head in the sand when confronted with danger. It's not a proactive way to confront competitive demands and mental obstacles that all athletes will face at one time.

How Do You Set Up an Imagery Training Program?

There are four phases in setting up the imagery program. First, the idea of using imagery must be sold to athletes. Second, the imagery ability of the athletes should be evaluated to help them understand their imagery abilities and areas that need improvement. Third, athletes must develop basic imagery skills. Fourth, a systematic program of imagery practice must be implemented and monitored.

Introduce Imagery to Athletes

Although you've learned that seeing is believing when it comes to imagery, you now have to sell this idea to your athletes. Imagery only works for athletes if they believe in it. At the same time that you must convince athletes that imagery can indeed help them perform better, you should avoid unnecessary hype or unrealistic claims. Make sure they understand that imagery will not guarantee success. It is simply a mental training technique that has been proven to enhance sport performance.

An approach that we have found useful in introducing imagery to athletes is the analogy of building a machine. When athletes continuously practice a sport skill over and over, they are in essence attempting to build a machine. Divers attempt to fine-tune their body to make their muscles react flawlessly in a dive. Shot putters work hours refining their technique in order to uncoil their body in maximum thrust. Coaches and athletes spend a great deal of time using drill and repetition attempting to build a flawless, automatic machine. Why not use imagery to help? Make the point that building a machine for optimal sport performance requires mental training as well as physical training.

The introduction of imagery can take place in an informal group setting if you are working with a team. We recommend that you spend no more than 20 to 30 minutes summarizing some important points about imagery. An introduction to imagery might include the following steps.

Hook 'em. You need to grab athletes' attention right away to get them interested in imagery. You could (a) discuss the concept of building a machine, (b) ask them to recall a time when they choked in a crucial situation (even have someone describe his or her experience), and then explain how imagery can be used to combat choking in sports, (c) ask them if they use imagery and have them describe how they use it, (d) explain how several famous and successful athletes see and believe by using imagery, and (e) anything you can think of to get their attention. Be creative! Also, it is critical that you are enthusiastic and model your confidence and strong belief in the power of imagery.

Define and give evidence. Briefly explain what imagery is by using a definition such as "practicing in your head" or "building your mental blueprint." Without bogging them down with scientific research, provide some brief evidence that imagery does work to enhance performance. It is helpful to use testimonials from famous coaches and athletes who believe in imagery. It is important at this point to make it clear that imagery is not magic but simply a mental technique that they can use to help their performance.

Explain how it works. You should provide a simple and brief explanation for how imagery works to enhance performance. The amount of detail you get into here depends on the level of the athletes. We usually explain that imagery creates a mental blueprint of a particular skill and that by using imagery they are ingraining or strengthening that mental blueprint to make their skills automatic or to build a machine. Although psychoneuromuscular theory has not been fully supported, athletes are always intrigued when they learn that their muscles are innervated during imagery similar to when they are performing the skill. Make sure you use the terms described earlier—muscle memory, mental blueprint, response set, or mental set—as opposed to scientific terminology.

To emphasize the way imagery works, you may want to take your athletes through one or both of the following exercises so they can immediately experience the power of imagery. If correctly done, these exercises are extremely helpful in convincing skeptical athletes of the merits of practicing imagery.

String and bolt. Give each athlete a string approximately 14 to 16 inches long threaded through a heavy bolt (a neck chain and heavy ring also will work). Stabilizing the elbow, ideally on a table top, have each athlete lightly hold the two ends of the string between the thumb and forefinger with the weight suspended directly below. Focusing on the weight, each athlete in his or her mind's eye should imagine the weight moving right and left like the pendulum of a clock. Once most athletes have at least some movement right and left, have them change the image so the weight swings directly away from and then toward the chest. Again, once successful, change the image so the weight moves in a clockwise circle and finally in a counterclockwise circle. In discussing this exercise, you will find most athletes are absolutely amazed at how imagining the movement ultimately translates to the actual physical movement of the pendulum. Once completed, you can explain to the athletes that the subtle muscle innervation in the arm and hand created by the imagery is responsible for the movement of the pendulum.

Arm as iron bar. Pair each athlete up with a partner who is of similar height and strength. While directly facing each other, one partner extends his dominant arm straight out, palm up, so the back of the wrist is resting on the partner's opposite shoulder. The other partner cups both of his hands above the bend in the partner's elbow. The person whose arm is extended then maximally tightens all the muscles in the arm, trying to make it as strong as possible. Then the partner tests for strength by pushing down at the elbow with both hands, trying to see how much strength it takes to bend the arm. Then switch roles and have the other partner tested for strength. Afterward, resume the initial position with the original partner. This time, to create strength, the partner is to close everything out of his mind and imagine that the arm is a thick steel bar. Not only is the arm a hard, steel bar, but it extends out through the opposite wall. Once the partner has created the image of an unbendable, strong steel bar, he indicates such by raising one of the fingers of the opposite hand. This signals the partner to again test for strength. Again, switch roles and have the opposite partner practice the image and be tested for strength. In follow-up discussion you will find that most athletes will be amazed at how much stronger their arm was with the iron bar image.

Give specifics about how imagery will be used.
At this point you want to let the athletes know
exactly how imagery will be incorporated in
their training. Apply the KISS principle here—keep
it simple and systematic. For example, a basketball
team could start by using mental practice for free
throws and imagery to mentally rehearse specific
team plays. It is a mistake to try to do too much too
soon. However, it is important for athletes to
quickly see how imagery can be applied to meet
their practical needs.

Help Athletes Evaluate Their Imagery Ability

After sparking athletes' interest in imagery, the
next step is to help them evaluate their imagery
abilities. One method of evaluation is to take the
athletes through some Basic Training imagery
exercises provided in this chapter. By discussing
their images with them, you could determine
whether certain areas need to be strengthened.
Another way to evaluate imagery ability is to
administer the Sport Imagery Evaluation, which
measures athletes' abilities to experience different
senses, emotions, and perspectives during
imagery. There are other inventories designed to
measure imagery ability, but this evaluation seems
to be most useful to the coach/practitioner. The
Sport Imagery Evaluation appears in Appendix C.

For best results, direct athletes through the
exercises in the evaluation. Encourage athletes
to answer honestly on the basis of their imagery
ability. Administering the evaluation should
take approximately 15 minutes. Afterward, discuss the results informally with athletes to better
understand their unique imagery abilities and
to target areas that can be improved through
practice.

Basic Training

Basic Training is similar to a preseason physical
conditioning program. By developing a foundation of strength and endurance, athletes are
better equipped to fine-tune their physical skills
when the season begins. By strengthening their
imagery muscle in Basic Training, athletes are

more likely to benefit from the use of imagery
during the season.

Basic Training includes three types of
imagery exercises. First, athletes need to develop
vivid images. Like using a fine-tuning control on
a television, increasing the vividness of images
sharpens the details of the image. The vividness
exercises are designed to strengthen the senses
that are important in sport performance. Second,
athletes must be able to *control* their images. Controllability exercises involve learning to manipulate images by will. Third, athletes need to
enhance their ability to engage in *self-awareness*.
It is a skill to use imagery to become more aware
of underlying thoughts and feelings that often
influence our performance without our realizing
it. Self-awareness exercises will also increase athletes' vividness of emotional imagery as they try
to graphically re-create their thoughts and feelings during competition.

It is important for athletes to gain proficiency
in all three types of imagery exercises. The example exercises purposely use vague descriptors to
encourage you to develop your own imagery exercises that are tailored specifically for your athletes.
It is also helpful to develop additional exercises in
areas in which athletes are having trouble.

Vividness

Exercise 1:

*Place yourself in a familiar place where you usually
perform your sport (gym, pool, rink, field, track,
etc.). It is empty except for you. Stand in the middle
of this place and look all around. Notice the quiet
emptiness. Pick out as many details as you can.
What does it smell like? What are the colors,
shapes, and forms that you see? Now imagine yourself in the same setting, but this time there are
many spectators there. Imagine yourself getting
ready to perform. Try to experience this image from
inside your body. See the spectators, your*

teammates, your coach, and the opponents. Try to hear the sounds of the noisy crowd, your teammates' chatter, your coach yelling encouragement, and the particular sounds of your sport (e.g., ball swishing through the net, volleyball spike hitting the floor). Re-create the feelings of nervous anticipation and excitement that you have before competing. How do you feel?

Exercise 2:

Choose a piece of equipment in your sport such as a ball, pole, racket, or club. Focus on this object. Try to imagine the fine details of the object. Turn it over in your hands and examine every part of the object. Feel its outline and texture. Now imagine yourself performing with the object. First, focus on seeing yourself very clearly performing this activity. Visualize yourself repeating the skill over and over. See yourself performing from behind your own eyes. Then step outside of your body and see yourself perform as if you were watching yourself on film. Now, step back in your body and continue performing. Next, try to hear the sounds that accompany this particular movement. Listen carefully to all the sounds that are being made as you perform this skill. Now, put the sight and the sound together. Try to get a clear picture of yourself performing the skill and also hear all the sounds involved.

Exercise 3:

Pick a very simple skill in your sport. Perform the skill over and over in your mind and imagine every feeling and movement in your muscles as you perform that skill. Try to feel this image as if you were inside your own body. Concentrate on how the different parts of your body feel as you stretch and contract the various muscles associated with the skill. Think about building a machine as you perform the

skill flawlessly over and over again and concentrate on the feeling of the movement.

Now try to combine all of your senses, but particularly those of feeling, seeing, and hearing yourself perform the skill over and over. Do not concentrate too hard on any one sense. Instead, try to imagine the total experience using all of your senses.

Once athletes have mastered these exercises, you might consider follow-up variations to imagine more complex skills, grouping skills together, or placing the skill in the context of competition (such as reacting to certain defenses, executing strategy, etc.).

Controllability

Exercise 1:

Choose a simple sport skill and begin practicing it. Now imagine yourself performing this skill either with a teammate or against an opponent. Imagine yourself executing successful strategies in relation to the movements of your teammate or opponent.

Exercise 2:

Choose a particular sport skill that you have trouble performing. Begin practicing the skill over and over. See and feel yourself doing this from inside your body. If you make a mistake or perform the skill incorrectly, stop the image and repeat it, attempting to perform perfectly every time. Re-create past experiences in which you have not performed the skill well. Take careful notice of what you are doing wrong. Now imagine yourself performing the skill correctly. Focus on how your body feels as you go through different positions in performing the skill correctly. Build a perfect machine!

Self-Awareness

Exercise 1:

Think back and choose a past performance in which you performed very well. Using all your senses, re-create that situation in your mind. See yourself as you were succeeding, hear the sounds involved, feel your body as you performed the movements, and reexperience the positive emotions. Try to pick out the characteristics that made you perform so well (e.g., intense concentration, feelings of confidence, optimal arousal). After identifying these characteristics, try to determine why they were present in this situation. Think about the things you did in preparation for this particular event. What are some things that may have caused this great performance?

Repeat this exercise, imagining a situation in which you performed very poorly. Make sure you are very relaxed before practicing this image, as your mind will subconsciously resist your imagery attempts to re-create unpleasant thoughts, images, and feelings. Attempt to become more self-aware of how you reacted to different stimuli (e.g., coaches, opponents, officials, fear of failure, needing approval from others) and how these thoughts and feelings may have interfered with your performance.

Exercise 2:

Think back to a sport situation in which you experienced a great deal of anxiety. Re-create that situation in your head, seeing and hearing yourself. Especially re-create the feeling of anxiety. Try to feel the physical responses of your body to the emotion and also try to recall the thoughts going through your mind that may have caused the anxiety. Now attempt to let go of the anxiety and relax your body. Breathe slowly and deeply and focus on your body as you exhale. Imagine all of the tension being pulled into

your lungs and exhaled from your body. Continue breathing slowly and exhaling tension until you are deeply relaxed. Now repeat this exercise imagining a situation in which you experienced a great deal of anger, and then relax yourself using the breathing and exhalation technique.

Exercise 3:

The purpose of this exercise is to help you to become more aware of things that happen during competition that bother you when you perform. Think about the times when your performance suddenly went from good to bad. Re-create several of these experiences in your mind. Try to pinpoint the specific factors that negatively influenced your performance (e.g., officials, teammates, opponents' remarks, opponent started to play much better). After becoming aware of these factors that negatively affected your performance, take several minutes to re-create the situations, develop appropriate strategies to deal with the negative factors, and imagine the situations again; but this time imagine yourself using your strategies to keep the negative factors from interfering with your performance. Reinforce yourself by feeling proud and confident that you were able to control the negative factors and perform well.

Additional sensory images. Remember, the exercises presented here are models to get you started. Be creative and provide meaningful images that are personally relevant to your athletes. Check the library for books on imagery if you would like other examples. Here are some additional sensory images that athletes may enjoy.

Try to see various colors in your mind. Pick out objects of certain colors (e.g., a tomato), and then try to paint the screen in front of your face with the color (red). To practice auditory imagery, try to hear the beat of rain against a window, an automobile horn, the sound of a clock striking, applause from a crowd, and the sound of a train whistle. To practice kinesthetic imagery, try to feel yourself running up stairs, lifting a heavy weight, stooping down to tie your shoe, suspending your weight by your hands, nodding your head, and rising up from sitting in a low chair. To practice tactile imagery, try to feel velvet, wool mittens, a hot bath, the clasp of someone's hand on yours, a soft, comfortable bed, a crisp dead leaf, and wet soap. To practice olfactory imagery, try to smell cigar smoke, roses, fresh paint, newly mown grass, leather, coffee, and your favorite cologne. To practice gustatory imagery, try to taste salt, chocolate, sugar, coffee, your favorite fruit, and a lemon. Although these images are not sport-specific in content, they are good practice in strengthening athletes' imagery muscles and also can be fun!

Implement a Systematic Program

Athletes are now ready to begin a *systematic* program of imagery. Imagery practice must be systematic to be effective, so always follow the KISS principle (Keep It Simple and Systematic)! Your first concern is to build the imagery program into the athletes' routine. The imagery program must *not* be something extra but should instead be an integral part of training and practice.

Another key is to fit the needs of the athlete. The imagery program does not need to be long and complex. In fact, when first starting it is a good idea to keep it concise and simple. Initially, choose a sport skill or strategy that is easy to control. That is, choose a movement in which the environment is stable rather than reactive. For example, in basketball you could start with free throw shooting and in racket sports with the serve. As your athletes become more proficient and accepting of the program, you can increase the variety of the program.

Imagery Cookbook for Coaches and Practitioners

It is impossible to design an imagery program that would be appropriate for all sports. For that reason, we have designed this section like a cookbook, in which the necessary ingredients of an imagery program are itemized. The ingredients listed include ways to use imagery, times in which imagery may be practiced, and strategies to enhance imagery practice. It is up to you to choose which ingredients are most relevant for the needs of your athletes.

Ways to Use Imagery

Athletes can use imagery in a number of ways to enhance sport performance. These include:

- Learning and practicing sport skills
- Correcting mistakes
- Learning and practicing performance strategies
- Preparing a mental focus for competition
- Automating preperformance routines
- Building and enhancing mental skills
- Aiding in the recovery from injuries

Learning and practicing sport skills. One of the best places for athletes to start using imagery is mental practice, or the repetitive practice of a sport skill in their minds. They should choose one or two skills in their sport, and mentally practice these skills. Athletes should be urged to mentally practice on their own, but they will be more inclined to do so if mental practice is incorporated as part of their regular training. Coaches can implement a volleyball serving drill in which athletes serve 10 balls and mentally practice each serve prior to physically performing it. This also could be applied to shooting free throws, executing wrestling moves, serving in tennis, sprinting over a set of hurdles, or hitting a baseball. Mental practice is also useful to aid beginners in learning sport skills by helping them to develop a "mental blueprint for perfect responses."

Athletes can strengthen or build their mental blueprints for perfect responses by using verbal triggers and symbolic images. **Verbal triggers** are words or phrases that help athletes focus on key aspects in an image to make their mental blueprint for performance correct. Triggers are used to program the proper image. Coaches use triggers all the time in teaching skills or as points of emphasis they want athletes to think about when performing. Softball players are told to "throw their hands" and focus on a "quick bat." Volleyball serving is taught by having athletes focus on the "bow and arrow" technique. Basketball players are taught to "plant" their inside foot and "square up" for perfect jump shot form. Cross-country skiers think "quick" for their uphill technique to trigger the quick, short kick technique needed on hills. Golfers use simple triggers such as steady head, balance, and rhythm to create the image of a perfect golf swing in their minds prior to hitting a shot. A famous golfer kept the word oooom-PAH written on her driver to program the image of an easy slow backswing and a strong and vigorous downswing.

Symbolic images are mental symbols or models for desired components of performance. Archers can envision a string extending from the center of the target that pulls their arrows directly into the bull's-eye. Sprinters may imagine the explosive energy in their legs as coiled springs that will catapult them from the starting blocks. U.S. biathletes have used the symbolic image *Rock of Gibralter* to program the steady body state they need to shoot effectively. Golfers can imagine turning their body inside a barrel to ensure proper body rotation on the swing and can imagine their arms as a pendulum swinging from the shoulders for the proper putting stroke. A gymnast may visualize her back against a cold, steel wall to perfect the image and movement of a perfectly straight body during a floor exercise routine.

As you read earlier in the chapter, imagery can only hurt performance if athletes imagine the wrong responses. Triggers and symbolic images help athletes lock in the proper responses so that the imagery is "programmed" in the right way. Mental practice using triggers and symbolic images may be helpful for athletes who are mired in a slump or who are having technique problems. They should imagine themselves performing perfectly and attempt to analyze how their present technique is different from their perfect performance. It may be helpful for athletes to view videotapes of themselves performing well and then internalize that performance by using

kinesthetic imagery. Always keep in mind that imagery helps athletes when it gives them "a mental blueprint for perfect responses." Coaches should help athletes identify the triggers and symbolic images that really lock in those perfect responses within a sound performance mental blueprint.

Correcting mistakes. A very simple use of imagery for athletes is in correcting mistakes. Athletes receive constant feedback and corrections from coaches that are provided to enhance their performance. Imagery is a great tool that athletes can use to gain the most benefit from corrections provided from their coaches. Athletes should listen to the feedback or correction provided by their coaches and then run it through their minds in a brief image of the skill now performed correctly. That is, athletes should receive the feedback, and then see it and feel it as they incorporate the information from the coach into their image and execution of the skill.

Remember how bioinformational theory says that imagery works to help athletes perform better? It does so by creating a mental blueprint for perfect responses. By using imagery to see and feel the correction in performance, athletes are retooling their mental blueprint for more perfect responses. Coaches should teach and expect athletes to use imagery each time they receive feedback by requesting them to imagine the desired correction in performance in terms of seeing it and feeling it. Coaches should ask each time: Can you see it? Can you feel it? Using imagery to correct mistakes is also helpful when watching videotape of performances. When athletes and coaches identify flaws or mistakes in athletes' performance when watching tape, athletes should be cued immediately to imagine the correction by seeing it and feeling it. Coaches also can help athletes build in triggers or symbolic images to help athletes lock in the mental blueprint for perfect responses.

Coaches can help athletes "calibrate" their images by observing athletes perform and then comparing their observations with what the athletes perceive is occurring in their performance (Simons, 2000). Simons describes how a high jumper attempts to recall the image of her jump immediately after each attempt. She describes her image of her jump to her coach, who then describes her observations of the jump. In this way, the coach is calibrating the athlete's image of the jump to ensure that the athlete's perception and image of what she is doing is indeed correct in form.

Learning and practicing performance strategies. Imagery is very useful in helping athletes learn and practice performance strategies, such as tactics, systems of play, and decision making. For example, football quarterbacks can mentally rehearse various plays in relation to specific defenses, even imagining reacting to blitzes and changing defensive formations to audible and complete the appropriate offensive counter to this defense. When introducing a new basketball offense or out-of-bounds play, coaches can direct athletes to walk through the new pattern and then immediately follow this physical practice by imagining their movements through the patterns. Then, before competition, coaches can lead athletes in the mental rehearsal of these previously learned offensive and defensive strategies and plays. Similarly, skiers may ski over a particular course in their mind to prepare for an upcoming downhill race. Softball outfielders may use imagery to practice throws from the outfield based on various situations that may arise in a game. Tennis players can mentally rehearse their planned strategy against a particular opponent. Tennis champion Chris Evert prepared for upcoming matches by systematically using imagery to mentally rehearse planned strategies based on the tendencies of specific opponents. Coaches frequently use imagery in this way as they think through strategies and formations.

Preparing a mental focus for competition. Imagery can be used by athletes to create and practice in their heads the strong, unshakable mental focus needed for specific competitions. Coaches should help athletes answer two questions: "What will it be like?" "How will I respond?" The first question, "What will it be like?" refers to the external factors of competition, or the physical and social environment. Research has shown that

huge championship events such as the Olympic Games create an environment full of distractions that athletes have never faced before (Greenleaf et al., 2001). For each competitive situation that athletes face, they should vividly imagine what it will be like in terms of the facilities, crowd, potential distracters, officials, weather, and so on.

The second question, "How will I respond?" is by far the most important question for athletes. Athletes should plan to respond, not react. Responding requires mental skill and toughness to manage one's thoughts and emotions and performance when faced with obstacles, surprises, and disappointments. Reacting doesn't take any skill at all—it is typically a raw emission of emotion (anger, anxiety, fear) in which athletes allow the competitive environment to control them and make them reactive. Imagery is the tool athletes can use to practice over and over in their heads the ways in which they will respond to any type of competitive pressure they might face, and even those that they can't anticipate. Think of these as "emotional fire-drills" (Lazarus, 1984), because using imagery in this way allows athletes time to practice rational and logical responses for situations that are unexpected and stressful.

Athletes should program the answers to the two questions into a short imagery routine that they practice over and over in their heads in the days and weeks leading up to a particular competition. Imagery used in this way is an attempt to help athletes gain "experience" in responding to competitive challenges. The idea is to create a sense of expectancy, so that athletes expect certain obstacles and pressures, and that they even expect the unexpected. If they have been mentally trained to expect the unexpected and to respond productively to the unexpected, they will be less likely to react emotionally in ways that will hurt their performances.

Coaches should attempt to simulate competitive conditions at times in practice so that athletes can practice their mental focus plan for competition. The best coaches are masters at simulation by creating all types of situations that athletes might face in competition. These "dress rehearsals" might include wearing uniforms, using clocks and officials, and simulating environmental conditions such as noise/distractions, heat, cold, and pressure. Peter Vidmar, collegiate national champion gymnast and Olympic gold medalist, describes how he and his teammates would simulate competition during practice:

> The team did really weird things to prepare for [the Olympics]. In practice, we would turn off the radio so it was silent in the gym. We would go through the dialogues, like this next routine is the Olympic Games and it's the team finals. It's the last event, and we were neck-and-neck with the Chinese. It was only make-believe when we did it, but what if we really were neck-and-neck with the Chinese during the Games and this routine was our only chance to beat them and win the gold? We'd set the whole thing up, and my heart would be pounding and I would be imagining I was in Pauley Pavilion at the Olympic Games with all the pressure and people watching. I would get really nervous, take those few deep breaths and imagine I was there at the meet and [Coach] was the head judge. Tim [Daggett] would be Mr. Loudspeaker. "Okay. Next up for the USA," he would say, "Mr. Peter Vidmar." We were dead serious when we were doing this.
>
> During the Olympics, a funny thing happened. It was the last event and the USA just happened to be on the high bar and . . . I just happened to be the last up. We just happened to be neck-and-neck with the Chinese. It's the same scenario we had gone through every day for the last six months and here we were actually living it. [Coach] said, "Okay, Pete. Let's go do it just like in the gym." So I imagined I was in the UCLA gym. Consciously, I knew I was at the Olympics, but I was able to put myself in the frame of mind that I was back at the gym. I was even able to geographically orient that bar to the gym as if there was a pit over there and the wall there, etc. I did my routine and landed successfully. . . . We won the gold. (Ravizza, 1993, pp. 94–95)

Automating preperformance routines. A **preperformance routine** is a preplanned, systematic sequence of thoughts and behaviors that an athlete engages in prior to performing a specific skill. Preperformance routines are typically used by athletes prior to the execution of specific sport skills, such as a golf shot, basketball free throw, gymnastics vault, volleyball or tennis serve, field goal kick in football, start in swimming, or any of the jumping and throwing events in track and field. Research has supported preperformance routines as facilitative to athletes' performances (Lidor & Singer, 2003).

Often, imagery is included in the preperformance routines of athletes (e.g., seeing the ball float softly over the front of the rim into the basket). Imagery also should be used to systematically practice preperformance routines to make them more automatic. Then, during the pressure of competition, these routines are used to lock athletes into "autopilot," where their best performances occur.

Building and enhancing mental skills. Imagery, as a mental training tool, can be used to build and enhance all types of mental skills important to an athlete's performance.

Self-confidence. Imagery is critical to athletes' self-confidence based on the importance of their self-image in shaping the way they think and act. Obviously, athletes should nurture a self-image of competence and success, and this can be done by re-creating past successful performances and the positive feelings associated with these successes. An imagery exercise called Ideal Self-Image (ISI) is useful to work on confidence. To practice the ISI exercise, athletes should imagine themselves displaying the skills and qualities that they would most like to have, such as more assertive communication skills, a confident posture after performance errors, or the ability to manage emotions during competition. Then, they should compare their ISI with their current self-image. This should enable them to understand specific behaviors and thoughts that they can actively engage in to begin to move toward their ISI. The ISI exercise should be used continuously to understand differences between their real and ideal selves. Imagery then can be used to practice new behaviors and ways of responding that move athletes toward their ISI.

Energy management. Athletes who need to increase their energy (arousal) to psych up for competition can imagine playing intensely and aggressively in front of a roaring crowd. Athletes who need to decrease their energy, or arousal, before competition can mentally recall their preparation and good performances in practice and previous competitions and then visualize themselves handling the pressure and performing successfully in the upcoming competition.

An imagery exercise called the Energy Room can help athletes regulate arousal from different competitive demands. The Energy Room image involves athletes walking down a dark tunnel to a door that leads them into a room that is very comfortable and pleasing. (You can create whatever type of room you wish.) The room is sealed and the idea is that special air is piped into the room that creates the type of energy that is needed for this specific athlete in his or her event. The athletes feel themselves become more (energized/relaxed) with each inhalation and feel increasing (focus/intensity/relaxation). The breathing continues until the athletes feel appropriately energized and walk back through the tunnel feeling (relaxed, focused, intense, centered/confidence). Whatever variation is used in this image, the main objective is for athletes to have an imaginary place that they can go to create optimal energy and use any mental strategies they want to employ. The room should become comfortable and familiar so it is an easy place for athletes to go in their minds to manage and control their physical and mental arousal levels.

Stress management. Energy management is usually needed just before or during competition. Imagery may also be helpful to reduce stress that occurs because of an overload of life demands (e.g., job pressure, exams, deadlines). Coaches and athletes both should have two or three relaxing images that they can use when they need to reduce stress and help them to relax and unwind. These images might be of a favorite place or a warm beach. An example stress reduction imagery script is provided below.

Sample Imagery Script for Relaxation/Stress Reduction (Fanning, 1988)

1. Get into a comfortable position and close your eyes. Take several deep, cleansing breaths to relax and center yourself. Take a moment to scan your muscles. If you feel tension anywhere, gently remind yourself to "let it go." Continue to scan the muscles of your body. Wherever you feel any tension, allow yourself to consciously "let it go." As you do this, repeat the words "let it go" to yourself.

2. I would like you to visualize a very thick rope that is tied into a big knot. See the knot in your mind's eye. Notice the tightly intertwined pieces of the rope that are stretched taut against each other. Now visualize the knot slowly loosening, slowly loosening—a little bit of slack at a time until it is slack, limp, and completely uncoiled.

3. Now visualize a candle that has burned out. Focus on the cold and hard wax that has accumulated at the base of the candle. Now visualize the wax slowly softening—becoming first gooey, then soft like butter, then totally liquid as the wax warms and melts.

4. Visualize yourself on a loud city corner. It's windy and cold, very busy, and very noisy. Feel people buffet you as they rush by, hear the noise of cars and trucks, and smell the bus fumes as they drive by. Right beside you is a construction site, and a jack-hammer goes off without warning. It is so loud that your ears hurt and your body vibrates with the noise and concussions as it tears up the concrete. Slowly, ease yourself away so you are lying on your back on a grassy knoll by a sparkling blue lake. The sun warms your face and body, and a gentle breeze creates small ripples on the water. Listen as the jackhammer fades into a woodpecker gently rapping on a tree.

5. Now focus inward on yourself. You have released the knots and relaxed your body. You have softened and then melted the tension of your day. You have transformed the bustle and noise in your life into pleasant sounds of nature. By doing this, you have gained control over your mind and body. Remind yourself now that you have the ability to gain control of your thoughts and feelings through creative visualization.

Affirm your personal power to choose to think and feel well, and to believe in your ability to transform your life in productive ways.

6. Refocus now on your breathing, and repeat the following affirmation each time you exhale: "My body is relaxed and open" (wait 30 seconds). Now change that affirmation (each time you exhale) to: "I choose to think and be well" (wait 30–50 seconds). Feel pride in yourself and your abilities, and reinforce to yourself now that you have the power each day to manage how you think and feel. Take time each day to relax your body, melt away the tension, and quiet the noise in your life.

Increasing self-awareness. By systematically practicing imagery, athletes can become more aware of what is taking place within and around them by relaxing and paying attention to sensory details. A runner may learn much about a previously run race by vividly re-creating it in her mind. A member of the U.S. Nordic ski team was having problems sustaining the level of concentration she needed throughout her races. By imagining her past races in vivid detail, she suddenly became aware that she was shifting attention to the wrong things at the end of her races. She made a tactical correction in her race plan, and then mentally practiced her new strategy using imagery.

Aiding in the recovery from injury. Because injured athletes typically cannot participate in physical training, imagery allows them to mentally practice skills and strategies during their recovery. Injured athletes should attend team training sessions and imagine themselves running through the drills and workouts just as though they were physically performing them. Athletes should be challenged to use their time recovering from injuries to engage in mental training, and to maintain a focused, productive-thinking, strong-willed mind-set toward recovery. Among other things, athletes can set progressive rehabilitation goals and vividly imag-

ine the attainment of these goals. They can also use the ISI exercise to work toward full recovery of their competitive self-image. Productive, goal-oriented imagery is essential to facilitate the critical mind-body link that has been shown to enhance the healing process. Consider the following quote from a professional (NHL) hockey goalie:

> The best example I've had . . . of the effects of positive imagery was the season with the lockout and then, being injured for eight weeks, and coming back, having to play in midseason form after a layoff of close to eight months. I came back and immediately played well that year, largely due to the visualization and my belief that I was going to be ready and I was going to play well with very little practice time. There is really no better proof than that. So I know it works . . . and if you start off slow, I know it will work for you. (Orlick, 1998, p. 74)

Times to Use Imagery

You now know some specific uses for imagery. But when is the most effective time to use it? Staying with our cookbook design, we offer three suggestions about when to use imagery.

Daily practice. A recurring theme throughout this chapter is the systematic use of imagery. To be systematic, daily imagery practice is advised. As you will see in the sample programs at the end of the chapter, this may require only 5–10 minutes per day.

First, imagery practice may be used before actual physical practice sessions. This fits imagery into the athletes' routine and may get them into the proper frame of mind for practice.

It may also be appropriate to practice imagery after actual physical practice sessions. This has been successful with groups in reaffirming the points emphasized in practice that day. Also, athletes are more relaxed at the end of practice and may be more receptive to imagery at that time.

There are certain times when imagery may be beneficial during practice. For example, if a basketball coach implements an imagery program to practice free throws, he or she may build in time for imagery practice prior to shooting free throws in practice. This is especially helpful in developing kinesthetic imagery ability.

Preperformance routine. As discussed earlier, it is helpful for athletes to go through a preperformance imagery routine *before every contest.* This routine should be individualized for each athlete and practiced in preperformance situations. To facilitate this, it is helpful to have a quiet, comfortable room available to all athletes prior to competition. However, if no room is available, imagery can be practiced anywhere. In this case, athletes could use the Energy Room image suggested earlier to mentally prepare for competition. Suggestions about the content of these precompetitive routines are included with the sample programs at the end of the chapter.

Also, certain skills in sport are conducive to a preperformance imagery routine before actually performing the skill. This is the type of routine that Annika Sorenstam practices before hitting each shot. Closed skills such as free throw shooting, field goal kicking, ski jumping, volleyball serving, or gymnastic vaulting are more easily practiced in this way, as opposed to open skills such as broken field running in football or executing a fast break in basketball.

Postperformance review. Another appropriate time to use imagery is after competition. Again, this should be an individual exercise, but coaches can monitor it by having the athletes complete postcompetitive evaluation sheets based on their postperformance imagery. Using imagery at this time facilitates increased awareness of what actually happened during the competition.

Strategies to Enhance Imagery Practice

Now that you understand what athletes can use imagery for and when they can use it, some additional strategies are offered in this section to make their imagery more effective.

Athletes should practice imagery in many different places and positions. Most people envision

mental training as something an athlete does when lying on a couch. Athletes may want to spend time developing their imagery skills in quiet, nondistractible settings but, once they have become proficient at imagery, they should engage in it in many different settings and positions. Athletes should be able to engage in imagery in the locker room, on the field, in the pool, during practice, during competition—in any type of setting! It helps if you as the coach incorporate imagery into practice sessions, as it will then become second nature to your athletes. Also, encourage athletes to practice imagery in many different positions. If they are mentally practicing a sport skill such as a gymnastics routine or high jump, it might be useful for them to stand up or even walk through and move their body in certain ways that match the different segments of their images. They may want to hold the bat, club, or ball in their hands to facilitate their images as they repeat their imagery triggers to themselves to cue in perfect responses.

Training the Inner Winner

> Tony DiCicco, former coach of the U.S. Women's Soccer national team, talks about the importance of developing the "inner winner" in athletes. He describes how he attempted to boost his athletes' confidence by helping them *feel* themselves being successful by using imagery:
>
> "In the middle of the day, with the sun beaming down after a hard training session, I would have the players lie down on the grass, relax and do imagery training. I had them visualize performing their unique abilities on the soccer field over and over again. I would say, 'Imagine in your mind what you do well. If you're a great header, visualize yourself winning headers. If you're a great defender, visualize yourself stripping the ball from an attacking player. If you're a great passer of the ball, visualize yourself playing balls in. If you've got great speed, visualize yourself running by players and receiving the ball.' I made a special point of saying, 'Visualize the special skills that separate you from the rest—the skills that make your team better because you possess them.'" (DiCicco, Hacker, & Salzberg, 2003, p. 112)

The timing in imagery should be the same as in the actual physical execution of the skill. Forget about slow motion and fast forward—imagery shouldn't be used for slow motion analysis nor should it be rushed. Athletes should make their images as realistic in timing as possible in relation to the actual timing of their physical performance. Timing is a critical performance factor in many sports; thus it becomes a key response characteristic that athletes want to stamp into their mental blueprint as a perfect timing response. Elite swimmers and runners are typically able to imagine their races down to the second in terms of their splits and final times.

Help athletes use technology to enhance their images. Some athletes find it useful to buy commercially produced imagery cassette tapes or make their own imagery tapes. Sport psychology consultants can make cassette tapes for athletes that combine the practice of physical and mental skills. When making imagery tapes for athletes, they should be highly individualized with specific verbal triggers and symbolic images that are meaningful to each athlete.

The use of personal highlight videotapes has been shown to enhance the confidence and performance of basketball (Templin & Vernacchia, 1995), ice hockey (Halliwell, 1990), and soccer (Lieber, 1999) players. Athletes' peak performance moments are edited from competitive videotape and integrated with special effects and motivational music. These highlight videos can then be used in conjunction with imagery to enhance confidence in returning from injury or slumps. Clearly, the equipment to produce these videotapes is not available to everyone but, as technology advances, this powerful method to see and believe should become more accessible.

Remember that athletes should imagine vivid mental, physiological, and behavioral responses to situations. Athletes must load their images with vivid responses. Remember that imagery works by helping athletes build and refine mental blueprints for perfect responses (bioinformational theory). Repeatedly remind athletes that their images should include their mental, physio-

logical, and behavioral responses to competition—not just the stimulus characteristics of the situation. That is, when they imagine a big crowd and lots of noise and distractions, make sure they imagine how they will respond to this (e.g., using the energy as positive fuel, keeping focused in the "cocoon," and exuding confidence as they physically warm up for competition).

Image performance and outcome. Tennis players should imagine executing sharply paced passing shots and then see these shots hit in the corners of their opponent's court. Baseball players should imagine a strong and compact swing, and then see the ball driven as a line-drive through the outfield. Golfers should envision and feel the swing they will use, and then "see" the trajectory the ball will take as well as exactly where it will land. Athletes should follow through on their imagery to see not only perfect performances, but also perfect outcomes.

Be specific in all uses of imagery. Imagery should be very specifically tailored to each athlete's individual needs. For example, consider a softball pitcher who generally pitches well until there are runners on base, which seems to distract her from throwing strikes. Although it would be somewhat helpful for her to engage in the repetitive mental practice of pitching, it would be better for her to set up many different situations to practice using imagery to build her confidence and concentration to pitch effectively in changing game situations. She should repeatedly envision herself in various situations with baserunners, different counts and number of outs, and different game scores to groove strong and consistent mental and physical responses to the pressure of these situations. Athletes must consider their exact performance needs, so that their imagery practice is specific in helping them develop thoughts and behaviors that can overcome performance problems.

Imagery logs. To monitor imagery practice and improvement, it is useful for athletes to keep a log or written record of their imagery experiences. The log can contain different types of imagery exercises and self-evaluation forms to monitor individual progress in the program. The postperformance review exercise discussed in the section on times to practice imagery could be included in the log. This is a means of emphasizing systematic practice and provides a way to monitor that practice.

Using the Imagery Cookbook

You now have all the ingredients (uses, times, strategies) to cook up an effective and systematic imagery program for your athletes. Remember the KISS principle—keep it simple and systematic instead of trying to do too much at first. Carefully consider the types and methods of imagery that will work for you in your particular situation. Remember that imagery is a creative experience, so have the confidence to experiment with different imagery ingredients to creatively implement imagery for your unique needs.

Sample imagery programs. Three sample imagery programs are provided here to give you a basic idea about the structure and progression of imagery programs for athletes. Although these program outlines are generic, you should of course modify them sport-specific and program-specific to the needs of your athletes.

Team Imagery Program

The coach or sport psychology consultant should begin the team imagery program well before the start of the competitive season so athletes are familiar with imagery and proficient in their imagery skills. Informational literature can be provided to more advanced athletes in the off-season to introduce them to imagery. This reading material should be motivational and interesting so the athletes are intrigued and ready to learn more about imagery in the preseason.

First three weeks of preseason

1. Introduce program (20 minutes).
2. Evaluate athletes' imagery ability (15 minutes).
3. Basic Training (three times per week for 10 minutes following practice). Begin Basic Training with the exercises suggested in this

chapter; then add exercises that are appropriate for your team and sport (team tactics and strategies).

4. Provide individual imagery sessions for athletes who are interested. Also, invite athletes to meet with you individually to discuss personalized imagery training they can do on their own. Continue to provide individual sessions for athletes throughout the season if they want them.

Remainder of season (three times per week 10 minutes before, following, or during practice)

1. Relaxation for optimal focus imagery*
2. Repetitive practice of simple sport skills*— perform them perfectly!
3. Repetitive practice of advanced sport skills*—perform them perfectly!
4. Competitive tactics and strategies in relation to specific needs of team and upcoming opponents*
5. Re-create past successful performance
6. Goal programming for future success

The imagery exercises marked with an asterisk should be included in *all* sessions. They are a warm-up for the other types of imagery. After these initial warm-up exercises, any types of imagery exercises can be used. Other suggested images might include the following:

- Confidence in fulfilling team role successfully
- Attentional focus (develop a team focus plan for different opponents)
- Using verbal triggers and symbolic images
- Energy management (Energy Room or similar image to feel control over arousal regulation)
- Correcting mistakes/practice refocusing plan
- Precompetitive routine (should be practiced at least twice a week)

Precompetitive imagery routine. The suggested practice outline (the first six steps listed under "Remainder of Season") could be incorporated into individual precompetitive routines. Encourage each athlete to develop his or her own routine, and make available a preevent imagery room or specified area in which imagery can be practiced privately.

Postgame imagery review. Devise an event evaluation sheet that athletes will complete after each game. This sheet should ask the athletes to evaluate their performance in the following areas: physical skills, strategies, fulfillment of role, achievement of goals, energy management, attentional focus, self-confidence, areas that need improvement, and strategies to improve these areas. Make the sheet concise and objective so the athletes will find it easy to complete (see Chapter 12 for a sample evaluation sheet).

Explain to the athletes that they should relax in a quiet setting, mentally re-create the competition, and complete the evaluation form. They can either keep the forms in a log book or turn them in to you after each competition.

Individual Imagery Program

1. Education about imagery to understand basics of imagery
2. Evaluation of imagery ability (use questionnaire)
3. Basic Training (once a day for 10 minutes). Basic Training should include imagery practice in all areas. Also, this training should emphasize imagery exercises in areas found to be weak in the imagery evaluation phase.
4. Regular imagery sessions (throughout competitive season)

    Prepractice (5 minutes):

    Technique work

    Goal programming for practice

    Postpractice (10 minutes):

    Re-create practice performance

    Mental skills practice (according to individual need)

    Practice precompetitive imagery program

5. Competition day

    Preevent imagery (10–20 minutes):

    Use format suggested in "Team Imagery Program"

    Postevent review (10–20 minutes):

    Design personal event evaluation sheet or log

Figure Skating Skill Acquisition Program

Skill acquisition exercises for an axel jump

1. Watch a skilled skater, either live or on videotape, perform an axel several times. Try to get a general idea of the timing and the movements involved. Now, close your eyes and imagine the other skater performing the axel. Next, try to put yourself in the other skater's body. Imagine what the timing and movements *feel* like.
2. Walk through the axel several times off the ice in sneakers. Notice how the jump feels. Pay attention to the timing and the rotation. Close your eyes and try to feel yourself performing the axel. Alternate between walking through the jump and imagining the jump. Try to feel balanced and in control during both activities.
3. Close your eyes and imagine yourself performing the axel. Concentrate on the feelings associated with performing the jump. Imagine yourself performing successfully and feeling confident. Now, physically perform the axel on the ice. Focus on creating the same feelings during the physical performance as in the mental practice.

Activity. Perform the axel 10 times, concentrating on feeling the timing, the rotation, and staying balanced.

Triggers for axel jump

1. Exhale and sit into the takeoff (proper takeoff position).
2. Kick a football and explode (bring free leg through as if you were kicking a football).

3. Step up, land backwards (shift weight to the free leg as if you were stepping up onto a step and landing on the step backwards).

4. Soft and hold (the landing motion should be soft and the landing position held).

Imagery practice with triggers. Use the triggers in conjunction with the imagery practice and physical practice of the axel jump. Imagine performing the axel five times using the triggers as a guide for proper technique.

Routine for each jump

1. Before physically performing the jump, imagine yourself successfully performing and landing the axel. Focus on the feeling and timing of the jump, as well as the sense of control over the jump. Use the triggers to re-create the proper technique.

2. When setting up the jump, take a deep breath and exhale. Focus on feeling balanced.

3. As you enter the jump, concentrate on sitting into the entry and exploding on the takeoff.

4. The jump happens quickly, so try to re-create the imaged feeling and timing of performing the jump.

5. On the landing, use the triggers soft and hold to achieve the proper landing position.

Imagery exercise. It is important to get to the point where the technique of the axel is automatic. Use imagery to mentally practice the axel so that it becomes consistent in feeling and timing. Develop some verbal trigger or symbolic images that help you achieve a consistent and automatic axel jump.

Case studies. Now that you've read the "cookbook" and some sample programs, let's try your hand at planning imagery training programs for athletes. In this section, three case studies are presented that describe athletes who are having performance problems. Read through each case and use your knowledge from the chapter to plan an imagery intervention to help that athlete perform better. Write your plan for each athlete down on paper, and then go on to read the hypothetical imagery interventions that we suggest for each case. Don't look ahead until you plan your own imagery interventions for each athlete!

Molly

Molly, a 13-year-old figure skater, is attempting her senior freestyle test for the third time. Molly needs to pass this test to qualify for the highest level of national competition. In practice, Molly has completed all of the elements of her freestyle program with ease, but she tends to choke during the test sessions. Her coach attempts to be patient and supportive by telling Molly that she just needs to try harder and practice more.

Mario

Mario is a collegiate ice hockey player who lacks consistency in his performance. He performs well until he becomes distracted by his anger in reaction to game events that he cannot control, such as poor officiating, rough play by opponents, or poor ice conditions. When asked about his inconsistency, Mario says, "I just can't concentrate on the game when things go wrong!" Mario's coach tells him that he'd better get a handle on his temper and focus on the game.

Dee

Dee is a gifted high school sprinter. She is in top physical condition and is expected to have a great senior season and earn a track scholarship to a major university. Dee injures her ankle before the first meet of the year, yet when she returns to competition a few weeks later, she does not perform as well as she or her coaches expected. Dee has recovered physically from the injury, but mentally she is worried about reinjury. She is not putting 100% effort into practice and her performance suffers as a result. Deep down, she is concerned that she will not make it back to her previous performance level, and she is worried that she will now fail to gain a scholarship.

Suggested Imagery Intervention Plans

Molly. Initially we got to know Molly and talked with her about her perceived strengths and weaknesses as a figure skater. We introduced the concept of imagery to her and guided her through imagery in which she imagined her performance during practice and during a test session. After imagining each scene, she wrote down the characteristics of the performances, including how she felt during the performance, what she said to herself, how she prepared for the performances, and how she responded to mistakes. Based on an evaluation of Molly's imagery ability, we recommended some Basic Training exercises with an emphasis on arousal control and refocusing after mistakes.

We worked with Molly to develop a pretest imagery program in which she saw herself performing well, achieving her goals (goal programming), and refocusing after mistakes in her program. We developed an imagery script for Molly to use before test sessions focusing on arousal control and self-confidence. Here is an example of Molly's imagery script:

> I am calm, confident, and in control. My muscles are loose and relaxed, like flexible springs. I am breathing easily, feeling my lungs fill with energizing air. During my warm-up, I feel focused and confident. My blades cut into the ice with ease, making a crisp cutting noise. My jumps are snappy and explosive. My spins are centered and tight. My muscles are warm and elastic. As I step onto the ice for my program, I feel balanced and in control. I take my beginning position with a confident posture, feeling excited anticipation to perform my best. I know that I'm ready.

Molly practiced this pretest imagery program during simulated test sessions and during practice sessions to re-create the testing experience. Through imagery, Molly developed the mental skills to become more mentally tough and focused during pressure performances.

Mario. We first got to know Mario and talked with him about his perceived strengths and weaknesses as a hockey player. We introduced the concept of imagery to him and guided him through an imagery session in which he visualized his performance being negatively affected by anger. After the imagery, we specifically worked with Mario to identify the specific characteristics of the situation, such as what triggered his anger, his attitude before and after the trigger event, and his focus before and after the trigger. We evaluated Mario's imagery ability and recommended various Basic Training exercises, especially focusing on self-awareness and controllability.

We worked with Mario to develop a refocusing imagery program in which he saw himself refocusing after negative events, directing the anger in a productive way, and performing well after negative events. Mario imagined several different scenarios in which he typically loses his temper and his focus, such as after a poor call from an official or rough play by the opposing team. We worked with Mario to develop several imagery scripts incorporating imagery triggers, so he could mentally practice emotional control and refocusing. An excerpt from his emotional control script follows:

> [Trigger event]. . . Deep breath . . . Squeeze stick . . . Let anger swell up from the bottom of your toes, into your legs, all the way through your trunk and chest. Feel the anger flowing down out of your arms, feel the hot emotions bursting out of your fingers. Squeeze all of that anger into your stick. Take a deep breath. Relax your hands.

Mario was able to use his imagery scripts to practice emotional control and refocusing skills. He became more consistent in his ability to focus after negative events during games and continued to use imagery for refocusing.

Dee. We first got to know Dee and discussed her physical and mental approach to competition. We guided her through several imagery sessions in which she imagined her performance both before and after her injury. We asked Dee to focus on how she felt, what she said to herself, and what her mental attitude was during both situations. We had her re-create through imagery the times before her injury in which she ran well, and also had her compare her thoughts, feelings, and behaviors to times after her injury. During this time, we also had Dee practice imagery to become more skilled at controlling her images.

We worked with Dee to develop an imagery program in which she re-created the feelings of confidence and competence she experienced prior to her injury. We had her keep a log of her mental states before, during, and after practices and meets. Additionally, Dee recorded any triggers that she associated with changes in her attitude or mood toward her ability. Initially, Dee's log indicated that she questioned her running ability. After a period of systematic and consistent use of imagery, Dee's attitude began to change. She began to feel more sure of herself and thus pushed herself harder during practice. The combination of her mental and physical training helped Dee to get back to her preinjury running level. Seeing *was* believing for Dee as she went on to become a successful collegiate runner and advocate for the power of imagery.

Summary

Imagery is defined as using all the senses to re-create or create an experience in the mind. It is a mental technique that programs the human mind to respond as programmed—to see and believe. The evidence supporting the positive influence of imagery on sport performance is impressive. Both scientific and experiential accounts of the use of imagery to enhance sport performance report positive results. Key considerations in using imagery include developing both internal and external perspectives and understanding that imagery is a supplement to, not a replacement for, physical practice. Also, imagery may be useful for both skilled and novice athletes, and the ability of athletes to engage in vivid and controlled images is critical to the effectiveness of imagery in enhancing performance.

Four conceptual explanations suggest how imagery may enhance performance. The psychoneuromuscular theory states that vivid imagined events produce innervation in the muscles that is similar to that produced by physical execution of the event. The symbolic learning theory suggests that imagery facilitates performance by helping individuals blueprint or code their movements into symbolic components, thus making the movements more familiar and perhaps more automatic. Bioinformational theory indicates that individuals respond to imagery with response characteristics that create psychophysiological changes in the body that positively influence performance. The attentional-arousal set explanation suggests that imagery causes athletes to optimize arousal and focus their attention on relevant cues prior to competition.

All athletes possess the ability to use imagery to improve their performance. However, like physical skill, the mental skill of imagery requires systematic practice to be effective. Setting up a systematic imagery program involves four steps. First, athletes should be introduced to imagery and convinced about the merits of practicing imagery. Second, athletes must evaluate their imagery abilities to understand their strengths and areas that need improvement. Just as athletes differ in physical skills, they will differ in their ability to develop vivid and controlled images. Third, athletes should engage in Basic Training to develop and enhance their imagery skills. It is important for athletes to use all appropriate senses and their emotions when practicing imagery. Finally, imagery should be integrated into a systematic program of physical and mental training. Major concerns include building the imagery program into the athletes' routine and fitting the program to the needs of the athlete. Coaches and athletes can incorporate many uses of imagery and different methods of practicing imagery in this four-step program.

Study Questions

1. Briefly describe some of the evidence supporting the positive influence of imagery on sport performance.

2. Describe the four phases of setting up an imagery training program.

3. Vividness, controllability, and self-awareness are three areas of Basic Training in the imagery training program. Define each of these and describe the role each plays in training an athlete to use an imagery program.

4. What are five different ways imagery can be used by athletes?

5. Identify and describe the four explanations provided in this chapter that address how imagery works to enhance sport performance.

6. Develop an imagery program for an athlete in your sport using the imagery cookbook.

7. Why is imagery a polysensory experience?

8. What are three different times imagery can be used optimally by athletes?

9. What is the difference between external and internal imagery, and how can each perspective be used by athletes?

10. Can imagery hurt athletes' performance? Explain and then identify how athletes can avoid this negative imagery effect.

References

Ahsen, A. (1984). ISM: The triple code model for imagery and psychophysiology. *Journal of Mental Imagery, 8,* 15–42.

Bakker, F. C., Boschker, M. S. J., & Chung, T. (1996). Changes in muscular activity while imagining weight lifting using stimulus or response propositions. *Journal of Sport & Exercise Psychology, 18,* 313–324.

Beauchamp, P. H., Halliwell, W. R., Fournier, J. F., & Koestner, R. (1996). Effects of cognitive-behavioral psychological skills training on the motivation, preparation, and putting performance of novice golfers. *The Sport Psychologist, 10,* 157–170.

Beilock, S. L., Afremow, J. A., Rabe, A. L., & Carr, T. H. (2001). "Don't miss!" The debilitating effects of suppressive imagery on golf putting performance. *Journal of Sport & Exercise Psychology, 23,* 200–221.

Bird, E. (1984). EMG quantification of mental rehearsal. *Perceptual and Motor Skills, 59,* 899–906.

Bird, L. (1989). *Drive: The story of my life.* New York: Bantam.

Callow, N., Hardy, L., & Hall, C. (2001). The effects of a motivational general-mastery imagery intervention on the sport confidence of high-level badminton players. *Research Quarterly for Exercise and Sport, 72,* 389–400.

Calmels, C., Berthoumieux, C., & d'Arripe-Longueville, F. (2004). Effects of an imagery training program on selective attention of national softball players. *The Sport Psychologist, 18,* 272–296.

Calmels, C., d'Arripe-Longueville, F., Fournier, J. F., & Soulard, A. (2003). Competitive strategies among elite female gymnasts: An exploration of the relative influence of psychological skills training and natural learning experiences. *International Journal of Sport & Exercise Psychology, 1,* 327–352.

Cogan, K. D., & Petrie, T. A. (1995). Sport consultation: An evaluation of a season-long intervention with female collegiate gymnasts. *The Sport Psychologist, 9,* 282–296.

Cumming, J., & Hall, C. (2002). Athletes' use of imagery in the off-season. *The Sport Psychologist, 16,* 160–172.

Daw, J., & Burton, D. (1994). Evaluation of a comprehensive psychological skills training program for collegiate tennis players. *The Sport Psychologist, 8,* 37–57.

DiCicco, T., Hacker, C., & Salzberg, C. (2003). *Catch them being good.* New York: Penguin.

Durand-Bush, N., & Salmela, J. H. (2002). The development and maintenance of expert athletic performance: Perceptions of world and Olympic champions. *Journal of Applied Sport Psychology, 14,* 154–171.

Efran, J. S., Lesser, G. S., & Spiller, M. J. (1994). Enhancing tennis coaching with youths using a metaphor method. *The Sport Psychologist, 8,* 349–359.

Evans, L., Jones, L., & Mullen, R. (2004). An imagery intervention during the competitive season with an elite rugby union player. *The Sport Psychologist, 18,* 252–271.

Fanning, P. (1988). *Visualization for change.* Oakland, CA: New Harbinger.

Feltz, D. L., & Landers, D. M. (1983). The effects of mental practice on motor skill learning and performance: A meta-analysis. *Journal of Sport Psychology, 5,* 25–57.

Feltz, D. L., Landers, D. M., & Becker, B. J. (1988). A revised meta-analysis of the mental practice literature on motor skill learning. In D. Druckman & J. Swets (Eds.), *Enhancing human performance: Issues, theories, and techniques* (pp. 1–65). Washington, DC: National Academy Press.

Garza, D. L., & Feltz, D. L. (1998). Effects of selected mental practice on performance, self-efficacy, and competition confidence of figure skaters. *The Sport Psychologist, 12,* 1–15.

Goss, S., Hall, C., Buckolz, E., & Fishburne, G. (1986). Imagery ability and the acquisition and retention of movements. *Memory and Cognition, 4,* 469–477.

Gould, D., Eklund, R. C., & Jackson, S. A. (1992). 1988 U.S. Olympic wrestling excellence: I. Mental preparation, precompetitive cognition, and affect. *The Sport Psychologist, 6,* 358–383.

Gould, D., Guinan, D., Greenleaf, C., Medbery, R., & Peterson, K. (1999). Factors affecting Olympic performance: Perceptions of athletes and coaches from more and less successful teams. *The Sport Psychologist, 13,* 371–394.

Gould, D., Tammen, V., Murphy, S. M., & May, J. (1989). An examination of U.S. Olympic sport psychology consultants and the services they provide. *The Sport Psychologist, 3,* 300–312.

Gould, D., Weinberg, R., & Jackson, A. (1980). Mental preparation strategies, cognitions, and strength performance. *Journal of Sport Psychology, 2,* 329–339.

Greenleaf, C. A., Gould, D., & Dieffenbach, K. (2001). Factors influencing Olympic performance: Interviews with Atlanta and Nagano U.S. Olympians. *Journal of Applied Sport Psychology, 13,* 154–184.

Hale, B. D. (1982). The effects of internal and external imagery on muscular and ocular concomitants. *Journal of Sport Psychology, 4,* 379–387.

Hale, B. D., & Whitehouse, A. (1998). The effects of imagery-manipulated appraisal on intensity and direction of competitive anxiety. *The Sport Psychologist, 12,* 40–51.

Hall, C. R. (1985). Individual differences in the mental practice and imagery of motor skill performance. *Canadian Journal of Applied Sport Science, 10,* 17S–21S.

Hall, C. R., & Rodgers, W. M. (1989). Enhancing coaching effectiveness in figure skating through a mental skills training program. *The Sport Psychologist, 2,* 142–154.

Hall, C. R., Rodgers, W. M., & Barr, K. A. (1990). The use of imagery by athletes in selected sports. *The Sport Psychologist, 4,* 1–10.

Hall, C. R., Schmidt, D., Durand, M., & Buckolz, E. (1994). Imagery and motor skills acquisition. In A. A. Sheikh & E. R. Korn (Eds.), *Imagery in sports and physical performance* (pp. 121–134). Amityville, NY: Baywood.

Hall, E. G., & Erffmeyer, E. S. (1983). The effect of visuo-motor behavior rehearsal with videotaped modeling on free throw accuracy of intercollegiate female basketball players. *Journal of Sport Psychology, 5,* 343–346.

Halliwell, W. (1990). Providing sport psychology consulting services in professional hockey. *The Sport Psychologist, 4,* 369–377.

Hanton, S., & Jones, G. (1999). The effects of a multimodal intervention program on performers: II. Training the butterflies to fly in formation. *The Sport Psychologist, 13,* 22–41.

Hardy, L., & Callow, N. (1999). Efficacy of external and internal visual imagery perspectives for the enhancement of performance on tasks in which form is important. *Journal of Sport & Exercise Psychology, 21,* 95–112.

Harris, D. V., & Robinson, W. J. (1986). The effects of skill level on EMG activity during internal and external imagery. *Journal of Sport Psychology, 8,* 105–111.

Hecker, J. E., & Kaczor, L. M. (1988). Application of imagery theory to sport psychology: Some preliminary findings. *Journal of Sport and Exercise Psychology, 10,* 363–373.

Hird, J. S., Landers, D. M., Thomas, J. R., & Horan, J. J. (1991). Physical practice is superior to mental practice in enhancing cognitive and motor task performance. *Journal of Sport and Exercise Psychology, 8,* 293.

Holmes, P. S., & Collins, D. J. (2001). The PETTLEP approach to motor imagery: A functional equivalence model for sport psychologists. *Journal of Applied Sport Psychology, 13,* 60–83.

Housner, L. D. (1984). The role of visual imagery in recall of modeled motoric stimuli. *Journal of Sport Psychology, 6,* 148–158.

Isaac, A. R. (1992). Mental practice—Does it work in the field? *The Sport Psychologist, 6,* 192–198.

Jacobson, E. (1931). Electrical measurements of neuromuscular states during mental activities. *American Journal of Physiology, 96,* 115–121.

Jowdy, D. P., & Harris, D. V. (1990). Muscular responses during mental imagery as a function of motor skill level. *Journal of Sport and Exercise Psychology, 12,* 191–201.

Kendall, G., Hrycaiko, D., Martin, G. L., & Kendall, T. (1990). The effects of an imagery rehearsal, relaxation, and self-talk package on basketball game performance. *Journal of Sport and Exercise Psychology, 12,* 157–166.

Kerr, G., & Leith, L. (1993). Stress management and athletic performance. *The Sport Psychologist, 1,* 221–231.

Lang, P. J. (1977). Imagery in therapy: An information processing analysis of fear. *Behavior Therapy, 8,* 862–886.

Lang, P. J. (1979). A bio-informational theory of emotional imagery. *Psychophysiology, 16,* 495–512.

Lazarus, A. (1984). *In the mind's eye: The power of imagery for personal enrichment.* New York: Guilford.

Lee, A. B., & Hewitt, J. (1987). Using visual imagery in a flotation tank to improve gymnastic performance and reduce physical symptoms. *International Journal of Sport Psychology, 18,* 223–230.

Lee, C. (1990). Psyching up for a muscular endurance task: Effects of image content on performance and mood state. *Journal of Sport and Exercise Psychology, 12,* 66–73.

Lidor, R., & Singer, R. M. (2003). Preperformance routines in self-paced tasks: Developmental and educational considerations. In R. Lidor & K. P. Henschen (Eds.), *The psychology of team sports* (pp. 69–98). Morgantown, WV: Fitness Information Technology.

Lieber, J. (1999, July 6). USA won't kick habit of believing. *USA Today,* July 6, pp. 1c–2c.

Mamassis, G., & Doganis, G. (2004). The effects of a mental training program on juniors pre-competitive anxiety, self-confidence, and tennis performance. *Journal of Applied Sport Psychology, 16,* 118–137.

Marks, D. F. (1983). Mental imagery and consciousness: A theoretical review. In A. A. Sheikh (Ed.), *Imagery: Current theory, research, and application* (pp. 96–130). New York: Wiley.

Martin, K. A., & Hall, C. R. (1995). Using mental imagery to enhance intrinsic motivation. *Journal of Sport and Exercise Psychology, 17,* 54–69.

Martin, K. A., Moritz, S. E., & Hall, C. R. (1999). Imagery use in sport: A literature review and applied model. *The Sport Psychologist, 13,* 245–268.

McCallum, J. (2004, May 24). It's that time again. *Sports Illustrated,* pp. 54–65.

McKenzie, A., & Howe, B. L. (1997). The effect of imagery on self-efficacy for a motor skill. *International Journal of Sport Psychology, 28,* 196–210.

Ming, S., & Martin, G. L. (1996). Single-subject evaluation of a self-talk package for improving figure skating performance. *The Sport Psychologist, 10,* 227–238.

Mumford, P., & Hall, C. (1985). The effects of internal and external imagery on performing figures of figure skating. *Canadian Journal of Applied Sport Sciences, 10,* 171–177.

Murphy, S. M., & Woolfolk, R. (1987). The effects of cognitive interventions on competitive anxiety and performance on a fine motor skill task. *International Journal of Sport Psychology, 18,* 152–166.

Nicklaus, J. (1974). *Golf my way.* New York: Simon & Schuster.

Noel, R. C. (1980). The effect of visuo-motor behavior rehearsal on tennis performance. *Journal of Sport Psychology, 2,* 221–226.

Orlick, T. (1998). *Embracing your potential.* Champaign, IL: Human Kinetics.

Orlick, T., & Partington, J. (1988). Mental links to excellence. *The Sport Psychologist, 2,* 105–130.

Page, S. J., Sime, W., & Nordell, K. (1999). The effects of imagery on female college swimmers' perceptions of anxiety. *The Sport Psychologist, 13,* 458–469.

Ravizza, K. (1993). An interview with Peter Vidmar, member of the 1994 U.S. Olympic gymnastics team. *Contemporary Thought in Performance Enhancement, 2,* 93–100.

Richardson, A. (1967). Mental practice: A review and discussion (Part 2). *Research Quarterly, 38,* 263–273.

Rodgers, W., Hall, C., & Buckolz, E. (1991). The effect of an imagery training program on imagery ability, imagery use, and figure skating performance. *Journal of Applied Sport Psychology, 3,* 109–125.

Rotella, R. J. (1995). *Golf is not a game of perfect.* New York: Simon & Schuster.

Rotella, R. J., Gansneder, B., Ojala, D., & Billing, J. (1980). Cognitions and coping strategies of elite skiers: An exploratory study of young developing athletes. *Journal of Sport Psychology, 2,* 350–354.

Ryan, D. E., & Simons, J. (1981). Cognitive demand, imagery, and frequency of mental rehearsal as factors influencing acquisition of motor skills. *Journal of Sport Psychology, 3,* 35–45.

Ryan, D. E., & Simons, J. (1983). What is learned in mental practice of motor skills: A test of the cognitive-motor hypothesis. *Journal of Sport Psychology, 5,* 419–426.

Ryska, T. A. (1998). Cognitive-behavioral strategies and precompetitive anxiety among recreational athletes. *Psychological Record, 48,* 697–708.

Sackett, R. S. (1934). The influences of symbolic rehearsal upon the retention of a maze habit. *Journal of General Psychology, 13,* 113–128.

Salmon, J., Hall, C., & Haslam, I. (1994). The use of imagery by soccer players. *Journal of Applied Sport Psychology, 6,* 116–133.

Savoy, C. (1993). A yearly mental training program for a college basketball player. *The Sport Psychologist, 7,* 173–190.

Savoy, C. (1997). Two individual mental training programs for a team sport. *International Journal of Sport Psychology, 28,* 259–270.

Shelton, T. O., & Mahoney, M. J. (1978). The content and effect of "psyching-up" strategies in weightlifters. *Cognitive Therapy and Research, 2,* 275–284.

Short, S. E., Bruggeman, J. M., Engel, S. G., Marback, T. L., Wang, L. J., Willadsen, A., & Short, M. W. (2002). The effect of imagery function and imagery direction on self-efficacy and performance on a golf-putting task. *The Sport Psychologist, 16,* 48–67.

Simons, J. (2000). Doing imagery in the field. In M. Andersen (Ed.), *Doing sport psychology* (pp. 77–92). Champaign, IL: Human Kinetics.

Slade, J. M., Landers, D. M., & Martin, P. E. (2002). Muscular activity during real and imagined movements: A test of inflow explanations. *Journal of Sport & Exercise Psychology, 24,* 11–67.

Smith, D., & Collins, D. (2004). Mental practice, motor performance, and the late CNV. *Journal of Sport & Exercise Psychology, 26,* 412–426.

Smith, D., Collins, D., & Holmes, P. (2003). Impact and mechanism of mental practice effects on strength. *International Journal of Sport and Exercise Psychology, 1,* 293–306.

Smith, D., & Holmes, P. (2004). The effect of imagery modality on golf putting performance. *Journal of Sport & Exercise Psychology, 26,* 385–395.

Smith, D., Holmes, P., Whitemore, L., Collins, D., & Devenport, T. (2001). The effect of theoretically-based imagery scripts on hockey penalty flick performance. *Journal of Sport Behavior, 24,* 408–419.

Suinn, R. M. (1980). Psychology and sport performance: Principles and applications. In R. M. Suinn (Ed.), *Psychology in sports: Methods and applications* (pp. 26–36). Minneapolis: Burgess.

Templin, D. P., & Vernacchia, R. A. (1995). The effect of highlight music videotapes upon the game performance of intercollegiate basketball players. *The Sport Psychologist, 9,* 41–50.

Thelwell, R. C., & Greenlees, I. A. (2001). The effects of a mental skills training program on gymnasium triathlon performance. *The Sport Psychologist, 15,* 127–141.

Tynes, L. L., & McFatter, R. M. (1987). The efficacy of "psyching" strategies on a weightlifting task. *Cognitive Therapy and Research, 11,* 327–336.

Vandall, R. A., Davis, R. A., & Clugston, H. A. (1934). The function of mental practice in the acquisition of motor skills. *Journal of General Psychology, 29,* 243–250.

White, A., & Hardy, L. (1998). An in-depth analysis of the uses of imagery by high-level slalom canoeists and artistic gymnasts. *The Sport Psychologist, 12,* 387–403.

Woolfolk, R. L., Murphy, S. M., Gottesfeld, D., & Aitken, D. (1985). Effects of mental rehearsal of motor task activity and mental depiction of task outcome on motor skill performance. *Journal of Sport Psychology, 7,* 191–197.

Woolfolk, R., Parrish, W., & Murphy, S. M. (1985). The effects of positive and negative imagery on motor skill performance. *Cognitive Therapy and Research, 9,* 235–341.

Wrisberg, C. A. (1990). An interview with Pat Head Summitt. *The Sport Psychologist, 4,* 180–191.

Wrisberg, C. A., & Anshel, M. H. (1989). The effect of cognitive strategies on the free throw shooting performance of young athletes. *The Sport Psychologist, 3,* 95–104.

Wrisberg, C. A., & Ragsdale, M. R. (1979). Cognitive demand and practice level: Factors in the mental rehearsal of motor skills. *Journal of Human Movement Studies, 5,* 201–208.

A

Sample Imagery Script for Competition Preparation

Get into a comfortable position and close your eyes. Focus on the center of your body and take several slow deep breaths. With each inhalation, imagine that you are pulling all of the tension from your body into your lungs. With each exhalation, imagine that you are releasing all of your tension and negative thoughts from your body. Continue this focused breathing until your body becomes relaxed and your mind is alert and open for productive thoughts. (Pause for 30 seconds.)

Imagine it is the night before an important competition or performance. You are preparing for the next day's event. As you are preparing to go to sleep, you are focusing on feeling calm, confident, and physically and emotionally in control. (Pause for 10 seconds.) You are excited and anticipatory about performing well tomorrow. (Pause for 10 seconds.) You sleep well and awaken feeling rested, excited, and focused. (Pause for 8 seconds.) You realize that you are well prepared, both physically and mentally, for the competition. Physically, you feel balanced and ready. Mentally, you are confident and focused. (Pause for 10 seconds.)

Now imagine that you are at home preparing to leave for the competition sight. (Pause for 10 seconds.) You take some time to run through your mental warm-up by visualizing several repetitions of a few basic skills in your sport, such as a warm-up drill. (Pause for 30 seconds.) Now in your mind's eye, focus on the specific goals and strategies for this particular competition. Imagine yourself performing perfectly, achieving your goals for the competition and successfully executing specific strategies for this opponent. (Pause for 60 seconds.)

Now imagine yourself arriving at the competition sight feeling confident in your physical and mental preparation. (Pause for 20 seconds.) You feel the nervous anticipation of competition and remind yourself that it is exhilarating to play your sport. You love it! (Pause for 10 seconds.) Imagine your feelings as you dress and go through any precompetitive preparations. (Pause for 20 seconds.) You feel confident in your preparation and clearly focused on your upcoming performance. Your breathing is calm and controlled. Your muscles feel warm and elastic, ready to explode with intensity and precision. You are ready! (Pause for 15 seconds.) Imagine going through your competition warm-up as you have done so many times in practice. (Pause for 30 seconds.) Your warm-up goes well, yet you remind yourself that you are ready for any unexpected problem or obstacle. You are confident in your refocusing ability and remind yourself that you are mentally tough. You feel optimally energized and ready to go. Enjoy it!

Sport Imagery Evaluation

As you complete this evaluation, remember that imagery is more than just visualizing something in your mind's eye. Vivid images may include many senses, such as seeing, hearing, feeling, touching, and smelling. Vivid images also may include feeling emotions or moods.

In this exercise you will read descriptions of general sport situations. You are to imagine the situation and provide as much detail from your imagination as possible to make the image as real as you can. Then you will be asked to rate your imagery in seven areas:

a. How vividly you *saw* or visualized the image.

b. How clearly you *heard* the sounds.

c. How vividly you *felt your body movements* during the activity.

d. How clearly you were aware of your mood or *felt your emotions* of the situation.

e. Whether you could see the image from *inside your body.*

f. Whether you could see the image from *outside your body.*

g. How well you could *control* the image.

After you read each description, think of a specific example of it—the skill, the people involved, the place, the time. Then close your eyes and take a few deep breaths to become as relaxed as you can. Put aside all other thoughts for a moment. Keep your eyes closed as you try to imagine the situation as vividly as you can.

There are, of course, no right or wrong images. Use your imagery skills to create the most vivid and clear image that you can. After you have completed imagining each situation, rate your imagery skills using the following scales.

For items a–f:

1 = no image present

2 = not clear or vivid, but a recognizable image

3 = moderately clear and vivid image

4 = clear and vivid image

5 = extremely clear and vivid image

For item g:

1 = no control at all of image

2 = very hard to control

3 = moderate control of image

4 = good control of image

5 = complete control of image

Practicing Alone

Select one specific skill or activity in your sport, such as shooting free throws, performing a parallel bar routine, executing a takedown, throwing a pass, hitting a ball, or swimming the butterfly. Now imagine yourself performing this activity at the place where you normally practice (gym, pool, rink, field, court) without anyone else present. Close your eyes for about one minute and try to see yourself at this place, hear the sounds, feel your body perform the movement, and be aware of your state of mind or mood. Try to see yourself from behind your eyes or from inside your body. Then, try to see yourself from outside your body, as if you were watching a videotape of yourself performing.

a.	Rate how well you *saw* yourself doing the activity.	1	2	3	4	5
b.	Rate how well you heard the sounds of doing the activity.	1	2	3	4	5
c.	Rate how well you *felt yourself* making the movements.	1	2	3	4	5
d.	Rate how well you were aware of your *mood*.	1	2	3	4	5
e.	Rate how well you were able to see the image from *inside* your body.	1	2	3	4	5
f.	Rate how well you were able to see the image from outside your body.	1	2	3	4	5
g.	Rate how well you *controlled* the image.	1	2	3	4	5

Practicing With Others

You are doing the same activity, but now you are practicing the skill with your coach and teammates present. This time, however, you make a mistake that everyone notices. Close your eyes for about one minute to imagine making the error and the situation immediately afterward as vividly as you can. First, try to experience the feelings you have as you make the mistake. Then, quickly try to re-create the situation in your mind and imagine yourself correcting the mistake and performing perfectly. Try to see the image from behind your eyes or from inside your body as you correct the mistake. Next, try to see the image as if you were watching through a video camera as you correct the mistake.

a.	Rate how well you *saw* yourself in this situation.	1	2	3	4	5
b.	Rate how well you *heard* the sounds in this situation.	1	2	3	4	5
c.	Rate how well you *felt yourself* making the movements.	1	2	3	4	5
d.	Rate how well you *felt the emotions* of this situation.	1	2	3	4	5
e.	Rate how well you were able to see the image from *inside* your body.	1	2	3	4	5

f. Rate how well you were able to see the image from *outside* your body. 1 2 3 4 5

g. Rate how well you *controlled* the image. 1 2 3 4 5

Playing in a Contest

Imagine yourself performing the same or similar activity in competition, but imagine yourself doing the activity very skillfully and the spectators and teammates showing their appreciation. As you imagine the situation, try to see the crowd and hear the noise they are making. Imagine yourself feeling confident in your ability to perform, as well as your ability to handle the pressure. Now close your eyes for about one minute and imagine this situation as vividly as possible. Try to image yourself performing from inside your body, as if you were actually performing, as well as from outside your body, as if you were a spectator.

a. Rate how well you *saw* yourself in this situation. 1 2 3 4 5

b. Rate how well you *heard* the sounds in this situation. 1 2 3 4 5

c. Rate how well you *felt yourself* making the movements. 1 2 3 4 5

d. Rate how well you *felt the emotions* of the situation. 1 2 3 4 5

e. Rate how well you were able to see the image from *inside* your body. 1 2 3 4 5

f. Rate how well you were able to see the image from *outside* your body. 1 2 3 4 5

g. Rate how well you *controlled* the image. 1 2 3 4 5

Recalling a Peak Performance

Recall one of your all-time best performances—a performance in which you felt confident, in control, in the zone. Close your eyes for about one minute and try to see yourself in that situation, feel your emotions, and re-create the experience. Imagine your performance and re-create the feelings you experienced, both mentally and physically, during that performance. Try to see the image from within yourself, and then try to imagine the situation from outside yourself.

a. Rate how well you *saw* yourself in this situation. 1 2 3 4 5

b. Rate how well you *heard* the sounds in this situation. 1 2 3 4 5

c.	Rate how well you *felt yourself* making the movements.	1	2	3	4	5
d.	Rate how well you *felt the emotions* of the situation.	1	2	3	4	5
e.	Rate how well you were able to see the image from *inside* your body.	1	2	3	4	5
f.	Rate how well you were able to see the image from *outside* your body.	1	2	3	4	5
g.	Rate how well you *controlled* the image.	1	2	3	4	5

Scoring

Now let's determine your imagery scores and see what they mean. Sum the ratings for each category and record them below.

Directions	Dimension	Score
Sum all *a* items	Visual	——
Sum all *b* items	Auditory	——
Sum all *c* items	Kinesthetic	——
Sum all *d* items	Emotion	——
Sum all *e* items	Internal perspective	——
Sum all *f* items	External perspective	——
Sum all *g* items	Controllability	——

Interpret your scores in the visual, auditory, kinesthetic, emotion, and controllability categories based on the following scale: excellent (20–18), good (17–15), average (14–12), fair (11–8), and poor (7–4). Notice the categories in which your scores were low and refer to exercises in the chapter to increase your imagery ability in those areas. All of these categories are important for imagery training, so don't just rely on your visual sense. Work to improve the others! Remember, it takes practice but you *can* increase your imagery ability. Good luck!

17

Cognitive Techniques for Building Confidence and Enhancing Performance

Nate Zinsser, *United States Military Academy*
Linda Bunker, *University of Virginia*
Jean M. Williams, *University of Arizona*

Whether you believe you can do something or believe you can't, you're probably right.

—unknown source

The most consistent finding in peak performance literature is the direct correlation between self-confidence and success (see Chapter 11). Athletes who are truly outstanding are self-confident. Their confidence has been developed over many years and is the direct result of effective thinking and frequent experiences in which they have been successful. Because developing confidence is such a high priority for athletes and coaches who wish to become successful, understanding confidence and how to enhance it is an equally high priority for sport psychologists working in applied settings. This chapter is devoted to that understanding.

Confident athletes think about themselves and the action at hand in a different way than those who lack confidence. They have discovered that what they think and say to themselves in practice and competition is critical to perfor-

mance. They have learned that the conscious mind is not always an ally, that it must be disciplined, just as their bodies have been disciplined, to respond effectively in the heat of competition. We all spend vast amounts of time talking to ourselves. Much of the time we are not even aware of this internal dialogue, much less its content. Nevertheless, thoughts directly affect feelings and ultimately actions:

THOUGHTS ➔ FEELINGS ➔ BEHAVIOR

Inappropriate or misguided thinking usually leads to negative feelings and poor performance, just as appropriate or positive thinking leads to enabling feelings and good performance (Kendall, Hrycaiko, Martin, & Kendall, 1990; McPherson, 2000; Van Raalte et al., 1995). The conscious mind—that remarkable, uniquely human instrument—is not automatically one's ally. It must first be trained to think effectively.

Athletes who are truly outstanding are self-confident, and this confidence is not an accident. This chapter's central thesis is that confidence in competitive sport is the result of particular thinking habits more so than physical talent, opportunity, or previous success. These thinking habits, when consistently practiced until they have become automatic and natural, enable athletes to both retain and benefit from the experiences in which they have been successful, and release or restructure the memories and feelings from the less successful experiences. The result of this selective perception is the priceless trait called confidence.

Confident athletes think they can, and *they do.* They never give up. They typically are characterized by positive self-talk, images, and dreams. They imagine themselves winning and being successful. They say positive things to themselves and hence never doubt their abilities. They focus on successfully mastering a task rather than worrying about performing poorly or the negative consequences of failure. This predisposition to keep one's mind on the positive aspects of one's life and sport performance, even in the face of setbacks and disappointments, is a hallmark of the successful athlete, a trait Seligman (1991) refers to as "learned optimism." Having learned to be optimistic, these confident athletes get the most from their abilities. Their confidence programs them for successful performance.

If confidence is so critical to successful performance and personal growth, what can coaches and sport psychologists do to help promote self-confidence within their athletes? Many of the earlier chapters in this book have provided, either directly or indirectly, some answers to this question. For example, seeing improvement in physical skill is an obvious way to build confidence. Providing for a history of successful experiences builds both confidence and the expectation of future success. Coaches who observe the learning and performance guidelines outlined in Chapters 2 and 3 will be more likely to maximize successful skill development in their athletes. Effective coach–athlete interactions, as illustrated in Chapters 6, 7, and 8, are likely to enhance each athlete's sense of self-worth and self-esteem. Practices that maximize such growth in athletes, whether the growth be in physical skills or personal development, lead to a more positive self-concept and increased self-confidence.

In this chapter we discuss techniques for improving confidence and performance by learning to use and control thoughts or cognitions appropriately. Developing and maintaining confidence for high-level competition requires that athletes recognize and then deliberately step away from many of the thinking habits that are often part of the socialization process. It is important that athletes understand how the mind works, how it affects their feelings and actions, and ultimately how it can be disciplined. Initially thoughts may appear to occur spontaneously and involuntarily—thus, beyond control. With the skills of intentional thinking, athletes can control their thoughts. They can learn to use self-talk to facilitate learning and performance. They can also learn to replace self-defeating thoughts with positive ones—thoughts that build confidence and the expectation of success. Such positive thought processes can become self-fulfilling prophecies.

Key Definitions: Confidence, Mental Toughness, Optimism, Self-Efficacy

Most dictionary definitions of confidence will include phrases such as "a state of assurance" and "a belief in one's powers." The image of any great athlete (e.g., Tiger Woods, Serena Williams, Tim Duncan) usually includes this assurance. Joe Morgan, the former major league baseball all-star, expressed this thought when he said, "To be a star and stay a star, I think you've got to have a *certain air of arrogance about you, a cockiness, a swagger on the field* [italics added] that says, 'I can do this and you can't stop me.' I know that I play with this air of arrogance, but I think it's lacking in a lot of guys who have the talent to be stars" (Ferguson, 1991, p. 425). For many, confidence can be thought of as a certain level of healthy arrogance.

The term "mental toughness" is certainly related to the concept of confidence. Through a series of interviews with international caliber athletes, Jones, Hanton, and Connaugton (2002) arrived at a definition of mental toughness as "the natural or developed psychological edge . . . that enables you to cope better than your competitors with the demands of performance . . . and to remain more determined, focused, confident, and in control." Furthermore they identified the most important attribute of mental toughness as "an unshakable belief in your ability to achieve your competitive goals." This study reinforces the importance of belief in oneself to the concept of confidence and also emphasizes that it can be developed through time and training.

A related concept important to the understanding of confidence is optimism, defined as "a tendency to expect the best possible outcome or dwell on the most hopeful aspects of a situation." In the world of sport and competitive performance, the propensity to look for opportunities to score, to win, to excel, regardless of the circumstances, is indispensable for success. Most important, any athlete or performer can systematically cultivate and develop this optimistic tendency, as the following pages will describe.

A fourth related concept is self-efficacy (Bandura, 1977), which refers to the conviction that one can successfully execute the specific behavior required to produce the desired outcome. It is useful to think of sport confidence as a relatively global concept, referring to one's overall attitude toward one's sport. Think of self-efficacy as more specific, referring to particular skills, techniques, and situations. Taken together, the concepts of confidence, mental toughness, optimism, and self-efficacy make up both a global and specific "I can do it" belief, which is essential for success, especially for athletic success. Without this belief, one automatically concedes an advantage to the opponent.

Perhaps the best example of the powerful impact of beliefs on performance occurred over a half century ago when Roger Bannister, a young English medical student, made history by breaking one of sport's most fabled physical and psychological barriers—running a mile in less than 4 minutes. Many today consider his run in Oxford, England, one of the defining athletic achievements of the 20th century. Until his 1954 race, it was considered physically and mentally impossible for the body to endure the punishment of such a feat. Individuals had even written treatises on why the body was physiologically incapable of running the mile in under 4 minutes. Bannister, however, believed that the mile could be run in under 4 minutes and, equally important, he was the person who would do it. He achieved the impossible not merely by physical practice but also by constantly rehearsing the event in his head, breaking through the 4-minute barrier so often and with so much emotional intensity that he programmed his mind and body to believe and do the impossible. What people do not realize, though, is that the greatest impact of his feat was on others. Within the next year, 37 runners broke the 4-minute barrier. The only thing that had changed was their belief system!

Common Misconceptions About Confidence

Misconception 1: Either You Have It or You Don't

Some people believe that confidence is an inherited disposition or trait that cannot be changed by training, practice, or experience. This belief implies that nothing can be done to enhance confidence, so why bother trying? It also takes well-deserved credit away from the athletes who have worked hard, often for years, to develop their confidence. The truth is that the high self-confidence seen in outstanding athletes is not an accident or a random occurrence over which athletes have no control. Instead, confidence is the result of a consistently constructive thinking process that allows athletes to do two things: (1) hang on to and thus benefit from their successful experiences, and (2) let go of or deemphasize their less successful experiences. Thus athletes gain confidence in the same way that they gain other skills or attributes—through practice and repetition of the proper habits. Making the commitment to systematically gain confidence must become one of an athlete's top priorities.

Misconception 2: Only Positive Feedback Can Build Confidence

Although positive feedback from teammates, parents, and coaches certainly helps to build confidence, it is possible to selectively perceive and reinterpret criticism, sarcasm, and negative comments as stimulating challenges and use them to build confidence. Instead of being mentally destroyed by what appears to be negative feedback, athletes who choose to respond by reinterpreting the comments or using active strategies to combat them may actually *gain* confidence. Thus, with the right attitude and thinking skills, athletes can gain confidence even when they are overlooked, underestimated, and disrespected, provided they selectively screen and reinterpret these experiences.

Misconception 3: Success Always Builds Confidence

It is generally true that "nothing succeeds like success," but this is not the whole story. Successful high school athletes do not always make an easy transition to college competition, despite their years of previous success. Other successful athletes may lose their confidence because their past success becomes a form of pressure from which they cannot escape. Still other athletes who experience great success use their perceptual abilities to focus only on their weaknesses and to remember only their failures. Thus, successful athletes may limit their future success because they do not have the level of confidence that their accomplishments would suggest.

Logic would assert that confidence follows competence, that after having performed and accomplished at a certain level, confidence inevitably follows. Although seemingly obvious, the "facts" do not support logic in this case. Success or competence in no way guarantees confidence. Take the example of Michael Strahan, All-Pro defensive end for the New York Giants. Despite making 10 sacks and playing at his all-time best during the 1998 season, Strahan was plagued by self-doubt: "I thought I sucked, and we were losing. It was like I had no hope" (King, 2001). How could a player of such obvious and demonstrated competence be so lacking in confidence? The answer lies in the often illogical and irrational nature of the human mind. Strahan's mind was apparently focused on his mistakes, misses, and losses, rather than on his sacks, tackles, and successes, even though he had ample successes in his immediate past to draw strength and optimism from. Only when he disciplined his thinking with regular mental training sessions that incorporated visualizations of success did Strahan's confidence come back, and with that confidence his Pro Bowl season, and his long-term dominance, were virtually assured.

Misconception 4: Confidence Equals Outspoken Arrogance

Certain confident individuals in the world of sport are outspoken and brash, but there are just as many who carry with them an equally powerful quiet confidence. Names such as Muhammad Ali, Charles Barkley, and Deion Sanders are associated with loud and often abrasive levels of confidence, but other great athletes such as Emmitt Smith, Joe Montana, and Jackie Joyner-Kersee are every bit as confident on the inside while conveying politeness and respect on the outside. For many athletes, difficulty in separating the quiet, internal, private confidence needed for success from the noisy, external, public confidence often portrayed in athletes by the media is a serious impediment. It is crucial for athletes to realize that they can be confident without being considered conceited or arrogant.

Misconception 5: Mistakes Inevitably Destroy Confidence

The greatest difficulty in gaining confidence is the fact that sports are played by imperfect human beings who periodically make mistakes. Too many athletes respond to their mistakes with weakened or diminished confidence. Ironically, these athletes actually *lose* confidence as they gain experiences playing their sport because they selectively attend more to the mistakes and errors that are inevitable in sport. Because of this shortcoming, many athletes become more cautious, more tentative, and more fearful as they advance from the beginning to the end of their years in competitive sport. Other athletes build confidence despite repeated failures because they use their perceptual abilities to selectively attend to whatever small improvements and positive experiences occur. In fact, such positive self-monitoring and focus provide the foundation for intervention programs that have successfully enhanced performance (e.g., Kirschenbaum, Owens, & O'Connor, 1999). Thus athletes can learn to gain confidence even while making mistakes, and this is what the greatest athletes have always done.

Taken collectively, the preceding points all indicate that confidence often has relatively little to do with what happens to an individual. Instead, *confidence is a result of how one thinks, what one focuses on, and how one reacts to the events in one's life.*

Prerequisites for Gaining Confidence

Now that we have dispelled several myths about confidence and shown that it is within anyone's grasp, how does one gain confidence? The following four prerequisites provide a solid foundation for building confidence:

1. Understand the interaction of thought and performance.

2. Cultivate honest self-awareness.

3. Develop an optimistic explanatory style.

4. Embrace a psychology of excellence.

Understand the Interaction of Thought and Performance

The thoughts we have of our ability, of the demands we face, and of the environment we happen to be in determine to a large extent the way we feel inside at any given moment. Think "I have done this many times before," and you feel confident. Think "I am being taken advan-

tage of," and you feel anger. Think "This practice is worthless," and you feel impatient. These immediate feelings, in turn, directly affect performance, because they produce objectively verifiable changes in muscle tension, blood flow, hormone production, and attentional focus. For example, thoughts that anticipate failure lead to feelings of anxiety and, among other things, overall muscle tension. When the wrong muscles are tense, or the right muscles are tense at the wrong times, coordination and timing are disrupted. The confident athlete deliberately directs his or her thoughts onto those aspects of the environment and onto those aspects of self that produce powerful, confident feelings, so as to produce better and better performance.

Cultivate Honest Self-Awareness

Striving for control over one's thoughts and feelings is a process demanding honest self-awareness. One must be willing to honestly pursue the question "Am I really thinking in a way that will give me the best chance of success?" For most people who play sport the real opponent is within themselves in the form of self-criticism, self-doubt, and hesitation, all of which are caused by ineffective cognitive habits. This means athletes with great confidence have simply learned to win the battle with themselves. This is the most difficult battle that anyone will ever try to win, and it is also the challenge that makes sport such a great experience with so much potential for self-development and satisfaction.

Develop an Optimistic Explanatory Style

The term **explanatory style** refers to the way an athlete internally responds to and explains both the good and bad events that occur in his or her life. According to Seligman (1991), explanatory style is the hallmark of whether an individual is an optimist or a pessimist. This habitual style of interpreting events is developed in childhood and adolescence and "stems directly from your view of your place in the world, whether you think you are valuable and deserving, or worthless and hopeless" (Seligman, 1991, p. 98). The concept of explanatory style is especially applicable to the competitive sport environment, in that sport participation inevitably involves setbacks, obstacles, and disappointments to which an athlete must respond optimistically if he or she is to retain confidence and continue investing time and energy. In the often hostile world of sport, explanatory style is a useful tool for helping athletes maintain optimism and confidence.

Explanatory style can be broken down into three dimensions. The first is **permanence**—the degree to which one feels events will repeat themselves and continue to affect one's life either negatively or positively. An athlete with an optimistic explanatory style will usually assume that the same good or positive event will repeat itself time and time again, rather than assume that the success was a fluke. This same athlete will tend to respond to bad events or setbacks with the explanation that they will not continue to occur, that they are isolated and rare. In contrast, the athlete with a negative explanatory style will tend to think that good events will not repeat themselves, but that bad events or misfortune will.

The second dimension is **pervasiveness**—the degree to which one feels that a particular experience will generalize to other contexts. The optimistic athlete will tend to assume that a good event or a success in one aspect of his or her game will positively affect other aspects, but that mistakes and difficulties will remain confined to their original context. A tennis player might assume on the basis of success with the first serve that the net game and ground strokes are also going to be successful. The more pessimistic athlete will tend to assume that a breakdown in one area of the game will spread to other areas and that successes will be limited to their original context.

The third dimension of explanatory style is **personalization**—the degree to which one sees him- or herself as the primary causal agent in events. Optimistic athletes will take personal credit for successes and progress and protect their confidence by explaining misfortune as the result of outside forces beyond their control (field conditions, referee's decisions, or exceptional play by the opponent). More pessimistic athletes will have the opposite tendency, to see successes as functions of luck and circumstance rather than

personal actions, but to see losses and setbacks as due to personal shortcomings.

Explaining events according to these guidelines and deliberately perceiving them selectively does not mean that one ignores mistakes entirely or adopts a totally unrealistic view of one's ability and circumstances. It means that one views mistakes and failures rationally, using them as aids to improvement rather than dwelling on them unproductively. Taking notice of one's errors or shortcomings is a great way to grow, as long as it is done with an eye to the bigger question, "How do I use this to help me improve *right now?*" Watching a game film and noting technical errors is a good idea, as long as the athlete (a) simultaneously makes note of the good points revealed on the film, (b) decides right then and there what to do about those errors, and (c) *while correcting those errors remains focused on his or her good points and bright future.* Athletes with great attitudes *do* criticize themselves occasionally, but this criticism is always kept in its proper perspective. The athlete with an effective explanatory style thinks, "It's just these few mistakes that I'll soon correct, they don't affect the rest of my game, and they are balanced out by all these other things I did well." Compare this with the less effective statement, "I made tons of errors, they spoiled every part of my game, and they're going to keep on happening." To summarize, an optimistic explanatory style is one in which errors are treated as temporary, specific to that one practice or game, and atypical of one's potential, whereas one looks at successes as more permanent, more general, and certainly more indicative of one's true abilities.

An athlete's tendency to interpret events along these dimensions is learned and reinforced through experience. By learning techniques of self-talk and selective perception, and then employing these techniques in practice and competition, athletes can systematically cultivate optimism and gain confidence.

One caveat, however, for excessive optimism comes from a golf study by Kirschenbaum, O'Connor, and Owens (1999). They found that individuals can be overly optimistic, having such *positive illusions* about their skill and control that they make poor decisions. For example, across all skill levels, they found performance suffered on challenging holes because of too aggressive shot selection. An intervention in which golfers were taught more conservative and realistic shot selection led to better performance. A useful guideline here is the phrase "conservative strategy and cocky execution" (Rotella, 1995). This refers to settings realistic, short-term expectations and game plans, and then totally, completely, and utterly committing oneself to following them through.

Embrace a Psychology of Excellence

As has been already mentioned, confidence in competitive performance is the result of a consistently constructive thinking process, a process in which one's thoughts about oneself, one's sport, and one's experiences in that sport are all aligned to produce energy, optimism, and enthusiasm. Here are a few components of this overall psychology of excellence:

1. *Go for your dreams.* Get excited about doing things that few people have ever done. Believe that great things are possible, even if they have never been accomplished before.

2. *Focus on your successes.* Deliberately use your capacity for free will to dwell on and emphasize your day-by-day accomplishments, improvements, and episodes of great effort. After every practice session or competition (not just after the successful ones), file away in a training journal at least one instance of success, one instance of improvement, and one instance of great effort.

3. *Be your own best friend, biggest fan, and greatest coach.* Give yourself the same helpful advice and total support you routinely give to your very best friends. At the end of each day create the image of the most positive and helpful person you have ever known and talk to yourself the way that person would.

4. *Create your own reality.* Interpret the events in your sport in a way that opens you up to greater and greater chances for success.

If your performance early in a contest (first at bat, first serving game, first field goal attempt) does not go well, take it as a signal that you are getting all the kinks out of your motion now and expect to do better as the game goes on. Conversely, if performance in the early rounds is good, take it as a signal that you are in a great groove and expect it all to continue.

Maintaining this confidence-building perspective can be problematic in today's world. Indeed, the socialization process that is part of our cultural fabric often encourages emerging athletes and performers to think in ways that inhibit the development of confidence. For example, the importance given during schooling to developing the ability to be self-critical can encourage students to emotionally hang on to failures and setbacks rather than fully embracing and dwelling on their strengths and successes. A failure focus also occurs when well-meaning teachers, coaches, and parents repeatedly ask questions such as "Why did you do that?" or "What went wrong?" after the athlete makes some mistake or fails to perform up to expectations.

All athletes searching for the "mental edge" that will take their game to the next level must honestly look inside and understand the source of their thinking habits, explanatory style, emotional tendencies, and beliefs about themselves. Are those habits of mind determined by a social perspective that encourages mediocrity, or are those habits of mind based on a personal perspective dedicated to success, achievement, and the realization of potential? This is an ongoing personal mental battle that each athlete must enter and win if the ultimate dream is to be realized. The remainder of this chapter is devoted to learning the skills that will make this possible.

Self-Talk

The key to cognitive control is **self-talk.** The frequency and content of thoughts vary from person to person and situation to situation. You engage in self-talk any time you carry on an internal dialogue with yourself, such as giving yourself instructions and reinforcement, stating your convictions, or interpreting what you are feeling or perceiving (Hackfort & Schwenkmezger, 1993). This dialogue can occur out loud (e.g., mumbling to yourself) or inside your head. Self-talk becomes an asset when it enhances self-worth and performance. Such talk can help the athlete stay appropriately focused in the present, not dwelling on past mistakes or projecting too far into the future. For example, Gould, Eklund, and Jackson's (1992a, 1992b) studies of Olympic wrestlers indicated that self-talk was a technique that the wrestlers used to foster positive expectancies and appropriately focus attention on the task. These wrestlers also reported more positive expectancies and task-specific self-talk prior to their best versus worst performances. In another qualitative study, Gould, Finch, and Jackson (1993) investigated the stress-coping strategies of U.S. national champion figure skaters and found that their two most common coping strategies were (a) rational thinking and self-talk and (b) positive focus and orientation maintenance.

Self-talk becomes a liability when it is negative, distracting to the task at hand, or so frequent that it disrupts the automatic performance of skills. For example, a study of observed self-talk and behavioral assessments with junior tennis players found that negative self-talk was associated with losing, but it failed to show a relationship of positive self-talk to better performance (Van Raalte, Brewer, Rivera, & Petitpas, 1994). The authors concluded that the tennis players may have internalized their positive self-talk and thus the researchers could not observe it as readily as negative self-talk. Other experimental studies found that positive self-talk led to better performance than negative self-talk for individuals completing fairly simple tasks (Dagrou, Gauvin, & Halliwell, 1992; Van Raalte et al., 1995) as well as complex tasks such as bowling and golfing (Johnston-O'Conner & Kirschenbaum, 1986; Kirschenbaum, Ordman, Tomarken, & Holtzbauer, 1982).

Negative self-talk becomes especially destructive when an athlete evaluates his or her performance and then engages in derogatory self-labeling or self-rating, by using labels such as

loser, choke artist, and the like. When athletes hold these negative perceptions of themselves, they will often behave in ways that will confirm these perceptions and thus prove to themselves that they are "right."

According to Albert Ellis and his colleagues (Ellis, 1988; Ellis & Dryden, 1987; Grieger & Boyd, 1980), evaluating and labeling oneself this way is both destructive to one's mental health and completely irrational. Although it is possible and often desirable to rate one's *behavior* (such as test performance or execution of a sport skill), there is no logical or rational reason to label *oneself,* because what we call our "self" is a very abstract, theoretical concept and impossible to confirm with any certainty. Furthermore, even if one's self could be empirically proven, it would include so many different traits, characteristics, and performances and would be so ever changing that rating and labeling it would be impossible. Athletes would be better off, Ellis argues, if they would eliminate self-rating and labeling altogether. This point will be further developed later in the discussion of irrational and distorted thinking.

The use of negative self-talk by athletes affects not only their immediate performance but also their overall self-esteem and, in extreme cases, can lead to acute depression. Seligman (1991) has described **depression** as nothing more than a disorder of conscious thought, and not a matter of brain chemistry or anger turned inward, as other theories maintain. Depressed people simply think awful things about themselves and their future; their symptom, negative self-talk, *is* their disease. Because depression results from consistently using negative thought, changing this habit will help cure the disease. The fastest way out of depression, and the fastest way to build one's self-esteem, is through consistently positive self-talk, in which the athlete continuously reminds him- or herself of past great performances, of skills and techniques that are performed well, and of a bright future ahead.

Raising self-esteem through effective self-talk, however, takes time and patience. A conscientious effort to screen out negative memories and statements, to ignore so-called experts when they set limits on how good teams and players can expect to be, and to focus the mind on present strengths and desired outcomes is required. Self-esteem, and confidence, begins and ends in the mind of the individual, with self-talk playing the primary and most powerful role in feeding the mind. Cognitive-behavioral techniques can be effectively used for enhancing and maintaining self-esteem (Branden, 1994; McKay & Fanning, 1994). By fostering healthy self-esteem, sport psychologists can enhance the personal growth and development of athletes as well as their performance.

Before we address the matter of how specific types of self-talk can be used in different situations to help achieve excellence in learning and performance and to promote confidence and self-esteem, we want to remind you that the interview research reported in Chapter 11 found many athletes stating that their best sport performances occurred when they had no thoughts at all. The athletes were so immersed in the action that it just seemed to happen without conscious thought. Tim Gallwey, author of *The Inner Game of Tennis* (1974), Bob Rotella, author of *Golf Is a Game of Confidence* (1996), and others have stressed that peak performance does not occur when athletes are thinking about it. They emphasize learning to turn performance over to unconscious or automatic functions—functions that are free from the interference of thought. This concept is supported by a rich literature from Eastern philosophical and martial arts traditions (Deshimaru, 1982; Leonard, 1992).

It may be desirable to strive for such thought-free performance, but athletes usually *do* think when performing. In fact, they engage in sport related self-talk outside of practice as well as before, during, and after both practice and competition (Hardy, Gammage, & Hall, 2001). There is even evidence that more self-talk occurs in competition settings than in practice settings and that the greatest use occurs *during* competition compared to before or after performance (Hardy, Hall, & Hardy, 2004a). In addition, individual sport and skilled athletes use self-talk more frequently than team sport and less skilled athletes (Hardy, Hall & Hardy, 2004b). Athletes' self-talk affects their self-concept, self-confidence, and

behavior. Therefore, it is important that coaches and sport psychologists teach athletes to recognize and control their thoughts. Once athletes have developed their abilities to recognize and control their thoughts, they are far more likely to experience those desirable episodes of unconscious immersion. If used properly, thinking can be a great aid to performance and personal growth. The question should not be whether to think but what, when, and how to think. The rest will take care of itself.

The uses for self-talk are almost as varied as are the different types of sports. The effective coach and sport psychologist can use self-talk to aid athletes in learning skills, correcting bad habits, preparing for performance, focusing attention, creating the best mood for performance, and building confidence and competence.

Self-Talk for Skill Acquisition and Performance

Researchers have found that planned self-talk can enhance skill acquisition (e.g., Perkos, Theodorakis, & Chroni, 2002; Siri & Martin, 1996). The nature of thoughts and self-talk should change as performers become more proficient. During early learning, skill acquisition is usually aided when self-instructional talk is used to remind the performer of certain key aspects of the movement. For example, cue words might be used to describe a particular movement phase or to help in learning the appropriate sequencing of actions. Simple cues such as "step, swing" in tennis, "step, drop, step, kick" for a soccer punt, and "arms straight, elbows in" for the golf address are designed to foster cognitive associations that will aid the athlete in learning proper physical execution. Even on the beginning level, self-talk should be kept as brief and minimal as possible. Oververbalization by the coach or athlete can cause paralysis by analysis.

As skills are mastered, self-talk becomes shorter, less frequent, and shifts from a focus on the mechanics of technique to a focus on strategies and optimal feelings. With learning, the goal is to reduce conscious control and promote the automatic execution of the skill. For most athletes this means less self-talk concerning the specific mechanics to be performed and more self-talk focusing on the desired feeling. Examples might be a distance runner using a phrase such as "smooth and fluid" to maintain a pace or a soccer player using the phrase "constant, accurate, and intense" to help her focus on the flow of play. Simple verbal cues like these may be used to trigger a desired, automatic action.

The effectiveness and content of self-talk while the athlete is learning skills also depend on the nature of the task. Skills that are self-paced—that is, initiated by the performer when he or she is ready—are positively influenced by thoughts just prior to performance. Examples include skills such as pitching, riflery, bowling, archery, golf, free throw shooting, and any kind of serve. Successful execution can be programmed by positive thoughts and images just prior to physical execution. If the skills are well learned, the nature of the self-talk should focus on what the performer is trying to achieve rather than the physical mechanics of the act. For example, in the book *The Courtside Coach,* Bunker and Young (1995) suggest that a server in tennis should think or see "deep outside corner" to specify the landing area of the serve. Similarly, a pitcher might think "high and inside," or a free throw shooter might simply say, "arch and swish."

Typically there is less time for this type of direct verbal-mental programming in reactive, externally paced skills such as spiking in volleyball, fast breaking in basketball, or volleying in tennis. With externally paced skills the performer needs to rely more on being able to automatically respond correctly, because there is not enough time to separately preprogram each movement. This being the case, athletes in these sports must learn to use the naturally occurring pauses in the game (changing sides of the court, time-outs, out-of-bounds) as opportunities to control their self-talk and set themselves up for success by focusing on what they want to achieve when the action begins again.

One study, however, did find that skilled tennis players improved their volleying performance after they were taught a two-word (split, turn) self-talk sequence in which they separately said the words and timed each to specific reactions and movement on the court (Landin & Hebert, 1999). The players attributed the success of the self-talk to its directing their attentional focus. They also reported increased confidence. Other studies found improved competitive performance in ice hockey goaltenders who participated in a mental skills program consisting of a centering and self-talk intervention (Rogerson & Hrycaiko, 2002) and improved soccer shooting performance for elite under-14 female soccer players who received a self-talk intervention (Johnson, Hrycaiko, Johnson, & Halas, 2004). These findings suggest that self-talk can enhance performance on externally paced skills as well as on self-paced skills.

Self-Talk for Changing Bad Habits

Experienced athletes may wish to use self-talk when they want to change a well-learned skill or habit. In such cases the athlete must unlearn an automatic response that is no longer effective and replace it with a new one. To change a bad habit, it is usually necessary to intentionally force conscious control over the previously automatic execution. Self-talk can be an effective way to deautomatize the old skill and make way for a new response.

The more drastic the change, the more detailed the demands of self-talk in the relearning phase. For example, if a tennis player is attempting to change from a two-hand to a one-hand backhand, considerable *self-instruction* may be required. In this case the athlete must verbally redirect the entire swing motion. However, if the change is merely to get behind the ball and hit it a little bit earlier with more weight on the front foot, then a simple cue may be all that is necessary.

When an athlete uses self-talk to redirect technique or strategy, it is essential that the content of the statements focus on the desired outcome rather than on what the athlete is trying *not* to do. If a coach or athlete fails to focus on the desired goal and instead talks about avoiding the undesirable, the head is merely filled with the negative image, making the appropriate actions even more difficult to execute. Upon reading the phrase "don't think of a blue elephant," nearly every reader will form the mental picture of a blue elephant, because it is virtually impossible to process the thought without performing the action. Sport skills operate in the same action-follows-thought sequence. For example, saying, "Don't stay on your back foot" when hitting a backhand gives no direction to the swing pattern and only emphasizes the negative. Effective self-talk would be using a cue such as "step-hit." The importance of keeping the content of one's self-talk focused on a desired outcome or a desired process is dramatized by research investigating the ironic effects of thought suppression in sport (Dugdale and Ecklund, 2002; Wenzlaff & Wegner, 2000; Janelle, 1999). These studies all demonstrate the difficulty of trying to suppress an unwanted thought (e.g., "Don't think about the umpire"). The problems that occur when trying to stop unwanted thoughts are discussed in more detail later in this chapter. In short, athletes should be trained to focus on what they want to happen not on what they want to avoid. An additional bonus with this type of short but "desired action" oriented self-talk is that it reinforces the habit of making thoughts positive. Remember, "Winners say what they want to happen, losers say what they fear might happen."

Self-Talk for Attention Control

Self-talk can also help athletes control their attention (e.g., Gould et al., 1992a, 1992b; Hardy et al., 2001; Landin & Hebert, 1999). It is often easy to be distracted during competition and practice. By using a specific set of verbal cues, athletes can keep their minds appropriately focused. Attention control is particularly important in helping athletes stay in the present. As Hay (1984) puts it, "The point of power is always the present moment." The future cannot be controlled and the past cannot be erased or replaced, so it is essential that athletes learn to remain in the present. If athletes allow themselves to wander into the past (e.g., "If I had only made that last putt") or focus on the future (e.g., "If I birdie the next hole, I'll be leading the field"), they will have difficulty executing the

present shot. Once again, focusing the mind on what is desired *right now* ("head down, smooth") gives the athlete the best chance of making the correct shot. Several books, including *Golf Is a Game of Confidence* (Rotella, 1996), have emphasized the importance of remaining in the present tense. (For further elaboration and specific examples, see Chapter 19.)

Self-Talk for Creating Affect or Mood

Researchers have found that affective cues can produce significant changes in performance. For example, runners who say "fast" or "quick" have been found to increase their speed (Meichenbaum, 1975). Golfers who use swing thoughts such as "smooth" or "oily" produce swings that appear smoother and more controlled (Owens & Bunker, 1989). Power words such as "blast," "hit," and "go" are important aids in explosive movements, helping to create the desired mood state (Owens & Bunker, 1989). As an example, a sprinter in the starting blocks will get a faster start by saying "go" or "explode" than by thinking about hearing the gun, because the appropriate self-talk will directly trigger the desired movement when the gun sounds (Silva, 1982). Otherwise, the athlete must process the fact that the gun went off and then start. For a long-distance run, an athlete may wish to shift word cues throughout the race. During the initial portion, words that encourage consistent pace and energy conservation may be most appropriate. During the middle portion of the run, words that encourage persistence and tuning in to the body are important, whereas the final portion requires speed and power. Corresponding cues might be "easy," "responding," and "sprint." Each word has an emotional quality that is linked to the movement quality or content (Meichenbaum, 1975). Use of the right affective cues can ultimately help lead to the best potential for peak performance.

Self-Talk for Changing Affect or Mood

In a similar manner, the use of appropriate self-talk can help an athlete change his or her mood to achieve a desired emotional state. For example, self-talk can help angry or overaroused athletes refocus their energy so that it can be used constructively, and it can help bored or fatigued athletes mobilize the energy necessary for intense play. Golf legend Sam Snead learned in high school that simply recalling the phrase "coolmad" helped him control his temper so that it worked for him rather than against him (Rotella, 1984). Hanton and Jones (1999a) demonstrated that competitive swimmers who perceived their precompetitive anxiety symptoms as debilitative could be taught to use self-talk interventions to reinterpret them as facilitative and thereby enhance their performance. Finn (1985) advises underaroused athletes to use a combination of self-talk and rapid breathing to reach a desired emotional state. Statements like "Come on, rev up, it's time to go all out!" alternated with rapid breathing or high-intensity running will increase the athlete's heart rate and produce a new mood state more favorable for peak performance. Use of the right affective cues can ultimately help lead to the best potential for peak performance.

Self-Talk for Controlling Effort

Self-talk can be an effective technique to help maintain energy and persistence. It may be difficult for some athletes to get started in the morning, at practice, or in the first few moments of a contest. Others may have difficulty changing tempo or maintaining effort. Phrases such as "go for it," "easy," "pace," "pick it up," "cool it," "hold onto it," "push," "stay," and so forth can be very effective in controlling effort (Harris & Harris, 1984).

Sustaining effort over a long training period is a typical problem for athletes. If practices become boring or fatigue sets in, athletes may begin to question their commitment or the value of that commitment. Athletes can use self-talk not only to direct action but also to sustain it (Tod, Iredale, & Gill, 2003; Thellwell & Greenlee, 2003). Such emphasis on effort control is essential because it helps athletes recognize the importance of hard work in achieving success. And if by chance the athletes do not succeed, they are more likely to attribute failure to insufficient effort and therefore want to work harder in the

future. Coaches should note that this is a much more productive attribution strategy than blaming lack of success on factors such as luck, poor officiating, or the weather.

Self-Talk for Building Self-Efficacy

As mentioned previously, the term *self-efficacy* refers to one's expectation of succeeding at a specific task or meeting a particular challenge (Schunk, 1995). Self-efficacy can be considered a very specific form of self-confidence, the confidence to win a specific race, to make a particular shot, or to defeat a certain opponent. Efficacy expectations affect performance because they determine how much effort athletes will expend on a task and how long they will maintain effort when confronted with setbacks and obstacles. Many studies have shown that athletes with high self-efficacy outperform those with lower self-efficacy on strength, endurance, and skill tasks (Kitsantas & Zimmerman, 2002; Mahoney, Gabriel, & Perkins, 1987; Weinberg, Gould, & Jackson, 1979; Weinberg, Gould, Yukelson, & Jackson, 1981). These studies illustrate how powerful efficacy expectations are and, just as important, demonstrate that an individual's preexisting expectations of efficacy can be enhanced to improve performance.

According to Bandura (1977), self-efficacy is influenced by verbal persuasion, both from others and from self in the form of self-talk. Mahoney (1979) also states that self-talk is a useful method for building the self-efficacy expectations of athletes, and Hanton and Jones (1999b) found that an intervention that included cognitive restructuring strategies led to increases in confidence levels just prior to competition. Gould and colleagues found that junior tennis coaches (Gould, Medberry, Damarjian, & Lauer, 1999) and elite college and national team coaches systematically encourage their athletes to develop positive self-talk (Gould, Hodge, Peterson, & Gianni, 1989). The coaches in the 1989 study also rated the encouragement of positive self-talk as the third most effective strategy for developing self-efficacy, ranking physical practice first and modeling confidence by the coach second. These sources of self-efficacy can be utilized by coaches in two important ways. First, coaches can provide feedback to athletes on their success through highlight videotapes (actual performance). Second, coaches can actively express (model) confidence in an athlete's ability to perform well before the entire team by referring to his or her previous successes and bright future. These studies indicate how effective positive self-talk is for enhancing self-efficacy.

A further area in which self-talk plays a crucial role in self-efficacy is rehabilitation from injury. Ieleva and Orlick (1991) found that athletes who recovered exceptionally fast from ankle and knee injuries had a significantly higher frequency of positive self-talk concerning the process of their recovery than did athletes who healed more slowly. Positive self-talk directly influences one's belief in the body's healing power and thus in the actual healing process itself.

Self-Talk for Increasing Adoption and Maintenance of Exercise Behavior

Many studies in the area of exercise behavior have implicated self-efficacy cognitions as a significant factor in predicting adoption and adherence to an exercise program (see McAuley and Blissmer, 2000, for a review). Self-efficacy cognitions may also serve as potential mediators in the relationship of social support to exercise adherence (Duncan & McAuley, 1993). These preliminary findings suggest that modifying self-efficacy cognitions toward exercise contribute to exercise adoption or adherence.

Although cognitive interventions hold promise for fostering exercise behaviors, these interventions have received little attention or research support. For example, Buffone, Sachs, and Dowd (1984) recommended modifying self-talk as a potential cognitive strategy for maintaining exercise behavior but did not provide any research support for its use. Gauvin (1990) hypothesized that persistent exercisers use positive and motivational self-talk whereas dropouts and sedentaries use self-defeating negative self-talk. Based on these recommendations and the preliminary research findings, a need exists for

more thorough study of the role of self-talk and the effectiveness of different cognitive intervention strategies for fostering exercise adoption and adherence.

Identifying Self-Talk

Appropriate use of the preceding kinds of self-talk will enhance self-worth and performance. The first step in gaining control of self-talk is to become aware of what you say to yourself. Surprisingly enough, most people are not aware of their thoughts, much less the powerful impact they have on their feelings and behavior. By getting athletes to review carefully the way in which they talk to themselves in different types of situations, the coach or sport psychologist will identify what kind of thinking helps, what thoughts appear to be harmful, and what situations or events are associated with this talk. Once athletes develop this awareness, they usually discover that their self-talk varies from short cue words and phrases to extremely complex monologues, with the overall content ranging from self-enhancing to self-defeating. The key is to know both when and how to talk to yourself.

Successful athletes have learned to identify the type and content of thought associated with particularly good and particularly bad performances. For example, are there any usual thought patterns or common themes during different situations? Most athletes find different thinking during successful and unsuccessful performances. Identifying the thoughts that typically prepare an athlete to perform well and to cope successfully with problems during performance can provide a repertoire of cognitive tools for the enhancement of performance. The use of these same thoughts in future performance environments should create similar feelings of confidence and direct performance in much the same way. When an athlete can re-create these positive thoughts and bring them to the new environment, the athlete can be said to be *taking control* of his or her mind.

Most athletes discover that during an unsuccessful performance their mind actually programmed failure through self-doubt and negative statements. The body merely performed what the mind was thinking. Examples include an athlete's thinking before a competition, "I never swim well in this pool" or "I always play poorly against this opponent" and then going on to swim or compete exactly as prophesied. Obviously, future performance would be enhanced if athletes could eliminate dysfunctional and self-defeating thoughts that lead to worry and poor performance. Before such thoughts can be eliminated, they need to be identified. Three of the most effective tools for identifying self-talk are retrospection, imagery, and keeping a self-talk log.

Retrospection

By reflecting on situations in which they performed particularly well or particularly poorly and trying to re-create the thoughts and feelings that occurred prior to and during these performances, many athletes are able to identify typical thoughts and thought patterns associated with both good and bad performance. It is also beneficial to recall the specific situation, or circumstances, that led to the thoughts and resulting performance. Viewing videotapes of actual past performances helps the athlete recount the action by heightening the memory of the event. If this technique is used, not only should the actual performance be taped but, ideally, the time before the contest begins, the time-outs or breaks during the contest, and even the time right after the contest ends. Thoughts during all of these times play a major role in determining the quality of one's present performance, one's expectations regarding future performance, and even one's feelings of self-esteem.

Imagery

Another technique is to have athletes relax as deeply as possible and then try reliving a past performance through visualization and remembering other sensory experiences, such as how a moment felt or sounded. This technique is much more effective if athletes have been previously trained in imagery (see Chapter 16 for suggestions). Athletes who are effective at imagery can usually describe exactly what happened during the competition and what thoughts and feelings preceded, accompanied, and followed the performance. After athletes have relived past performances through imagery, it may be helpful to have them write down the recalled thoughts, situations, and outcomes. If it is not disruptive, the athletes may even want to talk into a tape recorder as they are imaging.

Self-Talk Log

Not all athletes can use retrospection and imagery to remember accurately how they thought and felt or what circumstances triggered their thoughts and feelings. Even athletes who are comfortable using these tools run the risk that time and personal impressions may distort the memory of actual thoughts and circumstances. Keeping a daily diary or self-talk log of thoughts and performance situations is an excellent tool for accurately creating awareness of self-talk. Thoughts should be transcribed as soon after they occur as possible. Athletes in sports such as golf, archery, rowing, and running have found it beneficial to have a tape recorder present while they perform so they can directly tape their thoughts and a description of the situation as they occur.

When keeping a log, the athlete should address such questions as, When I talk to myself, what do I say? What thoughts precede and accompany my good performances? Not only what thoughts, but how frequently am I talking to myself? When playing poorly, do I deprecate myself as a person? Do I stay in the present moment, or revert to dwelling on past performance? Do I call myself names and wish I were still sitting on the bench? Does the content of my self-talk center on how I feel about myself, or how others will feel about me, or on letting down my friends and teammates, or on how unlucky I am?

If there is a problem in thinking, the goal is to identify the problem and its boundary points in specific terms. This means that each athlete must be able to answer maladaptive questions such as When do I have negative thoughts? Do I begin doubting myself even before I have a chance to perform? For example, when a whistle blows, do I automatically assume it is directed at me? If I have been fouled, do I start worrying from the moment the whistle blows until after I have shot the free throw, or do I begin worrying only after I walk to the free throw line? Athletes must be able to specify the initial cue that caused them to start worrying or thinking negatively to gain control over their thoughts. Also, when do they stop saying self-defeating things? Such detailed knowledge will help in planning an effective intervention. For instance, if worry begins with the referee's whistle, then this is the cue with which an alternate thought pattern should be linked.

It is as important to monitor self-talk during practice as it is during competition. The thoughts typically occurring prior to, during, and after practice play an important role in developing typical thought and behavior patterns. More specifically, the athlete should identify what is said after making mistakes, after teammates perform poorly, after having difficulty performing a new skill or strategy, when fatigued, and after the coach criticizes performance. Often the pattern of thoughts found during competition is merely a reflection of what occurs during practices. Learning to recognize and control the nature of self-talk during practices becomes the foundation for effective thinking during competition.

Techniques for Controlling Self-Talk

Using the preceding self-monitoring tools is an essential first step in the process necessary for producing performance-enhancing thoughts and eliminating disabling thoughts. However, the mere act of monitoring thoughts is usually not enough. In fact, paying too much attention to negative thoughts or thoughts associated with poor performance can be detrimental if they are not linked to some action or change process. Once awareness of negative talk and feelings is heightened, the coach or sport psychologist should immediately instruct the athlete in how to start dealing with these thoughts. Similarly,

when good performance is analyzed, it should be with the intent of capitalizing on the state of mind that existed during that performance in the hope of being able to purposefully duplicate it in the future. In this section we present techniques for controlling self-talk. The effectiveness of these techniques in enhancing sport performance has been well documented. In fact, a recent meta-analysis by Meyers, Whelan, and Murphy (1996) calculated a greater effect size for cognitive restructuring interventions ($n = 4$, $d = .79$, $SD = .36$) than that found for goal setting ($n = 3$, $d = .54$, $SD = .15$); mental rehearsal ($n = 28$, $d = .57$, $SD = .75$); and relaxation interventions ($n = 25$, $d = .73$, $SD = 1.65$). Techniques for controlling self-talk include:

Thought-stoppage

Changing negative thoughts to positive thoughts

Countering

Reframing

ABC cognitive restructuring

Affirmation statements

Mastery and coping tapes

Video technology

Thought Stoppage

If an athlete's self-talk is constant and thus distracting, or if the talk produces self-doubt, it must be terminated. Getting rid of negative thoughts often makes it possible to break the link that leads to negative feelings and behaviors, just as stopping excessive or task-irrelevant talk facilitates the athlete's regaining a more appropriate attentional focus. The technique of **thought stoppage** provides one very effective method for eliminating negative or counterproductive thoughts (Meyers & Schleser, 1980). The technique begins with awareness of the unwanted thought and uses a trigger to interrupt or stop the undesirable thought. The trigger can be a word such as *stop* or a physical action such as snapping the fingers or clapping one hand against the thigh. Each athlete should choose the most natural trigger and use it consistently. (Most athletes who use a verbal cue prefer the word *stop,* but almost any cue is acceptable if it is used consistently.)

Thought stoppage will not work unless the athlete first recognizes undesirable thoughts and then is motivated to stop them. Developing the commitment necessary to improve the quality of an athlete's self-talk is not as easy for the coach and sport psychologist to accomplish as it sounds. This process requires the athlete to invest some time in monitoring the frequency and content of his or her self-talk and then truly deciding to change this talk for the better. For example, even after using the typical tools for creating awareness of thoughts, one young professional golfer would not admit negative statements were affecting her golf. As a method to convince her of the severity of the problem, she was asked to empty a box of 100 paper clips into her pocket. Each time she had a negative thought, she had to move a clip to her back pocket. At the end of the golf round she had shot an 84 and had 87 paper clips in her back pocket! The process of actually counting paper clips, each of which represented a negative thought, made her dramatically aware of her problem and motivated her to try thought-stoppage (Owens & Bunker, 1989).

Thought-stoppage is a skill, and, as with any other skill, it is best to experiment with it first during practice and become comfortable with it before using it in actual competition. An effective way to practice thought-stoppage is to combine it with imagery. Athletes should be instructed to select a typical negative thought, or thought pattern, they would like to eliminate. Next they should close their eyes and as vividly as possible imagine themselves in the situation in which they usually have that negative thought. Once they have re-created the situation and negative thought, they should practice interrupting the thought with whatever trigger they have selected for thought stoppage. This practice should be repeated until the athletes can effortlessly and automatically eliminate negative talk and accompanying feelings of worry and anxiety. This will require time, patience, and a strong commitment to improving the quality of one's internal dialogue.

It is suggested that during the earlier stages of thought-stoppage practice, athletes should visibly use their trigger. Saying "stop" out loud not only makes athletes more conscious of their wish to stop excessive or negative talk but serves several additional functions. It helps the coach and sport psychologist to monitor whether athletes are doing what they were instructed to do. If an athlete's body language is showing frustration or disgust with play, his or her thoughts probably are, too. The coach and sport psychologist who sees no visible thought-stoppage trigger during these circumstances should directly confront the athlete by asking him or her what thoughts are occurring. This will serve to reinforce awareness and the need to stop negative talk immediately. The other advantage of visibly practicing the technique is that athletes realize they are not alone in their need to deal more effectively with self-talk. The technique is particularly effective when becoming more positive is a team effort and responsibility. Thus, this is a good time to encourage athletes to be supportive of one another rather than critical or sarcastic. When one high school basketball coach instituted such a program halfway through his season, he was so impressed with the outcome that he attributed a losing season's turning into a winning season to the athletes' learning to control negative talk and body language and becoming supportive rather than critical of one another.

Learning to turn off negative or inappropriate thoughts takes time, particularly when negative thought patterns have become the athlete's habitual mode of response to adversity (Cautela & Wisocki, 1977). Frustration over the recurrence of negative thoughts may be lessened if the coach or sport psychologist draws the parallel of trying to eliminate negative thoughts with trying to unlearn some well-established error in physical technique. Old habits change slowly, whether they are physical or cognitive, and they only change with considerable motivation and practice. The more practice an athlete employs, the less likely negative thought patterns are to recur.

Even with practice it may not always be possible to avoid negative thoughts. When such thoughts do occur, good advice would be to manage them or let them pass and concentrate on some positive thought or some specific cue that can serve to trigger what the athlete wants to do next. In fact, a series of studies by Wegner and his colleagues (Wegner & Erber, 1992; Wegner, Schneider, Knutson, & McMahon, 1991; Wenzlaff, Wegner, & Klein, 1991) have demonstrated that individuals deliberately trying to suppress unwanted thoughts often find themselves even more preoccupied by the thoughts they are trying to escape. Wegner, Ansfield, and Pilloff (1998) obtained similar results in an experiment designed to test the effect of trying to suppress action. That is, participants were more likely to overshoot the hole when putting, particularly under the stress of cognitive load, when they received instructions to *avoid* overhitting the ball. The researchers explained these failures (i.e., doing the opposite of what one intends) with the theory of ironic processes of mental control (Wegner, 1994, 1997). For an interesting discussion of the implications this theory has for sport psychology research and interventions, see Janelle (1999), Hall, Hardy, and Gammage (1999), and Taylor (1999).

These findings indicate how important it is for athletes to use negative or self-critical thoughts as the stimulus or trigger to deliberately focus the mind on a desired outcome. This leads to the next technique for controlling thoughts—changing self-defeating thoughts to self-enhancing thoughts.

Changing Negative Thoughts to Positive Thoughts

Although it makes sense to stop negative thoughts altogether, sometimes this cannot be accomplished. An alternative is to learn to couple any negative thought with a positive thought that either provides encouragement and support or appropriately redirects attention. The coach or sport psychologist should instruct athletes to extinguish unwanted thought as soon as it is recognized and then immediately practice switching to a positive or more appropriate thought. If, for example, a gymnast finds himself saying, "This new move is really hard—I'll never get it right!"

he should learn to follow this phrase immediately with "I've learned lots of hard moves before, so I know if I'm patient I can learn this one too."

Another advantage for teaching this technique along with thought stoppage is that it takes some pressure off athletes who initially doubt their ability to control their thoughts. Perhaps these athletes think they cannot control what thoughts enter their head, but they will accept their ability to control the last thoughts they have. For example, for the professional golfer who used the "paper clip" technique to become aware of the many negative thoughts that adversely affected her performance, her goal in working with cognitions was simply to reduce the negative statements that were not followed by self-enhancing statements. Not having to worry about the occurrence of a self-defeating statement took considerable pressure off of her. Each day she was able to reduce the number of paper clips that stood for negative thoughts not followed by positive thoughts, and in time she was able to get rid of the recurring pattern of negative talk.

Changing self-talk from negative to positive works best if coaches and sport psychologists have their athletes individually make a list of typical self-defeating things they say and would like to change. Athletes can often generate this list from the self-talk log discussed earlier. Meichenbaum (1977) has emphasized that it is important for athletes to specify when they make these self-defeating statements and what causes them to make such statements. The goal is to recognize what the situation involved and why the negative thought occurred. Athletes should then design a substitute positive statement. It may be helpful to make a table with the self-defeating thoughts on one side and the preferred self-enhancing statements directly opposite the negative thought (Table 17-1).

Notice that the self-enhancing statements in the table always bring the athlete back to the present time and personal control of the situation. The positive self-talker sees a possibility in every problem, not a problem in every possibility.

The coach or sport psychologist may also want to couple relaxation techniques with changing self-defeating thoughts to self-enhancing ones.

Table 17-1 **Examples of Changing Negative Thoughts to Positive Thoughts**

Self-Defeating Thoughts	Change to Self-Enhancing Thoughts
I can't believe it's raining. I have to play in the rain.	No one likes the rain, but I can play as well in it as anyone else.
You dumb jerk.	Ease off. Everyone makes mistakes. Sluff it off and put your mind on what you want to do.
There's no sense in practicing. I have no natural talent.	I've seen good players who had to work hard to be successful. I can get better if I practice correctly.
This officiating stinks; we'll never win.	There's nothing we can do about the officiating, so let's just concentrate on what we want to do. If we play well, the officiating won't matter.
Why did they foul me in the last minute of play—I'm so nervous, I'll probably choke and miss everything.	My heart is beating fast. That's OK, I've sunk free throws a hundred times. Just breathe and swish.
We'll win the meet only if I get a 9.0 on this routine.	Stop worrying about the score; just concentrate on how you're going to execute the routine.
The coach must think I'm hopeless. He never helps me.	That's not fair. He has a whole team to coach. Tomorrow I'll ask what he thinks I need to work on the most.
I don't want to fail.	Nothing was ever gained by being afraid to take risks. As long as I give my best, I'll never be a failure.
I'll take it easy today and go hard next workout.	The next workout will be easier if I go hard now.
Who cares how well I do anyway?	I care, and I'll be happier if I push myself.
This hurts; I don't know if it's worth it.	Of course it hurts, but the rewards are worth it.

Most negative thoughts occur when an individual is under stress and therefore usually overly aroused physiologically. Instruct athletes to stop their negative thought and then take a deep breath. As they feel relaxation spreading with the long, slow exhalation, they should repeat the substitute self-enhancing thought.

There is nothing unusual about having negative thoughts, and even the greatest athletes have anxious or negative thoughts on occasion. Tennis legend Arthur Ashe once feared "he wouldn't get a single serve in the court" just before his U.S. Open championship. Bobby Jones, the famous golfer, was standing over a 2-foot putt that would allow him to win the 1926 U.S. Open when he had the thought, "What if I stub my putter into the ground and miss the ball entirely and lose the tournament?" These champions, however, did not store their negative thoughts away where they could build themselves into a mental block. Instead, Ashe and Jones stopped those thoughts and replaced them with positive thoughts. The key is not to give in to these negative thoughts and allow them to control and dominate the mind. Make the last thought in any string or sequence of thoughts positive and self-enhancing. This is possible if you become aware of your negative self-talk and use it as a signal to *stop, cope,* and *take control.*

The information presented above is based on research conducted with athletes and nonathletes from individualistic cultures (e.g., the United States, Western Europe). Recent research suggests that the relationship of self-talk to performance is different for individuals from collectivist cultures (e.g., China, Singapore) and, therefore, self-talk interventions such as changing negative thoughts to positive thoughts may not be appropriate for all people. Peters and Williams (2004) found that Asians had significantly more negative self-talk than European Americans during dart-throwing performance and that their negative self-talk related to better performance. Conversely, as previously found, negative self-talk related to poorer performance for European Americans. Additionally, cross-cultural research suggests that a self-critical versus self-enhancing orientation is necessary for self-improvement and a characteristic of collectivist individuals' self-concepts (Kitayama, 2002; Kashiwagi, 1986). Assuming the present findings replicate, sport psychologists and coaches should consider an athlete's culture when designing self-talk interventions.

Countering

Changing negative to positive self-statements probably will not achieve the expected behavioral outcome if the athlete still *believes* in the negative statements. For example, an athlete might change his or her talk from "I will never be able to run this offensive pattern; I'm just not quick enough" to "I can too; I'm as quick as anyone else." The athlete is merely going through the outward motions of being positive if the real belief system is still saying, "No, I can't; I really am too slow." Dysfunctional thought patterns will keep recurring if they have strong underlying bases that are not identified and refuted.

Athletes will rarely be able to accomplish something if they truly believe they cannot.

Furthermore, the motivation even to try will be eroded if there is no belief that one's efforts will ultimately yield success. Bell (1983) proposes that in such instances merely directing one's thoughts toward desired actions may not be enough. Instead, the athlete may have to identify and build a case against the negative self-statements that are interfering with effective performance. Bell suggests using the tool of countering under these circumstances. **Countering** is an internal dialogue that uses facts and reasons to refute the underlying beliefs and assumptions that led to negative thinking. Rather than blindly accepting the negative voice in the back of the head, the athlete argues against it.

When learning to use counters, it is important that the athlete actually describe the evidence necessary to change an attitude or belief. In the preceding example, the coach or sport psychologist might try helping the athlete identify issues such as, What makes me think I am slow? Have I ever in the past played with good speed? Am I as fast as any of the other athletes? If yes, are they successful at running this offense? What might be causing my slowness, and can I do anything to change it? If I am not quite as fast as some of my teammates, do I have any other talents that might compensate for this, such as using my good game sense to read the situation faster so I can react more quickly? What other skills do I have that might help me learn this offensive pattern?

Any or all of the preceding approaches should provide some evidence for refuting either the athlete's slowness or the importance of only speed in being successful at the offensive pattern. The more evidence and logic there is to refute the negative belief structure, the more effective the counters will be in getting the athlete to accept the positive statement; and the more firmly the athlete believes in the counters, the less time it will take to turn the thinking around. Later it may be possible for the athlete to identify the negative or irrational thought and simply dismiss it with phrases such as "No, that's not right," "Who says I can't?" or just plain "Bull."

In his discussion of countering, Bell (1983) makes another excellent point. Sometimes thinking is neither right nor wrong—it cannot be verified. Bell suggests that what is more important is determining whether a given thought *helps* an athlete to reach his or her goals. Encourage athletes to ask themselves, "Is this thinking in my best interest? Does this thinking help me feel the way I want to or does it make me worry and be tense? Does this thinking help me perform better?" When athletes realize that thinking certain thoughts can only be detrimental, it becomes sensible, and thus easier, to use the tools of thought stoppage to change negative self-statements to positive ones. Helping athletes identify for themselves the value of these tools creates powerful motivation to use them.

Reframing

Another effective technique for dealing with negative self-talk is **reframing,** described by Gauron (1984) as the process of creating alternative frames of reference or different ways of looking at the world. Because the world is literally what we make it, reframing allows us to transform what appears at first to be a weakness or difficulty into a strength or possibility, simply by looking at it from a different point of view. Gauron encourages athletes to cultivate the skill of reframing because it helps athletes control their internal dialogue in a positive, self-enhancing manner. Almost any self-defeating statement or negative thought can be reframed, or interpreted from a different perspective, so that it aids rather than hinders the athlete.

An important element of reframing is that it does not deny or downplay what the athlete is experiencing or encourage the athlete to ignore something troublesome. Instead, by reframing, the athlete acknowledges what is happening and decides to use it to his or her best advantage. For example, if an athlete was saying, "I'm feeling tense and anxious about playing today," he can reframe the statement to "I'm feeling excited and ready." Similarly, an athlete dwelling on the *problems* of improving a skill or the *struggle* of a performance slump can turn these situations to his advantage and maintain a positive attitude by focusing on the *possibilities* of achieving a new level of skill and the *opportunity* present in each new performance.

Research support for the positive effects of reframing comes from a study that compared the mental preparation of teams who met or exceeded their goals in the 1996 Atlanta Olympics to teams who failed to meet expectations at the Games (Gould, Guinan, Greenleaf, Medbery, & Pederson, 1999). Gould et al. found that members of the more successful teams reported that they were able to "reframe negative events in a positive light." Additional support comes from research by Hanton and Jones (1999a). They taught nonelite swimmers to reframe their anxiety symptoms as facilitative rather than debilitative to performance. The end result was improved performance.

Identifying Irrational and Distorted Thinking

In addition to dealing with negative self-talk and self-doubt, athletes need to realize that they may also be engaging in cognitive distortions and irrational thinking. According to Ellis (1982), athletes fail to reach their goals and perform below their ability primarily because they accept and endorse self-defeating, irrational beliefs. Ellis identifies four basic irrational beliefs that negatively affect athletes' performance. If athletes accept any of these beliefs (let alone two or three of them), or any of their variations, their progress and satisfaction will be blocked. These four irrational beliefs are (1) I *must* at all times perform outstandingly well, (2) others whom I hold significant to me (e.g., teammates and coaches) *have to* approve and love me, (3) everyone has *got to* treat me kindly and fairly, and (4) the conditions of my life, particularly my life in sports, absolutely *must* be arranged so that I get what I want when I want.

Such thinking is counterproductive because it negatively influences self-concept, self-confidence, and performance. Once identified—a task that may take considerable soul-searching—these self-defeating types of beliefs need to be modified. Here are some irrational thoughts and cognitive distortions that are common among athletes (Gauron, 1984):

- Perfection is essential
- Catastrophizing

- Worth depends on achievement
- Personalization
- Fallacy of fairness
- Blaming
- Polarized thinking/labeling
- One-trial generalizations

Let's take a look at each of these thought patterns along with some suggestions for modifying such irrational and distorted thinking.

Perfection is essential. One of the most debilitating irrational ideas for an athlete is that he or she must be competent and near perfection in everything attempted. No one can consistently achieve perfection. Athletes who believe they should be perfect will blame themselves for every defeat, every setback. Their self-concept will likely suffer and they may start a fear-of-failure syndrome. Furthermore, they will put such pressures on themselves to do well that both their enjoyment and performance will likely suffer. There is always value in *striving* for perfection, but nothing is gained by *demanding* perfection. The same can be said for the thinking of the coach.

Catastrophizing. Catastrophizing often accompanies perfectionistic tendencies, as the athlete believes that any failure will be a humiliating disaster or that pleasing others (especially friends and parents) is the number one priority. Catastrophizers expect the worst possible thing to happen. Unfortunately, expecting disaster often leads to disaster! Individuals become plagued by what-ifs. "What if I lose today?" "What if my parents are embarrassed when I strike out?" "How will I ever be able to compete again?"

Perfectionistic thinking and catastrophizing can be combated by realistic evaluations of the actual situation and by setting appropriate goals. A careful assessment of the actual odds of success or failure as well as the objective nature of the possible outcomes or consequences is essential.

Worth depends on achievement. Another problem for some athletes is the belief that their worth depends on their achievements. Many young athletes believe they are only as good as what they win. Correspondingly, they think they must excel in order to please others. Try asking an athlete or coach to describe who he or she is without mentioning his or her sport or success rate! Athletes must learn to value themselves for more than what they do; worth as a human being is based on factors other than achievement outcome.

Personalization. The assumption that personal worth depends solely on achievement is often linked with the self-defeating tendency to personalize everything. People who do this believe they are the cause and focus of activities and actions around them. For example, when some athletes walk past a crowd that is laughing, they believe the crowd is laughing at them. Other athletes feel personally attacked and threatened when a coach criticizes or corrects their play.

Fallacy of fairness and ideal conditions. Some athletes believe they are entitled to fair treatment and ideal conditions. "Fair" is usually a disguise for just wanting one's personal preferences versus what someone else sees as being in the best interests of all concerned. "Ideal conditions" means that coaches should carve out the easiest possible path for athletes to follow. Athletes need to realize that it is irrational to think that things will come easily or that they will not need to be self-disciplined and to work hard. It is equally irrational to believe that the world of sport should somehow be fair—that each investment of time and energy should deliver an equitable level of success, or that everyone on a team or in a sport program should be treated the same. Holding these expectations will inevitably produce frustration, because in reality coaches do treat players differently; one's efforts, improvements, and achievements are not always noticed; and the breaks of the game often do seem to favor the opposition. Coming to grips with unfairness and learning to stay composed is one of sport's great lessons. Rarely will an athlete realize his or her potential without dealing with unfairness and tolerating sustained effort, pain, and sacrifice.

Blaming. Any feeling of unfair treatment can also produce blaming or external attributions. Nothing is gained by making excuses or assigning fault to others. This type of thinking allows athletes to abdicate all responsibility—an absolutely nonproductive form of cognition. Athletes must learn to replace external attributions with attributions that are within their control: "Success comes from effort and working hard to develop my full potential, whereas failure comes from lack of effort or insufficient practice of key fundamentals." Athletes often learn their attributions from coaches. If coaches usually blame failure on external factors, athletes will, too. This subtly leads athletes to expect failure under similar future circumstances—for example, bad weather or poor officiating. However, if coaches and sport psychologists provide appropriate internal attributions for individual athlete and team successes and failures, they will help athletes eliminate some of their feelings of external control and inappropriate, superstitious thinking. The more athletes realize they are personally responsible for and in control of their performance, the more their confidence will grow after good performance and the more confidence they will have in turning current failures into future successes.

If athletes accept complete responsibility for everything, however, they may be equally nonproductive. For example, some players are prone to taking sole responsibility for the entire team's performance. "We lost because I missed that last free throw." Accepting such irrational blame can lead to many potential problems, including further irrationalizations: "The coach and my teammates must really hate me." The answer to this kind of irrational thinking lies in helping athletes to be realistic and honest in evaluating performance outcome.

In the previous discussion of effective explanatory style, it was stated that optimistic (hence confident) athletes tend to make external attributions for failures and setbacks while making internal attributions for successes and improvements. At first this idea may seem to be at odds with the present point of taking responsibility for oneself and avoiding the tendency to blame outside forces for one's difficulties. A closer look at the issue reveals that a crucial part of taking responsibility for oneself is protecting one's confidence by refusing to deprecate oneself and engage in prolonged self-criticism. It is certainly irrational to consistently blame others for one's difficulties, but it is equally destructive to routinely blame oneself for everything that goes wrong and subsequently lose confidence. The resolution lies in taking responsibility to improve oneself in the face of adversity while simultaneously refusing to question one's potential, appropriateness, or adequacy. This means that the athlete does everything in his or her power to improve and develop, but never takes a loss or a setback as a statement that he or she is unworthy and undeserving of success.

Polarized thinking. The tendency to view things and people in absolute terms is called **polarized thinking.** All-or-nothing thinking can lead an athlete to categorize everything as either successful or unsuccessful, good or bad, rather than learning from each and every experience. Such thinking often leads to judgmental **labeling**—the identification or description of something or someone with a single evaluative word or phrase, such as "choker," "butterfingers," "airbrain," "loser." Athletes and people who work with athletes need to recognize that such negative labeling is very detrimental because these labels are often internalized and become, in a more or less permanent way, a part of self-concept and future expectations. Once established and internalized, these negative labels are difficult to erase—*labeling is disabling.* Coaches and sport psychologists should instead stress the avoidance of any kind of negative evaluative language, judgmentalism, and absolute thinking. The personal behavior of the coach and sport psychologist should set the example for what they expect from their athletes.

One-trial generalizations. Perhaps the cognitive distortion that has the greatest negative impact on performance comes from one-trial generalizations or superstitions. These are also among the easiest to desensitize. **Overgeneralizations** occur when a single incident causes athletes to link the situation with the outcome. Examples include statements such as "I never swim well in a pool without gutters" and "I can't golf well in the rain." If these conclusions are based on only one or two experiences, then some careful analysis can usually lead athletes to negate them. If they are based on many experiences, then they should merely be used to direct practice to overcome the apparent obstacle to performing well. Practicing under perceived negative conditions until success is achieved will often produce effective evidence to repudiate the initial negative generalization.

Modifying Irrational and Distorted Thinking: ABC Cognitive Prestructuring

Irrational beliefs and distorted thinking often underlie much of the stress and resulting negative thoughts and feelings athletes experience during athletic performance and in life in general. Unfortunately, athletes often are unaware that the culprit is maladaptive thinking. Instead they think the circumstance or event caused the deleterious emotional reaction and behavior. For example, a basketball player misses a critical free throw in the final seconds of a game and ends up feeling worthless being put in a similar circumstance in the future. The typical athlete probably thinks his thoughts and anxiety are caused by the missed free throw (see Figure 17-1). In actuality it was the *assumptions* the athlete made about the event. In this case, irrational assumptions such as perfectionism, worth-depends-on-achievement, or personalization may have been the culprit.

The coach or sport psychologist can help athletes reduce their self-caused pressure by getting them to identify and dispute their irrational assumptions. One excellent way to accomplish the preceding is to use Albert Ellis's rational emotive therapy procedure (Ellis & Dryden, 1987), sometimes referred to as ABC cognitive restructuring. The process begins by getting athletes to keep a daily record in which they record not only their upsetting thoughts but also the resulting feelings and behavior and the negative event that triggered them (see Figure 17-1). In column A they briefly describe the activating event in terms of what happened, what they saw and heard. In column B they record the exact content of their dysfunctional self-talk, that is, whatever they think or say out loud that could be interpreted as negative, irrational, or self-destructive. In column C they record the resulting emotional and behavioral consequences. To help determine what should be recorded, have the athletes use Steinmetz, Blankenship, and Brown's (1980) five criteria for deciding whether self-talk and underlying beliefs are rational or irrational, productive or unproductive.

1. Are the beliefs based on objective reality? That is, would a mixed group of people all agree that the event happened the way you perceived it, or do you exaggerate and personalize experiences?

2. Are they helpful to you? Self-destructive thoughts are usually irrational.

3. Are they useful in reducing conflicts with other people, or do you set up a me-versus-them situation?

4. Do they help you reach your short- and long-term goals, or do they get in the way?

5. Do they reduce emotional conflict and help you feel the way you want to feel?

After completing the ABC steps across a designated number of days, the athletes are now ready for the next critical step, which entails trying to rebut or dispute their self-criticism. The first step is to reexamine the self-talk under column B to determine the irrational beliefs or distortions in thinking that might underlie what appeared, on the surface, to be automatic dysfunctional statements. Record the underlying beliefs in column B after the self-talk statement. In many cases, more than one thinking error may have led to the self-talk. For example, see Figure 17-1 for what occurred when the athlete missed the free throw. Identifying the underlying irrational beliefs and thinking distortions helps athletes discover what was erroneous or

ABC Cognitive Restructuring

A. Activating Event	B. Beliefs or Interpretations	C. Consequences	D. Dispute
Briefly describe the actual event that led to the feelings and behavior	Record the actual dysfunctional self-talk and, if appropriate, include mental pictures	Identify feelings, bodily reactions, and behavior	Write rational response(s) to the automatic thoughts
Fouled in final ten seconds with game tied – missed free throw	"I lost the game for the team." (*personalization*) (*blaming*) "I always choke in pressure situations." (*overgeneralizations*) (*catastrophizing*)	Depressed, tensed up, blew defensive assignment after free throw	"Hey, I'm disappointed but that was just one point out of 40 minutes of play." "I missed this shot, but there are other times when I've come through under pressure. I'll put extra time into free throw practice and work on staying loose and positive."

Figure 17-1 **Example of how to use ABC cognitive restructuring to identify and modify irrational and distorted thinking**

illogical in the initial self-talk. Once done, the athletes are ready to substitute more rationale and productive thoughts in column D. If a particular dysfunctional thought often occurs (e.g., saying "I always screw-up" or something equivalent after every disappointment), the person may want to multiple-times daily repeat the substituted rational statement until it is believed. Incorporating one of the quick relaxation techniques discussed in Chapter 15 before saying the statement may increase susceptibility to believing the statement. For example, take a deep, complete breath and with the exhalation say, "Lighten up! It's human to make mistakes. Learn from it and move on." The preceding may be difficult to do, but it gets easier and easier with practice. The ultimate goal is to create such awareness in the athletes that when they have dysfunctional thinking, they immediately recognize and dispute it.

Less enlightened coaches and athletes might fear that modifying irrational beliefs such as perfectionistic demands and taking excessive responsibility for performance outcome may take the edge off an athlete's competitiveness. This fear is unfounded. Reflection back to an athlete's best moments in competition almost always reveals that he or she was experiencing a sense of unhurried, joyful abandon—the opposite of any perfectionistic demand or irrational thought.

Helping athletes eliminate irrational thinking and develop more adaptive thoughts will go a long way toward improving performance and, perhaps more important, personal growth.

Constructing Affirmation Statements

Feelings of confidence, efficacy, and personal control will be enhanced if coaches and sport psychologists assist athletes in constructing personal affirmation statements. **Affirmations** are statements that reflect positive attitudes or thoughts about oneself, or, stated differently, affirmations are statements about what you want, *phrased as if you already had it*. For example, in 1985 Ivan Lendl had a record of 9 wins and 12 losses against John McEnroe. Lendl then started writing each day in a notebook, "I look forward to playing John McEnroe." By early 1991 his record against McEnroe had improved to 19 wins and 15 losses, and Lendl had won the last 10 straight matches (Wishful Inking, 1991).

The most effective affirmations are both believable and vivid. They are also often spontaneous and thus capture the feelings of a particularly satisfying and successful experience (Syer & Connolly, 1984). "I am as strong as a bull," "I fly down the finish line," and "I really come through under pressure" are all good examples of positive affirmations. Note that each of these expresses a personal, positive message of something that is happening in the present.

Team slogans can also serve as affirmations: "Winners think they can and they do"; "See it, think it, believe it, do it"; "Say yes to success." Each slogan can become a recipe or formula for success provided it is internalized. As just noted, a good source of affirmations is positive statements that might naturally have occurred with previous successful performance. Another way to build affirmations is to have each athlete make a self-esteem list and a success list (Gauron, 1984). The **self-esteem list** contains all of the athlete's positive attributes—all of his or her perceived assets, strengths, and positive qualities. The **success list** contains all of the athlete's successes thus far. The goal is to use one's own personal history in an enabling way by reviewing, reexperiencing, and visualizing previous success experiences.

The self-esteem and success lists serve to remind the athlete of how capable he or she is and how deserving of being successful. This is not the time for modesty but for honest reflection on all of one's positive qualities and successes. Rushall (1979) has emphasized that once this positive frame of reference is established, the athlete should write specific affirmation statements that are *positive action-oriented* self-statements affirming his or her capabilities and what he or she would like to do. A positive action-oriented affirmation statement might be "I play well under pressure" rather than "I know I can play well under pressure." Affirmations should be in the present tense and worded in a way that avoids perfectionist statements that may be impossible to live up to, such as "I always . . ." or "I never. . . ."

Once formulated, how can these statements be maximally used to foster confidence and the desired goal of the affirmation? Gauron (1984) suggests having a number-one affirmation to work on each day, especially when feeling bummed or going into a slump. An athlete may want to write the statement 10 to 20 times each day on a piece of paper or on a card that can be carried around and pulled out and read during free moments. Once the affirmation becomes so integrated into the conscious mind that it is completely believed and made automatically, the athlete can select another affirmation to work on. Other techniques for utilizing affirmations are to post them (singularly or in combination) in places such as one's bedroom, bathroom, or locker. There is also merit in recording affirmations on cassette tapes and playing them whenever possible, such as between classes or before going to bed.

Designing Coping and Mastery Self-Talk Tapes

Every individual has the capacity to program his or her mind for successful thoughts. Some athletes do it naturally; others must learn how to be effective thinkers. One very effective method for training the mind to think in a confident, success-oriented way is through the use of mastery and coping audiotapes. These are tapes on which the athlete records his or her own voice describing an outstanding performance in which events proceed precisely as desired (mastery tape), and a performance in which the athlete successfully adjusts to, or copes with, a series of potentially distracting obstacles to achieve a desired level of performance (coping tape). Helping athletes design and produce these self-talk tapes is another strategy that coaches and sport psychologists can use to program confidence. According to Bell (1983), confident athletes focus their thoughts and images on coping with the environment and the opponent, on mastering the task, and on the rewards of success rather than worrying and catastrophizing about performing poorly and the consequences of failure. Mastery and coping tapes are tools that allow athletes to practice these specific skills.

To produce a **mastery tape,** an athlete first considers what a perfect performance would be like at his or her present level. Recalling a past great game or great day of competition may help the athlete get started with this process. It is advisable to get the coach's opinion on what this perfect performance might be like in order to make the resulting tape more believable. Next, the athlete writes out a script describing this perfect performance, recording all of the positive thoughts and phrases that might occur if he or she were actually performing perfectly in a competitive situation that is progressing exactly as the athlete would wish. The concept with the mastery tape is always to be playing perfectly and always to be in complete control of the situation. If feasible, the mastery tape should be approximately the same length as an actual performance. For example, if an athlete is trying to master a perfect routine for free throw shooting in basketball, he or she would want a segment of tape about 15 to 30 seconds long. If the athlete needs to build confidence in the ability to handle timeouts being called before shooting, the tape might be the length of a time-out and include desirable self-talk for both this time and the preparation time before actually shooting.

If it is not feasible to produce a tape as long as the actual performance (as would be the case with many sports), the mastery script should consist of descriptions of important moments occurring throughout the competition, beginning early in the day and proceeding all the way to the end of the competition. For example, a lacrosse player might describe waking up the day of an important game, traveling to the field or stadium, dressing for competition, warming up, the opening face-off, key segments of the first two quarters of play, half time, more key segments from the second half, and the game's end. At each of these moments, the athlete would describe his or her ideal thoughts, feelings, and emotions, making sure each moment proceeds exactly as desired. The greater the detail provided in these descriptions, the better, as this will enable the programming to work more quickly and effectively. Athletes should use sport-specific terms and include specific descriptions of the weather, how the field or arena looks, how teammates and opponents are dressed, and so on.

Once the athlete reviews this script with a coach, he or she records it onto an audiotape or compact disc with a musical background that will help create the desired emotions. When recording the tape, it is important to speak slowly and provide pauses to allow the mind time to fully visualize each of the scenes that is described. Listening over and over to a mastery tape rendition of the perfect performance should program the conscious and subconscious mind for success by helping the athlete become comfortable with positive statements and associating these statements with his or her own voice and performance; advances in digital and computer technology make this process easier than ever.

Since perfect performances are rare and because obstacles and setbacks are likely to occur in even the best of circumstances, producing and listening to a **coping tape** is an effective way of programming the mind to maintain one's confidence and focus in the face of difficulties. Coping tapes should allow the athlete to practice dealing with negative and anxious thoughts and situations. A coping tape is produced similarly to the mastery tape, but instead of imagining a performance in which the circumstances and conditions are perfect, an athlete producing a coping tape would imagine him- or herself in a difficult situation. The situation might be one in which the athlete makes a foolish mistake and loses mental or emotional control. The athlete then rehearses the strategies needed to regain control and confidence. This is an excellent opportunity to practice thought stoppage, reframing, or any of the other techniques mentioned in this chapter and in other chapters, such as the arousal control techniques in Chapter 15.

Producing a coping tape requires an athlete to imagine all of the potential problems to be faced and how they might be handled successfully. Concern over such things as practice time, physical conditioning, environmental conditions, performance situations, pressures from other people, lack of sleep, unfriendly officials, and tough competition should all be considered. The coping tape includes a description of the negative situations and initial negative self-talk followed by rehearsal of an appropriate strategy and self-statements for dealing effectively with the situation(s) and feeling an optimal arousal level. It should be stressed that the emphasis on a coping tape is not on the stressful or distracting situation described but on the process by which the athlete regains control and confidence when confronted with these situations. At the conclusion of each segment of a coping tape, the athlete should feel that the situation has been resolved and control gained.

Listening over and over to this type of self-talk will help create a sense of well-being so that if the same situation occurs in real life, the athlete will already have practiced coping with it successfully. Once the athlete learns the skill of imagery, he or she can listen to the tape and actually visualize him- or herself successfully coping with what is described on the tape. Further guidelines on producing and using mastery and coping tapes are provided by Rotella, Malone, and Ojala (1985).

Using Videotape to Enhance Performance

Modern video technology can also be used to help athletes gain confidence and improve skills (Ives, Straub, & Shelley, 2002). Just as mastery and coping audiotapes help an athlete feel that a victory is near at hand or that an obstacle can be overcome, videotapes can feed back to an athlete scenes of successful execution and steady improvement. Video cameras are now so easy to use, and so common, that almost any athlete has access to enough raw footage from which a personal highlight video can be created. All that is necessary is to identify the beginning and ending points of a few scenes of correct execution. These scenes can be spliced together to produce a personal or team highlight video. A video editing console makes this process easier, but linking two standard VCRs together will also produce a useful product. VCRs with an additional audio input allow an athlete's or team's favorite musical selection to serve as the sound track to their video images. Watching well-executed play on video while recalling the emotions and sensations that accompanied the scenes serves as a form of imagery rehearsal, which can affect the body in many positive ways (see Chapter 16).

Video can also be useful in helping to improve specific athletic skills. A single successful scene, such as driving to the basket and making a difficult shot, or pulling down the line of scrimmage and making a key block, can be isolated on video and recorded up to 10, 15, or 20 times onto a new video. Each repetition of the scene is separated by blank footage of equal time. This allows athletes to view the scene, and then, as the screen goes blank, close their eyes and produce the same scene from their own internal viewpoint, feeling the emotions and sensations that accompany that execution. This process can be especially effective in improving skill levels and thus confidence if the figure in the video is an accomplished or even world-class athlete with a similar build as the athlete who will view the video. Watching the expert execute, then closing the eyes and feeling that same execution, can help an athlete move toward that expert level.

Summary

There is a direct correlation between self-confidence and success. Confident athletes think about themselves and the action at hand in a different way than those who lack confidence. The difference is that the confident athlete's self-talk and internal imagery are consistently positive and enthusiastic. The positive thinking of confident athletes is likely to lead to enabling feelings and good performance, just as the inappropriate or misguided thinking of athletes lacking in confidence is likely to lead to negative feelings and poor performance. Athletes can learn to use self-talk to build confidence and to facilitate learning and performance. The first step in an athlete's gaining control of thinking is to monitor self-talk to become aware of what kind of thinking helps, what thoughts are occurring that appear to be harmful, and what situations or events are associated with the talk. Three of the most effective tools for identifying self-talk are retrospection, imagery, and keeping a self-talk log.

Once awareness of self-talk and feelings is heightened, particularly of negative talk, the coach or sport psychologist can instruct the athlete in how to start dealing with these thoughts. Techniques such as thought stoppage, changing negative thoughts to positive thoughts, countering, reframing, ABC cognitive restructuring of irrational and distorted thinking, and constructing affirmation statements are possible tools for producing performance-enhancing thoughts and eliminating disabling thoughts. Using mastery and coping tapes and video technology can also enhance confidence and performance.

Using these tools will require an investment of time and faith on the part of the athlete, and there is no guarantee that immediate improvements will result. As with any other training method that truly enhances performance, the results of training the mind to think effectively will emerge gradually, in precise correlation to the athlete's persistence and commitment (Brewer & Shillinglaw, 1992). Some athletes may be hesitant to take this step, just as there are athletes who do not use recent innovations in strength, endurance, and skill training. The athletes, however, who do invest that persistence and commitment to improving their self-talk will find their efforts well rewarded.

Study Questions

1. Describe how the self-talk of a successful athlete is different from that of an unsuccessful athlete. Give five examples of the self-talk from each.

2. What is the relationship between (a) self-talk and self-esteem and (b) self-confidence and self-efficacy?

3. Name and describe the six uses for self-talk. Using any sport setting, provide an example of each.

4. Susie, a varsity golfer, is concerned that her self-talk may be having an adverse effect on her play. What three techniques could she use to become more aware of her self-talk and how might she use them?

5. Describe how a coach or sport psychologist might help athletes use the techniques of thought stoppage and changing negative thoughts to positive thoughts.

6. How does countering a negative self-statement differ from reframing? Give examples of both in response to the statement "I'm always getting beaten on my opponent's first serve."

7. List and describe eight types of irrational and distorted thinking. Provide an example for how you can use the ABC cognitive restructuring intervention to help an athlete modify his or her irrational and distorted thinking.

8. When John monitors his self-talk, what five criteria should he use to determine whether his self-talk and underlying beliefs are rational or irrational?

9. What are the guidelines for writing and repeating affirmations?

10. How does a mastery tape help an athlete develop appropriate self-talk?

11. What is the purpose of a coping audiotape, and how is this purpose accomplished?

12. How might a videotape be designed and used to enhance an athlete's confidence and performance?

References

Bandura, A. (1977). Self efficacy: Toward a unifying theory of behavior change. *Psychological Review, 8,* 191–215.

Bell, K. E. (1983). *Championship thinking: The athlete's guide to winning performance in all sports.* Englewood Cliffs, NJ: Prentice-Hall.

Branden, N. (1994). *The six pillars of self-esteem.* New York: Bantam.

Brewer, B. S., & Shillinglaw, R. (1992). Evaluation of a psychological skills training workshop for male intercollegiate lacrosse players. *The Sport Psychologist, 6,* 139–147.

Buffone, G. W., Sachs, M. L., & Dowd, E. T. (1984). Cognitive-behavioral strategies for promoting adherence to exercise. In M. L. Sachs & G. W. Buffone (Eds.), *Running as therapy: An integrated approach* (pp. 198–214). Lincoln: University of Nebraska.

Bunker, L. K., & Young, B. (1995). *The courtside coach.* Charlottesville, VA: Links.

Cautela, J. R., & Wisocki, P. A. (1977). Thought stoppage procedure: Description, application and learning theory interpretations. *Psychological Record, 27,* 255–264.

Dagrou, E., Gauvin, L., & Halliwell, W. (1992). Effets du langage positif, négatif, et neutre sur la performance motrice. [Effects of positive, negative, and neutral language on motor performance.] *Canadian Journal of Sport Sciences, 17,* 145–147.

Deshimaru, T. (1982). *The zen way to the martial arts.* New York: Penguin Books.

Dugdale, J., & Ecklund, R., (2002). Do not pay attention to the umpires: Thought suppression and taste-relevant focusing strategies. *Journal of Sport and Exercise Psychology 24,* 306–320.

Duncan, T. E., & McAuley, E. (1993). Social support and efficacy cognitions in exercise adherence: A latent growth curve analysis. *Journal of Behavioral Medicine, 16,* 199–218.

Ellis, A. (1982). Self-direction in sport and life. In T. Orlick, J. Partington, & J. Salmela (Eds.), *Mental training for coaches and athlete's* (pp. 10–17). Ottawa, ON: Coaching Association of Canada.

Ellis, A. (1988). Can we legitimately evaluate ourselves? *Psychotherapy Theory, Research and Practice, 25,* 314–316.

Ellis, A., & Dryden, W. (1987). *The practice of rational emotive therapy.* New York: Springer.

Ferguson, H. (1991). *The edge.* Cleveland, OH: Getting the Edge Company.

Finn, J. (1985). Competitive excellence: It's a matter of mind and body. *Physician and Sports Medicine, 13,* 61–72.

Gallwey, W. T. (1974). *The inner game of tennis.* New York: Random House.

Gauron, E. F. (1984). *Mental training for peak performance.* Lansing, NY: Sport Science Associates.

Gauvin, L. (1990). An experiential perspective on the motivational features of exercise and lifestyle. *Canadian Journal of Sport Sciences, 15*, 51–58.

Gould, D., Eklund, R. C., & Jackson, S. A. (1992a). 1988 U.S. Olympic wrestling excellence: I. Mental preparation, precompetitive cognition, and affect. *The Sport Psychologist, 6*, 358–382.

Gould, D., Eklund. R. C., & Jackson, S. A. (1992b). 1988 U.S. Olympic wrestling excellence: II. Thoughts and affect occurring during competition. *The Sport Psychologist, 6*, 383–402.

Gould, D., Finch, L. M., & Jackson, S. A. (1993). Coping strategies used by national champion figure skaters. *Research Quarterly for Exercise and Sport, 64*, 453–468.

Gould, D., Guinan, D., Greenleaf, C., Medbery, R., & Pederson, K. (1999). Factors affecting Olympic performance perceptions of athletes and coaches from more or less successful teams. *The Sport Psychologist, 13*, 371–394.

Gould, D., Hodge, K., Peterson, K., & Gianni, J. (1989). An exploratory examination of strategies used by elite coaches to enhance self-efficacy in athletes. *Journal of Sport and Exercise Psychology, 11*, 128–140.

Gould, D., Medberry, R., Damarjian, N., & Lauer, L. (1999). A survey of mental skills training knowledge, opinions, and practices of junior tennis coaches. *Journal of Applied Sport Psychology, 11*, 28–50.

Grieger, R., & Boyd, J. (1980). *Rational emotive therapy.* New York: Van Nostrand.

Hackfort, D., & Schwenkmezger, P. (1993). In R. N. Singer, M. Murphey, and L. K. Tennant (Eds.), *Handbook of research on sport psychology* (pp. 328–364). New York: MacMillan.

Hall, C. R., Hardy, J., & Gammage, K. L. (1999). About hitting golf balls in the water: Comments on Janelle's (1999) article on ironic processes. *The Sport Psychologist, 13*, 221–224.

Hanton, S., & Jones G. (1999a) The effects of a multimodal intervention program on performers: II. Training the butterflies to fly in formation. *The Sport Psychologist, 13*, 22–41.

Hanton, S., & Jones, G. (1999b) The acquisition and development of cognitive skills and strategies: II. Training the butterflies to fly in formation. *The Sport Psychologist, 13*, 22–41.

Hardy, J., Gammage, K., & Hall, C. (2001). A descriptive study of athlete self-talk. *The Sport Psychologist, 15*, 306–318.

Hardy, J., Hall, C. R., & Hardy, L. (2004a). *Quantifying athletes' use of self-talk.* Manuscript submitted for publication.

Hardy, J., Hall, C. R., & Hardy, L. (2004b). A note on athletes' use of self-talk. *Journal of Applied Sport Psychology, 16*, 251–257.

Harris, D. V., & Harris, B. L. (1984). *The athlete's guide to sports psychology: Mental skills for physical people.* West Point, NY: Leisure Press.

Hay, L. (1984). *You can heal your life.* Santa Monica, CA: Hay House.

Ieleva, L., & Orlick, T. (1991). Mental links to enhanced healing: An exploratory study. *The Sport Psychologist, 5*, 25–40.

Ives, J. C., Straub, W. F., & Shelley, G. A. (2002). Enhancing athletic performance using digital video in consulting. *Journal of Applied Sport Psychology, 14*, 237–245.

Janelle, C. (1999). Ironic mental processes in sport: Implications for sport psychologists. *The Sport Psychologist, 13,* 201–220.

Johnson, J. J. M., Hrycaiko, D. W., Johnson, G. V., & Halas, J. M. (2004). Self-talk and female youth soccer performance. *The Sport Psychologist, 18,* 44–59.

Johnston-O'Conner, E. J., & Kirschenbaum, D. S. (1986). Something succeeds like success: Positive self-monitoring for unskilled golfers. *Cognitive Therapy and Research, 6,* 335–342.

Jones, G., Hanton, S., & Connaughton, D. (2002). What is this thing called mental toughness: An investigation of elite Sport Performers. *Journal of Applied Sport Psychology, 14,* 205–218

Kashiwagi, K. (1986). Personality development of adolescents. In H. W. Stevenson & H. Azuma (Eds.), *Child development and education in Japan* (pp. 167–185). New York: W. H. Freeman.

Kendall, G., Hrycaiko, D., Martin, G., & Kendall, T. (1990). Effects of an imagery rehearsal, relaxation, and self-talk package on basketball game performance. *Journal of Sport and Exercise Psychology, 12,* 157–166.

King, P. (2001, January 29). Who let this dog out? *Sports Illustrated,* 46–50.

Kirschenbaum, D. S., O'Connor, E. A., & Owens, D. (1999). Smart golf: Preliminary evaluation of a simple, yet comprehensive, approach to improving and scoring the mental game. *The Sport Psychologist, 12,* 271–282.

Kirschenbaum, D. S., Ordman, A. M., Tomarken, A. J., & Holtzbauer, R. (1982). Effects of differential self-monitoring and level of mastery on sports performance: Brain power bowling. *Cognitive Therapy and Research, 6,* 335–342.

Kirschenbaum, D. S., Owens, D., & O'Connor, E. A. (1999). Positive illusions in golf: Empirical and conceptual analyses. *Journal of Applied Sport Psychology, 11,* 1–27.

Kitayama, S. (2002). Cultural psychology of the self: A renewed look at independence and interdependence. In C. Hofsten & L. Backman (Eds.), *Psychology at the turn of the millennium* (Vol. 2, pp. 305–322). Florence, KY: Taylor & Frances/Routledge.

Kitsantas, A., & Zimmerman, B. J. (2002). Comparing self-regulatory processes among novice, non-expert, and expert volleyball players: A microanalytic study. *Journal of Applied Sport Psychology, 13,* 365–379.

Landin, D., & Hebert, E. P. (1999). The influence of self-talk on the performance of skilled female tennis players. *Journal of Applied Sport Psychology, 11,* 263–282.

Leonard, G. (1992). *Mastery.* New York: Viking.

Mahoney, M. J. (1979). Cognitive skills and athletic performance. In P. C. Kendall & S. D. Hollon (Eds.), *Cognitive-behavioral interventions: Theory, research and procedure.* New York: Academic Press.

Mahoney, M. J., Gabriel, T. J., & Perkins, T. S. (1987). Psychological skills and exceptional athletic performance. *The Sport Psychologist, 1,* 181–199.

McAuley, E., & Blissmer, B. (2000). Self-efficacy determinants and consequences of physical activity. *Exercise and Sport Sciences Reviews, 28,* 85–88.

McKay, M., & Fanning, P. (1994). *Self-esteem* (2nd ed.). Oakland, CA: New Harbinger.

McPherson, S. L. (2000). Expert-novice differences in planning strategies during collegiate singles tennis competition. *Journal of Sport and Exercise Psychology, 22,* 39–62.

Meichenbaum, D. (1975). Toward a cognitive theory of self-control. In G. Schwartz & D. Shapiro (Eds.), *Consciousness and self-regulation: Advances in research.* New York: Plenum.

Meichenbaum, D. (1977). *Cognitive behavior modification: An integrative approach.* New York: Plenum.

Meyers, A. W., & Schleser, R. A. (1980). A cognitive behavioral intervention for improving basketball performance. *Journal of Sport Psychology, 2,* 69–73.

Meyers, A. W., Whelan, J. P., & Murphy, S. M. (1996). Cognitive behavioral strategies in athletic performance enhancement. In M. Hersen, R. M. Eisler, & P. M. Miller (Eds.), *Progress in behavior modification* (pp. 53–65). New York: Plenum Press.

Owens, D., & Bunker, L. K. (1989). *Golf: Steps to success.* Champaign, IL: Human Kinetics.

Perkos, S., Theodorakis, Y., & Chroni, S., (2002). Enhancing performance and still acquisition in novice basketball players with instructional self-talk. *Sport Psychologist, 16,* 368–383.

Peters, H. J., & Williams, J. M. (2004). *Effect of culture on self-talk and the relationship of self-talk to performance.* Manuscript submitted for publication.

Rogerson, L. J., & Hrycaiko, D. W. (2002). Enhancing competitive performance of ice hockey goaltenders using centering and self-talk. *Journal of Applied Sport Psychology, 14,* 14–26.

Rotella, R. (1984). Untitled manuscript. University of Virginia, Charlottesville.

Rotella, R. (1995). *Golf is not a game of perfect.* New York: Simon & Schuster.

Rotella, R. (1996). *Golf is a game of confidence.* New York: Simon and Schuster.

Rotella, R. J., Malone, C., & Ojala, D. (1985). Facilitating athletic performance through the use of mastery and coping tapes. In L. K. Bunker, R. J. Rotella, & A. S. Reilly (Eds.), *Sport psychology: Psychological considerations in maximizing sport performance.* Ithaca, NY: Mouvement Publications.

Rushall, B. S. (1979). *Psyching in sports.* London: Pelham.

Schunk, D. H. (1995). Self-efficacy, motivation and performance. *Journal of Applied Sport Psychology, 7,* 112–137.

Seligman, M. (1991). *Learned optimism.* New York: Knopf.

Silva, J. (1982). Performance enhancement through cognitive intervention. *Behavioral Modification, 6,* 443–463.

Siri, S., & Martin, G. L. (1996). Single-subject evaluation of a self-talk package for improving figure skating performance. *The Sport Psychologist, 10,* 227–238.

Steinmetz, J., Blankenship, J., & Brown, L. (1980). *Managing stress before it manages you.* Palo Alto, CA: Bull.

Syer, J., & Connolly, C. (1984). *Sporting body sporting mind: An athlete's guide to mental training.* New York: Cambridge University Press.

Taylor, J. (1999). Isn't it ironic? Or irony is in the unconscious eye of the beholder. *The Sport Psychologist, 13,* 225–230.

Thellwell, R., & Greenlee, I. (2003). Developing competitive endurance performance using mental skills training. *Sport Psychologist, 17,* 208–225.

Tod, D., Iredale, F., and Gill, N. (2003). Psyching-up and muscular force production. *Sports Medicine, 33,* 47–59.

Van Raalte, J. L., Brewer, B. W., Lewis, B. P., Linder, D. E., Wildman, G., & Kozimor, J. (1995). Cork! The effects of positive and negative self-talk on dart throwing performance. *Journal of Sport Behavior, 18,* 50–57.

Van Raalte, J. L., Brewer, B. W., Rivera, P. M., & Petitpas, A. J. (1994). The relationship between observable self-talk and competitive junior tennis players' match performance. *Journal of Sport and Exercise Psychology, 16,* 400–415.

Wegner, D. M. (1994). Ironic processes of mental control. *Psychological Review, 16,* 34–52.

Wegner, D. M. (1997). When the antidote is the poison. Ironic mental control processes. *Psychological Science, 8,* 148–150.

Wegner, D. M., Ansfield, M., & Pilloff, D. (1998). The putt and the pendulum: Ironic effects of mental control of action. *Psychological Science, 9,* 196–199.

Wegner, D. M., & Erber, R. (1992). The hyperaccessibility of suppressed thoughts. *Journal of Personality and Social Psychology, 63,* 903–912.

Wegner, D. M., Schneider, D. J., Knutson, B., & McMahon, S. R. (1991). Polluting the stream of consciousness: The effect of thought suppression on the mind's environment. *Cognitive Therapy and Research, 15,* 41–152.

Weinberg, R. S., Gould, D., & Jackson, A. (1979). Expectations and performance: An empirical test of Bandura's self-efficacy theory. *Journal of Sport Psychology, 3,* 320–331.

Weinberg, R. S., Gould, D., Yukelson, D., & Jackson, A. (1981). The effects of pre-existing and manipulated self-efficacy on a competitive muscular endurance task. *Journal of Sport Psychology, 3,* 345–354.

Wenzlaff, R. M., Wegner D. M., & Klein, S. B. (1991). The role of thought suppression in the bonding of thought and mood. *Journal of Personality and Social Psychology, 60,* 500–508.

Wenzlaff, R. M., & Wegner, D. M. (2000). Thought suppression. *Annual Review of Psychology, 51,* 39–91.

Wishful Inking. (1991, January). *Special Report: On Sports,* p. 24.

CHAPTER

18

Concentration and Attention Control Training

Robert M. Nideffer, *Enhanced Performance Systems*
Marc-Simon Sagal, *The Winning Mind*

Eight runners are in the starting blocks for the final of the 100-meter sprint in the Olympics. Each of these runners on "their day," or with a little help from the other runners (e.g., a slow start), is capable of winning the gold medal.[1] Knowing those facts, what are the critical variables that will determine who wins the race?

There are three factors that will determine the winner of that race. The runners' focus of concentration, stride length, and speed of turn over. Concentration plays a role in several ways. Perhaps the most obvious is at the start of the race. If the individual does not get a good start, either because he was distracted by something going on around him, or wasn't ready because he was still going through a mental checklist, or caught up in thoughts or feelings, he will lose the race. It isn't concentration or mental energy, however, that actually propels the athlete down the track. It is the combination of stride length and speed of turn over (how rapidly the legs move). The athlete with the best ratio of

turn over to stride length will, given that he got a good start, win the race.

For a psychological intervention to have a difference on the outcome of the 100-meter sprint, it will have to directly affect one or more of those three critical variables. To convince the skeptical athlete or coach that you can help them improve their performance you have to demonstrate a connection between the services you offer and one or more of those variables. You will have to show how the techniques you are using affect concentration or the activation of muscles that control stride length and turn over, and the relaxation of the muscles that interfere with those variables.

The 100-meter sprint is a relatively simple sporting event. Simple in that very little in the way of thinking, strategizing, shifting of concentration, or making adjustments to one's performance is required. To quote a coach, "The sprints aren't rocket science. A gun goes off and you run as fast as you can." Other sports require a great deal more of the athlete when it comes to managing concentration and emotional or physiological level of arousal.

As simple as sprinting may be, however, if there is a concentration break that destroys a

---

[1]Final times for the men at the 2004 Olympics in Athens, Greece, were 9.85, 9.86, 9.87, 9.89, 9.94, 10.00, and 10.1. One of the runners was disqualified and did not finish.

sprinter's start, what caused it and what do you do to prevent it from happening again? If muscles tighten during the race interfering with the athlete's stride length and speed of turn over, what caused it, and what do you do about it? It's answering those questions in any critical performance situation, and demonstrating the relationship between an athlete's ability to shift his or her focus of concentration in response to changing performance demands, combined with the ability to control emotions that affect muscle tension, coordination, and timing, that attention control training (ACT) is all about.

Attention control training is more than a technique (e.g., centering). It is a complex process that involves the following elements: (1) education, defining concentration for coaches and athletes, and clarifying the relationship between focus of concentration, and various physiological parameters like breathing and muscle tension levels that affect performance; (2) assessment, identifying the concentration requirements of the performance setting and mapping those to the concentration skills of the athlete and measuring the personal and interpersonal characteristics that will allow us to predict both the types of situations likely to interfere with performance, and the athlete's most likely performance errors; (3) identification, of a situation specific focus for our training program, and (4) implementation and evaluation of the program.

Attention Control Training Principles

Attention control training is based on a theory of attentional and interpersonal style. The Attentional and Interpersonal Style (TAIS) inventory is an assessment tool based on the theory and used by us, in the development of attention control training programs (Nideffer, 1976; Nideffer & Sagal, 2001, and Nideffer, 2003).[2] The principles

underlying the application of ACT to performance enhancement are outlined here.

1. Athletes need to be able to engage in at least four different types of concentration.[3]

2. Different sport situations will make different attentional demands on an athlete. Accordingly, the athlete must be able to shift to the appropriate type of concentration to match changing attentional demands.

3. Under optimal conditions, the average person can meet the concentration demands of a wide variety of performance situations.

4. Attentional characteristics are at times traitlike, having predictive utility in any number of situations. At other times they are statelike, situationally determined and modifiable through training. Factors that determine the extent to which a given individual's attentional skills are traitlike include biological or genetic predispositions and alterations in arousal. As arousal moves out of the moderate range, the habit strength of the individual's more dominant attentional focus or style increases (Hull, 1951). Thus, the individual's dominant attentional style becomes more traitlike and more predictive of behavior when arousal levels are high.

5. The individual's ability to perform effectively as the dominant concentration style becomes more traitlike depends on two factors: (1) the appropriateness of the dominant attentional style, and (2) the level of confidence within the particular performance situation (Carver & Scheier, 1989).

6. The phenomenon of choking—of having performance progressively deteriorate—occurs as physiological arousal increases, causing attention to involuntarily narrow and become more internally focused. This results in alterations in perception; time

---

[2]TAIS is only one method for assessing the concentration and interpersonal skills required by different performance situations; behavior rating scales, observations, and other assessment tools measuring these characteristics also may be used.

[3]The words *concentration and attention* are used interchangeably in these discussions.

seems speeded up which contributes to a tendency to rush (e.g., start to throw the ball before completing the catch). Muscles antagonistic to performance begin to tighten, interfering with weight transfer, timing, and coordination.

7. Alterations in physiological arousal affect concentration. Thus, the systematic manipulation of physiological arousal is one way of gaining some control over concentration.

8. Alterations in the focus of attention will also affect physiological arousal. Thus, the systematic manipulation of concentration is one way to gain some control over arousal (e.g., muscular tension levels, heart rate, and respiration rate).

Different Types of Concentration

When a coach tells an athlete to concentrate, the athlete is more likely to respond to the instruction if the coach specifically defines the type of concentration that he or she would like the athlete to engage in. To do this, it is necessary to think of attention as requiring at least two different types of focus. First, the athlete will need to control the *width* of his or her attentional focus. Certain sports, such as basketball and hockey, require a broad focus of attention. Other sports, such as sprints, diving, and shooting, require a narrow focus. The second type of focus that needs to be controlled relates to the *direction* of the athlete's attention. In some situations, attention must be directed internally to make adjustments in muscle tension, or to problem solve and strategize. At other times, attention must be focused externally, on the opponent, or the flash of the starting gun. Figure 18-1 presents the four different types of concentration required by different sport situations that result when both width and direction of attention are controlled.

Shifting Attention

Recall the second principle underlying attention control training: Different sport situations make different attentional demands on athletes. Thus,

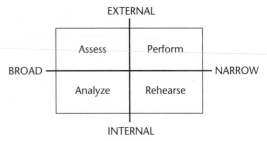

Figure 18-1 **Dimensions of attention**

a position such as quarterback in football places a greater demand on an athlete to be able to develop a broad external focus of attention (e.g., to be aware of the entire field) than a position such as guard, which requires a narrower type of concentration (e.g., to block a particular athlete on the other team). Beyond this difference, however, there are demands for shifting attention within a particular sport. An example from golf will illustrate the point.

When golfers step up to the ball prior to hitting a shot, they start off with a fairly broad external type of attention. Golfers need to take in several different kinds of information. They need to be aware of the placement of hazards (trees, sand traps, out-of-bounds markers, water, etc.) and course conditions (dryness of the grass, speed and direction of wind). Once they have gathered this external information, golfers shift attention to a broad internal focus to plan their shot. At this time they should try to recall past similar situations, remembering how they played them and what the results were. Then they must think about any changes they may have made in the meantime, changes that might modify how they should now play this similar situation (e.g., have they changed their swing, gotten new clubs; are they in a different tactical position such as needing to be conservative or to take a risk). Analyzing all of this information allows golfers to select a particular club and to determine how they want to hit the ball.

Once golfers have formulated a plan, they shift to a narrow internal type of concentration to monitor their own tension (e.g., making sure they are not too tight or too relaxed) and mentally rehearse the shot. They may picture in their mind what they want to feel and see as they execute the shot. Finally, golfers shift attention to a narrow external focus as they address the ball and begin their backswing. At this time concentration is on the ball. To attend to other external or internal cues would only interfere with their execution of the shot.

This basic model can be applied to a great many sports. Thus, athletes are continually required to shift attention across the different dimensions listed even though some sports require more of one type of attention than others. In addition, in some sport situations coaches and other athletes can make up for attentional deficiencies of some players. As an illustration, in football the coach can select the plays for the quarterback. This limits the need for the quarterback to develop a broad internal type of attention.

Individual Differences

The third and fourth principles underlying attention control training deal with an individual's ability to shift attention. The third principle indicates that if individuals are appropriately motivated and trained and if they have control over their level of arousal (so that it is neither too high nor too low), they are capable of effective concentration. They can control the width and direction of attention enough to be effective. The actual attentional demands of most sports are not so extreme that the average person cannot meet them. This means that there is hope for most athletes.

At the same time, the fourth principle indicates that it will be easier for some athletes to meet a given sport's attentional demands than for others. Just as we are willing to concede that there are physiological and biological differences among athletes, we should be willing to concede that there are attentional differences. As mentioned earlier, some of the differences seem to be learned (e.g., the result of social and environmental factors), whereas others seem to be genetic or biological. Research on attentional processes suggests the following differences, among others.

1. Different individuals have different capacities for developing a broad internal type of attention. Thus, some individuals are better suited to analyzing large amounts of information than others.

2. Certain individuals appear to be more sensitive to environmental (external) information than others. The former read and react to other people more effectively.

3. Some individuals are more capable of developing a narrow, nondistractible type of attention. This is especially true of world class performers in sport (Nideffer, Sagal, Lowry, & Bond, 2000).

There are superstars who seem to have been born for their particular event. There are sprinters with more fast-twitch muscle fibers than most other people, divers with a greater kinesthetic awareness, and so on. Likewise, some athletes are more attentionally suited to their sport. Their ability to focus narrowly makes it easier for them to be dedicated to follow through on a task, to be as selfish as they must be to make it to the top. Some athletes have the ability to deal with a great deal of information and not become overloaded and confused. This helps them to be more resistant to pressure and makes it easier for them to perform in critical situations.

Although a small percentage of the world's athletes may indeed have been born dedicated and resistant to choking, the majority have to learn to focus attention to achieve these goals. An increasingly important role for the sport psychologist and coach will be assisting athletes in recognizing the attentional demands of their sports, as well as helping athletes identify their own relative attentional strengths and weaknesses. The systematic assessment of attentional abilities and of the ability to shift from one type of attention to another will play a major role in the development of training programs. This assessment will aid the majority of athletes in developing concentration skills and compensating for any attentional problems they may have. Early attempts at this type of assessment have already begun and are listed in the references at the end of this chapter. For a quick assessment of your concentration skills, and to get an idea about how they affect performance, log on to the Internet and go to http://www.enhanced-performance.com/st_login.php.

Playing to One's Attentional Strength

The fifth principle underlying attention control training indicates that athletes have a tendency to play to their strengths as pressure increases. This is true of almost all of us. We have an unerring capacity to become our own worst enemies, to turn what are normally strengths into weaknesses. For example, outgoing people who are normally appreciated because they also have enough sensitivity to know when to leave other people alone occasionally lose their sensitivity and become pests.

There is an unproven assumption in sport that good coaches do not make good athletes and vice versa. If this is true, one of the reasons might be that coaching makes a very heavy demand on an individual to be able to think and analyze. Coaches must be able to develop a broad internal type of attention. In contrast, many sporting situations require athletes to shut off their analyzing. If they do not, we see the paralysis by analysis that coaches are so fond of talking about. The athletes think too much and fail to react to the sport situation. They are "in their head" at an inappropriate time. Athletes who ultimately become coaches are often the ones who were continually analyzing. They are not the brilliant broken-field runners who reacted instinctively.

Take the pressure off most coaches and athletes and they can be either analytical or instinctive. Put them under pressure, however, and they play to their strengths. Analytical coaches become *too* analytical. They go inside their head and lose sensitivity to the athletes and the game situation. Often they attempt to communicate their analysis to the athletes, overloading them with information, getting them to think too much.

Instinctive athletes have a tendency to react too quickly. They may fail to analyze and plan when they need to. They lose their capacity to make adjustments, getting faked out by the same moves time and time again, not learning from their own mistakes. If arousal reaches the point of causing narrowing of attention and of increasing internal distractions, the athletes' ability to process information deteriorates. At this time, coaches should be minimizing the amount of information they are giving their athletes. The coaches should be providing as much structure and support as possible. If coaches are playing to their own strength, they fail. Instead of calling the play for their athletes, unsuccessful coaches ask the athletes what they think or give them several possibilities.

Sport psychologists can help athletes and coaches *team build* and maintain effective communication under pressure. Sport psychologists do this by sensitizing coaches and athletes to their own and others' relative strengths and weaknesses. Sport psychologists help coaches and athletes identify the specific situations in which communication is likely to break down and help them plan alternative ways to behave. When no sport psychologist is available to help, coaches need to be sufficiently knowledgeable and aware to do this on their own.

As an example of the team-building process, consider a situation in which a coach tends to be more analytical and more assertive than the athletes (a normally ideal situation). As pressure increases, the coach becomes more analytical and more assertive and the athletes less so. At a certain point the athletes should be confronting the coach with the fact that they are being overloaded with instructions; they may behave in an even more outwardly compliant way, nodding their heads to show agreement even when they are not hearing or when they are confused. The coach, thinking that he or she has a willing, even enthusiastic, audience, feels encouraged to give still more information. The sport psychologist helps the athletes recognize their feelings of confusion and provides them with the support they need to confront the coach. Then all work together to develop ways of minimizing the problem. Perhaps insight is all the coach needs to decrease the amount of information he or she gives. Perhaps the coach's insight and an initial confrontation with the coach (e.g., "Coach, I can't take all of this right now") will provide all the encouragement the athletes need to be

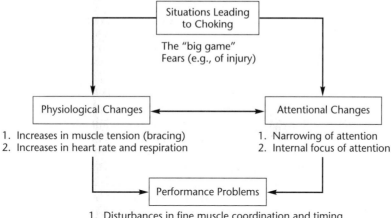

Figure 18-2 **Interaction between physiological and attentional processes under highly stressful conditions**

Operationally Defining Choking

Before we can examine the sixth principle underlying attention control training, we must define operationally the term **choking.** (Unfortunately, there is little agreement among most coaches and athletes regarding the definition of as critical a term as choking. Thus, when a coach tells an athlete not to choke, the athlete may have no idea of what he or she is supposed to avoid.)

Given what we do know about the interaction between thought process (what we attend to) and physiological process, it is possible to come up with a definition of choking that can be very useful to coaches, athletes, sport psychology practitioners, and researchers alike.

Behaviorally, we can infer that athletes are choking when their performance seems to be progressively deteriorating and when they seem incapable of regaining control over performance on their own, that is, without some outside assistance. Examples would be the baseball player who follows a bobbled catch with a throwing error, or the diver or gymnast who lets an early mistake (e.g., on a dive or particular move) upset him or her to the point of making additional errors on other maneuvers.

Figure 18-2 illustrates the interaction that occurs between physiological and attentional processes under highly stressful conditions. The figure also shows how the changes that occur affect performance. By using Figure 18-2 and the section that follows, coaches should gain a more useful understanding of the choking process—an understanding that can help increase their ability to understand, predict, and control behavior in sport situations.

Prevention and Treatment of Choking

The seventh and eighth principles underlying attention control training suggest that by creating changes in what is going on either physiologically or attentionally athletes can break the downward spiral associated with choking. Thus, if they eliminate the physical feelings associated with excessive tension (tight muscles, pounding heart), they will reduce the number of attentional distractions and improve their ability to concentrate. Likewise, if coaches can get the athletes to either ignore or reinterpret their physical feelings (e.g., if they give a positive interpretation to being aroused, such as "I'm ready"), gradually the physical changes will be reduced and tension levels and heart rate will return to what is normal for the competitive conditions.

Under ideal conditions, we would be able to prevent choking from ever occurring. One of the unrealistic goals of many sport psychology programs is to prevent choking by teaching athletes some type of relaxation or rehearsal procedure. In truth, we probably can reduce the frequency of choking through better training and through some type of relaxation and rehearsal process. We can reduce the tendency to choke, but we cannot eliminate it. In addition, we are likely to be successful only if our program has a performance-specific focus. That is, we should teach the athletes to use the relaxation at a particular time (e.g., at bat), and we should train them to rehearse a particular performance situation (e.g., hitting under certain conditions).

By teaching athletes to relax, to monitor their own muscle tension levels, and to use their tension levels as a signal to employ some brief type of relaxation procedure, we can help them improve the consistency of their performance. By getting them to mentally simulate anticipated performance conditions and to systematically rehearse what they will see and feel, we can begin to desensitize them and increase the likelihood that tension will not reach a level that will cause them to choke.

With a specific training focus we can reduce the frequency of choking and "season" athletes more quickly. Simulation and rehearsal can make up for some lack of experience. Nevertheless, there will always be unanticipated situations that we could not prepare for. If we tried to think of every contingency, we would overload ourselves and never make any progress. As a result, we must begin to train athletes to recover quickly from the unexpected. Learning to recover once tension has already gotten out

of control or once a mistake has been made is even more critical than trying to eliminate choking altogether.

Process Versus Outcome

Once athletes have made a mistake or once they become aware of the tension and the attentional distractions that are likely to interfere with performance, what they attend to becomes critical. In the prevention strategy discussed previously, emphasis is placed on training the athlete to recognize and reduce physical tension, thereby improving concentration. Once mistakes have been made, however, many athletes find it difficult to directly challenge what is going on in their bodies.

Imagine a situation in which you have just double-faulted away a game in a critical tennis match. You know you are tight and you try to counter it by saying, "It's all right, just relax; the game isn't that important anyway," and a little voice inside you immediately counters with, "Oh yes it is, you blew it, you can't do it."

Your lack of confidence created by the feelings and the failure causes you to doubt your own ability. Trying to take control directly only creates more distractions and frustration. If you had a great deal of confidence in yourself you could do that. You could challenge and confront yourself, using your frustration and anger to help you concentrate on the task. When you lack confidence, however, you must focus your attention on something else. You must become process focused rather than outcome focused.

During practice, especially in sports that require a great deal of training and sacrifice on the part of the athlete, individuals motivate themselves by thinking about outcome: "If we win the championship, I'll be a hero." "I am working this hard because I want to win a gold medal." "By making these sacrifices I can get the recognition and financial rewards I want." Once the competition begins, however, an outcome focus can become very negative.

To be thinking about how important the outcome of a contest is or about what one can win or lose during the actual competition typically generates additional physical and attentional changes that interfere with performance. One of the biggest contributors to choking is thinking about the outcome or the importance of a contest while involved in it. To help athletes break out of this thinking, sport psychologists are training them to recognize their tendency toward placing too much importance on outcome (during the competition) and to use those thoughts, when they occur, as signals to attend to the process. Coaches need to do the same thing. **Process cues** are related to the process of performing as opposed to the outcome. For example, swimmers might attend to some technical aspect of their stroke or the feeling of their body moving through the water. Often the focus is on generating a rhythm. Over time, people learn that if they maintain this type of focus, the outcome will take care of itself. Then, as they have success and as confidence builds, they can begin to attend to outcome to motivate themselves to try harder. Thus, the athlete who has a lot of success and who becomes a little lazy or too relaxed needs to think about outcome to get arousal levels up and to keep going.

In the next few pages, we will use case histories to illustrate the entire attention control training processes. Before doing that, however, we wish to address concerns raised by some researchers that question the factor structure of The Attentional and Interpersonal Style (TAIS) inventory, and whether sport specific measures of attentional processes might not be more useful than TAIS. These issues have been discussed in detail by Van Schyock and Grasha (1983), by Nideffer (1990; 2003), and by Ford and Summers (1992).

A review of the research on TAIS clearly indicates that the inventory, like every other psychological inventory, can be improved on. Research aside for the moment, it is equally important to point out that TAIS has been, and continues to be, used for the purposes described in this chapter, by professional staff at Olympic training centers and with professional athletes around the world. Clearly the tool is helpful for

the development of performance enhancement programs with elite level athletes. We have focused on TAIS in the chapter because TAIS is what we use. We are not trying to endorse TAIS; it is not what you use to measure critical performance relevant concentration skills and interpersonal characteristics that is important. What is important is that you pay attention to, and evaluate by whatever means you can, these characteristics. You may use interview techniques, behavior rating scales, other psychological assessment tools, performance observations, or all of the above.

The Process of Attention Control Training

In ACT, assessment of the athlete is an ongoing process. For us, that process begins with administration of The Attentional and Interpersonal Style inventory (TAIS), whether there is a specific reason for referral or not. A description of the attentional and interpersonal characteristics measured by TAIS is provided in Table 18-1. TAIS inventory is administered in advance of the training program, to both coach and athlete. Individuals are told the instrument measures the attentional and interpersonal characteristics that are important determinants of performance and that information from TAIS will be used to help design a training program. At this point, no attempt is made to control the individuals' response set (e.g., to ask them to respond in a sport-specific way, or to give them a comparison group).

Information from TAIS is used in two ways. First, it can help the workshop leader understand some of the factors that may be contributing to an already identified problem or, if a problem has not been identified, to provide direction for the trainer. Score patterns indicate areas of possible concern, helping to focus interview questions and behavioral observations. Second, information from TAIS is used in the design of a training program and to provide an educational focus for the subject.

Table 18-1 **Test of Attentional and Interpersonal Style Scales**

Scale	Scale Description
BET	*Broad External Attention:* High scores indicate good environmental awareness and assessment skills (street sense).
OET	*Overloaded by External Information:* High scores are associated with errors because attention is inappropriately focused on irrelevant external stimuli.
BIT	*Broad Internal Attention:* High scores indicate good analytical planning skills.
OIT	*Overloaded by Internal Information:* High scores are associated with errors due to distractions from irrelevant internal sources (e.g., thoughts and feelings).
NAR	*Narrow-Focused Attention:* High scores indicate the ability to remain task oriented, to avoid distractions, and to stay focused on a single job.
RED	*Reduced Attention:* High scores are associated with errors due to a failure to shift attention from an external focus to an internal one, or vice versa.
INFP	*Information Processing:* High scores are associated with a desire for and enjoyment of a diversity of activity.
BCON	*Behavior Control:* High scores are associated with an increased likelihood of acting out in impulsive ways and a tendency to establish one's own rules rather than strictly adhering to the rules of others.
CON	*Interpersonal Control:* High scores are associated both with needing to be in control in interpersonal situations and with actually being in control.
SES	*Self-Esteem:* High scores are associated with feelings of self-worth and self-confidence.
P/O	*Physical Orientation:* High scores are associated with having been physically competitive and with the enjoyment of competitive activities.
OBS	*Obsessive/Speed of Decision Making:* This scale reflects speed of decision making, worry, and anxiety. High scores are associated with increased worry and difficulty making decisions.
EXT	*Extroversion:* High scores indicate an enjoyment of social involvements and a tendency to assume leadership in social situations.
INT	*Introversion:* High scores indicate a need for personal space and privacy.
IEX	*Intellectual Expression:* High scores indicate a willingness to express thoughts and ideas in front of others.
NAE	*Negative Affect Expression:* High scores indicate a willingness to confront issues, to set limits on others, and to express anger.
PAE	*Positive Affect Expression:* High scores indicate a willingness to express support and encouragement to others.
DEP	*Depression:* A high score is associated with situational (transient) depression.
FOT	*Focus Over Time:* High scores indicate a willingness to make sacrifices to achieve long-term objectives.
PUP	*Performance Under Pressure:* High scores indicate a good ability to perform effectively in stressful conditions.

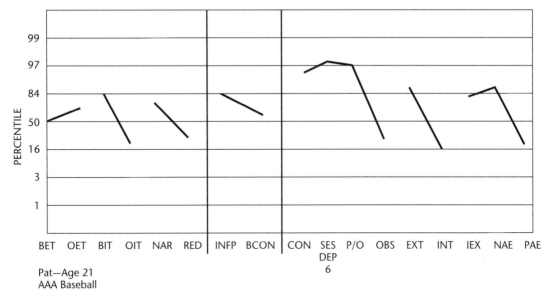

Pat—Age 21
AAA Baseball

Figure 18-3 **Pat's Attentional and Interpersonal Style (TAIS) inventory**

Scores on TAIS for two different athletes are presented in Figure 18-3 and Figure 18-4.[4] The individual whose scores are presented in Figure 18-3 (Pat) is a baseball player on a AAA team. This athlete was referred by the coach because of a particular problem. The athlete whose scores are presented in Figure 18-4 (Steve) is one of the best junior tennis players in the world. He participated in a 3-day ACT program for tennis players and at the outset of the program had no identified problem. Training programs differ when there are and are not specific problems or reasons for referral. By discussing the two cases separately, we can highlight those differences.[5]

Case I

Pat (see Figure 18-3) was described by his coach as a super kid. He has a great attitude, loves baseball and is all hustle. He tries harder than any other two kids on the team. Lately, his hitting has dropped off, particularly in situations where there are runners on the bases. He's trying too hard and it's affecting his confidence, though he says it isn't. I keep telling him to relax, but he can't seem to do it.

The coach had spoken to Pat about talking to an expert on concentration, and Pat was eager to cooperate. He knew that he wasn't performing as well as he or the coach wanted in big situations. The coach gave him a copy of TAIS and asked him to complete it and to mail it to me. Arrangements were then made for me to spend 3 days with Pat and the coach during spring training.

I met briefly with both of them, explaining that to be helpful I needed to observe Pat in a game situation. In this meeting I emphasized my desire to help and at the same time attempted to subtly increase the pressure Pat was feeling by letting him know that I would be analyzing him. I wanted to create additional stress, so I could consensually validate the problem the coach had identified and so I could see for myself the physical consequences of "trying too hard."

[4]These cases were completed prior to the development of TAIS scales measuring focus over time (FOT) and performance under pressure (PUP).

[5]These two case studies are based on work done by Robert M. Nideffer.

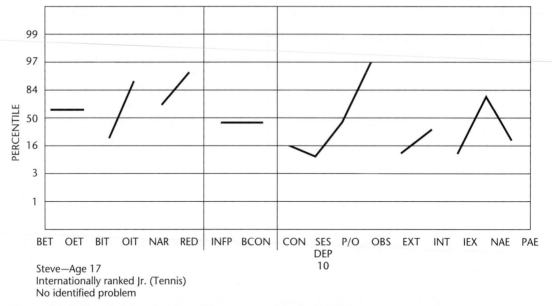

Steve—Age 17
Internationally ranked Jr. (Tennis)
No identified problem

Figure 18-4 **Steve's Attentional and Interpersonal Style (TAIS) inventory**

Looking at Pat's TAIS profile had given me some insight into the types of problems that might be occurring:

1. The general attentional profile was that of an effective, analytical athlete who might become too analytical under pressure.

2. Pat's high need for control (CON), high level of self-esteem (SES), and high score on the physical orientation scale (P/O) all indicated a high need to achieve. Thus, arousal would be likely to increase in any situation in which Pat was not performing at the level he expected of himself.

3. A high score on the negative affect expression scale (NAE) combined with his high scores on control and self-esteem suggested Pat could become his own worst enemy. Frustration at not performing well would be likely to lead to anger, which could cause him to tighten up and behave impulsively from time to time.

First observational session. The game provided partial support for the information provided by

TAIS and the coach's reason for referral. Throughout the game Pat was enthusiastic and supportive of his team. He hustled and seemed to be a positive force. At bat, however, the pressure he was feeling was obvious. In his first at bat he swung at the first pitch (a ball that was high), fouling out to the catcher. He knew he shouldn't have swung at the pitch and returned to the dugout mumbling about his stupidity.

In his second at bat there was no one on the bases. He concentrated a little better, waiting for "his pitch." He got on base with a walk. In his third at bat there was a runner on first. As Pat stepped into the batter's box, the tension in his neck and shoulders seemed much more noticeable. He continually moved his head and shoulders, trying to release some of the tension. He took the first pitch for a called strike (the third base coach had told him to take the pitch), and that increased the tension. He swung at the next pitch, a fast ball on the outside corner, but was very late. Then, he jumped at a pitch that was high and out of the strike zone.

First educational session. The opportunity to observe Pat in an actual playing situation was important for two reasons: (1) It served as another form of assessment, helping to consensually validate information gained through testing and from the coach; and (2) it provided Pat and me with a shared experience. Now I could use Pat's own behavior to make the points I wanted to make about the relationship between concentration, arousal, and performance. When talking about scores on TAIS (e.g., the tendency for Pat to become angry), I could relate them directly to things observed in the game.

To facilitate the education process and to further validate the information already gained from the referral, TAIS, and behavioral observations, I provide athletes with an ACT workbook that is sport specific (Nideffer, 1989). I hope to accomplish the following goals through education:

1. I make the athletes aware of the attentional requirements of their sport and of their own attentional strengths and weaknesses. This is accomplished through the use of the Inventory of Concentration and Communication Skills (ICCS) contained in the workbook. Athletes are asked a series of 15 questions relating to the four different attentional styles and to the different types of attentional distractions that can occur. In responding to the questions, they are asked to answer each item as "it relates to your particular sport" and to compare themselves to "the average athlete you compete against." Examples would include: "I am more capable of narrowing my attention, of shutting out distractions under pressure, of focusing my concentration on one thing, than ____% of the athletes I know." "____% of my mistakes due to external distractions occur because I get bored (e.g., stare at other players, fans, etc.)." "____% of my mistakes occur because I get angry (e.g., at a call or opponent) and lose concentration." "____% of my mistakes due to external distractions occur because I rush my performance, failing to set up properly (e.g., getting pressured by my opponent's move)."

2. I teach athletes about the relationship between focus of attention, physiological

arousal, and performance. My examples become highly situation specific based on actual behavioral observations. To make sure the information is being absorbed, the athletes are asked to fill in a table like that shown in Figure 18-5.

Pat's chart (Figure 18–5) is instructive because he has identified two problems or responses to the pressure he feels. First, he's aware of tightening up. That's important because his awareness can become a cue signaling him to use arousal control strategies. His thoughts at these times will also serve as cues. Not only does the awareness of change in tension tell Pat he needs to make adjustments, but he's been able to identify those areas of tension that are most important to him (e.g., grip on the bat). If he can relax his grip a little, he believes the rest of his body will relax as well.

To this point, Pat's attempts to give himself instructions have served as distractions, keeping him from attending to the ball. He can't be in his head, consciously giving himself instructions, trying to problem solve, and attend to the release of the ball at the same time. In addition, many of his instructions are negative (e.g., "Don't blow it"), making him tentative or defensive. The end result is that he reacts too slowly, and when he swings, his weight is on his back foot. If he were more aggressive and his timing was on, there would be a transfer of weight from his back foot to his front foot as his bat makes contact with the ball.

In a game, when Pat finds himself being tentative and thinking too much, he gets angry and jumps from one problem to another. Anger makes him too aggressive, causing him to rush and swing early. His weight transfer occurs before the ball arrives. If he makes contact with the ball, he must rely on the strength in his arms instead of being able to use the weight of his entire body.

Second observational session. Once Pat had learned about the relationship between concentration and arousal, there was a second observational session. The purpose of this session was to provide Pat, myself, and the coach with an opportunity to validate previous findings. This is an important session for several reasons.

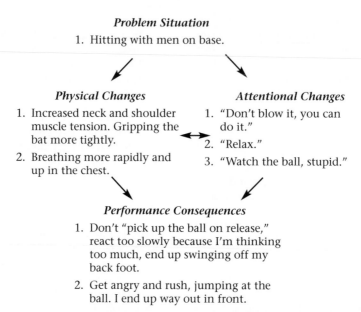

Figure 18-5 **Observation of case 1 problem response patterns**

First, athletes in ACT are attempting to rate their concentration skills for the first time and may never have thought about these attentional dimensions before. Likewise, they may never have made direct comparisons between their concentration skills and those of other players. The second session provides them with an opportunity to make those comparisons. As a result, their initial impressions may change (Pat's did not).

In addition, the second observational session and subsequent discussions with the coach help to pinpoint specific performance cues that should and should not be attended to. The second session answers questions like "What specific thoughts increase (or decrease) muscle tension and arousal?" "What are the particular stimuli that remind you about outcome and the possibility of failure?" "What technical or tactical process cues should the athlete be attending to so he can perform more effectively?" As you might imagine, the technical and tactical knowledge of most sport psychologists is more limited than that of the coach and athlete. For this reason, the assistance of the coach and athlete in identifying critical task-relevant cues is essential. This is especially true with ACT

because programs emphasize making specific behavioral changes within specific performance situations.

Pat's performance in the second observational session was different from the first, because he was observing his own behavior. He still did not have "good at bats." Mistakes were occurring, however, because he was too analytical and not watching the ball. Anger and rushing were not issues in the second session.

Pat learned that his coach and the third base coach had become distracting cues, causing him to tighten up. When there were runners on base, he was extremely sensitive to any anxiety on the part of the coach. He interpreted the coach's anxiety as a lack of confidence in his ability to get a hit. Thus, attending to the coach would increase muscle tension and doubts (internal distractions).

Second educational session. Following the second observational session, Pat filled out the information in Figure 18-6. His goal, confirmed by his coach, was to identify those feelings and thoughts that would result in a good at bat.

It's important to notice that as far as performance consequences are concerned, Pat didn't

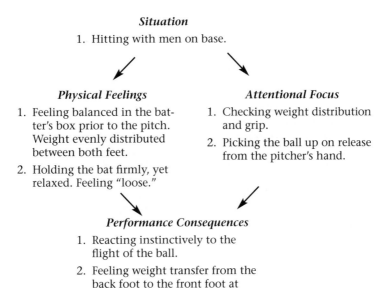

Figure 18-6 Case 1 response patterns after training

list "get a hit." To improve performance, Pat had to set reasonable goals. That meant controlling those things he has the power to control. A good at bat is one where you don't swing at bad pitches and do swing at good pitches. It is an at bat where you make good contact with the ball (e.g., hit a line drive), independent of whether the ball is caught and you are out or not.

Reasonable goal setting also means not expecting every single at bat to be a good one. Instead, Pat's goals involved reducing the frequency of errors due to not watching the ball, and rushing. It also involved learning to recover from errors more quickly (e.g., to avoid having one mistake lead to another).

Introduction of training techniques. In the second classroom session, Pat was introduced to the concept of centering as a means for controlling physiological arousal and for ignoring negative and task-irrelevant stimuli. To understand centering, you actually need to understand three terms: (1) center of mass, (2) centered, and (3) centering.

Draw a vertical line from your head to your toes, dividing your body into two equal parts. Next, draw a horizontal line through your body so

that 50% of your weight is above the line and 50% is below it. Where those two lines intersect (somewhere behind your navel) is your **center of mass.**

You are **centered** within a performance situation when your body weight is distributed about your center of mass in a way that feels comfortable (e.g., your body seems to communicate a physical readiness to perform). Exactly how your center of mass should be distributed varies from situation to situation. When you need to be more aggressive and alert, your center of mass is raised and slightly forward. The more relaxed and immovable you need to be, the lower your center of mass.

Centering is the process used to adjust weight about your center of mass so you feel centered. Alterations in breathing and tension levels in various muscle groups (e.g., breathing from your abdomen instead of up in your chest, and relaxing neck and shoulder muscle tension) are used to make these adjustments.

Pat was instructed to use the centering technique immediately prior to each pitch when he was hitting with men on base. He was to time the end of his centering breath so that it was as close to the time the pitcher began his windup as possible. On the exhale he used two words to create the physical feelings and mental focus he wanted. He used the word *loose* to remind him of the feelings he wanted in his hands as he held the bat. He used the word *focused* to remind him to "pick up the ball on release."

The coach served as a facilitator for Pat in two ways. First, he acted as an external reminder, signaling Pat to use the centering procedure when there were base runners. Second, he reinforced Pat for good at bats rather than hits.[6]

In addition to using the centering procedure in the games, Pat was encouraged to mentally rehearse. It's important to point out a couple of differences between mental rehearsal as used with ACT and mental rehearsal as used with other programs.

First, many mental rehearsal programs involve lengthy relaxation sessions before rehearsal. In ACT the athlete is shown how to use three deep breaths to quickly relax before rehearsal.

Second, many programs emphasize that the rehearsal perspective athletes use should be an *internal* one, as if they were actually engaging in the performance. Programs also emphasize that athletes should use all their senses (seeing, feeling, hearing, etc.) in the rehearsal process. Actual physical movements, however, are not overt in most programs. With ACT, athletes are encouraged to actually initiate and engage in the movements. This often facilitates imagery. In addition, some athletes are encouraged to rehearse with their eyes open. Many find this results in eye movements that also facilitate imagery.

Finally, athletes are encouraged to rehearse as frequently as they can, in the performance situation (when appropriate) and away from the performance situation. Pat, for example, was encouraged to rehearse in the dugout and in the on-deck circle.

Like many programs, rehearsal involved going through the entire situation, including (1) rehearsal of the thoughts and feelings associ-

ated with coming to bat with men on base, (2) rehearsal of tightening up, (3) rehearsal of remembering to center, (4) rehearsal of centering and redirecting attention, and (5) rehearsal of a successful experience.

The last thing accomplished in the second classroom session involves putting the athlete through a series of concentration tests designed to examine the athlete's ability to control arousal and focus attention. These tests include using centering to make it impossible for someone to bend his or her arm, using centering to keep two people from lifting him or her off the ground, and using centering to focus attention in order to break a 1-inch board.

The tests have two purposes. First, they provide athletes with support and motivation. Through the tests they can see the effectiveness of the procedure. Second, since few individuals master all three tests the first time, they demonstrate that centering to control concentration and arousal is a skill that must be continually practiced. Although the technique can be learned in a few minutes, the athletes cannot expect to execute successfully, particularly under pressure, without continued practice.

Third observational session. The final observational session provides the athlete with an opportunity to practice what he or she has learned under supervision. Emphasis is on providing support and encouragement and on making corrections when necessary (e.g., if the athlete is mentally rehearsing at the wrong time). Realistic goals are reemphasized, and, when appropriate, information from TAIS is used to facilitate communication between coach and athlete. For example, scores on TAIS might indicate the athlete is easily overloaded with information (not Pat's case) and that the coach is highly verbal (high BIT and IEX). Under these conditions, I would emphasize that coach and athlete need to find ways of keeping things simple, especially in the identified pressure situation.

Case 2

Steve, a 17-year-old tennis player, was one of the top juniors in the world and had been playing as a professional for over a year. He was

---

[6]We cannot overemphasize the importance of using other athletes or coaches to serve as external reminders to the individual to use centering and to refocus concentration. No matter how highly motivated an athlete, until centering skills are highly developed, high-pressure situations will interfere with the ability to remember to use them.

tested with five other top juniors, all taking part in a three-day ACT program. Steve's TAIS scores are presented in Figure 18-4. There was no identified problem. (All of the players were participating in the program because they had been told it would help them improve their concentration skills.)

The workshop format was similar to the program used with Pat and included the following:

1. Brief introduction and program outline (1 hour)

2. Mini-round-robin tennis tournament to create competitive pressure and provide an initial observation session

3. Classroom session to work through the ICCS, educating players about concentration on the tennis court and its relationship to arousal and performance

4. A second tournament to validate findings from the first tournament and the players' responses in the classroom

5. Second classroom session to develop individualized intervention programs that used centering and rehearsal procedures

6. Third performance session giving players an opportunity to practice their ACT programs during competition

7. Testing of attention control and individual feedback sessions with each player and his coach

TAIS results. Given that Steve was one of the best junior tennis players in the world, some of his scores on TAIS were surprising. Normally I'd expect an athlete performing at Steve's level to score around the 77th percentile on TAIS scales measuring control (CON), self-esteem (SES), and physical competitiveness (P/O). Steve's scores on these scales were quite low (16%, 10%, and 50%, respectively). In addition, Steve indicated he was internally overloaded (OIT) and not very expressive of thoughts and ideas. These scores generated several hypotheses:

1. Because Steve didn't express himself (IEX), had a low level of self-confidence, and was

more introverted than extroverted, I doubted Steve's coach would be aware of his feelings or the fact that he was overloaded.

2. Low scores on control, self-esteem, and physical orientation scales suggested Steve was not the competitor many other athletes were. It was my guess he needed a lot of support from the coach.

3. Relatively high overload scores, low scores on self-esteem and intellectual expressiveness, and a tendency to ruminate and worry (OBS) indicated Steve would not be an effective problem solver on court. He would need structure and direction. Instructions and discussions prior to a match would have to be fairly simple.

4. Finally, one of the things creating stress for athletes low in confidence is positive expectations on the part of others. The more positive the situation for Steve, the more likely he would be to feel pressure.

First observational session. Coming into the training session, both Steve and the coach anticipated that he would dominate the round-robin tournament. As it turned out, Steve seemed to feel more pressure than any of the other players. He would start out well (e.g., win the first three or four games easily) and then begin to tighten up. He responded to the loss of points or games by becoming angry at himself, saying negative things, and then beginning to behave as if he didn't care (e.g., not moving for balls). The coach was surprised by Steve's performance. At the same time, he mentioned Steve had a habit of getting ahead of opponents ranked higher than he was and then losing the match.

Educational sessions. Steve's TAIS profile indicated that he was not very expressive, and indeed, Steve was not particularly verbal during the classroom sessions. He listened and took notes but didn't contribute. He was uncomfortable and defensive in front of the other players, making it necessary to pull him aside in order to draw him out. In one-on-one conversations Steve was able to admit his anger when he wasn't "winning every point" against "people like these" (referring to the other five players). If he wasn't able to gain immediate control, he would "tank." When asked about playing against people better than he was, he indicated that he usually started out well, but as soon as he found himself in a winning position, he would begin playing not to lose rather than to win.

During these courtside talks, Steve was prepared for the material that would be presented in the classroom. He was told, for example, that we would be identifying a problem situation for each athlete and then trying to see exactly what happens physically and mentally. Steve was told that he should think about situations in which he found himself ahead at the end of the first set and then would begin to play conservatively during the second.

Though there were two different problems to be worked on, it was important to focus on one of them. Even if Steve didn't have a tendency to become overloaded, this would be true. The biggest factor keeping athletes from making significant changes is the fact that they don't stay focused on one problem. A good coach would never dream of asking an athlete to work on several different technical or biomechanical issues at the same time. The same should be true of psychological or concentration issues. From a motivational standpoint it was important to let Steve pick the problem he felt was most important. He chose to work on situations where he was ahead of someone that he wasn't really expected to beat. Figure 18-7 presents Steve's analysis of this problem.

Problem Situation

1. Winning the first set against an opponent ranked higher than me.

Physical Feelings

1. Steve was not aware of any physical changes.

Attentional Focus

1. In terms of thoughts, Steve would be saying things to himself like "Hang on," "Don't miss."

2. Mentally, Steve would feel rushed. "I don't seem ready on my opponent's serve."

Performance Consequences

1. Steve was aware of the performance consequences because he and the coach had discussed them several times. He would become less aggressive, playing more from the baseline. He would be conservative on all of his shots, tending to hit back to the center of the court. He would not close as much on volleys and play farther behind the baseline. Often, he would be hitting shots off his back foot. At times he would let balls go, hoping they would be out.

Figure 18-7 **Observation of case 2 problem response patterns**

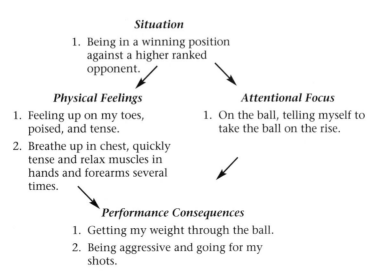

Situation

1. Being in a winning position against a higher ranked opponent.

Physical Feelings

1. Feeling up on my toes, poised, and tense.
2. Breathe up in chest, quickly tense and relax muscles in hands and forearms several times.

Attentional Focus

1. On the ball, telling myself to take the ball on the rise.

Performance Consequences

1. Getting my weight through the ball.
2. Being aggressive and going for my shots.

Figure 18-8 **Case 2 response patterns after training**

Second observational session. Watching Steve play, I sensed that his arousal level dropped too low in pressure situations. The pressure of possible success seemed to result in an emotional shutting down. Steve would begin to appear lazy and preoccupied. There wasn't any evidence of muscle tension (e.g., low ball toss on serve, the inability to generate racket head speed, difficulty bending). Instead, he simply didn't seem to be ready and attending to the task.

Steve was asked to imagine an arousal continuum:

> At one end of the continuum is a triangle standing on its base. The triangle represents the lowest level of arousal and the number you would assign to that arousal level is 1. When you're a 1, you are so relaxed you can't move. At the other end of the continuum is a triangle standing on its point. The number you assign to this triangle is a 10. When your arousal level is a 10, you are so wired your feet are hardly touching the ground. At a 10, your center of mass is too high; you don't feel solid. Where along this continuum are you when you are feeling most confident?

Steve indicated he felt most confident and ready when his arousal level was around a 7 or 8. When

he was ahead, his arousal level seemed to drop to a 4 or 5. On the basis of his observations the centering procedures were modified during the training phase to help him increase his level of arousal every time he was in winning position (e.g., at the start of the second set, when he had break points). Figure 18-8 provides a summary of the things that Steve was supposed to do in specific performance situations.

Because of Steve's tendency to become attentionally overloaded in pressure situations, however, and because he was alone on the tennis court, it was necessary to find ways to remind him to implement the ACT program. To help Steve remember and to encourage him to practice, he was given an intention arousing device (IAD). This is a small countdown timer that clips to a belt or pocket. The IAD can be set to time any interval from one minute to 24 hours. At the end of the time interval, it vibrates, then resets itself and starts timing the interval over again. Steve was instructed to wear the IAD in those matches in which he was playing opponents who were ranked higher than he was. He was also asked to wear it during the last half hour of each training session. This was to get him to focus on controlling concentration and arousal (e.g., to use the centering and attentional refocusing) for a short period during each training session.

In the final feedback session with Steve and his coach, emphasis was placed on (1) having the coach keep instructions relatively simple and structured, (2) getting the coach to draw Steve out to make sure he understood what was expected (e.g., by paraphrasing what the coach had said), and (3) encouraging Steve to do more of his own problem solving and to assume more responsibility in relatively nonstressful situations (such as practice).

Evaluation and Follow-Through

Because ACT programs are situation specific, it's easy to evaluate the effectiveness of training. For Pat, success could be measured by an increase in the frequency of good at bats. For Steve, positive change could be measured in terms of an increased frequency with respect to the number of times he would continue to go for shots, take the ball on the rise, and get his weight through the ball when he was ahead in a match. Or, to put it another way, progress was seen as occurring when there was a reduction in tentative shots.

Steve showed some immediate change, but the improvement was short-lived. Steve's lack of confidence meant that for lasting change to occur he would need considerable ongoing support from the coach. Unfortunately, the coach wasn't able to provide as much support as Steve needed.

Too often, athletes lacking in confidence are looking for a quick fix or a miracle that's going to make them believe in themselves. They seem unable to accept the fact that real confidence comes from real success. You need to be a winner to have the deep-seated conviction that you are a winner. Without that past history you can't expect to be free of doubts. To control those doubts under pressure requires practice. Athletes seeking to improve confidence or other concentration areas must use ACT or some other psychological training programs on a regular basis. They must practice the procedures just as they would practice anything else.

Several readings regarding the research, theory, and practice outlined in this chapter are listed at the end of the chapter. Specific techniques that coaches and sport psychologists can use to help train better concentration in athletes appear in Chapter 19.

The Impact of New Technology on Training

Advances in technology will play an increasing role in sport psychological assessment and training. Computers, the Internet, and other forms of multimedia are improving our ability to communicate, access information, perform complex statistical analyses, and provide novel ways of predicting and improving mental skills training.

Communication and Information Access

The World Wide Web allows effective and inexpensive flow of information around the world. Simple keyword searches on search engines such as http://www.yahoo.com and http://www. google. com can provide individuals with listings of sites containing relevant information. University sport psychology programs, as well as private consulting organizations, are discovering just how useful this mode of information exchange can be.

Web sites such as the Association for the Advancement of Applied Sport Psychology's at http://www.aaasponline.org offer a wide range of resources including articles, convention news, discussions of ethical issues, lists of certified consultants, and links to other sites. Professional and private Web sites such as ours at http://www. enhanced-performance.com, provide opportunities for individuals and groups to promote their ideas, research, and services. Web sites are being used to publish online articles and question-and-answer dialogues, as well as to provide online assessment tools. Students, professors, and practitioners are finding that e-mail has become an efficient and enjoyable way to communicate in an increasingly busy academic environment.

One particularly exciting development associated with the availability of more powerful and portable computers involves our ability to provide an improved range and quality of sport psychological services. Customization of the assessment process to particular athlete populations and competitive situations can be accomplished by collecting and storing various population databases (norm groups). The ability to go into the field to determine key performance factors and to almost instantaneously translate them into quantifiable measures means that we can begin the process of making positive changes that much sooner.

Summary

All training programs recognize that there is some optimal level of arousal and that problems can occur on either side of the optimal level. In practice, however, most programs are designed to deal only with problems that result when arousal is too high. In addition, concepts such as anxiety and arousal seem to be treated globally. It's as if a highly physiologically aroused individual is also anxious, worried, externally and internally distracted, and so forth.

The Importance of Greater Theoretical Specificity

ACT differs from other programs in that the underlying theory is much more explicit. For example, concentration (attention) is behaviorally defined and so are the different types of concentration errors. Individuals can be highly aroused physiologically without being anxious, worried, distracted, or impulsive. The greater differentiation allowed by ACT allows the practitioner to make predictions about the types of situations that are likely to be stressful to a given individual and to make predictions about the specific behaviors that are likely to occur under pressure.

The education phases of ACT teach participants to differentiate the types of concentration required within their particular sports. They are taught to think in terms of the width and direction of attention required. They learn to recognize when to shift from one focus to another. Greater definition allows them to be much more exact when it comes to describing problems and helps them learn more quickly. This behavioral specificity carries over into the assessment process, leading to the development of individualized, situation-specific training programs.

Assessment Differences

With ACT, assessment includes formal testing (use of TAIS and the ICCS) to gather information about those attentional and interpersonal processes that are predictors of performance. Assessment also includes a structured interview that covers past performance history and repeated behavioral observations in actual performance settings.

The analysis of attention into dimensions of width and direction of attentional focus leads identification and classification of the specific types of errors that occur within a performance situation (e.g., internal versus external distractions; rushing and overaggressive responses as opposed to becoming tentative). This analysis also leads to identification (with the assistance of coach and athlete) of the technical, tactical, and motivational cues that should be attended to in the identified performance situation.

Although the literature is generally supportive of a variety of mental skills training programs, some special features of ACT should encourage its use. First, in contrast to most other programs, ACT was designed to be used with healthy, high-functioning individuals. An assumption that underlies the use of ACT is that the individual functions quite well most of the time. Thus, when problems appear to be fairly chronic, or anxiety levels are high even in relatively low stress situations, ACT would be inappropriate.

ACT is especially appropriate when working with individuals for whom the bottom line, or performance outcome, is critical. Most professionals—and in fact most high school and college athletes—are more concerned about winning than they are about feeing good. In fact, for most of these athletes feeling good is tied to success. Because we are working with healthy, high-functioning individuals, the desire to be a winner is not an unreasonable goal. By the same token, healthy individuals are not likely to be so traumatized by failure that they can't confront it and grow. As you might imagine, the philosophy behind ACT, and to a lesser extent the procedures themselves, would appear to be less appropriate when working with younger athletes and recreational athletes.

Whenever possible, ACT programs involve the coach. First, the coach functions as a problem solver, identifying the most task-relevant cues the athlete should be attending to. Next, feedback from TAIS (both coach and athletes) facilitates communication. Finally, the coach is shown how the ACT program should be integrated into both practice and competitive settings. Throughout the training process, everything possible is done to maximize the likelihood that the coach will encourage and support the athlete's use of ACT procedures. Because ACT programs do involve the coach and because the first priority of the training program involves the improvement of performance, it is not the program of choice in clinical situations in which athletes have relatively severe emotional problems.

Finally, ACT would appear to be the program of choice when some type of arousal or concentration intervention is required within an actual performance situation. This may mean training an individual to react to unexpected events (e.g., to recover quickly from a mistake or an accident). It may mean training the individual to overcome a problem that consistently appears within a particular situation (e.g., the tendency to become tentative when leading). Too many programs create (or add to) an artificial mind–body split, which affects the way many athletes and coaches see sport psychology. Programs that are developed and applied outside of the actual practice or performance setting feed the misconception that mental training is somehow separate from physical training. ACT programs are designed for implementation within the performance setting.

Study Questions

1. Describe the eight principles that underlie attention control training.

2. Diagram the figure depicting the four different types of attentional focus, and then briefly describe and give an example of each.

3. What does it mean to play to one's attentional strength?

4. How is choking defined in terms of attentional focus?

5. Describe how to prevent and treat choking.

6. Explain the process versus outcome notion in regard to attentional phenomena.

7. In what types of situations and with what types of individuals might it be appropriate to use an ACT intervention?

8. Identify some specific problem in which ACT might be an appropriate intervention, and then briefly describe the different processes you might go through in implementing an ACT intervention.

9. Describe how advances in technology and communication may enhance the practitioner's ability to assess and train psychological skills and abilities.

References

Carver, C. S., & Scheier, M. F. (1989). A control-process perspective on anxiety. *Anxiety Research, 1,* 17–22.

Ford, S. K., & Summers, J. J. (1992). The factorial validity of the TAIS attentional-style inventory. *Journal of Sport and Exercise Psychology, 14,* 283–297.

Hull, C. L. (1951). *Essentials of behavior.* New Haven, CT: Yale University Press.

Nideffer, R. M. (1976). Test of attentional and inter-personal style. *Journal of Personality and Social Psychology, 34,* 394–404.

Nideffer, R. M. (1989). *Attention control training for sport.* Los Gatos, CA: Enhanced Performance Services.

Nideffer, R. M. (1990). Use of the test of attentional and interpersonal style in sport. *The Sport Psychologist, 4,* 285–300.

Nideffer, R. M. (1995). *Focus for success.* San Diego, CA: Enhanced Performance Systems.

Nideffer, R. M. (2003). Theory of attentional and interpersonal style vs. Test of Attentional and Interpersonal Style (TAIS). http://www.enhanced-performance.com/articles/tais.pdf

Nideffer, R. M., & Sagal, M.S. (2001). *Assessment in sport psychology.* Morgantown, WV: Fitness Information Technology.

Nideffer, R. M., Sagal, M. S., Lowry, M., & Bond, J. (2000). Identifying and developing world class performers. In *The practice of sport and exercise psychology: International perspectives.* Morgantown, WV: Fitness Information Technology.

Van Schyock, S. R., & Grasha, A. F. (1983). Attentional style variations and athletic ability: The advantage of a sport specific test. *Journal of Sport Psychology, 3,* 149–165.

CHAPTER

19

Strategies for Training Concentration

Vietta E. Wilson, *York University*
Erik Peper, *San Francisco State University*
Andrea Schmid, *San Francisco State University*

From the beginning, I realized you have to take one point at a time and lock into a kind of concentration zone. . . . If I concentrated, I could win a lot of points in a row while opponents were thinking about other things.

—*Chris Evert, 1988*

Concentration is essential for performing one's best. The major component of concentration is the ability to focus one's attention on the task at hand and thereby not be disturbed or affected by irrelevant external and internal stimuli. External stimuli may include an audience booing, music, bad officiating calls, and unsportsmanlike behavior from opponents. Internal stimuli include distracting body sensations and thoughts and feelings such as "I'm really tired," "Don't be nervous," "The pain is fierce," "My opponent is bigger and better," and "I blew it!"

Although external and internal stimuli appear to be separate categories, they continually affect each other. Almost every external event will trigger a cognitive and emotional shift in the athlete and a corresponding change in the responses of the body. Similarly, a change in one's thoughts and feelings changes what one attends to and how one attends. Because this interaction occurs all the time, coaches and sport

psychologists must train athletes to cope with these events under pressure situations such as a major competition. Unless this training has occurred and concentration skills have been mastered, performance will almost always suffer. Failure to develop or employ concentration skills has been the downfall of many athletes. According to Cox (2002), few areas in sport psychology are as important to the overall performance as the area of concentration or attention.

For example, a gymnast lost her poise and concentration and performed very poorly after she saw another competitor fall in the same event in which she was about to compete. Similarly, during the fifth game of a critical volleyball match the visiting team completely lost its composure when the home crowd began stamping their feet and clapping in unison whenever the away team was serving the ball, and a closely contested game ended overwhelmingly in favor of the home team. These examples illustrate the potential for distractions in a competitive environment. The ability not to react to or be disturbed by distractions such as these is achieved when athletes learn how to control their thoughts and appropriately focus their attention.

Many other performers, such as surgeons, artists, writers, and musicians, can equally achieve this kind of high level of concentration. For example, Walsh and Spelman (1983) reported that conductor Carlos Kleiber never noticed the earthquake rattling a giant chandelier when he was conducting Strauss's *Der Rosenkavalier* at La Scala. He was concentrating that intently! These examples illustrate how elite performers tend not to be disturbed by external factors, a skill not yet acquired by many developing performers.

Paradoxically, trying to concentrate is also not concentrating. Concentration means focusing, not forcing, one's attention on a task. At times this may be perceived as shielding ourselves from stimuli that might penetrate and disturb our focus of attention. Active shielding by itself would be a distraction. Thus, concentration is the learned skill of passively not reacting to or being distracted by irrelevant stimuli. Concentration also means being totally in the here and now, in the present. When our minds drift into the past or future, we are usually not as effective in our present performance. The ability to concentrate is a skill, and like any other skill it can be developed and improved through practice. We either learn to decrease attention to irrelevant stimuli or increase attention to relevant stimuli. In this process we learn **selective awareness**—the skill of selectively paying attention to relevant stimuli and ignoring irrelevant stimuli. In addition, when we become distracted, previous concentration training enhances our ability to rapidly refocus our attention on the task at hand without continuing to feel or think about the disturbance.

In Chapter 18, Nideffer and Sagal identified the different types of attention or concentration that seem to be required in athletic situations. These types were described along two dimensions: broad versus narrow and internal versus external. The most appropriate type of focus, or attentional style, depends on the sport skill, the demands of the specific situation, and the skill level of the athlete. In concentration training, knowing what to focus on is as critical as knowing how to control one's focus. Athletes may have excellent concentration skills, but if they are focusing on the wrong things, the skills will not be very helpful. Additionally, they must know when to switch from one attentional style to another in a very short time period. Fortunately, the brain is capable of responding in milliseconds (one thousands of a second) and extremely complex skills can be done almost instantaneously if switching attention is practiced correctly a sufficient number of times.

In addition to providing athletes with techniques that help train better control of concentration, coaches and sport psychologists need to assist athletes in identifying different attentional styles and those most appropriate for their specific sport involvement. An excellent technique for helping athletes experience the different attentional styles is an "expanding awareness" exercise developed by Gauron (1984). We present his exercise below but with minor modifications. Athletes can practice this exercise in its entirety or break the various segments into separate exercises. When practicing, athletes should sit or lie in a comfortable position. As you go through the steps yourself, you can see the relevance of the exercise for concentration training.

1. Focus on your breathing for a few breaths. As you exhale (let the air out) release all the muscle tension you can locate in your jaw, shoulders, and hands. Now make the time to exhale longer than the time to inhale. The air comes in, pause, then let the air effortlessly come out for a longer time than it took to get in. Notice how the abdominal region rises as the air comes in, and how it gently falls as the air goes out. It is as if the breathing is being done for you, and you are a mere spectator.

2. Now pay attention to what you hear by taking each separate sound, identifying it, and then mentally labeling it, such as footsteps, voices, or a cough. Next, broaden your focus by simultaneously listening to all the sounds without attempting to identify or

label them. Listen to the blend of sound as you would to music, while verbal thinking drops away. "Let them be. Let them go."

3. Now become aware of bodily sensations such as the feeling of where the chair or floor supports your body. Mentally label each sensation as you notice it. Before moving on to another sensation, let each sensation linger for a moment while you examine it; consider its quality and its source. Next, experience all these sensations simultaneously without identifying or labeling any particular one. This necessitates going into the broadest possible internal body awareness. "Let them be. Let them go."

4. Attend now only to your emotions or thoughts. Let each thought or emotion appear gently, without being forced. Identify the nature of your thoughts and feelings. Remain calm no matter how pleasant or unpleasant they may be. Feel one, then another, then another. Now try to empty yourself of all thoughts and feelings. "Let them be. Let them go." If this is not possible, tune in to only one and hold your attention there.

5. Open your eyes and pick some object across the room directly in front of you. While looking ahead, see as much of the room and the objects in the room as your peripheral vision will allow. Simultaneously observe the entire room and all the items in it. Picture now a broad funnel into which your mind is moving. Centered in the middle of the funnel is the object directly across the room from you. Gradually narrow your focus by narrowing the funnel so the only thing at the small end of the funnel is the object across from you. Expand your focus little by little, widening the funnel until you can see everything in the room. Think of your external focus as a zoom lens; practice zooming in and out, narrowing or broadening according to your wishes.

Besides helping athletes experience different attentional styles and the "parking" of unwanted

thinking, the preceding exercise illustrates what it is like to keep focus in one place and then to change across the internal to external dimension and the specific to panoramic focus. This type of experience provides an excellent foundation for clarifying the most appropriate focus for specific athletic skills and situations.

6. Do a movement very slowly. Slow down a movement by a factor of 10 or slower. Experience the movement as if you were moving through molasses. For example, stand up and very, very slowly walk for 5 feet. Take 5 minutes to cover the distance. First assess your body posture, your head position, where the weight is on your feet, and where your arms are located. Take a minute to absorb the feeling of this pre-movement position. Then feel the shift in weight on your feet, change in knee position, and postural changes as you *think* of moving. As you begin very slowly to make the first move, note how your arms begin to move. As you very slowly move one arm forward, where are your shoulders (down we hope)? Feel where your second arm is and how this arm movement is related to the beginning lift of your leg. Did you subconsciously hold your breath as you began the first movement? As you move, be aware how the pressure changes in your feet as you shift your weight, feel the weight transfer through the hips, notice the changes in pressure on the inside or outside part of the knee as well as the compensation by your spine and head position. Feel the shifting balance as you place weight on the other leg so your leg can swing free. Feel all sensations, such as the movement of the air, the shifting pressures and tensions in the body, and the rustling of your clothing. Let your attention be with the sensations of movement; if the attention drifts, bring it back.

Coaches should not assume that athletes automatically know where and how to look or focus when coaches tell them to pay attention. Tell athletes specifically what to focus on, then create drills so the athletes experience the optimal focus, if one exists. If it does not, coaches should create drills that help athletes find the focus that best suits them. For example, in football most coaches would agree that focusing on the hips, or center, of an opponent that one has to guard is more important when "faking" is involved than watching the head. However, in other sports such as running or swimming where speed out of the blocks is important, the specific attentional instructions are not so clear cut. Namely, some athletes have faster movement times out of the blocks by focusing on the sound of the gun (external focus), others react faster by focusing on some aspect of their movements (internal focus), and others are faster when they "go blank" (no focus). Such athletes need to try all possible attentional strategies while getting accurate feedback (e.g., reaction time and correct takeoff for runners and sprinters) to determine what is the best focus. Before reaching a final decision, athletes must test the attentional strategy at competitions as reactions often differ between practice and stress-filled conditions. In general, for all drills that train what to focus on, once the appropriate focus has been learned in a relatively stress-free environment, the coach or sport psychologist needs to add additional challenges in order for athletes to practice the skill in an overload situation.

The preceding sounds fairly straightforward, but the optimal attentional focus may not be what the coach and sport psychologist think. There is growing evidence that an internal attentional focus may be detrimental to performance because it constrains the motor system by interfering with natural control processes. In contrast, instructing individuals to focus on an external movement effect, as opposed to one's own movements or an external cue not related to the movement effect, led to the best learning and performance, probably by allowing movement to be mediated by automatic control processes. For example, researchers found that when learning to hit a pitch shot in golf, better results occur from focusing on the pendulum-like motion of the club (external movement effect focus) rather than the swing of their arms (internal focus) or the dimples on the ball (external focus not related to the effect). In tennis,

when hitting a backhand stroke cross-court, focusing on the trajectory of the ball and its landing point leads to greater accuracy than focusing on the backswing and the racket-ball contact point. The distance of the external movement effect also appears relevant. Best results occur with an external focus far enough away to be easily distinguishable from body movements, but not so far that the performer cannot relate the effect to the movement technique. See Wulf and Prinz (2001) for a review of this literature. Although the preceding results should prove helpful in determining an optimal attentional focus, we advise against universally applying them until research is conducted across a broader array of sport skills, specific situations, and skill levels.

In addition to the expanding awareness exercises already presented, we offer the following attentional exercises as additional aids in helping athletes attain skill at developing the appropriate focus.

1. **Broad-external drill.** In a team sport, a coach can enhance the experience of staying focused but open to picking up an array of important information by making a game of FREEZE out of many sport situations. During practice the coach can randomly yell FREEZE; players immediately stop, close their eyes, and then the coach asks the players or a selected player where everyone was on the floor or field and where was the ball or puck.

2. **Narrow-external drill.** A coach can place different numbers on a ball or puck and the athletes have to yell out the number as the ball/puck approaches them (e.g., receiving a served volleyball) as one way to enhance narrow focus. Another version is that the coach puts different colors on the balls/pucks and the players are instructed to hit with different techniques or to a different location depending on the color of the ball/puck. Because athletes have a tendency to become too aroused during these drills, we suggest that you remind them to relax the shoulder muscles and keep the knees bent so they are in a position to move quickly.

3. **Narrow-to-broad external drill.** Extend both arms in front of you with both thumbs up and approximately 4 inches apart framing some "main focus" in the distance. See the "main focus" in as much detail as you can. As you maintain that focus, begin to slowly move both extended arms to the side. Continue to see the "main focus" as well as both thumbs and everything in between. Do this in a passive manner. Relax and repeat two or three times. Many athletes report that this drill enables them to see the main focus while also clearly picking up the broader field.

4. **Narrow-internal drill.** Have athletes of similar height pair up and stand facing each other. One athlete will extend his/her dominant arm with the palm facing up and wrist resting on the other athlete's opposite shoulder. The athlete with the extended arm will focus his/her attention on contracting the muscles to make the arm as strong as possible while the other athlete cups his/her hands over the elbow and slowly pulls to bend the arm downward at the elbow. (Note: Palm must be up to prevent elbow injury.) Begin again and this time the athlete with the extended arm focuses on staying relaxed while imagining that his/her arm is like a stiff fire hose spraying energy out of the hand against the wall. Once the athlete with the extended arm signals that he/she is now imagining the energy spraying, the other athlete will begin slowly increasing force on the elbow trying to bend it. In most cases, the arm will not bend as easily as compared to not using the imagery. This exercise demonstrates the power of a focused mind to direct energy and create great strength. It also teaches the important principle that relaxation of the body is necessary in order to direct and maintain the flow of energy in the body.

5. **Broad-internal drill.** Have athletes perform one of their sport skills in a low stress environment. Instruct them to focus on every body sensation they are experiencing while simultaneously attending to what they might be feeling or thinking. Emphasize keeping a passive, open awareness. Repeat the exercise but do it when performing the skill in a high stress environment. Contrasting these two experiences can help athletes identify the subtle changes that sometimes occur in high stress condition and that can lead to poorer performance. It is okay if athletes, either during or after the exercise, shift to a narrow-internal focus in order to zoom in on a particularly relevant sensation.

6. **Intention leads to attention.** Intentions are psychological processes that affect our effort and attention and consequentially affect our performance and physiological responses. Goal setting is one example of intention. We suggest that equally important is the "intent" behind *every* drill, skill, and movement. The intent is what **primes** attention. To illustrate how intention leads to attention do the following: For one minute, scan the room or court and find everything that is green. . . . Now close your eyes and describe how many things in the room are blue. You may not remember any. The same effect occurs in sport. If we are "primed" by our attentional focus to look for something, we are more likely to see it, and see it in more detail. The preceding exercise also illustrates the danger of having the wrong intention and, ergo, attention.

In the remainder of this chapter we provide specific strategies and techniques that coaches and sport psychologists can use to train better concentration control in athletes. These strategies are divided into two sections: strategies to control distracting external factors and strategies to control internal distractions. The categorization is somewhat arbitrary, because external and internal stimuli continually affect each other. Because of this interaction, strategies in one category may be equally effective in correcting apparent lack of concentration in the other category.

External Factors: Strategies to Keep Concentration

Athletes need to be trained not to react (orient) to irrelevant external stimuli. In a competition these stimuli are situational factors that coaches often expect the athletes to have learned to control by trial and error in previous competitive experiences. This "previous experience" strategy for developing concentration control has obvious limitations and false assumptions. Coaches need to realize that athletes can be systematically trained before a competition to be situationally independent. The concept underlying training is based on Pavlovian conditioning. The novelty of the competitive environment, compared to the practice environment, tends to reduce performance. Through training, the novelty of the competitive environment can be minimized. In short, athletes need to experience simulated competition training in which they practice their physical skills while being exposed to all possible external stimuli that can occur during a real competition. This training follows similar procedures used by NASA and U.S. Air Force astronauts and pilots to cope with emergencies. For example, in flight training pilots practice dead stick landings, pulling out of spins, recovering from stalls, and so forth. For athletes, strategies that reduce the novelty effect upon performance by conditioning an appropriate response include dress rehearsal practice, general simulation of competition experiences, and mental rehearsal of concentration training. Also tell the athletes to expect some unusual event to occur that was not planned and be ready with a "coping plan" on how to deal with it.

Strategy 1: Dress Rehearsal

Dress rehearsal is a particularly effective strategy for sports such as gymnastics, diving, synchronized swimming, and figure skating. Dress rehearsal is based on the concept that ease in skillful competitive performance is unconsciously conditioned by the external and internal stimuli that surround athletes during practice. The greater the number of different stimuli present during competition compared to practice, the more likely the performance quality will decrease. Stimuli can include things such as the athletes' uniforms, background illumination, announcers' voices, and music. Ironically, to make a good impression during the competitive event, athletes usually wear uniforms or costumes different from the ones they wear during practice. This means that an unconscious stimulus (the practice uniform) associated with the performance of the skill (response) is not elicited during the competition. Wearing a different or new uniform is a new stimulus and may inhibit performance. This may be one reason some athletes tend to perform better during practice than during competition. Such athletes need to practice their complete competitive routines during practice in the same uniform they wear during actual competition. Dress rehearsal needs to be conducted frequently after athletes have mastered a new skill and are practicing the whole routine for performance. This concept is important for any performer. For example, Mark Braunstein (1991), a violist with the Cleveland Orchestra, reported that he felt somewhat uncomfortable performing in his tuxedo in the orchestra after having practiced in his jeans at home. When he started dress rehearsal at home wearing his tuxedo, he was able to concentrate more, feel more at ease, and improve his playing during concerts.

More commonly, beginning musicians often report that they have difficulty during a recital. Imagine, for example, playing the piano at home wearing sneakers and then playing the piano at a recital wearing high heels. With the unfamiliar high heels, the performer may have problems with the pedals. What is forgotten is that she never practices wearing high heels during rehearsal. When she performs her recital, her body cues are unfamiliar. Hence, practice for a performance needs to be rehearsed in the same way as it will actually be performed.

The reverse of this strategy can also be applied when an athlete is in a slump. In this case the athletes ceremoniously discard their uniforms and thereby symbolically disconnect from the slump associations and now practice with a new uniform. The athlete is metaphorically and ritualistically reborn. A coach can ritualistically change a warm-up or the order of performance.

Athletes and coaches should not lose sight of the fact that these "rituals" are not the underlying reasons for nonperformance. Often it is more productive for the coach and athlete to maintain their traditional patterns with an understanding that performance is typically not linear but, rather, up and down.

Strategy 2: Rehearsal of Simulated Competition Experiences

Simulated competition experiences enable athletes to become so familiar with the stimuli associated with competition that they are no longer distracting. This is the same concept that underlies dress rehearsal practice. Athletes are trained to concentrate and dissociate from the disruptive stimuli. Research by Orlick and Partington (1988) involving a study of Canadian Olympic athletes demonstrates the importance of reducing distractions. They report that the ability to control distractibility was closely associated with superior performance at the Olympic Games.

In gymnastics, athletes might rehearse their routines in practice while a loud tape recording of a previous meet is played over the public address system. This tape would include another gymnast's floor exercise music, audience applause, and so on. A similar example for team sports such as football, basketball, and volleyball would be holding the week's practice before an away game with the public address system loudly playing hostile crowd noises and the opposing team's fight song. Such exercises reduce the effect of meet-induced novelty, which tends to interfere with performance, and make the competitive experience seem just like practice workouts. We assume that a good example of not preparing for an extremely angry crowd was Zola Budd's slipping to a seventh-place finish after a strong lead during the 3000-meter finals in the 1984 Olympics. The thunderous booing of the hostile crowd must have demoralized her after the accident with Mary Decker from the United States.

When using this strategy, coaches and sport psychologists should overtrain athletes by including simulated practice of the worst possible scenario, such as having a basketball player ready to take a free throw shot and then having to wait the length of a time-out before shooting. "Wet ball" drills in football are based on the same concept. Many psychologically astute coaches turn the sprinklers on before practice and then soak the ball between plays when preparing for a football game during which rain is likely. As stated earlier, a similar approach is essential in training pilots and astronauts. They spend a significant amount of time practicing in very realistic flight simulators. In these simulators they are presented with numerous flight and equipment problems. The simulation trains pilots to maintain their concentration and appropriate responses in the face of disruptions or emergencies. Until equivalent simulators are available for sport, wise coaches can simulate many competition situations by judiciously "springing" novelty situations in practice. Athletes generally look forward to these challenges as long as they provide an opportunity for learning and are not used to punish or embarrass the athletes. Just as learning a physical skill takes time, learning the mental control of concentrating on the task while not reacting to external stimuli takes many hours of training.

Strategy 3: Mental Rehearsal

Most performers report that **visualization (mental rehearsal)** is an important ingredient in their success. Many discover this process serendipitously. A systematic training program was organized by Suinn (1980), who developed visual-motor behavioral rehearsal (VMBR) for Olympic biathlon, alpine, and Nordic skiers. He reported impressive perceived results. Scientific findings confirm that skilled performers using mental rehearsal programs such as VMBR perform better than control groups (see Chapter 16).

Using mental rehearsal to practice concentration and to learn not to react to purposely induced external distractions is another useful strategy for athletes. Obviously, athletes can only benefit from this strategy after they have learned relaxation and imagery skills. Such a strategy might involve having athletes form pairs in which one member of the pair relaxes and mentally rehearses his sport while the other member attempts to distract the performer from the mental rehearsal. The distraction can be anything except touching. After this type of mental rehearsal, the coach or sport psychologist might have the athlete rate his achieved concentration on a 0–6 scale. Thereafter the athletes reverse roles. In a study involving members of the U.S. national rhythmic gymnastic team (Schmid & Peper, 1982), the gymnasts practiced this pair distraction exercise daily for 5 days. On the first and fifth days they were asked to rate their concentration while mentally rehearsing their routine with a partner who attempted to distract them. They reported a significant increase in their concentration from the first day to the fifth day. Through this type of exercise, athletes learn how to detach and dissociate themselves from external distractions and resulting unwanted internal reactions (stimuli) while focusing on the task of mentally rehearsing their sport. Unestahl (1983), in his Basic Mental Training program, uses dissociation and detachment exercises. He teaches athletes to screen out distractions either by building a mental wall around themselves, a wall that cannot be penetrated, or by accepting the distraction but not judging it. Let it pass by and continue on its way.

Just as coaches or sport psychologists can train athletes to use mental rehearsal to attain concentration, they can also train athletes to use mental rehearsal to *regain* concentration. For example, as soon as athletes realize their concentration has been disrupted by external factors such as crowd noises, they should stop themselves, take a deep breath to relax, and then bring their attention back by mentally rehearsing what they should be doing next. The utility of attentional control training has been demonstrated in a study by Ziegler (1994) with four collegiate soccer players. A series of attentional shift drills were used, and all players were able to significantly improve their attentional focus.

These strategies can all be employed during regular physical practice sessions. Athletes are responsive to them and especially enjoy being involved in generating the distracting stimuli.

Internal Factors: Strategies to Stay Centered

The coach or sport psychologist must train the athlete's mind to exert control, because concentration inhibits distraction. Lapses in concentration invite fear and self-doubt, and the resulting worry and anxiety lead to further increases in lack of concentration, thus creating a vicious cycle that ultimately leads to failure. The effect of internal factors becomes more pronounced in high-pressure situations. As an analogy, consider what would happen if someone were to ask you to walk on a board 4 inches wide, 15 feet long, and 9 inches above the ground (like a practice beam in gymnastics). You would be able to do this without hesitation just by concentrating on the task of walking across the board. However, if the board were 60 feet off the ground, you might become paralyzed by the fear of falling. Such fear inhibits performance and increases the possibility of falling. Ironically, there is no difference in the physical skill required. The difference is in your psychological response to the perceived stressful event, and as a result, your attention is on trying not to fall instead of on walking across the beam. In addition, if you had previously fallen off a beam, then every time you thought about it or related the experience to someone, you might have unknowingly rehearsed all of the cognitive and motor events that led to failure.

Similar psychological processes occur during competition. For example, a field-goal kicker who normally hits his short kicks during practice may react quite differently during competition when he attempts to kick a short field goal and there are only a few seconds left on the clock and his team is behind by 2 points. He is even more likely to fear "blowing it" if he has recently missed a kick in similar circumstances. One professional football player, while kicking under such a high-pressure situation, described the goal posts as looking as though they had narrowed to less than a foot apart. It does not take much insight to figure out what happened to his kick!

One way to improve concentration is to reduce self-doubts and competitive anxiety and their resulting physical manifestations (i.e., increased arousal). (Arousal and cognitive control techniques are discussed in Chapters 15 and 17.) Unless an athlete has control over internal dialogue, his or her focus of attention will not be congruent with good performance, let alone peak performance. In addition to the specific arousal and cognition techniques found in preceding chapters, in our work with performers we have found the following strategies helpful in controlling internal dialogue and facilitating concentration and performance.

Strategy 1: Attentional Cues and Triggers

Athletes can use verbal and kinesthetic cues to focus their concentration and to retrigger concentration once it has been lost. These cues can help athletes center their attention on the most appropriate focus within the task at hand and thus help them to avoid distracting thoughts and feelings (Schmid, 1982). Similar observations have been confirmed by Nideffer (1981, 1987), who reported case histories in which athletes benefited from centering by using task-relevant cues.

Generally, it is best to find cues that focus on positives rather than negatives, the present (current or upcoming moment) rather than the past or future, and the process (proper form or execution) rather than the score or external movement effect. During a television interview on September 1, 1984, Greg Louganis, the Olympic diving champion, gave some excellent examples of effective attentional cues. He said, "I picture my dive as the judge will see it, then as I see it." In his forward three-and-one-half somersault dive, he uses the following word cues: "Relax, see the platform, spot the water, spot the water, spot the water, kick out, spot the water again." This helps him to concentrate and focus on the dive. Consequently, with his power to concentrate, he obtains a maximum result with a minimum of apparent effort. Coaches and sport psychologists should work with athletes to help them establish effective verbal and kinesthetic cues for triggering concentration. Such cues must be individualized, however. What is effective for one athlete may not be effective for another. Similarly, some athletes perform best with frequent cues and others with very few cues.

Strategy 2: TIC-TOC

Another effective strategy for switching attention from non-productive to productive thoughts, feelings, or actions is an exercise that uses the words TIC and TOC to trigger the response (Burns, 1993). Simply stated, any self-statement, thought, or idea that is irrelevant or off target to what you need to be doing right now is a TIC, and should be immediately recognized. Then you need to switch to a task relevant focus (one that focuses upon either the positive outcome or actions needed to move toward that outcome) or a TOC. In both sport and nonsport situations, become aware of TICs and immediately make them TOCs.

Strategy 3: Turning Failure into Success

Many athletes report that they commonly lose concentration after making a mistake. One way to deal with this problem is to train athletes to turn failure into success. This is a cognitive habit by which athletes mentally rehearse successful performance after a failure. As soon as possible after making an error (learning is only possible when errors occur), athletes should mentally rehearse executing the same skill perfectly rather than dwelling on the error. One component of successful performance is to avoid self-judgment or blaming others, which disrupts concentration, and to refocus on the performance. The power of not focusing on the failure and just taking the challenge is illustrated by Lasse Viren during the 1972 Munich Olympic Games (Benagh, 1976). He won the 10,000-meter race and broke the world record despite the fact that he fell flat on his face as another runner ran over him. Even though he was down for 3 full seconds, he got up, composed himself, ran, and came in first. Many others would have given up because they would have assumed that they would be defeated. When an error occurs, an accident happens, remember to use the TIC-TOC method. Move quickly from task irrelevant to what you need to be doing right now to get back on track for a successful outcome—TIC-TOC.

More harmful than making a performance error is ruminating on the failed event. Each time athletes recite (verbally or mentally) a previous failure, they condition their mind to make the failure the preferred motor pattern. The verbal retelling to others or the chronic rumination on why one made a mistake is a type of global visual-motor behavior rehearsal in which one is training the mind to perform the same failure behavior again. Instead of reciting the error, athletes might ask: "What was the problem?" "How could I have performed differently in the same situation?" or "What other skills do I need?" Then athletes can mentally rehearse the previous conditions leading to the error but now change their behavior so that they imagine themselves performing the skill perfectly.

The coach or sport psychologist can also encourage athletes to do the same thing after an injury. When concerned friends and others ask what happened, athletes should avoid recounting the accident and instead focus on describing a perfect performance the next time. For example, after a 16-year-old downhill skier ran off the course and was seriously injured, her skiing improved remarkably when she stopped telling other people how she got injured. Whenever people asked her what happened, she described how she would now ski the race successfully. (When she felt herself going too fast, she would sink down into her skis and continue to breathe while setting the edges as she was going through a gate.) As she talked, she unconsciously rehearsed how to react successfully to the conditions under which she had previously fallen (Peper & Holt, 1993).

Strategy 4 : Use of Biofeedback

At one time it was thought that physiological systems (heart rate, sweat response, blood flow, temperature, single motor units, etc.) were under subconscious control and not amenable to awareness or conscious control. Now we know that is not true as individuals can be trained to control their physiology through biofeedback. Biofeedback is the use of instruments to measure physiological systems and feed that information back to the athlete either in a visual display or through changes in sound (for more details go to the Web sites http://www.aapb.org or http://www.bfe.org).

The coach or sport psychologist can use biofeedback instruments to monitor and train athletes to improve their arousal control, thought control, and concentration. For example, Peper and Schmid (1983–1984) used electrodermal feedback in conjunction with other mental training skills to (1) illustrate how thoughts affect the body and performance, (2) monitor physiological arousal, (3) identify stressful components of the athletic performance during imagery rehearsal, and (4) facilitate concentration training. An electrodermal activity (EDA) feedback unit measures and feeds back changes in skin conductance—the amount of perspiration on the palmar surface of the hand. An increase in autonomic arousal usually results in an increase in skin conductance. An EDA unit reflects this change by increasing the pitch of the sound when conductivity and arousal increase, and decreasing the pitch when conductivity and arousal decrease. The latency of the EDA response is about 2 seconds. These devices are available from biofeedback companies such as Thought Technology, Ltd. Following are four exercises that show how electrodermal biofeedback can be used to train each of the aforementioned purposes.

Exercise A: Thoughts affect body. EDA feedback can be used to show that thoughts and feelings affect our performance. That is, each thought has a corresponding physiological effect—a concept that many athletes are unaware of. We often illustrate this concept in a group meeting in which one of the athletes is attached to a portable EDA feedback device. After the device is turned on, we ask the athlete to think of an anxiety-provoking event or we whisper something to him or her such as "You just blew your routine." Each time the person thinks of an embarrassing or anxiety-provoking situation, such as imagining a difficult move, the pitch of the sound increases. After demonstrating the EDA feedback device, we ask athletes to use it to experience how their thoughts and feelings affect their physiological state. This helps them to identify and stop disturbing thoughts and feelings, as well as to restructure their self-talk from negative to positive.

Exercise B: Regulating arousal level. As Nideffer and Sagal indicated in the previous chapter, having optimal activation is critical to enabling athletes to obtain and maintain an appropriate focus. Thus athletes need skill at both relaxing and energizing (see exercises presented in Chapter 15) depending upon whether their monitoring of activation states indicates under or over arousal. EDA instrumentation can be used to illustrate the individual effects of the different types of relaxation and activation exercises. Athletes often are amazed at how quickly and dramatically their sweat response goes down with relaxation and up with energizing exercises. Practicing these arousal regulation exercises, combined with EDA feedback, gives athletes the skill to raise or lower arousal into the ideal performance state.

Exercise C: Facilitating mental rehearsal. Athletes can use small portable EDA feedback units while they mentally rehearse their routines. These small feedback units fit in the palm of the hand, and the athletes receive auditory feedback. With the help of the feedback, athletes can more rapidly identify stressful, anxiety-provoking events or cues during imagery rehearsal of their routine or athletic event. In the case of the rhythmic gymnasts, some of their subjective experiences associated with the EDA feedback occurred during a hoop routine: "On a toss or catch that was risky, just when I was about to do a toss that I frequently miss, right before a toss, when I thought, 'You've got to make it!' so I tensed up just before the routine began." Most gymnasts who used EDA feedback reported it was helpful in learning to reduce their arousal during mental rehearsal. In fact, many of the gymnasts reported that within 2 weeks they had learned to inhibit the EDA feedback tone during imagery rehearsal.

Exercise D: Enhancing concentration training. EDA feedback can be used to facilitate concentration learning in an enjoyable dyadic practice similar to the one described earlier under the mental rehearsal strategy. In this practice athletes again form pairs, with one member of each pair mentally practicing some competitive situation while receiving EDA feedback. Simultaneously, the other partner attempts to distract and arouse him/her so that there will be a change in the EDA feedback signal. After 2 to 5 minutes of practice, the athletes reverse roles. Athletes enjoy this competitive practice and at the same time learn awareness of their own internal cues of anxiety, as well as strategies to control their EDA response through passive attention and relaxed breathing. Through this competitive practice, they learn the ability to detach and dissociate from external distractions and unwanted internal stimuli while focusing on the task.

It is important to note that EDA is a useful biofeedback tool with many athletes but not all athletes respond in this physiological way nor is the sweat response equally important for all sports. Other readily available biofeedback devices can be equally useful. Electromyography (sEMG) or muscle monitoring assists in helping athletes gain awareness and control of the necessary muscle tension in specific muscles. This is crucial to all sports. For example, in activities such as running or swimming where unnecessary and unnoticed tension in the shoulders slows down the athlete, shoulder sEMG biofeedback can be used to help athletes identify unnecessary tension and when they are relaxing the muscles. Heart rate biofeedback can assist the athlete in locating the heart rate zone wherein they are working at the maximum level but without risking hitting the wall, for example, marathon runners. Heart rate variability (HRV) biofeedback can also help athletes in shooting sports (e.g., pistol, archery) focus on the variability of their heart beat with the goal of slowing it down and learning to shoot between heart beats, thereby increasing their accuracy. Temperature biofeedback can be used to assess autonomic changes. As individuals become more aroused or stressed, the temperature in the hands and feet generally becomes lower. Although not as sensitive as a sweat response for autonomic arousal, it is less expensive and available at electronic stores. Most people can rapidly learn to increase their temperature 5–6 degrees Fahrenheit and when they see the temperature change, they know that they have more control (Peper & Gibney, 2003). Paradoxically, passive attention usually works much quicker than active striving to increase peripheral hand temperature. When an athlete consistently "tries too hard" temperature biofeedback can be used to learn to "try easier."

Strategy 5: Increasing Focusing and Refocusing Skills

Focus training teaches performers to gently hold their attention on a predetermined task and, if the attention wanders, to gently bring the attention back. As Landers, Boutcher, and Wang (1986) state, failure to develop refocusing skills has been the downfall of many athletes. The key to avoiding these pitfalls is to perform in the present; that is, focus awareness in the "now" rather than the past or future. One must learn how to pass quickly from negative thoughts to a constructive performance focus. The dynamics of this strategy are similar to those of meditative practices, such as Raja yoga meditation in which a person focuses on a mantra and each time the attention wanders from the mantra the person gently guides the attention back to it. Using a similar approach, the following exercises can help performers improve their focusing skills.

Exercise A: Mindfulness. Sit quietly, close your eyes, and see how long you can focus on a single thought. For many activities this is very important. Athletes can begin to enhance locking in their concentration by practicing focusing in the sport location. Some tennis players practice "locking in" by focusing only on their strings prior to a serve and then transfer this narrow focus to what they need to be doing in the next moment. For serve reception, some tennis players focus on the ball coming off the racket. For serving, they might focus on what is necessary for them to execute their ideal serve (cue word, feeling of power, looking at spot where ball is to go).

Exercise B: One pointing. Look at an action photo or an object from your sport. For example, if your sport is baseball, softball, or tennis, you might focus on the ball. If distracting thoughts enter your mind, bring your attention back to the ball. Don't shut out the thoughts or

continue to explore the disruptive thoughts or feelings. Just gently bring your attention back to the ball. This also can be done with watching a second hand on a watch tick each second off for one minute. How many times did you lose your concentration? What happens if you see the hand move and say tick at the same time for one minute? Some people with busy brains need to occupy both sides of the brain with visual and verbal cues.

Have athletes practice these two exercises daily for 5 minutes and chart their progress. Get them to time how long they can focus their attention on a single thought or on the picture. It is our experience that these home practices help athletes eliminate their concentration-breaking thoughts. Another similar exercise to practice focus training is Benson's relaxation response described in Chapter 15.

Exercise C: Grid exercise. Another training exercise for practicing focusing ability is the grid exercise (Harris & Harris, 1984). This exercise necessitates having a 10-by-10 block grid with each block containing a two-digit number ranging from 00 to 99. Figure 19-1 shows a sample grid. The purpose of this exercise is to scan the grid and within a given time (usually one minute) find and put a slash through as many numbers as possible in numerical sequence starting with number 00. The same form can be used several times by starting with a number just higher than the highest number reached on the first attempt. New grids can be developed easily by simply relocating the numbers. According to Harris and Harris, athletes who have the ability to concentrate, scan, and store relevant cues will usually score in the upper 20s and into the 30s during a 1-minute timed trial. Those who cannot disregard everything except the task at hand do poorly.

Try doing the grid immediately after you have done some relaxation exercises such as slowing your breathing or releasing your muscle tension. Then repeat the exercise after you have done a series of quick, sharp movements that elevate your heart rate (shadow box or Simon says, for example). Nideffer and Sagal predict

GRID CONCENTRATION EXERCISE

Directions:
Beginning with 00, put a slash through each number in the proper sequence.

84	27	51	78	59	52	13	85	61	55
28	60	92	04	97	90	31	57	29	33
32	96	65	39	80	77	49	86	18	70
76	87	71	95	98	81	01	46	88	00
48	82	89	47	35	17	10	42	62	34
44	67	93	11	07	43	72	94	69	56
53	79	05	22	54	74	58	14	91	02
06	68	99	75	26	15	41	66	20	40
50	09	64	08	38	30	36	45	83	24
03	73	21	23	16	37	25	19	12	63

Comments:

Figure 19-1 **Sample grid exercise form for training and assessing the ability to concentrate**

that most people would narrow with the arousal exercises and therefore perform better. Our experience with hundreds of students concurs with this, but it is not true for all people. Each athlete needs to find the optimum arousal level for all of the various situations in her or his sport.

After initial practice, you can increase the difficulty of the exercise by creating distractions such as loud noises and verbal harassment by a partner to see if the performer can block out everything and concentrate fully on the grid. Besides training focusing skills, Harris and Harris report that this exercise was used extensively in Eastern Bloc countries as a precompetition screening device for current level of concentration ability. Athletes are selected for competition on the basis of their performance.

Exercise D: Video games. There are many new video games that increase reaction speed, hand–eye coordination, and concentration. For example, Michele Mitchell, the 1984 and 1988 Olympic silver medalist in women's platform diving, attributed her consistent performance to good concentration enhanced by playing computer video games. As she said: "It helped me to be in the present." The advantage of the video games is that momentary lapses in concentration will result in immediate feedback—you *lose*. Because most games only involve hand movements, it is helpful if you can find a game with a slower speed. You then play the game but must first move both feet before you hit the keyboard with your hands. Some newer Gameboys have foot controls that would be better for sports in which total body movement is important. The more sport specific movement you can make, the more likely it will transfer to your sport setting. With boxers, for example, we have incorporated a specific right or left punch or a right or left block reaction time board that was attached to a brief time display (1/100 or 1/1000 of a second) of another boxer throwing a punch. Within a few weeks of practice, the lower-skilled boxers were almost as fast and accurate at seeing a punch as the Olympic-level boxers.

Strategy 6: Developing Performing Protocols

Many athletes develop the ability to tune in to their ideal performance state by associating concentration with certain performance rituals. Preset behavioral protocols should be established during warm-ups, practice, and the actual competition. These protocols should be designed to cue both body and mind. It will take time to help each athlete identify his or her own ideal preperformance concentration routine. Once a definite routine is developed, it should be practiced consistently. Over time these protocols will serve automatically to trigger the focused concentration athletes need for good performance. This is illustrated by the behavior of Eberhard Gienger, the 1974 world champion on the horizontal bar.

> To compete Gienger stood up, put on his suspenders, adjusted his gymnastic pants and slippers, chalked up, put on his hand guards, placed his warm-up jacket on his shoulders, turned his back to the competition apparatus, and concentrated on the upcoming routine with his eyes closed. . . . This ritual did not vary from event to event, nor from preliminaries to finals. (Salmela, 1976)

Systematic precompetitive behaviors enhance performance by getting the athlete ready for the task at hand. Working with two synchronized swimmers for the 1988 Olympic competition, we initially observed that their precompetition protocol was not well thought out. For example, when one swimmer put on her nose clip, it irritated the other and triggered thoughts about non–task-related matters. After helping them analyze, plan, and carry out with minute detail their precompetition protocol, we observed that the swimmers had increased their focus on the task at hand. Similarly, Boutcher and Crews (1987) demonstrated that the use of a preshot concentration routine can improve putting performance of female golfers.

Finally, if attention lapses, performers can use their personal idiosyncratic protocols to refocus their attention. The small procedural steps are the triggers for concentration on the task. A protocol for unexpected events also should be practiced.

Athletes need to consider what is the process of thinking if something totally unexpected occurs.

New Technologies for Assessment and Training

Our current understanding of the influence of attention and concentration on performance depends largely on actual behavioral observations, interview data, case studies, and self-report of performers. Ways to directly measure the brain activity, using electroencephalography (EEG), may now be used to determine how we attend to information from the outside display and how we attend or process information internally (for a review, see Wilson & Gunkleman, 2000).

Early work on the relationship between EEG and sport suggested that volleyball players who had good concentration during the stress of competition, as assessed by the coaches, had different EEG profiles than those who were not as able to concentrate (Wilson, Ainsworth, & Bird, 1984). Rossi and Zani (1991) noted that EEG taken during actual performance indicated different brain functioning, depending on the athlete's sport activity. Fontani, Voglino, and Girolami (1996) noted EEG differences in sports thought to represent different attentional demands (broad focus for basketball had a different EEG pattern than that for a narrow focus in swimming). Other researchers (Salazar et al., 1990; Crews & Landers, 1993) found EEG differences in several sports and attributed these differences to either arousal or attentional demands. Konttinen and Lyytinen (1993) used EEG and were able to distinguish between arousal demands and attention demands in shooting sports; and attributed the differences to extensive practice in the different skill requirements. They also noted that task, strategy, skill, and experience all affected the brain processing. This degree of complexity of the brain suggests that EEG training will have to be individualized!

Researchers (Kerick, Iso-Ahola, & Hatfield, 2000; Loze, Collins, & Holmes, 2001) have continued to use EEG with shooters to determine what the person was doing when performing. Their results suggest less cognitive brain activity for more highly skilled shooters; that is, the shooter thinks less. Additionally, there is less thinking during good versus poor shots. This confirms our clinical experience, "once skilled, don't think, just do!"

Sterman (1995) reports EEG changes were related to flight performance of pilots in laboratory and actual flying and was able to distinguish when pilots take "micro-breaks" in the heat of the fighting action, probably in order to regenerate. It is natural for someone to take a micro-break, but these are accomplished in a fraction of a second and the pilot (or athlete) knows when to take the break. One does not pay continuous attention for a 2-hour competition or even 5 minutes. We move in and out rapidly. Knowing when to not attend is as important as when and what to attend to in order to avoid fatigue.

In a noteworthy group research study (Landers et al., 1991), archers were trained to maintain a less busy mind (more alpha or slow wave activity). They learned the brain state and improved their actual archery scores! Elite musicians also showed that the learned changes from EEG training were accompanied by improvements in the quality of their music performance (Egner & Gruzelier, 2003). Interestingly, this improvement went above and beyond noted improvement from the typical imagery/relaxation/ cognition training that also was provided!

Although recent reports (Sime, 2004; Strack, 2004; Wilson & Thompson, 2003) encourage training both individual and team sport athletes with EEG, much more research needs to be conducted to determine the effects on actual competitive performance. Additionally, we still need to determine who should be trained, what areas of the brain to train, and how many sessions of training it takes before learning is established.

The cost of units, technical sophistication, and proven programs are rapidly advancing and we are optimistic that "attention trainers" will be take-home items for athletes in the near future just as heart rate monitors are now. We do caution that it is a complex skill that requires sophisticated equipment and a knowledgeable EEG trainer. Unwanted side effects, such as irritation, depression, or anger, have been found when individuals are not properly assessed and trained. Buyer Beware!

Summary

In summary, concentration is the ability to direct one's full attention to appropriate cues in the present task instead of being controlled by irrelevant external or internal stimuli. Most top athletes have developed their own mental strategies for doing this. These strategies are often perceived as a component of natural athletic ability. In fact, they are not totally innate; they are skills that athletes acquire through regular practice of attention control training. However, because of genetic makeup, early life experiences, and different opportunities of training the mind, every athlete will have individual attentional strengths and weaknesses, and the ability and time necessary to learn different attentional styles will vary among athletes. The consistent control over one's attentional focus before and during competition can be improved through practice, just as any difficult physical skill is learned.

The ability to control thoughts, arousal, and attentional focus appears to be the common denominator in the concentration of winning competitors. For example, an Olympic gold medal winner reported that her goal was to perform to the best of her ability. Specifically, she reported: "I went out to perform and not worry about my scores. In fact, it helped me more not to know my scores at all. That way I didn't have anything to worry about. . . . I didn't care what anyone else was doing and I didn't want to know at all" (Botkin, 1984). She won by 0.050 of a point because she did not focus on winning. She was able to hold on to the present and to focus on her routine, whereas the girl was who leading the competition all three days lost her composure and made major faults in her last routine.

Many other athletes also report that peak performances occurred when they eliminated all thoughts about winning and focused instead on the process—the task at hand. This type of mental control allows athletes to be in the present. They do not ruminate. To achieve consistency in performance, athletes need to develop and practice their concentration skills in practice sessions and then practice them in competitive settings. For some, the performance becomes so automatic they report becoming "brain dead" and do not remember "just doing"! Although automatic responses are desirable, they are not always achievable, but with systematic mental preparation it is more likely to occur. To achieve peak performance more consistently, a mental preparedness program should follow these steps to better concentration.

Mental Preparation Steps to Better Concentration

1. Learn personal strategies to attain optimal arousal for performance.
2. Learn to practice with a positive attitude and specified intention.
3. Learn which attentional focus is best for you, how to switch focus, and when to "park" thoughts.
4. Learn and practice the attentional strategies that are necessary for skill and strategies in your particular sport.
5. Associate concentration with certain triggers such as cue words or feelings. Practice finding TICs and making them TOCs.
6. Focus on the positive behaviors or outcomes.
7. Develop protocols or rituals to trigger concentration when you "lose it."

Study Questions

1. Describe the potential interaction between external and internal stimuli in distracting a performer.

2. Describe a technique for helping athletes experience and distinguish among Nideffer's four attentional styles.

3. Briefly describe and give one example each of how dress rehearsal, rehearsal of simulated competition, and mental rehearsal can be effective strategies to keep concentration.

4. How can attentional cues and triggers be used to either initially focus or retrigger concentration?

5. Provide an example of how the technique of "turning failure into success" might be used and a brief description of why the strategy might be effective.

6. Describe the three techniques that use electrodermal feedback to stay centered.

7. Briefly describe the four exercises under the section "Increasing Focusing and Refocusing Skills."

8. Provide two examples of when and how developing performing protocols might be used to improve concentration.

References

Benagh, J. (1976). *Incredible Olympic feats*. New York: McGraw-Hill.

Bernardi, L., Sleight, P., Bandinelli, G., Cencetti, S., Fattorini, L., Wdowczyc-Szulc, J., & Lagi, A. (2001). Effect of rosary prayer and yoga mantras on autonomic cardiovascular rhythms: Comparative study. *British Medical Journal, 323,* 1446–1449.

Botkin, M. (1984). Olympic gold makes topping oh so sweet. In *The 1984 Four Continents Rhythmic Sportive Gymnastics Championships Program* (pp. 4–5). Indianapolis, IN: USGF.

Boutcher, S. H., & Crews, D. J. (1987). The effect of a preshot attentional routine on a well-learned skill. *International Journal of Sport Psychology, 18,* 30–39.

Braunstein, M. (1991, October 21). *Interested in achieving peak performance?* Lecture/demonstration at San Francisco State University, San Francisco.

Burns, D. (1993). *Ten days to self esteem*. New York: William Morrow.

Cox, R. H. (2002). *Sport psychology: Concepts and applications*. Dubuque, IA: Brown.

Crews, D. J., & Landers, D. M. (1993). Electroencephalographic measures of attentional patterns prior to the golf putt. *Medicine and Science in Sports and Exercise, 25,* 116–126.

Egner, T., & Gruzelier, J. H. (2003). Ecological validity of neurofeedback: Modulation of slow wave EEG enhances musical performance. *Neuroreport, 14,* 1221–1224.

Evert, C. (1988). Concentrated effort. *World Tennis, 36*(3), 29–30.

Fontani, G., Voglino, N., & Girolami, L., (1996). EEG frequency variations during a test of attention in athletes. *International Journal of Sport Psychology, 17,* 68–78.

Gauron, E. F. (1984). *Mental training for peak performance.* Lansing, NY: Sport Science Associates.

Harris, D. V., & Harris. B. L. (1984). *The athlete's guide to sports psychology: Mental skills for physical people.* New York: Leisure Press.

Kerick, S., Iso-Ahola, S., & Hatfield, B. (2000). Psychological momentum in target shooting: Cortical, cognitive-affective and behavioral responses. *Journal of Sport and Exercise Psychology, 22,* 1–20.

Konttinen, N., & Lyytinen, H. (1993). Brain slow waves preceding time-locked visuomotor performance. *Journal of Sports Sciences, 11,* 257–266.

Landers, D. M., Boutcher, S. H., & Wang, M. Q. (1986). A psychological study of archery performance. *Research Quarterly for Exercise and Sport, 57,* 236–244.

Landers, D. M., Petruzzello, S. J., Salazar, W., Crews, D. L., Kubitz, K. A., Gannon, T. L., Han, M. (1991). The influence of electrocortical biofeedback on performance in pre-elite archers. *Medicine and Science in Sports and Exercise, 23,* 123–129.

Loze, G., Collins, D., & Holmes, P. (2001). Pre-shot EEG alpha-power reactivity during expert air-pistol shooting: A comparison of best and worst shots. *Journal of Sport Sciences, 19,* 727–733.

Nideffer, R. M. (1981). *The ethics and practice of applied sport psychology.* Ithaca, NY: Mouvement Publications.

Nideffer, R. M. (1987). Psychological preparation of the highly competitive athlete. *The Physician and Sports Medicine, 15*(10), 85–92.

Orlick, T., & Partington, J. (1988). Mental links to excellence. *The Sport Psychologist, 2,* 105–130.

Peper, E., & Gibney, K. H. (2003). A teaching strategy for successful hand warming. *Somatics, XIV*(1), 26–30.

Peper, E., & Holt, C. F. (1993). *Creating wholeness: A self-healing workbook using dynamic relaxation, images, and thoughts.* New York: Plenum.

Peper, E., & Schmid, A. B. (1983–1984). The use of electrodermal biofeedback for peak performance training. *Somatics, 4*(3), 16–18.

Peper, E., & Williams, E. A. (1981). *From the inside out: A self-teaching and laboratory manual for biofeedback.* New York: Plenum.

Rossi, B., & Zani, A. (1991). Timing of movement-related decision processes in clay-pigeon shooters as assessed by event-related brain potential and reaction times. *International Journal of Sport Psychology, 22,* 128–139.

Salazar, W., Landers, D. M., Petruzellow, S. J., Han, M., Crews, D. L., & Kubitz, K. A. (1990). Hemispheric asymmetry, cardiac response and performance in elite archers. *Research Quarterly for Exercise and Sport, 61,* 351–359.

Salmela, J. H. (1976). *Competitive behaviors of Olympic gymnasts.* Springfield, IL: Thomas.

Schmid, A. B. (1982). Coach's reaction to Dr. A. B. Frederick's coaching strategies based upon tension research. In L. D. Zaichkowsky & W. E. Sime (Eds.), *Stress management for sport* (pp. 95–100). Reston, VA: AAHPERD.

Schmid, A. B., & Peper, E. (1982). *Mental preparation for optimal performance in rhythmic gymnastics*. Paper presented at the Western Society for Physical Education of College Women Conference, Asilomar, CA.

Sime, W. (2004). *Attention enhancement for athletes: Optimal Performance Panel*. Unpublished panel at the 2004 Winter Brain Meeting, Palm Springs, CA.

Song, H., & Lehrer, P. (2003). The effects of specific respiratory rates on heart rate and heart rate variability. *Applied Psychophysiology and Biofeedback, 28*, 13–23.

Sterman, M. B. (1995). Concepts and applications of EEG analysis in aviation performance evaluation. *Biological Psychology, 40*(1–2), 115–130.

Strack, B. (2004). *Performance enhancement for athletes*. Unpublished workshop at the 2004 Winter Brain Meeting, Palm Springs, CA.

Suinn, R. M. (1980). Body thinking: Psychology of Olympic champs. In R. M. Suinn (Ed.), *Psychology in sports: Methods and applications*. Minneapolis, MN: Burgess.

Unestahl, L. E. (1983). *Inner mental training*. Orebro, Sweden: Veje.

Walsh, M., & Spelman, F. (1983, June 13). Unvarnished symphonies. *Time*, p. 75.

Wilson, V. E., Ainsworth, M., & Bird, E. I. (1984). Assessment of attentional abilities in male athletes. *International Journal of Sport Psychology, 16*, 296–306.

Wilson, V. E., & Gunkleman, J. (2000). Practical applications of psychophysiology and neurotherapy in sport. *Journal of Neurotherapy, 12*, 14–21.

Wilson, V. E., & Thompson, M. (2003, March). *The integration of biofeedback and neurofeedback in the assessment and training of high performing executives and athletes: Update*, Unpublished workshop. Association for Applied Psychophysiology and Biofeedback, Annual meeting in Jacksonville, FL.

Wulf, G., & Prinz, W. (2001). Directing attention to movement effects enhances learning: A review. *Psychonomic Bulletin & Review, 8*, 648–660.

Ziegler, S. G. (1994). The effects of attentional shift training on the execution of soccer skills: A preliminary investigation. *Journal of Applied Behavioral Analysis, 27*, 545–552.

Implementing Training Programs

Integrating and Implementing a Psychological Skills Training Program

Robert S. Weinberg, *Miami University*
Jean M. Williams, *University of Arizona*

The authors of Chapters 11 through 19 have discussed peak performance characteristics, psychological theory, and exercises for training specific psychological skills. When sport psychologists began employing psychological skills interventions in the early 1980s, there were not many empirical data or controlled studies to help guide these initial attempts to improve performance. However, the last 20–25 years have produced a number of field-based studies that have investigated the effectiveness of different psychological interventions to enhance performance. Although we have learned a great deal from these studies, many questions still remain. Some of the most important questions include the following: How old and skillful should athletes be before beginning psychological skills training? Who should conduct the training program—the sport psychologist or the coach? Is there an ideal time during the year for implementing a psychological skills training program? How much time is needed for psychological skills training? What specific components should be incorporated in training, and how should those components be sequenced and integrated? What ethical considerations should one be aware of when

implementing a program? In this chapter we address these questions and others, but first we must recognize that regarding some of these questions only preliminary data exist. Therefore, caution must be observed until more definitive studies are conducted.

Most comprehensive mental training programs stress the development of psychological skills and techniques such as anxiety management, imagery, goal setting, concentration, self-talk, thought stopping, routines, and confidence (just to name a few). The multitude of possibilities makes it very difficult to integrate all of the components into one comprehensive mental training program. In essence, situational constraints (e.g., the athlete or team only has a few weeks to learn and implement a psychological skills training program) do not always permit the implementation of a comprehensive mental training program, and thus it is often necessary to plan an abbreviated program. Furthermore, although a number of mental training programs have been developed (e.g., Gordon, 1990; Orlick, 1986, 1992; Ravizza & Hanson, 1995; Suinn, 1986), there still isn't general agreement among sport psychologists on how much time should be spent learning these techniques or what techniques are best for achieving certain objectives. For example, what technique should be used for an athlete who starts thinking ahead during competition to what might happen if he or she loses or wins the game?

Unfortunately, there are no ready-made solutions to questions of how coaches and sport psychologists can integrate and implement a psychological skills training program. The database is only recently being developed, and thus new information is constantly changing the way mental training programs are implemented. Nonetheless, if a mental training program is to be effective, strategies for putting all of the different components into place must be planned and well thought out. In this chapter we offer some suggestions and practical pointers for implementing mental skills training and for integrating various psychological skill components into these programs. Unless otherwise noted, these guidelines are the same for either the coach or sport psychologist, although we will discuss the pros and cons of taking on a dual role of coach/sport psychologist. Finally, we again caution you to view these recommendations only as suggested guidelines.

Before discussing the various aspects of psychological interventions to enhance performance, we feel it is instructive to note that there are several other approaches to intervention in sport and exercise psychology that are different from the focus of this chapter, which is psychological skills to enhance competitive performance. In fact, many of these approaches are similar to ones developed in the counseling literature that focus more on adjustment and personal growth. Many of these alternative interventions are discussed by Murphy (1995), and we recommend consulting his edited text to learn more about the details of these approaches. Examples of these psychological interventions include the following: (a) a life development model focusing on a psychoeducational–developmental approach over the life span; (b) a marital therapy model focusing on human relationships; (c) a family systems model, which makes the family central to helping athletes reach their potential; and (d) an organizational model, which focuses on how organizational dynamics influence the way psychological services are provided and received.

Are Psychological Interventions Effective in Improving Sport Performance?

Probably the most important question that sport psychology consultants need to ask themselves revolves around the effectiveness of their psychological interventions in enhancing performance and personal growth. It is the same problem that has plagued clinical psychologists and counselors over the years—demonstrating that what they do makes a difference in the behavior and well-being of their clients. Defending the effectiveness of psychological skills training programs in improving sport performance and well-being requires the accumulation of well-controlled, outcome-based intervention studies conducted in competitive sport environments. These are traditionally difficult to carry out because of time and money constraints, unwillingness of coaches and athletes to participate, and inability to adequately control the environment.

Fortunately, sport psychology researchers have been working hard to establish a database concerning the effectiveness of these psychological interventions in improving performance. Reviews by Greenspan and Feltz (1989), Vealey (1994), and Weinberg and Comar (1994) identified 45 studies employing psychological interventions in competitive sport settings, including such diverse sports as golf, karate, skiing, boxing, basketball, volleyball, gymnastics, baseball, tennis, and figure skating. Of the 45 studies, 38 (85%) found positive performance effects. Many of these studies employed a variety of psychological techniques as part of the total program package. See Meyers, Whelan, and Murphy (1996) for the most recent meta-analysis of psychological interventions to enhance sport performance. Their analysis of 90 interventions indicated moderate to large positive effects on performance for interventions such as goal setting, mental rehearsal, anxiety management, cognitive restructuring, attentional focusing, and multi-components. Had someone reviewed the intervention studies since 1996, there is every reason to assume that the findings would indicate equally strong effectiveness.

Who Will Benefit From Psychological Skills Training?

Many coaches and athletes misunderstand peak performance sport psychology. They think mental training strategies are only applicable to elite athletes or that these techniques can only fine-tune the performance of the already highly skilled. In actuality, mental skills training should be beneficial for a variety of people, although, as previously noted, we need more studies across different skill and age groups and special populations. If beginning athletes are taught to set realistic goals, increase self-confidence, visualize success, and react constructively, we can expect their performance and personal development to progress faster than the performance and personal development of athletes who do not receive similar mental training. Special adjustments may be needed, however, based on the population of athletes. For example, very young athletes may need adjustments such as fewer goals, shorter training sessions, simpler verbal instruction, and turning the exercises into games, but these athletes can still benefit from some sort of mental skills training provided they are interested in receiving it (Orlick & McCaffrey, 1991; Smith & Smoll, 1982; Weiss, 1991). Furthermore, Whelan, Meyers, and Donovan (1995) present a multisystemic model for intervention with the vast amount of competitive recreational athletes. Thus psychological skills training can be applied to sport participants at all levels of skill.

The ideal time for initially implementing training may be when individuals are just beginning to participate in sport. As any experienced teacher or coach knows, it is far easier to develop proper physical technique in a beginner than it is to modify poor technique in a more experienced athlete. Although never empirically tested, the same phenomenon may be true for psychological skills. Furthermore, early implementation ensures the laying of a psychological skills foundation that will facilitate future achievement of full athletic potential, enjoyment, and benefit.

Highly skilled athletes also can certainly benefit from systematic psychological skills training programs. As athletes get better, physical differences tend to become smaller. At this level, minute adjustments and differences can literally mean the difference between winning and losing. For example, Orlick (1986) was one of the first to provide a number of case studies of Olympic athletes who systematically employed a mental training program. The athletes report that their mental training and discipline were a critical component of their success. Their comments generally reflect the notion that everybody they were competing against was physically talented. The key difference was in their consistency of mental preparation and training. Let's look at an example of an Olympic skier in her second year of mental training:

> Last year I got angry with myself or so upset about not performing well. Initially if I didn't get angry or punish myself, I would feel guilty, as if I wasn't taking it seriously. This year I'm keeping it in perspective and reminding myself what it's for. Now I'm thinking about enjoyment as well as intensity. This year for the first time ever, I pushed during a whole training camp. I never let up. I stayed interested and motivated. When I started to coast I stopped and went free skiing. I don't want to practice skiing at low intensity. (Orlick, 1986, p. 148)

Who Should Conduct the Psychological Skills Training Program?

Ideally, a psychological skills training program should be planned, implemented, and supervised by a qualified consulting sport psychologist. The sport psychologist has the advantage of having more extensive special training and experience than a coach. Also, athletes may be more open in discussing difficulties with the psychological aspects of play because the sport psychologist does not decide who stays on the team and who gets to play. Even though it is desirable to have a sport psychologist administer the program, this is rarely feasible except perhaps at the highest levels of competition (and even here it is still a rarity for a sport psychologist to work and travel with a team throughout a season). The basic premise of this book is that it is also the responsibility of the coach to provide mental skills training and reinforce optimal psychological states; after all, who knows the athletes better and who works more closely with them? Thus, there are advantages to having mental skills training provided by the consulting sport psychologist *or* the coach.

When the mental training program is to be implemented by a sport psychologist, the selection of that person is critical. Who is qualified to be a sport psychologist? In 1991 the Association for the Advancement of Applied Sport Psychology (*AAASP Newsletter,* 1991) adopted criteria for certification for individuals working in the area of applied sport psychology. Basically, this certification requires individuals to have an extensive background in both the sport and psychological sciences as well as some practical supervised experience implementing psychological skills with sport and exercise participants (see Chapter 1 for a more detailed explanation of AAASP certification). The USOC now requires AAASP certification to become part of their sport psychology registry. Having an individual who is certified by AAASP ensures a certain experience, background, and competence in applied sport psychology. However, just because an individual is certified does not necessarily mean he or she has the type of orientation or experiential background that would best meet the needs of a specific team or coach. For example, will the person's focus be on dealing with personal and emotional problems (i.e., clinical approach) or teaching mental skills for enhancing performance (performance enhancement approach)? Does the person have experience with younger athletes or primarily elite athletes? Is he or she sufficiently knowledgeable about the sport in which the psychological skills are to be applied? How much time does the person have to spend with the team? Does the person have references from teams or individuals he or she worked with in the past developing psychological skills? These and other questions guide the selection of the sport psychologist who best suits the athletes' specific needs and goal.

If a sport psychology consultant conducts the program, we recommend that the coach, or coaching staff, attend most or all of the initial group training sessions. There are a number of reasons for this recommendation. First, the coach's presence tells the athletes that the coach thinks the sessions are important. Second, the sport psychologist will not be present during most of the physical practices and competitions; a knowledgeable coach can be a key person in ensuring the effectiveness of mental skills training by seeing that appropriate application of such training occurs. Ideally, the sport psychologist and coach should have special meetings to discuss ways for the coach to apply and reinforce whatever the sport psychologist emphasizes in mental skills training sessions. Third, misunderstandings regarding what the sport psychologist is doing will not occur because the coach will know exactly what is happening and will be providing feedback regarding what needs to be done. Ravizza (1990), in his work with professional baseball teams, notes that in the early stages a good portion of his work with coaches was done in the locker room, hotel lobby, or at meals. As the relationship progressed, they set aside mutually convenient times for formal meetings to discuss how individual players were performing, as well as any other relevant issues.

Our understanding about how to conduct psychological skills training programs with athletes has increased rapidly over the years. Along these lines, a number of sport psychologists have written about their consulting experiences with athletes and teams. In fact, as far back as 1989, separate issues of *The Sport Psychologist* (1989, #4; 1990, #4; 1991, #4) were devoted to psychological interventions with a variety of sports as well as with physically disabled and mentally retarded athletes.

As psychological skills training programs have been developed in recent years, it has also been suggested that it is important that we understand the sport psychologist–athlete relation to maximize the effectiveness of the intervention. For example, Petitpas, Giges, and Danish (1999) have argued that the effectiveness of psychological interventions is closely tied to the quality of the relationship between athlete and sport psychologist.

They draw on the counseling psychology literature, which has demonstrated that of all the techniques and variables examined the only one that has consistently related to positive therapeutic outcomes has been the counselor–client relationship (Sexton & Whitson, 1994). Thus, it would appear that sport psychologists should look closely at the counseling psychology literature to help facilitate a positive athlete–sport psychologist relationship. In fact, some sport psychology research has already indicated that the ability to build rapport, create a positive environment, and provide concrete suggestions is highly correlated with successful sport psychology interventions (e.g., Gould, Murphy, Tammen, & May, 1991; Martin, Wrisberg, Beitel, & Lounsbury, 1997). Therefore, it appears that having good counseling skills will facilitate the effectiveness of a sport psychology consultant administering mental training programs to athletes.

In addition to counseling skills, recently it also has been demonstrated that sensitivity to ethnic/racial diversity and sexual orientation (Barber & Krane, 2005) in applied sport psychology settings will enhance the quality of the relationship. Being sensitive to such multicultural concepts such as identity, enculturation, generalizations, and stereotyping has been shown to be helpful in dealing with a more and more diverse clientele (Kontos & Breland-Noble, 2002). Therefore, most probably there is a need for more sport psychologists of color to help with the increasing number of African American. Latino, and American Indian athletes. Along these lines, Butryn (2002) argues that there is a need for more multicultural training programs for sport psychology consultants working with diverse athlete populations.

Of course, the philosophy and implementation of mental training programs differ somewhat from one sport psychologist to the next. Each person has to understand the nature of the team or individual athletes he or she is working with and integrate that with his or her background, training, and orientation. It's important for the sport psychologist to communicate his or her philosophy to the athletes and coaches at the outset and to make sure that everyone understands the parameters of the consultation.

It was previously noted that one of the drawbacks of having a sport psychologist conduct a psychological skills program is the difficulty in being with the athletes on a day-to-day basis. In many cases the sport psychology consultant cannot provide continuous services, either because the organization is diffused over a wide geographical area or because the consultant or athletic group cannot make the time commitment necessary to provide ongoing services. Coaches, of course, have the best access to athletes on a daily basis and are thus in a position to administer psychological interventions over the course of a season. An innovative consultation model has been developed by Smith and Johnson (1990) in their work with the Houston Astros minor league player development program. They call this model "organizational empowerment," and we will discuss it in some depth since it serves as an excellent prototype for sport psychology consultation.

In this model of service delivery, the sport psychology consultant trains one or more qualified individuals within the sport organization to provide psychological services to athletes and coaches. The consultant then oversees the program and provides ongoing supervision of the actual trainers. This approach thus empowers a sport organization to provide its own sport psychology services under the supervision of the consultant.

In setting up this program, one of the major challenges was to provide continuity to a major league baseball club that has minor league teams in several cities over a wide geographical area. Smith and Johnson strongly believe one-shot or occasional psychological skills training, no matter how competently carried out, cannot be as effective as that provided on a continuous basis over an extended period of time. In addition, they feel there are real advantages to having someone identified with professional baseball as the service provider, given that the trainer has the requisite background in counseling and psychological skills training. A "baseball person" may have an easier time establishing credibility within what is still a very traditional baseball establishment and may find it easier to coordinate psychological skills training with the technical aspects of player development because of the deeper knowledge of the game.

In their specific case, Smith (the sport psychology consultant) trained Johnson (a manager in the Astros organization with a Master's degree in psychology). An intensive 6-week training program was established prior to spring training in which Johnson was given a set of extensive sport psychology reading materials and Smith met with Johnson for several days concerning the use of psychological interventions in sport. In addition, Smith accompanied Johnson to spring training for 10 days of hands-on training plus a series of orientation workshops for staff and players. Weekly and sometimes daily telephone supervision continued throughout the remainder of spring training and the regular season, along with two additional 4-day blocks of personal contact. Once Johnson felt comfortable with his new skills, Smith worked with him to help put together a psychological skills training program. Smith helped in overseeing the program, but it was Johnson who was in charge of implementing the day-to-day psychological exercises. With continued interaction and support between Smith and Johnson, the program enjoyed some initial success and is now ongoing.

Another alternative model has been proposed for the delivery of sport psychology services to athletes and coaches (Kremer & Scully, 1998). Briefly, this model identifies the coach rather than the athlete as the primary target for psychological intervention. Thus, the sport psychologist becomes more of a management consultant who is part of the team along with the coach and support staff. This challenges the myth that sport psychologists are "shrinks" who can provide instant solutions for athletes whose problems have baffled their coaches.

When Should You Implement a Psychological Skills Training Program?

It is generally agreed that the *least* desirable time to implement a psychological skills program is after the competitive season has started, when the athlete is facing a string of competitions in quick succession. At this time, mental training often amounts to no more than a quick-fix, bandage approach and consequently is rarely, if ever, effective. One of the underlying principles of this book is that psychological skills are learned and therefore need to be practiced systematically, just like physical skills.

To draw an analogy, golfers or tennis players would not change their grip on the club or racket right before a tournament without extensively using the new grip in practice for several weeks or even months. Similarly, we should not expect athletes to be able to learn new psychological skills in such a short period of time. And even if there are benefits, the influence may be only that of a short-term placebo—the athlete expects the psychological intervention to improve performance, and therefore it does.

For these reasons, most sport psychology consultants believe the best time to initially implement psychological skills training is during the off-season or preseason. During this period there is more time to learn new skills, and it is easier to try new ideas because this is the time of year when athletes are not so pressured with winning. Some athletes have reported that it took several months to a year to fully understand and integrate their new psychological skills into actual competitions. This underscores the importance of viewing mental training as an ongoing process that needs to be integrated with physical practice over a period of time.

When Should Athletes Practice Psychological Skills?

The rudiments of most psychological skills should first be taught and systematically practiced during special training sessions. The first or last 15 to 30 minutes of practice is often a good time for training. The content of the particular session will determine whether it is better held at the beginning or end of practice (see earlier chapters for suggestions on which training exercises are better practiced before or after physical workouts). Homework assignments also can be given, but unless the athletes are self-directed, it is better to have most mental training practice occur under someone's supervision.

As soon as possible the psychological skills practice should be integrated with physical skills practice. When integrating the two, the rehearsal of mental skills should have a performance-specific focus. For example, once athletes have learned the skill of relaxation and recognizing tension, they should be instructed to scan their muscles for harmful tension and practice appropriate differential relaxation while performing. Specific performance times should be identified—for example, always scan and relax before pitching, shooting a free throw, serving a tennis ball, or taking a shot in golf. Once relaxation skills have been effectively integrated into physical workouts, they should be tried during simulated or practice competition and later during actual competition. The same stepwise building of competence should occur for introducing and practicing other mental skills such as imagery and concentration. It is important not to proceed too quickly from learning to competition because the psychological skills may not be fully integrated and therefore performance decrements could occur.

This progressive method of practice is also psychologically sound from a learning standpoint because it allows athletes to gain knowledge and competence in using each mental skill as environmental demands slowly become more variable, challenging, and applicable. The ultimate goal is for the practice of mental skills to become such an integral part of all physical practices that the training program does not appear to be something extra. This type of systematic, consistent practice of mental skills is likely to achieve lasting optimal results rather than short-term placebo effects.

Let us provide some concrete illustrations of integrating psychological skills into actual physical practice. For example, let's say a tennis player is having trouble hitting the ball short, thus allowing his opponent to take the offensive. A practice drill can be set up where he has a goal to get 20 balls in a row over the net between the service line and baseline to work on his depth of shot. If he misses, he has to start over from zero. In addition, he may also use a cue word like "lift" when he swings to make sure that he follows through on the shot and lifts his racquet after impact. With this type of drill the player is practicing his concentration skills by using a concentrative cue and setting the conditions of practice to require extreme concentration. In addition, this drill creates pressure. The player will typically start to get a little tight as he approaches the goal of 20 consecutive shots because he doesn't want to miss and have to start all over at that point.

Another example would be a golfer who typically gets down on herself whenever she makes a poor shot. Specifically, she uses a lot of negative self-talk to put herself down and criticize herself. First, during practice rounds she could carry a small logbook and record the type of shots she hits and then her self-talk. Keeping a log will enable her to be more aware of exactly what she is saying and under what specific conditions. Then the coach can help her come up with a number of positive self-statements that are either motivational (e.g., "hang in there, you still have nine holes to play") or informational, if there is a technique error (e.g., "bring club head straight back"). These statements can then be used in practice in place of the negative self-talk until the player feels comfortable using them in competitive matches.

How Much Time Should Be Spent in Mental Training?

By now it should be obvious that the time needed for practicing mental skills varies according to what is being practiced and how well it is learned. If a new mental skill is being introduced, special 15- to 30-minute training sessions 3 to 5 days per week may be needed. Some weeks, no special sessions may be needed because all practice can occur along with physical workouts. As athletes become more proficient, fewer special training sessions are necessary. However, special sessions still may be advisable for individual athletes who are experiencing difficulty learning the mental skills.

When separate times are not being designated solely for mental training, it is very important that the coaching staff or sport psychologist provide verbal reminders for integrating mental skills practice with physical skills practice. In addition, appropriate reinforcement for the use of these mental skills during practice is crucial for athletes' motivation since they are attempting to develop new habits and possibly break some old bad habits. This can be a difficult task, and a positive approach is important to keep spirits up, as well as providing informative feedback to help athletes integrate the mental skills into their physical performance.

The time frame we have just recommended may not be desirable if a sport psychology consultant is implementing the training, particularly when the sport psychologist has to spend time traveling to reach the team. Under such circumstances, fewer and longer mental training sessions are usually held unless a coach or other organization member is trained to carry out the mental training program. Most of the initial meetings should be group sessions to best use the sport psychologist's time. However, research has indicated that individual sessions and individualized training programs are needed to optimize the effectiveness of mental training programs (Seabourne, Weinberg, Jackson, & Suinn, 1985). That is why most sport psychology consultants will typically start with some group or team sessions to lay down some general principles and state their philosophy before following up with individual meetings with athletes (e.g., Botterill, 1990; Halliwell, 1990). It is particularly critical that athletes be assigned training exercises to practice during the times the sport psychologist is not with the team. The same stepwise building of competence that we described earlier should be observed here.

The traveling sport psychology consultant must design practice exercises in such a way that maximum feedback occurs from participation and that adherence to training is likely to occur. As noted earlier, in the absence of the consultant, the coach or an individual designated by the coach can play a major role in ensuring compliance and feedback if he or she assumes responsibility for personally conducting the training exercises or at least provides the time for athletes to practice. If this is not possible, the coach or designated individual should remind athletes of their homework assignments and briefly discuss the athletes' reactions to the exercises once the homework has been completed. However, maximum effectiveness is likely only when this individual and the sport psychologist work together as a team.

A logical question that arises after a mental training program has been put in place is "When can athletes stop mental skills training?" In the truest sense, mental skills training continues as long as athletes participate in sport. In this sense, mental skills are no different from physical skills. Retention will not occur without continued practice. Athletes who during physical practice allow their concentration to be sloppy, their mental attitude to be negative, or their arousal level to be too high or low invariably find the same behaviors occurring during competition. When we hear the names of such athletes as Michael Jordan, Martina Navratilova, Tiger Woods, Tim Duncan, Jackie Joyner-Kersee, and Wayne Gretsky (just to name a few), we think of individuals who are highly skilled and great competitors. However, these same athletes are also known for their great practice habits, especially making sure that the mental aspects of their respective sports are integrated into their physical practice on an ongoing basis.

If athletes never stop mental skills training, what is the ideal length of time for their first exposure to a formal mental skills training program? Most sport psychology consultants would recommend an average of between 3 and 6 months because it takes time to learn these new mental skills, use them in practice, and then integrate them into actual competitive situations. The specific sport, time available, existing mental skills, and commitment of individuals are all factors that should be considered in determining actual length of time. For example, we have worked with athletes who simply needed to change a small part of their mental approach and were able to do that in under 2 months. In contrast, Orlick (1986) has noted that many of the Canadian Olympic athletes he has consulted with started practicing their mental training program a couple of years before the Olympic Games. Their psychological plans and mental preparation were extremely detailed and precise, as seen in the example provided in Table 20-1 for an Olympic alpine skier (Orlick, 1986, p. 34).

Table 20-1 **Prerace Mental Preparation Plan**

General Warm-Up	Start Preparation
Physical and Mental	*Physical and Mental*

Night Before Race

- Receive number, determine how many minutes after start I race.
- Figure out what time to awaken and leave for hill in the morning and approximately how many free runs or training course runs to have before start.
- Estimate how long to put number on, stretch inside lodge.
- Spend ideally no more than 20 to 25 minutes in start area.

Morning of Race

- Light run, exercises, begin the morning on a positive or high note.
- Wake up feeling good about myself, be optimistic, flow.
- Important for me not to project (e.g., about outcomes); just feel good about myself for myself.
- Free skiing and training courses to feel aggressive and pumped, yet calm and relaxed.
- Focused and concentrated while skiing.
- Mental imagery (to know course and feel good about myself on the course).

(Start Preparation)

- Arrive at start 20 minutes prior to my start.
- First get race skis in snow, check them to see if all is ready; see rep. (equipment person).
- Begin stretching, running; think happy, relaxed thoughts.
- Apply these comments to mental imagery.

- Heavier physical preparation.
- Get into skis, binding check.
- More imagery of race focus and feeling—include correction imagery if needed.
- Quicker physical activity.
- 1 minute: Take coat, warm-ups off, intense, focused on task.
- 30 seconds: Ready myself in start, think only of course and of myself.
- Explosive start.

Setting Up a Mental Skills Training Program

Thus far we have discussed some important questions surrounding the use of mental training programs, including who will benefit, who should conduct the program, when to implement the training program, when to actually practice the mental skills, and how much time to spend on mental training. Although this information is important in understanding mental training programs, it does not really tell us exactly what to do in setting up such a program. Therefore, we will attempt to outline some of the critical components of implementing a mental skills training program. To accomplish this, we will draw on our own research and experience in consulting with athletes as well as those of other sport psychologists.

Self-Regulation: A Key to Effective Mental Training

One of the critical aspects of successfully implementing a mental training program is the use of self-regulation. Self-regulation can be defined as the processes by which people manage their own behaviors that are directed toward specific goals. These processes include goal setting, planning, observing, and evaluating behaviors (Kirschenbaum, 1997). Being able to regulate and control one's behavior is an essential part of any athlete's mental training plan, and this process has six specific phases.

The first phase is *problem identification*. This phase encourages you to evaluate progress in your sport thoroughly and to remain open to new suggestions about all aspects of performance. Being open to, or seeking out, suggestions for improvement in your mental skills is a step in the right direction. For example, you might become aware that you lose your concentration by thinking negatively at critical junctures during competition. This awareness is a critical first step on the road to improvement. Once you have identified a problem and recognize that change is possible, the next step is to establish a *commitment to change*. This usually involves *developing specific plans* and *setting goals*. After problems are identified and commitments are made, *actions* must be initiated so that positive steps toward *goal attainment* can occur. This execution of self-regulated change can be viewed as a feedback loop with self-monitoring leading to self-evaluation, which in turn leads to self-consequence (Kirschenbaum, 1997). For example, you might monitor your progress toward a goal of improving your average golf score from 85 to 80. After several rounds, you could evaluate whether you achieved your goal. If you did, you might treat yourself to a great dinner; this would be an example of positive consequence. Although self-regulation implies a solitary pursuit of goals, in sport you also have to manage the environment, which might include teammates, friends, and coaches as well as specific playing and practice conditions. The long-term goal of self-regulation is to maintain behavior change over time and across different situations. This is called **generalization.** It is often difficult to achieve because it requires dedicated, consistent, systematic practice of mental skills over time.

Discuss Your Approach—What You Do and What You Don't Do

Many athletes are still fairly naive or uninformed about what sport psychology is and what sport psychologists do. Therefore, we believe it is important to spell this out right at the outset of the initial meeting. Although most athletes typically view sport psychology solely in terms of performance enhancement, they also should be made to understand its mental health aspects and potential for application outside of sport. In fact, as reflected in the title of this text, sport psychology has as much to do with personal growth issues as it does with achieving maximum performance. Therefore, these two different aspects need to be clearly communicated to athletes so they understand the broad focus that sport psychology can have.

In addition to conducting a brief discussion on what sport psychology is, it is equally critical that sport psychologists spell out their specific approach in dealing with psychological problems in sport and exercise. Sport psychologists use two approaches when working with athletes: clinical and educational. Research and experience have indicated that the large majority of athletes consulting with sport psychologists require an educational approach as opposed to a clinical approach. Athletes typically need to develop a psychological skill such as improving concentration or managing anxiety rather than to deal with a deep-seated, severe psychological problem. Therefore, we will focus on the educational approach, but it should be made clear that if an educational sport psychologist or coach comes across an athlete who has such a serious psychological problem that it is beyond his or her skills to treat, then the athlete should be referred to a qualified individual or counseling center. (See Chapter 22 for a discussion of when it may be appropriate to refer athletes for counseling or psychotherapy.)

Thus, the sport psychology consultant should tell the athlete what he or she does and does not do, as many people still believe that if athletes see a sport psychologist then something must be psychologically wrong with them. This is especially true of younger athletes, who can be extra sensitive to the idea that they "have to see a shrink." Rather, we try to emphasize that if an athlete stayed after practice to work with the coach on a particular move or physical technique most people would applaud this extra effort to improve. Similarly, if an athlete realizes that he or she needs to work on some aspect of the mental game such as concentration skills, then this also should be applauded. In essence, working to improve mentally should not be looked on as a weakness but rather as simply another way for an athlete to improve performance as well as enhance personal growth.

In discussing your philosophy or approach, a contemporary way of making initial contact with athletes is through electronic methods such as e-mail or Web pages. It appears that more and more people use the Internet as a communication tool, and are getting more and more comfortable using this medium. Along these lines, an interesting study by Zizzi and Perna (2002) comparing traditional versus electronic contact found that there were greater contacts and assessments completed in the electronic group compared to the traditional group 1 month after taking a workshop. In essence, results suggested that electronic contact methods are at least as good as, and in several cases superior to, traditional contact (e.g., phone, in-person contact methods regarding generating requests for service from athletes on a short-term basis).

Emphasize the Importance of Mental Training

Another important component to an initial meeting with athletes is convincing them of the need for systematic mental training and creating a positive belief structure regarding the effects of mental training. This can be done in many ways. One way to start is to have athletes identify how important their state of mind is in achieving success by having them decide what percentage of their game is mental. Then compare this percentage to the actual percentage of practice time spent training mental skills. The disparity is usually in the direction of the mental side of sport being very important, yet little or no time being spent specifically practicing these mental aspects.

Providing anecdotes about the importance of mental preparation from relevant, well-known amateur and professional athletes is another effective way to increase receptivity. The extensive coverage of the Olympic Games and other sport literature provide many personal stories of the positive effects of mental training. Such anecdotes are usually much more motivating than a recitation of the results of research studies on mental training. Along these lines, a study from the U.S. Olympic Training Center (Murphy, Jowdy, & Durtschi, 1990) revealed that more than 90% of Olympic athletes surveyed regularly used some sort of mental preparation and training in preparing for competition. This type of information can help athletes realize that mental training does work and is being used by many of our very best athletes, although athletes of all ability levels can benefit from such training.

Fortunately, the popularity of applied sport psychology has evolved to the point that it is becoming easier to sell a mental skills training program to most athletes. Nevertheless, some athletes still will refuse to accept mental skills training. Most sport psychologists recommend not forcing unreceptive athletes to participate. Conversely, there also can be problems with athletes who are highly enthusiastic about mental training. Occasionally this enthusiasm can lead to unreasonable expectations. Athletes, coaches, and sport psychologists must realize that no amount of mental training will substitute for poor mechanics, lack of practice, or limited physical aptitude. Also, good psychological skills cannot replace hard physical conditioning and training. Another problem may come from athletes who expect miracles from only a small investment of time. Excellent physical skills do not develop overnight and neither do mental skills.

Assess Psychological Strengths and Weaknesses

Once athletes are informed of the approach the sport psychologist plans to take and are convinced of the importance of mental training, the next step is to determine the athletes' psychological strengths and weaknesses as related specifically to sport. A needs assessment helps reveal those psychological skills that are deficient or appear to have the most adverse effect on performance and personal satisfaction. In addition, it should also reveal the strong points of each athlete from a mental perspective. When something is bothering athletes or they are struggling with a specific problem, they often overlook all the things that they do well, and these should not be forgotten.

In conducting the initial evaluation of athletes' psychological strengths and weaknesses, it is important that sport psychology consultants first understand that there are factors outside the psychological realm that influence performance. These include such things as physiological conditioning, biomechanics (technique), strategy, and equipment. For example, a golfer who has a major flaw in his or her swing may attribute the resulting poor performance to ineffective concentration, whereas the underlying problem is biomechanical. A gymnast who more frequently falls off the balance beam may not have developed an anxiety problem but experienced a growth spurt to which she has yet to adjust. The important point is that one must not try to interpret all aspects of performance from a psychological perspective. Thus, the need for input from experts such as coaches, biomechanists, and exercise physiologists must be recognized.

In terms of the actual psychological skills evaluation, one procedure we recommend is an oral interview as well as written psychological inventories and behavioral observation. In this way the athlete will have a chance to tell his or her story face to face as well as to respond to some objective questionnaires. This also helps the consultant in looking for consistencies (and inconsistencies) between oral and written statements.

There are various approaches to conducting an initial interview, but the one we recommend is the semistructured interview, which is outlined in detail by Orlick (1980). Some general questions provide structure to this type of interview, but there is leeway to use the athlete's responses to form other follow-up questions. For example, some key questions might include the following:

- Summarize your involvement in your sport, noting important events both positive and negative (this is a good starting point as it lets athletes talk about themselves and become more comfortable).

- Describe what you believe to be your greatest psychological strength and your biggest weakness.

- Describe the boundaries of any specific psychological problem you are currently having (i.e., when, why, how).

- What is your relationship with your coach?

It is our experience that this interview typically lasts approximately 1 hour. Of course, individual differences and time constraints can alter this time frame to some degree. The initial interview is very important not only to find out where the athlete needs help but also as a place to start building the trust that is critical for any therapeutic relationship. For a sport psychology consultant to be maximally effective, the athlete needs to feel comfortable and believe that the consultant not only is competent but cares about the athlete's particular situation. One thing that we have found important is that the consultant should have a good working knowledge of the sport even if he or she does not have much actual playing experience. This helps build credibility from the athletes' point of view because it gives them a sense that the consultant not only understands psychology but also understands the fine points of their sport.

In addition to the interview, most (although not all) sport psychology consultants use some paper-and-pencil psychological inventories to assess psychological skills related to sport as well as more general mood states. Although many different inventories are utilized, some of the more popular ones include the following: Profile of Mood States (McNair, Lorr, & Droppleman, 1971), Sport Competition Anxiety Test (Martens, 1977), Competitive State Anxiety Inventory-2 (Martens, Vealey, & Burton, 1990), Sport Anxiety Scale (Smith, Smoll, & Schutz, 1990), Test of Attentional and Interpersonal Style (Nideffer, 1976), Psychological Skills Inventory for Sport (Mahoney, Gabriel, & Perkins, 1987), Athletic Coping Skills Inventory-28 (Smith, Schutz, Smoll, & Ptacek, 1995), and Trait-State Sport Confidence Inventory (Vealey, 1986). A more recent scale, the Ottawa Mental Skills Assessment Tool (OMSAT-3), has been developed by Durand-Bush, Salmela, and Green-Demers (2001) to assist consultants and coaches in their designing of appropriate and individualized mental training programs as well as to help researchers assess the effectiveness of interventions with sport performers. In addition, a number of sport-specific inventories have been developed, such as the Tennis Test of Attentional and Interpersonal Style (Van Schoyck & Grasha, 1981) and the Anxiety Assessment for Wrestlers (Gould, Horn, & Spreeman, 1983), that provide more directed questions toward a specific sport.

It should be noted that applied sport psychology consultants should consider a number of factors before administering questionnaires or other formal assessments to athletes (Beckman & Kellmann, 2003). For example, to be used effectively, assessment instruments need to be reliable and valid for the individual athlete or sport group in question, be seen as useful by the athlete(s) completing the instrument, and be completed honestly by the athlete(s). In addition, sport psychology consultants need to provide athletes with a clear identification of the purpose of the assessment, and make sure that the athlete and coach (if applicable) are committed to the assessment.

Once the interview and psychological inventories have been completed, we recommend that written feedback be provided to each athlete that highlights his or her psychological strengths and weaknesses as they relate to sport performance and participation. This assessment should be given to athletes in a second one-on-one meeting,

and athletes should be provided with an opportunity to react to it. This provides an opportunity to get consensual validation from athletes in terms of the evaluation of the sport psychology consultant. At times we have found the oral interview and written assessments to be contrary, and this is a good time to bring any discrepancy up and have the athlete resolve it. The assessment should conclude with recommendations for the type of skills and intervention program that the consultant thinks would best suit the athlete's needs. Ideally, these recommendations are mutually decided and agreed upon by the athlete and the sport psychologist.

One weakness of using interviews, questionnaires, and behavioral observation to determine an athlete's psychological strengths and weaknesses is that the athlete plays a relatively passive role in the process. This often results in the sport psychology consultant having to convince athletes that they really need to work on particular psychological skills (Butler & Hardy, 1992). Motivation and adherence problems will occur in the psychological skills training program if the athlete does not fully accept the decisions reached in the needs assessment. Butler and Hardy propose that using performance profiling resolves this problem, and an increasing number of sport psychology consultants are using the approach and finding it very effective.

For these reasons, we recommend performance profiling as an alternative approach to assessing psychological strengths and weaknesses. When using performance profiling, the athlete, with his or her own labels and definitions, determines the psychological skills needed for success. Once done, the athlete rates him- or herself on each of the identified constructs. Butler and Hardy (1992) propose that the rating use a 0–10 scale anchored with "not at all" and "very much." The athlete's resulting constructs are then displayed in the form of performance profiles. See Figure 20-1 for one example of plotting and using a performance profile to determine psychological needs and goals.

In this particular example, an athlete client of one of the authors had the goal of making the national team. Four months before the qualifying

Figure 20-1 **Example of using performance profiling to determine psychological needs and goals**

competition, the athlete with the help of the sport psychologist determined what psychological skills he would need, and their relative importance, in order to make the national team (see dark bars depicting long-term goals). The athlete then assessed his present weakness/strength specific to each of the constructs he identified (see shaded bars). This information was displayed pictorially and together the athlete and the sport psychologist determined what progress the athlete wanted to make in the next month and exactly what he would have to do to reach each of his psychological skills goals. See the clear bars added later to represent the athlete's short-term goals. (Note: The athlete had previously received some psychological skills training and was adamant that he simultaneously work on all the constructs.)

The performance profiling sheet also has the advantage of providing one format for the athlete and sport psychology consultant to periodically assess and record the athlete's progress in

using interventions to reach his or her goals. This is done by using that same 10-point rating scale. Once done, draw a new bar to depict the rating, or you can extend or shade in the existing bar depicting starting status (labeled "present") and short-term goals. When using performance profiling in this way, we also recommend modifying the sheet in Figure 20-1 to allow sufficient room for comments after listing each construct.

The sport psychology consultant and coach can assess the psychological strengths and weakness of teams by using essentially the same procedure as that described for the individual athlete. We recommend putting the team members into groups of 3 to 5 players. Have each group take 5–10 minutes to identify the constructs that they perceive as important to reach the team's goal. Then have a team discussion regarding each construct identified by the groups, with the goal of reaching consensus regarding what psychological skills to include. After identifying the resulting constructs and their relative importance, have the small groups use the 10-point scale to rate the present status of the team on each of the constructs. Also ask the groups to provide a rationale for their decision. Once finished, have all team members discuss each group's ratings and rationale until some consensus is reached regarding a final rating. One bonus of using the preceding procedure is that the discussion of the rationale for the ratings often results in a clear identification of both the attitudes and behaviors that the team members want to encourage and those that they want to discourage.

The procedure of performance profiling has many uses besides assessing psychological strengths and weaknesses. See Butler and Hardy (1992) for a discussion of how coaches and sport psychologists can use performance profiling. We also recommend an article by Dale and Wrisberg (1996) in which they discuss how they used performance profiling to create a more open atmosphere for coach–athlete communication.

Regardless of the approach used to assess psychological strengths and weaknesses, if a sport psychology consultant is working with an entire team, it is essential that the coach be involved in the needs assessment because he or she is more likely to know the team's mental strengths and weaknesses over a period of time. This might, in turn, require different psychological approaches based on the team's history. For example, quite different psychological needs would probably be perceived for a team with a long history of losing compared to a team that climbed to the top and was currently experiencing the pressure of trying to maintain number-one status. A consultant working with the losing team might determine that the primary emphasis should be on developing a positive mental attitude. In such a case, strategies might be directed at getting the athletes to stop feeling like losers and begin thinking and feeling like they could win. Techniques for building confidence, monitoring and replacing self-defeating talk, and setting realistic goals should prove quite beneficial.

In contrast, the coach or sport psychology consultant working with the highly successful team might perceive a primary need to develop skills for regulating arousal and maintaining concentration. Techniques would need to be planned for coping with the stress of being expected to win consistently, even when playing against excellent competitors who always play their best against the defending champions. In addition, the team may need help to sufficiently energize and focus when playing against clearly inferior competitors.

An obvious implication of this discussion on needs assessment is that the coach should be wary of anyone who suggests a canned mental training program that does not provide for the specific needs of a given group of athletes. Although such a program may be better than nothing, the more attention that is paid to the individual needs and the maturation and experiences of the given group, the more likely it is that the program will be successful.

Analyze Demands of the Sport

As noted in Taylor's (1995) conceptual model for integrating athletes' needs and sport demands in the development of competitive mental preparation strategies, every sport has unique physical, technical, and logistical demands that require special preparation by participating athletes. These characteristics that distinguish different sports also affect the type of mental preparation and training an athlete may employ. Thus, sport psychologists need a detailed understanding of important aspects of the sport in which they are working.

As Taylor (1995) notes, sports that involve explosiveness and anaerobic power (e.g., 100-yard dash) will differ greatly from those requiring endurance and aerobic conditioning (e.g., long-distance running and cycling). Patrick and Hrycaiko (1998) used such an approach in developing a mental training package for endurance performance. Similarly, a sport requiring great precision (e.g., golf putting) might differ from one requiring more gross motor movements (e.g., power lifting). Furthermore, a sport or performance that lasts a very short time (figure skating) would require a different set of psychological skills than one that lasts hours (e.g., golf). Finally, the actual time between performances within a competition or between competitions also can vary greatly. For example, a gymnast or figure skater often only has a few competitions throughout the year, whereas a basketball or softball player will have many, many games. In essence, the demands of the sport need to be carefully analyzed and considered when devising a mental skills training program.

One example of a mental training program that took into consideration the nature of the task was conducted by Terry, Mayer, and Howe (1998). Specifically, they developed a mental training package for scuba diving, basing their work on the fact that this activity can be very anxiety producing and that the ability to respond effectively under stress is crucial to survival. Therefore, their mental training program emphasized relaxation and coping skills (both cognitively and somatically oriented) such as deep rhythmic diaphragmatic breathing, guided imagery, and attentional focus. Results revealed that the mental training group exhibited lower levels of cognitive anxiety, higher levels of self-confidence, and significantly better performance than did the control group.

Determining What Skills to Include and How to Sequence Them

Once the assessment is complete and all needed psychological skills have been listed, the coach or sport psychologist must decide how many of these skills to emphasize. This decision should be based on when the program is first being implemented (e.g., preseason, practice season, competitive season) and how much time the athletes and coach are willing to devote to mental skills training. Several questions are pertinent at this point:

- How much practice time will be given up on the average each week for mental skills training?

- How many weeks of practice are available?

- Will there still be time to practice mental skills after the competitive season starts, or after the first couple of losses?

- How interested are the athletes in receiving mental skills training?

The answers to these questions will help provide a realistic perspective on the commitment to mental skills training and the time available for accomplishing psychological skill objectives. When there is not adequate time or commitment for a comprehensive training program, it is better to prioritize objectives and emphasize a few to work on initially rather than work superficially on all of the needed skills. The coach or sport psychologist may even wish to develop a 2- to 3-year plan (Gould, 1983; Orlick, 1986). When there is time, interest, and need for a comprehensive mental training program, what should be the main components of the program and how should the coach or sport psychologist sequence the teaching of all the different psychological skill components?

Although there is certainly no definitive answer as to what a psychological skills training program should include or in what sequence these skills should be taught, Vealey (1988) provides a thoughtful analysis of the nature of psychological skills training programs. The first thing Vealey notes is the need to differentiate between psychological skills and methods. **Skills** are qualities to be obtained, as opposed to **methods,** which are procedures or techniques employed to develop these skills. Although sport psychology consultants certainly use different models, it is useful to differentiate between skills and methods. Consultants should focus on the skill to be obtained and then choose any method or combination of methods that will help attain this skill. At times, however, sport psychology consultants have become enamored with a particular method (e.g., relaxation) and used it indiscriminately instead of focusing on a skill that an athlete needs to develop. This type of approach may cause athletes to lose interest because the training is not directed specifically at meeting their individual needs.

Table 20-2 provides an overview of the methods that can be used to develop and enhance psychological skills. The basic psychological skills training methods include the four traditional techniques of goal setting (Chapter 13), imagery

Table 20-2 **Methods for Developing Psychological Skills**

Foundation Methods	Psychological Skills Methods
Physical Practice	Goal Setting
Education	Imagery
	Physical Relaxation
	Thought Control

Source: Vealey, 1988.

(Chapter 16), physical relaxation (Chapter 15), and thought control (Chapter 17). Physical practice and education are also included as foundation methods to emphasize that psychological skills are facilitated by productive physical practice and the understanding of the physical and mental processes that influence performance. In fact, most psychological skills training programs include an educational phase in which athletes are introduced to a number of basic sport psychology principles and concepts. This educational phase provides the needed information and background for athletes to move forward to the actual learning and implementation of specific psychological skills.

Using foundation and psychological skills methods, Vealey (1988) proposes a number of skills that can and should be developed in a well-rounded psychological skills training program (Table 20-3). It's important to note that these skills reflect areas related to personal development as well as performance enhancement. Such a human development model (Danish & Hale, 1981) focuses on human growth and change and assists individuals in gaining control of their lives. This framework is an example of a holistic and personal development approach that emphasizes the need to first develop some basic skills before moving on to other sport and life skills.

The most basic skills, termed **foundation skills,** represent those qualities that are basic and necessary psychological skills. The first foundation skill is **volition,** which is concerned with one's internal motivation. Without an individual's desire to achieve success, there is little hope that any psychological skills program would be successful because it takes commitment to practice the skills and carry out the program. One good way to enhance athletes' motivation is through the use of goal setting (see Chapter 13).

The second foundation skill is **self-awareness.** Before athletes can start changing some of their previous bad habits, they need to understand and become aware of exactly when and where their problem behaviors occur and what they are thinking and feeling at that time. In addition, athletes need to be aware of what they typically think and feel when performing at their best. That is, do they have an ideal performance state

Table 20-3 **Psychological Skills**

Foundation Skills	Performance Skills	Facilitative Skills
Volition	Optimal Physical Arousal	Interpersonal Skills
Self-Awareness	Optimal Mental Arousal	Lifestyle Management
Self-Esteem	Optimal Attention	
Self-Confidence		

Source: Vealey, 1988.

that is associated with peak performance? (See Chapter 11 for more detail on typical peak performance characteristics.) Keeping a sport journal is one way to increase awareness of performance states and to understand how different situations bring about different emotional reactions. (See Chapter 12 for suggestions regarding how to keep a journal and implement other techniques for increasing awareness.)

If athletes are sufficiently motivated and have become aware of the relationship between their thoughts and feelings and behavior, they can begin to develop their self-esteem and self-confidence. **Self-esteem** and **self-confidence** not only are critical to sport performance (see Chapters 11 and 17) but are also central to a wide array of behaviors outside the world of sport and physical activity (Bandura, 1986). Thus, it would appear inappropriate to begin specific psychological skills training methods (e.g., imagery) until individuals learn a certain level of proficiency in the foundation skills.

The **performance skills** in Vealey's (1988) model are the traditional psychological skills that most sport psychology consultants attempt to teach. These skills are addressed in detail in various chapters throughout the text. The premise is that exceptional performance is most likely to occur when these skills are learned and integrated into an athlete's actual competitive performance.

Facilitative skills have unfortunately been left out of many psychological skills training programs in the past. Although these skills do not always directly influence sport performance, once acquired they can facilitate behavior in sport as well as other areas of life. For example, **interpersonal skills** are important for both athletes and coaches to have as they can enhance coach–athlete communication, which is an often-cited problem. In addition, communication breakdowns are often the cause of problems at work and in relationships, and thus developing interpersonal skills can help in a number of areas (see Chapter 10). Likewise,

Table 20-4 A Sample of Psychological Skills Objectives and Outcomes

Objective 1	Objective 2	Objective 3
Positive Mental Attitude	*Coping With Mistakes and Failures*	*Handling the High-Stress Situation*
Don't make negative statements at games or practices.	Accept the fact that mistakes and failures are a necessary part of the learning process.	Learn to interpret the situation as a challenge rather than a threat.
Change "I can't" statements to "I can" statements.	Don't make excuses. Appropriately accepting responsibility will help turn failures into success.	Recognize too much tension. Achieve appropriate differential relaxation.
Always give 100% effort.	Stay positive even after a stupid mistake.	Keep thoughts positive and focused on the task at hand.
Don't talk while coaches talk.	Be supportive of teammates even when they are making mistakes.	Image goal of performing well under high-stress situations.
Hustle during all plays and drills.	Keep focused concentration rather than dwelling on mistakes.	Focus concentration on appropriate cues.

lifestyle management skills stress the personal development approach to psychological skills training (see Chapter 10). Providing athletes with lifestyle management skills allows them to organize and manage their lives more effectively by becoming more responsible for their actions, by managing their time, and by setting up career goals.

Regardless of the specific methods and skills to be included in any psychological skills training program, it will be more effective if psychological objectives appropriate to the athletes are identified and if these objectives are defined in easily understood and measurable terms; Table 20-4 provides some examples. Such definitions help clarify exactly what is meant by the objective and what outcomes are expected once the objective is achieved. The definitions also provide a clear foundation for planning strategies to accomplish the objectives and for assessing how effective the strategies were in achieving the objectives.

Evaluation of Program Effectiveness

It is not easy to evaluate the impact of a psychology skills training program, yet evaluation is essential for improving a training program and the skills of the person in charge of the program. In fact, evaluation should be an essential feature of any organizational as well as individualized intervention. Aside from the accountability demands that ethically oblige sport psychology consultants to evaluate the effectiveness of what they do (see Smith, 1989), practical considerations are also important.

First, program evaluation provides consultants and coaches with the information needed to gauge the effectiveness of the various components of their programs and to make modifications where needed. Second, an evaluation provides consumers with an opportunity to provide feedback concerning areas that they feel weren't included or to suggest changes in the way the program was conducted. Third, evaluation is the only way we can objectively judge whether the program achieved its intended goals

in changing some aspects of the individual's or team's behavior/performance.

It is important to note that evaluation should be a continuous process. Sport psychology consultants should assess the strengths and weaknesses of the content and delivery of their sessions, especially team sessions. Questions such as the following might be addressed: Did the session accomplish its objective(s)? Were explanations of psychological concepts and directions for practicing the training exercises adequate? What techniques appeared to work best? Was time allotted appropriately during the session? Are any additions or deletions warranted? How responsive did the athletes appear to be? Writing a critique is more beneficial than simply trying to remember strengths and weaknesses. Plans for future sessions may need to be modified on the basis of the results of each session evaluation.

A more formal, total evaluation should occur at the end of the mental skills training program. This evaluation might include team and individual discussions as well as written evaluations by the athletes and coaches. The evaluation should focus on the players' assessment of the value of the program from both a psychological and performance perspective. Objective performance data should be used in addition to subjective reports from coaches and athletes. For example, one recommended objective data system entails behavioral assessment which involves the collection and analysis of information and data to identify and describe target behaviors, identify possible causes of the behaviors, select appropriate treatment strategies to modify the behaviors, and evaluate treatment outcomes (Tkachuk, Leslie-Toogood, & Martin, 2003). In addition, athletes should be asked how often they actually practiced their skills. When psychological skills programs don't work, one of the major reasons is simply because athletes do not systematically practice what they have learned. Information should also be obtained on different aspects of the program, such as group sessions, individual sessions, and written materials. Additional questions can be asked, such as, What did athletes see as the major strengths and weaknesses of the mental skills training? What mental skills improved the most? What exercises were the most helpful? What suggestions do athletes have to make the program even better in the future? To help out new sport psychology consultants, Partington and Orlick (1987a, 1987b) provide a sample sport psychology evaluation form as well as data on what makes a consultant effective from both the coaches' and athletes' point of view. In addition, Poczwardowski, Sherman, and Henschen (1998) provide additional suggestions on the key points when conducting programs and making evaluations. It is important to remember that we are continually learning, and our programs will continue to change and evolve.

A recent article (Anderson, Miles, Mahoney, & Robinson, 2002) suggests that a practitioner administered case study approach to evaluation should be employed, which uses a number of effectiveness indicators to accommodate the constraints of a practice setting and fulfill the functional criteria for evaluating practice. More specifically, they break down effectiveness indicators into four distinct categories. These include the quality of support (e.g., consultant effectiveness), psychological skill and well-being (e.g., anxiety control, happiness), response to support (e.g., changes in knowledge and attitude), and performance (objective, subjective). This presents a more well-rounded view of evaluation than simply performance (bottom line), which is the focus of many interventions.

Practical Pointers for Teaching Mental Skills

In the preceding chapters on mental skills training the authors have presented many excellent pointers for teaching specific mental skills. The following pointers apply either to the entire psychological training program or to its components.

Provide the What, Why, When, and How of Training

For mental skills to be of maximum value, the athlete must consciously and continually choose to utilize mental training methods. This necessitates a high level of commitment, an understanding of

proper execution, and ultimately the ability to be self-sufficient in mental preparation. This can be accomplished in a number of ways. Athletes who are taught the what, why, when, and how of mental skills training are much more likely to acquire the necessary knowledge base to become self-sufficient in mental training as well as the motivation to follow through with the program. At the beginning of each special mental training session, the coach or sport psychologist should outline for the athletes the purpose, content, and approximate length of the session. The educational aspect of the program is critical to provide athletes with an understanding of what principles the program is based on and how it works. Similarly, before initiating practice on a new exercise or technique, the coach or sport psychologist should first explain the entire procedure so athletes know exactly what to expect and any questions can be answered. It is also a good idea to allot time for discussion and questions after practicing each exercise and at the end of each session. In addition to enhancing forthright self-examination and the learning process, the sharing that occurs in these discussions often improves communication and understanding among teammates and leads to better group support and more team cohesiveness.

Stress Personal Responsibility

When it comes to performance, some athletes have the attitude "When you're hot, you're hot, and when you're not, you're not." These athletes view peak performance as more a consequence of fate than something under their own personal control. Implementors of mental skills training should teach the opposite attitude. Peak performance is not mysterious; it is a product of the body and mind, both of which can be controlled. This is why, with the right physical and mental training, athletes can learn to repeat their best performances more consistently. This means learning to be in control of oneself instead of letting the environment or others do the controlling. The athlete must ultimately accept the fact that only he or she can take responsibility for being physically and mentally ready to compete. Therefore, no matter what mental skills are being taught or practiced, the coach and sport psychology consultant should continually emphasize that athletes must assume personal responsibility for their thoughts, feelings, and actions—because ultimately, in the heat of competition, athletes will have to rely on themselves to make positive things happen.

Be Flexible and Individualized

When teaching mental skills to a group of athletes, the best approach is to be flexible and individualized. All athletes do not learn mental skills in the same way and at the same pace any more than they do physical skills. Within reasonable time constraints, a variety of techniques should be introduced and practiced. Do not force everyone into a fixed pattern. Instead, encourage athletes to modify or combine techniques until they derive the most effective method for them. A backup technique should also be identified and practiced for those times when the preferred one fails to accomplish its objective. Once a basic foundation of mental skills has been established, it is critical that the application of these skills be individualized on the basis of the specific psychological skill needs of the athlete and the requirements of his or her performance situation. Thus, the most effective coaches and sport psychology consultants will be those who can work simultaneously with the group and with individuals within the group.

Providing handouts and cassette or CD recordings of exercises and specific concepts, including the ones in this book, is another way to ensure that athletes have a variety of exercises with which to work and the knowledge base for making modifications and application. Although many athletes like to use recordings and handouts when they practice, be sure they do not become so dependent on them that they cannot practice the mental skills without such props.

Use Goal Setting and Journal Assignments

You can also enhance and individualize the teaching of specific mental skills by using goal setting and journal assignments. This is one reason many sport psychology consultants suggest

that athletes be encouraged to keep a journal (see Chapter 12) and set goals (see Chapter 13) early in a training program. The following is an example of their use.

A runner, after having been taught to recognize tension and to relax, identifies that he grimaces and his neck and shoulder muscles tighten when he is running under poor weather conditions, after experiencing the first signs of fatigue, and when a steep hill is coming up. He records this in his journal. Next, the runner sets a reasonable goal for correcting the problem: "In one week I will run a workout over hilly terrain keeping my face, neck, and shoulder muscles relaxed throughout the run." After he records the goal, he plans and records a strategy for reaching the goal: "(1) Do five minutes of progressive relaxation (PR) each day on just the face, neck, and shoulder muscles. (2) After PR practice, visualize running fluidly over hilly terrain. (3) When running, frequently scan the face for tension—if needed, relax the face so the forehead is smooth as glass and the jaw is slack. When the face is relaxed, scan neck and shoulders for unwanted tension. If tense, relax by slowly rolling the head and/or dropping the shoulders." Each day the runner records his progress in achieving the goal. Once the runner feels he is consistently achieving the goal, he may want to establish a slightly more difficult goal and repeat the process.

Precompetition and Competition Plans

The ultimate goal of psychological skills training is for each athlete to learn how to create consistently at competition time the ideal performance state (thoughts, feelings, bodily responses) typically associated with peak performance. Rarely will this occur if precompetition preparation and competition behaviors are left to chance or good and bad breaks. Athletes get ready for competition in a variety of ways, but more often than not they do not have a consistent pattern of readying procedures. Performance is likely to be enhanced if an athlete's preparation becomes more systematic. Implementors of psychological skills training programs can help athletes develop effective behavioral plans that can be used regularly as precompetition and competition readying procedures.

One of the objectives of precompetition planning is to arrange the external and internal world in a way that maximizes the athlete's feelings of control. The athlete's **external world** consists of the actual physical surroundings, what is happening in these surroundings, and the physical things the athlete does. The **internal world** is the athlete's physical states, thoughts, feelings, mental images, and attentional focus. The greater the familiarity, routine, and structure in the external environment, the easier it is for the athlete to be in control of his or her internal world. The external world can be stabilized in a number of ways—for example, eating similar meals with the same time lapse before each competition; always arriving at the contest site with a set amount of time for precompetition preparation; establishing a set dressing ritual; and following the same equipment check, taping, and warm-up procedures.

Maintaining a constant and familiar external world is even more critical with away competitions. This is more easily accomplished when athletes diligently adhere to elaborate and consistent precompetition plans before both home and away games. The coach can also increase familiarity with the site of away games by taking the athletes to the site before the competition begins, ideally at least a day before. Some coaches and sport psychology consultants even advocate getting films of the away facility, including the locker rooms, and showing these films to their athletes well before a competition (see Chapters 16 and 18 for further elaboration on how such films can be used and why they are effective in improving performance).

The best precompetition and competition plans consist of procedures that ready the athlete physically and mentally for competition. Most coaches already prepare their athletes well physically for competition by tapering heavy workouts on the days prior to competition and conducting warm-up exercises and technique drills before the start of a competition. However, these physical preparations should be supplemented with emotional and cognitive readying procedures if athletes are to maximize their chances of being ready to peak at competition time. This entails planning procedures for monitoring and controlling the task at hand as competition nears. It also means

monitoring and controlling emotions so that the energy and excitement for competing build slowly. But this should be done without the athlete becoming energized too soon or becoming overenergized and thus producing feelings of anxiety and worry rather than excitement and challenge.

Mental monitoring and readying procedures should be integrated with certain external markers such as waking up the morning of competition, traveling to the competition, arriving at the competition site, getting dressed, doing warm-up exercises and technique drills, and dealing with the short time between physical warm-ups and the beginning of competition. For example, some athletes have found it effective to wake up slowly in the morning and then, before getting out of bed, to relive through imagery a previous best performance. These athletes believe this type of imagery starts the competition day with a winning feeling and expectancy of success. When some athletes arrive at a competition site, they like to find a quiet place where they can practice 5 to 10 minutes of relaxation exercises such as deep breathing or passive progressive relaxation. Such athletes believe these relaxation procedures have the benefit of bringing them to the same starting point prior to each competition before they begin the rest of their on-site preparation. Other athletes combine their dressing ritual with cognitive focusing techniques designed to narrow attentional focus to what the athletes want to do during the competition. Often athletes end their dressing ritual or precede their physical warm-up with a 5- to 10-minute imagery exercise of exactly what they want to feel and perform during competition. Some athletes even use *all* of these readying procedures.

The most effective readying procedure is individual; this means that the length, content, and sequencing of behavioral protocols vary greatly from one player to another—even when the players are on the same team. Such variability stems partly from different needs in creating an ideal performance state and different preferences for the mental training exercises. Much trial-and-error experimentation, accompanied by consultations with a coach or sport psychology consultant, may be necessary before each athlete identifies the most effective precompetition ritual for performing well.

Some interesting qualitative research by Gould, Eklund, and Jackson (1992) and Eklund, Gould, and Jackson (1993) on thoughts and cognitions of Olympic wrestlers highlights the importance of precompetition and competition plans as well as individual variability. First, some between-group differences among medalists and nonmedalists revealed that medalists had competition plans firmly in their minds and did not spontaneously second-guess these plans during matches, whereas nonmedalists reported that spontaneous deviations from competition plans developed for matches and often had negative consequences (i.e., poorer performance). In addition, medalists had very systematic preperformance routines that they consistently adhered to throughout the Olympics, whereas nonmedalists reported deviating from their preperformance routines, especially in matches that they considered less challenging or less important.

Despite these differences between medalists and nonmedalists, interviews revealed individual differences and variations among the medalists. For example, one medalist placed great importance on prematch focus. "I just try to think about the techniques I am going to use and what strategies I am going to do and get that into my mind before I go out on the mat so I am focused on what I am going to do" (Eklund et al., 1993, p. 43). Conversely, another medalist deemphasized preperformance routines and strategy, feeling that they made them "too programmed." This orientation is captured in the following quotation: "I don't worry about strategy and technique. I try to keep my mind clear of getting caught up in all that stuff. If I have watched a wrestler and what he does—that is all I need to know. I don't go over what I am going to do or what different strategies I am going to try to use. I just keep my mind clear, and when I get out there I just react" (Eklund et al., 1993, p. 44).

Ultimately, it is important that each athlete develop a definite routine that he or she systematically goes through for every competition. The particular routine should be the one that best helps the athlete to get in touch with thoughts, feelings, and bodily responses and to make whatever adjustments are necessary so that when the time for competition arrives, the athlete is as near

his or her ideal performance state as possible. A good starting point in developing a routine is to examine what athletes are already doing in their precompetition preparation. The more experienced, successful athlete may already have an effective preparation ritual, although it may not be identified as such or be used systematically. It may be best to leave this athlete alone, except to have him or her consciously identify existing preparation behaviors that are effective and then commit to using these procedures consistently before each competition.

No athlete should be forced to use precompetition or competition readying procedures. Although most athletes find such structured rituals to be an effective way to enhance their level and consistency of performance, some athletes are not comfortable with such techniques or feel they are not beneficial. Other athletes may need only a very abbreviated readying procedure. For example, Jimmy Connors has said, "Because I'm familiar with the games of most players on tour, I never think far ahead about what I'm going to try to do in a match. . . . Before playing a tournament match, I just like to go off by myself somewhere private for five minutes or so to collect my thoughts" (Connors, 1984, p. 34). One important implication of the diversity in effective readying preferences is that many coaches may need to allow athletes much more flexibility in precompetition preparation procedures than is currently observed in many sports.

Some excellent examples of precompetition and competition planning come from the work of Orlick (1986) with Canadian Olympic athletes. Orlick has the athletes he works with develop very specific precompetition and competition plans. However, in addition, his athletes develop precompetition and competition *refocusing* plans in case things don't go exactly as they originally planned. This is extremely important because things out of an athlete's control can throw off his or her plans at the last second. And, as Jack Donohue, Canadian Olympic basketball coach, says, "What happens to you is nowhere near as important as how you react to what happens to you." A refocusing plan is aimed at helping athletes refocus away from unwanted external distractions or internal distractions such as worries, self-doubt, and self-put-downs. A good example of precompetition and competition refocusing plans for an Olympic speedskater is provided in Table 20-5.

Table 20-5 Refocusing Plans for an Olympic Speedskater

Worries About Competitors Before the Race

- They are human just like me. We'll see what they can do in the race, not in warm-ups or in training. I need to focus on my *own* preparation.

- All I can do is my best. Nobody can take that away from me. If my performance is good, I'll be happy. If it's not so good and I try, I shouldn't be disappointed.

- I'm racing for *me*. It's *my* max that I want.

Worry About Competitors During the Race

- If I start to think about others during the race, I'll shift my concentration to *my* race, *my* technique—"Stay low, race your race."

- "I have the potion—I have the motion."

Pre-Event Hassles

- Skate blades don't cut the ice—carry a small sharpening stone to pass over the blades.

- Delay in start—if I'm already on the ice and it's likely to be a short delay, jog around, keep moving, stay warm, do a mini warm-up with some accelerations. Follow normal prerace plan when approaching the line.

- Windy or snowy conditions—it's the same for everyone. Just go out and do what you can do.

Worries During Competition

- Poor start—no problem, it can happen. It's not the start that determines the final results. Follow your race plan. Push your max.

- Not hearing a split time—it's okay. Just skate well and race your race.

- Pain in legs—shift focus to the specifics of the task to be done, the steps in the turn, pushing the blade to the side, pushing hard to the finish line.

Source: Reprinted by permission from T. Orlick, 1986, *Psyching for Sport* (Champaign, IL: Human Kinetics Publishers), pp. 165–166.

Stress Application to Other Life Pursuits

One tremendous bonus that comes from implementing a mental training program is that the skills learned are applicable to life in general as well as to athletics, and the benefits last long after the competitive year is over. The training program can assist athletes in applying their new mental skills by suggesting relevant uses in nonathletic settings. For example, suggest that athletes learn to do their homework more quickly by using mental training concentration skills. With these skills, athletes can become more aware of when their mind is wandering and can bring their focus of attention back to the task at hand. If an athlete gets so uptight before tests that he or she cannot remember what was learned, the same relaxation and positive thinking skills that athletes are taught to control competitive anxiety can be used for test-taking anxiety and many other stressful situations people face in life. Another application of mental training is to visualize a speech or an important job or TV interview in advance to give oneself confidence. When athletic programs offer both physical and mental skills training, they provide a better argument that participating in competitive sport can also be a valuable educational experience. For example, Danish, Petitpas, and Hale (1993) describe a life skills program that uses skills developed in sport as a basis for developing and learning basic life skills. This type of approach is becoming more popular within applied sport psychology.

A recent issue of the *Journal of Applied Sport Psychology* (2002, 4) focused on the application of psychological skills typically used in sport and exercise settings to other settings and endeavors such as business, medicine, space travel, and special forces. More and more sport psychology consultants are practicing in areas outside of sport, fueled in part by the renewed interest in the psychology of excellence. For example, Loehr and Schwartz (2001) have discussed the similarities of high performers, whether they be elite athletes or CEOs working for a Fortune 500 company. Similarly, Murphy (1996) discusses the transfer from working with elite athletes at the Olympic Training Center to working with performers in the corporate arena. Murphy reports that his clients (whether sport or nonsport) tell him that the skills they are taught help them to achieve their best under pressure, allow them to stay focused during difficult tasks, and enable them to enjoy even the most challenging assignments. Thus, the transfer from sport to other areas of life seems to be a fertile ground for future practitioners and researchers.

Practice It Before Teaching It

Before teaching any of the mental training exercises to athletes, sport psychology consultants and coaches should take the time to practice each technique themselves. Personally experiencing an exercise is an excellent way to increase one's ability to teach a specific technique and to answer any questions athletes may have about it. An additional bonus of practicing the exercises, particularly if the practice is systematic and long term, is that the practitioner will accrue psychological benefits similar to those that the athletes receive from the practice. After all, athletes are not the only people who can benefit from learning skills such as effectively setting goals, planning strategies for goal achievement, handling stress, and maintaining concentration and confidence under even the most demanding situations.

Teach by Example

In regard to psychological control—or any type of behavior—good coaches and sport psychology consultants teach and lead by example. If the person leading the mental training program does not exemplify what he or she is teaching, it is highly unlikely the athletes will model it either. The coach who appears calm, confident, and in control during a competition usually has athletes who act the same way. Players are more likely to offer encouragement and support to one another when they have a leader who models encouragement (Wescott, 1980). But research on modeling need not be cited to illustrate the importance of teaching by example. All one has to do is watch a ball game. The next time you see athletes consistently losing control and concentration after poor officiating calls, look to the bench, and you probably will see the coach behaving similarly. Watch how athletes react to poor performance. Athletes who become negative or rattled after mistakes are often led by coaches who react similarly. For psychological training to be maximally effective, the coaches and sport psychology consultants must exemplify in practice and competition the behavior they expect from athletes.

Observe Practices and Competitions Whenever Possible

As noted earlier, one of the disadvantages of sport psychology consultants conducting mental training programs with teams is their lack of day-to-day availability. Despite this limitation, it is critical that consultants attempt to attend some practices and competitions. We have found that this is particularly important at the beginning stages of the intervention. Listening and reading about an athlete's problem cannot substitute for actually being there to observe it. This firsthand view can provide consultants with critical information that might not be evident from an interview or paper-and-pencil measure. As noted earlier, the problem might be biomechanical or physical in nature rather than psychological, and this would not likely show up in an interview or a test. Perhaps even more important than the information the consultants gain is the trust that will be built up as athletes know that they really care about them, because they are taking the time to see them perform. In surveys evaluating the effectiveness of sport psychology consultants (Gould, Tammen, Murphy, & May, 1989; Partington & Orlick, 1987a), a critical component to the perceived effectiveness of sport psychology consultants that directly affected building trust between athletes and consultants was the amount of time the consultants spent being with and observing the athletes.

Emphasize Strengths as Competition Nears

Behavior by the coach and sport psychology consultant prior to and during competition is particularly critical. The nearer the time to competition, the more important it is that they are reassuring and complimentary toward athletes. This is not the time to be critical of technique or anything else. Besides, it is too late to change weaknesses, so there is no reason to focus on them. Instead, if at all possible, get athletes to think they are looking great and help build their confidence. In short, now is the time to build from what is positive, to play to strengths rather than weaknesses. Such behavior by the coach and sport psychology consultant will help athletes build and maintain confidence rather than self-doubt prior to competition. This usually means better performance.

The preceding recommendation is particularly critical with athletes who have higher anxiety and lower self-confidence. Williams et al. (2003) found that when these athletes perceived the coach to lose emotional control, become negative, or fail to be supportive, this was likely to lead to poorer performance and more difficulty maintaining optimal mental states and focus. Using the self-monitoring or outside monitoring described in the next section should help coaches and sport psychology consultants assess their behavior prior to and during competition.

Monitor Your Behavior

In Chapter 12, Ravizza suggests that athletes become more aware of their behavior, thoughts, and feelings through self-monitoring. The same awareness on the part of coaches and sport psychology consultants can help them become more effective in working with athletes. For example, by means of self-monitoring, coaches and sport psychology consultants can become more conscious of how they communicate with athletes during different situations. They should monitor what they say as well as what they communicate with their body language. They should ask themselves such questions as "How is my behavior likely to change in certain situations?" "Am I a good role model for the mental discipline and psychological control I wish to teach?" "Am I behaving in a way that facilitates the personal growth and performance of my athletes, or is my behavior toward them disabling?" The awareness created by conscientious and objective self-monitoring is a necessary first step in becoming more effective in working with athletes.

There is also merit in having someone else observe and evaluate one's behavior. For example, if a coach has a sport psychology consultant working with the team, he or she would be an ideal person to observe the coach's behavior during practices and games. Coaching behaviors should be analyzed on the basis of the principles for desirable behavior elaborated in earlier chapters. Evaluation would be facilitated if special forms were employed (e.g., Smith, Smoll, & Hunt, 1977; Tharp & Gallimore, 1976). The information presented in earlier chapters can be used to help plan a specific strategy for modifying a coach's behavior in a direction that is more likely to facilitate the performance and personal growth of his or her athletes. A prospective sport psychology consultant's behavior could be assessed through a supervised internship working with athletes on mental skills training.

Ethical Considerations for the Coach and Sport Psychology Consultant

Sport psychology is a relatively young profession, and the people practicing applied sport psychology in the 1970s and early 1980s had little to guide them in terms of ethical issues. The purpose of this section is to call attention to some basic ethical concerns involved in implementing mental skills training. This brief discussion should not be construed as a complete presentation of the many complex ethical issues and interrelationships involved in psychological skills training. A more thorough discussion of these topics can be found in Moore (2003); Whelan, Meyers, and Elkin (1996); and Sachs (1993).

To better understand what specific situations and circumstances applied sport psychologists perceive as particularly difficult and possibly controversial from an ethical perspective, Petitpas, Brewer, Rivera, and Van Raalte (1994) administered surveys to individuals practicing applied sport psychology. Respondents were asked to report their own behavior and belief concerning 47 ethical situations as well as to provide a brief description of difficult ethical situations they had personally experienced in applied sport psychology. Results revealed that four classifications of behaviors were identified as requiring the most difficult ethical judgments or were perceived as controversial. These included (a) conflicts with confidentiality (e.g., reporting recruiting violations to appropriate officials); (b) conflicts between personal values and professional ethics (e.g., working with an athlete who uses steroids); (c) conflicts with dual relationships (e.g., socializing with clients); (d) conflicts with self-presentation or advertising (e.g., including athlete testimonials in advertising). Ethics in any profession have many gray areas, making decisions extremely difficult at times.

To help guide professionals working in applied sport psychology settings to more effectively deal with ethical dilemmas, sport psychology associations such as the Association for the Advancement of Applied Sport Psychology, the North American Society for the Psychology of Sport and Physical Activity, and the Canadian Society for Psychomotor Learning and Sport Psychology have developed modifications of the American Psychological Association's Ethical Standards (1992). At the core of these standards is the general philosophy that sport psychology consultants respect the dignity and worth of the individual and honor the preservation and protection of fundamental human rights. In addition, consultants are committed to increasing the knowledge of human behavior and of people's understanding of themselves and others in sport environments. The essence of this philosophy is that the athlete's welfare must be foremost. For a more detailed discussion of ethical principles please consult the American Psychological Association's ethical guidelines (1992). In addition, McCann, Jowdy and Van Raalte (2002) provide ethical guidelines especially for assessments.

Potential Problem Areas

Although the potential benefits of implementing a psychological skills training program are clearly demonstrable, there are of course some problems that a consultant or coach will have to deal with throughout the process. Each situation, naturally, will offer its own unique set of problems. For example, working one on one with individual athletes is quite different from working with an entire team. Working with Olympic athletes or professional athletes might present an entirely different set of problems than working with high school athletes. However, a number of common problems have been identified by athletes, coaches, and consultants when it comes down to practically implementing these mental training programs. If not adequately dealt with, these problems can severely reduce the effectiveness of the program. Some examples of common problems include the following:

- Overcoming player reluctance about participating in a mental training program
- Lack of time spent with individual athletes in a team setting
- Gaining the trust of the athletes
- Making sure athletes systematically practice their skills
- Consultant's lack of knowledge about the specific sport
- Maintaining contact with athletes throughout a competitive season
- Getting full cooperation from coaching staff/organization

A sport psychology consultant needs to be aware of these potential problem areas and be ready to deal with them if necessary. It has taken most of us several years to learn many of these things by trial and error. Many of us made mistakes in our early years of consulting because we simply weren't aware of, or hadn't experienced, many of these nuances of setting up and implementing a mental training program. A lot of homework and planning should be a prerequisite for any sport psychology consultant considering working with athletes and teams. However, with good preparation, careful thought, and a sense of commitment, this can be a very rewarding experience. After all, helping individuals reach their potential both inside and outside the world of sport is what it's all about.

Summary

In this chapter we have addressed many general issues relating to the integration and implementation of a psychological skills training program. In summary: (1) there are advantages to having either a coach or a sport psychologist implement a psychological skills training program, (2) athletes of all types and age and skill levels can benefit from mental training, (3) mental skills training should continue for as long as an athlete participates in sport, (4) the initial mental skills training program should probably last 3 to 6 months and start in the off-season or preseason, (5) a psychological skills needs assessment should be made to determine the specific components to be incorporated in training and the psychological objectives to be achieved, (6) there is no one best way to sequence and integrate psychological components even though one was proposed, (7) once basic mental skills are acquired they should have a performance-specific focus and be integrated with practice of physical skills, and (8) real benefits from psychological skills training will only occur with long-term systematic practice.

We have also suggested practical teaching pointers that apply either to the entire psychological training program or to many of its components. Stress that athletes accept self-responsibility for their mental state. Be flexible, eclectic, and individualized in planning training techniques. Stress personal growth and how to use mental skills in nonathletic settings. Practice techniques before teaching them. Teach by personally exemplifying the mental skills being taught. Finally, we concluded the chapter with ethical considerations that all psychological training implementors need to be aware of and observe in their own behavior.

This chapter and the earlier chapters on psychological skills training have emphasized that the rewards are many for those who choose to teach and practice mental training in their dedication to the pursuit of excellence. Benefits will accrue not only in athletic performance but in performance outside of the athletic setting and, perhaps more important, in general personal growth and in enhanced sense of self-worth.

Study Questions

1. Discuss who will benefit most from psychological skills training.

2. Are psychological skills intervention programs effective in enhancing performance? Provide evidence to support your answer.

3. What are some advantages and disadvantages of a coach or sport psychology consultant conducting a mental training program?

4. How much time should be spent in mental training?

5. When is the best time to practice psychological skills?

6. When is the best time to implement a psychological skills training program?

7. Discuss what would be covered in a first interview with an athlete.

8. Discuss the use of psychological inventories to help assess athletes' psychological skills.

9. Discuss Vealey's distinction between psychological methods and psychological skills. What are the different categories of psychological skills? What impact does this distinction between methods and skills have on the implementation of a psychological skills training program?

10. John, a golfer, goes to a sport psychologist because his play is "erratic." One of the sport psychologist's observation is that he has no consistent preshot readying procedure. How might the sport psychologist help John develop a preshot routine, what might it include, and why should this intervention improve John's performance?

11. Discuss how a psychological skills program might be evaluated.

12. Discuss five practical pointers that may help make a psychological skills program more effective. Cite specific practical examples and research to support your points.

References

American Psychological Association. (1992). Ethical principles and code of conduct. *American Psychologist, 47,* 1597–1611.

Anderson, A., Miles, A., Mahoney, C., & Robinson, P. (2002). Evaluating the effectiveness of applied sport psychology practice: Making the case for a case study approach. *The Sport Psychologist, 16,* 432–453.

Association for the Advancement of Applied Sport Psychology Newsletter (Winter 1991, vol. 6).

Bandura, A. (1986). *Social foundations of thought and action: A social cognitive theory.* Englewood Cliffs, NJ: Prentice Hall.

Barber, H., & Krane, V. (2005). The elephant in the lockerroom: Opening the dialogue about sexual orientation on women's sports teams. In M. Andersen (Ed.). *Sport psychology in practice.* Champaign, IL: Human Kinetics.

Beckman, J., & Kellmann, M. (2003). Procedures and principles of sport psychological assessment. *The Sport Psychologist, 17,* 338–350.

Botterill, C. (1990). Sport psychology and professional hockey. *The Sport Psychologist, 4,* 369–377.

Butler, R. J., & Hardy, L. (1992). The performance profile: Theory and application. *The Sport Psychologist, 6,* 253–264.

Butryn, T. (2002). Critically examining white racial identity and privilege in sport psychology consulting. *The Sport Psychologist, 16,* 316–336.

Connors, J. (1984, December). *Tennis,* pp. 33–35.

Dale, G. A., & Wrisberg, C. A. (1996). The use of a performance profiling technique in a team setting: Getting the athletes and coach on the "same page." *The Sport Psychologist, 10,* 261–277.

Danish, S., Petitpas, A., & Hale, B. (1993). Life development intervention for athletes: Life skills through sports. *Counseling Psychologist, 21,* 352–385.

Durand-Bush, N., Salmela, J., & Green-Demers, I. (2001). The Ottawa mental skills assessment tool (OMSAT3). *The Sport Psychologist, 15,* 1–19.

Eklund, R. C., Gould, D., & Jackson, S. A. (1993). Psychological foundations of Olympic wrestling excellence: Reconciling individual differences and nomothetic characterization. *Journal of Applied Sport Psychology, 5,* 35–47.

Gordon, S. (1990). A mental skills training program for the Western Australia cricket team. *The Sport Psychologist, 4,* 386–399.

Gould, D. (1983). Developing psychological skills in young athletes. In N. Wood (Ed.), *Coaching science update*. Ottawa, ON: Coaching Association of Canada.

Gould, D., Eklund, R. C., & Jackson, S. A. (1992). 1988 U.S. Olympic wrestling excellence: I. Mental preparation, precompetition cognition, and affect. *The Sport Psychologist, 6,* 358–382.

Gould, D., Horn, T., & Spreeman, J. (1983). Competitive anxiety in junior elite wrestlers. *Journal of Sport Psychology, 5,* 58–71.

Gould, D., Murphy, S., Tammen, V., & May, J. (1991). An evaluation of Olympic sport psychology consultant effectiveness. *The Sport Psychologist, 5,* 111–127.

Gould, D., Tammen, V., Murphy, S., & May, J. (1989). An examination of the U.S. Olympic sport psychology consultants and the services they provide. *The Sport Psychologist, 3,* 300–312.

Greenspan, M. J., & Feltz, D. F. (1989). Psychological interventions with athletes in competitive situations: A review. *The Sport Psychologist, 3,* 219–236.

Halliwell, W. (1990). Providing sport psychology consulting services to a professional sport organization. *The Sport Psychologist, 4,* 369–377.

Kirschenbaum, D. (1997). *Mind matters: 7 steps to smarter sport performance*. Carmel, IN: Cooper Publishing.

Kontos, A., & Breland-Noble, A. (2002). Racial/ethnic diversity in applied sport psychology: A multicultural introduction to working with athletes of color. *The Sport Psychologist, 16,* 296–315.

Kremer, J., & Scully, D. (1998). What applied sport psychologists often don't do: On empowerment and independence. In H. Sternberg, I. Cockerill, & A. Dewey (Eds.), *What sport psychologists do* (pp. 21–27). Leichester: The British Psychological Society.

Loehr, J., & Schwartz, T. (2001, January). The making of the corporate athlete. *Harvard Business Review,* pp. 120–128.

Mahoney, M. J., Gabriel, T. J., & Perkins, T. S. (1987). Psychological skills and exceptional athletic performance. *The Sport Psychologist, 1,* 181–199.

Martens, R. (1977). *Sport competition anxiety test*. Champaign, IL: Human Kinetics.

Martens, R., Vealey, R. S., & Burton, D. (1990). *Competitive anxiety in sport*. Champaign, IL: Human Kinetics.

Martin, S. B., Wrisberg, C. A., Beitel, P. A., & Lounsbury, J. (1997). NCAA Division 1 athletes' attitudes toward seeking sport psychology consultation: The development of an objective instrument. *The Sport Psychologist, 11,* 201–218.

McCann, S., Jowdy, D., & Van Raalte, J. (2002). Assessment in sport and exercise psychology. In J. Van Raalte and B. Brewer (Eds.), *Exploring sport and exercise psychology* (2nd ed., pp. 291–305). Washington, DC: American Psychological Association.

McNair, D. M., Lorr, M., & Droppleman, L. F. (1971). *EDITS manual for POMS*. San Diego, CA: Educational and Industrial Testing Service.

Meyers, A. W., Whelan, J. P., & Murphy, S. M. (1996). Cognitive behavioral strategies in athletic performance enhancement. In M. Hersen, R. M. Eisler, & P. M. Miller (Eds.), *Progress in behavior modification* (Vol. 30, pp. 137–164). Pacific Grove, CA: Brooks/Cole.

Moore, Z. E. (2003). Ethical dilemmas in sport psychology: Discussion and recommendations for practice. *Professional Psychology: Research and Practice, 34,* 601–610.

Murphy, S. (1995). *Sport psychology intervention.* Champaign, IL: Human Kinetics.

Murphy, S. (1996). *The achievement zone.* New York: Putnam.

Murphy, S., Jowdy, D., & Durtschi, S. (1990). *Imagery perspective survey.* Colorado Springs, CO: U.S. Olympic Training Center.

Nideffer, R. M. (1976). Test of attentional and interpersonal style. *Journal of Personality and Social Psychology, 34,* 394–404.

Nideffer, R. M. (1989). Psychological services for the U.S. track and field team. *The Sport Psychologist, 3,* 350–357.

Orlick, T. (1980). *In pursuit of excellence.* Champaign, IL: Human Kinetics.

Orlick, T. (1986). *Psyching for sport: Mental training for athletes.* Champaign, IL: Human Kinetics.

Orlick, T. (1992). The psychology of personal excellence. *Contemporary Thought on Performance Enhancement, 1,* 109–122.

Orlick, T., & McCaffrey, N. (1991). Mental training with children for sport and life. *The Sport Psychologist, 5,* 322–334.

Partington, J., & Orlick, T. (1987a). The sport psychology consultant: Olympic coaches' views. *The Sport Psychologist, 1,* 95–102.

Partington, J., & Orlick, T. (1987b). The sport psychology consultant evaluation form. *The Sport Psychologist, 1,* 309–317.

Patrick, T. D., & Hrycaiko, D. W. (1998). Effects of a mental training package on an endurance performance. *The Sport Psychologist, 12,* 283–299.

Petitpas, A., Brewer, B., Rivera, P., & Van Raalte, J. (1994). Ethical beliefs and behaviors in applied sport psychology: The AAASP ethics survey. *Journal of Applied Sport Psychology, 6,* 135–151.

Petitpas, A. J., Giges, B., & Danish, S. J. (1999). The sport psychologist–athlete relationship: Implications for training. *The Sport Psychologist, 13,* 344–357.

Poczwardowski, A., Sherman, C. P., & Henschen, K. P. (1998). A sport psychology service delivery heuristic: Building on theory and practice. *The Sport Psychologist, 12,* 191–207.

Ravizza, K. (1990). Sportpsych consultation issues in professional baseball. *The Sport Psychologist, 4,* 330–340.

Ravizza, K., & Hanson, T. (1995). *Heads up baseball: Playing the game one pitch at a time.* Indianapolis, IN: Masters Press.

Sachs, M. (1993). Professional ethics in sport psychology. In R. N. Singer, M. Murphey, & L. K. Tennant (Eds.), *Handbook of research in sport psychology* (pp. 921–932). New York: Macmillan.

Seabourne, T., Weinberg, R. S., Jackson, A., & Suinn, R. M. (1985). Effect of individualized, nonindividualized and package intervention strategies on karate performance. *Journal of Sport Psychology, 7,* 40–50.

Sexton, T. L., & Whitson, S. C. (1994). The status of the counseling relationship: An empirical review, theoretical implications, and research directions. *The Counseling Psychologist, 22*, 6–78.

Smith, R. E. (1989). Applied sport psychology in the age of accountability. *Journal of Applied Sport Psychology, 1*, 166–180.

Smith, R. E. & Johnson, J. (1990). An organizational empowerment approach to consultation in professional baseball. *The Sport Psychologist, 4*, 347–357.

Smith, R. E., Schutz, R. W., Smoll, F. L., & Ptacek, J. T. (1995). Development and validation of a multi-dimensional measure of sport-specific psychological skills: The Athletic Coping Skills Inventory–28. *Journal of Sport and Exercise Psychology, 17*, 379–387.

Smith, R. E., & Smoll, F. L. (1982). Psychological stress: A conceptual model and some intervention strategies in youth sports. In R. A. Magill, M. J. Ash, & F. L. Smoll (Eds.), *Children in sport* (pp. 153–177). Champaign, IL: Human Kinetics.

Smith, R. E., Smoll, F. L., & Hunt, E. (1977). A system for the behavioral assessment of athletic coaches. *Research Quarterly, 48*, 401–407.

Smith, R. E., Smoll, F. L., & Schutz, R. W. (1990). Measurement and correlates of sport-specific cognitive and somatic trait anxiety: The Sport Anxiety Scale. *Anxiety Research, 2*, 263–280.

Suinn, R. M. (1986). *Seven steps to peak performance*. Toronto, ON: Luber.

Taylor, J. (1995). A conceptual model for integrating athletes' needs and sport demands in the development of competitive mental preparation strategies. *The Sport Psychologist, 9*, 339–357.

Terry, P. C., Mayer, J. L., & Howe, B. L. (1998). Effectiveness of a mental training program for novice scuba divers. *Journal of Applied Sport Psychology, 10*, 251–267.

Tharp, R. G., & Gallimore, R. (1976, January). What a coach can teach a teacher. *Psychology Today*, 75–78.

Tkachuk, G., Leslie-Toogood, A., & Martin, G. (2003). Behavioral assessment in sport psychology. *The Sport Psychologist, 17*, 104–117.

Van Schoyck, S. R., & Grasha, A. F. (1981). Attentional style variations and athletic ability. The advantages of a sports-specific test. *Journal of Sport Psychology, 3*, 149–165.

Vealey, R. S. (1986). Conceptualization of sport-confidence and competitive orientation: Preliminary investigation and instrument development. *Journal of Sport Psychology, 8*, 221–246.

Vealey, R. S. (1988). Future directions in psychological skills training. *The Sport Psychologist, 2*, 318–336.

Vealey, R. (1994). Current status and prominent issues in sport psychology interventions. *Medicine and Science in Sport and Exercise*, 495–502.

Weinberg, R. S., & Comar, W. (1994). The effectiveness of psychological interventions in competitive sport. *Sports Medicine Journal, 18*, 406–418.

Weiss, M. R. (1991). Psychological skill development in children and adolescents. *The Sport Psychologist, 5*, 335–354.

Wescott, W. L. (1980). Effects of teacher modeling on children's peer encouragement behavior. *Research Quarterly, 51*, 585–587.

Whelan, J. P., Meyers, A. W., & Donovan, C. (1995). Competitive recreational athletes: A multisystemic model. In S. Murphy (Ed.), *Sport Psychology Interventions* (pp. 71–116). Champaign, IL: Human Kinetics.

Whelan, J. P., Meyers, A. W., & Elkin, D. (1996). Ethics in sport and exercise psychology. In J. L. Van Raalte and S. Brewer (Eds.), *Exploring sport and exercise psychology* (pp. 431–447). Washington, DC: American Psychological Association.

Williams, J. M., Jerome, G. J., Kenow, L. J., Rogers, T., Sartain, T. A., & Darland, G. (2003). Factoring structure of the coaching behavior questionnaire and its relationship to athlete variables. *The Sport Psychologist, 17,* 16–34.

Zizzi, S., & Perna, F. (2002). Integrating web pages and e-mail into sport psychology consultations. *The Sport Psychologist, 16,* 416–431.

Development and Implementation of Coach-Training Programs: Cognitive-Behavioral Principles and Techniques[1]

Frank L. Smoll, *University of Washington*
Ronald E. Smith, *University of Washington*

I try never to plant a negative seed. I try to make every comment a positive comment. There's a lot of scientific evidence to support positive management.

—Jimmy Johnson, former National Football League coach

The most heavily publicized area of sport psychology tends to be interventions for enhancing performance of elite athletes. However, youth sports is another domain that is equally worthy of attention. **Youth sports** refers to "adult-organized and controlled athletic programs for young people in the age range 6 to 18 years. The participants are formally organized into teams and leagues, and they attend practices and scheduled competitions under the supervision of an adult leader" (Smoll & Smith, 2002, p. xi). An estimated 41 million youngsters participate in nonschool sports, and approximately 6 to 7 million more take part in interscholastic athletics (Ewing & Seefeldt, 2002). There has been continued growth over the past

several decades, which has been accompanied by a greater degree of adult involvement as well (Martens, 1988; Weiss & Hayashi, 1996). These programs have become extremely complex social systems that have attracted the attention of researchers interested in studying the impact of competition on psychosocial development (see Brustad, Babkes, & Smith, 2001; Cahill & Pearl, 1993; Malina & Clark, 2003; Smoll & Smith, 2002; Weiss, 2004).

Youth sports are regarded as potentially important in child and adolescent development, and participation is believed to have direct relevance to the acquisition of prosocial attitudes and behaviors, such as respect for authority, cooperation, self-discipline, risk-taking, and the ability to tolerate frustration and to delay gratification (Coakley, 1993; Ewing, Seefeldt, & Brown, 1996; Martens, 1993; Scanlan, 2002; Smoll, 1989). Yet a

[1]Preparation of this chapter was supported in part by Grant 2297 to Ronald E. Smith and Frank L. Smoll from the William T. Grant Foundation.

realistic appraisal indicates that participation does not automatically result in these outcomes. The most important determinant of the effects of participation lies in the relationship between coach and athlete (Ewing, Seefeldt, & Brown, 1996; Martens, 2004; Smoll & Smith, 1989). Most coaches are fairly well versed in the technical aspects of the sport, but they rarely have had any formal training in creating a healthy psychological environment. It is here that sport psychologists are capable of making significant contributions, by developing and conducting educational programs that positively affect coaching behaviors and thereby increase the likelihood that youngsters will have positive sport experiences.

This chapter begins with an overview of the development of an intervention designed to assist coaches in relating more effectively to young athletes. Consideration is then given to cognitive-behavioral principles and techniques for implementing psychologically oriented coach-training programs. Although the focus throughout is on youth sports, the various methods and approaches are applicable to sport psychology workshops for coaches at virtually all levels of competition, including the professional ranks (Smith & Johnson, 1990).

Developing a Coach-Training Program

A crucial first step in developing a training program is to determine *what* is to be presented. In addressing this issue, our work was guided by a fundamental assumption that a training program should be based on scientific evidence rather than on intuition or what we "know" on the basis of informal observation. An empirical foundation for coaching guidelines not only enhances the validity and potential value of the program, but also increases its credibility in the eyes of consumers.

Theoretical Model and Research Paradigm

Our approach to generating an empirical database for a coach-training program was guided by a mediational model of coach–athlete interactions, the basic elements of which are represented as follows:

COACH'S BEHAVIORS → ATHLETES' PERCEPTIONS
AND RECALL → ATHLETES' EVALUATIVE REACTIONS

This model stipulates that the ultimate effects of coaching behaviors are mediated by the athletes' recall and the meaning they attribute to the coach's actions. In other words, what athletes remember about their coach's behaviors and how they interpret these actions affect the way athletes evaluate their sport experiences. Furthermore, a complex of cognitive and affective processes is involved at this mediational level. These processes are likely to be affected not only by the coach's behaviors but also by other factors, such as the athlete's age, what he or she expects of coaches (normative beliefs and expectations), and certain personality variables such as self-esteem and anxiety. The basic three-element model was expanded to reflect these factors (Smoll & Smith, 1989). The more comprehensive model specifies a number of situational as well as coach and athlete individual difference variables that are expected to influence coach behaviors and the perceptions and reactions of athletes to them.

In accordance with the model we have sought to determine how observed coaching behaviors, athletes' perception and recall of the coach's behaviors, and athlete attitudes are interrelated. We have also explored the manner in which athlete and coach individual difference variables might serve as moderator variables and influence basic behavior–attitude relations.

Measurement of Coaching Behaviors

Several research groups have used behavioral assessment techniques to observe the actual behaviors of youth coaches and their effects on young athletes (see Smith, Smoll, & Christensen, 1996). To measure leadership behaviors, we developed the Coaching Behavior Assessment System (CBAS) to permit the direct observation and coding of coaches' actions during practices and games (Smith, Smoll, & Hunt, 1977). The behavioral categories, derived from content analyses

Table 21-1 **Response Categories of the Coaching Behavior Assessment System**

Response Category	Behavioral Description
Class I: Reactive (Elicited) Behaviors	
Responses to desirable performance	
Reinforcement	A positive, rewarding reaction (verbal or nonverbal) to a good play or good effort
Nonreinforcement	Failure to respond to a good performance
Responses to mistakes	
Mistake-contingent encouragement	Encouragement given to a player following a mistake
Mistake-contingent technical instruction	Instructing or demonstrating to a player how to correct a mistake
Punishment	A negative reaction (verbal or nonverbal) following a mistake
Punitive technical instruction	Technical instruction following a mistake given in a punitive or hostile manner
Ignoring mistakes	Failure to respond to a player's mistake
Responses to misbehavior	
Keeping control	Reactions intended to restore or maintain order among team members
Class II: Spontaneous (Emitted) Behaviors	
Game related	
General technical instruction	Spontaneous instruction in the techniques and strategies of the sport (not following a mistake)
General encouragement	Spontaneous encouragement that does not follow a mistake
Organization	Administrative behavior that sets the stage for play by assigning, for example, duties, responsibilities, positions
Game irrelevant	
General communication	Interactions with players unrelated to the game/practice

Source: Adapted from Smith, Smoll, and Hunt, 1977.

of observers' verbal descriptions of coach behavior–situation units using a time-sampling procedure, are shown in Table 21-1.

The 12 CBAS categories are divided into two major classes of behaviors. **Reactive** (elicited) behaviors are responses to immediately preceding athlete or team behaviors, whereas **spontaneous** (emitted) behaviors are initiated by the coach and are not a response to a discernible preceding event. Use of the CBAS in observing and coding coaching behaviors in a variety of sports indicates that the scoring system is sufficiently comprehensive to incorporate the vast majority of overt leader behaviors, that high interrater reliability can be obtained, and that individual differences in behavioral patterns can be discerned (Chaumeton & Duda, 1988; Cruz et al., 1987; Horn, 1984, 1985; Jones, Housner, & Kornspan, 1997; Krane, Eklund, & McDermott, 1991; Rejeski, Darracott, & Hutslar, 1979; Sherman & Hassan, 1986; Wandzilak, Ansorge, & Potter, 1988).

Coaching Behaviors and Children's Evaluative Reactions

Following development of the CBAS, a systematic program of research was carried out over a period of several years (Curtis, Smith, & Smoll, 1979; Smith & Smoll, 1990; Smith, Smoll, & Curtis, 1978; Smith, Zane, Smoll, & Coppel, 1983; Smoll, Smith, Curtis, & Hunt, 1978). This involved pursuing several questions concerning the potential impact of youth coaches on athletes' psychological welfare. For example, how frequently do coaches engage in behaviors such as encouragement, punishment, instruction, and organization, and how are observable coaching behaviors related to children's reactions to their organized athletic experiences? Answers to such questions not only were a first step in describing the behavioral ecology of one aspect of the youth sport setting, but also provided an empirical basis for the development of a psychologically oriented intervention program.

The results indicated that the typical baseball or basketball coach engages in more than 200 codable actions during an average game. We were thus able to generate behavioral profiles of up to several thousand responses over the course of a season. In large-scale observational studies, we coded more than 80,000 behaviors of some 70 male youth coaches, then interviewed and administered questionnaires after the season to nearly 1,000 children in their homes to measure their recall of their coaches' behaviors and their evaluative reactions to the coach, their sport experiences, and themselves. We also obtained coaches' postseason ratings of how frequently they engaged in each of the observed behaviors.

These data provided clear evidence for the crucial role of the coach. We found that won-lost records bore little relation to our psychosocial outcome measure (i.e., reactions to coach, enjoyment, and self-esteem); virtually all of the systematic variance was accounted for by differences in coaching behaviors. Not surprisingly, we found that the most positive outcomes occurred when children played for coaches who engaged in high levels of positive reinforcement for both desirable performance and effort, who responded to mistakes with encouragement and technical instruction, and who emphasized the importance of fun and personal improvement over winning. Not only did the children who had such coaches like their coaches more and have more fun, but they also liked their teammates more.

Another important issue concerns the degree of accuracy with which coaches perceive their own behaviors. Correlations between CBAS-observed behaviors and coaches' ratings of how frequently they performed the behaviors were generally low and nonsignificant. The only actions on their self-report measure that correlated significantly (around .50) with the observational measures were the punitive behaviors. Overall, we found that children's ratings on the same perceived behavior scales correlated much more highly with CBAS measures than did the coaches' own reports! It thus appears that coaches were, for the most part, blissfully unaware of how they behaved and that athletes were more accurate perceivers of actual coach behaviors. Because behavior change requires an awareness of how one currently is behaving, this finding clearly indicated the need to increase coaches' self-awareness when developing an intervention program.

The data from one of our field studies were also used to test a hypothesis derived from a self-enhancement model of self-esteem (Smith & Smoll, 1990). This model posits that people who are low in self-esteem are particularly responsive to variations in supportiveness from others because they have a strong need for positive feedback from others (or, alternatively, because they find a lack of support to be highly aversive). This hypothesis was strongly supported by the data; the greatest difference in liking for supportive (reinforcing and encouraging) versus nonsupportive coaches was found for children who were low in self-esteem. Also consistent with a self-enhancement model, boys with low self-esteem showed the greatest difference in attraction toward (i.e., liking for) coaches who were either quite high or quite low on a behavioral dimension identified through factor analysis as instructiveness (general technical instruction and mistake-contingent technical instruction *versus* general communication and general encouragement). Instructiveness should be relevant to self-enhancement because such behaviors are likely to be perceived by athletes as contributing to skill increments that would increase positive self-regard.

Assessing the Efficacy of a Coach-Training Program

Sweeping conclusions are often drawn about the efficacy of intervention programs in the absence of anything approximating acceptable scientific evidence. We therefore felt it was important not only to develop an empirical foundation for a coach-training program but also to measure its effects on coaches and the youngsters who play for them.

The results from the observational studies formed the basis for a cognitive-behavioral intervention designed to train coaches to provide a more positive and socially supportive athletic environment for their young athletes. In an initial field experiment (Smith, Smoll, & Curtis, 1979), 31 Little League Baseball coaches were randomly assigned either to an experimental (training) group or to a no-treatment control group. During a preseason workshop, which is known as Coach Effectiveness Training (CET), behavioral guidelines derived from our earlier research were presented and modeled by the trainers. In addition to the information-modeling portion of the program, behavioral feedback and self-monitoring procedures were employed in an attempt to increase the coaches' self-awareness of their behaviors and to encourage them to comply with the coaching guidelines. To provide behavioral feedback, observers trained in the use of the CBAS observed experimental group coaches for two complete games. Behavioral profiles for each coach were derived from these observations and

were then mailed to the coaches so that they were able to see the distribution of their own behaviors. Trained coaches were also given brief self-monitoring forms that they completed immediately after the first 10 games of the season.

To assess the effects of the experimental program, CBAS data were collected throughout the season, and behavioral profiles were generated for each coach in the experimental and control groups. Postseason outcome measures were obtained from 325 children in individual data collection sessions in their homes. On both observed behavior and player perception measures, the trained coaches differed from the controls in a manner consistent with the coaching guidelines. The trained coaches gave more reinforcement in response to good performance and effort, and they responded to mistakes with more encouragement and technical instruction and with fewer punitive responses. These behavioral differences were, in turn, reflected in their players' attitudes. Although the average won-lost percentages of the two groups of coaches did not differ, the trained coaches were better liked and were rated as better teachers. Additionally, players on their teams liked one another more and enjoyed their sport experiences more. These results seemingly reflect the more socially supportive environment created by the trained coaches. Perhaps most encouraging was the fact that children who played for the trained coaches exhibited a significant increase on a measure of general self-esteem compared to scores obtained a year earlier, while those who played for the untrained coaches showed no significant change.

Replication of our research on the efficacy of CET has been conducted with the inclusion of several additional outcomes measures. The study included 18 coaches and 152 children who participated in three Little League Baseball programs. Using a quasi-experimental design, one league (8 teams) was designated as the experimental group. The no-treatment control group included 10 teams from two other leagues. Prior to the season, the experimental group coaches participated in CET. The control coaches participated in a technical skills training workshop conducted by the Seattle Mariners baseball team. To assess the effects of CET, preseason and postseason data were collected for 62 and 90 children in the experimental and control groups, respectively.

The study yielded four major results. First, the CET intervention resulted in player-perceived behavioral differences between trained and untrained coaches that were consistent with the behavioral guidelines. Thus, as in previous research (Smith et al., 1979), the experimental manipulation was successful in promoting a more desirable pattern of coaching behaviors. Second, the behavioral differences resulting from the CET program were accompanied by player evaluative responses that favored the trained coaches. The trained coaches were better liked and were rated as better teachers by their players. Moreover, their players reported that they had more fun playing baseball, and a higher level of attraction among teammates was again found, despite the fact that their teams did not differ from controls in won-lost records. Third, consistent with a self-esteem enhancement model, children with low self-esteem who played for the trained coaches exhibited a significant increase in general self-esteem over the course of the season; youngsters with low self-esteem in the control group did not change (Smoll, Smith, Barnett, & Everett, 1993). Fourth, the children who played for the CET coaches manifested lower levels of performance anxiety than did the control children (Smith, Smoll, & Barnett, 1995).

An extension of the above study was completed one year after the CET intervention. At the beginning of the next baseball season dropout rates were assessed for youngsters who had played for the two groups of coaches. The results showed a 26% dropout rate among the control group, a figure that was quite consistent with previous reports of 22% to 59% annual attrition rates in youth sport programs (Gould, 1987). In contrast, only 5% of the children who had played for the CET-trained coaches failed to return to the sport program in the next season (Barnett, Smoll, & Smith, 1992).

In summary, the results obtained from experimental field research indicate that cognitive-behavioral methods can be employed to train coaches to relate more effectively to young athletes and that this psychological intervention can have a positive impact on a social system that is an important part of the lives of many children.

Implementing Sport Psychology Workshops for Coaches

Creating a Positive Learning Environment

The most basic objectives of CET and other sport psychology training programs are to communicate coaching principles in a way that is easy to understand and to maximize the likelihood that coaches will adopt the information. Because of this, the importance of creating a positive learning environment cannot be overemphasized. Even the very best program is of little value if presented in a way that creates antagonism and defensiveness on the part of coaches.

There are several considerations in setting the stage for a successful session. The primary key is to convey respect for the participating coaches. They really deserve it! We point out to them that even though they may not be explicitly told so, people are aware of the valuable contributions they are making and that their efforts are appreciated. Indeed, without their unselfish involvement, there could be no organized youth sports.

Next, at the very outset of a training session we always emphasize that the coaches themselves have a great deal to offer as a result of their own experiences and associated practical knowledge. We attempt to take advantage of their expertise by encouraging them to share it with the group. In conducting a CET workshop as a two-way sharing of information, coaches are treated as an integral part of the session rather than a mere audience. The open atmosphere for exchange promotes active rather than passive learning, and the dialogue serves to enhance the participants' interest and involvement in the learning process.

A final key to successful program implementation is to put a considerable amount of sincere enthusiasm into leading the session. When a trainer truly enjoys his or her pedagogical role, the pleasurable feeling ultimately carries over to the coaches. In such an atmosphere attention and audience involvement is likely to be enhanced, increasing the enjoyment of coaches and trainer alike.

In contrast to the above, three strategies are virtually guaranteed to create hostility and resistance from coaches. One is to approach coaches in a condescending manner. In other words, the thing not to do is communicate how much you think you know and how little they know. An associated implication concerns the way a trainer is introduced at the beginning of a session. We recommend against presenting an extensive list of credentials and professional accomplishments, which tends to convey an air of elitism. Another contraindicated approach is to intimate that your training program is designed to protect athletes from coaches. Indeed, most volunteer coaches have commendable motives for coaching (Martens & Gould, 1979; Smith et al., 1978), and they generally make positive contributions to children's well-being. A final breach is to convey the impression that what the coaches have been doing is incorrect. Rather, we emphasize that many options are available for dealing with particular coaching situations, and although all of these tactics may work in *some* cases, certain procedures have a greater likelihood than others of being successful. By counteracting the notion of "right versus wrong," we stress the importance of flexibility and thus attempt to make coaches receptive to alternative ways of responding to specific circumstances.

Orientation to the Psychology of Coaching

In introducing the psychology of coaching, workshop participants should first be made aware of the importance of their role as coaches. Some coaches underestimate their influence, and they must be reminded of the many ways they can affect young athletes. Information and increased awareness of what they are doing can help them to optimize the desirable effects they can have on young athletes.

An orientation to the psychology of coaching includes consideration of the topic of winning.

The conventional notion of success in sports involves achieving a victorious outcome. But when winning games becomes the sole or primary goal, athletes can be deprived of important opportunities to develop their skills, enjoy participation, and grow as people. Because of the educational potential of sport, youngsters can learn from both winning and losing. But for this to occur, winning must be placed in a *healthy* perspective. We have therefore developed a four-part philosophy of winning that is taught in CET (Smith & Smoll, 2002, pp. 16–18):

1. *Winning isn't everything, nor is it the only thing.* Young athletes cannot get the most out of sports if they think that the only objective is to beat their opponents. Although winning is an important goal, it is not the most important objective.

2. *Failure is not the same thing as losing.* It is important that athletes do not view losing as a sign of failure or as a threat to their personal value.

3. *Success is not equivalent to winning.* Neither success nor failure need depend on the outcome of a contest or on a won-lost record. Winning and losing pertain to the outcome of a contest, whereas success and failure do not.

4. *Athletes should be taught that success is found in striving for victory (i.e., success is related to effort).* Athletes should be taught that they are never "losers" if they give maximum effort.

This philosophy is designed to maximize young athletes' enjoyment of sport and their chances of deriving the benefits of participation, partly as a result of combating competitive anxiety (Smith, Smoll, & Passer, 2002). Although seeking victory is encouraged, the ultimate importance of winning is reduced relative to other participation motives. In recognition of the inverse relation between enjoyment and postcompetition stress, *fun* is highlighted as the paramount objective. The philosophy also promotes separation of the athlete's feelings of self-worth from the game's outcome, which serves to help overcome fear of failure.

Because they tend to project adult values onto children, many coaches seem to believe that how their athletes feel about them hinges on how successfully the team performs. Yet, as noted earlier, our own research has shown that coaches for whom players enjoyed playing most, and who were most successful in enhancing youngsters' self-esteem, actually had won-lost records that were about the same as coaches who were less liked and less effective in promoting feelings of self-worth (Smith et al., 1978). Differences in coaching behaviors consistently accounted for significantly more variance in player attitudes toward the coach than did won-lost records. Stressing this finding to coaches tends to make them more receptive to the philosophy of winning that we espouse.

Presenting an Empirical Basis for the Program

We believe in the importance of establishing an empirical foundation for training guidelines, but we also feel that the ability to present supportive data increases the credibility of the guidelines for the coaches. A CET workshop therefore includes a description of the development and testing of the program. As a prelude to presenting behavioral guidelines, we describe the Coaching Behavior Assessment System. This provides coaches with a set of perceptual categories for organizing their own experiences and self-perceptions, and it sets the stage for the presentation of coaching guidelines.

A number of considerations underlie our commitment to presenting empirical results. First of all, expertise (special knowledge) and trustworthiness (the quality of meriting confidence) are two critically important variables in communicating credibility (Hovland, Janis, & Kelley, 1953; Petty & Wegener, 1998). Both are enhanced when data are presented rather than intuitive beliefs. Coaches have greater confidence in a training program when they know the content is not merely composed of armchair psychology or athletic folklore. Second, the presence of empirical data arouses the curiosity and involvement of the participants. Coaches show a

great deal of interest in the research, which stimulates their active involvement in the workshop. Also, presentation of unexpected results prevents either the trainer or the coaches from believing they already know all the answers. Third, the research findings form a useful frame of reference for the behavioral guidelines. Better understanding as well as increased credibility of the guidelines seem to result when coaches know how they were derived. Fourth, the ability to demonstrate empirically that certain behaviors have positive effects on children serves to arouse the expectation that the coaches can produce similar effects if they themselves apply the behavioral guidelines. This may increase their motivation to learn and apply the information.

There are some practical points to be aware of in presenting empirical results. Trainers should use lay terms and avoid scientific jargon. It is best to present data as simply as possible and to avoid technical details. In addition, appropriate use of visual aids enhances any presentation. Diagrams and cartoons illustrating certain concepts, and tables summarizing important principles, serve to facilitate comprehension and retention.

Behavioral Guidelines and Their Presentation

CET was conceptualized and designed within a cognitive-behavioral framework (Bandura, 1986). The core of the program consists of a series of empirically derived behavioral guidelines (i.e., coaching *do's* and *don'ts*), which are summarized in Appendix A. The coaching guidelines are based primarily on (a) social influence techniques that involve principles of positive control rather than aversive control, and (b) the philosophy of winning discussed above.

In the academic realm, Ames (1992a, 1992b), Dweck (1999), and Epstein (1988, 1989) have described specific methods that can be used to create a motivational climate that supports a task-orientation (also termed a mastery or learning orientation). These principles are designed to foster an orientation toward developing new skills, intrinsic motivation for learning, a focus on effort rather than social comparison, reduced fear of failure, and improved competence based on self-referenced standards. The current literature on motivational climate in both academic and sport domains strongly supports the hypothesis that a task-orientated climate is associated with a wide range of salutary motivational, self-evaluative, affective, and behavioral outcomes (see McArdle & Duda, 2002; Smith & Smoll, 2005). Although derived independently from different theoretical systems, striking similarities exist in the goals and behavioral guidelines derived from CET and achievement goal theory. Both are designed to create a task-oriented motivational climate that focuses on the learning process rather than on outcome. Sport is viewed as a personal development arena, and the emphasis is on becoming "your best" rather than "the best." CET guidelines explicitly define "winning" as exerting maximum effort and commitment to learning the skills of the sport, a position that is highly consistent with a mastery-based motivational climate. Likewise, mistakes are conceived as stepping-stones to achievement that provide the feedback needed to improve performance. That is, mistakes are viewed as an important part of the learning process, rather than something to be feared. CET guidelines emphasize that to the extent that athletes are focused on effort and preparation and freed from unnecessary performance anxiety, winning as an outcome will take care of itself within the limits of their abilities. A desired outcome of both CET and achievement goal theory is the creation of a positive interpersonal and athletic environment that fosters intrinsic enjoyment of the activity.

Didactic procedures. In a CET workshop, which lasts approximately 2½ hours, behavioral guidelines are presented both verbally and in a printed manual given to the coaches. The manual (Smoll & Smith, 2005) supplements the guidelines with concrete suggestions for communicating effectively with young athletes, gaining their respect, and relating effectively to their parents. The importance of sensitivity and being responsive to individual differences among athletes is also stressed. The manual eliminates the need for coaches to take notes; it facilitates their

understanding of the information; and it gives coaches a tangible resource to refer to in the future.

Audiovisual aids to a presentation are necessary for providing a multisensory stimulus and for countering the potential influence of "verbalism"—the tendency to place excessive reliance on words. In CET, PowerPoint slides and cartoons illustrating important points are used to present key principles and add to the organizational quality of the session. A word of caution is in order here. We have witnessed the collapse of several commendable presentations because of the failure of one or more electronic devices. Murphy's Law—if anything can go wrong it will—should be taken seriously when preparing to give a coaching workshop that includes audio or visual aids. An essential *preworkshop* procedure should thus include an operational check of each piece of equipment. (See Howell and Borman [1997] for an overview of audio and visual aids and their use.)

In introducing coaching guidelines, we emphasize that they should not be viewed as a "magic formula" and that mere knowledge of the principles is not sufficient. We stress that the challenge is not so much in learning the principles; they are relatively simple. Rather, the challenge is for the coach to integrate the guidelines into his or her own coaching style. When coaches believe that adoption of the guidelines is a result of their own dedication and effort, they are more likely to attribute behavioral changes to themselves rather than to the trainer. This approach is supported by evidence that self-attributed behavioral changes are more enduring than those attributed to some outside causal agent (Deci & Ryan, 1987).

As noted earlier, CET workshops are conducted with an interactive format to encourage active participatory learning (Brookfield, 1998). Efforts are made to draw coaches into a discussion of the guidelines as opposed to using an exclusively lecture-type approach. This is accomplished by directing questions to the coaches and then relating their responses to the written materials. To use this instructional style, a trainer must be well versed in the practical ramifications of the guidelines, their applicability to various kinds of coaching situations, and the kinds of questions they are likely to elicit from coaches.

A practical problem occurs when coaches ask questions that are unrelated to the topic being covered. For example, during a discussion of principles of reinforcement, a coach might inquire about formulating team rules. Our experience indicates that answering such questions disrupts the sequencing and continuity of concepts, which causes confusion for some coaches. A tactful procedure is to politely ask the coach to write down the question and to indicate on the program outline where he or she should repeat the query.

What are the secrets of effective, engaging presentations? In answering this question, Chamberlin (2000) interviewed six university faculty, each of whom was known for delivering outstanding lectures. Their recommendations are presented here, along with comments by the professors.

- *Prepare, prepare, prepare.* Practicing the workshop is an excellent way to thoroughly learn the material and feel comfortable speaking and answering questions about the content. "Saying it out loud will highlight the sticky points and give you a chance to smooth those out beforehand. It feels like you run the risk of making the lecture stale, but the energy in the classroom will bring it to life and you feel like you are doing it for the first time" (p. 63). Some experienced teachers bring notes or a script to every class—even for those they have done dozens of times—and advise against trying to conduct a session cold. As stated by one expert, "I may never look at my typed notes, but I always have them there as a security blanket" (p. 63).

- *Find your style.* Seasoned lecturers warn about the mistake of emulating a mentor or favorite instructor. Rather, they emphasize the importance of performing in a way that reflects your own style. "Your personality is a part of your lecturing, so you have to lecture in a way that is comfortable to your personality" (p. 63). In other words, do what feels right. And, as noted earlier, whatever your approach, make enthusiasm a big part of it.

"Enthusiasm is infectious. If you're not excited about the material, they're not going to be either" (p. 63).

- *Spice it up.* The use of intermittent stories and anecdotes can enliven your presentation. Weaving in personal sport stories or linking coaching principles to current research and events helps keep workshop participants engaged. One trap to avoid is relying solely on computer graphics and technology to add flavor to a workshop. As stated by a master teacher, "I have sat through far too many sleep-inducing PowerPoint presentations that have had a lot of power and no point" (p. 63).

- *Cover less, not more.* Another pitfall is packing too much content into a workshop, because of the fear that coaches will not learn certain material if it is not included in the session. Trainers who try to cover too much inevitably end up going too fast. In this regard, "Less is more. . . . Go slowly and thoughtfully through the material" (p. 64). Additionally, one of the benefits of providing participants with a workshop manual is that they can obtain considerable information by reading on their own.

- *Make improvements.* Avoid doing the same thing over and over, even though it is not working. If your presentation style is not effective, be committed and courageous enough to change it. An initial step toward improvement is to find out how you are doing by asking coaches for feedback, especially if you feel they are not responding well to your style or are not learning. Furthermore, do not get discouraged when you have a bad workshop. With sufficient dedication and effort, you will nail it and feel great the next time.

Credibility and persuasiveness. A primary goal of our instructional approach is to change coaches' attitudes about some of their roles and responsibilities and about their use of certain coaching behaviors. Several aspects of the persuasion process, such as credibility, trustworthiness, likability, and novelty, are utilized and have proven to be effective in a variety of intervention contexts (see Petty & Wegener, 1998; Taylor, Peplau, & Sears, 2003; Worchel, Cooper, & Goethals, 1991). In terms of personal characteristics, a highly *credible* communicator is more effective in changing attitudes than one with low credibility. As emphasized by Galbraith (1998), "common sense tells us that being technically proficient in the content area within the teaching and learning encounter is paramount if it is going to have some meaning and value" (p. 4). We strongly believe individuals who are best qualified to conduct psychologically oriented coach-training programs are sport psychologists/consultants who have been certified by a professional organization (e.g., Association for the Advancement of Applied Sport Psychology). In addition, competent trainers often have a formal affiliation with an academic institution. Such qualifications and the associated prestige provide some degree of credibility. It is not surprising, then, that coaches seem to be more receptive and responsive to recommendations presented by a sport psychologist rather than a recreation director or a youth league administrator.

Credibility is a multifaceted concept that seems to be a function of at least *expertise* and *trustworthiness*. As stated earlier, we endeavor to establish expertise in CET by substantiating the content with empirical evidence from our own work and from the research of other sport psychologists as well. With respect to trusting a communicator's intentions, credibility increases when the communicator does not appear to be purposefully trying to persuade the target (i.e., coaches in this case). We therefore present information and coaching guidelines objectively, and as noted earlier, we specifically avoid a "right versus wrong" orientation. In addition, because unexpected positions are generally seen as more trustworthy, we inform coaches that although we have been studying coach–athlete interactions for more than 20 years we simply do not have all the answers, and in some cases one must be willing to say, "I don't know." The honesty of such disclosures likely contributes to credibility.

The perceived similarity between a communicator and the target of the message affects the power of persuasion. To increase the degree of perceived similarity with coaches, we customarily dress in a fairly casual style. More important, while leading discussions, we share examples from our own experiences as athletes and coaches, and we often phrase comments with a "we" versus "you" perspective.

The communicator's likability also affects the efficacy of persuasion. Because liking works by identification, we try to create a warm, friendly rapport with coaches—partly by showing enjoyment in being with them and by expressing caring for them. Empirical work from the communication studies literature suggests that teachers' behavioral cues of interpersonal warmth and students' perceptions of those behaviors are predictive of a variety of desirable learning outcomes, including students' liking for the material and their intentions to act on what they have learned (Friedrich & Douglass, 1998). Accordingly, we strive to be more persuasive agents by honestly and sincerely engaging in behaviors that are known to communicate caring for learners, such as gesturing while lecturing, modulating one's voice, making eye contact, smiling, and self-disclosing. Reciprocity is another factor that increases liking: People tend to like those who like them. We communicate our high esteem for coaches by praising their commitment to providing high-quality sport experiences for young athletes. Listening ability is yet another factor in being likable. By encouraging coaches to express themselves freely, and by listening attentively to them when they do, we are better able to conduct a CET workshop as a mutual sharing of information.

In addition to characteristics of the communicator, several facets of the message affect its persuasiveness. Coaches are generally not opposed to the points of view advocated in CET, so we usually present *one-sided* communications. In some instances, however, a *two-sided* presentation is utilized. This involves more than just acknowledging that another side exists. Rather, contrary approaches are analyzed to point out their deficiencies and thus strengthen our position. For example, in discussing recommendations relative to reinforcement, the coaching guidelines are developed fully, and their beneficial effects are substantiated with empirical evidence. Then, when aversive control is considered, we proceed to point out the disadvantages of using punitive coaching behaviors. (See Chapter 3 for a discussion of the negative side effects of punishment.)

Using *rhetorical questions* is another way of influencing attitudes. We ask coaches rhetorical questions (questions to which no answer is expected) to stimulate their thinking and to make them pay closer attention to a communication. For example, "What is the best way to maintain order and teach self-discipline?"

Novelty of information also affects the message's impact. Some coaches may have had previous exposure to some of CET's behavioral guidelines. We attempt to make the principles seem unique by using diagrams, charts, and cartoons for their presentation.

Finally, *humor* can enhance the persuasiveness of messages. If used properly, humor can loosen up a potentially tense atmosphere, make people feel good, increase their responsiveness, and reveal a more human side of the speaker (Barker & Gaut, 2002). We use humorous anecdotes whenever possible—not primarily for entertainment but as an educational tool to help emphasize certain points and make concepts memorable. This objective is best accomplished by strongly establishing the link between humor and the point to be made such that coaches remember the key point, not just the good joke or story (Farrah, 1998).

Modeling. The instructional procedures described above contain many *verbal* modeling cues that essentially tell coaches what to do. Information is also transmitted through *behavioral* modeling cues (i.e., demonstrations showing coaches how to behave in desirable ways). In CET such cues are presented by a live model (the trainer) and by symbolic models (coach cartoons), as many forms of modeling have been shown to be highly effective in changing behavior (Bandura, 1986; Perry & Furukawa, 1986).

Role playing. Modeling is frequently used in CET in conjunction with later role playing of positive behaviors. Coaches are kept actively involved in the training process through presentation of critical situations and opportunities for them to role-play appropriate ways of responding. This form of behavioral rehearsal has great promise in enhancing acquisition of desired behaviors, in providing the opportunity to practice the behaviors, and in establishing an increased level of participant involvement during the workshops.

Increasing Self-Awareness and Compliance With Coaching Guidelines

One of the striking findings from our basic research was that coaches had very limited awareness of how often they behaved in various ways (Smith et al., 1978). Thus, an important goal of CET is to increase coaches' awareness of what they are doing, for no change is likely to occur without it. CET coaches are taught the use of two proven behavioral-change techniques, namely, behavioral feedback and self-monitoring.

Behavioral feedback. To obtain feedback, coaches are encouraged to work with their assistants as a team and share descriptions of each other's behaviors (Edelstein & Eisler, 1976; McFall & Twentyman, 1973). They can discuss alternate ways of dealing with difficult situations and athletes and prepare themselves for dealing with similar situations in the future. Other potential feedback procedures include coaches soliciting input from athletes and provision of feedback by a league committee.

Self-monitoring. Another behavioral-change technique that has the potential for increasing coaches' awareness of their own behavioral patterns and encouraging their compliance with the guidelines is self-monitoring (observing and recording one's own behavior). This method of self-regulation has proved to be an effective behavioral-change procedure in a variety of intervention contexts (Kanfer & Gaelick-Buys, 1991; Kazdin, 1974; McFall, 1977). Because it is impractical to have coaches monitor and record their own behavior during practices or games, the workshop manual contains a brief self-monitoring form. Coaches are encouraged to complete the form immediately after practices and games (see Appendix B). Self-monitoring is restricted to desired behaviors in light of evidence that tracking undesired behaviors can be detrimental to effective self-regulation (Cavior & Marabotto, 1976; Gottman & McFall, 1972; Kirschenbaum & Karoly, 1977). Coaches are encouraged to engage in self-monitoring on a regular basis to achieve optimal results.

Additional procedures. In addition to feedback and self-monitoring some other procedures might be valuable for increasing awareness and compliance with guidelines. For example, one or more follow-up meetings might be held with coaches during which they discuss their experiences in utilizing the guidelines and the effects that the behaviors seem to be having on their athletes. Follow-up may also occur through telephone contacts with individual coaches by the trainer. Finally, brief questionnaires may be designed and sent to coaches. Such questionnaires may be used not only to elicit information from the coaches but also to provide refresher points that will help maintain or increase compliance with coaching guidelines.

The Continuing Need for Coach-Training Programs

Given the ever-expanding nature of youth sports, the need for effective coach-training programs is obvious. Likewise, the large coach turnover from year to year creates a continuing demand for intervention. Our experience in offering CET has shown that youth coaches are committed to providing positive experiences for youngsters. It is also reassuring to note that coaches are willing to spend time to acquire additional information, and they do take advantage of the availability of workshops. An important feature of the CET approach is that it is a brief program that focuses on a relatively small number of critical principles and guidelines that clearly make a difference.

Unlike other countries, the United States does not have a national coaching association that provides a unified system for training and certification of coaches. Rather, three commercially

distributed programs are widely available that include curricular components designed to influence coach–athlete interactions: the American Coaching Effectiveness Program (ACEP), the National Youth Sports Coaches Association (NYSCA), and the Program for Athletic Coaches' Education (PACE). ACEP, NYSCA, and PACE are relatively lengthy (8- to 16-hour) programs. They offer broad-spectrum workshops that cover an array of topics, including those subsumed under the rubric of sport psychology (e.g., goal setting, motivation, stress management). Unfortunately, however, these three programs share two shortcomings in common, First, they lack a core theoretical or empirical foundation on which their sport psychology components are based. Rather, the eclectic nature of their content is generally derived by borrowing principles from educational and psychological literature. Second, there is an absence of systematic research attempting to validate the efficacy of these programs. Consequently, very little is known about their impact on coaches or the athletes who play for them. In essence, ACEP, NYSCA, and PACE "have provided coaching workshops to thousands of individuals involved in community-based and school-sponsored sports, but evaluation research is essential to determine the effectiveness of these training programs on increasing sport science knowledge and applications" (Weiss & Hayashi, 1996, p. 53).

The Positive Coaching Alliance, which was developed in 1998, is a recent entry into the psychologically oriented coach-intervention domain. Like CET, this program has important links with achievement goal theory and with social-cognitive approaches to behavior change. The Positive Coaching program appears promising but, to this point, it has not been evaluated in terms of its ability to change coaching behaviors or affect athletes' sport outcomes. Indeed, CET is the only program that has been subjected to systematic evaluation to determine its influence on coaches' behaviors and the effects of such behaviors on youngsters' psychosocial development (Brown & Butterfield, 1992).

In concluding this chapter, it is appropriate to restate our firm belief that extended efforts to improve the quality and value of coach-training programs are best achieved via well-conceived and properly conducted evaluation research. Future collaboration between sport psychologists and youth sport organizations not only will serve to advance understanding of the effects of competition but also will provide for enriched opportunities for children and youth in sport.

Summary

We have described the development and evaluation of an empirically supported intervention designed to assist coaches in providing a more positive and growth-inducing athletic experience for athletes. This chapter provides guidelines in how to present such a program. We describe the principles and ways we have found successful in presenting them with maximum positive impact. As noted in the chapter, there are several virtues of presenting a program that is based on scientific data rather than on "experiential knowledge" or speculation. First, you can have greater confidence in the principles you are presenting. Even more important is the approach you can take in presenting the principles. You can present your workshop as informational in nature. In other words, you can play to their desire to provide the best possible experience for youngsters (the prevailing motivation for most volunteer coaches). You are not telling them what they "should do," but rather what research has shown to be effective in helping them meet their goals and how they can incorporate these findings into their own coaching style. We have always found coaches receptive to this approach. By communicating simple but sound principles and showing coaches how to implement them and become more self-aware, you provide tools that they can apply immediately. Once they begin doing so, the positive responses from athletes and the reduced need to maintain discipline through punitive means provide powerful sources of reinforcement that strengthen and maintain the new behaviors. Many a coach has reported that applying the CET principles resulted in the most enjoyable season they had experienced in their coaching tenures, an outcome that is highly reinforcing to the trainer as well.

Study Questions

1. Describe the three basic elements of the mediational model of coach–athlete interactions that served to guide coaching-behaviors research.

2. What are the two major classes of behaviors included in the CBAS, and what is the difference between them?

3. Following development of the CBAS, field studies were conducted to establish relations between coaching behaviors and children's evaluative reactions. Describe the basic research procedures, and discuss the major findings with respect to (a) the role of winning relative to athletes' psychosocial outcome measures, (b) relations between coaching behaviors and athletes' attitudinal responses, (c) the degree of accuracy with which coaches perceived their own behaviors, and (d) the role of self-esteem as a mediator variable in coaching behavior–athlete attitude relations.

4. Describe the research design and methodology incorporated in the studies that tested the efficacy of CET. What were the results with respect to (a) behavioral differences

between trained and untrained coaches, (b) won-lost records, (c) players' evaluative reactions to trained and untrained coaches, (d) self-esteem effects, (e) competitive anxiety differences between youngsters who played for trained and untrained coaches, and (f) dropout rates?

5. In implementing sport psychology workshops for coaches the trainer should create a positive learning environment. What are some ways to foster a receptive and cooperative attitude on the part of coaches? What approaches should be avoided?

6. Describe the components of the healthy philosophy of winning that is taught in CET, and indicate how this orientation is designed to combat competitive anxiety.

7. In conducting a CET workshop, what is the rationale/justification for presenting empirical results to coaches?

8. Briefly describe the major behavioral guidelines (i.e., coaching *do's* and *don'ts*) that form the core of CET.

9. What are the advantages of conducting coach-training programs with an interactive format, and how might this be accomplished?

10. Discuss the key points associated with the following recommendations for making effective presentations: (a) prepare, prepare, prepare; (b) find your style; (c) spice it up; (d) cover less, not more; and (e) make improvements.

11. With respect to changing coaches' attitudes during a training program, explain how the following aspects of the persuasion process might be taken into account: (a) credibility (expertise and trustworthiness) of the trainer, (b) perceived similarity between the trainer and the coaches, (c) likability of the trainer, (d) one-sided versus two-sided communications, (e) use of rhetorical questions, (f) novelty of information, and (g) use of humor.

12. Describe the procedures that can be utilized to increase coaches' self-awareness and their compliance with coaching guidelines.

References

Ames, C. (1992a). Classrooms: Goals, structures, and student motivation. *Journal of Educational Psychology, 84,* 261–271.

Ames, C. (1992b). Achievement goals and adaptive motivational patterns: The role of the environment. In G. C. Roberts (Ed.), *Motivation in sport and exercise* (pp. 161–176). Champaign, IL: Human Kinetics.

Bandura, A. (1986). *Social foundations of thought and action: A social cognitive theory.* Englewood Cliffs, NJ: Prentice Hall.

Barker, L. L., & Gaut, D. A. (2002). *Communication* (8th ed.). Boston: Allyn and Bacon.

Barnett, N. P., Smoll, F. L., & Smith, R. E. (1992). Effects of enhancing coach–athlete relationships on youth sport attrition. *The Sport Psychologist, 6,* 111–127.

Brookfield, S. D. (1998). Discussion. In M. W. Galbraith (Ed.). *Adult learning methods: A guide for effective instruction* (2nd ed., pp. 169–186). Malabar, FL: Krieger.

Brown, B. R., & Butterfield, S. A. (1992). Coaches: A missing link in the health care system. *American Journal of Diseases in Childhood, 146,* 211–217.

Brustad, R. J., Babkes, M. L., & Smith, A. L. (2001). Youth in sport: Psychosocial considerations. In R. N. Singer, H. A. Hausenblas, & C. M. Janelle (Eds.), *Handbook of sport psychology* (2nd ed., pp. 604–635). New York: John Wiley & Sons.

Cahill, B. R., & Pearl, A. J. (Eds.). (1993). *Intensive participation in children's sports.* Champaign, IL: Human Kinetics.

Cavior, N., & Marabotto, C. M. (1976). Monitoring verbal behaviors in a dyadic interaction. *Journal of Consulting and Clinical Psychology, 44,* 68–76.

Chamberlin, J. (2000, December). Stand and deliver. *Monitor on Psychology, 31,* 62–64.

Chaumeton, N. R., & Duda, J. L. (1988). Is it how you play the game or whether you win or lose?: The effect of competitive level and situation on coaching behaviors. *Journal of Sport Behavior, 11,* 157–173.

Coakley, J. (1993). Social dimensions of intensive training and participation in youth sports. In B. R. Cahill & A. J. Pearl (Eds.), *Intensive participation in children's sports* (pp. 77–94). Champaign, IL: Human Kinetics.

Cruz, J., Bou, A., Fernandez, J. M., Martin, M., Monras, J., Monfort, N., & Ruiz, A. (1987). Avaluacio conductual de les interaccions entre entrenadors i jugadors de basquet escolar. *Apunts Medicina de L'esport, 24,* 89–98.

Curtis, B., Smith, R. E., & Smoll, F. L. (1979). Scrutinizing the skipper: A study of leadership behaviors in the dugout. *Journal of Applied Psychology, 64,* 391–400.

Deci, E. L., & Ryan, R. M. (1987). The support of autonomy and the control of behavior. *Journal of Personality and Social Psychology, 53,* 1024–1037.

Dweck, C. S. (1999). *Self-theories and goals: Their role in motivation, personality, and development.* Philadelphia: Taylor & Francis.

Edelstein, B. A., & Eisler, R. M. (1976). Effects of modeling and modeling with instructions and feedback on the behavioral components of social skills. *Behavior Therapy, 7,* 382–389.

Epstein, J. (1988). Effective schools or effective students? Dealing with diversity. In R. Haskins & B. MacRae (Eds.), *Policies for America's schools* (pp. 89–126). Norwood, NJ: Ablex.

Epstein, J. (1989). Family structures and students motivation: A developmental perspective. In C. Ames & R. Ames (Eds.), *Research on motivation in education: Vol. 3. Goals and cognitions* (pp. 259–295). New York: Academic Press.

Ewing, M. E., & Seefeldt, V. (2002). Patterns of participation in American agency-sponsored youth sports. In F. L. Smoll & R. E. Smith (Eds.), *Children and youth in sport: A biopsychosocial perspective* (2nd ed., pp. 39–56). Dubuque, IA: Kendall/Hunt.

Ewing, M. E., Seefeldt, V. D., & Brown, T. P. (1996). Role of organized sport in the education and health of American children and youth. In A. Poinsett (Ed.), *The role of sports in youth development* (pp. i–157). New York: Carnegie Corporation.

Farrah, S. J. (1998). Lecture. In M. W. Galbraith (Ed.), *Adult learning methods: A guide for effective instruction* (2nd ed., pp. 143–168). Malabar, FL: Krieger.

Friedrich, J., & Douglass, D. (1998). Ethics and the persuasive enterprise of teaching psychology. *American Psychologist, 53,* 549–562.

Galbraith, M. W. (1998). Becoming an effective teacher of adults. In M. W. Galbraith (Ed.), *Adult learning methods: A guide for effective instruction* (2nd ed., pp. 3–19). Malabar, FL: Krieger.

Gottman, J. M., & McFall, R. M. (1972). Self-monitoring effects in a program for potential high school dropouts: A time series analysis. *Journal of Consulting and Clinical Psychology, 39,* 273–281.

Gould, D. (1987). Understanding attrition in children's sport. In D. Gould & M. R. Weiss (Eds.), *Advances in pediatric sport sciences: Vol. 2. Behavioral issues* (pp. 61–85). Champaign, IL: Human Kinetics.

Horn, T. S. (1984). Expectancy effects in the interscholastic athletic setting: Methodological considerations. *Journal of Sport Psychology, 6,* 60–76.

Horn, T. S. (1985). Coaches' feedback and changes in children's perceptions of their physical competence. *Journal of Educational Psychology, 77,* 174–186.

Hovland, C. I., Janis, I. L., & Kelley, H. H. (1953). *Communication and persuasion.* New Haven, CT: Yale University Press.

Howell. W. S., & Borman, E. G. (1997). *The process of presentational speaking* (2nd ed.). Boston: Allyn and Bacon.

Jones, D. F., Housner, L. D., & Kornspan, A. S. (1997). Interactive decision making and behavior of experienced and inexperienced basketball coaches during practices. *Journal of Teaching in Physical Education, 16,* 454–468.

Kanfer, F. H., & Gaelick-Buys, L. (1991). Self-management methods. In F. H. Kanfer & A. P. Goldstein (Eds.), *Helping people change: A textbook of methods* (4th ed., pp. 305–360). Boston: Allyn and Bacon.

Kazdin, A. E. (1974). Self-monitoring and behavior change. In M. J. Mahoney & C. E. Thoresen (Eds.), *Self-control: Power to the person* (pp. 218–246). Pacific Grove, CA: Brooks/Cole.

Kirschenbaum. D. S., & Karoly, P. (1977). When self-regulation fails: Tests of some preliminary hypotheses. *Journal of Consulting and Clinical Psychology, 45,* 1116–1125.

Krane, V., Eklund, R., & McDermott, M. (1991). Collaborative action research and behavioral coaching intervention: A case study. In W. K. Simpson, A. LeUnes, & J. S. Picou (Eds.), *The applied research in coaching and athletics annual 1991* (pp. 119–147). Boston, MA: American Press.

Malina, R. M., & Clark, M. A. (Eds.). (2003). *Youth sports: Perspectives for a new century.* Monterey, CA: Coaches Choice.

Martens, R. (1988). Youth sport in the USA. In F. L. Smoll, R. A. Magill, & M. J. Ash (Eds.), *Children in sport* (3rd ed., pp. 17–23). Champaign, IL: Human Kinetics.

Martens, R. (1993). Psychological perspectives. In B. R. Cahill & A. J. Pearl (Eds.), *Intensive participation in children's sports* (pp. 9–17). Champaign, IL: Human Kinetics.

Martens, R. (2004). *Successful coaching* (3rd ed.). Champaign, IL: Human Kinetics.

Martens, R., & Gould, D. (1979). Why do adults volunteer to coach children's sports? In G. C. Roberts & K. M. Newell (Eds.), *Psychology of motor behavior and sport, 1978* (pp. 79–89). Champaign, IL: Human Kinetics.

McArdle, S., & Duda, J. K. (2002). Implications of the motivational climate in youth sports. In F. L. Smoll & R. E. Smith (Eds.), *Children and youth in sport: A biopsychosocial perspective* (2nd ed., pp. 409–434). Dubuque, IA: Kendall/Hunt.

McFall, R. M. (1977). Parameters of self-monitoring. In R. B. Stuart (Ed.), *Behavioral self-management: Strategies, techniques and outcomes* (pp. 196–214). New York: Brunner/Mazel.

McFall, R. M., & Twentyman. C. T. (1973). Four experiments on the relative contributions of rehearsal, modeling, and coaching to assertion training. *Journal of Abnormal Psychology, 81*, 199–218.

Perry, M. A., & Furukawa, M. J. (1986). Modeling methods. In F. H. Kanfer & A. P. Goldstein (Eds.), *Helping people change: A textbook of methods* (3rd ed., pp. 66–110). New York: Pergamon.

Petty, R. E., & Wegener, D. T. (1998). Attitude change: Multiple roles for persuasion variables. In D. T. Gilbert, S. T. Fiske, & G. Lindzey (Eds.), *The handbook of social psychology, Vol. I* (4th ed., pp. 323–390). Boston: McGraw-Hill.

Rejeski, W., Darracott, C., & Hutslar, S. (1979). Pygmalion in youth sport: A field study. *Journal of Sport Psychology, 1*, 311–319.

Scanlan, T. K. (2002). Social evaluation and the competition process: A developmental perspective. In F. L. Smoll & R. E. Smith (Eds.), *Children and youth in sport: A biopsychosocial perspective* (2nd ed., pp. 393–407). Dubuque, IA: Kendall/Hunt.

Sherman, M. A., & Hassan, J. S. (1986). Behavioral studies of youth sport coaches. In M. Pieron & G. Graham (Eds.), *The Olympic Scientific Congress proceedings: Vol. 6. Sport pedagogy* (pp. 103–108). Champaign, IL: Human Kinetics.

Smith, R. E., & Johnson, J. (1990). An organizational empowerment approach to consultation in professional baseball. *The Sport Psychologist, 4*, 347–357.

Smith, R. E., & Smoll, F. L. (1990). Self-esteem and children's reactions to youth sport coaching behaviors: A field study of self-enhancement processes. *Developmental Psychology, 26*, 987–993.

Smith, R. E., & Smoll, F. L. (2002). *Way to go, coach! A scientifically-proven approach to coaching effectiveness* (2nd ed.). Portola Valley, CA: Warde.

Smith, R. E., & Smoll, F. L. (2005). Assessing psychosocial outcomes in coach training programs. In D. Hackfort, J. L. Duda, & R. Lidor (Eds.), *Handbook of research in applied sport and exercise psychology* (pp. 295–318). Morgantown, WV: Fitness Information Technology.

Smith, R. E., Smoll, F. L., & Barnett, N. P. (1995). Reduction of children's sport performance anxiety through social support and stress-reduction training for coaches. *Journal of Applied Developmental Psychology, 16*, 125–142.

Smith, R. E., Smoll. F. L., & Christensen, D. S. (1996). Behavioral assessment and interventions in youth sports. *Behavior Modification, 20*, 3–44.

Smith, R. E., Smoll, F. L., & Curtis, B. (1978). Coaching behaviors in Little League Baseball. In F. L. Smoll & R. E. Smith (Eds.), *Psychological perspectives in youth sports* (pp. 173–201). Washington, DC: Hemisphere.

Smith, R. E., Smoll, F. L., & Curtis, B. (1979). Coach effectiveness training: A cognitive-behavioral approach to enhancing relationship skills in youth sport coaches. *Journal of Sport Psychology, 1*, 59–75.

Smith, R. E., Smoll, F. L., & Hunt, E. B. (1977). A system for the behavioral assessment of athletic coaches. *Research Quarterly, 48,* 401–407.

Smith, R. E., Smoll, F. L., & Passer, M. P. (2002). Sport performance anxiety in young athletes. In F. L. Smoll & R. E. Smith (Eds.), *Children and youth in sport: A biopsychosocial perspective* (2nd ed., pp. 501–536). Dubuque, IA: Kendall/Hunt.

Smith, R. E., Zane, N. W. S., Smoll, F. L., & Coppel, D. B. (1983). Behavioral assessment in youth sports: Coaching behaviors and children's attitudes. *Medicine and Science in Sports and Exercise, 15,* 208–214.

Smoll, F. L. (1989). Sports and the preadolescent: "Little league" sports. In N. J. Smith (Ed.), *Common problems in pediatric sports medicine* (pp. 3–15). Chicago: Year Book Medical Publishers.

Smoll, F. L., & Smith. R. E. (1989). Leadership behaviors in sport: A theoretical model and research paradigm. *Journal of Applied Social Psychology, 19,* 1522–1551.

Smoll, F. L., & Smith, R. E. (Eds.). (2002). *Children and youth in sport: A biopsychosocial perspective* (2nd ed.). Dubuque, IA: Kendall/Hunt.

Smoll, F. L., & Smith, R. E. (2005). *Coaches who never lose: Making sure athletes win, no matter what the score* (2nd ed.). Palo Alto, CA: Warde.

Smoll, F. L., Smith, R. E., Barnett. N. P., & Everett, J. J. (1993). Enhancement of children's self-esteem through social support training for youth sport coaches. *Journal of Applied Psychology, 78,* 602–610.

Smoll, F. L., Smith, R. E., Curtis, B., & Hunt, E. (1978). Toward a mediational model of coach–player relationships. *Research Quarterly, 49,* 528–541.

Taylor, S. E., Peplau, L. A., & Sears, D. O. (2003). *Social psychology* (11th ed.). Upper Saddle River, NJ: Prentice Hall.

Wandzilak, T., Ansorge, C. J., & Potter, G. (1988). Comparison between selected practice and game behaviors of youth soccer coaches. *Journal of Sport Behavior, 11,* 78–88.

Weiss, M. (Ed.). (2004). *Developmental sport and exercise psychology: A lifespan perspective.* Morgantown, WV: Fitness Information Technology.

Weiss, M. R., & Hayashi, C. T. (1996). The United States. In P. De Knop, L-M. Engstrom, B. Skirstad, & M. R. Weiss (Eds.), *Worldwide trends in youth sport* (pp. 43–57). Champaign, IL: Human Kinetics.

Worchel, S., Cooper, J., & Goethals, G. R. (1991). *Understanding social psychology* (5th ed.). Pacific Grove, CA: Brooks/Cole.

Summary of Coaching Guidelines

I. Reacting to Athlete Behaviors and Game Situations

A. Good plays

Do: Provide *reinforcement!* Do so immediately. Let the athletes know that you appreciate and value their efforts. Reinforce effort as much as you do results. Look for positive things, reinforce them, and you will see them increase. Remember, whether athletes show it or not, the positive things you say and do remain with them.

Don't: Take their efforts for granted.

B. Mistakes

Do: Give *encouragement* immediately after mistakes. That's when the youngster needs your support the most. If you are sure the athlete knows how to correct the mistake, then encouragement alone is sufficient. When appropriate, give *corrective instruction,* but always do so in an encouraging manner. Do this by emphasizing not the bad things that just happened but the good things that will happen if the athlete follows your instruction (the "why" of it). This will make the athlete positively self-motivated to correct the mistakes rather than negatively motivated to avoid failure and your disapproval.

Don't: Punish when things are going wrong! Punishment isn't just yelling. It can be tone of voice, action, or any indication of disapproval. Athletes respond much better to a positive approach. Fear of failure is reduced if you work to reduce fear of punishment. Indications of displeasure should be limited to clear cases of lack of effort; but, even here, criticize the lack of effort rather than the athlete as a person.

Don't: Give corrective instruction in a hostile, demeaning, or harsh manner. That is, avoid *punitive instruction.* This is more likely to increase frustration and create resentment than to improve performance. Don't let your good intentions in giving instruction be self-defeating.

C. Misbehaviors, lack of attention

Do: Maintain order by establishing clear expectations. Emphasize that during a game all members of the team are part of the activity, even those on the bench. Use reinforcement to strengthen team participation. In other words, try to prevent misbehaviors by using the positive approach to strengthen their opposites.

Don't: Get into the position of having to constantly nag or threaten athletes to prevent chaos. Don't be a drill sergeant. If an athlete refuses to cooperate, deprive him or her of something valued. Don't use physical measures, such as running laps. The idea here is that if you establish clear behavioral guidelines early and work to build team spirit in achieving them, you can avoid having to repeatedly *keep control.* Youngsters want clear guidelines and expectations, but they don't want to be regimented. Try to achieve a healthy balance.

II. Getting Positive Things to Happen and Creating a Good Learning Atmosphere

Do: Give *technical instruction.* Establish your role as a caring and competent teacher. Try to structure participation as a learning experience in which you are going to help the athletes become the best they can be. Always give instruction in a positive way. Satisfy your athletes' desire to improve their skills. Give instruction in a clear, concise manner and, if possible, demonstrate how to do skills correctly.

Do: Give encouragement. Encourage effort, don't demand results. Use encouragement selectively so that it is meaningful. Be supportive without acting like a cheerleader.

Do: Concentrate on the activity. Be "in the game" with the athletes. Set a good example for team unity.

Don't: Give either instruction or encouragement in a sarcastic or degrading manner. Make a point, then leave it. Don't let "encouragement" become irritating to the athletes.

Note: These guidelines were excerpted from the manual that is given to CET workshop participants (Smoll & Smith, 2005).

Coach Self-Report Form

Complete this form[2] as soon as possible after a practice or game.

For items 1, 2, and 3, not only think about what you did, but also consider the kinds of situations in which the actions occurred and the kinds of athletes who were involved.

1. Approximately what percent of the time they occurred did you respond to good plays with

   REINFORCEMENT? _____

2. Approximately what percent of the time they occurred did you respond to mistakes with each of the following communications?

   A. ENCOURAGEMENT only _____

   B. CORRECTIVE INSTRUCTION given in an encouraging manner _____
      (Sum of A plus B should not exceed 100%)

3. About how many times did you reinforce athletes for effort, complying with team rules, encouraging teammates, showing "team spirit," etc.? _____

4. How well did your team play tonight? (Check one)

_____	_____	_____	_____	_____
Very poorly	*Not very well*	*Average*	*Quite well*	*Very well*

5. How positive an experience *for the kids* was this practice/game?

_____	_____	_____	_____	_____
Very negative	*Somewhat negative*	*Neutral*	*Somewhat positive*	*Very positive*

6. How positive an experience *for you* was this practice/game?

_____	_____	_____	_____	_____
Very negative	*Somewhat negative*	*Neutral*	*Somewhat positive*	*Very positive*

[2]This form was excerpted from the manual that is given to CET workshop participants (Smoll & Smith, 2005).

7. Is there anything you might do differently if you had a chance to coach this practice/game again? (If so, briefly explain.)

_____

_____

_____

_____

_____

_____

Psychological Issues: Referral, Drug Abuse, Burnout, Injury, Termination from Athletics, and Exercise

When to Refer Athletes for Counseling or Psychotherapy

Mark B. Andersen, *Victoria University*
David Tod, *University of Wales, Aberystwyth*

Canst thou not minister to a mind diseas'd, Pluck from the memory a rooted sorrow, Raze out the written troubles of the brain, And with some sweet oblivious antidote Cleanse the stuff'd bosom of that perilous stuff Which weighs upon the heart?

—*Macbeth, act 5, scene iii*

A sport psychologist had been working with a gifted collegiate male hammer thrower for about 3 months. A close trusting relationship had formed, and together they had addressed a number of performance and communication issues. Recently, however, the thrower started to miss sessions, although he always contacted the consultant and rescheduled. The consultant was concerned because he also had noticed the athlete had been losing weight. One day when the young man failed to attend a session and did not call, the practitioner tried to contact him and left a message. After not hearing from the thrower for 2 days, the sport psychologist attended practice and found out from the coach (who knew the athlete had been seeing the consultant) that the thrower had missed the last 2 days of training because of the flu. Later that evening the practitioner finally made contact with the athlete via the telephone. The thrower was very apologetic

and also scared because he had not had the flu but had lied to his coach. On further discussion, the athlete admitted that he had not been able to train, go to school, or even bring himself to eat. He had fallen into a dark place, and he wanted to go to sleep without waking up. The consultant, recognizing the signs of depression and realizing the associated risk of suicide, managed to convince the athlete to come to his office straight away.

Depression is a common complaint among the general population and sport psychology consultants will probably come across athletes displaying the signs, such as those in the above case example. Athletes often experience depressed moods following a loss or a failure to perform as hoped or expected. If depressed moods are particularly severe or seem to last longer than typical, athletes may need help to get through the sense of loss or disappointment. In many cases, individuals hide their depression from others or may self-medicate through the use of alcohol or other substances. Individuals experiencing depression may show personal or social withdrawal, hopelessness, or loss of self-esteem. Lethargy is also a common symptom and may prevent sports participants from training (Faulkner & Biddle, 2004). Verbalizations indicating depression, hopelessness, or poor self-esteem should be red flags for coaches and sport psychologists alike. Overt and covert signs may signal a call for help. With depression there is always the possibility of suicide, which may take the form of unusual risk-taking (see Barney & Andersen, 2000, and Cogan, 2000, for examples of working with suicidal athletes). Treatment may include psychotherapy and antidepressant medication, and unless the sport psychology consultant is qualified to deal with depressed athletes, a referral to another professional is needed. Referral is a sensitive issue, and consultants need to show compassion and care (refer to Andersen & Van Raalte, in press, to see how the above case example was successfully resolved).

In the space of a chapter it is impossible to describe the precise methods for the assessment of depression and all the other possible mental health issues that athletes present and the ways to resolve them. Readers are referred to the American Psychiatric Association's (2000) *Diagnostic and statistical manual for mental disorders: Text revision (DSM-IV-TR)*. The goal of this chapter is to provide a set of guidelines that people working with athletes and exercise participants can use for referring individuals for professional psychotherapy. We also will provide suggestions about making suitable referrals for varying circumstances, and we will present dialogue from a referral session as well. Referring athletes to mental health practitioners does not mean sport psychologists need to stop working with their clients. There are no ethical violations or professional problems when a performance enhancement sport psychologist and a clinical or counseling psychologist work with an athlete at the same time, as long as all parties are informed with the client's consent. In many cases, a team approach can be the optimal way to deliver services.

Counseling and Sport Psychology

The fields of counseling, clinical, and applied sport psychology are becoming closer as practitioners begin to recognize the extensive overlap of sport performance and mental health. Recent examples, including Hays's (2002, Hays & Smith, 2002) work on bringing exercise into psychotherapy, Robertson and Newton's (2001) recent chapter directed to mainstream counselors on issues related to male athletes, and Lesyk's (1998) book on bringing sport psychology into clinical practice, show just how blurry and artificial are the lines drawn between sport and exercise psychology and clinical practice. Poczwardowski, Sherman, and Henschen's (1998) article on a model for sport psychology service is solidly grounded in counseling psychology principles, and an emerging area in applied sport psychology emphasizes the relationships between sport psychologists and athletes and coaches (Andersen, 2000; Petitpas, Danish, & Giges, 1999; Tod & Andersen, 2005). Examining practitioner-client relationships is a core feature of clinical and counseling psychology that is now also a part of applied sport psychology (see also Strean & Strean, 1998).

Over the last two decades, increased attention in the sport psychology literature has been paid to the psychosocial and mental health problems affecting sport participants (Andersen, Denson, Brewer, & Van Raalte, 1994; Brewer & Petrie, 2002; Carr & Murphy, 1995; Grove, Lavallee, Gordon, & Harvey, 1998; Thompson & Sherman, 1993; Tricker & Cook, 1989). This emphasis is also reflected in the strong clinical and counseling themes found in edited books (Andersen, 2000, in press; Etzel, Ferrante, & Pinkney, 1996; Murphy, 1995; Ray & Bjonstal, 1999; Van Raalte & Brewer, 2002) and in the writings of individuals showing the overlap between sport, counseling, and clinical psychology (see Lent, 1993; Petrie, Diehl, & Watkins, 1995; Petrie & Watkins, 1994). In addition, over a decade ago, the July 1993 issue of *The Counseling Psychologist*, along with the first issue of *Professional Psychology: Research and Practice* in 2001, were dedicated primarily to sport psychology practice.

Although sport psychology is embracing more and more clinical and counseling concerns, for some sport psychologists this is a lamentable development that is moving the field away from its unique area of inquiry and service (e.g., Rotella, 1992). For others, however, this trend represents the future direction of applied service (see Andersen, 2000; Simons & Andersen, 1995). Even though the gap between performance enhancement sport psychologists and those more interested in athletes' clinical or counseling issues is decreasing, it still exists and can create some difficulties. For example, the majority of individuals working in sport psychology have received their graduate degrees from kinesiology programs, whereas many others graduated from counseling or clinical psychology programs. Most of these individuals received training across both disciplines, but great diversity exists in qualifications for dealing with certain types of problems. Because of training in different departments, sport psychologists have received different emphases on performance enhancement and skills regarding psychological assessment, psychopathology, and counseling/psychotherapy.

Although Western society at large has become more psychologically minded in the last 50 years, and many issues of psychosocial distress are recognized as issues requiring help, stigmas are often still attached to those in counseling or therapy. Athletes who seek the services of sport psychologists, even if merely to enhance performance, are no exception. For example, Linder, Pillow, and Reno (1989) and Linder, Brewer, Van Raalte, and De Lange (1991) found that athletes who consulted a sport psychologist to improve performance were derided by the public as compared to athletes who attempted to resolve the same issues by working with their coaches. But a later study (Van Raalte, Brewer, Brewer, & Linder, 1992) found that other athletes (rather than the general public) did not think less of athletes who consulted with sport psychologists. As sport psychology becomes a more accepted part of service delivery for athletes, the negative associations with the word *psychologist* and the stigma that accompanies it will diminish.

It is important to understand that we all experience difficulties and that counseling or psychotherapy, particularly if intervention is sought early enough, can be an important part of personal growth and development, not a mark of personal failure. Athletes and sport participants, who may be subjected to particularly strong personal and interpersonal stressors, should have access to resources to help them deal with the issues they confront as part of their growth and development. We hope resources continue to grow not only for performance enhancement but also for personal growth and development (Rejeski & Brawley, 1988).

Differentiating Performance Enhancement From More Problematic Personal Issues

Many sport psychologists, usually those trained in sport science, argue that they focus only on performance enhancement issues, and if personal issues arise they refer their athletes onto other professionals. In taking such a stance, these performance enhancement consultants recognize that they may not be equipped to help athletes with concerns for which they have not received any training (e.g., eating disorders, identity issues). There is, however, a limitation inherent in their arguments: Performance is central to the lives of many athletes and often can be tied to their self-worth. In addition, performance may be interwoven within athletes' family dynamics. Given the interdependence of sport in many athletes' lives, performance can be a decidedly personal issue. Imagine that a sport psychologist, who focuses on performance enhancement, has worked with an athlete for several months and the client's skill level has improved to the point that making an international team is now a realistic possibility. The athlete's life may have changed considerably; she is now living her dream, her self-worth has risen, and her relationships with her coach, parents, and siblings have improved. She has become a happier person. The performance enhancement versus personal issues debate overlooks the important question: "How does performance fit in the rest of the athlete's life?" Performance enhancement techniques may be of limited value if the athlete's life is a jumble of confusion and conflict. For an athlete experiencing prerace anxiety that is intimately tied to parental love and acceptance, or feelings of worthiness as a human being, then relaxation may prove to be an inadequate Band-Aid for what are deeper issues than prerace nerves.

In much of the performance enhancement literature, problems in performance are related to issues such as competition anxiety, motivational problems, and poor self-talk and concentration (Greenspan & Feltz, 1989; Straub & Williams, 1984). Determining whether other factors might be involved requires understanding a number of interrelated issues.

An athlete coming to a coach or sport psychologist may be uncomfortable if an interview probes personal areas. Likewise, the sport counselor may be reluctant to ask highly personal questions. It is possible, however, to get at least a feel for some of the salient issues in typical discussions of sport performance factors. It is natural for the sport psychology consultant or coach to build rapport by asking athletes about themselves. Getting athletes to talk about their lives can lead not only to understanding their performance or motivational problems but also to an understanding of the whole person.

Fortunately, an overwhelming majority of requests for assistance with performance will be just what they appear to be. In the next sections we will try to identify those less common requests that reflect issues that might require additional professional assistance to help the athlete grow and develop.

First, how long a problem has existed, its severity, and its relationship to other issues in the person's life become important. A problem that is more recent, that is not severe in its emotional implications, and that does not have strong overlaps with other aspects of a person's life is less likely to require professional assistance. Thus, an athlete who is facing a tough competitive situation and who experiences mild to moderate anxiety, fear, and negative self-talk is not likely to require referral. A person for whom each athletic competition becomes an all-or-nothing battle for a sense of self, whose emotional state is dependent on performance outcomes, and where strong anxiety, depressive states, or substance abuse may also be involved is more likely to need a referral, although certainly performance-related issues can still be addressed by the performance enhancement sport psychologist.

Second, unusual emotional reactions may also need to be considered. Anxiety that generalizes to situations beyond the athletic arena may signal that other issues are present and that interventions may be needed to help deal with other areas of the person's life.

Anger or aggression is likely to be an issue presented by an athlete only if it has become a problem to others. Unfortunately, it may take the form of fights with strangers, which sometimes involve legal complications, as well as familial abuse issues. In other cases an athlete may lose control within the competitive context. This emotional reaction may inhibit otherwise good performance or be a performance threat, in that the person becomes a liability in terms of penalties or ejections from the game.

Third, it may also be important to examine the effectiveness of more traditional performance enhancement interventions. For example, perhaps an athlete has not disclosed the full extent of the issue or is not aware of it. It may be that the person working with the athlete did not come to understand the nature and extent of the problem. If more traditional interventions, such as working on self-talk and visualization, do not seem to be working, there are several possibilities to consider. Perhaps the athlete did not respond to the particular intervention—for example, not all individuals can visualize. It may also be that the sport-related problem was not accurately assessed or was stronger than initially assumed. It may also be, however, that the sport-related issue is, in fact, related to other issues in the person's life and may have deeper, stronger, or more chronic patterns. These possibilities should be investigated.

One can frame questions about other aspects of athletes' lives by reminding athletes that performance can be influenced by many factors, some of which are not connected with the playing field (e.g., family and relationship problems, school issues). Also, a not uncommon development in performance enhancement consultation is that after the athlete has become comfortable with the sport psychologist and has built up trust the athlete one day says, "I don't really want to talk about sport today; I want to talk about . . . ," and then a story comes out about some personal issue. I recall a bright senior year college swimmer I worked with on performance enhancement for several months. Suddenly one day the swimmer said, "Doc, I gotta talk to you about girls." Out came a story of being shy, nervous, self-conscious, and "feeling like a dork" around young women. The disclosure made a substantial shift in focus of the service delivery to concentrating on relieving the swimmer's anxiety and changing his self-defeating negative cognitions associated with meeting and talking to women. Within a short time he got up the nerve to ask a young woman out on a date and ended up having a good time. The swimmer continued to date throughout the rest of his senior year. The focus of the performance enhancement sessions returned to swimming, but I kept tabs on how his social life was progressing. He did not swim all that much faster that season, but he certainly seemed happier. A case like this probably does not require a referral, but it does illustrate how personal and emotional issues can emerge long after a performance enhancement consulting relationship has developed. What would one do, for example, if the story that emerged was about how the athlete had hit his girlfriend?

The referral process is not always a straightforward one. If trust and rapport have been built between the sport psychologist and the athlete, sending the athlete away to someone else when material comes up that the sport psychologist does not feel competent to handle may not be the optimal choice. Instead of referring *out*, referring *in* may be the better choice (see Van Raalte & Andersen, 2002). Bringing in a qualified professional and having all three parties sit down and discuss a plan may be less threatening to the athlete and help ease him or her into the therapeutic process. Actually, the therapeutic process had already begun with the rapport building and the athlete telling the sport psychologist about a personal concern. Referring *in* may be the best way to keep that therapeutic process going.

Most articles on referring athletes to other practitioners (e.g., Van Raalte & Andersen, 2002) focus on what to do (and what not to do) and what should happen. The question I (First author) get from many of my students is, "That's all fine, but *how* do you do it?" There is probably no better way (except for a live role play) to demonstrate how to do a referral than through dialogue and commentary. Here is an example from my files from a time when I knew I was not qualified to handle an athlete with an eating disorder. I had been seeing a swimmer, Angela, for about 2 months, working with her primarily on self-talk and arousal regulation. When she arrived at our eighth meeting, I could see something was wrong. We had built a strong working alliance, so when she answered my question about how things were going with a very flat "OK, I guess," I jumped in:

Mark (M): From over here, it doesn't look like things are OK. It looks like something not very good is going on.

Angela (A): I don't know Doc, I'm just kind of worried. [I kept silent to see if she would go on, but she just sighed.]

M: So, what's troubling you, Angela?

A: [beginning to have tears in her eyes] I am just outta control [now full tears flowing].

M: I can see that this is really painful; tell me what's going on.

A: You'd be disgusted with me.

M: We've worked together for about 2 months, and I think we've built up a good relationship. I don't know everything about you, but what I know is that you are a fine person. I can't imagine that anything you could tell me would put me off. So let's look at what's going on and see if we can figure out what to do.

At this point, I know something big is coming. Angela is having trouble talking to me about the problem for a variety of reasons. First, she is disgusted with herself and thinks I will be disgusted too. Because of our strong working alliance and her positive transference to me, she does not want to say anything that will disappoint me (see Andersen, 2004c, for a discussion on transference and countertransference). I am trying to reassure her of my unconditional positive regard and to remind her that we are in this endeavor together and that we will look for solutions. Angela then began to tell me of being stressed with swimming, weight, and school pressures and how her long-standing once a week binge–purge episodes had turned into an almost daily occurrence.

A: How can I do that to myself? Don't you think it's terrible?

M: No, I don't think it's terrible. In fact, right now I am feeling really proud of you for having the courage to talk about all this. I know it's gotta be one of the harder things you've done. . . . I want to do everything I can to help, but Angela, to tell you the truth, I am not trained in eating problems. I think we need to talk to an expert.

A: But I don't want to talk to anyone else. I want to talk to you. Those people over in Student Health don't understand athletes.

M: I know what you mean, but I know a great psychologist over there who is a runner herself and competed in college. She is a major sweetheart and really understands eating problems and weight concerns in sport.

A: I just hate going over there, and I don't want to go to sports medicine. If I did that, I know it would get back to the coach.

M: Nothing is going to get back to the coach unless you want it too. I have an idea. How about if I ask Dr. Kerstner [the expert] to come over here and you and she and I all sit down together? We could meet right here in my office just like our usual appointment. How's that sound?

A: I guess that would be OK. I just feel comfortable with you.

M: I'll be there with you all the way, and I know you and Dr. Kerstner will hit it off.

A: Can I still keep seeing you?

M: Of course! I am your sport psychologist as long as you want me to be. We can keep working on your swimming, and I'll be checking in with you and Dr. Kerstner occasionally on how things are going. How's that?

A: OK, ask her to come over.

M: I'll get hold of her right after our session.

A: Doc, could we do a nice long autogenic thing today? I'm kind of frazzled.

M: You bet, you know the drill. All right, get yourself in a comfortable position and take a nice deep breath. . . .

This interchange contains many different processes, all directed at making the referral an acceptable option. First, I assure Angela that instead of seeing her problem as terrible (and disgusting) I am proud of her. I am letting her know that my opinion of her has only changed for the better because of what she has told me. Next, I introduce the idea of referral, but she is quite resistant. Athletes at large North American universities (from my experience) often feel that services on "main campus" are not geared for their needs. I attempt to overcome the resistance by telling her a little bit about the psychologist's sport background and by letting her know that I think quite highly of Dr. Kerstner. This last point illustrates the importance of having a referral network of health care professionals who are sensitive to athletes' issues. Angela is coming around, but she still wants to stay with me. Her reaction is understandable; our relationship has been built to this intimate point, a point where she is able to talk about truly painful issues in her life. Getting here was a long process, and she may not want to tell her problems to a stranger. I address her lingering resistance by suggesting that we refer Dr. Kerstner *in* to familiar turf (my office) and by letting her know I will be with her all the way.

At the end of this emotionally draining session (for athlete and psychologist both), Angela wants to return to the familiar and the soothing, so we do something together that we have done several times before—we relax. In time, other professionals (e.g., physician, nutritionist) would be called in to help Angela (see Petrie & Sherman, 2000, for a description of a team approach to eating disorders). This first, and largest, referral step helped Angela get on the path of treatment. No two referrals are alike, and some referrals are easier than others. But all referrals are complex and sensitive in nature.

When Enhancement Approaches Bring Up Deeper Issues

When an individual is not responding to a more traditional performance enhancement intervention, there may be a number of issues to consider. Sometimes, a more serious situation emerges. In medical terms there are "iatrogenic complications." This means that the *treatment itself* causes additional problems.

Some of the interventions most commonly used in educational sport psychology are clearly drawn from cognitive-behavioral psychology (see Straub & Williams, 1984). These include cognitive restructuring and self-talk. Usually these techniques address more conscious issues and can be evaluated and responded to by an athlete fairly quickly and directly. Other approaches, however, such as visualization, relaxation, and hypnosis, require that a person loosen conscious controls, allowing preconscious or unconscious material more access to consciousness. Although problems with these approaches are rare, someone working with these techniques over time with a large number of individuals should be sensitive to the possibilities. First, a person may become uncomfortable with memories or associations that emerge. For example, an athlete had a particularly negative relationship with a coach when the athlete's performance slumped. The coach, using visualization and imagery, unknowingly activated memories of childhood physical abuse that had been denied and repressed. The athlete at first tried to hide these but became increasingly fearful of the relaxation and imagery sessions. It was necessary to locate a professional who could work with the athlete on the childhood issues. Other reactions such as anxiety,

depression, anger, and the release of bottled up memories or emotions should be noted if they seem to result from more traditional performance enhancement interventions. The sport psychologist—or anyone else working with an athlete—must be able to talk with the athlete about these reactions and to have a sense of when a consultation or referral might be appropriate.

More Specific Athlete-Related Issues

Sometimes, in addition to performance issues, or related to them, other issues confronting athletes may surface. Let's look at some of these issues in more detail.

Identity Issues

One of the most problematic issues for many athletes is that their whole sense of self has revolved around their role as an athlete (Balague, 1999). This overidentification may be particularly true for those at elite levels or in more glamorous sports, but it can occur for any person in any sport. Often the athlete's hopes for the future and social support from others may revolve around the sport and the athlete's success at it. For someone working with these issues, attempts at performance enhancement may take on an extreme urgency, as the athlete's sense of self may well be riding on the outcome. When athletes identify with the role of athlete exclusively, they are said to have *foreclosed* their identity (Miller, 2003). Petitpas and Danish (1995) have discussed psychological identity foreclosure:

> In psychological foreclosure people rigidly adhere to their identities to maintain security or to cope with intrapsychic anxiety. This might be seen in athletes who are adult children of an alcoholic parent. They may be resistant to change and more vulnerable to threats of identity loss because their method of coping with their life situations is to seek approval through their athletic successes. The loss of their athletic role would compromise their entire defensive structure. (p. 263)

Major threats to identity can come through athletic injury (Brewer, 1994; Brewer, Van Raalte, & Linder, 1991, 1993; Kolt, 2004; Chapter 25 of this text) and through career terminations (Baillie & Danish, 1992; Grove et al., 1998; Lavallee & Andersen, 2000; Chapter 26 of this text). Brewer and Petrie (2002) have reported that 5% to 24% of athletes who sustain an injury experience clinically significant levels of psychological distress. For a more thorough discussion of issues in athletic injury, refer to Chapter 25 in this book, Udry and Andersen (2002), and Brewer and Petitpas (in press). The last reference contains an in-depth case study about an international skier who has experienced repeated knee injuries.

Negative Identities

Although we normally think of the identity of athlete as something both individuals and peer groups see as positive, valuable, and rewarding, there are also versions of this that become negative identities (Balague, 1999; Erikson, 1968). In essence, a **negative identity** is the acceptance and valuing of an identity that is generally disapproved of by society. For example, the dumb jock is one such negative identity. Individuals and subgroups may determine that athletes shouldn't care about school or shouldn't do well, and so forth. This negative identity, although disapproved of by many, may become important to an individual or subgroup.

Similarly, the tough jock identity is problematic. Being an athlete—most commonly for men but increasing for women—means being tough, and it often involves intimidating others verbally or physically.

Substance abuse issues also can become part of negative identity patterns. To be a successful jock one may need to be able to consume a great deal of alcohol or other drugs. In some cases this is done covertly, with an eye to the clean-cut image that has to be maintained for public relations purposes.

As with many other human issues, unless a person sees these as areas that are problematic and that he or she would like to change, it may only be possible for the coach or educational sport psychologist to communicate concern for these areas and to point a person in the direction of someone who can help him or her work on these issues.

Sexual Orientation and Homophobia

There are a number of lesbian sport psychologists who have "come out of the closet" regarding their sexual orientation, but the same cannot be said about gay male practitioners. The absence of visible gay male academics and consultants may indicate that homophobia is still alive and well in the discipline (Martens & Mobley, in press). With respect to athletes, sexual orientation, particularly of gay men, has only received a smattering of attention in the sport psychology literature (Andersen, Butki, & Heyman, 1997; Cogan & Petrie, 2002; Krane, 1995; McConnell, 1995; Rotella & Murray, 1991), and one must go to sociological and popular writings to learn about the experiences of gay male athletes. Although gay and lesbian athletes may struggle with the "coming out" process, for most of these sports participants their sexuality is not their primary issue. The homophobia present in the sporting world is usually a far more serious concern, and it raises fears in athletes about getting less playing time, being kicked off teams, being harassed, and being physically abused if their orientations were made public (Martens & Mobley, in press).

Sport psychology consultants need to be comfortable with interacting with gay and lesbian athletes (see the case vignette in Martens and Mobley [in press] for how a student consultant, receiving effective supervision, was able to help a gay male athlete). In recent years U.S. society has been trying to deal with gender role issues and with homophobia. One might ask, how do these relate to the issues of when to refer? A regrettable example was reported by Garnets, Hancock, Cochran, Goodchilds, and Peplau (1991) in a report on issues in psychotherapy with lesbians and gay men.

> A 19 year old male client . . . had been receiving therapy from a University athletic department's sport psychologist. . . . The student-client developed transference toward

the psychologist and in the seventh session shared with the psychologist his affection/ positive feelings—referring to being "surprised that he could feel love for a man that way." The psychologist became angry, immediately terminated the session and all therapy. (p. 967)

If the above report is accurate, there would certainly be clear ethical issues about the psychologist's behavior. Even worse, the original report of this incident (APA Committee on Lesbian and Gay Concerns, 1990) went on to state that the sport psychologist "broke confidentiality by telling the client's coach he was gay. The client sat out the rest of the games that season and was asked not to return the next season as 'his problem was unacceptable'" (p. 34).

A coach or a sport psychologist who is homophobic or who has biases about gender role behaviors (for example, negative attitudes toward women who are assertive) may have great difficulty when encountering issues of sexual orientation or gender roles. If so, such a person should seek help; he or she cannot truly be of help to others who have conflicts with these issues. A person who is open and accepting of others, however, will convey an important message to the athlete and will increase the likelihood of the athlete's accepting an appropriate referral.

Referral of gay and lesbian athletes may be advisable when sport psychologists know little about issues concerned with sexual orientation or they are uncomfortable in dealing with such sport participants. Also, if athletes are currently confused about their sexuality referral to knowledgeable practitioners will help athletes explore such issues in a safe environment.

Sex and Health-Related Issues

Most athletic careers start seriously sometime during adolescence and usually end somewhere in the mid-20s to late 30s. In Eriksonian terms (Erikson, 1968) many athletes are in the middle of the challenge of either "identify versus role confusion" or "intimacy versus isolation." Both these times are periods of experimentation,

exploration, and finding out about oneself. For some athletes the exploration of self and intimate relationships may involve risk-taking behavior, especially in the realm of sex. The number of sexually transmitted diseases (STDs) is bewildering. HIV is only the most obvious. Other potentially lethal or debilitating STDs include hepatitis B and C, gonorrhea, and syphilis (making a comeback in many urban centers). Athletes may approach sport psychologists to talk about risky sexual behaviors they have engaged in that have made them quite anxious about their health status. If a sport psychologist is uncomfortable discussing intimate behavior or is just not knowledgeable about STDs, referral to a counselor with expertise in sexual health is most appropriate.

A study by Butki, Andersen, and Heyman (1996) revealed that collegiate athletes and nonathletes alike use condoms irregularly, but athletes in general engage in sexual behavior more frequently and have more partners than their nonathlete peers. Thus, student athletes may be at greater risk for a variety of sexually transmitted diseases than students in general. At the same time, it must be understood that sharing needles, in addition to sexual behaviors, is a high-risk factor for hepatitis B and C and HIV infection. Steroids can be injected, and often in gyms or locker rooms several athletes may use the same syringe. Again, athletes or sport participants may need to talk with someone about their behaviors and their fears. This person should be knowledgeable and should also be able to make referrals for more specific issues.

Eating Disorders

Because of the complexities of eating disorders and the psychological, physical, and physiological effects that accompany them, referral to a variety of health care professionals (e.g., dieticians, gastroenterologists, psychologists, and team doctors) is becoming the norm. Eating disorders among athletes have received much attention in the sports medicine and sport psychology fields (Brewer & Petrie, 2002; Brownell, Rodin, & Wilmore, 1992; Martin & Hausenblaus, 1998; National Collegiate Athletic Association, 1989;

Petrie & Sherman, 2000; Putukian, 1994; Swoap & Murphy, 1995; Thompson & Sherman, 1993). Prevalence rates for eating disorders among athletes are quite variable depending on the sport and who is doing the study. For example, Sundgot-Borgen (1994) found that 8% of elite female Norwegian athletes were diagnosable as eating disordered, but Burckes-Miller and Black (1988) found a huge prevalence rate—39%—for female college athletes.

Although estimates of eating disorder incidence in men vary greatly, from 0.2% to 20% depending on the study cited, the rate may be increasing (Braun, Sunday, Huang, & Halmi, 1999). Eating disorders historically have been considered a "female" concern, and so there is probably significant underreporting of the prevalence and incidence in males. Compared to women, however, men may have a higher age of onset (Braun et al., 1999; Carlat, Camargo, & Herzog, 1997), seek therapeutic help less often (Olivardia, Pope, Mangweth, & Hudson, 1995), and have less chance of successful outcomes (Oyebode, Boodhoo, & Schapira, 1988). In controlling weight, men may be more likely to use saunas, steam baths, and exercise (Davis & Cowles, 1991; Drewnowski & Yee, 1987; Johnson, Powers, & Dick, 1999), whereas women may resort to purging, diet pills, and laxatives (Braun et al., 1999; Johnson et al., 1999).

A central feature of eating disorders is often a disturbance in body image, and over the last two decades there has been increased interest in the ways men view their physiques. Increasingly, men are feeling as if they need to attain a highly muscular mesomorphic body shape (Pope, Phillips, & Olivardio, 2000). In addition to eating disorders, body dissatisfaction has been related with body dysmorphia, some forms of somatic delusional disorders, poor self-esteem, depression, social anxiety, inhibition, sexual dysfunction, and a variety of health risk behaviors, such as excessive exercise and steroid use (Blouin & Goldfield, 1995; Brower, 1992; Buckley, Yesalis, Friedl, Anderson, Streit, & Wright, 1988; Cash & Grant, 1995; Cash & Syzmanski, 1995; McMurray, Bell, & Shircore, 1995; McMurray & Gazis, 1995; Yates, 1991).

The etiologies for eating disorders and body dissatisfaction in the general public and in athletes are probably, in some cases, dissimilar. The psychodynamic issues of warding off sexual maturity, conflicts with parents, and dual diagnosis with borderline disorders (Sours, 1980) are probably not at the core of the problem for many athletes. Andersen and Fawkner (in press, Chapter 5 of the book also has a case study of a male diver with an eating disorder) identified a number of reasons why athletes may experience disturbed eating and body dissatisfaction. First, although poor body image might motivate exercise and sports participation, there may be no changes in some anatomical features, and, hence, the source of the dissatisfaction may not be alleviated. Second, some sports and types of exercise may be unable to produce desired body changes. Participation in aerobic sports, for example, may lead to fat loss but does not substantially increase muscle mass. Third, participation in sport and exercise may raise expectations beyond what is realistically or genetically possible. For example, weight training may not lead to hypermuscularity. Fourth, comparing oneself against others may result in a negative evaluation. The chance of dissatisfaction may be heightened in sports where comparisons are part of the competitive process, especially in sports such as diving or gymnastics. Fifth, participants may be reinforced for developing an excessive preoccupation with their weight and physique, notably those whose coaches dwell on body appearance. Disturbed body image may continue past an athletic career into retirement (Stephan, 2003). Sixth, individual, psychosocial, and cultural factors also need consideration. For example, men with stronger affiliations to the gay community experience greater body dissatisfaction compared to those with weaker affiliations (Beren, Hayden, Wifley, & Grillo, 1996). Andersen and Fawkner suggested that individual, psychosocial, and cultural factors need more empirical and clinical examination if a better understanding of the relationships between exercise participation, sports involvement, body dissatisfaction, and eating disorders is to be achieved.

Should an athlete with eating disorders be referred for treatment? Yes, certainly, if the sport psychologist is not knowledgeable regarding eating disorders and how best to treat them. A more important question in sports, however, is should the pathogenic sport environment be the object of treatment? I worked with a collegiate gymnast whose disordered eating was essentially environmentally dependent. When she was away from school and away from the coach and the gym, her bulimic behavior dropped to zero. After returning from semester break, she said, " I was just fine at home; it didn't happen, not even once. But as soon as I get back here—Blam!—it's starting all over again." I met this gymnast in her senior year and we worked together on some cognitive-behavioral interventions to decrease the frequency of her bulimic behavior. She was successful at reducing the behaviors, but the eating disorder did not go into full remission until she finished her competitive career and left the sport at the end of her senior year.

Eating disorders are difficult to treat, and eating disorders among athletes, more than many other referrals, bring up the question of who or what is really in need of referral. Stimulated by the previously mentioned case (and others), the Eating Disorders Team at my university (composed of general practitioners, a psychiatrist, psychologists, a dietician, and a sport psychologist from the student mental health center) ran educational seminars in the athletics department. These seminars were aimed at increasing the awareness of coaches, administrators, and sports medicine personnel to the signs and symptoms of eating disorders and helping them make referrals to appropriate services. The athletics department was receptive to these interventions, in part, because they and the university were facing litigation from a former student athlete who claimed she arrived at the university healthy and left with an eating disorder directly related to her sport.

Some warning signs of eating disorders to watch for include a marked loss in weight, preoccupation with weight, avoidance of team and other socially related functions involving food, eating very little if at such functions, visits to the bathroom after meals, bloodshot eyes after bathroom visits, a decrease in energy level and ability to concentrate, chronic gastrointestinal complaints, and increased emotionalism. Eating disorders among athletes is a topic deserving an entire chapter on its own, and entire books have been written on the subject (see Black, 1991; Thompson & Sherman, 1993). For further information also consult the following: Swoap and Murphy (1995), Petrie and Sherman (2000), and Seime and Damer (1991).

Alcohol and Substance Abuse Issues

Due to the public attention to celebrities' problems with alcohol and drugs, this is one domain in which athletes' problems have received extensive attention (see Stainback & Taylor, in press, for an in-depth case study of a college football player). Authors in this book (Anshel, Chapter 23) and in other volumes (Murphy, 1995; Tricker & Cook, 1989) have considered these areas. The association in U.S. culture between masculinity and drinking (as well as the ability to consume large amounts of other substances) may make some athletes more vulnerable to developing problems in this area. Research suggests that student-athletes consume more alcohol, start drinking earlier, and engage more frequently in alcohol-related risk behaviors (e.g., driving after drinking) than their nonsporting counterparts (Hilderbrand, Johnson, & Bogle, 2001). In addition, individuals inclined to take risks, or "sensation seekers," as Zuckerman (1979) has called them, are also likely to indulge in greater amounts of alcohol and drug use. Certain sports may disproportionately attract sensation seekers.

Someone working with athletes should recognize the general symptoms of excessive alcohol or drug use. Most commonly these involve chronic use or binges, a centering of life events around this usage, personality changes during usage, and usage interfering with other life activities or relationships. Unfortunately, high school and college life in general, and often the athletic environment, will cloak problem usage with different forms of social acceptability. Given denial and defensiveness around issues of alcohol and drug use, a coach or sport psychologist concerned about these issues can note his or her concern, but not in a lecturing or threatening manner. It is important to have sources for referral available, particularly if the athlete becomes concerned about this usage and would like to seek help.

Anger and Aggression Control

In many competitive sports we encourage psychological attitudes of toughness and competitiveness and see the opponent as an enemy to be defeated. In contact sports in particular, but in other sports as well, physical aggression is sanctioned. Most athletes are able to control their anger and aggression both on the field and off, although some require a little time after competition for the behavioral controls to reset.

There are individuals, however, who experience difficulty with anger or aggression control and for whom a referral might be appropriate. Some individuals may have always had a reputation for conflict. For men, this may have a negative identity component that cloaks the problem in an acceptable way for a peer group. The athlete may be tough on and off the field, someone "not to mess with." Unfortunately, the frequency and severity of conflicts may escalate to harmful levels.

In other cases, someone going through a personally difficult time may be less able to control anger or aggression. This may be expressed either on or off the field. Particularly when anger and aggression have not been issues for a person before, they might be discussed with the athlete and a referral made.

Alcohol and drug use may also be related to such behaviors. In general, when people are intoxicated, bottled-up anger or rage may be expressed more easily. In recent years, in addition, *roid rages,* or violent reactions in some individuals who are taking steroids, have been noted (Gregg & Rejeski, 1990).

There are ways to help individuals deal with anger (e.g., Novaco, 1975) as well as with aggression (Heyman, 1987). It is easier to help someone resolve conflicts and reestablish controls if he or she has had a reasonably good history of anger and aggression control. Helping athletes with

more problematic histories is possible, but it may be a slower process.

Relationship Issues

Athletes and sport participants are likely to have relationship problems similar to those of others in their peer groups. Some problems, however, might be somewhat unique to athletes, although similar to others who are celebrities or who are dedicated to a demanding activity in which the partner may not be involved.

Many athletes have to be away from friends or family for extended periods of time. This absence can cause loneliness, anxiety, and depression, for both the athlete and the family members. There may be conflicts in the relationship, or fears or suspicions, and these can manifest themselves in decreased performance, increased anger or aggression, or a number of other ways.

At the same time, practice and competition place demands on the athlete's time at home, and this, too, may be problematic for the partner. For many marathoners, who may not be elite or competitive athletes, for example, the months taken to train may disrupt family or relationship patterns. Someone who spends years involved in training and competition may need a very understanding or mutually involved partner.

The glamour and celebrity status that can surround athletes, as well as long travels away from home, offer opportunities for infidelity. Even when an athlete is not unfaithful, the partner may have fears about this when the athlete is away, or the athlete may have fears about the partner left behind.

It is not always easy to identify these issues. In some cases, when performance becomes problematic, the athlete will indicate the source is interpersonal or a relationship problem. In other cases, a relationship problem may manifest itself in changes in mood; the expression of anger, depression, or anxiety; or increases in alcohol or drug use. Often teammates will be told of the situation, and they may discuss it with a coach or others.

The athlete or sport participant may need to talk with someone individually to understand personal reactions better and to make decisions about commitments and behaviors. In other cases marital, relationship, or family counseling or therapy might be required.

When Referrals Don't Go Smoothly

Athletes may not always follow their sport psychology consultants' advice to seek assistance from other professionals. Van Raalte and Andersen (2002) presented a list of *do's* and *don'ts* for the referral process, and these provide some indications to why athletes do not always follow their consultants' suggestions. First, there might not be a sound working alliance between consultants and athletes. In the absence of close relationships, athletes may not trust that their sport psychologists have their best interests at heart. Consultants' recommendations, for example, might be interpreted as attempts to rid themselves of their athletes and pass them onto other professionals. From such interpretations, athletes might infer they are damaged goods and possibly unworthy.

Second, if handled insensitively, athletes might feel unsupported and believe their trepidations regarding referral have been ignored. One fear might be that the mental health practitioners will take away from athletes what made them high sporting achievers. Confidentiality is important as well; if word gets around that athletes are seeing other practitioners, they might feel they have lost some of their dignity. Although society has become more psychologically aware in recent years, there are those who still stigmatize people seeking counseling.

Third, consultants may not have prepared athletes adequately for the referral process. Consultants need to educate athletes about what referrals involve, whom the other helpers include, why they might help, and what the implications are for the existing sport psychologist-athlete relationships. Practitioners can begin preparation right from the start by signaling to athletes in their first sessions together that referral might be a possibility in the future. Athletes poorly prepared for referral may have unrealistic expectations about how helpful the new practitioners might be, particularly if sport psychologists have oversold the benefits to convince athletes to seek help.

Fourth, in the absence of any follow-up or facilitation, athletes might never contact the recommended practitioners or may not persist after the initial meetings. The match between the athlete and the helper may not be sufficient enough for benefits to accrue. Also, it may have been a huge step for athletes to share sensitive material with their sport psychologists, who may be one of the few trusted people in their lives. Athletes may not be ready to establish new relationships with other strangers.

When faced with referrals that do not appear to be working well, consultants can still keep in contact with athletes. To maintain a close relationship, the perception that the sport psychologist's continued help is conditional on the athlete meeting with the external helper needs to be avoided. It is probably inadvisable, and impractical, to force athletes to meet with other professionals if they are uncomfortable, except in situations where there is a threat of harm to self or others. Then consultants have legal obligations to consider. Sport psychologists who maintain their relationships with their athletes can continue to provide performance enhancement assistance and can still initiate referral process in the future if athletes change their minds.

Professional Development Tasks for Practitioners and Students

There are a number of ways that practitioners and students can engage in professional development so that referral processes are more likely to occur smoothly and ensure that athletes feel accepted and supported. Becoming familiar with the psychopathology of various mental health problems is a valuable first step, particularly for those individuals without clinical backgrounds. Practitioners with knowledge about the origins and manifestations of mental and behavioral disorders will be better placed to recognize when athletes are experiencing serious difficulties and be able to direct them to suitable professionals. Knowledge of psychopharmacology is also relevant because practitioners need to be familiar with what drugs are prescribed for various disorders and the typical side effects. For example, some anxiolytic drugs may lower blood pressure, and if relaxation treatment is also being used, blood pressure may drop to unhealthy levels. Sport psychologists well informed about psychopathology and pharmacology may have greater appreciations of what life is like for people with mental health concerns, and they may be able to use that empathic understanding to maintain helpful working relationships with their athletes. Being able to talk knowledgeably and nonjudgmentally about mental disorders with athletes will help sport psychologists better support their clients and prepare them for referrals to recommended mental health professionals. Texts and chapters, such as the *DSM-IV-TR* (APA, 2000) and Andersen (2004a, 2004b), contain useful information for practitioner continuing education, and sport psychologists can supplement their technical knowledge by reading biographies of athletes who have experienced mental health issues such as depression or drug dependency (Hadlee & Francis, 1985; Louganis & Marcus, 1996).

Another way students and practitioners can prepare themselves for future referrals is by identifying professionals they know and trust. There is a range of practitioners from whom sport psychologists can select suitable individuals depending on athletes' needs. These professionals include psychiatrists, clinical and counseling psychologists, social workers, pastoral care providers, marriage and family therapists, substance abuse counselors, and career guidance experts. Athletes' concerns may not always be related to mental health, but instead to other domains such as nutrition or physical well-being. Sport psychologists' networks could include nutritionists, biomechanists, sports medicine specialists, and exercise physiologists. Understanding the sporting backgrounds of the individuals in sport psychologists' networks will help practitioners suggest professionals who are best suited to helping and forming working alliances with athletes. For example, a clinical psychologist who has participated in track and field events may be a good choice for the depressed hammer thrower mentioned at the start of this chapter.

Sport psychology practitioners and students also can engage in role-plays to prepare themselves for making referrals. By rehearsing the referral process, sport psychologists can practice ways to interact with athletes in a caring and compassionate manner. For example, an athlete may feel threatened by meeting a clinical or counseling psychologist, and role-playing helping the athlete overcome those anxieties adds another dimension to the sport psychologist's repertoire. Peer-group supervision is an ideal place to conduct role-plays because fellow practitioners can receive feedback from their colleagues in a safe, problem-solving environment.

Summary

Referral: When?

Throughout this chapter, we have tried to address a variety of issues involved in deciding when to refer an athlete for professional counseling or psychotherapy. In most situations, referral will not be necessary. We hope that this chapter has provided helpful clues for recognizing when an athlete presents issues beyond the scope of the usual sport psychologist–client interaction. It is also important, however, for individuals working on performance-enhancement issues, whether sport psychologists, coaches, or others, to recognize the need for sensitivity to the athlete's personal issues in making appropriate referrals. These helping individuals must also be sensitive to their own issues and values because they might affect their ability to work with and to be sensitive to the issues others might have.

Referral: To What?

Early in the chapter it was suggested that even though we have become more accepting of personal and psychosocial conflicts, society in general and the sport world more particularly might have difficulty acknowledging and dealing with some issues.

Early in this century, as the nature of human conflict was recognized, there was a shift from blaming individuals or family backgrounds for problems to a "medicalization" of problems. In an attempt to understand people and treat them more compassionately, psychiatry and psychoanalysis (led by physicians) came up with the concept of mental illnesses, diagnosis, and treatment. In the 1960s, Thomas Szasz (1961) suggested, rather, that we again shift perspective to see conflict issues as problems in living.

There are many different theories of personality and approaches to counseling and psychotherapy. Individuals may have conflicts ranging from mild through severe. These problems do not have to be seen as illnesses or personal failings, but they may require the help of a trained professional. Increasingly, the medical model is fading, as models of growth and development replace it.

At the same time, it must be recognized that a small percentage of athletes, much like a small percentage of the general population, will have severe problems that may seriously affect their own functioning and their interpersonal relationships but that may not interfere with the performance of their athletic activities. As Giges (1998) reminds us, just because there is pathology present, that does not mean that it *has* to be treated. Many therapists have worked with individuals who are highly successful in some domains of their lives but have significant personal problems or disturbances in other domains.

Referral: To Whom?

There are many different types and levels of professional counselors, psychologists, psychiatrists, and psychotherapists. If a coach, trainer, athlete, or sport psychologist has not developed a working relationship with someone to whom he or she can refer, it may be necessary to investigate resources within the community. Most colleges have counseling centers, and many high schools have counseling personnel. It is possible to meet with them to find who may have a particular background in working with athletes or who might be interested in developing such a specialization. Similarly, individuals in private practice within a community or working at community mental health centers may be well suited for sport referrals.

Individuals who are licensed or certified by a state as counselors, psychologists (clinical or counseling), psychiatrists, or social workers have met certain educational requirements, although this does not speak to the quality of their work. In many states, however, the term *psychotherapist* is not legally defined. In essence, therefore, anyone can take out an advertisement and declare himself or herself to be a therapist. Some individuals will be trained, usually at the master's level. Perhaps the best advice for someone who is not familiar with these complex issues is to consult a licensed or certified psychiatrist, counselor, social worker, or psychologist for help in locating appropriate individuals to whom to refer.

To make things even more complicated, it may be necessary to know more than one professional. For example, a psychotherapist may work well with certain personal or interpersonal issues but might not be skilled with eating disorders or substance abuse. Perhaps one person works well with anxiety and depression but not with patterns of anger or aggression. In many cases counselors and therapists know the areas in which they are not as well trained or experienced and are able to refer to others. In other situations, however, the coach or educational sport psychologist may want to develop a personal listing of individuals with different skills.

It is important to understand the nature of *confidentiality* in counseling relationships. The coach or person referring the athlete to the professional may want feedback, but the professional may not be able to report much, or even any, information. There are very clear ethical issues on confidentiality that the person referring the athlete and the professional should discuss in developing a working relationship. The therapist likely cannot disclose the issues discussed with the athlete or even whether progress is being made.

Similarly, the athlete may not want to discuss the general or specific issues being explored in counseling or therapy. Over time, however, it is likely that a sense will develop of how helpful a therapist is and perhaps with what types of problems. A significant hallmark is the referral of one athlete by another to a person he or she has found helpful.

Final Thoughts

This has been a difficult chapter to write because there are many complex issues to discuss, or at least to acknowledge. Many of these topics could easily merit chapters on their own. For example, referral for career termination counseling issues (Lavallee & Wylleman, 2000; Lavallee & Andersen, 2000; Chapter 26) or for psychological treatment during injury rehabilitation (e.g., Kolt, 2000, 2004; Chapter 25) have not been discussed. This chapter has explored ways to help those not trained in counseling or psychotherapy to recognize these issues and to facilitate such referral.

Study Questions

1. From the dialogue in the chapter, what are some important issues to be sensitive to when making a referral?

2. What are three patterns someone might note as indicating more serious problems when working with an athlete on performance enhancement?

3. What are some reasons why the hammer thrower presented at the beginning of this chapter may not meet with a mental health practitioner?

4. How does homophobia in society and in the sport world contribute to problems for athletes who may be struggling with identity issues around their sexuality?

5. How might a concern with food or making weight reflect more serious eating disorder problems?

6. What can sport psychologists do to prepare themselves for making referrals?

7. What are some signs that aggressiveness in an athlete has become problematic? Is it likely that an athlete who has been driven by anger will become less successful if underlying conflicts are resolved?

8. What factors related to sport can cause or exacerbate relationship problems for athletes?

9. How might a coach or sport psychologist find professionals to whom to refer athletes for counseling or psychotherapy?

10. What might you do if an athlete currently does not want to take your referral advice?

References

American Psychiatric Association. (2000). *Diagnostic and statistical manual of mental disorders: Text revision* (4th ed.). Washington, DC: Author.

American Psychological Association. (1989). Ethical principles of psychologists and code of conduct. *American Psychologist, 46*, 1597–1611.

Andersen, M. B. (Ed.). (2000). *Doing sport psychology.* Champaign, IL: Human Kinetics.

Andersen, M. B. (Ed.). (in press). *Sport psychology in practice.* Champaign, IL: Human Kinetics.

Andersen, M. B. (2004a). Recognizing psychopathology. In G. S. Kolt, & M. B. Andersen (Eds.), *Psychology in the physical and manual therapies* (pp. 81–92). Edinburgh, UK: Churchill Livingstone.

Andersen, M. B. (2004b). Personality disorders. In G. S. Kolt, & M. B. Andersen (Eds.), *Psychology in the physical and manual therapies* (pp. 321–332). Edinburgh, UK: Churchill Livingstone.

Andersen, M. B. (2004c). Transference and counter transference. In G. S. Kolt, & M. B. Andersen (Eds.), *Psychology in the physical and manual therapies* (pp. 71–80). Edinburgh, UK: Churchill Livingstone.

Andersen, M. B., Butki, B. D., & Heyman, S. R. (1997). Homophobia and sport experience: A survey of college students. *Academic Athletic Journal, 12*(1), 27–38.

Andersen, M. B., Denson, E. L., Brewer, B. W., & Van Raalte, J. L. (1994). Disorders of personality and mood in athletes: Recognition and referral. *Journal of Applied Sport Psychology, 6*, 168–184.

Andersen, M. B., & Fawkner, H. J. (in press). The skin game: Extra points for looking good. In M. B. Andersen (Ed.), *Sport psychology in practice.* Champaign, IL: Human Kinetics.

Andersen, M. B., & Van Raalte, J. L. (in press). Over one's head: Referral processes. In M. B. Andersen (Ed.), *Sport psychology in practice.* Champaign, IL: Human Kinetics.

APA Committee on Lesbian and Gay Concerns. (1990). *Bias in psychotherapy with lesbians and gay men.* Washington, DC: American Psychological Association.

Baillie, P. H. F., & Danish, S. J. (1992). Understanding the career transitions of athletes. *The Sport Psychologist, 6*, 77–98.

Balague, G. (1999). Understanding identity, value, and meaning when working with elite athletes. *The Sport Psychologist, 13*, 89–98.

Barney, S. T., & Andersen, M. B. (2000). Looking for help, grieving love lost: The case of C. In M. B. Andersen (Ed.), *Doing sport psychology* (pp. 139–150). Champaign, IL: Human Kinetics.

Beren, S. E., Hayden, H. A., Wifley, D. E., & Grillo, C. M. (1996). The influence of sexual orientation on body dissatisfaction in adult men and women. *International Journal of Eating Disorders, 20*, 135–141.

Black, D. (Ed.). (1991). *Eating disorders among athletes: Theory, issues, and research.* Reston, VA: American Alliance for Health, Physical Education, Recreation, & Dance.

Blouin, A. G., & Goldfield, G. S. (1995). Body image and steroid use in male bodybuilders. *International Journal of Eating Disorders, 18*, 159–165.

Braun, D. L., Sunday, S. R., Huang, A., & Halmi, K. (1999). More males seek treatment for eating disorders. *International Journal of Eating Disorders, 26,* 413–424.

Brewer, B. W. (1994). Review and critique of models of psychological adjustment to athletic injury. *Journal of Applied Sport Psychology, 6,* 87–100.

Brewer, B. W., & Petitpas, A. J. (in press). Returning to self: The anxieties of coming back after injury. In M. B. Andersen (Ed.), *Sport psychology in practice.* Champaign, IL: Human Kinetics.

Brewer, B. W., & Petrie, T. A. (2002). Psychopathology in sport and exercise. In J. L. Van Raalte, & B. W. Brewer (Eds.), *Exploring sport and exercise psychology* (2nd ed. pp. 307–324). Washington, DC: American Psychological Association.

Brewer, B. W., Van Raalte, J. L., & Linder, D. E. (1991). Role of the sport psychologist in treating injured athletes: A survey of sports medicine providers. *Journal of Applied Sport Psychology, 3,* 183–190.

Brewer, B. W., Van Raalte, J. L., & Linder, D. E. (1993). Athletic identity: Hercules' muscles or Achilles heel. *International Journal of Sport Psychology, 24,* 237–254.

Brower, K. J. (1992). Addictive potential of anabolic steroids. *Psychiatric Annals, 22,* 30–34.

Brownell, K. D., Rodin, J., & Wilmore, J. H. (Eds.). (1992). *Eating, body weight, and performance in athletes.* Malvern, PA: Lea & Febiger.

Buckley, W. E., Yesalis, C. E., Friedl, K. E., Anderson, W. A., Streit, A. L., & Wright, J. E. (1988). Estimated prevalence of anabolic steroid use among high school seniors. *Journal of the American Medical Association, 260,* 3441–3445.

Burckes-Miller, M., & Black, D. (1988). Male and female college athletes: Prevalence of anorexia nervosa and bulimia nervosa. *Athletic Training, 23,* 137–140.

Butki, B. D., Andersen, M. B., & Heyman, S. R. (1996). Knowledge of AIDS and risky sexual behavior among athletes. *Academic Athletic Journal, 11*(1), 29–36.

Carlat, D., Camargo, C. A., & Herzog, D. B. (1997). Eating disorders in males: A report on 135 patients. *American Journal of Psychiatry, 154,* 1127–1132.

Carr, C. M., & Murphy, S. M. (1995). Alcohol and drugs in sport. In S. M. Murphy (Ed.), *Sport psychology interventions* (pp. 283–306). Champaign, IL: Human Kinetics.

Cash, T. F., & Grant, J. R. (1995). The cognitive-behavioral treatment of body-image disturbances. In V. V. Hasselt & M. Hersen (Eds.), *Sourcebook of psychological treatment manuals for adults* (pp. 567–614). New York: Plenum.

Cash, T. F., & Syzmanski, M. L. (1995). The development and validation of the Body-Ideals Questionnaire. *Journal of Personality Assessment, 64,* 466–477.

Cogan, K. D. (2000). The sadness in sport: Working with a depressed and suicidal athlete. In M. B. Andersen (Ed.), *Doing sport psychology* (pp. 107–119). Champaign, IL: Human Kinetics.

Cogan, K. D., & Petrie, T. A. (2002). Diversity in sport. In J. L. Van Raalte & B. W. Brewer (Eds.), *Exploring sport and exercise psychology* (2nd ed., pp. 417–436). Washington, DC: American Psychological Association.

Davis, C., & Cowles, M. (1991). Body image and exercise: A study of relationships and comparisons between physically active men and women. *Sex Roles, 25*(1–2), 33–44.

Drewnowski, A., & Yee, D. K. (1987). Men and body image: Are males satisfied with their body weight? *Psychosomatic Medicine, 49*, 626–634.

Erikson, E. (1968). *Identity: Youth and crisis.* New York: Norton.

Etzel, E. F., Ferrante, A. P., & Pinkney, J. W. (Eds.). (1996). *Counseling college student-athletes: Issues and interventions* (2nd ed.). Morgantown, WV: Fitness Information Technology.

Faulkner, G., & Biddle, S. J. H. (2004). Exercise and depression: Considering variability and contextuality. *Journal of Sport & Exercise Psychology, 26*, 3–18.

Garnets, L., Hancock, K., Cochran, S., Goodchilds, J., & Peplau, L. A. (1991). Issues in psychotherapy with lesbians and gay men: A survey of psychologists, *American Psychologist, 46*, 964–972.

Giges, B. (1998). Psychodynamic concepts in sport psychology: Comment on Strean and Strean (1998). *The Sport Psychologist, 12*, 223–227.

Greenspan, M. J., & Feltz, D. L (1989). Psychological interventions with athletes in competitive situations: A review. *The Sport Psychologist, 3*, 219–236.

Gregg, E., & Rejeski, W. J. (1990). Social psychologic dysfunction associated with anabolic steroids: A review. *The Sport Psychologist, 4*, 275–284.

Grove, J. R., Lavallee, D., Gordon, S., & Harvey, J. H. (1998). Account-making: A model for understanding and resolving distressful reactions to retirement from sport. *The Sport Psychologist, 12*, 52–67.

Hadlee, R., & Francis, T. (1985). *At the double: The story of cricket's pacemaker.* Auckland, New Zealand: Arrow.

Hays, K. F. (2002). *The workout therapy workbook: Move your body, tone your mood.* Oakland, CA: New Harbinger.

Hays, K. F., & Smith, R. J. (2002). Incorporating sport and exercise psychology into clinical practice. In J. L. Van Raalte, & B. W. Brewer (Eds.), *Exploring sport and exercise psychology* (2nd ed., pp. 479–502). Washington, DC: American Psychological Association.

Heyman, S. R. (1987). Counseling and psychotherapy with athletes: Special considerations. In J. R. May & M. J. Asken (Eds.), *Sport psychology: The psychological health of the athlete.* New York: PMA.

Hilderbrand, K. M., Johnson, D. J., & Bogle, K. (2001). Comparison of patterns of alcohol use between high school and college athletes and non-athletes. *College Student Journal, 35*, 258–365.

Johnson, C., Powers, P. S., & Dick, R. (1999). Athletes and eating disorders: The National Collegiate Athletic Association study. *International Journal of Eating Disorders, 26*, 179–188.

Kolt, G. (2004). Injury from sport, exercise, and physical activity. In G. S. Kolt, & M. B. Andersen (Eds.), *Psychology in the physical and manual therapies* (pp. 247–267). Edinburgh, UK: Churchill Livingstone.

Kolt, G. S. (2000). Doing sport psychology with injured athletes. In M. B. Andersen (Ed.), *Doing sport psychology* (pp. 223–236). Champaign, IL: Human Kinetics.

Krane, V. (1995). Performance related outcomes experienced by lesbian athletes. *Journal of Applied Sport Psychology, 7*(suppl.), S83.

Lavellee, D., & Andersen, M. B. (2000). Leaving sport: Easing career transitions. In M. B. Andersen (Ed.), *Doing sport psychology* (pp. 249–260). Champaign, IL: Human Kinetics.

Lavallee, D., & Wylleman, P. (Eds.). (2000). *Career transitions in sport: International perspectives.* Morgantown, WV: Fitness Information Technology.

Lent, R. (1993). Sports psychology and counseling psychology: Players in the same ball park? *The Counseling Psychologist, 21,* 430–435.

Lesyk, J. L. (1998). *Developing sport psychology within your clinical practice: A practical guide for mental health professionals.* San Francisco: Jossey-Bass.

Linder, D. E., Brewer, B. W., Van Raalte, J. L., & De Lange, N. (1991). A negative halo for athletes who consult sport psychologists: Replication and extension. *Journal of Sport & Exercise Psychology, 13,* 133–148.

Linder, D. E., Pillow, D. R., & Reno, R. R. (1989). Shrinking jocks: Derogation of athletes who consult a sport psychologist. *Journal of Sport & Exercise Psychology, 11,* 270–280.

Louganis, G., & Marcus, E. (1996). *Breaking the surface.* New York: Penguin Putnam.

Martens, M. P., & Mobley, M. (in press). Homophobia and sport psychology service: "Straight" guys working with "Gay" guys. In M. B. Andersen (Ed.), *Sport psychology in practice.* Champaign, IL: Human Kinetics.

Martin, K. A., & Hausenblaus, H. A. (1998). Psychological commitment to exercise and eating disorder symptomatology among female aerobic instructors. *The Sport Psychologist, 12,* 180–190.

McConnell, K. E. (1995). Homophobia in women's intercollegiate athletics: A case study. *Journal of Applied Sport Psychology, 7*(suppl.), S89.

McMurray, N. E., Bell, R., & Shircore, J. (1995, July). *Psychological factors influencing positive and negative health behaviors in a community sample of men and women.* Paper presented at the 9th European Congress of Psychology, Athens, Greece.

McMurray, N. E., & Gazis, J. (1995). *Factors associated with sexual risk taking in gay and bisexual men.* Paper presented at the 19th Annual Conference for the Advancement of Behavior Therapy, Houston, TX.

Miller, P. S. (2003). The role experimentation of intercollegiate student athletes. *The Sport Psychologist, 17,* 196–219.

Murphy, S. M. (Ed.). (1995). *Sport psychology interventions.* Champaign, IL: Human Kinetics.

National Collegiate Athletic Association. (1989). *NCAA eating disorders project, Part 1, Afraid to eat: Eating disorders and student athletes* (Video). Overland, KS: Author.

Novaco, R. (1975). *Anger control: The development and evaluation of an experimental treatment.* Lexington, MA: Heath.

Olivardia, R., Pope, H. G., Jr., Mangweth, B., & Hudson, J. J. (1995). Eating disorders in college men. *American Journal of Psychiatry, 152,* 1279–1285.

Oyebode, F., Boodhoo, J.-A., & Schapira, K. (1988). Anorexia nervosa in males: Clinical features and outcome. *International Journal of Eating Disorders, 7,* 121–124.

Petitpas, A., & Danish, S. J. (1995). Caring for injured athletes. In S. M. Murphy (Ed.), *Sport psychology interventions* (pp. 255–281). Champaign, IL: Human Kinetics.

Petitpas, A. J., Danish, S. J., & Giges, B. (1999). The sport psychologist–athlete relationship: Implications for training. *The Sport Psychologist, 13,* 344–357.

Petrie, T. A., Diehl, N. S., & Watkins, C. E., Jr. (1995). Sport psychology: An emerging domain in the counseling psychology profession. *The Counseling Psychologist, 23,* 535–545.

Petrie, T. A., & Sherman, R. T. (2000). Counseling athletes with eating disorders: A case example. In M. B. Andersen (Ed.), *Doing sport psychology* (pp. 121–137). Champaign, IL: Human Kinetics.

Petrie, T. A., & Watkins, C. E., Jr. (1994). Sport psychology training in counseling psychology programs: Is there room at the inn? *The Counseling Psychologist, 22,* 335–341.

Poczwardowski, A., Sherman, C. P., & Henschen, K. P. (1998). A sport psychology service delivery heuristic: Building on theory and practice. *The Sport Psychologist, 12,* 191–207.

Pope, H. G., Jr., Phillips, K. A., & Olivardia, R. (2000). *The Adonis complex: The secret crisis of male body obsession.* New York: Free Press.

Putukian, M. (1994). The female triad: Eating disorders, amenorrhea, and osteoporosis. *Medical Clinics of North America, 78,* 345–356.

Ray, R., & Wiese-Bjornstal, D. M. (Eds.). (1999). *Counseling in sports medicine.* Champaign, IL: Human Kinetics.

Rejeski, W. J., & Brawley, L. R. (1988). Defining the boundaries of sport psychology. *The Sport Psychologist, 2,* 231–242.

Robertson, J. M., & Newton, F. B. (2001). Working with men in sports settings. In G. R. Brooks & G. E. Good (Eds.), *The new handbook of psychotherapy and counseling with men: A comprehensive guide to settings, problems, and treatment approaches* (Vol. 1, pp. 92–125). San Francisco: Jossey-Bass.

Rotella, R. J. (1992, Fall). Sport psychology: Staying focused on a common and shared mission for a bright future. *AAASP Newsletter, 7,* 8–9.

Rotella, R., & Murray, M. M. (1991). Homophobia, the world of sport, and sport psychology consulting. *The Sport Psychologist, 5,* 355–364.

Seime, R., & Damer, D. (1991). Identification and treatment of the athlete with an eating disorder. In E. F. Etzel, A. P. Ferrante, & J. W. Pinkney (Eds.), *Counseling college student-athletes: Issues and interventions* (pp. 175–198). Morgantown, WV: Fitness Information Technology.

Simons, J. P., & Andersen, M. B. (1995). The development of consulting practice in applied sport psychology: Some personal perspectives. *The Sport Psychologist, 9,* 449–468.

Sours, J. A. (1980). *Starving to death in a sea of objects: The anorexia nervosa syndrome.* New York: Jason Aronson.

Stainback, R. D., & Taylor, R. E. (in press). Facilitating change: Alcohol and violence among athletes. In M. B. Andersen (Ed.), *Sport psychology in practice.* Champaign, IL: Human Kinetics.

Stephan, Y. (2003). Repercussions of transition out of elite sport on body image. *Perceptual and Motor Skills, 96,* 95–104.

Straub, W. F., & Williams. J. M. (1984). *Cognitive sport psychology.* Lansing, NY: Sport Science Associates.

Strean, W. B., & Strean, H. S. (1998). Applying psychodynamic concepts in sport psychology practice. *The Sport Psychologist, 12,* 208–222.

Sundgot-Borgen, J. (1994). Risk and trigger factors for the development of eating disorders in female elite athletes. *Medicine and Science in Sports and Exercise, 26,* 414–419.

Swoap, R. A., & Murphy, S. M. (1995). Eating disorders and weight management in athletes. In S. M. Murphy (Ed.), *Sport psychology interventions* (pp. 307–329). Champaign, IL: Human Kinetics.

Szasz, T. (1961). *The myth of mental illness.* New York: Harper & Row.

Thompson, R. A., & Sherman, R. T. (1993). *Helping athletes with eating disorders.* Champaign, IL: Human Kinetics.

Tod, D., & Andersen, M. (2005). Success in sport psychology: Effective sport psychologists. In S. Murphy (Ed.), *The sport psych handbook* (pp. 305–314). Champaign, IL: Human Kinetics.

Tricker, R., & Cook, D. L. (1989). *Athletes at risk: Drugs and sport.* Dubuque, IA: Brown.

Udry, E., & Andersen, M. B. (2002). Athletic injury and sport behavior. In T. S. Horn (Ed.), *Advances in sport psychology* (2nd ed., pp. 529–553). Champaign, IL: Human Kinetics.

Van Raalte, J. L., & Andersen, M. B. (2002). Referral processes in sport psychology. In J. L. Van Raalte & B. W. Brewer (Eds.), *Exploring sport and exercise psychology* (2nd ed., pp. 325–337). Washington, DC: American Psychological Association.

Van Raalte, J. L., & Brewer, B. W. (Eds.). (2002). *Exploring sport and exercise psychology* (2nd ed.). Washington, DC: American Psychological Association.

Van Raalte, J. L., Brewer, B. W., Brewer, D. D., & Linder, D. E. (1992). NCAA Division II college football players' perceptions of an athlete who consults a sport psychologist. *Journal of Sport & Exercise Psychology, 14,* 273–282.

Yates, A. (1991). *Compulsive exercise and the eating disorders: Towards an integrated theory of activity.* New York: Brunner/Mazel.

Zuckerman, M. (1979). *Sensation seeking: Beyond the optimal level of arousal.* Hillsdale, NJ: Erlbaum.

Drug Abuse in Sport: Causes and Cures

Mark H. Anshel, *Middle Tennessee State University*

Athletes who think they're immortal are playing Russian roulette with their health by toying with drugs. Experts warn of heart disease and tumors. Ask the friends of former NFL stud Lyle Alzado, who blamed his death from cancer at 42 on steroids.

—*Sandy Grady, USA Today*

The French have an interesting adage: "The more things change, the more they stay the same." I have been writing about and studying drugs in sport since 1989 when the International Olympic Committee (IOC), United States Olympic Committee (USOC), and other sporting organizations were becoming increasingly concerned about the illicit use of banned substances. For good reason. At the 1988 Olympic Games in Seoul, the Canadian world-class sprinter Ben Johnson tested positive for steroids. Even in the 1970s, it was widely thought that so-called performance-enhancing drugs were used among medal winners from the Soviet Union and other Eastern European countries, most notably East Germany. The results of subsequent investigations indicated that these allegations turned out to be true. The former Olympic medal winner and hurdler Edwin Moses wrote in an October 1988 issue of *Newsweek* magazine: "Drug use definitely is rampant. In Seoul we had a community of people ravaged by steroids and other banned substances" (p. 57). What were officials doing about it? Despite evidence of drug use among elite athletes, official reaction to drug use has been inconsistent. Indeed, the absence of assertive and consistent responses to drug abuse by sport administrators and coaches has likely contributed to its proliferation. As Strauss (1987) points out, "Sports officials voice unequivocal disapproval of performance-enhancing drugs and formally ban them. Yet, when violations are uncovered, punishment is inconsistent" (p. 13).

Perhaps this type of response is at least partly because of society's obsession with obtaining "the edge" and reflects the views of most athletes that the end—performance success—justifies the means.

The word *drug* means different things to different people. The two most common categories of drug use among competitive athletes are performance-enhancing drugs, such as anabolic steroids, and recreational drugs, such as cocaine, heroin, or marijuana. The reasons for ingesting recreational and performance-enhancing drugs vary. The objective of recreational drug users is to alter the state of mind, with no intention of improving performance. Users of drugs such as steroids, in contrast, feel a need to improve performance to gain a competitive advantage. These different rationales for ingesting drugs must be taken into account when developing strategies to reduce or eliminate such behaviors.

Why are certain substances banned from competitive sport, and why should sport administrators, coaches, parents of athletes, and athletes themselves be concerned about the use of drugs categorized as "performance-enhancing"? Yesalis and Cowart (1998) state that the use of steroids by athletes (a) may cause physical and psychological harm, (b) violates state and federal laws if used for nonmedical purposes, (c) is cheating and violates the team rules and organizational policies of almost every sport, and (d) contaminates performance results, which are obtained by unnatural means.

What drugs are banned by sport organizations? Why break the rules and chance expulsion from a team and sport organization? Why risk severe health problems? The purpose of this chapter is to address these questions and to suggest cognitive and behavioral strategies that coaches, parents, and sport psychology consultants can use to combat drug abuse in sport. Only when causes for drug usage are identified can cognitive and behavioral strategies be devised to help prevent and perhaps eliminate this problem. First, however, a brief history of drug use in sport is warranted.

Brief Historical Review

Efforts to use performance-enhancing drugs and ways to prevent their use has a long history. Greek athletes competing in the Olympic games in the third century B.C. tried to improve performance by ingesting certain plants, as did swimmers and cyclists in the 1860s. The first drug-related fatality occurred in 1886 when an English cyclist succumbed to a fatal dose of a stimulant during a race. American cyclists used strychnine in the 1904 Olympic games. And another cyclist died during the 1952 Olympic games in Helsinki due to an overdose of amphetamines. But it was not until the 1950s amid allegations of cheating at track and field competitions and athlete fatalities that the IOC passed a resolution against "doping." In 1967, a medical commission was established by the IOC to control drug use.

Penalties for drug use were first implemented during the 1976 Olympics in Montreal. Illegal drug use was found with 2.9% urine specimens testing positive. Two gold medal winners and one silver medal winner were disqualified. In 1983, the USOC concluded that drug education alone, even 20 years worth, was ineffective in preventing drug abuse among competitors. A USOC Drug Control Program was established that year, and it included disciplinary action toward coaches, trainers, and physicians if they were found to aid or abet drug use. In more recent years, the combination of positive drug tests for Olympic Games medal winners, accusations of cheating by athletes and their coaches, and the deaths of selected high profile athletes has resulted in an all-out effort at monitoring drug use in sport. It is not just Olympic athletes who have turned toward artificial means of performance enhancement. The use of drugs in professional sport is yet an additional challenge to sports administrators. The publicized deaths and high rates of heart disease and cancer among professional athletes, for example, Lyle Alzado, a former well-known football player with the Denver Broncos (discussed later), lend further credence to the widespread use of banned substances in sport at the highest levels. In more recent times, we are seeing one particularly troubling outcome from widespread steroid use in sport—the use of steroids by adolescent males to improve physical appearance (Ringhofer & Harding, 1996).

Yesalis and Cowart (1998) contend there has been a significant increase in steroid use in the middle schools due, primarily, to the well-known steroid habits of elite athletes. Steroid use is now ubiquitous in the school system, from college to middle school. A study by the University of Michigan in 2003 indicated that 3.5% of high school seniors, all nonathletes, had used illegal steroids, a 2% increase from 10 years earlier. Apparently, failing to control the availability of performance-enhancing drugs is taking a toll on our society beyond competitive sport.

Review of Drugs Banned in Sport

Drugs have the common characteristic of altering a physiological process within the body, usually for medicinal purposes to treat, prevent, or diagnose disease. However, a drug that is classified as "performance-enhancing" does not fit this definition. Instead, substances that are intended to affect the quality of movement are more compatible with the concept of doping.

The IOC refers to the act of ingesting banned drugs as "doping" (Prokop, 1990). **Doping** has been defined as "the administering or use of substances in any form alien to the body or of physiological substances in abnormal amounts and with abnormal methods by healthy persons with the exclusive aim of attaining an artificial and unfair increase of performance in competition" (p. 5). The IOC has classified five doping categories that are banned from international competition: anabolic androgenic steroids, stimulants (including hallucinogens), narcotic analgesics, beta-adrenergic blockers, and diuretics (Chappel, 1987; Park, 1990). Central nervous system depressants that serve to reduce anxiety (e.g., alcohol, barbiturates, and sedative hypnotics), local anesthetics, and corticosteroids (anti-inflammatory drugs that relieve pain) are not on the IOC list but are tested for in selected international competitions (Chappel, 1987). Typically, however, these substances are considered illegal. In addition, as an ergogenic aid, the technique of blood doping is also banned. The reasons for banning such drugs in sport are understandable given their psychophysiological effects (Mottram, 1988; Park, 1990; Strauss, 1987; Weinhold, 1991; Williams, 1998). Not banned by the IOC and therefore not against policies of national and international sport organizations, at least for mature-age athletes, are depressants (e.g., alcohol), nicotine, diet regimens (e.g.,

carbohydrate loading or any other food-ingestion habits), amino acids, and vitamins (Williams, 1998). However, it may only be a matter of time before certain nutritional supplements are also on the banned list.

Williams (1994) cites the IOC doping legislation that stipulates that any physiologic substance taken in abnormal quantities with the intention of artificially and unfairly increasing performance should be construed as doping, violating the ethics of sport performance. Williams suggests that perhaps athletic-governing organizations should consider the legality and ethics that accompany the use of ergogenic nutraceuticals in sport.

Before reviewing the different types of banned substances, it is important to briefly describe the concept of **addiction.** Addiction is, by definition, characterized by an inability on the part of the individual to control his or her chemical use. A person who is addicted to a drug is chemically and, for some types of drugs, psychologically dependent on the substance to maintain a sense of normality, or homogeneity. Probably the key diagnostic feature of addiction is the withdrawal syndrome, in which physiological and psychological processes become dysfunctional or may even temporarily terminate. Although some substances are more addictive and destructive than others, ultimately those in both mind-altering (recreational) and performance-enhancing categories affect the same nerve pathways (Nardo, 1992). In other words, there is no such thing as a safe drug.

Anabolic Steroids

As discussed later, ergogenic drugs consist of any agent that is used for the intended purpose of enhancing physical performance. Anabolic steroids are one type of ergogenic aid and the best-known category of performance-enhancing drug. As indicated throughout this chapter, any potential benefit of steroid use to sport performance depends on the type of skills and physical demands required of that sport. Briefly, if steroids improve strength and power, for instance, then athletes of sports in which strength is an important component (e.g., U.S. football, track and field) might find steroids advantageous to performance, whereas competitors of sports not requiring strength and power (e.g., golf, archery) will not.

Benefits of steroid use. Perhaps the most salient advantage of steroid use on sport performance is improved strength and power (Yesalis & Cowart, 1998). This is because the function of anabolic steroids is to increase the male hormone androgen and decrease the female hormone estrogen. These effects explain why steroids have a masculinizing effect for females (e.g., increased facial and body hair, lowered voice, increased muscular bulk and strength, interference with reproductive function), whereas males experience increased feminine characteristics (e.g., reduced facial and body hair, reduced sperm production and impotence), although testosterone and strength do increase in males. Strength gain is optimal when an intensified training program accompanies steroid intake. These benefits primarily occur because steroids promote the synthesis of proteins that are used to build skeletal muscle tissue (Yesalis & Cowart, 1998). Anabolic steroids also are used for medicinal purposes, most notably, to promote muscle growth and tissue repair as part of injury rehabilitation.

Harmful effects. The harmful side effects of prolonged steroid use are extensive (see Cohen, Noakes, & Benade, 1988; Lubell, 1989; Mottram, Reilly, & Chester, 1997; Strauss, 1987; Yesalis & Cowart, 1998). When testosterone levels become too high, the hypothalamus in the brain starts to shut down the body processes involving the hormone. These processes include stimulation and maintenance of the sex organs for males, and the development of masculine body characteristics for women. Both genders may experience temporary or permanent sterility. Ringhofer and Harding (1996) assert that production of the male's "naturally occurring hormones, like testosterone, may be decreased (which may) result in shrinking of the testes, low sperm counts, and infertility" (p. 175). These negative side effects are even greater for individuals who have not yet reached physiological maturity. Because tendons and ligaments may not strengthen at the same rate

that muscle tissue develops, there are often more injuries of muscles, tendons, and ligaments among steroid users (Wright & Cowart, 1990).

More ominously, prolonged heavy steroid users risk cancerous liver cell tumors, high blood pressure (i.e., hypertension), premature heart disease, myocardial infarction (heart attack), and stroke. Related behavioral outcomes include child abuse, domestic violence, suicide, and attempted murder or death. When chronic steroid use is suddenly stopped, clinical depression often results. Adolescent abusers may suffer the additional effect of reduced bone growth because of premature fusion of the epiphysis of long bones. The result is permanently stunted growth.

Another undesirable effect of prolonged steroid use is heightened, uncontrolled aggression and temper, often referred to as "roid rage." Roid rage is a condition in which a behavioral manifestation of chronic steroid users is increased aggressiveness. In his review of related studies, Branch (2002) found that the change in temperament is likely because of a marked increase in testosterone, a chemical produced naturally in the body but also taken artificially. Anabolic steroids increase the rate at which the body manufactures testosterone, which, in turn, is associated with higher than normal rates of concomitant high-risk behaviors, such as drinking and driving, unsafe sex, nonuse of seat belts, suicidal behavior, and heightened aggression level.

Another concern about steroid use is their addictive properties, both psychologically and physiologically (Weinhold, 1991). From a psychological perspective, the individual may feel dependent on steroids for maintaining a sense of well-being, strength, increased musculature, and improved performance. Failing to maintain the steroid regimen may result in lost confidence, fear of failure, and depression. Physiological addiction may reflect the body's dependence on molecular substances for protein synthesis, which build skeletal tissue. Symptoms of sudden withdrawal of prolonged steroid ingestion include changes in heart rate, blood pressure, tension, and fatigue (Leccese, 1991).

According to Schlaadt and Shannon (1994), athletes may attempt to overcome these problems by taking "drug holidays" between periods of use by "pyramiding" or "stacking." Pyramiding consists of beginning with a lower dose, then increasing the amount progressively until the maximum dose is reached, then tapering the dosage until the drug is completely withdrawn. Stacking consists of using numerous drugs and varying the dosage throughout the cycle. The authors conclude, however, that "no scientific evidence supports the idea that 'stacking' or 'pyramiding' the drugs is more effective than other methods of using them or that it minimizes the harmful side effects of steroid use" (p. 50).

Taken together, it is apparent that the costs of taking anabolic steroids may far outweigh the benefits. According to Voy (1991), a physician who tested for drugs as a consultant with the U.S. Olympic Committee, "there isn't an anabolic-androgenic steroid an athlete can take to increase muscle mass, endurance, or speed without risking dangerous hormonal side effects" (p. 14).

To find detailed information about steroids and their effects, read the National Institute on Drug Abuse Research Report Series, which is sponsored by the National Institutes of Health and can be obtained on the Internet: http://www.nida.nig.gov/ResearchReports/Steroids/anabolicsteroids3.html

Stimulants

Stimulant drugs increase the rate and, hence, the work capacity of the heart, central nervous system, and respiratory system. Stimulants are divided into three groups: **psychomotor** (e.g., amphetamines, cocaine, and most diet suppressants); **sympathomimetic amines,** which stimulate the sympathetic and autonomic nervous systems; and miscellaneous **central nervous system (CNS) stimulants** (e.g., drugs such as ephedrine that are found in many prescription and over-the-counter cold remedies). Ostensibly these drugs improve athletic performance by increasing alertness through inhibition of mental and physical fatigue. However, on the minus—and very dangerous—side, some stimulants (e.g., cocaine) may result in death due to seizures, damage to the heart muscle, or stroke (Doweiko, 1996).

Another category of stimulant is **hallucinogens.** Often referred to as recreational, mind-altering, or street drugs (Bell & Doege, 1987; Julien, 1981), hallucinogens alter the perceptions of incoming stimuli. The IOC does not place hallucinogens in a separate banned drugs category because they are stimulants or narcotic analgesics, both banned by the IOC. Because they inhibit response and decision-making time and attentional focus, these drugs impair rather than enhance sport performance. Marijuana (a sedative) and LSD, PCP, and cocaine (stimulants) are examples. The use of these drugs is also against the federal laws of most countries.

Caffeine is another type of central nervous system (CNS) stimulant that is banned by the IOC if ingested beyond moderation. How much caffeine intake is too much? Moderate caffeine intake commensurate with less than 18 ounces of coffee is not prohibited by the IOC. Caffeine increases alertness and arousal, thereby preventing or overcoming mental and physical fatigue. These effects may improve forms of athletic performance that depend on heightened CNS activity. Used in excessive amounts, caffeine has been shown to prolong endurance performance and high-intensity short-duration exercise performed in a clinical setting, creating an unfair advantage in competitive sport. However, excessive caffeine may adversely affect thermoregulation (i.e., internal body temperature) because of its diuretic effect. Increased urination with insufficient water intake raises the internal body temperature, inducing premature fatigue and, at dangerous levels, heat-related illnesses.

Narcotic Analgesics (Anti-Inflammatories)

Narcotic analgesics are used by athletes for their pain-killing properties, to slow or stop the inflammation and swelling of tissue, to reduce fever, and to produce feelings of well-being or invincibility. As pain suppressants, these drugs enable an injured competitor to continue playing despite tissue damage and injury. Anti-inflammatories can actually reduce performance effectiveness in some sports due to their sedative effect.

All analgesics are toxic in large doses. Examples of narcotic analgesics include codeine, heroin, morphine, and opium. Harmful effects of analgesics include gastrointestinal disturbances, physical and psychological dependence, and depressed respiration—including respiratory arrest. Nonnarcotic analgesics such as aspirin and acetaminophen, which are not habit forming and do not affect the central nervous system, are not banned. Sadly, according to research in the United States, 90% of narcotics addicts return to the use of drugs within 6 months of achieving sobriety (Doweiko, 1996). Wagner (1991) provides a superb overview of the literature on banned performance-enhancing drugs.

Beta-Adrenergic Blockers

Perhaps best known for the treatment of high blood pressure and some forms of heart disease, **beta blockers** are among the few drugs banned by the IOC that do not induce dependence. They aid performance by slowing the heart rate, decreasing anxiety, and steadying natural body tremors. These are desirable outcomes in sports such as rifle and pistol shooting, archery, bowling, and golf. Adverse effects of beta blockers include bronchospasms, CNS disturbances, hypotension, and impotence. In addition, beta blockers may negatively affect high-intensity, longer endurance tasks.

Diuretics

Diuretics increase the rate at which water and salts leave the body as urine. Athletes such as jockeys, wrestlers, and boxers use diuretics to make weight for a competition. Other athletes use diuretics to overcome fluid retention—often to modify the excretion rate of urine in order to alter the urinary concentrations of banned drugs such as anabolic steroids. The rapid depletion of body fluids in general and of potassium in particular can produce heart arrhythmias. Nausea, heat exhaustion or stroke from impaired thermoregulatory control, blood clotting, reduced blood volume, and muscle cramps are other possible outcomes (Russell, 1990).

Depressants

Depressants relieve tension, reduce anxiety, and have a steadying effect on the nervous or fearful athlete, such as reducing arm tremor in shooters. They also, however, impair reaction time, hand–eye coordination, balance, and judgment. Thus, for the most part, depressants inhibit rather than enhance sport performance. Because they are addictive, the heavy and prolonged use of depressants may result in withdrawal symptoms. Barbiturates, sedative-hypnotics, and alcohol are examples of this form of drug.

Ergogenic Aids

The word *ergogenic* refers to "an increase in the rate of work output" (Williams, 1998). Ergogenic aids, also called sports ergogenics, refers to the use of any technique that "improves athletic performance beyond what would be possible through natural ability (genetics) and training alone" (pp. 9–10). There are five categories of sports ergogenics: nutritional (e.g., vitamins, creatine, amino acids), pharmacological (e.g., anabolic steroids, anti-inflammatory agents, caffeine), physiological (e.g., blood doping, oxygen inhalation), psychological (e.g., mental skills for emotional control, anxiety management, establishing optimal arousal), and biomechanical (e.g., sportswear, sports equipment). This section is not about evaluating the effectiveness of sports ergogenics (see Williams, 1998, for this information). However, I will briefly examine the factors that separate legal and ethical ergogenic aids, such as mental skills, updated equipment, and nutritional supplements, from illegal and unethical ergogenic aids, such as anabolic steroids and blood doping.

Williams (1998) lists four considerations, other than cost and availability, that determine whether athletes should consider using a specific sports ergogenic: (1) Is the substance legal? (2) Is it ethical? (3) Is it safe? (4) Is it effective? The issues of legality and ethics are important considerations, because substances are banned by the governing body of a particular sport, such as antidoping legislation, to protect athletes' health and prevent cheating. In addition to putting their short- and long-term health at risk, athletes who are found to have ingested banned substances may be prevented from future sport participation. Very rarely do athletes get away with cheating, especially if they are among the top finishers.

Common sense would dictate that the third consideration about using a sports ergonomic aid—is the substance safe?—is the most important factor. Is sport so important that some athletes would actually put their health at risk just to win? Sadly, yes they would. If athletes' self-identify and self-worth are defined by their success as sports competitors, they are more likely to engage in risky behaviors to enhance performance. In addition, Yesalis and Cowart (1998) contend that "the benefits outweigh the risks" (p. 13). They surmise that the typical steroid user's relatively low education level—high school or less—and poor knowledge about the harmful effects of prolonged steroid use may also influence the athlete's decision to ingest these substances. This is particularly likely among adolescent *nonathletes* who take steroids to improve their physique, a phenomenon called "The Adonis Complex" (Pope, 2002). Either steroid takers are in a state of denial or, perhaps, they are characterized by the "Superman Complex," a psychological characteristic of individuals who feel impervious to the harmful effects of certain risky behaviors despite acknowledging that these behaviors might harm others (Anshel, 1993). Two common forms of sport ergonomic aids need additional review, blood doping, used for many years and first tested in Scandinavian countries, and creatine, receiving extensive attention more recently. Readers are referred to reviews of related literature by Mottram (1999), Mottram et. al. (1997), and Branch (2002) concerning the etiology of anabolic steroids and ergogenic aids.

Blood Doping

Blood doping involves removing approximately one liter (about two units) of the athlete's blood one to two months before the competition and appropriately freezing and storing it. The athlete's frozen red blood cells are then infused back into the competitor shortly before competition, thus producing increased red cell mass and hemoglobin of up to 15%. The effect may last as long as 2 weeks. This technique increases oxygen uptake—the blood's oxygen-carrying capacity—thereby improving aerobic (endurance) performance. Despite these apparent benefits, the results of studies on the effects of blood doping on actual endurance performance have been equivocal. However, the failure to find beneficial performance occurred primarily in studies employing improper procedures. There are few medical dangers if doping is performed by a careful and knowledgeable physician. Still, an ominous sign of the times in which we live concerns the possible contamination of blood with hepatitis B, hepatitis C, and HIV (AIDS) infection. Equally serious is the occasional mishandling or mislabeling of blood products. As Williams (1998) indicates, "an incompatible blood transfusion could be fatal" (p. 143). Blood doping is unethical and falls into the IOC's definition of banned drugs by ingesting a substance in an abnormal quantity or the improper route of entry into the body for the purpose of artificially fostering physical performance. One form of blood doping, which increases the secretion of red blood cells, may occur by ingesting the hormone erythropoietin, or Epo.

Erythropoietin (Epo)

Epo is a hormone that is secreted by the kidneys in response to hypoxia—a lack of oxygen in the blood—and stimulates production of red blood cells. Typically, Epo is used clinically to treat anemia in hemodialysis patients. However, world-class athletes have been known to ingest Epo (see http://sportsillustrated.cnn.com/cycling/1998/tourdefrance/news/1998/07/22/financial_impact/ for a story on the 1998 Tour de Force scandal involving Epo).

Any substance that promotes the circulation of red blood cell mass will provide two advantages to performing cardiovascular endurance tasks (e.g., distance running) by enhancing two processes: the content of oxygen in arterial blood, and the body's ability to transport oxygen to exercising muscles. Epo, then, reduces the onset of muscular fatigue, providing an unfair advantage to distance runners. There is additional evidence that Epo may improve regulation of the runner's internal body temperature, referred to as thermoregulation. The American College of Sports Medicine (ACSM) considers blood doping unethical, and sports-governing bodies have banned its use. Readers are referred to Sawka et al. (1996) for the ACSM's position paper on the use of blood doping.

Creatine

Creatine has become increasingly popular since St. Louis Cardinals' home run slugger Mark McGuire admitted using it during the 1998 season in which he hit 70 home runs (he has since discontinued using creatine, according to media reports). Creatine is classified as a physiological sports ergogenic, although it is also regarded as a nutritional sports ergogenic (Williams, 1998; Williams et al., 1999). It is naturally found in vertebrates. Ostensibly, its function is to increase muscular power and speed in sports events (Williams, 1998). It is currently a very popular substance, for three reasons: (1) it is not considered an anabolic steroid; (2) it is not, at this writing and in the absence of scientific research on its long-term effects, considered unsafe in reasonable amounts; and (3) it is legally available in drug and health food stores and fitness clubs around the world. Although banned by the National Football League, creatine is still allowed by the International Olympic Committee (IOC) and Major League Baseball, and is used by many athletes at virtually all levels of competition (Williams et al., 1999). Creatine is considered a natural dietary substance, and the IOC currently classifies creatine as a food: "creatine is a popular dietary supplement among public school, college, Olympic, and professional athletes; one estimate is that 80% of the athletes at the 1996 Summer Olympics in Atlanta used creatine" (p. 7).

How effective is it? The results of studies are equivocal. Based on an extensive review of related research, Williams et al. (1999) concluded that "short-term creatine supplementation may contribute to increased total body mass, at least in males, although much of the increase in body mass may be attributed to water retention rather than increased contractile protein. Chronic creatine supplementation, combined with resistance training, may increase (lean body mass), but more supportive research is desirable to determine efficacy and the possible underlying mechanism" (p. 194). Williams (1998), however, also reports that "creatine supplementation might be detrimental to performance in events dependent primarily on the oxygen energy system. Creatine phosphate is not a very important energy source for prolonged aerobic exercise" (p. 180). Williams concludes that creatine supplementation may have an ergogenic effect only in certain types of performance (e.g., repetitive, high-intensity, very short-term tasks with brief recovery periods). For more information on this controversial issue, visit the following Web sites: http://sportsillustrated.cnn.com/olympics/news/1998/12/14/olympics_creatine/ and http://sportsmedicine.about.com/library/weekly/aa042199.htm

Human Growth Hormone (hGH) and Gamma-Hydroxybutyrate (GHB)

This hormone, banned by the IOC, is naturally secreted by the pituitary gland, although, more recently, it has been created by recombinant DNA technology, but remains very expensive. Clinically, hGH is prescribed to overcome pituitary deficiency in children. In adults, hGH increases lean body mass and decreased fat mass. *hgH* was the primary steroid used by the late professional football player Lyle Alzado, discussed earlier, who died at age 42 of two brain tumors. Banned by the IOC, hgH is medically used to treat dwarfism by stimulating growth (Goldberg, 1998). Although this anabolic outcome may appear to have an ergogenic effect related to sport performance, the results of past studies have indicated that similar increases in strength and lean body mass occur following resistance training with and without hGH supplementation. The effect of hGH on physical performance has been limited, at best.

A related hormone that ostensibly has an ergogenic effect is *gamma-hydroxybutyrate (GHB)*. Although the body produces this substance naturally, too much can lead to distorted physical characteristics (e.g., "Frankenstein's syndrome") and death. *GHB* stimulates the release of human growth hormone and can lead to a coma. The IOC also bans *GHB*.

Rationale for an Antidrug Policy in Sport

Why do antidrug policies exist in competitive sport? Why not allow all athletes to take whatever substances they wish? Typical reasons for banning drugs concern legal considerations, ethical issues related to cheating and creating an unfair performance advantage, and medical problems. Equally important is the need to protect athletes from themselves—that is, many athletes will take any drug, no matter how harmful, to enhance their performance. This issue will be discussed later.

Legal Considerations

Certain drugs, particularly in the hallucinogens category, are against federal law and are usually addictive. For example, smoking marijuana or ingesting cocaine can result in a fine or incarceration. With respect to sports competitors, banning hallucinogens also has safety implications. These drugs slow information processing and distort visual perception, and they can slow the athlete's reactions and movements, thereby endangering the athlete's safety. Substance abuse also is often accompanied by criminal activity, violence, and a drain of personal and community financial resources (Anshel, 1990a).

The proliferation of anabolic steroids, and their recently discovered dangerous effects on physical and mental health, has resulted in legislation against their distribution in many countries. In the United States, for example, the Steroid Trafficking Act of 1990 (Report No. 101-433), in which anabolic steroids were added to the earlier legislated Controlled Substances Act, bans the illegal use of steroids by (1) increasing

steroid trafficking penalties similar to those for distributing cocaine; (2) imposing tight record-keeping and regulating control of steroid production to prevent diverting legally produced steroids into the black market; (3) giving the Drug Enforcement Administration the authority to investigate violations involving illegal production, distribution, or possession with intent to distribute; and (4) requiring that information about steroids be placed in all federally supported drug abuse prevention, education, and treatment programs. As this chapter was being written, two U.S. Senators, Joe Biden (D-Del.) and Orrin Hatch (R-Utah), were sponsoring a bill to ban the steroid Androstenedione, or "Andro," because it promotes muscle growth and is not currently illegal (*USA Today*, 3/12/2004, p. 8c). The legal implications of abusing and distributing steroids is far greater than ever before.

Ethical Issues

One important reason drugs have been banned by sport organizations is because they may facilitate athletic performance (Weinhold, 1991). But should there be limits to an athlete's decision to seek advantages to improve performance? Some of the ways athletes try to improve performance include special training regimens, exercise machines, types of equipment and clothing, nutritional supplements and diets, and steroids. From one perspective, Wright and Cowart (1990) quote Norman Frost, M.D., a professor of pediatrics and director of the program in medical ethics at the University of Wisconsin School of Medicine: "Taking steroids cannot be distinguished from other tortures, deprivations, and risks to which athletes subject themselves to achieve success" (p. 144). Another view, however, comes from Thomas H. Murray, Ph.D., director of the Center for Biomedical Ethics at the School of Medicine at Case Western Reserve University, and is supported by most sports medicine experts: "The use of performance-enhancing drugs is a form of cheating, counter to the quest for physical excellence that sport is supposed to honor . . . the purpose of sport is the encouragement and reward of excellence" (p. 144). Thus, athletes who ingest performance-enhancing banned drugs are cheating by gaining an unfair competitive advantage (Strauss, 1987). This is an ethical issue.

Also, "athletes may feel compelled to use drugs which have been shown to compromise the user's physical and psychological well-being" (Albrecht, Anderson, & McKeag, 1992b, p. 350). Without strict control of these substances, organized sport is providing the athlete with a license to self-destruct.

Medical Problems

Perhaps the most important problem with drug use in sport is its potential lethal effect. The literature abounds with research indicating unequivocal evidence on the detrimental medical effects of drug taking (e.g., Chappel, 1987; Donald, 1983; Julien, 1981; Strauss, 1987). Anecdotal evidence has shown that athletes are literally dying from using so-called performance-enhancing drugs. For example, as reported in the *Sydney Daily Telegraph* (October 26, 1989), a 23-year-old bodybuilder died of cardiac arrest hours before entering the Mr. Australia contest. Police reports indicated he ingested 20 tablets of potassium chloride and 11 diuretic tablets within 24 hours. This incident shows the extent to which some athletes will go to succeed, literally at all costs.

Another source of evidence about the medical effects of drugs on the organism is a type of research called a case (single-subject) study. This type of information varies markedly from a newspaper report; data from the individual subject are scientifically gathered, based on valid tests and a proper research design, and reported in scholarly journals. There have been numerous single-subject studies on the effects of anabolic steroids. For example, Appleby, Fisher, and Martin (1994) identified the link between a 31-year-old bodybuilder who collapsed with a myocardial infarction (i.e., a heart attack) and his history of taking anabolic steroids. Because the patient survived the infarct, he was able to disclose to the researchers his long-term and extensive drug-taking habits and his lack of awareness about the effects of the drugs on the heart. In another single-subject study, Wemyss-Holden, Hamdy, and Hastie (1994) found

that steroids had a profound (enlarged) effect on the prostate gland and (reduced) urinary flow of a white male athlete who routinely used steroids. Other researchers worldwide have also found strong links of heart disease with prolonged abuse of doping agents, for example, Delbeke, Desmet, and Debackere (1995) with Belgium bodybuilders, Nakatani and Udagawa (1995) among Japanese users, and Kennedy and Lawrence (1993) with Australian rugby players. The Australian researchers found an enlarged heart (hypertrophic cardiomyopathy) and the anabolic steroid oxymesterone in the urine of two deceased athletes, only 18 and 24 years old, who sustained fatal cardiac arrests at training sessions. Both were considered fit and healthy. This is one area where cultural differences are virtually nonexistent. The causes of death from sport-related drug abuse are both acute (e.g., dehydration, heatstroke, cardiac arrest) and chronic (e.g., liver cancer, lymphoma, cardiovascular disease). Less lethal physical maladies (e.g., kidney stones, irregular heartbeat, sterility, hypertension) and psychological problems (e.g, heightened anxiety, suicidal tendencies, short attention span, depression, aggression, and schizophrenia) have been reported as well (Corrigan, 1988; Donald, 1983; Lamb, 1984; Weinhold, 1991).

Pope and Katz (1994) examined the psychiatric and medical effects of anabolic steroid use on a group of athletes—88 athletes who were using steroids and 68 nonusers. They found that steroid users, compared to nonusers, suffered from higher levels of "bad" cholesterol and major mood syndromes and disorders such as mania and depression. The researchers concluded that these major mood disturbances associated with anabolic steroids represent an important public health problem, not only for the athletes but also for the victims of their heightened aggression and irritability. Results of another study (Meilman, Crace, Presley, & Lyerla, 1995) indicated that nonathlete steroid users also reported consuming significantly more alcohol, engaging in higher rates of binge drinking, and using more tobacco products, marijuana, and other illegal drugs. Clearly, society has an obligation to protect the public in general and sport participants in particular by prohibiting certain practices that sooner or later may lead to serious physical and mental problems.

As if existing medical problems are not enough to worry about, we are seeing two additional epidemics related to drug injections—HIV and hepatitis B and C infections. Injecting anabolic steroids with a syringe directly into the muscle or throughout the bloodstream is not uncommon. Consequently, steroid takers are at risk of contracting any virus that spreads through an exchange of body fluids, similar to the spread of HIV and hepatitis. Currently no published research exists measuring the onset of viral infections such as HIV and hepatitis due to injecting anabolic steroids. However, the problem may exist. According to one Australian newspaper account (*Sydney Morning Herald,* Sept. 3, 1996, p. 9), "Drug workers say a big problem is that steroid users do not perceive themselves to be at risk of diseases such as hepatitis C and HIV from their drug-injecting habit. The fact that large batches of veterinary steroids are now being used also increased the risk of cross-contamination."

How Widespread Is Drug Abuse in Sport?

It is impossible to determine the exact extent of drug abuse in sport. The two primary sources of drug usage, anecdotal evidence and scientific research studies, have serious limitations. Anecdotal reports, among other serious shortcomings, fail to provide concrete evidence documenting the usage of drugs. Scientific studies suffer from underreporting because ethical and legal considerations make drug taking a largely clandestine behavior. Keep these limitations in mind when examining the following information.

Anecdotal Evidence

Anecdotal evidence consists of information provided by individuals based on their own experiences or perceptions. For example, former U.S. Olympic gold medal hurdler Edwin Moses (1988) asserts that "at least 50 percent of the athletes in high-performance sports such as track and field,

cycling, and rowing would be disqualified if they weren't so adept at beating the tests" (p. 57).

Not surprisingly, steroid abuse has been traditionally rampant in professional (U.S.) football. Testimony given to the Committee on the Judiciary in amending the Controlled Substances Act (Steroid Trafficking Act of 1990) included the following: "Recognized as a sport plagued by alarming levels of steroid use, football has always favored those players that are bigger, bulkier and more aggressive than their opponents." The National Football League now has a policy of random periodic testing. The first violation results in a four-game suspension (see Table 23-2).

In another example of self-reported drug use, a story in *Sports Illustrated* (Chaikin & Telander, 1988) detailed the effects of prolonged steroid use on Tommy Chaikin, a skilled football lineman with the University of South Carolina. His prolific steroid taking almost took his life. The result was heightened chronic aggression, severe acne, backache, insomnia, testicular shrinkage, hair loss, depression, poor vision, inability to cope with stress, chronic anxiety, poor concentration, and, even more serious, hypertension, heart murmur, and benign tumors. Surgery, immediate cessation of taking steroids, and counseling saved his life.

In a self-effacing report on the factors that led to his addiction to anabolic steroids, Chaikin provides significant insight into numerous psychological and social pressures that foster drug use in sport. According to Chaikin, "I felt I had the coaches' encouragement . . . he told me 'do what you have to do, take what you have to take'" (p. 88). He contends that "college athletes feel tremendous pressure to succeed" due to the expectations of others. "Nobody wants to sit on the bench and be a failure" (p. 88). Unspoken sanctioning of drug use by coaches and sport administrators is reflected by the absence of team rules and other forms of communication that discourage drug taking. Perhaps not surprisingly, Chaikin says the coaches never called him in the hospital, nor did the university offer to pay any medical expenses. The university claimed his health problems were not related to playing for the team.

Other anecdotal evidence exists to show that some coaches actually sanction drug use, either *passively* by failing to warn their athletes against drug use, or *actively* by encouraging athletes to use steroids and ways to avoid positive drug tests. Other forms of encouragement to take banned substances were direct (e.g., advising, "Taking steroids is the only way to stay competitive") or indirect (e.g., requiring that the participant reach an unrealistic body weight by a certain time; requiring a particularly demanding performance goal; or ignoring drug-taking behavior, thus sanctioning its use). For example, Canadian world-class sprinter Ben Johnson, after having his gold medal taken away, strongly asserted to a Canadian government inquiry that his coach knowingly gave him a substance that was banned by international sport organizations (*Time*, 1989). "Charlie [Francis] was my coach. . . . If Charlie gave me something to take, I took it" (p. 57). In fact, this coach's testimony at the same inquiry supported Johnson's contention. Francis told Johnson (and other sprinters) that "drugs marked the only route to international success and admitted that he provided such chemicals to his charges" (*Time*, June 26, 1989, p. 57).

Anecdotal evidence indicates team physicians also have contributed to drug abuse among athletes. For example, Ye Qiaobo, a Chinese speed skater, was sent home in disgrace from the 1988 Olympics after testing positive for steroids. A later inquiry revealed that she unknowingly had been taking steroids prescribed by the team doctor. Television's coverage of the 1992 (Madrid), 1996 (Atlanta), and 2000 (Sydney) Olympics revealed the extensiveness, as far back as preparation for the 1976 Olympics, of experimentation with steroids by many countries. In the former East Germany, for example, team doctors, under orders from the highest political powers, prescribed steroids for athletes, even 13-year-old girls, and then kept careful records regarding the effects of different dosages on performance and the length of time needed to test clean.

Scientific Evidence

Scientific research on drug use in sport has centered primarily on performance-enhancing drugs, particularly anabolic steroids. One limitation in obtaining accurate information about an athlete's use of banned substances is underreporting. For example, Pope, Katz, and Champoux (1988) investigated the prevalence of anabolic steroid use in American college males. Of the 1,010 respondents, only 17 (2%) reported using steroids. Four individuals used steroids primarily to improve personal appearance, and the goal of the other respondents, all competitive athletes, was to improve sport performance. The authors admit to the problem of underreporting in comparing their results with other studies in which a far higher percentage of steroid use—as high as 20%—is reported among university competitors (e.g., Dezelsky, Toohey, & Shaw, 1985; Heitzinger et al., 1986).

A study of over 3,000 male American high school seniors found 6.6% used anabolic steroids, with over two thirds of the user group first taking drugs when they were 16 years of age or younger (Buckley et al., 1988). Out of 4,064 Australian athletes surveyed by the Australian Sports Drug Agency over a 3-year period, only 39 respondents (1.0%) admitted to using anabolic steroids (Australian Sports Medicine Federation, 1989).

Other studies of specific sport populations, particularly ones involving strength or endurance, report higher drug usage. For example, in one study Anshel (1991a) conducted personal interviews with U.S. university athletes, 94 males and 32 females, competing in nine sports. To overcome the inherent dangers of underreporting found in related literature, information about the participants' personal use of drugs was not solicited. Of the 126 athletes surveyed, 81 (64%) revealed "known" drug use on their team. More specifically, 68 (72%) of the 94 males and 13 (40%) of the 32 females contended that teammates took a drug that the user knew was illegal or banned from their sport. Forty-three percent (494 of the athletes' 1,156 responses) acknowledged that athletes use drugs for the purpose of enhancing performance as opposed to recreational use.

Melia, Pipe, and Greenberg (1996) attempted to determine the prevalence of use of anabolic steroids and other performance-enhancing drugs among 16,119 Canadian students from grades 6–12 representing five regions of Canada. They found that 2.8% of this sample ($N = 4{,}513$) ingested these banned substances in attempts to improve sport performance or to improve body build. To some extent, there appears to be a gender gap in drug taking among athletes. Doweiko (1996), supporting earlier findings by Anshel (1991a), concluded from his review of literature that more males than females abuse anabolic steroids.

Sadly, researchers also report widespread use of steroids well beyond the sport venue. For example, in an early study, Taylor (1987) reports at least 1 million Americans have used or are currently using steroids for nonmedical purposes, to either increase athletic performance or improve physical appearance. His data revealed that steroid use among high school students is nearly as common as the use of crack cocaine. A brief review of this literature in the United States Steroid Trafficking Act of 1990 report concluded that "up to 500,000 male high school students use, or have used, steroids (with) more than one-third of the users (starting) at the age of 15 or younger; two-thirds had started by the age of 16" (p. 4). Similarly disturbing is a study by Whitehead, Chillag, and Elliott (1992), who examined the use of steroids among 3,900 male high school students in a rural (U.S.) state. The most common reason for using steroids, among 205 students (5.3%) who admitted to drug use, was to *improve physical appearance* (43%). In addition, steroid use was closely associated with illicit drug and cigarette use. Apparently, the abuse of anabolic steroids is not restricted to metropolitan areas.

Likely Causes of Drug Abuse in Sport

Athletes abuse many types of drugs, and for different reasons. Hence, any discussion on the likely causes of drug abuse in sport should differentiate among the types of substances ingested. With respect to anabolic steroids, Nardo (1992) reported one study of high school males that found reasons for ingesting steroids included improving athletic performance (48%), to look better (28%), to prevent sports injuries (10%),

social reasons (6%), and "other reasons" (8%). Based on a review of the anecdotal and scientific literature and on my own professional interaction with athletes as a sport psychology consultant in the U.S. and Australia, I have concluded that the causes of drug use lie within three categories: physical, psychological/emotional, and social.

Physical Causes

Given the extensive pressure on skilled athletes to succeed and be competitive, a view held and often communicated by their coaches and corporate sponsors, it is not surprising that performers explore all possible avenues to reach—perhaps even go beyond—their performance potential. The sources of this pressure are rarely identified in combating drug use. As indicated earlier, coaches and sponsors can and often do contribute to the competitors' dilemma by reinforcing the need to win at any cost. The expectations of parents, media, and peers only fuel the pressure to maximize performance by artificial substance abuse (Chappel, 1987; Lamb, 1984; Williams, 1989).

Enhance sport performance. The most common physical cause for ingesting drugs is attempting to enhance performance. Depending on the drug being taken, the athlete may be seeking benefits such as increased strength, endurance, alertness, and aggression, or decreased reaction time, fatigue, anxiety, and muscle tremor. (See the earlier discussion of banned drugs for a more comprehensive list of potential physical and performance effects of specific types of drugs.)

In a rare study in this area, Laure and Reinsberger (1995) attempted to identify the reason for using anabolic steroids among elite race walkers. Increasing performance, the wish to win, and financial incentive (e.g., commercial contracts and product endorsements) were the three principal motives to use banned performance-enhancing drugs. Forty-one percent of these athletes had heard of endurance walkers using such drugs. Apparently, the pressure of performing well in international events, especially the Olympic Games, exacerbates the problem.

Cope with pain and injury rehabilitation. Athletes also ingest drugs to cope psychologically with physical discomfort and to expedite recovery from injury (English, 1987; Goldman, Bush, & Katz, 1984). For example, athletes may feel that medical treatment is not sufficient to eliminate pain. They will take drugs to attenuate pain with no prescription and without the coach's knowledge (Donald, 1983), usually for the reason of not disappointing the coach or to avoid losing starting status (a tendency more typical of the male athletes) (Anshel, 1991a; Donald, 1983).

Weight control. Amphetamines are often used to control appetite and diuretics to reduce fluid weight. These drugs quickly reduce weight, allowing the athlete to compete in a lower, more favorable weight group (Donald, 1983) or at a weight deemed more facilitative to success.

Psychological Causes

By far the most common rationale for using recreational drugs among athletes is psychological and emotional (Anshel, 1991a). For some athletes, mind-altering drugs provide the most convenient escape from unpleasant emotions. There also are psychological causes for taking drugs believed to be ergogenic aids.

Stress and anxiety. Emotions such as stress, tension, and anxiety may be antecedent causes of ingesting drugs, particularly hallucinogens and beta blockers. Drug taking attenuates the stress and tension associated with the pressures to succeed over a prolonged time period, such as a full season or longer. Thus, recreational drug use may reflect a short-term approach to managing stress and anxiety or be a vehicle for escaping an unpleasant present situation (Donald, 1983; Egger, 1981).

Boredom. For many individuals, experimentation with recreational drugs, often ingested in group (social) situations, can help overcome boredom (Julien, 1981). This type of drug use appears to be more prevalent on weekends or when team-related activities are unplanned, especially when traveling. Athletes also can become bored by

redundancy in the team's practices or in some other aspect of their participation (Anshel, 1991b; Egger, 1981).

Personal problems. Drug taking may be a response to a personal problem independent of sport involvement. The athlete's personal life can be a potential source of support—or of extreme stress. Orlick and Partington's (1986) interviews with 16 Canadian Olympic athletes showed that elite athletes, like any other individuals, need the love, acceptance, and support of their immediate family. When this support is lacking, the competitor may be less capable of coping with sport demands and more susceptible to the mental escape that certain drugs provide.

Low self-confidence. Many athletes use drugs to build self-confidence (Anshel, 1991a; Nardo, 1992). This use reflects the athlete's doubt about his or her own skills ("They make me feel better about my ability") or concern about staying competitive ("I'm sure 'so and so' are taking them" or "If I'm going to perform at 'X' speed, I have to take these"). As an example, competitors may use steroids to foster aggressive behavior and increase body size and strength to overcome low self-confidence, especially in contact sports.

The Superman complex/experimentation. Some athletes feel impervious to any potential negative side effects of drugs (Collins, Pippenger, & Janesz, 1984). According to Don Weiss, executive director of the National Football League: "It is not easy to convince pro football players that they are vulnerable to the negative health effects of steroids. Some of these young men are such great physical specimens with such great athletic ability that they think they'll be like that forever" (Shroyer, 1990, p. 115). According to Nicholson and Agnew (1989), athletes who exhibit the Superman complex do not feel constrained by the deleterious effects of drugs, even after obtaining valid information about possible detrimental effects to their health.

Perfectionism. Some individuals are never pleased with their accomplishments, even with the appropriate recognition and adulation of others. For these people, "good" is never quite good enough. A **perfectionist** is someone who has trouble discriminating between realistic and idealized standards (Flett & Hewitt, 2002). He or she bypasses attainable excellence in pursuit of unattainable perfection. It would appear that the perfectionist athlete is ripe for drug abuse, a concept called negative, or neurotic, perfectionism. In a sport context, some athletes may be driven to seek consistent, perfect performance through anabolic steroids or other performance-enhancing drugs. Inversely, these individuals may need to mentally escape the pressures of their unrealistically high goals, or to cope with their fear of performance failure. Using performance-enhancing drugs provides a means to overcome the self-doubt and anxiety associated with failing to meet excessively high standards (Hewitt & Flett, 2002). Although perfectionism has not been studied among athletes who take drugs, it would not be surprising to find that certain drug-taking competitors fit the profile of this unhealthy psychological state.

Self-esteem. Two related conceptual frameworks, often used interchangeably, that might help explain drug use in sport are self-concept and self-esteem. *Self-concept* is the collection of ideas, or the picture, that persons hold about themselves. *Self-esteem* is the evaluation they place on this picture (Sonstroem, 1997). For example, an athlete's self-concept may be derived from the joy and satisfaction they derive from their participation and success in sport, and the extent to which these positive feelings contribute to life satisfaction. The athletes' self-evaluation as a successful sports competitor comprises their self-esteem. Because self-esteem reflects the extent to which individuals value themselves, being successful in competitive sport would be of significant importance to any skilled athlete. The perception of failure is painful, humiliating, and unacceptable. Success is the only viable outcome, even if it means cheating.

Of course, this is not healthy thinking. Any individual who identifies too strongly with only one form of self-concept, at the omission of others, is walking on thin ice. Success is never guaranteed and the ability to cope effectively with not meeting self-expectations is very important to mental health. Nevertheless, unless athletes are able to separate sport performance outcomes from sport participation as a primary source of their self-esteem, and perhaps being less judgmental in juxtaposing their sport success with their value as a person, the attraction to performance-enhancing drugs will likely persist. Failure to find reward and gratification in other areas of life outside of sport, and dealing effectively with disappointment in sport settings, may lead to depression and other forms of self-destructive, often illegal, behavior.

Competitiveness and pressures for success. Meeting the expectations of others (e.g., spectators, coaches, teammates, media, corporate sponsors), especially in elite sport, creates substantial pressure to excel and to remain competitive. If anabolic steroids favorably affect sports performance, then certain athletes will search for anything, even using banned substances, that will give them a competitive edge over their opponents. Perhaps the pivotal point for athletes about their decision to use steroids is whether they can control the temptation to cheat and, instead, to respond to internal and external sources of pressure with hard training, confidence, high-quality coaching, proper nutrition (including vitamin supplements), and social support from friends and family.

Social Causes

Perhaps there is no greater cause of succumbing to drug ingestion than response to social—and societal—pressures.

Peer pressure and acceptance. Pressure from peers, or the need to gain group acceptance, is a likely cause of drug taking among some sport participants (Nicholson, 1989; Wragg, 1990). From the perspective of psychological maturation and development, the need for social acceptance and pressure to conform make adolescents particularly susceptible to peer influence.

Wragg (1990) describes the peer group as "a critical agent of socialization as dependence on the family is reduced and the young person seeks to belong and fit into new relations with peers" (p. 237). In their eagerness to attain social acceptance, adolescents become aware of the types of approval-earning behaviors—the need to please other people—that will facilitate popularity. Wragg (1990) concludes that these developmental characteristics, "coupled with a setting or contest where (drugs) are readily available, clearly implies that adolescence is a time of increased susceptibility to risk from drug use" (p. 238). Newman (1994) concluded, in his study of Canadian adolescents, that the lure of steroids is too strong for many teens due to extreme demands on conformity, particularly among males. Attitudes of strongly rejecting drug use should be developed early in life, *before* drug taking occurs.

Models. Modeling occurs when we learn by demonstration or change our behavior to imitate behaviors we have observed (Gill, 1986). Modeling has a particularly influential effect during adolescence. Accordingly, the development of appropriate (e.g., training and effort) and inappropriate (e.g., cheating, drug taking) behavior of young athletes is often derived from the modeling of older, more experienced counterparts (Chu, 1982). The modeling effect is reinforced by media reports that publicize incidences of drug abuse by professional athletes (Collins et al., 1984). It is highly likely that reports of drug use by established sports stars influence the use of performance-enhancing drugs among interscholastic and intercollegiate athletes, many of whom aspire to compete at higher (i.e., Olympic or professional) levels. Perceptions are common that elite athletes ingest drugs, and "if it doesn't hurt so and so, it won't hurt me", a reflection of the "Superman Complex" (Nicholson, 1989; Nicholson & Agnew, 1989). Thus, for many athletes, drug use is sanctioned through observing their elite models.

Social support. Athletes may ingest a banned substance to gain social support. For example, the increase in muscle size and strength from steroid use may result in acceptance and approval among peers and coaches. Social support is a primary need of athletes, particularly from teammates. Rosenfeld, Richman, and Hardy (1989) operationally define **social support** in a sport context as involving a network of personal ties to meet a recipient's needs for venting feelings, providing companionship and reassurance, reducing uncertainty during stressful times, aiding mental and physical recovery from stress and fatigue, and improving communication skills. Their findings indicate that coaches in particular are not providing listening support, emotional support, or shared social support. Statements from athletes such as "No one ever tells me I'm doing a good job" or "There's no one to turn to when I need to talk to somebody" indicate the lack of social support. Perhaps more than any other rationale for drug use among athletes, the absence of social support can create drug dependency in athletes either for enhancing performance (i.e., to gain needed recognition from others) or as a vehicle to cope with stress or relieve boredom (i.e., reasons to use recreational drugs).

Strategies for Controlling Drug Abuse

The effectiveness of strategies to prevent or eliminate drug taking in sport is often a function of factors such as the individual's perceived needs for using drugs (e.g., gaining self-confidence, overcoming pain, improving strength); the type of drug usage (e.g., performance-enhancing versus mind-altering); the sport's physical demands (e.g., those requiring improved aerobic capacity, strength, or steadiness); and situational factors (e.g., boredom, stress, or the high expectations of others). However, athletes share similar types of experiences, psychological demands, and performance requirements. Therefore, many of the issues described here can be applied to most competitors.

An array of techniques is available in the antidrug arsenal (see Anshel, 1993, for an extensive review of drug prevention and control strategies). However, these techniques are only as effective as the individuals who implement them. It is important to recognize the role of coaches, parents, teachers, and sport psychology consultants in providing initiative, leadership, and expertise for successfully using these strategies. Coaches, in particular, have a far greater influence in regulating athlete behavior and attitude than any other individuals in the competitor's sport domain (Orlick & Partington, 1986). Anshel (1986, 1990a) and Smith (1983) contend that the coach is the most important agent in preventing drug use on the team—yet coaches tend not to be concerned with the athlete's behaviors away from the competitive environment in general and with drug-taking behaviors in particular (Anshel, 1986; Rosenfeld et al., 1989). Coaches' reluctance to engage in actions that they believe might constitute intrusiveness into the private lives of others is understandable. However, the coaches' feelings would be more justifiable if drug use among athletes was not so common and medically unsafe. Appropriately trained sport psychology consultants might assist coaches by helping them develop and implement their team's drug policy and by providing guidance on how to meet privately and confidentially with team members to discuss these delicate issues. Consultants have the additional role of helping athletes modify certain feelings and behaviors that might predispose them to drug use.

The two approaches taken in this chapter for combating drug use in sport center on cognitive and behavioral strategies. **Cognitive** strategies deal with influencing the athlete's behaviors and attitudes intellectually and psychologically through verbal and nonverbal communication. **Behavioral** techniques involve two components: (1) setting up situations that foster certain desirable responses from the athletes, and (2) using verbal and nonverbal techniques that reinforce favorable behaviors or performance outcomes (Martin & Lumsden, 1987). The following suggestions were derived from anecdotal and scientific literature, media reports, and my own experiences as a sport psychology consultant.

Cognitive Approaches

The primary objective of cognitive strategies in controlling substance abuse in sport is to appeal to the participants' maturity, intellect, and need for self-actualization and personal fulfillment, both individually and collectively as a group of competitors (Donald, 1983; Egger, 1981). Individual issues concern the health and well-being of the competitor, and team issues reflect social support and group success.

Provide education. Education is the most widely used strategy for preventing drug abuse. Traditionally, the primary objective of drug education programs was to disseminate accurate information about the negative consequences of drug taking. However, the effectiveness of drug education programs on drug-taking behaviors has been less than optimum. For example, data gathered from 1981 to 1986 on 9,891 U.S. college athletes by the drug education consulting firm Heitzinger and Associates (1986) indicated that "drug education deterred [only] about 5% of the regular users from experimenting with drugs; drug testing and knowledge of punishment deterred 5% of the social users" (p. 158).

Marcello, Danish, and Stolberg (1989) initiated a drug prevention program for university student-athletes in the United States. Their program, directed toward performance-enhancing and recreational drugs, consisted of skill training in the areas of decision making, risk assessment, stress management, assertiveness training, resisting peer pressure, and transferring learned skills to outside settings. The findings indicated that the program did not lead to reduced drugs use. The program developers later decided the amount of time spent teaching resistance to peer pressure was overemphasized. Apparently, "pro-usage attitudes are influenced by parental modeling, media advertising, cultural, ethnic and religious factors, and peer influences prior to their arrival at college," as opposed to the assumption that the school environment fosters drug abuse (p. 208). Assessment of other knowledge-based approaches also shows no significant effect on the frequency or extent of drug use (Hanson, 1980; Kinder, Pope, & Walfish, 1980; Stuart, 1974).

Two underlying factors may explain the limited success of educational programs in controlling drug use. First, education is based on the tenet that people use drugs because they have no knowledge of any deleterious effects (Nicholson & Agnew, 1989). Supposedly, after being educated about these deleterious effects, the individual is expected to develop a negative attitude toward drug use that, in turn, will dictate desirable behavior. However, although the learner's knowledge increases after education programs, it has not been shown conclusively that this new knowledge leads to a change in the learner's attitude about drug taking (Reilly, 1988). In fact, the person's curiosity about the effect of drugs may be awakened by these programs, possibly leading to increased drug experimentation (Marcello et al., 1989; Stuart, 1974). Anshel and Russell (1997) found no relationships between knowledge about the long-term physical and psychological effects of anabolic steroids and athletes' attitudes toward steroid ingestion among 291 state-level Australian track and field athletes. The results held constant for both males and females of all age groups, from ages 14 to 40 years.

The problem with the argument against educational programs on drug taking is that drug users do not usually make rational judgments based on the advantages and disadvantages of drug use. This conclusion is partially supported by a study of college athletes, showing that athletes having lower grade point averages were less likely to believe that anabolic steroids are a threat to health, are a problem in their sport, and are addictive (Perko, Cowdery, Wang, & Yesalis, 1995).

It has become apparent that educational programs should be only one of several components in drug prevention programs (Marcello et al., 1989; Strauss, 1988). Still, Ryan (1982) suggests that the "education of athletes to prevent them from starting drug abuse or to reclaim them from it has probably been successful to some degree. It is impossible to measure the effects exactly, but without drug education the situation would probably be much worse" (p. 50).

Bell and Doege (1987) feel that physicians, particularly, should have a primary role in the drug education effort. They also feel that physicians should refrain from prescribing anabolic steroids, amphetamines, and other potentially harmful substances; should educate colleagues and the public about the problem; and should support the development of programs to reduce the illegal prescription and distribution of drugs.

Potteiger and Stilger (1994) argue that athletic trainers and physical therapists are probably in the best position of any team member, including physicians, to detect steroid use because players usually trust them, and they maintain contact with players throughout the season—often year-round. In addition, athletic trainers and physical therapists are often in a position to identify anabolic steroid users and know the clinical signs and symptoms.

An educational model is needed that identifies a program aimed to prevent steroid ingestion. One Portland, Oregon, program, called Adolescents Training and Learning to Avoid Steroids (ATLAS), has been described by Yesalis and Cowart (1998). This program was a follow-up to an earlier attempt by its founders at the Oregon Health Sciences University in which providing information to football players about the deleterious effects of prolonged steroid use, in both verbal and written forms, resulted in unchanged or *increased* steroid-taking. In explaining the results, the researchers claimed that educational strategies that provide factual information alone fail to alter behavior. The ATLAS program involves 14 sessions with three information modules: weight training skills, nutritional information for sports, and anabolic steroids education. The program teaches safe and effective weight-training techniques to build adolescent athletes' self-esteem and to experience a "normal" and healthy means of improving musculature and physique, provides proper guidelines for sports nutrition that facilitates muscular development and performance quality, and includes both the benefits and negative effects of taking steroids. Program planners contend that providing information about the potential benefits of anabolic steroids provides greater credibility for disclosing its harmful effects. Only depicting bad effects of steroids without acknowledging its potential benefits "appeared to be too biased to be credible" (p. 94). Yesalis and Cowart (1998) report that the program's director states that "this fairly labor-intensive program . . . works to reduce interest in steroids" (p. 95).

Here are some suggestions for educational programs: Invite specialists to discuss topics of current or future interest to the athletes, such as stress management (preventive measures, coping with pressure), assertiveness training (how to deal with pressure from peers, sponsors, and others to experiment with drugs), and academic tutoring (to reduce stress from demands of classes). Professional athletes would find discussions on financial investment, legal issues, and facts about retirement of great interest. Other appropriate topics might come from specialists in the fields of medicine (e.g., the short- and long-term somatic responses to drug use or a discussion of different types of drugs); law (e.g., the legal implications in sport and the community in general); psychology (e.g., addiction, dependency, anorexia, bulimia, or the psychological causes of drugs use); and nutrition (e.g., proper food intake for optimal energy without ingesting artificial substances). Another source of information could be former athletes whom the athletes can identify with, such as members of previous teams or well-known university or professional athletes.

Discuss ethical issues. According to media reports, world champion track and field athlete Carl Lewis contends that drug taking has three negative effects: (1) The athlete will never know his or her real full potential, (2) there is a health risk, and (3) the drug-induced athlete is quitting on himself or herself. Coaches must inform their athletes that drug taking is depriving them of knowing their performance potential. What does cheating reflect? What is the purpose? Where is the satisfaction? Parents in particular have a role in teaching proper ethics of sports competition and reducing performance expectations, which adds pressure for success—and possible steroid use to gain a competitive edge.

Athletes need to know that drug use is cheating. In one study of Australian adolescent athletes, Martin and Anshel (1991) found that athletes were more likely to use a banned performance-enhancing drug if it was not detectable by drug testing.

Provide communication outlets. Often the head coach cannot be readily accessible to all team members, and supervising all player behavior on and off the field is virtually impossible for one person. Yet, athletes often need—and warrant—personal contact and communication with team leaders. Coach availability may help players deal more effectively with personal and sport-related issues. The risk for ingestion of recreational and other types of drugs may increase from a lack of such contact. Assistant coaches, athletic trainers, team counselors, other school teachers or professors, team captains, and even spouses or close acquaintances of the coaching staff can act as an athlete's communication outlets for emotional support or as a liaison with the team's head coach. Parents also play a vital role in this communication process. Parent–athlete communication should primarily consist of allowing the athlete, son or daughter, to set the agenda of items for conversation and to do most of the talking. Active listening is an important skill here for parents as well as the rest of these providers (see Chapter 9).

Recognize the athletes' use of drugs. To conclude that "it can't happen on my team (or to me)" is not only naive but also irresponsible. To be effective, coaches or parents must detect signs and symptoms of drug ingestion—even drugs that are legal but the intake of which is against team rules, such as alcohol and tobacco—before it becomes addictive and has long-lasting negative consequences to good health. Unfortunately, according to at least one study (Hanson & Gould, 1988), this is not usually the case, at least with coaches. The researchers found that coaches are somewhat minimally aware of the attitudes, feelings, and overall mental status of their players, particularly before a contest. Because it is unlikely that the student-athlete will admit experiencing drug-related problems, coaches and team consultants (e.g., athletic trainers, sport psychology consultants, academic tutors) should be sensitive to various aspects of athletes' lives. Examples include a newly divorced or deceased parent, poor school grades or attendance, a lack of social fulfillment, a personal crisis, frequent illness, changing physical features of the athlete (knowing the physical signs of anabolic steroid use is especially important), development of new associations with individuals who use or condone drug use, unwarranted challenges to authority, and even detecting the occasional rumor that may provide a tip-off of a possible problem (Damm, 1991). Personal information can also be obtained simply by asking the athlete.

According to Damm, "when drug abuse is suspected in the student-athlete, referral should be made to a trained professional (e.g., drug counselor, physician, psychologist) who can confirm or deny its existence" (p. 159). If suspicion of drug abuse has been confirmed, the next step is to determine the appropriate treatment as soon as possible. In addition, attempts to stop the drug-taking behavior must be enacted immediately. Sensitivity toward the athlete's condition is needed at this time, and strict limit setting about the offending—and perhaps illegal—action is also required. On this point I respectfully disagree with Damm (1991) who "believes that the student-athlete alone has the right to decide whether or not to use drugs" (p. 163). Although drug education and counseling strategies may have limited influence on drug-taking habits (discussed earlier), my belief is that there is no choice about ingesting substances that have very dangerous short- and often long-term effects and may be illegal. The legal ramifications notwithstanding, the only choice an athlete has is whether to stop taking these substances and remain with the team or to continue taking them and be banned from the team. This is why a team policy on drug taking is so necessary (discussed later in the chapter). Signs of drug use can take physical, emotional, behavioral, and cognitive forms. These are listed in Table 23-1.

Build confidence and self-esteem. According to Tobler's (1986) personal development program model, low self-esteem and low self-confidence are other reasons for drug ingestion. Athletes who doubt their ability to succeed are more susceptible to performance-enhancing drugs than their more confident counter parts.

Table 23-1 Physical, Behavioral, Emotional, and Cognitive Signs of Drug Use

Physical Signs
- Bloodshot eyes
- Dark circles under eyes
- Profuse sweating
- Heightened sensitivity to touch, smell, and sound
- Chronic fatigue
- Trouble maintaining normal body temperature (always feeling too hot or cold)

Behavioral Signs
- Unusually secretive behavior
- Increased tardiness to practice and school
- Apathetic attitude about school
- Poor school performance
- Social isolation
- Often broke or out of money
- Irresponsible
- High risk-taking behaviors
- Change in dress style
- New circle of friends
- Marked changes in usual or normal ways of behaving (e.g., unwarranted challenges to authority, isolation, increased arguments, new friends)

Emotional Signs
- Extreme mood swings
- Irritability
- Highly reactive
- Less affectionate
- Chronic physical fatigue
- Heightened aggression/hostility
- Recurrent depressive episodes

Cognitive Signs
- Decreased mental capabilities
- Disordered thinking
- Increased forgetfulness
- Thinks that others are out to get him or her
- Denial of problems
- Superman complex (i.e., sense of invulnerability)
- Shortened attention span
- Thoughts of suicide

Coaches and parents can play key roles in helping athletes feel better about their ability and performance by having realistic expectations, providing instruction and informational feedback on skill execution, showing concern, and offering praise for both desirable outcomes and optimal effort. Anshel (1997, chap. 8) provides guidelines for effectively conducting these strategies in sport settings. The key objective is increasing and solidifying the participant's self-esteem, which in turn will decrease the athlete's self-appraisal of inadequacy. At the same time, threats, sarcasm, and other forms of negative communication have a counterproductive influence on the player's mental status and self-esteem (Anshel, 1990b). Sport psychologists can help athletes with low self-esteem and self-confidence by teaching them the cognitive techniques found in Chapter 17.

Professional counseling. An athlete's decision to ingest steroids, particularly over a prolonged period of time, usually has a psychological explanation. Low self-esteem, high competitiveness, chronic anxiety, pressure to achieve, need for peer approval and acceptance by others, or feelings of hopelessness and low personal control are all reasons for athletes to obtain professional counseling. If athletes are unable to control their need for steroids, the source of their drug-taking habit must be addressed (Ringhofer & Harding, 1996).

Coaches do not typically have training in counseling, but the coach is often the first—and most important—person to whom an athlete comes to discuss personal or team-related concerns (Anshel, 1990b; Rosenfeld et al., 1989). Team members need private and confidential access to their coach. Coach–athlete discussions can help reduce the many pressures and other factors that underlie the athlete's need to ingest drugs. The sport psychology consultant, who should have training in at least basic counseling skills, can be another effective confidant and facilitator in helping athletes deal with their pressures and problems. The availability of counseling from a licensed psychologist or counselor is also important. Coaches and parents of athletes should identify a person who may offer professional psychological guidance to team members

who need it (see Chapter 22 for guidelines on referral). However, it must be understood that all issues discussed in counseling sessions are confidential.

Professional counselors, sport psychologists, nurses, physicians (particularly in the sports medicine area), and other medically trained personnel should be available either to work with the team on a consistent basis or to respond to a drug crisis, whether it is an acute drug response (emergency) or acknowledgment of a positive drug test.

Promote the perception of a meaningful team role. Athletes who perceive themselves as valued team members will more likely remain loyal to the coach and maintain proper health (Anshel, 1991a). Conversely, feelings of irrelevance and the absence of a clearly identified team role may lead to feelings of group detachment. Athletes who feel detached may be more likely to engage in rule-breaking behaviors due to reduced coach loyalty. And, in their view, they have less to lose by engaging in risk-taking behaviors. Ideally, each player should feel wanted and needed.

One approach to enhancing team-role meaningfulness is to solicit input from the participants on making decisions about various issues directly affecting them (e.g., team policy or game strategies)—or at least to discuss issues with the coach before decisions are made. These strategies would likely promote team loyalty and athletes' accountability for their actions. It also reflects a coach's respect for his or her players, a perception that is very important in promoting team cohesion and a supportive team climate (Fisher, Mancini, Hirsch, Proulx, & Staurowsky, 1982).

Behavioral Strategies

As indicated earlier, the primary objective of a behavioral approach is to shape the environment to control and influence subsequent behavior, a system referred to as "contingency management" (see Martin & Lumsden, 1987, and Rushall & Siedentop, 1972, for explanations and guidelines). Specifically, behavioral techniques involve (1) setting up situations that foster certain desirable responses from the athletes, and (2) using verbal or nonverbal techniques that reinforce favorable behaviors or performance outcomes.

Teach sport skills. Athletes, perhaps more than most other individuals, are driven to achieve the virtually impossible task of performing consistent and error-free skilled movements. It is in the athletes' best interests to acknowledge the boundaries of human performance in general and perhaps their own capabilities and limitations in particular. If most athletes who take drugs do so to facilitate their performance, then this objective can be met without drugs if they make use of properly implemented conditioning programs and are taught sport skills and strategies. Good coaches are good teachers (Anshel, 1997). Athletes will feel they can stay competitive and be less in need of artificial means to perform at superior levels when they experience quality conditioning and instructional programs. The key objectives for the coach are (1) to make skill and conditioning improvement apparent to the athlete, and (2) to positively reinforce desirable performance changes by verbally and nonverbally communicating approval (Martin & Lumsden, 1987).

Avoid boredom. Boredom usually leads to inappropriate actions. For example, my own confidential discussions with elite competitive skiers reveal that redundant and prolonged skiing and conditioning drills lead many competitors to engage in recreational drug use at private parties (Anshel, 1987). Egger (1981) suggests that sports should be "an alternative high" (p. 26), by planning exciting practice sessions and to work with athletes to set and reach challenging performance goals (e.g., "I think you can run 0.5 seconds faster after another month of training").

My informal discussions with more than 200 college athletes revealed that more nonsport recreational opportunity—and relatively less practice time, especially during the last half of the season—is highly desirable. Thus, coaches can reduce boredom by providing alternative activities for their players away from team-related events.

Be aware of athletes' lives away from sport. What type of activities do the athletes engage in during off hours, and with whom? If the athletes' peers take drugs, there is an increased likelihood that the athletes will do so as well. Other questions about athletes that team leaders and sport psychologists should ask include, How are they doing in school? Do they have any friends? Do they have a satisfying family and social life or is it in turmoil? Are they receiving proper attention and recognition from others? Are they nearing the end of their playing career? If any of these issues are unpleasant or stressful, how are they coping? Problems can be avoided if action is taken relatively soon. Coaches, particularly, can help create a supportive environment away from sport to reduce the probability of drug use.

Develop and implement a drug policy and plan of action. The widespread information about the dangers of drugs in sport requires teams and sport organizations to develop a drug policy and a vehicle to inform athletes about banned drugs and the consequences of taking them. Failure to do so, in effect, actually sanctions drug use—or gives the impression that sport leaders do not care. For example, a study conducted by *USA Today* (February 1, 1990) showed that "only 54 percent of coaches said their school has an anti-steroids drug policy" (p. 1B). However, this habit may be changing, at least among U.S. universities. Fields, Lange, Kreiter, and Fudala (1994) examined current and proposed drug testing policies from 288 athletic directors across the United States. Among the 288 athletic directors surveyed, 245 (85%) responded, an unusually large return rate for a mailed survey and perhaps one indicator of the perceived seriousness of this problem among university administrators. Of the respondents, 29% reported drug testing of their student athletes, mostly conducted on a random basis. Surprisingly, however, most of the tests covered cocaine (85%) and amphetamines (83%), with only 56% of tests for using performance-enhancing drugs such as anabolic steroids. Referral for treatment rather than immediate termination from the team or school was the most common consequence for testing positive.

Athletes need to know the boundaries between acceptable and unacceptable behaviors. The coach and parents must jointly assert that taking drugs is not allowed. Responsible, mature individuals in secure and nonthreatening situations can often make this distinction themselves. However, many others—athletes among them—cannot, particularly when they are self-centered, psychologically immature, or have low self-esteem.

Strict limit setting is equally important for responding effectively to an infringement of the policy. This is especially relevant following a positive drug test. The team's response to breaking team rules is the most important element in protecting each player and maintaining the coach's (and organization's) integrity. Probably the toughest response to drug abuse in sport has been recently introduced by the British Olympic Association. According to a report appearing in *The Australian* newspaper (November 2, 1991), "anyone caught using illegal substances will be banned for life from British Olympic teams" (p. 64). This policy, announced in advance, alerts athletes to the dire risks of engaging in behaviors that are inappropriate and will not be tolerated. The policy also relieves athletes of feeling pressured to engage in behaviors that are illegal, unethical, and detrimental to their physical and mental health. Drug policies have become more stringent at the professional level as well. The drug policy of the National Basketball Association (NBA), according to *Sports Illustrated* (June 3, 1991, p. 83), is this: "If a player who used drugs came forward voluntarily, the NBA would quietly help him find treatment, without recrimination. The league, however, had the right to administer random drug tests to players if there was "reasonable cause." Table 23-2 lists the policies of elite sports organizations for steroid use.

If a drug-taking incident occurs, coaches should know whom to call—physicians, school administrative personnel, a counselor, legal advice, perhaps a religious leader, and so on. For example, should parents be notified if their son or daughter is involved in drugs? All team leaders and athletes should know *in advance* the necessary steps in responding to a player's drug problem. This policy should be an integral part of an overall crisis management plan. Medical and psychological support services should be in place and ready to respond in an emergency 24 hours a day. A management-by-crisis approach must be avoided.

Respecting the competitor's confidentiality and privacy is another important ingredient to an effective plan of action. Cases of drug abuse need not be publicized nor handled publicly.

Table 23-2 **Policies for Steroid Use Among Elite Sports Organizations**

Organization	Policy	Penalty
Olympics (USOC)	Regular testing year-round	A violation brings a 2-year ban
National Football League	Year-round testing	First violation brings a four-game suspension
NCAA	Year-round testing in football and track & field; testing at postseason championships for all sports	Violators lose a year of eligibility
National Basketball Association	Periodic testing	First violation brings a five-game suspension
Major League Baseball	Random testing started 2004	First violation results in treatment, education, and more testing. A fifth violation brings a 1-year suspension.
National Hockey League	No testing program	

Source: USA Today, 12/8/2003, p. 22A.

The objective of an effective response to drug abuse is to extinguish the probability of future undesirable behaviors by responding efficiently to an emergency. Effective crisis management consists of anticipating the likelihood of a drug problem and being ready to react accordingly (Wilkerson, 1995).

Have a continuous random drug testing program. Drug policies and educational programs should also emphasize drug testing. Drug testing programs in sports organizations have heretofore been infrequent, but it has now become a more common reality for intercollegiate and elite athletes—probably so much so that, in some settings, drug testing programs and sanctions now contribute to the effective prevention of drug use. Drug testing, especially if offered randomly to the athletes so that they are not anticipated, can be a particularly powerful behavioral controller when the threat of dismissal or some other serious penalty accompanies a positive drug test.

The results of studies show that drug testing effectively reduces the likelihood of drug abuse among athletes. For example, Albrecht, Anderson, McGrew, McKeag, and Hough (1992a) found, in their study of 2,282 college athletes, that "among those athletes participating at college and universities with institutionally based drug-testing programs, individuals who are aware of the fact they are susceptible to periodic testing are more inclined to view such procedures as an effective deterrent to drug use" (p. 245). These results can be generalized to younger athletes as well. In an Australian study, Martin and Anshel (1991) examined the attitudes of 94 elite adolescent male and female Australian athletes toward ingesting various drugs (e.g., anabolic steroids, anti-inflammatories, hallucinogens, alcohol) related and unrelated to sport performance. The authors found that athletes voiced disagreement with the use of anabolic steroids, but not unconditionally. If these athletes were offered a performance-enhancing drug, they were more likely to avoid drug taking if the substance was detectable by testing. These results suggest that the athletes' knowledge about upcoming drug tests markedly inhibits ingesting banned drugs.

Perhaps nowhere has drug testing become more expected, persistent, and sophisticated than at the Olympic Games. Drug testing programs at the Olympics include short- or no-notice testing during training periods, testing at qualifying competitions, and testing at the Olympic Games. In their review of these procedures, Catlin and Murray (1996) report that the 1996 Games in Atlanta included testing urine samples for stimulants, narcotics, anabolic agents (particularly steroids), diuretics, peptides, and glycoprotein hormones, as well as prohibited methods of enhancing performance, including blood doping and pharmacological, chemical, and physical manipulation of urine. Also on the banned substance list of the U.S. Olympic Committee is a drug called **clenbuterol.** This is a new popular drug used by athletes for its purported tissue-building, fat-reducing effects (Prather, Brown, North, & Wilson, 1995). The researchers review animal research literature that shows the drug will inhibit the storage of fat and increase the deposit of lean body mass. To date, no human data are available.

Three principles contribute to an effective drug testing program (see Uzych, 1991, for a review of flaws in programs and guidelines for effective drug testing):

1. *Announce the policy in advance.* All team personnel should become aware of the team's or league's rules and guidelines from the first day of participation. Only in this way can participants effectively be held accountable for their actions. However, the actual testing procedure should *not* be announced in advance. To reduce costs, **random testing**—in which only a percentage of the team's athletes, rather than all players, are selected—has been shown to deter, though not eliminate, drug abuse (*Drugs in Sport,* 1990).

2. *Be consistent in implementing the policy.* The least effective approach to enacting a drug policy is responding to one athlete differently than to others. Unfortunately, team rules will likely be tested by group members. If the coach or league officials are serious about drug abuse prevention and control, they must react vigorously and consistently to the team's most and least talented players. Otherwise, any credibility the policy has will be destroyed.

3. *Link test results to sanctions.* The coach's or league's responses to positive drug tests can be very restrictive (e.g., player dismissed from the team) or more flexible (e.g., counseling and monitoring). However, the least appropriate response is to have a policy that includes sanctions that are not implemented or used inconsistently. Athletes, not unlike others in a subordinate position, need to realize that behaviors that are illegal, unethical, and medically unsafe cannot be tolerated.

Use behavioral contracting. A **contract system,** often called a performance contract, is among the most sophisticated forms of contingency management. It is a preplanned agreement between two parties (the coach or administrative unit and athlete in this case) that a specified reinforcement will occur to the athlete following the occurrence of a particular action (Martin & Lumsden, 1987; Rushall & Siedentop, 1972). Contracts can be verbal or, perhaps more effectively, be in written form and signed by the parties involved. Of course, in professional sports in the United States, player unions and team contracts stipulate drug testing procedures and penalties.

Use a support group. Palmer's (1989) study on the effectiveness of educational programs on drug use revealed that high school seniors served as excellent peer educators and role models in drug prevention among fellow student athletes and nonathletes. Among the first structured attempts at dealing with drug abuse on a sports team, particularly at the elite level, was one conducted by the Cleveland Browns football team (Collins et al., 1984). In addition to medical and psychological treatment programs, the team owner hired a psychiatrist to conduct group and individual therapies and to establish self-help meetings for players and their wives. The core of the program consisted of a subgroup called The Inner Circle, which consisted of a group of identified drug-involved players. According to Collins et al.:

> Group discussions typically dealt with who was relapsing and why and the need for changes in the individual's lifestyle to support staying "clean. . . ." Rather than participating

in cover-ups and deceptions, the players saw that relapses were "contagious," and that when one member was in trouble, others would soon follow. . . . The group eventually became responsible for much of its own therapeutic work in keeping its individual members away from drugs. (p. 490)

Invite guest speakers. Sometimes athletes become *coach deaf*—they are so accustomed to the voice of their coach (or, for that matter, their parents) that they tune him or her out. Guest speakers bring to the team a renewed sense of authority, expertise, credibility, and respect. Examples of guest speakers include pharmacists, retired athletes, former coaches, physicians, lawyers, religious leaders, and individuals whose personal history may benefit the listeners (e.g., the medical problems of a former steroid abuser, former champion athletes who can reveal their commitment and dedication to become successful).

A Values-Based Intervention Model

The pressures to succeed in sport, especially at elite levels, are too great to expect athletes to regulate their own personal behavior. And, as indicated earlier, frequently the athletes' self-esteem is dependent on their sport success—at virtually any cost. In addition, typical of human nature, most athletes do not associate a negative, unhealthy habit with longer-term harmful outcomes. Short-term benefits prevail over long-term consequences. Previous experience as a consultant has included a unique approach to behavioral change among athletes and nonathletes that appeals to the very core of the athletes' reasons for competing—their deepest values and beliefs—what I call the *Disconnected Values Model* (Anshel, 2003).

The primary purpose of the model is to assist athletes in acknowledging that taking drugs, whether it is for performance-enhancing or "recreational" purposes, is a negative habit that has benefits but also has dire costs and long-term consequences (Strelan & Boeckman, 2003). The model is "driven" by the athlete's willingness to become aware of the "disconnect," or contradiction, between their deepest values and beliefs and their actions—negative habits—in this case, taking

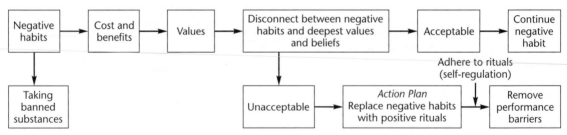

Figure 23-1   **The disconnected values intervention model for drug use in sport**

banned substances. For example, athletes may acknowledge a "disconnect," or inconsistency, between their values of competitiveness, integrity, fairness, health, honesty, and integrity. Yet, they make a conscious decision to ingest substances that they know to be illegal in society, unhealthy to long-term health, or against the team's or sport organization's rules. Does the athlete find this disconnect acceptable? If the athlete acknowledges the "disconnect," yet deems it acceptable, for whatever reason, the negative habit (i.e., drug-taking) will continue. The ability to act in a way that is consistent with one's deepest values and beliefs is referred to as expanding spiritual capacity (Groppel, 2000; Loehr & Schwartz, 2003). The model, presented in Figure 23-1, depicts the intervention stages.

An Overview of the Disconnected Values Model

It is widely acknowledged in the previous literature that drug education programs among athletes and nonathletes are not usually effective. In one study, for example, reviewed earlier, Anshel and Russell (1997) found that greater knowledge about the harmful effects of drugs, including anabolic steroid use, does not appear to affect the athletes' attitudes toward taking these drugs. If attitudes are not strongly influenced by increased knowledge about the harmful effects of drugs, it is hardly surprising that drug education does not influence drug-taking behaviors. Therefore, future attempts at changing anabolic steroid use and other performance-enhancing drugs should consist of addressing the athletes' most deeply held beliefs and values (Loehr & Schwartz, 2003).

Athletes who cheat by ingesting substances that they know are against the rules or are illegal, and, therefore, risk their future participation in sport, are misaligned with their values of fairness, health, and integrity." Athletes whose actions are self-serving and contradictory to their values and deeply held beliefs, are being selfish and self-destructive. Athletes who are selfish in this way are often driven by insecurity, low self-esteem, and unhappiness. The question now becomes how to assist the athlete to identify their values, to acknowledge this disconnect between the negative habit of drug-taking and their values, and to create the energy and commitment needed to act in a way that is consistent with their values, that is, to expand their spiritual capacity. Each component of the model is now discussed.

Negative habits. The model begins with identifying thoughts, emotions, or behaviors that are consistent, yet compromise health, energy, or performance, called negative habits. The athlete's choice to ingest performance-enhancing drugs that are illegal, contrary to the rules and policies of their sport organization or team (cheating), or lead to poorer health is a negative habit. Why would a person persist at any negative habit that they knew was bad for them? The reason is that there are benefits to every negative habit. The benefits of negative habits provide added incentive to persist in these behaviors or thoughts (Loehr & Schwartz, 2003). For example, the perceived benefits of taking banned substances that are purported to enhance performance are greater than the costs.

Benefits of negative habits. The next process in the model is to help the individual (athlete) acknowledge the benefits of his or her negative habits, in this case, the perceived benefits of taking performance-enhancing illegal substances. See earlier sections of this chapter for an explanation of these benefits. There are perceived benefits to taking "recreational" (hallucinogens, etc.) drugs as well. These include peer acceptance and approval, immediate pleasure, reduced tension and anxiety, more comfort in social settings, and "numbing out." The importance of recognizing the perceived benefits of any negative habit is (a) to acknowledge that the individual engages in these behaviors for one or more plausible reasons and (b) to increase the contrasts against the *costs* of these same habits. To provide only the disadvantages of inappropriate behaviors without recognizing their advantages is to discredit the individual's thinking and decision-making capability that explain these behaviors. Respecting the athlete allows us to expect him or her to think rationally and to willingly change behavior.

Costs of negative habits. Central to the change process is the ability of the athlete to detect the costs of his or her negative habit(s). Taking hallucinogenic drugs is replete with costs to one's physical health and mental well-being, as well as reduced sport performance. The costs of ingesting anabolic steroids and other performance-enhancing illegal substances have been identified earlier.

Long-term consequences. Long-term consequences of any negative habit are difficult for younger, relatively healthy individuals to recognize because the advantages of short-term benefits often seem to far outweigh the long-term costs. The tendency to delay gratification is typical of individuals who possess poor "self-regulation" skills, the ability to initiate and persist at behaviors that encourage self-control. Individuals differ in their ability to avoid short-term, impulsive behaviors that result in immediate benefits but poor long-term consequences. In the "delay of gratification paradigm," for example, researchers often find that when individuals are given a choice between a small reward that is immediately available or a large reward that requires a period of waiting, most individuals choose the former, especially for children. With normal development, however, this

tendency changes, planning behaviors emerge, and longer term, strategic forms of self-regulating behaviors form.

Another reason that explains the difficulty of changing behavior based on reviewing the long-term consequences is that athletes often suffer from a condition called "The Superman Complex"; also called the "Adonis Complex," this is a condition in which some athletes feel impervious to the known harmful effects to health that most drugs are known to cause (Anshel, 1993). What does appear to change these perceptions are the publicized stories of high profiled athletes whose health has significantly deteriorated, or death has occurred, because of the prolonged use of anabolic steroids. This was the exact reaction to the death of former Denver Broncos football player Lyle Alzado, who in 1989 died from cancer that he (and his doctors) attributed to prolonged, extensive use of steroids and human growth hormone (hgH). In an article published in *Sports Illustrated* (July 8, 1991) entitled, "I'm sick and I'm scared," Alzado decided to discuss his brain lymphoma and its likely causes in order to help save other athletes from a similar fate. At the time, he was receiving chemotherapy and rapidly losing weight. Alzado, at just 42 years of age, soon lost the battle to beat his disease. As Alzado said before his premature death, "If I had known that I would be this sick now, I would have tried to make it in football on my own—naturally. Whoever is doing this stuff, if you stay on it too long or maybe if you get on it at all, you're going to get something bad from it. . . . It is a wrong thing to do" (*Sports Illustrated*, 1991, p. 25).

Values. This stage is the heart of the model; the primary process by which change in thinking and acting occurs. Values represent a self-statement about what is really important to the individual. What are the passion, the purpose, and the mission that ignite energy needed for establishing and meeting our goals and experiencing a high quality of life? To Groppel (2000), "a value is anything on which you place worth . . . whatever your value system is, you should emotionally connect to it" (p. 147). Examples of values for athletes might include commitment, character, fairness, competitiveness, perseverance, family, respect for others, loyalty, happiness, health, excellence, and compassion. At this stage, the athlete selects his or her most important values.

Disconnects between values and negative habits.

The model now requires the athlete to engage in very deep and personal self-reflection in identifying any incompatibilities between the values they hold in high esteem and their drug-taking behavior. If an athlete's values include health, family, competitiveness, and fairness, yet he or she has decided to ingest a banned substance, then the athlete is acting in a way that is inconsistent with these values. One way to communicate this outcome to the competitor is as follows: "Joe, you say that maintaining good health is one of your most important values. Yet you admit to taking steroids, which you believe will improve your performance. You also acknowledge that steroids have health-related risks. There appears to be a 'disconnect,' or inconsistency, between the high value you place on your health and maintaining a habit that has serious health-related side effects. Would you agree?" Another example would be to point out the "disconnect" between the athlete's value of competitiveness or fairness and his or her decision to use banned substances that will give an unfair advantage; a contradiction between values and behaviors.

Acceptable or not acceptable.

At this stage, the athlete makes a crucial decision about future actions. If they accept the apparent contradiction between their deepest values and their self-destructive (negative) habits, perhaps as the "price they must pay" for competing at elite levels in sport, then their drug taking will continue. Until they no longer compete, or they become sick or test positive, these athletes will continue to ingest these substances. However, if the athlete concludes that this contradiction is *not* acceptable, that their drug-taking behaviors are inconsistent with what really matters to them, it is likely they will voluntarily decide to stop taking the banned substances and, instead, to rely on their training and ability to succeed at their highest level. Coaches and sport psychology consultants must provide as much support and encouragement during the decision-making process as possible. The athlete is now prepared to engage in an "action plan" that replaces the negative habits with positive routines consisting of both thoughts and actions.

Research on the model's effectiveness continues. However, the results of one study of male and female adult nonathletes indicated that adherence to a prescribed exercise program was significantly superior for the intervention group as compared to the control group in which the model was not used (Anshel, 2003).

Summary

The causes of drug taking among athletes are multidimensional, as evidenced by the taking of different performance-enhancing and recreational drugs. Although personal characteristics and sport demands play a relevant role in drug taking, situational and environmental issues also contribute by exacerbating the pressures placed on athletes to achieve sport success. Examples include unreasonable expectations by others, particularly the coach; defining success as a function of outcome rather than performance improvement; peer pressure; the perception of social acceptance through media reports of high-profile athletes who take drugs; and, at the elite level, the financial incentives for success. Given the extent and persistence of pressures to win, perhaps it is not surprising that education, threats, and even drug testing alone are not efficient means of eliminating drugs in sport.

Winning should not be at the expense of the athletes' health and psychological well-being. It is true that athletes, rather than their coaches and other sport leaders, must take the primary responsibility for their actions, particularly when those actions are illegal and unethical. However, athletes also need protection and a support network to help cope with sport-related pressure and stress (Rosenfeld et al., 1989). When a player attaches his or her self-esteem to sport success, the probability of using drugs increases. Such players need help in meeting the responsibilities of competition because they often do not have the psychological resources to cope. Protection from this pressure must come from team coaches, sport psychology consultants, parents, and other team and organizational personnel (e.g., athletic trainers, counselors, teammates).

It is unrealistic to expect athletes to eliminate the problem of drug abuse without external support. Particularly warranted are implementation of team and league drug policies; drug educational programs; drug testing; psychological skills training; counseling; activities to counter boredom; and closer monitoring of the athletes' attitudes and behaviors by coaches, sport psychology consultants, and sport administrators. Sadly (and surprisingly), research on the effectiveness of cognitive and behavioral strategies and educational programs in reducing drug use among athletes is lacking. I hope this will change as drug policies and educational/intervention programs become more commonplace.

Lawrie Woodman of the Australian Sports Commission (see Anshel, 1990a) places the problem of drug abuse in perspective. He says,

> The root of the problem is people. The misuse of drugs in sport is a people problem; it is not just the system or the rules. The issue is ultimately one of codes of conduct or standards and it is people who set standards. If we fail to recognize and confront the drug problem in sport, the concept of athletic competition will change as we now know it. Nothing less than the integrity of sport is at stake. (p. 51)

Study Questions

1. How does the IOC define doping?

2. List the five doping categories banned by the IOC. Give an example of drugs under each category and indicate why athletes might take such a drug.

3. Identify the different health concerns for ingesting drugs from the different doping categories.

4. What is the rationale for an antidrug policy in sport?

5. Using both anecdotal reports and evidence from scientific studies, give some indication of the extensiveness of drug abuse in sport.

6. Discuss the physical, psychological/emotional, and social causes of drug abuse in sport.

7. Distinguish between cognitive approaches and behavioral strategies in controlling drug abuse in athletes. Provide examples of both types of interventions.

8. If you were the team's head coach, describe the cognitive and behavioral strategies you would use on your team to prevent and respond to the use of anabolic steroids.

9. Discuss the three main components of an effective drug testing program and how to help ensure an effective testing program.

10. What are the advantages and disadvantages of using ergogenic aids? Should creatine be banned in competitive sport? Why or why not?

11. What strategies can parents of athletes use to reduce the chance their child athlete will use anabolic steroids?

References

Albrecht, R. R., Anderson, W. A., McGrew, C. A., McKeag, D. B., & Hough, D. O. (1992a). NCAA institutionally based drug testing: Do our athletes know the rules of *this* game? *Medicine and Science in Sport and Exercise, 24,* 242–246.

Albrecht, R. R., Anderson, W. A., & McKeag, D. B. (1992b). Drug testing of college athletes: The issues. *Sports Medicine, 14,* 349–352.

Alzado, L. (1991, July 8). I'm sick and I'm scared. *Sports Illustrated, 75,* 21–25.

Anshel, M. H. (1986, May/June). The coach's role in preventing drug abuse by athletes. *Coaching Review, 9,* 29–32, 34–35.

Anshel, M. H. (1987, November 15). *Coaching strategies for managing drug abuse in sport.* Presentation to coaches of the United States Olympic Ski Team, Colorado Springs, CO.

Anshel, M. H. (1990a). Commentary on the national drugs in sport conference—1989. Testing the causes and symptoms. *Australian Journal of Science and Medicine in Sport, 22,* 49–56.

Anshel, M. H. (1990b, January). *Suggested cognitive and behavioral strategies for reducing/preventing drug abuse in sport.* Paper presented at the 1990 Commonwealth Games Conference, Auckland, New Zealand.

Anshel, M. H. (1991a). Causes for drug abuse in sport: A survey of intercollegiate athletes. *Journal of Sport Behavior, 14,* 283–307.

Anshel, M. H. (1991b). Cognitive and behavioral strategies for combating drug abuse in sport: Implications for coaches and sport psychology consultants. *The Sport Psychologist, 5,* 152–166.

Anshel, M. H. (1993). Psychology of drug use in sport. In R. N. Singer, M. Murphey, & L. K. Tennant (Eds.), *Handbook of research on sport psychology* (pp. 851–876). New York: Macmillan.

Anshel, M. H. (2003). *Sport psychology: From theory to practice* (4th ed.). San Francisco: Benjamin-Cummings.

Anshel, M. H. (2003, August). *A values-based model for enhancing exercise adherence.* Paper presented at the American Psychological Association Convention in Toronto, Ontario, Canada.

Anshel, M. H., & Russell, K. (1997). Effect of an educational program on knowledge and attitudes toward ingesting anabolic steroids among track and field athletes. *Journal of Drug Education, 27,* 172–187.

Appleby, M., Fisher, M., & Martin, M. (1994). Myocardial infarction, hyperkalaemia and ventricular tachycardia in a young male body-builder. *International Journal of Cardiology, 44,* 171–174.

Australian Sports Medicine Federation. (1989, October). *Survey of drug use in Australian sport* (2nd ed.). Canberra, A.C.T. (Australia): Australian Sports Drug Agency.

Bell, J. A., & Doege, T. C. (1987). Athletes' use and abuse of drugs. *The Physician and Sportsmedicine, 15,* 99–106, 108.

Branch, J. D. (2002). Performance-enhancing drugs and ergogenic aids. In L. L. Mostofsky & L. D. Zaichkowsky (Eds.), *Medical and psychological aspects of sport and exercise* (pp. 55–71). Morgantown, WV: Fitness Information Technology.

Buckley, W. E., Yesalis, C. E., Friedl, K. E., Anderson, W. A., Streit, A. L., & Wright, J. E. (1988). Estimated prevalence of anabolic steroid use among male high school seniors. *Journal of the American Medical Association, 260,* 3441–3445.

Catlin, D. H., & Murray, T. H. (1996, July 17). Performance-enhancing drugs, fair competition, and Olympic sport. *Journal of the American Medical Association, 276,* 231–237.

Chaikin, T., & Telander, R. (1988, October 24). The nightmare of steroids. *Sports Illustrated,* pp. 84–93, 97–98, 100–102.

Chappel, J. N. (1987). Drug use and abuse in the athlete. In J. R. May & M. J. Asken (Eds.), *Sport psychology: The psychological health of the athlete* (pp. 187–212). New York: PMA.

Chu, D. (1982). *Dimensions of sport studies.* New York: Wiley.

Cohen, J. C., Noakes, T. D., & Benade, A. J. S. (1988). Hypercholesterolemia in male power lifters using anabolic-androgenic steroids. *The Physician and Sportsmedicine, 16,* 49–50, 53–54, 56.

Cohen, S. (1979). Doping: Drugs in sport. *Drug Abuse and Alcoholism Newsletter, 8*(1), pp. 2–4.

Collins, G. B., Pippenger, C. E., & Janesz, J. W. (1984). Links in the chain: An approach to the treatment of drug abuse on a professional football team. *Cleveland Clinic Quarterly, 51,* 485–492.

Corrigan, B. (1988, October–December). Doping in sport. *Sports Coach, 12,* 11–17.

Damm, J. (1991). Drugs and the college student-athlete. In E. F. Etzel, A. B. Ferraute, & J. W. Pinkney (Eds.), *Counseling college student-athletes: Issues and interventions* (pp. 151–174). Morgantown, WV: Fitness Information Technology.

Delbeke, F. T., Desmet, N., & Debackere, M. (1995). The abuse of doping agents in competing body builders in Flanders (1988–1993). *International Journal of Sportsmedicine, 16,* 66–70.

Dezelsky, T. L., Toohey, J. V., & Shaw, R. S. (1985). Non-medical drug use behavior at five United States universities: A 15-year study. *Bulletin of Narcotics, 37,* 49–53.

Donald, K. (1983). *The doping game.* Brisbane, Australia: Boolarang.

Doweiko, H. E. (1996). *Concepts of chemical dependency* (3rd ed.). Pacific Grove, CA: Brooks/Cole.

Drugs in sport: Second report of the Senate Standing Committee on Environment, Recreation and the Arts. (1990, May). Canberra, ACT: Australian Government Publishing Service.

Egger, G. (1981). *The sport drug.* Boston: George, Allen & Unwin.

English, G. (1987). A theoretical explanation of why athletes choose to use steroids, and the role of the coach in influencing behavior. *National Strength and Conditioning Association Journal, 9,* 53–56.

Fields, L., Lange, W. R., Kreiter, N. A., & Fudala, P. J. (1994). *Medicine and Science in Sports and Exercise, 26,* 682–686.

Fisher, A. C., Mancini, V. H., Hirsch, R. L., Proulx, T. J., & Staurowsky, E. J. (1982). Coach–athlete interactions and team climate. *Journal of Sport Psychology, 4,* 388–404.

Flett, G. L., & Hewitt, P. L. (2002). Perfectionism and maladjustment: An overview of theoretical, definitional, and treatment issues. In G. L. Flett & P. L. Hewitt (Eds.), *Perfectionism: Theory, research, and treatment* (pp. 5–32). Washington, DC: American Psychological Association.

Forman, S. G. (1997). *Coping skills interventions for children and adolescents.* San Francisco: Jossey-Bass.

Galper, D. I. (1996, March). *Anabolic steroid beliefs and attitudes: Differences between users and non-users.* Paper presented at the 17th Annual Society of Behavioral Medicine Conference, Washington, DC.

Gerslick, K., Grady, K., Sexton, E., & Lyons, M. (1981). Personality and sociodemographic factors in adolescent drugs use. In D. J. Lettiers & J. P. Ludford (Eds.), *Drug abuse and the American adolescent* (pp. 81–116). Rockville, MD: U.S. Department of Health and Human Services, National Institute on Drug Abuse, Research Monograph No. 38.

Gill, D. (1986). *Psychological dynamics of sport.* Champaign, IL: Human Kinetics.

Goldberg, R. (1998). *Taking sides: Clashing views on controversial issues in drugs and society* (3rd ed.). New York: McGraw-Hill.

Goldman, B., Bush, P., & Katz, R. (1984). *Death in the locker room: Steroids and sports.* South Bend, IN: Icarus Press.

Groppel, J. (2000). *The corporate athlete.* New York: John Wiley & Sons.

Hanson, D. (1980). Drugs education, does it work? In F. Scarpitti & S. Datesman (Eds.), *Drugs and youth culture: Annual reviews of drug and alcohol abuse* (Vol. 4, pp. 212–236), Beverly Hills, CA: Sage.

Hanson, T. W., & Gould, D. (1988). Factors affecting the ability of coaches to estimate their athletes' trait and state anxiety levels. *The Sport Psychologist, 2,* 298–313.

Harris, R. C., Soderlund, K., & Hultman, E. (1992). Elevation of creatine in resting and exercised muscle of normal subjects by creatine supplementation. *Clinical Science, 83,* 367–374.

Heitzinger & Associates. (1986). *1981–1986 data collection and analysis: High school, college, professional athletes alcohol/drug survey.* 333 W. Miflin, Madison, WI.

Hewitt, P. L., & Flett, G. L. (2002). Perfectionism and stress processes in psychopathology. In G. L. Flett & P. L. Hewitt (Eds.), *Perfectionism: Theory, research, and treatment* (pp. 255–284). Washington, DC: American Psychological Association.

Hughes, R., & Coakley, J. J. (1991). Positive deviance among athletes. *Sociology of Sport Journal, 8,* 307–325.

Julien, R. M. (1981). *A primer of drug action* (3rd ed.). San Francisco: Freeman.

Kandel, D. B. (1978). *Longitudinal research on drug use: Empirical findings and methodological issues.* Washington, DC: Hemisphere-Wiley.

Kennedy, M. C., & Lawrence, C. (1993). Anabolic steroid abuse and cardiac death. *Medical Journal of Australia, 158*, 346–348.

Kinder, B. N., Pope, N. E., & Walfish, S. (1980). Drug and alcohol education programs: A review of outcome studies. *International Journal of the Addictions, 15*, 1035–1054.

Lamb, D. R. (1984). Anabolic steroids in athletics: How well do they work and how dangerous are they? *American Journal of Sports Medicine, 12*, 31–38.

Laure, P., & Reinsberger, H. (1995). Doping and high-level endurance walkers—knowledge and representation: A prohibited practice. *Journal of Sports Medicine & Physical Fitness, 35*, 228–231.

Leccese, A. P. (1991). *Drugs and society: Behavioral medicines and abusable drugs*. Uper Saddle River, NJ: Prentice Hall.

Loehr, J., & Schwartz, T. (2003). *The power of full engagement*. New York: Free Press.

Lombardo, J. (1993). The efficacy and mechanisms of action of anabolic steroids. In C. E. Yesalis (Ed.), *Anabolic steroids in sport and exercise* (pp. 89–106). Champaign, IL: Human Kinetics.

Lubell, A. (1989). Does steroid abuse cause—or excuse—violence? *The Physician and Sportsmedicine, 17*, 176, 178–180, 185.

Marcello, R. J., Danish, S. J., & Stolberg, A. L. (1989). An evaluation of strategies developed to prevent substance abuse among student-athletes. *The Sport Psychologist, 3*, 196–211.

Martin, M. B., & Anshel, M. H. (1991). Attitudes of elite junior athletes on drug-taking behaviors: Implications for drug prevention programs. *Drug Education Journal of Australia, 5*, 223–238.

Martin, M. B., & Anshel, M. H. (1999). Attitudes of elite adolescent Australian athletes toward drug taking: Implications for effective drug prevent programs. *Drug Education Journal of Australia, 5*, 223–238.

Martin, G. L., & Lumsden, J. A. (1987). *Coaching: An effective behavioral approach*. St. Louis, MO: Times Mirror/Mosby.

Meilman, P. W., Crace, R. K., Presley, C. A., & Lyerla, R. (1995). Beyond performance enhancement: Polypharmacy among collegiate users of steroids. *Journal of American College Health, 44*, 98–104.

Melia, P., Pipe, A., & Greenberg, L. (1996). The use of anabolic-androgenic steroids by Canadian students. *Clinical Journal of Sport Medicine, 6*, 9–14.

Moses, E. (1988, October 10). An athlete's Rx for the drug problem. *Newsweek*, p. 57.

Mottram, D. R. (1999). Banned drugs in sport: Does the International Olympic Committee (IOC) List need updating? *Sports Medicine, 27*, 1–10.

Mottram, D. R., Reilly, T., & Chester, N. (1997). Doping in sport: The extent of the problem. In R. Reilly & M. Orne (Eds.), *The clinical pharmacology of sport and exercise* (pp. 3–12). Amsterdam: Excerpta Medica.

Mottram, D. R. (Ed.). (1988). *Drugs in sport*. London: Spon.

Nakatani, Y., & Udagawa, M. (1995). Anabolic steroid abuse and mental disorder. *Arukoru-Kenkyuto-Yakubutsu, 30*, 333–347.

Nardo, D. (1992). *Drugs and sports*. San Diego, CA: Lucent Books, Inc.

Newman, S. (1994). Despite warnings, lure of steroids too strong for some young Canadians. *Canadian Medical Association Journal, 151,* 844–846.

Nicholson, N., (1989, July). The role of drug education. In S. Haynes & M. H. Anshel (Eds.), *Proceedings of the 1989 National Drugs in Sport Conference—Treating the causes and symptoms.* University of Wollongong, Wollongong, NSW, Australia.

Nicholson, N., & Agnew, M. (1989). *Education strategies to reduce drug use in sport.* Canberra, ACT: Australian Sports Drug Agency.

Orlick, T. (1990). *In pursuit of excellence* (2nd ed.). Champaign, IL: Human Kinetics.

Orlick, T., & Partington, J. (1986). *Psyched: Inner views of winning.* Ottawa, ON: Coaching Association of Canada.

Palmer, J. (1989, Fall). High school senior athletes as peer educators and role models: An innovative approach to drug prevention. *Journal of Alcohol and Drug Education, 35,* 23–27.

Park, J. (1990). Analytical methods to detect dope agents. In J. Park (Ed.), *Proceedings of the International Symposium on Drug Abuse in Sports (doping)* (pp. 51–70). Seoul: Korea Institute of Science and Technology.

Perko, M. A., Cowdery, J., Wang, M. Q., & Yesalis, C. S. (1995). Associations between academic performance of Division I college athletes and their perceptions of the effects of anabolic steroids. *Perceptual Motor Skills, 80,* 284–286.

Polich, J., Ellickson, P., Reuter, P., & Kahan, P. (1984). *Strategies for controlling adolescent drug use.* Santa Monica, CA: The Rand Corporation.

Pope, H. G., & Katz, D. L. (1994). Psychiatric and medical effects of anabolic-androgenic steroid use. A controlled study of 160 athletes. *Archives of General Psychiatry, 51,* 375–382.

Pope, H. G., Katz, D. L., & Champoux, R. (1988, July). Anabolic-androgenic steroid use among 1,010 college men. *The Physician and Sportsmedicine, 16,* 75–77, 80–81.

Pope, H. G., Jr. (2002). *The Adonis complex: How to identify, treat, and prevent body obsession in men and boys.* New York: Free Press.

Potteiger, J. A., & Stilger, V. G. (1994). Anabolic steroid use in the adolescent athlete. *Journal of Athletic Training, 29,* 60–62, 64.

Prather, I. D., Brown, D. E., North, P., & Wilson, J. R. (1995). Clenbuterol: A substitute for anabolic steroids? *Medicine and Science in Sports and Exercise, 27,* 1118–1121.

Prokop, L. (1990). The history of doping. In J. Park (Ed.), *Proceedings of the International Symposium on Drug Abuse in Sport (doping)* (pp. 1–9). Seoul: Korea institute of Science and Technology.

Radakovich, J., Broderick, P., & Pickell, G. (1993). Rate of anabolic-androgenic steroid use among students in junior high school. *Journal of American Board of Family Practice, 6,* 341–345.

Reilly, C. (1988). *An evaluation of the peer support program.* (Report No. A 88/5). Sydney, NSW (Australia): NSW Department of Health.

Ringhofer, K. R., & Harding, M. E. (1996). *Coaches guide to drugs and sport*. Champaign, IL: Human Kinetics.

Rosenfeld, L. B., Richman, J. M., & Hardy, C. J. (1989). Examining social support networks among athletes: Description and relationship to stress. *The Sport Psychologist, 3,* 23–33.

Rushall, B. S., & Siedentop, D. (1972). *The development and control of behavior in sport and physical education*. Philadelphia: Lea & Febiger.

Russell, D. G. (1990). *Drugs and medicines in sport*. Wellington, NZ: Royal Society of New Zealand.

Ryan, A. J. (1982). Advantage, drug-free athletes. *The Physician and Sportsmedicine, 10,* 50.

Sawka, M. N., Joyner, M. J., Miles, D. S., Roberson, R. J., Spriet, L. L., & Young, A. J. (1996). *American College of Sports Medicine position stand*: The use of blood doping as an ergogenic aid. *Medicine and Science in Sports and Exercise, 28,* i–viii.

Schlaadt, R. G., & Shannon, P. T. (1994). *Drugs: Use, misuse, and abuse*. Upper Saddle River, NJ: Prentice Hall.

Shroyer, J. (1990). Getting tough on anabolic steroids. Can we win the battle? *The Physician and Sportsmedicine, 18,* 106, 108–110, 115, 118.

Smith, G. (1983). Recreational drugs in sport. *The Physician and Sportsmedicine, 11,* 75–76, 79, 82.

Sonstroem, R. J. (1997). Physical activity and self-esteem. In W. P. Morgan (Ed.), *Physical activity and mental health* (pp. 127–143). Washington, DC: Taylor & Francis.

Steroid Trafficking Act of 1990 (1990, August 30). Committee of the Judiciary, 101st Congress, 2nd Session, Report No. 101–433.

Strauss, R. H. (1987). Anabolic steroids. In R. H. Strauss (Ed.), *Drugs and performance in sports* (pp. 59–68). Philadelphia: Saunders.

Strauss, R. H. (1988, October–December). Drug abuse in sports: A three-pronged response. *Sports Coach,* pp. 12, 23.

Strelan, P., & Boeckman, R. J. (2003). A new model for understanding performance-enhancing drug use by elite athletes. *Journal of Applied Sport Psychology, 15,* 176–183.

Stuart, R. (1974). Teaching facts about drugs: Pushing or preventing? *Journal of Educational Psychology, 66,* 189–201.

Taylor, W. N. (1987). Synthetic anabolic-androgenic steroids: A plea for controlled substance status. *The Physician and Sportsmedicine, 15,* 140–150.

Tobler, N. (1986). Meta-analysis of 143 adolescent drug prevention programs: Quantitative outcome results of program participants compared to a control or comparison group. *Journal of Drug Issues, 16,* 537–567.

Uzych, L. (1991). Drug testing of athletes. *British Journal of Addictions, 86,* 5–8.

Voy, R. (1991). *Drugs, sport, and politics*. Champaign, IL: Leisure Press.

Wagner, J. C. (1991). Enhancement of athletic performance with drugs. An overview. *Sports Medicine, 12,* 250–265.

Weinhold, L. L. (1991). Steroid and drug use by athletes. In L. Diamant (Ed.), *Psychology of sport, exercise, and fitness: Social and personal issues*. New York: Hemisphere.

Wemyss-Holden, S. A., Hamdy, F. C., & Hastie, K. J. (1994). *British Journal of Urology, 74*, 476–478.

Whitehead, R., Chillag, S., & Elliott, D. (1992). Anabolic steroid use among adolescents in a rural state. *Journal of Family Practice, 35*, 401–405.

Wilkerson, L. A. (1995). Taking a strong stance against anabolic steroid use [editorial]. *Journal of the American Osteopathic Association, 95*, 468–470.

Williams, M. H. (1989). *Beyond training: How athletes enhance performance legally and illegally*. Champaign, IL: Leisure Press.

Williams, M. H. (1994). The use of nutritional ergogenic aids in sports: Is it an ethical issue? *International Journal of Sport Nutrition, 4*, 120–131.

Williams, M. H. (1998). *The ergogenics edge: Pushing the limits of sports performance*. Champaign, IL: Human Kinetics.

Williams, M. H., Kreider, R. B., & Branch, J. D. (1999). *Creatine: The power supplement*. Champaign, IL: Human Kinetics.

Wright, J. E., & Cowart, V. S. (1990). *Anabolic steroids: Altered states*. Carmel, IN: Cooper Publishing Group.

Yesalis, C. E., & Bahrke, M. S. (1995). Anabolic-androgenic steroids. Current issues. *Sports Medicine, 19*, 326–340.

Yesalis, C. E., & Cowart, V. S. (1998). *The steroids game*. Champaign, IL: Human Kinetics.

Burnout in Sport: Understanding the Process—From Early Warning Signs to Individualized Intervention

Kate Goodger, *Loughborough University*
David Lavallee, *Loughborough University*
Trish Gorely, *Loughborough University*
Chris Harwood, *Loughborough University*

Maybe 14 is too young to handle everything emotionally and I needed to escape from the expectation of being able to win every tournament I entered. I was always expected to be at the top and if I didn't win, to me that meant I was a loser. If I played terrible I thought I could handle it, but really I couldn't. I felt no one liked me as a person. I was depressed and sad and lonely and guilty. . . . I burned out. After the U.S. Open I spent a week in bed in darkness, just hating everything. When I looked in the mirror I saw this distorted image. I just wanted to kill myself. I'm not addicted to drugs, but you could say I was an addict to my own pain. I had this sarcasm about everything. I was depressed and sad and lonely and guilty.

—Jennifer Capriati, in 2001, reflecting on an earlier time in her tennis career

Introduction

Burnout as an academic construct within the field of sport psychology, and burnout framed in the anecdotal accounts of athletes, coaches, parents, athletic directors, and trainers, appears to present two very different situations in terms of familiarity and understanding. Sport psychology journal articles and book chapters on the topic explain that there is a paucity of research in the field (Dale & Weinberg, 1990; Fender, 1989; Gould, Tuffey, Udry, & Loehr, 1996a), and that this limited empirical base has resulted in the concept being little understood as an applied area (Raedeke, Lunney, & Venables, 2002). In contrast, burnout as a lay term used by members of the sport community has experienced widespread colloquial use and been greeted with enormous public appeal. In the 1990s, it was described as a "hot" topic (Gould et al., 1996a), a "buzzword" within this environment (Raedeke, 1997), and significant media attention followed—and continues today. In turn, the latter has served to further popularize it among the wider public. Burnout, thus, has become a term used in everyday language by both members of the sport community (Vealey, Armstrong, Comar, & Greenleaf, 1998) and sports fans alike and, as such, appears as a concept that is readily understood and observable in day-to-day practice.

The chapter begins by providing an overview of the historical development of the term *burnout*. A definition of burnout is then provided, in comparison to the related concepts of dropout, overtraining, and staleness. The signs, symptoms, and consequences of burnout are then considered, along with traditional theories and models of burnout in sport. We then review research conducted on both athletes and coaches and highlight tools used for monitoring burnout and potential intervention strategies. Finally, the chapter closes with a case study.

The Historical Development of Burnout

The term *burnout* within sporting contexts has been borrowed from the professional literature in which it originated. The founding father of burnout is generally considered to be Herbert Freudenberger (1974), through his introduction of the term in his influential paper on burnout of volunteers at a New York Free Clinic for drug addicts. At the same time, however, research was being undertaken by a social psychologist named Christina Maslach, who was examining how human services employees coped with the emotional demands of the job. She and her co-workers heard the term burnout being used colloquially by Californian poverty lawyers and chose to adopt it because interviewees in her study appreciated and understood it. The apparent simultaneous establishment of the term *burnout* by Freudenberger, a clinician, and Maslach, a researcher, marked the beginning of two traditions within the field—a practical approach primarily concerned with assessment, prevention, and treatment, and a scientific approach mainly focused on research and theory. Schaufeli and Buunk (2003) explain that these two traditions developed relatively independently of one another

with the practical approach prevailing during the earlier pioneering phase, in which interest was influenced more by pragmatic than scholarly concerns.

Defining Burnout

A significant challenge to professional practice and the advancement of empirical research into burnout across a range of domains has been the attainment of a universal definition. The similarity of symptoms that the individual experiencing burnout may display to those of related conditions, such as anxiety and depression, has resulted in gray areas surrounding the terms boundaries. Within the professional literature there are numerous theories of burnout spanning individual, interpersonal, and organizational approaches (Schaufeli & Buunk, 2003). Although a range of definitions has been proposed as part of these theories, one of the most accepted is one of the first that was put forward—that of Maslach and Jackson (1981, 1984). Burnout was originally defined by Maslach and Jackson (1981) with specific reference to helping professions such as nursing, teaching, childcare work, and poverty lawyers. The authors described these professions as those who do *people work*, and in developing a model of burnout, explained how the everyday nature of these professions made individuals working within them susceptible to burnout. They suggested that helping professionals are required: ". . . to spend considerable time in intense involvement with other people . . . [and that the] . . . staff-client interaction is centered around the client's current problems (psychological, social, and/or physical) and is therefore charged with feelings of anger, embarrassment, fear or despair. Solutions for these problems are not always obvious and easily obtained, thus adding ambiguity and frustration to the situation" (p. 99). In addition, the result of continuous exposure to such circumstances leads to chronic stress that not only is emotionally draining but also increases vulnerability to burnout. Maslach and Jackson (1984) later extended their definition of burnout so that it consisted of three distinct dimensions by proposing that burnout is a "psychological syndrome of emotional exhaustion, depersonalization, and reduced sense of performance accomplishment that can occur among individuals who work with people in some capacity" (p. 134). According to this definition, and as proposed within their stage model, an individual experiencing burnout over time initially becomes emotionally exhausted and experiences extreme fatigue, and this further reduces their resources to be able to cope with the demands of the situation. A consequence of these feelings of exhaustion is the second dimension of depersonalization, which is characterized by negative and cynical attitudes toward the source of stress. Although such a defensive coping strategy may help to deal with the initial feelings of emotional exhaustion, they also can serve to place more emotional strain on the individual—and, in turn, lead to further (and often greater) feelings of exhaustion. Combined emotional exhaustion and depersonalization cause the individual to evaluate themselves negatively, and they become unhappy and dissatisfied. This leads them to experience a sense of reduced performance accomplishment, and it is proposed that this dimension exacerbates the feelings of emotional exhaustion and depersonalization further.

Maslach and Jackson (1981, 1984) originally defined burnout as a construct that was limited to occur within individuals working in helping professions. Since then, they have broadened the definition to relate to other types of work and now see burnout as a crisis in one's relationship with work in general, rather than a crisis in one's relationship with people at work. As a result exhaustion now refers to fatigue irrespective of the cause. Depersonalization also has become known as *cynicism* as denoted by a distant and indifferent attitude toward others at work, and performance accomplishment is now described as *professional efficacy* and incorporates both social and nonsocial aspects of occupational accomplishment (Schaufeli & Buunk, 2003).

Defining Burnout in Sport

A striking feature of the burnout in sport literature is the widespread agreement that there is no agreement on a universal definition (Dale &

Weinberg, 1990; Fender, 1989; Gould, 1997; Raedeke et al., 2002). Dale and Weinberg identify five common features of definitions of burnout, including (1) exhaustion, (2) negative change in response to others, (3) attitudes toward performance accomplishment, (4) results of chronic stress, and (5) occurs at the individual level.

Generally, the most widely accepted definition of burnout within the sport domain is that offered by Smith (1986), who defines burnout as "a psychological, emotional and at times physical withdrawal from a formerly pursued and enjoyable activity in response to excessive stress or dissatisfaction" (p. 39). The individual here has become worn down over time by their involvement in sport. The activity they once loved has become something they now dislike and from which they wish to be distanced. Distancing behavior that may result can include absence from training or competition, lateness to or early departure from sessions, as well as a distancing and social disengagement from others in the sport environment such as peers and teammates. Recently, Raedeke and colleagues (Raedeke, 1997; Raedeke et al., 2002; Raedeke & Smith, 2001) have returned to Maslach and Jackson's (1984) definition from the professional literature to offer a sport-specific, athlete-focused definition. This definition is framed in the delineating signs and symptoms of burnout and adopts the three dimensions of burnout (i.e., emotional exhaustion, depersonalization, and reduced sense of performance accomplishment) originally proffered by Maslach and Jackson (1984). To facilitate the use of these dimensions in the sport domain, Raedeke et al. (2002) examined what is central to the athletic experience and modified the dimensions relative to that context. Emotional exhaustion is associated with intense training and competition. The experience of a reduced sense of accomplishment for the athlete is in terms of skills and abilities. The athlete may be unable to achieve personal goals or performs below expectations. Raedeke and Smith (2001) report that depersonalization has not been identified as a salient dimension in athlete burnout, but that devaluation has. As a result, they have coined this dimension as *sport devaluation*, and it is associated with characteristics of burnout such as loss of interest, "don't care" attitude, and resentment. In the context of swimming, Raedeke et al. (2002) offer the following sport specific definition of burnout: "A withdrawal from swimming noted by a reduced sense of accomplishment, devaluation/resentment of sport, and physical/psychological exhaustion" (p. 181).

Burnout, Dropout, Overtraining, and Staleness

Providing a clear definition of burnout has been compounded in part by the close association and key characteristics which this syndrome shares with the related concepts of dropout, overtraining, and staleness. There is considerable overlap among them, and historically the boundaries seem always to have been blurred. These concepts also are considered to form a sequence of events in that the overtrained may begin to experience feelings of staleness that, in turn, may lead to burnout and eventual dropout.

The end product of burnout, if not managed effectively, is withdrawal or dropout from the activity. However, not all dropout in sport is the result of burnout (Gould & Dieffenbach, 2002). There are many reasons for attrition in sport, and burnout is just one of them. Individuals may simply want to try something new, or aspects of their life change and other priorities emerge. Gould (1997) explains that athletes who discontinue sport as a result of burnout do so because of prolonged, excessive stress. Other athletes who dropout have not experienced this prolonged stress.

The conditions of overtraining and staleness and their relationship with burnout will be discussed in more detail within the *Theories and Models of Burnout in Sport* section later in the chapter, but some recent definitions of the terms are offered here. In a review chapter of overtraining, Raglin and Wilson (2000) comment that the use of terminology within the literature has been inconsistent. They explain that overtraining has been defined in both positive and negative terms and as a stimulus, response, or process. A distinction is also made between the use of the term by European coaches and sport scientists, and in North America. In Europe, it is considered to reflect the detrimental effects of excessive training, and, in North America to be a beneficial, prescribed period of training but which sometimes results in reduced performance. More recently, Gould and Dieffenbach (2002) offer that a consensus definition of overtraining now exists through the work of a special task force formulated by the U.S. Olympic Committee (comprising elite coaches and sport scientist specialists in the field). This committee defines overtraining as "a syndrome that results when excessive, usually physical, overload on an athlete occurs without adequate rest" (p. 25). In other words, the athlete is unable to sufficiently recover from the overload. The consequences of this overload are performance decrements, an inability to train, and potentially staleness and even burnout.

Staleness often has been used synonymously with the term burnout, but more recent research has begun to provide a clearer distinction for the term (Kentta, Hassmen, & Raglin, 2001; Raglin, Sawamura, Alexiou, Hassmen, & Kentta, 2000). Staleness is generally associated with a negative outcome of overtraining that is the result of the athlete's failure to adapt to the prescribed training regimen (Raglin & Wilson, 2000). Raglin et al. explain that a hallmark of staleness "is an unexpected and long-term loss of performance that cannot be attributed to factors such as illness or injury" (p. 61). A range of symptoms has been associated with staleness but the most consistent include loss of appetite, mood disturbance, depression, and increased perceptions of effort (Kentta et al., 2001; Raglin et al., 2000).

Distinguishing burnout from related conditions such as overtraining and staleness is difficult, but one of the key differences is that burnout has a broader range of possible antecedents. Overtraining and staleness both result from too much physical training. Burnout, though, results from chronic stress that could be induced by both training and nontraining parameters (e.g., coach interactions, restrictions on other activities).

Signs, Symptoms, and Consequences of Burnout

Symptoms of burnout have been well documented. Although burnout has been described as a unique and personal experience, in that the experiences of no two individuals are the same (Gould, Tuffey, Udry, & Loehr, 1997), its symptomology is highly similar to related conditions and a number of physical disease processes. Through the sharing of symptoms with conditions such as depression, job stress, anxiety, overtraining, and chronic fatigue, burnout is less distinctive as a term, and this has in part led to the lack of clarity surrounding a definition of the term. It has been suggested that the first step in diagnosis is to rule out physical conditions such as anemia and cardiac problems.

A Practitioner's Model of Burnout

In an attempt to provide an overview of burnout in athletes for medical practitioners and other consultants, Cresswell and Eklund (2003a) present a model of the athlete burnout syndrome stemming from their work with professional rugby players. These authors offer a summary of early signs, symptoms, potential consequences of athlete burnout, as well as potential intervention strategies. A brief overview of this model will be provided here in order to examine signs, symptoms, and consequences of burnout in sport.

The early signs that precede burnout are indicative of athletes who are *at risk* to experiencing burnout, and include key characteristics of the syndrome such as enduring negative mood shifts, an athlete struggling to meet professional and personal obligations, feelings of disappointment and frustration, feeling physically tired, difficulty in communicating or unhappiness with social life (this may include failure to get on with others in an usual manner or abruptness in social interactions), and feeling that they are receiving insufficient support from support staff. Cresswell and Eklund (2003a) make the important distinction that these early warning signs may be subjective signs (relating to the athletes' own perceptions) or objective signs (observable by others). They

explain that it is the athletes' own perceptions that determine if elements actually indicate burnout or not, although the signs that are observable by others also may aid the role of those who are responsible for the athletes' welfare. Identification of these early warning signs permits the employment of proactive management strategies to prevent or reduce the incidence of burnout.

In their applied article the authors present two contrasting examples of an athlete who is experiencing burnout against one who is not, in order to outline burnout symptoms (Cresswell & Eklund, 2003a). Typically, the types of symptoms displayed by the burned-out athlete include mental and physical exhaustion, feelings of isolation, low confidence, difficulty in concentrating during performance, and feelings that their career is not moving forward and that their own contribution to the team is small or not valued by teammates, coaches, and management. Although the contrasting examples provide a useful means through which to discuss the symptomology, the authors acknowledge that such clear examples are rare because of the large variations that exist between individuals' stress perceptions and personal experiences. The range of experiences and associated symptoms has made burnout a complex and multifaceted syndrome, and in describing its complexity, Edelwich and Brodsky (1980) summarize the situation in arguing that "burnout is easier to observe and describe than it is to explain" (p. 13).

Consequences of Burnout

In their review of 25 years of burnout research within the work domain, Schaufeli and Buunk (2003) classify the consequences of burnout into five categories. The categories are consequences associated with (1) affective (e.g., feeling gloomy, tearful, and depressed); (2) cognitive (e.g., helplessness, hopelessness, and powerlessness); (3) physical (e.g., emotional exhaustion and somatic complaints); (4) behavioral (e.g., smoking, consumption of medication, impaired performance, and absenteeism); and (5) motivational (e.g., lack of zeal, enthusiasm, and interest) aspects. Within the sport context, the impact of burnout echoes much of what has been experienced in the work domain. Referring again to Cresswell and Eklund's (2003a) model of athlete burnout, potential consequences include decreased commitment to the sport, which may be reflected in the loss of enthusiasm for preparation and competition, or reluctance/lack of motivation to self-initiate work in training sessions, performance decrements that may in turn impact selection/ nonselection and the subsequent implications of this to funding and athlete confidence, increased susceptibility to injury and illness, and the requirement of extended recovery periods to return to fitness. The burned-out individual also may experience mood changes that affect social consequences in that they are difficult to be around, or prefer to distance themselves from others. The social distancing behavior may ultimately end in withdrawal from the sport entirely. With regard to these social consequences Cresswell and Eklund (2003a) also discuss the wider implications of burnout to significant others within the athlete's social network. Burnout may lead to relationship problems and family or marital issues. Antisocial behaviors in the form of drug and alcohol abuse may occur in more progressive cases of burnout.

Theories and Models of Burnout in Sport

Within the burnout literature there have been four traditional theories that have sought to explain how burnout is caused and subsequently develops in sport. For practitioners, these theories offer the opportunity to propose or implement intervention strategies that may both prevent the incidence of burnout among both athletes and coaches, and manage the condition more effectively to reduce its debilitative effects on the individual's well-being and performance.

Silva's (1990) Negative Training Stress Response Model

Much confusion has existed as to where the boundaries of the concepts of burnout, overtraining, and staleness start and finish, and how

exactly they are related to each other. They have often been used interchangeably to essentially mean one and the same, and as a consequence have been applied inaccurately in some instances. Silva (1990) attempted to offer some clarification of these terms in his negative training stress response model. The model proposes that burnout is a negative product of excessive training. Physical training places stresses on the athlete that can be both positive and negative. Although positive stress results in positive adaptations and training gains, negative stresses such as too much training lead to negative adaptation and negative training responses. Silva states that these responses include staleness ("an initial failure of the body's adaptive mechanisms to cope with psycho-physiological stress," p. 10), overtraining ("detectable psycho-physiological malfunctions characterized by easily observed changes in the athletes' mental orientation and physical performance," p. 10), and burnout ("an exhaustive psycho-physiological response exhibited as a result of frequent, sometimes extreme, but generally ineffective efforts to meet excessive training and sometimes competitive demands," p. 11). These responses are hypothesized to lie on a continuum from staleness experienced as a result of overtraining, and which if unmanaged, progresses to the more severe state of burnout (Gould & Dieffenbach, 2002). Although there was initially limited support for Silva's model (Gould et al., 1996a), recent developments in research that incorporate aspects of this perspective have emerged (e.g., Kallus & Kellmann, 2000; Kentta et al., 2001; Tenebaum, Jones, Kitsantas, Sacks, & Berwick, 2003), and we will address these later in the chapter.

Smith's (1986) Cognitive–Affective Stress Model

Smith (1986) offered a four-stage cognitive-affective stress model to explain stress-induced burnout. The model proposes that burnout is a process that involves physical, psychological, and behavioral components. An overarching feature of these components is that they are influenced by motivation and personality factors.

The first stage of the model refers to situational demands that the athlete is placed under, and may include such factors as intense training schedules. The second stage involves cognitive appraisal of the situation. Some athletes may perceive the situation as threatening and that the demands outweigh their resources to cope with them. This appraisal governs the nature and intensity of emotional responses, and negative appraisal may lead to stress. In the third stage of physiological responses, if the situation has been perceived as threatening, physiological changes occur such as increased tension and fatigue, insomnia, lethargy, and illness. The fourth and final stage, behavioral responses, is characterized by types of coping and task behavior such as performance decrements and withdrawal that result from the physiological responses. An additional feature of this model is that the burnout process is considered to be circular and continuous, where behavioral responses feed back into the situational demands stage. Reciprocal relationships also are hypothesized between the four stages (Gould et al., 1996a).

Smith (1986) also asserts, however, that not all withdrawal from sport is burnout-related. In an attempt to differentiate between burnout-induced withdrawal and other-determinant withdrawal (i.e., dropout), Smith applied Thibaut and Kelley's (1959) social exchange theory as a framework. The principles of this theory propose that human behavior is governed by the desire to maximize positive experiences and to minimize negative. Individuals participate in activities as long as they are favorable, and this favorability is determined by the balance of costs and rewards and how these compare to the outcomes of alternative activities (Weinberg & Gould, 2003). If activities fall below the comparison level for alternatives, individuals are likely to withdraw in the hope of pursuing alternative activities.

Smith (1986) reports that the most prevalent reason for dropout in youth sport is the attraction of alternative activities. These alternatives are perceived to be above the outcomes of participation in their current sport. For the individual who experiences burnout, however, withdrawal results from an increase in stress-induced costs for the present activity. The previously enjoyed activity becomes an aversive source of stress.

Coakley's (1992) Unidimensional Identity Development and External Control Model

Although stress-induced perspectives such as Smith's (1986) model have dominated the literature, alternative approaches have also been advanced and supported. Coakley's (1992) unidimensional identity development and external control model postulates that stress is a symptom of burnout rather than a cause. Through a sociological perspective, this model asserts that burnout is a social problem that is the product of the organization of sport. Specifically, organizational constraints prevent the development of a multifaceted identity. Exclusive involvement in sport means that the young performer is unable to explore and develop other aspects of their identity. They become identified and recognized by others through sport, and their identity becomes hinged upon success in sport. Furthermore, the organization of the sport results in limited autonomy for the young person. Decision making is in the hands of others. According to the model, burnout in athletes results from stress associated with the creation of a unidimensional identity and a lack of control over one's own life.

Schmidt and Stein's (1991) Sport Commitment Model

Another divergent approach to the stress-induced perspective of burnout is Schmidt and Stein's (1991) sport commitment model of burnout. This model suggests that burnout is more than a simple reaction to stress, and that, although everyone can experience stress, not everyone who experiences stress burns out (Raedeke, 1997). Schmidt and Stein initially contended that there are three primary determinants that influence athlete commitment, and that athletes who experience burnout are committed to sport for reasons that differ from those who do not experience burnout. The determinants of athlete commitment are satisfaction based on rewards and costs associated with sport, attractiveness of alternative options, and resources athletes have invested in sport. The model proposes that burnout is likely to occur in athletes who display an entrapment profile, where they are participating in the sport because they have to rather than want to. This occurs when the athlete experiences high costs and low rewards but remains in the sport because they feel that they have invested a lot in terms of resources, and perceive a lack of attractive alternatives (high investment and low alternatives). This contrasts with the dropout athlete who is not committed to the sport. The perspective has received more recent attention through the work of Raedeke and colleagues (e.g., Raedeke, 1997; Raedeke & Smith 2001), who highlight different commitment profiles which may predispose individuals to burnout. To illustrate, Raedeke (1997) describes the entrapped swimmer who is participating in their sport because they "have to" as opposed to "wanting to," and, as such, is more susceptible to burnout.

Stress and Recovery Perspectives of Burnout

Burnout research has seen a rejuvenated interest in the field from the late 1990s and since the millennium. Alongside the new measurement tools that have been developed during this time, some new theoretical perspectives have now emerged. In particular, there has been a fresh perspective from Europe that has aimed to explain the complex relationships among staleness, overtraining, recovery, stress, burnout, coping, and mood through psychological, sociological, and physiological frameworks. A key text that the reader is referred to for an overview of this work is *Enhancing Recovery: Preventing Underperformance in Athletes* (Kellmann, 2002). This stress-recovery approach suggests that burnout is the product of accumulating stress (which is both training and nontraining based) without appropriate recovery. Stress is defined within this model as an:

> . . . unspecific reaction syndrome characterized by deviation from the psychobiological homeostatic state of the organism. Stress is accompanied by emotional symptoms such as anxiety and anger as well as elevated autonomic and central activation, humoral responses, changes in immune function, and behavioural changes. Stress sends processes of adaptation and coping into action. (Kallus & Kellmann, 2000, p. 209)

The authors explain that recovery is less well defined but it is complementary to the concept of stress. Strategies included in recovery are goal-oriented regeneration, physiological and behavioral processes, social activities, and elements of coping responses. Overtraining occurs when an athlete is exposed to stress and is unable to recover sufficiently from this exposure. Progressively, this imbalance of stress and recovery leads to staleness and then burnout. This approach advocates a multidimensional perspective to the treatment of conditions such as burnout, which encompasses physiological, emotional, cognitive, behavioral/performance, and social aspects of the problem.

A second perspective that has adopted a multidimensional conceptualization of burnout and emphasized the importance of sufficient (and quality) recovery in preventing burnout is that of Kentta and Hassmen (1998). These authors have advanced a conceptual model of underrecovery and overtraining, as well as a new approach to the monitoring of recovery (Total Quality Recovery). Central to this approach is the concept of staleness, which is referred to as a "severe outcome resulting from an imbalance between total stressors and total recovery, which is largely determined by the overall capacity (stress tolerance) of the individual" (Kentta, 2001, p. 41). The psychosociophysiological perspective adopted suggests that conditions such as overtraining, staleness, and burnout are a product of three subsystems—physiology, psychology, and sociology. An individual's adaptation or maladaptation to training is affected by stress (training and nontraining), recovery (quality of), and stress tolerance (capacity of the individual to cope with stress). Findings from research that has examined the prevalence of staleness among young performers by Kentta et al. (2001) have reported that 35% of subjects had experienced staleness at least once. Of these, a further 41% had experienced burnout as indicated by motivational loss toward training (Kentta et al., 2001).

To the practitioner working with overtrained, stale, or burned-out athletes, the multidimensionality of these new perspectives provides a framework through which to explore both training and competition environments that may highlight contributory factors that have brought about these states of underperformance. Furthermore, they present opportunities to reflect on current practices and assess athlete responses to them, and through the development of such instruments as the RESTQ (discussed later) it may be possible to intervene earlier with athletes who are showing warning signs associated with overtraining, staleness, and burnout.

Theories of Coach Burnout

At present, there is only one published model of coach burnout (Kelley, 1994), although this model has also been extended for use in examining burnout among athletic directors. In testing this model, Kelley hypothesized that the personal and situational variables of coaching issues, social support, hardiness, gender, and win/loss record would predict stress appraisal. Types of coaching issues include budget management, coach athlete relationships, and role conflict. Stress appraisal would then, in turn, predict burnout. The model is loosely based upon that of Smith (1986) but has been developed specifically to target burnout in coaches. Research findings have reported partial support for the model in that both coaching issues and hardiness were found to be predictive of stress appraisal in both male and female coaches. Social support was found to be predictive of perceived stress in males but not in females, and winning percentage was not found to predict burnout in either gender. Perceived stress was shown to be a predictor of all three dimensions of burnout (emotional exhaustion, depersonalization, and reduced performance accomplishment).

Examining Burnout in Sport

Research interest in burnout in sport really began in earnest during the early 1980s. The professional literature and popular media had seen a boom in the popularity of the term, and from the beginning it seemed to be a term to which everyone could relate. Although the image associated with the incidence of burnout in sport is generally that of the exhausted athlete who is marred by underperformance and the loss of their former passion for their sport, initial research actually focused on coach burnout. Referring directly to findings in the professional domain, Caccese and Mayerberg (1984) drew comparisons between the role of the coach and individuals in helping professions. They proposed that human relationships were a central feature of the coaching profession, and this, together with the stressful and volatile nature of the coaching environment, made coaches a prime candidate for burnout. Since the publication of this original study, burnout has been examined empirically in other individuals working in sport, including athletic trainers, athletic directors, officials, and, of course, athletes.

Much of what has been written about burnout in athletes appears to focus on exposure to chronic stress in both the training and competition environment. Weinberg and Gould (2003) explain that unrelenting training regimes have led to an increase in the incidence of conditions such as overtraining and burnout in sport. They describe that through the pressure to win, there has resulted a blurring of the season and off-season. Emphasis has been placed on "more training is better," "starting training earlier," and "you have to train year round if you are to compete at a high level." The pursuit of athletic excellence has driven performers and support teams to try to gain the edge, but for some hopefuls their experience has led Gould and Dieffenbach (2002) to warn others: "Be careful in trying to get the edge that you don't over do it and lose the edge" (p. 25).

Within both research and anecdotal accounts, analogies frequently are used to describe burnout in athletes and a recurrent sentiment of these analogies is of "a candle that once glowed brightly, began to flicker, and eventually extinguished" (Raedeke et al., 2002, p. 182). Here burnout is considered to be a phenomenon that leads to the curtailment of the careers of bright and promising young athletes before their potential has been fulfilled. From this standpoint, young athletes are becoming the victim of these increasing demands, and withdrawal from sport as a result of burnout is the endpoint. In terms of optimizing performance standards within sporting systems, the impact of burnout on both training and competitive performances and the retention and continued development of sporting excellence, presents a very real concern. Feigley (1984) summarizes these implications to national performance standards further in the following statement: "Athletes, particularly female athletes, often retire from their sport during their mid-teens, long before they have reached their physical and psychological prime. The losses created by this early attrition rate are great in terms of unfulfilled human potential and a lowered quality of our national team programs" (p. 109). Research examining coach burnout suggests that these concerns also could be extended to the loss or early departure of young coaches from the profession (Kosa, 1990). Withdrawal from the activity or sport is not the only consequence of burnout; rather, it is the end result of a chronic process (see Situation Study 1).

Research on Athletes

A review of the literature reveals that less than 25 studies have been conducted examining burnout among athletes (these include Coakley, 1992; Cohn, 1990; Gould et al., 1996a, 1996b, 1997; Harlick & McKenzie, 2000; Kellmann & Gunther, 2000; Kentta et al., 2001; Lai & Wiggins, 2003; Price & Weiss, 2000; Raedeke, 1997; Raedeke & Smith, 2001; Raglin et al., 2000; Silva, 1990; Tenebaum et al., 2003; Udry, Gould, Bridges, & Tuffey, 1997; Vealey et al., 1998).

This research has sought to understand more about the factors that cause burnout, and its subsequent consequences. As yet no causal relationships have been established between the variables examined but there are a number of potential correlates of burnout that have shown reproducible associations across a small number of studies. These correlates can be divided into two broad categories of psychological (e.g., trait anxiety and commitment) and demographic or situational (e.g., age and training loads). In examining potential causes and consequences of burnout, researchers have tended to focus more on psychological than demographic or situational factors.

Burnout has been positively associated with the following variables: amotivation, anxiety, training stress/underrecovery and failure adaptation, mood disturbance, and staleness (e.g., Gould et al., 1996a, 1996b, 1997; Harlick & McKenzie, 2000; Vealey et al., 1998; Kentta et al., 2001; Raglin et al., 2000; Tenebaum et al., 2003). Motivation, intrinsic motivation, enjoyment, coping, and social support are all negatively associated with burnout (e.g., Gould et al., 1996a, 1996b, 1997; Harlick & McKenzie, 2000; Raedeke, 1997; Raedeke & Smith, 2001; Udry et al., 1997). Research has shown that athletes who experience burnout are lower in intrinsic motivation or are amotivated, perceive less enjoyment or fail to enjoy their involvement in sport, possess ineffective coping strategies, have low or negative social support, and may exhibit signs of stress and anxiety that can be the result of intense physical training or insufficient recovery. Episodes of staleness may also precede burnout. The association between burnout and extrinsic motivation and parental involvement is indeterminate at this time as findings are conflicting. In studies of parental involvement in burnout among junior tennis players, Udry et al. (1997) and Harlick and McKenzie (2000) report both positive and negative effects of parents. That is, parents may contribute to feelings of being burned out through acting as an additional stressor, or—conversely—may take on the role of a buffer or mediator who helps to reduce their son or daughter's exposure to stress (see Situation Study 2). The following are comments made by players about the high-stress environment that negative parents created, and, in

Situation Study 1

The Problem Kid, or the Kid with the Problem?

Mark had been swimming his whole life. He couldn't remember a time when he hadn't been in the water. He loved it; it was that simple. From early on, Mark's talent and natural ability for swimming also were apparent. He was enthusiastic to join a swimming club when his parents were approached by a coach at the local pool; swimming fast and faster still became his drive. At age 14, he secured his place on the national team, and had been representing his country ever since.

At age 18, Mark elected to take a year or two out of education to train full time, and swimming had become a very different place for him. His life was swimming. He was known by everyone as "Mark the swimmer" and was introduced to new people with that title. People had high hopes of him and an Olympic campaign was expected to figure prominently in his future career. Mark, however, no longer felt the same about swimming. The sport he had loved he had now grown to hate. Each day was the same routine and he was constantly being pushed. He would wake up exhausted and go to sleep exhausted. He had not felt like the old Mark for more months than he could remember. Where he once had found solitude in the water, a place to forget about the rest of the world, he now found the sound of the water against him deafening and was desperate for each session to be over. He no longer attacked his races, and even when he tried to put all that he had left into the race, the results failed to come. The passion and hunger had died, and what was left was anger, hurt, and frustration. Swimming was eating away at him and he was becoming the "problem athlete" that he had always despised. This was the kind of athlete who strode around poolside, with an I don't care and can't be bothered attitude. Coaches didn't like them, and teammates resented them. He withdrew from people and found it easier to just disappear. Things had gone from a few almost unbearable days to a procession of them, rolling from one long week into the next. There was no escape. His coping strategy was to spend as little time as possible around swimming and other swimmers. He was now last in and first out, and absent when possible. Happiness only came when he was away from the pool. The hardest part of all, however, was the realization that he wanted out, and that no one could hear or see that this was what he wanted and desperately needed.

contrast, the supportive behaviors that positive parents demonstrated (Udry et al., 1997):

> I always felt like I was supposed to win, and I never felt like anything I did was ever enough for him [father], you know. Even after I'd win a tournament or I'd do something well, even—on that same day—he'd already want something else, and I never felt like he was really satisfied with how well I did, like he was really, you know, proud of me. I always felt like I wasn't meeting his expectations. (p. 375)

> They [parents] pushed me to work, but I don't think that is wrong either. When somebody wants to do something and you think that they have the opportunity to achieve what they want, then you should do all that you can to help them. (p. 376)

Several studies have employed a qualitative research approach to the study of athlete burnout (e.g., Coakley, 1992; Cohn, 1990; Gould et al., 1996b, 1997; Harlick & McKenzie, 2000; Tenebaum et al., 2003; Udry et al., 1997). The use

Situation Study 2

Parental Pressure—Whose Dreams?

Christine is an enthusiastic and talented young soccer player who has been on national age group teams and development squads since she was 12 years old. Recently, though, she has been complaining of the pressure and expectations from home. She says her parents aren't interested in how she plays and only want to know if she's scored or been on the winning team. When she loses, her parents mutter about the time and money that it is costing them to support her soccer. Her younger brother and sister complain that everything revolves around Christine's soccer and they're sick of being dragged around to watch her play or train. Christine says that even the family's holidays are centered on soccer and she feels she can never escape it. All of this makes Christine feel pressured to succeed and that nothing will ever be good enough to pay back her family.

of these types of methods has enabled researchers to gain a better understanding of the individual nature of burnout and factors contributing to it. For example, Cohn (1990) was able to examine sources of stress and perceived causes of burnout by interviewing 10 active high school golfers. The results identified too much playing/practice, lack of fun and enjoyment, no new goals to strive for, going into a slump, and pressure to do well from self, coaches, and parents as the primary causes of their burnout. Coakley's (1992) qualitative study with 15 adolescent athletes reported that burnout is caused by the social organization of high performance sport interfering with their development of autonomy and independence, and also individuals constraining the development of the athlete's identity outside of sport. This is illustrated in the case of Mark (see Situation Study 1), who had developed a strong and exclusive athletic identity through his participation in swimming. The foreclosure of other aspects of his identity in order to train on a full-time basis, which could have occurred as a result of the demands and expectations of his environment or be the result of his own choice, put Mark at risk of burnout.

In their series of studies, Gould and colleagues (Gould et al., 1996b; Udry et al., 1997) interviewed 10 former elite tennis players who experienced high levels of burnout during their junior tennis careers. The interviews focused on the signs and symptoms of burnout, how players responded to these signs and symptoms, factors perceived to lead to burnout, suggestions for preventing burnout, and involvement of significant others. This research identified both physical (injuries, illness, or being physically asymptomatic) and mental (lacking energy/motivation, negative feelings, feelings of isolation, concentration problems, and high and low mood) characteristics of burnout. These characteristics, in turn, also formed the basis of different strains and substrains of burnout. Gould and colleagues (1997) initially identified two main types of burnout for those athletes who had withdrawn from the sport completely, and those who were *active burnouts* in that they continued to participate despite experiencing burnout but had curtailed their involvement. From the identification that different types of burnout seemed to exist, further inquiry led to the establishment of different strains of burnout based upon their antecedents, symptoms, and consequences. Two major strains emerged: *physically driven* and *social-psychologically driven*. Physically driven burnout is essentially the result of overtraining, and heavy training and competition loads. Social-psychologically driven burnout is the

Situation Study 3

Pressure in Tennis—It's Not Just the Players

Stephen was a gifted coach who had developed a good track record in producing high-level junior tennis players. Most of these players, however, were naturally passed on through the system to other coaches, and had failed to make an impact on the game. Stephen was disappointed with this lack of follow through and wanted to coach his players from grassroots to their full potential within the senior game. Stephen worked with one such player who was now making the transition from the junior to the senior game. This player wanted his support on a one-to-one basis, yet did not have the funds for a traveling coach on a year-round basis. Stephen was then in the position of running an entire tennis program for a developing club, which meant long and arduous hours on court, inevitable administration loads, and phone calls from pushy parents 6 days a week. He could only devote segments of coaching time to his protégé who deeply valued his input, and was unable to travel away with the player for long periods on the lonely tournament circuit. Nevertheless, Stephen made an effort to do everything possible and greatly enjoyed the in-depth work, video analysis, and high-performance coaching details that would make the difference at the highest levels of the game. Over time, Stephen began to pay the price physically of trying to manage multiple roles, and became resentful and frustrated that he could not maximize his performance role with the senior player. He felt added pressure from his home life as his girlfriend began to resent the total amount of time he spent at the tennis club or away at tennis events. He also felt pressure from his upcoming players at the club to devote more individual time to their programs. Stephen began to struggle sleeping at nights, felt forced to work through colds as he was largely self-employed, felt disillusioned, and physically worn out, yet could not see an easy solution to what may turn out to be a destructive pattern of behavior.

result of athlete perfectionism and situation pressure such as parental or coach pressure. The identification of these different strains of burnout suggests the need to consider carefully the structure and nature of interventions for individuals who become affected by the condition.

Research on Coaches

In a similar fashion to athlete burnout studies, investigations into coach burnout have explored factors contributing to coach burnout (see Situation 3). Two studies, however, also have sought to examine how coach burnout affects athlete burnout and psychological responses of athletes (Price & Weiss, 2000; Vealey, Armstrong, Comar, & Greenleaf, 1998). Price and Weiss (2000)

assessed coach burnout (via the *Maslach Burnout Inventory*; Maslach & Jackson, 1981), coaching behaviors, and athletes' psychological responses among a sample of 193 female soccer players and 15 head coaches of high school teams. By examining both players and coaches, these researchers assessed how levels of coach burnout can impact perceptions of behavior by their players. In addition, they examined how coach behavior can impact psychological outcomes in athletes (e.g., anxiety, enjoyment, and burnout). Coaches higher in emotional exhaustion were perceived by their teams as providing less training/instruction and social support, while making fewer autocratic (and more democratic) decisions. Depersonalization and reduced personal accomplishment were not found to be significantly related to coaching behaviors. Results also revealed that lower perceived competence and enjoyment, and higher anxiety and burnout, were associated with coaches who exhibited less frequent training/instruction, social support, and positive feedback. These were generally characteristics of coaches experiencing high levels of burnout.

Vealey et al. (1998) examined the influence of perceived coaching behavior and burnout and competitive anxiety in female college athletes. Findings reported that coach burnout was significantly related to perceived coaching behaviors, perceived coaching behavior was predictive of athletes' burnout, and athletes' anxiety and athlete burnout were significantly related. What emerges from this research, as well as the study by Price and Weiss (2000), is the need for coaches to consider their behavior in both contributing to their own feelings of burnout from coaching, as well as potentially adding to burnout among their athletes. As a result of the multiple roles that the coach undertakes, and also the often intense nature of the coach-athlete relationship, coaches are in a crucial position to safeguard against athlete burnout. Furthermore, coaches also need to be mindful of their own susceptibility to burnout. See Situation Study 4 for coaching behaviors that can lead to situations where burnout is more likely.

Perceived stress (Kelley, 1994), coaching issues (Kelley & Gill, 1993), role conflict (Capel, Sisley, & Desertrain, 1987), role ambiguity (Quigley, Slack, & Smith, 1987) and gender (Pastore & Judd, 1993) have all been found to be positively associated with burnout across research with coaches. Coaches who experienced coaching issues such as budget considerations, coach-athlete relationship, role conflict, and so forth are considered to experience higher levels of perceived stress, which in turn predicts burnout (Kelley, 1994). In studies that have reported gender differences, females have been shown to have higher levels of emotional exhaustion and a greater sense of reduced performance accomplishment compared to their male counterparts (Kelley & Gill, 1993; Pastore & Judd, 1992). Causes of these dimensions of burnout are attributed to female coaches feeling overloaded with work, experiencing role conflict often between home life and coaching (Drake & Herbert, 2002), and the tendency for female sport to be marginalized over the male sport program and feeling undervalued in their job. Male coaches are, however, higher generally in depersonalization than females (Dale & Weinberg, 1989; Pastore & Judd, 1992). The negativity that becomes associated with the activities coaches undertake with depersonalization has been suggested to possibly reflect the socialization process and the business-like "win orientated" focus of sport today, causing male coaches to be more impersonal toward their athletes (Vealey et al., 1998).

Much of what appears to contribute to coach burnout is contained within the coaching environment, and reflects the time-demanding nature of the role and the intense pressure that coaches find themselves under to produce results. Although the final performance is with the athlete on the day of competition, coaches are often the ones who are accountable long after the final whistle has been blown. In the case of Stephen (in Situation Study 3), the conflicting roles of performance director and coach have caused a considerable amount of stress in his life. The secondary effect could hinder the continued development and performance of his athletes. As performance standards become higher, together with the mass spectatorship of modern sport, demands on coaches are likely to increase as they have with athletes. It may be worthwhile in the future for governing bodies of sport to consider helping coaches develop appropriate skills through coach education, continued professional development, and mentoring schemes in order to develop effective coping strategies to handle these pressures and reduce or prevent the incidence of burnout among coaches.

Monitoring Burnout

Traditionally, self-report measures have been the popular research tool for measuring burnout within both the professional domain and the sport domain. More recently, developments

Situation Study 4

A combination of some or all of the following behaviors by coaches may lead to a situation in which burnout is more likely:

- *Year-round training with few rest periods, making the season artificially long*
- *Little variety in the type and intensity of training*
- *A "more is better" philosophy*
- *A focus on winning or normative comparison rather than on performance or improvement*
- *Expecting athletes to excel in all competitions, even those in which they may not have tapered*
- *Only seeing the individual as an athlete and giving little recognition to other aspects such as school or work commitments*
- *Autocratic decision making and failure to share goals or reasons for training and so on with athletes*
- *Treating second-tier players as "invisible"*
- *Making sure the athlete is aware that "my [coach] career is dependent on your performance"*
- *Failure to acknowledge and deal with postcompetition emotions in an effective way*

have taken place within sport psychology research that have seen the advancement of new instruments not only to facilitate more effective assessment of burnout for empirical enquiry but also for the monitoring of burnout by practitioners such as coaches and sport psychology consultants. These instruments are the Athlete Burnout Questionnaire and Recovery Stress Questionnaire.

Athlete Burnout Questionnaire

Raedeke and Smith (2001) have revisited Maslach and Jackson's (1984) original conceptualization of burnout as three separate dimensions in order to develop a specific tool for assessing athlete burnout, the *Athlete Burnout Questionnaire* (ABQ). The ABQ consists of 15 items relating to 3 subscales of emotional exhaustion, performance accomplishment, and sport devaluation. Responses are recorded using a 5-point Likert scale from *almost never* to *almost always*. Use of the ABQ in

empirical research to date is limited, but in a study comparing the construct validity of the ABQ with the more widely known *Maslach Burnout Inventory* (MBI-GS), Cresswell and Eklund (2003b) reported acceptable validity and satisfactory divergence, and supported the use of the ABQ in assessing sport burnout. The results of the ABQ provide a profile of athlete burnout based on the three dimensions, for which a separate score is recorded. This becomes important in terms of intervention in that one athlete at the early stages of burnout may appear to be experiencing greater emotional exhaustion, and hence in need of effective recovery strategies or physical rest, whereas another may be experiencing a significant sense of reduced accomplishment and, in turn, low self-confidence. The development of the profile can enable the coach, sport psychology consultant, or support staff working with the athlete to devise a tailored intervention that is likely to be more effective to the needs of the affected individual.

Recovery Stress Questionnaire

In an attempt to monitor in greater detail the relationship between stress and recovery and provide a means of enabling early identification of individuals who are experiencing stress or insufficient effective recovery, Kellmann and Kallus (2001) developed the *Recovery Stress Questionnaire* (RESTQ). This instrument contains subscales relating to stress and recovery aspects, and scores are provided for both. The aim is to assess the recovery state of individuals, which indicates the extent that they are physically or mentally stressed, whether or not they are capable of using individual strategies for recovery, as well as which strategies are used. A version has been developed for athletes (RESTQ-Sport; Kellmann & Kallus, 2001) and coaches (RESTQ-Coach; Kallus & Kellmann, 1995). Two subscales within the instrument refer specifically to burnout; these are emotional exhaustion and personal accomplishment. Applications of the RESTQ-Sport have been used successfully to monitor and screen athletes to identify incidences of stress and underrecovery in the lead up and during major competitions (Kellmann & Gunther, 2000), assess the effects of a yearly improved training schedule, and provide concrete recommendations for interventions (Kellmann & Gunther, 2000). The development of such a tool has created an excellent opportunity to bring together multidisciplinary support services to work collaboratively on the development and preparation of athletes across the range of performance standards.

Interventions

An interesting feature of the burnout literature is the lack of intervention studies to combat this condition. As discussed earlier, it appears to be a concept that athletes, practitioners in sport, and sports fan alike are able to relate to. Web-based searches using burnout as a keyword will produce hundreds of hits that advise the "Top Ten" ways to beat burnout, and periodicals and magazines providing further strategies aimed at the target audiences of athletes, coaches, and parents. Despite this information being readily available,

there is still much that we do not know and understand about burnout. Moreover, we do not know as yet how prevalent the incidence of burnout in youth sport truly is. This is something that there is no present way to gauge (Gould & Dieffenbach, 2002). The only current estimate that appears to exist is that by Gould and Dieffenbach (2002), which is based on a sample of 236 swimmers from Raedeke's (1997) research. It is estimated that 1–5% of these youth swimmers were experiencing burnout. Although this figure may not be high, there are athletes out on the playing court, practice field, running track, in the gymnasium, or in the pool who just don't want to be in the game anymore. The activity that once made them happy is now a negative experience, and is possibly one which they feel unable to leave.

One study that did seek to gain advice on how athletes with burnout may be helped and how the incidence of burnout might be reduced is that by Gould et al. (1996b). In this study, the authors asked junior tennis players who had experienced burnout for their recommendations on how burnout might be prevented. Their results were divided into three sections: Advice for Other Players, Advice for Parents, and Advice for Coaches.

Advice for Other Players

The players offered the following advice for other tennis players

- Play for your own reasons
- Balance tennis with other things
- No fun—no play
- Try to make it fun
- Relax
- Take time off

Advice for Parents

- Recognize optimal amount of "pushing needed"
- Lessen involvement
- Reduce importance of outcome

- Show support/empathy
- Parent–coach role separation/clarification
- Solicit player input

Advice for Coaches

- Cultivate personal involvement with player
- Have two-way communication with player
- Utilize player input
- Understand player feelings

This advice provides a very useful means of organizing potential intervention strategies in the sense that there are several key persons involved who can help prevent this condition from occurring. It is not simply about the player's response to training and competition, and how they manage the balance of their sport with other aspects of their life. Parents and coaches have an important role to play, and, as such, intervention also should look at developing awareness among these individuals possibly through the delivery of parent and coach education sessions.

Another publication that offers useful advice for consideration in the development of interventions is Cresswell and Eklund's (2003a) paper presenting research findings in professional rugby. This paper was discussed earlier in the section on signs, symptoms, and consequences of burnout, in which a practitioner's model of burnout was described. In the last tier of this model, the authors highlight a range of potential strategies, including the following:

- Time off training
- Time away from rugby
- Relaxation
- Life and Career Counseling (i.e., to attain more balance)
- Player rotation (scheduled rest from training and games)
- Increased involvement in decision making
- Specialized counseling (e.g., relationship counselor)
- Social support—teammates and family

- Ways to deal with stress
- Talk things over with someone
- Try a new approach to increase enjoyment

The authors make the distinction that intervention strategies can consist of a preventative or management focus on burnout. It is important to make this distinction in order to tailor interventions to the needs of the individual. Furthermore, and building on the notion of tackling burnout from a range of levels through different key persons (i.e., coach, athlete, and parent), Cresswell and Eklund (2003a) suggest that prevention and management of burnout may happen at the personal (e.g., skills and relaxation training) or organizational (e.g., player rotation, increased involvement in decision making) level. A significant point they make for the management of burnout is the assumption that individuals experiencing characteristics of burnout are motivated enough to learn and implement new strategies. This may be a key determining factor influencing the relative success of an intervention.

Although research on interventions is limited, what little information is available (together with recent advances in the field) suggests a number of common themes that may serve to prevent and manage burnout in sport, including:

- *Identify early warning signs—prevention is better than cure.* Coaches, parents, and athletes need to become aware and monitor periods of underperformance. It is more common that individuals will experience performance slumps than burnout, but the process of burnout has to start somewhere. Look out for the early warning signs.

- *Involve athletes in decision making.* This not only aids motivation but provides a sense of ownership, which can raise confidence.

- *Schedule time-outs.* Doing too much too soon, or not resting enough, can become a fast track to burnout if not handled effectively. Time-outs give athletes the opportunity to have time away from the sport, experience quality recovery, and return fresh and ready to go.

- *Quality recovery and management of training regimes.* Athletes who are driven to succeed (or driven by others) may not rest enough to satisfy the needs of their body. They are desperate to get better and improve, and feel that time off may set them back in training. By failing to rest and enable the body to recover more fully, they gradually become more fatigued and performance starts to slip. Initially, overtraining may occur in a bid to return their performance to its original standards, but staleness and burnout can be the end result.

- *Utilize athlete input—listen.* The athlete is the expert and they must feel comfortable enough with the coach and support staff to be open about how they feel they are performing or responding to competition and training. A more open dialogue could enable the warning signs to be picked up sooner.

- *Coach and parent support.* Social support is a key vehicle in both the prevention and management of burnout. By educating significant others within the athlete's social network (such as the parent or coach), these individuals may become effective buffers, able to mediate potential causes of burnout, as well as supporting an athlete who is experiencing burnout. The burned-out athlete may not always be an easy individual to deal with, or be around, and this can influence the quality of support (or the athletes' perception of it).

- *Make it fun—enjoyment is crucial.* Athletes that experience burnout probably once started out as athletes that loved their sport. They ate it, breathed it, and slept it, but over time that passion steadily ebbed away. By making training and competition fun and motivating, the love of the sport is more likely to continue. Equally, unhappy athletes are unlikely to produce their best performances. The variability principle of training is particularly important in endurance sports such as swimming where the mundane nature of trudging up and down the training pool may easily become boring and tiresome. Variety is the spice of life.

- *Time and lifestyle management.* Burnout is the result of exposure to chronic stress and this stress may be training or nontraining related. It is essential that athletes maintain a healthy balance in their life between work and play, and have time away from the sport environment. They come back revitalized and more eager to train and compete. This balance in lifestyle is not just a preventative measure for burnout but also ensures the enjoyment continues and that young performers move into adulthood with varied life experiences.

Case Study

Within the positive drive to help a normal, healthy, and talented athlete to reach his/her potential, it might be understandable that the rather negative topic of burnout is rarely the main or natural focus of a sport psychology consultant's work. Clearly, the sport psychology practitioner has a role in providing informational support and advice to coaches on psychological dimensions of the training and coaching environment as well as a means to monitor and support the athlete as they move through stressful transitions in their sport (Wylleman & Lavallee, 2004).

An actual case example may illustrate the potential roles of the practitioner more clearly. Molly is a 13-year-old British tennis prodigy whose success is such that few girls in her peer group have produced a similar level of success. Her physical training, on-court practice, and tournament programs lie under the control of the national governing body of coaches. The intensity of this program, in keeping up with world-class standards in the women's game, has resulted in diminished schooling and the employment of private tutors outside of a normal educational environment. Thus, Molly does not possess a normal lifestyle and her opportunities to socialize with other girls and boys in extracurricular activities are limited. There is also great media interest in Molly and agents have been interested in signing her up as a prospective British champion.

Within this case lie many of the potential antecedents to burnout that have been discussed in this chapter. From a psychological perspective, it is vital for a sport psychology practitioner to focus on some of the motivational issues that may arise. This includes monitoring player expectations given the various sources of pressure placed on the player to win as well as creating a system of prematch goal setting and postmatch reviewing, which helps Molly to develop and maintain a high-task orientation (Duda & Hall, 2001, plus see Chapter 4 of this book). Such an achievement goal orientation will help her to learn and develop from each match regardless of the result, as opposed to being entirely driven by the high ego orientation that is likely, given the nature of the situation in which she is placed. Working with Molly's parents and her coach in addressing how their behavior will help develop a positive motivational climate (Ames, 1992) around the player is also a critical process in preventing burnout. Such a climate carefully transmits the value that coach and parents place upon learning, effort, improvement, and enjoyment, as opposed to simply winning and comparisons with others. Moreover, this climate is perceived by the player not only in training and tournaments, but in the behaviors of others in the car on the way to matches, after matches, and at home.

From a social perspective, the presence and quality of social support systems and the presentation of opportunities for Molly to develop a more multidimensional identity are important checkpoints for a consultant to address. Planning a structure in which Molly can gain some benefit from opportunities as a normal teenager and developing valued friendships within and outside of the sport will help her to become more than just "Molly the tennis player." For example, Internet correspondence with friends when on tour to break up the boredom of waiting between matches can play an important social and identity-building function. Self-determination theory (Deci & Ryan, 1985) suggests that the construct of relatedness carries a great deal of motivational value, and helping Molly to develop a healthy sense of belonging with the constant support of others should help the formation of her identity and guard against burnout symptoms.

From a physiological point of view, a consultant (with the support of coaches) might encourage Molly to self-monitor certain lifestyle parameters, including sleep, waking heart rate, diet, illness, mood, and training stress as potential indicators of overtraining. This also will help Molly to develop a high level of responsibility and achievement motivation if these dimensions of self-monitoring were part of a system where she rated herself on a variety of skills/qualities and set weekly goals.

In sum, proactive work exists for the sport psychology consultant to put preventative burnout strategies in place. Careful consideration needs to be given to assessing the psychological demands and sources of stress placed on the athlete, the motivational characteristics of the athlete, and the quality of the support environment available to the athlete. Assimilating this information should aid practitioners in developing a well-considered and integrated plan for monitoring and preventing the symptoms of burnout.

Summary

The term burnout within sporting contexts has been borrowed from the professional literature where it originated. The founding father of burnout generally is considered to be Herbert Freudenberger (1974), through the publication of his experiential encounters and observations of burnout as a clinical practitioner. Empirical inquiry began around the same time through the work of the social psychologist Christina Maslach. A significant challenge to professional practice and the advancement of empirical research into burnout across a range of domains has been the lack of agreement on a universal definition. This is also true of the sport domain. The most popular definition within the sport context has been Smith's (1986) definition. More recently, however, Raedeke and colleagues (Raedeke, 1997; Raedeke et al., 2002; Raedeke & Smith, 2001) have offered a return to original conceptualizations of burnout from the professional domain, and in particular the work of Maslach and Jackson (1984). Based upon their approach, burnout within sport is characterized by a withdrawal from an activity denoted by a reduced sense of accomplishment, devaluation/resentment of sport, and physical/psychological exhaustion. The debate surrounding the agreement of a universal definition of burnout in sport has been confounded further by the similarity of the symptoms it shares with the related concepts of overtraining, staleness, and dropout.

Within the sport psychology literature, there are four main theories that can be described as *traditional* theories. These, together with more recent theoretical perspectives, can be divided into two broad categories: stress-induced burnout and non-stress-induced burnout. The stress-induced perspectives have tended to dominate and continue to do so, but more recent approaches have advanced the field by offering more multidimensional conceptualizations of burnout across physiological, social, and psychological subsystems.

From Caccese and Mayerberg's (1984) initial research on coach burnout, empirical research has expanded to incorporate work examining burnout among athletic trainers, athletic directors, officials, and athletes also. Research on coaches and athletes has, however, received the majority of the research attention. In addition to the difficulties in establishing a universal definition of burnout, the development of a valid and reliable research tool has also been problematic. A breakthrough has occurred, however, with the advent of the Athlete Burnout Questionnaire by Raedeke and Smith (2001), which assesses perceived burnout across the three dimensions of physical/emotional exhaustion, sport devaluation, and reduced performance accomplishments.

Despite the popularity with which burnout has been received and its use as a colloquial term within the everyday sport context, there remains much to be understood about the construct. One of the areas in which our lack of knowledge and understanding is most significant is in the development of effective intervention strategies. To date their remains a significant gap in the literature in terms of intervention studies. What little is known is reliant upon the recall of individuals who have previously experienced burnout (Gould et al., 1996b), and therefore intervention approaches must be addressed as an important area for future research efforts.

Study Questions

1. List and define the three dimensions of burnout proposed by Maslach and Jackson (1984), and compare these with those proposed in the definition of athlete burnout by Raedeke, Lunney, and Venables (2002).

2. Describe the principal tenets of Silva's (1990) negative training stress response model.

3. List the principal components of Smith's (1986) cognitive-affective stress model and discuss each component.

4. Describe Coakley's (1992) unidimensional identity development and external control model. Discuss the principal differences between this model and Smith's (1986) or Silva's (1990) models.

5. Discuss how sport commitment can be used to investigate burnout.

6. Describe the differences between staleness, overtraining, and burnout.

7. Describe an athlete who is at risk of burnout and design an intervention program that will hopefully prevent burnout in the athlete.

References

Ames, C. (1992). Classrooms: Goals, structures, and student motivation. *Journal of Educational Psychology, 84*, 261–271.

Caccese, T. M., & Mayerberg, C. K. (1984). Gender differences in perceived burnout of college coaches. *Journal of Sport and Exercise Psychology, 6*, 279–288.

Capel, S. A., Sisley, B. L., & Desertrain, G. S. (1987). The relationship of role conflict and role ambiguity to burnout in high school basketball coaches. *Journal of Sport Psychology, 9*, 106–117.

Coakley, J. A. (1992). Burnout amongst adolescent athletes: A personal failure or social problem? *Sociology of Sport Journal, 9*, 271–285.

Cohn, P. (1990). An exploratory study on sources of stress and athlete burnout in youth golf. *The Sport Psychologist, 4*, 95–106.

Cresswell, S. L., & Eklund, R. C. (2003a). The athlete burnout syndrome: A practitioner's guide. *New Zealand Journal of Sports Medicine, 31*(1), 4–9.

Cresswell, S. L., & Eklund, R. C. (2003b). The construct validity of two burnout measures in sport. In R. Stelter (Ed.), *New approaches to exercise and sport psychology: Theories, methods and applications* (p. 45). Copenhagen: European Congress of Sport Psychology.

Dale, J., & Weinberg, R. S. (1989). The relationship between coaches leadership style and burnout. *The Sport Psychologist, 3*, 1–13.

Dale, J., & Weinberg, R. S. (1990). Burnout in sport: A review and critique. *Journal of Applied Sport Psychology, 2*, 67–83.

Deci, E. L., & Ryan, R. M. (1985). The general causality orientations scale: Self-determination in personality. *Journal of Research in Personality, 19*, 109–134.

Drake, D., & Herbert, E. P. (2002). Perceptions of occupational stress and strategies for avoiding burnout: Case studies of two female teacher coaches. *The Physical Educator, 59*(4), 170–183.

Duda, J. L., & Hall, H. (2001). Achievement goal theory in sport: Recent extensions and future directions. In R. N. Singer, H. A. Hausenblas, & C. M. Janelle (Eds.), *Handbook of sport psychology* (2nd ed.). New York: John Wiley & Sons.

Edelwich, J., & Brodsky, A. (1980) *Burnout: Stages of disillusionment in the helping professions.* New York: Human Sciences.

Feigely, D. A. (1984). Psychological burnout in high-level athletes. *The Physician and Sportsmedicine, 12*, 109–119.

Felder, D., & Wishnietsky, D. (1990). Role conflict, coaching burnout and the reduction in the number of female interscholastic coaches. *The Physical Educator, 47*(2), 7–13.

Fender, L. K. (1989). Athlete burnout: Potential for research and intervention strategies. *The Sport Psychologist, 3,* 63–71.

Freudenberger, H. J. (1974). Staff burnout. *Journal of Social Issues, 30,* 159–165.

Gould, D. (1997). Burnout: Personal motivation gone awry. *Journal of Applied Sport Psychology, 7,* 176–189.

Gould, D., & Dieffenbach, K. (2002). Overtaining, underrecovery, and burnout in sport. In M. Kellman (Ed.), *Enhancing recovery: Preventing underperformance in athletes* (pp. 25–35). Champaign IL: Human Kinetics.

Gould, D., Tuffey, Udry, E., & Loehr, J. (1996a). Burnout in competitive junior tennis players: I. Quantitative psychological assessment. *The Sport Psychologist, 10,* 322–340.

Gould, D., Tuffey, Udry, E., & Loehr, J. (1996b). Burnout in competitive junior tennis players: II. Qualitative analysis. *The Sport Psychologist, 10,* 341–366.

Gould, D., Tuffey, Udry, E., & Loehr, J. (1997). Burnout in competitive junior tennis players: III. Individual differences in the burnout experience. *The Sport Psychologist, 11,* 257–276.

Harlick, M., & McKenzie, A. (2000). Burnout in junior tennis: A research report. *New Zealand Journal of Sport Medicine, 28,* 36–39.

Kallus, K. W., & Kellmann, M. (1995). The Recovery-Stress-Questionnaire for coaches. In R. Vanfraechem-Raway & Y. Vanden Auweele (Eds.), *Integrating laboratory and field studies* (pp. 26–33). Brussels, Belgium: European Federation of Sports Psychology.

Kallus, K. W., & Kellmann, M. (2000). Burnout in athletes and coaches. In Y. L. Hanin (Ed.), *Emotions in sport* (pp. 209–230). Champaign IL: Human Kinetics.

Kelley, B. C. (1994). A model of stress and burnout in collegiate coaches: Effects of gender and time of season. *Research Quarterly for Exercise and Sport, 65,* 48–58.

Kelley, B. C., & Gill, D. L. (1993). An examination of personal and situational variables, stress appraisal, and burnout in collegiate teacher–coaches. *Research Quarterly for Exercise and Sport, 64,* 94–102.

Kellmann, M. (Ed). (2002). *Enhancing recovery: Preventing underperformance in athletes.* Champaign, IL: Human Kinetics.

Kellmann, M., & Gunther, K. (2000). Changes in stress and recovery in elite rowers during preparation for the Olympic Games. *Medicine and Science in Sport and Exercise, 32,* 676–683.

Kellmann, M., & Kallus, K.W. (2001). *Recovery-Stress Questionnaire for athletes: User manual.* Champaign, IL: Human Kinetics.

Kentta, G. (2001). *Overtraining, staleness and burnout in sports.* Unpublished Ph.D. thesis, Stockholm Universitet, Psykologiska Institutionen.

Kentta, G., & Hassmen, P. (1998). Overtraining and recovery: A conceptual model. *Sports Medicine, 26,* 1–16.

Kentta, G., Hassmen, P., & Raglin, J. S. (2001). Training practices and overtraining syndrome in Swedish age-group athletes. *International Journal of Sports Medicine, 22,* 460–465.

Kosa, B. (1990). Teacher-coach burnout and coping strategies. *The Physical Educator, 47,* 153–157.

Lai, C., & Wiggins, M. S. (2003). Burnout perceptions over time in NCAA Division I soccer players. *International Sports Journal, 7*(2), 120–127.

Maslach, C., & Jackson, S. E. (1981). The measurement of experienced burnout. *Journal of Occupational Behavior, 2,* 99–113.

Maslach, C., & Jackson, S. E. (1984). Burnout in organizational settings. In S. Oskamp (Ed.), *Applied social psychology annual: Applications in organizational settings* (Vol. 5, pp. 133–153). Beverly Hills, CA: Sage.

Pastore, D. L., & Judd, M. R. (1992). Burnout in two-year college coaches of women's team sports. *Journal of Physical Education, Recreation, and Dance, 63,* 74–79.

Pastore, D. L., & Judd, M. R. (1993). Burnout and gender differences in two year college coaches of women's athletic teams. *Sociology of Sport Journal, 10,* 205–212.

Price, M.S., & Weiss, M.R. (2000). Relationships among coach burnout, coach behaviors, and athletes psychological responses. *The Sport Psychologist, 14,* 391–409.

Quigley, T. A., Slack, T., & Smith, G. J. (1987). Burnout in secondary school teacher-coaches. *The Alberta Journal of Educational Research, 33,* 260–274.

Raedeke, T. D. (1997). Is athlete burnout more than just stress? A sport commitment perspective. *Journal of Sport & Exercise Psychology, 19,* 396–417.

Raedeke, T.D., Lunney, K., & Venables, K. (2002). Understanding athlete burnout: Coach perspectives. *Journal of Sport Behavior, 25,* 181–201.

Raedeke, T. D., & Smith, A .L. (2001). Development and preliminary validation of an athlete burnout measure. *Journal of Sport & Exercise Psychology, 23,* 281–306.

Raglin, J., Sawamura, S., Alexiou, S., Hassmen, P., & Kentta, G. (2000). Training practices and staleness in age-group swimmers: A cross-cultural study. *Pediatric Exercise Science, 12,* 61–70.

Raglin, J. S., & Wilson, G. S. (2000). Overtraining in athletes. In Y. L. Hanin (Ed.), *Emotions in sport* (pp. 191–207). Champaign, IL: Human Kinetics.

Schaufeli, W. B., & Buunk, B. P. (2003). Burnout: An overview of 25 years of research and theorizing. In M. J. Schabracq, J. A. M. Winnubst, & C. L. Cooper (Eds.), *The handbook of work and health psychology* (2nd ed., pp. 383–425). London: John Wiley and Sons.

Schmidt, G. W., & Stein, G. L. (1991). Sport commitment: A model integrating enjoyment, dropout, and burnout. *Journal of Sport & Exercise Psychology, 8,* 254–265.

Silva, J. M. (1990). An analysis of the training stress syndrome in competitive athletics. *Journal of Applied Sport Psychology, 2,* 5–20.

Smith, R. E. (1986). Toward a cognitive-affective model of athlete burnout. *Journal of Sport Psychology, 8,* 36–50.

Tenebaum, G., Jones, C. M., Kitsantas, A., Sacks, D. N., & Berwick, J. P. (2003). Failure adaptation: An investigation of the stress response process in sport. *International Journal of Sport Psychology, 34,* 27–62.

Thibaut, J. W., & Kelley, H. H. (1959). *The social psychology of groups.* New York: Wiley.

Udry, E., Gould, D., Bridges, D., & Tuffey, S. (1997). People helping people? Examining the social ties of athletes coping with burnout and injury stress. *Journal of Sport & Exercise Psychology, 19,* 368–395.

Vealey, R. S., Armstrong, L., Comar, W., & Greenleaf, C. A. (1998). Influence of perceived coaching behaviors on burnout and competitive anxiety in female college athletes. *Journal of Applied Sport Psychology, 10,* 297–318.

Weinberg, R. S., & Gould, D. (2003). *Foundations of sport and exercise psychology* (3rd ed.). Champaign, IL: Human Kinetics.

Wylleman, P., & Lavallee, D. (2004). A developmental perspective on transitions faced by athletes. In M. R. Weiss (Ed.), *Developmental sport and exercise psychology: A lifespan perspective* (pp. 503–524). Morgantown, WV: Fitness Information Technology.

CHAPTER

25

Injury Risk and Rehabilitation: Psychological Considerations

Jean M. Williams, *University of Arizona*
Carrie B. Scherzer, *University of Arizona*

I knew I was in trouble when I heard snap, crackle and pop, and I wasn't having a bowl of cereal.
—Nick Kypreos, Toronto Maple Leaf player (in McDonell, 2004, p. 96)

Although many of the causes for injury are undoubtedly physical in nature (e.g., body build, level of conditioning, equipment failure, poor playing surface, or faulty biomechanics) or just plain bad luck, psychosocial factors also play a role. When the original draft of this chapter was completed in 1986, relatively few studies had tried to identify psychological factors that might predispose athletes to injury (e.g., Bramwell, Masuda, Wagner, & Holmes, 1975; Coddington & Troxell, 1980; Passer & Seese, 1983) and researchers had not attempted to integrate them in a meaningful way for the athlete, coach, sport psychologist, or athletic trainer. In the intervening years, more than four dozen studies have been completed (see Williams, 2001, and Williams and Andersen, 1998, for reviews), and models have been generated (e.g., Andersen & Williams, 1988) and even revised (Williams & Andersen, 1998) to counter the narrow scope and atheoretical nature of early research.

Also, although some clinical articles appeared before 1986 discussing athletes' psychological reactions to injury (e.g., Nideffer, 1983; Yaffe, 1983), the practical implications were not clear. Knowledge has expanded considerably in recent years regarding psychological reactions to injury, how to facilitate psychological adjustment once injured, and the role of selected psychological interventions in enhancing physical healing and rehabilitation.

This chapter will review the research on the psychology of injury and will provide examples of how to implement psychological interventions to reduce injury risk and to enhance the physical and psychological recovery of the injured athlete. We assume in this chapter that the injured athletes plan on returning to their sport. We recognize, however, that in some cases injuries will be so severe, or the damage so permanent, that an athlete cannot return to her or his sport. It is beyond the scope of this chapter to discuss the psychological issues involved when this happens,

565

but the reader is directed to Chapter 26 in this volume, as well as to several chapters in psychology of injury books edited by Heil (1993) and Pargman (1999).

Psychological Readiness to Return After Injury

> Athletes are stronger, quicker, and presumably sturdier than the rest of us. They seem blessed. We forget that what they do is hard. We so rarely see them at their most vulnerable—in pain and out of commission. And we almost never hear, from their perspective, about those injuries that disrupt their existence and play havoc with their futures.
>
> Harry Stein, "Brought to His Knees," *Sport*, September 1984, p. 64

Historically, sport medicine specialists have concerned themselves primarily with the physical aspects of injury rehabilitation—largely because of the assumption that attaining a prescribed level of physical rehabilitation prepared the athlete for a safe and successful return to competition. Gradually it has become clear that this assumption is not valid for all athletes. Certainly, many athletes psychologically adapt to injury quite readily. When these athletes receive appropriate physical rehabilitation combined with support, encouragement, and the assurance that it is safe to return to competition, they are ready for a confident return.

Other athletes, however, despite physical readiness, are not psychologically ready to return to competition. To them even the suggestion of returning creates unmanageable stress. Doubts, fears, and anxieties surface. Despite assurances from trainers, physicians, and coaches, these athletes do not feel ready. Fears mount concerning the possible risk of returning too quickly. The mind and body get overloaded with thoughts and images of further injury. Sleep is interrupted by dreams of a disastrous return to the playing field or by vivid recall of the feelings and consequences of the original injury.

It appears that the frequency with which these apprehensive responses occur has increased

as (1) surgical techniques have reduced the time period required for physical rehabilitation, thereby reducing the time frame available for psychological adjustment; and (2) athletes have become more aware of the importance of taking care of their bodies. As a result, optimal injury rehabilitation often demands that injury rehabilitation include both physical and psychological components. It will no longer suffice to argue that athletes who appear to be physically ready to return but who do not feel prepared psychologically are malingerers, mentally weak, or lacking in toughness. The old-school approaches of challenging desire and commitment to the team; inducing guilt for letting the team down; or using scare tactics to foster fear, shame, and embarrassment will have to change. These strategies cause more problems than they cure. For example, upon an athlete's initial return to competition, anxiety and tension can lead to one or more of the following:

- Reinjury
- Injury to another body part
- Lowered confidence resulting in a temporary performance decrement
- Lowered confidence resulting in a permanent performance decrement
- General depression and fear of further injury, which can sap motivation and the desire to return to competition

Today's athletes are well educated. They usually see through coercive strategies and will distrust individuals who use such approaches. The athletes may respond by simply refusing to return to competition by confidently claiming that they are not ready or by finding other indirect ways to undermine their performance or physical rehabilitation. As a result, everyone suffers—the athletes, the team, the coach, and the sport psychologist.

Old, purely physical approaches to rehabilitation need to be replaced by theoretically sound and broad-based educational approaches. Such approaches will result in coaches, athletic trainers, and sport psychologists teaching athletes how to respond psychologically to injury in a positive and growth-oriented way rather than in a negative and self-defeating way. We discuss some of these newer rehabilitation theories and approaches later in this chapter.

Factors That Predispose Athletes to Injury

Research with recreational and nonelite to elite competitive athletes has found that certain psychosocial factors predispose individuals to injury, whereas other psychosocial factors help protect them from injury. Andersen and Williams (1988) proposed that most psychosocial variables, if they influence injury outcome at all, probably do so through a linkage with stress and a resulting stress response. The central hypothesis of their stress-injury model is that individuals with a history of many stressors, personality characteristics that exacerbate the stress response, and few coping resources will, when placed in a stressful situation such as a demanding practice or crucial competition, be more likely to appraise the situation as stressful and to exhibit greater physiological activation and attentional disruptions (see Figure 25-1). The severity of the resulting stress response, caused by the increased stress reactivity, is what predisposes the athletes to injury. Considerable support exists for all facets of the stress-injury model (see Williams, 2001, and Williams and Andersen, 1998, for a more thorough review of research testing the model).

The central core of the stress-injury model, the stress response, is a bidirectional relationship between the person's cognitive appraisal of a potentially stressful external situation and the physiological and attention aspects of stress. In terms of sport participation, the individual makes some cognitive appraisal of the demands of the practice or competitive situation, the adequacy of his or her ability to meet those demands, and the consequences of failure/success in meeting the demands. For example, if an athlete views competition as challenging, exciting, and fun, the resulting "good" stress (eustress) may help the athlete stay focused and successfully "flow"

with the competition. Injury risk in this situation would be lower than when the athlete feels "bad" stress (distress), such as appraising the competition as ego threatening or anxiety producing. Such an interpretation most likely occurs when athletes perceive that they do not have the resources to meet the demands of the situation and it is important to do so because failure will result in dire consequences.

Whether the cognitive appraisal is accurate or distorted by irrational beliefs or other maladaptive thought patterns (see Chapter 18) is unimportant in the generation of the stress response. If the athlete perceives inadequate resources to meet the demands of the situation, and it is important to succeed, the stress response activates and manifests itself physiologically, attentionally, and in the perception of higher state anxiety. Correspondingly, these cognitive appraisals and physiological and attentional responses to stress constantly modify and remodify each other. For example, a relaxed body can help calm the mind just as anxious thoughts can activate the physical stress response. The resulting individual differences in stress responsivity due to differences in psychosocial variables may either help inoculate the athlete against injury or exacerbate his or her risk.

Of the myriad physiological and attentional changes that occur during the stress response, Andersen and Williams (1988) hypothesized that increases in generalized muscle tension, narrowing of the visual field (revised model added auditory cues, Williams and Andersen, 1998), and increased distractibility were the primary culprits in the stress-injury relationship. For example, generalized muscle tension can lead to fatigue and reduced flexibility, motor coordination difficulties, and muscle inefficiency, thereby creating a greater risk for incurring injuries such as sprains, strains, and other musculoskeletal injuries. Narrowing of peripheral vision could lead to not picking up or responding in time to dangerous cues in the periphery such as when a quarterback does not see or react fast enough to a defensive player running in from the periphery. Attention disruptions, often due to attention to task-irrelevant cues, may also result in failure to detect or respond quickly enough to relevant cues in the

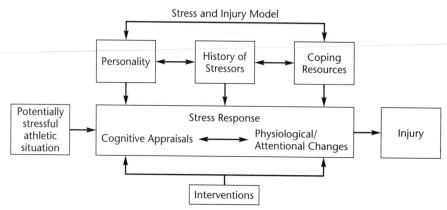

Figure 25-1　Revised version of the stress and injury model. From Williams and Andersen (1998)

Note: The original model had only directional arrows from personality to history of stressors and from coping resources to history of stressors, and it had no bidirectional arrow between personality and coping resources.

central field of vision such as when a batter with a high-risk psychosocial profile fails to avoid a pitch coming directly at his head.

When comparing performance under stressful and nonstressful laboratory conditions, considerable support (five studies) exists for athletes with a high-risk psychosocial profile experiencing greater peripheral narrowing when performing under stress compared to athletes with a low-risk profile. Only one study (Williams & Andersen, 1997) examined perception in the central field of vision (e.g., missing or delayed response to important visual cues, responding to irrelevant cues), and it too found a greater susceptibility to attention disruptions for athletes with a high injury risk profile when they performed under higher stress. The one study that examined the connection between psychosocial factors and muscle tension found increased muscle tension during the stress condition for the total group, but failed to support the stress-injury model's hypothesis of even greater muscle tension for individuals with a high-risk psychosocial profile. The failure to do so may have resulted from Andersen studying the general population rather than a high-risk subpopulation.

Before addressing the implications of these findings for designing interventions to decrease

injuries due to psychosocial factors, we will discuss how the history of stressors, personality factors, and coping resources influence stress and injury. These variables may contribute interactively or in isolation in influencing the stress response and, ultimately, injury occurrence and severity. The original stress-injury model hypothesized that an athlete's history of stressors contributes directly to the stress response, whereas personality factors and coping resources act on the stress response either directly or through a moderating influence on the effects of the history of stressors. In addition to these directional relationships, when Williams and Andersen (1998) critiqued and revised their stress-injury model 10 years after its initial publication, they added bidirectional arrows between personality and history of stressors, coping resources and history of stressors, and personality and coping resources.

History of Stressors

This category of injury risk variables includes life change events, daily hassles, and previous injury. Of these, the most support exists for the detrimental effects of the presence of major life events—typically the amount of change and upset that athletes experienced in the year prior to a competitive season. Examples of general life events are incidents such as the breakup of a relationship, change in residence, and death of a loved one, whereas major events related to sports include eligibility difficulties, trouble with coaches, and change in playing status.

A review by Williams (2001) reported that 30 out of 35 studies that assessed life events found at least some type of positive relationship between high life stress and injury. The best evidence involves football (six studies), but similar findings have occurred across other physical activities as diverse as Alpine skiing, race walking, figure skating, baseball, gymnastics, soccer, field hockey, wrestling, track and field, and ballet. The new studies supported an earlier review by Williams and Roepke (1993) that reported injuries tended to occur 2 to 5 times more frequently in athletes with high compared to low life stress and that the risk of injury tended to increase in direct proportion to the level of life stress.

Most research efforts failed to support daily hassles (e.g., minor daily problems, irritations, or changes) as a contributor to injury risk (Blackwell & McCullagh, 1990; Hanson, McCullagh, & Tonymon, 1992; Smith, Smoll, & Ptacek, 1990; Van Mechelen et al., 1996), but the results are suspect because of assessing hassles only once. In contrast, a study that measured hassles on a weekly basis (the more appropriate methodological approach) found that injured athletes had a significant increase in hassles for the week prior to injury compared to no significant increases for the noninjured athletes (Fawkner, McMurray, & Summers, 1999).

Personality and Coping Resources

The presence of desirable personality attributes and coping resources may buffer individuals from stress and injury by helping them to perceive fewer situations and events as stressful or by helping them cope more effectively with their history of stressors. Conversely, the lack of desirable personality characteristics and coping resources, or the presence of undesirable ones,

may leave individuals vulnerable to higher stress (acute and chronic) and, presumably, greater injury risk.

It would be very useful to have a specific personality test to predict the more injury-prone athlete. Unfortunately, from those studies that have used measures of more basic, stable personality patterns (with instruments such as Cattel's 16 Personality Factors Questionnaire or the California Personality Inventory) no consistent results have emerged. Still, some support does exist for selected personality variables possibly influencing injury risk.

Fields, Delaney, and Hinkle (1990) reported that runners scoring high (e.g., more aggressive, hard-driving) on a Type A behavior screening questionnaire experienced significantly more injuries, especially multiple injuries, compared to runners scoring lower on this measure. Similar results occurred in Japan with a large sample of college athletes ($N = 2,164$). Athletes with a high Type A behavior pattern incurred more injuries than those with a low Type A pattern (Nigorikawa et al., 2003). Wittig and Schurr (1994) determined that being tough-minded (i.e., more assertive, independent, and self-assured) predicted the likelihood of more severe injuries but not the occurrence of injury, and Thompson and Morris (1994) found that high anger directed outward, but not inward, increased injury risk.

Mixed results occurred when researchers examined locus of control and trait anxiety. **Locus of control** is a concept that deals with the degree to which individuals view their lives and environment as under their personal control. **Trait anxiety** is a general disposition or tendency to perceive situations as threatening and to react with an anxiety response. Pargman and Lunt (1989) reported that a higher injury rate correlated with an external locus of control in a sample of freshman college football players. In contrast, Kolt and Kirkby (1996) found a more internal locus of control significantly predicted injury in elite gymnasts, but not with nonelite gymnasts. Other researchers who used nonsport tools to assess locus of control (Blackwell & McCullagh, 1990; Hanson, McCullagh, & Tonymon, 1992; Kerr & Minden, 1988; McLeod &

Kirkby, 1995) and trait anxiety (Kerr & Minden, 1988; Lysens, Auweele, & Ostyn, 1986; Passer & Seese, 1983) found no relationship between these variables and the incidence of injury. When researchers used sport-specific tools, athletes who scored high on either external locus of control (Dalhauser & Thomas, 1979), competitive trait anxiety (Blackwell & McCullagh, 1990; Hanson et al., 1992; Passer & Seese, 1983; Petrie, 1993), or somatic trait anxiety (Smith, Ptacek, & Patterson, 2000) had more injuries, more severe injuries, or more time-loss due to injury than athletes with the opposite profile.

In Petrie's (1993) study, the finding occurred for football starters but not nonstarters. Petrie also found that competitive trait anxiety moderated the effects of positive life stress such that higher levels of anxiety and stress were associated with more days missed because of injury. He conjectured that the combination of starting and having high life stress and competitive trait anxiety "may have negatively influenced these athletes' appraisals such that they either viewed practices and competitions as threatening/uncontrollable or believed they did not have the resources to cope. Such appraisals may have corresponded with attentional and physiological disruptions that would have increased the starters' vulnerability to injury" (p. 272).

Other researchers also have tested whether personality variables might interact with history of stressors or with other personality and coping variables in influencing injury risk. Smith et al. (2000) found that the combination of high daily life stress and high cognitive or somatic anxiety predicted high injury time-loss in ballet dancers affiliated with a major ballet company. In another study that tested whether a personality variable might moderate the stress-injury relationship (Smith, Ptacek, & Smoll, 1992), only athletes who scored low in sensation seeking had a significant positive relationship between major negative life events and subsequent injury time-loss. According to Zuckerman (1979), sensation avoiders, unlike sensation seekers, have a lower tolerance for arousal and, therefore, do not care for change, avoid the unfamiliar, and stay away from risky activities. Smith and his colleagues (1990)

found no support for a competing hypothesis that the risk-taking characteristics of high sensation seeking would constitute an injury vulnerability factor. Also, although they found that sensation avoiders reported poorer stress management coping skills, no support existed for differences in coping skills mediating the injury vulnerability differences.

In other promising personality research, defensive pessimism, dispositional optimism, and hardiness aggression influenced injury risk. Perna and McDowell (1993) found that athletes who scored high on defensive pessimism, and who also experienced a high degree of life stress, experienced more illness/injury symptoms than did athletes scoring low on defensive pessimism and having fewer stressful life events. Meyer (1995), however, failed to replicate their results, but Ford, Eklund, and Gordon (2000) found that athletes high in optimism and hardiness experienced less injury time-loss when positive life change increased, compared to athletes low in optimism or hardiness.

In addition to the preceding findings for personality traits, mood states also influence injury risk. For example, Williams, Hogan, and Andersen (1993) concluded that intercollegiate football, volleyball, and cross-country athletes who experienced positive states of mind (e.g., ability to stay focused, keep relaxed, share with others) early in the season incurred significantly fewer injuries during their athletic season compared to athletes who had less positive states of mind. Whereas positive states of mind might buffer the effects of potentially stressful sport situations, thereby creating less stress and fewer injuries, the presence of negative states might do the opposite. Fawkner (1995) found just that when she assessed team and individual sport athletes' mood states (five negative and one positive) over the course of the competitive season. She noted significant increases in mood disturbance in the measurement immediately prior to injury. Lavallee and Flint (1996) also reported a relationship of negative mood states to injury vulnerability. A higher degree of tension/anxiety correlated with a higher rate of injury and a higher degree of tension/anxiety, anger/hostility, and total negative mood

Situation Study 1

Athlete at Risk of Injury

John is in his second season as the starting quarterback for his university's football team. He is under a lot of pressure because of a new coaching staff and many changes in the offensive plays. In addition, he is very worried about his mother who just began treatment for breast cancer. Both his academics and football performance are suffering because he is so stressed out. Normally he talks his troubles out with his girlfriend, but she broke up with him over the summer. He used to love game days, but now he dreads them because he has so much anxiety about playing well. He fears losing his starting position and, more important, letting his teammates down. Although normally an upbeat person, he's become very moody and pessimistic.

state correlated with higher severity of injury. In a related study Van Mechelen et al. (1996) stated that persons who reported vital exhaustion, which represented more feelings of depression, malfunctioning, apathy, and anxiety, were more likely to sustain an injury.

Compared to research on personality factors, coping resources have received less attention but more consistent results. An athlete's coping resources, particularly social support, appear to influence injury outcome directly and by lessening the negative effects of high life-event stress (e.g., Hardy, O'Connor, & Geisler, 1990; Petrie, 1992; Williams, Tonymon, & Wadsworth, 1986). These findings suggest that increasing social support from family, friends, and significant others—a group likely to include coaches and teammates—is one way to reduce injury risk. Richman, Hardy, Rosenfeld, and Callahan (1989) is an excellent source for a variety of strategies coaches and sport psychologists could implement to affect this type and level of social support in student athletes.

Although a greater number of supportive relationships may be desired, the *quality* of such relationships is also important. For example, on one football team a young man with fairly strong religious values felt he had to go out, drink, and chase women with his teammates to receive their support and friendship. Although he achieved an external measure of support, the relationships were unfulfilling for him and added to his level of stress. It was, in fact, through a classroom discussion of stress that the athlete sought out someone with whom to discuss his conflicts. Both his coach and his teammates were unaware of the nature and range of his stress. After he successfully resolved the conflicts, his coach commented that he was a "much freer person and player." This probably resulted from increased flexibility because of decreased stress. The athlete may well have been an accident that *did not* happen.

In addition to the merits of increasing social support, the findings of Smith, Smoll, and Ptacek (1990) and Andersen and Williams (1999) suggest that increasing psychological coping skills (e.g., the ability to stay focused under pressure, to be confident, to self-regulate activation) might also decrease injury risk. Smith and colleagues found that the most injuries occurred in athletes who experienced high negative life events and who lacked both social support and psychological coping skills (see Situation Study 1). Andersen and Williams found that for their athletes who scored low in social support, high in life stress and attentional disruptions—more specifically, peripheral narrowing under stress—accounted for 25% of the injury variance. Also, Kerr and Goss (1996) found less injury time-loss for gymnasts taught psychological coping skills.

Interventions to Reduce Injury Vulnerability

The stress-injury model proposes a two-pronged approach to prevent injuries from the increased stress reactivity of individuals at risk of injury due to their psychosocial profile. One set of interventions aims to change the cognitive appraisal of potentially stressful events (see Chapter 18 for techniques to eliminate or modify cognitions that cause stress) and the second set to modify the physiological/attentional aspects of the stress response. Chapter 15 describes relaxation techniques such as progressive muscle relaxation, meditation, autogenics, and breathing exercises, and Chapters 18 and 19 explain techniques to decrease distractibility and to keep an appropriate attentional focus. Also included on the cognitive appraisal side of the stress response are interventions for fostering realistic expectations, a sense of belonging (e.g., team cohesiveness), and optimal coach–athlete communication. For example, if coaches provide better communication with their athletes regarding their capabilities and potential, athletes will have a more realistic appraisal of the demands and resources available in potentially stressful athletic situations (see Chapter 9 for suggestions to enhance coach–athlete communication). In addition, the interventions presented in these chapters can be used to directly influence some of the variables under coping resources and personality factors.

Partial support for the interventions portion of the model comes from a study in which DeWitt (1980) found that her basketball and football players detected a noticeable decrease in minor injuries after participation in a cognitive and physiological (biofeedback) training program. Murphy (1988) describes another psychological intervention program in which injuries were not the specific focus, but there may have been some injury benefits from the program. Murphy conducted relaxation sessions with 12 members of a team at the 1987 Olympic Sports Festival, 5 of whom had minor injuries and 2 serious injuries. They conducted relaxation sessions after every workout until competition and found that all 12 athletes were able to compete.

Davis (1991) reported an archival review of injury data collected by athletic trainers before and after two university teams practiced progressive relaxation and technique/strategy imagery during team workouts. Major findings included a 52% reduction in injuries to the swimmers and a 33% reduction in injuries to the football players during the athletic season in which they practiced relaxation and imagery skills. Another favorable intervention study comes from May and Brown (1989) who used techniques such as attention control, imagery, and other mental practice skills in their delivery of interventions to individuals, pairs, and groups of U.S. alpine skiers in the Calgary Olympics. In addition to their mental skills training, they also employed team building, communication, relationship orientations, and crisis interventions. May and Brown reported that their interventions led to reduced injuries, increased self-confidence, and enhanced self-control.

A recent prospective injury prevention study conducted by Kerr and Goss (1996) offers more experimentally sound support for reducing life stress and injuries through a stress management program. Participants included 24 gymnasts who competed on the national and international level. They were matched in pairs according to sex, age, and performance and then randomly assigned to a control or experimental group. Across an 8-month time period, each gymnast in the experimental group met individually with one of the experimenters for 16 one-hour, biweekly stress management sessions. Meichenbaum's stress inoculation training program provided the framework for the stress management program, which included skills such as cognitive restructuring, thought control, imagery, and simulations. The stress management group reported less negative athletic stress, less total negative stress, and half the amount of time injured (5 versus 10 days) compared to the participants in the control group. In a similar randomized, single-blind clinical trial with collegiate athletes, a seven-session cognitive behavioral stress management program that used a stress-inoculation training format found that athletes assigned to the intervention group experienced significant reductions in the number of injury and illness days compared to athletes in the control group (Perna, Antoni, Baum, Gordon, & Schneiderman, 2003).

The injury benefits from the preceding intervention programs are even more impressive considering that none of them targeted athletes at risk of injury (they targeted athletes in general) and many of the programs did not include cognitive or concentration training interventions. A recent study (Johnson, Ekengren, & Andersen, 2005), however, did identify and target at-risk athletes and then employed an experimental-control group design to offer six intervention sessions and two telephone contacts consisting of treatments such as stress management skills, somatic and cognitive relaxation, goal-setting skills, and attribution and self-confidence training. The results showed that 10 of 13 in the experimental group remained injury free, in contrast to only 3 of 16 in the control group.

Although more research is needed, the success of these interventions in reducing injuries suggests that coaches, sport psychologists, and athletic trainers may want to employ screening instruments, such as the questionnaires used in research studies, to identify athletes predisposed to injury. Before using them, however, these individuals should understand the nature of psychological tests. Otherwise, they may misinterpret and misuse the tests. For example, coaches who are aware of an individual athlete's high level of stress and minimal coping resources might add additional pressure with their concerns, comments, expectations, or actions. They may even help to create a *self-fulfilling* prophecy if they have not been trained in the use and interpretation of tests.

It also is important to recognize the implications of the use of the word "predispose." Although we cannot predict with accuracy who will or will not suffer from a particular problem, we can reasonably predict the group from which those likely to have a problem will come.

Identifying populations of athletes most predisposed to injury allows us to target specific interventions to the group most likely to benefit from them. It also enables us to watch for the earliest signs of the particular problem concerning us. It would be most egregious, however, to think that all individuals in an at-risk group will experience an injury or that no individuals in a low-risk group will experience injury. In addition, some individuals cope with stress by denial or repression—in essence trying to make believe the stressors are not there. An outside observer, or someone who had results from a stress inventory, might conclude that "There's no problem" whereas, in fact, the opposite may be true.

Coaches also should consider reducing exposure to high-risk activities, such as learning a new and potentially dangerous vault or dive, for athletes who have experienced many recent stressors and who appear to be in a high-stress or distracted state. Finally, where levels of stress appear to be extreme and coping skills minimal, professional counseling may be necessary (see Chapter 22).

Athletes' Reactions to Injury

Regardless of the best efforts of coaches and athletic trainers, injuries still occur, and the resulting consequences are both physical and mental. For example, when injury keeps athletes from performing or causes performance at a lower skill level, it may be difficult for some athletes to see themselves as worthwhile people. Such a reaction to injury is just one way injury can have a significant impact on the psychological well-being of injured athletes. Injury rehabilitation thus becomes both a mental and physical process. The seriousness of an injury does not necessarily determine the ease or difficulty of psychological rehabilitation. One factor that seems to play a role in the psychological impact of injury is the athlete's prior involvement in sport. Athletes who are more involved before injury may be confused as they progress through rehabilitation and also may perceive a lesser degree of recovery at the end of rehabilitation (Johnston & Carroll, 2000). Good psychological rehabilitation helps ensure a healthy future for athletes, a future that must include more than just their playing careers. Therefore, the second step involved in serving the athlete's best interests entails gaining an understanding and appreciation of the psychology of injury rehabilitation.

Psychological Reactions to Injury

Athletes perceive injury in various ways. Some view it as a disaster; some see it as an opportunity to display courage; others welcome it as a relief from the drudgery of practice or the embarrassment and frustration of poor performance, lack of playing time, or a losing season; and still others see it as an opportunity to focus on other aspects of their life. It is not uncommon for injured athletes to feel concerned about whether they will ever completely recover and return to their previous form. Injured athletes are often uncertain if they will be facing a quick return to action, a long rehabilitation process, or the end of their career. Athletes have good reason to be upset when they get injured but, as one athletic trainer stated, "I know it's frustrating for athletes to be injured, but I found that those who have the negative attitudes or poor mood state, that they are the ones who are continuously in rehab, and having problems making it to rehab" (Granito, 2001, p. 78). A positive and enthusiastic response will ensure the best possible chance of complete rehabilitation both physically and mentally.

According to a survey of 482 certified athletic trainers, 47% responded that they believed every injured athlete suffers negative psychological effects (Larson, Starkey, & Zaichkowsky, 1996). The most common in order of frequency were stress/anxiety, anger, treatment compliance problems, depression, problems with concentration/attention, and exercise addiction. It is helpful for athletes to realize that the thoughts and feelings associated with injury are a normal and even useful part of an effective rehabilitation process. Larson and colleagues also indicated that 24% of the certified athletic trainers reported that they have referred an athlete for counseling for

situations related to their injury, and 25% reported that they have a sport psychologist as a member of their sports medicine team. Unfortunately, 75% of athletic trainers in the United States do not have access to a sport psychologist (Cramer Roh & Perna, 2000).

Initially, many sport psychologists (e.g., Pederson, 1986; Rotella, 1984) believed that, following injury, athletes commonly experienced a sequence of predictable psychological reactions similar to those outlined by Kubler-Ross in her classic *On Death and Dying* (1969). These reactions include (1) disbelief, denial, and isolation; (2) anger; (3) bargaining; (4) depression; and (5) acceptance and resignation while continuing to remain hopeful about the eventual return to competition.

Although some individuals still advocate these stage or grief models as a helpful approach to explaining athletes' responses to injury (e.g., Henderson & Carroll, 1993), a review and critique of models of psychological adjustment to athletic injury concluded that grief models in which injured athletes proceed sequentially through a series of stages on the way to recovery lacked consistent empirical support (Brewer, 1994). In fact, Quinn and Fallon (1999) found that athletes experience a myriad of emotions postinjury. Initially, athletes tend to report negative mood states (e.g., tension, depression, anger), and all of these moods improve as rehabilitation progresses. The major disadvantage to grief models is that no room exists for individual differences in the structure of the model. Additionally, extrapolating from the death and dying literature may not work because, in most cases, athletes have every intention of returning to sport once the rehabilitation process is complete (Botterill, Flint, & Ievleva, 1996). Instead, Brewer argued that, based on existing research findings, cognitive appraisal models provide a more viable conceptualization of the process of coping with athletic injury. For individuals still inclined toward a grief approach, we recommend reading an article by Evans and Hardy (1995) to gain both a better understanding of grief models and suggestions on better empirical assessments of the application of this concept

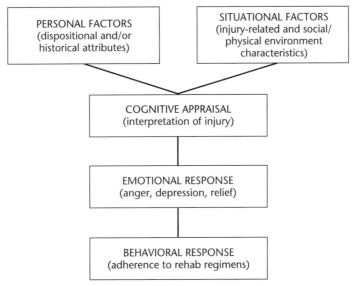

Figure 25-2 **Cognitive appraisal model of psychological adjustment to athletic injury**
Source: B. W. Brewer, 1994. *Journal of Applied Sport Psychology, 6,* 87–100. Used with permission of the publisher.

to clarifying psychological responses of injured athletes.

Cognitive Appraisal Models

Brewer (1994) identified five cognitive appraisal models relevant to psychological responses to athletic injury. Each model (Figure 25-2) has its roots in the literature on stress and coping; athletic injury is conceptualized as a stressor to the athlete, who then evaluates or *appraises* the stressor in accordance with personal and situational factors. According to Brewer, the advantage of cognitive appraisal models over grief models is that they account for individual differences in response to athletic injury. Consistent with stress and coping models, heavy emphasis is put on cognition. Thus, the response to injury comes not so much from the injury itself but from how the athlete interprets or perceives the injury. This cognitive appraisal determines the emotional response (e.g., anger, depression, relief), which, in turn, determines the behavioral response to

injury rehabilitation (e.g., adherence to rehabilitation regimens).

Personal factors. Many personal factors have been identified as contributing to cognitive appraisal and emotional and behavioral responses to athletic injury. For example, Brewer (1994) reported that Shaffer (1992) found that a prior injury history of successful rehabilitation positively affected assessments of ability to manage a subsequent injury. This rehabilitation self-efficacy, in turn, related positively to physical recovery over the course of rehabilitation. Grove, Stewart, and Gordon (1990) documented a positive relationship between pessimistic explanatory style and depression and anger for the first month of knee rehabilitation. In contrast, hardiness was negatively associated with total mood disturbance. Brewer (1993) found that physical self-esteem may buffer the negative effects of athletic injury on mood. Brewer (1994) reported that adherence to injury rehabilitation programs had been linked to personal factors such as self-motivation (Duda, Smart, & Tappe, 1989; Fisher, Domm, & Wuest, 1988), task involvement (Duda et al., 1989), pain tolerance, and perceived exertion (Fisher et al., 1988). In addition, Daly, Brewer, Van Raalte, Petitpas, and Sklar (1995) found that when athletes have emotional responses that are negative they may be less motivated to work at their rehabilitation.

Regarding personal factors, perhaps the most support exists for the influence an athlete's psychological investment in sport has on his or her adjustment to athletic injury (e.g., Brewer, 1993; Brewer, Van Raalte, & Linder, 1993; Kleiber & Brock, 1992; Meyers, Sterling, Calvo, Marley, & Duhon, 1991). Interestingly, after surveying 30 injured athletes, Green and Weinberg (2001) found no relationship between athletic identity and mood disturbance following injury. However, the athletes in this study were recreational athletes and may not have had as much stake in their athletic abilities. For many athletes, but particularly for those who are intensely involved with their sport and those who achieve notable success, the whole focus of their identity, their sense of self, may be in this role as an athlete (see Situation Study 2). Many of the issues faced with athletic injury parallel those that occur with career termination or retirement (see Chapter 26). Perhaps a case can illustrate the points.

If someone has only one basis for a sense of self or the different components of identity are tied to one sphere (Erikson, 1968), if that sphere is threatened, so will be the entire person. What we can expect is that the more narrowly focused an injured athlete's sense of self is, the more threatened the athlete will be. Such a person, depending on the severity of the injury, appears more likely to appraise his or her injury in terms of threat or loss (Brewer et al., 1993) and to experience feelings of anxiety, depression, or hopelessness (Brewer, 1993; Smith, Scott, O'Fallon, & Young, 1990). He or she might be more motivated to return to sport and possibly might also try to return prematurely. Eric Lindros, a player in the national hockey league (NHL), is a prime example of this. He was a standout player in juniors and, when he finally played in the NHL for the

Philadelphia Flyers, he was a dominant force who was named the league's most valuable player for the 1994–1995 season. Lindros, though, has had a career marred with injuries, concussions in particular. In January 2004, playing for the New York Rangers, he suffered his eighth concussion. Rather than taking a cue from his younger brother Brett, who retired from the NHL because of multiple concussions, Eric has repeatedly returned to the game. He also has had public feuds with his former team over the treatment he received and pressure to return to the game. The coach, athletic trainer, or others involved in the rehabilitative process should be sensitive to these issues. It may be appropriate to help the athlete to come to see himself or herself as more fully a person, with many potentials, and to explore other possibilities—not to replace the sport or athlete identity, but to complement it. The development of the NCAA CHAMPS/Life Skills program and books to help athletes plan for careers, such as the one by Petitpas, Champagne, Chartrand, Danish, and Murphy (1997), are helping athletes develop in other realms as well. Highlighting past athletes' success in establishing careers after sport may be helpful. For example, Tim Horton, a former NHL player, opened one doughnut shop that has expanded into one of the most recognized chains in Canada. Other athletes have gone on to careers in sport broadcasting (e.g., Bill Walton, Sean Elliot), owning a business (e.g., ex–Cleveland Brown Clay Matthews's Ford dealership), and law (e.g., ex-NHL player Ken Dryden).

In comparing the perceptions of the seriousness of illness of athletes and trainers, Crossman and Jamieson (1985) found that athletes in general perceived injury as more serious. A group they defined as "overestimators" experienced even greater pain, more anger, loneliness, and apathy. They noted: "Such athletes might benefit from psychological support and counselling about how to cope with their injury" (p. 1133).

Although referral for counseling or therapy may not be necessary as part of reframing the athlete's understanding of and reaction to an injury (Smith, Scott, & Wiese, 1990), there may be the opportunity to discover *positive* implications of the injury (Ermler & Thomas, 1990), not in a

Situation Study 2

Athlete Reacting to Injury

Beth was a two-time all-state performer who had already accepted a full athletic scholarship to a major college soccer powerhouse. During the winter months, Beth was a starter on the varsity basketball team. During the third game of the season she severely injured her right knee diving for a loose ball. The injury required surgery to repair torn ligaments, and the doctors told Beth that with hard work she would be as good as new in a few months.

This was Beth's first major injury. She was afraid, and she was angry at herself for getting injured because she felt it was a stupid play on her part. She also felt that she had let her parents and friends down because of what might happen if she didn't fully recover. She asked herself many of the same questions she heard her friends asking: Would she lose her scholarship? Would she be able to play as well as before? Did she make a mistake by playing basketball this year?

Up to this point, it seemed that the anger, guilt, and other feelings that resulted from the injury caused Beth to doubt herself and her ability to cope with the situation. She found it easier to be alone than to deal with family and friends. Although withdrawing from people brought her temporary relief from her feelings, it also kept her away from the support she needed to get through this unexpected transition.

During her rehabilitation, Beth refused to go to basketball games or social events that she normally attended. She was very moody and seemed to become angry at the smallest thing. Her boyfriend would come over to visit, but these meetings usually ended in a fight because Beth would say he didn't know what she was going through. She was becoming frustrated at her progress in physical therapy, even though she was reaching her therapist's treatment goals. She would be particularly demanding of her therapist if her strength or range of motion had not improved from day to day. Her frustration led her to ignore her therapist's recommendations. She pushed her exercises so hard that she cried from the pain and then became angry at herself for not being tough enough. Instead of getting better, Beth suffered a setback.

Although Beth was trying to deal with her feelings, she found herself pushing away the people who were trying to help her. At the same time her fear caused her to make some poor decisions about her rehabilitation program. Fortunately, Beth was able to get the support she needed to work through her feelings.

Beth's physical therapist introduced her to a counselor who was working in the training room. The counselor listened to Beth's story and tried to understand what she was going through. For the first time Beth was able to voice her anger and sadness. After this, the counselor helped Beth identify the skills that she had used to become a good athlete and showed her how to use them to deal with her injury. Beth had not been prepared for her injury, and her emotions kept her from using the goal-setting and imagery techniques that she used to improve her sport skills.

Beth had also failed to seek help from others. Before her injury, she had always sought out the best coaches for advice and had often talked with players she admired to learn more about game strategies and techniques. She withdrew from this type of support while she was injured. Once Beth learned to use her skills and the support of others, she made better decisions about her rehabilitation and made a quick recovery. (Reprinted by permission from Petitpas, Champagne, Chartrand, Danish, & Murphy, 1997, Athlete's Guide to Career Planning. Champaign, IL: Human Kinetics, 11–12.)

Pollyannaish way but as a source of self-understanding, self-growth, and discovery. Ermler and Thomas note that individuals who can develop positive meanings from injury adjust and cope significantly better than those who do not.

A more recent study by Udry, Gould, Bridges, and Beck (1997) assessed the possible benefits of season-ending injuries in elite skiers. They did so by interviewing skiers who had returned to skiing after sustaining a season-ending injury in a previous season. Four general dimensions of possible benefits were identified: personal growth benefits, psychologically based performance enhancements, physical/technical development benefits, and no benefits (Udry et al., 1997). Examples of these dimensions included clarified priorities, increased mental toughness, better/smarter technical skiing, and nothing, respectively. Udry and colleagues (1997) concluded that individual athletes did grow in positive ways from their injury experiences. The implication for working with injured athletes is that we should help them see that a silver lining exists for every cloud.

The question of referral for counseling and psychotherapy can be problematic (see Chapter 22 for a detailed discussion of when to refer). Not all sport psychologists are trained as counselors or psychotherapists, and not all counselors and psychotherapists will be sensitive to the particular issues confronting athletes. One alternative to referring athletes for counseling that is gaining attention is having athletic trainers take a more active role in the delivery of sport psychology in the athletic training room. Several authors have suggested that athletic trainers are in a perfect position to train athletes to use psychological skills (e.g., goal-setting, imagery), as they are in frequent contact with the injured athlete and possess a wealth of knowledge about the injury itself (e.g., Cramer Roh & Perna, 2000; Ford & Gordon, 1997; Misasi, Redmond, & Kemler, 1998; Tuffey, 1991). In fact, Misasi et al. (1998) point out that "the athletic therapist cannot avoid the need to be an effective counselor or helper" (p. 36). A recent study by Scherzer (2004) found that, when athletic trainers are given additional training in sport psychology, they perceive themselves as more skilled at using

the various techniques and they think that they use the skills more.

Situational factors. Cognitive appraisal models have identified many potential situational factors that influence cognitive appraisal and emotional and behavioral responses to injury. For example, in their revised model, Wiese-Bjornstal, Smith, Shaffer, and Morrey (1998) enumerated three types of situational factors: (1) sport factors, including time in season and playing status; (2) social factors, including coach influences and sports medicine team influences; and (3) environmental factors, such as accessibility to rehabilitation. Granito (2001) sought to provide empirical support for Wiese-Bjornstal et al.'s (1998) model. He conducted focus groups with injured athletes and found that athletes' responses and reactions to injury fell into seven categories: (1) personal factors, such as the personality of the athlete and role on the team; (2) effects on relationships (e.g., with coaches, parents, teammates); (3) sociological aspects (i.e., gender differences, athletic subculture); (4) physical factors, such as pain and use of painkillers; (5) daily hassles (i.e., stress); (6) feelings associated with injury (e.g., frustration, depression, tension); and (7) rehabilitation (i.e., adherence, ease of receiving treatment). Thus, Granito's investigation supports the notion that many factors contribute to an athlete's response to injury, including the personal and situational factors that are part of the cognitive appraisal model of psychological adjustment to athletic injury.

Combined with grief model. Considerable research support exists for the cognitive appraisal models (see Brewer, 1994; Wiese-Bjornstal et al., 1998). Other researchers (Striegel, Hedgpeth, & Sowa, 1996) have proposed a model that incorporates both the grief stage model by Kubler-Ross (1969) and the individual nature of the stress response as encompassed in cognitive appraisal models. Striegel and colleagues' model is composed of three levels: (a) short-term rehabilitation (level one), which they defined as the first 2 weeks of recovery; (b) long-term rehabilitation (level two), which they defined as any duration of rehabilitation longer than 2 weeks but less than permanent withdrawal from sport; and (c) termination of participation (level three), defined as withdrawal from sport. Cognitive appraisal is incorporated in levels one and two, and the model by Kubler-Ross (1969) is incorporated in level three, indicating that there may be differences in the psychological reaction of athletes who will be injured for 2 weeks versus athletes who will never be able to compete again (Striegel et al., 1996). In terms of treatment, each level of the model is made up of the treatments of the previous level along with new treatments. For example, level one treatment is focused on stress management and systematic rationalization, whereas level two treatment adds goal setting and joining a support group. Level three adds career counseling to the treatments of levels one and two. At this point in time, support for this model is theoretical rather than empirical.

More recently, Harris (2003) proposed that integrating the Kubler-Ross stage model and the Chickering and Reisser psychosocial developmental theory may provide insight with regard to working with injured collegiate athletes. The integration of the Kubler-Ross stage model and Chickering and Reisser psychosocial development theory enables athletic trainers to relate to and better understand collegiate athletes, who are in the midst of developmental growth that is different from adults. In addition, Junge (2000) proposed an integrative theoretical model based on stress theory to explain the relationship between psychological factors and sports injuries. This model is based on that of Andersen and Williams (1988); however, it requires empirical support.

Reacting to Injured Athletes

How others react to an injured athlete can play a role in the athlete's own interpretation of his or her injury. Reaction to an injured athlete can spring thoughtlessly from old-school attitudes about toughness in sport or can proceed naturally from a philosophy that embraces the concept of the athlete as a whole person, not just a sport participant. The first reaction not only can impede an athlete's recuperation from injury; it

can arguably *predispose* an athlete to sport accidents. The second reaction deals with short- and long-term aspects of an injury situation in a way that greatly increases the chances of an athlete's return to healthy sport participation.

Potentially Dangerous Attitudes

In an effort to help athletes develop into successful competitors, many coaches and athletic trainers have unknowingly fostered erroneous attitudes concerning successful injury rehabilitation. A clear understanding of these potentially dangerous attitudes is crucial to a complete appreciation of the psychological aspects of injury and rehabilitation.

Act tough and always give 110%. Athletes have been systematically taught that mental toughness and giving 110% all the time are necessary for success in sports. Although mental toughness and giving one's best are important to success, we must realize that when taken to *extremes* these actions can foster injury and failure.

Certainly, athletes must be capable of "playing through" some kinds of pain. Seldom, however, do we educate athletes about the necessity of learning which kinds of pain to ignore and which kinds of pain to listen to and respond to appropriately. The same holds true for learning the amount of pain one should tolerate.

Many highly motivated athletes learn to endure almost any amount or kind of pain. This ability may make for a tough athlete, but it may also make for a vulnerable, often injured athlete who never plays in a fully healthy state. Such athletes often have short-lived careers and a lifetime of suffering.

Especially in many contact sports, tough athletes are given bountiful rewards. Unfortunately, the rewards often lead to an extreme psychological reaction by athletes wishing to win the admiration and respect of coaches, athletic trainers, teammates, and fans. The athletes may thoroughly enjoy the rewards, and they may become increasingly involved in earning more rewards by proving and continually displaying their dedication.

With time, the well-intentioned appearance of dedication and commitment develops into the projection of a false image of invulnerability. As athletes attempt to live up to this impossible image, both psychologically and physically, problems begin to appear. Soon, it is accepted as fact that tough athletes never need a rest, never miss a play, never go to the athletic training room, and never let an injury keep them from playing. Failure to live up to the expectations fostered by this image is judged as a sign of weakness. Following his seventh concussion, Eric Lindros said "there might be more bumps in the road, there might not be . . . " (AskMen.com, 2004). He has since sustained an eighth concussion playing hockey, and continues to play.

Eventually, athletes begin to believe in the image of invulnerability off, as well as on, the playing field. They believe they only deserve the right to feel proud if they give 110%. No one points out to them that giving 110% is impossible or that trying to do so can lead to performing at 50% of optimal ability. This belief system persists in spite of the fact that most athletes who adhere to these attitudes are unable to perform at their best because they are chronically overtired, playing in pain, and adjusting their style of play to their injuries.

Finally, the athletes become extremely vulnerable and totally unprepared for the incapacitating injury or lifelong pain that will likely follow. A major change in attitude is required to ensure a healthy adaptation to injury and life. Without this change in attitude, athletes will not be able to accept injuries and respond positively to them. As a result, athletes will fail to develop to their fullest potential, and in so doing their coaches and athletic trainers will also fail. True professionals must realize the hazards of these mistaken attitudes of the past before they can use to the fullest the specific psychological strategies that we present later in this chapter.

Injured athletes are worthless

Montreal Expo's President John McHale attempted to describe Andre Dawson's response to the injury and pain in his knee. "Andre is a very unusual man. . . . I'll tell you what's happening here. What's happening is that even with the year he's had, his pride and his commitment to his job are such that he won't take himself out or even excuse himself."

Andre's view was "I'm just not the sort to throw in the towel. I don't know, maybe that's just the way I was raised."

Harry Stein, "Brought to His Knees,"
Sport, September 1984, pp. 64, 66

Some coaches have been led to believe the best way to foster a rapid recovery from injury is to make injured athletes feel unimportant as long as they are injured. This is, to say the least, a counterproductive approach. Coaches who hold this view clearly communicate to their athletes that they only care for them as performers. Some coaches communicate this message by isolating injured athletes from healthy team members. Some refuse any form of verbal communication while using body language to suggest that injured athletes should feel guilty for being injured and not helping the team win. Others talk behind the injured athletes' backs and suggest that the athletes are malingerers, lack mental toughness and desire, or are not fully committed to the success of the team.

Leaders in sport must realize that the time during which athletes are recovering from injury is crucial for either developing or destroying trust. It is during this time that leaders have a chance to demonstrate care and concern and show that they are as committed to their athletes as they ask their athletes to be to them.

Most contemporary athletes are intelligent and sophisticated. They realize that actions speak louder than words. Athletes have learned to respect their precious physical gifts, and they expect their coaches and athletic trainers to do likewise.

Successful leaders of athletes must help the athletes realize that attitudes such as desire, pride, and commitment are beneficial at the right time and place but that these attitudes may also be hazardous to present and future health if taken to the extreme. The key is for leaders to do what is in the *best interest* of injured athletes. When this approach is followed, athletes, coaches, athletic trainers, and teams alike will have the best possible chance of attaining their fullest potential. When this approach is not followed, there is still a chance that the athletes themselves will put sport in a proper perspective. But they will do so out of *distrust* rather than trust. This will often lead athletes to decide that sport is unimportant and a place for personal abuse rather than positive growth and fulfillment.

Whole-Person Philosophy

"I went to the doctor with Andre Dawson a couple of times," Pete Rose was saying now. . . . The conversation rapidly turned to the gruesome but unavoidable subject of permanent injury. "Listen," said Rose, "I know a guy who fought the whole organization because he didn't want to jeopardize his health—Johnny Bench. He told them, 'I will not catch anymore, period. I don't plan to be a cripple when I'm through.'"

Rose paused . . . "And I'm not gonna sit here and tell you that someone who says that is wrong. I mean, hell, when you finish playing this game, you've still got half your life in front of you."

Harry Stein, "Brought to His Knees,"
Sport, September 1984, p. 63

Danish (1986) makes an excellent point when he reminds us to respond to athletes as people, not just injuries. An athlete with an injury is no less of an athlete, no less of a person than before the injury. As such, it is unwise to treat the athlete as the injury. That is to say, a whole-person approach is preferable. Danish describes a helping skill model that can be of use to those working with athletes.

Social support. Social support, as mentioned previously, is critical in the rehabilitation process, particularly with moderate to severe injuries. If the athletic identification has been strong, family and friends may have come to respond to the athletes primarily through their role as athletes. In many cases friendships are based exclusively along these lines, particularly with other teammates or with other athletes. Suddenly these important ties may be ruptured. Injured athletes may no longer be seen and may no longer see themselves as athletes. Activities around which their lives centered now

move along without them. No one quite knows how to relate to these athletes except perhaps in terms of their past glory or possible future—but not to the injured people in the present.

Too often, when athletes are kept away because of injury, they feel that their teammates and time have marched on. There are new jokes, new alignments—in essence a new situation that excludes injured athletes and into which they must try to reintegrate themselves. By being there, other athletes have grown and developed with the situation.

We would go so far as to say that as soon as athletes can rejoin a team—even if on crutches or bandaged—they should do so. It is sometimes too much to ask someone to get back on a horse after being thrown, but a modified approach allows a gradual remount while preventing the consolidation of fears of overwhelming obstacles.

Asking an injured athlete to help the coaching staff or to mentor younger players are ways in which an injured athlete can still be a contributing member of the team.

Coaches and sport psychologists must help ensure that normal contacts are maintained. They should be as reassuringly optimistic about recovery of past abilities as possible, and they should also encourage injured athletes to discover other bases of support for themselves. Athletes need support from their coaches as they move from injury through rehabilitation to recovery (Peterson, 2001). In particular, athletes will benefit from informational support (i.e., relevant information about the injury) and emotional support (i.e., helping the athlete express emotions and feel understood) from coaches and athletic trainers throughout the injury and recovery processes.

Although social support and the reintegration of the injured athlete are important parts of the rehabilitation process, there are two problems with this "double-edged crutch" that may need confronting. First, an injured athlete may present a conscious or unconscious threat to others: "If it could happen to them, it could happen to me." This fear may evoke anything from a mild feeling of discomfort to an almost phobic avoidance of the injured player. This effect may even be exacerbated when a physical disfigurement or highly visible disability is present.

Second, although cooperation and cohesion are part of teamwork, so is competition. An athlete's injury may present an opportunity to another person. The second-string player, for example, may have a chance for glory. There may be mixed feelings by some team members in terms of providing emotional support and encouragement for a rapid return. This is what happened within the New England Patriots organization. Early in the 2000–2001 football season, the Patriots' starting quarterback, Drew Bledsoe, was injured. The starting job was turned over to an unknown, Tom Brady. With Brady as quarterback, the Patriots won seven games and were in contention for the playoffs. And then Bledsoe was cleared to play. Coach Bill Belichick decided to keep Brady in the starting lineup. Then, he got hurt in the AFC championship game and Bledsoe stepped in and carried the team to victory. With one game left, the Super Bowl, Coach Belichick had a tough decision on his hands. Should he start his high-profile, high-salary quarterback (Bledsoe) or his young breakout star who had been great all season? Brady was deemed healthy to play in the big game, got the start, and the Patriots won the first of what would be three NFL championships in four years, all with Brady as quarterback. Bledsoe has since been traded to the Buffalo Bills.

There is no easy way for a coach, trainer, sport psychologist, or athlete to proceed. The first scenario is probably easier to manage. Modeling warmth, openness, and acceptance will be very helpful. Showing at conscious and unconscious levels that the injured person should not be feared will set an important tone in the athletic environment. At the same time, the message "You will recover and rejoin us" is a powerful message for all concerned.

The second situation is more difficult. Even where it is recognized, it may be difficult to respond to it. Where possible, the competition should be appropriately focused on the athletic situation and not personalized. Tensions within the system (a polarization of teammates into factions around the competing athletes) should be brought to the surface and discussed. If not, the situation may fester and grow worse. One cannot ignore the realities of competition. One can, however, try to maintain as positive a climate as possible.

> To treat a knee and ignore the brain and emotions that direct the choreography of that knee is not consistent with total care of the patient.
>
> G. J. Faris, "Psychological Aspects of Athletic Rehabilitation," *Clinics in Sports Medicine, 4,* 1985, p. 546

Addressing the whole person. When dealing with an injured athlete, one of the most crucial aspects entails understanding what the athlete is going through before trying to "fix" him or her (Petitpas & Danish, 1995). An injured athlete may experience all, some, or none of the following feelings: grief, identity loss, separation and loneliness, fear and anxiety, and loss of confidence and performance decrements. If you try to address all of these issues, or some of them, without assessing what the individual athlete is experiencing, you risk frustrating the athlete further. When treating a physical ailment, there is often a protocol or guiding steps to follow. It can sometimes be difficult to remember that the injured athlete is a person and not just a broken leg. As Andersen (2000) put it, "We do not treat knees; we treat people" (p. 46). Thus, it is important to talk to the athlete about him/herself and not only about the injury.

Petitpas and Danish suggest a series of steps to follow when working with an injured athlete. The first step is to build rapport with the athlete. This step also allows you to develop a clear understanding of what the athlete is experiencing with his or her injury. Education is the next phase, during which the athlete learns more about the actual injury as well as what the rehabilitation process is likely to entail. This phase helps the athlete become a more active participant in the rehabilitation process. The phases of skill development and practice and evaluation follow the general education phase. The opportunity to learn and use skills (e.g., goal setting, imagery) not only help athletes with rehabilitation but also help them once they are "back in the game."

Heil, Wakefield, and Reed (1998) suggest that conceptualizing rehabilitation as an athletic challenge may help athletes through the rehabilitation process. By using this metaphor, the rehabilitation process encompasses familiar skills such as taking personal responsibility, an orientation toward achieving goals, readiness to pursue physical training with intensity and precision, and a willingness to move one's mental and physical skills to a higher level of performance. By likening rehabilitation to an injured athlete's familiar sport routine, rehabilitation becomes just another part of training for excellence rather than a setback in achieving athletic goals.

With athletes whose rehabilitation will take longer than 2 weeks, Striegel, Hedgpeth, and Sowa (1996) suggest two additional forms of social support: peer mentors and injury support groups. Peer mentor relationships are one-on-one opportunities for an injured athlete to talk with an athlete who has successfully rehabilitated a similar injury and, therefore, knows what the injured athlete is going through. Injury support groups provide injured athletes with a forum to talk about their injury, rehabilitation, and anything else with others who are in the same position. The injury support groups may focus on counseling, education, or both and are typically facilitated by a sport psychologist. Both of these forms of support may help motivate injured athletes as rehabilitation continues and also may give the athletes a sense that they are not alone. These forms of support can be formal or informal. As one athlete interviewed by Granito (2001) stated, "Anyone who is in the training room, it doesn't matter what sport, supports you. It's the same faces everyday. It's almost like you go through this whole process with people. It's like a support group" (p. 73).

Teaching Specific Psychological Rehabilitation Strategies

More and more, coaches and athletes are recognizing the mental aspects of sport performance and of the rehabilitation process. The same mental skills and techniques (e.g., goal-setting, mental imagery) that help athletes succeed in their sport can play a role in successful rehabilitation from injury. Helping athletes see the opportunity for personal learning and growth will enhance the process of recovering from an injury. Coaches, sport psychologists, and athletic trainers may also need to teach athletes that when an injury occurs it is reasonable and appropriate to think the injury is unfortunate, untimely, and inconvenient and to feel irritated, frustrated, and disappointed. It is *unreasonable* for athletes to convince themselves that the situation is hopeless, that injuries are a sign of weakness and should be hidden, or that their season or career is over.

Part of the learning is about the injury itself and the rehabilitation process. After all, it is difficult, if not impossible, for intelligent athletes to be positive and relaxed if they lack knowledge, are anxious, and wonder why they are doing what they are doing in the athletic training room. Much anxiety results from uncertainty, misconceptions, or inaccurate information. In addition, athletes who realize the purpose of rehabilitation are more likely to work hard and to provide useful information about their progress. A collaborative relationship between the athlete and athletic trainer can help foster a positive rehabilitation experience.

Athletes must also be helped to realize it is acceptable and appropriate to honestly express distressing emotions. When athletes are experiencing depressed mood, coaches or sport consultants must not negate disturbing feelings by urging athletes to "pick their spirits up." They should honestly explain to athletes that these feelings are normal and actually a sign of progress toward recovery psychologically and emotionally. To help get over these feelings, athletes may benefit from sharing experiences with other athletes who have successfully recovered from similar injuries and effectively returned to competition. As mentioned earlier, for more seriously injured athletes, support groups for sharing and discussing concerns, fears, and difficulties may be helpful (Granito, 2001; Silva & Hardy, 1991; Striegel et al., 1996; Wiese & Weiss, 1987). If, in spite of such support, prolonged detachment, lack of spontaneity, and disinterest in activities and people persist, professional counseling or therapy may be necessary (Wehlage, 1980).

Two comprehensive survey studies that examined psychosocial factors that might relate to sports injury rehabilitation, in this case ankle and knee injuries, found that athletes who possess certain mental attributes and who use certain mental skills may recover faster from injury. In the first study by Ievleva and Orlick (1991), athletes who used more goal setting, healing mental imagery, and positive self-talk recovered faster than athletes who failed to do so. A follow-up study by Loundagin and Fisher (1993) revealed a similar pattern of results and also that focus of attention and stress reduction significantly enhanced recovery time. In contrast, a study by Scherzer (1999) failed to find any correlation between using mental skills and recovery from knee surgery except for goal setting predicting one outcome measure. In a review of research on both preventive and rehabilitative psychological interventions for sport injury, Cupal (1998) concluded that psychological interventions significantly altered the rehabilitation outcome for injured athletes in terms of earlier gains in strength, increases in functional ability, and reduction of pain, state anxiety, and reinjury anxiety. Both research and extensive anecdotal information from consulting experiences offer support for teaching the following psychological interventions to injured athletes.

Thought-Stoppage and Cognitive Restructuring

What athletes say to themselves following an injury helps determine their subsequent behavior. Athletes can be taught coping skills to control their inner thoughts. Then when faulty or self-defeating internal dialogues occur, the athletes can use an intervention strategy such as thought-stoppage or cognitive restructuring. (See Chapter 18 for more information on these and other techniques for controlling thoughts.) Another way to conceptualize thought-stoppage and cognitive restructuring is to think of them in terms of "self-talk" or how we speak to ourselves. Positive self-talk is

thought to contribute to personal well-being and the enhancement of healing (Ievleva & Orlick, 1991), possibly because of such self-statements being under the athlete's control or because the statements enhance motivation.

As an example of the importance of inner dialogue, consider an injury-related situation in which an athlete is in the athletic training room receiving treatment and going through rehabilitation exercises while experiencing a great amount of pain and little apparent improvement in the injured area. If her inner dialogue becomes self-defeating, the athlete worries and questions the benefit of treatment and exercise.

> This is awful. This hurts too much to be beneficial. These exercises will probably cause me more harm. Besides, I've been doing this for three days now, and I can't see any progress. It would be a lot easier to just let the injury heal on its own. I don't think I'll come tomorrow. If it's really important, the coach will call me. If she doesn't, it will mean I was right. It really doesn't matter if I get treatment.

The athlete does not get much out of today's treatment and begins to develop excuses for not continuing therapy.

On the other hand, if the athlete's inner dialogue is self-enhancing, she worries and questions the benefits of treatment and exercise but then thinks:

> Stop. These exercises hurt, but it's okay—they'll pay off. I'm lucky to have knowledgeable people helping me. I'll be competing soon because I'm doing these exercises. If the pain gets too severe, I'll ask my rehabilitation trainer if I am doing it right and, if I am, I'll live with it and think about how happy I'll be to be competing again.

The athlete has a good treatment session and prepares herself to continue for as long as necessary. She develops rapport with her athletic trainer and coach, both of whom feel good about the athlete. By using cognitive techniques that promote positive self-talk and attitude, athletes can often shorten the time period needed to rehabilitate from injury (Ievleva & Orlick, 1991; Loundagin & Fisher, 1993).

Imagery

When Philadelphia Phillies pinch-hitter Len Matuszek unloaded against the Chicago Cubs Tuesday night, he released six weeks of frustration.

In his second at bat since coming off the disabled list, Matuszek cracked a leadoff, pinch-hit home run in the seventh inning to give the Phillies a 3–2 victory over the Cubs. He hit the first pitch into the right-field bull pen. "That was all I had on my mind during my time on the disabled list. I kept envisioning some ways to help this team win a game. Even with the injury, my attitude has been good."

"Phillie Unloads Frustration on Cubs,"
The Daily Progress, July 24, 1984, p. D3

Athletes' imaginations can greatly influence their response to injury. Many imagine the worst that could happen. Athletes can be taught to control their visual images and to direct them productively to reduce anxiety and to aid in rehabilitation and successful return to the performance arena. See Chapter 16 for more detailed information on what imagery is and techniques that can be used to teach and enhance imagery skills.

Mastery imagery can be used to foster motivation for rehabilitation and confidence on return to competition. While disabled, athletes may visually rehearse returning to competition and performing effectively. For athletes who experience difficulty viewing themselves vividly in their mind, relaxation exercises should precede the imagery session. Some athletes visualize better with the aid of recordings or video replays of their most effective game performances.

Injured athletes also can use coping rehearsal to visually rehearse anticipated problematic situations or obstacles that may stand in the way of their successful return to competition and then rehearse effectively overcoming these obstacles. Coping rehearsal is very realistic in that it prepares athletes for difficulties that might occur. Such visual rehearsal methods can effectively prepare injured athletes for any number of competitive or practice situations, thereby helping them to maintain physical skills, retain confidence in their ability, and dissipate any lingering fears they may have of reinjury on return to competition (Ievleva & Orlick, 1993).

Injured athletes can use emotive imagery to help feel secure and confident that rehabilitation will be successful. The athletes rehearse various scenes that produce positive self-enhancing feelings such as enthusiasm, self-pride, and confidence. Athletes may, for instance, rehearse feeling excited about their first game following injury or rehearse thoughts of the admiration coaches, teammates, and friends will have for them on their return from injury. Athletes can also be instructed to think of other athletes like themselves who have overcome similar injuries and then generate other scenes that produce positive feelings.

Athletes can use healing imagery to vividly envision what is happening to the injury internally during the rehabilitation process. To do this, athletes must receive a detailed explanation of their injury. Whenever possible, color pictures should be used to help athletes develop a mental picture of the injury. The healing process and purpose of the rehabilitation techniques are then explained. After visualizing the healing process, athletes are asked to imagine in vivid color the healing occurring during treatment sessions and at intervals during the day. For example, athletes can imagine increased blood flow and warmth going to the injured area, or they can imagine the stretching necessary for enhancing range of motion. Although there is need for further research to determine the effectiveness of healing rehearsal, it appears to be a beneficial strategy for aiding the healing process.

Despite research findings that imagery can help with recovery (e.g., Ievleva & Orlick, 1991), many athletes do not use imagery as extensively during rehabilitation as they do for training and competition (Sordoni, Hall, & Forwell, 2000). Cupal and Brewer (2001) found that for people recovering from ACL reconstruction, practicing mental imagery was associated with gains in strength, less reinjury anxiety, and less pain. These benefits were observed even though participants practiced visualization less often than expected.

Goal-Setting

Throughout the rehabilitation process, it is most helpful for the rehabilitation team to work actively with the injured athlete at setting specific short- and long-term goals for recovery, return to practice and competition, and day-to-day rehabilitation that include time, place, and activities (DePalma & DePalma, 1989). Athletes should be actively involved in this process as much as possible, with more seriously injured athletes more actively involved. (See Chapter 13 for specific suggestions on how to effectively set goals and implement a goal-setting program.)

The following example highlights the effective use of goals in the rehabilitation process. A university-age athlete was drafted out of high school by a professional baseball team but chose to go to college before turning professional. In the fall of his freshman year in college he tore ligaments in his throwing arm, which required surgery. The following advice and program were outlined for him as he psychologically prepared for his return to practice the following spring. The program was designed to facilitate a safe return and a successful future.

The athlete, a pitcher, was reminded of how excited he would be on the first day of spring practice to find out if he still "had it," if he could still throw hard. He was reminded of the need to be smart, emotionally controlled, disciplined, and patient in order to control himself when his personal excitement over being back on the field with his teammates was combined with the high of a beautiful spring day following a long winter. He also was told that he would feel great and have an almost overpowering urge to overthrow on the first day his arm felt good. In addition, he would want to try all of his different pitches. The desire to help his teammates be successful and the thrill of getting back on stage and becoming a star again would be highly motivating. He was told of the importance of realizing the

temptation of these feelings and cautioned not to fall victim to them.

Together, this athlete, his coaches, and his athletic trainers outlined a specific goal plan. They decided on a set number of throws each day, the distance of the throws, the approximate speed of the throws, and the kinds of throws. For the first 3 weeks the athlete's catcher and a coach would help make sure that the plan was adhered to on a daily basis. Short- and long-term goals were detailed so that by the fifth game of the year the athlete would be ready to return to the pitching mound for three innings of relief pitching. It is essential that these goals are important to the athlete (Danish, 1986), and this is best accomplished if time is taken to explain to the athlete the relationship between staying focused on and committed to agreed-on goals and successful rehabilitation and return to competition.

A similar plan was detailed for physical treatments. Both plans were reinforced by coaches, athletic trainers, and teammates, as well as by daily visualization of the good feelings and results that would occur from sticking to the plan. Despite many days of questioning, doubt, and uncertainty, the athlete generally remained positive, stayed with the plan, and made a highly successful return to competition one week later than planned.

As with many other athletes, the process from injury to return to competition was a challenge to this athlete's mind and body. Because the process was managed properly, it allowed for a positive and bright future. Research by Filby, Maynard, and Graydon (1999) found support for the notion that setting multiple goals (e.g., outcome, process, and performance goals) improved task performance. Wayda, Armenth-Brothers, and Boyce (1998) further explain that if the injured athlete feels that he or she is part of the process (i.e., by taking an active role in goal-setting), he or she is more likely to be committed to the rehabilitation program.

Relaxation

Practicing any of the relaxation techniques (see Chapter 15) can play a potential role in reducing stress and speeding injury rehabilitation and recovery (Loundagin & Fisher, 1993). These results may have occurred for a number of reasons. Relaxation helps open the mind–body channels that regulate the body, thereby enabling inner control over the body (Botterill et al., 1996). Tension levels often increase in the injured area, owing to the stress of being injured (Brewer, Van Raalte, & Linder, 1991). This tension can increase pain and work against the effectiveness of the rehabilitation exercises by, for example, reducing blood flow and range of motion. Practicing a relax-ation routine can relieve the tension and enhance blood circulation. The greater the blood flow, the faster injured tissues are repaired (Ievleva & Orlick, 1993). Injured athletes who participated in stress inoculation training (i.e., deep breathing, progres-sive muscular relaxation, imagery) experienced less anxiety, less pain, and fewer days to recovery than counterparts who received only physical therapy, demonstrating the effectiveness of adding relaxation training to physical rehabilita-tion protocols (Ross & Berger, 1996).

Summary

Sport psychologists have made great advances in understanding the psychological rehabilita-tion of athletes and the psychological factors that put athletes at risk of injury. Although some athletes have effective psychological responses, others do not. This chapter focuses on factors that may predispose athletes to injuries, patterns of negative reactions to injuries, and ways in which coaches and sport psychologists can help athletes respond psychologically to injuries in positive, growth-oriented ways.

Although no clear injury-prone personality has been identified, some factors such as high life stress and low social support and psychological coping skills are predictive of injury. These and other factors related to injury are described, and possible preventive interventions are pre-sented. More and less adaptive responses to injury are illustrated. Using a cognitive appraisal model, we identify personal and situational factors that might influence an athlete's cognitive appraisal of the injury and his or her resulting emotional and behavioral responses to both the injury and injury rehabilitation. We agree with Brewer's (1994) conclusion that cognitive appraisal models offer a useful framework to guide both future empirical efforts and rehabili-tation practice. Crisis intervention responses, systems of social support, treatment of the whole person, and cognitive-behavioral interventions are discussed as ways to help injured athletes respond to injury in a more positive psychological way.

Study Questions

1. What are key factors that may predispose some athletes to injury? How can the athlete and the sport or team environment be modified to reduce risk factors and enhance buffering factors?

2. List five responses that may occur as a result of anxiety and tension associated with an injury on an athlete's initial return to competition.

3. How and why might personal growth possibilities become an important part of the psy-chological rehabilitation of the injured athlete?

4. List five problematic results of an athlete returning to competition following an injury if not psychologically prepared.

5. Diagram the cognitive appraisal model of psychological adjustment to athletic injury and discuss the different components.

6. Explain the differences among mastery imagery, coping rehearsal, emotive imagery, and healing imagery.

7. Describe what other psychological strategies might be used to hasten rehabilitation and to prepare for returning to competition.

References

Andersen, M. B. (2000). Supervision of athletic trainers; counseling encounters. *Athletic Therapy Today, 5*, 46–47.

Andersen, M. B., & Williams, J. M. (1988). A model of stress and athletic injury: Prediction and prevention. *Journal of Sport and Exercise Psychology, 10*, 294–306.

Andersen, M. B., & Williams, J. M. (1999). Athletic injury, psychosocial factors, and perceptual changes during stress. *Journal of Sports Sciences, 17*, 735–741.

AskMen.com. (2004). *Eric Lindros*. Retrieved September 29, 2004, from http://www.askmen.com/men/sports/45_eric_lindros.html

Blackwell, B., & McCullagh, P. (1990). The relationship of athletic injury to life stress, competitive anxiety and coping resources. *Athletic Training, 25*, 23–27.

Botterill, C., Flint, F. A., & Ievleva, L. (1996). Psychology of the injured athlete. In J. E. Zachazewski, D. J. Magee, & W. S. Quillen (Eds.), *Athletic injuries and rehabilitation* (pp. 791–805). Philadelphia: W. B. Saunders.

Bramwell, S. T., Masuda, M., Wagner, N. N., & Holmes, T. H. (1975). Psychosocial factors in athletic injuries. *Journal of Human Stress, 2*, 6–20.

Brewer, B. W. (1993). Self-identity and specific vulnerability to depressed mood. *Journal of Personality, 61*, 343–364.

Brewer, B. W. (1994). Review and critique of models of psychological adjustment to athletic injury. *Journal of Applied Sport Psychology, 6*, 87–100.

Brewer, B. W., Van Raalte, J. L., & Linder, D. E. (1991). Role of the sport psychologist in treating injured athletes: A survey of sport medicine providers. *Journal of Applied Sport Psychology, 3*, 183–190.

Brewer, B. W., Van Raalte, J. L., & Linder, D. E. (1993). Athletic identity: Hercules' muscles or Achilles heel? *International Journal of Sport Psychology, 24*, 237–254.

Coddington, R. D., & Troxell, J. R. (1980). The effects of emotional factors on football injury rates—a pilot study. *Journal of Human Stress, 7*, 3–5.

Cramer Roh, J. L., & Perna, F. M. (2000). Psychology/counseling: A universal competency in athletic training. *Journal of Athletic Training, 35*, 458–465.

Crossman, J., & Jamieson, J. (1985). Differences in perceptions of seriousness and disrupting effects of athletic injury as viewed by athletes and their trainer. *Perceptual and Motor Skills, 61*, 1131–1134.

Cupal, D. D. (1998). Psychological interventions in sport injury prevention and rehabilitation. *Journal of Applied Sport Psychology, 10,* 103–123.

Cupal, D. D., & Brewer, B. W. (2001). Effects of relaxation and guided imagery on knee strength, reinjury anxiety, and pain following anterior cruciate ligament reconstruction. *Rehabilitation Psychology, 46,* 28–43.

Dalhauser, M., & Thomas, M. D. (1979). Visual disembedding and locus of control as variables associated with high school football injuries. *Perceptual and Motor Skills, 49,* 254.

Daly, J. M., Brewer, B. W., Van Raalte, J. L., Petitpas, A. J., & Sklar, J. H. (1995). Cognitive appraisal, emotional adjustment, and adherence to rehabilitation following knee surgery. *Journal of Sport Rehabilitation, 4,* 23–30.

Danish, S. J. (1986). Psychological aspects in the care and treatment of athletic injuries. In P. E. Vinger & E. F. Hoerner (Eds.), *Sports injuries: The unthwarted epidemic* (pp. 345–353). Littleton, MA: PSG.

Davis, J. O. (1991). Sports injuries and stress management: An opportunity for research. *The Sport Psychologist, 5,* 175–182.

DePalma, M. T., & DePalma, B. (1989). The use of instruction and the behavioral approach to facilitate injury rehabilitation. *Athletic Training, 24,* 217–219.

DeWitt, D. J. (1980). Cognitive and biofeedback training for stress reduction with university athletes. *Journal of Sport Psychology, 2,* 288–294.

Duda, J. L., Smart, A. E., & Tappe, M. K. (1989). Predictors of adherence in the rehabilitation of athletic injuries: An application of personal investment theory. *Journal of Sport Psychology, 11,* 367–381.

Erikson, E. (1968). *Identity: Youth and crisis.* New York: Norton.

Ermler, K. L., & Thomas, C. E. (1990). Interventions for the alienating effect of injury. *Athletic Training, 25,* 269–271.

Evans, L., & Hardy, L. (1995). Sport injury and grief responses. A review. *Journal of Sport & Exercise Psychology, 17,* 227–245.

Faris, G. J. (1985). Psychologic aspects of athletic rehabilitation. *Clinics in Sports Medicine, 4,* 545–551.

Fawkner, H. J. (1995). *Predisposition to injury in athletes: The role of psychosocial factors.* Unpublished master's thesis, University of Melbourne, Australia.

Fawkner, J. J., McMurray, N. E., & Summers, J. J. (1999). Athletic injury and minor life events: A prospective study. *Journal of Science and Medicine in Sport, 2,* 117–124.

Fields, K. B., Delaney, M., & Hinkle, S. (1990). A prospective study of type A behavior and running injuries. *The Journal of Family Practice, 30,* 425–429.

Filby, W. C. D., Maynard, I. W., & Graydon, J. K. (1999). The effect of multiple-goal strategies on performance outcomes in training and competition. *Journal of Applied Sport Psychology, 11,* 230–246.

Fisher, A. C., Domm, M. A., & Wuest, D. A. (1988). Adherence to sports-injury rehabilitation programs. *The Physician and Sportsmedicine, 16,* 47–52.

Ford, I. A., Eklund, R. C., & Gordon, S. (2000). An examination of psychosocial variables moderating the relationship between life stress and injury time-loss among athletes of a high standard. *Journal of Sports Sciences, 18,* 301–312.

Ford, I., & Gordon, S. (1997). Perspectives of sport physiotherapists on the frequency and significance of psychological factors in professional practice: Implications for curriculum design in professional training. *Australian Journal of Science and Medicine in Sport, 29,* 34–40.

Granito, V. J. (2001). Athletic injury experience: A qualitative focus group approach. *Journal of Sport Behavior, 24,* 63–82.

Green, S. L., & Weinberg, R. S. (2001). Relationships among athletic identity, coping skills, social support, and the psychological impact of injury in recreational participants. *Journal of Applied Sport Psychology, 31,* 40–59.

Grove, J. R., Stewart, R. M. L., & Gordon, S. (1990, October). *Emotional reactions of athletes to knee rehabilitation.* Paper presented at the annual meeting of the Australian Sports Medicine Federation, Alice Springs, Australia.

Hanson, S. J., McCullagh, P., & Tonymon, P. (1992). The relationship of personality characteristics, life stress, and coping resources to athletic injury. *Journal of Sport & Exercise Psychology, 14,* 262–272.

Hardy, C. J., O'Connor, K. A., & Geisler, P. R. (1990). The role of gender and social support in the life stress injury relationship. *Proceedings of the Association for the Advancement of Applied Sport Psychology, Fifth Annual Conference (Abstract),* 51.

Harris, L. L. (2003). Integrating and analyzing psychosocial and stage theories to challenge the development of the injured collegiate athlete. *Journal of Athletic Training, 38,* 75–82.

Heil, J. (Ed.). (1993). *Psychology of sport injury.* Champaign, IL: Human Kinetics.

Heil, J., Wakefield, C., & Reed, C. (1998). Patient as athlete: A metaphor for injury rehabilitation. In K. F. Hays (Ed.), *Integrating exercise, sports, movement and mind: Therapeutic unity.* Binghamton, NY: Haworth Press.

Henderson, J., & Carroll, W. (1993). The athletic trainer's role in preventing sport injury and rehabilitating injured athletes: A psychological perspective. In D. Pargman (Ed.), *Psychological bases of sports injuries* (pp. 15–31). Morgantown, WV: Fitness Information Technology.

Ievleva, L., & Orlick, T. (1991). Mental links to enhanced healing: An exploratory study. *The Sport Psychologist, 5,* 25–40.

Ievleva, L., & Orlick, T. (1993). Mental paths to enhanced recovery from a sports injury. In D. Pargman (Ed.), *Psychological bases of sport injuries* (pp. 219–245). Morgantown, WV: Fitness information Technology.

Johnson, U., Ekengren, J., & Andersen, M. B. (2005). Injury prevention in Sweden: Helping soccer players at risk. *Journal of Sport and Exercise Psychology, 27.*

Johnston, L. H., & Carroll, D. (2000). The psychological impact of injury: Effects of prior sport and exercise involvement. *British Journal of Sports Medicine, 34,* 436–439.

Junge, A. (2000). The influence of psychological factors on sports injuries. *American Journal of Sports Medicine, 28,* S10–S15.

Kerr, G., & Goss, J. (1996). The effects of a stress management program on injuries and stress levels. *Journal of Applied Sport Psychology, 8,* 109–117.

Kerr, G., & Minden, H. (1988). Psychological factors related to the occurrence of athletic injuries. *Journal of Sport and Exercise Physiology, 37,* 1–11.

Kleiber, D. A., & Brock, S. C. (1992). The effect of career-ending injuries on the subsequent well-being of elite college athletes. *Sociology of Sport Journal, 9,* 70–75.

Kolt, G., & Kirkby, R. (1996). Injury in Australian female competitive gymnasts: A psychological perspective. *Australian Physiotherapy, 42,* 121–126.

Kubler-Ross, E. (1969). *On death and dying.* New York: Macmillan.

Larson, G. A., Starkey, C., & Zaichkowsky, L. D. (1996). Psychological aspects of athletic injuries as perceived by athletic trainers. *The Sport Psychologist, 10,* 37–47.

Lavallee, L., & Flint, F. (1996). The relationship of stress, competitive anxiety, mood state, and social support to athletic injury. *Journal of Athletic Training, 31,* 296–299.

Loundagin, C., & Fisher, L. (1993, October). *The relationship between mental skills and enhanced injury rehabilitation.* Paper presented at the annual meeting of the Association for the Advancement of Applied Sport Psychology, Montreal, Quebec.

Lysens, R., Auweele, Y. V., & Ostyn, M. (1986). The relationship between psychosocial factors and sports injuries. *Journal of Sports Medicine and Physical Fitness, 26,* 77–84.

May, J. R., & Brown, L. (1989). Delivery of psychological services to the U.S. alpine ski team prior to and during the Olympics in Calgary. *The Sport Psychologist, 3,* 320–329.

McDonald, S. A., & Hardy, C. J. (1990). Affective response patterns of the injured athlete: An exploratory analysis. *The Sport Psychologist, 4,* 261–274.

McDonell, C. (2004). *Shooting from the lip.* Buffalo, NY: Firefly Books.

McLeod, S., & Kirkby, R. J. (1995). Locus of control as a predictor of injury in elite basketball players. *Sports Medicine, Training and Rehabilitation, 6,* 201–206.

Meyer, K. N. (1995). *The influence of personality factors, life stress, and coping strategies on the incidence of injury in long-distance runners.* Unpublished master's thesis, University of Colorado, Boulder.

Meyers, M. C., Sterling, J. C., Calvo, R. D., Marley, R., & Duhon, T. K. (1991). Mood state of athletes undergoing orthopaedic surgery and rehabilitation: A preliminary report. *Medicine and Science in Sports and Exercise, 23,* S138.

Misasi, S. P., Redmond, C. J., & Kemler, D. S. (1998). Counseling skills and the athletic therapist. *Athletic Therapy Today, 3,* 35–38.

Murphy, S. M. (1988). The on-site provision of sport psychology services at the U.S. Olympic Festival. *The Sport Psychologist, 2,* 337–350.

Nideffer, R. M. (1983). The injured athlete: Psychological factors in treatment. *Orthopedic Clinics of North America, 14,* 374–385.

Nigorikawa, T., Oishi, E., Yasukawa, M., Kamimura, M., Murayama, J., & Tanaka, N. (2003). Type A behavior pattern and sports injuries. *Japanese Journal of Physical Fitness and Sports Medicine, 52,* 359–367.

Pargman, D., (Ed.). (1999). *Psychological bases of sports injuries* (2nd ed.). Morgantown, WV: Fitness Information Technology.

Pargman, D., & Lunt, S. D. (1989). The relationship of self-concept and locus of control to the severity of injury in freshman collegiate football players. *Sports Medicine, Training and Rehabilitation, 1,* 201–208.

Passer, M. W., & Seese, M. D. (1983). Life stress and athletic injury: Examination of positive versus negative events and three moderator variables. *Journal of Human Stress, 10,* 11–16.

Pedersen, P. (1986). The grief response and injury: A special challenge for athletes and athletic trainers. *Athletic Training, 21,* 312–314.

Perna, F. M., Antoni, M. H., Baum, A., Gordon, P., & Schneiderman, N. (2003). Cognitive behavioral stress management effects on injury and illness among competitive athletes: A randomized clinical trial. *Annals of Behavioral Medicine, 25,* 66–73.

Perna, F., & McDowell, S. (1993, October). *The association of stress and coping with illness and injury among elite athletes.* Paper presented at the annual meeting of the Association for the Advancement of Applied Sport Psychology, Montreal, Quebec.

Peterson, K. (2001). Supporting athletes during injury rehab. *Olympic Coach, 11,* 7–9.

Petitpas, A., Champagne, D., Chartrand, J., Danish, S., & Murphy, S. (1997). *Athlete's guide to career planning.* Champaign, IL: Human Kinetics.

Petitpas, A., & Danish, S. J. (1995). Caring for injured athletes. In S. M. Murphy (Ed.), *Sport psychology interventions* (pp. 255–281). Champaign, IL: Human Kinetics.

Petrie, T. A. (1992). Psychosocial antecedents of athletic injury: The effects of life stress and social support on female collegiate gymnasts. *Behavioral Medicine, 18,* 127–138.

Petrie, T. A. (1993). Coping skills, competitive trait anxiety, and playing status: Moderating effects of the life stress-injury relationship. *Journal of Sport & Exercise Psychology, 15,* 261–274.

Quinn, A. M., & Fallon, B. J. (1999). The changes in psychological characteristics and reactions of elite athletes from injury onset until full recovery. *Journal of Applied Sport Psychology, 11,* 210–229.

Richman, J. M., Hardy, C. J., Rosenfeld, L. B., & Callahan, A. E. (1989). Strategies for enhancing social support networks in sport: A brainstorming experience. *Journal of Applied Sport Psychology, 1,* 150–159.

Ross, M. J., & Berger, R. S. (1996). Effects of stress inoculation training on athletes' postsurgical pain and rehabilitation after orthopedic injury. *Journal of Consulting and Clinical Psychology, 64,* 406–410.

Rotella, R. (1984). Psychological care of the injured athlete. In L. Bunker, R. J. Rotella, & A. S. Reilly (Eds.), *Sport psychology: Psychological considerations in maximizing sport performance.* Ithaca, NY: Mouvement Publications.

Scherzer, C. B. (1999). *Using psychological skills in rehabilitation following knee surgery.* Unpublished master's thesis, Springfield College, Springfield, MA.

Scherzer, C. B. (2004). *Training athletic trainers in the delivery of sport psychology rehabilitation interventions.* Unpublished doctoral dissertation, University of Arizona, Tucson.

Shaffer, S. M. (1992). *Attributions and self-efficacy as predictors of rehabilitative success*. Unpublished master's thesis, University of Illinois, Champaign.

Silva, J. M., Hardy, C. J. (1991). The sport psychologist: Psychological aspects of injury in sport. In F. O. Mueller & A. Ryan (Eds.), *The sport medicine team and athletic injury prevention* (pp. 114–132). Philadelphia: Davis.

Smith, R. E., Ptacek, J. T., & Patterson, E. (2000). Moderator effects of cognitive and somatic trait anxiety on the relation between life stress and physical injuries. *Anxiety, Stress & Coping, 13*, 269–288.

Smith, A. M., Scott, S. G., O'Fallon, W. M., & Young, M. L. (1990). Emotional responses of athletes to injury. *Mayo Clinic Proceedings, 65*, 38–50.

Smith, A. M., Scott, S. G., & Wiese, D. M. (1990). The psychological effects of sports injuries. *Sports Medicine, 9*, 352–369.

Smith, R. E., Ptacek, J. T., & Smoll, F. L. (1992). Sensation seeking, stress, and adolescent injuries: A test of stress-buffering, risk-taking, and coping skills hypotheses. *Journal of Personality and Social Psychology, 62*, 1016–1024.

Smith, R. E., Smoll, F. L., & Ptacek, J. T. (1990). Conjunctive moderator variables in vulnerability and resiliency research: Life stress, social support and coping skills, and adolescent sport injuries. *Journal of Personality and Social Psychology, 58*, 360–369.

Sordoni, C., Hall, C., & Forwell, L. (2000). The use of imagery by athletes during injury rehabilitation. *Journal of Sport Rehabilitation, 9*, 329–338.

Stein, H. (1984, September). Brought to his knees. *Sport,* 63–66.

Striegel, D. A., Hedgpeth, E. G., & Sowa, C. J. (1996). Differential psychological treatment of injured athletes based on length of rehabilitation. *Journal of Sport Rehabilitation, 5*, 330–335.

Thompson, N. J., & Morris, R. D. (1994). Predicting injury risk in adolescent football players: The importance of psychological variables. *Journal of Pediatric Psychology, 19*, 415–429.

Tuffey, S. (1991). The role of athletic trainers in facilitating psychological recovery from athletic injury. *Athletic Training, 26*, 346–351.

Udry, E., Gould, D., Bridges, D., & Beck, L. (1997). Down but not out: Athlete responses to season-ending injuries. *Journal of Sport and Exercise Psychology, 19*, 229–248.

Van Mechelen, W., Twisk, J., Molendijk, A., Blom, B., Snel, J., & Kemper, H. C. G. (1996). Subject-related risk factors for sports injuries: A 1-yr prospective study in young adults. *Medicine and Science in Sports and Exercise, 28*, 1171–1179.

Wayda, V. K., Armenth-Brothers, F., & Boyce, B. A. (1998). Goal setting: A key to injury rehabilitation. *Athletic Therapy Today, 3*, 21–25.

Wehlage, D. F. (1980). Managing the emotional reaction to loss in athletics. *Athletic Training, 15*, 144–146.

Wiese-Bjornstal, D. M., Smith, A. M., Shaffer, S. M., & Morrey, M. A. (1998). An integrated model of response to sport injury: Psychological and sociological dynamics. *Journal of Applied Sport Psychology, 10*, 46–69.

Wiese, D. M., & Weiss, M. R. (1987). Psychological rehabilitation and physical injury: Implications for the sport medicine team. *The Sport Psychologist, 1,* 318–330.

Williams, J. M. (2001). Psychology of injury risk and prevention. In R. N. Singer, H. A. Hausenblas, & C. M. Janelle (Eds.), *Handbook of research in sport psychology* (2nd ed.) (pp. 766–786). New York: Wiley.

Williams, J. M., & Andersen, M. B. (1997). Psychosocial influences on central and peripheral vision and reaction time during demanding tasks. *Behavioral Medicine, 26,* 160–167.

Williams, J. M., & Andersen, M. B. (1998). Psychosocial antecedents of sport injury: Review and critique of the stress and injury model. *Journal of Applied Sport Psychology, 10,* 5–25.

Williams, J. M., Hogan, T. D., & Andersen, M. B. (1993). Positive states of mind and athletic injury risk. *Psychosomatic Medicine, 55,* 468–472.

Williams, J. M., & Roepke, N. (1993). Psychology of injury and injury rehabilitation. In R. N. Singer, M. Murphy, & K. Tennant (Eds.), *Handbook of research in sport psychology* (pp. 815–839). New York: Macmillan.

Williams, J., Tonymon, P., & Wadsworth, W. A. (1986). Relationship of stress to injury in intercollegiate volleyball. *Journal of Human Stress, 12,* 38–43.

Wittig, A. F., & Schurr, K. T. (1994). Psychological characteristics of women volleyball players: Relationships with injuries, rehabilitation, and team success. *Personality and Social Psychology Bulletin, 20,* 322–330.

Yaffe, M. (1983). Sports injuries: Psychological aspects. *British Journal of Hospital Medicine, 27,* 224–232.

Zuckerman, M. (1979). *Sensation seeking: Beyond the optimal level of arousal.* Hillsdale, NJ: Erlbaum.

Career Transition among Athletes: Is There Life after Sports?

Jim Taylor, *San Francisco, California*
Bruce Ogilvie, *Los Gatos, California, deceased*
David Lavallee, *Loughborough, England*

I can't do it physically anymore, and that's really hard for me to say. It's hard to walk away. I can't explain in words how much everyone has meant to me. I'll never be able to fill the void of playing a football game. I don't look at it as a retirement. I look on it as graduation. You graduate from high school and you graduate from college. I'm graduating from pro football.

—*John Elway, two-time Super Bowl–winning quarterback*

During the course of athletes' careers, the primary focus of most sports administrators, coaches, and sport psychologists is on assisting athletes to maximize their competitive performances. This emphasis is expected, as athletes are their responsibilities during their competitive tenures and, when the athletes leave the team or sport organization, their attention has to turn to the current athletes under their charge. This system, unfortunately, tends to neglect what happens to athletes when they retire and must make the transition to another career and lifestyle.

Fortunately, there has been a growing interest at many levels of sport and among many groups involved in sport in the issue of what has become known as "career transition" (Baillie & Danish, 1992). Popular accounts of this issue over the years have provided anecdotal depictions of professional athletes adjusting to life after sport (Hoffer, 1990; Putnam, 1991). These have most often recounted difficulties that athletes have had following the conclusions of their careers (Bradley, 1976) with a few exceptions of athletes who had successful transitions (Batten, 1979). These accounts also have suggested that athlete retirement is a pervasive problem, but the accuracy of these observations comes into question as these writings lack empirical rigor and the ability to generalize to the larger population of athletes experiencing the end of their sports careers.

History and Background

It was only three decades ago that the issue of career transition gained the attention of sport psychologists. Leading professionals in the field in Europe such as Miroslav Vanek, Paul Kunath, Ferruccio Antonelli, Lars-Erik Unestahl, and John Kane who were consultants for their various national teams began to discuss this issue, describe experiences they had in their work with athletes, and express concern about the athletes' adjustment to a life after sport. Additionally, the media (e.g., Bradley, 1976; Plimpton, 1977) and early scholarly, although anecdotal, writings (Broom, 1982; McPherson, 1980; Ogilvie & Howe, 1982) brought to light some of the significant concerns associated with career transition among athletes. Soon after these preliminary discussions began, research emerged investigating the issues raised by these professionals (e.g., Haerle, 1975; Hill & Lowe, 1974). These researchers studied the impact of career transition on athletes in different sports and at various levels of competition.

Professionals from Eastern Europe were the leaders in these investigations. The nature of their sports organizations made the study of career transition more conducive to this process. Eastern European nations appeared to be accepting more responsibility for preparing their national athletes for a career beyond sport. The team psychologists in these countries typically had long-term relationships with the team members beginning early in their athletic development and enduring throughout their athletic careers.

Also, the centralized structure of the Eastern European sports organizations allowed for educational and vocational training to be an integral part of the developmental process of athletes. Many of these athletes studied in fields that were related to sports participation such as coaching, exercise physiology, and physical therapy, thus enabling them to combine their love of sport with a professional career after retirement. In addition, European elite athletes typically had a longer competitive history because of population size and the relatively limited pool of talent from which they had to draw. Outside of the former Soviet Union, most of these countries did not have the vast talent pool available in the United States, resulting in European athletes competing longer and retiring at a later age.

The decentralized nature of sports in many Western countries has often made it more difficult to examine the adjustment difficulties of elite athletes and to address them in an organized manner. Additionally, unlike other countries that often have national training centers for elite sports preparation, the primary development pools leading to most world-class and professional competition in the United States are the collegiate athletic programs and private sports clubs such as those found in swimming, figure skating, and gymnastics.

The opportunity to study and address career transition needs of elite athletes has proven to be difficult for a variety of reasons. Typically, trained professionals such as sport psychologists and career counselors have had limited contact with athletes during their competitive careers much less after they leave their sport. Until recently, sport administrators had little concern for athletes after they retire and sport psychologists rarely had the occasion to evaluate the need for such services to elite athletes. Additionally, the contact time that professionals had with athletes was not conducive to exploration of postcareer concerns. For example, sport psychologists usually work with elite athletes at training camps and competitions, neither of which provide opportunities for discussion of career transition issues.

Divergent perspectives held by administrators and coaches with respect to career transition also may have hindered further exploration of these concerns. For example, administrators either didn't see the need for career-transition services for their athletes or were limited because of budgetary constraints. Head coaches may have sabotaged career counseling programs because they interpreted them as distracting the athletes from their primary focus of winning. During the last 20 years, however, national sports federations in countries around the world have been establishing ongoing career counseling programs available to elite athletes (Anderson & Morris, 2000;

Sinclair & Hackfort, 2000; Wylleman, Lavallee, & Aflermann, 1999). For example, the Olympic Athlete Career Centre was launched in Canada in 1985 to assist their elite-level athletes in preparing for their life after sport. The United States Olympic Committee initiated the Career Assistance Program for Athletes in 1988 to provide support to retiring athletes during the career transition process. In addition, the Lifeskills for Elite Athletes Program was launched in Australia in 1989, and has since merged with the Athlete Career and Education (ACE) Program to provide a consistent career and education service for Australia's elite athletes. Although there is a dearth of research examining the value of these programs, one recent evaluation of the Australian ACE Program has shown that the program is effective in assisting active athletes in the areas of career planning and professional development (Gorely, Lavallee, Bruce, Teale, 2001).

Professional sports teams also appear to be responding to these concerns. The players' associations of the National Football League (NFL) and the National Basketball Association (NBA) have recently offered career counseling services to their members. However, the extent of use by these athletes is unclear. In fact, research indicates that relatively few elite athlete consider postathletic career concerns (Allison & Meyer, 1988; McInally, Cavin-Stice, & Knoth, 1992). It may be that the high salaries accorded these athletes may provide them with a false sense of security.

In recent years, the academic interest in career transitions has expanded. Whereas McPherson reported in 1980 that an extensive literature search generated 20 references pertaining to this area, over 270 references were identified that were related to sports career transition in 2000 by Lavallee, Wylleman, and Sinclair. In addition, an inspection of the conference proceedings from the 2001 International Society of Sport Psychology reveals that more than 10% of the program was dedicated to topics related to career transition. An international special-interest group of the European Federation of Sport Psychology (FEPSAC) has recently been initiated to exchange information on applied and

investigative work in the area, and this organization recently has published Position Statements on Sports Career Termination and Sports Career Transitions as well as a monograph on the topic (Wylleman et al., 1999).

Theoretical Perspectives on Career Transition

Since the onset of interest in the area of career transition for elite athletes, attempts have been made to provide a formal conceptualization of this process. Most investigators have drawn on retirement research outside of sport and tried to apply these models to the concerns of athletes.

Thanatology. Rosenberg (1982) originally suggested that retirement from sports is akin to social death, which is characterized as social isolation and rejection from the former in-group. This explanation has received support from anecdotal and fictitious accounts of athletes who have experienced similar reactions on retirement (Deford, 1981). However, the concept of social death also has been widely criticized and there has been little empirical support for this position (Blinde & Greendorfer, 1985; Blinde & Stratta, 1992).

Social gerontology. This view focuses on aging and considers life satisfaction as being dependent upon characteristics of the sports experience. Four social gerontological perspectives have been offered as the most applicable to sports retirement (Greendorfer & Blinde, 1985; Rosenberg, 1982). Disengagement theory (Cummings, Dean, Newell, & McCaffrey, 1960) posits that the person and society withdraw for the good of both, enabling younger people to enter the workforce and for the retired individuals to enjoy their remaining years. Activity theory (Havighurst & Albrecht, 1953) suggests that lost roles are replaced by new ones, so that people may maintain their overall level of activity. Continuity theory (Atchley, 1980) states that, if people have different roles, the time and energy from the earlier role may be reallocated to the remaining roles. Finally, social breakdown theory (Kuypers & Bengston, 1973) proposes that retirement becomes associated with negative evaluation, which causes individuals to withdraw from the activity and internalize the negative evaluation.

Despite their intuitive appeal, these views have been criticized as inadequate when applied to athletic retirement. Specifically, early research by Arviko (1976), Greendorfer and Blinde (1985), and Lerch (1982) provided little support for any of the social gerontological approaches.

Retirement as transition. A criticism of both thanatology and social gerontology theories is that they view retirement as a singular, abrupt event (Blinde & Greendorfer, 1985). In contrast, other researchers characterize retirement as a transition or process that involves development through life (Stambulova, 1994). Greendorfer and Blinde (1985) suggest that the focus should be on the continuation rather than cessation of behaviors, the gradual alteration rather than relinquishment of goals and interests, and the emergence of few difficulties in adjustment. Data collected from former collegiate athletes support their view of retirement as transition (Blinde & Greendorfer, 1985; Greendorfer & Blinde, 1985).

Building on this perspective, theorists have offered models of career transition considering the specific needs and concerns of the athletic population. Hill and Lowe (1974) applied Sussman's (1971) analytic model to sport, which stressed the roles that personal, social, and environmental factors have in the transition process. Schlossberg (1981) offered a similar model that emphasized athletes' perceptions of the transition, characteristics of the pre- and posttransition environments, and the attributes of the individuals in their roles in the adaptation to the transition. Research by Sinclair and Orlick (1993) and Swain (1991) have supported this model. Both Hopson and Adams (1977) and Kubler-Ross (1969) also offer models that can help describe the steps through which athletes progress after leaving their sport with a particular emphasis on the emotional implications of career transition.

Conceptual Model of Career Transition

To continue the evolutionary process in our understanding of career transition among elite athletes, Taylor and Ogilvie (1994) developed a conceptual model that attempted to integrate the theoretical and empirical investigations to date by incorporating aspects of earlier theorizing, taking into account the findings of previous empirical research, and considering their own applied work with athletes in career transition. What emerged was a model that addresses all relevant concerns from the initiation of career transition to its ultimate consequences (see Figure 26-1).

Stage 1: Causes of Career Termination

The causes for termination of an athletic career are found most frequently to be a function of four factors: age, deselection, the consequences of an injury, and free choice. These factors influence a variety of psychological, social, and physical issues that contribute to the likelihood of distress because of career transition.

Age

Age or, more specifically, the decline in performance because of advancing age is a primary cause of retirement. Although anecdotal accounts of former elite athletes underscore the importance of age in retirement, empirical evidence also has shown that a substantial proportion of elite athletes retire because of decreased performance associated with age (e.g., Alfermann, 1995; Allison & Meyer, 1988).

The influence of age on career termination is a function of physiological, psychological, and social factors and has significant ramifications for both young and older athletes. For athletes competing in sports in which high-level performance occurs during adolescence, career termination may result when they are still teenagers. This will be particularly evident for those sports such as gymnastics in which puberty, and the accompanying physical

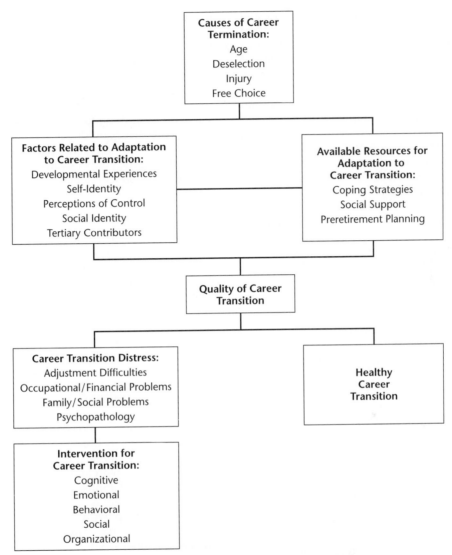

Figure 26-1 Conceptual model of adaptation to career transition

changes, can restrict rather than contribute to motor development and performance.

Similar difficulties with older athletes also are evident in sports such as baseball, football, and tennis that require size, strength, and precise motor skills. Athletes' ability to continue to perform at an elite level depends on whether they can maintain their physical capabilities at a competitive level. Athletes can often compete effectively into their 30s or later. However, because of the natural physical deterioration that accompanies approaching middle age, athletic performance will decline commensurately (Fisher & Conlee, 1979).

Age also has psychological influences on retirement. As athletes become older, they may lose their motivation to train and compete, and conclude that they have reached their competitive goals (Werthner & Orlick, 1986). Athletes' values may also change. In an early study, Svoboda and Vanek (1982) found that Czechoslovakian world-class athletes shifted their priorities away from a self-focus involving winning and traveling toward an other-focus with an emphasis on family and friends.

Finally, age possesses a social element. "Aging" athletes, particularly those whose performances begin to diminish, can be devalued by fans, management, media, and other athletes. This loss of status further contributes to the difficulties that may arise in the career transition process. Sinclair and Orlick (1993) reported that elite-amateur athletes who retired because of declining competitive performance tended to have the most difficulties with loss of status and a lack of self-confidence.

Deselection

One of the most significant contributors to career termination is the nature of the selection process that occurs at every level of competitive sports (Munroe & Albinson, 1996). This process, which follows a Darwinian "survival of the fittest" philosophy, selects only those athletes capable of progressing to the next level of competition and disregards those who do not meet the necessary performance criteria. Organized youth programs still place the highest priority on winning and this same philosophy predominates throughout high school, university, and professional sport. Data indicates that only one in 10,000 scholastic athletes receives college scholarships and only 1% of those play professionally. Moreover, the typical career length of a professional player in sports such as football, basketball, and baseball is only 4 to 5 years (National Collegiate Athletic Association, 2003).

Injury

Research has shown that the occurrence of serious or chronic injury often forces athletes to end their athletic careers prematurely (e.g., Allison & Meyer, 1988; Werthner & Orlick, 1986). Furthermore, it has been suggested that severe injuries may result in a variety of psychological difficulties including fear, anxiety, loss of self-esteem, depression, and substance abuse (Ogilvie & Howe, 1982).

Injury also has significant ramifications as retired athletes consider postsport careers. It is not uncommon for elite athletes to leave their sport permanently disabled to varying degrees. These physical disabilities can influence retired athletes negatively, producing a range of psychological and emotional problems. Injuries sustained during their athletic careers also may limit them in their choices of new careers.

Free Choice

An often neglected cause of career termination is that of the free choice of the athlete (Coakley, 1983). Research has indicated that it is a common cause of retirement among elite amateur and professional athletes (Alfermann & Gross, 1997). The impetus to end a career by choice is the most desirable of causes of retirement, because the decision resides wholly within the control of the athlete. Athletes choose to end their careers voluntarily for a variety of personal, social, and sport reasons. Athletes may choose to embark on a new direction in their lives (Lavallee, Grove, & Gordon, 1997). They may experience a change in values, motivations, and the desire to pursue new interests and goals (Greendorfer & Blinde, 1985).

Athletes in career transition may wish to spend more time with family and friends or seek out a new social milieu in which to immerse themselves (Schmid & Schilling, 1997). Lastly, their relationship with their sport also may change, for example, when athletes may have reached their sport-related goals (Sinclair & Orlick, 1993) or found that their sports participation was no longer enjoyable and rewarding (Werthner & Orlick, 1986).

Athletic careers that end voluntarily do not necessarily preclude athletes from having transition difficulties. Kerr and Dacyshyn (2000) reported that some athletes who chose to retire described their retirement as difficult. They also suggested that "voluntary" retirement is not always truly voluntary. Although athletes may decide to retire of their own volition, their decision may be in response to a difficult situation such as conflict with a coach or the high stress of competition.

A similar issue was raised in a study of Australian elite-amateur athletes in which nine causes of retirement emerged: work/study commitments, lost motivation, politics of sport, decrease in performance, finance, decrease in enjoyment, age, injury, and deselection (Lavallee et al., 1997). Although the authors suggested that only the latter three causes were involuntary, it could be argued that all of the causes could be interpreted as outside of the control of the athletes. For example, the athletes retired because of dissatisfaction (politics of sport), a forced change in priorities (work/study commitments, finance), or a decline in ability to be competitive (decrease in performance). The athletes who seemed to have retired voluntarily may be more appropriately characterized as "reluctant dropouts" (Kerr & Dacyshyn, 2000).

Other Causes of Career Termination

Other factors have been either suggested or reported to contribute to career termination. These causes include family reasons (Mihovilovic, 1968), problems with coaches or the sports organization (Werthner & Orlick, 1986), and financial difficulties (Lavallee et al., 1997).

Stage 2: Factors Related to Adaptation to Career Transition

Athletes experiencing career transition may face a wide range of psychological, social, financial, and occupational changes. The extent of these changes and how athletes perceive them may dictate the quality of the adaptation they experience as a function of their retirement.

Developmental contributors. The presence and quality of adaptation to career transition may depend on developmental experiences that occurred since the inception of their athletic careers. The nature of these experiences will affect the emergence of self-perceptions and interpersonal skills that will influence how athletes adapt to retirement.

The often single-minded pursuit of excellence that accompanies elite sports participation has potential psychological and social dangers, and this quest is rooted in the earliest experiences athletes have in their youth sports participation. The personal investment in and the pursuit of elite athletic success, although a worthy goal, may lead to a restricted development.

Although there is substantial evidence demonstrating the debilitating effects of deselection self-esteem among young athletes (e.g., Alfermann, 1995; Webb, Nasco, Riley, & Headrick, 1998), little consideration has been given to changing this process in a healthier direction. Most organized youth programs still appear to place the highest priority on winning with less concern for the positive development of young athletes.

To alleviate these difficulties at their source, the adoption of a more holistic approach to sports development can be beneficial early in the lives of athletes (Pearson & Petitpas, 1990; Petitpas & Champagne, 2000). This perspective relies on a primary prevention model that emphasizes preventing problems prior to their occurrence (Conyne, 1987). The first step in the prevention process is to engender in parents and coaches involved in youth sport a belief that long-term personal and social development is more important than short-term athletic success (Ogilvie, 1987).

It has been further argued that high school and college athletic programs restrict opportunities for personal and social growth such as the development of self and social identities, social roles and behaviors, and social support systems (Remer, Tongate, & Watson, 1978). Early intervention in these areas will decrease the likelihood that the factors related to the quality of the adaptation in career transition will contribute to distress because of retirement later in their lives.

Self-identity. Most fundamental of the psychological issues that influence adaptation to career transition is the degree to which athletes define their self-worth in terms of their participation and achievement in sports (Blinde & Greendorfer,

1985; Svoboda & Vanek, 1982). Athletes who have been immersed in their sport to the exclusion of other activities will have a self-identity that is composed almost exclusively of their sports involvement (Brewer, Van Raalte, & Petitpas, 2000). Without the input from their sport, retired athletes have little to support their sense of self-worth (Pearson & Petitpas, 1990).

Athletes who are disproportionately invested in their sports participation may be characterized as "unidimensional" people, in which their self-concept does not extend far beyond the limits of their sport (Coakley, 1983; Ogilvie & Howe, 1982). These athletes often have few options in which they can gain meaning and fulfillment from activities outside their sport (McPherson, 1980).

It has been suggested that athletes with overly developed athletic identities are less prepared for postsport careers (Baillie & Danish, 1992), have restricted career and educational plans (Blann, 1985), and typically experience retirement from sport as something very important that is lost and can never be recovered (Werthner & Orlick, 1986). The finality of the loss seems impossible to bear and herein lies a significant threat to healthy adaptation to athletic career transition.

Athletes who struggled with retirement held fast to their athletic identities and were most anxious about how it would affect their lives (Ungerleider, 1997). Grove, Lavallee, and Gordon (1997) found that athletes who overly identified with their sports careers were most vulnerable to transition distress. Finally, how effectively athletes adapted their identities in a healthy way following retirement is necessary to a positive reaction to distress over career termination (Lavallee et al., 1997).

Kerr and Dacyshyn (2000) suggest that the demands athletic retirement places on adolescent athletes can be excessive and destructive. Instead of adolescence being a time of identity formation (Erikson, 1963), it can actually be deconstructed, which may slow the identity-formation process. They further assert that transition of young female athletes can be particularly difficult. Retirement at an early age, which is common among female athletes such as gymnasts, figure skaters, and swimmers, inhibits their ability to try out different roles and relationships, interferes with the development of autonomy and decision-making skills (Chickering & Reisser, 1993), and can distort perceptions related to body weight, body image, and eating habits (Piphers, 1994). They conclude that these issues have the cumulative effect of interfering with the healthy development of a mature self-identity in young female athletes.

Perceived control. Central to the issue of perceived control in career transition is whether athletes chose to leave their sport or were forced to retire (Kerr & Dacyshyn, 2000; Lavallee et al., 1997). The degree of perceived control that the athletes have with respect to the end of their careers also can impact how they respond to career transition (McPherson, 1980). Of the four primary causes of athletic retirement discussed earlier, namely, age, deselection, injury, and free choice, the first three are predominantly outside the control of the individual athlete (Lavallee et al., 1997). This absence of control related to an event so intrinsically connected to athletes' self-identities may create a situation that is highly aversive and threatening (Blinde & Greendorfer, 1985; Brewer et al., 2000).

Both early and contemporary research examining Olympic-caliber and professional athletes has indicated that the causes of retirement for many athletes were beyond their control and that they experienced a decrease in their sense of personal control following retirement (Mihovilovic, 1968; Svoboda & Vanek, 1982; Webb et al., 1998). Although this issue has not been addressed extensively in the sports literature, there is considerable research from the areas of clinical, social, and physiological psychology demonstrating that perceived control is related to many areas of human functioning including sense of self-competence (White, 1959) and the interpretation of self (Kelly, 1967) and other (Jones & Davis, 1965) information. In addition, perceptions of control may influence individuals' feelings of helplessness (Friedlander, 1984–1985), motivation (Wood & Bandura, 1989), physiological changes (Tache & Selye, 1985), and self-confidence (Bandura & Adams, 1977). Loss of control has been associated with a variety of pathologies including depression (Alloy &

Abramson, 1982), anxiety (Garfield & Bergin, 1978), substance abuse (Shiffman, 1982), and dissociative disorders (Putnam, 1989).

Social identity. The diversity of athletes' social identities can affect their adaptation to career transition (Gorbett, 1985). Researchers have associated retirement with a loss of status and social identity (Tuckman & Lorge, 1953). McPherson (1980) suggests that many athletes define themselves in terms of their popular status, although this recognition is typically short-lived. As a result, retired athletes may question their self-worth and feel the need to regain the lost public esteem (Webb et al., 1998).

In addition, athletes whose socialization process occurred primarily in the sports environment may be characterized as "role restricted" (Ogilvie & Howe, 1982). That is, these athletes have only learned to assume certain social roles specific to the athletic setting and are only able to interact with others within the narrow context of sports. As a result, their ability to assume other roles following retirement may be severely inhibited (Blinde & Greendorfer, 1985). Studies by Chamalidis (1997), Haerle (1975), Mihovilovic (1968), and Werthner and Orlick (1986) indicate that athletes with a broad-based social identity that includes family, friendship, educational, and occupational components demonstrated better adaptation following sports career termination. Recent research examining the career transition process for teams also highlights similar issues (Danish, Owens, Green, & Brunelle, 1997; Zaichkowsky, King, & McCarthy, 2000) with regard to social identity.

Tertiary contributors. In addition to the above intrapersonal factors, there are personal, social, and environmental variables that may influence athletes' adaptation to retirement. These factors may be viewed as potential stressors whose presence will likely exacerbate the primary adaptive factors just discussed (Coakley, 1983).

Socioeconomic status may influence the adaptation process (Menkehorst & van den Berg, 1997). Athletes who are financially dependent on their sports participation and possess few skills to earn a living outside of sport or have limited financial resources to fall back on may perceive retirement as more threatening and, as a result, may evidence distress (Lerch, 1982; McPherson, 1980; Werthner & Orlick, 1986).

It also has been argued that minority status (Blinde & Greendorfer, 1985; Hill & Lowe, 1974) and gender (Coakley, 1983) will affect the adaptation process because of what are perceived as fewer postathletic career opportunities (Haerle, 1975). These factors are likely to be most significant when interacting with socioeconomic status and preretirement planning. The health of athletes at the time of retirement will further affect the quality of the adaptation (Gorbett, 1985; Hill & Lowe, 1974). Athletes with chronic disabilities incurred during athletic careers may, as a result of the injuries, have limited choices in their postathletic careers. Also, marital status, as an aspect of social support, will influence the adaptation process (Curtis & Ennis, 1988). Athlete characteristics including age, years competing, and level of attainment also will influence adaptation in the retirement process.

Stage 3: Available Resources for Adaptation to Career Transition

Athletes' adaptation to career transition depends largely on the resources that they have available to surmount the difficulties that arise. Two of the most important factors that can influence people's ability to respond effectively to these problems include coping skills (Lazarus & Folkman, 1984; Meichenbaum, 1996) and social support (Sarason & Sarason, 1986). In addition, research indicates that another valuable resource, preretirement planning, may significantly influence adaptation to career transition (Parker, 1994; Pearson & Petitpas, 1990).

Coping strategies. During the course of retirement, athletes are faced with dramatic changes in their personal, social, and occupational lives. These changes will affect them cognitively, emotionally, and behaviorally. The quality of the adaptation to career transition experienced by athletes will depend on the manner in which they respond to these changes. The availability of effective coping strategies may facilitate this process and reduce the likelihood of difficulties. Sinclair and Orlick (1993) reported that finding another focus of interest to replace their sports participation, keeping busy, maintaining their training/exercise regimens, talking with someone who listens, and staying in touch with their sport and friends in their sport were effective coping strategies for facilitating the transition process.

Cognitively, retiring athletes must alter their perceptions related to the career transition process, specifically with respect to self-identity, perceived control, and social identity (Williams-Rice, 1996). Athletes can use cognitive restructuring (Lazarus, 1972) and mental imagery (Smith, 1980) to reorient their thinking in a more positive direction, self-instructional training (Meichenbaum, 1996) to improve attention and problem solving, and goal-setting to provide direction and motivation in their postathletic careers (Bruning & Frew, 1987). These techniques have been used successfully to enhance adaptation in a variety of populations and activities (Labouvie-Vief & Gonda, 1976; Meichenbaum & Cameron, 1973; Moleski & Tosi, 1976; Trexler & Karst, 1972).

Similarly, relevant techniques could be used for emotional/physiological stressors. Specifically, athletes in transition could employ anger and anxiety strategies such as time-out (Browning, 1983), relaxation training (Bruning & Frew, 1987; Delman & Johnson, 1976; May, House, & Kovacs, 1982), and health, exercise, and nutritional counseling (Bruning & Frew, 1987) to alleviate these difficulties. Finally, a regimen of behavior modification could deal with overt manifestations of distress associated with career transition. Techniques such as assertiveness training (Lange & Jakubowski, 1976), time management training (Bruning & Frew, 1987; King, Winett, & Lovett, 1986), and skills assessment and development (Taylor, 1987) could be effective in overcoming behavioral difficulties caused by retirement.

One study of elite athletes reported that commonly used coping strategies included acceptance, positive reinterpretation, planning, active coping, and seeking social support (Grove et al., 1997).

These researchers also found that athletes who had strong athletic identities tended to use avoidance-based coping strategies such as denial, mental and behavioral disengagement, and venting of emotions, rather than more problem-focused techniques. This evidence, suggesting that athletes in transitions may employ various coping strategies as a function of their self-identity, provides a link between Step 2 and Step 3 of the present model.

Social support. Because of athletes' total psychological and social immersion in the sports world, the majority of their friends, acquaintances, and other associations are found in the sports environment and their social activities often revolve around their athletic lives (Petitpas & Champagne, 2000). Thus, athletes' primary social support system often will be derived from their athletic involvement (Coakley, 1983; Rosenfeld, Richman, & Hardy, 1989).

When the athletes' careers end, they are no longer an integral part of the team or organization. Consequently, the social support that they received previously may no longer be present. In a sample of athletes with international competitive experience, Sinclair and Orlick (1993) reported that missing the social aspects of their sport was a frequently reported difficulty during career transition. Moreover, because of their restricted social identity and the absence of alternative social support systems, they may become isolated, lonely, and unsustained socially, thus leading to significant distress (Alfermann, 1995; Blinde & Greendorfer, 1985; Schmid & Schilling, 1997).

Early research by Mihovilovic (1968), Reynolds (1981), and Werthner and Orlick (1986) reported that athletes who received considerable support from family and friends had easier transitions and those who had the most difficulties indicated that they felt alone as their careers ended and expressed the desire for support during that period. Additionally, other authors (Gorbett, 1985; Sinclair & Hackfort, 2000) suggest that athletes also need institutional support during the retirement process, best provided through preretirement counseling programs.

Ungerleider (1997) reported that ex-Olympic athletes received support from coaches, parents, and significant others. In addition, the 20% of athletes who reported experiencing serious difficulties following career termination received help from a mental health professional. Another study of retired world-class athletes indicated that they received considerable support from family and friends and little institutional support from the national governing body or their former coaches (Sinclair & Orlick, 1993). In a study of retiring disabled athletes, Wheeler, Malone, Van Vlack, and Nelson (1996) found that retirement was facilitated by having family interests outside of sport.

Preretirement planning. Of the available resources that are being discussed, preretirement planning appears to have the broadest influence on the quality of the career transition process (Murphy, 1995). Preretirement planning may include a variety of activities including continuing education, occupational and investment opportunities, and social networking. As a result, preretirement planning may significantly affect most of the factors previously discussed that are related to the adaptation process. For example, preretirement planning would broaden an athlete's self-identity, enhance perceptions of control, and diversify his or her social identity (Grove et al., 1997). As for the tertiary contributors, socioeconomic status, financial dependency on the sport, and postathletic occupational potential would all be positively influenced. Substantial research involving both elite-amateur and professional athletes supports this position (e.g., Haerle, 1975; Sinclair & Orlick, 1993).

Perna, Ahlgren, and Zaichkowsky (1999) found that collegiate athletes who could state a postcollegiate occupational plan indicated significantly more life satisfaction that those who did not have such a plan. Similarly, disabled athletes have indicated that their retirement was easier if they had job interests outside of sport (Martin, 1996; Wheeler et al., 1996).

Despite these benefits, a common theme that emerges from the literature on retirement outside of sports is the resistance on the part of individuals to plan for their lives after the end of their careers (Petitpas & Champagne, 2000). Gorely et al. (2001) found that athletes often do not consider their career termination until it draws near. Yet, it is likely that this denial of the inevitable will have serious, potentially negative, and long-term implications for the athletes. A wide range of difficulties have been reported because of athletes' resistance to preretirement planning.

Structured preretirement planning that involves reading materials and workshops (Anderson & Morris, 2000) is a valuable opportunity for athletes to plan for and work toward meaningful lives following retirement. In addition, effective money management and long-term financial planning can provide athletes with financial stability following the conclusion of their careers (Menkehorst & van den Berg, 1997).

The incorporation of preretirement planning is becoming increasingly a part of collegiate, elite-amateur, and professional organizations (Sinclair & Hackfort, 2000). The research clarifying the extent to which these services have been used by the elite athletes indicates that only a small proportion take advantage of these services (Gorely et al., 2001; Sinclair & Orlick, 1993). There is also still no empirical evidence of how effective these programs are for athletes in career transition.

Stage 4: Quality of Career Transition

Based on the present model to this point, it may be concluded that career transition from sports will not necessarily cause a distressful reaction on the part of athletes (Coakley, 1983). Rather, the quality of adaptation to career transition by athletes will depend on the previous steps of the retirement process. It is at the present juncture that the athlete's reaction to career transition will become evident. There are a variety of psychological, social, and environmental factors that will determine the nature of the response. Specifically, the presence or absence of the contributing variables described in the early steps of the model will dictate whether athletes undergo a healthy transition following retirement or experience distress in response to the end of their competitive career.

The question is often raised as to the incidence of those individual athletes who exhibit some form of distress when forced from their sport. In fact, the extant literature has not produced widespread evidence of transition difficulties at all levels of sports participation. Notably, there is little evidence of distress in athletes concluding their scholastic and collegiate careers (Williams-Rice, 1996). This may be because of the fact that the completion of high school and college athletic careers as dictated by eligibility restrictions may be seen as a natural part of the transition to entering college or the workforce, respectively (Coakley, 1983).

At the same time, another group of researchers assert that career transition may cause distress that manifests itself in a wide variety of disruptive ways. Sinclair and Orlick (1993), for example, reported that about one third of a sample of elite-amateur athletes experienced fair to serious problems with missing the social aspects of their sport, job-school pressures, and finances. In addition, 11% felt dissatisfied with their lives since retirement and 15% felt that they did not handle the transition well.

Kerr and Dacyshyn (2000) reported that 70% of their sample of elite female gymnasts experienced distress when their careers ended. These athletes described feelings of disorientation, void, and frustration, and struggled with issues such as self-identity, personal control, and body image. A recent review of 12 studies, which included 2,665 athletes representing a wide range of sports and participation levels, also has reported that 20% of the athletes studied required considerable psychological adjustment on their career termination (Lavallee, Nesti, Borkoles, Cockerill, & Edge, 2000).

Other researchers over the years also have reported more serious manifestations of transition difficulties consisting of incidences of alcohol and drug abuse, participation in criminal activities, and significant anxiety, acute depression, and other emotional problems following retirement (e.g., Chamalidis, 1997; Mihovilovic, 1968). The emergence of distress among elite-amateur and professional athletes is likely because of the significantly greater life investment in their sports and their commitment to their sports participation as a career into adulthood.

Stage 5: Intervention for Career Transition

Career transition may be characterized as a complex interaction of stressors. Whether the stressors are financial, social, psychological, or physical, their effects may produce some form of distress when athletes are confronted with the end of their careers. Despite the best efforts made in the prevention of career transition distress, difficulties may still arise when the reality of the end of an athletic career is recognized. The experience of career transition crises may adversely affect athletes cognitively, emotionally, behaviorally, and socially. As a result, it is important to address each of these areas in an active and constructive manner.

Unfortunately, as discussed earlier, there are significant organizational obstacles to the proper treatment of career transition difficulties (Sinclair & Hackfort, 2000; Thomas & Ermler, 1988). In particular, the limited involvement of sport psychologists at the elite level, where problems are most likely to occur, inhibits their ability to provide for the career transition needs of athletes. Also, the team psychologists typically associated with national governing bodies, collegiate teams, or professional organizations rarely have the opportunity to develop an extended relationship with team members. This limited contact rarely presents an opportunity to discuss issues related to career transition. Also, because retired athletes are no longer a part of a sports organization, treatment of the athletes may not be seen as being within the purview of the organization's psychologist (Sinclair & Hackfort, 2000).

The retiring athletes themselves also may present their own obstacles to intervention. Surveys of former world-class amateur athletes indicate that they do not perceive personal counseling as a useful coping strategy during the career transition process (e.g., Sinclair & Orlick, 1993).

The treatment of distress related to career transition may occur at a variety of levels. As discussed earlier, the changes that result from retirement may detrimentally impact a person psychologically, emotionally, behaviorally, and socially. As a consequence, it is necessary for the sport psychologist to address each of these areas in the intervention process.

Perhaps the most important task in the transition process is to assist athletes in maintaining their sense of self-worth when establishing a new self-identity. The goal of this process is to adapt their perceptions about themselves and their world to their new roles in a way that will be maximally functional. The sport psychologist can assist them in identifying desirable nonsport identities and experiencing feelings of value and self-worth in this new personal conception.

Also, sport psychologists can aid athletes in working through any emotional distress they may experience during retirement (Grove, Lavallee, Gordon, & Harvey, 1998). Specifically, they can provide the athletes with the opportunity to express feelings of doubt, concern, or frustration relative to the end of their careers (Gorbett, 1985). Constantine (1995) reported that a group counseling experience comprised of supportive counseling techniques and psychoeducational exercises for retired female collegiate athletes who were experiencing adjustment difficulties indicated higher levels of satisfaction from participation in the group.

On a manifest level, the sport psychologist can help the athletes cope with the stress of the transition process (Gorbett, 1985). Traditional therapeutic strategies such as cognitive restructuring (Garfield & Bergin, 1978), stress management (Meichenbaum & Jaremko, 1983), and emotional expression (Yalom, 1980) can be used in this process. It also has been recommended that Shapiro's (1995) eye movement desensitization and reprocessing (EMDR) can be employed as a psychomotor technique to ameliorate undesirable beliefs and images associated with career-ending injuries (Sime, 1998). Also, athletes can be shown that the skills they used to master their sport can be used as effectively in overcoming the challenges of a new career and lifestyle (Meichenbaum & Jaremko, 1983).

Grove et al. (1998) have adapted Horowitz's (1986) model of coping with loss to retirement from sport. This perspective stresses a working-through process in the form of the construction of a narrative about the career termination experience, termed *account-making*. This account enables athletes to better understand their career transition, allows them to gain closure on their athletic careers, and encourages the adoption of an evolving self- and social identity that will foster growth in their postathletic lives. Preliminary research indicates that account-making was directly related to athletes' success in coping with career termination (Lavallee et al., 1997).

Finally, the professional can help athletes at a social level. This goal may be accomplished by having athletes explore ways of broadening their social identity and role repertoire (Brewer et al., 2000). Additionally, athletes can be encouraged to expand their social support system to individuals and groups outside of the sports arena. The use of group therapy and the articulation of the athletes' potential social networks can be especially useful in aiding them in this process. Wolff and Lester (1989) propose a three-stage therapeutic process comprised of listening/confrontation, cognitive therapy, and vocational guidance to aid athletes in coping with their loss of self-identity and assist them in establishing a new identity.

There has been little empirical research examining the significant factors in this process. Outside of sport, Roskin (1982) found that the implementation of a package of cognitive, affective, and social support interventions within didactic and small-group settings significantly reduced depression and anxiety among a high-stress group of individuals composed partly of retirees.

Intervention at the organizational level also can be a useful means of facilitating the career transition process. As indicated earlier, many elite-amateur and professional organizations offer some form of preretirement and career transition assistance. Reece, Wilder, and Mahanes (1996) suggest that such programs should emphasize the transferability of skills from sport to a new career.

They further highlight the importance of identifying specific transferable skills and successful role models, and clarifying interests, values, and goals that will promote an effective career transition.

Sinclair and Orlick (1993) also support intervention at the organizational level as having a positive impact on career transitions of elite athletes. They recommend that sports organizations can facilitate the transition process by continuing financial support for a short time following retirement, encourage sports organizations to stay in contact with retired athletes, offer seminars on career transition issues, and establish a resource center for athletes in transition. Additionally, retired athletes should be provided with opportunities to stay involved in their sport and shown how mental skills training can be used in their new pursuits (Sinclair & Hackfort, 2000).

Summary

This chapter has reviewed the relevant literature pertaining to career transition among athletes. From this overview, several conclusions can be drawn. First, the extant research suggests that career transition difficulties are more likely to emerge with elite-amateur and professional athletes than with scholastic or collegiate athletes. This finding appears to be because of the greater ego-involvement and personal investment of the former group of athletes and because transition from world-class and professional sports participation typically occurs outside of the normal developmental process. Second, distress because of career transition will not necessarily occur. Rather, the emergence of difficulties is because of a variety of developmental, psychological, and social factors including early life experiences, coping strategies, perceptions of control, self and social identities, social support, and preretirement planning. Third, addressing career transition issues can begin at the earliest stages of sports participation. This process involves having parents, coaches, and youth sports administrators create an environment that will enable young athletes' sports involvement to be a meaningful vehicle that will engender healthy personal and social development. Finally, despite the best efforts to eliminate distress that may arise because of career transition, it may still occur when athletes fully recognize that their sports careers are over. This distress can manifest itself psychologically, emotionally, behaviorally, and socially. It is important that each of these areas is addressed directly and constructively by a trained professional.

Study Questions

1. Compare the Eastern European and Western methods of athlete development and their implications for career transition.

2. Briefly describe the causes of career termination and indicate how each factor would affect athletes' adaptation to career transition.

3. Discuss the most prevalent factors to adaptation to career transition.

4. Discuss the interpersonal factors that affect athletes' reactions to career transition and how they are related to the athletes' adaptation.

5. Indicate the role that early development has on athletes' reactions to career transition and give an example of an ideal upbringing for healthy transition.

6. Describe the three primary resources available to athletes to help them during the career transition process and give examples of how they influence retiring athletes.

7. Discuss the difficulties that retiring athletes most often experience and what types of athletes are most likely to have these difficulties.

8. Provide the primary areas that sport psychologists must address in working with a retiring athlete and describe some of the techniques that could be used.

Case Study

Sarah is a 25-year-old softball player who was informed earlier in the week that she was not selected for the Olympic Team. In terms of her deselection, she does not think that it is fair that the selectors suddenly decided that she could no longer do what she had trained so long and hard for. Sarah feels very frustrated and angry because this was going to be her first Olympics, and also disappointed that she will not compete alongside her teammates, who are some of her best friends. She also is concerned about what she is going to do next, as her philosophy has always been that she shouldn't concentrate on anything other than softball if she wanted to be the best and retain her place on the team.

1. Based on the model presented in this chapter, what kind of reaction might you expect from her and why?

2. What are the primary issues that might affect the quality of her retirement?

3. What could she have done to alter her reaction?

4. Create an intervention plan to help Sarah through her transition.

References

Alfermann, D. (1995). Career transitions of elite athletes: Drop-out and retirement. In R. Vanfraechem-Raway & Y. Vanden Auweele (Eds.), *Proceedings of the 9th European Congress of Sport Psychology* (pp. 828–833). Brussels: European Federation of Sports Psychology.

Alfermann, D., & Gross, A. (1997). Coping with career termination: It all depends on freedom of choice. In R. Lidor & M. Bar-Eli (Eds.), *Proceedings of the IX World Congress on Sport Psychology* (pp. 65–67). Netanya, Israel: International Society of Sport Psychology.

Allison, M. T., & Meyer, C. (1988). Career problems and retirement among elite athletes: The female tennis professional. *Sociology of Sport Journal, 5,* 212–222.

Alloy, L. B., & Abramson, L. Y. (1982). Learned helplessness, depression, and the illusion of control. *Journal of Personality and Social Psychology, 42,* 114–1126.

Anderson, D., & Morris, T. (2000) Athlete lifestyle programs. In D. Lavallee and P. Wylleman (Eds.), *Career transitions in sport: International perspectives* (pp. 59–81). Morgantown, WV: Fitness Information Technology.

Arviko, I. (1976). *Factors influencing the job and life satisfaction of retired baseball players.* Unpublished master's thesis, University of Waterloo, Ontario.

Atchley, R. C. (1980). *The social forces in later life.* Belmont, CA: Wadsworth.

Baillie, P. H. F., & Danish, S. J. (1992). Understanding the career transition of athletes. *The Sport Psychologist, 6,* 77–98.

Bandura, A. (1977). Self-efficacy: Toward a unifying theory of behavior change. *Psychological Review, 84,* 191–215.

Bandura, A., & Adams, N. E. (1977). Analysis of self-efficacy theory of behavioral change. *Cognitive Therapy and Research, 1,* 287–308.

Batten, J. (1979, April). After the cheering stops can athletes create new life in the business world? *The Financial Post Magazine,* pp. 14–20.

Blann, F. W. (1985). Intercollegiate athletic competition and students' educational and career plans. *Journal of College Student Personnel, 26,* 115–119.

Blinde, E. M., & Greendorfer, S. L. (1985). A reconceptualization of the process of leaving the role of competitive athlete. *International Review of Sport Sociology, 20,* 87–94.

Blinde, E. M., & Stratta, T. M. (1992). The "sport career death" of college athletes: Involuntary and unanticipated sports exits. *Journal of Sport Behavior, 15,* 3–20.

Bradley, B. (1976). *Life on the run.* New York: Quadrangle/The New York Times.

Brewer, B. W., Van Raalte, J. L., & Petitpas, A. J. (2000) Self-identity issues in sport career transitions. In D. Lavallee & P. Wylleman (Eds.), *Career transitions in sport: International perspectives* (pp. 29–43). Morgantown, WV: Fitness Information Technology.

Broom, E. F. (1982). Detraining and retirement from high level competition: A reaction to "retirement from high level competition" and "career crisis in sport." In T. Orlick, J. T. Partington, & J. H. Salmela (Eds.), *Proceedings of the Fifth World Congress of Sport Psychology* (pp. 183–187). Ottawa: Coaching Association of Canada.

Browning, E. R. (1983). A memory pacer for improving stimulus generalization. *Journal of Autism and Developmental Disorders, 13,* 427–432.

Bruning, N. S., & Frew, D. R. (1987). Effects of exercise, relaxation, and management skills on physiological stress indicators: A field experiment. *Journal of Applied Psychology, 72,* 515–521.

Chamalidis, P. (1997). Identity conflicts during and after retirement from top-level sports. In R. Lidor & M. Bar-Eli (Eds.), *Proceedings of the IX World Congress of Sport Psychology* (pp. 191–193). Netanya, Israel: International Society of Sport Psychology.

Chartrand, J. M., & Lent, R. W. (1987). Sports counselling: Enhancing the development of the student-athlete, *Journal of Counseling and Development, 66,* 164–167.

Chickering, A., & Reisser, L. (1993). *Education and identity* (2nd ed.). San Francisco: Jossey-Bass.

Coakley, J. J. (1983). Leaving competitive sport: Retirement or rebirth *Quest,* 35 1–11.

Curtis, J., & Ennis, R. (1988). Negative consequences of leaving competitive sport? Comparison findings for former elite-level hockey players. *Sociology of Sport Journal, 5,* 87–106.

Danish, S. J., Owens, S. S., Green, S. L., & Brunelle, J. P. (1997). Building bridges for disengagement: The transition process for individuals and teams. *Journal of Applied Sport Psychology, 9,* 154–167.

Deford, F. (1981). *Everybody's All-American*. New York: The Viking Press.

Delman, R., & Johnson, H. (1976). Biofeedback and progressive muscle relaxation: A comparison of psychophysiological effects. *Psychophysiology, 13,* 181–189.

Erikson. E. (1963). *Childhood and society*. New York: Norton.

Fisher, A. G., & Conlee, R. K. (1979). *The complete book of physical fitness* (pp. 119–121). Provo, UT: Brigham Young University Press.

Friedlander, S. (1984–1985). Learned helplessness in children: Perception of control and causal attributions. *Imagination, Cognition, and Personality, 4,* 99–116.

Garfield, S., & Bergin, A. (1978). *Handbook of psychotherapy and behavior change: An empirical analysis* (2nd ed.). New York: Wiley.

Gorbett, F. J. (1985). Psycho-social adjustment of athletes to retirement. In L. K. Bunker, R. J. Rotella, & A. Reilly (Eds.), *Sport psychology: Psychological considerations in maximizing sport performance* (pp. 288–294). Ithaca, NY: Mouvement Publications.

Gorely, T., Lavallee, D., Bruce, D., & Teale, B. (2001). An Evaluation of the Athlete Career and Education Program. *Athletic Academic Journal, 15,* 11–21.

Greendorfer, S. L., & Blinde, E. M. (1985). "Retirement" from intercollegiate sport: Theoretical and empirical considerations. *Sociology of Sport Journal, 2,* 101–110.

Grove, J. R., Lavallee, D., & Gordon, S. (1997). Coping with retirement from sport: The influence of athletic identity. *Journal of Applied Sport Psychology, 9,* 191–203.

Grove, J. R., Lavallee, D., Gordon, S., & Harvey, J. H. (1998). Account-making: A model of understanding and resolving distressful reactions to retirement from sport. *The Sport Psychologist, 12,* 52–67.

Haerle, R. K., Jr. (1975). Career patterns and career contingencies of professional baseball players: An occupational analysis. In D. Ball & J. Loy (Eds.), *Sport and social order* (pp. 461–519). Reading, MA: Addison-Wesley.

Havighurst, R. J., & Albrecht, R. (1953). *Older people*. New York: Longmans, Green.

Hill, P., & Lowe, B. (1974). The inevitable metathesis of the retiring athlete. *International Review of Sport Sociology, 4,* 5–29.

Hoffer, R. (1990, December 3). Magic's kingdom. *Sports Illustrated,* 106–110.

Hopson, B., & Adams, J. (1977). Toward an understanding of transition: Defining some boundaries of transition. In J. Adams & B. Hopson (Eds.), *Transition: Understanding and managing personal change* (pp. 3–25). Montclair, NJ: Allenhald & Osmund.

Horowitz, M. J. (1986). *Stress response syndromes* (2nd ed.). Northvale, NJ: Jason Aronson.

Jones, E. E., & Davis, K. E. (1965). From acts to dispositions: The attribution process in person perception. *Advances in Experimental Social Psychology, 2,* 219–266.

Kelly, H. H. (1967). Attribution in social psychology. In D. Levine (ed.), *Nebraska symposium on motivation*. Lincoln: University of Nebraska Press.

Kerr, G., & Dacyshyn, A. (2000). The retirement experiences of elite, female gymnasts. *Journal of Applied Sport Psychology, 12,* 115–133.

King, A. C., Winett, R. A., & Lovett, S. B. (1986). Enhancing coping behaviors in at-risk populations: The effects of time-management instruction and social support in women from dual-earner families. *Behavior Therapy, 17,* 57–66.

Kubler-Ross, E. (1969). *On death and dying.* New York: Macmillan.

Kuypers, J. A., & Bengston, V. L. (1973). Social breakdown and competence: A model of normal aging. *Human Development, 16,* 181–120.

Labouvie-Vief, G., & Gonda, J. (1976). Cognitive strategy training and intellectual performance in the elderly. *Journal of Gerontology, 31,* 327–332.

Lange, A. J., & Jakubowski, P. (1976). *Responsible assertive behavior.* Champaign, IL: Research Press.

Lavallee, D., Gordon, S., & Grove, J. R. (1997). Retirement from sport and the loss of athletic identity. *Journal of Personal and Interpersonal Loss, 2,* 129–147.

Lavallee, D., Grove, J. R., & Gordon, S. (1997). The causes of career termination from sport and their relationship to post-retirement adjustment among elite-amateur athletes in Australia. *Australian Psychologist, 32,* 131–135.

Lavallee, D., Nesti, M., Borkoles, E., Cockerill, I., & Edge, A. (2000). Intervention strategies for athletes in transition. In D. Lavallee & P. Wylleman (Eds.), *Career transitions in sport: International perspectives* (pp. 111–130). Morgantown, WV: Fitness Information Technology.

Lavallee, D., Wylleman, P., & Sinclair, D. A. (2000). Career transitions in sport: An annotated bibliography. In D. Lavallee & P. Wylleman (Eds.), *Career transitions in sport: International perspectives* (pp. 207–258). Morgantown, WV: Fitness Information Technology.

Lazarus, A. A. (1972). *Clinical behavior therapy.* New York: Brunner/Mazel.

Lazarus, A. (1972). *Behavior theory and beyond.* New York: McGraw-Hill.

Lazarus, R. S. (1975). The self-regulation of emotion. In L. Levi (Ed.), *Emotions—Their parameters and measurement* (pp. 47–68). New York: Ravel.

Lazarus, R. S., & Folkman, S. (1984). *Stress, appraisal, and coping.* New York: Springer.

Lerch, S. H. (1982). Athletic retirement as social death: An overview. In N. Theberge & P. Donnelly (Eds.), *Sport and the sociological imagination* (pp. 259–272). Fort Worth: Texas Christian University Press.

Manion, U. V. (1976). Preretirement counseling: The need for a new approach, *Personnel and Guidance Journal, 55,* 119–121.

Martin, J. J. (1996). Transitions out of competitive sport for athletes with disabilities. *Therapeutic Recreation Journal, 30,* 128–136.

May, E., House, W. C., & Kovacs, K. V. (1982). Group relaxation therapy to improve coping with stress. *Psychotherapy: Theory, research and practice, 19,* 102–109.

McInally, L., Cavin-Stice, J., & Knoth, R. L. (1992, August). *Adjustment following retirement from professional football.* Paper presented at the annual meeting of the American Psychological Association, Washington DC.

McPherson, B. P. (1980). Retirement from professional sport: The process and problems of occupational and psychological adjustment. *Sociological Symposium, 30,* 126–143.

Meichenbaum, D. (1996). Stress inoculation training for coping with stressors. *The Clinical Psychologist, 49*, 4–7.

Meichenbaum, D., & Jaremko, M. (1983). *Stress reduction and prevention.* New York: Plenum.

Meichenbaum, D. H., & Cameron, R. (1973). Training schizophrenics to talk to themselves: A means of delivering attentional controls. *Behavior Therapy, 4*, 515–534.

Menkehorst, G. A. B. M., & van den Berg, F. J. (1997). Retirement from high-level competition: A new start. In R. Lidor & M. Bar-Eli (Eds.), *Proceedings of the IX World Congress on Sport Psychology* (pp. 487–489). Netanya, Israel: International Society of Sport Psychology.

Mihovilovic, M. (1968). The status of former sportsman. *International Review of Sport Sociology, 3*, 73–96.

Moleski, R., & Tosi, E. J. (1976). Comparative psychotherapy: Rational-emotive therapy versus systematic desensitization in the treatment of stuttering. *Journal of Consulting and Clinical Psychology, 44*, 309–311.

Munroe, K. J., & Albinson, J. G., (1996, April). *Athletes' reactions immediately after and four months following involuntary disengagement at the varsity level.* Paper presented at the Joint Conference of the North American Society for the Psychology of Sport and Physical Activity and the Canadian Society for Psychomotor Learning and Sport Psychology, Ontario, Canada.

Murphy, S. M. (1995). Transition in competitive sport: Maximizing individual potential. In S. M. Murphy (Ed.), *Sport psychology interventions* (pp. 331–346). Champaign, IL: Human Kinetics.

National Collegiate Athletic Association (2003). *1981–2002 Sponsorship and participation report.* Indianapolis, IN: Author.

Ogilvie, B. C. (1987). Traumatic effects of sports career termination. *Proceedings National Conference of Sport Psychology, U.S. Olympic Committee.* Washington: DC.

Ogilvie, B. C., & Howe, M. (1982). Career crisis in sport. In T. Orlick, J. T. Partington, & J. H. Salmela (Eds.), *Proceedings of the Fifth World Congress of Sport Psychology* (pp. 176–183). Ottawa: Coaching Association of Canada.

Parker, K. B. (1994). "Has-beens" and "wanna-bes": Transition experiences of former major college football players. *The Sport Psychologist, 8*, 287–304.

Pearson, R., & Petitpas, A. (1990). Transition of athletes: Pitfalls and prevention. *Journal of Counseling and Development, 69*, 7–10.

Perna, F. M., Ahlgren, R. L., & Zaichkowsky, L. (1999). The influence of career planning, race, and athletic injury on life satisfaction among recently retired collegiate male athletes. *The Sport Psychologist, 13*, 144–156.

Petitpas, A., & Champagne, D. (2000). Practical considerations in implementing sport career transition programs. In D. Lavallee & P. Wylleman (Eds.), *Career transitions in sport: International perspectives* (pp. 81–93). Morgantown, WV: Fitness Information Technology.

Piphers, M. (1994). *Reviving Ophelia: Saving the selves of adolescent girls.* New York: Ballantine Books.

Plimpton, G. (1977, January). The final season. *Harpers,* pp. 63–67.

Putnam, F. W. (1989). Pierre Janet and modern views of dissociation. *Journal of Traumatic Stress, 2,* 413–429.

Reece, S. D., Wilder, K. C., & Mahanes, J. R. (1996, October). *Program for athlete career transition.* Paper presented at Association for the Advancement of Applied Sport Psychology annual meetings, Williamsburg, Virginia.

Remer, R., Tongate, R. A., & Watson, J. (1978). Athletes: Counseling for the overprivileged minority. *The Personnel and Guidance Journal, 56,* 622–629.

Reynolds, M. J. (1981). The effects of sports retirement on the job satisfaction of the former football player. In S. L. Greendorfer & A. Yiannakis (Eds.), *Sociology of sport: Perspectives* (pp. 127–137). West Point, NY: Leisure Press.

Rosenberg, E. (1982). Athletic retirement as social death: Concepts and perspectives. In N. Theberge & P. Donnelly (Eds.), *Sport and the sociological imagination* (pp. 245–258). Fort Worth: Texas Christian University Press.

Rosenfeld, L. B., Richman, J. M., & Hardy, C. J. (1989). Examining social support networks among athletes: Description and relationship to stress. *The Sport Psychologist, 3,* 23–33.

Roskin, M. (1082). Coping with life changes: A preventive social work approach. *American Journal of Community Psychology, 10,* 331–340.

Schlossberg, N. (1981). A model for analyzing human adaptation to transition. *The Counseling Psychologist, 9,* 2–18.

Schmid, J., & Schilling, G. (1997). Self-identity and adjustment to the transition out of sports. In R. Lidor & M. Bar-Eli (Eds.), *Proceedings of the IX World Congress on Sport Psychology* (pp. 608–610). Netanya, Israel: International Society of Sport Psychology.

Shapiro, F. (1995). *Eye movement desensitization and reprocessing: Basic principles, protocols, and procedures.* New York: Guilford Press.

Shiffman, S. (1982). A relapse-prevention hotline. *Bulletin of the Society of Psychologists in Substance Abuse, 1,* 50–54.

Sime, W. E. (1998). Injury and career termination issues. In M. A. Thompson, R. A. Vernacchia, & W. E. Moore (Eds.), *Case studies in applied sport psychology: An educational approach* (pp. 195–226). Dubuque, IA: Kendall/Hunt.

Sinclair, D. A., & Hackfort, O. (2000). The role of the sport organization in the career transition process. In D. Lavallee & P. Wylleman (Eds.), *Career transitions in sport: International perspectives* (pp. 131–142). Morgantown, WV: Fitness Information Technology.

Sinclair, D. A., & Orlick, T. (1993). Positive transitions from high-performance sport. *The Sport Psychologist, 7,* 138–150.

Smith, R. E. (1980). A cognitive-affective approach to stress management training for athletes. In C. Dadeau, W. Halliwell, K. Newell, & G. Roberts (Eds.), *Psychology of motor behavior and sports* (pp. 55–71). Champaign, IL: Human Kinetics.

Stambulova, N. B. (1994). Developmental sports career investigations in Russia: A post-perestroika analysis. *The Sport Psychologist, 8,* 221–237.

Sussman, M. B. (1971). An analytical model for the sociological study of retirement. In F. M. Carp (Ed.), *Retirement* (pp. 29–73). New York: Behavioral Publications.

Svoboda, B., & Vanek, M. (1982). Retirement from high level competition. In T. Orlick, J. T. Partington, & J. H. Salmela (Eds.), *Proceedings of the Fifth World Congress of Sport Psychology* (pp. 166–175). Ottawa, Canada: Coaching Association of Canada.

Swain, D. A. (1991). Withdrawal from sport and Schlossberg's model of transitions. *Sociology of Sport Journal, 8,* 152–160.

Tache, J., & Selye, H. (1985). On stress and coping mechanisms. *Issues in Mental Health Nursing, 7,* 3–24.

Taylor, J. (1987, September). *The application of psychological skills for the enhancement of coaching effectiveness.* Presented at the Association for the Advancement of Applied Sport Psychology annual meetings, Newport Beach, California.

Taylor, J., & Ogilvie, B. C. (1994). A conceptual model of adaptation to retirement among athletes. *Journal of Applied Sport Psychology, 6,* 1–20.

Thomas, C. E., & Ermler, K. L. (1988). Institutional obligations in the athletic retirement process. *Quest, 40,* 137–150.

Trexler, L. D., & Karst, T. O. (1972). Rational emotive therapy, placebo, and no treatment effects on public speaking anxiety. *Journal of Abnormal Psychology, 79,* 60–67.

Tuckman, J., & Lorge, I. (1953). *Retirement and the industrial worker.* New York: Macmillan.

Ungerleider, S. (1997). Olympic athletes' termination from sport to workplace. *Perceptual and Motor Skills, 84,* 1287–1295.

Webb, W. M., Nasco, S. A., Riley, S., & Headrick, B. (1998). *Journal of Sport Behavior, 21,* 338–362.

Werthner, P., & Orlick, T. (1986). Retirement experiences of successful Olympic athletes. *International Journal of Sport Psychology, 17,* 337–363.

Wheeler, G. D., Malone, L. A., Van Vlack, S., & Nelson, E. R. (1996). Retirement from disability sport: A pilot study. *Adapted Physical Activity Quarterly, 13,* 382–399.

White, R. W. (1959). Motivation revisited: The concept of competence. *Psychological Review, 66,* 297–333.

Williams-Rice, B. T. (1996). After the final snap: Cognitive appraisal, coping, and life satisfaction among former collegiate athletes. *Academic Athletic Journal,* Spring, 30–39.

Wolff, R., & Lester, D. (1989). A theoretical basis for counseling the retired professional athlete. *Psychological Reports, 64,* 1043–1046.

Wood, R., & Bandura, A. (1989). Social cognitive theory of organizational management. *Academy of Management Review, 14,* 361–384.

Wylleman, P., Lavallee, D., & Aflermann, D. (Eds.). (1999). *Career transitions in competitive sports.* Biel, Switzerland: European Federation of Sport Psychology Monograph Series.

Yalom, I. D. (1980). *Existential psychotherapy.* New York: Harper/Collins.

Zaichkowsky, L., King, E., & McCarthy, J. (2000). The end of an era: The case of forced transition involving Boston University football. In D. Lavallee & P. Wylleman (Eds.), *Career transitions in sport: International perspectives* (pp. 195–205). Morgantown, WV: Fitness Information Technology.

CHAPTER

27

Exercise Psychology

Rod K. Dishman, *The University of Georgia*
Janet Buckworth, *The Ohio State University*

Muscular vigor will . . . always be needed to furnish the background of sanity, serenity, and cheerfulness to life, . . . to round off the wiry edge of our fretfulness, and make us good-humored and easy of approach.

—William James, 1899

Physical inactivity during leisure time is a burden on public health in the United States and many other developed and developing nations (McGinnis, 1992; Varo et al., 2003; NIH Consensus Conference, 1996; U.S. Department of Health & Human Services, 1996, 2000). Although chronic organic diseases (e.g., cardiovascular disease, diabetes, cancer) and obesity have received most of the attention, the importance of understanding whether physical activity has a role in preventing depression, anxiety, and sleep disorders, as well as promoting positive emotional health and cognitive function, has grown during the past decade. This has resulted, in part, from results of the Global Burden of Disease study (Murray & Lopez, 1996), conducted by the World Health Organization (WHO), the World Bank, and Harvard University, which revealed that mental illness, including suicide, ranks second to cardiovascular disease in the burden of disease worldwide (Murray & Lopez, 1999). In addition, 4 of the 10 leading causes of disability for persons aged 5 and older are mental disorders (Murray & Lopez, 1996).

In the United States, mental disorders collectively account for more than 15% of the overall burden of disease from all causes, only slightly less than the burden of cardiovascular diseases (18.5%) and slightly more than the burden associated with all forms of cancer (15%) (Murray & Lopez, 1996). Despite the potential benefits for health associated with being physically active, about 25% of adults in the United States are sedentary during their leisure time, and another 35% are not active enough to meet the levels of participation recommended for health and fitness (Centers for Disease Control and Prevention, 2004; U.S. Department of Health & Human Services, 1996; 2000). About a third of adolescents do not meet recommended levels of physical activity (Grunbaum et al., 2004). Hence, understanding what motivates people to exercise has become a high priority for public health.

The primary focus of exercise psychology has been to explain the antecedents and consequences of exercise behavior (Buckworth & Dishman, 2002; Dishman, 2000). Efforts have been made to identify the determinants of adoption and adherence to regular exercise and the effects of physical activity on psychological attributes. We have organized this chapter into four sections in which we describe the evidence for positive effects on mental health, discuss concerns over risks to psychological health associated with excessive amounts of exercise, examine the hypothesis that exercise training leads to modifications in responses to nonexercise stress, and address issues in physical activity behavior change and exercise adherence.

Research in these four areas has implications for public health. First, there is evidence that physical activity positively affects depression, anxiety, sleep, self-esteem, and cognitive performance, and can be an effective adjuvant to traditional interventions used in counseling, clinical psychology, or psychiatry. Second, benefits of exercise notwithstanding, it is also important to consider potential psychological risks of excessive exercise. Third, evidence for physiological adaptations to exercise that generalize to nonexercise stress may have implications for modifying the risk of cardiovascular diseases and may reveal mechanisms by which physical activity reduces that risk. Finally, understanding the dynamics of physical activity behavior over time is critical to the development of interventions to increase the initiation and maintenance of a physically active lifestyle.

Exercise and Mental Health

The potential for exercise to have a positive effect on mental health has been addressed in numerous reviews and meta-analyses (Dishman, 1998; Fox & Stathi, 2002; Morgan, 1997; Lawlor & Hopker, 2001; North, McCullagh, & Tran, 1990; O'Connor, Raglin, & Martinsen, 2000; O'Neal, Dunn, & Martinsen, 2000; Petruzzello, Landers, Hatfield, Kubitz, & Salazar, 1991; Sonstroem, 1998). There is an international consensus among exercise scientists that acute exercise is associated with reduced state anxiety and that chronic exercise and physical fitness are associated with reduced trait anxiety (Landers & Petruzzello, 1994), reduced depression (Morgan, 1994), and increased self-esteem (Fox, 2000; McAuley, 1994).

However, the strength of the scientific basis for the role of exercise in mental health has been controversial. The U.S. Preventive Services Task Force of the U.S. Office of Disease Prevention and Health Promotion concluded in 1989 that the quality of the available evidence linking exercise with anxiety and depression was poor and that the role of exercise in the primary prevention of mental health problems was poorly understood (Harris, Caspersen, DeFriese, & Estes, 1989). The 1994 Physical Activity, Fitness, and Health international consensus text edited by Bouchard, Shephard, and Stephens gives more support to the link between mental health and physical activity, but acceptance of the role of exercise in mental health is illustrated by the omission of any reference to physical activity or exercise in the Practice Guideline for Major Depressive Disorder in Adults (American Psychiatric Association, 1993, 2000) and by the public health view that the strongest evidence on exercise comes from studies of self-esteem. In this section, we will discuss the evidence for exercise positively affecting anxiety, depression, sleep, self-esteem, and cognition. We will also present some of the proposed psychobiological mechanisms for these effects and discuss research issues.

Anxiety and Depression

Anxiety and depression are serious, prevalent diseases in the United States. Annually, they each affect 6–10% of the adult population and cost about $45 billion. They not only affect the quality of life, but also increase the risks for other chronic diseases, such as coronary heart disease, asthma, ulcers, rheumatoid arthritis, and headaches (Friedman & Booth-Kewley, 1987; Kessler et al., 1994). In their meta-analyses of exercise and anxiety, Petruzzello et al. (1991) and Landers and Petruzzello (1994) found a one fourth to nearly one half SD average effect size for decreases in state anxiety; effects were a little larger when exercise lasted from 20 to 30 minutes. An effect of one standard deviation is comparable to increasing a grade from a C to a B in a course graded using a normal or bell-shaped curve. About 150 small sample studies reviewed show a small to moderate reduction in self-rated trait anxiety with exercise in a variety of subjects (–0.25 to 0.60 *SD*) (McDonald & Hodgdon, 1991). Although intense, acute exercise can temporarily increase state anxiety (O'Connor, Petruzzello, Kubitz, & Robinson, 1995), moderate intensities of exercise lasting at least 30 minutes are generally associated with the largest reductions in self-rated state anxiety and resting measures of electromyographic and brain electrocortical activity. Petruzzello et al. (1991) also reported a one third *SD* effect size for decreases in trait anxiety with exercise training. Studies of endurance athletes have shown that chronic exercise is associated with lower state anxiety at rest, but the conflicting research provides little evidence to believe exercise can change temperament, contrary to what meta-analyses have found. Also, we are unaware of randomized controlled trials that have shown a reduction in anxiety after exercise training among people who have an anxiety disorder (O'Connor, Raglin, & Martinsen, 2000), although some training studies have demonstrated reductions in symptoms but not better than standard drug treatment (e.g., Broocks et al., 1998).

Exercise has been recommended as helpful in treating depression for several centuries. Hippocrates prescribed exercise for depression, and clinical reports about using exercise in the psychiatric treatment of depression appeared as early as 1905 (Dishman, 2000). However, the first research efforts to discover the potential impact of exercise on depression did not begin until the early 1960s (Dunn & Dishman, 1991; Morgan, 1994). Since then, a number of correlational, quasi-experimental, and experimental studies have been conducted. A meta-analysis by North et al. (1990) summarized 80 cross-sectional, longitudinal, published, and unpublished studies on exercise and depression as measured by self-report. They found a significant effect for all forms of depression, aerobic and nonaerobic exercise, and exercise programs of varying length. Their overall results, which included both chronic and acute exercises, found that exercise groups decreased depression scores .53 *SD* more than comparison groups. A more recent meta-analysis of randomized trials with patients diagnosed with depression reported an average reduction of about

1 *SD* in symptoms (Lawlor & Hopker, 2001), but the authors noted several methodological limitations of the studies that precluded a clear conclusion that exercise caused the reductions. There also are about 30 population-based studies (e.g., Farmer et al., 1988; Paffenberger, Lee, & Leung, 1994) that agree that exercise is associated with a moderate reduction in the risk of developing depression (physically inactive people have about twice the prevalence of depression compared with active people) in adults (Dishman, 1998; O'Neal et al., 2000) and reduced symptoms of depression during adolescence (Motl, Birnbaum, Kubik, & Dishman, 2004). Experimental studies with rats (Dishman et al., 1997; Yoo, Bunnell, Crabbe, Kalish, & Dishman, 2000) and randomized controlled trials in humans diagnosed with depression (e.g., Blumenthal et al., 1999; Babyak et al., 2000) have demonstrated that exercise training can reduce signs or symptoms of depression to a degree comparable to antidepressant drugs. There is no consensus, however, on the exercise prescription that is most effective for treating depression or anxiety. Dunn, Trivedi, and O'Neal (2001) reviewed 37 studies that examined varying amounts of leisure-time and occupational physical activity on levels of depression and anxiety, and found benefits from physical activity but little evidence for dose-response effects. They concluded that this lack of consistent results was likely more because of the quantity and quality of the studies. We know of only one published study that addressed the dose response issue in depressed individuals. Dunn, Trivedi, Kampert, Clark, and Chambliss (2005) found that greater weekly energy expenditure (17.5 kcal/kg/wk) produced greater decreases in depressive symptoms after 12 weeks of aerobic training compared to a lower dose (7.0 kcal/kg/wk) and to an equal contact control.

Sleep

Sleep disorders and sleep restrictions have a profound effect on public health. According to reports from the National Institutes of Health's conference on sleep and sleep disorders (*Frontiers of Knowledge in Sleep & Sleep Disorders: Opportunities for Improving Health and Quality of Life,* March 2004), each year 50 to 70 million Americans experience some effects on their health from sleep disorders, sleep deprivation, and excessive daytime sleepiness. The annual prevalence of insomnia is nearly one third of the adult population in the United States. The financial cost is approximately $65 billion, $50 billion of that in costs to industry from lost productivity. Only about 5% to 20% of people who suffer sleep disturbances will seek help from a primary care physician, and many will purchase over-the-counter sleep aids. Early studies reported that acute exercise was followed by increased slow wave sleep (SWS–deep sleep) on the exercise evening (see Dishman, 1986, for a review). When the exercise was of vigorous intensity (e.g., 50–70% of cardiorespiratory fitness, i.e., VO$_2$ peak) and continued to exhaustion, the increase in SWS occurred early in the night's sleep and was accompanied by a decrease in REM sleep (when most dreaming occurs). Although these effects occurred for untrained but moderately active individuals, the most consistent SWS changes were seen for moderately or highly trained people (Youngstedt, O'Connor, Crabbe, & Dishman, 2000).

A meta-analysis of English-language literature on the acute effects of physical activity on sleep (Youngstedt, O'Connor, & Dishman, 1997) found statistically significant increases in total sleep time, slow wave sleep, and REM latency (the time before REM onset), with a decrease in REM, after an exercise session. The changes in REM sleep may be important for treating or preventing depression. Many people with typical major depression have reduced REM latency and increased REM and respond with reduced depression after REM deprivation therapy. However, the effects in the meta-analysis ranged from about .20 to .50 standard deviations, which are small-to-moderately large effects statistically, but that equate to only a few minutes of sleep in each case, well within normal night-to-night variation. The subjects studied were good sleepers, so the effects of exercise gauged by this analysis of studies may be underestimates of the potential efficacy of exercise among people with sleep disorders, who have been understudied. Although a few epidemiological studies have reported an association between physical activity and good sleep based on questionnaires administered to population samples, few studies have examined the long-term effects of exercise on sleep among people with sleep disorders. There is some evidence that higher levels of usual physical activity appear to be protective against incident and chronic insomnia in older adults (Morgan, 2003), and a few randomized controlled trials have found that both aerobic (King et al., 1997) and resistance (Singh et al., 1997) exercise training led to improvements in self-rated sleep among older adults who had sleep problems. The long-term effects of exercise on polysomnographic measures of sleep among poor sleepers are not known (see Youngstedt, 2000, for a review).

Self-Esteem

From a public health perspective, the strongest evidence for the positive effects of exercise on mental health is for self-esteem (Harris et al., 1989). Enhanced self-esteem has significance for mental health because it provides a feeling of value or worth and it is a generalized indicator of psychological adjustment. Symptoms of anxiety and depression often are associated with low self-esteem. Because self-esteem is relatively enduring or stable, changes are more likely to be seen after prolonged involvement (e.g., training) than during or following an acute period of exercise. Positive changes in physical self-concept after exercise training are more likely than changes in self-esteem but may contribute to enhanced self-esteem (Fox, 2000). Changes in self-esteem with exercise are also more likely in children than adults, for whom self-esteem is more multidimensional. In a meta-analysis of exercise and self-esteem in children, Gruber (1986) found a moderately large effect size (one half *SD*) for increased self-esteem with exercise. A recent meta-analysis of about 50 studies published from 1967 through 2004 also found moderately large increases of about a half standard deviation in global self-esteem and in physical, but not academic, self-concept among youth who participated in exercise or sport programs (Dishman, 2004).

When increases in fitness or ability occur, there is a co-occurring change in body image or self-perceptions (Fox, 2000; Sonstroem, 1998). Enhanced body image or physical competence can contribute to global self-esteem in individuals for whom physical attributes are highly valued relative to other aspects of self-concept. However, it is not clear whether it is exercise itself that increases self-esteem, or something in the social context of the exercise setting. In one study, only those subjects who exercised and were told they were in a study of exercise and psychological well-being demonstrated an increase in self-esteem (Desharnais, Jobin, Cote, Levesque, & Godin, 1993). Subjects not told the study's purpose had no increase in self-esteem despite an increase in fitness similar to that of their informed peers. The potential effectiveness of physical activity appears to depend on facilitating self-perceptions of personally valued attributes either directly, by inducing biological or behavioral change, or indirectly, by augmenting social reinforcement. The greatest gains in self-esteem can be expected for individuals with low initial levels, and for whom physical attributes have a relatively high value as a part of global self-concept.

Cognitive Function

Cognitive function changes during maturation in childhood and declines after middle age. Hence, there has been an interest in whether exercise or physical fitness moderates cognitive function during the lifespan. Although early studies yielded mixed evidence about the benefits of regular exercise or cardiorespiratory fitness on cognitive functioning as a result of regular exercise (e.g., Tomporowski & Ellis, 1986), the cumulative evidence has indicated a small positive effect of about a one third *SD* of both acute and chronic exercise or physical fitness on several indicators of cognitive performance (Etnier et al., 1997; Sibley & Etnier, 2003). Reevaluations of that evidence and more recent research suggest some positive effects of both acute and chronic exercise on selected features of cognitive function in children (Tomporowski, 2003) and older adults (McAuley, Kramer, & Colcombe, 2004). First, the influence of fitness on cognitive performance among older adults seems to depend on features of the cognitive tasks. Fitness is more related to performance on tasks that are novel, complex, and require attention and fast processing speed (Chodzko-Zajko & Moore, 1994). Second, recent studies have shown that cardiorespiratory fitness and chronic aerobic exercise training facilitate executive control functions of cognition among older adults (Colcombe et al., 2004). Executive control functions include response inhibition, attentional control, working memory, and rule discovery and are mainly regulated by neural activity in the orbitofrontal, dorsolateral, and mesiofrontal (including the anterior cingulate) prefrontal cortexes of the brain, areas that are further modulated by activity in the temporal and parietal cortexes, the basal ganglia, thalamus, nucleus accumbens, amygdala, hippocampus, and entorhinal cortex (Royall et al., 2002).

Animal studies also indicate that exercise has a beneficial, moderately strong effect on some aspects of learning and memory, such as contextual conditioning (Van Hoomissen et al., 2004) and spatial memory (Fordyce & Farrar, 1991a; Fordyce & Farrar, 1991b; Fordyce & Wehner, 1993; Van Praag et al., 1999; Anderson et al., 2000), which depend largely on hippocampal function.

Potential Biopsychological Mechanisms

The mechanisms for explaining how physical activity reduces self-rated depression or generalized anxiety are unknown. Cognitively based explanations include distractions from worries or symptoms, increased sense of mastery, or improved perceptions of the self, including self-esteem or self-efficacy. Exercise also may decrease anxiety by redefining the subjective meaning of arousal or by offering a way to manage symptoms of anxiety. Increases in physical work capacity are accompanied by increased self-efficacy, which can generalize to increased confidence beyond the exercise setting. Improvements in self-esteem from increased self-efficacy might reduce anxiety and depression. Improvements in mental health also may stem from increased opportunities for social interaction (North et al., 1990).

Exercise as an intervention for improving mental health is unique because it is a biologically based behavior. Some of the acute and chronic physiological changes that occur with exercise training also have psychological effects. Hypotheses about biological mechanisms for explaining reduced anxiety and depression after exercise include increased body temperature and brain blood flow, increased endorphins, and altered autonomic, endocrine, and brain monoamine systems. However, biologically oriented hypotheses have been incompletely developed (Crews & Landers, 1987; Morgan & O'Connor, 1988) and understudied (Dishman, 1997, 1998). This is largely because there are very few exercise psychologists trained in biological psychology. This is ironic, given that the parent of psychology, Wilhelm Wundt, was trained as a physiologist.

The thermogenic hypothesis that reduced anxiety after exercise is dependent on the increased body temperature typical of moderate-to-heavy exertion seems plausible but has received little support (Koltyn & Morgan, 1992; Petruzzello, Landers, & Salazar, 1993; Youngstedt, Dishman, Cureton, & Peacock, 1993). The hypothesis that increased brain blood flow during acute exercise can explain changes in mood or anxiety has not been developed in a way consistent with current evidence. Brain blood flow and metabolism are increased by various stressors in humans and rats (Bryan, 1990), but the effects of exercise seem mainly limited to regions involved with motor, sensory, and cardiovascular regulation, rather than emotional responses (Nybo & Secher, 2004). Although both acute and chronic exercise has influenced blood flow in the anterior cingulate and insular cortexes (areas that are involved with emotional processing and cardiovascular control) (Colcombe et al., 2004; Williamson, McColl, & Mathews, 2003), it remains to be determined whether such responses to exercise reflect emotional responding to exercise or sensory and cardiovascular responses to increased arousal.

Endorphins play a role in removing tonic inhibition of dopamine release in parts of the brain involved with pleasure and could thus indirectly influence positive moods. The hypothesis that endorphins are responsible for changes in mood or anxiety following exercise remains plausible, but it has been perpetuated without much consideration of available evidence. Plasma β-endorphin is reliably elevated during intense exercise, but a plausible link between peripheral β-endorphin or enkephalins and mood or analgesic responses to acute exercise has not been established. In nearly all studies, opioid antagonists, which block the effects of endorphins, have not blocked mood changes after exercise. The influence of blood β-endorphin on the brain is probably limited by the blood brain barrier to peptides at the body temperatures characteristic of typical exercise. There is no evidence that brain opioids in humans are influenced by exercise. Studies with rats and mice show increased levels of endorphins or enkephalin receptor binding in the brain after acute exercise, but the effects of the levels on behavior, emotion, or physiology are unknown. Although opioid-mediated analgesia (Cook & Koltyn, 2000) could indirectly influence mood, peripheral opioid responses to acute exercise apparently inhibit catecholamine influences on cardiovascular, respiratory, and endocrine responses during exercise. A direct influence by peripheral opioid levels on mood is implausible at present.

Sympathetic and parasympathetic nervous system changes associated with exercise training deserve study, as the dysregulation of the sympathetic nervous system has been implicated in anxiety and depression. Evidence from animal models of depression and anxiety points to exercise-induced changes in brain norepinephrine (NE) and serotonin as potential mechanisms for the positive effects on mood. NE and serotonin are major modulators of brain neural activity. There is strong evidence of their involvement in pituitary hormone release, cardiovascular functioning, sleep, and analgesic responses. In rats, chronic physical activity induces positive alterations in brain levels of NE and serotonin and major metabolites in regions known to be involved in integrating behavioral and endocrine responses to stressors other than exercise (Chaouloff, 1997; Dishman et al., 1997; Dunn, Reigle, Youngstedt, Armstrong, & Dishman, 1996; Soares, Holmes, Renner, Edwards, Bunnell, & Dishman, 1999). Interestingly, these changes in

NE were not dependent on traditionally defined increases in fitness (Dishman, 1997), and a therapeutic dose of physical activity for antidepressant and antianxiety effects has not been identified (Dunn et al., 2001). Human studies indicate that exercise training does not alter plasma levels of NE or muscle sympathetic nerve activity measured under resting conditions.

It is also important to consider the effects of exercise training on the hypothalamic-pituitary-adrenal (HPA) cortical axis because it is involved in models of the pathogenesis of cardiovascular disease, anxiety disorders, and major depression. Moderate exercise training results in a diminished HPA response during the same absolute exercise intensity, but heavy exercise training can be associated with either a suppressed or elevated HPA response under resting conditions in humans or after stress in animals, which can interact with reproductive hormones, suggesting gender differences (White-Welkley, Bunnell, Mougey, Meyerhoff, & Dishman, 1995; White-Welkley et al., 1996). Limited correlational evidence suggests that altered HPA cortical responses that can accompany increases in negative moods with overtraining in athletes are consistent with those typically observed in patients diagnosed with major depression (O'Connor, Morgan, Raglin, Barksdale, & Kalin, 1989).

The spinal Hoffmann reflex (H-reflex) has been studied in respect to exercise to locate evidence for moderating effects of exercise on central nervous system activation. The H-reflex is a monosynptic reflex at the level of the S1-S2 sacral spinal roots that is mainly viewed as an index of the efficacy of synaptic transmission at the alpha motor neuron. However, ascending and descending supraspinal tracts exist that would permit it to be modulated by the central nervous system. A series of studies conducted by deVries (deVries, Simard, Wiswell, Heckathorne, & Carabetta, 1982) and others (Bulbulian & Darabos, 1986) showed a reduction in the H-reflex after exercise and hypothesized that the reduction was indicative of a tranquilizing effect of exercise. Recent research, however, has found that there is no generalizability in the reduction of the H-reflex after exercise beyond the specific spinal segments involved with the limbs involved in the exercise

(Motl & Dishman, 2003). Also, the reduction in the H-reflex after acute exercise does not appear dependent on motor efferents activity in the alpha frequency band and hemispheric asymmetry in anterior recording sites, as a correlate or possible mechanism for anxiety reduction or mood changes in response to acute exercise (e.g., Petruzzello, Hall, & Ekkekakis, 2001). However, the cumulative evidence from studies of acute exercise and brain electrocortical activity indicates that activity in all frequency bands increases in response to exercise regardless of hemispheric site (Crabbe & Dishman, 2004). The evidence suggests that acute exercise increases brain electrocortical activity in a general way consistent with increased arousal, possibly from increased sensory and cardiovascular neural traffic to the thalamus processed through the brain stem.

There are new areas of research that implicate other potential biological mechanisms for positive effects of exercise on mental health. For example, brain-derived neurotrophic factor (BDNF) enhances the growth and maintenance of several neuronal systems, and also may have an important role in the neuropathology and treatment of depression (Russo-Neustadt, 2003). Recent animal studies have demonstrated increases in BDNF in the hippocampus, which is involved with contextual memories (e.g., Adlard & Cotman, 2004), and the ventral tegmental area of the meso-limbic system, which helps modulate appetitive or hedonic behaviors (Van Hoomissen, O'Neal, Holmes, & Dishman, 2003) after chronic exercise in rats.

Three plausible mechanisms to explain enhanced cognitive function in response to exercise have included enhancements in brain blood flow, neurotransmitter systems, and neuronal plasticity (Chodzko-Zajko & Moore, 1994). A recent brain neuroimaging study demonstrated decreased blood flow in the anterior cingulate cortex among fit older adults during an executive function task requiring error detection, which was associated with their better performance (Colcombe et al., 2004). However, animal studies have shown that acute increases in blood flow during exercise (Vissing, Andersen, & Diemer, 1996) and adaptations in oxidative capacity after chronic exercise (McCloskey, Adamo, & Anderson, 2001) are mainly restricted to brain regions involved with sensory processing and motor control than with cognition. A large animal literature shows a strong effect of both acute and chronic physical activity on neural plasticity and the expression of neurotrophic growth factors in the hippocampal formation (Cotman & Berchtold, 2002), especially brain derived neurotrophic factor (BDNF), which appears dependent on noradrenergic function (Garcia et al., 2003; Ivy et al., 2003). Galanin, a neuropeptide that serves as both a neurotrophin and a neurotransmitter and is responsive to chronic exercise (O'Neal, Van Hoomissen, Holmes, & Dishman, 2001), has been hypothesized to be more important than BDNF for some types of learning (Van Hoomissen et al., 2004).

Research Issues in Exercise and Mental Health

Some of the inconsistency in links between exercise and mental health can be traced to the quality of the research. Many studies did not quantify physical activity and exertion adequately, examine clearly defined clinical groups, control for subject expectancy or social interaction effects, or consider health and activity history of the participants (Tieman, Peacock, Cureton, & Dishman, 2001). Most studies of exercise and anxiety or depression have not used clinical diagnostic criteria or concomitantly measured biological signs that are common features of standard clinical diagnosis. Theoretically based studies of how changes in mood after exercise might affect negative and positive emotional responding have received little study (Crabbe, Smith, & Dishman, 1999; Smith & Crabbe, 2000; Smith, O'Connor, Crabbe, & Dishman, 2002).

Current knowledge about dose-response relationships and biological plausibility for effects of exercise on mental health is limited (Dunn et al., 2001). Published studies usually have weak experimental control, in which people who did not have clinical conditions were tested. Hence, the internal validity and generalizability of the experimental studies are weak. Difficulties in defining a dose-response relationship also come from inconsistencies in mode, intensity, and duration of exercise treatment, and confounding effects from a variety of psychotherapeutic or pharmacological

treatments. Of the population studies reported, only one (Paffenbarger, Lee, & Leung, 1994) suggested a dose-dependent reduction in depression with increasing exercise. However, this occurred at high levels of leisure-time physical activity (i.e., 2,500 weekly calories expended), which is atypical of most Americans. There is also no experimental evidence of dose-dependent reductions in anxiety and depression with increasing exercise intensity. We know of no studies that varied frequency or duration of exercise, and one study that accounted for total energy expenditure to evaluate the effects of exercise training on depressive symptoms (Dunn et al., 2005). The absence of a consistent dose-gradient decrease in symptoms of depression with increasing levels of physical activity may reflect limited published evidence, or may suggest that the observed associations between exercise and depression are a consequence of increased depressive symptoms with inactivity, and not positive effects of high physical activity levels on lowering depression scores (Farmer et al., 1988).

Studies generally show a moderate reduction in the risk for depression among the physically active that is not dependent on exercise intensity, and that both moderate and vigorous intensities can reduce symptoms of depression (Dunn et al., 2001). Substantial reductions in trait anxiety and depression reportedly require about 4 months of exercise training (North et al., 1990; Petruzzello et al., 1991), but most evidence suggests that changes in self-ratings of self-esteem and depression following exercise training occur independently of increases in aerobic capacity (e.g., Doyne et al., 1987; Desharnais et al., 1993; King, Taylor, & Haskell, 1993; Martinsen, Hoffart, & Solberg, 1989a, 1989b). More studies of other types of exercise (e.g., resistance training) are needed. Although evidence does not indicate that the mental health benefits of physical activity depend upon changes in aerobic fitness, recommendations by the American College of Sports Medicine (ACSM) for exercise that increases or maintains fitness among healthy adults offer prudent guidelines for a graduated exercise program that can enhance mental health among people who have no other medical contraindications for physical exertion. People who do not desire to exercise for the purpose of marked gains in fitness may benefit from the complementary recommendation by the ACSM and the Centers for Disease Control and Prevention (CDC) that people engage in moderate-intensity physical activity (e.g., walking) for at least 30 minutes each day, possibly accumulated in multiple sessions, most days of the week.

Psychological Risks of Exercise

A maximal exercise bout can be followed by a small and temporary increase in state anxiety (O'Connor et al., 1995; Tieman, Peacock, Cureton, & Dishman, 2000). However, few scientific studies have tested whether extreme amounts of physical activity, or its social context, increase anxiety or depression to an extent that is clinically meaningful. Morgan, Brown, Raglin, O'Connor, and Ellickson (1987) proposed that the increased anxiety or depression that frequently accompanies the staleness resulting from overtraining in endurance sports represents a model for a paradoxical dose-response gradient with heavy exertion. Staleness occurs when uninjured athletes cannot maintain their normal level of performance, despite being motivated to do so. Some evidence shows that increased negative moods with overtraining in athletes can be accompanied by altered hypothalamic-pituitary-adrenal cortical responses consistent with those typically observed in patients diagnosed with major depression (O'Connor et al., 1989). However, the incidence and prevalence rates, risk factors, and the etiology of increased anxiety and depression because of overtraining are not established according to epidemiological or medical traditions, and the volume of exercise training that precedes athletic staleness far exceeds the amount engaged in by the vast majority of leisure-time exercisers.

Clinical parallels, including elevated anxiety and depression, also have been drawn between highly committed runners and patients diagnosed as suffering from anorexia nervosa or bulimia. There is some concern by mental health professionals that the disciplined training and social climate in sports that emphasizes a lean body composition and dietary restriction promotes the development of eating problems or adds to existing eating problems. Despite recognition of abusive exercise more than 20 years ago, it is still not known whether excessive exercise and disordered eating share a common course that is motivated by common goals and followed by common medical outcomes (Davis, 2000; Dishman, 1998). Results from nearly 100 studies on the topic are inconclusive because the studies were correlational, generally not controlling for subject selection biases, and lacking standard definitions or measures validated for excessive exercise. Anorexics often augment food restriction by hyperactivity, but their cardiorespiratory fitness is well below average compared with the above-average fitness of habitual runners and overtrained athletes. In addition, cross-sectional studies have not revealed a common psychopathology between excessively committed runners and anorexic patients.

Anorexia and bulimia are characterized by distortion of body image, and excessive preoccupation with body shape and distortion of body image has taken a new form. Harvard affiliated researchers have identified a variant of body dysmorphic disorder (see criteria below) they call *muscle dysmorphia*, in which both men and women develop a pathological preoccupation with their muscularity (Phillips et al., 1997). This preoccupation is manifested in the individual's behavior (excessive weight-lifting, excessive attention to diet, social impairment), and can include severe subjective distress, impaired social and occupational functioning, and abuse of anabolic steroids and other substances (Gruber & Pope, 2000; Pope et al., 1997).

Diagnostic Criteria for Body Dysmorphic Disorder[1]

A. Preoccupation with an imagined defect in appearance. If a slight physical anomaly is present, the person's concern is markedly excessive.

B. The preoccupation causes clinically significant distress or impairment in social, occupational, or other important areas of functioning.

[1]From the American Psychiatric Association. (1994). *Diagnostic and statistical manual of mental disorders* (4th ed.), p. 468.

C. The preoccupation is not better accounted for by another mental disorder (e.g., dissatisfaction with body shape and size in anorexia nervosa).

Pope et al. (2000) measured height, weight, and body fat in college-aged men in Austria (N = 54), France (N = 65), and the United States (N = 81), and asked them to choose a pictorial body image that they felt represented (1) their own body, (2) the body they ideally would like to have, (3) the body of an average man of their age, and (4) the male body they believed women would prefer. Men from all three countries demonstrated a wide discrepancy between their ideal body image and actual muscularity, choosing an ideal body that was 12.7 kg more muscular, on average, than themselves. In another study, 24 men classified as having muscle dysmorphia reported higher body dissatisfaction, risky eating attitudes, prevalence of anabolic steroid use, and lifetime prevalence of *Diagnostic and Statistical Manual of Mental Disorders,* 4th edition (DSM-IV), mood, anxiety, and eating disorders when compared with 30 normal comparison weight-lifters. The men with muscle dysmorphia also reported frequent feelings of shame and embarrassment and impaired function at work and in social situations (Olivardia, Pope, & Hudson, 2000). Several cases of body dysmorphia also have been documented among 75 women bodybuilders (Gruber & Pope, 2000).

Although eating disorders and muscle dysmorphia can have serious and debilitating symptoms, based on available scientific evidence, the potential risk that sedentariness poses for increased depression or anxiety in the U.S. population clearly represents a greater concern for public health than does the potential risk of excessive exercise for poor mental health.

Exercise and Cross-Stressor Tolerance

Exaggerated physiological responsiveness to mental stress is an established model for studying the etiology of coronary heart disease, atherosclerosis, and essential hypertension. Hyperresponsiveness is associated with transient increases in heart rate, blood pressure, and plasma catecholamines, which can contribute to increased risk of heart disease. Risk of hypertension may be increased with heightened sympathetic drive to the heart during mental stressors. A body of literature is founded on the idea that adaptations to the stress of exercise could translate to nonexercise stress (Dishman & Jackson, 2000). That is, people who are more physically fit would experience less strain during exercise but also would demonstrate attenuated physiological responsiveness during mental stress. A diminished stress response would have immediate benefits but, over time, also could decrease the risk of stress-linked diseases. Exercise-induced decreases in cardiovascular responsiveness may be one mechanism by which disease risk is reduced.

For the most part, the evidence for changes in the stress response due to exercise training is ambiguous. Crews and Landers's (1987) meta-analytical review reported a significant effect size of .48 *SD*, implying that aerobically fit subjects had a reduced response to psychosocial stress response. However, more recent reviews offer no consensus that exercise or physical fitness is accompanied by decreased physiological responsiveness to psychosocial stressors under nonexercise conditions (Dishman & Jackson, 2000; Peronnet & Szabo, 1993; Sothmann, 1991; Sothmann et al., 1996) or after acute exercise. A recent meta-analysis of the cumulative evidence published from 1965 to 2004 found that cardiorespiratory fitness was weakly associated with increased physiological reactivity, but quicker recovery, from laboratory stress (Jackson & Dishman, 2004). Effects seem to depend on the type and intensity of the stressor, the use of fitness or physical activity as an independent variable, and subject characteristics. Similar to the studies on anxiety and depression, the studies of the effects of fitness on stress responsiveness have generally suffered from several critical design and measurement limitations. We will address potential mechanisms for cross-stressor tolerance in light of the limitations of the research.

The few longitudinal exercise studies of physiological responsiveness to stressors (e.g., reviewed by Crews & Landers, 1987) typically did not use standardized measures of physical fitness or physical activity. Fitness/activity assessments in these studies often were based on heart rate–based estimates of cardiorespiratory fitness (i.e., VO$_2$ peak) (which have standard errors of 10–15%) or on unvalidated self-reports of activity. Heart rate (HR) has been the most commonly utilized stress response measure. This presents a serious problem. When HR defines both independent and dependent variables, independent tests of their association cannot be performed. In addition, some stressors, such as passive coping tasks or tasks requiring attention to nonthreatening external events, induce a decreased heart rate. Not taking into account the type of stressor or defining cardiovascular responsiveness only by an increase in heart rate, as is often done, also can confound results.

Most published studies used cross-sectional designs. Thus, low fitness might merely be correlated with a third factor, such as gender or psychological characteristics, which is actually responsible for increased responsiveness. There is some evidence that mood and catecholamine and endocrine responses to stressors are associated with menstrual status (Mills & Berry, 1999; Saab, 1989), but how exercise and fitness moderate these responses is not known. It has been reported that individuals characterized by the Type A behavior pattern (TABP; i.e., time urgency, impatience, extreme competitiveness, self-involvement) or hostility have exaggerated cardiovascular responsiveness to stressors presumably mediated mostly by task-evoked β-adrenergic activity (Harbin, 1989). Exaggerated sympathetic activity might oppose the influence of increased aerobic fitness on increased cardiac vagal tone, but studies have not concomitantly measured fitness, TABP, hostility, and sympathetic and cardiac vagal activity using direct measures.

We have attempted to address some of these issues in our research on responsiveness and physical activity. In a correlational study of responsiveness in men, we found that physical fitness and low hostility each were independently related to cardiac vagal tone (Graham, Zeichner, Peacock, & Dishman, 1996), which is associated with lowered heart rate and lowered risk for heart disease.

For women with parental history of hypertension, heart rate response demonstrated an interaction between self-report of physical activity and TABP (Buckworth, Zeichner, Lating, & Dishman, 1996). Active Type A women had a greater heart rate response compared to less active and Type B women during the Structured Interview, an active coping stress used to identify TABP. In black American women, fitness was positively related to increases in either total peripheral resistance (TPR) or calf vascular resistance during passive and active mental stressors (Jackson & Dishman, 2002). In contrast, fitness was positively related to blunted blood pressure during or after passive stress and enhanced recovery of blood pressure and TPR after an active stressor. In addition, the effects of fitness on the vascular responses during and after the active stressor were stronger among women having a negative history of parental hypertension. We also have found that cardiorespiratory fitness is associated with increased cardiac vagal tone in young women (Buckworth, Dishman, & Cureton, 1994) and men (Graham et al., 1996). Increased vagal tone may explain the fit subjects' lower tonic levels of heart rate that are maintained during mental stressors.

None of the hypothesized physiological mechanisms, such as change in baroreflex function or altered autonomic nervous system functioning (Crews & Landers, 1987), for the reductions in human responsiveness to stressors have been verified. There is evidence that sympathetic and parasympathetic systems are modified with regular exercise, but we do not know the mechanisms by which these adaptations would transfer to modifications in the response to mental stress. An increase in sensitivity of the baroreflex or a decrease in sympathetic nervous system activity has not been shown using direct measures common in the field of applied physiology. A few studies using respiratory sinus arrhythmia or the rapid heart rate response to carotid hypertension have converged to suggest that fitness is associated with increased cardiac vagal tone at rest and during mental stress (Buckworth et al., 1994; Buckworth, Convertino, Cureton, & Dishman, 1997; Graham et al., 1996; Sothmann et al., 1996). Proposed changes in β-adrenergic receptors have not been specified in ways that are consistent with current knowledge in neuroscience (Fillenz, 1990) or with evidence from exercise studies (Maki, Kontula, & Harkonen, 1990; Mazzeo, 1991; Yoo, Tackett, & Dishman, 1996). Some recent evidence suggests that the inverse relationship between cardiorespiratory fitness and blood pressure responses during cold pressor stress in women is explainable by mitigation of central nervous system outflow to the vasculature as measured by muscle sympathetic nerve activity (Dishman, Nakamura, Jackson, & Ray, 2003).

Plasma levels of norepinephrine have been measured in attempts to evaluate changes in sympathetic nervous system functioning, one of the potential mechanisms of a cross-stressor tolerance effect. Among exercise trained men, plasma NE levels are lower at a given absolute exercise intensity, unchanged at the same relative intensity but higher than normal at maximal exercise. Nonetheless, studies consistently have found that aerobic fitness does not attenuate plasma or urine levels of catecholamines measured during mild laboratory mental stressors. Sympathetic nerve discharge was not measured in those studies. Because levels of circulating catecholamines can rise because of reduced clearance from the blood, in addition to release from sympathetic nerves or the adrenal gland, it is premature to conclude that fitness or physical activity has no effect on sympathetic nervous system responses during mental stress (Dishman, Hong, Soares, Edwards, Bunnell, Jaso-Friedmann, & Evans, 2000; Dishman, Warren, Hong, Bunnell, Mougey, Meyerhoff, Jaso-Friedmann, & Evans, 2000).

There is some consistency in the fitness and NE literature for decreased responses to familiar stress and augmented responses to intense and novel stressors with high levels of fitness (Sothmann et al., 1996). A cross-stressor adaptation from exercise training to nonexercise stress might be delimited to intense exercise (i.e., 60–90% VO$_2$ peak) and to intense mental stressors that result in blood levels of norepinephrine (1800 pg/ml) and epinephrine (50–100 pg/ml) high enough to initiate systemic physiological activation. It is also necessary to measure cardiac vagal tone or activity during mental stressors in order to interpret fully the contribution of sympathetic activity to autonomic balance and the regulation of cardiovascular responses during stress (Dishman, Nakamura, Garcia, Thompson, Dunn, & Blair, 2000; Dishman, Nakamura, Jackson, & Ray, 2003).

Physical Activity Behavior Change

It is important for exercise psychologists to understand the effects of exercise on mental health and the stress response, but it may be more important to study the dynamics of exercise behavior and the factors necessary to increase physical activity and exercise adherence. Increased physical activity and cardiorespiratory fitness can make significant contributions to public health, but efforts to increase adoption and maintenance of an active lifestyle are not working. The proportion of adults who participated in regular moderate or vigorous physical activity stayed at 30% from 1997 to 2002, and remained below the Healthy People 2010 goal of 50%. Although there has been a significant decline from 1994 to 2002 in the proportion of adults reporting no leisure time physical activity (30% to 25%) (Grunbaum et al., 2004), this is still above the Healthy People 2010 goal of 20%. In addition, rates of overweight and obesity are steadily increasing to epidemic proportions.

There is a significant decrease in physical activity in late adolescence after high school and college. Seventy percent of 12-year-old children report vigorous physical activity, but by age 21, only 42% of men and 30% of women continue vigorous activity (NIH Consensus Conference, 1996), and the participation rate continues to decrease with increasing age. Traditional interventions have not addressed the cyclical or dynamic nature of exercise behavior, and the dropout rate from structured exercise programs has remained at 50% for the past 20 years (Dishman, 1994a).

To clarify the literature in this area, we conducted a quantitative meta-analysis of 127 studies that examined the efficacy of interventions for increasing physical activity among 130,000 people in community, worksite, school, home, and health care settings (Dishman & Buckworth, 1996). The estimated population effect, weighted by sample size, was about three fourths of a standard deviation, which is comparable to increasing adherence from 50%, the rate typically observed in exercise programs without a behavior change component, to a success rate of about 85% with the intervention. We examined moderators to establish practical information about which interventions worked, with whom, and under what conditions. The largest effects were found when interventions employed the principles of behavior modification and were delivered to healthy people in a community, particularly when the interventions were delivered to groups using media (e.g., telecommunication, print mailings, motivating signage), rather than face-to-face counseling by a professional. The best adherence was for unsupervised, low-intensity, leisure-time physical activity. The duration and frequency of participation were not significant influences on intervention effectiveness. Although the interventions with the largest effect size were based on behavior modification, it is difficult to assess the effectiveness of cognitive-behavior modification strategies because multiple interventions were used in many of the more recent studies. Nonetheless, it is surprising, given the evidence supporting the effectiveness of behavior modification for increasing physical activity, at least in the short term, that most contemporary interventions have not been based in behaviorism (Epstein, 1998) but, rather, have used mainly cognitively based interventions. There is also an emerging focus on environmental manipulations that increase opportunities and decrease barriers to physical activity.

Physical inactivity is a serious and pervasive public health concern, but there are gaps in our knowledge about exercise determinants and no consensus of guidelines for interventions to increase and maintain physical activity. In this section, we will describe theories that have guided adherence research, present some of the issues in research, discuss the current consensus on correlates of exercise, and provide examples of practical applications for influencing exercise behavior.

Theories of Exercise Behavior

Several theories have been used to predict and explain exercise behavior (see Biddle & Nigg, 2000, for a review). Many studies of exercise determinants and interventions have been based on social cognitive theories, behavior modification, and cognitive behavior modification. The transtheoretical model, or the stages of change model, has been applied to exercise behavior over the past 13 years and has been used successfully to guide intervention development. The ecological model is gaining support through efforts to implement multilevel multidimensional interventions with a focus on environmental influences.

Social cognitive theories. Social cognitive theories conceptualize cognition, affect, and value related variables as mediators in the choice of goals, and thus exercise behavior. The theories assume that personal factors, environmental events, and behavior function as interacting and reciprocal determinants of each other. Bandura (1986) emphasized the influence of self-efficacy, expectations about behavioral outcomes, and values placed on those outcomes as determinants of behavior. He proposed that self-change operates through self-initiated reactions. These reactions are stimulated by a discrepancy between personal goals or standards and knowledge of personal achievement. For example, individuals dissatisfied with their current exercise or fitness who adopt challenging goals and are confident (i.e., have high self-efficacy) that they can attain their goals would presumably have optimal motivation for maintaining exercise.

Behavior modification. Behavior modification is the planned, systematic application of principles of learning to the modification of behavior. According to behavior modification theory, changes in behavior result from associations between external stimuli and the consequences of a specific behavior. The role of thoughts, motives, and perceptions is minimized. What precedes and what follows a behavior will influence the frequency of that behavior—that is, behavior is cued and reinforced. According to behavior modification, the key to behavior change lies in the identification of the target behavior, for example, walking at lunch or doing aerobics when the children take gymnastics, and effective cues and reinforcers. Behavioral approaches, such as written agreements, behavioral contracts, lotteries, and stimulus and reinforcement control, have been successful in exercise intervention studies.

Cognitive-behavior modification. Cognitive-behavior modification is based on the assumption that psychological variables are the mediators of behavior. A wide range of dysfunctional or maladaptive behaviors results from the individual's irrational, unproductive thoughts and incompletely formed cognitions. Learning or insight can serve to restructure, augment, or replace faulty thoughts with behaviorally effective beliefs and cognitive skills. Simply put, cognitions moderate behavior, and cognitions can be changed. Clients are educated about the relationship between cognitions, feelings, and behaviors and are taught skills to identify and control antecedents and consequences that prompt and reinforce behavior. Cognitive-behavioral approaches, including self-monitoring, goal-setting, feedback, and decision making, have been effective in increasing exercise adherence when used alone or when combined in intervention packages.

Transtheoretical model. The transtheoretical model, also known as the stages of change model, has been used to describe the processes of health behavior change and has been applied to exercise (Marcus, Pinto, Simkin, Audrain, & Taylor, 1994; Marshall & Biddle, 2001). Behavior change is seen as a dynamic process that occurs through a series of five interrelated stages (Marcus & Simkin, 1994; Prochaska & Marcus, 1994). People in precontemplation are not thinking about starting an exercise program. Those in the contemplation stage are considering starting an exercise program. During the preparation stage, a plan has been made but not implemented. People in the action stage have started regular exercise within the past 6 months but are at greater risk of not adhering than someone in the maintenance stage, for whom exercise behavior is more established. Three components of the transtheoretical

model that are proposed mediators of behavior change are self-efficacy, decisional balance (i.e., pros and cons), and processes of change. The processes of change include application of both cognitive (e.g., self-reevaluation) and behavioral (e.g., stimulus control, reinforcement management) strategies to different degrees depending on the stage of change.

Ecological Models. Some scholars contend that the lack of progress in increasing physical activity may be a consequence of targeting mainly individuals using motivational and educational approaches to behavior change. Ecological models acknowledge that behavior can be influenced by intrapersonal, social environment, physical environment, and public policy variables. Sallis and Owen (1999) applied this model to physical activity and defined the "behavioral setting" to describe environmental factors that can facilitate the decisions to be more active and can support that behavior. Social environmental factors are supportive behaviors, social climate, culture, policies governing incentives for activity/inactivity, and policies governing resources and infrastructures related to activity/inactivity. Physical environmental factors are divided into natural and constructed environment. Natural environmental factors are weather and geography. Constructed environment includes information, level of urbanization, architecture, transportation environments, and the entertainment and recreation infrastructures. Using this model, physical activity is targeted through changing the environmental and public policies. For example, administrators at the Centers for Disease Control and Prevention have begun to address physical activity behavior change through establishing relationships with a variety of nontraditional partners, including city planners, architects, environmental psychologists, and specialists in transportation and recreation.

Research Issues in Exercise Behavior

There are weaknesses and gaps in this research that have characterized exercise adherence research in general, regardless of the theoretical perspective. For example, factors controlling adoption and maintenance of different types and intensities of exercise have not been explored, and specific determinants of adopting, maintaining, or resuming exercise after dropping out have not been identified (Sallis & Hovell, 1990). Most interventions have not determined whether the intervention actually changed the social-cognitive mediators presumed by theory to mediate the effects of the intervention on physical activity (Baranowski et al., 1998; Dishman, Motl et al., 2004).

In our meta-analysis of interventions to increase exercise adherence, only 20% of the 127 studies and 14 dissertations published from January 1965 through August 1995 reported a follow-up of the intervention (Dishman & Buckworth, 1996). Effects were smaller as time passed after the interventions. As health benefits of physical activity accrue over time, we need to know what facilitates and hinders long-term participation (Dishman & Sallis, 1994). There is some longitudinal evidence that exercise self-efficacy increases as one moves from an established sedentary lifestyle to long-term maintenance of regular exercise (Dishman, Motl et al., 2004; McAuley & Blissmer, 2000), and we are beginning to study the mediators of stage transitions in physical activity (Wallace & Buckworth, 2003), which may differ from other health behaviors (Rosen, 2000).

In general, level of physical activity in intervention studies has been quantified using self-report data gathered through questionnaires, interviews, and activity diaries, and with more objective methods, such as motion sensors and observation. However, activities at moderate and low intensities are easily forgotten and difficult to measure, calling to question the validity of self-report. The lack of concurrent validity with physiological measures can be a problem when we attempt to associate a change in exercise stage or self-report of physical activity with a change in health risk. If we want people to exercise so their risk of disease will decrease, we need to know if reports of increased activity are accompanied by beneficial physical changes.

Most studies of moderators and mediators of exercise behavior change have targeted social and psychological variables, but physiological characteristics of individuals also can play a critical role in decisions and habits, and may interact significantly with psychosocial constructs (Trost, Owen, Bauman, Sallis, & Brown, 2002). For example, body mass index, obesity, and physical discomfort have been negatively correlated with self-report of physical activity (Trost et al., 2002), and those who perceive their health as poor are unlikely to adopt and adhere to an exercise program (Dishman & Buckworth, 1997). Physiological influences on physical activity may be more basic, as proposed by Rowland (1998), who describes an anatomical-physiological entity that regulates the amount of daily physical activity as does analogous brain centers that control behavioral-physiological processes such as hunger and temperature regulation.

Correlates of Physical Activity

The known correlates of physical activity can be categorized as past and present personal attributes, past and present environments, and aspects of physical activity itself. Identifying factors associated with physical activity and exercise that reside in the individual is important because researchers can identify population segments that may be responsive or resistive to physical activity interventions. Personal attributes such as smoking, education, income, and ethnicity can be markers of underlying habits or circumstances that reinforce sedentary living. Identifying environmental factors in exercise behavior demonstrates the need to look beyond the individual and small group in developing interventions. The target of interventions should include policy and facility planning at the international, national, and community level and should include educational-behavioral applications in schools, churches, and health care and recreational settings (Blair et al., 1996; Dishman & Sallis, 1994). Identifying specific aspects of physical activity that enhance adoption and adherence is especially important to practitioners prescribing exercise in a variety of settings (Buckworth, 2003; Dishman & Buckworth, 1996; Kahn et al., 2002).

The significance of specific correlates also must be considered in the context of other personal and environmental influences. Determinants of physical activity are not isolated variables but influence and are influenced by each other as they contribute to the behavioral outcome. Personal attributes include cognitions, beliefs, attitudes, emotions, and values that can interact with environmental variables, such as social support and the weather. For example, someone who values physical fitness and is self-motivated may be less influenced by the weather and thus more likely to exercise when it is cold than someone whose fitness is less important and needs more external support and prompts.

Past and present personal attributes. Demographics such as low education and income, age, smoking, and female gender are consistent correlates of physical inactivity. There is no experimental evidence, however, that those factors cause inactivity. Obviously there are many women, smokers, and older people who are very active physically.

Being active in the recent past predicts present and future participation, but playing sports when young has not influenced adult physical activity patterns in reported studies. No prospective study has shown a relationship between interscholastic or intercollegiate athletics and free-living physical activity in adults, and there is mixed evidence that activity patterns in childhood are predictive of later physical activity (Barnekow-Bergkvist, Hedberg, Janlert, & Jansson, 1998; Seefeldt, Malina, & Clark, 2002). As mentioned earlier, vigorous physical activity significantly decreases during adolescence and young adulthood. However, participation in moderate-intensity activity seems to be stable with increasing age.

The cognitive variable with the most support as a determinant is self-efficacy, accounting for 25–35% of the variation in physical activity in most studies. It is difficult to determine, though, from most of the research, if self-efficacy causes physical activity. Active people may report a high self-efficacy because of past success in physical activity, but other factors may have actually caused the exercise habit. Other cognitive variables positively associated with physical activity are self-schemata (see self as an exerciser) (Kendzierski, 1994), expectations of benefits, self-motivation,

enjoyment, and behavioral intentions (Trost et al., 2002). Like self-efficacy, attitudes and intentions commonly account for about 25% of variations in people's self-ratings of their physical activity (Dzewaltowski, 1994; Godin, 1994; Godin & Shephard, 1990), but past physical activity habits can be more strongly related to contemporary exercise behavior (Trost et al., 2002). Mood disorders are negatively associated with physical activity. There has been little research on traits and states and exercise adherence, although there is some promise in linking personality variables, such as extroversion, with exercise behavior, motives, barriers, and preferences (Courneya & Hellsten, 1998).

Past and present environments. Social influences in the form of social support (i.e., encouragement or help from someone) and prompting (e.g., images of exercise) appear to be strong correlates of physical activity. Climate or season has a consistent relationship with physical activity in adults, whereas there is weak or contradictory evidence of association between cost and access to home exercise equipment with physical activity (Trost et al., 2002). Objectively measured access to facilities is a reliable predictor of physical activity, but evidence on perceived access is mixed (Dishman, 1994c). The reason most often given for dropping out of a supervised exercise program is lack of time, but it is not clear if this represents a true determinant, a perceived determinant, poor time-management skills, or a rationalization for lack of motivation to exercise (Dishman & Buckworth, 1996).

Physical activity. In terms of the exercise behavior itself, there seems to be better adherence for walking programs, but we do not know if there are different determinants for different types of exercise, such as aerobic dance versus swimming. Some studies have examined the influence of different frequencies and durations on adherence in light of the public health recommendation for physical activity that suggests health benefits from accumulating at least 30 minutes of moderate intensity physical activity daily through several short bouts of exercise. Jakicic, Winters, Lang, and Wing (1999) randomized 148 sedentary, overweight women to three interventions: long-bout exercise (LB), multiple short-bout exercise (SB), or multiple short-bout exercise with home exercise equipment (SBEQ) using a treadmill. After 18 months, women in the SBEQ group demonstrated better adherence that those in the LB and SB groups, and there were no group differences in weight loss or improvements in cardiorespiratory fitness. Schmidt, Biwer, and Kalscheuer (2001) also tested the effects of different combinations of short bouts compared to continuous exercise in overweight college women, and reported no differences in adherence or weight loss among the groups after eight weeks of training.

Both adoption and maintenance of exercise programs are inversely associated with exercise intensity (Pollock et al., 1991; Trost et al., 2002), and the largest effect for physical activity characteristics from the authors' meta-analysis was for low-intensity leisure-time activity. Although adherence was similar in a 1 year randomized exercise trial with middle-aged adults in groups assigned to low or high intensities based on percentage peak heart rate, each group selected intensities during the year that regressed toward a moderate intensity level (King, Haskell, Taylor, & DeBusk, 1991). Perceived effort has a strong negative association with physical activity, so it is possible that prescriptions based on preferred intensities might increase adherence to exercise programs (Dishman, 1994b).

Interventions

The theories we presented support several interventions that have been applied to physical activity behavior change. The effectiveness of interventions has been mixed, partly because of the research issues discussed above and the unique characteristics of physical activity itself. Physical activity is a health behavior that encompasses a wide range and complexity of dynamic behavioral demands. Physical activity is also perceived as requiring more time and effort than other health behaviors (Turk, Rudy, & Salovey, 1984). However, interventions, particularly those based on behavior modification, can be effective in changing exercise behavior. Although a wide variety of interventions have been applied to exercise behavior change (Dishman & Buckworth, 1996; Kahn et al., 2002), stimulus control, reinforcement control, self-efficacy enhancement, and goal-setting will be presented as examples of strategies that can be used to modify physical activity. We also will discuss the application of the transtheoretical model to intervention selection. Planning for participation, initial adoption of physical activity, continued participation or maintenance, and overall periodicity of participation (e.g., relapse, resumption of activity, and seasonal variation) are characteristics of physical activity that can involve different mediators and may warrant different interventions.

Example strategies. Stimulus control involves manipulating antecedent conditions, or cues, which can prompt a behavior. Prompts can be verbal, physical, or symbolic. The goal is to increase cues for the desired behavior and decrease cues for competing behaviors. Examples of cues to increase exercise behavior are posters, slogans, posted notes, placement of exercise equipment in visible places, recruitment of social support, and performance of exercise at the same time and place every day (Knapp, 1988). Exercising first thing in the morning is an example of timing exercise when the risk of distracting cues is less.

Reinforcement control entails understanding and modifying the consequences of target behavior to increase its occurrence. When we think of reinforcement, we commonly think of rewarding a behavior to increase its frequency. An aerobics instructor praising a participant for finishing an especially hard routine is an example of positive reinforcement in which something positive to the person is added during or immediately after the target behavior. Contracts with consequences, positive feedback, tokens, and group lotteries are examples of reinforcement control.

There is consistent evidence that self-efficacy is a mediator of behavior change, that is, the mechanism by which an intervention has its effect (e.g., Dishman et al., 2004). Interventions that do not change proposed mediating variables are unlikely to change behavior. There are four sources of efficacy information that can be manipulated in interventions: performance accomplishments, vicarious experiences, verbal persuasion, and physiological/psychological states. Performance accomplishments refers to mastering a difficult or previously feared task, and is the most potent strategy for increasing self-efficacy (Bandura, 1991). Breaking the target behavior into components that are easy to manage helps individuals to develop and refine skills and develop coping mechanisms. Someone who is successful meeting a reasonable but challenging short-term exercise goal will have a sense of accomplishment and increased efficacy. Vicarious experiences enable learning via observation of events or other people. Modeling is an effective strategy if the model is similar to the subjects and succeeds through effort with clear rewarding outcomes. An overweight teenager will develop more confidence for playing soccer if he sees another overweight teen score a goal. Verbal persuasion entails encouragement or support to reinforce progress toward reaching the target behavior and fosters the attribution of accomplishments to the person's own behavior. Finally, the physiological response to exercise can be interpreted by sedentary individuals as negative feedback about their performance. Because high arousal impairs performance and decreases efficacy expectations, understanding that heavy breathing, increased heart rate, fatigue, and muscle discomfort are normal responses to exercise can help manage psychological arousal during exercise.

Goal-setting is used to attain a specific task in a specific period of time. Goals can be as simple and time limited as completing a set of bench presses or as complicated and encompassing as participating in a triathlon. Goals serve as immediate regulators of human behavior, providing direction, mobilizing effort, and fostering persistence in the search for task strategies. Goal-setting provides a plan of action that focuses and directs activity and emphasizes a clear link between behavior and outcome. Specific, measurable goals make it easier to monitor progress, make adjustments, and know when the goal has been accomplished. Goals must be reasonable and realistic. A goal might be achievable, but personal and situational constraints can make it unrealistic. For example, losing 2 lb (1 kg) a week through diet and exercise is reasonable, but almost impossible for the working mother of three who has minimal time for exercise and cooking. Unrealistic goals set the participant up to fail, which can damage self-efficacy and adherence to the behavior-change program.

Stage-specific interventions. Most interventions try to fit the participant to an exercise program or behavioral intervention, rather than fit a program to the characteristics and needs of the participant. A major contribution of the transtheoretical model lies in the assertion that interventions should be targeted, that is, matched to an individual according to his or her activity history and readiness for change (Prochaska & Velicer, 1997; Marcus & Forsyth, 2003). For example, the goal in working with people in the precontemplation stage is to get them to begin thinking about changing. The personal benefits and barriers of exercise should be identified, and ways to overcome the barriers should be created. Strategies that help them develop a personal value for exercise and understand the importance of exercise in a healthy lifestyle are useful in helping them consider exercise (Marcus & Forsyth, 2003; Gorely & Gordon, 1995). Health-risk appraisals and fitness testing are examples of interventions that can prompt contemplation and enhance motivation to become more active (King, 1994).

The goal with contemplators is to help them take action. Marketing and media campaigns promoting exercise, as well as accurate, easy-to-understand information about how to start an exercise program, can help move people into the action stage. Other elements that can affect the intention to start exercising are role models, perceived barriers and benefits, and psychosocial variables, such as self-efficacy. Integrating decision theories with social marketing strategies may be helpful for increasing knowledge, attitudes, and intentions to adopt physical activity (Kahn et al., 2002).

Behavioral factors come into play more in moving from preparation to action. Fitness assessments and self-monitoring can be useful strategies at this juncture to help specify the variables that must be considered to change exercise behavior. For example, a fitness assessment can establish mode and intensity of exercise necessary to accomplish certain goals, and self-monitoring can help identify scheduling changes that must be made to fit in an exercise routine.

Goal-setting is another important strategy to use with individuals in the preparation stage. Manageable short- and long-term goals that are consistent with capabilities, values, resources, and needs should be set. Self-efficacy predicts adoption and maintenance of exercise, and can be increased with mastery experiences. Initial goals should thus be challenging but realistic in order to foster increases in exercise self-efficacy. Environmental and social supports and barriers also should be evaluated and modified to promote the new behaviors.

Individuals in the action phase are at a high risk of dropping out of an exercise program. Social support is critical in this stage. Instruction in self-regulatory skills, such as stimulus control, reinforcement management, and self-monitoring of progress, and training in relapse prevention are also useful strategies. Relapse prevention is based on the premises that the impact of interruptions and life events on exercise can be diminished if the individual anticipates and plans for their occurrence, recognizes them as only temporary obstructions, and develops self-regulatory skills for preventing relapses to inactivity (Marlatt & Gordon, 1985).

Movement from the action phase to the maintenance phase follows a decrease in the risk of relapse and an increase in self-efficacy. Interventions will be more effective if they involve reevaluation of rewards and goals, and promotion of strategies to cope with potential lapses from relocation, travel, or medical events. Social support, self-motivation, self-regulatory skills, and interventions such as relapse prevention seem necessary to maintain or resume exercise.

Summary

Determining the consequences of exercise, whether they are improvements in mood, sleep, self-concept, and cognitive performance, or diminished physiological responses to mental stress, has been an important area of research in exercise psychology. A few population studies using cross-sectional or prospective epidemiological designs have reported moderately higher proportions of self-rated symptoms of depression among sedentary men and women. The population studies of exercise and depression demonstrate some independence of the exercise effects, and some consistency across gender, age, and race. Studies show that small-to-moderate decreases in self-rated anxiety and depression accompany acute and chronic exercise. This has been reported in a large number of poorly controlled studies of small nonclinical samples, and in a very few well-controlled studies of clinical samples. Thus, the internal and external validity of most studies has been limited. The few large sample experiments have not confirmed a lasting independent reduction in depression or anxiety after chronic exercise (e.g., King et al., 1993; Stern & Cleary, 1981, 1982). Also, the effects of exercise usually are smaller compared with psychotherapy or drug therapy, which have effects of about 1 and 3 SD, respectively. One randomized controlled trial found similar reductions in depression symptoms after either exercise or antidepressant drug treatment, but the therapeutic benefits occurred more slowly after exercise than drug treatment (Blumenthal et al., 1999). People report the largest benefits when the exercise program lasts about four to five months, but without behavior modification, nearly 50% of people drop out of an exercise program within 3 months. Nonetheless, despite the low statistical power resulting from poor experimental control, measures of often questionable reliability, and usually small samples of people with test scores in the normal range, there are optimistic reviews (Landers & Petruzzello, 1994; Morgan, 1994) that hold that the observation of effects of exercise on anxiety and depression is evidence for strong, true effects of exercise.

Anecdotal reports support the effectiveness of regular exercise as a way to manage mental stress, and the evidence that exercise training can moderate responses to familiar psychosocial stressors implies a generalized modification of the stress response with exercise training. To establish the true role of exercise for modifying the stress response, more controlled, experimental studies that consider specific subject and stressor characteristics should be conducted using sophisticated tests of biologically plausible explanatory mechanisms.

Clarifying the factors that affect physical activity habits over time is a major focus in exercise psychology. Although considerable research has been conducted over the past 25 years to identify determinants of exercise adoption and adherence and to apply interventions to increase initiation and maintenance of regular exercise, results have been mixed. Recent research has focused on environmental factors that may be associated with physical activity in adults, such as heavy traffic and neighborhood safety (Trost et al., 2002).

From the authors' meta-analysis, we identified characteristics of effective interventions, such as the use of strategies based an behavior modification principles applied in a community setting, but evidence of effectiveness has not translated into public health gains. The lack of success in maintaining increases in sustained physical activity within the U.S. population can be attributed to the complexity of exercise behavior and gaps and weaknesses in the research discussed earlier. Social support, self-motivation, self-regulatory skills, and interventions such as relapse prevention, including alternative fitness programming and exercise planning, are probably necessary to maintain or resume a physical activity pattern, but empirical evidence verifying these relationships is needed. The origin and time course for intrinsic reinforcement of physical activity remains unknown, so persistent interventions at the personal and population level, including community, school, worksite, and clinical settings, are required along with national policy initiatives. The application of dynamic theories, such as the transtheoretical model, and broader models of behavior change, such as the social ecological model, also may help to reverse the disturbing trend toward increased physical inactivity in this country.

Study Questions

1. What are the effects of acute and chronic exercise in anxiety and depression? Why do we say there is not a dose-response for decreases in anxiety and depression with exercise?

2. What characteristics should an individual have in order to gain the greatest increase in self-esteem from exercise?

3. List and discuss three plausible explanations or mechanisms for changes in mental health with exercise training.

4. What is executive control function and what evidence suggests that regular exercise affects it?

5. What are potential public health benefits from exercise-induced decreases in responses to mental stress?

6. List the three major research areas in exercise psychology, and discuss public health implications of each.

7. List the primary factors involved in behavior change according to social-cognitive, behavior modification, and cognitive-behavior modification theories.

8. Describe the major differences between the transtheoretical model and the other theories of behavior change.

9. What are the three general categories of physical activity correlates? Give examples of correlates in each category. Discuss why it is important to consider how different correlates might interact.

10. A sedentary friend wants to "get in shape" and started walking after work 2 weeks ago. He missed walking for the past 3 days and asked for your help to get his program going. What exercise stage is he in, and what are some interventions you would suggest to help him with his exercise program?

11. Describe cues that prompt you to exercise and some of the ways your exercise is reinforced.

References

Adlard, P. A., & Cotman, C. W. (2004). Voluntary exercise protects against stress-induced decreases in brain-derived neurotrophic factor protein expression. *Neuroscience, 124,* 985–992.

Ajzen, 1. (1985). From intentions to actions: A theory of planned behavior. In J. Kuhl & J. Beckman (Eds.), *Action-control: From cognition to behavior* (pp. 11–39). Heidelberg: Springer.

American Psychiatric Association. (1993). *Practice guideline for major depressive disorder in adults.* Washington, DC: Author.

American Psychiatric Association. (1994). *Diagnostic and statistical manual of mental disorders* (4th ed.). Washington, DC: American Psychiatric Association.

American Psychiatric Association. (2000). Practice guidelines for the treatment of patients with major depressive disorders (revision). *The American Journal of Psychiatry, 157* (4 Suppl), 1–45.

Anderson, B. J., Alcantara, A. A., & Greenough, W. T. (1996). Motor-skill learning: Changes in synaptic organization of the rat cerebellar cortex. *Neurobiology of Learning and Memory, 66,* 221–229.

Anderson, B. J., Rapp, D. N., Baek, D. H., McCloskey, D. P., Coburn-Litvak, P. S., & Robinson, J. K. (2000). Exercise influences spatial learning in the radial arm maze. *Physiology and Behavior, 70,* 425–429.

Babyak, M., Blumenthal, J. A., Herman, S., Khatri, P., Doraiswamy, M., Moore, K., et al. (2000). Exercise treatment for major depression: Maintenance of therapeutic benefit at 10 months. *Psychosomatic Medicine, 62,* 633–638.

Bandura, A. (1986). *Social foundations of thought and action.* Englewood Cliffs, NJ: Prentice Hall.

Bandura, A. (1991). Social cognitive theory of self-regulation. *Organizational Behavior and Human Decision Processes, 50,* 248–287.

Baranowski, T., Anderson, C., & Carmack, C. (1998). Mediating variable framework in physical activity interventions: How are we doing? How might we do better? *American Journal of Preventive Medicine, 15,* 266–297.

Barnekow-Bergkvist, M., Hedberg, G., Janlert, U., & Jansson, E. (1998). Prediction of physical fitness and physical activity level in adulthood by physical performance and physical activity in adolescence—an 18-year follow-up study. *Scandinavian Journal of Medicine and Science in Sports, 8,* 299–308.

Biddle, S. J. H., & Nigg, C. R. (2000). Theories of exercise behavior. *International Journal of Sport Psychology, 31,* 290–304.

Blair, S. N., Booth, M., Gyarfas, I., Iwane, H., Marti, B., Matsudo, V., Morrow, M. S., Noakes, T., & Shephard, R. (1996). Development of public policy and physical activity initiatives internationally. *Sports Medicine, 21,* 157–163.

Blumenthal, J. A., Babyak, M. A., Moore, K. A., Craighead, W. E., Herman, S., Khatri, P., Waugh, R., Napolitano, M. A., Forman, L. M., Appelbaum, M., Doraiswamy, P. M., & Krishnan, K. R. (1999). Effects of exercise training on older patients with major depression. *Archives of Internal Medicine, 159,* 2349–2356.

Broocks, A., Bandelow, B., Pekrun, G., George, A., Meyer, T., Bartmann, U., et al. (1998). Comparison of aerobic exercise, clomipramine, and placebo in the treatment of panic disorder. *American Journal of Psychiatry, 155,* 603–609.

Bryan, R. M. (1990). Cerebral blood flow and energy metabolism during stress. *American Journal of Physiology, 259*(28), H269–H280.

Buckworth, J. (2003). Behavior modification. In E. T Howley & B. D. Franks (Eds.), *Health fitness instructor's handbook* (4th ed.). Champaign, IL: Human Kinetics.

Buckworth, J., Convertino, V., Cureton, K. J., & Dishman, R. K. (1997). Increased finger arterial blood pressure after exercise detraining in women with parental hypertension: autonomic tasks. *Acta Physiologica Scandinavica, 160,* 29–41.

Buckworth, J., & Dishman, R. K. (2002). *Exercise Psychology.* Champaign, IL: Human Kinetics Publishers, Inc.

Buckworth, J., Dishman, R. K., & Cureton, K. J. (1994). Autonomic responses of women with parental hypertension: Effects of $VO2_{2peak}$ and physical activity. *Hypertension, 24,* 576–584.

Buckworth, J., Zeichner, A., Lating, J., & Dishman, R. K. (1996). The effects of physical activity and type A behavior pattern and cardiovascular responses to the structured interview. *Medicine and Science in Sports and Exercise, 28,* S29 (abstract).

Bulbulian, R., & Darabos, B. L. (1986). Motor neuron excitability: The Hoffmann reflex following exercise of low and high intensity. *Medicine and Science in Sports and Exercise, 18,* 697–702.

Centers for Disease Control and Prevention. (2004). Prevalence of no leisure-time physical activity—35 states and the District of Columbia, 1988–2002. *Morbidity and Mortality Weekly Reports, 53*(04), 82–86.

Chaouloff, F. (1997). Effects of acute physical exercise on central serotonergic systems. *Medicine and Science in Sports and Exercise, 29,* 58–62.

Chodzko-Zajko W. J., & Moore K.A. (1994). Physical fitness and cognitive functioning in aging. *Exercise and Sport Sciences Reviews, 22*, 195–220.

Colcombe, S. J., Kramer, A. F., Erickson, K. I., Scalf, P., McAuley, E., Cohen, N. J., Webb, A., Jerome, G. J., Marquez, D. X., & Elavsky, S. (2004). Cardiovascular fitness, cortical plasticity, and aging. *Proceedings National Academy of Sciences U S A, 101*(9), 3316–3321.

Cook, D. B., & Koltyn, K. F. (2000). Pain and exercise. *International Journal of Sport Psychology, 31*, 256–277.

Cotman C. W., & Berchtold N. C. (2002). Exercise: A behavioral intervention to enhance brain health and plasticity. *Trends in Neuroscience, 25*(6), 295–301.

Courneya, K. S., & Hellsten, L. M. (1998). Personality correlates of exercise behavior, motives, barriers, and preferences: An application of the five-factor model. *Personality and Individual Differences, 24*, 625–633.

Crabbe, J. B., & Dishman, R. K. (2004). Brain electrocortical activity during and after exercise: A quantitative synthesis. *Psychophysiology, 41*, 563–574.

Crabbe, J. B., Smith, J. C., & Dishman, R. K. (1999). EEG and emotional response after cycling exercise. *Medicine and Science in Sports and Exercise, 31*(Suppl.), S173, 767.

Crews, D. J., & Landers, D. M. (1987). A metaanalytic review of aerobic fitness and reactivity to psychosocial stressors. *Medicine and Science in Sports and Exercise, 19*(Suppl.), S114–S120.

Davis, C. (2000). Exercise abuse. *International Journal of Sport Psychology, 31*, 278–289.

Desharnais, R., Jobin, J., Cote, C., Levesque, L., & Godin, G. (1993). Aerobic exercise and the placebo effect: A controlled study. *Psychosomatic Medicine, 55*, 149–154.

deVries, H. A., Simard, C. P., Wiswell, R. A., Heckathorne, E., & Carabetta, V. (1982). Fusimotor system involvement in the tranquilizer effect of exercise. *American Journal of Physical Medicine, 61*, 111–122.

Dishman, R. K. (1986). Mental health. In V. Seefeldt (Ed.), *Physical activity and well-being*. Washington, DC: American Alliance for Health, Physical Education, and Recreation.

Dishman, R. K. (Ed.). (1994a). *Advances in exercise adherence*. Champaign, IL: Human Kinetics.

Dishman, R. K. (1994b). Prescribing exercise intensity for healthy adults using perceived exertion. *Medicine and Science in Sports and Exercise, 26*, 1087–1094.

Dishman, R. K. (1994c). The measurement conundrum in exercise adherence research. *Medicine and Science in Sports and Exercise, 26*, 1382–1390.

Dishman, R. K. (1997). Brain monoamines, exercise and behavioral stress: Animal models. *Medicine and Science in Sports and Exercise, 29*, 63–67.

Dishman, R. K. (1998). Physical activity and mental health. In H. S. Friedman (Ed.), *Encyclopedia of Mental Health* (Vol. 3, pp. 171–188). San Diego, CA: Academic Press.

Dishman, R. K. (2000). Introduction: Special issue on exercise psychology, *International Journal of Sport Psychology, 31*, 103–109.

Dishman, R. K. (2004). *Self-concept and physical activity among youth: A quantitative synthesis*. Unpublished manuscript, University of Georgia, Athens.

Dishman, R. K., & Buckworth, J. (1996). Increasing physical activity: A quantitative synthesis. *Medicine and Science in Sports and Exercise, 28,* 706–719.

Dishman, R. K., & Buckworth, J. (1997). Adherence to physical activity. In W. P. Morgan (Ed.), *Physical activity and mental health.* Washington, DC: Taylor & Francis.

Dishman, R. K., & Jackson, E. M. (2000). Exercise, fitness, and stress. *International Journal of Sport Psychology, 31,* 175–203.

Dishman, R. K., Motl, R. W., Saunders, R., Felton, G., Ward, D. S., Dowda, M., & Pate, R. R. (2004). Self-efficacy partially mediates the effect of a school-based physical-activity intervention among adolescent girls. *Preventive Medicine, 38,* 628–636.

Dishman, R. K., Nakamura, Y., Garcia, M. E., Thompson, R. W., Dunn, A. L., & Blair, S. N. (2000). Heart rate variability, trait anxiety, and perceived stress among physically fit men and women. *International Journal of Psychophysiology, 37,* 121–133.

Dishman, R. K., Nakamura, Y., Jackson, E. M., & Ray, C. A. (2003). Blood pressure and sympathetic nerve activity during cold pressor stress: Fitness and gender. *Psychophysiology, 40,* 370–380.

Dishman, R. K., Hong, S., Soares, J., Edwards, G. L., Bunnell, B. N., Jaso-Friedmann, L., & Evans, D. L. (2000). Activity-wheel running attenuates suppression of natural killer cell cytotoxicity after sympathectomy and footshock. *Physiology & Behavior, 71,* 297–304.

Dishman, R. K., Renner, K. J., Youngstedt, S. D., Reigle, T. G., Bunnell, B. N., Burke, K. A., Yoo, H. S., Mougey, E. H., & Meyerhoff, J. L. (1997). Activity wheel running reduces escape latency and alters brain monoamine levels after footshock. *Brain Research Bulletin, 42*(5), 399–406.

Dishman, R. K., & Sallis, J. F. (1994). Determinants and interventions for physical activity and exercise. In C. Bouchard, R. J. Shephard, & T. Stephens (Eds.), *Physical activity, fitness and health: International proceedings and consensus statement* (pp. 214–238). Champaign, IL: Human Kinetics.

Dishman, R. K., Warren, J. M., Hong, S., Bunnell, B. N., Mougey, J. L., Meyerhoff, L., Jaso-Friedmann, L., & Evans, D. L. (2000). Treadmill exercise training blunts suppression of natural killer cell cytolysis after footshock. *Journal of Applied Physiology, 88,* 2176–2182.

Doyne, E. J., Ossip-Klein, D. J., Bowman, E. D., Osborn, K. M., McDougall-Wilson, I. B., & Neimeyer, R. A. (1987). Running versus weightlifting in the treatment of depression. *Journal of Consulting and Clinical Psychology, 55,* 748–754.

Dunn, A. L., & Dishman, R. K. (1991). Exercise and the neurobiology of depression. *Exercise and Sport Sciences Reviews, 19,* 41–98.

Dunn, A. L., Reigle, T. G., Youngstedt, S. D., Armstrong, R. B., & Dishman, R. K. (1996). Brain norepinephrine and metabolites after treadmill training and wheel running in rats. *Medicine and Science in Sports and Exercise, 28,* 204–209.

Dunn, A. L., Trivedi, M. H., Kampert, J. B., Clark, C. G., & Chambliss, H. O. (2005). Exercise treatment for depression efficacy and dose response. *American Journal of Preventive Medicine, 28,* 1–8.

Dunn, A. L., Trivedi, M. H., & O'Neal, H. A. (2001). Physical activity dose-response effects on outcomes of depression and anxiety. *Medicine and Science in Sports and Exercise, 33,* S587–S597.

Dzewaltowski, D. A. (1994). Physical activity determinants: A social cognitive approach. *Medicine and Science in Sports and Exercise, 26*, 1395–1399.

Epstein, L. H. (1998). Integrating theoretical approaches to promote physical activity. *American Journal of Preventive Medicine, 15*, 257–265.

Etnier, J. L., Salazar, W., Landers, D. M., Petruzzello, S. J., Han, M., & Nowell, P. (1997). The influence of physical fitness and exercise upon cognitive functioning: A meta-analysis. *Journal of Sport and Exercise Psychology, 19*, 249–277.

Farmer, M., Locke, B., Moscicki, E., Dannenberg, A., Larson, D., & Radloff, L. (1988). Physical activity and depressive symptoms: The NHANES I epidemiologic follow-up study. *American Journal of Epidemiology, 128*(6), 1340–1351.

Fillenz, M. (1990). *Noradrenergic neurons.* New York: Cambridge University Press.

Fordyce, D. E., & Wehner, J. M. (1993). Physical activity enhances spatial learning performance with an associated alteration in hippocampal protein kinase C activity in C57BL/6 and DBA/2 mince. *Brain Research, 619*, 111–119.

Fordyce, D. E., & Farrar, R. P. (1991a). Enhancement of spatial learning in F344 rats by physical activity and related learning-associated alterations in hippocampal and cortical cholinergic functioning. *Behavioral Brain Research, 46*, 123–133.

Fordyce, D. E., & Farrar, R. P. (1991b). Physical activity effects on hippocampal and parietal cortical cholinergic function and spatial learning in F344 rats. *Behavioral Brain Research, 43*, 115–123.

Fox, K. R. (2000). Self-esteem, self-perceptions and exercise. *International Journal of Sport Psychology, 31*, 228–240.

Fox, K. R., & Stathi, A. (2002). Physical activity and mental health in older adults: Current evidence and future perspectives. *Psychology: The Journal of the Hellenic Psychological Society, 9*, 563–580.

Friedman, H. S., & Booth-Kewley, S. (1987). The "disease-prone personality." A meta-analytic view of the construct. *American Psychologist, 42*, 539–555.

Garcia, C., Chen, M. J., Garza, A. A., Cotman, C. W., Russo-Neustadt, A. (2003). The influence of specific noradrenergic and serotonergic lesions on the expression of hippocampal brain-derived neurotrophic factor transcripts following voluntary physical activity. *Neuroscience, 119*, 721–732.

Godin, G. (1994). Social-cognitive models. In R. K. Dishman (Ed.), *Advances in exercise adherence* (pp. 113–136). Champaign, IL: Human Kinetics.

Godin, G., & Shephard, R. J. (1990). Use of attitude-behavior models in exercise promotion. *Sports Medicine, 10*(2), 103–121.

Gorely, T., & Gordon, S. (1995). An examination of the transtheoretical model of exercise behavior in older adults. *Journal of Sport and Exercise Psychology, 17*, 312–324.

Graham, R. E., Zeichner, A., Peacock, L. J., & Dishman, R. K. (1996). Bradycardia during baroreflex stimulation and active or passive stressor tasks: Cardiorespiratory fitness and hostility. *Psychophysiology, 33*(5), 566–575.

Gruber, A. J., & Pope, H. G., Jr. (2000). Psychiatric and medical effects of anabolic-androgenic steroid use in women. *Psychotherapy and Psychosomatics, 69*, 19–26.

Gruber, J. (1986). Physical activity and self-esteem development in children: A meta-analysis. In G. A. Stull & H. M. Eckhardt (Eds.), *Effects of physical activity an children: Papers of the American Academy of Physical Education, 19* (pp. 30–48). Champaign, IL: Human Kinetics.

Grunbaum, J. A., Kann, L., Kinchen, S., Ross, J., Hawkins, J., Lowry, R., Harris, W. A., McManus, T., Chyen, D., & Collins, J. (2004). Youth risk behavior surveillance—United States, 2003. *Morbidity and Mortality Weekly Reports: Surveillance Summaries, 53*(2), 1–96.

Harbin, T. J. (1989). The relationship between the type A behavior pattern and physiological responsivity: A quantitative review. *Psychophysiology, 26*, 110–119.

Harris, S. S., Caspersen, C. J., DeFriese, G. H., & Estes, E. H. (1989). Physical activity counseling for healthy adults as a primary preventive intervention in the clinical setting. *Journal of the American Medical Association, 261*, 3590–3598.

Ivy, A. S., Rodriguez, F. G., Garcia, C., Chen, M. J., & Russo-Neustadt, A. A. (2003). Noradrenergic and serotonergic blockade inhibits BDNF mRNA activation following exercise and antidepressant. *Pharmacology, Biochemistry, and Behavior, 75*, 81–88.

Jackson, E. M., & Dishman, R. K. (2002). Hemodynamic responses to stress among black women: Fitness and parental hypertension. *Medicine and Science in Sports and Exercise, 34*, 1097–1104.

Jackson, E. M., & Dishman, R. K. (2004). The effects of cardiorespiratory fitness on cardiovascular responses during and after stress: A quantitative synthesis. *Medicine and Science in Sports and Exercise, 36*(5 Suppl.), 1097.

Jakicic, J. M., Winters, C., Lang, W., & Wing, R. R. (1999). Effects of intermittent exercise and use of home exercise equipment on adherence, weight loss, and fitness in overweight women: A randomized trial. *Journal of the American Medical Association, 282*, 1554–1560.

Kahn, E. B., Ramsey, L. T., Brownson, R. C., Heath, G. W., Howze, E. H., Powell, K. E., et al. (2002). The effectiveness of interventions to increase physical activity. A systematic review. *American Journal of Preventive Medicine, 22*, 73–107.

Kendzierski, D. (1994). Schema theory: An information processing focus. In R. K. Dishman (Ed.), *Advances in exercise adherence* (pp. 137–159). Champaign, IL: Human Kinetics.

Kessler, R. C., McGonagle, K. A., Zhao, S., Nelson, C. B., Hughes, M., Eshleman, S., Wittchen, H., & Kendler, K. S. (1994). Lifetime and 12 month prevalence of DSM-III-R psychiatric disorders in the United States. *Archives of General Psychiatry, 51*, 8–19.

King, A. C. (1994). Community and public health approaches to the promotion of physical activity. *Medicine and Science in Sports and Exercise, 26*, 1405–1412.

King, A. C., Haskell, W. L., Taylor, H. C., & DeBusk, R. F. (1991). Group- vs. home-based exercise training in healthy older men and women. *Journal of the American Medical Association, 266*, 1535–1542.

King, A. C., Oman, R. F., Brassington, G. S., Bliwise, D. L., & Haskell, W. L. (1997). Moderate-intensity exercise and self-rated quality of sleep in older adults. A randomized controlled trial. *Journal of the American Medical Association, 277*, 32–37.

King, A. C., Taylor, C. B., & Haskell, W. L. (1993). Effects of differing intensities and formats of 12 months of exercise training and psychological outcomes in older adults. *Health Psychology, 12,* 292–300.

Knapp, D. N. (1988). Behavioral management techniques and exercise promotion. In R. K. Dishman (Ed.), *Exercise adherence: Its impact on public health* (pp. 203–236), Champaign, IL: Human Kinetics.

Koltyn, K. F., & Morgan, W. P. (1992). Influence of underwater exercise on anxiety and body temperature. *Scandinavian Journal of Medicine, Science and Sports, 2,* S41.

Landers, D. M., & Petruzzello, S. J. (1994). Physical activity, fitness, and anxiety. In C. Bouchard, R. J. Shephard, & T. Stephens (Eds.), *Physical activity, fitness and health: Proceedings and consensus statement* (pp. 868–882). Champaign, IL: Human Kinetics.

Lawlor, D. A., & Hopker, S. W. (2001). The effectiveness of exercise as an intervention in the management of depression: Systematic review and meta-regression analysis of randomized trials. *British Medical Journal, 322,* 1–8.

Maki, T., Kontula, K., & Harkonen, M. (1990). The beta-adrenergic system in man: Physiological and pathophysiological response. *Scandinavian Journal of Clinical Laboratory Investigation, 50*(Suppl. 201), 25–43.

Marcus, B. H., & Forsyth, L. H. (2003). *Motivating people to be physically active.* Champaign, IL: Human Kinetics.

Marcus, B. H., Pinto, B. M., Simkin, L. R., Audrain, J. E., & Taylor, E. R. (1994). Application of theoretical models to exercise behavior among employed women. *American Journal of Health Promotion, 9,* 49–55.

Marcus, B. H., & Simkin, L. R. (1994). The transtheoretical model: Applications to exercise behavior. *Medicine and Science in Sports and Exercise, 26,* 1400–1404.

Marlatt, G. A., & Gordon, J. (1985). *Relapse prevention.* New York: Guilford Press.

Marshall, S. J., & Biddle, S. J. H. (2001). The transtheoretical model of behavior change: A meta-analysis of applications to physical activity and exercise. *Annals of Behavioral Medicine, 23,* 229–246.

Martinsen, E. W., Hoffart, A., & Solberg, O. (1989a). Aerobic and non-aerobic forms of exercise in the treatment of anxiety disorders. *Stress Medicine, 5,* 115–120.

Martinsen, E. W., Hoffart, A., & Solberg, O. (1989b). Comparing aerobic and non-aerobic forms of exercise in the treatment of clinical depression: A randomized trial. *Comprehensive Psychiatry, 30,* 324–331.

Mazzeo, R. S. (1991). Catecholamine responses to acute and chronic exercise. *Medicine and Science in Sports and Exercise, 23*(7), 839–845.

McAuley, E. (1994). Physical activity and psychosocial outcomes. In C. Bouchard & R. J. Shephard (Eds.), *Physical activity, fitness, and health: International proceedings and consensus statement* (pp. 551–568). Champaign, IL: Human Kinetics.

McAuley, E., & Blissmer, B. (2000). Self-efficacy determinants and consequences of physical activity. *Exercise and Sport Sciences Reviews, 28,* 85–88.

McAuley, E., Kramer, A. F., & Colcombe, S. J. (2004). Cardiovascular fitness and neurocognitive function in older adults: A brief review. *Brain Behavior and Immunity, 18*(3), 214–220.

McCloskey, D. P., Adamo, D. S., & Anderson, B. J. (2001). Exercise increases metabolic capacity in the motor cortex and striatum, but not in the hippocampus. *Brain Research, 891,* 168–175.

McDonald, D. G., & Hodgdon, J. A. (1991). *Psychological effects of aerobic fitness training: Research and theory.* New York: Springer Verlag.

McGinnis, J. M. (1992). The public health burden of a sedentary lifestyle. *Medicine and Science in Sports and Exercise, 24*(Suppl), S196–S200.

Mills, P. J., & Berry, C. C. (1999). Menstrual cycle, race and task effects on blood pressure recovery from acute stress. *Journal of Psychosomatic Research, 46,* 445–454.

Morgan, K. (2003). Daytime activity and risk factors for late-life insomnia. *Journal of Sleep Research, 12,* 231–238.

Morgan, W. P. (1994). Physical activity, fitness, and depression. In C. Bouchard, R. J. Shephard, & T. Stephens (Eds.), *Physical activity, fitness and health: International proceedings and consensus statement* (pp. 851–867). Champaign, IL: Human Kinetics.

Morgan, W. P. (Ed.). (1997). *Physical activity and mental health.* Washington, DC: Taylor & Francis.

Morgan, W. P., Brown, D. R., Raglin, J. S., O'Connor, P. J., & Ellickson, K. A. (1987). Psychological monitoring of overtraining and staleness. *British Journal of Sports Medicine, 21,* 107–114.

Morgan, W. P., & O'Connor, P. J. (1988). Exercise and mental health. In R. K. Dishman (Ed.), *Exercise adherence: Its impact on public health* (pp. 91–121). Champaign, IL: Human Kinetics.

Motl, R. W., Birnbaum, A., Kubik, M., & Dishman, R. K. (2004). Naturally occurring changes in physical activity are inversely related to depressive symptoms during early adolescence. *Psychosomatic Medicine, 66*(3), 336–342.

Motl, R. W., & Dishman, R. K. (2003). Acute leg-cycling exercise attenuates the H-reflex recorded in soleus but not flexor carpi radialis. *Muscle & Nerve, 28,* 609–614.

Motl, R. W., & Dishman, R. K. (2004). Effects of acute exercise on the soleus H-reflex and self-reported anxiety after caffeine ingestion. *Physiology & Behavior, 80,* 577–585.

Motl, R. W., Knowles, D., & Dishman, R. K. (2003). Acute bouts of active and passive leg cycling attenuate the amplitude of the soleus H-reflex. *Neuroscience Letters, 347,* 69–72.

Motl, R. W., O'Connor, P. J., & Dishman, R. K. (2004). Effects of cycling exercise on the soleus H-reflex and state anxiety among men with low or high trait anxiety. *Psychophysiology, 41,* 96–105.

Murray, C. J., & Lopez, A. D. (1999). On the comparable quantification of health risks: Lessons from the Global Burden of Disease Study. *Epidemiology, 10,* 594–605.

Murray, C. J., & Lopez, A. D. (1996). *The global burden of disease: A comprehensive assessment of mortality and disability from diseases, injuries, and risk factors in 1990 and projected to 2020.* Boston, MA: World Health Organization World Bank, Harvard: Harvard School of Public Health.

NIH Consensus Conference. (1996). Physical activity and cardiovascular health. *Journal of the American Medical Association, 276,* 241–246.

North, T. C., McCullugh, P., & Vu Tran, Z. (1990). Effect of exercise an depression. *Exercise and Sport Sciences Reviews, 18,* 379–415.

Nybo, L., & Secher, N. H. (2004). Cerebral perturbations provoked by prolonged exercise. *Progress in Neurobiology, 72,* 223–261.

O'Connor, P. J., Morgan, W. P., Raglin, J. S., Barksdale, C. N., & Kalin, N. H. (1989). Mood state and salivary cortisol levels following overtraining in female swimmers. *Psychoneuroendocrinology, 14,* 303–310.

O'Connor, P. J., Petruzzello, S. J., Kubitz, K. A., & Robinson, T. L. (1995). Anxiety responses to maximal exercise testing. *British Journal of Sports Medicine, 29,* 97–102.

O'Connor, P. J., Raglin, J. S., & Martinsen, E. W. (2000). Physical activity, anxiety and anxiety disorders. *International Journal of Sport Psychology, 31,* 136–155.

Olivardia, R., Pope, H. G., Jr., & Hudson, J. I. (2000). Muscle dysmorphia in male weightlifters: A case-control study. *American Journal of Psychiatry, 157,* 1291–1296.

O'Neal, H. A., Dunn, A. L., & Martinsen, E. W. (2000). Depression and exercise. *International Journal of Sport Psychology, 31,* 110–135.

O'Neal, H. A., Van Hoomissen, J. D., Holmes, P. V., & Dishman, R. K. (2001). Prepro-galanin messenger RNA levels are increased in rat locus coeruleus after treadmill exercise training. *Neuroscience Letters, 299*(1–2), 69–72.

Paffenbarger, R. S., Jr., Lee, I.-M., & Leung, R. (1994). Physical activity and personal characteristics associated with depression and suicide in American college men. *Acta Psychiatrica Scandinavica* (Suppl. 377), 16–22.

Peronnet, F., & Szabo, A. (1993). Sympathetic response to acute psychosocial stressors in humans: Linkage to physical exercise and training. In P. Seraganian (Ed.), *Exercise psychology: The influence of physical exercise on psychological process* (pp. 172–217). New York: John Wiley.

Petruzzello, S. J., Hall, E. E., & Ekkekakis, P. (2001). Regional brain activation as a biological marker of affective responsivity to acute exercise: Influence of fitness. *Psychophysiology, 38*(1), 99–106.

Petruzzello, S. J., Landers, D. M., Hatfield, B. D., Kubitz, K. A., & Salazar, W. (1991). A meta-analysis on the anxiety reducing effects of acute and chronic exercise: Outcomes and mechanisms. *Sports Medicine, II,* 142–182.

Petruzzello, S. J., Landers, D. M., & Salazar, W. (1993). Exercise and anxiety reduction: Examination of temperature as an explanation for affective change. *Journal of Sport and Exercise Psychology, 15,* 63–76.

Phillips, K. A., O'Sullivan, R. L., & Pope, H. G., Jr. (1997). Muscle dysmorphia. *Journal of Clinical Psychiatry, 58,* 361.

Pollock, M. L., Carroll, J. F., Graves, J. E., Leggett, S. H., Braith, R. W., Limacher, M., & Hagberg, J. M. (1991). Injuries and adherence to walk/jog and resistance programs in the elderly. *Medicine and Science in Sports and Exercise, 23,* 1194–1200.

Pope, H. G., Jr., Gruber, A. J., Choi, P., Olivardia, R., & Phillips, K. A. (1997). Muscle dysmorphia: An underrecognized form of body dysmorphic disorder. *Psychosomatics, 38,* 548–557.

Pope, H. G., Jr., Gruber, A. J., Mangweth, B., Bureau, B., deCol, C., Jouvent, R., et al. (2000). Body image perception among men in three countries. *American Journal of Psychiatry, 157,* 1297–1301.

Prochaska, J. O., & Marcus, B. H. (1994). The transtheoretical model: Applications to exercise. In R. K. Dishman (Ed.), *Advances in exercise adherence* (pp. 161–180). Champaign, IL: Human Kinetics.

Prochaska, J. O., & Velicer, W. F. (1997). The transtheoretical model of behavior change. *American Journal of Health Promotion, 12,* 38–48.

Rosen, C. S. (2000). Is the sequencing of change processes by stage consistent across health problems? A meta-analysis. *Health Psychology, 19,* 593–604.

Rowland, T. W. (1998). The biological basis of physical activity. *Medicine and Science in Sports and Exercise, 30,* 392–399.

Royall, D. R., Lauterbach, E. C., Cummings, J. L., Reeve, A., Rummans, T. A., Kaufer, D. I., LaFrance, W. C., Jr., & Coffey, C. E. (2002). Executive control function: A review of its promise and challenges for clinical research. A report from the Committee on Research of the American Neuropsychiatric Association. *Journal of Neuropsychiatry and Clinical Neuroscience, 14*(4), 377–405.

Russo-Neustadt, A. (2003). Brain-derived neurotrophic factor, behavior, and new directions for the treatment of mental disorders. *Seminar in Clinical Neuropsychiatry, 8,* 109–118.

Saab, P. G. (1989). Cardiovascular and neuroendocrine responses to challenge in males and females. In N. Schneiderman, S. M. Weiss, & P. G. Kaufman (Eds.), *Handbook of research methods in cardiovascular behavioral medicine* (pp. 453–481). New York: Plenum Press.

Sallis, J. F., & Hovell, M. F. (1990). Determinants of exercise behavior. *Exercise and Sport Sciences Reviews, 11,* 307–330.

Sallis, J. F., & Owen, N. (1999). *Physical activity and behavioral medicine.* Thousand Oaks, CA: Sage Publications.

Schmidt, W. D., Biwer, C. J., & Kalscheuer, L. K. (2001). Effects of long versus short bout exercise on fitness and weight loss in overweight females. *Journal of the American College of Nutrition, 20,* 494–501.

Seefeldt, V., Malina, R. M., & Clark, M. A. (2002). Factors affecting levels of physical activity in adults. *Sports Medicine, 32,* 143–168.

Sibley, B. A., & Etnier, J. L. (2003). The relationship between physical activity and cognition in children: A meta-analysis. *Pediatric Exercise Science, 15,* 243–256.

Singh, N. A., Clements, K. M., & Fiatrone, M. A. (1997). A randomized controlled trial of the effect of exercise on sleep. *Sleep, 20,* 95–101.

Smith, J. C., & Crabbe, J. B. (2000). Emotion and exercise. *International Journal of Sport Psychology, 31,* 156–174.

Smith, J. C., O'Connor, P. J., Crabbe, J. B., & Dishman, R. K. (2002). Emotional responsiveness after low- and moderate-intensity exercise and seated rest. *Medicine and Science in Sports and Exercise, 34*(7), 1158–1167.

Soares, J., Holmes, P. V., Renner, K., Edward, G., Bunnell, B. N., & Dishman, R. K. (1999). Brain noradrenergic responses to footshock after chronic activity wheel running. *Behavioral Neuroscience, 113*, 558–566.

Sonstroem, R. J. (1998). Physical self-concept: Assessment and external validity. *Exercise and Sport Sciences Reviews, 26*, 133–164.

Sothmann, M. S. (1991). Catecholamines, behavioral stress, and exercise—introduction to the Symposium. *Medicine and Science in Sports and Exercise, 23*, 836–838.

Sothmann, M. S., Buckworth, J., Claytor, R. P., Cox, R. H., White-Welkley, J. E., & Dishman, R. K. (1996). Exercise training and the cross-stressor adaptation hypothesis. *Exercise and Sport Sciences Reviews, 24*, 267–287.

Stern, M. J., & Cleary, P. (1981). The national exercise and heart disease project: Psychosocial changes observed during a low-level exercise program. *Archives of Internal Medicine, 141*, 1463–1467.

Stern, M. J., & Cleary, P. (1982). The national exercise and heart disease project: Long term psychosocial outcome. *Archives of Internal Medicine, 142*, 1093–1097.

Tieman, J. G., Peacock, L. J., Cureton, K. J., & Dishman, R. K. (2001). Acoustic startle eyeblink response after acute exercise. *International Journal of Neuroscience, 106*, 21–33.

Tomporowski, P. D. (2003). Cognitive and behavioral responses to acute exercise in youths: A review. *Pediatric Exercise Science, 15*, 348–359.

Tomporowski, P. D., & Ellis, N. R. (1986). The effects of exercise on cognitive processes: A review. *Psychological Bulletin, 99*, 338–346.

Trost, S. G., Owen, N., Bauman, A., Sallis, J. F., & Brown, W. J. (2002). Correlates of adults' participation in physical activity: Review and update. *Medicine and Science in Sports and Exercise, 34*, 1996–2001.

Turk, D. C., Rudy, T. E., & Salovey, P. (1984). Health protection: Attitudes and behaviors of LPNs, teachers, and college students. *Health Psychology, 3*, 189–210.

U.S. Department of Health & Human Services. (1996). *Physical activity and health: A report of the Surgeon General.* Atlanta, GA: U.S. Department of Health & Human Services, Centers for Disease Control, National Center for Chronic Disease Prevention and Health Promotion.

U.S. Department of Health and Human Services. (2000). *Healthy people 2010: Understanding and improving health.* Washington, DC: U.S. Government Printing Office.

Van Hoomissen, J. D., Chambliss, H. O., Holmes, P. V., & Dishman, R. K. (2003). Effects of chronic exercise and imipramine on mRNA for BDNF after olfactory bulbectomy in rat. *Brain Research, 974*, 228–235.

Van Hoomissen, J. D., Holmes, P. V., Zellner, A. S., Poudevigne, A., & Dishman, R. K. (2004). Effects of beta-adrenoreceptor blockade during chronic exercise on contextual fear conditioning and mRNA for galanin and brain-derived neurotrophic factor. *Behavioral Neuroscience, 118*, 1378–1390.

Van Praag, H., Christie, B. R., Sejnowski, T. J., & Gage, F. H. (1999). Running enhances neurogenesis, learning, and long-term potentiation. *Proceedings of the National Academy of Sciences, 96*(23), 13427–13231.

Varo, J. J., Martinez-Gonzalez, M. A., De Irala-Estevez, J., Kearney, J., Gibney, M., & Martinez, J. A. (2003). Distribution and determinants of sedentary lifestyles in the European Union. *International Journal of Epidemiology, 32*, 138–146.

Vissing, J., Andersen, M., & Diemer, N. H. (1996). Exercise-induced changes in local cerebral glucose utilization in the rat. *Journal of Cerebral Blood Flow and Metabolism: Official Journal of the International Society of Cerebral Blood Flow and Metabolism, 16*, 729–736.

Wallace, L. S., & Buckworth, J. (2003). Longitudinal shifts in exercise stages of change in college students. *Journal of Sports Medicine and Physical Fitness, 43*, 209–212.

White-Welkley, J. E., Bunnell, B. N., Mougey, E. H., Meyerhoff J. L., & Dishman, R. K. (1995). Treadmill exercise training and estradiol differentially modulate hypothalamic-pituitary adrenal cortical responses to acute running and immobilization. *Physiology & Behavior, 57,* 533–540.

White-Welkley, J. E., Warren, G. L., Bunnell, B. N., Mougey, E. H., Meyerhoff, J. L., & Dishman, R. K., (1996). Treadmill exercise training and estradiol increase plasma ACTH and prolactin after novel footshock. *Journal of Applied Physiology, 80,* 931–939.

Williamson, J. W., McColl, R., Mathews, D. (2003). Evidence for central command activation of the human insular cortex during exercise. *Journal of Applied Physiology, 94*(5), 1726–1734.

Yoo, H. S., Bunnell, B. N., Crabbe, J. B., Kalish, L. R., & Dishman, R. K. (2000). Failure of neonatal clomipramine treatment to alter forced swim immobility: Chronic treadmill or activity-wheel running and imipramine. *Physiology and Behavior, 70,* 407–411.

Yoo, H. S., Tackett, R. L., & Dishman, R. K. (1996). Brain β-adrenergic responses to wheel running. *Medicine and Science in Sports and Exercise, 28*(5, Suppl.), S109.

Youngstedt, S. D. (2000). The exercise-sleep mystery. *International Journal of Sport Psychology, 31,* 241–255.

Youngstedt, S. D., Dishman, R. K., Cureton, K. J., & Peacock, L. J. (1993). Does body temperature mediate anxiolytic effects of acute exercise? *Journal of Applied Physiology, 74,* 825–831.

Youngstedt, S. D., O'Connor, P. J., & Dishman, R. K. (1997). The effects of acute exercise on sleep: A quantitative synthesis. *Sleep, 20,* 203–214.

Youngstedt, S. D., O'Connor, P., Crabbe, J. B., & Dishman, R. K. (2000). Effects of acute exercise on caffeine-induced insomnia. *Physiology & Behavior, 68,* 563–570.

SUBJECT INDEX